Sri Lanka

the Bradt Travel Guide

Philip Briggs

edition
6

www.bradtguides.com

Bradt Travel Guides Ltd, UK
The Globe Pequot Press Inc, USA

KEY

■ Capital
● City
● Major town
○ Other town
Expressway
Main road
Other road
✈ International airport
∴ Ancient site
⚲ Beach
≋ Zoo/sanctuary
❀ Waterfall
❀ Gardens
● Nature reserve

Jaffna: the little-visited but vibrant Tamil city of Jaffna is the gateway to a low-lying peninsula and archipelago studded with ancient temples and forts
pages 299–318

The Cultural Triangle: this archaeological circuit comprises four UNESCO World Heritage Sites, at Anuradhapura, Polonnaruwa, Sigiriya, and Dambulla
pages 209–84

Horton Plains National Park: day hikes through moorland and dwarf forest lead to the magnificent World's End Viewpoint and two of the country's three tallest peaks
pages 430–5

I N D I A N

O C E A N

Bradt

N

0   50km
0   30 miles

Kokkilai Lagoon

Pigeon Island National Park
Nilaveli
Trincomalee
Koddiyar Bay

Jaffna Peninsula

Elephant Pass

Chundikulam National Park

A12

A6

Gal Oya

Habarana

Ghitale

Minneriya National Park

Jaffna Lagoon

Mankulam

Vavuniya

Madawachchi

A9

Mihintale

Kankesanturai
Jaffna
Karaitivu

Punguditivu

Iranaitivu

Our Lady of Madhu Shrine

Aruvi Aru

Anuradhapura

A12

Palk Bay

Delft

Mannar

Thalaimannar

Karaitivu

Kalo

Wilpattu National Park

Kalpitiya

Puttalam

Puttalam Lagoon

G u l f   o f
M a n n a r

A11

A9

Galle Face Green: a popular evening promenade spot in the heart of Colombo
pages 101–2

Adam's Peak: the island's most imposing natural feature attracts hundreds of thousands of pilgrims between December and May
pages 413–17

Sinharaja Forest: the biodiverse rainforests of Sinharaja protect 830 endemic plant and animal species, including all but two of the 33 bird species unique to the island
pages 471–82

Galle Fort: recognised as a World Heritage Site, the fort is the best-preserved colonial sea fortress in Asia
pages 572–8

Kandy: the lovely highland city of Kandy is renowned for its sacred Temple of the Tooth and fabulous century-old botanical garden
pages 390–1 & 396–8

Arugam Bay: the east coast's hippest resort combines a chilled-out vibe with fine surfing and a gorgeous sun-kissed beach
pages 351–63

Yala National Park: Sri Lanka's premier safari destination supports dense populations of elephant, leopard, water buffalo and sloth bear
pages 508–15

Weligama Bay: this large oval bay combines attractive swimming beaches and fine surfing with top-notch whale-watching and the iconic sight of stilt fishermen
pages 545–58

Laccadive Sea

Chilaw
Munneswaram
Negombo
Colombo
Dehiwala
Mt Lavinia
SRI JAYAWARDENEPURA
KOTTE
Ragama
Gampaha
Ambepussa
Avissawella
Pinnawela
Polgahawela
Kurunegala
Ambalangoda
Beruwala
Kalutara
Ratnapura
Kitulgala
Peradeniya
Kandy
Matale
Ukuwela
Hikkaduwa
Hikkaduwa Marine National Park
Galle
Koggala
Kannetiya Forest Reserve
Sinharaja Forest Reserve
Adam's Peak 2243m
Horton Plains National Park
World's End
Belihuloya
Nanu Oya
St Clair Falls
Nuwara Eliya
Hakgala Botanical Garden
Pusselawa
Knuckles Forest Reserve
Knuckles Range
Knuckles 1862m
Madura Oya National Park
Kehelula
Batticaloa
Matara
Dondra Head
Tangalle
Kalametiya
Hambontota
Bundala National Park
Kirinda
Tissamaharama
Kataragama
Yala National Park
Kumana National Park
Udawalawe National Park
Lunugamwehera National Park
Tanamalwila
Kirindi
Wellawaya
Bandarawela
Haputale
Ella
Badulla
Mahiyanganaya
Victoria-Randenigala-Rantambe Sanctuary
Gal Oya National Park
Lahugala Kithulana National Park
Pottuvil
Ampara
Arugam Bay
Mahaweli
Walawe
Maduru Oya

A2 A1 A8 A4 A5 A6 A7 A9 A26 A3 A4 E1

Sri Lanka
Don't miss...

Cultural Triangle

Home to four of Sri Lanka's eight UNESCO World Heritage Sites, the Cultural Triangle is a treasure trove of ancient monasteries, decorated cave temples, magnificent dagobas and archaeological reserves whose collective history spans 2,500 years
pages 209–84

Yala National Park

Sri Lanka's most popular and rewarding safari destination is renowned for its dense populations of elephant, leopard and other wildlife, including more than 200 bird species
pages 508–15

Temple of the Tooth, Kandy

Spiritual centre of Kandy's Sacred City — inscribed as a UNESCO World Heritage Site — the Dalada Maligawa is one of the world's most venerated Buddhist shrines

pages 390–1

Indian Ocean beaches

Sri Lanka's tropical Indian Ocean coastline boasts endless swathes of beautiful beaches — Kirinda's unspoilt, boulder-strewn sands are breathtaking

pages 507–8

Sinharaja Forest Reserve

An important biodiversity hotspot, this UNESCO World Heritage Site is Sri Lanka's number-one birdwatching destination and offers fantastic hiking opportunities within its magnificent rainforest interior

pages 471–82

Sri Lanka in colour

left   Historic Fort District's best-known landmark is the Lighthouse Clock Tower — or 'Big Ben of Colombo' — built in 1857
page 104

below   Occupying an impressive red-and-white stone, colonial-era building, iconic Cargills is Colombo's oldest store
pages 104–5

bottom   Notable for its Thai-inspired Buddha statues, the stilted temple of Seema Malaka juts out on to Lake Beira and provides a rare religious showcase for the uncluttered aesthetic and clean lines typical of architect Geoffrey Bawa's secular work
page 109

above left Each year Gangaramaya Temple becomes the focal point of Colombo's spectacular Navam Perahera (February Parade) pages 109 and 57

above right Pettah District's narrow streets are a jostling open-air bazaar crammed with a colourful mix of street vendors, bargain hunters, bullock carts and tuktuks pages 105–8

right & below Prestigious Cinnamon Gardens is home to the Colombo National Museum and Independence Memorial; the museum houses a collection of 100,000 artefacts reflecting Sri Lankan architecture, history and culture from prehistoric times to the Kandyan era pages 111–12

above Sunset at Flag Rock Bastion, Galle Fort — the best-preserved colonial sea fortress in Asia and a UNESCO World Heritage Site pages 572–8

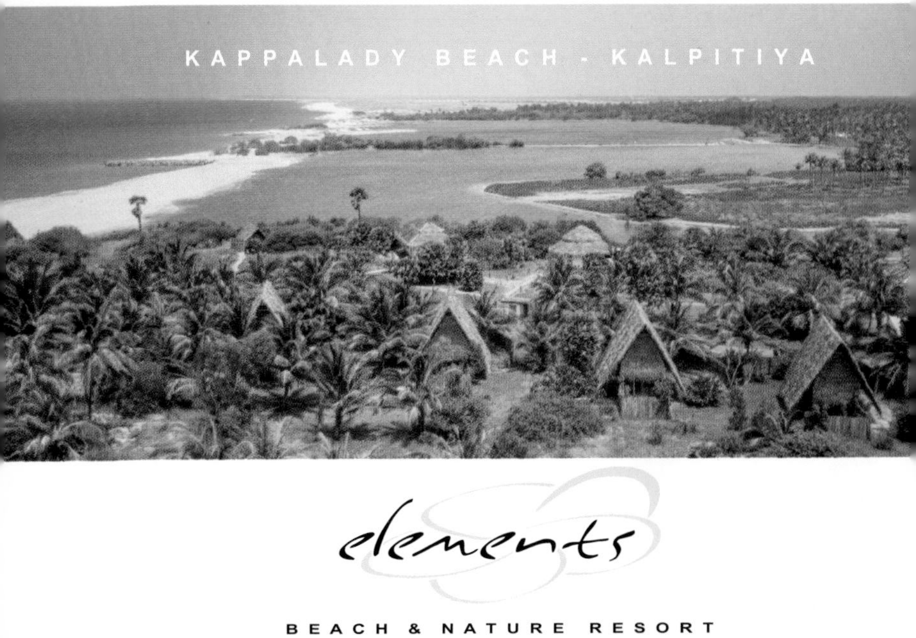

KAPPALADY BEACH · KALPITIYA

elements

BEACH & NATURE RESORT

AUTHOR

Philip Briggs (**e** *philip.briggs@bradtguides.com*) is one of the world's most experienced and knowledgeable guidebook writers having been researching and writing guides for Bradt and other well-known publishers for almost 30 years. He undertook his first major backpacking trip in 1986, when he spent several months travelling overland from Nairobi to Cape Town. In 1991, he wrote the *Bradt Guide to South Africa*, the first such guidebook to be published internationally after the release of Nelson Mandela. Over the rest of
the 1990s, Philip wrote a series of pioneering Bradt travel guides to destinations that were then – and in some cases still are – otherwise practically uncharted by the travel publishing industry. These included the first dedicated guidebooks to Tanzania, Uganda, Ethiopia, Malawi, Mozambique, Ghana and Rwanda, new editions of which have been published regularly ever since. More recently, he authored the first dedicated English-language guidebook to Somaliland, as well as a new guide to The Gambia, both published by Bradt. Turning his attention now to both South America and Asia, he has authored the Bradt guide to Suriname and now this new edition of *Sri Lanka*. Philip spends at least four months on the road every year, usually accompanied by his wife, travel photographer Ariadne Van Zandbergen, and spends the rest of his time battering away at a keyboard in the sleepy coastal village of Wilderness in South Africa's Western Cape.

CONTRIBUTOR

Royston Ellis (**w** *roystonellis.com*), who wrote the first five editions of this guide, is a novelist, travel writer and erstwhile beat poet, born in Britain, who has lived in Sri Lanka since 1980. He is also the author of the Bradt guides *Sri Lanka by Rail* and *India by Rail* (both out of print) and original author of Bradt's *Maldives* and *Mauritius, Rodrigues & Réunion*. As Richard Tresillian, he is the author of a score of historical novels, some of which are set in Sri Lanka, and he is currently working on a Ceylon tea plantation saga. *Gone Man Squared*, a collection of beat poetry he wrote and performed in England in the 1960s, and several novels under his own name have been published as paperbacks by Kicks Books of New York. When he is not writing, Royston relaxes at his colonial-period cottage near Bentota on the island's west coast.

PUBLISHER'S FOREWORD   *Adrian Phillips, Managing Director*

Sri Lanka offers one of the best all-round travel experiences in the world – from UNESCO-listed archaeological sites and colourful festivals to lazy beach breaks. Its wildlife in particular is spectacular, featuring bucket-list species like leopards and blue whales, and this sixth edition includes a dedicated wildlife chapter that you won't find in any other general guidebook to the country. Indeed, there's much in this book you won't find elsewhere. When Philip Briggs, Bradt's flagship author, agreed to take on this sixth edition, he did so with the determined aim to make it the leading guidebook on the market. And he hasn't disappointed. Philip has retained the best of former author Royston Ellis's tourist advice, of course, but he's also significantly overhauled and added to it. I don't recall any new edition receiving such a comprehensive facelift. Sri Lanka has come a long way since its tsunami and civil war; the Land of Smiles really does seem to be smiling. Philip's book will ensure tourists travel happy too.

Sixth edition published January 2018   First published 2002

Bradt Travel Guides Ltd
IDC House, The Vale, Chalfont St Peter, Bucks SL9 9RZ, England
www.bradtguides.com
Print edition published in the USA by The Globe Pequot Press Inc,
PO Box 480, Guilford, Connecticut 06437-0480

Text copyright © 2018 Philip Briggs
Maps copyright © 2018 Bradt Travel Guides Ltd. Includes map data © OpenStreetMap contributors
Photographs copyright © 2018 Individual photographers (see below)
Project Manager: Susannah Lord
Cover research: Ian Spick

ISBN: 978 1 78477 057 0 (print)
e-ISBN: 978 1 78477 522 3 (e-pub)
e-ISBN: 978 1 78477 423 3 (mobi)

British Library Cataloguing in Publication Data
A catalogue record for this book is available from the British Library

Photographs All photos in main colour sections by Ariadne Van Zandbergen; all photos in Natural World chapter (pages 13–36) by Gehan de Silva Wijeyeratne; Shutterstock.com: Eduard Kyslynskyy (EK/S), eXpose (e/S), feathercollector (f/S), maheshg (m/S), milosk50 (m50/S), PhilipYb Studio (PYS/S); Ariadne Van Zandbergen (www.africaimagelibrary.com) (AVZ)
Front cover Dancers at the Kandy Lake Club – Cultural Dance Show (AVZ)
Back cover Reclining Buddha, Isurumuniya Temple, Anuradhapura (AVZ), Leopard in the wild (EK/S)
Title page Jami Ul-Alfar (Red) Mosque, Pettah District, Colombo (AVZ), Traditional drummer, Full Moon Poya festival, Weligama (AVZ), Asian elephant (*Elephas maximus*), Udawalawe National Park (AVZ)
Part openers Boats in Bentota port (page 71; m50/S), Thuparama dagoba, Anuradhapura (page 209; e/S), Statue of god Shiva, Koneswaram Temple, Trincomalee (page 285; m/S), Sri Lanka blue magpie (*Urocissa ornata*) (page 365; f/S), Stilt fishermen, Koggala (page 485; PYS/S)

Maps David McCutcheon FBCart.S; relief map base by Nick Rowland FRGS

Typeset by Ian Spick, Bradt Travel Guides Ltd
Production managed by Jellyfish Print Solutions; printed in the UK
Digital conversion by www.dataworks.co.in

Acknowledgements

My thanks go out to the immense numbers of Sri Lankans and others who contributed to or supported the research and writing of this guide. Top of the list is my wife, Ariadne Van Zandbergen, who retained a sense of humour on those many days that turned into one long slog looking at hotel after restaurant after hotel. We were very fortunate to be allocated a succession of local drivers whose positive attitude, enthusiasm for and engagement with my work, not to mention willingness to work unusually long hours, made my task all the more easier and led to the inclusion of several places I might otherwise have missed – big thanks to Jeewa H Kumar, Manjula Prabath, Ananda Dissanayeka and Lakshman Ashoka, I hope you feel the end result justifies the hard work!

Our gratitude also extends in no particular order to the following: Emil van der Poorten, Lars Sorensen, Nathasha Abhayarathne, Manjula Susantha Kumara, Seraj Mohamed, Channa Perera, Melisha Yapa, Prasanna Welangoda, Jennie Harrison, Noel Rodrigo, Gomida Jayasinghe, Nevanka Fernando, Himali Wijesekara, Dilshan Soodin, Noel Jayasekera, Henri Tatham, Kevin Gray, Jonas Marainen, Michelle Fernando Weerasinghe, Mr Munas (Stardust Beach Hotel), Harsha Fernando, Prasanna (Mountain Heavens), Danushka (Elephant Stables), Karen Robertson, Hassan Refeek, Dirk (Ceylon Escapes), Sydney Wickramathilake, Ayanthi Samarajewa, Sandrine Debruyne, Devan de Mel, Sylvie Bobay, Oshaan Weerasekera, Ajith Rathnayake, Harshi Hewage, Milinda Samaranayake, Lakmal Perera, Dil and Leo (Kitesurfing Lanka), Jeanette Kangas, Champika De Silva, Roland Galka, Ravindra Wickramasekera, Pali (Sinharaja Rest), Karen Banister, Dilshan Gnanapragasam, Jonathan (Colombo Haven) and Charith Fernando.

I'm also very grateful to Gehan de Silva Wijeyeratne, author of Bradt's companion guide *Sri Lankan Wildlife*, for his generous provision of photos for the Natural World chapter.

Contents

LIST OF MAPS

HOW TO USE THIS GUIDE

AUTHOR'S FAVOURITES Finding genuinely characterful accommodation or that unmissable off-the-beaten-track café can be difficult, so the author has chosen a few of his favourite places throughout the country to point you in the right direction. These 'author's favourites' are marked with a ✳.

SIGHTS AND PLACES OF INTEREST
Entrance fees Unless otherwise stated, admission to the places of interest described in this guide is free.

Opening times The opening times given are daily, unless otherwise stated.

LISTINGS
🏠 **Where to stay** In this guide, meals included in the rate are indicated as B&B (bed & breakfast), HB (half-board, ie: dinner, bed and breakfast), or FB (full-board). Where none of these symbols appears, the rate quoted is room only. See also pages 51–3.

✖ **Where to eat and drink** Note that restaurant opening hours provided in this book are daily unless otherwise stated, though many places are closed or keep shorter hours on poya days, and very few serve alcohol as it is illegal. See also pages 53–5.

MAPS
Keys and symbols Maps include alphabetical keys covering the locations of those places to stay, eat or drink that are featured in the book. Note that regional maps may not show all hotels and restaurants in the area: other establishments may be located in towns shown on the map.

On occasion, hotels or restaurants that are not listed in the guide (but which might serve as alternative options if required or serve as useful landmarks to aid navigation) are also included on the maps; these are marked with accommodation (🏠) or restaurant (✖) symbols.

Grids and grid references Several maps use gridlines to allow easy location of sites. Map grid references are listed in square brackets after the name of the place or site of interest in the text, with page number followed by grid number, eg: [103 C3].

FOLLOW BRADT

For the latest news, special offers and competitions, subscribe to the Bradt newsletter via the website **w** bradtguides.com and follow Bradt on:

f BradtTravelGuides
🐦 @BradtGuides
📷 @bradtguides
𝒫 bradtguides

Introduction

Sri Lanka is a fantastic all-round travel destination. Most people know about the sumptuous surf-lapped palm-lined beaches that line the island's long tropical Indian Ocean coastline. But the small Asian country formerly known as Ceylon – extending over an area comparable to the Republic of Ireland – has so much more to offer curious travellers than a stock beach holiday.

There are the ancient Sinhalese capitals of Anuradhapura and Polonnaruwa, where handsome domed dagobas, the tallest of which were built in pre-Christian times on a scale to rival the Egyptian pyramids, tower over jungle-bound monastic ruins adorned with centuries-old Buddhist statues and engravings. There are exquisitely painted cave temples at Dambulla and Budugehinna, towering stone Buddha engravings at Avukana and Buduruvagala, and magnificent boulder-top royal citadels at Sigiriya and Yapahuwa. The pretty inland city of Kandy, the most recent of Sri Lanka's dozen or so erstwhile royal capitals, is renowned for its Temple of the Tooth, which stands as a living symbol of the island's 2,400 years of Buddhist history. Contemporaneous with Kandy, yet contrasting with it in almost every respect, is the port city of Galle, a former colonial trade entrepôt – possessed in turn by the Portuguese, the Dutch and the British – whose characterful old town is protected within the largest and best-preserved of the country's time-warped European-built fortresses.

This impressive collection of cultural gems – many inscribed as UNESCO World Heritage Sites – contrasts with some lovely scenery and great wildlife viewing. The Hill Country running south from Kandy supports a cover of neat tea plantations interspersed misty moorlands and dense rainforests teeming with plants and animals found nowhere else in the world. An ever-growing network of national parks protects Asia's densest elephant and leopard populations, and an abundance of peacocks (often seen performing their spectacular fan-tailed mating dance on the roadside), as well as sloth bears, wild boars and plentiful deer and monkeys. The forests of Sri Lanka are home to 33 unique bird species, an alluring selection of endemics that includes the magnificent Sri Lanka blue magpie, several colourful parakeets and barbets, and the striking cockerel-like Sri Lanka junglefowl (the national bird). Meanwhile, the offshore waters support coral gardens swirling with colourful reef fish and giant marine turtles, as well as a great opportunity to see blue whales and spinner dolphins in their natural marine habitat.

When it comes to everyday practicalities, Sri Lanka stands among the most approachable and straightforward of Asian travel destinations. People are genuinely hospitable, English is spoken widely and to a high standard, and the relatively short distances and good road and rail network make it easy to get around, even on a limited budget. An ever-growing choice of accommodation caters to all tastes and budgets: traditional beach resorts with blasting air conditioning and eager young stewards to propel you towards the groaning buffet table, more exclusive boutique hotels with contemporary décor and fusion cuisine, and an abundance of cheap-'n'-cheerful guesthouses and homestays serving tasty homemade curries. Whether you prefer to take in the acknowledged sites or explore off the beaten track, whether your tastes veer towards beach holidays, wildlife viewing, cultural sightseeing or montane hikes, whether your priority is upmarket luxury, mid-range value for money, or affordability above all else, Sri Lanka has it all in abundance.

ATTENTION WILDLIFE ENTHUSIASTS

For more on wildlife in Sri Lanka, why not check out Bradt's *Sri Lankan Wildlife* by Gehan de Silva Wijeyeratne? Visit **w** bradtguides.com/shop for a 10% discount on all our titles.

FEEDBACK REQUEST AND UPDATES WEBSITE

Administered by author Philip Briggs, Bradt's *Sri Lanka* update website (**w** *bradtupdates.com/srilanka*) is an online forum where travellers can post and read the latest travel news, trip reports and factual updates from Sri Lanka. The website is a free service to readers, or to anybody else who cares to drop by, and travellers to Sri Lanka and people in the tourist industry are encouraged to use it share their comments, grumbles, insights, news or other feedback. These can be posted directly on the website, or emailed to Philip (**e** *philip.briggs@bradtguides.com*).

It's easy to keep up to date with the latest posts by following Philip on Twitter (**🐦** *@philipbriggs*) and/or liking his Facebook page (**f** *fb.me/ pb.travel.updates*).

You can also add a review of the book to **w** bradtguides.com or Amazon.

SEND US YOUR SNAPS!

We'd love to follow your adventures using our *Sri Lanka* guide – why not send us your photos and stories via Twitter (*@BradtGuides*) and Instagram (*@bradtguides*) using the hashtag #srilanka? Alternatively, you can upload your photos directly to the gallery on the Sri Lanka destination page via our website (**w** *bradtguides.com/srilanka*).

Part One

GENERAL INFORMATION

SRI LANKA AT A GLANCE

Country The Democratic Socialist Republic of Sri Lanka, formerly Ceylon. It became Sri Lanka – and a republic – in 1972, with the addition of 'Sri', meaning 'resplendent', to an ancient name for the island, 'Lanka'.

Location An island off the southern tip of India, 880km north of the Equator; latitude 5°55' to 9°50'N, longitude 70°42' to 81°52'E

Area 65,525km² (25,299 square miles)

Topography Flat on the coastal areas and northern half of the island with the central and south-central areas being hilly and mountainous

Climate Tropical in lowlands with average temperatures of 27°C. Cooler in hills with average of 16°C. Monsoon in southwest May–July; in northeast, December–January.

Capital The official administrative capital is Sri Jayawardenepura Kotte, an otherwise rather obscure satellite of the commercial capital and largest city, Colombo

Government The directly elected president serves as head of state, commander-in-chief of the armed forces, and head of the cabinet of ministers drawn from a parliament of 225 elected members

Population 21 million (2017 estimate), of whom 74.9% are Sinhalese, 11.2% Sri Lankan Tamil, 4.2% Indian Tamil, 9.2% Moors, with the balance being Malays, Burghers (descendants of Dutch colonists) and others

Population distribution Urban 21.5%, rural 72.2%, estate 6.3%

Literacy rate 92.6%

Life expectancy at birth Males 71 years; females 78 years

Economy Main foreign-exchange earners: emigrants' remittances, tea, tourism (more than 2 million visitors in 2016) and locally manufactured garment exports

Gross domestic product (GDP) US$80 billion

Average per capita income US$1,100 per annum

Languages Official languages are Sinhala (spoken by 74% of the population) and Tamil (18%). English as the official link language

Religion Theravada Buddhist 70.2%, Hindu 12.6%, Muslim 9.7%, Christian 7.4%

Currency Sri Lankan rupee (Rs)

Rate of exchange £1 = Rs200, US$1 = Rs154, €1 = Rs179 (November 2017)

International dialling code +94

Time GMT +5 hours 30 minutes

Electricity 230 volts AC

Weights and measures Metric

Flag Two equal stripes of green and yellow alongside the Lion Flag of King Sri Vikrama Rajasinha

Public holidays See pages 55–8

1

History and Background

HISTORY   *By Royston Ellis, updated by Philip Briggs*

EARLY HISTORY It is probable that Sri Lanka was inhabited 500,000 years ago. Since it was a lush and fertile island of forests, plains and animals, with rivers abundant with fish, it would have been an attractive place for wandering prehistoric man to settle. The domestication of plants, broadening the food supply of hunting people, may have occurred some 12,000 years ago.

If Southeast Asia was the cradle of human civilisation, Sri Lanka would have benefited from the development of agriculture, pottery making and the fashioning of stone tools introduced by seafarers from neighbouring archipelagos such as the Philippines and Indonesia. Archaeological evidence suggests that reclusive Stone Age hunter-gather societies survived in the island's unexplored jungles up to 1,000 years ago. Today the Veddas (see box, page 7) are regarded as a living link with the original inhabitants.

Sri Lanka's recorded history began 2,500 years ago. There exist texts, begun 1,500 years ago by Buddhist monks, called the *Mahavamsa* and its sequel, the *Culavamsa*, containing details of a rich and colourful past. The *Mahavamsa* confidently determines the coming of the Sinhalese race with the arrival of Vijaya, 1,000 years earlier.

Sri Lanka was actively involved in trading with other countries long before the birth of Christ, and was regarded as an island of great bounty. For traders, the island was regarded as the granary of Asia. Greek merchants came during the time of Alexander the Great (r335–323BC) to trade in precious stones, muslin and tortoise shells, and the island was known as a source of ivory as well as rice. Buddhism was introduced to the island 250 years before the birth of Christ, a century after the foundation of Anuradhapura, which flourished as capital for 14 centuries until 1017.

Anuradhapura was overrun by the Chola army, which had conquered southern India under Raja-Raja the Great (r985–1014). This resulted in the setting up of a new power base, with Polonnaruwa as the centre of the kingdom. Conquest of the Cholas eventually came under forces led by Vijayabahu I (r1055–1110), who restored Buddhism to prominence after the Cholas' Hinduism.

Vijayabahu I's nephew, Parakramabahu I (r1153–86), is remembered not only for unifying the island but also for his splendid buildings (now in ruins at Polonnaruwa) and his irrigation work. His death led to dynastic disputes, and gradually the island fractured. There were five different capitals from 1253 to 1400. Eventually a new kingdom grew from a power base at Sri Jayawardenepura Kotte, which is where the modern parliament of Sri Lanka is located, on the outskirts of Colombo. With the death of Parakramabahu VI (r1412–67) there was a scramble for control that was diverted by the arrival in 1505 of the Portuguese.

PORTUGUESE, DUTCH AND BRITISH ERAS Whether it was due to a premonition about the impact of foreign rule, or simple caution, the King of Kotte led the first of the Portuguese invaders a merry dance. Hearing reports of these strange people who were dressed in iron clothes (armour), appeared to eat stones (bread), drank from bottles of blood (wine) and had sticks that cracked like thunder and lightning (firearms), the king must have been desperate to delay any encounter with them. He directed the strangers be brought to him by a roundabout route so they would not realise how close (13km) and vulnerable to attack his kingdom was from the harbour at Colombo. The ruse did not work since the noise of cannons fired from the ship, and the seamen's knowledge of navigation, let the reconnoitring party know its position. To this day, the Sri Lankan expression for 'taking people for a ride' is 'like taking the Portuguese to Kotte'.

At the time, the Portuguese were interested only in trade, wanting to take over the shipment of camphor, sapphires, elephants and cinnamon controlled by the King of Kotte. That might have been the end of Portuguese involvement but for internal dissensions among the Sinhalese. The rulers of Kotte hoped to take advantage of the presence of the Portuguese, so they allowed them to settle and build strategic forts along the coast. This resulted in the Portuguese entrenchment throughout the island, with the notable exception of the inland Kingdom of Kandy. In 1617, the Kandyan king agreed to a treaty with the Portuguese, but this led to Portuguese incursions into the Kandyan ports of Batticaloa and Trincomalee. Then King Rajasinha II (r1635–87) formed an alliance with the Dutch against the Portuguese.

The Dutch were powerful in the region through their pursuit of the spice trade in the East Indies. They were not slow to take advantage of the promise of a monopoly of the island's spice trade in return for help in ridding the island of the Portuguese. They took Batticaloa and Trincomalee for the Kingdom of Kandy, but kept the ports of Galle and Negombo, which they captured in 1641, for themselves. In 1656 they took over the fort in Colombo from the Portuguese and, with the capture of Jaffna in 1658, brought the Portuguese occupation to an end. The Dutch, to the dismay of the Kandyan monarchy, were not keen to leave Sri Lanka and contrived to stay for 138 years.

A breach between the Dutch and the British during the Napoleonic Wars resulted in the annexation of Dutch settlements in the East by Great Britain. The first phase of British takeover began with a siege of Colombo in 1796. The Dutch surrendered and ceded their other possessions in Ceylon to Britain. However, the Kingdom of Kandy atop the Central Highlands defied British attempts to tidy up the country into a neat package they could call their own.

The British tried, and failed disastrously, to conquer the kingdom by military means in 1803. Diplomacy and duplicity were then employed as weapons to connive with disaffected Kandyan chiefs and enable the British to take the kingdom. King Vikrama Rajasinha, the last monarch of Kandy (1798–1815), was bundled off to India and a convention was signed between British rulers and the Kandyan chiefs.

Having a convention did not mean the British had Kandy, and resistance was marshalled into organised rebellion in 1817–18. The British retaliated ruthlessly and at last the administration was set on a neat and tidy course of government. For the first time since the kingdoms of Parakramabahu I (r1153–86) and Nissanka Malla (r1187–96), Sri Lanka was governed in its entirety by one power.

Having conquered the island, the British energetically set about colonising it. It became a plantation economy, first with coffee and then tea, with young Britons (many from Scotland) emigrating to open up the countryside to tea plantations. The first 100 years of the colonial era went by without any major traumatic local crises, and fostered the emergence of a new indigenous aristocracy through involvement in capitalist enterprises.

TOWARDS INDEPENDENCE The first harbinger of change came in 1915, the centenary of the fall of Kandy, with riots that stemmed from the development of radical movements of protest. Moderate attitudes were developing too and the Ceylon National Congress, a political party of a conservative nature, was founded in 1919. Under the leadership of Don Stephen Senanayake the Congress lobbied steadily for constitutional reforms. The British complied by granting a system of territorial representation as an initial measure for internal self-rule. In addition, the British introduced universal adult suffrage, with every Sri Lankan over the age of 21, male or female, entitled to vote. This was the first time that such suffrage was permitted in a British colony, and came only two years after Britons themselves achieved it.

With all over-21s in Sri Lanka entitled to vote, a new freedom of expression and responsibility was in the air. Buddhist nationalism emerged, as did some working-class movements. The British hoped for a gradual transition to independence in a manner that would not antagonise those who were not part of the Sinhalese Buddhist dominance. In 1944, a new constitution was proposed by Senanayake that was intended to guarantee the state's religious neutrality. A commission led by Lord Soulbury arrived at a similar conclusion and espoused internal self-government. However, popular feeling was for complete independence and this was granted, so avoiding the traumas experienced by India. The British presence remained until 4 February 1948, when the Duke of Gloucester, representing King George VI, ceremonially conferred independence on Ceylon.

Senanayake, as leader of the United National Party (UNP), formed a coalition government with members of independent groups, to become the first prime minister of independent Ceylon, after 152 years of British rule. The country became a member of the Commonwealth of Nations and, in 1955, a member of the United Nations. In 1956, Mr S W R D Bandaranaike, leader of the opposition Mahajana Eksath Peramuna (MEP) party, became prime minister after a general election. He pursued a nationalisation programme, forming state monopolies, but was assassinated in 1959. His widow, Mrs Sirimavo Bandaranaike, as leader of the Sri Lanka Freedom Party, became prime minister in 1960, the first woman in the world to hold such a post. She continued the policy of nationalisation until an election defeat in 1965, but was returned to power in 1970.

THE MODERN ERA The Republic of Sri Lanka came into existence on 22 May 1972 following the adoption of a new constitution ending Ceylon's dominion status. At the same time, Buddhism was made the official religion, catalysing the Tamil-speaking Hindu minority's long-held resentment at Sinhala having been made the country's only official language back in 1956. It also led to the emergence of the Liberation Tigers of Tamil Eelam (LTTE), a militant secessionist organisation, popularly known as the Tamil Tigers, which advocated the creation of a self-determining Tamil state extending over much of the island's northeast.

The 1977 general election resulted in the UNP gaining power under J R Jayewardene, who subsequently amended the constitution and became the first executive president of the Democratic Socialist Republic of Sri Lanka. In July 1983 the LTTE killed 13 government security personnel, which led to ethnic clashes in Colombo, Jaffna and several other cities, and is regarded as the date Sri Lanka's sweet future turned sour. Despite attempts at both conquest and peace, the LTTE actively survived with a culture of assassinations and bombings. In 1988, Ranasinghe Premadasa was elected as president while his party, the UNP, won the general election held a year later. In 1993, President Premadasa was assassinated by an LTTE suicide bomber at a May Day rally in Colombo.

In 1994, the People's Alliance (PA) won the general election and formed the government under the leadership of Mrs Chandrika Bandaranaike Kumaratunga, daughter of two prime ministers and who herself became prime minister. She was elected as president in 1995 and was re-elected in 1999. Her party won a slim majority at the general election the next year, losing its majority by the crossing over to the opposition of some members of one of her coalition parties in June 2001. In the same year, the LTTE struck one of its most dramatic blows with a bomb attack that claimed 14 lives and resulted in the destruction of 11 military and civilian aircraft at Bandaranaike International Airport.

The general election held in December 2001 resulted in a win for the UNP and its allies, who had previously been the opposition, and Ranil Wickremesinghe, a former prime minister and nephew of J R Jayewardene, became prime minister. He immediately set up negotiations to achieve a political solution to end the terrorism initiated by the LTTE.

As a result of the new government's efforts a formal truce was signed in February 2002. Gradually tensions eased, roadblocks were removed and life throughout the country returned almost to normal. Foreign investment and tourism picked up. However, having a president (and cabinet head) from one side of the great political divide and a government from the other eventually resulted in a showdown, with President Kumaratunga dissolving parliament and new elections being held in April 2004.

Although the president's party and its Janathā Vimukthi Peramuṇa (JVP; Marxist) allies did not win an outright majority, they were able to form a government while the UNP and allies formed the opposition, headed by Ranil Wickremesinghe. A presidential election held in November 2005 resulted in victory over Wickremesinghe for then prime minister Mahinda Rajapaksa. Rajapaksa's party and its allies went on to form the new government in February 2007, having, with more than 50 ministers, the world's largest cabinet. With members of the opposition joining the government as ministers, and government MPs joining the opposition, party politics continued to be a nebulous affair into 2008.

An increase in terrorist activity in 2007 brought about the reintroduction of vigorous security checks at police and military roadblocks throughout the country, especially in Colombo. The formal ceasefire agreement (which had by then collapsed) was abrogated by the government in January 2008 and military action against the LTTE was intensified. Random bombing, said to be by LTTE terrorists, took place in the southeastern interior of the country, as well as in Colombo and its suburbs.

A surge in the military effort under General Sarath Fonseka and government determination resulted in the annihilation of the LTTE militarily in 2009. This was followed by a presidential election in which Mahinda Rajapaksa was returned to power, beating the opposition candidate, General (by then retired) Fonseka. Rajapaksa's party and allies won the subsequent general election while Fonseka was court-martialled, stripped of his rank and jailed. He was released in 2012. The most recent presidential election, held in January 2015, resulted in the defeat of Rajapaksa, a confident incumbent running for his third term of office, by the unfancied Maithripala Sirisena, a former Minister of Health fielded by a UNP-led opposition coalition. This shock victory was generally seen as a reaction to a culture of rampant corruption and nepotism that took hold under the Rajapaksa administration. The country's sixth executive presidency has started promisingly enough, with Sirisena having voluntarily transferred significant presidential powers to parliament, committed to a reformist programme aimed at reducing

VEDDAS   *Royston Ellis*

The Veddas (literally 'hunters') are the aboriginals of Sri Lanka. They survive in defiance of government attempts to assimilate them, and tourists' attempts to patronise them. Their culture has been affected by the interest of tourists who sometimes turn up at their settlements in coachloads to gaze at – and be photographed with – near-naked men armed with axes and bows. Naturally, this involves a reward of money (or even alcohol) with its corresponding effect. Instead of relying on the jungle that they once considered their home – and to which access is often restricted – many have become virtual performance artists to satisfy the local and foreign tourists. There are thought to be only a few hundred Veddas left, although their community comprises a few thousand families as many have become mixed through marriage with Sinhalese. While the Veddas and their close-to-nature lifestyle may seem fascinating to us, it is probably better to leave them in peace than make a sport of visiting them.

corruption and repealing a controversial Rajapaksa-era constitutional amendment that allowed a president to seek re-election an unlimited number of times, and pledging to serve only one six-year term himself.

GOVERNMENT AND POLITICS

The executive is headed up by the president, who serves as both head of state and commander-in-chief of the armed forces, and is directly elected by the people at a presidential election held every five years The president is responsible to parliament and is a member and head of the cabinet of ministers. Parliament consists of 225 members elected every six years following a complicated system that includes majority winners, proportional representation winners and nominated members. The person who is most likely to command the confidence of parliament is appointed by the president as prime minister. The chief justice, who is appointed by the president, heads the judiciary.

ECONOMY

The country is primarily agricultural, with the chief crop being rice, in which it is almost self-sufficient. However, the national income is based mainly on the non-agricultural sectors, for instance the manufacture and export of garments, on remittances from Sri Lankans working overseas, on the production and export of tea, and on tourism. The emphasis in recent years has been to diversify the economy by increasing the export of manufactured goods and exporting agricultural commodities in processed forms.

The main export markets for goods from Sri Lanka are the USA, the UK and Japan. (The main source countries for imports are Japan, India and China.) Sri Lanka is the world's largest exporter of black tea. Other agricultural exports include: areca nuts (betel nuts), baby corn, baby okra, betel leaf, cantaloupe melon, cardamom, cashew nuts, cinnamon, citronella oil, cloves, cocoa, coconut, coffee, cut flowers, decorative foliage plants, fresh fruits, fresh vegetables, gherkins, mace, mushrooms, nutmeg, oil of cinnamon bark and leaf, pepper, rice, rubber, sesame seeds and tobacco.

Tea was first grown in Ceylon in 1824 at the Peradeniya Royal Botanical Gardens when a few plants were brought from China. In 1867 (the year the railway reached Peradeniya), a Scottish planter, James Taylor, planted tea seedlings on 8ha of forest land which had been cleared for coffee growing. Taylor's foresight was remarkable because two years later a blight wiped out the country's coffee crop. The island's planters turned to tea and had 400ha flourishing by 1875. In 1965, Ceylon displaced India as the world's biggest tea exporter, and tea is still one of the major foreign-exchange earners for Sri Lanka. The large tea (and other) estates were nationalised in 1972, leaving individual owners with only 20ha. The process was reversed 20 years later and plantations were leased to management companies and the private sale of tea allowed (instead of exclusively through the weekly tea auction). The industry is going through a period of streamlining, with the result that more specialist (single estate, organic and green) teas are available.

Climate has a crucial effect on quality. The finest Ceylon teas are 'High Grown' in plantations set at 1,200m or higher in Uva District, and are produced mid year when the sweeping dry winds cause the leaves to take on their characteristic refreshing flavour. Teas from Nuwara Eliya and other western parts of Hill Country show their best quality in January and February after the northeast monsoon, when dry weather and cold nights predominate. Though Uva and Nuwara Eliya are close neighbours, the teas they produce have quite distinct flavours, illustrating how sensitive tea is to soil, environment and climate. Elsewhere, 'Low Grown' teas, grown below 600m at private estates in Matara, Galle and Ratnapura districts, are bought more for leaf appearance than taste, while 'Medium Grown' teas produce a rich, mellow-tasting brew with good colour.

Tea comes from the evergreen tree Chinese camellia (*Camellia sinensis*), which could grow 10m high if not pruned every two or three years to encourage the repeated growth of a 'flush' of fresh young shoots. These shoots, of two top leaves and a tender bud, are plucked every six to ten days. On arrival at the tea factory, the leaves are spread out in troughs until they lose their moisture and go limp, losing almost half their weight in the process. The withered leaves are fed into a rolling machine, which crushes their cell structure, releasing the natural juice and enzymes that give tea its flavour. The leaves emerge from the machine in twisted, sticky lumps. Oxidisation or fermentation then takes place in about 3 hours, changing the pulverised green leaf into a light, coppery shade through the absorption of oxygen. Firing (drying) in a hot-air chamber for about 20 minutes halts the 'fermentation', kills off any bacteria, dries the tea and preserves it, reducing the weight by another 50%.

The fired leaf is left to cool before being sifted. The main commercial leaf grades are Orange Pekoe (OP), Pekoe (Pek) and Flowery Pekoe (FP). Broken leaf grades are Broken Orange Pekoe (BOP), Broken Pekoe (BP), Fannings (F) and Dust (D). BOP grades are used in traditional packet blends, while Fannings and Dust find their way into tea bags. CTC tea, so called because the leaf is cut, torn and curled by machine instead of rolled, is also produced in Sri Lanka as tea-bag-quality tea. Tea is then auctioned in Colombo to traders who buy different grades and qualities for export and blending (though it is now possible to buy pure unblended estate teas in shops in Colombo and elsewhere).

Industrial products that are exported include aviation and marine fuels, canned fruit, cement, ceramic ware, chemicals, computer software, cosmetic accessories, dairy products, diamonds (re-exported cut and polished), electric and electronic appliances, fertiliser, footwear, fruit juices, furniture, garments, gloves, handicrafts, industrial pumps, jewellery, leather goods, machinery, paper, paper products, petrol, pharmaceuticals, plywood, porcelain figurine ornaments, PVC pipes, refrigerators, rubber goods, silk flowers, steel, sugar, textiles (cotton/synthetic), toys/sports requisites, tyres, water purification units, wooden products and yarns (cotton/synthetic).

Also exported are gems and minerals, timber (ebony, mahogany, satinwood and teak), and marine products such as aquarium fish, bêche-de-mer, crab, fish maws, lobsters, prawns, seashells, shark fin and shrimps.

Sri Lanka supplies the export services of bunkering, cargo transhipment, computer data entry, computer software development, construction/consultancy, entrepôt trade, lapidary, manpower, printing, ship chandlery, ship registry, ship repair/maintenance and tourism.

The **Colombo Stock Exchange** (w *cse.lk*) is the country's sole stock exchange. There are no taxes imposed on share transactions, except for a 15% withholding tax on dividends for non-residents.

NATIONAL FLAG

The national flag of Sri Lanka has an ancient link. To the design of the Lion Flag of Sri Vikrama Rajasinha, the last King of Kandy, which was taken to Britain in 1815, were added two stripes, one green and the other yellow, to form the national flag. Each of these stripes is equal to one-seventh of the size of the flag.

When Sri Lanka became a republic in 1972, the traditional Bo leaves depicted on the national flag were changed to resemble natural Bo leaves. This version of the flag was first unfurled at the Republic Day celebration held on 22 May 1972. The flag continues in use today, its design incorporated in the constitution.

PEOPLE

The official census of 2012 recorded 20.36 million people spread over nine provinces with the Western Province being the most populated (5.8 million) and the Northern Province the least (just over one million). The annual growth rate is roughly 1% so the population now probably stands at around 21 million. The majority (74.9%) are Sinhalese, with 11.2% Sri Lankan Tamils and 4.2% Indian Tamils. The majority of the remainder (9.2%) are Moors, being descendants of Arab settlers. There are also Sri Lankans of Malaysian, Chinese, Dutch (the Burghers) and distant Portuguese ancestry, plus a few Eurasians and some small Indian communities such as Parsis. The Veddas were originally a forest-dwelling aboriginal group, now numbering a few hundred since most have intermarried with Sinhalese. The Sinhalese are of Aryan stock while the Tamils are Dravidian. There is no easy visible way for a visitor to distinguish between a Sinhalese and a Tamil. For visitors, all are Sri Lankan.

LANGUAGE

Sinhala, a language in the same Indo-Aryan family as Hindi, is the first tongue of around 80% of the island's population. The language is unique to Sri Lanka and has its own alphabet derived from an ancient Brahmi script related to the obsolete Kadamba alphabet used to write Sanskrit (the primary liturgical language of Hindu). Sri Lanka's main minority tongue, most widely used in the north and east of the island, is Tamil, which belongs to the Dravidian family along with most other languages associated with southern India. The constitution now designates Sinhala and Tamil as the official languages and English as the link language. English is becoming more widely spoken, after a lull when it was not used as a medium of education; it is the main language of the mercantile sector and the hospitality industry. Place names and signboards are usually in English and Sinhala or English and Tamil; sometimes all three.

RELIGION

The majority religion on Sri Lanka, Buddhism is practised by roughly 70% of the population. Buddhism arrived on the island around 2,300 years ago, during the reign of King Devanampiya Tissa, and it evidently gave birth to a cultural revolution. In the wake of this cultural revolution came an era of unsurpassed achievement. Buddhism fashioned lifestyles, fostered the arts and inspired the creation of dagobas, temples, monasteries, statues, and vast manmade reservoirs and irrigation systems. Even 23 centuries after its arrival on the island, Buddhism is still preserved in its purest Theravada form on Sri Lanka, based on the *Tripitaka* or Pali canon, which was first transcribed, based on 500-year-old orally transmitted teachings, at Aluvihara Cave north of Kandy in 29BC, during the reign of Kutakanna Tissa.

Buddhism was founded by the Gautama Buddha, who was born Prince Siddhartha c624BC. A member of a noble North Indian family, Siddhartha was married and had a son, but decided to renounce his life of ease and luxury out of compassion for human suffering. He took up a life of self-denial and, at the age of 35, on the full-moon day of Vesak, seated under a Bodhi-tree at Bodh-Gaya (in India), he realised the Ultimate Truth. He became known thereafter as the Buddha, the Enlightened or Awakened One, and began to teach the Dharma (truth) to the world.

Buddha taught that a human being is constantly reborn into the world as a result of desire, and this is the root cause of suffering. The cycle can only be broken when one reaches nirvana or the State of Supreme Enlightenment. The Noble Eightfold Path of right belief, right aims, right speech, right action, right means of livelihood, right effort, right concentration and right meditation is the way to deliverance.

If a Buddhist renounces his home, his family and the world, he can join the Sangha (the order of monks). There is an equivalent order for women. Traditionally a monk should own only eight items of property, earn his living through donations, and follow the rules of the order rigorously. In Sri Lanka there are days that are special to Buddhists, and important events are started at auspicious times as determined by a monk. Since Buddhism rejects the notion of a personal god, it is often asked whether it should be treated as a religion or philosophy. The best answer is probably that it is both. On the one hand, the principles of Buddhism blend into a way of life with an ideal (nirvana) that is attainable without establishing a relationship with a divine being. Equally, however, Buddhists in Sri Lanka are generally deeply 'religious', often slavishly following rituals and beliefs in their devotion to the Buddha, not as a god, but as a supremely enlightened being who shows them the way to the ideal.

The second most important religion in Sri Lanka is Hinduism, which is practised by around 12.5% of the population, mostly among the Tamils of the north and east. Hinduism actually has a longer historical pedigree in Sri Lanka than Buddhism, having been the dominant religion of Anuradhapura and earlier kingdoms prior to the 3rd-century BC conversion of Devanampiya Tissa. Even since then, Hindu has re-emerged as the dominant state religion at several points in the island's history, for instance during the early days of Polonnaruwa, which was founded by Chola invaders from South India. As a result, Sri Lankan Buddhism and Hinduism possess an unusually syncretic relationship epitomised by their mutual worship of the island's guardian deity, Kataragama/Skanda, and the frequent depiction of Hindu deities such as Vishnu and Shiva in many Buddhist temples. Despite this, the contemporary Hindu presence on Sri Lanka is linked to two relatively recent migrations from South India, the first associated with the foundation of the Jaffna Kingdom in the early 13th century and the second with the importation of Tamil tea plantation workers during the British colonial period.

The next most numerically significant minority religion is Islam, which accounts for 9.7% of the population, most of them so-called Moors descended from Arab traders who settled on the island between the 6th century and the arrival of the Portuguese in the 16th century. In Sri Lanka, Muslims are mainly concentrated along the east coast, in the vicinity of Trincomalee, Batticaloa and Arugam Bay, but some west- and north-coast settlements also have a strong Islamic presence.

Christianity is practised by roughly 7.5% of the population. Of these, 6.1% are Roman Catholics whose forefathers were converted during the Portuguese occupation, and the remaining 1.3% are Anglican or Protestant, relics of a short-lived Dutch and British influence reversed in the 19th century by a swell of Buddhist revivalism. The main stronghold of Christianity in Sri Lanka is Negombo, on the west coast a short distance north of Colombo, but there are also significant Catholic strongholds elsewhere on the west coast.

EDUCATION

Education is important in Sri Lanka, and it is said to have begun informally in Buddhist *pirivenas* (schools attached to temples) centuries before the birth of Christ and eventually formalised by the British until independence. Now it's overseen by a Ministry of Education and one of Higher Education. The proud boast that the literacy rate is around 92% does not take into account that this would be in Sinhala or Tamil and not in English, although some schools do teach through the medium of English.

Education is free at government schools and there are also fee-charging kindergarten and 'international' schools. Primary education lasts for five to six years, after which children proceed to the junior secondary level for four years, followed by two years in preparation for the General Certificate of Education exams at Ordinary Level. At 16, children can leave school or stay on to study for Advanced Level.

Top students in the A-level examinations can apply to proceed to undergraduate education in one of the country's 15 state universities.

CULTURE

The mixed heritage of today's Sri Lanka results in a varied and vibrant culture, combining influences from Buddhist, Hindu and Islamic cultures, as well as colonial lifestyles. There is a thriving artistic tradition in painting, music, dance and theatre and, perhaps surprisingly, architecture. The varied building styles are easily visible on any drive through the country and add diversity to the city, suburban, coastal, agricultural and forest landscapes.

Individual Sri Lankans, whatever cultural background has influenced them, appear dedicated and determined, while preserving a somewhat orthodox outlook on life. Agriculture is regarded as a respected profession and many Sri Lankans are lifelong vegetarians or decline to eat a particular meat because of individual belief. Cricket is followed religiously. Sri Lankan culture is enhanced by frequent rest days either for religious or government-decreed holidays.

SRI LANKAN CRICKET   *Adrian Phillips, updated by Philip Briggs*

In Sri Lanka, cricket is embraced with a rare intensity. When the national team is playing, the whole island is enthralled; when it isn't, flat pieces of wasteland are dotted with children immersed in fiercely competitive games using any equipment which comes to hand. Successful players attract adulation, and significant victories are met with lively celebration and dancing in the streets. If you visit during the cricket season (January and April), take the opportunity to watch a live match in Colombo, Kandy, Galle or elsewhere, and experience the colourful atmosphere for yourself.

Sri Lankans' unfettered passion for cricket belies its roots in the more refined and stolid English version of the game. You are unlikely to come across stands full of trilbied spectators wrapping themselves around salmon and champagne. Nevertheless, England has played a conspicuous role in many defining moments in Sri Lanka's cricketing history. The sport was introduced by British officers in 1832, and it was against the team of an Englishman, G F Vernon, that the All Ceylon Eleven competed in their first 'unofficial Test' at Kandy in 1889. England were also the opponents when finally Sri Lanka contested their first official test match in 1982. It was several years before the newcomers won a test match (against India in 1985). But in 1996 they emphatically, gloriously, announced themselves as a force on the world stage by winning the ODI World Cup Final in Lahore. More recent milestones include being Joint Winners of the 2002 ICC ODI Champions Trophy, Winners of the 2014 ICC Twenty20 World Cup, and a historic 3–0 Test whitewash of Australia (then ranked the world No. 1 team) in 2016.

Sri Lanka not only play with an extravagance ideally suited to the one-day game, but have had some truly outstanding players. In the island's early days as a Test-playing nation, the courageous Anura Tennekoon, elegant Aravinda de Silva and nonchalant Arjuna Ranatunga all brought lustre and swagger to the team. Later players do not suffer by comparison. The beguiling off-spinner Muttiah Muralitharan retired in 2010 as the bowler with the highest number of career Test wickets of any player in the game's history (his tally of 800 easily surpassing the closest contenders, Australian Shane Warne and Indian Anil Kumble, with 708 and 619 respectively). More recently, batsmen Kumar Sangakkara and Mahela Jayawardene, whose careers spanned 2000–15 and 1997–2014 respectively, retired with career tallies of 12,400 and 11,814 Test runs, placing them fifth and eighth on the all-time list.

Despite this, the path has not always been smooth for Sri Lankan cricket. Its board has been dogged by accusations of financial mismanagement. Muralitharan was at one point branded a cheat and a 'javelin thrower' by some for his unorthodox bowling action. In more recent times, the retirement of Sangakkara and Jayawardene initiated a major slump in the national team's form and ranking in all three formats of the game. Yet one senses that the spirit with which the islanders approach the game will prevail in the face of such difficulties. It is just this spirit – this combination of flair and grit, commitment and pleasure – which has made the Sri Lankan team so popular abroad, as well as at home.

2

The Natural World

For more on wildlife in Sri Lanka, check out Bradt's Sri Lankan Wildlife, *by Gehan de Silva Wijeyeratne. Get 10% off at* **w** *bradtguides.com/shop.*

GEOGRAPHY AND CLIMATE

Extending over 65,525km², Sri Lanka is a large island but a relatively small country, roughly the same size as the Republic of Ireland, Lithuania, or the US state of Florida. Its length from north to south is 435km, and its greatest width is 240km. In prehistoric times the island was contiguous with mainland Asia and even today the 48km-wide Palk Strait that separates it from India is so shallow that ocean-going vessels cannot pass through it. Most of the island is low-lying and flat, and 90% of its surface comprises ancient Precambrian gneiss, quartzite and other strata that formed up to two billion years ago. It is geologically stable and seldom experiences earthquakes or other volcanic events because it sits at the centre of the Deccan tectonic plate.

The mountainous south-central highlands of Sri Lanka incorporates nine peaks that rise to above 2,133m (7,000ft), the tallest being the 2,524m Pidurutalagala (also known as Mount Pedro) overlooking Nuwara Eliya, and the best known the 2,243m Sri Pada (Adam's Peak). Of the many rivers, the longest is the Mahaweli Ganga at 335km, double the length of the next longest, the Aruyi Aru at 164km. The island has about 100 waterfalls, of which the highest is Bambarakanda at 263m, followed by Diyaluma at 220m and Kurundu Oya at 206m. Sri Lanka has 113 islands dotted around its coast. An unusual hydrological feature of Sri Lanka is the presence of

Horton Plains National Park

hundreds of artificial lakes, known locally as a tank or *wewa*, that were constructed for irrigation purposes by the Sinhalese kings of ancient Anuradhapura and Polonnaruwa. Many of these tanks date back more than 2,000 years and most have since been maintained, sometimes consistently, sometimes more sporadically, to survive largely unchanged into the 21st century.

In common with most low-lying tropical countries, Sri Lanka is typically hot and humid throughout the year, so seasons are vaguely defined and there is no winter. Daylight hours are almost regular in duration throughout the year, the difference in Colombo being only 48 minutes between 22 June and 22 December. The average annual rainfall varies from about 1,000mm over a small region in the arid northwest to over 5,000mm at a few places in the highlands. Climatically, the island can be divided into three broad zones, influenced by the prevailing monsoon and altitude. The northern half of the country and much of the southeast comprise the low dry zone, which is the hottest part of the country and displays a strong seasonal rainfall pattern, with Jaffna and the far north usually experiencing dry conditions from February to September and the east coast and north-central interior from May to August. Much of the southwest, including Colombo, Galle, Sinharaja Forest and popular resorts such as Bentota and Hikkaduwa, fall into the low wet zone, which has a more solid year-round rainfall pattern, though December–March is relatively dry. Finally, there's the high wet zone comprising the Hill Country around Kandy, Nuwara Eliya and Ella, which is relatively temperate owing to its altitude, and is pretty wet all year round, dipping somewhat over January–March. For climate charts and details of when to visit, see pages 38–9.

NATURAL HISTORY AND CONSERVATION

A few hundred years ago, almost the entire island was covered by natural forest complemented by an abundance of flora and fauna common to a tropical monsoon climate. Unfortunately, very little thought was given to conservation by

Kangaroo lizard

Grey-headed fish eagle

Pitcher plant

the pioneers of the plantation development of the country. As a result, total forest cover today comprises less than 30% of the island's area. This includes around 15,800km^2 of closed-canopy or dense natural forest, and 4,500km^2 of sparser forest cover. Despite this, Sri Lanka is one of the most world's most biodiverse eco-travel destinations, with at least 242 butterfly, 450 bird, 120 mammal, 107 freshwater fish, 120 amphibian and 200 reptile species recorded. In addition, 830 flowering plant species are endemic to the island, including 230 so rare that they are in danger of extinction.

Sri Lanka has designated 13% of its land area to a network of more than 100 conservation areas, a remarkable proportion for a country with a relatively high population density. This figure includes 26 national parks, almost half of which have been gazetted since the turn of the millennium. Several of these national parks – notably Wilpattu, Yala, Udawalawe, Gal Oya, Minneriya and Kaudulla – protect savannah and woodland habitats inhabited by elephants, leopards, sloth bears and other large mammals. Others protect more specialised habitats: hiker-friendly Horton Plains comprises a vast tract of misty highland moors and forests on the southwest escarpment, Pigeon Island and Hikkaduwa both protect coral reefs teeming with marine life, while Galway's Land in Nuwara Eliya is a tiny suburban island of montane forest famed for its birdlife. Of the other nature reserves and sanctuaries, the most important in terms of global biodiversity is undoubtedly Sinharaja Forest Reserve, which protects the country's largest extant tract of wet-zone rainforest, and forms the zoological showpiece of the southwestern lowlands, where more than 90% of the island's endemic species are concentrated in a 15,000km^2 region that ranks as the richest not merely in Sri Lanka but in all of south Asia.

Outside of formal reserves, the strong conservation ethic inherent to Buddhism and large number of wetland habitats mean that wildlife remains prolific, and birds in particular are a ubiquitous feature of Sri Lanka's non-urban landscapes. Wild peacocks strut splendidly around suburban lanes; outsized monitor lizards

Tailed jay

crash through riverine undergrowth; paddy fields support a proliferation of egrets, herons, spoonbills and other wading birds; marine turtles and dolphins cavort in offshore waters; hotel gardens are alive with colourful bee-eaters, parakeets, kingfishers and barbets; and there are still parts of the country where elephants perambulate on the roadside as they migrate between conservation areas.

Rhododendron

The text that follows makes regular reference to the Red Data List maintained by the International Union for Conservation of Nature and Natural Resources (IUCN; w *iucnredlist.org*). This classifies species according to their perceived level of threat as Extinct, Extinct in the Wild, Critically Endangered, Endangered, Vulnerable, Not Threatened, and Least Concern.

Asian elephant

MAMMALS Sri Lanka is home to around 120 indigenous mammal species, of which 92 can be classified as terrestrial – a list dominated by bats, rodents and other small creatures – and the remainder as marine. The island provides an important stronghold for several charismatic large mammal species, notably Asian elephant, leopard, sloth bear, water buffalo, wild boar and several species of deer and small carnivore, allowing national parks such as Yala, Wilpattu, Udawalawe, Minneriya and Gal Oya to rank among the best safari destinations in Asia. Outside of national parks, monkeys are very common, often in the vicinity of Buddhist temples, where their mischievous presence is tolerated by monks and visitors.

The Big Four Just as Africa has its Big Five, so can Sri Lanka claim a Big Four, namely Asian elephant, water buffalo, leopard and sloth bear.

***Asian elephant* (Elephas maximus)** Sri Lanka is an important stronghold for the world's second-largest land mammal, which is now IUCN red-listed as Endangered, with a total global population of wild animals estimated at 35,000–40,000. Sometimes regarded as a distinct subspecies (*Elephas maximus maximus*), Sri Lankan elephant numbers declined throughout most of the 20th century, from an estimated 10,000 individuals in 1900 to a nadir of around 2,000 in 1969. Since then, strong conservationist policies and the expansion of the national park network have allowed numbers to recover to around 3,500 in 2000 and as many as 6,000 today, a figure that represents the densest wild elephant population in Asia, if not anywhere in the world. Sri Lankan elephants, though appreciably smaller than their African counterparts, tend to be slightly larger and somewhat darker than those found on mainland Asia, and less than 5% of the population (mostly males) bear tusks, which reduces their vulnerability to ivory poaching. Elephants can be seen in most Sri Lankan national parks, with Udawalawe being the most reliable year-round destination, though it is outranked in the dry season by Minneriya, where several hundred individuals gather to drink every evening in the dry season, with numbers usually peaking over August–September.

Elephant herd, Minneriya National Park

Leopard

Leopard (Panthera pardus) No tigers, lions or cheetahs occur on Sri Lanka, but the island does support its own endemic subspecies of leopard, *Panthera pardus kotiya*, which is IUCN red-listed as Endangered, though the total population of almost 1,000 individuals is actually pretty healthy by modern standards. The Sri Lanka leopard is claimed to be the bulkiest physically of any of several African and Asian subspecies, and it also seems to be less secretive and arboreal, presumably because it has evolved as the island's alpha predator and thus has no real need to drag kills up trees. It is now largely confined to national parks and a few other protected areas, where it is often quite common and conspicuous – Yala National Park, which hosts the world's densest leopard population, can offer excellent leopard watching, and other parks such as Udawalawe and Wilpattu also often throw up good sightings.

Sloth bear (Melarsus ursinus) A solitary nocturnal omnivore whose range is centred on mainland India, this distant descendant of the brown bear is named for its heavy sickle-shaped claws, vacuum-like mouth, unusual dentition, and occasional custom of hanging upside-down in trees – adaptations all to a diet

Sloth bear

dominated by termites, ants and other insects, but which also includes beehives and fruit. Easily recognised by its considerable heft and shaggy black coat, it grows up to 2m long, sometimes weighing in at 150kg, and is far more agile and quick – and, if cornered, potentially dangerous – than its name or customary shambling gait might suggest. The Sri Lankan sloth bear is thought to be a distinct subspecies (*Melarsus ursinus inoratus*), and is IUCN red-listed as Endangered, with a population estimated at around 500 individuals. It is thinly distributed in most suitable national parks, with Wilpattu having the best reputation for regular sightings, though Yala and Udawalawe also have their moments, usually just before dusk.

Water buffalo

Water buffalo* (Bubalus bubalis)** A large ox-like bovid often seen wallowing in muddy pools, the water buffalo is now IUCN red-listed as Endangered in its undiluted wild form, with a global population estimated at around 3,500 centred almost entirely on India. The status of water buffalo in Sri Lanka is controversial. Domestic buffalo, which are probably descended from water buffalo, are common in rural areas, but zoologists suspect that the buffalo populations that occur conspicuously in several Sri Lankan national parks are not actually the real thing, but represent the progeny of domestic animals that went feral at some point in the last couple of thousand years.

Other ungulates
The water buffalo, described above, is the heftiest of eight even-toed ungulate species recorded in Sri Lanka. Of four true deer, the largest, weighing up to 280kg, with antlers that grow up to a metre long, is the shaggy grey-brown **Sri Lankan sambar** (*Rusa unicolor unicolor*), an endemic subspecies most common in grassland habitats in Horton Plains National Park, but also present at low densities in many other protected areas. Far more numerous in lowland national parks such as Yala and Wilpattu, as well as in some suburban parks, the medium-large **spotted deer** (*Axis axis*) has a white-on-chestnut spotted coat and large antlers. The widespread but secretive **red muntjac** (*Muntiacus muntjak*) is a smaller and plainer red-brown undergrowth-dweller also known as the barking deer on account of its harsh alarm call. The **hog deer** (*Hyelaphus porcinus*) is a small introduced species named for its low-slung appearance when running and is restricted to a few marshy areas along the west coast. Two species of chevrotain or mouse-deer are endemic: the widespread **Sri Lankan spotted chevrotain** (*Moschiola meminna*) of the dry zone and the more localised **yellow-striped chevrotain** (*Moschiola kathygre*) of the wet zone. Both

Sri Lankan sambar

19

Eurasian wild boar

Indian muntjac

Spotted deer

are secretive forest-dwellers distinguished from true deer by the combination of smaller size, slightly hunchbacked build and spotted coat. Finally, the **Eurasian wild boar** (*Sus scrofa*) is a bulky and unmistakeable swine that might be encountered in any terrestrial national park.

Smaller carnivores In addition to leopard and sloth bear, 14 relatively small Carnivora species are present on Sri Lanka. The **golden jackal** (*Canis aureus*), the island's only wild dog, has a speckled grey-brown coat, weighs in at up to 7kg, and is quite likely to be seen in most national parks, especially towards dusk. Of four rather similar-looking mongoose species, the **Indian grey mongoose** (*Herpestes edwardsii*) is commonly seen along the roadside both inside and outside protected areas in the north, but is more or less replaced by the equally conspicuous **ruddy mongoose** (*Herpestes smithii*) in the south. The larger **Indian brown mongoose** (*Herpestes fuscus*) is more nocturnal in habits and is less likely to be seen, while the **stripe-necked mongoose** (*Herpestes vitticollis*), the largest Asian species, can be distinguished by its stout built and short black tail contrasting with the red-brown coat. The island supports a trio of seldom-seen small-to-medium felids. The long-legged, plainish-brown, lynx-like **jungle cat** (*Felis chaus*) and heavily spotted wetland-associated **fishing cat** (*Prionailurus viverrinus*) are both significantly larger than a domestic cat, whereas the descriptively named **rusty-spotted cat** (*Prionailurus rubiginosus*) is the world's second-smallest felid. Also present are the semi-aquatic **common otter** (*Lutra lutra*), the highly secretive small **Indian civet** (*Viverricula indica*) and five seldom-seen and difficult-to-distinguish species of **palm civet** (*Paradoxurus* spp.), all but one of which are a Vulnerable or Endangered national endemic.

Golden jackal

Fishing cat

Common otter

Golden palm civet

Ruddy mongoose

Purple-faced langur, highland race
Trachypithecus vetulus nestor

Primates Probably the most conspicuous mammals in Sri Lanka are its trio of bold Old World monkey species. The most widespread of these, often seen in the vicinity of Buddhist temples both active and ruined, is the **toque macaque** (*Macaca sinica*), whose light reddish-brown coat is offset by a bald pink face and funky near-Mohican hairstyle. Also very widespread is the much larger and more spindly **grey langur** (*Semnopithecus priam*), whose black face is offset by a white face-ruff and tall, tufted hairstyle. Replacing it in the wet zone is the **purple-faced langur** (*Trachypithecus vetulus*), which has a similar build and blackish face, but is more brown in general coloration, and far more strictly arboreal, being seen most likely in forests and other well-wooded areas in the southwest. While the grey langur is also widespread on the Indian mainland, the toque macaque and purple-faced langur (also known as purple-faced leaf monkey) are both island endemics and IUCN red-listed as Endangered. The shaggy-coated highland race of purple-faced langur, *Trachypithecus vetulus monticola*, is often called the bear monkey, while the Critically Endangered wet-zone lowland race, *Trachypithecus vetulus nestor*, was included in the 2010 list of the World's 25 Most Endangered Primate Taxa. Sri Lanka is also home to two nocturnal species of **slender loris** (*Loris* spp.), tiny but endearingly wide-eyed relatives of the lemurs of Madagascar and galagos (bushbabies) of mainland Africa. These are seldom seen unless actively sought, which can be done by joining a loris walk at the Jetwing Vil Uyana hotel near Sigiriya (page 235).

Grey langur

Purple-faced langur

Toque macaque

Rodents Of 23 rodent species recorded in Sri Lanka (including seven endemics), most are small mice, rats, gerbils and the like. The island's largest rodent is the **Indian crested porcupine** (*Hystrix indica*), a widespread but seldom-seen nocturnal creature that weighs up to 16kg and is covered in sharp, hollow, foot-long quills that protect it from predators. Of six species of squirrel, the most widespread is the ubiquitous and often very tame **Indian palm squirrel** (*Funambulus palmarum*), while the closely related **Layard's palm squirrel** (*Funambulus layardi*) and **dusky palm squirrel** (*Funambulus obscurus*) are both restricted to a few forested habitats in the wet zone and hill country. The impressive **grizzled giant squirrel** (*Ratufa macroura*), which grows to more than 1m in length including the tail, is quite common in forest and dense woodland all over the island. A highly arboreal creature, it is represented by three distinct subspecies: the widespread brownish *Ratufa macroura dandolena* of the dry-zone lowlands, and the part-black *Ratufa macroura melanochra* and *Ratufa macroura macroura* associated respectively with wet-zone lowland forests such as Sinharaja and with the highlands hill country around Horton

Indian palm squirrel

Layard's palm squirrel

Grizzled giant squirrel
(*Ratufa macroura dandolena*)

Plains and Nuwara Eliya. The **giant flying squirrel** (*Petaurista philippensis*) and smaller **Travancore flying squirrel** (*Petinomys fuscocapillus*) are present but localised and seldom seen.

Bats Placed in the order Chiroptera, bats are the most diverse mammal group in Sri Lanka, with at least 30 species represented, none of them endemic. Most are small and rather inconspicuous, but not so the **Indian flying fox** (*Pteropus giganteus*), a spectacular creature with a 1.4m wingspan and a rather vulture-like appearance as it flies over the treetops at dusk. The Indian flying fox is common in urban habitats, where it aggregates in noisy communal daytime roosts in large leafy trees.

Indian flying fox

Striped dolphin

Marine mammals Of the world's 90 species of cetacean (whales, dolphins and allies), a full 27 have been recorded off the shores of Sri Lanka. Indeed, the island is one of the world's finest destinations for whale watching, with **blue whale** (*Balaenoptera musculus*; the world's largest extant creature, at up to 30m long), as well as **fin whale** (*Balaenoptera physalus*), **Bryde's whale** (*Balaenoptera edeni*) and **sperm whale** (*Physeter macrocephalus*) commonly sighted on boat trips offshore of Mirissa (November–April) and Trincomalee (May–October). Half a dozen dolphin species might also be seen on these whale-watching trips, or indeed elsewhere on the coast, but the finest place to see these charismatic creatures is offshore of Kalpitiya, where playful schools of several hundred **spinner dolphin** (*Stenella longirostris*) are resident. Other cetaceans commonly observed in Sri Lankan waters include **orca** (*Orcinus orca*), **bottlenose dolphin** (*Tursiops truncatus*), **Risso's dolphin** (*Grampus griseus*) and **striped dolphin** (*Stenella coeruleoalba*).

Once quite common in Sri Lankan marine waters, the **dugong** (*Dugong dugon*) is a bulky (up to 1,000kg) marine mammal that feeds mainly on sea-grass and has suffered a drastic population decrease in the past few decades, probably because so many are trapped in fish nets, and is now IUCN red-listed as Vulnerable. Also known as the sea-cow, the dugong is one of only four species placed in the family Sirenia, whose name refers to the Sirens of Greek legend, in keeping with the theory that these odd creatures gave rise to the mermaid myth. The dugong is now quite scarce in Sri Lankan waters, but a population is known to be resident in the Palk Strait, which separates the island from India, and it is occasionally sighted by divers and snorkellers in Hikkaduwa Marine National Park.

Sperm whale

Blue whale

25

Indian peafowl

BIRDS Sri Lanka is one of Asia's most rewarding birdwatching destinations. True, the number of species recorded isn't particularly high – roughly 450 in total, of which 238 are breeding residents, 144 regular migrants, and the remainder irregular or vagrant – but it still impressive for an area a quarter the size of the UK, especially when you consider that it includes 33 full endemics (species whose range is restricted to the island; see box, pages 32–3), 43 further species regarded as endemic to South Asia, and 68 endemic subspecies. This relatively modest national checklist also makes Sri Lanka a great starting point for first-time visitors to Asia, since most genera are represented by a few species only, meaning you don't face the daunting identification challenges inherent to countries where 1,000-plus species have been recorded. In other words, it is easy enough to get to grips with Sri Lanka's avifauna even within the duration of a normal holiday, which would ideally be timed between the start of November and the end of March, the core season for migrant species (though some arrive as early as mid-August or stay on into early May).

Even those with no particular interest in birds might be struck by their sheer abundance in Sri Lanka, certainly when compared to most of Europe or many other countries in mainland Asia. In part, this is due to a proliferation of natural and artificial wetlands ranging from paddy fields and lakes to rivers and coastal flats, most of which host good numbers of resident pelicans, storks, ibises, herons, egrets, kingfishers and rallids, supplemented seasonally by influxes of migrant waterfowls and waders. But even away from water, birds seem to enjoy an unusually high presence in Sri Lanka. A good case in point is the magnificent Indian peafowl, which is far more common and conspicuous here than in the country for which it is named – and, in its wild state, an utterly magnificent sight, especially when the male (peacock) fans up its iridescent trailing feathers in a courtship display.

Black-necked stork

1 The colourful **blue-tailed bee-eater** (*Merops philippinus*) is a common winter migrant often seen perching or hawking insects in national parks and other savannah habitats. **2** The **Indian roller** (*Coracias benghalensis*) is a striking and common lowland bird named for the acrobatic twisting aerial breeding display performed by males over March–June. **3** An easily overlooked nocturnal relative of the nightjar, the bizarre-looking **Sri Lanka frogmouth** (*Batrachostomus moniliger*) is often located by guides in Sinharaja, who know its favoured perching sites. **4** The **black-hooded oriole** (*Oriolus xanthornus*) is a widespread woodland and garden bird easily located by its rather beautiful loud fluting call.

1 Easily distinguished by its large ivory-coloured bill, the **Sri Lanka grey hornbill** (*Ocyceros gingalensis*) is one of the most widespread of the island's endemic birds, found in wooded habitats from gardens to forests. **2** The **crimson-backed goldenback** (*Chrysocolaptes stricklandi*), also known as the greater Sri Lanka flameback, is a large and boldly marked woodpecker regarded by some authorities as an endemic species and others as a race of the mainland greater goldenback. **3** The **Sri Lanka hill myna** (*Gracula ptilogenys*) is a vocal and locally conspicuous red-billed species whose range is confined to the hill country of southern Sri Lanka. **4** The **orange-billed babbler** (*Turdoides rufescens*), also known as the Sri Lanka rufous babbler, is a very localised island endemic most likely to be seen in forest interiors at Sinharaja and Kitulgala.

1 Common in most national parks, the **Sri Lanka junglefowl** (*Gallus lafayettii*), the national bird of Sri Lanka, is closely related to red junglefowl, the mainland ancestor of the domestic chicken, and similarly vocal in the morning. **2** Endemic to the moist southeast, **yellow-fronted barbet** (*Psilopogon flavifrons*) is one of four colourful barbets resident in Sri Lanka. All are frequently observed in the vicinity of fruiting trees. **3** Inconspicuous except for its trademark whistling call, the **Sri Lanka green pigeon** (*Treron pompadora*) is a large and subtly coloured resident of wooded lowland and mid-altitude habitats. **4** The **Sri Lanka drongo** (*Dicrurus lophorinus*), or Ceylon crested drongo, formerly listed as a subspecies of the greater racket-tailed drongo, is a Sri Lanka endemic restricted to forest interiors in the moist southwest. **5** Depicted on the 1,000-rupee note, the endemic **Sri Lanka hanging parrot** (*Loriculus beryllinus*) is far smaller than the island's other four parrot species, all of which are long-tailed parakeets whose males have a black cut-throat marking.

1 Probably the bird most eagerly sought by visitors, **Sri Lanka blue magpie** (*Urocissa ornata*) is a dazzling member of the crow family most likely to be seen in Sinharaja Forest. **2** An inconspicuous, shy and rare endemic of the island's far south, the gorgeous **red-faced malkoha** (*Phaenicophaeus pyrrhocephalus*) might be seen skulking in riparian forest of Yala National Park, but is more common in the jungles of Sinharaja. **3** Confined to highland forests, where it generally forages on or close to the ground, the **spot-winged thrush** (*Geokichla spiloptera*) is one of three endemic thrush species found in the tiny but bird-rich Galway's Land National Park. **4** The **Sri Lanka scaly thrush** (*Zoothera imbricata*) is another terrestrial bird mainly associated with high and medium-altitude forest interiors. **5** An uncommon endemic restricted to forests in the southwest, the **green-billed coucal** (*Centropus chlororhynchos*) is distinguished from the more widespread and common greater coucal by its bold ivory-green (as opposed to dull black) beak.

1 Endemic to the southern half of Sri Lanka, **Layard's parakeet** (*Psittacula calthrapae*) is a handsome long-tailed parrot distinguished from the island's three other parakeets by the extensive grey back and facial feathering. **2** A widespread resident of forest and woodland, the handsome **black-capped bulbul** (*Pycnonotus melanicterus*) is an island endemic sometimes treated as a subspecies of the extralimital black-crested bulbul. **3** The endemic **Sri Lanka scimitar-babbler** (*Pomatorhinus melanurus*) is named for the long yellow decurved bill that distinguishes it from the island's other seven babbler species. **4** A stout little bird that bears a superficial resemblance to the longer-billed sunbirds, the nectar-loving **Legge's flowerpecker** (*Dicaeum vincens*) is a southwestern endemic often seen near flowering trees in Sinharaja. **5** Among the most widespread of Sri Lanka's endemic birds is the **brown-capped babbler** (*Pellorneum fuscocapillus*), a rather inconspicuous skulker that might be seen in undergrowth anywhere but the far north and High Hill Country.

Name (Latin name)	Status and habitat	Most easily seen
Sri Lanka spurfowl (*Galloperdix bicalcarata*)	U, forest interiors countrywide	Sinharaja
Sri Lanka junglefowl (*Gallus lafayetii*)	Q, all forest, woodland and clearings	Yala, Wilpattu, Udawalawe
Sri Lanka wood pigeon (*Columba torringtoniae*)	U, highland and wet-zone forests*	Hakgala, Horton Plains
Sri Lanka green pigeon (*Treron pompadora*)	Q, most wooded habitats	Yala, Wilpattu, Sinharaja
Sri Lanka hanging parrot (*Loriculus beryllinus*)	Q, Wet-zone woodland and forest	Sinharaja, Bentota
Layard's parakeet (*Psittacula calthrapae*)	U, Wet-zone and highland forest	Sinharaja, Udawattekele
Red-faced malkoha (*Phaenicophaeus pyrrhocephalus*)	R, Wet-zone and riverine forest *	Sinharaja, Kitulgala
Green-billed coucal (*Centropus chlororhynchos*)	R, wet-zone lowland forest/bamboo*	Sinharaja, Kitulgala
Chestnut-backed owlet (*Glaucidium castanotum*)	U, wet-zone and highland woodland	Sinharaja, Kitulgala
Serendib scops owl (*Otus thilohoffmanni*)	R, wet-zone forest interior**	Sinharaja, Kitulgala
Yellow-fronted barbet (*Megalaima flavifrons*)	Q, wet-zone and highland forest	Sinharaja, Udawattekele
Crimson-fronted barbet (*Megalaima rubricapillus*)	Q, all forest and woodland	Fruiting Bo & other ficus trees
Sri Lanka grey hornbill (*Ocyceros gingalensis*)	C, most woodland, even gardens	Yala, Wilpattu, Sinharaja
Crimson-backed goldenback (*Chrysocolaptes stricklandi*)	C, all wooded habitats	Yala, Wilpattu, Sinharaja
Sri Lanka wood-shrike (*Tephrodornis affinis*)	Q, any dry-zone wooded habitats	Yala, Wilpattu, Udawalawe
Sri Lanka blue magpie (*Urocissa ornate*)	R, wet zone rainforest interiors*	Sinharaja, Kitulgala
Sri Lanka swallow (*Hirundo hyperythra*)	U, forest fringe, grass and cultivation	Might be seen anywhere
Sri Lanka drongo (*Dicrurus lophorhinus*)	Q, wet zone forest	Sinharaja, Kitulgala

Dedicated birdwatchers will place a high priority on seeking out the 33 endemic species recognised in Pamela Rasmussen and John Anderton's definitive two-volume *Birds of South Asia* (Lynx, 2005). This ambition more or less enforces a visit to the Sinharaja Forest Reserve, which harbours almost all the national endemics and is the main stronghold for those associated with wet-zone and other rainforests. Other good sites for endemics are the low-lying Makandawa Forest Reserve at Kitulgala, the mid-altitude Udawattekele Reserve in the heart of Kandy, the highland Hakgala National Park on the outskirts of Nuwara Eliya, and the hiking trail through Horton Plains National Park.

Name (Latin name)	Status and habitat	Most easily seen
Black-capped bulbul (*Pycnonotus melanicterus*)	U, any riverine and moist forest	Sinharaja, Kitulgala, Wilpattu
Yellow-eared bulbul (*Pycnonotus penicillatus*)	Q, wet-zone, mid-/ high-altitude forest	Hakgala, Horton Plains
Sri Lanka bush-warbler (*Bradypterus palliseri*)	U, hill country forest undergrowth	Hakgala, Horton Plains
Brown-capped babbler (*Pellorneum fuscocapillus*)	U, forest undergrowth and scrub	Sinharaja, Kitulgala, Wilpattu
Sri Lanka scimitar babbler (*Pomatorhinus melanurus*)	U, forest interior and fringes	Sinharaja, Udawattekele
Orange-billed babbler (*Turdoides rufescens*)	C, wet zone and highland forest fringe	Sinharaja, Kitulgala
Ashy-headed laughing thrush (*Garrulax cinereifrons*)	Q, wet-zone forest interior*	Sinharaja, Kitulgala
Sri Lanka hill myna (*Gracula ptilogenys*)	C, wet-zone and highland forest fringe	Sinharaja, Hill Country
White-faced starling (*Sturnus albofrontatus*)	U, wet-zone forest interior and fringe*	Sinharaja, Kitulgala
Sri Lanka whistling thrush (*Myophonus blighi*)	R, highland forest**	Hakgala, Horton Plains
Spot-winged thrush (*Zoothera spiloptera*)	R, wet-zone and highland forest	Sinharaja, Hakgala, Kitulgala
Sri Lanka (scaly) thrush (*Zoothera imbricata*)	R, wet-zone and highland forest	Hakgala, Sinharaja, Peradeniya
Dull-blue flycatcher (*Eumyias sordidus*)	U, highland and wet-zone forest	Horton Plains, Knuckles Range
Legge's flowerpecker (*Dicaeum vincens*)	U, wet-zone and mid-altitude forest	Sinharaja, Kitulgala
Sri Lanka white-eye (*Zosterops ceylonensis*)	C, high-/mid-altitude forest and gardens	Hakgala, Peradeniya, Knuckles

R = Rare or very localised/secretive, U = Uncommon, Q = Quite common, C = Common (in suitable habitats); *IUCN red-listed as Vulnerable; **IUCN red-listed as Endangered

Before detailing all 33 endemic species, it should be noted that the taxonomic status of some is still in flux and arguably has been since 1880, when W V Legge published the first full bird list to what was then Ceylon. Legge recognised a full 47 endemics, only 17 of which are listed as such by Rasmussen and Anderton. Most other works published in the 20th century have treated between 20 and 25 species as endemic to Sri Lanka, and even the Helm Field Guide published in 2012 (page 606) and used as the basis for bird names in this guidebook limits itself to 27 species, partly because the other six have yet to be recognised as endemic in formal papers. However, for the convenience of visiting birders, all 33 probable endemics are listed as such in the box above, following the order of appearance in the Helm Guide.

Muggar crocodile

REPTILES At least 200 species of reptile are known from Sri Lanka, roughly half of them endemic to the island, and new species are still being discovered on a regular basis, with 17 lizards alone having first been described in 2006. The largest non-marine reptiles are the **estuarine crocodile** (*Crocodylus porosus*), which can grow up to 6m long, and the slightly smaller **muggar crocodile** (*Crocodylus palustris*), which are respectively associated with saltwater and freshwater habitats, though they often occur alongside each other in brackish lagoons and swamps. Both are opportunistic predators that feed mainly on fish and other aquatic creatures, but will also attack larger creatures when they swim or drink, and the estuarine crocodile in particular vies with Africa's Nile crocodile as the most dangerous species to humans.

Lizard diversity in Sri Lanka extends to 97 described species, and includes the hulking 1.75m-long **Indian land monitor** (*Varanus bengalensis*), which is often seen crossing roads at its own sweet pace, oblivious to passing traffic, and the scarcer but larger (up to 3m) and more stripy **Indian water monitor** (*Varanus salvator*). Other striking species include the **green forest lizard** (*Calotes calotes*) often seen in Sinharaja Forest Reserve, the familiar **common house gecko** (*Hemidactylus frenatus*), which often darts around hotel room walls snaffling mosquitoes and other bugs, the **rhino-horned lizard** (*Ceratophora stoddartii*), found in highland forests around Nuwara Eliya, and the smallish but habitat-tolerant **Indian chameleon** (*Chamaeleo zeylanicus*).

Indian land monitor

At least 96 snake species occur in Sri Lanka, roughly half of them endemic. The island's largest snake is the non-venomous **Indian rock python** (*Python molurus*), which typically grows to about 3m long and kills its prey by strangulation. Just as long but far less bulky, the **Indian rat snake** (*Ptyas mucosa*) is a non-venomous colubrid often seen in the vicinity of human

Loggerhead turtle

habitations, where it is tolerated owing to the important role it plays in controlling numbers of rats and other vermin. Six terrestrial species found in Sri Lanka are potentially deadly to humans: the hooded and spectacled **Indian cobra** (*Naja naja*), **common krait** (*Bungarus caeruleus*), **Sri Lankan krait** (*Bungarus ceylonicus*), **saw-scaled viper** (*Echis carinatus*), **hump-nosed pit-viper** (*Hypnale hypnale*) and **Russell's viper** (*Daboia russelii*).

Nine species of chelonid (shelled reptile) are documented in Sri Lanka. This includes five types of marine turtle, all IUCN red-listed as Vulnerable or worse, that inhabit the waters off the island and lay their eggs on its beaches with varying degrees of regularity. Most common is the **green turtle** (*Chelonia mydas*), which is roughly 1.5m long, weighs upwards of 300kg, and is easily identified by its small head tipped by a short, rounded snout, and smooth shell with horny plates. Also quite common is the **olive ridley turtle** (*Lepidochelys olivacea*), which is the world's smallest marine chelonid, with an average length of 65cm and a weight of up to 50kg. Rather less common are the hefty **leatherback** (*Dermochelys coriacea*), the world's largest turtle with a length of up to 2m and body mass topping 500kg, the **hawksbill** (*Eretmochelys imbricata*), and the **loggerhead** (*Caretta caretta*). In freshwater habitats, look out for the **Indian pond terrapin** (*Melanochelys trijuga*), which is often seen sunbathing on rocks or logs. The commonest terrestrial chelonid, the **Indian star tortoise** (*Geochelone elegans*) grows up to 25cm long and is named for the yellow geometric patterns that decorate its hard, black shell.

Indian star tortoise

Reticulated shrub-frog

AMPHIBIANS Documentation of Sri Lanka's amphibians is still something of a work in progress. The earliest scientific review of class Amphibia, undertaken in the 1950s, listed just 35 species for the island, but a comprehensive field survey undertaken in 1998 proposed more than 250 species, many of which are controversial and await formal recognition. Even so, Sri Lanka has the highest rate of amphibian endemicity in Asia, with roughly 120 species described, 90% of which are unique to the island. As is often the case elsewhere, many of these are small tree frogs and dwarf toads with a very limited range that makes them highly vulnerable to extinction. Indeed, as many as 20 amphibian species described for Sri Lanka are IUCN red-listed as Extinct, another 23 are listed as Critically Endangered, and only 25 as Least Concern.

3

Practical Information

WHEN TO VISIT

Sri Lanka can be visited at any time of year, provided that you tweak your itinerary to allow for regional seasonal variations that are unusually divergent for such a small country. Climatically, the popular west and south coast of Sri Lanka are at their best during the winter months (December–April), when the sea is calm and rainfall is relatively low. By contrast, the less feted but increasingly popular east coast, from Trincomalee south to Arugam Bay, is driest and most agreeable to visit during the summer months (late April–September), while the little-visited north receives the bulk of its precipitation over the stormy months of October to December, leaving the rest of the year quite dry. Rainfall patterns are less of a consideration when it comes to visiting Kandy and the archaeological sites of the Cultural Triangle, but ideally you would want to avoid the wettest months of October to December. The Hill Country around Nuwara Eliya and Ella has a more even monthly rainfall spread than the rest if the country, but the wettest months are again October and November, while the driest are January to March

Sri Lanka has a near equatorial location and it mostly stands at altitudes of below 100m, which means that it tends to be hot and humid throughout the year, seldom dropping much below 25°C, even at night. Because it lies in the northern hemisphere, conditions are slightly cooler and more pleasant over the northern winter, especially from December to March. The only part of Sri Lanka to diverge significantly from this sweltering tropical climate is the temperate Hill Country around Nuwara Eliya and Ella, which stands at altitudes of over 1,000m and is almost always moderate by day and cool by night.

Another important factor in deciding when to visit is the extent to which you want to avoid the crowds. December to late April is the peak season in most parts of the country, but accommodation tends to be much cheaper from May to November (indeed, many establishments drop their rates by 50% out of season, and will negotiate even lower rates). The more popular archaeological sites and temples in the Cultural Triangle also tend to be far less crowded and more enjoyable out of season. By contrast, visitors with a strong interest in wildlife will find the country to be at its best from November to April, when resident birds are supplemented by 100-odd migratory species from India and further afield.

ITINERARIES

Many visitors to Sri Lanka are quite content to book into one or other beach resort for up to a fortnight, and to spend their days sunbathing, swimming and otherwise relaxing, possibly broken up with the odd excursion to the likes of Galle, Kandy or Yala National Park. For more active travellers, the standard 10- to 14-day itinerary offered by most operators first takes you from Colombo or Negombo

CLIMATE CHARTS

COLOMBO *Southwest coast, altitude 3m*

	Jan	Feb	Mar	Apr	May	Jun	Jul	Aug	Sep	Oct	Nov	Dec
Max (°C)	31	31	32	32	32	30	30	30	30	30	30	30
Min (°C)	27	27	27	28	28	28	28	28	27	27	27	26
Rain (mm)	60	75	125	245	390	185	120	120	245	365	415	180

GALLE *Southwest coast, altitude 0m*

	Jan	Feb	Mar	Apr	May	Jun	Jul	Aug	Sep	Oct	Nov	Dec
Max (°C)	29	29	30	31	31	30	29	28	28	28	29	29
Min (°C)	23	23	24	25	26	25	25	25	25	24	24	23
Rain (mm)	125	80	130	175	225	240	230	230	265	265	225	175

JAFFNA *North coast, altitude 15m*

	Jan	Feb	Mar	Apr	May	Jun	Jul	Aug	Sep	Oct	Nov	Dec
Max (°C)	29	30	32	33	33	32	32	32	32	31	29	28
Min (°C)	23	22	23	25	26	26	25	25	25	24	24	24
Rain (mm)	70	35	25	60	50	15	20	35	45	240	370	265

ARUGAM BAY *East coast, altitude 0m*

	Jan	Feb	Mar	Apr	May	Jun	Jul	Aug	Sep	Oct	Nov	Dec
Max (°C)	28	29	30	31	32	33	33	32	32	31	29	28
Min (°C)	23	23	23	24	25	25	24	24	24	24	23	23
Rain (mm)	285	180	90	90	45	15	30	25	35	130	255	300

ANURADHAPURA *Cultural Triangle, altitude 80m*

	Jan	Feb	Mar	Apr	May	Jun	Jul	Aug	Sep	Oct	Nov	Dec
Max (°C)	29	31	33	33	33	32	32	33	33	31	30	29
Min (°C)	21	21	22	24	25	25	25	25	25	24	22	22
Rain (mm)	100	50	80	165	90	10	35	45	70	235	250	230

to the Cultural Triangle, where you could spend anything from one to four days exploring the likes of Anuradhapura, Dambulla, Sigiriya and Polonnaruwa. Many tour operators use one hotel, usually centrally located in Dambulla or Sigiriya, as a base for exploring the triangle, an approach that saves the hassle of moving hotel every day, but also means that you tend to end up exploring more outlying sites in the midday heat rather than the cooler and more photogenic early morning or late afternoon. Heading south from the Cultural Triangle, it is normal to spend a couple of nights in Kandy, then to head to the High Hill Country around Nuwara Eliya, Ella and Adam's Peak, and on to Yala or Udawalawe National Park for a half-day safari, before settling into one of the beach resorts along the southwest coast for the rest of the duration. Travelling between April and August, a sensible variation on this route would be to slot in your beach stay on the east coast, which is far more amenable at this time of year.

The route above also makes sense for independent travellers using public transport, though with longer than two weeks to spare, you could slot in additional diversions north to little-visited Mannar or Jaffna, spend a little more time exploring some of the less publicised sites that dot the Cultural Triangle, head east to the likes of Trincomalee and Arugam Bay, or settle into Ella or Dalhousie for a few days'

KANDY *Northern Hill Country, altitude 500m*

	Jan	Feb	Mar	Apr	May	Jun	Jul	Aug	Sep	Oct	Nov	Dec
Max (°C)	28	30	31	31	30	28	28	28	28	29	28	28
Min (°C)	23	24	25	26	26	25	24	24	24	24	24	24
Rain (mm)	80	75	70	190	145	135	130	115	160	265	295	200

NUWARA ELIYA *Southern Hill Country, altitude 1,865m*

	Jan	Feb	Mar	Apr	May	Jun	Jul	Aug	Sep	Oct	Nov	Dec
Max (°C)	20	20	23	23	21	19	19	19	19	20	20	19
Min (°C)	15	15	16	17	16	16	16	16	16	16	15	15
Rain (mm)	105	75	70	150	180	180	175	160	175	230	215	195

DENIYAYA *Low Hill Country, altitude 175m*

	Jan	Feb	Mar	Apr	May	Jun	Jul	Aug	Sep	Oct	Nov	Dec
Max (°C)	28	29	30	30	29	29	28	28	28	28	28	28
Min (°C)	20	20	21	21	22	22	22	22	22	21	21	20
Rain (mm)	155	150	260	310	360	280	175	195	240	370	214	275

TANGALLE *South coast, altitude 25m*

	Jan	Feb	Mar	Apr	May	Jun	Jul	Aug	Sep	Oct	Nov	Dec
Max (°C)	30	30	31	31	30	30	30	30	30	30	30	30
Min (°C)	22	23	24	25	25	25	24	25	25	24	23	23
Rain (mm)	90	65	75	120	140	80	70	80	105	185	230	175

walking in lovely hill country. Indeed, with Sri Lanka being such a small country (about a quarter the size of the UK or Colorado), and well equipped with cheap and reasonably efficient bus and train services, it is very easy to explore whimsically, cutting across the country – from beach to town or archaeological site to national park – as the mood takes you.

TOUR OPERATORS

A number of large international tour operators sell package holidays to Sri Lanka, while several more specialised international and local operators focus on bespoke itineraries.

INTERNATIONAL OPERATORS
Asian Pacific Adventures ☎+1 800 825 1680; e info@asianpacificadventures.com; w asianpacificadventures.com; see ad, page xii
Audley Travel ☎+44 (0)1993 838000; e mail@ audleytravel.com; w audleytravel.com

CaroLanka ☎+44 (0)1822 810230; e carolanka@ btconnect.com; w carolanka.co.uk
Cox & Kings ☎+44 (0)20 3813 9384; e cox. kings@coxandkings.co.uk; w coxandkings.co.uk
First Choice ☎+44 (0)20 3451 2720; w firstchoice.co.uk

Hayes & Jarvis ☎+44 (0)1293 762404; w hayesandjarvis.co.uk

Indus Tours & Travel ☎+44 (0)20 8901 7320; e holidays@industours.co.uk; w industours.co.uk

Kuoni Travel ☎+44 (0)800 140 4920; w kuoni.co.uk

Natural World Safaris ☎+44 (0)1273 691642; tf +1 866 357 6569 (USA), tf +1 800 066 8890 (Australia); w naturalworldsafaris.com

Red Dot Tours Ltd ☎+44 (0)870 231 7892; e enquiries@reddottours.com; w reddottours.com

Steppes Travel ☎+44 (0)1285 601770; w steppestravel.co.uk

Thomas Cook ☎+44 (0)1733 224808; w thomascook.com

Thomson Holidays ☎+44 (0)20 3451 2688; w thomson.co.uk

TravelLocal w travellocal.com. This UK-based website allows you to book directly with selected local travel companies without using a 3rd-party travel operator or agent but with full financial protection. Travel to the destination is not included.

LOCAL OPERATORS

Aitken Spence Travels ☎011 230 8308; e astonline@aitkenspence.lk; w aitkenspencetravels.com. A major tour & hotel operator; soft adventure, birdwatching, nature trails, trekking, culture & wildlife ecotourism.

Bird & Wildlife Team ☎011 318 1519; e birdteam@sltnet.lk; w birdandwildlifeteam.com. Specialising in nature tours with both birding & wildlife watching, this outfit can also arrange pelagic tours to watch marine wildlife, including whales.

Camlo Lanka ☎011 575 2485; e camlolanka@gmail.com; w camlolanka.com; see ad, page 123. Customised wildlife & cultural tours of Sri Lanka catering to visitors on a tighter budget.

Ceylon Escapes m 0772 380003; e info@ceylonescapes.com; w ceylonescapes.com; see ad, page 122. Responsive & well-organised company offering chauffeured trips on & off the beaten track.

Columbus Tours ☎011 268 7719; e info@columbustourssrilanka.com; w columbustourssrilanka.com. Trekking, mountain biking, rafting, rock climbing & wilderness camping.

Diethelm Travel ☎011 231 3131; e inquiries@lk.diethelmtravel.com; w hemtours.com. For birdwatching, trekking, rafting, cultural heritage & rainforest programmes.

Ecowave Travels ☎063 373 0404; e info@ecowavetravels.lk; w ecowavetravels.lk. Based in Arugam Bay, this social benefit enterprise offers cultural tours that bring direct benefits to local communities.

J F Tours & Travels ☎011 258 9402; e inquiries@jftours.com; w jftours.com; see ad, page 68. This well-established operator runs tours on the Viceroy Special steam train, as well as private rail, wildlife & nature tours in 4x4 vehicles.

Jetwing Eco Holidays ☎011 238 1201; e enquiries@jetwingeco.com; w jetwingeco.com. Affiliated to the upmarket Jetwing chain of boutique hotels, this operates bespoke tours with an emphasis on eco-friendly wildlife viewing.

Noel Rodrigo's Leopard Safaris m 0713 314024; e reservations@leopardsafaris.com; w leopardsafaris.com. Wildlife specialist offering safaris in unique mobile tented camps with gourmet camp & especially adapted 4x4s, usually escorted by personable wildlife photographer Noel Rodrigo or a similarly capable & enthusiastic guide.

Quickshaws Tours Ltd 3 Kalinga Pl, Colombo 5; ☎011 258 3133; e tours@quickshaws.com; w quickshaws.com; see ad, page 69. Established in 1950, this offers a good selection of bespoke nature & cultural tours.

Red Dot Tours ☎011 789 5810; e enquiries@reddottours.com; w reddottours.com; see ad, page 70. Top-of-the-range operator providing individually planned tours to suit all tastes, staying at many little-known but charming retreats.

Sri Lanka In Style ☎011 239 6666; e enquiries@srilankainstyle.com; w srilankainstyle.com. Bespoke holidays taking in the best of Sri Lanka, whether by Viceroy Special or balloon, staying in luxury private villas or tented camps.

Walkers Tours ☎011 230 6306; e info@walkerstours.com; w walkerstours.com. Long-serving tour operator with programmes for trekking, birdwatching, deep-sea fishing, diving & cycling.

Wayfarers Ltd ☎011 232 4343; e info@wayfarers.lk; w wayfarers.lk. A small family company good for cycling, hiking & other outdoorsy activities.

TOURIST INFORMATION

In addition to its useful website, Sri Lanka Tourism (*80 Galle Rd, Colombo;* \ *011 243 7055;* e *info@srilanka.travel;* w *srilankatourism.org*) operates a domestic tourist information hotline (dial 1912 from anywhere within Sri Lanka) and information centres in Colombo and Kandy and at Bandaranaike International Airport.

RED TAPE

VISAS Nationals of all countries except for the Maldives, Singapore and the Seychelles require an Electronic Travel Authorisation (ETA), which amounts to the same thing as a visa. The ETA costs US$35 at the time of writing and can be applied and paid for by credit card at w eta.gov.lk. The application must be made within 30 days of your intended date of arrival and usually takes up to one day to process, whereupon you'll be emailed a letter that you can print out and show upon arrival at Bandaranaike International Airport to guarantee entry. If you don't have an ETA, you can buy a visa on arrival, but this means joining a tiresome queue at a special desk in the airport, and carries a small risk of being refused entry for some or other reason. Until recently, the online ETA application process was exclusively for tourist visits, but as of November 2016, business travellers can evidently apply on the same website.

The immigration desk customarily stamps in visitors for 30 days. If you intend to stay longer, the conservative option would be to obtain a visa covering the full duration of your visit from a Sri Lankan embassy or high commission (to see a full list of consulates abroad, visit w mfa.gov.lk and click on the 'missions' tab). Alternatively, you can extend your stay to 90 days at the Department of Immigration and Emigration in Colombo (page 100) at any point within the original 30-day period.

GETTING THERE AND AWAY

BY AIR Practically all international flights to Sri Lanka land at Bandaranaike International Airport [map, page 74] (CMB; \ *011 225 2861;* w *airport.lk*), which stands in Katunayake some 30km north of central Colombo and 10km southeast of the popular resort town of Negombo. Bandaranaike is serviced by a good selection of international airlines offering non-stop and/or reasonably direct one-stop flights to most capital cities in Europe, Asia and the Middle East. These include the national carrier SriLankan Airlines (w *srilankan.com*), which operates direct services to London, Paris, Rome, Frankfurt, Moscow, Singapore, Bangkok, Hong Kong, Shanghai, Beijing, Canton, Kuala Lumpur, Tokyo, Karachi, Kuwait, Riyadh, Jeddah, Doha, Abu Dhabi, Muscat, Dubai, Malé and several cities in India. Coming from Africa or the Americas, the flight of least resistance is generally a one-stop routing through the Middle East with Emirates, Qatar or Etihad. From Australia or New Zealand, the most convenient option is through Asian cities such as Tokyo or Singapore.

Major airlines that fly to Bandaranaike include: Aeroflot (w *aeroflot.ru*), Air India (w *airindia.in*), British Airways (w *britishairways.com*), Cathay Pacific (w *cathaypacific.com*), Emirates (w *emirates.com*), Etihad Airways (w *etihad.com*), Fly Dubai (w *flydubai.com*), KLM (w *klm.com*), Malaysia Airlines (w *malaysiaairlines.com*), Qatar Airways (w *qatarairways.com*), Singapore Airlines (w *singaporeair.com*), Thai Airways (w *thaiairways.com*) and Turkish Airlines (w *turkishairlines.com*). For a full list of airlines and flights servicing Bandaranaike, visit w airport.lk.

Opened in March 2013 by President Mahinda Rajapaksa, the Mattala Rajapaksa International Airport (HRI) on the south coast 18km from Hambantota has proved to be something of a white elephant, serviced as it is only by two domestic airlines and Fly Dubai, which offers connecting flights to the United Arab Emirates.

Arrival On the plane you should be given an Arrivals Card prior to disembarkation. If not, you will find one in the arrivals hall and must fill it out while passengers with ready-filled cards queue ahead of you. If you have a pre-approved ETA, head straight to the main row of immigration desks, where you're unlikely to wait longer than a few minutes to be stamped through. If not, then you need to queue at a special desk signposted 'visas' on arrival, which takes longer. Having collected your luggage, you pass through customs, where you may need to put your luggage through an X-ray scanner. The duty-free allowance for tourists is: 1½ litres of spirits and two bottles of wine; 2oz perfume and ¼ litre of eau de toilette; no tobacco products. The smuggling of drugs can lead to the death penalty and the authorities are very watchful. From here you exit into the main arrivals hall, which has several foreign exchange bureaux, a few ATMs (Commercial Bank is most reliable for foreign cards), a tourist information counter, and a Mobitel desk, where you can buy a local SIM card for your phone and load it with data and/or airtime. This is also where travellers

AYURVEDA   *Royston Ellis*

Ayurveda (pronounced *ae-ur-vay-dah*) is the natural medicine of Sri Lanka – an alternative to Western medical lore – which has an efficacy proven by 3,000 years of care and cure. It is nature's way to good health because of its reliance on natural plants, herbs and oils.

As the name implies (*ayur* = life; *veda* = knowledge), Ayurveda is the 'Knowledge of Life' or 'the art of healthy living'. According to the leaflet provided by the Neptune Ayurveda Village, it is the oldest complete medical system in the world.

These traditional medications were developed by ancient sages through keen observation of life and its functions. Ayurvedic philosophy postulates that the development of each of us from birth is governed by the varied combination of the five basic forces of nature: Water, Fire, Air, Earth and Ether.

Treatment comprises not only potions made from fresh, natural ingredients, but also oil massages, steam baths and bathing in herbal waters. Treatments are particularly beneficial for patients suffering from migraine, insomnia, arthritis and gastritis, but can also help in cases of paralysis and practically any affliction. The Panchakarma method has a great distinction in Ayurveda as it uses the five elements of medicinal herbs – leaves, flowers, barks, roots and berries – to cleanse the blood and the body's system of impurities.

Ayurveda treatment not only cures, it provides immunity too, so patients are both those in need of a cure for a particular ailment, and those who want to follow a course to stimulate and maintain good health. Treatment by nature cannot be hurried; it is not nature's aspirin.

While locals are likely to consult a renowned village practitioner, tourists can have a course of treatment from a government-licensed practitioner while staying at a holiday resort. There are also several exclusively Ayurveda hotels, with treatment supplemented by specially prepared meals recommended by a resident physician, in the vicinity of Bentota (pages 174–5).

with pre-booked hotel transfers will find representatives of hotels or tour operators waiting with their or your name on a board. If you are going independently to Colombo, best to head to one of the semi-official taxi agencies, which charge around US$15–20 for a transfer to Colombo, depending on where exactly you are headed, whether you want an air-conditioned or ordinary vehicle, and whether you opt to take the Colombo–Katunayake Expressway, which usually reduces the travel time by at least 50%. A transfer to Negombo will cost about half that.

SECURITY AND SAFETY

Sri Lanka is a remarkably safe country, with relatively low levels of crime and – now that the protracted civil war has drawn to a close – few security issues. Indeed, the main concerns for most travellers are probably road accidents associated with the manic local driving style, drowning in the ocean, and insect-borne diseases such as dengue fever (pages 63–7). It should also be pointed out that, as is the case almost anywhere in the world, breaking the law – in particular the usage of illegal drugs – could land you in serious trouble.

To check the latest security situation, but as seen by government officials who have to be cautious, go to either the UK gov.uk website (w *gov.uk/foreign-travel-advice/sri-lanka*), or the US version (w *travel.state.gov*).

CRIME Theft is not as rampant in Sri Lanka as some might expect, and street or beach muggings are almost unheard of. However, pickpockets sometimes operate on buses, especially when passengers are standing close to each other, while razor blades are occasionally used to slash holes in bags or to cut the strap. Overall, though, Sri Lanka is certainly safer than most countries in Asia, and crime is far less prevalent than in most Western countries. Still, while there's no call to be paranoid about personal safety, you shouldn't be too casual about your possessions, and action such as leaving your handbag open on a train seat or your wallet peeping out of your hip pocket might be viewed as inviting trouble. Single travellers should avoid dark alleys and beaches at night. When in doubt, it is usually safest to leave valuables sealed in the hotel safe or in the mini-safe in your room. If you do get robbed and intend to claim from your insurance company, make a report to the police and get a copy of the report from them as proof of your loss.

WOMEN TRAVELLERS On the whole, women travelling alone have little to fear on a gender-specific level, and they will generally be treated with respect and kindness by protective locals. That said, single women travellers often attract unwanted male attention, mostly nothing more inappropriate than persistent staring, but also sometimes flirtatiousness and even groping. Wearing a wedding ring and telling anyone who wants to know that you have a husband at home or waiting for you in the next town helps deflect attention. And while dress codes are relaxed enough in Colombo and other recognised resort areas, elsewhere – especially in strongly Muslim areas – it pays to dress modestly, which means covering your knees and shoulders, and wearing loose tops and skirts or trousers.

GAY TRAVELLERS Homosexuality is illegal in Sri Lanka, a law is that has seldom been enforced in recent decades, but which reflects a widespread stigmatisation of local gays and lesbians. Still, while Sri Lanka isn't a destination suited to single travellers in search of any kind of gay scene, homosexual couples are unlikely to encounter any problems with discrimination in hotels and other tourist institutions, provided they exercise some public discretion.

TRAVELLERS WITH A DISABILITY There are few of the facilities for disabled travellers that exist in some countries, although public buildings are now supposed to be accessible to wheelchair users. At the international airport, wheelchairs and assistance in boarding and disembarking from planes are available. Because of the difficulties in boarding trains and lack of space within carriages, train travel by people with a disability would be difficult. Yet beggars without limbs know how to get on board, and blind singers – usually with a child as guide – patrol the aisles. Sri Lankans are generally very considerate to a foreigner who has special needs and one could expect help from strangers in an emergency.

The UK's gov.uk website (w *gov.uk/guidance/foreign-travel-for-disabled-people*) provides general advice and practical information for travellers with a disability (and their companions) preparing for overseas travel.

TRAVELLING WITH CHILDREN Travellers with babies will attract a lot of friendly attention since Sri Lankans love kids. However, babies may feel the heat. Children should be watched in case they wander off alone. There are half-price entrance tickets to most places for children.

WHAT TO TAKE

When packing for so-called developing countries, many Western travellers devote considerable thought and effort to finding the right balance between bringing everything they might possibly need and keeping down weight and bulk. So a few general points are worth stressing. First, almost all genuine and borderline necessities – from batteries and light clothing to over-the-counter medication and toiletries – are easy to get hold of in Colombo and most resorts and other large towns, so no need to over-pack. Second, the vast majority of those ingenious outdoor gadgets sold to neophyte tropical travellers in travel and camping shops turn out to be gimmicky dead weight once on the road. Third, wherever and whenever you travel, Sri Lanka tends to be very hot and you can expect to be caught in the occasional tropical downpour, so bring plenty of light quick-dry clothing as well as waterproofing for your luggage and electronic gear.

CARRYING LUGGAGE Unless you plan on using a lot of public transport, any solid suitcase or duffel bag should suffice. For those expecting to use public transport or to walk a lot, a rucksack, or other bag that can be carried on the back, would be the best choice. Either way, make sure your bag is designed in such a way it can easily be padlocked; this won't prevent a determined thief from slashing it open, but it will be a real deterrent to more casual theft. For regular travellers, an excellent option, pre-empting most climatic and other travel conditions, is the Base Camp series of duffel-bags-with-back-straps produced by North Face (the only disadvantage of these rugged, waterproof and easily padlocked bags being that they have only one single compartment).

CLOTHES Sri Lanka's sweaty tropical climate is ideally suited to light summery clothing that dries quickly. Minimum requirements might be two pairs of long trousers or long skirts, two sets of shorts, half a dozen T-shirts, a bathing costume, enough socks and underwear to last a week, one solid pair of walking shoes with decent ankle support, and one pair of sandals, thongs, or other light shoes. Socks and underwear should ideally be made from natural fabrics as these are less likely to encourage fungal infections such as athlete's foot, or prickly heat in the groin region. With sufficient clothes to last a week, it should be easy enough to arrange laundry at any decent hotel, but if you do run short, it is easy enough to top up by buying a few cheap supplementary items. Most of Sri Lanka is too hot for you to be likely to require heavier clothing even at night, but a poncho or similar waterproof windbreaker will come in handy in storms or on windy beaches at night, and you will almost certainly want a sweatshirt or similarly warm clothing if you head to the High Hill Country around Nuwara Eliya and Ella.

OTHER USEFUL ITEMS The case for bringing camping equipment to Sri Lanka is all but non-existent, as there are so few campsites. If you're interested in natural history, it's difficult to imagine anything that will give you such value-for-weight entertainment as a pair of binoculars, which these days needn't be much heavier or bulkier than a pack of cards. Binoculars are essential if you want to get a good look at birds, or monkeys and other wildlife high in the trees. For most purposes, 7x or 8x magnification will be fine, but serious birdwatchers will find a 10x magnification more useful.

All the toiletry bag basics (soap, shampoo, conditioner, toothpaste, toothbrush, deodorant, basic razors) are very easy to replace as you go along – so there's no need to bring family-sized packs – but women planning on longer stays might want to stock up on some heavy-duty, leave-in conditioner to minimise sun damage to their hair. If you wear contact lenses, be aware that many people find the intense sun irritates their eyes, so you might consider reverting to glasses. Almost all hotels provide toilet paper and many also provide towels and have mosquito nets.

You should carry a small medical kit. Two other important items of tropical toiletry are mosquito repellent of a type suitable for skin application, and high-factor sunscreen. A pack of wet-wipes or antibacterial gel is a good way of making sure you don't make yourself sick with your own grime if you're eating on the move.

Other useful items include a padlock for your bag, a torch, a penknife, and (if you don't have one on your phone) a compact alarm clock. A twisted no-peg washing line is great for hanging clothes out. Some people wouldn't travel without a good pair of earplugs to help them sleep at night, and a travel pillow to make long journeys that bit easier to endure.

MONEY

The unit of currency is the Sri Lanka rupee (LKR or Rs) and it comes in bank note denominations of Rs10, Rs20, Rs50, Rs100, Rs200, Rs500, Rs1,000, Rs2,000 and Rs5,000, as well as disproportionately heavy coins worth Rs1, Rs2, Rs5 and Rs10. The exchange rate fluctuates daily and is given in daily newspapers or on the website w xe.com. In November 2017, the rates were approximately £1 = Rs200; US$1 = Rs154; €1 = Rs179.

Assuming you have a debit or credit card issued by Visa or MasterCard, the easiest way to obtain local currency is through 24-hour ATMs, which can be found outside almost all banks in all towns of any size, as well as in standalone kiosks at several beach resorts. Most ATMs operated by the country's main private chains – Commercial, Hatton National, Seylan and Sampath Bank – will accept foreign cards and issue up to Rs400,000 (around US$270) per transaction, with the Commercial Bank ATMs being the most widespread and reliable option. By contrast, while ATMs operated by the state-run banks, including the ubiquitous Bank of Ceylon (BOC) and Peoples Bank, often indicate that they accept Visa and MasterCard, this usually extends to locally issued cards only. Finally, be conscious of the fact that, unlike in most Western countries, ATMs in Sri Lanka generally dispense cash and issue a slip *before* they regurgitate the card, which makes it all too easy to walk away with a fistful of rupees and forget to wait for your card.

Credit cards do occasionally play up abroad, so it is a good idea to carry a back-up card and/or a small stash of hard currency cash (say up to US$500 in value), which can be exchanged for local currency during banking hours (*typically ⊕ 09.00–14.30 Mon–Fri*) at most branches of all the banks mentioned above. Outside banking hours, hard currency cash can also be exchanged at private bureaux de change where they exist (Bandaranaike International Airport, central Colombo and a few other larger towns). Travellers' cheques are all but obsolete in Sri Lanka these days.

Most prices in Sri Lanka are quoted in local currency, and are best paid for that way. A significant minority of hotels and restaurants quote rack rates in a hard currency, most often US dollars and more occasionally euros, but will still accept payment in Sri Lanka rupees. In this guide, however, prices are generally given in hard currency (US dollars by default, except where the establishment itself quotes its rates in euros), using the conversion rate at the time of writing. This may result in slight inconsistencies as exchange rates fluctuate up and down, but sticking with US dollars throughout does help facilitate comparison between establishments that quote rates in different currencies, and it will also accommodate any price rises associated with the ongoing devaluation of the Sri Lanka rupee against hard currencies in recent years.

BUDGETING

Because there are so many options in Sri Lanka, whether it's transport, meals or accommodation, it is very difficult to predict what to budget per day as it depends to what extent you choose to operate within the very inexpensive local economy and more inflated tourist economy. Bus and train travel won't cost more than a few dollars a day, whereas you'd be looking at upwards of US$50 a day for a hired car with driver. Accommodation ranges from US$15 for two in a small-town homestay to more than US$500 in a modern boutique-style hotel. A vegetarian rice-and-curry in a local eatery might cost as little as US$1 per person, while a buffet lunch in a more touristy venue might be in the US$6–10 range, and a three-course dinner in Colombo's finest might set you back US$50 per person. Bottled mineral water costs the equivalent of about US$0.50, and soft drinks about half that from a shop but double and more if ordered in a hotel or restaurant. Local beers are relatively expensive – about US$1.50 from a shop and upwards of US$3 in a restaurant – and wine is even pricier. That said, if you stick to local homestays and restaurants, focus on sites and activities that don't attract hefty entrance fees or other charges, travel out of season, and take it easy on the booze front, Sri Lanka can be a very cheap place and it should be possible for a rigidly parsimonious couple to get around on about US$25–30 a day. A more generous but still quite tight daily budget for two sharing would be around US$50, while a figure of US$80–100 would be around the minimum for those who require a room with air conditioning and want to enjoy some meals and a few drinks in proper restaurants.

When thinking of how much to budget, remember that hotels as well as restaurants are obliged to add various government and local taxes, which push the bill up by about 17%. On top of that there is the customary 10% service charge. Some places absorb the taxes in their menu prices, in which case it advertises that prices are Nett. Where a price is written as, for instance, Rs1,000++ (spoken out loud as 'one-thousand-plus-plus'), it indicates that taxes and service charge will be added to the quoted price.

TIPPING Most restaurants add a 10% service charge to the bill and in theory the staff shares the accumulated total at the month end (on a points basis linked to tenure of service) as an essential supplement to their meagre take-home pay. If you want to reward the person who served you directly, add another 5–10% to the bill, and hand it to them directly in cash (even if you are paying the rest of the bill by credit card). If you travel with a car and driver, it is customary to tip them about US$5–10 per day. Tip in rupees, not foreign currency, as it could be difficult for the recipient to change. When dealing with official (or indeed unofficial) guides, it is best to agree a fee in advance, but you might want to add a small tip if the service justifies it.

GETTING AROUND

Distances in Sri Lanka are relatively short and the limited but useful rail system is supplemented by a network of well-maintained surfaced roads connecting all major towns and most other points of interest. This means it is very easy to get around, whether you travel with a rented car and driver, or depend on public transport, which includes an inexpensive and all-but-comprehensive bus service and an equally affordable rail network. In addition, a plethora of reasonably priced three-wheeler tuktuks can be found almost everywhere for short urban hops or local excursions.

BY AIR A limited network of domestic flights is available but seldom used by tourists, except to travel between Colombo and the far north- or east-coast resorts such as Trincomalee and Batticaloa. The main domestic carriers are SriLankan Airlines (**w** *srilankan.com*), Helitours (**w** *helitours.lk*), FitsAir (**w** *fitsair.com*) and Cinnamon Air (**w** *cinnamonair.com*).

BY RAIL Established in the colonial era and vastly upgraded following the end of the civil war in 2009, Sri Lanka has a useful rail network comprising four main lines out of Colombo (see map, page 48). These are the South Coast line running to Matara via Bentota, Hikkaduwa, Galle and Weligama, the Hill Country line running to Badulla via Kandy, Hatton and Ella, the East Coast line running to Trincomalee via Kurunegala, Maho and Gal Oya Junction as well as to Batticaloa via Kurunegala, Maho, Gal Oya Junction and Polonnaruwa, and the Northern line to Jaffna and Mannar via Kurunegala, Maho and Anuradhapura. This means that most of the country's established highlights are accessible by train, or lie within a couple of hours of the nearest railway station by bus.

On routes covered by both forms of public transport, trains tend to be safer and more comfortable than buses, as well as being more interesting scenically, but, with the exception of the express services to Kandy, Galle, Anuradhapura, Jaffna and Mannar, they tend to be significantly slower. Fares on public passenger trains are very low: the country's longest trip, a 400km ride from Colombo to Jaffna, costs around US$2.50 third class or US$10 first class, and most other routes are significantly cheaper. Reservations can be made up to 30 days in advance, either by visiting any railway station in person, or by phone, contacting the central reservation office at Colombo Fort Railway Station (\ *011 243 2908*), or by dialling \365 from a Mobitel or Etisalat mobile number, or \1365 from a local land line.

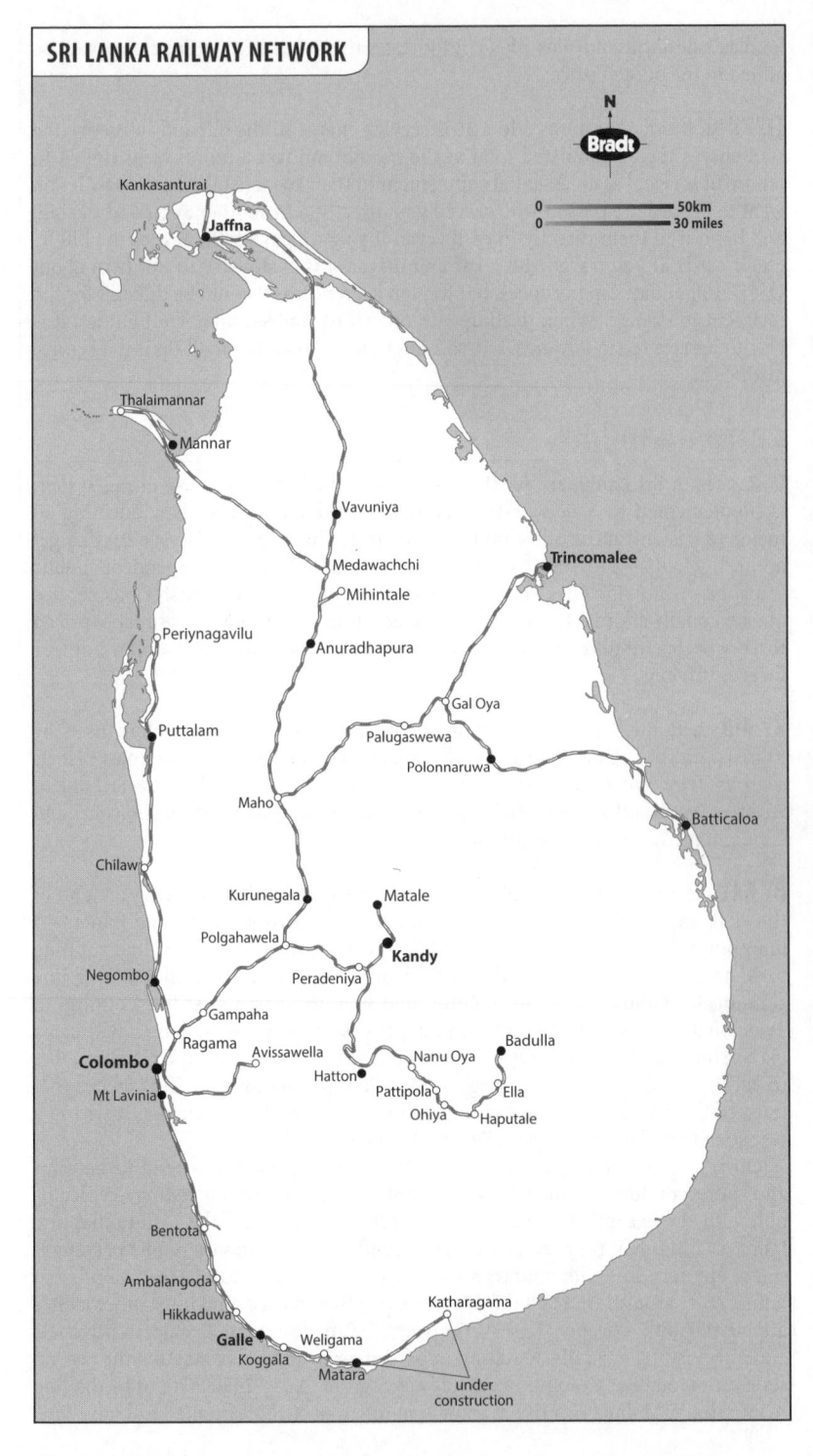

VICEROY SPECIAL: STEAM TRAIN TOURS   *Ariadne Van Zandbergen*

Sometimes travelling is about the journey more than the destination. This is especially true when taking a train trip through scenic Sri Lanka. The national railway system is well equipped for getting from A to B, but a journey on the Viceroy Special is all in all a more memorable experience. Depending on demand, up to four luxury coaches, painted in the bright red livery of the former Ceylon Government Railway, and outlined in gold with the CGR crest displayed on the body panels, are hauled by a steam or diesel engine along railway tracks dating back to the 19th century.

Four steam engines, all British built, have been brought out of retirement to pull the Viceroy Special. The main one, Sir Thomas Maitland, No 251, was built in 1928; the oldest, No 213, in 1922; No 240 in 1927; and the newest, No 340, in 1945. The name Viceroy Special was inspired by a special locomotive called the SEAC Special used by Lord Louis Mountbatten, the last Viceroy of India and Supreme Commander of All Forces in the South East Asian Command, to travel between Colombo and his headquarters in Kandy during World War II.

The most popular trips run from Colombo to Kandy and the tea plantations of the Hill Country, but the chartered train is available for tour group holidays around the country. J F Tours pioneered luxury train travel in Sri Lanka in 1986. They leased the carriages and refurbished them using antiques to re-create the charm of train travel in its heyday. Some of the period fittings include wood panelling, little fans and overhead luggage racks. For comfort the carriages have modern reclining seats and air conditioning. High-speed Wi-Fi is available throughout the train. Each seat has a little table, and three-course meals are served along the way. There is also a bar/dining carriage, and a good selection of drinks is available.

The scenery is fabulous. The tracks cut through an ever-changing series of vistas that include villages, forests, cascading waterfalls, cultivated lands with paddy fields and coconut palms, and endless beaches, occasionally disappearing into darkness in tunnels carved out of solid rock. The train can be stopped on request and guests can photograph scenic beauty spots along the way.

Individuals wishing to travel on the Viceroy Special need to consult the J F Tours website as far in advance as possible and can book scheduled tours online. It is also possible for groups to book the entire train for their own private trips. For further information and details, contact the train operators, J F Tours & Travels (*189 Bauddhaloka Rd, Colombo;* 011 258 9402; e *inquiries@ jftours.com;* w *jftours.com; see ad, page 68*).

Details of more popular routings are included in the appropriate regional chapters of this guidebook, but a good map of the rail network and full schedules are posted at w railway.gov.lk, or you can search for trains on your route of choice at w eservices.railway.gov.lk/schedule.

A recent and very welcome development are the exclusive first-class carriages with air conditioning, power points, private TV and on-board snacks operated by two private companies that also offer user-friendly online booking services now. These are more expensive than normal carriages, but still represent great value for money at around US$7 one-way from Colombo to Galle or Matara, or US$8 from Colombo to Kandy. The more extensive network is operated by Rajadhani Express (☎ *011 574 7000;* m *0710 355355;* e *info@rajadhani.lk;* w *rajadhani.lk*), which runs daily in either direction between Colombo and Kandy and six times weekly between Colombo and Matara (via Galle) and Colombo to Badulla (via Ella). Meanwhile, ExpoRail (☎ *011 422 5050/522 5050;* e *reservations@exporail.lk;* w *exporail.lk*) operates daily in either direction between Colombo and Galle, and Colombo and Badulla via Ella. *Note that both these services reported all services to be suspended in late 2017 and it is unclear whether or when they will resume – check the websites for the latest news!*

Altogether more exclusive and a must-do for genuine train buffs are the Viceroy Special steam trains operated by J F Tours & Travels (see box, page 49).

BY ROAD The road network is good and extensive, and the main highways are generally well maintained, although country lanes are bumpier. There are also two excellent multi-lane toll roads in the southwest: the 160km Southern Expressway connecting the southern Colombo suburb of Kottawa to Matara via Bentota and Galle, and the 35km Katunayake Expressway linking the northern Colombo suburb of Kelani to Bandaranaike International Airport. A third expressway connecting Colombo to Kandy is likely to open during the lifespan of this edition.

Buses The Sri Lanka Transport Board (SLTB) operates a comprehensive network of red buses covering pretty much every road countrywide, though most travellers prefer to use trains where the choice exists. SLTB buses adhere loosely to formal timetables, stop wherever passengers want to embark or disembark, and are seldom packed full. On longer hauls, buses generally depart every 30 minutes to 2 hours starting at around 05.00, but services tend to peter out in the late afternoon so as not to be driving into the night. On shorter routes, the buses typically depart every 15–60 minutes throughout daylight hours. On more popular routes, the SLTB bus service is supplemented by more comfortable and modern private express coaches. These are usually painted blue as opposed to red, and they generally cover the distance more quickly than their government counterparts, but not necessarily with greater regard for road safety. Fares on all buses are very low (around US$1–2 per 100km), reservations are seldom required (the one exception being some long-haul air-conditioned coach services between Colombo and the likes of Jaffna and Trincomalee), and all routes are assigned numbers that are displayed on the front of the bus along with the destination, usually in English but sometimes only in Sinhala. Some towns have separate stations for SLTB and private buses, but where this is the case, they are usually close together. Within each station, there are set departure points for all routes, so where in doubt just ask someone to point you to the right place. People at bus stations are very helpful and, unlike in some countries, the overcharging or deliberate misdirection of tourists by push touts isn't a cause for concern. Further details of individual routes are given in the relevant regional chapter of this guide, and full timetables for all intercity routes are posted online at w ntc.gov.lk/Bus_info/time_table.php.

Car hire Unless you have experience driving in Asia, a self-drive car rental probably isn't a good idea. Far better to rent a car or minibus with a driver, either from one of the operators listed on page 40, or directly through a hotel or guesthouse. Rates vary and are to some extent negotiable, but you are typically looking at around US$50–80 per day inclusive of fuel. Some hotels offer complimentary rooms and meals to drivers, but where they don't, it is customary to provide the driver with a daily allowance equivalent to US$15 per day. A tip of US$5–10 per day will also be expected. Some drivers will try to dissuade their clients from making side excursions in order to save fuel costs, and will also try to steer them towards shops and other establishments that offer commissions, so where possible it is worth 'test driving' any given driver before you commit to spending a long time with them. Bearing this in mind, rather than committing to one vehicle at the start of a trip, it might actually be cheaper and less stressful to hire one as the need presents itself on a day-by-day basis (any hotel or guesthouse can put you in touch with a suitable self-employed driver).

By tuktuk Also known as three-wheelers and ground-helicopters, motorised tuktuks are the most ubiquitous form of transport in Sri Lanka, swarming and weaving between larger vehicles in every town and village, and usually sitting waiting at any strategic junction countrywide. In Colombo, most tuktuks are metered and the first kilometre incurs a charge of Rs50, with subsequent kilometres at Rs32. Elsewhere, tuktuks are unmetered and rates are negotiable, but you shouldn't be paying more than around US$1 per 3–4km, though in some cases you might need to factor in waiting time, or the fare for the driver to return empty. In addition to serving as cheap taxis for urban transfers, tuktuks are an excellent and affordable way to get to out-of-town sites not accessible by bus, and they can even be used for travel between towns by single travellers or couples who don't have too much luggage. The driver will often start a long journey by pulling into a petrol station and asking you to give him an advance on the fare to pay for fuel. It's fine to do this, but remember to deduct the advance when you pay the final amount.

By motorbike Motorbikes and scooters can be hired, usually on an informal basis, in several resort towns. If you do rent one, be sure to check it thoroughly, perhaps with a test drive. As well as the fee in advance, by negotiation, you will be asked to leave your passport as security. If you have an accident, the repair bill will be at your expense, which you'll have to pay to get back the passport. Crash helmets are compulsory both for the driver and for any pillion rider.

By bicycle Bicycles can be hired in resort areas and are great for discovering what lies down the country lanes away from the beach, or for pedalling around Anuradhapura or Polonnaruwa. Unfortunately, they are often real bone-shakers and, if they do have brakes that work, then something else will be wrong. Visitors who bring their own bikes seem to fare well enough and, on country lanes away from the madness of the main roads, may even enjoy it.

ACCOMMODATION

Accommodation is plentiful in Sri Lanka and caters to all tastes and budgets. At the one extreme is a generous scattering of US$300-plus beach resorts, boutique hotels, colonial villas and city hotels that attain or approach international five-star standards and come with all mod cons, from world-class restaurants and spacious well-appointed rooms to large swimming pools and attentive service. At the other end of the spectrum, budget travellers are catered for by an ever-growing number of small family-run guesthouses, unpretentious homestays and laid-back backpacker hostels typically charging around US$15–30 for a double room. In between, you will find plenty of no-frills but comfortable mid-range to upmarket resorts, hotels and guesthouses charging anything from US$50 to US$200 for a double.

Most accommodation entries in this guidebook are categorised under one of five main headings: exclusive/luxury, upmarket, moderate, budget and shoestring. Typically, establishments listed under the exclusive or luxury header are world-class institutions that offer the highest standards of comfort and/or exude a strong air of exclusivity. Upmarket hotels also meet international standards but with a more mainstream feel and slightly less flair. The moderate bracket embraces comfortable and perfectly respectable lodgings that don't quite make the upmarket grade but often still possess considerable character and would be comfortable enough for all but the most demanding tourists. Almost all hotels listed in these first three categories would have air conditioning, sat TV, and en-suite hot showers in all rooms. Accommodation in the budget category is typically aimed at the local or backpacker market, but is still reasonably comfortable with en-suite facilities and, in the majority of cases, air conditioning. Shoestring accommodation consists of the cheapest rooms around, which may or may not be en suite, may or may not provide amenities such as towel and soap, and will most often have a fan but seldom air conditioning.

ACCOMMODATION PRICE CODES

Codes are based on the standard rate for a double room in high season (west coast, December–April; east coast, May–October; Hill Country, August):

$$$$$+	US$300+
$$$$$	US$170–299
$$$$	US$86–169
$$$	US$46–85
$$	US$25–45
$	up to US$24

The categorisation of accommodation is designed to help readers identify those establishments that best suit their taste and budget, for which reason it isn't based rigidly on prices, but an overall evaluation that takes into account the broad feel of the hotel, its location and setting, and where it sits price-wise in relation to other nearby options. A breakdown of rates is included in italics at the end of every accommodation entry, followed by a price-range symbol (see box, above) intended as a quick visual navigational aid. As a rule, breakfast is included in the standard room rates for hotels in the moderate, upmarket and exclusive categories, but not at budget and shoestring places. In the listings in this book, meals included in the rate are indicated as B&B (bed and breakfast), HB (half-board, ie: dinner, bed and breakfast, or FB (full-board). Where none of these symbols appears, the rate quoted is room only, and all meals are extra. Where a hotel has seasonal rates, we quote the high-season price (December–April in most of the country, but May–October on the east coast) and indicate what sort of seasonal discount is offered. Finally, a ✳ at the start of any given entry indicates that it is an author's pick, this being an establishment that stands out from the crowd owing to its exceptional location, character, management style, good value or a combination of these factors.

Wherever possible, listings include a landline, mobile number, email address and website (or, in lieu of that, Facebook page). While we've made every reasonable effort to verify these contact details, it is often the case that the numbers and email address given to us on the spot are different from those provided on the website, and we have generally gone with the former, a judgement call that depended to some extent on the seniority of the staff member we dealt with *in situ*. Where strong discrepancies exist between the rate advertised online and the walk-in rate we were offered on the ground, the higher rate is generally quoted. In this context, it is worth noting that most budget hotels are open to some negotiation out of season, especially for longer stays, when business is slack, and when dealing with last-minute walk-in clients. Also, before you contact any given establishment directly, try shopping around at sites such as w booking.com, w hotels.com, w agoda.com, w expedia.com and w tripadvisor.com, which often offer substantially discounted rates, especially when it comes to last-minute bookings.

EATING AND DRINKING

RESTAURANTS Most restaurants in Sri Lanka slot into one of four broad categories. Most expensive, and largely confined to Colombo and to a lesser extent Galle, are genuine international restaurants that deal in specific cuisines, be it Japanese, French or Bavarian, and cater almost entirely to a clientele of business people, tourists and affluent locals. Middling in price, with mains typically falling into the US$5–10 bracket, is a rather generic selection of 'proper' tourist-oriented restaurants that tend to offer predictable menus comprising a combination of grilled meat and seafood, pasta dishes, fried noodles and rice, possibly pizzas and/or burgers, and local dishes such as rice-and-curry or devilled chicken or fish. Also generally associated with larger towns and more touristy areas are deli-style places serving tea, coffee, juices, sandwiches, pastries, cake and the like. Finally, every town, no matter how small, will boast at least one and usually several dozen little local holes-in-the-wall serving rice-and-curry buffets and other Sri Lankan staples for around US$1–2 per head. Although the first three categories of establishment inevitably dominate listings in this guidebook, it is worth pointing out that the overwhelming majority of restaurants in Sri Lanka fall into the fourth category, and while the sheer number of options renders it near-impossible to make individual recommendations, we took quick lunch breaks at many such places during the course of researching this book, and almost invariably the food was delicious and fabulous value, assuming you have some tolerance for spiciness.

Note that restaurant opening hours provided in this book are daily unless otherwise stated, though many places are closed or keep shorter hours on poya days, and very few serve alcohol as it is illegal.

LOCAL CUISINE Sri Lanka has a unique cuisine whose manifest South Indian roots are infused with various Malay, Portuguese, Dutch and Arab influences, and make far greater use of coconuts and seafood, as might be expected of a low-lying island with such a long tropical coastline. Sri Lankan dishes tend to be rather hot and spicy, but most tourist-oriented hotels and restaurants will modify their recipes to account for less fire-resistant Western palates. In addition to the dishes listed below, Chinese-style fried rice and noodles are a greasy staple on many local menus, while lighter snacks include fiery meat or vegetable samosas, and various deep-fried meat and vegetable cutlets. Fresh seafood is ubiquitous on the coast, and usually of a very high standard.

Rice-and-curry The staple diet is rice-and-curry, which differs from its Indian namesake-in-reverse in that a heap of rice is loaded on to a central plate, then surrounded by anything from five to 15 different curry dishes, each usually in a separate bowl. The exact origin of this dish is unclear, but it is essentially a local variation of the banquet-like Dutch *rijstafel* (rice table) – itself heavily influenced by the Sumatran smorgasbord called *nasi padang* – introduced to the island during the colonial era. The accompaniments are distinctly Sri Lankan, however, and usually include a hot chicken or fish curry, together with a milder paste-like dhal (lentil) curry, and a variety of other plants, tubers and leaves – from sweet mango and stodgy potato to meaty jackfruit and spinach-like kankun – often with a couple of small crunchy poppadoms, chopped sambal and mallung (a spicy mix of stir-fried gotukola leaves and ground coconut) on the side. Many Sri Lankan curries are spicy hot, but not all, since the word 'curry' refers to the sauced accompaniment rather than to something fiendishly fiery. But if they should be too hot for your palate, the addition of coconut milk will tame them a bit. You could also try a slice of pineapple or a banana, which will remove the pieces of chilli where they have settled between your teeth. Either way, curries are actually best savoured when they are not hot in temperature, which makes them ideal for buffet service, or when the dishes are allowed to remain on the dining table to cool before you are called to eat. Almost all local eateries serve a lunchtime curry buffet, typically charging around US$1 for a vegetarian-only selection and up to US$2 with fish or meat. In tourist areas, particularly around the Cultural Triangle, more elaborate (and, as a rule, considerably milder) rice-and-curry buffets at restaurants aimed mainly at passing tourist buses typically cost around US$5–10 per person. Most other restaurants in Sri Lanka serve curries, but more often than not as less elaborate à la carte dishes rather than buffets.

Devilled dishes Another typical Sri Lankan dish is devilled meat, most often chicken or fish, which is smothered in chillies and served in a flame-red sweet-and-sour sauce with chopped leeks, tomatoes and other vegetables. It is usually cooked fresh, so can be as spicy or mild as you request, and served with rice.

String hoppers Most often eaten at breakfast with an accompaniment of fish or chicken curry and dhal, a string hopper (or *iddyappa*) is a light-textured tangle of thin noodles usually made with rice flour, but sometimes also with wheat flour. It came to Sri Lanka from China via South India.

Hopper Also known as appa, a hopper is a type of steamed or fried pancake made with a fermented rice-flour and coconut-milk batter. It is cooked in a bowl-shaped pan that causes the batter to pool at the bottom, so the sides are crispy and thin, while the base is thicker and softer. As with string hoppers, it is generally a breakfast dish, eaten with fish or chicken curry, though an intriguing variation incorporates an egg, fried sunny side up.

Lamprais Boasting the most overt Dutch influence of any Sri Lankan dish, lamprais consists of rice boiled in a yellow stock, then mixed with a combination of *frikadellen* (meatballs) or meat curry, various vegetable curries and sambal, and wrapped in a banana leaf and baked in an oven.

Roti Now a popular staple at many local restaurants catering to budget-conscious backpackers, a roti (often spelt *rotty*, and also known as paratha) is a tortilla-like flat bread that can be filled with anything from curry and dhal to pineapples and bananas to create a wide range of savoury wraps. A filled roti is generally very inexpensive though you might need to order two servings to fill up.

Kottu Also known as kottu roti, this fast-food dish – as its name implies – consists of a chopped up roti stir-fried together with an assortment of sliced vegetables and (optionally) large shreds of chicken, egg, fish or meat. It's a popular dinner dish, particularly in Colombo, and is normally quite spicy, though you can usually ask for it to be cooked mild. If it is too dry for your taste, ask for a bowl of curry sauce to moisten (and spice) it up.

Sweets Wattalapam is a kind of crème caramel. Curd, similar to yoghurt but made from buffalo milk, is eaten with a type of treacle made from the natural sweet sap from a kitul palm tree. Particularly in Hindu areas, you find plenty of shops selling a colourful array of hand-crafted Indian sweets. Quality ice cream is widely available. Fresh seasonal fruits are in good supply and make a healthy supplement to cooked meals. Depending to some extent on season, the fruits most frequently served in hotels and restaurants are bananas, pineapples, papayas, watermelon, mango, avocado and less familiar items such as durian (jackfruit), mangosteen and rambutan.

RESTAURANT PRICE CODES	
$$$$$	most mains US$15+
$$$$	most mains US$10–15
$$$	most mains US$6–10
$$	most mains under US$6
$	should be able to fill up for under US$2.50

DRINKS Locally produced mineral water costs around US$0.50 per 1.5-litre bottle. The usual selection of international fizzy drinks is equally inexpensive, as is soda water, a refreshing alternative to its sugary counterparts. Also very refreshing is *thambili*, the golden-hued coconut you'll see on sale at stalls around the country. The vendor will chop off the top of the coconut so you can drink the liquid from within. Freshly prepared fruit juices and smoothies are also widely available in cafés and restaurants, but you might want to ask to have it prepared with only a small amount of sugar, or none at all. Tea, as might be expected, is ubiquitous and generally of superb quality, and good coffee is served in smarter cafés, usually at a price.

Good locally brewed lager-style beer is widely available, with the main brands being Lion, Carlsberg, Anchor and Three Coins, all of which come in recreational standard (around 5% alcohol) and industrial strong (upwards of 8%) varieties. These are available in 500ml cans and recyclable 750ml bottles, and usually cost around US$1.50 in so-called Wine or Beer Shops (a few of which can be found clustered on the main road through most towns) but double or more in restaurants and hotels. Imported wine, often of mediocre quality, is widely available but quite pricey. Retail prices for a 750ml bottle start at around US$10, while restaurants typically ask US$4–5 for a small glass and upwards of US$20 for a bottle. The main local tipple is arrack, a strong (30–50% alcohol) rum-like spirit made from distilled toddy (coconut palm sap) but often diluted with less pure spirits. Many brands are available, starting at around US$6 for a 750ml bottle, though purer varieties are a bit more expensive. Connoisseurs drink arrack neat or on the rocks, while others drown it with cola and other fizzy drinks.

Alcoholic drinks are generally served at mid-range and upmarket hotels and restaurants, but not at cheaper family-run guesthouses and eateries. The main reason for this is the high cost of liquor licences, a consideration that also tends to push up prices in licensed establishments. It is usually acceptable to bring your own beer or wine to an unlicensed restaurant, but you should ask first, as some smaller places – especially in Islamic areas – will be uncomfortable with the idea. Many unlicensed restaurants that depend mainly on tourist custom will also discreetly go out to buy a couple of beers for diners who ask nicely.

PUBLIC HOLIDAYS AND FESTIVALS

PUBLIC HOLIDAYS Sri Lanka has only five fixed-date public holidays but another 20 (or in some years 21) variable-date ones associated with the Buddhist, Hindu, Christian or Muslim calendars. These include 12 (or in some years 13) 'poya' days, the Sri Lankan equivalent of the full-moon Uposatha observed in other Buddhist countries, held at full moon every lunar month (ie: every 29 or 30 days, depending on when exactly the moon is at its fullest; see box, opposite). In addition to being a bank and civil holiday, the monthly poya is the one day when many restaurants otherwise open seven days a week stay locked up, as do some museums and other secular attractions. The sale of alcoholic beverages is illegal on poya, which means that all liquor shops are closed and most hotels lock up the bar for the day; but it is permitted to consume any drinks bought in advance (or stocked in the minibar) in the privacy of your room. Poya is a great day to visit active Buddhist shrines and soak up the atmosphere, but it can be a mixed blessing as historical temples tend to be overrun with domestic tourists. Oddly, although poya days are aligned with the lunar cycle, they are named according to the Sinhala name for the calendar month wherein they fall. In other words, if a poya day takes place in January, which is known as Duruthu in Sinhala, it is referred to as the Duruthu Poya. About once every three years, two poya days will occur at the start and end of the same calendar month, in which case the name of the second one will be prefixed with the word *Adhi* (literally 'Extra'). The most important poya is the one in May (Vesak), which is commemorated as the birthday of the Buddha, and thus celebrated over two days (both public holidays) rather than the usual one day. When the official holiday falls on a Saturday or Sunday, other days may be given as additional holidays.

Fixed holidays

4 February	National Day (Anniversary of independence from Britain in 1948)
13 April	Sinhala and Tamil New Year's Eve
14 April	Sinhala and Tamil New Year's Day
1 May	May Day (also known as Labour Day)
25 December	Christmas Day

Variable-date holidays See also box, opposite.

	2018	2019	2020
Thai Pongal (Tamil Thanksgiving)	14 January	15 January	15 January
Maha Sivarathri (Hindu festival dedicated to Shiva)	24 February	4 March	21 February
Good Friday (Christian holiday)	14 April	19 April	10 April
Eid al-Fitr (Muslim, End of Ramadan)	26 June	4 June	23 May
Eid al-Adha (Muslim, Hadji Festival)	1 September	11 August	30 July
Deepavali (Diwali, Hindu Festival of Lights)	18 October	27 October	14 November
Milad un-Nabi (Muslim, Holy Prophet's Birthday)	1 December	9 November	28 October

FESTIVALS

Sri Pada Pilgrimage Season Tens of thousands of multi-denominational pilgrims climb the 2,243m-high Sri Pada (Adam's Peak) to pay homage and make observance over a four-month season that runs from the Unduvap (December) Poya to the Bak (April) Poya. The Buddhapada at the summit reputedly enshrines the footprint of the Gautama Buddha. Hindus, Muslims and Christians make the pilgrimage for their own religious reasons.

MONTHLY POYA

	2018	2019
Duruthu (January) Poya	12 January	20 January
Navam (February) Poya	10 February	19 February
Madin (March) Poya	12 March	20 March
Bak (April) Poya	10 April	19 April
Vesak (May) Poya	10/11 May	18/19 May
Poson (June) Poya	8 June	16 June
Esala (July) Poya	8 July	16 July
Nikini (August) Poya	7 August	15 August
Binara (September) Poya	5 September	13 September
Vap (October) Poya	5 October	13 October
Ill (November) Poya	3 November	12 November
Unduvap (December) Poya	3 December	11 December

Duruthu Perahera A colourful religious pageant, complete with caparisoned elephants, torch-bearers and dancers, takes place at Kelaniya Temple, on the outskirts of Colombo, the day before the Duruthu (January) Poya to mark the start of the first of the Buddha's three visits to Sri Lanka.

Galle Literary Festival (w *galleliteraryfestival.com*) Sri Lanka's premier arts festival takes place over three days in mid-January and attracts dozens of writers and performers from all over Asia and the rest of the world

Tamil Thai Pongal Thai Pongal is an ancient thanksgiving harvest festival celebrated by Tamils and other Hindus the world over. Houses are decorated with mango and plantain leaves and the hearth is decorated with rice flour. Dates vary slightly from one year to the next, but usually it takes place over four days starting between 12 and 15 January.

Navam Perahera (w *gangaramaya.com/perahara-processing*) Focused on Gangaramaya Temple in Colombo, this spectacular perahera with parades of dancers, elephants, whip crackers and hundreds of Buddhist monks was first staged in 1979 but is now a major fixture on the Colombo calendar, taking place over two days building up to the Navam (February) Poya.

Sinhalese and Tamil New Year The island's two main ethnic groups, Sinhalese and Tamil, celebrate a common traditional New Year at what was originally a harvest thanksgiving festival that marks the passage of the sun from Pisces to Aries. It occurs on 13 and 14 April. Games customary to the time and other rituals take place, and it is two days of fun for everyone.

Vesak (May) Poya This is a thrice-blessed day for Buddhists as it commemorates three important events in the life of the Gautama Buddha: his birth as Prince Siddhartha, his attainment of enlightenment, and his death. The day is devoted to religious observances and charity, as well as being celebrated with illuminations, pageants and *pandals* (decorated and electrified hoardings). Celebrants set up wayside stalls to distribute food and refreshment to pilgrims and passers-by.

Galle/Jaffna Music Festival (GalleMusicFestival; JaffnaMusicFestival) This two-day festival of local and international music is held in Jaffna in odd-numbered years and Galle in even-numbered years, usually in late May.

Poson (June) Poya Second in importance only to the Vesak Poya, Poson commemorates the advent of Buddhism in Sri Lanka and is celebrated with religious observances in addition to illuminations and processions.

Esala Perahera Sri Lanka's oldest and most spectacular Buddhist festival, held over ten nights in Kandy, honours the Buddha tooth relic preserved in the Dalada Maligawa (Temple of the Tooth), as well as its four guardian deities: Natha, Vishnu, Kataragama and Pattini. During the preliminary five days, the perahera is held within the precincts of each of these five temples. The public perahera then begins, taking place over five spectacular nights with men cracking whips leading the parade, followed by men bearing flags of the various provinces of the former Kandyan kingdom. You will also see jugglers and fire-eaters as well as elephants of varying stature. The nightly parade lasts at least 3 hours. The Esala Perahera takes place over the build-up to the Esala (July) or Nikini (August) Poya and focuses on the Temple of the Tooth. Check out w sridaladamaligawa.lk for more background, and dates for any given year. There are also Esala festivals at Kataragama and Munneswaram, both associated with daring displays of fire-walking, and at Dondra and Bellanwila.

Vel Though not an official holiday, Vel is Colombo's main Hindu festival, with the ornately decorated Vel Chariot making its annual trip between ancient temples in the suburbs of Pettah, Wellawatta and Bambalapitiya. It takes place over July or August.

Deepavali The festival of lights celebrated by all Hindus takes place in late October or early November and commemorates the return from exile of the heroic deity Rama.

Ill Poya The last poya of the rainy season, the November poya also marks the end of the Vassana Samaya, a period of retreat practised by Bhikkhu monks, who stay indoors to meditate for the duration. At many temples it is marked by the Katina Cheeva ceremony, a colourful procession during which the Katina Robe and other clothes intended for the monks are carried to the temple by beneficent locals.

Unduvap Poya Also known as Sangamitta, the year's final poya commemorates the arrival in Sri Lanka of the shoot of the sacred Bo Tree under which Gautama Buddha attained enlightenment.

SHOPPING

The best shops are in Colombo but most resorts have a few souvenir shops specialising in batiks, lace, woodwork and other crafts. Gem shops are most prolific in Ratnapura but there are also plenty in Colombo, Galle, Kandy and the larger resorts. Other less tourist-oriented towns and villages are a wonderful jumble of local shops from bakeries and sweet vendors to jewellers and florists (actually, funeral parlours). A visit to a village market is fascinating, and great for photography of odd goods and characters, but be prepared to haggle, as prices are often inflated

UNUSUAL SOUVENIRS

Colombo resident Rehan Mudannayake lists ideas for unusual local souvenirs easily obtainable at stores in Colombo and certain tourist resorts.

JEWELLED ELEPHANTS Wooden elephants dexterously covered with colourful beads, mirrors and sparkling colours make a bright pachyderm present.

WOODEN SPOONS Spoons made of sanded coconut shell with painted wooden handles are fun for the kitchen.

DOOR STOPPERS Wooden door stoppers amusingly decorated with figures of Ceylon colonials bedecked in moustaches, sarongs and saris.

FLOATING CANDLES Flower-shaped candles in yellow and white modelled on the (araliya) frangipani blossom and purple and yellow lotus shapes, to light and float in a bowl of water.

KITUL PLACE MATS Mats made from polished strips of *kitul* (sugar palm) wood.

HANDMADE NATURAL SOAP Soap made and scented with natural ingredients such as cinnamon, sandalwood, coconut, eucalyptus, aloe and peppermint.

HAND-WOVEN SARONGS Hand-woven sarongs make a startling fashion statement in glorious colours, particularly the vibrant orange matching the colour of a monk's robe, and deep greens and blues.

SOFT TOYS Locally made cuddly geckos, monkeys and elephants make a tropical alternative to the teddy bear.

BEERALU LACE Lace tray- and tablecloths with daintily decorated edges which tourist souvenir purchasing will keep alive.

for foreigners. In catering specifically for tourists the prices quoted could be triple what the vendor is prepared to accept.

CRAFTS Sri Lankan handicrafts are the products of age-old techniques and tools, and of natural, indigenous raw materials, fashioned in the cottages of craftsmen and women, or in rural craft centres, and incorporate a legacy of centuries of skill. The ancient Indo-Aryan social system assigned certain trades and pursuits to specific socio-economic groups, or castes. It was within these castes that historical skills were preserved with a high degree of purity and a distinct ethnic identity. Traditional handicrafts have vivid colour combinations (mainly red, green, yellow and black) and bold design. Items are made of silver and brass; reed, rush, bamboo and rattan; coir (coconut fibre); lacquer ware; batik, handloom fabrics and lace. Also there are drums and other musical instruments, pottery, wood carvings including demonic masks, papier mâché dolls, embroidered garments and linen.

BOOKS AND MAPS If you are looking for reading matter relating to Sri Lanka, there are some very good bookshops in Colombo and Galle, and there are also adequate ones in some smaller towns and certain major hotels. For general holiday reading, most hotels that regularly cater to tourists maintain a useful library where you can trade in your finished novels for something unread. A useful map book for people spending time in Sri Lanka is the excellent A4 *Sri Lanka Road Atlas* (Sarasavi Publishers) which covers the entire island at 1:250,00 and also has street maps of a few major towns. Also useful is the 112-page *Arjuna's A–Z Street Guide*, which has indexed colour street maps not just of Colombo and suburbs but also of Galle, Kandy, Nuwara Eliya, Negombo, Anuradhapura, Polonnaruwa, Trincomalee, Batticaloa and Jaffna.

SUPERMARKETS The most consistently reliable supermarket chain is the iconic Cargills Food City, which operates more than 300 branches countrywide, including one or more in most towns of any substance. Most branches stock a fair selection of imported and local packaged goods, fresh fruit and vegetables, fresh and frozen meat and fish, and stationery and toiletries, while larger branches often include a liquor outlet and pharmacy. Opening hours are generally ⊕ 08.00–20.00 daily (some branches keep slightly shorter hours) and the website **w** cargillsceylon.com incorporates a useful store locator. Smaller supermarkets can also be found in most towns, but seldom are they comparable to the local Cargills.

MEDIA AND COMMUNICATIONS

INTERNET The internet is as ubiquitous in Sri Lanka as it is elsewhere. With a handful of exceptions countrywide, pretty much every hotel and guesthouse listed in this guidebook now offers Wi-Fi access to guests, usually for free but occasionally at a nominal charge, as do many restaurants. For a more-or-less permanent connection, buy a local SIM card and data bundle for your mobile phone (see below).

POST International post is cheap and reasonably reliable, but slow. To help speed things up, best send all post from Colombo's General Post Office, at the back entrance of Fort railway station. The philatelic bureau here sells a collection of intriguing first-day covers.

NEWSPAPERS Three major daily newspapers are published in English: the government-owned *Daily News* (**w** dailynews.lk), and *Island* (**w** island.lk) and the *Daily Mirror* (**w** dailymirror.lk), which are independent. All carry agency and English newspaper reports. Sunday newspapers include the *Observer* (part of the same government group as the *Daily News*), the *Sunday Times* (part of the same group as the *Daily Mirror*) and the *Sunday Island*. International news magazines are available at hotel bookshops and Colombo supermarket outlets.

TELEPHONE Sri Lanka has a reliable landline phone network. All landline numbers are ten digits long, and begin with a three-digit area code that starts with a zero and is followed by any number other than zero (since '00' is the international dialling out code) or seven (which is reserved for mobile numbers). There are also half a dozen mobile networks, all of which use ten-digit numbers starting with '07'. If you're going to be in Sri Lanka for any length of time, rather than roaming on your home number, which can be very costly, it is worth buying a SIM card from a local provider and inserting it in your phone (assuming it isn't locked). This is a simple procedure – it takes 5 minutes at the airport on arrival – and an outlay of

EMERGENCY NUMBERS

Directory Assistance ☎1231 (national), 1234 (international)
Police emergency number ☎118/119
Emergency, fire & ambulance service ☎110
Accident service (Colombo General Hospital) ☎011 269 1111
Police Emergency ☎011 243 3333
Tourist Police ☎011 242 1052
Flight information ☎019 733 2677/011 225 2861

less than US$10 should also get you all the airtime you'd need for a week or two in the country, as well as a data bundle providing direct access to internet, emails and all your apps via the local network. The national provider Mobitel (**w** *mobitel.lk*) is generally regarded to be the most reliable, and it has the most widespread network countrywide (though reception can be spotty in the vicinity of Sinharaja Forest Reserve). Dialog (**w** *dialog.lk*) is the largest operator in terms of subscribers but tends to be strongest in major urban areas.

International calls When phoning abroad from Sri Lanka, dial 00 followed by the international dialling code (eg: 44 for the UK) and then the number you want to call but dropping any leading zero. Calling Sri Lanka from overseas, the country code is +94, and you need to drop the leading zero from the local number, so that 011 234 5678 would become +94 11 234 5678.

TELEVISION AND RADIO The state television service is of limited interest to tourists, but most hotels supplement this with a vast satellite bouquet including the likes of CNN, BBC World and various sports and movie channels. The Colombo-based government-owned Sri Lanka Broadcasting Corporation serves the whole island through various channels in English, Sinhala and Tamil. There are several independent radio stations that broadcast local and international pop music.

CULTURAL ETIQUETTE

Sri Lankans are tolerant of breaches in social etiquette by foreigners, so do not let your anxiety to conform and not give offence deter you from enjoying your holiday. It is accepted that you, as a foreigner, might not be privileged to know very much about local habits. The major culture shock will come when you are invited to eat in a Sri Lankan home or local eatery, and find there is no cutlery. Thus you discover that the technique of eating with your fingers is not as easy as it looks. You use only your right hand (the left hand is reserved for ablutions), letting your fingers and thumb mix the food together into a convenient-sized morsel, which you then pop into your mouth using your thumb as a guide. If you can't manage, you won't cause offence if you ask for a spoon and use that instead.

The Sri Lankan all-purpose greeting is *ayubowan*, uttered while keeping one's own hands with palms together at chest height. It means 'may you have long life' and, if you are greeted in that manner, respond in kind. Handshaking is an acceptable greeting, but do not offer your hand to a monk.

Other breaches of local etiquette include kissing or hugging in public, skimpy clothing and nudity (in resort towns, beachwear should be reserved for the beach, and women should never go topless), and displays of brashness or anger. It is

TEMPLE TIPS

The following rules and guidelines should be observed when visiting Buddhist temples both active and historical.

COVER UP Knees, shoulders and cleavage should be covered in all temples and religious sites. Wear long trousers, or failing that a medium-length skirt or trousers that fall below the knee, as well as a shirt or scarf that covers your shoulders.

REMOVE SHOES AND HEADGEAR Shoes, hats and other head coverings should always be removed and left outside the main worship area when you enter a temple. A pile of shoes is an obvious indication of where to leave them. Some more sprawling temple sites are seated on rocky outcrops or stone platforms that become intolerably hot underfoot below the tropical sun, so either visit in the early morning, or make a habit of carrying a pair of socks – which are permissible foot attire – as a fall-back. Shoes must also be taken off before entering a Hindu temple – and, more surprisingly, some Christian churches.

SHOW RESPECT Turn off mobile phones, remove headphones, lower your voice and avoid inappropriate conversation. Eating, smoking and chewing gum are also frowned upon at religious sites. Public demonstrations of intimate behaviour such as kissing and hugging are considered impolite in Sri Lanka at the best of times and would be totally unacceptable during a temple visit.

RESPECT THE STATUES Never touch, sit near, or climb on a statue. Pointing at statues and other temple artefacts is considered to be extremely rude. It is usually more than acceptable to take documentary photographs of Buddha and other temple statues, but not to take selfies or other photographs of people posing in front of them. This is because of a strong taboo against showing your back to a Buddha icon. It is conventional to walk around dagobas in a clockwise direction in order that your left hand (the one used for ablutions) always faces the other way.

CHOOSE YOUR TIMING The ideal time to visit a temple is when few other tourists are around and a puja service – often accompanied by drums and horns – is under way. Tour groups tend to arrive after breakfast (08.00 onwards and the last ones are usually gone by late afternoon (after 17.00). Puja timings vary from one shrine to the next, but typical hours are 06.30–07.00, 10.45–11.15 and 18.30–19.00. Temperature-wise, the most pleasant time to be out and about is shortly after sunrise or just before sunset, times that also often offer the best photographic light. All things considered, then, the ideal time to visit a popular temple is early morning (before 07.00) or late afternoon (arriving at 17.00 and holding on for any evening puja). Temples tend to be busiest with domestic tourist and worshippers on poya days, which can be a mixed blessing – things tend to be more lively, but also more crowded.

particularly important to observe local etiquette in and around religious temples of all types: Buddhist, Hindu, Muslim or Christian.

People generally don't mind having their photograph taken, but do ask first – although asking permission will often have them posing like mad, instead of the natural shot you were hoping for.

4

Health and Safety

with Dr Felicity Nicholson

Sri Lanka is home to several tropical diseases unfamiliar to those living in more temperate and sanitary climates. However, with adequate preparation, the chances of serious mishap are small, especially now that malaria has been eradicated. And in the unlikely event you are taken ill, decent hospitals and pharmacies exist in most large towns, consultation fees and laboratory tests are relatively inexpensive, and doctors and pharmacists almost invariably speak good English. Commonly required medicines such as broad-spectrum antibiotics, painkillers and antihistamines are widely available, but anybody who has specific needs relating to a less common medical condition should bring the necessary treatment with them.

PREPARATIONS

Sensible preparation will go a long way to ensuring your trip goes smoothly. Particularly for first-time visitors to Asia, this includes a visit to a travel clinic to discuss vaccinations. A full list of travel clinic websites worldwide is available at w istm.org. For other journey preparation information, consult w travelhealthpro.org.uk (UK) or w wwwnc.cdc.gov/travel (US). Information about various medications may be found on w netdoctor.co.uk/travel. All advice found online should be used in conjunction with expert advice received prior to or during travel.

The following summary points are worth emphasising:

- Don't travel without comprehensive medical **travel insurance** that will fly you home in an emergency.
- Make sure all your **immunisations** are up to date. A yellow fever certificate is not required unless you are coming from a yellow fever endemic zone. It's also reckless to travel in the tropics without being up to date on tetanus, polio and diphtheria (now given as an all-in-one vaccine, Revaxis) and hepatitis A. Immunisation against, typhoid, hepatitis B, rabies, Japanese encephalitis and TB may also be recommended.
- The biggest health risk used to be **malaria**, but this is no longer the case. Indeed, in 2016 the World Health Organization finally declared Sri Lanka to be malaria-free after a 3½-year period when no locally transmitted cases were recorded. Hence there is no reason to take anti-malarial drugs, though you might want to confirm the situation before you travel, and should still take precautions against being bitten by mosquitoes, which also carry dengue fever and the like.
- Though advised for everyone, a **pre-exposure rabies vaccination**, involving three doses taken over a minimum of 21 days, is particularly important if you intend to have contact with animals, or are likely to be 24 hours away from medical help.
- Anybody travelling away from major centres should carry a **personal first aid kit**. Contents might include a good drying antiseptic (eg: iodine or potassium

Any prolonged immobility, including travel by land or air, can result in deep-vein thrombosis (DVT) with the risk of embolus to the lungs. Certain factors can increase the risk and these include:

- History of DVT or pulmonary embolism
- Recent surgery to pelvic region or legs
- Cancer
- Stroke
- Heart disease
- Inherited tendency to clot (thrombophilia)
- Obesity
- Pregnancy
- Hormone therapy
- Older age
- Being taller than 6ft (1.8m) or shorter than 5ft (1.5m)

A DVT causes painful swelling and redness of the calf or sometimes the thigh. It is only dangerous if a clot travels to the lungs (pulmonary embolus). Symptoms of a pulmonary embolism – which commonly start three to ten days after a long flight – include chest pain, shortness of breath, and sometimes coughing up small amounts of blood. Anyone who thinks that they might have a DVT needs to see a doctor immediately.

PREVENTION OF DVT
- Wear loose comfortable clothing
- Do anti-DVT exercises and move around when possible
- Drink plenty of fluids during the flight
- Avoid taking sleeping pills unless you are able to lie flat
- Avoid excessive tea, coffee and alcohol
- Consider wearing flight socks or support stockings

If you think you are at increased risk of a clot, ask your doctor if it is safe to travel.

permanganate), Band-Aids, suncream, insect repellent, aspirin or paracetamol, antifungal cream (eg: Canesten), ciprofloxacin or norfloxacin (for severe diarrhoea), antibiotic eye drops, tweezers, condoms or femidoms, a digital thermometer and a needle-and-syringe kit with accompanying letter from a health-care professional.
- Bring any **drugs or devices relating to known medical conditions** with you. That applies both to those who are on medication prior to departure, and those who are, for instance, allergic to bee stings, or prone to attacks of asthma.
- Prolonged immobility on long-haul flights can result in **deep vein thrombosis**; for further information, see box, above.

COMMON MEDICAL PROBLEMS

TRAVELLERS' DIARRHOEA Many visitors to unfamiliar destinations suffer a dose of travellers' diarrhoea, usually as a result of imbibing contaminated food or water. Rule one in avoiding diarrhoea and other sanitation-related diseases is arguably to wash your hands regularly, particularly before snacks and meals, and after handling banknotes (small denominations in particular are often engrained in filth). As for what food you can safely eat, a useful maxim is:

PEEL IT, BOIL IT, COOK IT OR FORGET IT.

This means that fruit you have washed and peeled yourself should be safe, as should hot cooked foods. However, raw foods, cold cooked foods, salads, fruit salads prepared by others, ice cream and ice are all risky. It is rarer to get sick from drinking contaminated water but it happens, so stick to bottled water, which is widely available.

If you suffer a bout of diarrhoea, it is dehydration that makes you feel awful, so drink lots of water and other clear fluids. These can be infused with sachets of oral rehydration salts, though any dilute mixture of sugar and salt in water will do you good, for instance a bottled soda with a pinch of salt. If diarrhoea persists beyond a couple of days, it is possible it is a symptom of a more serious sanitation-related illness (typhoid, cholera, hepatitis, dysentery, worms, etc), so get to a doctor. If the diarrhoea is greasy and bulky, and is accompanied by sulphurous (eggy) burps, one likely cause is giardia, which is best treated with tinidazole (four x 500mg in one dose, repeated seven days later if symptoms persist).

RABIES This deadly disease can be carried by any mammal and is usually transmitted to humans via a bite or deep scratch. Beware village dogs and habituated monkeys, but assume that *any* mammal that bites or scratches you (or even licks you, whether or not you have an obvious wound) might be rabid. First, scrub the wound with soap under a running tap, or while pouring water from a jug, then pour on a strong iodine or alcohol solution, which will guard against infections and might reduce the risk of the rabies virus entering the body. Whether or not you underwent pre-exposure vaccination, it is vital to obtain post-exposure prophylaxis as soon as possible after the incident. However, if you have had at least two of the three pre-exposure vaccines, then you won't need to get Rabies Immunoglobulin which is often in short supply and expensive. Death from rabies is probably one of the worst ways to go, and once you show symptoms it is too late to do anything – the mortality rate is 100%.

JAPANESE ENCEPHALITIS Japanese encephalitis is a viral infection which is transmitted by mosquitoes that live and breed around rice fields which bite the pigs and wading birds that carry the disease. As the name suggests, the virus causes an inflammation to the brain. Although cases in Western travellers are rare, there is a 30% mortality meaning that it has a high impact if you contract the disease, for which there is no treatment. There are two peak seasons in Sri Lanka, October to January and May to June. It is possible to get cases outside of these times but they are very rare. Travellers who will be remote, or who are spending a month or more in Sri Lanka, or those who are often bitten and would feel safer having had the vaccine should consider vaccination. The Ixiaro vaccine used in the UK is ideally given as a two-dose course at least 24 days apart. This gives good protection for about two years. A shorter course of just seven days apart can be used when time is short but lasts for a year. A subsequent booster given before the age of 65 will give a further ten years' protection.

4

TETANUS Tetanus is caught through deep dirty wounds, including animal bites, so ensure that such wounds are thoroughly cleaned. Immunisation protects for ten years, provided you don't have an overwhelming number of tetanus bacteria on board. If you haven't had a tetanus shot in ten years, or you are unsure, get a booster immediately.

HIV/AIDS Rates of HIV/AIDS infection are not particularly high but it and other sexually transmitted diseases are present. Condoms (or femidoms) greatly reduce the risk of transmission.

SKIN INFECTIONS Any mosquito bite or small nick is an opportunity for a skin infection in warm humid climates, so clean and cover the slightest wound in a good drying antiseptic such as dilute iodine, potassium permanganate or crystal (or gentian) violet. Prickly heat, most likely to be contracted at the humid coast, is a fine pimply rash that can be alleviated by cool showers, dabbing (not rubbing) dry and talc, and sleeping naked under a fan or in an air-conditioned room. Fungal infections also get a hold easily in hot moist climates, so wear 100% cotton socks and underwear and shower frequently.

EYE PROBLEMS Bacterial conjunctivitis (pink eye) is a common infection in the tropics, particularly for contact-lens wearers. Symptoms are sore, gritty eyelids that often stick closed in the morning. They will need treatment with antibiotic drops or ointment. Lesser eye irritation should settle with bathing in salt water and keeping the eyes shaded. If an insect flies into your eye, extract it with great care, ensuring you do not crush or damage it, otherwise you may get a nastily inflamed eye from toxins secreted by the creature.

SUNSTROKE AND DEHYDRATION Overexposure to the sun can lead to short-term sunburn or sunstroke, and increases the long-term risk of skin cancer. Wear

AVOIDING MOSQUITO AND INSECT BITES

Mosquitoes tend to be most active at dusk and after dark. Most bites can thus be avoided by covering up at night. This means donning a long-sleeved shirt, trousers and socks from around 30 minutes before dusk until you retire to bed, and applying a DEET-based insect repellent (ideally around 50% DEET) to any exposed flesh. It is best to sleep under a net, or in an air-conditioned room, though sleeping under a fan will also reduce (though not entirely eliminate) bites. Travel clinics usually sell a good range of nets and repellents, as well as Permethrin treatment kits, which will render even the tattiest net a lot more protective, and helps prevent mosquitoes from biting through a net when you roll against it. These measures will also do much to reduce exposure to other nocturnal biters. Bear in mind, too, that most flying insects are attracted to light: leaving one on in a poorly screened hotel room will greatly increase the insect presence in your sleeping quarters.

It is also advisable to think about avoiding bites when walking in the countryside by day, especially in wetland habitats, which often teem with the diurnal mosquitoes that sometimes carry dengue fever. Wear a long loose shirt and trousers, preferably 100% cotton, as well as proper walking or hiking shoes with heavy socks (the ankle is particularly vulnerable to bites), and apply a DEET-based insect repellent to any exposed skin.

a T-shirt and waterproof sunscreen when swimming. When visiting outdoor historical sites or walking in the direct sun, cover up with long, loose clothes, wear a hat, and use sunscreen. The glare and the dust can be hard on the eyes, so bring UV-protecting sunglasses. A less direct effect of the tropical heat is dehydration, so drink more fluids than you would at home.

OTHER SAFETY CONCERNS

WILD ANIMALS There are still a few parts of Sri Lanka where you might stumble across a wild elephant, the most dangerous of the country's terrestrial creatures. Elephants almost invariably mock charge and indulge in some hair-raising trumpeting before they attack in earnest. Provided that you back off at the first sign of unease, they are unlikely to take any further notice of you. If you see them before they see you, give them a wide berth, bearing in mind they are most likely to attack if surprised at close proximity. If an animal charges you, the safest course of action is to head for the nearest tree and climb it.

There are a few places where monkeys (in particular toque macaques) have become pests. Feeding these animals is highly irresponsible, since it encourages them to scavenge and lose their fear of humans. Although monkeys can give a nasty bite (one that should treated for rabies), they are unlikely to do serious damage except perhaps to young children.

Leopards and sloth bears are both large enough to kill a person, and have occasionally been known to attack one, but such events are too rare to be considered a real cause for concern.

SNAKE BITES All manner of venomous snakes occur in Sri Lanka, but they are unlikely to be encountered since they generally slither away when they sense the seismic vibrations made by a walking person. Wearing good boots when walking in the bush will protect against the 50% of snake bites that occur below the ankle, and long trousers will help deflect bites higher up on the leg, reducing the quantity of venom injected. In the unlikely event of a bite, medical attention should be sought immediately.

CAR ACCIDENTS Dangerous driving is probably the biggest threat to life and limb. On a self-drive visit, drive defensively, being especially wary of stray livestock and reckless overtaking manoeuvres. Try to avoid driving at night. On a chauffeured tour, don't be afraid to tell the driver to slow or calm down if you think he is too fast or reckless.

MARINE DANGERS Although many beaches in Sri Lanka offer safe swimming conditions in season, most also shelve rapidly, and swimmers risk being dragged away from shore by riptides and strong undertows out of season or in rough conditions. Never swim when red warning flags are flying and, bearing in mind that most beaches lack for dedicated lifeguards, don't swim when conditions look rough, at any time of year. Even in calm conditions, it is best to ask local advice on any beach that isn't obviously regarded as safe for swimming, and to avoid going in too deep unless you have some sort of flotation device with you. Never swim under the influence of alcohol. Once in the water, if you sense the presence of a strong undertow, get out immediately. If you are caught in a riptide, it is generally advisable not to fight the current by trying to swim directly to shore, but rather to save your strength by floating on your back or swimming parallel to shore until the tide weakens, and only then to try to get back to land.

Viceroy Special
A journey of distinction

Viceroy II - An odyssey in luxury redefined

T1 Diesel Deluxe Railcar - An intimate rail experience

Part Two

COLOMBO AND SURROUNDS

Overview of Part Two

The main port of arrival to Sri Lanka – indeed, to all intents and purposes, the only one – is Bandaranaike International Airport, which stands a short distance inland of the west coast 30km north of the country's largest city and ipso facto capital, Colombo. This section covers Colombo, the coastal strip either side of it and Bandaranaike International Airport, and a few major routes running inland from the coast to the Cultural Triangle, Kandy and other more remote regions covered later in this book. It is split into four reasonably self-explanatory chapters.

The first deals with Colombo and its immediate suburban environs, including the adjacent municipality of Dehiwala–Mount Lavinia. The next chapter deals with the west coast running north from Colombo, most notably the large seaside town of Negombo, only 8km from the airport, and the more remote and rustic Kalpitiya Peninsula. The next chapter deals with routes inland, covering a number of attractions that could be visited *en route* to the likes of Kandy or Dambulla, but that are also close enough to Colombo and Negombo to be visited as day trips from them. The last chapter in this section deals with Sri Lanka's best-established and most developed stretch of coastal resorts, which run south from Colombo towards Galle and include Bentota, Kosgoda and Hikkaduwa. Logistically, most visitors to Sri Lanka will take one of two approaches to the region covered in this section of the book. Many holidaymakers will spend their entire vacation at one or two of the resorts covered in this section, possibly heading inland or south to Galle for the odd day excursion, in which case distances are sufficiently small that you could transfer straight from the airport to your resort of choice and bypass the capital altogether if you so choose. By contrast, most independent travellers will spend a night or two in the area at the start and/or end of their trip, in which case it is a straight choice between the urban buzz of Colombo or Mount Lavinia, the slightly greater convenience of less-built-up Negombo, or the more genuinely resort-like environs of Bentota and Hikkaduwa.

HIGHLIGHTS

COLOMBO FORT AND PETTAH (pages 102–8) These two adjacent districts inland of the harbour form the historical hub of the capital, dotted as they are with old colonial churches and hotels, colourful Hindu and Buddhist temples, low-key museums and thronging open-air bazaars – as well as the cosmopolitan culinary scene centred on the restored and revitalised Old Dutch Hospital.

COLOMBO NATIONAL MUSEUM (pages 111–12) Established in a purpose-built Neoclassical building in 1877, Sri Lanka's finest museum houses a collection of 100,000 artefacts (not all on display) including some superb Buddha statues, beautiful bronzes of Hindu deities, and a Kandyan Hall dominated by King Vimaladharmasuriya II's throne.

MOUNT LAVINIA (pages 113–20) Situated just 30 minutes' tuktuk ride from Colombo's central Fort District, leafy Mount Lavinia possesses an uncontrived beach resort atmosphere, a likeably time-warped Edwardian architectural ambience, and no shortage of down-to-earth guesthouses and beach restaurants offering good value to backpackers.

NEGOMBO (pages 124–34) There are prettier resorts in Sri Lanka, but lagoonside Negombo – on the doorstep of Bandaranaike International Airport, and serviced by more than a hundred resorts and guesthouses, as well as a great selection of beachfront restaurants – makes for an ideal first or last port of call for visitors who prefer to avoid the capital.

THE KALPITIYA PENINSULA (pages 137–43) This flat, sandy and emphatically rustic sliver of land dividing the vast Puttalam Lagoon from the open sea is Sri Lanka's premier kitesurfing hotspot, as well as an emerging marine wildlife destination offering some fine snorkelling, diving, and dolphin and whale watching.

KURUNEGALA (pages 153–87) Easily visited *en route* to the Cultural Triangle, the 14th-century capital of Dambadeniya has a pretty lakeside location below a gigantic 320m-high whaleback known as Elephant Rock and is usefully positioned for visits to half a dozen off-the-beaten-track archaeological sites.

YAPAHUWA (page 161) Reminiscent of a scaled-down version of Sigiriya, the short-lived but spectacular rock fortress at Yapahuwa was built by King Bhuvanaikabahu I in c1271 and is renowned for the lively cast of deities, dwarves and mythical creatures that adorn its long, granite stairwell.

KELANI VALLEY RAILWAY (pages 161–3) Serviced by four trains daily, this non-electrified single-track line running inland from Colombo was established in 1902 and offers train buffs fabulous views as it cautiously ascends 60km of sharp curves to terminate at Avissawella, from where buses continue to Low Hill Country landmarks such as Kitulgala and Sinharaja via Ratnapura.

BENTOTA (pages 171–87) The most developed beach resort on Sri Lanka's west coast is the all-but-contiguous 10km band of tourist development that flanks the Bentota river mouth some 65km south of Colombo and centres on the surprisingly gritty north-bank town and transport hub of Aluthgama.

HIKKADUWA (pages 195–208) Protected by a calming offshore reef, Hikkaduwa beach offers ideal swimming and snorkelling conditions from December to April, while the adjacent Wewala and Narigama beaches are good for surfing and bodyboarding. A non-stop strip of hotels and guesthouses lines this relatively urbanised resort, and several venerable Buddhist shrines can be found in the vicinity.

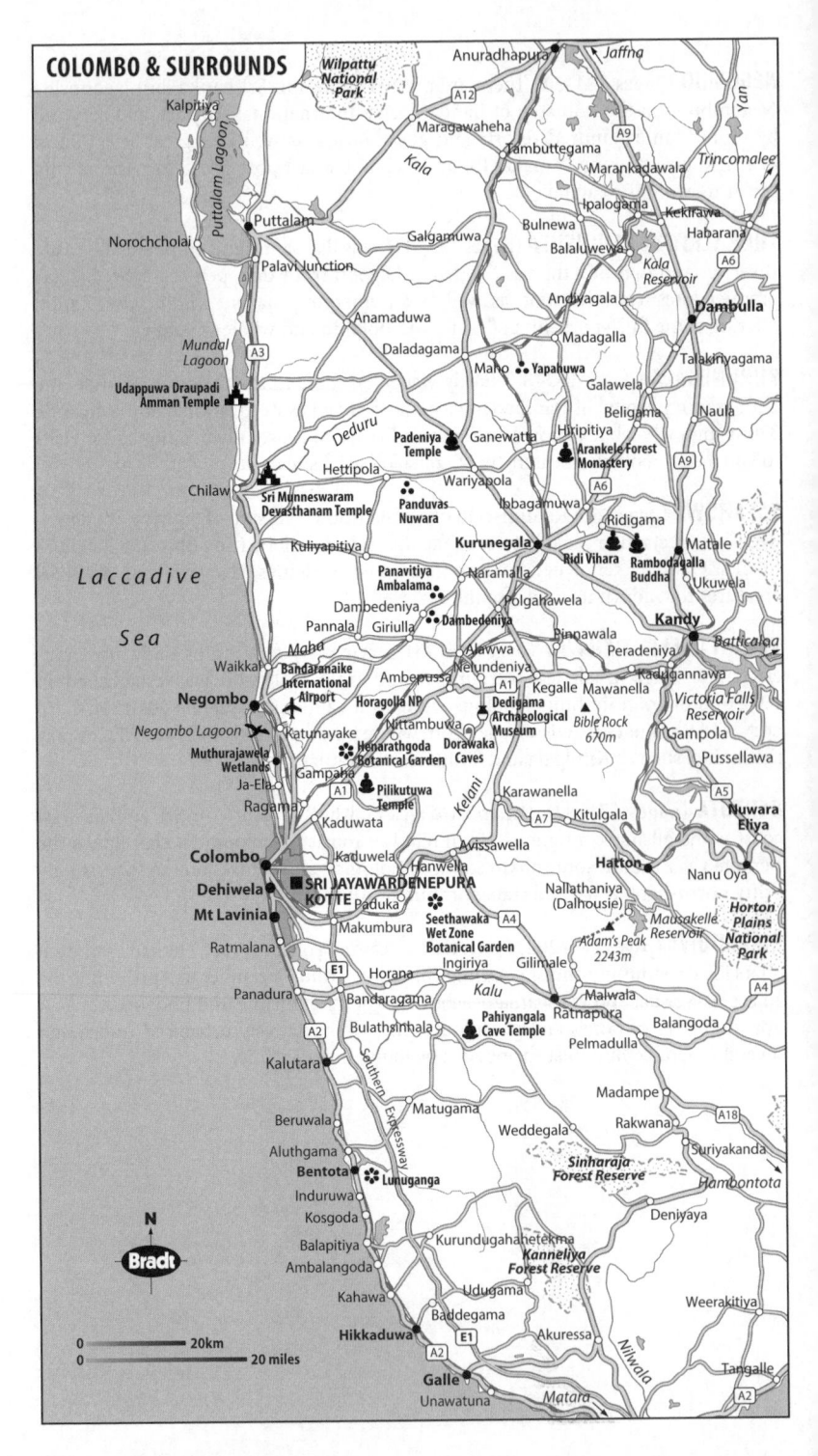

5

Colombo

Set on a fine natural harbour on the island's west coast, Sri Lanka's largest city (population 800,000) and main commercial hub is the focal point of a metropolitan area that incorporates Sri Jayawardenepura Kotte (which replaced Colombo as official administrative capital in 1982) and whose population of five million represents about a quarter of the national total. From a travel perspective, Colombo is a difficult city to pin down. Boasting an extensive Indian Ocean frontage just 30km south of Bandaranaike International Airport, it might look, on paper, to be the obvious place to start and/or end an extended trip around Sri Lanka. In practice, however, Colombo's exhaust-infused cocktail of congested horn-blasting traffic, crowded pavements and sticky coastal humidity – combined with a lack of usable beach frontage and paucity of genuinely must-see attractions – makes it unlikely to win over conventional holidaymakers seeking the tranquil escapism of a beach resort.

That said, Colombo, in its favour, is an unusually safe, affordable and welcoming metropolis, with much to occupy travellers wanting to explore urban Sri Lanka on its own terms. The National Museum offers a fine introduction to the country's main archaeological sites, while the engaging inner-city districts of Fort and Pettah are steeped in history, and a growing coterie of art galleries and boutique shops lend the city an appealingly cosmopolitan aura. Elsewhere, multi-cultural Colombo hosts an astonishing urban variety: historical monuments and towering modern skyscrapers, colonial churches and ancient Buddhist temples, gleaming hotels and trendy restaurants, tree-lined boulevards and mysterious lanes, glittering casinos and state-of-the-art 3D cinemas, traditional produce markets and 21st-century shopping malls … it's a fascinating place to explore at whim.

Either way, whether or not you opt to include Colombo in your itinerary is a matter of preference rather than logistics. The popular resort town of Negombo, situated only 10km from Bandaranaike, forms an even more convenient first-/last-night stopover. More southerly beach resorts such as Bentota and Hikkaduwa are easily reached from the airport in a couple of hours after skirting around Colombo. For those who want to move straight on from the airport to the likes of Kandy or Galle, air-conditioned daytime and overnight trains out of Colombo Fort provide a quick getaway. And for the undecided? Well, there's always Mount Lavinia, an attractive seafront suburb whose pleasant swimming beach and host of well-priced budget and mid-range hotels represent a best-of-both-worlds scenario just 30 minutes by tuktuk from central Colombo.

HISTORY

The fine natural harbour running south from the mouth of the Kelani River has attracted maritime trade from the Asian mainland for at least two millennia. Little is known about its specific history until the 8th century, when it was settled by Arab traders whose Muslim descendants are now integrated into the island's so-called Moor community. Two events initiated Colombo's rise to modern pre-eminence. The first, in 1415, was the relocation of the Sinhala capital to Sri Jayawardenepura Kotte (aka Kotte) under the popular King Parakramabahu VI, whose 55-year reign was renowned as an era of island-wide unity, stability and literary prowess. The second was the arrival of the Portuguese at Colombo Harbour in 1505. The Portuguese insisted on visiting Kotte, which was by this time ruled by its founder's grandson Parakramabahu VIII, and were taken there along a long, convoluted route in the hope it would fool them into thinking the Sinhala capital – actually only 5km inland of the modern coastal suburb of Bambalapitiya – was too deep in the interior for a naval attack. Unfortunately, this cunning plan was bamboozled when those Portuguese sailors who had stayed in the harbour fired off a round of cannons that were clearly audible to their compatriots at Kotte.

In 1515, Parakramabahu VIII's successor, Vijayabahu VI, reluctantly granted the military superior Portuguese permission to establish a fortified trade outpost at Colombo. This fort became the first European stronghold on the island, and an important export centre for cinnamon grown in the immediate interior. Vijayabahu VI's unpopular decision created an atmosphere of dissent among the royal family, and in 1521 he was murdered and succeeded by his oldest son, Bhuvanaikabahu VII. Despite this, economic and political ties between Kotte and the expanding Portuguese fort at Colombo were cemented during the 30-year reign of Bhuvanaikabahu VII, who allowed his oldest grandson and chosen heir to be educated by Franciscan monks and convert to Catholicism, rendering him ineligible as a successor to his Buddhist subjects. Following Bhuvanaiekabahu VII's death in 1551, King Mayadunne exploited this rupture to annex much of Kotte to the rival state of Sitawaka. Mayadunne then initiated a series of attacks on Colombo Fort, to be repelled by reinforcements from the Indian headquarters at Goa. Only when Sitawaka collapsed in 1593 was Bhuvanaikabahu VII's grandson installed as a puppet king of Kotte under the name Don Juan Dharmapala. The Portuguese ceased the pretence after Dharmapala's death in 1597, when Kotte officially became a crown territory of King Philip I. This annexation led not only to the entrenchment of Colombo as a colonial capital and base for missionary activity further afield, but also to Kandy's emergence as the country's main stronghold of Sinhala sovereignty.

Colombo was one of the few major Sri Lankan ports to remain in Portuguese hands following the Dutch–Kandyan treaty of 1638 and the fall of Batticaloa, Trincomalee, Galle and Negombo over 1639–40. A protracted Dutch siege led to the capture of Colombo in 1656, two years before the expulsion of the Portuguese from Jaffna signalled the end of the Portuguese Era. Shortly afterwards, the Dutch relocated their military headquarters from Galle to Colombo. By this time, the monopolistic economic nature of the 1638 treaty, which more or less forced Kandyan farmers and producers to sell their produce to appointed Dutch agents at fixed (in both senses of the word) prices, together with the colonial power's refusal to cede control of the island's richest cinnamon-growing regions, had created strong political tensions between the two signatories. As a result, the ramparts of Colombo Fort were expanded and strengthened to protect it from naval and terrestrial incursions, then tested with some regularity during periods of conflict with the Kandyan monarchy. The city grew significantly under the Dutch, who created an extensive network of canals to reclaim the surrounding swampland. This process continued under the British, who captured Colombo in 1796, built the Hamilton Canal to Negombo in 1804, and extended the city south and east beyond the fort's limits, leaving a prescient legacy of wide streets and spacious buildings that now accommodate far more traffic than existed back then.

Over the second half of the 19th century, several old Dutch buildings were replaced by newer and grander British edifices, while the ageing Dutch fortifications, by then militarily redundant, were demolished to make way for urban expansion and development. By the late Victorian era, Colombo had evolved into an attractive modern metropolis, often dubbed the 'Garden City of the East'. Perhaps the most significant post-independence event in Colombo was the Black July Riots of 1983, when ongoing ethnic tensions erupted as a Sinhalese mob burned every last Tamil-owned building and business in Fort District to the ground, and murdered hundreds, possibly thousands, of innocent civilians. The city shed much of its former glister in the aftermath of the riots, and went on to experience a prolonged economic slump exacerbated during the long years of civil war by a combination of LTTE bombings and plain neglect. In more recent times, the end of the war in 2009 initiated a new era of urban regeneration in Colombo, one epitomised by a host of official projects implemented by the Urban Development Authority, and a flurry of private development including the construction of several modern international-class hotels. With some historical poignance, Colombo was officially replaced by Sri Jayawardenepura Kotte as administrative capital of Sri Lanka in 1982, but it remains the island's economic and cultural pulse.

ORIENTATION

Colombo, or at least that subset of the city regularly frequented by tourists, has an uncomplicated layout. **Fort District**, the old city centre (often referred to locally as **Colombo 01**, its postal designation), is set on a small island separated from the mainland by Lake Beira and several narrow canals, but also linked to it by around half a dozen road bridges. Most of Fort District comprises the off-limits Colombo Harbour and the Naval Headquarters, but the remainder of the small island (an area of about 500m by 500m) supports a dense urban huddle of colonial-era buildings, staid upmarket hotels and modern skyscrapers such as the twin-towered World Trade Centre.

Immediately east of Fort, **Pettah** (aka **Colombo 11**) is a compact but densely populated commercial hub focused around the famous Pettah Market. Pettah is Colombo's most important transport hub, housing as it does all the main intercity bus stations, as well as Colombo Fort railway station, the terminus for

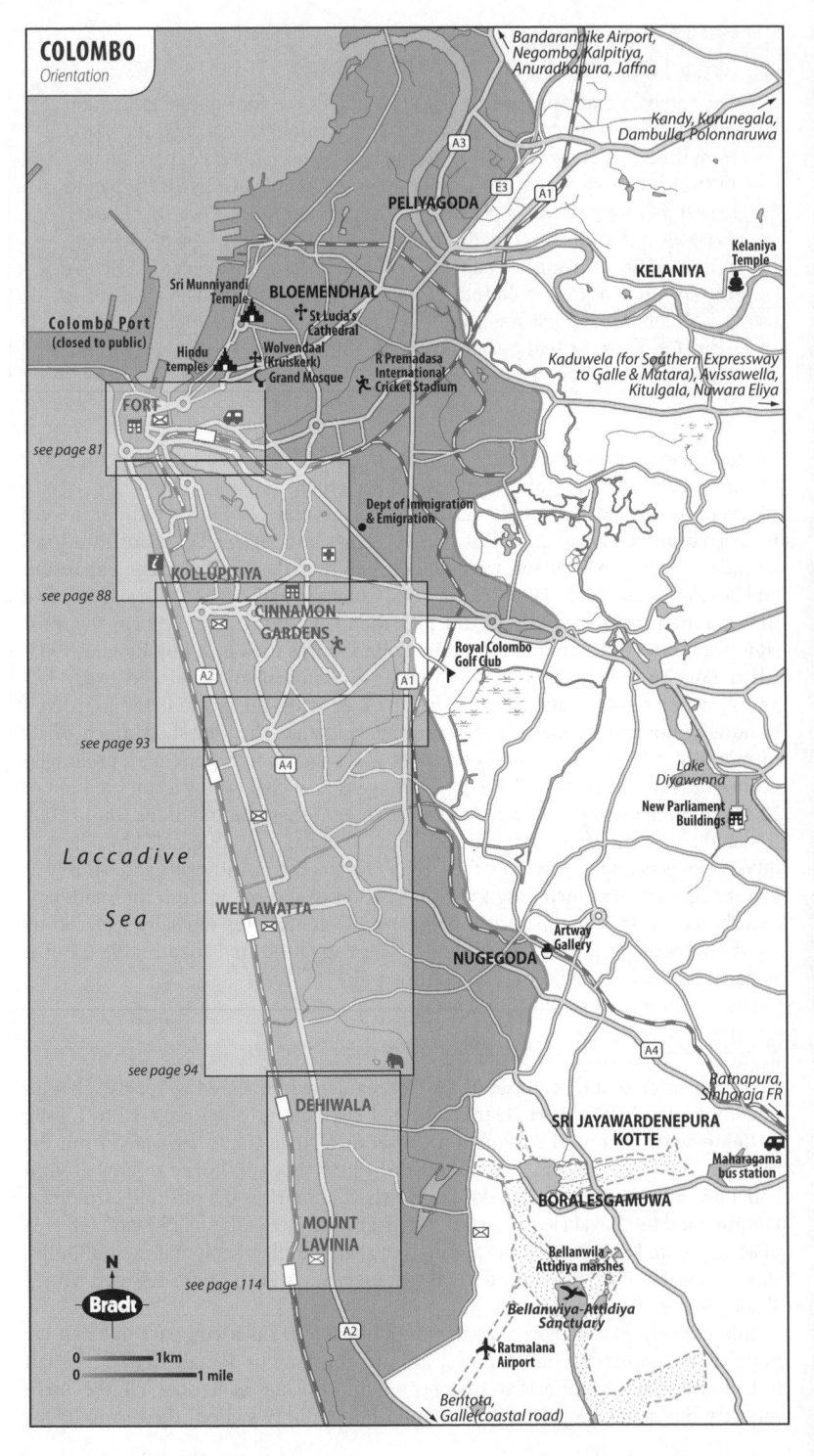

COLOMBO
Orientation

Bandaranaike Airport,
Negombo, Kalpitiya,
Anuradhapura, Jaffna

Kandy, Kurunegala,
Dambulla, Polonnaruwa

A3
E3 A1

PELIYAGODA

KELANIYA

Kelaniya
Temple

Sri Munniyandi
Temple

BLOEMENDHAL

St Lucia's
Cathedral

Colombo Port
(closed to public)

Hindu
temples

Wolvendaal
(Kruiskerk)

Grand Mosque

R Premadasa
International
Cricket Stadium

Kaduwela (for Southern Expressway
to Galle & Matara), Avissawella,
Kitulgala, Nuwara Eliya

FORT

see page 81

Dept of Immigration
& Emigration

KOLLUPITIYA

see page 88

**CINNAMON
GARDENS**

Royal Colombo
Golf Club

see page 93

A2

A4

A1

*Lake
Diyawanna*

**New Parliament
Buildings**

Laccadive

Sea

WELLAWATTA

Artway
Gallery

NUGEGODA

see page 94

A4

Ratnapura,
Sinharaja FR

DEHIWALA

**SRI JAYAWARDENEPURA
KOTTE**

Maharagama
bus station

BORALESGAMUWA

**MOUNT
LAVINIA**

see page 114

Bellanwila-
Attidiya marshes

*Bellanwiya-Attidiya
Sanctuary*

N

Bradt

0 ――――― 1km
0 ――――― 1 mile

Ratmalana
Airport

Bentota,
Galle (coastal road)

78

all northbound intercity trains. Southbound trains leave from Maradana railway station, which lies in the much larger district of **Maradana** (aka **Colombo 10**) to the southeast of Pettah. Maradana is also the site of the Visa Extension office and sprawling Colombo General Hospital.

Immediately south of Fort District, **Galle Face** is a 700m-long beachfront green lined by several of the city's most prominent hotels, among them the Galle Face, Taj Samudra and Cinnamon Grand. Galle Face is the most northerly part of **Kollupitiya** (aka **Colombo 03**), a long narrow suburb that follows the coast south of Fort for about 3.5km past Kollupitiya railway station almost as far as Bambalapitiya railway station. Kollupitiya is known as Colombo's main upmarket shopping area and it supports several malls and moderate-to-upmarket hotels and restaurants. South of Kollupitiya, two further suburbs follow the coast to the boundary with the separate municipality of Dehiwala–Mount Lavinia (pages 113–20). These are the more northerly **Bambalapitiya** (aka **Colombo 04**) and southerly **Wellawatta** (aka **Colombo 06**), both of which share a name with a seaside railway station that stands closest to their northern boundary. Somewhat seedier in character than Kollupitiya, Bambalapitiya supports a wealth of budget hotels and eateries, while Wellawatta is a lively and down-to-earth commercial area dominated by small Tamil shops and family businesses.

The most important thoroughfare through Kollupitiya, Bambalapitiya and Wellawatta, **Galle Road** runs from Galle Face all the way south to Dehiwala–Mount Lavinia (and then on towards Galle itself). **R A de Mel Road**, also known as Duplication Road, runs parallel to and inland of Galle Road south to Wellawatta, while **Marine Drive**, also known as Colombo Plan Road, follows the coast parallel to Galle Road to the municipal boundary with Dehiwala–Mount Lavinia. Almost everything of note in these suburbs either stands alongside one of these three main roads, or a few minutes' walk away. It is worth knowing that, while Marine Drive is a two-way road for its entire length, much of Galle Road is one way running north, while R A de Mel Road is one way running south.

Three smarter inland suburbs are of interest to tourists. The most northerly, **Slave Island** (aka **Colombo 06**), situated inland of Galle Face and west of Lake Beira, is the site of the popular Gangaramaya Temple. Immediately south of this, **Cinnamon Gardens** (aka **Colombo 07**) is a prestigious residential suburb whose landmarks include Viharamahadevi Park, the National Museum and Independence Memorial. Further south still, **Havelock Town** (aka **Colombo 05**) is another posh residential area that incorporates the trendily genteel suburb of Thimbirigasyaya.

GETTING THERE AND AWAY

BY AIR The terminus for all international and many domestic flights, Bandaranaike International Airport stands 30km north of central Colombo along the nippy multi-lane Katunayake Expressway. For details of flights and arrival procedures, see pages 42–3. Fresh arrivals can pick up a taxi from one of the semi-official agencies that line the arrivals hall and charge around US$15–20 for a city transfer. Any hotel or guesthouse in Colombo can arrange a taxi to the airport for a similar rate. If you place any value whatsoever on your time, it is emphatically worth paying the nominal toll fee (around US$2 per car) to use the expressway. Note that domestic flights operated by the likes of Cinnamon Air and Helitours leave from Ratmalana Airport, which lies 18km south of central Colombo in Dehiwala–Mount Lavinia.

BY RAIL There are two major stations: Colombo Fort [81 D3] and Maradana [81 G3]. All northbound trains originating in Colombo start at Fort while southbound trains start at Maradana, but in practice you can board at either station, with Fort almost invariably being the more convenient. Reservations for trains to Anuradhapura, Badulla, Kandy, Trincomalee and Batticaloa can be made up to 14 days in advance at Fort's Berth Reservations Office (↘ *011 243 2908;* w *railway. gov.lk;* ⏀ *06.00–14.30 Mon–Sat, 06.00–noon Sun & holidays*), which is also where passengers who book online with ExpoRail or Rajadhani (assuming they have resumed their services) can collect their tickets. For further details of online and phone bookings countrywide, see pages 47–50.

BY ROAD Regular government and private buses connect Colombo to all towns and resorts regularly visited by tourists. Details of regularity and other route-specific information are provided in the *Getting there and away* section of the relevant destination deeper into this book. Locating the bus service you need is usually quite straightforward, since all three main intercity bus stations are huddled close together in Pettah a few hundred metres east of Colombo Fort railway station and Manning Market. Running from south to north, **Bastian Road bus stand** [81 F3] (*south side of Olcott Rd, opposite Pettah Floating Market*) is the main departure point for private buses to most destinations countrywide (the main exception being Negombo and buses that use the Southern Expressway to reach the likes of Galle, Matara and resorts in between), while the **Central bus stand** [81 F2] (*north side of Olcott Rd, next to the Pettah Bo Tree;* ↘ *011 232 8081*) is reserved for all government SLTB buses, and **Gunasinghepura bus stand** [81 F1] (*Bodiraja Rd*) is used by private buses to more local destinations such as Negombo and Aluthgama. About 15km southeast of the city centre (US$3–4 by tuktuk), **Maharagama bus stand** [map, page 78] is the place to pick up private express buses that use the Southern Expressway to the likes of Galle, Matara and the far southeast. Most air-conditioned private buses to Jaffna leave Colombo from **Wellawatta Market** (*Galle Rd*); see page 50 for details.

GETTING AROUND

Colombo is a flat city so short distances are walkable, though fresh arrivals may find that they tire quickly in the heat and humidity, especially in congested areas. Tuktuks putter around ubiquitously and often stop when they see a tourist, even before you hail them. Most tuktuks are metered and charge Rs50 for the first kilometre and Rs32 for every subsequent kilometre, which means a short hop (up to 4km) shouldn't cost more than US$1 and you can cross the city for US$3–4. If you use an unmetered taxi, the fare should be agreed in advance and will depend on your bargaining powers, but you're unlikely to come out on top. Far more expensive but more convenient for those with luggage are taxis, which generally charge fixed rates and come with air conditioning, and are available through all major hotels. Buses traverse the whole city, and regular commuter trains follow the coastal line from Colombo Fort to Mount Lavinia via Kollupitiya, Bambalapitiya, Wellawatta and Dehiwala. However, with tuktuks being so affordable, and pickpockets posing a small but real risk, few travellers make the effort to get to grips with public transport.

CRIME AND SAFETY

Colombo must rank among the world's safest cities. Violent crime against tourists is almost unknown, but as is the case in many cities, pickpockets are known to frequent crowded public transport during rush hour. Be wary of any individual, no matter how well dressed or well spoken, who approaches you in the street talking

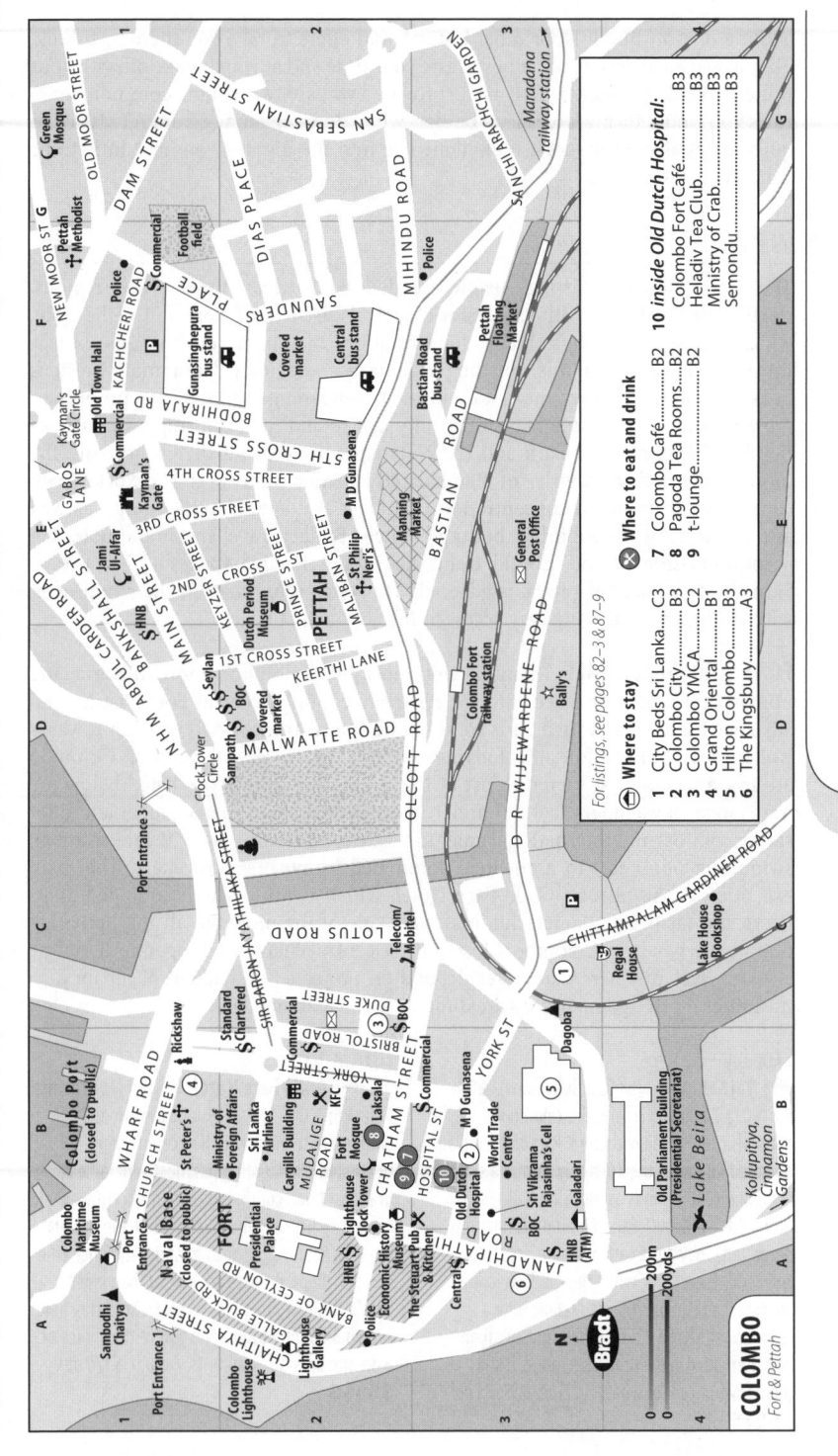

COLOMBO
Fort & Pettah

For listings, see pages 82–3 & 87–9

Where to stay

1　City Beds Sri Lanka.....C3
2　Colombo City.....B3
3　Colombo YMCA.....C2
4　Grand Oriental.....B1
5　Hilton Colombo.....B3
6　The Kingsbury.....A3

Where to eat and drink

7　Colombo Café.....B2
8　Pagoda Tea Rooms.....B2
9　t-lounge.....B2

10　inside Old Dutch Hospital:
　　Colombo Fort Café.....B3
　　Heladiv Tea Club.....B3
　　Ministry of Crab.....B3
　　Semondu.....B3

about a one-off Buddhist or other festival, and offers to take you there by tuktuk. They are scam artists who'll at best waste your time and at worst make off with your wallet or pocket contents. That aside, provided you apply the same common-sense rules you would in any large city – be alert when drawing money from ATMs, avoid quiet alleys after dark, don't walk alone late into the night – you have little to be concerned about.

WHERE TO STAY

The accommodation listings below are divided between three broad regions, starting in the north with the historic central districts of Fort and Galle Face, which house Colombo's main concentration of upmarket business hotels. Immediately south of this, bustling Kollupitiya and leafy Cinnamon Gardens boast a good selection of more individualistic mid-range to upmarket properties, most well located for day trips to the city centre and for exploring around Lake Beira, Viharamahadevi Park and the National Museum. Further south still, the more downmarket suburbs of Bambalapitiya, Wellawatta and Havelock Town support the city's main concentration of budget and shoestring lodgings, as well as a few worthwhile suburban boutique hotels. Budget travellers should note that accommodation in and around Dehiwala–Mount Lavinia (pages 115–17), only 5km south of Bambalapitiya, is generally far better value than in the city proper, with the bonus of offering easy access to Mount Lavinia beach.

FORT AND GALLE FACE Many, if not most, of Colombo's more historic and upmarket hotels are packed into the relatively confined central Fort District and adjacent Galle Face, which runs south along the seafront for about 2km towards Kollupitiya. More affordable lodgings in this most central part of Colombo are few and rather scattered. Most of the 'Upmarket' properties listed below are impersonal skyscrapers that fall under international chain management and offer sterile comfort and international amenities (air conditioning, sat TV, safe, minibar, swimming pool, etc) to a clientele dominated by business travellers. The main exception is the historic Galle Face Hotel, which is no less well equipped as its peers, but far more characterful, making it one of the most tantalising upmarket options anywhere in Colombo. Most of these central chain hotels operate an online booking system where daily rates depend on projected and actual occupancy, so meaningful price comparisons are difficult without actual dates.

Luxury

🏠 **Taj Samudra** [88 B2] (300 rooms) Galle Rd; ☎011 244 6622; e samudra.colombo@ tajhotels.com; w tajhotels.com. Part of the Indian-operated Taj Group, the 10-storey Samudra stands in magnificent grounds overlooking Galle Face Green & the Indian Ocean. The bright & ornately decorated lobby has a coffee lounge, sports bar & several restaurants, while the spacious rooms are very well equipped & many come with a sea view. Although it's marginally plusher than any alternative in the upmarket range, it still seems overpriced for what it is. *From US$325 dbl.* **$$$$$+**

Upmarket

✳ 🏠 **Galle Face Hotel** [88 B3] (158 rooms) Galle Rd; ☎011 254 1010; e reservations@ gallefacehotel.net; w gallefacehotel.com. Opened in 1864, Colombo's most venerable & grandest hotel commands a magnificent view of Galle Face Green & the ocean, while the colonial interiors retain a gracious historic ambience (the wooden-floored suites are bigger than most hotels' dining rooms). It's a real treat to stay here, even if only for 1 night, and you've the choice of 6 on-site bars & restaurants. *From US$170 dbl.* **$$$$$**

🏠 **Cinnamon Grand** [88 B3] (501 rooms) Galle Rd; 📞011 243 7437; e grand@cinnamonhotels.com; w cinnamonhotels.com. A favourite of British visitors, this once rather staid 5-star hotel has been revamped to cater to the demands of a sophisticated leisure clientele. A sparkling selection of trendy restaurants & bars complement the new-look rooms. It is close to the tourist office & US Embassy. *From US$180 dbl.* **$$$$$**

🏠 **Cinnamon Lakeside** [88 B1] (346 rooms) Sir Chittampalam A Gardiner Rd; 📞011 249 1000; e lakeside@cinnamonhotels.com; w cinnamonhotels.com. This popular fortress-like hotel overlooking Lake Beira has a bright lobby, a large swimming pool, a garden courtyard fringed by an avenue of excellent restaurants, & well-equipped AC rooms with private terraces furnished in a dignified gentleman's-club style. *From US$170 dbl.* **$$$$$**

🏠 **The Kingsbury Hotel** [81 A3] (229 rooms) Janadhipathi Rd; 📞011 242 1221; e info@thekingsburyhotel.com; w thekingsburyhotel.com. Established in 1973 as the Ceylon Intercontinental & refurbished in 2013, this 9-storey not-quite-seafront hotel is central Colombo's flashiest option, ostentatious but also fun. A trio of restaurants is completed by a large harbour-facing swimming pool, the rooftop Sky Lounge, & a ground-floor bar that serves good-value daily specials. Standard rooms are smallish but come with all the usual amenities. *From US$184 dbl B&B.* **$$$$$**

🏠 **Hilton Colombo** [81 B3] (384 rooms) Off Lotus Rd; 📞011 249 2492; e colombo.reservations@hilton.com; w colombo.hilton.com. Though rather corporate & soulless, the Hilton is Colombo's best-known international chain hotel, with a useful location for business travellers, & well-equipped AC rooms affording a view of Lake Beira or the city. *Online rates start at US$175.* **$$$$$**

🏠 **Shangri-La Hotel Colombo** [88 A1] (466 rooms) Galle Rd; 📞+94 11 788 8288; e slcb@shangri-la.com; w shangri-la.com/colombo/shangrila. This massive & highly anticipated new chain hotel was scheduled to open as we went to print. Expect high levels of comfort & good value. *From US$180 dbl.* **$$$$$**

Moderate

🏠 **Grand Oriental Hotel** [81 B1] (80 rooms) York St; 📞011 232 0320; e info@grandoriental.com; w grandoriental.com. This low-rent counterpart to the Galle Face Hotel was built as an army barracks outside the port gates in 1837, opened as a hotel in 1875, & remained a popular place to stay upon arrival in the days of sea travel. Strongly recommended to those who put a high premium on historical ambience, it has decent amenities but could be sharper on the service & maintenance front. *US$101/110 sgl/dbl B&B.* **$$$$**

🏠 **Colombo City Hotel** [81 B3] (50 rooms) Canal Row; 📞011 534 1962; e cmb_cityhotels@sltnet.lk; w colombocityhotel.com. Boasting a historic façade alongside the Dutch Hospital complex, this is a simple & well-run hotel that would be unremarkable in any other setting but stands out as a good-value lower mid-range option in the heart of Colombo. All rooms have AC, fan, TV & safe. *US$85/96 sgl/dbl B&B.* **$$$$**

Budget

🏠 **City Beds Sri Lanka** [81 C3] (5 rooms) Parsons Rd; 📞011 238 3420; m 0777 733747; e info@citybedssrilanka.com; w citybedssrilanka.com. This small backpacker-oriented lodge stands in Regent Building (opposite Lake House) close to several restaurants & within 500m of the railway & bus stations. Small AC rooms are brightly decorated, clean & comfortable, & the friendly staff is a great source of local travel information. A good budget choice for new arrivals. *US$50 dbl.* **$$$**

Shoestring

🏠 **Colombo YMCA** [81 C2] (40 rooms) Bristol Rd; 📞011 232 5252; e ymcacbo@sltnet.lk. Founded in 1882, the habitable but rundown YMCA is by far the city centre's cheapest option, but has few other merits. *US$14/18 sgl/dbl fan & shared bathroom, US$30/40 en-suite dbl with fan/AC.* **$–$$**

KOLLUPITIYA AND CINNAMON GARDENS These relatively smart suburbs to the south of Galle Face and Slave Island host some of the city's most attractive moderate to upmarket boutique hotels, notably the well-established Tintagel Paradise Road,

Zylan Luxury Villa and Lake Lodge, and newly opened Maniumpathy. It also boasts some very good properties at the upper end of the budget range, but those seeking cheaper rooms are better off heading south to Bambalapitiya or Dehiwala–Mount Lavinia.

Luxury

✳ 🏠 **Tintagel Paradise Road** [93 E1] (10 suites) Rosmead Pl; ☎ 011 460 2122; e reservations@tintagelcolombo.com; w paradiseroadhotels.com. The former home of 3 prime ministers of the Bandaranaike family, this colonnaded 2-storey 1930s villa – which hosted the Prince of Wales & Duchess of Cornwall in 2013 – has been restored with taste & style as perhaps the most covetable boutique address in Sri Lanka. The original ceramic tile & wooden floors are intact, classic furnishings include crystal chandeliers, antique gilded mirrors & a library of 500 leather-bound volumes, while contemporary touches include the courtyard swimming pool & a fabulously gloomy bar with red lacquered walls hung with vintage maps. The décor of the lavishly appointed AC bedrooms is rich in relaxing hues & delightful objets d'art. The food, served in the outdoor courtyard or indoor dining room, is equally sophisticated. *From US$320 dbl.* **$$$$$+**

🏠 **Maniumpathy** [93 G1] (8 rooms) Kynsey Rd; ☎ 011 269 6988; e reservations@maniumpathy.com; w maniumpathy.com; see ad, 2nd colour section. Named after the Manipay district of Jaffna, whence hails the family that have owned it for 5 generations, this newly opened boutique hotel is set in a beautifully maintained 19th-century villa decorated in magnificent period style. The individually decorated rooms all have parquet floors & Jaffna-style antique furniture, as well as modern touches such as AC, sat TV & minibar. Most rooms also have a standing tub & small private garden. Common areas include a cigar room decorated with vintage maps & engravings, an opulent dining room serving meals to order, & a garden with terrace seating & swimming pool. *From around US$300 dbl B&B, with 25% discount out of season.* **$$$$$+**

Upmarket

🏠 **Zylan Luxury Villa** [93 F1] (7 rooms) Rosmead Pl; ☎ 011 268 6885; e res@zylan.lk; w zylan.lk. This popular & elegant boutique hotel is owned & managed by a renowned artist from Hong Kong & her family. Tastefully decorated rooms come with AC, fan, safe, TV, DVD player & minibar. Other amenities include a lovely 1st-floor open-air garden, a rooftop swimming pool & an unlicensed sushi restaurant. *From US$168/189 sgl/dbl B&B.* **$$$$$**

Moderate

✳ 🏠 **Lake Lodge** [93 B1] (13 rooms) Alvis Tce; ☎ 011 242 4246; m 0770 751128; e lakelodge@taruvillas.com; w taruvillas.com. Tucked away at the end of a quiet cul-de-sac, this modern boutique hotel offers a winning combination of professional & flexible management, crisp contemporary décor & very reasonable rack rates. The 1st-floor terrace restaurant, hung with abstract art, serves a varied selection of meals & snacks, & offers a glimpse over the garden to nearby Lake Beira. Handsome AC rooms come with polished concrete floors & walls, darkwood furniture including a king-size bed, colourful wall hangings & stylish modern bathroom. *From US$117 dbl B&B.* **$$$$**

🏠 **Cinnamon Red** [93 B1] (242 rooms) Ananda Coomaraswamy Rd; ☎ 011 214 5145; e infored@cinnamonhotels.com w cinnamonhotels.com. Conveniently located about halfway between Kollupitiya Junction and the National Museum, this comfortable & efficiently managed 26-storey hotel has a bright contemporary feel reflecting the bold use of reds, blacks & whites in the décor. Rooms with twin or king-size beds come with AC, minibar, tall windows offering good views & naff inspirational message emblazoned on the back wall. There are 2 restaurants & a rooftop infinity pool offering sensational views over the city to the ocean. Very good value. *US$113 dbl.* **$$$$**

🏠 **Renuka City Hotel** [93 A2] (99 rooms) Galle Rd; ☎ 011 257 3598; e renukaht@renukahotel.com; w renukahotel.com. Set bang in the main Galle Rd shopping area, this bland business hotel offers a decent combination of comfort, convenience & value for money. All rooms have AC, TV & 24-hr room service, & amenities include 2 restaurants & a rooftop swimming pool. *US$109/112 sgl/dbl B&B.* **$$$$**

Budget

★ 🏠 Black Cat B&B [88 G4] (5 rooms) Wijerama Rd; 📞 011 267 5111; **e** blackcatcolombo@gmail.com; **w** blackcatcolombo.com. Set above the funky Black Cat Café, the spacious tall-ceilinged 1st-floor rooms at this attractive villa come with AC & fan, & are beautifully but simply decorated with wood & wrought-iron furniture & vintage posters. In addition to the downstairs café, there's a shared guest lounge. A bit out of the way but quiet & good value. *From US$50 dbl.* **$$$**

★ 🏠 YWCA International Guesthouse [88 E3] (10 rooms) Colvin De Silva Rd; 📞 011 232 4181; **e** ywcacolombo@gmail.com; **w** ywcacolombo. com. Converted to a guesthouse in 1942, this undersubscribed gem (open to men & couples, as well as women) inhabits a fabulous colonnaded Dutch building that started life as a hospital more than 200 years ago, was acquired by the YWCA in 1913, & retains a strong period feel thanks to wooden floors, tall ceilings & vintage furniture. Add to this a dynamic & friendly manageress, & a useful location 500m north of Viharamahadevi Park (technically in Slave Island rather than Cinnamon Gardens), & it adds up to one of the city's best budget deals. *US$33 small dbl with fan & net, US$46 dbl with AC.* **$$–$$$**

🏠 Colombo Haven [93 A1] (4 rooms) Galle Rd; 📞 011 230 1672; **m** 0777 905559; **e** colombohaven@gmail.com; **w** colombohaven. com. Tucked away unsignposted at the end of a quiet alley behind the well-known Carnival Ice-cream, this low-key lodging in the heart of bustling Kollupitiya has spacious colourfully painted rooms with AC, TV, fridge & tea/coffee.

Managed by a welcoming & knowledgeable former guide & his wife (who cooks excellent b/fasts), it is both a secure budget introduction to Colombo & a good source of travel advice & assistance further afield. *US$60 dbl, plus US$5 pp b/fast.* **$$$**

🏠 Ivy Lane [93 B3] (16 rooms) Galle Rd; 📞 011 257 5733; **e** info@ivylane.lk; **w** ivylane.lk. Part of the Clock Inn chain, this budget not-quite-boutique hotel has a useful location & comfortable attractively decorated rooms with queen-size beds, AC & TV. Some noise seeps into the road-facing rooms. *US$55/60 sgl/dbl B&B.* **$$$**

🏠 ACA by Riamim [93 B3] (9 rooms) Alfred Pl; 📞 011 257 6677; **m** 0777 748022; **e** info@ alfredcourt.lk; **w** alfredcourt.lk. Formerly called Alfred Court Accommodation, this adequate & reasonably priced hotel opposite Durdans Hospital has brightly decorated AC rooms, friendly staff & a usefully central location close to plenty of restaurants, but it lacks character & maintenance appears to be a low priority. *US$60 dbl B&B.* **$$$**

Shoestring

🏠 Backpack Lanka [93 B1] (11 rooms, 3 dorms) R A de Mel Rd; 📞 011 438 8889; **m** 0770 300900; **e** admin@backpacklanka. com; **w** backpacklanka.com. The most central backpackers in Colombo, this welcoming owner-managed lodge spans several stories of a tall building opposite the prominent Liberty Mall. Small & unadorned rooms have AC & use a shared bathroom & kitchen, as do the 3- & 4-bed dorms. There's a pool bar downstairs, but no alcohol served. *US$36 dbl, US$14.50 pp dorm bed, dropping to US$22/US$10 out of season.* **$–$$**

BAMBALAPITIYA, WELLAWATTA AND HAVELOCK TOWN This most southerly part of the Colombo Municipality boasts a varied selection of accommodation including several good moderate-to-luxury hotels. It also hosts the city's largest concentration of backpacker-friendly budget and shoestring options, though better value is available further south in the more attractive beachside environs of Mount Lavinia.

Luxury

★ 🏠 Casa Colombo [94 A2] (12 suites) Galle Rd; 📞 011 452 0130; **e** reservations@casacolombo. com; **w** casacolombo.com. Describing itself as a 'retro-chic designer hotel', this 200-year-old Moorish mansion has been converted into a breathtaking & playfully individualistic lodge

where original ceramic tiled floors & tall ornate ceilings are offset by contemporary lighting, fittings & furniture. Suites are all individually decorated & equipped with AC, Wi-Fi, laptops & other gadgets, & every guest is attended by a personable, personal 'casa domo'. With an alfresco Mexican restaurant, grand dining room, tea garden, stylish spa & pink swimming pool, Casa Colombo is a surprising, inspiring find. *From US$400 dbl B&B.* **$$$$$+**

Upmarket

✳ 🏠 Havelock Place Bungalow [94 C3] (7 rooms) Havelock Pl; 📞 011 258 5191; 📱 0772 112199; e info@havelockbungalow.com; w havelockbungalow.com. In contrast to the slick modern hotels typical of central Colombo, this charming & characterful boutique property, set in a lovingly tended garden down a quiet cul-de-sac only 1km east of the seafront, feels like a misplaced hill-country bungalow. Amenities include a swimming pool with jacuzzi & gourmet Asian fusion restaurant, while the comfortable & stylish rooms & suites all have AC, wooden floors & private terraces. *From US$155 dbl B&B, dropping by up to 50% out of season.* **$$$$**

🏠 Ozo Colombo [94 A3] (158 rooms) Cnr Clifford Pl & Marine Dr; 📞 011 255 5570; w ozohotels.com. An imaginatively decorated modern variation on a standard business hotel, this efficiently managed 12-storey edifice is also one of the few in Colombo with a genuine seafront location. Comfortable AC rooms have full-length windows that make the most of the view & large built-in TV. There's a good 1st-floor restaurant but the crowning glory is the rooftop swimming pool & cocktail/snack bar, which offers fabulous views over the waterfront to the city skyscrapers about 5km to the north. Good value. *From US$133 dbl.* **$$$$**

🏠 Colombo Courtyard [94 A1] (32 rooms) Cnr R A de Mel Rd & Alfred Hse Av; 📞 011 464 5333; e info@colombocourtyard.com; w colombocourtyard.com. Situated within easy reach of everything the business or leisure visitor needs to see & do in Colombo, this modern hotel has a refreshingly different feel, with décor that includes a climbing sculpture of old bicycle parts, the walls of shaved railway sleepers & a cobbled entrance courtyard. Large light rooms are decorated with monochrome prints & come with AC, fan, massive TV & modern bathroom. Amenities include an L-shaped swimming pool in the back courtyard, a spa & a good Italian restaurant. *Rack rates are unduly hefty at US$220/235 sgl/dbl B&B; online bookings seem to be up to 50% cheaper.* **$$$$$**

Moderate

🏠 Fairview Hotel [94 B6] (50 rooms) Ramakrishna Rd; 📞 011 205 8843; e reservations@ fairviewhotel.lk; w tangerinehotels.com. Set on a quiet suburban thoroughfare connecting Galle Rd to Marine Dr, this efficiently run modern 8-storey hotel provides agreeable accommodation at very reasonable rates. Spacious & comfortable rooms all have AC, TV & tea/coffee. There's a good restaurant & TV lounge too. Good value. *US$75 dbl B&B.* **$$$**

🏠 Mirage Hotel [94 B5] (60 rooms) Marine Dr; 📞 011 236 3471; e reservations@ miragecolombo.com; w miragecolombo.com. This smart business hotel has a waterfront setting, in-house swimming pool, rooftop restaurant ideally positioned to catch the sunset over the sea, & large modern rooms with AC, TV, minibar, tea/coffee & private balcony. *US$90/95 sgl/dbl B&B.* **$$$$**

Budget

🏠 Clock Inn Colombo [94 A1] (8 rooms, 7 dorms) Galle Rd; 📞 011 250 0588; e info@ clockinn.lk; w clockinncolombo.lk. This conveniently located & deservedly popular backpackers haunt has small but well-maintained & brightly decorated en-suite rooms with AC, TV, writing desk, soundproofing & plenty of cupboard space, as well as a range of 3- to 6-bed dorms, also with AC, reading lights & lockers. A sociable lounge/dining area with TV, sofas & scatter cushions makes it a good place to hook up with other travellers, or pick their brains, at the start of a trip. Rates include a filling b/fast & there's a shared fridge for guests' use. *US$50/55 sgl/dbl, US$16 pp dorm bed.* **$$–$$$**

🏠 Drift B&B [94 A1] (12 rooms, 2 dorms) Galle Rd; 📞 011 250 5536; e driftbnb@gmail.com; 🅵 driftbnb. This state-of-the-art backpackers lodge, its walls hung with arty photographic prints, offers the choice of a spacious private room with wooden floor, TV, writing desk & tea/coffee, or a 4-bed female or 6-bed mixed dorm with private reading lights & locker. All rooms & dorms are soundproofed & come with AC. Overall it's a very nice set-up that provides a spotless & secure introduction to Colombo, but pricey. *Walk-in B&B rates: US$92 dbl, US$21 pp dorm bed; much better deals available through online booking agencies.* **$$–$$$$**

🏠 Moss Colombo [94 B1] (14 rooms) Bauddhaloka Rd; 📞 011 255 3929. Tucked away behind the giant banyan tree near Thunmulla Circle, this clean, quiet & friendly backpacker-oriented lodge offers AC rooms with a modern minimalist look & TV in a small garden hemmed in by clumps of bamboo. *US$60 dbl B&B.* **$$$**

Shoestring

🏠 **Mrs Settupathy's** [94 A3] (5 rooms) Shrubbery Gdn; ☎ 011 258 7964; e jbs@slt.lk. Situated on the left at the end of a short alley running behind the Church of Christ, this unsignposted homestay has been hosting travellers for years & offers comfortable en-suite accommodation with fan & optional AC, as well as a common lounge & kitchen. *From US$20 dbl.* **$**

🏠 **Hotel Sunshine** [94 A3] (29 rooms) Shrubbery Gdn; ☎ 011 401 7676; m 0777 732735; e sunshine.shrubbery@gmail.com; w hotelsunshine.lk. This unpretentious hotel has simple but clean double rooms in two categories. *Walk-in rates are excellent value at US$15 dbl with cold water & fan only, US$23 with hot water, TV & AC; online rates start at US$36 dbl.* **$–$$**

🏠 **Eestee Rest** [94 A3] (27 rooms) Jaya Rd; ☎ 011 259 9190; m 0777 226886; e gajen1988@hotmail.com. Set in an attractive old house built around a central courtyard, this pleasant family-run place offers simple but clean rooms with fan, hot water & optional AC. It is close to the seafront & several budget restaurants. *US$21 dbl with fan only, US$27 with AC.* **$–$$**

🏠 **Greenlands Hotel** [94 A3] (16 rooms) Shrubbery Gdn; ☎ 011 258 5592; e greenlandshotel@gmail.com. Better known for its vegetarian restaurant & bar than its accommodation, this bizarrely time-warped set-up, complete with statues of Hindu gods & Edwardian fashion models on the stairwell, has spacious but rundown twin rooms with fan, AC, peeling paint & furniture that looks like it hasn't shifted since the 1960s. *Fair value at US$28 dbl, assuming the AC works.* **$$**

🏠 **Sea View Holiday House** [94 B7] (8 rooms) Galle Rd; m 0710 815636. Quite possibly the cheapest rooms in Colombo, but very scruffy & only some have fans. Only for the desperate. *US$7 dbl.* **$**

✖ WHERE TO EAT AND DRINK

Colombo is blessed with a huge number and variety of restaurants and cafés representing practically every world cuisine and conceivable travel budget. Indeed, while wine-loving foodies with deep pockets could easily blow US$50 plus per head at some of the city's top culinary addresses, backpackers will find plenty of perfectly acceptable local eateries where a filling rice-and-curry or vegetarian buffet will set them back US$2 or less. A wide cross section of Colombo's best and/or most affordable restaurants is listed below, but Colombo is also scattered with numerous international fast-food franchises – the likes of Pizza Hut, KFC, Burger King, Subway and McDonald's – and local coffee-shop chains such as Java Lounge and Coffee Bean & Tea Leaf. Immediately south of Colombo, less than 30 minutes distant by tuktuk, a row of attractive beachfront restaurants can be found in Dehiwala–Mount Lavinia (pages 117–18).

FORT The culinary focal point of Colombo's most historic district is the **Old Dutch Hospital** [81 B3] (*Hospital St;* ☎ *011 528 8002;* ☐ *DutchHospital*), a converted 17th-century building that officially refers to itself as a shopping precinct but actually feels more like an upmarket food court, housing half a dozen restaurants including several described below.

✳ ✖ **Ministry of Crab** [81 B3] Old Dutch Hospital; ☎ 011 234 2722; w ministryofcrab. com; ☉ 11.30–15.30 & 18.00–22.30. Colombo's most celebrated (& probably most expensive) restaurant is co-owned by cricketers Kumar Sangakkara & Mahela Jayawardene & renowned restaurateur Darshan Munidasa. The AC interior

retains 17th-century features such as a high-beamed ceiling, wooden shutters & flagstone floor, & there's also terrace seating. Prawns, chicken & fish all feature on the menu, but the speciality is crabs, delivered fresh from the northern lagoons daily & cooked in any of half a dozen styles using fresh ground local herbs

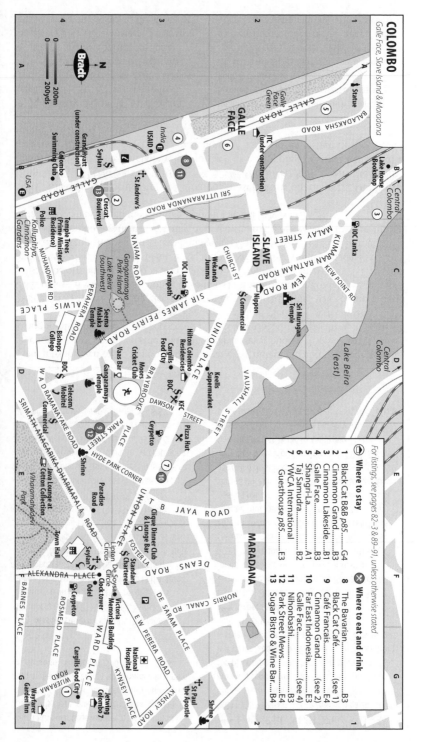

COLOMBO
Galle Face, Slave Island & Maradana

Bradt

N

0 ——— 200m
0 ——— 200yds

A · B · C · D · E · F · G

1 · 2 · 3 · 4

GALLE FACE

Galle Face Green

Statue

GALLE ROAD

BALADAKSHA ROAD

Lake House
Bookshop

Central
Colombo

India

USAID

ITC
(under construction)

IOC Lanka

SRI UTTARANANDA ROAD

MALAY STREET

KUMARAN RATNAM ROAD

KEW ROAD

KEW POINT RD

SLAVE ISLAND

Central
Colombo

Lake Beira
(east)

Grand Hyatt
(under construction)

Colombo
Swimming Club

USA

Seylan

St Andrew's

Crescat
Boulevard

Police

Temple Trees
(Prime Minister's
Residence)

Kollupitiya,
Cinnamon
Gardens

MUHANDIRAM RD

NAVAM ROAD

Wekanda
Jumma

CHURCH ST

IOC Lanka

Sampath

Seema
Malaka
Temple

Gangaramaya
Park Island

Lake Beira
(southwest)

Nippon

SIR JAMES PEIRIS ROAD

Commercial

Sri Murugan
Temple

VAUXHALL ST

UNION PLACE

PERAHERA ROAD

ALWIS PLACE

Bishops
College

Gangaramaya
Temple

BOC

Telecom/
Mobitel

W A D RAMANAYAKE ROAD

Commercial

SRIMATH ANAGARIKA DHARMAPALA ROAD

Hilton Colombo
Residences

Moors'
Cricket Club

Vyas Bar

Cargills
Food City

BOC

KFC

DAWSON
STREET

BRAYBROOKE

Keells
Supermarket

Ceypetco

PARK STREET PLACE

HYDE PARK CORNER

Pizza
Hut

Shrine

Java Lounge at
Cotton Collection

Viharamahadevi
Park

Town Hall

Paradise
Road

UNION PLACE

FOSTER LA

Clique Dinner Club
& Lounge Bar

Lipton De Soysa
Circus Circle

U T B JAYA ROAD

DEANS ROAD

Seylan

Standard
Chartered

Odel

Clock tower

ALEXANDRA PLACE

Ceypetco

ROSMEAD PLACE

BARNES PLACE

WARD PLACE

Victoria
Memorial Building

National
Hospital

DE SARAM PLACE

NORRIS CANAL RD

E W PERERA ROAD

KYNSEY PLACE

WIJERAMA ROAD

Cargills Food City

St Paul
the Apostle

Shrine

Jetwing
Colombo 7

Wayfarer
Garden Inn

MARADANA

For listings, see pages 82–3 & 89–91, unless otherwise stated

Where to stay

1 Black Cat B&B p85.........G4
2 Cinnamon Grand........B3
3 Cinnamon Lakeside......B1
4 Galle Face...........B3
5 Shangri-La...........A1
6 Taj Samudra.........B2
7 YWCA International
Guesthouse p85......E3
8 The Bavarian..........B3
9 Black Cat Café..........(see 1)
10 Cinnamon Grand.........(see 2)

Where to eat and drink

8 The Bavarian.............B3
9 Black Cat Café.........(see 1)
10 Cinnamon Grand........(see 2)
  Far East Indonesia......E3
  Galle Face.............(see 4)
11 Nihonbashi.............B3
12 Park Street Mews.......B3
13 Sugar Bistro & Wine Bar....B4

& spices. There's no doubting the quality of the food & service, but the prices will terrify anyone who considers themselves to be vaguely budget conscious. $$$$

✳ ✖ **Pagoda Tea Rooms** [81 B2] Chatham St;☎011 232 3086; ⏱ 07.30–17.30 Mon–Fri, 07.30–13.30 Sat. At the very opposite end of the price spectrum, this venerable Colombo institution occupies the ground floor of the ornate 1880s De Mel Building. The fabulously time-warped interior, little changed since it featured prominently in Duran Duran's 'Hungry Like the Wolf' video (check it out on YouTube), is complemented by colonial-era paintings & stylish wooden features. It serves authentic & inexpensive lamprais & curries, as well as a selection of Mongolian dishes, together with a range of sub-US$1 savoury & sweet snacks to wash down with freshly brewed tea or coffee. No alcohol. Snacks $, mains $$

✖ **Colombo Fort Café** [81 B3] Old Dutch Hospital;☎011 243 4946; w colombofortcafe. com; ⏱ 09.00–23.00. A modern pub-like venue with terrace seating spilling out into the main courtyard, this place has a meat-dominated Mediterranean menu supplemented by cheaper pizzas & burgers in an informal atmosphere. Cocktails & beers are sensibly priced. $$$–$$$$

✖ **Colombo Café** [81 B2] Chatham St;☎011 233 7783; ⏱ 08.00–20.00 Mon–Sat. An ideal central venue for a budget-friendly lunch or early dinner, this brightly decorated AC café dishes up a supremely affordable lunchtime buffet (*US$2.50 per head*) as well as à la carte wraps, sandwiches & burgers. Good fresh juices but no alcohol. $$

✖ **t-Lounge** [81 B2] Chatham St;☎011 244 7168; w dilmaht-lounge.com; ⏱ 11.00–23.00. This bright & funky AC-chilled 2-storey café serves (& sells) a dazzling variety of teas produced by Dilmah (*US$2–3 per pot*) along with tea-based mocktails & a selection of tasty & reasonably priced burgers, pizzas, filled crêpes & other substantial snacks. $$

✖ **Heladiv Tea Club** [81 B3] Old Dutch Hospital;☎011 575 3377; w heladivteaclub.com; ⏱ 08.30–midnight. Boasting a sophisticated ambience with plush sofas & terrace seating for enjoying mocktails, cocktails, beers, wines, coffee & – last but not least – tea produced by the Heladiv estate, this convivial bar also serves a great selection of cakes & desserts, as well as tasty but rather small burgers, sandwiches & salads. $$$

✖ **Semondu** [81 B3] Old Dutch Hospital;☎011 244 1590; w semondu.com; ⏱ noon–15.00 & 19.00–23.00. Managed by SriLankan Airlines & serving a long menu of mostly Asian dishes based loosely on in-flight cuisine & presented on a tray, this works surprisingly well for those seeking an uncomplicated meal. Wine & beer available at a counter with a view of the kitchen. $$$$

GALLE FACE A few well-established upmarket restaurants are scattered around Galle Front, immediately south of the Fort District.

✖ **Sugar Bistro & Wine Bar** [88 B4] Galle Rd;☎011 244 6229; w sugarcolombo.com; ⏱ 08.00–23.30. Situated at the entrance to the Crescat Boulevard Mall 200m south of Galle Face, this contemporary bistro has simple & striking décor, with air ducts coated in silver foil & 9 odd clocks on the back wall, as well as terrace seating. The cosmopolitan menu includes b/fast, lunch, dinner & everything in between, while an extensive wine list is supplemented by reasonably priced cocktails & beers. $$$

✖ **Nihonbashi** [88 B3] Galle Face Tce;☎011 232 3847; w nihonbashi.lk; ⏱ noon–14.30 & 18.00–22.30. Founded in 1995 by a Sri Lankan with a mixed Japanese heritage, this world-class restaurant specialises in teriyaki, yakitori, sushi & fusion cuisine in a minimalist Japanese setting complete with Zen garden. Sampler & degustation menus are available for those who want to try a bit of several dishes. $$$$$

✖ **The Bavarian** [88 B3] Galle Face Ct;☎011 242 1577; ❚ TheBavarianSL; ⏱ noon–15.00 & 18.00–midnight. Established in 1983, this German restaurant has a pub-like atmosphere & serves draft beer, as well as the usual bottled drinks. Seafood & vegetarian fare is well represented, but the menu's main focus is meat, ranging from whole pork knuckle & Bavarian steak stack to chicken Kiev & mixed sausage platters. Quality is high & portions are generous. $$$$

✖ **Cinnamon Grand** [88 B3] Galle Rd;☎011 243 7437; w cinnamonhotels.com. This sprawling hotel is home to a dozen restaurants, bars & coffee shops, including some of the finest Colombo has to offer. The Lagoon specialises in seafood chosen by guests from an iced fish-market counter for lunch & dinner. The London Grill has the time-warped feel of a 1950s English steakhouse, making it a popular dining spot with nostalgic British expats. Chutneys specialises in South Indian dishes that are as good as, if not better than, any in India (**$$**), while the garden Nuga Gama serves rural Sri Lankan food in a reproduction of a village. **$$$$–$$$$$**

✗ **Galle Face Hotel** [88 B3] Galle Rd, Colombo 3; ☎011 254 1010; w gallefacehotel.com. This historic seafront hotel incorporates several good restaurants. The most affordable is Seaspray, a populist open-air restaurant renowned for its seafood, while the pricier 1864 (the year the hotel was founded) is a fine dining venue with the anachronistic feel of an English gentlemen's club & an impressive wine cellar. **$$$$–$$$$$**

KOLLUPITIYA Most of the restaurants listed below lie alongside or within a few minutes' walk of Galle and R A de Mel roads, the main north–south thoroughfares through Kollupitiya.

✳ ✗ **Mitsi's Coffee Shop** [93 C3] Bagatelle Rd; ☎011 438 7376; m 0777 163090; ⏱ 09.00–23.00. Set in an early 20th-century villa with a fan-cooled contemporary interior & limited terrace seating in a pretty small garden, this owner-managed restaurant specialises in meaty Balkan & Mediterranean fare such as smoked beef tenderloins, ćevapčići stew (made with homemade skinless sausages) & grilled meatballs. It also serves pasta, burgers, excellent coffee & possibly the best cakes in Sri Lanka. Cakes **$**, mains **$$$**

✳ ✗ **Navayuga Indian Restaurant** [93 B2] Abdul Caffoor Rd; ☎011 230 1302; m 0727 527444; ⏱ 11.00–15.00 & 19.00–23.00. Set in a restored early 20th-century mansion complete with Kandyan-style roof, wooden floor & stylishly minimalist interior, this good-value restaurant specialises in North Indian cuisine, with the special thali & ½-chicken tandoori being menu highlights. No alcohol served but you can bring your own. Good value. **$$$**

✗ **Manhattan Fish Market** [93 B2] Cnr R A de Mel Rd & Deal Pl; ☎011 230 1901; w manhattanfishmarket.com; ⏱ noon–23.00 Mon–Thu, 13.30–midnight Fri, noon–midnight Sat–Sun. The Sri Lankan franchise of this pan-Asian chain is a busy, modern, family-friendly set-up that serves 5 different types of fish to your taste – poached, grilled, baked or fried – as well as other seafood & mixed platters. No alcohol. Standard mains **$$$**, platters **$$$$$**

✗ **Café Alfresco** [93 B4] Cnr R A de Mel & Bagatelle rds; ☎011 521 9432; ⏱ 10.00–19.00. With its neatly cropped lawn & frilly garden seating, this small outdoor café brings an old-fashioned English village aesthetic to one of Colombo's busiest thoroughfares. A huge selection of local teas is served along with juices, smoothies, shakes & light meals such as burgers, filled crêpes, subs & fresh strawberries with cream. **$$**

✗ **Nara Thai** [93 B2] Deal Pl; ☎011 257 7655; w naracuisine.com; ⏱ 13.30–midnight. This Colombo franchise of a popular Thai restaurant chain is set in an old colonial villa with a beautiful red-dominated AC interior & massive Thai bells outside. A lengthy menu of typical Thai fare includes a good vegetarian selection. No alcohol. **$$$–$$$$**

✗ **Hazari's** [93 B3] Marine Dr; m 0773 363600; ⏱ hazaris.restaurant; ⏱ 11.00–23.00. Recently relocated to a seafront property on Marine Dr, this specialist Middle Eastern restaurant serves tasty couscous, shwarmas, pizza Arabica, hummus, falafel & the like at pocket-friendly prices. No alcohol. **$$**

✗ **The Sizzle** [93 B3] Walukarama Rd; ☎011 257 5237; m 0716 888777; w thesizzle.lk; ⏱ 11.00–midnight. Despite its orange-&-black diner-like interior, this place specialises in grilled meat & seafood, all served on a sizzling hot griddle with your choice of sauce. The steak & seer fish are particularly recommended. No alcohol. **$$$–$$$$**

✗ **Hotel de Pilawoos** [93 B3] Galle Rd; ☎011 257 4795; m 0777 417417; w pilawoos.lk; ⏱ 24hrs. Situated around the corner from Durdans Hospital, the original Pilawoos, easily confused with several namesakes elsewhere on Galle Rd, is one of the city's landmark downmarket eateries, renowned for its cheesy kottu roti & mean whole fish or chicken barbecue. No alcohol. **$$**

✖ **Amaravathi Restaurant** [93 A2] 2 Mile Post Av;✆011 257 7418; ⊕ 11.30–15.30 & 18.30–23.00. Established in 1980, this stalwart Indian restaurant serves a huge range of meat & vegetarian dishes from both north & south. No alcohol. Good value. $$$

CINNAMON GARDENS Set a short distance inland of Kollupitiya, the posh suburb of Cinnamon Gardens is studded with some excellent moderate-to-upmarket eateries, most of which lie within walking distance of the National Museum and Viharamahadevi Park.

✳ ✖ **Café Kumbuk** [93 E1] Horton Pl;✆011 268 5310; m 0771 581333; e cafekumbuk@gmail. com; w cafekumbuk-lk.com; ⊕ 08.00–17.00. Set in a restored villa with a wide ceramic-tiled terrace & wooden-floored & high-ceilinged interior, this beautifully decorated café promotes healthy eating & the use of seasonal & organic ingredients. The small & regularly changing menu includes a cosmopolitan selection of imaginative grills, salads, curries, b/fasts & artisan sandwiches, with gluten-free, dairy-free, vegan & vegetarian selections. Good coffee, smoothies & coolers. $$$

✳ ✖ **Black Cat Café** [88 G4] Wijerama Rd;✆011 267 5111; w blackcatcolombo.com; ⊕ 08.00–18.00 Tue–Sun. Set in a beautifully restored 2-storey mansion with a light airy exterior, retro décor, reading rooms full of quirky old books & terrace seating in the garden, this chilled café greets you with the aroma of freshly roasted coffee & delivers superb homemade juices & a small but imaginative selection of delicious salads, sandwiches, filled pancakes & light lunches. $$$

✳ ✖ **Far East Indonesia Restaurant** [88 E3] Vauxhall St; m 0777 578533; 𝐟 fareastindonesian; ⊕ 09.30–18.30 Mon–Fri. Situated around the corner from the YWCA, this tiny eatery has a helpful English-speaking proprietor & dishes up generous portions of tasty nasi goreng, beef rendang & other authentic Indonesian dishes (which are generally less spicy than Sri Lankan food). Primarily a take-away but there is some seating. No alcohol but great iced coffee. Top value. Vegetarian $, meat $$

✖ **Park Street Mews** [88 E4] Park St;✆011 230 0133; w parkstreetmewsrestaurantcolombo. com; ⊕ 11.00–23.00. This action-packed café, set in a chic converted warehouse, has armchairs for lounging over a coffee or beer, as well as more formal seating to enjoy tapas or a full meal from the regularly overhauled tropical-fusion menu. The 3-course set lunch is a bargain at US$8. $$$–$$$$

✖ **Café Francais** [88 E4] Park St;✆011 450 2606; w cafefrancaisbypourcel.com; ⊕ 09.00–23.00. Complete with Montpellier-trained chef, Colombo's top French restaurant has a varied menu of well-presented & generous seafood & vegetarian dishes along with the likes of veal, duck & steak tartare. The experience is enhanced by the tasteful contemporary-classic ambience, good wine list & on-the-ball service. $$$$

✖ **Upali's by Nawaloka** [93 D1] C W W Kannangara Rd;✆011 269 5812; m 0710 888666; w upalis.com, ⊕ 11.30–10.30. Situated opposite Viharamahadevi Park only 500m from the National Museum, this Colombo institution has an extensive menu of Sri Lankan specialities, including several you'll struggle to find elsewhere in the country, at prices that are slightly higher than usual for local eateries, but will feel like good value to most tourists, considering it feels like a proper restaurant rather than a hole in the wall. $$

✖ **The Mango Tree** [93 B1] S A Dharmapala Rd;✆011 762 0620; w themangotree.net; ⊕ noon–23.00. Situated just 600m inland of Kollupitiya Junction, this large & busy Indian restaurant lacks for ambience, but the menu is long & varied, with plenty of vegetarian & tandoor options, & it's all tasty & quite reasonably priced. Fully licensed, unlike many Indian restaurants. Vegetarian $$$, meat & fish $$$$

✖ **Grande Gourmet at Nirj's** [93 E1] Horton Pl;✆011 268 9111; m 0773 527978; w nirjs. com; ⊕ noon–15.00 & 19.00–23.00. Set in an attractive villa furnished in formal 19th-century Parisian style & hung with contemporary portraits of prominent families in colonial Ceylon, this pricey fine-dining restaurant, manned by an award-winning chef, serves up a predominantly French selection including Provençal fish stew, mushroom & asparagus risotto, truffles & orange-glazed duck. No licence but you can bring your own bottle. $$$$$

✗ Cricket Club Café [93 B1] Flower Rd; ☎011 250 1384; ⏲ 11.00–23.00. Established in 1996 (the same year Sri Lanka won the Cricket World Cup), this recently relocated café comprises a terrace, an AC dining room, & a bar where TVs replay endless cricket matches. The quickly served & moderately priced pub grub is consistently good. $$$

✗ Dottie's English Tea Room [93 F1] Rosmead Pl; m 0719 956 204; f dottiesenglishtearoom; ⏲ noon–19.00 Tue–Fri, 09.00–19.00 Sat–Sun. Dressed up like the set of an Edwardian costume drama, this determinedly eccentric recreation of a vintage tea room comes complete with frilly laced tablecloths, imported bone china, & small indoor pond & garden. A range of single-estate hill-country teas are served up along with scones, tarts, sandwich plates, heaped b/fasts & the self-proclaimed 'best pork sausages in Sri Lanka'. $–$$$

✗ Laksala Museum Gallery Café [93 D2] Nelum Pokuna Rd; ☎011 269 8263; ⏲ 06.30–23.00. This well-stocked AC craft shop & bough-shaded terrace café is a great place to stop for an inexpensive snack, juice or coffee after exploring the adjacent National Museum. $$

BAMBALAPITIYA AND WELLAWATTA

Colombo's main centre of budget accommodation, Bambalapitiya is also suitably well endowed when it comes to affordable local eateries, many of them specialised in vegetarian fare, but is also home to two of the city's most iconic upmarket cafés: Barefoot Garden and the Gallery.

＊✗ Barefoot Garden Café [94 A1] Galle Rd; ☎011 258 9305; w barefootceylon.com/cafe; ⏲ 10.00–19.00 Mon–Sat, 11.00–17.00 Sun. Set in a shady bamboo-clumped courtyard behind the Barefoot Gallery (Colombo's funkiest souvenir shop), this informal outdoor eatery is a great place to escape the hectic tempo of the city for a beer, coffee or juice. A varied selection of sensibly priced light meals includes salads, sandwiches, rice-&-curry & daily specials. A pub quiz is held at 20.15 every Wed, & it often hosts live music & cultural events outside normal hours. $$$

＊✗ Gallery Café [94 A1] Alfred House Rd; ☎011 258 2162; w paradiseroad.lk; ⏲ 10.00–midnight. Set in the garden & patio of Geoffrey Bawa's former studio, this elegant café, liberally adorned with contemporary artworks, is the brainchild of the designer Shanth Fernando. The imaginative Asian–continental fusion menu is especially strong on seafood & complemented by a fine dessert selection & globetrotting wine list that includes several iconic labels, albeit it at a price. $$$$

＊✗ Dwaraka [94 A3] Cnr Jaya Rd & Marine Dr; ☎011 208 1168; m 0778 510499; w dwaraka. lk; ⏲ 07.30–15.00 & 18.00–22.30. The colourful décor & blasting AC give this 1st-floor vegetarian restaurant specialising in North & South Indian cuisine a bright modern feel, but the food & prices are both admirably down to earth. Highlights of a long, varied menu are pancake-like filled dosas, smorgasbord-like South & North Indian thalis & hot & sour soup. No alcohol. $–$$

＊✗ VOC Café [94 B1] Bauddhaloka Rd; ☎011 533 1661; ⏲ 09.00–22.00. Set on the shady terrace & leafy courtyard of the historic gabled Dutch Burghers Union building, this quiet, unpretentious & affordable café is renowned for its lamprais (a dish associated with Sri Lanka's Burgher community), but it also serves good rice-&-curry, along with the likes of fish & chips, pork chops, bangers & mash, cottage pie & sandwiches. One of the few central budget eateries to serve wine & beer. $$

✗ Pagoda Green Cabin [94 A1] Galle Rd; ☎011 258 8811; m 0773 786144; f; ⏲ 11.30–15.00 & 18.30–23.00. Established in the 1950s, this is basically an upscale take on a standard local eatery, complete with the choice of eating in the clean AC interior or leafy fan-cooled courtyard. The rice-&-curry vegetarian buffet lunch is a bargain at US$2 (add US$1.50 for a fiery chicken or fish curry) while the à la carte menu embraces lamprais, kottu roti, Mongolian dishes & burgers. Great dessert & cake selection. No alcohol. Exceptional value. $$

✗ Shanmugas Vegetarian Restaurant [94 B6] Ramakrishna Rd; ☎011 236 1384; w shanmugas.com; ⏲ 10.00–22.00 Mon–Fri, 07.30–22.30 Sat–Sun. This iconic restaurant tucked away off Marine Dr has an old-fashioned family feel, characterful AC interior & long menu of South Indian vegetarian fare including expansive thalis. The Sun buffet lunch is legendary. No alcohol. À la carte $$, Sun buffet $$$

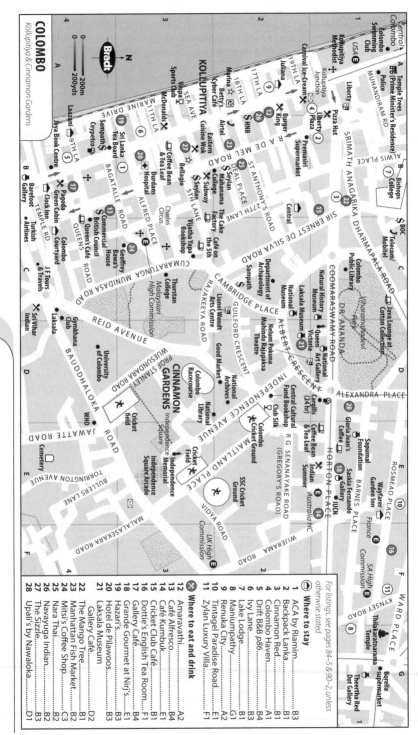

COLOMBO
Kollupitiya & Cinnamon Gardens

For listings, see pages 84–5 & 90–2, unless otherwise stated

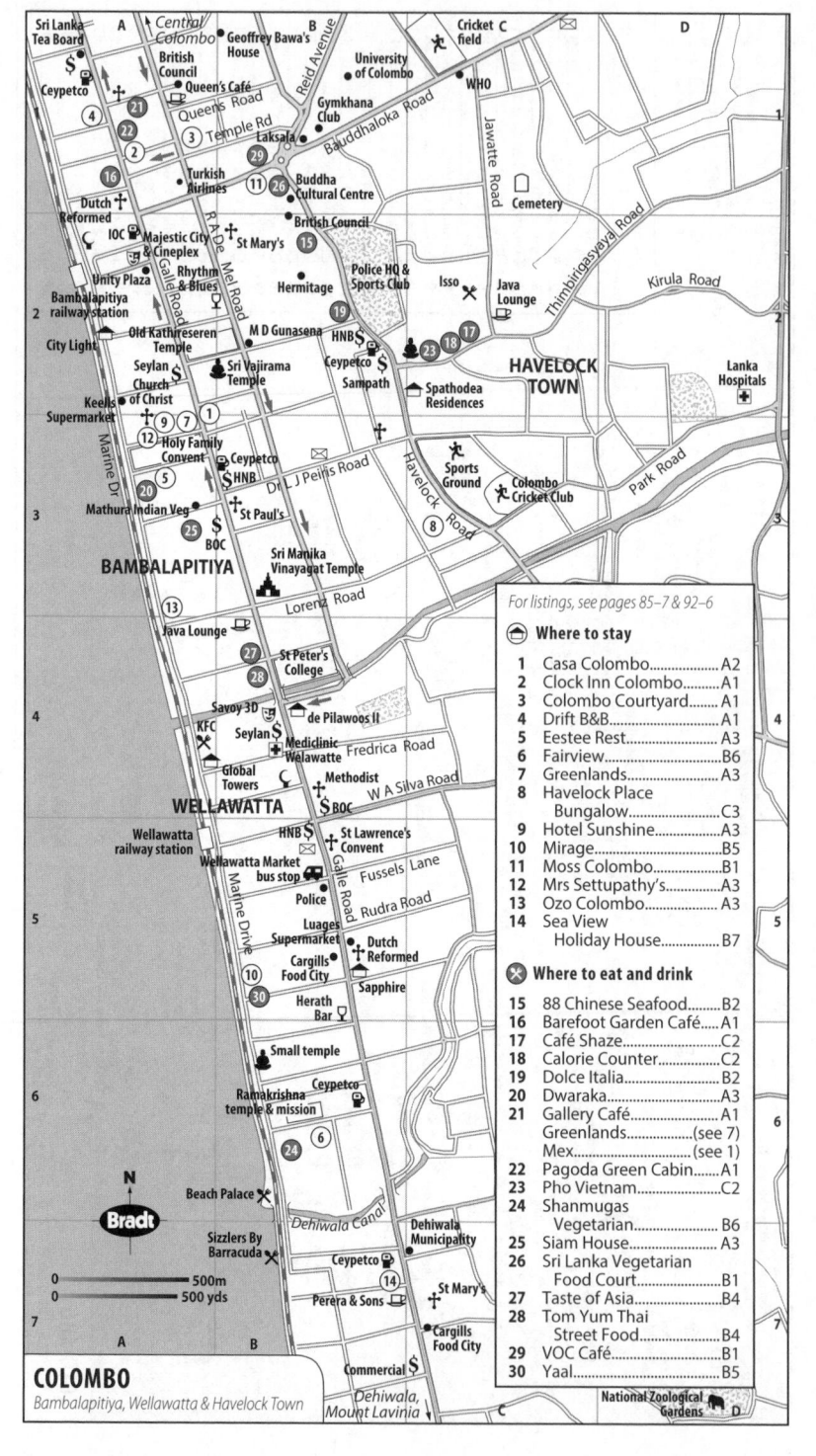

For listings, see pages 85–7 & 92–6

🛏 Where to stay

1 Casa Colombo.....................A2
2 Clock Inn Colombo...........A1
3 Colombo Courtyard.........A1
4 Drift B&B.............................A1
5 Eestee Rest........................A3
6 Fairview..............................B6
7 Greenlands........................A3
8 Havelock Place
   Bungalow.......................C3
9 Hotel Sunshine................A3
10 Mirage................................B5
11 Moss Colombo..................B1
12 Mrs Settupathy's.............A3
13 Ozo Colombo................... A3
14 Sea View
   Holiday House...............B7

✴ Where to eat and drink

15 88 Chinese Seafood.........B2
16 Barefoot Garden Café......A1
17 Café Shaze.........................C2
18 Calorie Counter................C2
19 Dolce Italia.......................B2
20 Dwaraka.............................A3
21 Gallery Café......................A1
   Greenlands...............(see 7)
   Mex...........................(see 1)
22 Pagoda Green Cabin.......A1
23 Pho Vietnam.....................C2
24 Shanmugas
   Vegetarian................... B6
25 Siam House....................... A3
26 Sri Lanka Vegetarian
   Food Court...................B1
27 Taste of Asia.....................B4
28 Tom Yum Thai
   Street Food...................B4
29 VOC Café............................B1
30 Yaal....................................B5

COLOMBO
Bambalapitiya, Wellawatta & Havelock Town

X Taste of Asia [94 B4] Galle Rd; ☎011 438 9908; ⏰ 07.00–22.00. This sanitised variant on the hole-in-the-wall eateries you'll see on any high street in Sri Lanka serves excellent northern cuisine, including chicken poriyal (a spicy dry dish from Jaffna, usually eaten with roti) in a clean AC environment. There's a good cake & juice menu, but no alcohol. Great value. $

X Tom Yum Thai Street Food [94 B4] Galle Rd; ☎011 259 4458; ⏰ noon–15.00 & 18.30–22.30. Prepared fresh by the Thai owner-manager couple, this is probably the most authentic Thai restaurant in Colombo, serving excellent & well-priced (but convincingly spicy) tom yum soup, red & green curries, & grills such as chicken in basil leaves & garlic squid. The contemporary décor – painted wooden furniture, open kitchen & modern art on the walls – is equally refreshing. No alcohol. $$$

X Siam House [94 A3] Melbourne Rd; ☎011 259 5966; ⏰ 11.00–23.00. Above-average Thai restaurant with blasting AC indoors, terrace seating facing a neat green garden, & a long menu of meat & vegetarian dishes supplemented by a fully licensed bar. $$$

X Yaal Restaurant [94 B5] Marine Dr; ☎011 566 1212; ⏰ 07.30–21.00. Decidedly unpretentious but very good value, this place specialises in Jaffna cuisine & is particularly good for crab curry, biriani & chicken poriyal. No alcohol. $$

X Greenlands Restaurant [94 A3] Shrubbery Gdn; ☎011 258 5592; ⏰ 08.00–22.00. The fan-cooled dining room at the Greenlands Hotel, though rather canteen-like in feel, serves excellent Indian vegetarian fare at rock-bottom prices. No alcohol, even though a bar is attached. $

X Mex Restaurant [94 A2] Galle Rd; ☎011 259 9766; w casacolombo.com/eateries.htm; ⏰ 11.00–23.30. Providing a relatively affordable opportunity to experience the ambience of the city's quirkiest boutique hotel, this surreally decorated Mexican restaurant is high on quality but portions tend to be on the meagre side. $$$–$$$$

HAVELOCK TOWN Set within walking distance of Bambalapitiya, the junction of Thimbirigasyaya and Havelock roads is rapidly emerging as a low-key culinary centre dotted with good-value modern eateries that cater primarily to Colombo's young and trendy crowd, but also likely to appeal to travellers on a moderate budget.

✳ **X Calorie Counter** [94 C2] Thimbirigasyaya Rd; ☎011 258 0980; w caloriecounter.lk; ⏰ 07.00–22.00 Mon–Fri, 08.00–22.00 Sat–Sun. Overhung with the aroma of freshly roasted herbs, this health-oriented restaurant, with calorie counts listed for all menu items & an emphasis on organic ingredients, might feel a little oppressive were it not that the food – whether you're after a nutritious b/fast, an imaginative lunchtime salad or sandwich (on rye or wholemeal bread), or a more filling grilled chicken, salmon or steak dinner – is so delicious & well presented. Vegetarians are exceptionally well catered for, too. No alcohol but plenty of choice on the juice front. $$$

X Pho Vietnam [94 C2] Thimbirigasyaya Rd; ☎011 738 6565; 🅕 phovietnamcolombo; ⏰ 09.00–23.00. This family-run restaurant matches bright & pleasant AC ambience with a long menu of authentic lemongrass-tinged Vietnamese meat, fish & vegetarian dishes. No alcohol, but you can bring your own. Excellent value. $$

X Dolce Italia [94 B2] Havelock Rd; ☎011 255 9900; m 0772 944567; 🅕 Dolceltaliarestaurant; ⏰ 07.00–22.00. This Italian-owned & -managed bakery-cum-bistro has a light pastel-shaded interior with AC, as well as limited terrace seating on the front courtyard. A great spot for a quick coffee, croissant, cake, artisan ice cream or crusty panini sandwich, it also serves a wide range of well-priced homemade Italian fare, from ravioli & pasta to risotto & lasagne. $$$

X Sri Lanka Vegetarian Food Court [94 B1] Havelock Rd; m 0776 655800; 🅕 ParadiseColomboSriLanka; ⏰ 07.00–22.00. The inexpensive (*around US$1.50*) self-service buffet here is a treat for budget-conscious vegetarians & it also serves a varied selection of snacks, juices & desserts. $

X Café Shaze [94 C2] Thimbirigasyaya Rd; m 0768 433122; w cafeshaze.com; ⏰ 08.00–midnight. With clean architectural lines offset by the eclectic off-the-wall décor, this coffee lounge & restaurant is an attractive spot for a drink or light meal. The menu has a strong Italian flavour (pasta, lasagne, risotto, filled ciabattas) but also incorporates Malay & Mongolian dishes, as well as salads & burgers. Excellent dessert menu. **$$–$$$**

✘ **88 Chinese Seafood** [94 B2] Havelock Rd; ☏011 451 6488; ⏲ 11.30–14.45 & 18.00–22.45. One of Colombo's best & most authentic Chinese restaurants, offering quick service & a lengthy menu of vegetarian & meat dishes in an uncluttered almost canteen-like interior. **$$$**

BARS AND NIGHTLIFE

Colombo isn't generally regarded as much of a party city. If you are looking for somewhere to enjoy a few relaxed drinks, most of the hotels and restaurants listed on the preceding pages will suffice, assuming they serve alcohol. The Kingsbury, Galle Face and Grand Oriental hotels are attractive spots for a central drink with a sea (or port) view, but a touch pricey, while other good central restaurants that double as bars include the Bavarian, Colombo Fort Café, Cricket Club Café and Park Street Mews. Overall, though, if you feel like imbibing in a tropical seaside setting as opposed to a more conventional indoor bar, you'd be best hopping on a tuktuk to Mount Lavinia (page 119), whose sandy beach is lined with lively bars and restaurants serving beer, wine and cocktails at reasonable prices.

♀ **Vespa Sports Club** [93 A3] Sea Av; ☏011 257 4229; ⏲ 11.00–14.00 & 17.00–22.00. A haven for drinking & dining alfresco, this dilapidated old building in Kollupitiya has a small bar & disproportionately large car park where people usually sit. Though very friendly, it's male-dominated & a touch sketchy, so females should be accompanied by a man. Drinks & bites are relatively cheap, & Fri or Sat night attracts a host of loud customers blasting chart music out of their jeeps. A great place to pre-lash before a club!

♀ **Rhythm & Blues** [94 A2] R A de Mel Rd; m 0770 552335, 0773 088600; 🅵 rhythmandbluescolombo; ⏲ 19.00–04.00. More wine bar than nightclub, this popular

& long-serving venue hosts live music some evenings, & the pool tables are a draw. Hang out indoors, or in an outside area with tables & chairs.

♀ **Club Silk** [93 D2] Maitland Cres; ☏011 268 2122; w sugarcolombo.com/club-silk; ⏲ 21.00–02.00 Wed–Sat. Sophisticated & pricey nightclub with salsa on Thu, more conventional DJs on other nights, & regular theme events.

♀ **Clique Supper Club & Lounge Bar** [88 F3] Union Pl; m 0767 254783; ⏲ 19.00–01.00 Tue–Thu, Sun, 19.00–04.00 Fri–Sat. Split across 2 floors of a high-rise overlooking De Soysa Circle, this sophisticated upmarket nightspot serves cocktails, champagne & wine to a backdrop of contemporary dance & jazz music.

CASINOS While few gamblers jet into Sri Lanka just to try their luck at the gaming tables, Colombo is home to several classy casinos that operate 24/7, closing only on the monthly poya days. Drinks and food are free to players, so some tourists have been known to take the money they would spend on drinks and dinner, and gamble it in a casino, where a buffet dinner is served at around 21.00, together with premium-quality drinks. As well as roulette, there are blackjack, baccarat and other gaming tables. The following casinos are easy-going and enjoyable places for gambling and run to a high standard: **Bellagio** [93 B3] (*R A De Mel Rd;* ☏ *011 257 5271;* w *bellagiocolombo.com*), **Bally's** [81 D3] (*D R Wijewardene Rd;* ☏ *011 233 1150;* w *ballyscolombo.com*), and the newer **Marina** [93 A2] (*Marine Dr;* ☏ *011 421 9988*).

SHOPPING

BOOKS Colombo has some very good bookshops, most of which have sections dedicated to books on Sri Lanka.

Barefoot Bookshop [94 A1] Galle Rd; ☎011 258 9305; w barefootceylon.com; ⊕ 10.00–20.00 Mon–Sat, 11.00–18.00 Sun. Set in the same building as the eponymous café & gift shop, the Barefoot Bookshop has the most comprehensive selection of books about Sri Lanka, ranging from field guides & travel guides to novels, historical works & coffee-table tomes.

Central Cultural Fund Bookshop [93 D2] Independence Av; ⊕ 08.30–16.00 Mon–Sat. Situated in Cinnamon Gardens only 500m from the National Museum, this book & craft shop stocks a decent selection of inexpensive booklets & glossier books focused on the main sites of the Cultural Triangle.

Lake House Bookshop [81 C4] Sir Chittampalam Gardiner Rd/[93 B1] Liberty Plaza, R A de Mel Rd; ☎011 473 4137/257 4418; w lakehousebookshop.com; ⊕ 10.00–18.00 Mon–Sat. Massive bookshop with a wide-ranging selection of books about Sri Lanka.

M D Gunasena [81 B3] Olcott Rd; ☎011 232 3981; w mdgunasena.com; ⊕ 09.00–18.00 Mon–Sat. This popular family bookseller is also a well-respected publisher of notable Sri Lankan books. It has several branches countrywide & in suburban Colombo.

Odel [88 F4] De Soysa Circle; ☎011 472 2200; w odel.lk. On this department store's mezzanine floor is an attractive layout of illustrated books with a large section devoted to books about Sri Lanka.

Vijitha Yapa Bookshop [94 A2] Unity Plaza, Galle Rd; ☎011 259 6960; w vijithayapa.com. An innovative bookseller, with branches at Crescat Bd & at the airport transit lounge often featuring bargain-priced books, as well as their own published works.

CRAFTS, CLOTHS AND CURIOS

Good Market [93 D2] Colombo Racecourse, Gunawardena Rd; m 0773 772122; w goodmarket.lk; ⊕ 10.00–18.00 Sat. This socially aware, volunteer-driven weekly market in Cinnamon Gardens hosts dozens of stalls selling fair-trade handicrafts, organic foodstuffs & natural health & beauty products.

Barefoot [94 A1] Galle Rd; ☎011 258 9305; w barefootceylon.com; ⊕ 10.00–20.00 Mon–Sat, 11.00–18.00 Sun. Renowned for its dedication to local hand-woven fabrics in colourful hippy-style designs, this fabulous boutique has expanded to include all manner of bright & beautiful craft & curios, as well as books, vintage posters & delightful household items.

Paradise Road [88 E4] S A Dharmapala Rd, Colombo 7; ☎011 268 6043; w paradiseroad.lk/shops; ⊕ 10.00–19.00. Walk into this converted 19th-century mansion, & you'll feel as though you have found Aladdin's cave. You can amble through avenues of candles & crazy cutlery, discover basketry & sculpture, go upstairs for stylish sarongs & modern versions of Victoriana, & even find genuine antiques, as well as copies. A branch in the affiliated Gallery Café (page 92) stays open until 22.00.

Laksala [94 B2] York St; ☎011 232 3513; w laksala.gov.lk; ⊕ 09.00–21.00. The most central branch of the official souvenir shop stands in Fort, just south of the old Cargills Building, but there are also branches in the National Museum gardens & on Bauddhaloka Rd just inland of Bambalapitiya station. All stock a fabulous selection of well-priced goods, from fabrics & handicrafts, to tea & spices, gems & jewellery, & CDs of Sri Lankan music.

LUV SL [81 B3] Old Dutch Hospital; ☎011 244 8872; w odel.lk/odel-dutch-hospital; ⊕ 10.00–19.00. Colourful Sri Lanka-branded modern souvenirs ranging from T-shirts & caps to mugs, fridge magnets & toiletries.

Hermitage [94 B2] Gower St; ☎011 250 2196; w hermitart.com; ⊕ 09.00–18.00. A good place to browse & buy colonial reproduction furniture, as well as genuine antique prints, maps & postcards, & beautiful things from India.

Sri Lanka Tea Board [93 B4] Galle Rd; ☎011 255 3652; m 0714 334243; w pureceylontea.com; ⊕ 09.00–19.00 Mon–Sat. A must for tea buffs, the national tea board's shop in Kollupitiya stocks a vast, diverse & well-priced selection of top Ceylon teas, as well as many pricier difficult-to-find single-estate specialities, all in easily transported packets.

SHOPPING MALLS The city's first shopping mall, the two-storey **Liberty Plaza** [93 A1] (*R A de Mel Rd*; ☎*011 257 5935*), opened in the 1980s and it shows its age, containing shops that specialise mostly in imported items. The newer **Majestic City** [94 A2] (*Station Rd;* ☏ *011 250 8673*) is livelier and has a better standard of shop. More upmarket is **Crescat Boulevard** [88 B4] (*Galle Rd*), whose food court offers low-priced self-service meals from different themed outlets.

SUPERMARKETS Numerous branches of the reliable **Cargills Food City** (w *cargillsceylon.com*) are dotted around the city. Most are open at least from 08.00 to 22.00 (some keep longer hours) and stock a good selection of packaged goods, fresh produce (bread, meat, fish, fruit and vegetables), and have a pharmacy and beer and wine counter. The more strategically located branches are shown on our maps, but a useful store locator can be found on their website. Similar in standard and only slightly less ubiquitous, **Keells Supermarket** (w *keellssuper. com*) also has a dozen or more branches citywide, and an online store locator. Another excellent option, conveniently located for those staying in Kollupitiya or Bambalapitiya, is the 60-year-old **Premasiri Supermarket** [93 B2] (☏ *011 233 1477;* w *premasiristores.lk*), which is known for its varied and well-priced selection of wine, beer and other liquor.

OTHER PRACTICALITIES

ART GALLERIES In addition to the three places listed below, the national gallery and several private galleries are clustered in Cinnamon Gardens near the National Museum, and described in the box on page 110.

Artway Gallery [map, page 78] Old Kesbewa Rd; ☏011 285 2606; m 0755 958301; w artgallery. lk; ⏰ 10.00–18.00. The suburban location in a fine old mansion in Nugegoda makes this rather inconvenient for travellers, but it displays a vast & diverse selection of contemporary & traditional Sri Lankan art.
Barefoot Gallery [94 A1] Galle Rd; ☏011 258 9305; w barefootceylon.com/gallery; ⏰ 10.00–20.00 Mon–Sat, 11.00–18.00 Sun. Established in

1967 as the Colombo Gallery, this extension of the Barefoot Café hosts regular exhibitions featuring local & overseas artists, as well as occasional music concerts, poetry readings & film nights.
Gallery Café [94 A1] Alfred House Rd; ☏011 258 2162; w paradiseroad.lk; ⏰ 10.00–midnight. This popular upmarket restaurant is adjoined by a small gallery displaying contemporary art curated by owner Shanth Fernando.

BANKS AND ATMS Foreign credit and debit cards (Visa and MasterCard) can be used to withdraw local currency from 24-hour ATMs outside any branch of the Commercial, Hatton National (HNB), Seylan, Sampath or Standard Chartered banks. These are liberally scattered around the city, with the most convenient branches being marked on the maps in this book. Hard currency cash can be also exchanged for local currency at most banks during banking hours (*typically* ⏰ *09.00–14.30 Mon–Fri*). Outside banking hours, if you need cash urgently, head to Bandaranaike International Airport, where foreign exchange counters operate at all hours.

CINEMA AND THEATRE
Lionel Wendt Art Centre [93 C2] Guildford Cres; ☏011 269 5794; w lionelwendt.org; ⏰ 09.00–19.00 Mon–Fri, 10.00–noon & 14.00– 19.00 Sat–Sun. Founded in 1953 & named after the pioneering photographer Lionel Wendt, this

600-seat auditorium hosts regular dance, English-language theatre & music performances.
Nelum Pokuna Mahinda Rajapaksa Theatre [93 D2] Ananda Coomaraswamy Rd; ☏011 269 0932; w lotuspond.lk. Opened in

2011, this ultramodern building next to the National Museum is worth visiting just for its striking architecture, inspired by the 12th-century Nelum Pokuna (Lotus Pond) built in Polonnaruwa by Parakramabahu I. The 1,270-seat auditorium hosts sporadic one-off concerts & other events, but overall it seems to be rather under-utilised.

Majestic Cineplex [94 A2] Majestic City, Galle Rd; 011 258 1759; w ceylontheatres.lk. This complex incorporates 2 3D cinemas & 2 normal ones. Both usually screen recent US & Indian movies.

Regal Cinema [81 C4] Sir C A Gardiner Rd; 011 243 2936; w ceylontheatres.lk. Another multiscreen complex showing recent international blockbusters.

Savoy 3D Cinema [94 B4] Galle Rd, Wellawatta; 011 744 4466; w eapmovies.com. 2-screen cinema screening a mixture of Sri Lankan, Bollywood & Hollywood flicks. Beer is available; clean bathrooms too.

Liberty Cinema [93 A1] Dharmapala Rd; 011 744 4477; w eapmovies.com. Overlooking Kollupitiya Junction, this is the oldest English-language cinema in Colombo, with a stench to prove it. 2 screens show a range of Sinhala, Hindi & Hollywood action & horror films.

CRICKET Cricket is to Sri Lanka what football is to most other countries, and there must be at least a dozen school or club cricket pitches within a few kilometres of Fort District. Most important is the Sinhalese Sports Club Ground (SSC) [93 E2], which has a capacity of 10,000 and is sometimes referred to as the 'Lords of Sri Lanka', having hosted more than 40 test matches and 60 one-day internationals since 1984. In recent years, however, the favoured ground for internationals has been the suburban Ranasinghe Premadasa Stadium [map, page 78], which was expanded to hold a capacity of 35,000 for the 2011 ICC World Cup. Check w espncricinfo.com or w srilankacricket.lk for details of upcoming international and domestic fixtures in Colombo.

EMBASSIES Consular representatives in Colombo include the UK High Commission [93 F3] (*Bauddhaloka Rd;* 011 539 0639) and US Embassy [93 A1] (*Galle Rd;* 011 249 8500). A full list with current contact details is maintained at w sltda.lk/embassies_in_sri_lanka.

GOLF
Royal Colombo Golf Club [map, page 74] Model Farm Rd; 011 269 5431; w rcgcsl.com. This flat 18-hole, par-71 course, complete with broad fairways, water hazards & bunkers, stands in amazing contrast to the clutter of the city. Temporary membership costs US$70/85 per day on weekdays/weekends. You can rent a set of clubs for around US$27 & arrange a caddy for around US$6 per round.

MEDICAL There are many hospitals and clinics scattered around Colombo but health-care standards tend to be far lower than in most Western countries. For non-urgent requirements, best ask your hotel to recommend a good local doctor or dentist. In case of an emergency, highly regarded hospitals with 24-hour ICU facilities include **Durdans** [93 B3] (*Alfred Pl, Kollupitiya;* 1344 (emergency helpline), 011 214 0000; w durdans.com), **Lanka Hospitals** [94 D2] (*Evitigala Rd, Havelock Town;* 011 543 0000/553 0000; w lankahospitals.com) and the state-run **National Hospital** [88 G3] (*Regent St, Maradana;* 011 269 1111; w nhsl.health.gov.lk).

POST OFFICE The **General Post Office** [81 D3] (011 232 6203; ⊕ 24hrs for the sale of stamps) is located on D R Wijewardene Road, behind the Colombo Fort railway station.

TOURIST INFORMATION The **central tourist information office** [88 B3] (*Galle Rd;* ✆ *011 242 6900;* w *srilanka.travel;* ⊕ *08.00–21.00*) is just south of Galle Face, more or less opposite the Cinnamon Grand Hotel, and stocks a useful selection of brochures and booklets to the whole country.

SPAS AND SALONS A reliable chain of hair and beauty salons, **Ramani Fernando** (w *ramanifernando.com*) operates around ten branches in Colombo, most usefully in the Cinnamon Grand, Hilton Colombo, Taj Samudra and World Trade Centre. Good salons can be found at several of the city's other upmarket hotels, including the Galle Face and Mount Lavinia. Ayurveda spas are more sparse on the ground in Colombo than they are at the resorts of the southwest coast, but the chain operated by **Spa Ceylon** (w *store.spaceylon.com*) comes highly recommended and includes branches in the Old Dutch Hospital [81 B3] (✆ *011 244 1931;* ⊕ *10.00–23.00*), Park Street Mews [88 E4] (✆ *011 534 0011;* ⊕ *10.00–23.00*), Crescat Boulevard [88 B4] (✆ *011 554 4398;* ⊕ *10.00–19.00*), Barefoot Café [94 A1] (✆ *011 558 9305;* ⊕ *10.00–19.00*) and several other localities citywide. There are also good spas in the Casa Colombo and Colombo Courtyard hotels.

SWIMMING The only swimming beach in the immediate vicinity of Colombo is Mount Lavinia, about 12km south of the city centre (page 119). If there is no swimming pool at your hotel, several upmarket hotels, notably the Ramada, Ozo, Kingsbury and Taj Samudra, open their pool to day-visitors for a fee, typically around US$5–7.

VISA EXTENSIONS Immigration at Bandaranaike International Airport usually stamps in visitors for 30 days. This can be extended to 90 days at any point prior to expiry, even your day of arrival, at the Department of Immigration and Emigration [map, page 78] (*41 Ananda Rajakhruna Rd, Maradana;* ✆ *011 532 9000;* w *immigration.gov.lk;* ⊕ *08.30–14.00 Mon–Fri*). Arrive as early as you can, bring your passport, one passport photo and a pen, and allow for at least 3 hours to complete the formalities. The first step is to fill in the visa extension form, which is available on the spot, or downloadable in advance at w immigration.gov.lk, and paste on a passport photo. Hand in this form at reception, where you will be issued with a number. Depending on how busy the office is, you might wait up to 2 hours for your number to be called, when you'll be interviewed briefly by an immigration officer. From here on in, factor in another 30-minute wait for payment details to be processed, then up to 15 minutes to queue to make the payment, then another 30 minutes or so for the visa extension to be issued. The extension costs US$30–100 depending on your nationality (*charges are listed at* w *immigration.gov.lk*) and can be paid in local currency.

WHAT TO SEE AND DO

Colombo is liberally studded with colonial architectural gems, museums, galleries and other points of interest, most clustered in the city centre or the southern suburbia of Slave Island and Cinnamon Gardens. Few if any of these individual sites fall into the 'must-visit' category, but collectively they add up to a couple of days of solid sightseeing. Most worthwhile for archaeology enthusiasts is the National Museum, which provides an excellent primer to the likes of Anuradhapura, Polonnaruwa and Kandy. The bustling bazaars of Pettah and more staidly historic Fort District are ideal for casual urban exploration. When it comes to Buddhist-related sites, the historic out-of-town Kelaniya Temple contains some fine Kandyan-era paintings, while Gangaramaya Temple dazzles in its own rather kitschy way. There's no shortage of fine colonial edifices, while more contemporary architectural highlights include the traditionally inspired Independence Memorial, the pied-à-terre designed and lived in by the celebrated Geoffrey Bawa, and the same architect's Parliament Building in Sri Jayawardenepura Kotte.

Colombo also provides easy access to Dehiwala–Mount Lavinia, a contiguous municipality whose main attractions are the lovely Mount Lavinia beach, the underwhelming National Zoological Gardens, and more worthwhile but rather esoteric Bellanwila-Attidiya Sanctuary. Potential goals for day trips out of Colombo include the Muthurajawela Wetland Sanctuary and substantial resort town of Negombo, respectively set at the southern and northern ends of the Negombo Lagoon, as well as Pinnawala Elephant Orphanage and other sites described on pages 148–50.

Central Colombo is easy enough to get around on foot, while sites further afield can be explored using a combination of walking and tuktuk hops. No entrance fee is charged to sites described below unless otherwise stated.

GALLE FACE GREEN The largest green space (or, much of the time, brown space) in central Colombo, Galle Face Green – not, as might be supposed, named after the more southerly port of Galle, but a derivative of the Sinhalese word *gal* (rock) – is an obvious place to start or end any walking tour of the city. Measuring almost a kilometre from north to south, this elevated seafront promenade was initially laid out by the Dutch, who lined the ramparts above the rocky coastline with a battery of cannons to fend off Portuguese and other maritime attacks. During the British colonial period, Galle Face Green was much larger than it is today, sprawling inland to Lake Beira, and it served as a recreational ground complete with horse-racing track, golf course and other sporting fields. The construction of the present Galle Face Walk was initiated by Sir Henry Ward in 1856 and completed three years later, when (states a stone inscription now stowed in the Old Town Hall) it was 'recommended to his successors in the interest of the Ladies and Children of Colombo'. The green is prettiest and most atmospheric at dusk, being ideally located to catch the sun setting over the Indian Ocean while locals promenade companionably in the sea breeze, catch up on gossip, fly kites or knock around balls, or buy fresh snacks from night-time hawkers. Two of Colombo's most

COLOMBO BY DOUBLE-DECKER

A straightforward and enjoyable way to explore the city is one of the bus tours operated by Colombo City Tours in conjunction with Ebert Silva Holidays. These take place on a genuine 1950s London Transport double-decker bus, with the roof removed from the upper deck for easy viewing, and takes guests on a delightful ramble taking in the central Fort District, Lake Beira, a Buddhist and Hindu temple, and visits to Independence Square and the National Museum. An expert guide is on board with a running commentary in English and to answer questions; sandwiches and mineral water are included, and umbrellas are available. Tours leave from the Old Dutch Hospital [81 B3] (*16.00 Mon–Fri, 08.30 & 16.30 Sat–Sun*), but weekday tours are shorter and cheaper (*2½ hrs; US$25 pp*) than weekend itineraries (*3½ hrs; US$30 pp*). For further details and bookings, contact: 011 281 4700; m 0777 599963; e info@colombocitytours.com; w colombocitytours.com.

imposing colonial relicts bookend the long narrow green: the Galle Face Hotel, the city's oldest hostelry, built in 1864, and a fine place for a sundowner or snack; and the Old Parliament Building described below.

FORT DISTRICT The most historic quarter of Colombo, Fort is traditionally regarded as the city's CBD, and it remains an important banking and commercial centre, despite having been superseded in many respects by booming suburbs such as Kollupitiya and Cinnamon Gardens. The district's titular fortifications, built by the Portuguese in 1510 and expanded by the Dutch after 1656, were later demolished, almost without trace, by the British colonists. Following a prolonged economic slump in the late 20th century, Fort District has experienced a remarkable post-millennial revival, one boosted significantly by the end of the civil war in 2009. Once-faded colonial-era architectural gems are now restored to their former glory, streets formerly barricaded for security reasons have reopened to the public, and a host of newly established shops, restaurants and other business are thriving, partly due to an increase in tourist traffic. All the same, much of the island's northwest still comprises a naval base, and several roads remain closed. These include Galle Buck Road and Flagstaff Street, along with the stretch of Church Street west of St Peter's Church [81 B1] and Chatham Street west of the Lighthouse Clock Tower [81 B2].

A recommended walking route through Fort, starting from the circle in front of the Old Parliament Building, entails heading north along Chaitya Street to the Maritime Museum then returning the same way to the circle, and turning north on to Janadhipathi Road. Here you could divert east along Bank of Ceylon Road to the Old Dutch Hospital, then continue north along Janadhipathi past the Presidential Palace before taking an obligatory right turn that brings you to York Street. Here you will see the Cargills Building to your immediate south, and can then head north for 150m to the junction of York and Church streets. This route involves about 3km of walking and sites of interest within Fort are described following it. Those with sufficient energy could continue eastward from the junction of York and Church streets to the neighbouring district of Pettah (pages 105–8).

Old Parliament Building [81 B4] (*Galle Face Dr*) Standing sentinel over the north end of Galle Face, the Old Parliament is the first building to the right as you cross from the Galle Road Bridge into Fort. An imposing forum-style neo-Baroque brownstone, it was constructed in 1930 and now houses the Presidential Secretariat, while forming a sedate antidote to the glaring mirror-glass of the sky-scraping Bank of Ceylon headquarters behind. In its front gardens stand statues of several former Sri Lankan presidents and other leaders.

Colombo Lighthouse [81 A2] (*Chaitya St*) Built in 1951 as an emblem of the port development scheme initiated by Prime Minister Senanayake a year earlier, this granite lighthouse stands on a stone platform overlooking the harbour, where it is guarded by a quartet of lions. Below it, the Governor's Bath, restored in 1991, is a natural seawater rock pool where colonial governors and their ladies were wont to bathe back in the day.

Sambodhi Chaitya [81 A1] (*Chaitya St*) Supported by two interlocked arches bridging Chaitya Street, this unusual white concrete dagoba, built in 1956 to commemorate the 25th centennial of Gautama Buddha, reaches almost 80m into the sky above Colombo Port. The hollow interior can be reached by walking (barefoot) up a 260-step outdoor staircase that surrounds an 11-storey tower connected to it by a short metal bridge. The Buddhist paintings that decorate the dome's interior aren't of overwhelming interest (you'll see similar in hundreds of other temples countywide) but it is an interesting and unusual structure, and the views over the city and port are fantastic.

Colombo Maritime Museum [81 A1] (*Chaitya St;* \ *011 242 1201;* ◷ *10.00–19.00*) Situated alongside Sambodhi Chaitya, this moderately diverting museum is housed in what is probably Fort District's oldest building, a barrel-roofed Dutch *pakhuizen* (warehouse) constructed in 1676, the date inscribed above its eastern entrance. In 1951, when all the other old port buildings were demolished, the old warehouse was spared, finally to be renovated in 1998 by the Sri Lanka Ports Authority, which also founded the museum. Displays mostly relate to the maritime history and old trade routes of Colombo and the island, and include depictions of key historical events from the arrival of Prince Vijaya to the British occupation. Also of interest is a series of maps and illustrations that chart the development of the island and evolution of the port from pre-colonial times to the 21st century.

Old Dutch Hospital [81 B3] (*Bank of Ceylon Rd*) Vying with the maritime museum as Fort's oldest building, the Old Dutch Hospital is clearly recognisable from two watercolour paintings made in 1771, but it is most likely a century older than this. Almost certainly, this building is the 'well-built hospital where sick Dutchmen are well-served by surgeons and slaves with medicine and plasters', as recorded by German solider Christopher Schweitzer in 1681, and the same hospital where Paul Hermann – a VOC surgeon whose vast collection of dried plants and drawings earned him the sobriquet 'Father of Ceylonese botany' – worked in the 1670s. It served as a hospital and apothecary throughout the British colonial era, but was converted to a police station in the early 1980s, and suffered heavy damage in 1996 when the Central Bank opposite was destroyed in a suicide bombing that killed at least 91 people and left more than a hundred bystanders blind. Following the end of the civil war, the timeworn building was restored under the supervision of the Department of Archaeology, to reopen as the Dutch Hospital Shopping Precinct in 2011. Now one of the main tourist draws in Colombo, it contains several restaurants and souvenir shops, but it is also of interest as a fine example of functional Dutch colonial architecture, comprising two sets of former wards and barracks, with 50cm-thick walls and red-tiled roofs supported by massive teak beams, whose wide verandas enclose a pair of large courtyards.

World Trade Centre [81 B3] (*Bank of Ceylon Rd;* w *wtc.lk*) Dominating the skies above the courtyard of the Old Dutch Hospital, Colombo's own World Trade Centre (WTC) is the city's tallest building, comprising identical east and west 40-storey towers that stand 152m tall. It was inaugurated by President Chandrika Kumaratunga on 12 October 1997, and only three days later formed the target of an LTTE bombing that left the skyscrapers unscathed, but killed 15 people and wounded more than a hundred. The twin towers are soon likely to be surpassed in altitude by the Grand Hyatt and Lotus Tower, which respectively overlook Galle Face Green and Lake Beira, and will stand 230m and 305m tall once complete.

Sri Vikrama Rajasinha's Prison Cell [81 B3] (*Cnr Bank of Ceylon & Janadhipathi rds*) Tucked away behind railings in the parking lot of the Ceylinco Building is a small half-barrel building where the British colonial administration reputedly imprisoned King Vikrama Rajasinha after he was deposed in 1815 but prior to deporting him to

Madras. A plaque in English and Sinhala confirms that the king was held here for a period, and his effigy glowers from behind bars at passers-by who seldom notice it. With its mustard-painted exterior and a distinctive red-scalloped tile roof topped by chimney-like protrusion, the tiny edifice is difficult to miss, but whether anybody was ever imprisoned here is a matter some of debate – sceptics insist that it was built after 1815 and most likely served as a store or sentry room.

Lighthouse Clock Tower [81 A2/B2] (*Cnr Janadhipathi Rd & Chatham St*) Fort's best-known landmark, the 'Big Ben of Colombo' was constructed in 1857, when it was the tallest edifice in the city centre, standing 29m high. Initially, it served purely as a clock tower, topped by a four-faced clock commissioned by Governor Brownrigg in 1814 and held in storage ever since. In 1867, following the demolition of the Dutch ramparts and older lighthouse that stood upon them, it was converted to a dual-purpose lighthouse, emitting a triple flash visible for up to 25km out at sea. The original kerosene light was upgraded to gas in 1907 and then electrified in 1933. Things came full circle in 1951, when the new Colombo Lighthouse (page 102) was erected on the waterfront 250m further west, and it reverted to being a clock tower only.

Economic History Museum [81 B2] (*Cnr Janadhipathi Rd & Chatham St;* ❧011 247 7257; ⌚ *09.00–17.00 Mon–Sat*) This modern installation spans two storeys of the former National Mutual Building, a stately colonial relict built over 1911–14 and briefly the city's tallest landmark. Damaged by the Central Bank bombing in 1996, it had become very dilapidated by 2011, when it was acquired by the Central Bank of Sri Lanka, and renamed the Central Point Building. Since then, the fabulous arched and colonnaded façade has been fully restored, as has the interior, which is dominated by a grand circular stairwell. The museum itself is more engaging than its insomnia-cure of a name might suggest. Colourful and well-annotated displays cover the various themed banknote series issued over the decades, including the current ones from 2011, each of which features an architectural landmark and endemic bird on the front, and a different traditional drummer and dancer on the back. A section of older currencies displays coins from the likes of Rome and China, as well as those minted locally in Anuradhapura. The refreshing air conditioning furthers the case for escaping the city street to give it a quick look over.

Presidential Palace [81 A2] (*Janadhipathi Rd*) This magnificent two-storey residence was built in c1790 by Johan van Angelbeek, the last Dutch governor of Ceylon, on the site of a freshly demolished 16th-century Portuguese church. Van Angelbeek's granddaughter sold it to the British colonial administration in 1804, since when it has served as the residence of 29 British governors and six presidents. Known as King's or Queen's House during the colonial era, it is hidden behind a wealth of trees and heavily guarded, but you can catch a glimpse of the grand façade through the foliage. In front of the palace stands a statue of Sir Edward Barnes (the governor responsible for much of island's development between 1820 and 1831), from which all distances ex-Colombo are measured.

Cargills Building [81 B2] (*York St*) One of Fort's most iconic landmarks, Cargills is a two-storey department store whose striking red-and-white puce stone exterior incorporates plaster horns-of-plenty bursting with bounty, and a shady multi-arched ground-floor walkway and balustrade typical of Colombo's older buildings.

The property was acquired by Cargills – Colombo's oldest store – in 1888, and the present-day building was constructed over 1902–06. It stands on the site of a one-storey house that quite possibly started life as the first Dutch governor's residence in Colombo (the foundation stone is dated 1684) and that was occupied by Frederick North, the first British governor of Ceylon, c1798. It is unclear to what extent elements of these older structures were incorporated into the present-day building. The interior is just as impressive as the façade, with its dark wooden floors, tall ceilings and ornate arches, and it houses what must surely be the world's only colonial-style KFC outlet!

Grand Oriental Hotel [81 B1] (*Cnr York & Church sts*) This imposing building was constructed as an army barracks in 1837 and upgraded to become a hotel in 1875. It thrived in the days of sea travel, when its location outside the port gates made it a popular and convenient place to spend one's first few nights on tropical terra firma (a bronze statue outside depicts a smartly attired new arrival being rickshawed to its shady sanctuary). These days it feels somewhat past its prime, but it's still worth dropping in for impressive colonial architecture and period décor, or to enjoy an early evening drink in the balcony bar, which offers fine views over the port.

St Peter's Church [81 B1] (*Church St*) Tucked away along an alley that looks to be off limits on first inspection, this Anglican church 50m west of the Grand Oriental Hotel is yet another Colombo landmark that reputedly started life as a Dutch governor's residence. It was consecrated as an Anglican church and dedicated to St Peter in 1821, but the plaque outside suggests that it might have been converted to a church (presumably Dutch Reformed) as early as 1680. The interior is rather sombre and plain, but the original wooden ceiling is intact, the hardwood pews look equally antiquated, and several 19th-century memorial stones commemorate parishioners and sailors who succumbed to various tropical ailments.

PETTAH DISTRICT Situated immediately east of Fort and separated from it by a 50m wide channel, Pettah started life during the Dutch and early British periods as a select residential area, but it later came to be regarded as the 'native quarter'. The name Pettah is often said to derive from *pettai*, a Tamil word used loosely to describe a colony or place, but a more likely etymology is the Sinhala word *pitiya* (village) or phrase *pita kotuwa* ('outside the fort'). Today, Pettah is Colombo's haunt of the streetwise, a hectic and sprawling inner-city open-air bazaar where everything you ever wanted, and many things you never will, can be found in a motley assortment of hardware shops, garment stores and grocery stalls, all stacked high with goods that flow over on to the pavement. Reminiscent of parts of Cairo or Mumbai, the narrow streets (or, if you prefer, wide alleys) of Pettah are jammed with bargain hunters, herds of trucks, cars and bullock carts, explosive klaxons of tuktuks, and porters barking instructions to move out of their way. Indeed, such is the human throng that, in peak shopping hours, pedestrians for once actually get to stall vehicular traffic, rather than having to make way for it. An exciting and engaging area to explore on foot, Pettah is also largely free of hassle and there's little to worry about security-wise, though it would be sensible to leave valuables at home or buried somewhere out of reach of the light-fingered.

Coming from Fort, two bridges span the channel with Pettah. The more northerly leads from the port entrance on Church Street via Sir Baron Jayathilaka Vidyalaya Street to a traffic circle – crowned by a clock tower erected in 1923 to commemorate the 45th anniversary of the death of one Framjee Bhikkajee Khan – at the entrance to Pettah Main Street. The more southerly follows Olcott Road to Pettah's best-known landmark, Fort railway station. A good walking route through Pettah would entail following Olcott Road east to the Pettah Floating Market, then trailing through the inner alleys via the Dutch Period Museum to the Pettah Methodist Church via Main Street and the Old City Hall. On the way, you will pass along, or can easily divert to, roads that specialise in certain types of goods: stores on 1st Cross Street, for instance, mostly sell watches and bags, while 2nd Cross Street is known for leatherware and electric goods, 3rd Cross Street for textiles, 4th Cross Street for wholesale goods, etc.

Colombo Fort Station [81 D3] (*Olcott Rd*) Sri Lanka's busiest single transport hub, Colombo Fort is the starting point for most of the country's commuter and intercity rail services, and carries an estimated daily traffic of 200,000 passengers. Modelled on Manchester Victoria, the station opened in 1917 on land reclaimed from Lake Beira to replace the original Fort Station built a short distance to the west 40 years earlier. In the car park stands a statue of Henry Steel Olcott, the US-born Buddhist crusader for whom Olcott Road is named.

St Philip Neri's Church [81 E2] (*Olcott Rd;* ✆ *011 242 1367;* f *PhilipNerisPettah*) Founded by Benedictine monks in 1858 and consecrated four years later, this most central of Colombo's catholic edifices has a handsome colonnaded and arched Corinthian façade modelled loosely on Rome's Arch-basilica of St John in Lateran. With a capacity of 600 worshippers, it was one of the city's largest buildings at the time of its construction, and it remains Colombo's most popular Catholic shrine.

Manning Market [81 E2/3] (*Olcott Rd*) Colombo's principal fresh-produce market, sandwiched between Colombo Fort station and Bastian Road bus stand on the south side of Olcott Road, is named after Governor Manning, who was responsible for the construction of a row of warehouses there over 1918–25. Today it comprises more than a thousand stalls and incorporates several fine Dutch-era buildings with wooden doors and roof timbers. It's an interesting place to wander around, but how long it will remain *in situ* is an open question, following the announcement in 2016 of a controversial plan to relocate it to Peliyagoda, 10km to the east.

Pettah Floating Market [81 F3] (*Bastian Rd;* ✆ *011 287 3640;* ⊕ *08.00–20.00;* f *pettahfloatingmarket*). Not quite as exotic as it sounds, this low-key waterfront-type Urban Development Authority development opened in 2014 on a small (and, in some conditions, distinctly whiffy) northern extension of Lake Beira. The 92 stalls cater mainly to local tastes, and it is difficult to imagine too many travellers will leap at the opportunity to take a swan-shaped pedal-boat out on the small patch of open water (*less than US$1*). On the other hand, it's a pleasant enough spot to pause your exploration of Pettah and stop for a reviving drink or snack at any of a dozen inexpensive bakeries and roti stands.

Dutch Period Museum [81 E2] (*Prince St;* ✆ *011 244 8466;* w *museum.gov. lk;* ⊕ *09.00–17.00 Tue–Sat; entrance US$3.50, photography US$1.75*) A rather improbable apparition amid the hubbub of central Pettah, this well-preserved relic of the Dutch colonial era was built in the 1690s as a townhouse for Governor van Rhee, and subsequently served as a seminary orphanage, a hospital, the headquarters of the Ceylon Volunteers, a police training school and a post office. It was abandoned in 1972 after a monsoon precipitated the collapse of one of the exterior walls, only to be restored as a museum over 1977–82, with financial assistance from the Netherlands government. From an architectural perspective, the two-storey main house ranks among the country's finest surviving Dutch buildings, with its dark wooden floors and stairwells, and colonnaded whitewashed façade. Two single-storey annexes surround a pretty courtyard garden with a well. The museum's contents are poorly labelled and less engaging than the building itself, but the ground-floor room stuffed with miscellaneous Kandyan artefacts – bronze Buddhas, ornamental traditional dancers' costumes, painted wood beads *et al.* – justifies the moderate entrance fee.

Jami Ul-Alfar Mosque [81 E1] (*Cnr 2nd Cross St & Main Rd;* w *redmasjid.com*) Built in 1908 as a place of worship for Tamil immigrants, the striking Jami Ul-Alfar is also known prosaically as Samman Kottu Palli (Mosque for Indian Muslims) and more descriptively as Rathu Palliya (Red Mosque), owing to the giddying assortment of red-and-white stripes, chequers, jags and spirals that enliven the interior. A tall and ornate building, it has the slightly surreal appearance of a fairy-tale candy castle, with a façade of barbershop-pole columns supporting boldly patterned arches and windows, all topped by a trio of plump minarets whose shape was inspired by the pomegranate fruit. Outside of prayer times, respectfully dressed non-Muslim visitors are usually allowed inside, but women may have more difficulty gaining access.

Kayman's Gate [81 E1] (*Cnr 4th Cross St & Main Rd*) This easily missed roadside belfry, complete with bell and nesting crows, marks the site of Queen's Gate, the principal eastern entrance to the Portuguese fort built at Colombo in 1554. Reached via a drawbridge and tunnel, the gate was later renamed after the plentiful mugger crocodiles ('kaymans' in Dutch) that scavenged in the enclosing moat. The last vestiges of the Portuguese ramparts were destroyed by the British in c1870, and the moat was filled in at the same time. The belfry, which probably dates to the Dutch occupation, was spared demolition, and it remained the site for public executions for some decades after. The bell itself is one of Colombo's few surviving relics of the Portuguese occupation, salvaged as it was from the ruins of a church they built at the then-Sinhalese capital Kotte prior to 1565.

Old Town Hall [81 E1] (*Kayman's Gate Circle*) Overlooking the traffic circle at the east end of Main Street, this grandly rundown Gothic town hall was built in 1873 and served as the seat of city government until 1928, when its yard became a public market. In 1984, it was reinvented as a **Municipal Museum** featuring various quirky bygones of city life: cast-iron water pumps and drinking fountains, a manhole cover, a signpost, a city father's official robes, bits of machinery, a massive steamroller, an ancient steam lorry emblazoned with the council's crest, and a bizarre recreation of a 1906 council meeting featuring life-size mannequins sitting around a wooden table. Officially, the museum is closed, but if you wander around outside, you should find someone to let you in for a 'fee' of around US$1.50.

Gabos Lane [81 E1] This short narrow lane running west from the circle 100m north of the Old Town Hall is lined with several remarkable shops specialising in the ingredients of Ayurvedic (herbal) remedies. Outside the New Royal Fireworks & Medical Store and its neighbouring Ayurvedic merchants are sacks of twigs, strips of bark, dried herbs and leaves that, properly mixed, offer an age-old alternative to modern Western medicine. Sea Street, running north from the same circle, is lined with small gold and jewellery dealers.

Pettah Methodist Church [81 F1] (*Dam St*) The Wesleyan Mission House built on Dam Street in 1816 is said to be the oldest Methodist Church in Asia (though its counterpart in Mount Lavinia is dated two years earlier). A rather plain building, it is reputedly modelled on Brunswick Wesleyan Church in Liverpool, but the resemblance between the two buildings isn't particularly strong.

Wolvendaal Church [map, page 78] (*Wolvendaal Ln;* m *0779 976295;* w *wolvendaal.org; no fee but a nominal donation is asked*) Named after a marshy area known to the Dutch as Wolvendaal (Valley of Jackals), Sri Lanka's oldest surviving Dutch Reformed Church was founded in 1749 under Governor Julius Valentijn Stein Van Gollenesse, whose initials are inscribed on the foundation stone. The site chosen was on a small hill that then offered views to the harbour and stood within easy walking distance of Kayman's Gate, the original eastern entrance to the Fort. The church is built in the classical Greek Doric style, with fluted columns on the thick outer walls and tall ornate gables above each of the four façades, and is also known as the Kruiskerk (Cross Church) owing to its cruciform shape. Five Dutch governors were buried here, and the courtyard is lined with 18th-century Dutch memorial stones, many translated into English.

St Lucia's Cathedral [map, page 78] (*St Lucia St;* f *StLuciasKotahena*) Located at Kotahena about 1km northeast of Pettah, St Lucia's Cathedral, seat of the Archbishop of Colombo, is the city's largest Christian shrine, with a capacity of 6,000. Its origins can be traced to 1760, when Catholic Fathers belonging to the apostolic Congregation of the Oratory of Saint Philip Neri built a rudimentary palm-roof church on the site. This was superseded by a modest brick-and-mortar church constructed in 1782 and elevated to cathedral status in 1838. The present-day church, a Gothic replica of St Peter's Basilica in the Vatican, with a massive silver dome crowned by the cross and colonnaded façade topped with seven statues of Biblical figures, was built over 1872–81 and received a papal visit in 1995. The interior contains many beautiful stained-glass windows and statues, notably Our Lady of Kotahena, a unique dark-skinned Madonna-and-child paraded during the annual procession through Kotahena held every May.

SLAVE ISLAND Situated inland of Galle Face Green to the immediate south of Fort and Pettah, this large unfocused suburb is encircled by Lake Beira and associated canals on three sides, and bounded by Viharamahadevi Park to the south. Its unsavoury name alludes to the many thousands of Mozambican slaves imported to serve both as labourers and as soldiers in service to the Portuguese. When the Dutch captured Colombo in 1656, they continued to use these African slaves as cheap labour, leading to an uprising during which a VOC official was killed. After this, slaves were forbidden from staying overnight in the fort, but were instead ferried south across the crocodile-infested Lake Beira to their rudimentary purpose-built quarters. In Dutch times, the area across-the-water was known informally as the Kaffir Veldt (Kaffir being a derogatory term for an African), a name that mutated to Slave Island during the British colonial era, by which time most of the slaves to which it refers had either returned to Africa or become integrated into local Sinhalese and Tamil communities. Over the course of the 20th century, ongoing land reclamation has caused the not-quite island to increase in area by around 100ha, while murky green Lake Beira has shrunk to about a third of its original size.

Sri Murugan Temple [88 C2] (*Kew Rd*) Built in the late 19th century for South Indian troops stationed in the area, this Murugan (or Sivasubramania Swami) Temple, dedicated to the eponymous deity also known as Kataragama, has a 25m seven-tier central Raja Gopuram embellished with the usual colourful assemblage of Hindu deities. A modern construction, dating to the mid-1990s, the gopuram is flanked by a pair of more modest and sombre clock towers. There are more significant and beautiful Hindu temples in Sri Lanka, but this is a lively and interesting place to visit, especially during the morning and evening puja, which start at around 08.00 and 17.00.

Gangaramaya Temple [88 D4] (*Sri Jinarathana Rd;* ☏ *011 243 5169;* w *gangaramaya.com;* ⊕ *06.00–21.00; entrance US$2*) Established in the late 19th century on reclaimed swampland bordering Lake Beira, Gangaramaya is the most important Buddhist temple in central Colombo, and the focal point of the city's spectacular annual Navam Perahera (February Parade). Architecturally, it's a disjointed and atypical affair, centred on a tall image house whose mustard exterior is propped up by the spread hands (or, in some upside-down instances, the rounded buttocks) of a row of plump dwarves, while the chaotically colourful interior is dominated by seated, standing and sleeping Buddhas painted bright yellow and red, and attended by an assortment of worshippers, including a flock of apsaras that look like they winged across from the nearest church. The sense of clutter extends to the adjoining museum, where a cosmopolitan collection of Buddha statues, some very valuable, fights for display space with a miscellany of unlabelled bric-a-brac: dusty old typewriters, portraits of the British royal family c1950, rocking horses, and the like. Rather more serene is the large tangled Bo Tree towards the back of the complex, and the prayer hall alongside it. Compared with many other more historic temples in Sri Lanka, Gangaramaya attracts a disproportionate volume of tourists, so it is best visited early in the day, before the coaches arrive.

Seema Malaka Temple [88 D4] (*Sir James Pieris Rd;* ⊕ *06.00–21.00; entrance inc in fee for Gangaramaya Temple*) Situated on Lake Beira just around the corner from Gangaramaya, the stilted temple Seema Malaka is perhaps the most beautiful and serene Buddhist shrine in Colombo. Built in the late 1970s, it was designed by Geoffrey Bawa, and provides a rare religious showcase for the uncluttered aesthetic and clean lines typical of his secular work. The temple comprises a trio of stilted platforms connected by wooden walkways, and is used primarily to ordain monks from Gangaramaya and to conduct other rituals that some Buddhist sects insist must be performed at a site that doesn't touch the ground and is surrounded by water on three or more sides. In contrast to Gangaramaya, adornments are few, but the Thai-inspired Buddha statues that line the railing of the central platform are both sublime and – juxtaposed against a backdrop of the lake and city skyscrapers – splendidly photogenic.

CINNAMON GARDENS Cinnamon Gardens (also known as Colombo 07) is the city's most prestigious suburb, a leafy residential area where private colonial-era mansions and villas rub shoulders with – or peer across hedges towards – boutique hotels, art galleries, foreign embassies and lofty edifices of officialdom such as the

Cinnamon Gardens houses most of the city's top art galleries. The following all stand with easy walking distance of the National Museum and of each other. None charges an entrance fee.

NATIONAL ART GALLERY [93 D1] (*Ananda Coomaraswamy Rd;* ⏀ *11.00–20.00*) Situated next to the National Museum, the National Gallery displays a mixed bag of artworks, ranging from a long line of mundane busts of politicians to some more interesting modern works. Could be better, but still worth popping past should you be visiting the museum.

LIONEL WENDT ART CENTRE [93 C2] (*Guildford Cres;* ☎ *011 269 5794;* w *lionelwendt. org;* ⏀ *09.00–19.00 Mon–Fri, 10.00–noon & 14.00–19.00 Sat–Sun*) This 600-seat auditorium (page 98) has two galleries that regularly host powerful art and photographic exhibitions.

SAPUMAL FOUNDATION [93 E1] (*Barnes Pl;* ☎ *011 269 5731;* w *artsrilanka.org/ sapumalfoundation;* ⏀ *10.00–13.00 Wed–Sun*) Set in the former home of the late great Harry Pieris, this is arguably the finest art gallery in Sri Lanka, peculiar opening hours notwithstanding. It traces the development of Sri Lankan art from the 1920s onwards, displaying more than 200 paintings and drawings by Pieris and other members of the '43 group', whose work laid the foundations of contemporary Sri Lankan art, along with more recent works by leading local artists.

SASKIA FERNANDO GALLERY [93 E1] (*Horton Pl;* ☎ *011 742 9010;* w *saskiafernandogallery.com;* ⏀ *10.00–18.00*) Established in 2009, this is now Sri Lanka's largest art gallery, focusing mainly on contemporary local artists, with around 300 different works hanging in the main gallery. Two smaller galleries are used for temporary exhibitions by individual local and international artists.

THEERTHA RED DOT GALLERY [93 G1] (*Off D S Senanayake Rd;* ☎ *011 269 8130;* w *theertha.org*) Dedicated to the thriving 1990s and post-millennial art scene, this gallery prides itself on hosting exhibitions that display the country's most experimental, innovative and sometimes challenging new art.

Town Hall, National Museum and Independence Memorial. The name Cinnamon Gardens dates to 1789, when the city bailiff Cornelis de Cock planted a 94ha tract of land, roughly corresponding to the modern suburb, with the cinnamon trees whose aromatic bark was the island's most important export crop. The gardens were tended carefully under Frederick North, the first British governor of Ceylon, but fell into neglect thereafter, due partly to the administration's focus on the ongoing war with Kandy, and partly to the decline in the value of cinnamon as cultivation spread to other parts of Asia and other crops such as coffee and cacao outgrew it in popularity. By the 1850s, the old cinnamon gardens became the site of a racing track and a popular residential area with the rich and powerful. Few if any cinnamon trees remain here today, but the old name has endured, as has a relatively garden-like feel in and around Viharamahadevi Park.

Town Hall [88 F4] (*F R Senanayake Rd*) Built over 1924–28 to replace the original town hall in Pettah, this most imposing of Colombo's British colonial structures was designed by S J Edwards, who modelled it on the Capitol in Washington DC. Long and narrow, it has a Neoclassical façade incorporating 16 tall columns, a central dome and clock tower that stand more than 50m high, and a large open front lawn that runs southwest to Viharamahadevi Park. The hall doubles as the headquarters of the Colombo Municipal Council and mayoral office.

Viharamahadevi Park [93 C1/D1] (*Ananda Coomaraswamy Rd*) Extending over 20ha between the Town Hall and National Museum, Colombo's largest and most popular green space occupies a tract of land donated to the city by the wealthy industrialist and philanthropist Charles Henry de Soysa in the 1880s. It staged the island's first first-class international cricket match, against a touring English team, in 1927, and was occupied by the British army during World War II. Originally called Victoria Park, it was renamed after independence to honour a more ancient indigenous monarch – Queen Viharamahadevi of 2nd-century BC Ruhuna. Crisscrossed with footpaths, it's a popular haunt of courting couples and promenading families, and provides a precious urban refuge to woodland birds such as rose-ringed parakeet, brown-headed barbet, black-hooded oriole and yellow-billed babbler.

Colombo National Museum [93 C2] (*Sir Marcus Fernando Rd;* ☎ *011 269 4366;* w *museum.gov.lk;* ⊕ *09.00–17.00; entrance US$4, photography US$2*) Sri Lanka's premier museum houses a collection of 100,000 artefacts reflecting various aspects of the island's architecture, history and culture from prehistoric times to the Kandyan era. It was established by Governor Gregory in 1877 with just 800 exhibits, but rapidly expanded to fill up a purpose-built palatial Neoclassical building set in large grounds bounded to the north by Viharamahadevi Park. The museum also houses the most important library on the island, and its green gardens incorporate a rather stuffy natural history museum (entrance included in National Museum ticket), the National Gallery (see box, opposite), and a statue of Queen Victoria erected to commemorate her diamond jubilee in 1897. The agreeable Laksala Museum Gallery Café (page 92) is a pleasant place to break up the sightseeing for a drink or snack, or a dose of retail therapy. The Nelum Pokuna Theatre (page 98) stands right next door.

The museum is split across two floors and contains 16 galleries, several of which were closed for refurbishment at the time of research but should reopen during the lifespan of this edition. The museum is entered through a grand lobby dominated by one of its most celebrated treasures: the 8th-century Toluvila Buddha, a masterfully serene 1.75m-tall crystalline-limestone statue unearthed during excavations at Anuradhapura in 1900. Most of the other ground-floor galleries focus on a specific archaeological subject, for instance cast Hindu and Buddhist bronzes, granite statues, exotic and local ceramic items, and Brahmi, Sinhalese, Portuguese and Dutch rock inscriptions spanning a period of more than 2,000 years. Among the many striking bronzes here are an ingenious lamp from Dedigama that dispenses oil into a bowl via an elephant's penis, and a fantastic 90cm-high Polonnaruwa depiction of a four-armed flowing-haired Shiva performing the tandava dance in a tiruvasi circle. An immense collection of granite statues is dominated by Buddha figures that more or less replicate the type of thing you'll see *in situ* at most of the ancient monasteries of the Cultural Triangle, but it also includes some more unusual carvings of Hindu deities such as the elephant-like Ganesh and buxom Parvati, and an exceptional frieze of dancers and dwarves. Another important ground-floor exhibit is the Kandyan Hall, whose focal point is the throne donated by Governor van Rhee to King Vimaladharmasuriya II c1693 and used by six subsequent Kandyan monarchs. At the time of writing, the first floor has a more limited and mundane selection of exhibits, dealing mainly with rural practices and the colonial and modern eras, but this may change as and when galleries dedicated to paintings, textile and traditional rituals reopen.

Independence Memorial [93 E3] (*Independence Av*) Set in the parklike Independence Square about 1km southeast of the National Museum, this impressive and attractive memorial hall was erected to commemorate the country's formal declaration of independence on 4 February 1948, and it remains the focal point of annual celebrations on the anniversary of that historic event. Perched on a raised granite plinth and guarded by rows of stone lions, the memorial is based on Kandy's 18th-century Magul Madhuwa. However, where the engraved pillars of the original hall were made of wood, the memorial is made entirely of stone, except for the typical Kandyan tiled roof. A statue of D S Senanayake stands at the head.

Independence Square Arcade [93 E3] (*Bauddhaloka Rd*; m *0713 456789*; w *arcadeindependencesquare.com*) The latest and smartest addition to Colombo's growing collection of malls occupies a stately old building immediately south of the Independence Memorial. The two-storey building was constructed over 1879–82 and served as the Jawatta Lunatic Asylum until 1926, when the last of its inmates were relocated to the larger Angoda Mental Hospital 7km to the east. It was then taken over by the colonial administration and for many years housed the Auditor General's offices. In 2012, a joint venture by the Urban Development Authority and Ministry of Defence set about restoring the handsome domed and multiple-arched building to its former glory, and in 2014 it opened as an upmarket shopping mall comprising around 40 boutiques, shops and restaurants.

FURTHER AFIELD
Geoffrey Bawa's House [93 C3] (*33rd Ln, Kollupitiya*; ℡ *011 433 7335*; w *geoffreybawa.com*; guided tours ⊕ *10.00 daily & also at noon, 14.00 & 15.30 Mon–Sat*; entrance *US$7 pp*). Describing itself as 'an essay in architectural bricolage', the Colombo residence of Sri Lanka's most celebrated architect was created over 1958–70, as Bawa gradually bought out a row of four small bungalows on a short cul-de-sac running off Bagatelle. He converted his first acquisition to a small apartment with bedroom, living room and tiny kitchen, his second to a dining room and second living room, and eventually demolished the last to make way for a four-storey tower. For students of architecture, the resultant warren of rooms, outdoor spaces and passages is a delightful and fascinating Bawa-in-miniature, and the interior is also adorned with some excellent modern artworks. Although set departure tours are advertised, it is advisable to call first to make an appointment.

New Parliament Building [map, page 78] (*Parliament Rd, Sri Jayawardenepura Kotte*; ℡ *011 277 7473*; w *parliament.lk*; ⊕ *09.30–15.30 Mon–Fri*) Situated about 10km southeast of Fort District (and the original parliament building) as the crow flies, Sri Lanka's Parliament Building has an attractive location on a 5ha island reclaimed from the historic Lake Diyawanna, an artificial 120ha reservoir constructed to service the 16th-century Sinhalese capital of Kotte. Commissioned by President Jayawardene in 1979, it is one of Geoffrey Bawa's finest works, comprising an asymmetric cluster of stilted terraces and colonnaded pavilions modelled on the traditional architecture of Kandy and the more ancient temples of the Cultural Triangle. The building was inaugurated in 1982, when Sri Jayawardenepura Kotte took over from Colombo as the official administrative capital of Sri Lanka. Advance permission must be obtained to visit parliament (see the above website for the full formidable procedure), but not to view it from across the lake.

Kelaniya Temple [map, page 78] (✆ *011 291 1505*; w *kelaniyatemple.org*) The most historic temple in the immediate vicinity of Colombo stands on the forested north bank of the Kelani River in the suburb of Kelaniya about 7km east of Fort District as the crow flies. Kelaniya is mentioned in the *Ramayana* as the primary site of the Buddha's third visit to Sri Lanka some 2,500 years ago, and also claimed as the birthplace of the illustrious Queen Viharamahadevi of Ruhuna. A temple was built on the site shortly after the Buddha's visit, but it has been destroyed by invaders – most recently the Portuguese – several times since. However, the present-day dagoba, though modestly proportioned, is probably the renovated original, and it reputedly enshrines a gem-studded throne on which the Buddha sat to preach. The extant temple was built in the mid 18th century under the patronage of King Kirti Sri Rajasinha of Kandy, and incorporates several retouched Kandyan paintings from that time. It was greatly expanded in the 1920s with funds provided by the philanthropist Helena Wijewardene, who commissioned Walimuni Solias Mendis, probably the finest temple artist of the era, to produce the exceptional artwork that adorns the interior. Worth a visit at any time, Kelaniya is at its most festive during the Duruthu Perahera (January Pageant), which takes place the day before the January poya.

DEHIWALA–MOUNT LAVINIA

Sri Lanka's second-largest municipality (population 250,000), Dehiwala–Mount Lavinia lies immediately south of Colombo and integrates into the neighbouring city so seamlessly it comes across as a suburban extension of Bambalapitiya and Wellawatta. Home to the National Zoological Gardens, Dehiwala–Mount Lavinia is of greater interest to most travellers for Mount Lavinia beach, a 2km-long swathe of palm-lined white sand that comes close to replicating the holiday mood of more celebrated resorts such as Bentota and Negombo. Indeed, from the perspective of a newly arrived tourist who wants to explore Colombo, or has business to conduct there, Mount Lavinia offers something of a best-of-both-worlds proposition: an attractive and well-equipped beach resort situated barely 30 minutes' drive from the central Fort District, and only 5 minutes on foot from bustling Galle Road. True, Mount Lavinia might lack the glamorous façade of those Sri Lankan resorts that exploded into being to cater to an international tourist boom, but it also possesses an altogether more uncontrived atmosphere: an enclave of genteel Edwardian suburbia that has evolved organically into an unpretentious weekend and evening refuge catering to local city-dwellers seeking respite from the 21st-century rat race. The quiet leafy avenues of Mount Lavinia are lined with old colonial relics, not only the grandiose Mount Lavinia Hotel, but also a more modest 200-year-old Methodist church, the prestigious 19th-century St Thomas's College, and dozens of restored villas dating to the early 20th century. This middle-class suburb also has a reputation for liberality, among other things being host to the annual Rainbow Kite Festival, the country's only gay pride march, held every July. Not least among its merits, Mount Lavinia is well endowed with accommodation and beach restaurants suited to budget-conscious travellers, much of it far better value for money than comparable lodgings within the municipal bounds of Colombo proper.

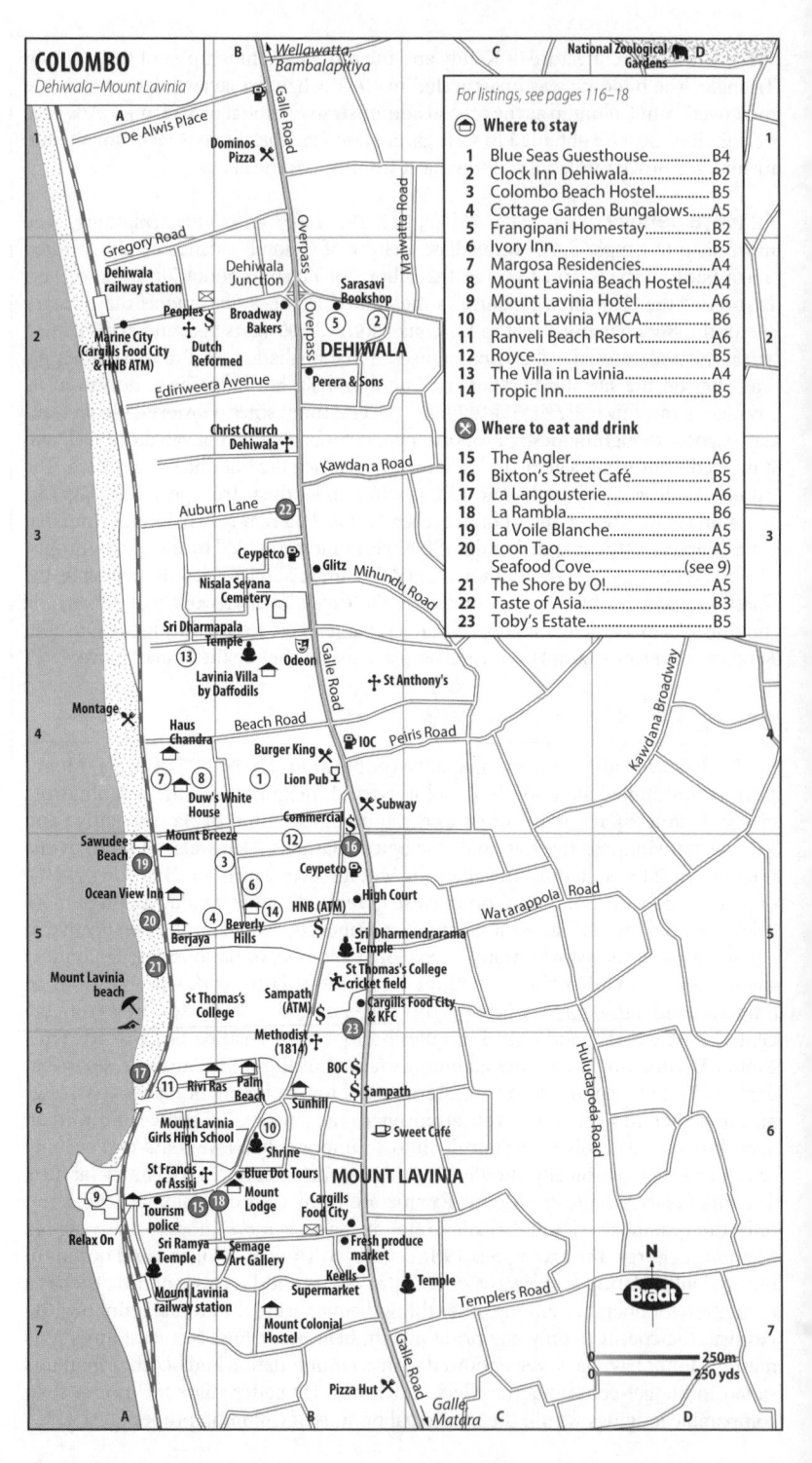

COLOMBO
Dehiwala–Mount Lavinia

Wellawatta,
Bambalapitiya

National Zoological
Gardens

For listings, see pages 116–18

Where to stay

1	Blue Seas Guesthouse................B4
2	Clock Inn Dehiwala.....................B2
3	Colombo Beach Hostel...............B5
4	Cottage Garden Bungalows......A5
5	Frangipani Homestay..................B2
6	Ivory Inn.......................................B5
7	Margosa Residencies..................A4
8	Mount Lavinia Beach Hostel.....A4
9	Mount Lavinia Hotel...................A6
10	Mount Lavinia YMCA...................B6
11	Ranveli Beach Resort..................A6
12	Royce...B5
13	The Villa in Lavinia....................A4
14	Tropic Inn.....................................B5

Where to eat and drink

15	The Angler...................................A6
16	Bixton's Street Café....................B5
17	La Langousterie..........................A6
18	La Rambla.....................................B6
19	La Voile Blanche.........................A5
20	Loon Tao.......................................A5
	Seafood Cove.......................(see 9)
21	The Shore by O!...........................A5
22	Taste of Asia................................B3
23	Toby's Estate................................B5

De Alwis Place

Dominos
Pizza

Galle Road

Malwatta Road

Gregory Road

Dehiwala
railway station

Dehiwala
Junction

Sarasavi
Bookshop

Overpass

Peoples

Marine City
(Cargills Food City
& HNB ATM)

Broadway
Bakers

Dutch
Reformed

DEHIWALA

Ediriweera Avenue

Perera & Sons

Christ Church
Dehiwala

Kawdana Road

Auburn Lane

Ceypetco

Glitz

Mihundu Road

Nisala Sevana
Cemetery

Sri Dharmapala
Temple

Odeon

Lavinia Villa
by Daffodils

Galle Road

St Anthony's

Kawdana Broadway

Montage

Beach Road

Haus
Chandra

Burger King

IOC

Peiris Road

Duw's White
House

Lion Pub

Subway

Mount Breeze

Commercial

Sawudee
Beach

Ceypetco

Ocean View Inn

Berjaya

Beverly
Hills

HNB (ATM)

High Court

Watarappola Road

Sri Dharmendrarama
Temple

Mount Lavinia
beach

St Thomas's
College

Sampath
(ATM)

St Thomas's College
cricket field

Cargills Food City
& KFC

Huludagoda Road

Methodist
(1814)

BOC

Sampath

Rivi Ras

Palm
Beach

Sunhill

Sweet Café

MOUNT LAVINIA

Mount Lavinia
Girls High School

Shrine

St Francis
of Assisi

Blue Dot Tours

Mount
Lodge

Cargills
Food City

Tourism
police

Relax On

Sri Ramya
Temple

Semage
Art Gallery

Fresh produce
market

Keells
Supermarket

Temple

Templers Road

Mount Lavinia
railway station

Mount Colonial
Hostel

Bradt

N

Pizza Hut

Galle,
Matara

Galle Road

0 _____ 250m
0 _____ 250 yds

KING TOM AND LADY LAVINIA

Prior to the 19th century, Mount Lavinia was known as Galkissa, a name that is still in local use and which translates loosely as 'Place of the Boulder'. The rock in question is the low promontory bought in 1805 by Sir Thomas Maitland, a 45-year-old military officer and bachelor freshly appointed as the second British Governor General of Ceylon. Here, King Tom, as locals knew him, built himself a one-storey bungalow that was described by one early British visitor as 'rustic on the outside, but handsomely laid out, and furnished beautifully'. According to legend, Maitland named the house Mount Lavinia, in sly reference to Lovina Aponsuwa, a beguiling dancer of mixed Portuguese-Sinhala descent who regularly sneaked into the governor's residence for a night of clandestine romance via a 300m-long secret tunnel that linked the wine cellar to her father's house. The relationship between King Tom and Lady Lavinia endured until 1811, when Maitland was recalled against his will to serve in the Mediterranean (he would be appointed as Governor of Malta in 1813). The fate of Lady Lavinia is less certain. Some say she was so distressed at her abandonment that she flung herself into the ocean and drowned, others that she retired to a large property bought for her by Maitland in nearby Attidiya, others still that she lived out her days in Galle, supported by her former paramour until his death in Malta in 1824. As for the one-storey bungalow used by the secret lovers, it went on to serve as the primary residence of three further governors, Sir Robert Brownrigg, Sir Edward Paget and Sir Edward Barnes, and was expanded frequently prior to being auctioned in 1842, and converted to a lunatic asylum. In 1877, following the construction of the railway line between Colombo and Galle, which passed right in front of the neglected mansion, Mount Lavinia was bought by private developers for conversion to a luxurious hotel, which it has remained ever since, barring a six-year interval during World War II, when it served as an Allied hospital. And while more prosaic explanations have been put forward for the name Mount Lavinia, for instance that it derives from the Sinhalese Lihiniya Kanda (Seagull Rock), romantics will forever associate it with the beautiful Lady Lavinia, a statue of whom can be seen in the water fountain at the entrance of the grand old hotel that bears her name.

GETTING THERE AND AWAY The two main landmarks in Dehiwala–Mount Lavinia are Dehiwala Junction, which lies on Galle Road about 10km south of the central Fort District, and the Mount Lavinia Hotel, which lies at the end of Hotel Road about 2.5km further southwest. Both can easily be reached by slow train (hop off at Dehiwala station 500m west of Dehiwala Junction or Mount Lavinia station next to the eponymous hotel) or by taking any bus (including numbers 100, 101 and 102) headed south along Galle Road. However, the easiest way to travel between Mount Lavinia and elsewhere in Colombo is by metered tuktuk, which should cost around US$3–4 coming from the city centre and around US$2 from the vicinity of Kollupitiya or Bambalapitiya.

WHERE TO STAY When it comes to a pay-off between cost, quality and character, the landmark Mount Lavinia Hotel stands out as one of the most attractive upmarket offerings in the vicinity of Colombo. Otherwise, accommodation is geared mainly towards budget travellers, who will find that – in addition to easy beach access –

the area generally offers far better value than Colombo proper. The beach at Mount Lavinia is separated from neighbouring suburbia by a railway track that carries traffic throughout the night, so light sleepers might prefer to look for a hotel a couple of hundred metres inland rather than right on the beach.

Upmarket

☀ 🏠 **Mount Lavinia Hotel** [114 A6] (210 AC rooms) Hotel Rd; ☏ 011 271 1711; e info@ mountlaviniahotel.com; w mountlaviniahotel. com. Established as a governor's residence in 1806, this splendidly ostentatious & characterful colonial edifice later gave its name to the surrounding suburb and went on to feature as the hospital in the 1957 movie *The Bridge on the River Kwai*. It is the only hotel situated on the right (ie: seaward) side of the railway track as it runs through Mount Lavinia, & stands on a rocky beachfront prominence draped in fussily attractive gardens whose trimmed hedges & manicured lawns are endearingly subverted by a juxtaposition of windward-leaning tropical palms & temperate conifers. Amenities include several theme restaurants & a deck-style swimming pool with views that embrace the coast. Good value in its range. *US$150/160 standard sgl/dbl B&B*. **$$$$**

🏠 **Margosa Residencies** [114 A4] (6 apts) Samudra Rd; m 0772 228821, 0776 044555; e margosa.residencies@fitsair.com; w fitsair. com/the-margosa-residencies.html. This lovingly restored 1930s villa, set only 50m from the beach, has been split into stylish 1-, 2- & 3-bedroom apartments with terracotta tile floors, wood furniture & traditional crafts, & contemporary artworks on the walls. All apartments incorporate an AC bedroom with 4-poster bed & net, a private balcony, & a spacious open-plan kitchen/lounge with fridge, washing machine, cooking facilities & TV/DVD player. The only drawback with this otherwise excellent & well-priced set-up is the bed-shaking proximity to the railway track – bring earplugs! *US$105 dbl, US$135/147 2-/3-bedroom apt*. **$$$$**

Moderate

☀ 🏠 **Royce Hotel** [114 B5] (14 rooms) Barnes Rd; ☏ 011 271 6653; e enquiry@ roycehotelgroup.com; w roycehotelgroup.com. Situated in a quiet & compact fern-draped garden 200m from the beach, this beautifully restored 1906 villa ranks among the best value in its range anywhere in Colombo, offering boutique-style colonial comfort at rates that only just nudge above the budget category. Characterful, bright & well-maintained rooms all have AC, fan, 4-poster bed with net, large TV, original floor & walls hung with modern art. *From US$50 dbl b&b*. **$$$**

🏠 **The Villa in Lavinia** [114 A4] (10 rooms) Sri Dharmapala Rd; ☏ 011 273 7879; m 0718 814452; e thevillainlavinia@gmail.com. Only 200m from the north end of Mount Lavinia beach, this is another hotel offering near-boutique standard accommodation at budget rates. It's set in a stylishly restored old house whose compact but neat-as-a-pin rooms have slate-tile floors, old monochrome photos on the walls, AC, fan, TV & fridge. There is a plunge pool in the small back courtyard & the restaurant serves a BBQ catch of the day in the US$10–15 range. *US$50 dbl B&B*. **$$$**

Budget

☀ 🏠 **Cottage Garden Bungalows** [114 A5] (5 cottages) College Av; ☏ 011 271 9692; m 0777 947804; e cottageg42@yahoo.com; w cottagegardenbungalows.com. Set in a walled green garden only 100m from the beach, these modern brickface self-catering cottages all come with good natural ventilation, AC, fan, net, private balcony & small but well-equipped kitchen with gas cooker & fridge. Exceptional value. *US$40 dbl, dropping to US$35 out of season*. **$$**

🏠 **Frangipani Homestay** [114 B2] (4 rooms) Hill St; m 0718 357427; w frangipanihomestay. bookings.lk. This cosy & well-priced homestay boasts an indifferent location 100m east of Dehiwala Junction & 2km from Mount Lavinia beach, but it is set close to a bustle of unpretentious local shops & restaurants, & the energetic & obliging owner-manager is a fount of local travel advice. Inconspicuously signposted behind the Sarasavi Bookshop, it spans 2 apartments in a 5-storey building & the individually decorated rooms come with AC, fridge & kitchenette. *From US$38 dbl*. **$$**

🏠 **Clock Inn Dehiwala** [114 B2] (8 rooms, 8 dorms) Hill St; ☏ 011 271 0002; e dehiwala@ clockinn.lk; w clockinn.lk. Situated 200m uphill of Dehiwala Junction, the newest & largest member of the growing Clock Inn chain has the same locational drawbacks as Frangipani, but nevertheless it's a comfortable, friendly & well-equipped hostel. Large spic-&-span rooms with AC & TV have a contemporary beach-house feel, while the 8-bed mixed dorms & 4-bed female-only dorm come with AC, personal reading lights, locker & bedding. *Good value at US$35/40 sgl/dbl, US$9 pp dorm bed, all B&B.* **$–$$**

🏠 **Ranveli Beach Resort** [114 A6] (28 rooms) Off De Saram Rd; ☎ 011 271 7385; **m** 0777 575452; **e** ranvelibeach@ymail.com; **w** ranvelibeachmountlavinia.com. The large & well-maintained swimming pool & close proximity to the beach are the main selling points of this hotel, which also has a good travel desk & pleasant terrace restaurant. Rooms are a bit dark & cluttered, lack a sea view, & seem overdue a facelift, but they all have fan, net, TV & fridge, & some also have AC. *US$35/40 sgl/dbl with fan only, US$45/55 with AC, all rates B&B.* **$$–$$$**

🏠 **Ivory Inn** [114 B5] (13 rooms, 2 dorms) De Saram Rd; ☎ 011 271 5006; **e** ivoryinn@hotmail. com. This long-serving & friendly budget hotel comprises a 3-storey brickface building & attractive open-sided garden b/fast area only 200m from the beach. Spacious rooms have modern furnishings, AC, fan, net & private balcony (best view from the top floor). The 4-bed dorms lack AC but all beds have a private mini-fan, reading light, net & locker. The adjacent nightclub can be disruptive Fri & Sat night. *US$44 dbl B&B, US$10 pp dorm bed.* **$–$$**

🏠 **Tropic Inn** [114 B5] (16 rooms) College Av; ☎ 011 273 8653; **e** info@tropicinn.com; **w** tropicinn.com. Solid but perhaps slightly overpriced 3-storey hotel whose bright little rooms come with AC, fan, TV & fridge. Rooms are variably sized & some have a private balcony, so look before

you check in. *US$46/56 sgl/dbl B&B, dropping to US$30/40 out of season.* **$$**

Shoestring

☀ 🏠 **Blue Seas Guesthouse** [114 B4] (14 rooms) Off De Saram Rd; ☎ 011 271 6298; **m** 0777 530918; **e** info@blueseas.com; **w** blueseasguest. com. This friendly family-owned & -managed guesthouse stands at the end of a quiet cul-de-sac only 350m from the beach. Common areas are decorated with vintage furniture while the brightly decorated & spacious guest rooms all have fan, net, optional AC & twin or dbl bed. Very good value. *US$24 dbl, plus US$7 for AC.* **$–$$**

🏠 **Colombo Beach Hostel** [114 B5] (5 rooms, 4 dorms) De Saram Rd; **m** 0777 871393; **e** desaramroad@gmail.com; **w** colombobeachhostel.com. This well-priced & well-managed hostel with equipped kitchen 200m from the beach has spacious private rooms with tall ceiling, simple modern décor, fan & net (but no AC or hot water), as well as 4- to 8-bed dorms with nets & fans. *US$30 dbl, US$10 pp dorm bed.* **$–$$**

🏠 **Mount Lavinia Beach Hostel** [114 A4] (11 rooms, 3 dorms) Samudra Rd; ☎ 011 573 1306; **m** 0713 251716; **e** laviniahostel@gmail.com; 📘 LaviniaBeachHostel. Although it feels more like a homestay than a backpacker hostel, this friendly owner-managed lodge boasts a pleasant garden setting 150m from the beach & comfortable well-maintained rooms & 5- to 6-bed dorms with décor, fan, net & private balcony. The slightly fuddy-duddy vibe & secure feel will be reassuring to nervous single females. *US$13/28 sgl/dbl, US$9.50 pp dorm bed.* **$–$$**

🏠 **Mount Lavinia YMCA** [114 B6] (4 rooms) Hotel Rd; ☎ 011 271 3786. Simple but dirt-cheap shoestring rooms with en-suite bathroom & fan but no nets or AC. Usefully located close to several shops & just 300m from the beach. *US$11 dbl.* **$**

Colombo DEHIWALA–MOUNT LAVINIA

5

🍴 **WHERE TO EAT AND DRINK** Cooled by a steady sea breeze, a string of agreeable restaurants – most specialising in seafood and pasta – lines the beach at Mount Lavinia. A few good restaurants can also be found inland. These include branches of Subway [114 B4], KFC [114 B5] and Pizza Hut [114 B7] on Galle Road as it skirts a few hundred metres inland of the beach.

Beachfront

🍴 **Seafood Cove** [114 A6] ☎ 011 271 1711; ⏱ 07.00–22.30. This excellent seafood restaurant in the Mount Lavinia Hotel has a wonderful

beachfront location & an unexpectedly informal atmosphere & reasonable prices, whether you go for the straight fish & chips, or grilled tuna, prawns or whole fish. There's 50% off selected cocktails

& local beers during happy hour (*18.00–19.00*).
$$$-$$$$

✗ La Voile Blanche [114 A5] **m** 0717
645459; **w** lavoileblanche.lk; ⏰ 09.00–23.00.
With its white beach-house décor & outdoor
seating spilling out on to the sand, this Mount
Lavinia landmark is a fine place for a sundowner
cocktail or beer, & it also serves homemade pasta
& substantial salads in the US$5–6 range & an
imaginative selection of seafood & meat dishes for
$$$-$$$$.

✗ La Langousterie [114 A6] ☎ 011 271
7786; **w** lalangousterie.com; ⏰ 10.00–22.00.
Established in the 1960s & relaunched in 2016, this
beachfront stalwart dishes up some of the best-
value seafood in the Colombo area, along with
well-priced beers & cocktails. The thatched open-
sided restaurant building is fronted by a hedge that
shields patrons from the wind in rough weather
but creates a sense of separation from the beach in
more clement conditions. **$$$**

✗ The Shore by O! [114 A5] ☎ 011 438 9428;
f TheShoreByO; ⏰ 11.00–14.00 & 17.00–23.00.
Mount Lavinia's most popular beach bar is a two-
storey wooden construction set on a palm-shaded
stretch of sand & scattered with wooden seating &
beanbags. The well-stocked bar serves cocktails &
beer on tap, while eating options range from soups
& snacks to pizzas, burgers & seafood. **$$$**

✗ Loon Tao [114 A5] ☎ 011 272 2723;
w loontao.com; ⏰ 11.00–15.00 & 18.00–23.00.
Although it bills itself as a Chinese seafood
restaurant, this long-serving beachfront eatery
also serves plenty of meat & vegetarian dishes,
while the menu extends to Thailand, Indonesia &
elsewhere in Southeast Asia. There's gentle live
music most nights. **$$$**

Inland

✱ ✗ The Angler [114 A6] Hotel Rd; ☎ 011 271
6626; ⏰ 08.00–22.00. This unpretentious small
mom-&-pop 1st-floor restaurant serves delicious
local curries & seafood, all home-cooked by the
friendly owner-manager couple. There's terrace
seating with a view to the church opposite. No
alcohol, but you can bring your own. **$$$**

✗ La Rambla [114 B6] Hotel Rd; ☎ 011 272
5403; **m** 0763 291483; **w** tastycaterers.lk;
⏰ 11.00–22.30. Set in a renovated colonial villa
opposite a church, the stylish AC interior of this
specialist Thai restaurant provides welcome refuge
from the coastal heat. Antique Thai furniture
& a chef from Thailand boost the authenticity.
No alcohol served, but you can bring your own.
Vegetarian **$$$**, meat & fish **$$$$**

✗ Taste of Asia [114 B3] Galle Rd; ☎ 011 438
9908; ⏰ 07.00–22.00. A branch of the eponymous
Jaffna-style eatery described on page 95. Great
value. **$**

✗ Toby's Estate [114 B5] Galle Rd; ☎ 011 271
6495; **f** TobysEstateCMB; ⏰ 08.30–23.00. Easily
the best café in Mount Lavinia, this Australian
franchise serves organic teas & coffees, an
imaginative selection of blended fruit & vegetable
juices, yummy desserts, and a wide selection
of light meals ranging from salads & soups to
vegetable lasagne & pork schnitzel. **$$$**

✗ Bixton's Street Café [114 B5] Entrances
on Galle & Hotel rds; ☎ 011 406 3200;
w bixtonstreetcafe.com; ⏰ 11.00–23.00. This
contemporary café is a bit lacking in character but
the blasting AC is welcome in the midday heat
& the extensive menu – everything from wraps
& gourmet burgers to Italian & Thai – claims to
be free of MSG & other artificial ingredients. No
alcohol, but good coffee & juices. **$$$**

OTHER PRACTICALITIES All the main **banks** are represented on the stretch of Galle
Street running through Mount Lavinia, including a Commercial Bank [114 B4]
next to the junction with Hotel Road. Standalone HNB and Sampath **ATMs** can be
found on Hotel Road. For self-caterers, a well-stocked **Cargills Food City** [114 B6]
(⏰ *08.00–23.00*), complete with liquor and pharmacy counters, stands on Galle
Street 500m south of the junction with Hotel Road. The junction of Galle and
Station roads hosts an informal **produce market** [114 B7] selling fresh fish, fruit
and vegetables. The closest **bookshop** is Sarasavi [114 B2] on Hill Road about 100m
east of Dehiwala Junction.

WHAT TO DO In addition to the sites listed below, the city of Colombo is easily
explored using Dehiwala–Mount Lavinia as a base. The historic Fort District lies

about 10km north along Galle Road, while the National Museum and associated sites in Cinnamon Gardens can be reached turning right off the Galle Road at Kollupitiya Junction. It is straightforward enough to reach either by buses or train, but far easier to catch a metered tuktuk, which shouldn't set you back more than US$3–4 one way.

Mount Lavinia beach [114 A5] The main attraction of Mount Lavinia is its swimming beach, which runs for about 2km north of the Mount Lavinia Hotel, offering distant views of central Colombo to the north, as well as being perfectly sited to enjoy the sunset. Far less touristy than other developed beaches in Sri Lanka, Mount Lavinia is usually busiest in the evening and over weekends, when local couples and families stroll past, stopping to enjoy a fresh fruit juice or ice cream, while enthusiastic youngsters play beach cricket or volleyball. Despite this, the sheltered beach at Mount Lavinia, with its relatively gentle incline, offers some of the most reliably safe (though not necessarily unpolluted) swimming conditions in Sri Lanka, and it is also usually watched over by lifeguards, though you might want to check this before you take the plunge. Towards dusk, a seaside sprawl of acceptable-to-good restaurants (including those listed on pages 117–18) serves chilled beers, cocktails and other drinks, as well as fresh seafood and other meals at relatively moderate prices that reflect the predominantly local clientele.

National Zoological Gardens [94 D1] (*Anagarika Dharmapala Rd;* \ *011 271 2752;* e *zoosl@slt.lk;* w *nationalzoo.gov.lk;* ⊕ *08.00–18.00; entrance US$17 foreign adults, children half-price*) Founded in 1936, the Colombo or Dehiwala Zoo is seldom patronised by foreigners, not least due to the inordinately hefty entrance fee, but the predominance of exotic (as opposed to indigenous) creatures, rundown state of many of the cages, noisy children's activities and abysmal treatment of elephants (several Asian and one African specimen chained up in an abject row) all count against it. Near-redeeming features are the presence of some caged local wildlife (sloth bear, muntjac, purple-faced langur and the like) and the plentiful birds and 2m-long brown rat snakes (hefty but harmless, unless you're a suitably sized rodent) that flap and slither untethered in the jungle-like grounds. You can easily walk the 1km from Dehiwala Junction, but a metered tuktuk from there or elsewhere in Dehiwala–Mount Lavinia shouldn't cost more than US$1, while one from further afield in Colombo might work out at US$2–3.

Bellanwila-Attidiya Sanctuary [map, page 78] Extending over 3.7km² of marshy terrain about 3km inland of Mount Lavinia beach, the Bellanwila-Attidiya Sanctuary was set aside in 1990 to protect a precious fragment of the once extensive wetlands that used to surround Colombo. It is run through by the Weras River, which forms part of the Bolgoda drainage system, along with parts of the Nedimala Canal and several substantial sheets of open water. Although it has suffered from some encroachment in recent years, it ranks as the top birdwatching site in the immediate vicinity of Colombo, with more than 150 species recorded. A 2–3-hour session might yield up to 40 species when migrants are present, including the relatively unusual cinnamon bittern, black bittern, yellow bittern, glossy ibis, purple swamphen, ruddy-breasted crake, pheasant-tailed jacana, stork-billed kingfisher, blue-tailed bee-eater, crimson-fronted barbet, rusty-rumped warbler and Loten's sunbird. Rather less likely to be seen are secretive resident mammals such as Eurasian otter, fishing cat and various mongooses. Other wildlife includes 39 species of fish, 52 butterflies (including nine endemics) and the often conspicuous water monitor lizard.

The best access point is the Wildlife Department office situated on the south side of Kahawita Road immediately west of where it crosses the Nedimala Canal some 600m east of Attidiya Post Office. Rough foot trails follow either side of the canal as it runs north from the wildlife office, but there are plans to develop more and better footpaths. To get there, either bus the 3km from Dehiwala Junction to Attidiya, then walk the last 600m, or catch a tuktuk, which should cost around US$1–2 from Dehiwala–Mount Lavinia or US$2–4 from further afield in Colombo.

MUTHURAJAWELA WETLAND SANCTUARY

[map, page 74] Situated about halfway between Colombo and Negombo, the Muthurajawela Wetland comprises a roughly 7km² peat bog at the southern end of the Negombo Lagoon. Their proximity to Sri Lanka's largest two towns means the wetlands are under constant threat of development, but while some tracts were lost during the construction of the new Airport Expressway, the remainder was set aside as a sanctuary in 1996. Dominated by reeds and mangroves, the marsh is perhaps the most important refuge for waterbirds close to Colombo, with 102 species recorded. These include purple heron, intermediate egret, black bittern, yellow bittern, lesser whistling duck and painted stork. Favourites with visitors are the dazzling kingfishers, with common, white-throated, stork-billed and pied kingfishers likely to be seen, and the scarce migrant black-capped kingfisher also recorded. Other common birds in the surrounding scrub include ring-necked parakeet, common hawk cuckoo, pied cuckoo, greater coucal, shikra and Brahminy kite.

The most conspicuous of 34 recorded mammal species is toque macaque, which is likely to be seen on every boat ride, but the endemic painted bat and threatened otter are also present, along with slender loris, rusty-spotted cat, fishing cat, common jackal and Sri Lanka spotted chevrotain. Other wildlife includes 73 fish species (51 endemic), 15 amphibians (two endemic) and 37 reptiles (five endemic). The endangered estuarine crocodile may, with luck, be seen. A study has shown the presence of about six of them, 3–5m in length, as well as 60 smaller individuals. The snake *Gerarda prevostiana*, though widespread on the Asian mainland, was only known in Sri Lanka from a single specimen collected about a hundred years ago from the Kelani River, until a second was recently collected in the northern part of Muthurajawela, close to the Negombo Lagoon. Occasionally, tidal fluctuations result in high salinity and then jellyfish may be seen in the rivulets that crisscross the marsh.

GETTING THERE AND AWAY The Muthurajawela Visitor Centre in Pamunugama stands on the east bank of the Hamilton Canal, 500m from the main coastal road between Colombo and Negombo. Pamunugama lies about 20km north of central Colombo and a similar distance south of Negombo, and can be reached from either by taking a bus along the coastal road. Alternatively, catch a train or bus along the old Negombo Road to Ja-Ela railway station, then charter a tuktuk for the last 5km. Most hotels in Colombo or Negombo can arrange an all-inclusive round trip to Muthurajawela, travelling there by taxi or tuktuk, for around US$15–25 per person.

WHAT TO SEE AND DO The Muthurajawela Visitor Centre (\ *011 083 0150;* m *0777 043447;* e *info@muthurajawelavisitorcentre.org;* w *muthurajawelavisitorcentre. org;* ⊕ *07.00–16.00*) operates 2-hour boat rides through the canals and rivulets for around US$8 per person. Boats follow the Hamilton Canal to the southern end of the Negombo Lagoon, then proceed to the Matiwala Bokka (literally 'Clay Pit Ditch'), an open area of 1.5m-deep water created by the excavation of clay. The boat

MEDICINAL PLANTS OF MUTHURAJAWELA

Of the 129 plant species recorded in Muthurajawela, 40 are known to have medicinal properties. The banks are lined with a reed locally known as *val bata* (*Phragmites carca*). Also found is the wetland plant *Achrosticum aureum*, whose tender leaves are rich in vitamin E and cooked as a vegetable. As the boat glides through the rivulets, you may see a mangrove tree with green, apple-like fruits. This is *Cerbera manghas*, locally known as *diya kadura*. The fruits are poisonous. Many plants are harvested by the local folk. One is the *wetakeiya*, a kind of pandanus with thorny leaves, used to make mats.

then goes on to the Dandugam River, which is 15m deep in places, before returning back along the Hamilton Canal. Boat trips are accompanied by knowledgeable trained guides, most with at least an A-level in biology, to talk visitors through the flora, fauna and history of the marshes. Birdwatching is usually most productive in the early morning or late afternoon, which are anyway the nicest times to be out on the water in terms of heat and exposure. The centre also has a small souvenir shop selling publications on the marsh's fauna and flora, while a video presentation is available in the auditorium.

UPDATES WEBSITE

Go to **w** bradtupdates.com/srilanka for the latest on-the-ground travel news, trip reports and factual updates. Keep up to date with the latest posts by following Philip on Twitter (**y** *@philipbriggs*) and via Facebook (**f** *fb.me/ pb.travel.updates*). And, if you have any comments, queries, grumbles, insights, news or other feedback, you're invited to post them directly on the website, or to email them to Philip (**e** *philip.briggs@bradtguides.com*) for inclusion.

CAMLO LANKA TOURS
WE MAKE YOUR DREAMS COME TRUE

Camlo Lanka Tours is one of Sri Lanka's leading tour management companies. We specialise in personalised tour arrangements, guaranteeing the highest level of experience and satisfaction.

Camlo Lanka is your reliable partner for inbound travels to Sri Lanka and the Maldives. With hand-picked luxury and budget hotels, we create unique and affordable tour packages that cater to travellers' individual requirements. As a full-service company, multi-lingual representatives will meet you at the airport and look after all your needs during your stay - a professional and personal approach providing excellent service that reflects the warmth and hospitality of the beautiful island of Sri Lanka.

CAMLO LANKA TOURS (PVT) LTD
No 52.Level 02 Galle Road, Colombo 03, Sri Lanka
Email: bookings@camlolanka.com / info@camlolanka.com
Mobile: +94 773666999/Landline+94 115752485
Web: www.camlolanka.com

6

The Coast from Negombo to Kalpitiya

The closest stretch of Indian Ocean frontage to Bandaranaike International Airport runs for 140km north of the Negombo Lagoon to the tip of the Kalpitiya Peninsula on the west bank of the Puttalam Lagoon. It is a region of strong contrasts. Negombo, on the north bank of the eponymous lagoon, is a large and busy seaside town that doubles as one of the country's most popular beach resorts thanks primarily to its proximity to the airport. Only 10km further north, well-wooded Waikkal is studded with a few undersubscribed and low-key resort hotels that offer something of a wilderness feel only 30 minutes drive from the airport. Further north still, Kalpitiya is a tranquil emergent ecotourism destination famed for its seasonal kitesurfing but that also offers something to engage wildlife enthusiasts throughout the year.

NEGOMBO

The historic ocean port of Negombo stands on the west coast immediately north of the eponymous lagoon mouth, only 40km north of Colombo and 8km by road from Bandaranaike International Airport. It is the second-largest town in Sri Lanka after Greater Colombo, with a population of more than 130,000, supplemented by another 80,000 living in the airport suburb of Katunayake. Nicknamed 'Little Rome', it is also the most Christian-dominated Sri Lankan settlement of comparable size, with almost two-thirds of its population being Roman Catholic, as evidenced by the presence of several historic churches dating to colonial times. And while the town centre is a rather workaday place with little to attract tourists, not so the beach that stretches for several kilometres to its north and south, which now ranks among the country's best-developed tourist sites, serviced by more than 100 resorts, hotels and guesthouses.

Less than 15 minutes' drive from Sri Lanka's main international airport, Negombo has largely supplanted the busier and more intimidating capital as a one-night-stand venue catering to freshly arrived tourists or those leaving on early flights. Whether it can be plugged as a beach destination in its own right is another matter. Though superficially pretty, especially at sunset, Negombo beach tends to be a lot dirtier than southern counterparts such as Bentota and Hikkaduwa, while the sea is typically less blue and the vegetation not quite so lush. Furthermore, the steep incline and rough waves mean that swimming is generally unsafe, especially but by no means exclusively during the monsoon months (May–November). In Negombo's favour, the town centre, with its busy markets, historic churches and plethora of modern shops, has a harder-working and less resort-like atmosphere than Bentota and Hikkaduwa. It also has a lively culinary scene and nightlife, with scores of restaurants and bars lining the main beach road. Other attractions around Negombo include the birdlife associated with the Muthurajawela Wetlands, and the partially restored Dutch Canal that runs from the town centre all the way north to Puttalam.

HISTORY Back in the 2nd century BC, according to legend, Queen Viharamahadevi, while pregnant with the child that would grow up to become King Dutugamunu of Anuradhapura, developed an insatiable craving for honey. Her husband King Kavan Tissa dispatched a giant called Welusumana in search of a beehive large enough to satisfy her longing, and he located one on a beached canoe at a village that became known by the Sinhala name Migamuva (literally 'Place of Bees'). In the 8th century AD, Migamuva became the site of an Arab trading post dealing mainly in the export of the cinnamon that grew wild there more profusely than anywhere else in the world. By this time, the area had also been settled by the predominantly Tamil Karava people, who traditionally make their living as fisherman using the catamaran-like twin canoes that can still be seen plying the waters of the Negombo Lagoon today.

In the early 16th century, Migamuva was captured by the Portuguese, who took over the lucrative cinnamon trade, built a small wooden fort at the lagoon mouth, and corrupted the original Sinhalese name to Negombo. The town and its fort were captured by the Dutch in February 1640, retaken by the Portuguese in December the same year, then recaptured by the Dutch in January 1644. The Portuguese tenure, though it lasted little more than a century, had an oddly enduring evangelical impact: almost four centuries later, today some 65% of Negombo's residents are Catholic, whereas fewer than 4% subscribe to the Protestant beliefs of the Portuguese's Dutch successors, and only 15% retain the Islamic faith introduced by Medieval Arabs. Negombo developed into a much larger town under the Dutch, who built a stronger fort on the site originally used by the Portuguese, and – more important in economic terms – constructed a 90km canal north to Puttalam Lagoon, allowing for easy boat transportation of cinnamon and other goods along the coastal belt.

Although cinnamon remained the main product exported from Negombo throughout the Dutch occupation, export volumes declined rapidly during the last two decades of the 18th century, partly due to the deliberate obstruction of the trade by King Vikrama Rajasinha of Kandy, and despite failed attempts to establish plantations in the immediate vicinity. In 1796, Fort Negombo was captured by the British, who proceeded to improve transportation links to Negombo by constructing the 15km Hamilton Canal between Colombo and the south bank of the Negombo Lagoon over 1802–04. Despite this, further declines in cinnamon exports meant that Negombo had become somewhat sidelined by 1815, when Kandy fell to the British. Despite this, their proximity to Colombo meant that the rich fishing grounds of the Negombo Lagoon, and the small town on its northern shore, lay at the heart of the island's seafood trade throughout the colonial era. The economic modern rise of Negombo started in 1907, when the arrival of the railway line connecting Colombo to Puttalam prompted the creation of several coconut and other plantations in the vicinity. During World War II, the suburb of Katunayake became the site of an RAF airfield that was expanded to become the country's main international airport over 1964–67.

GETTING THERE AND AWAY Most of Negombo's beach hotels actually lie outside the centre, alongside or close to the 4km road that runs parallel to the beach north of town. This road is known as Lewis Place for the first 2km or so of its length, then it becomes Porutota Road. If you arrive by rail or bus, the stations lie right in the town centre so, unless you fancy a longish walk, grab one of the tuktuks waiting outside. Expect to pay US$1–2, depending on how far out of town your hotel is.

By air Negombo being the closest town to Bandaranaike International Airport, quite a number of people effectively leave or arrive here by air. Official taxi rates

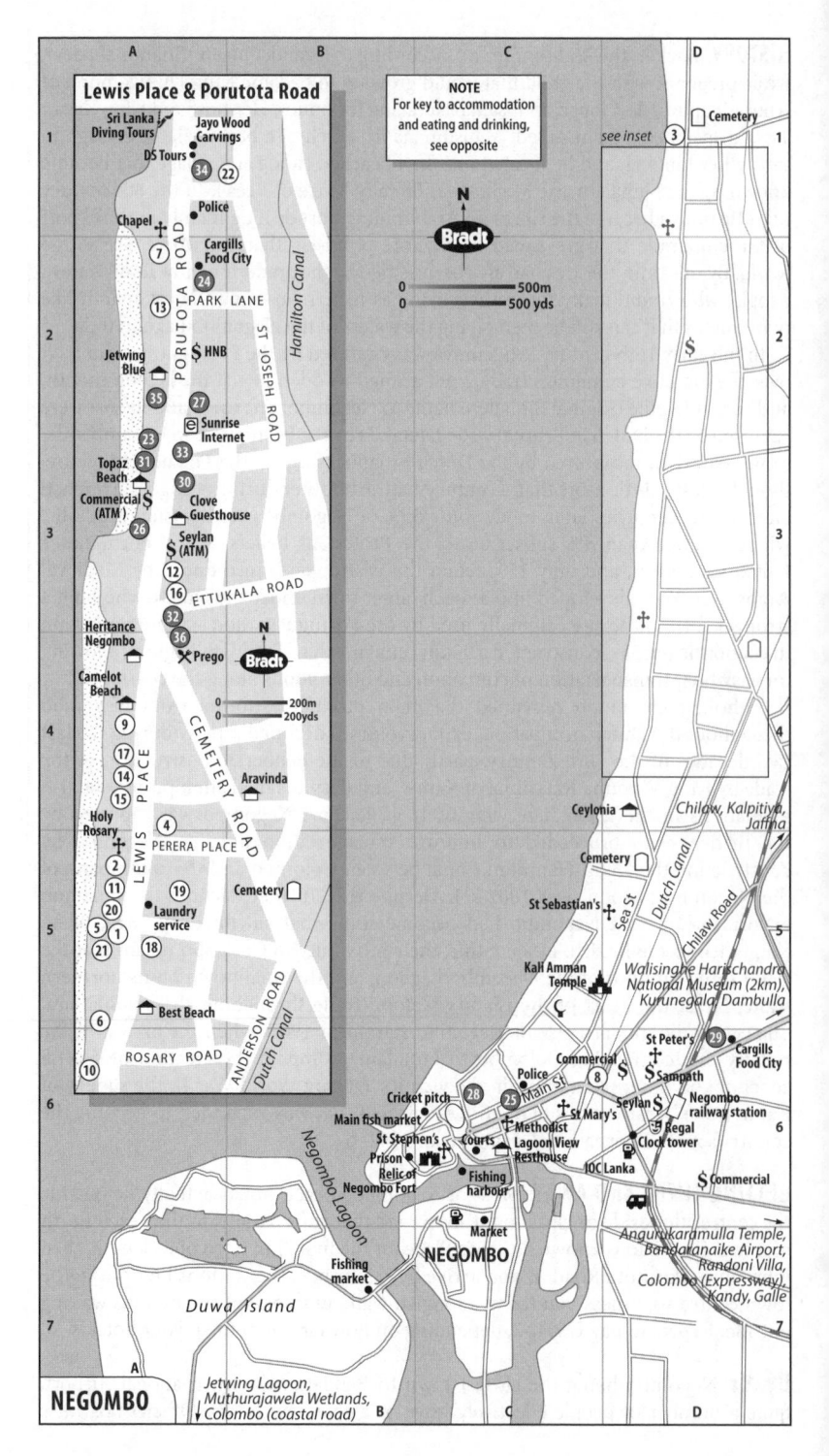

NOTE
For key to accommodation
and eating and drinking,
see opposite

Lewis Place & Porutota Road

NEGOMBO

Sri Lanka Diving Tours
Jayo Wood Carvings
DS Tours
Chapel
Police
Cargills Food City
PARK LANE
PORUTOTA ROAD
ST JOSEPH ROAD
Hamilton Canal
HNB
Jetwing Blue
Sunrise Internet
Topaz Beach
Commercial (ATM)
Clove Guesthouse
Seylan (ATM)
ETTUKALA ROAD
Heritance Negombo
Prego
Camelot Beach
CEMETERY ROAD
LEWIS PLACE
Aravinda
Holy Rosary
PERERA PLACE
Cemetery
Laundry service
Best Beach
ROSARY ROAD
ANDERSON ROAD
Dutch Canal

Cemetery
see inset

Ceylonia
Chilaw, Kalpitiya, Jaffna
Cemetery
Dutch Canal
St Sebastian's
Sea St
Chilaw Road
Kali Amman Temple
Walisinghe Harischandra National Museum (2km), Kurunegala, Dambulla
St Peter's
Commercial
Sampath
Cargills Food City
Cricket pitch
Main St
Police
Seylan
Negombo railway station
Main fish market
Methodist
St Mary's
Regal
St Stephen's
Courts
Lagoon View Resthouse
Clock tower
Prison
Relic of Negombo Fort
Fishing harbour
IOC Lanka
Commercial
Negombo Lagoon
Market
NEGOMBO
Angurukaramulla Temple, Bandaranaike Airport, Randoni Villa, Colombo (Expressway), Kandy, Galle
Duwa Island
Fishing market

Jetwing Lagoon,
Muthurajawela Wetlands,
Colombo (coastal road)

Bradt

0   500m
0   500 yds

0   200m
0   200yds

NEGOMBO
For listings, see pages 128–32

🛏 Where to stay

⊗ Where to eat and drink

between the airport and Negombo work out at around US$8/9 without/with air conditioning. Private operators often charge more to flustered new arrivals, but equally taxis operating out of Negombo might well charge less. Expect to pay around US$5 for a tuktuk.

By rail Around 15 trains daily connect Colombo Fort to Negombo, most continuing on north to Chilaw and many on to Puttalam. Depending on where it stops, the journey can take up to 90 minutes. The centrally located railway station [126 D6] was rebuilt in 1978; outside is a huge silver-painted statue of a buxom fishwife, with a fish rampant in her hand.

By road Negombo lies about 40km north of Colombo by road. If you are driving or taking a taxi, there are three options: the old Negombo Road running inland of the lagoon, the much faster Expressway also inland of the lagoon, and the less-used Pamunugama Road running between the lagoon and the ocean (via Jetwing Lagoon Hotel). Allow at least an hour on the Expressway, depending greatly on congestion as you exit Colombo, and at least 2 hours on either of the other routes. The main bus station [126 D6] is on St Joseph's Road, the main thoroughfare leading out to the Colombo and airport roads. Buses run along all three routes to Colombo throughout the day, but it is well worth paying the slight extra for one using the Expressway. There are also regular buses running north to Chilaw and Puttalam (for Kalpitiya, Mannar and Wilpattu National Park), northeast to Kurunegala (for Dambulla and Anuradhapura), and east to Kandy. For destinations further south you must change buses either at Colombo or Kandy.

By boat Once the current restoration project on the Hamilton Canal is complete, it should be possible to take a boat all the way from Colombo to Negombo along the canal and the Negombo Lagoon.

WHERE TO STAY Negombo offers the choice of more than a hundred lodgings, ranging from mass-market hotels and boutique guesthouses to small guesthouses and homestays. These places cater mostly to a transit clientele of freshly arrived or about-to-depart air passengers who choose to stay in Negombo over Colombo, thanks to the former's beachfront location, relatively unbuilt-up resort-like feel, and proximity to the airport. With a very few exceptions, Negombo's myriad

6

accommodation options all lie alongside or within a stone's throw of Lewis Place, the main beachside strip running north out of the town centre, or its more northerly extension Porutota Road. Of the places listed below, the only exceptions are Hamilton House, set in the heart of the old town centre, and the lovely Jetwing Lagoon 5km south of town.

Upmarket

Jetwing Lagoon [126 A7] (55 rooms) Pamunugama Rd; 031 222 7272; e resv. lagoon@jetwinghotels.com; w jetwinghotels. com. Sandwiched idyllically between the lagoon & open sea 5km south of Negombo, this top-notch spa resort was the first resort hotel built specifically for tourists in Sri Lanka, & also one of Geoffrey Bawa's earliest works. Reopened in 2012 following extensive renovations, the spacious low-rise design reflects Bawa's love of simple lines, most evidently in the view from reception of Sri Lanka's longest swimming pool extending into a U-shaped plaza. Management places a strong emphasis on eco-friendly water, waste & energy management, without compromising on comfort. Spacious AC rooms & suites have a contemporary feel & all the amenities you'd expect, & the restaurant is excellent. Activities include lagoon boat trips, kayaks for rent, waterskiing, tours along the Negombo lagoon & visits to Muthurajawela Wetlands Sanctuary. *From US$260/280 sgl/dbl B&B, dropping to under US$100 out of season, when it represents fantastic value.* $$$$$

Jetwing Beach Hotel [126 A2] (78 rooms) Porutota Rd; 031 227 3500; e resv.beach@ jetwinghotels.com; w jetwinghotels.com. A stylish option for a night before departure or a night on arrival, this grand beachfront hotel in Ethukala 4km north of the town centre has huge public areas & bedrooms & a feel halfway between a package hotel & a boutique one. The AC rooms have modern facilities & a view of the pool, beach & ocean. *From US$220/240 sgl/dbl B&B, dropping by around 50% out of season, when it represents very good value.* $$$$$

Goldi Sands Beach Hotel [126 A2] (71 rooms) Porutota Rd; 031 227 9021; e goldi@ eureka.lk; w goldisands.com. Set on a golden-sanded beach fringed by loungers shaded by palms & a swimming pool, this unabashed package hotel has spacious modern rooms with a sea or beach view, AC, fan, cable TV & a crisp contemporary feel. *US$150/160 sgl/dbl B&B, dropping by up to 40% out of season.* $$$$

Pledge 3 Lodge [126 A3] (14 rooms) Kattuwa Rd, off Porutota Rd; 031 222 4005; m 0766 908687; e reservation@hotelpledge3. com; w hotelpledge3.com. Far from being your average beach resort, this funky urban-feeling boutique hotel has boldly colour-themed rooms with pale wood laminate floors, queen-size beds, modernist furniture, AC, fan, cable TV & tea-/ coffee-making facilities. Only 5mins' walk from the beach, the high-roofed open-air restaurant leads out to a small bamboo-dominated garden with a swimming pool set on a wooden deck. *Online rates are all over the park, but walk-ins pay US$150/165 sgl/dbl B&B, with low-season discounts.* $$$$

Moderate

Beach All-Suite Hotel [126 A5] (16 suites) Lewis Pl; m 0772 667667; e reservations@ thebeachhotel.com; w thebeachhotel.com. Boasting a superb beachfront location next to the Holy Rosary Church, this new 4-storey offers accommodation in modern 1- & 2-bedroom suites with direct sea view, well-equipped kitchen, washing machine, spacious dining & sitting area, private balcony & large bedrooms. Amenities include a gym, rooftop restaurant & swimming pool. *From US$115 dbl, with significant seasonal discounts.* $$$$

Jetwing Ayurveda Pavilions [126 A3] (36 rooms) Porutota Rd; 031 227 6719; e resv.ayurveda@jetwinghotels.com; w jetwingayurvedapavilions.com. Aimed mainly at those seeking the excellent multiple-day Ayurvedic spa treatments, this lovely & very well-priced spa hotel is also open to normal holidaymakers. It lacks beach frontage but the neat gardens are well wooded & have a swimming pool. The stylish rooms range from simple doubles with AC & fan to large private villas. A good restaurant is attached. *From US$72/96 B&B, exc spa treatments, with solid low-season discounts.* $$$

Randoni Villa [126 D6] (3 rooms) Off Kotugoda Rd; m 0716 829669; e randonivilla66@ gmail.com; w authenticceylon.com. Situated 2km east of the Negombo Lagoon & 7km south of the airport, this pleasant owner-managed lodge stands in small, isolated & well-wooded riverside grounds with a swimming pool & plenty of birdlife. Spacious & brightly decorated rooms have AC, fitted nets, TV & writing desk, & excellent local-style meals can be prepared on request. The antithesis of a beach resort, this is a convenient & tranquil place to start or end a Sri Lanka trip. *US$95 dbl B&B, with 30% low-season discounts.* **$$$**

🏠 **Hotel J** [126 A4] (40 rooms) Lewis Pl; 📞 031 223 2999; e reservations@hotelj.lk; w hotelj.lk. This budget-friendly subsidiary of the upmarket Jetwing chain has a contemporary urban feel with décor dominated by bright colours & pop-art quirkiness. The AC rooms are well-equipped, the ground-floor restaurant has an imaginative menu & the beachfront location is enhanced with a small garden & swimming pool. Good value. *US$75/80 sgl/dbl B&B, with attractively hefty low-season discounts.* **$$$**

🏠 **Paradise Beach Hotel** [126 A4] (60 rooms) Lewis Pl; 📞 031 223 8154; e paradisebeach@ sltnet.lk; w paradisebeachsrilanka.com. This well-managed, well-priced & unpretentious 4-storey resort hotel has an alluring 3-part swimming pool, great beachfront location & comfortable AC rooms with balcony & sea view. *US$100 dbl B&B, dropping to US$80 out of season.* **$$$$**

🏠 **Rani Beach Resort** [126 A4] (34 rooms) Lewis Pl; 📞 031 222 3101; e info@ ranibeachresorts.com; w ranibeachresorts.com. This smart, sensibly priced & relatively intimate resort is centred on neat lawns & a swimming pool leading right down to the beach. Spacious & tastefully decorated rooms come with AC, TV & private sea-facing balcony. *US$93/102 sgl/dbl B&B.* **$$$$**

🏠 **Villa Araliya** [126 B1] (14 rooms) 150m east of Porutota Rd; 📞 031 227 7650; m 0712 728504; e villaaraliya@sltnet.lk; w villaaraliya-negombo.com. Though it lacks beach frontage, this popular suburban-feeling brickface guesthouse stands in small green gardens with a swimming pool & restaurant. The modern AC rooms, though slightly cramped, come with 4-poster king-size bed with fitted net, but no TV. Reasonably priced. *US$80/85 sgl/dbl B&B.* **$$$**

Budget

☀ 🏠 **The Icebear Guesthouse** [126 A6] (9 rooms) Lewis Pl; m 0714 237755; e icebearhotel@yahoo.com; w icebearhotel. com. This long-serving Swiss-owned boutique guesthouse is probably Negombo's most characterful lodging, inhabiting a busy tropical beachfront garden, shaded by palms hung with creepers, about 1km north of the town centre. The highly regarded seafood restaurant (*mains US$9–12*) has something of a colonial feel with its wide balconies, while rooms range from compact no-frills singles with ¾ beds to smart & funky beachfront units with 4-poster beds & private balcony. *From €23/46 sgl/dbl B&B.* **$$$**

☀ 🏠 **The Beach Lodge** [126 D1] (10 rooms) Porutota Rd; 📞 031 227 3363; m 0777 724067; e present@sltnet.lk; w thebeachlodgenegombosl. com. This laid-back & friendly little lodge has a terrace restaurant with rustic wooden furniture that spills out on to the sandy palm-shaded beach & small but smart rooms with AC, fan & TV. *US$41/48 dbl B&B without/with sea view.* **$$**

☀ 🏠 **Dephani Guesthouse** [126 A5] (12 rooms) Lewis Pl; 📞 031 223 4349. Set in a pretty & well-tended palm-shaded garden with a gate opening right out on to the beach, this characterful 2-storey building has terracotta tiled floors, wood shutters & awnings, & a breezy ground-floor terrace restaurant serving tasty Sri Lankan meals, with plenty of vegetarian selections, in the US$4–5 range. All rooms have a king-size bed with fitted net, & rooms 12 & 14 have balconies with a sea view. *US$26/35 dbl with fan/AC; prices drop slightly in the low season.* **$$**

🏠 **Silver Sands Hotel** [126 A5] (20 rooms) Lewis Pl; 📞 031 222 2880; e silversands@sltnet. lk; w silversandsnegombo.com. This agreeably quirky beachfront hotel is set in a colonial-style building with wide arched balconies set around a courtyard leading through a palm-shaded garden down to the sea. Cheerful no-frills rooms have pale blue floor tiles, net, fan & private balcony. A breezy rooftop restaurant serves Sri Lankan, Western & Chinese food. *From US$17–26 dbl with fan, US$35 dbl with AC, with small low-season discounts, b/fast US$3.75 pp extra.* **$**

🏠 **Blue Elephant Guesthouse** [126 A4] (7 rooms) Lewis Pl; 📞 031 222 4744; m 0773 978168; e darshana@blueelephantguest.com; w blueelephantguest.com. This stylish gem of a guesthouse has bright & cheerful high-ceilinged rooms, decorated with colourful batiks & local

6

fabrics, & equipped with AC & cable TV. Good value. *US$33/38 sgl/dbl.* **$$**

🏠 **Angel Inn Guesthouse** [126 A5] (12 rooms) Lewis Pl; ✆ 031 223 6187; m 0777 647585; e angelinn-negombo@hotmail.com; w angelinnlk.com. Owned & managed by the well-travelled family that lives on the ground floor, this above-par budget lodge has large, clean tiled AC rooms with a king-size bed & fitted net. There's plenty of outdoor seating on the courtyard balcony to encourage socialising with other guests. *From US$30 dbl B&B.* **$$**

🏠 **Star Beach Hotel** [126 A5] (14 rooms) Lewis Pl; ✆ 031 222 2606; m 0714 172067; e starbeachhotelnegombo@gmail.com; w starbeachhotelnegombo.com. This pleasant budget hotel has a seafront restaurant opening out to a shady, well-maintained garden separated from the beach by a low picket fence. Rooms are on the small side but brightly decorated in a modern style & come with AC, cable TV, fan & tea-/coffee-making facilities. *From US$26 ground-floor dbl to US$45 1st-floor dbl with sea view, with rates dropping by 20% out of season.* **$$**

🏠 **Dion's Guesthouse** [126 A5] (5 rooms) Lewis Pl; ✆ 031 223 7373; e info@ dionsguesthouse.com; w dionsguesthouse.com. Situated in a small garden 100m from the beach, this service-oriented owner-managed guesthouse has simple but clean & very well-maintained rooms with AC, fan, net & large cable TV. *US$35 dbl; rates drop 20% out of season & long stays are negotiable.* **$$**

🏠 **Hamilton House** [126 C6] (10 rooms, 3 dorms) Asarappa Ln; ✆ 031 222 7703; m 0777 888484; e aldnegombo@sltnet. lk; w hamiltonhouse.bookings.lk. The only accommodation of note in central Negombo, this characterful owner-managed colonial-style property stands on the west bank of the Dutch Canal about 600m from the railway or bus station. Spacious & bright rooms all have AC & darkwood furniture, while there's a choice of male-only, female-only or mixed dorm, with all beds being allocated a private locker. It's a pleasant enough budget set-up & convenient if you are just looking for somewhere central to crash, but feels a touch overpriced. *US$39/49 sgl/dbl B&B, US$15/25 pp bed in dorm with fan/AC, all rates inc b/fast; discounts of up to 30% available off season.* **$–$$**

Shoestring

🏠 **Marshall Guesthouse** [126 A4] (9 rooms) Lewis Pl; ✆ 031 223 11555; m 0714 268303; e marshal_1958@yahoo.com; w negombo. wordpress.com. Only 20m from the beach, this unpretentious little guesthouse has a friendly owner-manager who lives on site & has years of experience in tourism. Clean, spacious rooms all have nets & fan, & some come with AC. A characterful ground-floor restaurant serves home-cooked rice-&-curry & other local dishes in the US$2–3 range. *US$23/33 dbl B&B with fan/AC.* **$**

🏠 **Seetha's Hostel** [126 A5] (6 rooms) Peter Mendis Rd; m 0771 899017; e info@ seethashostelnegombo.com; w seethashostel. com. The closest thing in Negombo to a conventional backpacker hostel, this friendly little place, set on a side road 5mins' walk from the beach, has a few private rooms & 4-bed dorms, all with net & fan, & some with AC. The owner isn't always around, but she can prepare great local food when she is. *US$5 pp dorm bed, US$17/24 dbl with fan/AC.* **$**

🏠 **Jeero Guesthouse** [126 A5] (4 rooms) Lewis Pl; ✆ 031 223 4210; m 0776 161619. Occupying the upper floor of a family home, this friendly & well-priced guesthouse has clean & spacious rooms with twin bed, fan, net & private balcony (with a sea view at the rear of the house). There's also a breezy rooftop pavilion. *US$15 dbl, US$24 with AC.* **$**

🏠 **Sea Joy Guesthouse** [126 A5] (8 rooms) Lewis Pl; ✆ 031 222 1659. This well-established & friendly owner-managed eatery also has a few inexpensive en-suite rooms at the back, with prices depending on whether they have hot water & fan or AC. *US$10–20 dbl.* **$**

✗ **WHERE TO EAT AND DRINK** The main hotel strip running for 4km along Lewis Place and Porutota Road is lined with bars and restaurants that throb with action at night. During the day, though, places tend to be quieter as guests (and staff) recover from the night before. Most of Negombo's hotels have restaurants attached, with the Icebear Guesthouse and Hotel J being well-established upper range options, while the Marshall Guesthouse is recommended for inexpensive local food.

Eating-out options in the town centre are rather more limited but do include the superb Icebear Century Café and super-affordable Red Chilli.

Expensive

❋ ✖ **Lords Restaurant** [126 A2] Porutota Rd; m 0772 853190; e martin@lordsrestaurant. net; w lordsrestaurant.net; ⊕ 15.30–23.30. At once Negombo's grungiest & most upmarket offering, incongruously named after the famous English cricket ground, Lords has an industrial look enhanced by a black floor, twisted wrought-iron sculptures & other works by contemporary Sri Lankan artists. Renowned for its Thai & other Asian platters, this perennial favourite is also strong on seafood, steak & burgers. An extensive cocktail menu & wine list is supplemented by the usual local beers. Most mains **$$$**, seafood **$$$$**

✖ **Bacco Wine Bar & Bistro** [126 A3] Porutota Rd; ✆031 227 6533; m 0766 147136; e prego. bacco@yahoo.com; w pregosuites.com/bacco-wine-bar-bistro. Excellent Mediterranean-style restaurant specialising in southern Italian cuisine, with an open kitchen & the choice of dining in the stylish interior or a small outdoor courtyard offering a glimpse of the beach & occasional puff of sea breeze. There's an extensive dessert menu & Italian wine list. Thin-crust pizzas & pasta dishes **$$$**, grilled seafood & meat **$$$$**. The nearby Prego Restaurant, under the same management & with an almost identical menu, is equally good.

✖ **Sunny's Restaurant** [126 A1] Porutota Rd; m 0776 544095; ⊕ 14.00–23.00. Unpretentious licensed family-run restaurant renowned for its pricey but generous seafood platter & grilled jumbo prawns (**$$$$**) & tasty rice-&-curry dishes (**$$$**).

✖ **Sushi Bar Samurai** [126 A2] Porutota Rd; ✆031 227 9500; ⊕ 11.00–15.00 & 18.00–23.00. Excellent & well-priced fresh sushi & other Japanese cuisine in a minimalistic modern setting. Alcoholic drinks & mocktails served. **$$$**

✖ **Restaurant Bijou** [126 A3] Porutota Rd; ✆031 227 4710; ⊕ 08.30–22.00. Established in the early 1980s, this licensed Swiss restaurant with cosy indoor & terrace seating is known for its steaks, shellfish & fondue but it also serves a few Italian & Chinese dishes. Most mains **$$$**, but fondue is a lot pricier.

Medium

❋ ✖ **Serendib Pub & Seafood Restaurant** [126 A3] Porutota Rd; ✆031 227 9129; e serendib_neg@yahoo.com; w serendibnegombo.com; ⊕ 11.00–23.00. One of the few bespoke Negombo restaurants with proper sea frontage (& associated breeze), this is ideally placed for sundowners – good cocktail menu & wine list, & affordable beers – but it also serves great seafood & pan-Asian cuisine, as well as pasta & meat grills. **$$$**

✖ **Rodeo Pub** [126 A3] Porutota Rd; ✆031 227 4713; m 0777 746474; e janaka@rodeopub.com; w rodeopub.com; ⊕ 09.00–late. Under the same hands-on management since it opened in 1996, Negombo's oldest pub has an appropriately lived-in look, a good cocktail menu, inexpensive beers, shisha pipes, DJs from 19.00 onwards, energetic & engaged waiters, & a carb-heavy menu that includes all-day b/fasts, sandwiches, wraps & paninis (**$$**) & more substantial mains (**$$$**).

✖ **Scandic Restaurant** [126 A3] Porutota Rd; m 0754 215161. Furnished with wood tables, pastel orange walls & pot plants, this small modern restaurant serves tasty wraps, sandwiches & salads (**$$**), as well as an imaginative chalk menu of chef's specials, many with a fusion twist (**$$$**). The food is excellent & good value, but the owner-manager has been known to take loquaciousness to intrusive extremes.

✖ **Tusker Restaurant** [126 A4] Porutota Rd; ✆031 222 6999; m 0777 344357; e tuskerrestaurant@yahoo.com; ⊕ noon–22.30. This airy Belgian-owned/-managed restaurant, with overhead fans in place to assist the good natural ventilation, has an outdoorsy bistro-like feel. Seafood & pasta are the main fields of speciality, but it also serves good continental meat & poultry dishes. Preparation can be slow, but it's worth the wait. **$$$**

✖ **Coffee Bean & Tea Leaf** [126 A2] Porutota Rd; m 0769 133440; ⊕ 07.00–21.00. This cheerful modern coffee shop has comfortable sofas & stool seating & blasting AC. The menu includes freshly brewed coffee, a selection of cakes, muffins & the like (**$$**) & more substantial snacks such as salads, wraps & sandwiches (**$$$**).

✖ **King Coconut Restaurant** [126 A3] Porutota Rd; ✆031 227 8043; e info@kingcoconutnegombo.com; w kingcoconutnegombo.com; ⊕ 11.00–23.00.

This is arguably Negombo's most visually appealing restaurant, with an open-plan look somewhere between warehouse & beach house, & a superb location right on the beach. Unfortunately, the food – an unremarkable selection of seafood, steak, pizzas & Chinese – doesn't quite match up, but it is a great spot for watching the sun set above the sea over a chilled cocktail or beer. **$$$**

Cheap

✳ ✖ **Icebear Century Café** [126 C6] Main St; ☎ 031 223 8097; ⊕ 09.00–18.00. The top eatery in central Negombo, this fabulous café – set in the Kirthi Nawase (Century Townhouse) built by a prominent local businessman in 1904 – is worth visiting for its museum-like ambience alone. Adorned with period furniture & old photographs of the mansion in its halcyon days, it also serves delicious cakes, pastries & fair-trade coffee, along with light meals such as goulash & seafood pasta. **$$–$$$**

✳ ✖ **Sea Joy Restaurant** [126 A5] Lewis Pl; ☎ 031 222 1659; ⊕ 07.00–22.00. Negombo's best-value budget eatery, this fan-cooled mom-&-pop enterprise with indoor or pavement seating serves excellent chicken, fish or vegetarian rice-&-curry for US$2–3, along with chilled beers & fruit juices, & a varied selection of grills, salads & Chinese dishes. **$$**

✖ **Red Chilli** [126 D6] Main St; m 0777 750688; ⊕ 07.00–20.00. In refreshing contrast to the touristy restaurants that line the beach roads, this clean cafeteria-like centrally located eatery serves tasty & very inexpensive rice-&-curry & other local dishes. **$**

✖ **New Negombo Resthouse** [126 C6] King George Dr; ☎ 031 222 2299. Situated near the fish market & fort, this potentially stunning government resthouse is anything but new – it's been trading under that name for longer than a century! – & you'd have to be something of a masochist to try the rooms or even the food. The bar, by contrast, is a fabulously characterful spot for a chilled beer or arrack. **$**

OTHER PRACTICALITIES Central Negombo is well equipped with supermarkets, and there is a branch of Cargills Food City [126 D6] (⊕ 08.00–20.00) on Porutota Road, more or less opposite Jetwing Beach Hotel. If you need to change money, all the main banks are represented in the town centre, including branches of the Commercial Bank, both with ATMs, on Fernando and St Joseph's roads (both [126 D6]). More convenient to tourists staying at the beach will be the Commercial Bank ATM [126 A3] outside the Topaz Hotel on Porutota Road.

TOUR OPERATORS A good option for day and overnight tours out of Negombo is **DS Tours** [126 A1] (*Porutota Rd; m 0776 544095; e dstourssrilanka@gmail.com; w dstourssrilanka.com*), which is under the same management as the neighbouring Sunny's Restaurant.

WHAT TO SEE AND DO Although the beach running north of town is the main centre of tourist activity in Negombo, it doesn't compare to the country's finest, and swimming is discouraged due to the rough surf.

Town centre The old town centre has surprisingly little to show for its long colonial history. The largest and oldest of several Catholic shrines is the grandiose **St Mary's Church** [126 C6] (*Main St;* 🛐 *StMarysChurchNegombo*), which was established by the Portuguese in 1603, though the present building – the fifth – was constructed between 1874 and 1922. The subject of a postage stamp sequence released in 2014, the church has a striking colonnaded Neoclassical pink façade, while the interior is decorated with alabaster statues of various saints and ceiling murals depicting the life of Christ by the aptly named local Buddhist painter N S Godamanne. The stretch of main street running southwest of the church is lined with **old colonial homesteads** adorned with ornate wood balconies, most of which are rather rundown lawyer's offices, the one exception being the splendid 1904 homestead that has been restored as the Icebear Century Café [126 C6].

The most interesting part of Negombo is the old quarter set on a peninsula at the lagoon mouth. This is the site of **Negombo Fort** [126 C6], established during the Portuguese occupation but rebuilt by the Dutch in 1672. The pentagonal Dutch construction was entered via a drawbridge spanning a dry moat. The British administration later demolished the fort to make way for a prison still in use today. The most significant relic of the old fort is a recessed arched gateway topped by a granite slab inscribed with the year 1678. Close by, **St Stephen's Church** [126 C6], a pretty hilltop Anglican edifice with whitewashed walls and tile roofs, was constructed in 1879 and now offers fine views over the fishing harbour. On the opposite side of Circular Road, the spectacularly rundown **New Negombo Resthouse** [126 C6] is a fine double-storey building that must surely date back to the late 18th century, possibly earlier.

The lagoon mouth running inland from the Old Fort to Kothalawala Bridge serves as the colourful main **fishing harbour** [126 C6], and is lined with literally hundreds of brightly painted wooden boats. These include the square-sailed *oruva* outriggers traditionally used by local Karava fishermen, as well as more modern motorised boats. The ugly and untidy looking metal structures that dominate the central **fish market** [126 C6], on the seashore immediately northeast of the lagoon mouth, wouldn't win any architectural awards, but they ares a hive of photogenic activity in the morning, especially between 07.00 and 10.00.

Dutch Canal [126 D5] The most enduring Dutch legacy in Negombo is the long canal that bisects the town starting at the Negombo Lagoon about 300m east of the fishing harbour and Kothalawala Bridge. The canal originally ran all the way to the Puttalam Lagoon, 90km to the north, and it was recently restored as far as the Maha River, about 8km north of the town centre. To get a glimpse of life along the canal, you can follow the towpaths that run along either side of it as it passes through the town centre. A more rewarding option would be to charter one of the distinctive flat-bottomed *padda* cargo boats traditionally used to navigate and carry cinnamon and other agricultural produce to the port. Depending on how long you go out for, expect to pay around US$10 for a boat.

Negombo Lagoon [map, page 74] Extending over 29km^2 and with a mean depth of only 1.5m, the vast saline lagoon that shares its name with Negombo has long been one of the country's most important fisheries. It's also a very pretty body of water, and rich in birdlife, particularly in the south where it merges into the protected Muthurajawela Wetland. To see birds and other wildlife, the best option is a boat trip from the Muthurajawela Visitor Centre halfway back to Colombo (pages 120–1), but boats can also be chartered from Negombo Fishing Harbour [126 C6] for around US$10.

Duwa Island [126 A7–B7] Not actually an island but a small peninsula connected to the southern mainland by a sliver of land only 100m wide, Duwa is also passed through by the main coastal road to Colombo about 1km south of Kothalawala Bridge. It hosts a daily fish market smaller but far more picturesque than its counterpart in the town centre. If you are here over Easter weekend, the Duwa Passion Play, held on Good Friday, is Sri Lanka's oldest and most famous Catholic pageant, dating back 400 years to the Portuguese occupation, and frequently involving more than 200 actors.

6

Diving The sea off Negombo incorporates several dive sites which are at their best from late November to March. The most experienced operator in town is Sri Lanka Diving Tours [126 A1] (*Porutota Rd*; m *0777 648459*; e *felicianfernando@hotmail. com*; w *srilanka-divingtours.com*). The best time to dive is generally early morning, when the sea tends to be smooth and visibility is highest.

Walisinghe Harischandra National Museum [126 D5] (*Mirigama Rd*; ⤷ *031 223 3644*; w *museum.gov.lk*; ⏲ *08.00–16.00 exc Tue*) This low-key museum preserves the house where Buddhist revivalist leader Walisinghe Harischandra was born in 1876 and lived until his death, aged only 37, in 1913. With its wide colonnaded balcony, whitewashed walls and tile roof, the house is one of the finest remaining examples of colonial architecture in Negombo, and the interior preserves the original furniture, household objects, books and diaries used by Harischandra, who played a vital role in the preservation of the ancient Buddhist shrines at Anuradhapura and Mihintale. The museum lies on the south side of the Mirigama Road, more or less opposite the Cargills Food City at a major Y-junction 3km east of the town centre.

Angurukaramulla Temple [126 D6] Situated on Temple Road about 3km east of the town centre, Angurukaramulla is the most important Buddhist shrine in a part of the country where the country's majority religion is numerically outranked by Catholicism and Islam. The abundant and often quite graphic artwork includes a large seated Buddha shrine built in the 1980s, as well as a long frieze comprising life-size images of every last Sinhalese monarch, from the founding Prince Vijaya to the ill-fated King Vikrama Rajasinha of Kandy, who was deposed by the British in 1815. It also incorporates a ruined colonial-era library which, according to the on-site plaque, was declared open in 1941 by Sir Andrew Caldecott, then the Governor of Ceylon.

WAIKKAL

Situated 10km north of Negombo, Waikkal – sometime spelt Wayikkala – is a small coastal village flanked to the north by the forest-fringed Maha River and to the south and east by various tentacles of the mangrove-lined Ging River. The beach at Waikkal supports a scattering of resorts that tend to be more rustic and characterful than their counterparts in Negombo, but – being no more than an hour's drive from Bandaranaike International Airport – also form a useful stopover for freshly arrived or soon-to-depart visitors, or a convenient weekend break from the capital.

GETTING THERE AND AWAY Waikkal lies 45km north of Colombo and 20km from Bandaranaike International Airport. Most buses and trains between Colombo and Chilaw stop there. From the airport, you'll need to charter a taxi or arrange a transfer with your hotel.

⌂ WHERE TO STAY
Upmarket
⌂ **Ranweli Holiday Village** (90 rooms) ⤷ *031 227 7359*; m *0771 096739*; e *ranweli@ slt.lk*; w *ranweli.com*. Reached via a punt across the Ging River, this isolated eco-resort is set in jungled gardens run through by a nature trail & teeming with birds & butterflies. It's a good choice for active nature lovers, since the room rate includes free canoeing, kayaking & paddle-boating, & an activity desk can also arrange bicycle & boat tours. The rocky coastline is less well suited to conventional beach holidays, but a large palm-shaded swimming pool compensates. Small but stylish rooms & larger bungalows all come with AC, TV & fan. *From US$179/199 sgl/dbl B&B.* **$$$$$**

Suriya Resort (58 rooms) 031 227 7775; e suriyaresort@yahoo.com; w suriyaresort.com. Set in lovely 5ha grounds bounded by the Ging River on two sides and the ocean on a third, this luxurious resort is centred on a 50m-long beachfront swimming pool and massive colonial-style main building with whitewashed walls & wooden floors & frames. It offers a choice of stilted wooden bungalows on a lagoon reached via a wooden walkway, or more conventional hotel rooms in the main building, all with AC, fan, darkwood furniture, cable TV, large bathroom & balcony. Avoid poolside rooms as they lack privacy. *From US$150 dbl B&B.* **$$$$**

Moderate

✽ ⌂ Ging Oya Lodge (7 rooms) 031 227 7822; m 0718 739541; e info@gingoya.com; w gingoya.com. Set in large densely jungled grounds alongside the creek-like Ging River, this superb down-to-earth lodge is the perfect antidote to the larger coastal resort, thanks to its friendly hands-on Belgian owner-managers & proliferation of birds & small mammals. The stylishly decorated colonial-style bungalows come with AC, fitted nets, fridge, private balcony & solar-heated showers, while amenities include free kayaking & canoeing, an attractive swimming pool, a good library in the cosy lounge, & excellent continental & Sri Lankan meals for US$7 (lunch) or US$12 (3-course dinner). Diving & riverboat trips, & Ayurvedic massage can be arranged, & it's about 20mins on foot from the beach. Excellent value. *€50/57 sgl/dbl B&B.* **$$$**

Budget

⌂ Rico Shadow (25 rooms) 031 227 7486; m 0772 987842; e ricoshad@bluewin.ch; w rico-shadow.com. This likeably quirky family-run guesthouse offers a variety of rooms & suites, all with AC, nets, & tub or shower. Ground-floor rooms open out on to a terrace in the large tropical garden, while 1st-floor rooms have a private balcony. There's also tasty Sri Lankan cuisine with a home-cooked flair. *From US$44/50 sgl/dbl B&B.* **$$$**

CHILAW AND SURROUNDS

A substantial but little-touristed seaside town of around 27,000 inhabitants, Chilaw, also known as Chilao, is bisected by the lagoon of the same name 80km north of Colombo. With a sea breeze billowing over the lagoon to ruffle the hundreds of fishing boats moored along its banks between the fish market and railway station, it is a colourful if sleepy town whose main historical claim is that it hosted Mahatma Ghandi in November 1927 on what was to be the venerated Indian's only visit to Sri Lanka. As with many ports on the west coast of Sri Lanka, Chilaw was captured by the Portuguese in 1632, and it retains a strong Catholic influence most evident in the impressive yellow-painted Our Lady of Mount Carmel Cathedral (032 222 2343) constructed on the east bank on the lagoon in 1861. Also of interest are two venerable out-of-town Hindu shrines: Sri Munneswaram Devasthanam 2.5km to the east and Draupadi Amman at Udappuwa 25km to the north.

GETTING THERE AND AWAY Chilaw lies 80km north of Colombo along the main road to Puttalam and Kalpitiya, a trip that usually takes around 2 hours on account of the traffic around Colombo. At least two buses every hour connect Chilaw to Colombo via Negombo and Waikkal, and the lagoon-front railway station is serviced by at least half a dozen trains from Colombo and Negombo daily. Most accommodation lies on the beach side of town, which is reached along a bridge spanning the lagoon 200m north of the railway station. Tuktuks are available to take you across.

⌂ WHERE TO STAY

⌂ Chilaw City Hotel (60 rooms) Ambakandawila Rd; 032 222 4000; e chilawcityhotel@yahoo.com; w chilawcityhotel. com. Nestled between the beach & lagoon about 1km south of the bridge, this unexciting but well-managed hotel has comfortable modern rooms with AC & cable TV. The restaurant overlooks a swimming pool. *From US$38/47 sgl/dbl B&B.* **$$$**

🏠 **Chilaw Resthouse** (15 rooms)
Beach Rd; ☎ 032 222 2299; 📱 0716
837453; e chilawresthouse@gmail.com;
w chilawresthouse.com. Originally built in the late
19th century, this former government resthouse
on the beachfront 100m east of the bridge could
do with a revamp, but it has a perfect location & a
certain faded charm. All rooms have AC, cable TV,
minibar & Wi-Fi. *From US$20 dbl.* **$**

AROUND CHILAW

Sri Munneswaram Devasthanam Temple [map, page 74] The Shiva temple at Munneswaram, on the north side of the Wariyapara Road a quick 2.5km tuktuk hop east of Chilaw, is one of Sri Lanka's oldest and most important Hindu shrines. Its date of foundation is unknown, but one Tamil legend asserts that it was founded in prehistoric times by Rama, the hero of the epic *Ramayana*, while some Sinhalese believe that Munneswaram is where the evil human-eating goddess Kali landed upon her arrival from India and was forced to settle by the more benevolent Pattini. As with so many Hindu shrines in this part of Sri Lanka, the temple was destroyed during the Portuguese occupation, and rebuilt several times after that, most recently c1875, when the current building was established. Owing to its reputed antiquity, Munneswaram is a popular pilgrimage site with Hindus and Buddhists alike, and worth a diversion at any time for its atmospheric and colourfully decorated interior, which incorporates five separate shrines including a very old Shiva lingam. The temple really comes to life during the nine-day Navaratri festival, which is held on moveable dates over August and September, and should be classed as a 'must-see' if you are in the area at the right time.

Udappuwa Draupadi Amman Temple [map, page 74] The small sandy seaside town of Udappuwa, whose local economy is based on shrimp farming, is the site of an ancient temple dedicated to the Hindu goddess Draupadi Amman and dominated by a striking and ornately decorated nine-tier gopuram that towers some 25m above the modest homesteads that surround it. As with Munneswaram, it is worth a diversion at any time, but comes into its own during the festival of Draupadi Amman, which is held over 18 days in late July to early August, and concludes with a fire-walking ceremony wherein every male in Udappuwa walks barefoot over a bed of red hot coals. To get here, follow the Puttalam Road north out of Chilaw for 19km, then turn left on to a road flanked by shrimp farms and continue for another 6km to Udappuwa, where the shrine dominates the local skyline.

PUTTALAM

The northern terminus of the coastal railway line through Negombo and Chilaw, Puttalam is a substantial town of around 50,000 inhabitants set on the east bank of the eponymous lagoon 130km from Colombo. During the civil war, it had the end-of-the-line air of a forgotten frontier town, but in recent years it has emerged as an important route crossroads, situated close to the junction of the coastal road from Colombo to Wilpattu National Park and Anuradhapura, and the side roads running northwest to Kalpitiya and north to Mannar Island. For all that, it is the sort of place that many travellers pass through *en route* to somewhere else, but few grace it with an overnight stay.

GETTING THERE AND AWAY

By rail The railway line north from Colombo Fort to Negombo reached Chilaw in 1916 and Puttalam ten years later. The track was removed in 1943 as the rails were needed due to shortages caused by World War II, but relaid in 1964. Three trains now cover the route in either direction daily, but they are very slow, taking at least 4 hours one way.

By road Regular buses run between Colombo and Anuradhapura (and points further north) via Puttalam. These buses can be used to reach Wilpattu National Park. In addition, at least half a dozen buses run back and forth between Puttalam and Kalpitiya daily, and two buses run from Puttalam to Mannar daily, one leaving in the morning and one in the afternoon.

WHERE TO STAY A few budget hotels are dotted around town. The picks are the **Senatilake Guesthouse** (*Kurunegala Rd;* ☏ *032 567 4467;* **$$**) and **Sea Bay Resort** (*Beach Rd;* **$$**), both of which have air-conditioned rooms with TV and hot water for around US$30.

THE KALPITIYA PENINSULA

Connected to the rest of Sri Lanka by a 2km-wide isthmus, Kalpitiya is a flat, sandy and low-lying sliver of terra firma flanked by the 330km^2 Puttalam Lagoon to the east and the open sea to the west. The area is entrenched as Sri Lanka's premier kitesurfing site, but it is also a great emerging destination for wildlife enthusiasts, offering some of the country's finest snorkelling, diving, and dolphin and whale watching, as well as good birding and the opportunity to go on safari in nearby Wilpattu National Park. Extending northward for 60km but nowhere more than 5km wide, the peninsula is named after the historic small town of Kalpitiya, which stands on a small protrusion towards the northern end of the lagoonside shore. South of its principal town, the narrow tongue is one solid landmass, interspersed with seaside villages, small lagoons, salt extraction pools, agricultural smallholdings, coconut plantations, mangroves and wind-turbine plants. Further north, it disintegrates into a confusing patchwork of small islands, narrow sandbars and shallow watery expanses – namely Kalpitiya Lagoon, Dutch Bay and Portuguese Bay – before terminating at the main lagoon mouth opposite Kudiramalai Point.

Kalpitiya's proximity to war-torn Northern Province meant that until recently it was one of the most unknown and least developed parts of Sri Lanka in touristic terms. That has changed greatly since 2010, when the government established the 20km^2 Kalpitiya Tourist Zone, which incorporates the northern peninsula fringing Kalpitiya Lagoon, as well as 14 islands in Dutch and Portuguese bays. Even so, Kalpitiya still feels a little too scruffy and down-to-earth to be regarded as a conventional beach resort, and it certainly lacks for the kind of culinary scene or party vibe associated with the likes of Negombo, Bentota or Arugam Bay. Nevertheless, at least two dozen beach lodges are now dotted around the peninsula, most of them small rustic camps or boutique resorts catering to kitesurfers and other travellers who seek to engage actively with the ocean and its wildlife rather than just lounging around on the beach.

GETTING THERE AND AWAY Kalpitiya town lies about 165km from Colombo via Negombo (135km) and Chilaw (90km). Allow 4 hours to drive from Colombo and three coming directly from Negombo or Bandaranaike International Airport. To get here from Colombo, follow the A3 north for 125km to Palavi Junction (about 5km before Puttalam), then turn left and continue in a broadly northerly direction for another 40km. If you are heading to one of the resorts at Alankuda, turn left at the well-signposted junction at Norochcholai 16km past Palavi Junction, then

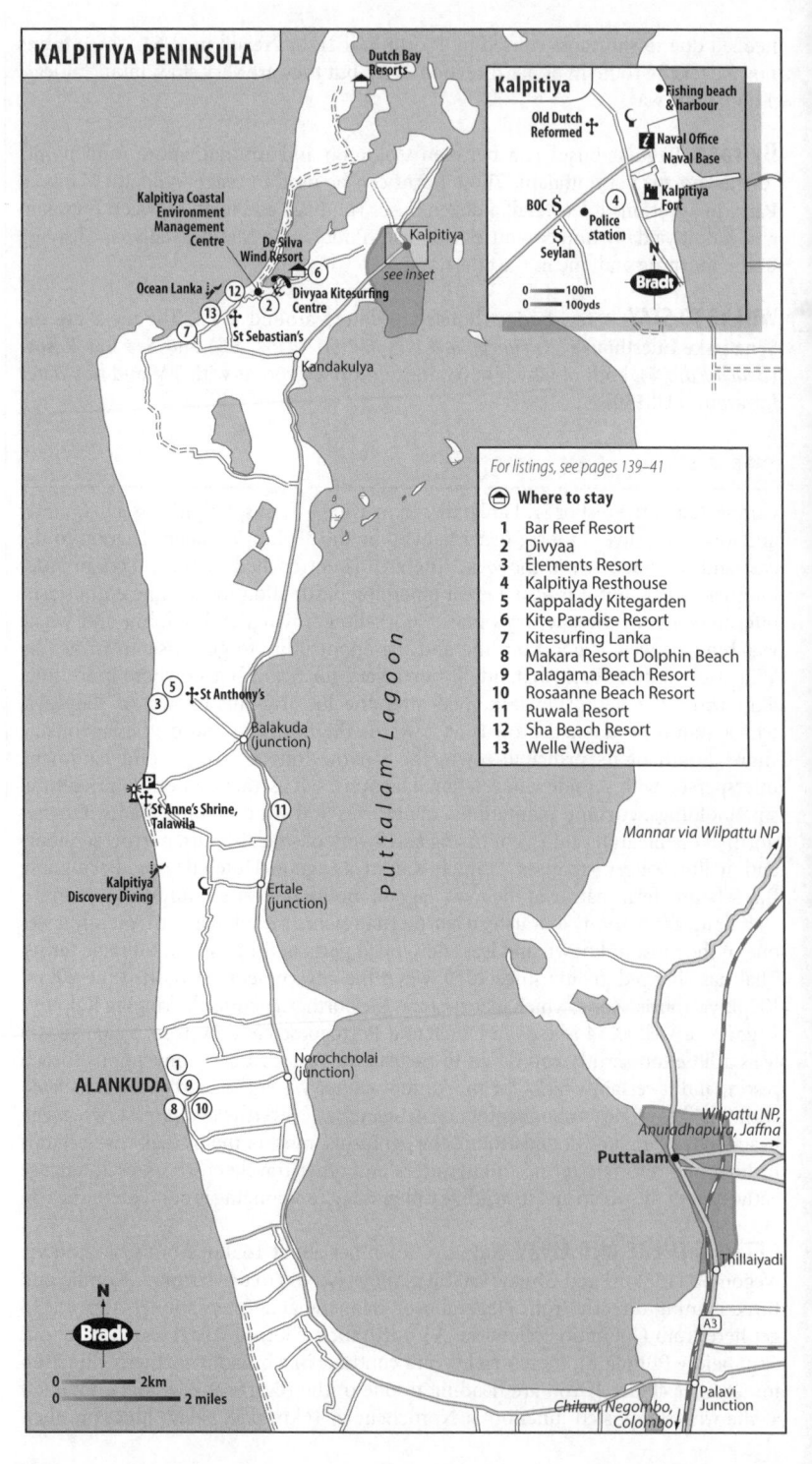

KALPITIYA PENINSULA

Dutch Bay Resorts

Kalpitiya

- Fishing beach & harbour
- Old Dutch Reformed †
- Naval Office
- Naval Base
- BOC $
- Police station
- $ Seylan
- 4 Kalpitiya Fort

N

Bradt

0 ——— 100m
0 ——— 100yds

Kalpitiya Coastal Environment Management Centre

De Silva Wind Resort 6

Ocean Lanka 12
Divyaa Kitesurfing Centre 2
13
7
St Sebastian's

Kalpitiya
see inset

Kandakulya

For listings, see pages 139–41

🏠 **Where to stay**

1 Bar Reef Resort
2 Divyaa
3 Elements Resort
4 Kalpitiya Resthouse
5 Kappalady Kitegarden
6 Kite Paradise Resort
7 Kitesurfing Lanka
8 Makara Resort Dolphin Beach
9 Palagama Beach Resort
10 Rosaanne Beach Resort
11 Ruwala Resort
12 Sha Beach Resort
13 Welle Wediya

5 † St Anthony's
3

Balakuda (junction)

P
† St Anne's Shrine, Talawila

11

Kalpitiya Discovery Diving

Ertale (junction)

Puttalam Lagoon

Mannar via Wilpattu NP

Norochcholai (junction)

1
ALANKUDA 9
8 10

Wilpattu NP, Anuradhapura, Jaffna

Puttalam

N

Bradt

0 ——— 2km
0 ——— 2 miles

Thillaiyadi

A3

Chilaw, Negombo, Colombo

Palavi Junction

continue westward for about 2km. For Kappalady Kitegarden or Elements, take the (poorly signposted) second of two close-together left turns at Balakuda, 26km past Palavi Junction. For any of the more northerly resorts on the Kalpitiya Lagoon, look for the relevant signpost to the left about 3km before Kalpitiya town. Using public transport, half a dozen direct buses daily run back and forth between Colombo and Kalpitiya, and there are also regular buses to/from Puttalam, which has onward connections to Wilpattu National Park, Anuradhapura, Trincomalee, Mannar and Jaffna. Tuktuks are available in Norochcholai, Balakuda and Kalpitiya to transport you to the resort of your choice.

WHERE TO STAY, EAT AND DRINK *Map, opposite*

There are three main accommodation clusters on the peninsula. The oldest and most tightly clustered of these is Alankuda, near the southern end of the peninsula. A few more isolated resorts stand on the central part of the peninsula, in the vicinity of Talawila and the famous St Anne's Shrine. Further north, a larger and more varied selection of resorts can be found abutting the Kalpitiya Lagoon a few kilometres west of Kalpitiya town. There is also a simple but well-priced government resthouse in Kalpitiya town.

Alankuda

The 4 resorts below all lie within a few hundred metres of each other at Alankuda & maintain a collective website (w *alankuda.com*). In all cases, the quoted rates rise significantly over mid-Dec–mid-Jan, & are discounted Apr– Nov.

Upmarket

✳ 🏠 **Bar Reef Resort** (12 rooms) m 0777 219218; e info@barreefresort.com; w barreefresort.com. This down-to-earth eco-resort is set in lush tropical gardens dominated by a chlorine-free saltwater swimming pool & running down to a sandy beach where evening meals are served, weather permitting. Well spaced out for maximum privacy, the well-ventilated Mediterranean-meets-Asia garden & beach cabanas have adobe-style walls, earthy pastel colours, palm leaf roofs, fan, fitted nets, outdoor shower & large private balcony. *US$125/150 sgl/dbl B&B, plus US$15 pp per lunch/dinner.* **$$$$**

🏠 **Makara Resort Dolphin Beach** (9 rooms) 📞032 738 8050; m 0777 723272; e reservations@ dolphinbeach.lk; w dolphinbeach.lk. This small family-oriented beach resort has a relaxed vibe in the mould of its well-travelled owner-manager, whose Italian heritage is reflected in a varied menu specialising in pizza & homemade pasta. Accommodation is in stylish tent-like units with canvas sides, treated concrete floor, AC, fan & private balcony. Sandy palm-shaded gardens run down to a beach that offers safe swimming

in season, & there's also a swimming pool. *US$125/150 sgl/dbl B&B, plus US$15 pp per lunch/ dinner.* **$$$$**

🏠 **Palagama Beach Resort** (13 rooms) m 0777 818970; e info@palagamabeach. com; w palagamabeach.com. Set in landscaped beachfront gardens next to Bar Reef Resort, this unsignposted boutique retreat offers accommodation in tile-roofed villas or more rustic beach & garden cabanas, all of which are individually decorated & have good natural ventilation supplemented by a fan. Good seafood & an extensive cocktail menu can be enjoyed on the beach or by the swimming pool. *From US$159 dbl B&B.* **$$$$**

Moderate

🏠 **Rosaanne Beach Resort** (9 rooms) 📞032 720 0434; m 0778 788242; e rosaannebeach@ gmail.com; w rosaannebeach.lk. Set in a sandy palm grove on the opposite side of the road to the beach, this friendly family-owned & -managed set-up has clean, comfortable & brightly decorated cabanas with AC, fan, net & small balcony. Amenities include a restaurant serving mains for around US$7 & a swimming pool. *US$80/100 sgl/ dbl B&B, with low-season discounts.* **$$$$**

Central resorts
Upmarket
✳ 🏠 **Elements Resort** (10 rooms) m 0777 377387; e reservations@elements-resort.com;

w elements-resort.com; see ad, 1st colour section. One of the most beautiful resorts on the peninsula, rustic but smart Elements is carved into a patch of coastal bush sandwiched between a fabulous swimming beach & a smallish lagoon that offers ideal conditions for novice kitesurfers. Amenities include a beachfront saltwater infinity pool, a breezy open-sided 1st-floor bar with sea views, a kitesurfing & watersports centre manned by on-site instructors from the UK in season & an adventure centre operating snorkelling & dolphin-watching excursions & day safaris to Wilpattu. Accommodation is in attractive A-frame bungalows with palm-frond roof, good natural ventilation, walk-in nets & a minibar. *€199 dbl HB, with substantial discounts out of season.* **$$$$$**

🏠 **Ruwala Resort** (16 rooms) 📞032 329 9299; **m** 0777 141714; **e** reservations@ruwalaresort.com; **w** ruwalaresort.com. Set in sprawlingly beautiful palm-shaded gardens on the west shore of the Puttalam Lagoon, this slick resort has modern double or twin cottages with good quality furnishing & finishes, walk-in nets, large flatscreen cable TV, large balcony & outdoor shower. Seems a bit overpriced. *US$215/260 sgl/dbl FB, with substantial low-season discounts.* **$$$$$**

Budget

🏠 **Kappalady Kitegarden** (11 rooms) **m** 0722 313129, 0723 787999; **e** jonas@kappaladykitegarden.com; **w** kappaladykitegarden.com. Set in lush well-tended gardens 500m from a good swimming beach & only 100m from a lagoon that offers ideal kitesurfing conditions, this chilled-out low-key resort feels a bit like a superior backpacker hostel, with delicious buffet meals being eaten communally at a long wooden table, & plenty of hammocks & corners where you can chill out. Kitesurfing is the core activity in season, but it also offers sensibly priced group day tours to Wilpattu National Park & Anuradhapura, snorkelling excursions, & whale & dolphin tours offshore. Rooms are simple but come with nets, fan & optional AC. *From €25 pp FB in a fan room using shared bathroom to €70/90 en-suite sgl/dbl FB with AC.* **$$$**

Kalpitiya Lagoon

The resorts below are spread out along the south bank of the Kalpitiya Lagoon & the shallow oceanic beach running to its south.

Moderate

☀ 🏠 **Kitesurfing Lanka** (28 rooms) **m** 0773 686235, 0770 038467; **e** info@kitesurfinglanka.com; **w** kitesurfinglanka.com. The main hub of kitesurfing activity in Kalpitiya, this superior backpackers' lodge has a vibe that reflects the laid-back but dynamic French & Sri Lankan owner-management team. It has a great location on the edge of a shallow lagoon only 200m from the beach & offers the choice of large standing tents with fan, bedding & palm-leaf shelter for shade, or en-suite wooden bungalows with fan, net & private balcony with hammock. Room rates include free use of kayaks, paddle-boards, bicycles & storage space for kitesurfers, while a well-equipped adventure centre offers the full range of activities associated with Kalpitiya, including kitesurfing, safaris to Wilpattu, snorkel & dive excursions, & dolphin & whale watching. Tasty & reasonably priced à la carte or buffet meals are eaten in a large open-sided dining room with Wi-Fi. *€35/57 pp FB in tent/bungalow May–Oct or Dec–Feb, €20/40 dbl B&B in tent/bungalow Mar, Apr & Nov.* **$$$**

🏠 **Welle Wediya** (6 rooms) 📞011 432 2288; **m** 0770 112929; **e** info@wellewediya.com; **w** wellewediya.com. This small isolated resort consists of a 2-storey building set in compact but well-tended gardens that run right down to a good swimming beach. Brightly decorated modern rooms with queen-size bed, net & fan but no AC all have a private balcony with a sea view. The stylish modern restaurant majors in seafood & local curries, & can also arrange evening beach barbecues. A little bland perhaps but comfortable, professionally managed & very good value. *US$85 dbl B&B, dropping to US$65 in low season.* **$$$**

🏠 **Divyaa** (11 rooms) 📞011 438 4704; **m** 0715 678326; **e** info@divyaa.com; **w** divyaa.com. This boutique resort has a superb location in large gardens set around a beautiful swimming pool fronting the Kalpitiya Lagoon & large rooms with 4-poster bed, walk-in net, AC & private balcony. Suites also have their own small walled garden with deckchairs & plunge pool. It is ideally located for kitesurfing & has equipment to rent. *From US$95 dbl B&B.* **$$$$**

Budget

🏠 **Sha Beach Resort** (12 rooms) ✆031 227 7722; m 0777 488746; e suranga007@yahoo. com; w shabeachcabana.com. This cosy & relaxed backpacker-oriented set-up stands 100m from a becalmed shallow oceanic beach at the southwest end of the sandbar that hems in the Kalpitiya Lagoon. Simple rooms without fan or hot water but with nets & good natural ventilation are set in a bamboo, wood & palm-dominated 2-storey building, & there are also separate AC rooms with hot water. A breezy open-sided restaurant with sand underfoot serves a varied selection of local dishes in the US$3–4 range. *From US$20 dbl using common showers to US$50 en-suite dbl with AC.* **$**

🏠 **Kite Paradise Resort** (19 rooms) m 0777 770074, 0727 659000; e kiteparadise2014@yahoo.

com. Set in a sandy & shady palm plantation run through by neat gravel paths, this simple lodge offers the choice of cramped backpacker rooms with ¾ beds using common showers, or more spacious en-suite rooms with net & private balcony. Tasty & inexpensive local meals are served. There's no sea view but it's only a 10min walk to the lagoon. *US$17/20 sgl/dbl using common ablutions, US$40 en-suite dbl, US$84 AC family room sleeping 5.* **$**

Kalpitiya town

🏠 **Kalpitiya Resthouse** (3 rooms) ✆032 226 0705. Set in large dusty gardens on the main road 200m before the fort, this time-warped colonial lodge has adequate twin & family rooms with net & fan, as well as bar & restaurant. *US$15/18 twin/ family room.* **$**

WHAT TO SEE AND DO

Kitesurfing The Kalpitiya Peninsula is Sri Lanka's premier kitesurfing destination. The Kalpitiya Lagoon offers ideal conditions for beginners, as do several similar but smaller flat water bodies, while the shallow Indian Ocean shore to the immediate west is perfect for intermediate and experienced kitesurfers. The season runs from May to October, when monsoon conditions generate winds of 20–25 knots, making the beaches unpleasant for more conventional beach tourists but ideal for kitesurfing. Almost all resorts and hotels on the peninsula can rent out equipment, typically for around US$40–45 for 1 or 2 hours, so serious kitesurfers might prefer to bring their own gear. A dedicated kitesurfing shop selling spares and offering limited repair facilities can be found at Kitesurfing Lanka (see opposite), and there is also a good kitesurfing centre at Elements (pages 139–40). Probably the most usefully located operator, perched on the edge of the Kalpitiya Lagoon, is **De Silva Wind Resort** (✆ *032 493 4076;* m *0777 047817;* e *office@surfschool-srilanka.com;* w *surfschool-srilanka.com*).

Diving and snorkelling Protected within a 300km² marine sanctuary since 1992, the relatively pristine Bar Reef off the west coast of Kalpitiya has the highest biodiversity of any coral formation in Sri Lankan waters, with more than 200 coral species and almost 300 fish species recorded alongside a wide selection of marine invertebrates. The main 2ha reef lies at the northern tip of the peninsula about 40–60 minutes by boat from most resorts on Kalpitiya (depending on where exactly you start) and it incorporates several exceptional snorkelling and dive sites, with a good chance of encountering manta rays, marine turtles and reef sharks. Often combined with dolphin-watching tours, diving and snorkelling excursions can be arranged indirectly through any hotel or resort on the peninsula, or directly through two recommended companies: **Kalpitiya Discovery Diving** (m *0770 030033;* e *bookings@kalpitiyadiving.lk;* w *kalpitiyadiving.lk*) and **Ocean Lanka** (m *0710 822231;* w *oceanlankainfo.com*). For snorkelling, expect to pay around US$100 per boat for up to six people inclusive of gear. Single dives start at around US$85 per person, but packages and courses are also available. A Department of Conservation entrance fee of around US$8 per person is also levied. Snorkelling conditions are good from October to April, but best over February and March.

Dolphin and whale tours The shallow shelved waters off the Kalpitiya Lagoon support large numbers of resident dolphin all year round, along with migrant whales whose numbers peak over November, December, March and April. The most reliable attraction is hundred-strong schools of spinner dolphins, which are named for their ability to rotate on their longitudinal axis several times as they leap through the air. The reason for these acrobatic displays is unclear. Some behavioural zoologists believe it is to help rid themselves of parasites, part of a courtship ritual, or to eject water from their respiratory tract, but it's tempting to think it might simply express a *joie de vivre* reminiscent of an unleashed dog on a run. Other cetacean species regularly observed off Kalpitiya are bottlenose dolphin, Risso's dolphin, Indo-Pacific humpback dolphin, sperm whale and blue whale. The common minke, melon-headed whale, dwarf sperm whale and orca (killer whale) have also been spotted in the area.

Kalpitiya town [map, page 138] The small town at the north end of the peninsular mainland is the site of Kalpitiya Fort, which was built by the Dutch in 1666 as an extension of an older Portuguese chapel, whose gables are still visible. A well-maintained square structure with tall coral rag walls, the fort has a single entrance topped by an arch of yellow bricks imported from Holland and a tall belfry whose bell was later removed to an Anglican church in Puttalam. Known to the Dutch as Calpetty, the fort was strategically important insofar as it allowed them to monitor access to Puttalam harbour and to control the Muslim-dominated trade out of the region. In 1795, the fort was surrendered to the British, who renovated it in 1840 and actively occupied it until 1859. It is now part of a naval base, which means that you need to ask permission to visit, a straightforward procedure though you might be asked to produce your passport. There's no charge, and you will probably be guided around by an English-speaking naval officer, but photography is forbidden. Look out for the massive whale skeleton preserved in the open air as you enter the naval compound, and the engraving of two elephants and a palm tree above the entrance gate. The former is said to be a symbol of strength, the latter of the region's fertility, but it seems just as likely they represent the two main items of export from Kalpitiya, namely ivory and coconuts. On Muthuwella Street, about 200m outside the fort and naval compound, stands the oldest extant building on the peninsula: a whitewashed Dutch Reformed Church with handsome gables, a red tiled roof, and a colonnaded balcony. Built in 1642, the church now only opens to the public during services, which are held at 09.30 on Wednesdays and Sundays. The subterranean tunnel that once connected the fort and the church was blocked up many years ago.

St Anne's Shrine, Talawila [map, page 138] One of the most important Christian shrines in Sri Lanka, St Anne's Church is also reputedly the oldest, though the provenance of its sanctified status is somewhat vague. Some say that St Anne appeared here in person to a poor Portuguese traveller who fell asleep under the massive multi-rooted banyan tree that still stands at the site today. Another story has it that a newly shipwrecked visitor from Europe placed a statue of St Anne salvaged from the wreck at the base of the shady banyan, vowing to built a church there if his business prospered. Either way, the shrine and surviving statue of St Anne both reputedly date back to 1703, the first church was built here in 1762, and the present-day structure – a large rectangular building with a plain tiled roof supported by carved wooden pillars – was constructed between 1837 and 1843.

The most spectacular times to visit are on or around the annual feast of St Joseph (second Sunday in March) or the Talawila St Anne's Church Festival (first week of August) when thousands of pilgrims converge on the site. But it remains a very busy shrine throughout the year. Try to be here just before mass, which is held at 17.00 daily, or at 07.00 and 11.00 on Sunday. Mass at Talawila is an enchantingly peculiar Asiatic variation on the conventional Catholic service – there are no chairs, and the wearing of shoes is forbidden, so worshippers sit barefoot on the floor, performing a lilting Sinhalese call-and-response with a distinctive Indo-Lankan sing-song intonation. After mass, head out to the nearby St Anne's Lighthouse, which was built in 2012 to mark the 250th anniversary of the church's foundation. If the lighthouse is unlocked, you can climb to the top for a view, but even if not, the location is fabulous, especially at sunset.

Getting there St Anne's Shrine stands in the fishing village of Talawila about 3km from the main Palavi–Kalpitiya road, along a surfaced side road branching southwest at Balakuda Junction. It also lies about 3km south of Kappalady Kitegarden and Elements by road. Using public transport, any bus heading between Palavi and Kalpitiya can drop you at Balakuda, where you can charter a tuktuk for US$1–2. It is also possible to walk along the lovely 2.5km beach running south from Kappalady Kitegarden and Elements to the (very conspicuous) St Anne's Lighthouse.

Wilpattu National Park
Sri Lanka's largest national park (pages 281–4) borders the east shore of Puttalam north of Kalpitiya, while the main road entrance gate at Hunuvilagama is only 50km by road from Palavi Junction via Puttalam. Most resorts and operators on the Kalpitiya Lagoon offer half-day safaris to Wilpattu, either travelling by road or using a recently opened western entrance gate that can be reached by boating across the lagoon. Rates start at around US$100 per group exclusive of guide and entrance fees. Given the choice, late afternoon drives tend to be most productive for mammals but early morning is also good and usually better for birds.

6

7

Inland of Colombo

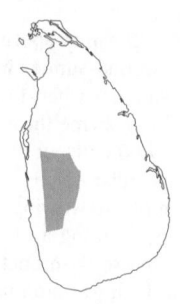

This chapter covers a varied scattering of inland sites that are most often passed through *en route* between Colombo and the likes of Kandy, Dambulla, Anuradhapura and Kitulgala, but might as easily be visited as a day or overnight trip from the coast. With the noteworthy exception of the popular Pinnawala Elephant Orphanage, most of these sites, though certainly not very far from the beaten tourist track, remain low-key and relatively little-visited. You could, for instance, easily spend a couple of days exploring the various diversions along the main road to Kandy, while the substantial town of Kurunegala, *en route* to the Cultural Triangle, lies at the heart of an area rich in ancient monasteries and archaeological sites. More obscure still is the narrow gauge railway that runs through the Kelani Valley from Colombo to Avissawella, a potential gateway to Kitulgala, Hatton and other parts of the Hill Country.

THE A1 TOWARDS KANDY AND KURUNEGALA

Kandy lies 120km northeast of Colombo along the A1 via the small towns of Gampaha, Ambepussa, Mawanella and Kadugannawa, and 100km east of Negombo (or Bandaranaike International Airport) along a relatively minor 40km road through Mirigama that connects with the A1 at Ambepussa. The first 60km of the A1 also form the start of the main route from Colombo to Kurunegala, Dambulla and Trincomalee, which branches northeast at Ambepussa to become the A6. In a private vehicle, the non-stop drive from Colombo (or Negombo) to Kandy (or Kurunegala) shouldn't take longer than 3 hours, depending on traffic, and there are also plenty of direct buses and trains between the two cities. Equally, there are plenty of opportunities to break up the trip. The most popular and established among these is Pinnawala and its famous elephant orphanage, which lie only 6km north of the A1. Heading more off the beaten track, the little-visited Horagolla National Park provides a great introduction to Sri Lanka's forest birds, while Utuwankanda Hill and Bible Rock near Mawanella form attractive goals for short hikes, and history buffs might consider a diversion to the sprawling Pilikutuwa Rajamaha Temple, the rather more compact dagoba and archaeological museum at Dedigama, or the ruined 16th-century Balana Fort near Kadugannawa.

GAMPAHA Best known as the site of the Henarathgoda Botanical Gardens, Gampaha (literally 'Five Villages') is a well-equipped town of 10,000 inhabitants situated just off the Kandy Road 28km inland of Colombo. The surrounding area was an important cinnamon-harvesting centre along the old Kandy Road back in the Portuguese and Dutch eras, but Gampaha – originally known as Henarathgoda – was established only after 1828, when a Catholic church dedicated to St Sebastian was constructed at nearby Moragoda. In 1866, Henarathgoda became the site of one of the initial trio of railway stations along the 60km track between Colombo

Fort and Ambepussa. A year later, the first rubber plantation in South Asia was established in what later became the botanical garden.

Getting there and away Gampaha is easily visited as a day trip out of Colombo or Negombo, or *en route* from either to destinations further inland. By road, the town centre stands about 2km north of Yakkala Junction, 30km from Colombo on the A1 to Kandy. Gampaha lies along more than ten different bus routes running out of the capital, and it is also connected to Negombo, 30km to the northwest, by regular buses. Gampaha is a major railway station and more than 40 trains daily in either direction stop here on various lines running north and east from Colombo Fort. The trip takes less than 1 hour.

What to see and do The two oldest buildings in the vicinity of Gampaha are St Sebastian's Church, which still stands in Moragoda 2km to the south of town, and the original Henarathgoda Old Railway Station, which is fenced off a couple of minutes' walk from its expanded 1926 modern counterpart, right next to the bus station.

Henarathgoda Botanical Gardens [map, page 74] \ 033 222 2316; w botanicgardens.gov.lk; ⊕ 07.30–17.00; entrance US$10) One of five botanical gardens in Sri Lanka, Henarathgoda started life as the first rubber nursery and plantation established in South Asia. Rubber seedlings smuggled out of Brazil and nurtured at Kew Gardens were planted at Henarathgoda in 1867 and blossomed 13 years later to form the founding stock of all other such plantations not only in Sri Lanka but also in Malaysia, Indonesia and India. Later expanded and diversified to become a 17ha botanical garden, Henarathgoda now also incorporates an orchid garden, a fernery (where the toilets are hidden), a Japanese garden, and several ponds fed by the Attanagalu River as it courses along the southern boundary. The first rubber tree planted in Sri Lanka can still be seen, as can several other exotic trees planted in the 19th century. The toque macaque, purple-faced langur and giant squirrel are among the most conspicuous of 17 known mammal species, while the bird checklist of 68 species includes the endemic Sri Lankan hanging parrot and crimson-fronted barbet along with various kingfishers and bee-eaters. Overall, it's a pleasant enough spot for a stroll, but the hefty foreigners' entrance fee is difficult to justify. The gardens lie about 1km west of the town centre and plenty of tuktuks are available to take you there.

Pilikutuwa Temple [map, page 74] Sprawling across a lushly forested rocky outcrop 5km southeast of Gampaha, this ancient 100ha monastery dates back to the reign of King Devanampiya Tissa, as documented by several Brahmi rock inscriptions from the 3rd century BC. Though still an active monastery, the complex has a tangled jungle setting, and its collection of 99 drip-ledged kuti caves is among the largest in the country. The main cave temple and vestibule includes some fine Kandyan-era paintings. Look out for a rare depiction of four nuns (despite their butch appearance, the dress covering both shoulders indicates their gender), as well as an oddly Egyptian-looking bodhisattva flanked by a group of blue-robed women. Pilikutuwa's proximity to Colombo has led to two unexpected and possibly unique features with European associations. These are a Dutch-era wooden bridge that spans a subterranean waterway between two caves, and an intriguing not quite life-size painting of two Portuguese soldiers – draped in green and brandishing cutlasses – that guards the entrance to the main image house. Another point of interest is a chart showing the 12 Buddhist astrological signs on an arched wooden roof above the main door. To get to Pilikutuwa, branch east from the A1 at Miriswatta, then drive east for about 4.5km until you see the signpost to your left just before the village of Buthpitiya. Buses between Gampaha and Kindiriwela run past this signposted junction, from where it's a 1km walk or tuktuk ride to the temple.

HORAGOLLA NATIONAL PARK [map, page 74] (⊕ *06.30–18.00; entrance US$10 pp plus 12% tax*) Proclaimed as a wildlife sanctuary in 1973 and upgraded to become Sri Lanka's smallest national park in 2004, Horagolla protects a 13ha patch of dense evergreen forest named after the hora tree *Dipterocarpus zeylanicus*, an endemic hardwood that can grow to be 60m tall. Although small mammals such as giant flying squirrel and Sri Lankan spotted chevrotain are present, the park is primarily of interest for its forest birdlife, which includes several endemic and localised species, among them Sri Lankan hanging parrot, Layard's parakeet, Oriental dwarf kingfisher, Sri Lanka grey hornbill, yellow-fronted barbet and black-capped bulbul. It also harbours an interesting selection of butterflies. Allow at least 2 hours to explore the roughly 5km network of trails that runs through the park.

Horagolla National Park is easily visited as a day trip from Colombo or Negombo, or *en route* from either of them to Kandy. The park entrance is 1.5km by road from Nittambuwa, a small town straddling the A1 to Kandy 40km inland of Colombo. Coming from the direction of Colombo, turn left on to the Veyangoda Road at Nittambuwa, follow it for 1km, then turn left on to the Pinnagolla Road and you'll see the entrance gate to your left after a few hundred metres. Coming from Negombo, it's about 32km via Veyangoda, turning right on to the Pinnagolla Road 1km before you reach Nittambuwa. Using public transport, any bus headed in the direction of Kandy can drop you at Nittambuwa, or you could catch any of 40-plus trains daily between Colombo Fort and Veyangoda, from where plenty of tuktuks are available for the last 4km to the park entrance.

AMBEPUSSA The small but significant junction town of Ambepussa straddles the A1 some 60km inland of Colombo, only 2km past the intersection with the most direct road coming from Negombo, and right where the A6 branches northeast to Kurunegala and Trincomalee. It also has some claim to historical fame as the inland terminal of the country's maiden rail voyage, a ten-carriage train that steamed out of Colombo Fort on 2 October 1865 and ended its journey at a then newly built station about 5km west of the present-day junction of the A1 and A6. Ambepussa is also the site of the roadside Heritage Ambepussa Hotel (*formerly Ambepussa Resthouse;* \ *035 493 3084*), which is Sri Lanka's oldest purpose-built hostelry, comprising an English-style bungalow with chubby columns constructed in 1828 when Sir Edward Barnes was opening up the interior with roads, and a popular place to stop for a snack or lunch between Colombo and Kandy or Dambulla.

DEDIGAMA The birthplace of Parakramabahu I, Dedigama formed part of the regional Dakkhinadesa Kingdom and served as the capital of some of its rulers. Its most famous landmark, built by Parakramabahu to mark the exact spot of his birth, is the Suthigara Dagoba, an unusual flat-topped construction that stands 15m high and has a diameter of 80m. The adjacent **Dedigama Archaeological Museum** [map, page 74] (⊕ *045 222 3035; ⊕ 08.00–16.00; no photography*) was established in 1954 to display a wealth of items discovered during excavations of the dagoba's ten relic chambers. These include a fine gold Buddha and some exquisite bronze miniatures of bodhisattva figures and Hindu goddesses. There's also a copy of the unique Eth Pahana (Elephant Lamp), the original of which was unearthed here but is now displayed in the National Museum in Colombo. The dominant figure of this rather ingenious bronze – an elephant ridden by a Hindu goddess – serves as a reservoir that releases oil through its penis into the receptacle below when a gauge in its feet detects the burning liquid has dropped below a certain level.

The museum also incorporates some tantalising displays about rock art sites dotted around the Kegalle District. The most important of these, situated around 5km southwest of Dedigama via Menikkadawara, is Dorawaka, where an isolated cave has been created by two massive rectangular rocks that lean in on each other. First excavated in the 1940s, Dorawaka shows signs of human habitation dating back more than 8,000 years, and its walls are inscribed with Neolithic engravings of animals (possibly elephants or cows), as well as a very ancient Brahmi script that incorporates several mysterious characters unknown from elsewhere in Sri Lanka.

PINNAWALA Set on the east bank of the shallow and meandering Maha River, Pinnawala is the most established tourist focus between Colombo and Kandy, thanks to the presence of the popular but controversial Pinnawala Elephant Orphanage and its captive herd of 90-odd elephants. The village is also home to a few newer and less well-known but similarly contrived tourist attractions, most of which are elephant-related and feel rather unedifying compared with the experience of seeing these magnificent creatures in their wild state. Most organised tours stop for a couple of hours at Pinnawala *en route* between Colombo and Kandy or Dambulla, but it is also possible to stay overnight, or to visit as a day trip out of Colombo or Kandy. Aim to be here between 10.00 and noon or 14.00 and 16.00, when the orphanage's elephants are released from their confines and walked through the village to a pretty bathing spot on the Maha River.

Getting there and away Pinnawala and its elephant orphanage lie alongside the Rambukkana Road about 6km north of the A1. The junction is clearly signposted 80km northeast of Colombo, 35km west of Kandy, and 3km east of the substantial town of Kegalle. Coming by public transport, any bus heading between Colombo and Kandy can drop you at Kegalle, from where you can pick up another bus to Rambukkana and ask to be dropped at Pinnawala. By rail, the closest station is Rambukkana, which is serviced by around 20 trains from Colombo daily (typically around 2½ hours) and ten from Kandy (around 1½ hours). From Rambukkana, you could either bus or charter a tuktuk for the 3.5km drive to Pinnawala.

Where to stay, eat and drink   *Map, page 148*

Moderate

Hotel Elephant Park (14 rooms) \035 226 6171; m 0776 275215; e pinn@sltnet.lk; w hotelelephantpark.com. This pleasant modern hotel overlooking the elephant bathing spot has large rooms with AC & cable TV. Superior rooms are larger and have a direct view over the bathing pool from their private balcony. There are also great views from the restaurant. *From US$48/55 sgl/dbl B&B.* **$$$**

Budget

Suwani Pinnawala Homestay (3 rooms) m 0717 272709. This likeable small guesthouse opposite the elephant orphanage has simple but clean rooms with fan, net & free Wi-Fi access. *US$30 dbl.* **$$**

Greenland Guesthouse (10 rooms) \035 226 5668; m 0773 316979; e pinnawala@ msn.com; w greenlandguest.com. Situated alongside the side road connecting the elephant orphanage to the bathing spot, this guesthouse has comfortable rooms with AC or fan, cable TV & private balcony. A restaurant serves adequate Sri Lankan & Western fare. *US$30/40 dbl with fan/ AC.* **$$**

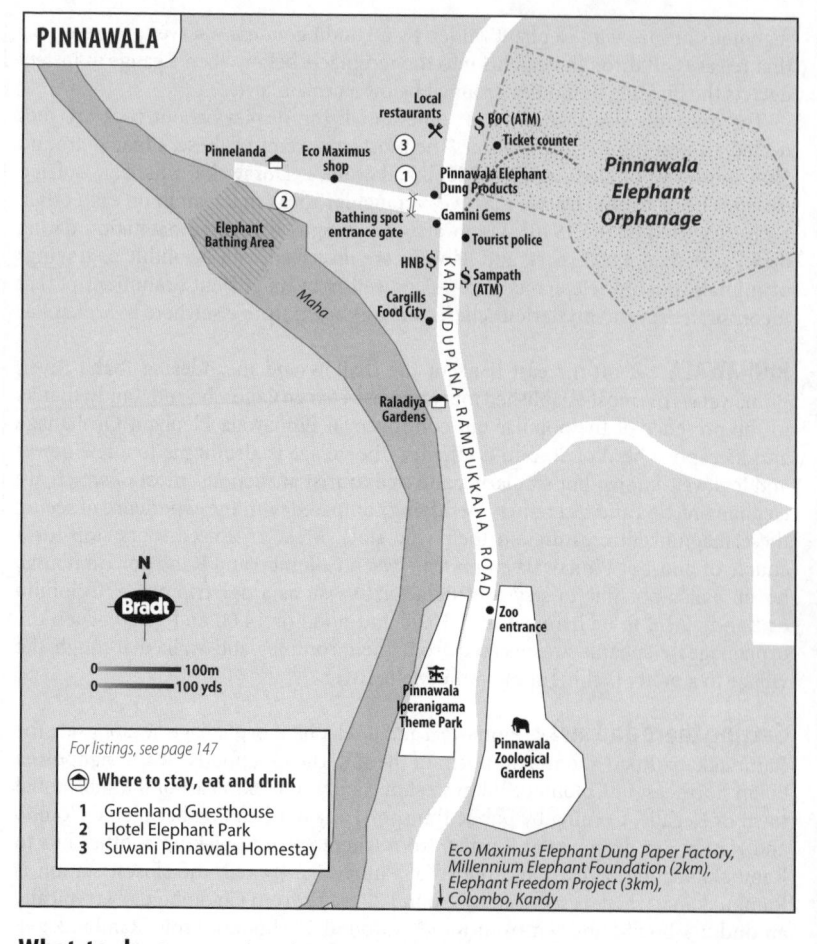

PINNAWALA

Local restaurants
BOC (ATM)
Ticket counter
Pinnelanda
Eco Maximus shop
③
①
Pinnawala Elephant Dung Products
Gamini Gems
②
Bathing spot entrance gate
Tourist police
Elephant Bathing Area
HNB $
Sampath (ATM)
Cargills Food City
Pinnawala Elephant Orphanage

Maha

KARANDUPANA-RAMBUKKANA ROAD

Raladiya Gardens

N

Bradt

Zoo entrance

0 — 100m
0 — 100 yds

Pinnawala Iperanigama Theme Park

For listings, see page 147

⊖ **Where to stay, eat and drink**
1 Greenland Guesthouse
2 Hotel Elephant Park
3 Suwani Pinnawala Homestay

Pinnawala Zoological Gardens

Eco Maximus Elephant Dung Paper Factory,
Millennium Elephant Foundation (2km),
Elephant Freedom Project (3km),
↓ Colombo, Kandy

What to do Sites are listed below starting with the main Pinnawala Elephant Orphanage in the north then working back south towards the junction with the A1. In addition, several spice and herb gardens are open to visitors along the 6km feeder road to Pinnawala.

Pinnawala Elephant Orphanage (📞 035 226 6116; e *zoosl@slt.lk*; w *nationalzoo.gov.lk/elephantorphanage*; ⏱ 08.30–18.00, feeding times 09.15, 13.15 & 17.00; entrance US$17 pp, with reductions for children & SAARC country residents) Set on a 10ha former coconut plantation, Pinnawala Elephant Orphanage was established in 1975 to shelter and care for five young elephants abandoned by their mothers or orphaned. It has since established itself as one of the most popular tourist attractions in the Sri Lankan interior, offering a thrilling opportunity to get up close to the world's second-largest land mammal (exceeded in bulk only by its African counterpart). A popular time to visit is when the young elephants are being fed, or when the whole herd troops eagerly through the village, guided by a team of green-uniformed mahouts, to a wonderfully scenic bathing spot on the forest-fringed Maha River (bathing times are 10.00–noon and 14.00–16.00). This pool lies about 300m outside the orphanage, and can be viewed from the balcony of

PINNAWALA: ORPHANAGE OR ZOO?

Pinnawala has attracted considerable controversy in recent years and is now excluded from the itineraries of several more ecologically aware operators. The reason for this is that, while the orphanage pursued its original aim until 1995, hand-rearing a steady stream of new arrivals and using older elephants as substitute family members, it has since mutated into something closer to a zoo, or at least a breeding centre for captive elephants. Today, around two-thirds of Pinnawala's 93 elephants – the world's largest captive herd – were born on site, and no attempt has been made to introduce any animals reared there back into the wild. Furthermore, a report compiled by the highly regarded animal welfare organisation Born Free (w *bornfree.org.uk*) cited several unethical practices, including the training of young elephants with a sharp spike known as an ankus, the chaining up of potentially aggressive male elephants during 'musth' and causing wounds to their legs, allowing the animals to be used as photo props to bring in tourist revenue, and the transfer of several individual elephants to private collections, zoos or temples offering far lower standards of care. Born Free concluded that Pinnawala 'is certainly much better than many captive elephant facilities in Asia' but that it nevertheless fails when it comes to 'putting the welfare and care of the animals as its highest priority', instead making many decisions based on 'the convenience of the management, or for the benefit of tourists, the local tourist industry, and the captive animal industry'.

the Elephant Park or neighbouring Pinnalanda Hotels, but do note that foreigners without an admission ticket are forbidden entrance to the lane leading to these two hotels between sunrise and 16.00, when the elephants return home for the night.

Pinnawala Zoological Gardens (◊ 035 226 6116; e *zoosl@slt.lk*; w *nationalzoo. gov.lk/pinnawalazoo*; ⊕ 08.30–18.00; entrance US$7 per adult) An extension of the elephant orphanage 500m to its north, Pinnawala Zoo opened in April 2015 but still feels like something of a work in progress. It is a conceptually admirable establishment insofar as animals are housed in large open enclosures typical of modern European zoos, but at the time of research it houses a very limited range of wildlife – leopards, a few species of deer and monkey, a children's zoo with donkeys, ducks and the like – and seems unrealistically overpriced for foreigners.

Pinnawala Iperanigama Theme Park (◊ 035 226 2288; e *iperanigama@ gmail.com*; ⊕ 08.30–18.00; entrance US$6 per adult) Strung out along the banks of the Maha River on the opposite side of the main road to the zoo, this new 2ha open-air museum is intended to replicate a traditional 18th-century Sinhalese village. Exhibits range from a village headman's and farmer's house to a traditional healer's practice, a blacksmith's workshop, a small Buddhist temple and a traditional coffee house. The entrance fee includes an informative guided tour, which takes up to 1 hour.

Millennium Elephant Foundation (◊ 035 226 3377; e *millenniumelephantfoundation@gmail.com*; w *millenniumelephantfoundation. com*; ⊕ 08.30–16.00; entrance US$7 per adult, elephant rides US$14) As with the more famous government orphanage 3km to its north, this private foundation, founded in 1999, gets mixed feedback. Though it's not quite an orphanage, the half-dozen adult elephants to which it provides sanctuary are all former working animals whose owners could no longer afford their upkeep. It also allows for a more direct interaction with the animals, as visitors get to feed, wash or walk with the elderly pachyderms, and can also go on a bareback elephant ride for a small fee. Despite this, the elephants spend much of their time in chains, and the sanctuary feels quite cramped.

Eco Maximus Elephant Dung Paper Factory (✆ *011 238 2341*; w *ecomaximus. com*) Established in 1999, this eco-friendly company specialises in manufacturing elephant-dung paper, an attractively fibrous and rough-hewn – and perfectly sanitary – product whose colour and texture depend on the food consumed. Eco Maximus has earned several awards for its dedication to social entrepreneurship and environmentalism, and its innovative range of products ranges from notebooks and other stationery to jewellery and miniature elephant sculptures. The workshop stands next to the Millennium Elephant Foundation and visits are incorporated into the ticket price. Products can also be bought at the Eco Maximus shop on the side road connecting the Pinnawala Elephant Orphanage to the bathing pool.

Elephant Freedom Project (w *volunteersatwork.org*) Generally regarded to be the most ethical and rewarding of the various elephant-related concerns around Pinnawala, the Elephant Freedom Project offers visitors the opportunity to spend a full day accompanying, grooming and feeding one of two elderly female elephants to which it provides sanctuary. This costs US$100 per person per day, numbers are strictly limited, and advance booking must be made on the website. Overnight accommodation costs an additional US$20 per night.

MAWANELLA The last major town passed through by Kandy-bound travellers before the A1 starts its ascent into Hill Country, Mawanella is also flanked by two striking natural landmarks: Utuwankanda Hill and Bible Rock. The town is strongly associated with Deekirikevage Saradiel, the so-called Robin Hood of Sri Lanka (see box, opposite).

Getting there and away Mawanella straddles the A1 13km east of Kegalle and 9km past Pinnawala Junction. Any bus travelling between Colombo and Kandy can drop you here. Tuktuks are available to travel from town to the base of Utuwankanda Hill or Bible Rock.

What to see and do Mawanella doesn't have much to offer tourists, its only notable landmark, situated alongside the A1 as it passes through town, being a conspicuous memorial to Constable Sabhan and the other victims of the two raids that took place here in 1864. The bridge spanning the Maha River is a good place to look for giant flying foxes, which hang head down from riverside tree branches like giant black fruit. Out of town, the nearby Utuwankanda Hill and more distant Bible Rock both form worthwhile goals for scenic walks.

Utuwankanda Also known as Castle Rock, Utuwankanda is a distinctive 430m-high hill whose prominent rocky pinnacle, rising 3km northwest of Mawanella, looks remarkably like a manmade fortress from a distance. Its eastern base can be reached along a 1.5km dirt feeder road that runs north from the A1 about 2.5km west of Mawanella. As you approach the hill, you'll see a quirky little

THE ROBIN HOOD OF SRI LANKA

Deekirikevage Saradiel was born in Mawanella in 1832, and used the rocky caves of nearby Utuwankanda as a hideout from where he and his heavily armed gang preyed on wealthy carriage passengers travelling between Colombo and Kandy in the 1850s and early 1860s. Despite his notorious standing with the authorities, Saradiel was something of a folk hero locally, not only because he routinely distributed his plunder to the poor and needy, but also because the main victims of his hold-ups were the detested colonial administration and its lackeys. Although he was arrested for robbery or murder on several occasions, Saradiel repeatedly managed to escape before any punitive action was taken.

His last lucky break occurred on 17 March 1864, when a posse led by Special Constable George van Haght surrounded him in his mother's house in Mawanella. Saradiel and his right-hand man Mammala Marikkar came out guns blazing, killing van Haght and his father-in-law, Christian Appu, and wounding three other police officers, before they fled the scene. Only four days later, on 21 March 1864, the two highwaymen were once again apprehended in Mawanella, leading to a shoot-out, during which Constable Tuan Sabhan became the first native Sri Lankan policemen to be killed in the line of duty. This time, however, Saradiel and Marikkar were captured and taken under military escort to Kandy, where they were tried for and found guilty of murder, to be hanged at Gallows Hill on 7 May 1864.

theme park called Saradiel Village Resort (m *0722 220308*; w *robinhoodofceylon. com*; *entrance US$1.50*) to your right. Opposite this, a short but steep path to the left leads after 30–45 minutes to the open summit, which offers spectacular views over the surrounding countryside, though the rocky pinnacle is difficult to scale without local guidance. You'll need a guide to locate the caves where Saradiel and his gang once hid out.

Bible Rock   Known locally as Bathalegala, this striking flat-topped granite outcrop, which rises to an elevation of 670m about 8km south of Mawanella, is named for its rather tenuous resemblance to an open book on a lectern. Bible Rock is distantly visible from several points along the Kandy Road, but to see it up close, you need to divert south from the A1 at Mawanella and continue for 10km to the small junction village of Gevilipitiya. To climb to the top of the rock, which offers tremendous views in all directions, turn west on to the Hettimulla Road at Gevilipitiya, then continue for another 2.5km to Hathgampala Temple, where a 2.5km track to Bathalegala is clearly signposted to the right. The first few hundred metres of this track are motorable, but the last part of the ascent is quite steep and entails climbing some rock-hewn steps. Regular buses connect Mawanella to Gevilipitiya, but public transport from there to Hathgampala is infrequent, so you may need to walk or catch a tuktuk. Allow up to 3 hours for the round hike from Hathgampala.

KADUGANNAWA   The 10km ascent along the A1 from Mawanella to Kadugannawa is one of the most spectacular in the county, offering wonderful views across to Bible Rock as the sweltering coastal lowland air gives way to the more rarefied atmosphere of the highlands around Kandy. Most travellers pass through without stopping, but the town does boast a few minor landmarks including the 19th-century Dawson

7

Tower and Kadugannawa Ambalama, the tourist-friendly Kadugannawa Tea Factory, and the recently opened National Railway Museum.

Getting there and away Straddling the A1 exactly 100km inland of Colombo and 17km west of Kandy, Kadugannawa is where the main road to Kandy and railway line reconverge for the first time after having parted ways at the outskirts of Colombo. Any bus between Colombo and Kandy can drop you here, and most trains between the two towns stop at Kadugannawa railway station.

What to see and do All but two of the sites described below flank a 3km stretch of the A1 west of Kadugannawa railway station, and are listed in the same sequence that you'd pass them coming by road from the direction of Kandy. The exceptions are Balana Fort, a 6km drive north of the railway station, and Bulumgala Rock overlooking Kadugannawa Pass.

Kadugannawa Ambalama Built during the early 19th-century reign of King Sri Vikrama Rajasinha, this excellent example of a Kandyan-era ambalama (an open-sided wayside rest for travelling pilgrims and traders) was faithfully restored by the Department of Archaeology in 2009 and has been repaired again after being hit by a truck in 2011. Coming from Colombo, it stands on the left side of the A1 about 1km before the largest hairpin curve in the Kadugannawa Pass.

Kadugannawa Tea Factory (✆ *081 257 1350;* e *kadugannawatea@gmail.com;* w *kadugannawatea.com;* ⊕ *09.30–17.30 Mon–Fri*) Situated on the right side of the A1 just after you complete the hairpin curve referred to above, this small tea factory offers free tours, including a complementary cup of homegrown tea with jaggery, and it also has a shop where you can buy a range of different teas processed on site.

Dawson Tower This 40m-high tower was constructed in 1932 in memory of Captain W F Dawson, the engineer who was chiefly responsible for designing and constructing the modern road between Colombo and Kandy, but died in 1929 before it could be completed. Coming from Colombo, it stands like a misplaced lighthouse on the right side of the A1 about 100m before the central Ceypetco filling station. Inside, a spiral case of 110 wooden steps leads to the top, which offers fabulous views over the town and its environs.

National Railway Museum (⊕ *09.00–16.00; entrance US$3.50*) Occupying a former goods shed next to the railway station, this museum was relocated from Colombo to Kadugannawa in December 2014 to mark the 150th anniversary of Sri Lanka's railway service. It focuses strongly on the early days of steam trains, but also has some more modern exhibits, as well as a short subtitled video presentation about the history of the country's railway network. A must-do for train buffs, it's probably a bit esoteric for more general visitors, especially at the difficult-to-justify admission fee.

Bulumgala Rock This massive granite outcrop on the escarpment overlooking the Kadugannawa Pass provides a good pretext for an extended leg stretch on the outskirts of town. It was used as a lookout point in the colonial era, and the views across the road pass to the lowlands below remain stupendous. To get here from Kadugannawa, head south along the Gampola Road (opposite the Ceypetco filling station) for about 1km, then follow a footpath to the right through a tea estate for about 3km.

Balana Fort Located on the Alagalla Hills north of Kadugannawa, the 16th-century Balana Fort was constructed to forewarn the Kandyan monarchy of any military advances made by the acquisitive Portuguese who controlled the lowlands running west towards Colombo. It played an important role stalling failed Portuguese campaigns to capture Kandy in 1594, 1603 and 1630. In 1638, the Portuguese captured Balana, but their plan to retreat to the fort when a fresh assault on Kandy met with yet another failure was thwarted by King Rajasinha II, whose army defeated them, with the loss of more than 4,000 lives, in the Battle of Gannoruwa. Balana Fort retained its role as the Watchtower of Kandy until the early 19th century, after which it fell into disuse. The little-visited but atmospherically overgrown ruin still offers the all-encompassing views that made it so strategically important 500 years ago. To get here from Kadugannawa, follow the Pottepitiya Road, which starts immediately behind the railway station, as it curves northeast then northwest out of town. Turn left after 4.5km, then take the fork to the right after another 1.25km. The fort stands on the left side of the road about 800m past this second junction.

KURUNEGALA AND SURROUNDS

The capital of Northwestern Province and main road gateway to the ancient cities of the Cultural Triangle, Kurunegala doesn't lack for historical pedigree itself, having served as one of several short-lived capitals of the Dambadeniya Kingdom in the early 14th century. The town's outstanding feature is the enormous rock formations – named after the animals whose shapes they resemble, for instance Ibbagala (Tortoise Rock), Elugala (Goat Rock) and Wanduragala (Monkey Rock) – that dominate its northeastern skyline. Most impressive among these is Athugala – Elephant Rock – a gigantic 320m-high whaleback topped by a temple and large white Buddha statue. Sometimes spelt Ethagala, this imposing boulder overlooks Lake Kurunegala, a pretty 40ha reservoir that runs northward from the town centre and is lined by several budget hotels and restaurants. According to the 2011 census, Kurunegala supports a population of roughly 30,000, but it comes across as far larger and more urbanised than this figure suggests. It is also very much a town of two halves. The attractively leafy old administrative suburb to the north of the lake stands in sedate contrast to the rather charmless town centre, with its bustling sidewalks and hooting traffic. For all that, budget travellers escaping Colombo might find that this unpretentious and prettily located town makes for a surprisingly agreeable first overnight stop *en route* to more touristy centres such as Anuradhapura, Dambulla or Sigiriya. Kurunegala is also a useful springboard for day trips to several little-visited but worthwhile archaeological sites, notably the secular hilltop sentinels of Dambadeniya and Yapahuwa, both of which preceded Kurunegala as the capital of Dambadeniya, and the Buddhist shrines at Ridee and Arankele.

HISTORY Kurunegala is probably synonymous with Hastinapura, an ancient city founded by followers of Vijaya who migrated to Sri Lanka from India in the 5th century BC. Its modern name is generally said to derive from the compound Tamil–Sinhala 'Kurunai-gala', meaning 'Elephant Rock', but it might also derive from Kurujangala, the Indian region from where its ancient founders hailed. The area around Kurunegala was the main centre of Sinhalese power during the Dambadeniya period, which was bookended by the fall of Polonnaruwa in 1220 and relocation of the capital to Gampola in the 1340s. Three sites around Kurunegala served as capital during this period, all of them rocky outcrops fortified as citadels. The first, 30km southwest of

Kurunegala, was Dambadeniya, established by Vijayabahu III c1232, and also used by his son Parakramabahu II. In 1272, Bhuvanaikabahu I, following the assassination of his brother and predecessor Vijayabahu IV, relocated his capital to Yapahuwa, 45km north of Kurunegala. Yapahuwa was abandoned in 1284 following the death of King Bhuvanaikabahu and capture of the tooth relic by Pandyan invaders. Following a brief revival of the former capital Polonnaruwa, Bhuvanaikabahu II relocated the capital to Kurunegala in 1293. In more modern times, Kurunegala received a major economic boost when the railway line from Colombo reached it in 1894. It is now a bustling provincial capital set at the heart of a flourishing coconut industry.

GETTING THERE AND AWAY Kurunegala is one of the best-connected towns in Sri Lanka. Linked to Colombo Fort by a 94km railway line since 1894, it is a pivotal stop on all train services running further north or northeast, as well as being an important crossroads town served by regular buses in all directions.

By rail Kurunegala lies on the Northern line and is serviced by more than a dozen trains from Colombo Fort daily. There is also at least one direct connection daily north to/from Anuradhapura, Mannar and Jaffna, and northeast to Polonnaruwa, Batticaloa and Trincomalee. The main railway station lies 150m south of the Kandy Road, about 2km southeast of the clock tower. The secondary Muththettugala railway station, situated along the Dambulla Road about 1.5km out of town, is closer to the hotels on North Lake Road, but relatively few trains stop there.

By road Kurunegala lies about 90km by road from Colombo along the A1 and A6 via Ambepussa, and 70km inland of Negombo and Bandaranaike International Airport via Dambadeniya and Narammala. Either way, allow about 2 hours to drive through directly, or a bit longer if there's heavy traffic around the capital. Kurunegala is also an important route crossroads, situated along the main roads connecting Colombo to Dambulla, Sigiriya, Polonnaruwa, Trincomalee, Pasikuda and Batticaloa. It also lies on an important route north to Anuradhapura, Mannar and Jaffna, and it lies just 45km northwest of Kandy. As such, it is serviced by regular government and private buses to/from almost anywhere that's likely to be of interest to tourists, and all buses arrive at and leave from the central bus station 50m east of the railway station.

WHERE TO STAY *Map, oppposite*
Moderate

Littlemore Estate Bungalow (3 rooms) Pellandeniya, 7km northwest of town; m 0768 249350; f littlemoreestate. This tranquil boutique bungalow comprises a mock-colonial house set on a coconut plantation about 2.5km from Pellandeniya along a dirt road running southwest of the A10 just before St Anthony's Church. The stylish accommodation is complemented by obliging staff, excellent local buffets (*US$10 pp*), an infinity pool & a lovely garden alive with birdsong. *US$75 dbl B&B.* **$$$**

Kandyan Reach Hotel (40 rooms) Kandy Rd; 037 222 4218; e kandyanreachhotel@ gmail.com; w kandyanreach.com. Situated close to the railway station about 1km east of the

town centre, this modern hotel, built in 1997 but recently refurbished, is Kurunegala's finest central option. Large comfortable rooms come with AC, wooden floor, modern art & private balcony, & there's a good restaurant serving local & international cuisine. *US$62/82 sgl/dbl B&B.* **$$$**

Budget

Seasons Hotel (3 rooms) North Lake Rd; 037 222 3452; e diyadahara@sltnet.lk. This rather grandiose 3-storey building stands opposite the lakeshore Diya Dahara Restaurant & falls under the same management. It's a peaceful set-up & the spacious modern rooms have AC & cable TV. Decent value. *US$29 dbl.* **$$**

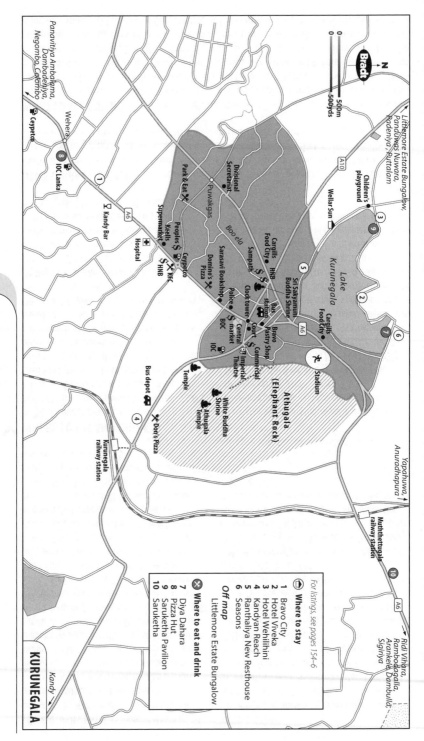

KURUNEGALA

For listings, see pages 154–6

Where to stay
1 Bravo City
2 Hotel Viveka
3 Hotel Wehilihini
4 Kandyan Reach
5 Ranthaliya New Resthouse
6 Seasons

Off map
Littlemore Estate Bungalow

Where to eat and drink
7 Diya Dahara
8 Pizza Hut
9 Saruketha Pavilion
10 Saruketha

Panavitiya Ambalama,
Dambadeniya,
Negombo, Colombo

Littlemore Estate Bungalow,
Panduwas Nuwara,
Padeniya, Puttalam

Yapahuwa,
Anuradhapura

Ridi Vihara,
Rambodagalla,
Arankele, Dambulla,
Sigiriya

Wehera

Ceypetco

IOC Lanka

Kandy Bar

Hospital

Park & Eat

Divisional
Secretariat

Puwakgas

Peoples
Supermarket

Keells

Ceypetco

KFC

HNB

Cargills
Food City

Sampath

HNB

Sarasavi Bookshop

Domino's
Pizza

Police

Clock tower

Bus
station

Sri Sakyamuni Buddha Shrine

Bravo
Pastry Shop

Cargills
Food City

BOC

Court

Central
market

Commercial

IOC

Imperial
Theatre

Temple

White Buddha
Shrine

Athugala
Temple

Athugala
(Elephant Rock)

Stadium

Lake
Kurunegala

Wellar Sun

Children's
playground

Bus depot

Don's Pizza

Kurunegala
railway station

Muththettugala
railway station

Kandy

Boo ela

N

Bradt

0 500m
0 500yds

🏠 **Bravo City Hotel** (5 rooms) Colombo Rd; 📞 037 223 1800; m 0777 937677; e info@bravocityhotels.com; w bravocityhotels.com. Set above an affiliated restaurant & bakery, this medium-rise doesn't have the most convenient location, 1.5km from the town centre along the Colombo Rd, and the traffic can also be quite noisy, but the modern rooms with AC, cable TV & Wi-Fi are comfortable & well maintained. *US$33 dbl.* **$$**

🏠 **Ranthaliya New Resthouse** (10 rooms) South Lake Rd; 📞 037 222 2298; e ranthaliyarest@gmail.com; w kurunegalaranthaliyaresthouse.com. Set on a low rise on the west shore of the lake, this creaky old resthouse offers wonderful views across the water to the rocky hills further east from the balcony restaurant & bar. Less praiseworthy are the tired-looking rooms, which come with cable TV & fan or AC, but seem quite pricey compared with the competition. *US$23 dbl with fan, US$38 with AC.* **$$**

Shoestring

❋ 🏠 **Hotel Viveka** (5 rooms) North Lake Rd; 📞 037 222 2897; e vivekahotel64@sltnet.lk; w hotelviveka.com. Set in a restored 1890s villa, this low-key but attractive hotel has a wide lake-facing veranda, restaurant serving Sri Lankan & Chinese dishes in the US$3–4 bracket & bar serving inexpensive beers. The tall-ceilinged rooms are furnished in period style & decorated with old black-&-white photos, & come with cable TV & choice of fan or AC. Great value. *US$13.50 dbl with fan, US$20.50 with AC.* **$**

🏠 **Hotel Wehilihini** (6 rooms) North Lake Rd; 📞 037 223 3505; m 0776 447096. A definite step down from the Viveka, this is still a very acceptable shoestring option with gardens overlooking the lake & clean rooms with fan (but no AC) & cable TV. *US$17 dbl.* **$**

🍴 **WHERE TO EAT AND DRINK** *Map, page 155*

❋ 🍴 **Saruketha Pavilion** North Lake Rd; 📞 037 223 3869; w saruketha.lk; ⏰ 09.00–23.00. This newer & more central branch of the out-of-town Saruketha is set in attractive gardens on a peninsula jutting into the lily-covered northwest corner of Lake Kurunegala. You can eat in the rather stylish interior, on the wide terrace, or under the lakeshore trees. A varied selection of Western, Chinese & Sri Lankan dishes mostly costs around US$5–6. Alcohol is served. **$$$**

🍴 **Diya Dahara Restaurant** North Lake Rd; 📞 037 222 3452; e diyadahara@sltnet.lk; ⏰ 07.00–23.00. This well-established eatery on the northeast lakeshore lacks the ambience of the Saruketha Pavilion, but there's a varied menu of grills & local dishes in the US$5-6 range,

& the choice of sitting indoors or at the lake. The lunchtime buffet comes highly recommended (*US$7 pp*) and alcohol is served. **$$$**

🍴 **Saruketha Restaurant** 3km along the Dambulla Rd; 📞 037 469 1123; m 0713 950022; e info@saruketha.lk; w saruketha.lk; ⏰ 09.00–21.00. Set among the paddy fields & bamboo 500m past the Muththettugala railway station, this out-of-town garden restaurant is popular with tour groups for its tasty local buffets & international à la carte selection. Mains in the US$5–6 range. **$$$**

🍴 **Pizza Hut** Colombo Rd; w pizzahut.lk; ⏰ 11.00–23.00. Situated about 2km along the Colombo Rd, this branch of the international chain has an AC interior & a varied selection of pizzas for US$3–4. **$$**

OTHER PRACTICALITIES All the main banks have branches in Kurunegala, including the Commercial Bank, which is on the Kandy Road about 200m east of the clock tower, and has an ATM outside. The best supermarket is the Cargills Food City on the Narammala Road 500m west of the clock tower.

WHAT TO SEE AND DO Several relatively off-the-beaten-track archaeological sites and temples lie within easy striking distance of Kurunegala. The most spectacular, and only one to charge an admission fee, is the rock fortress of Yapahuwa, which resembles a scaled-down version of Sigiriya but without the masses of tourists. The most inherently interesting Buddhist temple in the area is Ridi Vihara, which also has the advantage of being easy to reach on public transport. That said, the more remote and relatively inaccessible Arankele Monastery, brooding deep within the jungle-swathed lower slopes of Mount Dolukanda, offers more of an immersion experience to those seeking a more extended walk in a stimulating natural environment. Aside from Yapahuwa, none of the sites described below charges admission fees, or has restrictive opening hours unless otherwise noted.

Around town Mount Athugala, on the northern outskirts of the town centre, can be ascended by car or on foot along a 2km road that switchbacks uphill from the Kandy Road 200m east of the clock tower and just before the Imperial Theatre. Up on top, Athugala Temple contains a replica of the Buddhapada on Adam's Peak, and there's a prominent 26m-high white Samadhi Buddha statue built between 1993 and 2012. The summit affords a magnificent view of the town, the lake and the surrounding countryside. The town's other significant attraction is Lake Kurunegala, whose construction is attributed to King Bhuvanaika Bahu II in the late 13th century. It is a lovely spot, especially when viewed from the west side with Athugala as a backdrop, and a footpath runs all the way around its 3.5km circumference, offering some good birding and the opportunity to stop for a meal or drink at the lakeside Saruketha Pavilion or Diya Dahara Restaurant.

Southwest of Kurunegala The two sites below both stand close to the main road connecting Kurunegala to Negombo and Bandaranaike International Airport. They could also be accessed by diverting northward from the A1 between Colombo and Kandy.

Panavitiya Ambalama [map, page 74] This fine example of a Kandyan-era wooden ambalama (wayside rest) was constructed in the 18th century along what was then the main road from Colombo to Anuradhapura. A sophisticated construction whose tiled roof is supported by 28 timber columns, it is unusual insofar as it resembles a tampita (stilted temple), though the elevated wooden base is supported not by columns or stilts, but by four large boulders. The inner pillars and upper rafters are adorned with intricate and beautifully executed Kandyan-era carvings depicting musicians, dancers, wrestlers and acrobats, along with various deities and a menagerie of creatures real and mythical. The junction village for Panavitiya is Metiyagane, which lies on the Negombo Road about 25km southwest of Kurunegala and 4km before Dambadeniya. From Metiyagane, follow the dirt Kasungama Road north for about 1.8km, then turn left and you'll see a small white dagoba to your right after another 1km. The ambalama is just 50m behind the dagoba.

Dambadeniya [map, page 74] Now little more than an overgrown village, the original capital of the Dambadeniya Kingdom lies about 30km southwest of Kurunegala along the main road to Negombo, where it is easily accessed by bus. Dambadeniya was chosen as the capital of King Vijayabahu III in c1232, but it is most strongly associated with his son and successor Parakramabahu II (r1234–69), an illustrious and long-serving monarch whose many achievements included the authorship of the *Kavsilumina*, a poetic epic that ranks among the greatest works of Sinhalese literature.

The royal palace at Dambadeniya is a hilltop citadel perched on a prominent 200m-high granite outcrop called Maligagala, 1.5km southeast of the modern town. Back in the days of Parakramabahu II, the base of the hill was protected by stone walls and a moat of which few traces remain. By contrast, the steep and easily defensible stone staircase that leads to the hilltop palace is still in good shape.

Having hauled yourself to the top, there's not a great deal to see archaeologically – a ruined palace courtyard, large bathing pool and boulder engraved with rock-hewn steps – but further excavations are under way, and the atmospheric jungle setting and spectacular views over the surrounding paddies and coconut plantations go a long way to justifying the climb.

Also of interest, only 300m from the town centre along the Maligagala Road, Dambadeniya Vijaya Sundara was founded by Vijayabahu III as a Dalada Maligawa to replace its abandoned counterpart in Polonnaruwa. The original stone base now supports an attractive double-storeyed Kandyan-era temple with a balconied exterior decorated with carved wooden columns and faded paintings that must date back several hundred years. As is so often the case, the temple complex is dotted with ancient columns, engraved stones and foundations of outbuildings. Outside the temple, a small site museum (⊕ *08.30–16.00; no photography*) displays a 13th-century bodhisattva sculpture and other artefacts of a similar vintage.

Northeast of Kurunegala The three sites described below are most easily visited from the main road running northeast from Kurunegala towards Dambulla. Ridi Vihara and the Rambodagalla Buddha could also be accessed via a northward diversion from the main road between Kurunegala and Kandy.

Arankele Forest Monastery [map, page 74] The ancient monastery lies at the forested base of Mount Dolukanda, the highest peak in this part of Sri Lanka at around 600m. According to local legend, this rocky crag is a massive fragment of Himalayan rubble carried across to Sri Lanka by Hanuman, and it also reputedly served as the hideout of the future King Silameghavanna, a rebellious royal sword-bearer who seized the throne after killing his predecessor and former employer Moggallana III in the early 7th century. Today, the isolated massif forms the centrepiece of a 20km² nature reserve that supports plenty of small to medium-sized mammals along with a prolific forest avifauna including Alexandrine parakeet, crested treeswift, crimson-fronted barbet, bar-winged flycatcher-shrike, Jerdon's leafbird, greater racquet-tailed drongo, white-rumped shama and Tickell's blue flycatcher.

The history of Arankele is shrouded in mystery. Some say it was founded in the 3rd century BC, others that it dates to the 6th century AD. Either way, it is unclear by what name the hermitage was known in its heyday (the name Arankele, a derivative of *arahant kale*, 'forest of the enlightened', in reference to the ascetic Pansukulika monks who lived there, was coined by outsiders). The oldest and most remote part of the still partially occupied monastery is a tiny built-up cave temple set below a massive protruding rock engraved with a drip-ledge and two lines of round holes that presumably once supported a wooden canopy. This is reached via a long straight meditation walkway running through the thick forest. A unique feature of the main monastic ruins at the start of the walkway is a cluster of low shelters, each comprising a massive horizontal granite slab supported by six standing megaliths – the purpose of these unusual structures is unknown but most likely they were some sort of meditation cell. The main ruins also incorporate the remains of a 550m² heated pool used for therapeutic purposes.

Arankele lies about 28km from Kurunegala, and can be reached by following the Dambulla Road out of town for 15km as far as Ibbagamuwa, where you need to turn left on to the Kumbukgete Road opposite the Food City Supermarket. Follow the Kumbukgete Road north for 8.5km, then turn left on to the Arankele Road, and right after another 500m, and continue north for 4km until you see the archaeological site signposted to your left. Using public transport, you'll have no problem finding a bus from Kurunegala or Dambulla as far as Ibbagamuwa, but most likely you'll need to charter a tuktuk from there.

Ridi Vihara [map, page 74] Situated 22km northeast of Kurunegala, Ridi Vihara (Silver Temple) legendarily dates to the 2nd-century BC reign of Dutugamunu, who built it around the silver mine that funded the construction of Anuradhapura's Ruwanweli Dagoba. According to this legend, the gold-plated Buddha statue – held in a casket adorned with swashbuckling carvings of Hindu goddesses – at the centre of the main cave temple is an original feature that marks the exact spot where the vein of silver ore was discovered, while the leftmost statue on the back wall is a contemporaneous image of Dutugamunu.

More recent features of the main cave temple – which resembles a scaled-down version of its more famous counterpart at Dambulla – includes a collection of Buddha statues, a well-preserved 8th-century moonstone, and an abundance of faded Kandyan-era wall and ceiling paintings. To the left of the main entrance, an uncharacteristically cheerful-looking 9m-long sleeping Buddha is set on a base inlaid rather incongruously with blue Delft ceramic tiles depicting rural Dutch activities and Biblical scenes – evidently a gift presented to the 18th-century Kandyan court which somehow ended up at Ridi. When you exit through the rightmost door, look behind the glass panel to your left and you'll see an extraordinary ivory 'Pancha Naari Getaya' (Knot of Five Maidens), a floral vase-shaped Hindu-style engraving which on closer inspection actually depicts a gymnastic formation of four bare-breasted women balancing on the hands of a fifth.

The suspicion that Ridi Vihara started life as a Hindu shrine is reinforced by the South Indian architecture of the small but perfectly formed Varakha Valandu (Jackfruit Treat) Temple situated just inside the entrance to the complex. Thought to date to the 11th century, this extended cave temple has a built-up exterior supported by six stone pillars. It was closed in 2016 in order that the Kandyan-era wall paintings could be restored by a team of specialists from the Department of Archaeology.

Ridi Vihara is most easily reached from the main road between Kurunegala and Dambulla. Coming from Kurunegala, follow the Dambulla road past Muththettugala railway station for 12km, then turn right on to the Dodangaslanda Road, follow that for 5km, turn right again, and continue for 2km to Ridigama village. From here, it's another 2km to Ridi Vihara along a feeder road signposted to the left. At least one bus per hour runs directly between Kurunegala and Ridigama, taking up to 45 minutes.

Rambodagalla Buddha [map, page 74] Easily tagged on to a visit to Ridi Vihara, the 20.5m high Rambodagalla Samadhi Buddha (w *samadhibuddhastatue. lk*) claims to be the tallest rock-hewn granite sculpture of its type anywhere in the world. It was carved between 2003 and 2014 to commemorate the destruction – by the Taliban, in 2001 – of a renowned pair of 4th- and 5th-century Buddha statues carved into a rock face in Afghanistan's Bamiyan Valley. It stands about 5km from Ridi Vihara along a clearly signposted road running south about halfway between the temple and Ridigama village.

Northwest of Kurunegala
The three sites described below all lie within striking distance of the main road from Kurunegala to Anuradhapura via Padeniya.

Panduvas Nuwara [map, page 74] Legend has it that Panduvas Nuwara (literally 'Panduvas's Town') dates back to the 5th century BC, when it served as the capital of King Panduvasudeva of Upatissa Nuwara, the ancient kingdom that preceded and eventually morphed into Anuradhapura. According to the same legend, Panduvasudeva also constructed several of the ponds around his erstwhile capital, making them the country's oldest artificial reservoir, while the ruined dagoba at Medagama Kanda, 3km to the southeast, was constructed as the tomb of Panduvasudeva's uncle and predecessor King Vijaya, the earliest Sinhalese monarch named in the *Mahavamsa*. Truth be told, there isn't much in the way of archaeological evidence to support Panduvas Nuwara's claims to pre-Buddhist antiquity; the ruins you see here today all date to the 12th century, when it was constructed as the capital of King Parakramabahu I prior to his capture of Polonnaruwa from the Pandyan interlopers, and it was also visited by King Nissanka Malla, who left one of his trademark inscriptions there.

The city Parakramabahu I constructed at Panduvas Nuwara is rather low key by comparison with his later and more aesthetically inspired work at Polonnaruwa, and much of it still awaits excavation, but the scale is impressive all the same. Before you explore the ruins, the small archaeological museum close to the entrance (⊕ *08.30–16.30 exc Tue*) is worth checking out both for its interpretive displays and to see some of the artefacts unearthed during excavations. South of the museum, a rhomboid 1.2km stone wall and now dry moat encloses a 10ha compound centred on the stone platform that supported the original two-storey wooden palace. Elsewhere, drifting further south, the vast and largely overgrown site incorporates three ruined temples marked by small or medium-sized dagobas, while the active Panduvas Nuwara Monastery 1km southeast of the palace ruins incorporates a restored Dalada Maligawa (Temple of the Tooth) dating to Parakramabahu I's time, as well as an attractive little Kandyan-era tampita (stilted temple). On foot, it's another 45-minute walk south from here to the jungle-bound Medagama Kanda Dagoba, which legendarily forms Sri Lanka's oldest royal grave.

Panduvas Nuwara stands 38km from Kurunegala and is most easily reached by following the Puttalam Road northeast for 22km to Wariyapola (4km before Padeniya), then turning left on to the Chilaw Road and continuing for 16km until you see the archaeological site and museum signposted to your left, just after a large school sports field. The museum stands about 100m from the main road and the rest of the archaeological site sprawls south from that. Using public transport, at least one bus hourly runs between Kurunegala and Chilaw, stopping on the main road almost alongside the museum.

Padeniya Temple [map, page 74] The small town of Padeniya, 26km northwest of Kurunegala at the junction of the roads to Puttalam and Anuradhapura, is the site of an unusual temple, possibly built in the 15th century, which combines features associated with the architecture of Gampola and Kandy with elements that suggest a Chinese influence. Set on a large boulder, the temple has a two-tiered tile and wood-strut roof supported by around 50 interior and exterior wood columns engraved in a manner that resembles the famous 14th-century Embekke Temple near Kandy. The front entrance consists of an ornate engraved wooden Kandyan door flanked on both sides by two large sculptures of Hindu deities alongside an unusual bare-chested dark-skinned midget. More striking still is the colourful frieze of toothy, floppy-lipped and rather oriental-looking seated lion sculptures that perch on top of all four sides of the outer wall. Padeniya Temple stands within the prominent wooded compound on the west side of the Y-junction of the Puttalam and Anuradhapura roads, and any bus heading between Kurunegala and either of these towns can drop you here.

Yapahuwa [map, page 74] (☉ *08.00–18.00; entrance US$7*) Probably the shortest lived of Sri Lanka's former capitals, but also one of the most spectacular, the rock fortress at Yapahuwa is reminiscent of Sigiriya in many respects, and while it may be smaller in scale, it is also less overrun with tourists and more tranquil as a consequence. Yapahuwa served as the seat of Bhuvanaikabahu I from 1271 until his death in 1283, and the hilltop citadel created by this beleaguered king displays a level of architectural ambition and aesthetic craftsmanship at odds both with its ephemeral fate and with the precarious state of the Sinhalese monarchy at the time. Yapahuwa's most impressive feature is the well-preserved ornamental stone stairway that climbs almost 100m from the base to the bald granite summit that once housed Bhuvanaikabahu's palace and the Temple of the Tooth. The stairs are flanked by some fine engravings and sculptures depicting a lively cast of deities, dwarves, entertainers and real and mythical creatures. Most famous among these is the Yapahuwa Lion, a Chinese-looking stone sculpture reproduced on the Rs10 banknote. Chinese ceramics unearthed at the site suggest that Bhuvanaikabahu maintained strong links with that country during his short reign. Little is known about the history of Yapahuwa after it was abandoned as capital, but it evidently continued as a monastery. Other features include a Kandyan-era wooden temple and cave temple at the base, and a small dagoba (about 3–4m high) and pond at the summit. The views from the top are stupendous.

One reason why Yapahuwa sees relatively few visitors is its remoteness from the other main sites of the Cultural Triangle. By road, the springboard village is Daladagama, which lies on the main road to Anuradhapura some 45km from Kurunegala. From Daladagama, it's a 9km drive east to Yapahuwa, passing Maho railway station about halfway. Using public transport, you could either get a bus between Kurunegala and Anuradhapura to drop you at Daladagama, or catch any train heading north from Colombo or Kurunegala (or indeed south from Anuradhapura, Jaffna, Mannar, Polonnaruwa or Trincomalee) and ask to be dropped at Maho, then cover the last stretch by tuktuk.

AVISSAWELLA AND THE KELANI VALLEY RAILWAY

Of special interest to train buffs, Avissawella – terminus of the 60km single-track Kelani Valley Line that runs inland from Colombo – is also a substantial town and potential springboard for bus travel on to Kitulgala, Ratnapura and elsewhere in the southwestern interior. The Kelani Valley Line was established in 1902 as part of a narrow-gauge line to service the rubber plantations around nearby Yatiyanthota, and it reopened in 1996 as a single-track broad-gauge line that was originally intended to continue to Ratnapura, but now stops at Avissawella. Though it is no longer a steam service, it remains non-electrified, and the diesel trains offer some fabulous views as they ascend the sharp curves slowly and with justified caution. The town itself is of limited interest, though the suburb of Seethawaka (or Sitawaka), 800m from the railway station, is said to be where Rama's wife Sita was held captive by King Ravana in prehistoric times. The legend is also alluded to in the name of the Seethawaka Wet Zone Botanical Garden, which recently opened 8km south of Avissawella on the Labugama Road.

GETTING THERE AND AWAY The most attractive way to travel to Avissawella, and most likely *raison d'être* for any tourist visit, is the Kelani Valley rail service. Up to four trains cover the route daily in either direction, taking around 2½–4 hours, depending on the specific service and which direction it is going. Unfortunately, for anybody thinking of visiting Avissawella as a return day trip from Colombo, the single track precludes trains from travelling simultaneously in opposite directions. So, because the line is aimed mainly at commuter traffic, it has been scheduled so that all trains headed inland from Colombo Fort leave between 16.10 and 20.00, while coast-bound trains from Avissawella depart between 04.55 and 12.35. So, in order to use the train, you are more or less forced to overnight in Avissawella before or after your trip, or to bus the 45km road from Colombo and catch the last train back at 12.35. Buses are plentiful and include an intercity service every 10 minutes from Colombo to Ratnapura via Avissawella.

🏠 WHERE TO STAY

🏠 **Seethawaka Regency** (10 rooms) 📞036 222 2711; m 0776 448442; e info@ seethawakaregency.com; w seethawakaregency. com. Situated 1km out of town along the Puwakpitiya Rd, this modern hotel has smart rooms with AC, cable TV, minibar, tea-/coffee- making facilities, Wi-Fi & private terrace. Amenities

include a restaurant & swimming pool. No alcohol served. *US$65 dbl B&B*. **$$$**

🏠 **Avissawella Resthouse** (8 rooms) Main Rd; 📞036 222 2299. Situated 300m east of the railway station, this simple resthouse has a bar & serves good meals, but the rooms are quite rundown. *US$10 dbl*. **$**

WHAT TO SEE AND DO

Seethawaka Wet Zone Botanical Garden [map, page 74] 📞 *036 379 5295;* w *botanicgardens.gov.lk;* ⊕ *07.30–17.00; entrance US$10*) Sri Lanka's newest botanical garden was established on an abandoned rubber plantation in 2008 and opened to the public in 2014. Extending over 42ha, its primary function is as a repository for rare and endemic plant species associated with the tropical lowland flora of Sinharaja and other wet-zone forests. A perennial stream runs through the sloping garden,

---

PAHIYANGALA

Also known as Fahiyangala (Faxian's Cave), this prehistoric archaeological site and venerated temple lies about 60km southeast of Colombo and could be visited as a day trip in its own right or as a diversion *en route* to Ratnapura or the west-coast resorts running south towards Galle. Situated on a wooded slope at an altitude of 400m, it is the largest natural cave in Sri Lanka, measuring about 90m deep, 60m wide and 50m high, and its name refers to an unverified legend that the Chinese monk Faxian (or Fa Hien) rested up here on his pilgrimage to Adam's Peak in the early 5th century AD. Pahiyangala has a more verifiable claim to fame as one of the country's most important prehistoric sites, having yielded an abundance of microlithic stone tools, prehistoric fireplaces, fossilised human remains and other artefacts suggesting it was inhabited from around 35,000 years ago, making it the oldest and probably most important site of its type on the island. All these ancient finds have been removed from the site for safekeeping, so there's not much to see in the way of archaeological remains, but the steep walk uphill from the car park is enjoyable and the cave – now partially incorporated into a temple – is impressive enough. The most straightforward route from Colombo is to follow the Southern Expressway to Bandaragama, then head inland along the Ratnapura Road for 26km to Ingiriya, where a right turn leads after 15km to Bulathsinhala. From here it is 5km to the cave along a signposted track.

which also contains a large lake, stands of bamboo, and tracts of kumbuk (*Terminalia arjuna*) forest. It is most rewarding in the rainy season, when the flowers come into bloom. Wildlife includes purple-faced langur, toque macaque, and a decent selection of wet-zone birds associated with the bordering Indikada-Mulukana Forest Reserve. To get to the botanical garden from Avissawella, follow the A4 south for 3km to Puwakpitiya (also the site of a railway station on the Kelani Valley Line to Colombo) then branch south on to the rougher Labugama Road and continue for 6km to the signposted entrance. Buses between Avissawella and Kalatuwewa run right past the entrance, while tuktuks charge around US$3–4 one way.

SRI LANKA ONLINE

For additional online content, articles, photos and more on Sri Lanka, why not visit **w** bradtguides.com/srilanka?

SEND US YOUR SNAPS!

We'd love to follow your adventures using our *Sri Lanka* guide – why not send us your photos and stories via Twitter (*@BradtGuides*) and Instagram (*@bradtguides*) using the hashtag #srilanka? Alternatively, you can upload your photos directly to the gallery on the Sri Lanka destination page via our website (**w** *bradtguides.com/srilanka*).

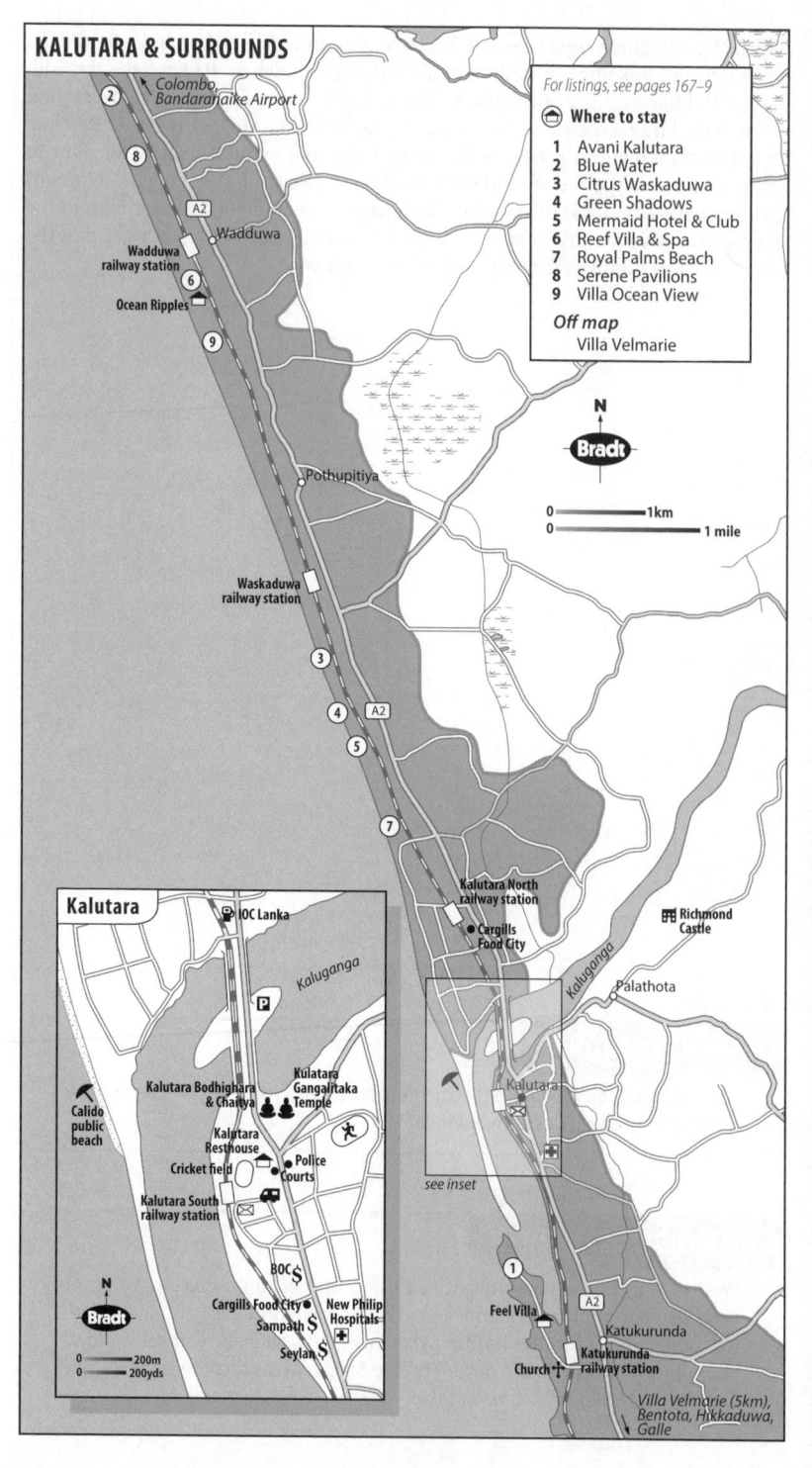

KALUTARA & SURROUNDS

Colombo, Bandaranaike Airport

A2

Wadduwa

Wadduwa railway station

Ocean Ripples

Pothupitiya

Waskaduwa railway station

A2

Kalutara North railway station

Cargills Food City

Richmond Castle

Kaluganga

Palathota

Kalutara

see inset

Feel Villa

A2

Katukurunda

Katukurunda railway station

Church

Villa Velmarie (5km), Bentota, Hikkaduwa, Galle

For listings, see pages 167–9

Where to stay

1   Avani Kalutara
2   Blue Water
3   Citrus Waskaduwa
4   Green Shadows
5   Mermaid Hotel & Club
6   Reef Villa & Spa
7   Royal Palms Beach
8   Serene Pavilions
9   Villa Ocean View

Off map
    Villa Velmarie

N

Bradt

0 ———————— 1km
0 ———————— 1 mile

Kalutara

IOC Lanka

Kaluganga

P

Calido public beach

Kalutara Bodhighara & Chaitya

Kulatara Gangatitaka Temple

Kalutara Resthouse

Cricket field

Police
Courts

Kalutara South railway station

BOC $

Cargills Food City

New Philip Hospitals

Sampath $

Seylan $

N

Bradt

0 ———————— 200m
0 ———————— 200yds

8

The Western Resort Coast: Bentota, Kosgoda and Hikkaduwa

The sublime 120km stretch of coastline between Colombo and Galle traditionally lies at the heart of the island's beach tourism industry, partly due to its proximity to the capital and the country's main international airport. And while improved roads and increased political stability have seen a recent mushrooming of tourist amenities on the south and east coast, the southwest still hosts several of Sri Lanka's most accessible and popular resort towns, most notably Bentota/Aluthgama, a popular package destination situated about halfway between Colombo and Galle, and more southerly Hikkaduwa, which was formerly a legendary hippy hang-out and is still renowned today for its fine seasonal snorkelling and surfing opportunities. Now almost fully recovered from the tsunami that struck it with such tragic effect on Boxing Day of 2004, the southwest coast is dominated by its beaches – a truly fantastic sequence of palm-lined white-sanded vistas – but it also hosts several interesting old temples, bird-rich lagoons and other wetlands, and small workaday ports with vibrant fishing harbours and markets. And more perhaps than anywhere in Sri Lanka, the coast between Colombo and Galle has an astonishingly seasonal tourist industry – bustling mad between December and April, when the weather is driest and the waves are calmest, but almost deserted of tourists at other times, when hotel rates drop by as much as 50% and are often negotiable beyond that.

8

KALUTARA AND SURROUNDS

Set on the west coast 40km south of Colombo, the eponymous capital of Kalutara District flanks the wide mouth of the Kalu (Black) River from which its name derives. It's a substantial and historic settlement, with a population estimated at 40,000 and a pedigree stretching back to the 11th century, when King Vikrama Pandu of Ruhuna made it his temporary capital. Back then, the river mouth housed an important spice-trading centre, and the lagoon was well known to Arab sailors, who took shelter there during the southwest monsoon, and traded with boats and rafts from as far upstream as Ratnapura. In the early 16th century, Kalutara was taken by the Portuguese, who demolished the original Kalutara Gangatilaka Temple on the south bank of the river and built a small fort there. The fort was captured by the Dutch in 1655, who expanded it significantly before ceding it to the British in 1797. Economically, the district is the country's most important source of arrack, a spirit distilled from toddy (palm sap) tapped from coconut plantations, established in the 13th century at the order of King Parakramabahu II.

It is not just the beaches that make the west coast attractive for a holiday. Surprisingly perhaps, traditional village life continues at its own tempo close to the resorts, down palm-shaded side roads and footpaths that lead past coconut groves, paddy fields, colonial mansions, rural homesteads, village shops, antique shops and local craftsmen practising their trade. Indeed, while many village families have sons and daughters who are employed in the modern beach hotels, home life beyond the tourist belt remains remarkably unchanged, and you need only amble along a few inland byways to find villagers still practising crafts and a lifestyle handed down for generations, and who will be pleased to share it with an interested tourist.

Village houses range from the rustic wattle-and-daub hut with roof of palm thatch, to simple buildings with a veranda, wooden columns and a clay-tiled roof. These have wooden shutters and bars on the windows, instead of glass panes and air conditioning. Cool air flows into the house through ornately carved wooden transoms. Life in many coastal villages centres around a river. Where there are no bridges, children must paddle themselves to school in slender, dugout canoes. River fishing is done using sunken wooden fences to form funnels that lure fish and freshwater prawns into bamboo cages, where they can be netted from the water with ease.

Itinerant vendors are common. Salesmen can be seen walking along the road carrying tables and chairs on their heads; man-powered carts sell fish or vegetables; and strolling craftsmen offer to repair rattan chairs and cane blinds at home. Ice cream sellers on bicycles call children by blowing on horns, while lottery-ticket sellers ring bells vigorously to attract attention. The fish salesman's lusty shout of '*maalu, maalu!*' (fish, fish!) brings housewives hurrying out of their homes to buy.

The making of batik is a village craft that has benefited from foreign demand. Bolts of cloth are put through several stages of waxing and dyeing in village workshops. Designs done by untutored but talented village artists result in bright wall hangings, dress and shirt lengths, and sarongs. Batik is popular for souvenirs because of its exotic, colourful patterns and light weight, which makes it easy to pack.

During the British colonial era, Kalutara's proximity to Colombo made it a popular resort with the city's elite, and it earned the sobriquet 'Richmond of Ceylon' because of its similarity to that Thames-side town. The coastal strip 10km either side of Kalutara North is still dotted with seaside hotels, running south via Katukurunda to Maggola and north via Waskaduwa to Wadduwa (a smaller town whose name is reputedly truncated from Veda Duva, literally 'Land of Doctors', a reference to the traditional healers for which the area was once famed). Unfortunately, however, the rough sea and nasty undertow offshore of Kalutara and nearby resorts makes for potentially dangerous swimming conditions, so holiday life tends to focus less on the beach than on hotel swimming pools. Other points of interest near Kalutara are the recently revived Gangatilaka Temple and the quirky 19th-century Richmond Castle.

GETTING THERE AND AWAY

By road Kalutara lies about 40km south of Colombo along the main coastal road through Mount Lavinia and Panadura, a drive of at least 1 hour (longer in heavy traffic). The main bus station is on the Colombo–Galle Road about 300m south of Gangatilaka Temple. Buses to/from Colombo depart every 15 minutes and take

On the beach by Induruwa (page 185), near the 68km post, are fishing boats that look as old as time. Called *paruwa*, these boats are made to a traditional design out of tree trunks bound and stitched together with coir rope. They carry a dozen men to row and cast the nets that are gradually drawn into the shore, where the fish are gathered up and carried off by villagers.

The odd sight of a pair of men sawing wood over a roadside pit might herald the district around Ambalangoda, whose wood-turners and cabinet-makers are renowned worldwide for their skill in making reproduction antiques. To saw a huge tree into suitable planks, the trunk is positioned over a pit. One man crouches on a frame above the pit opening, while the other stands below, smothered in sawdust. The two men pull the large-toothed saw blade backwards and forwards until the trunk is reduced to boards suited to making furniture.

Coconut palms provide the material for traditional crafts, as well as for villagers' livelihoods. *Gokkala* is an ephemeral but artistic craft involving the making of elaborate designs from young, green palm fronds. Nimble-fingered villagers fashion the split fronds into headdresses or decorations for community occasions. Since these creations soon wither away, they are not made as souvenirs, but for the villagers' own delight.

A thriving industry in several villages is the production of coir, a yarn made from coconut husks, and preferred by many locals to modern synthetic fibres. To make coir, the husks are soaked for days in pens in the shallow waters of the river, then beaten with wooden mallets to extract the brown fibrous threads. These are dried in the sun and then spun by village women into rope. Loose coir is used as the stuffing for mattresses whose natural ingredients make them environmentally correct.

Elsewhere, wayside vendors in tiny *cadjan* (plaited palm-frond thatch) shelters entice motorists with bunches of thambili (fresh golden-hued coconuts). They chop off the top of the coconut, stick in a straw, and sell it as a natural and refreshing drink. Other common sights close to modern resorts are housewives scavenging for wood for cooking fires, and herdsmen driving buffaloes to graze.

about 90 minutes, stopping at Wadduwa and Waskaduwa *en route*. Heading south, buses also run several times per hour to/from Galle and all major towns in between.

By rail The busiest railway station in the vicinity is Kalutara South, which stands on the coast about 200m west of the bus station. At least 25 trains daily connect Colombo to Kalutara South, typically taking about 90 minutes, and slower services stop *en route* at Wadduwa, Waskaduwa and Kalutara North stations. Several trains daily run between Kalutara and Aluthgama (for Bentota), Hikkaduwa and Galle, with around half a dozen continuing all the way to Matara. If you are heading to Katukurunda or Maggola, some southbound trains stop at these railway stations, or you could hop off at Kalutara South and catch a tuktuk.

WHERE TO STAY   Map, page 164

Exclusive

✱ ⌂ Serene Pavilions (12 rooms) Upali Rd, 1km north of Wadduwa railway station; **☎** 038 229 6890; **m** 0776 229545; **e** fom@www. serenepavilions.com; **w** serenepavilions.com. This stylish beachfront boutique hotel has a lovely reception area with koi ponds & a large free-form swimming pool set in well-vegetated gardens alive with birdsong. Accommodation is in luxurious secluded ocean or garden pavilions all with their own private garden & plunge pool, dining & sitting room, & AC, fan, TV & hardwood 4-poster bed with fitted net. *From US$460 dbl B&B.* $$$$$+

🏠 **Reef Villa & Spa** (7 suites) Samanthara Rd, 400m south of Wadduwa railway station; ☎038 228 4442; m 0777 595400; e info@ reefvilla.com; w reefvilla.com; see ad, 2nd colour section. A haven of fantasy that begins with a walk through an impressive miniature botanical garden & leads to a spread of palatial AC suites whose sophisticated décor – Kerala terracotta & hand-crafted floor tiles, Jacobean 4-poster beds from Calcutta, vintage furniture based on original East India Company designs, blissful bathroom with a bathtub hewn from a single block of stone – is emphatically 'fit for a Maharaja'. The garden swimming pool has a view of the beach & sea, & menus are prepared to guests' demands. Lavish tropical tranquillity of superior quality, & priced accordingly. *US$495–825 dbl B&B depending on season.* $$$$$+

Upmarket

✴ 🏠 **Avani Kalutara** (105 rooms) St Sebastian Rd, 1km from Katukurunda railway station; ☎034 429 7700; e kalutara@avanihotels. com; w minorhotels.com. This chic low-rise hotel boasts the best location in the area, at the north end of a long narrow peninsula, flanked by the open sea to the west & the more serene Kalutara Lagoon to the east, making it ideally positioned to catch both sunset & sunrise. The spacious & stylish rooms all come with AC & private sea- or lagoon-facing balcony. The large grounds contain a swimming pool & a multitude of palms. *From US$210 dbl B&B.* $$$$$

🏠 **Mermaid Hotel & Club** (81 rooms) Samanthara Rd, 2km south of Waskaduwa railway station; ☎034 720 0478; e resv@ mermaidhotelnclub.com; w mermaidhotelnclub. com. The blandly modern 3-storey hotel is run as a 'club' where all drink & food is included in the room rate, & seems like excellent value on its own terms, attracting many a repeat visitor year after year. Spacious & brightly furnished rooms have AC, TV, writing desk, minibar, tea/coffee & wide balcony overlooking small palm-studded gardens & swimming pool that run down to the beach. Staff are cheerful & engaged, & a wide variety of excursions further afield can be arranged. *US$139/185 sgl/dbl (non-sea view) or from US$167/213 (sea-view* rooms) all-inclusive; substantial seasonal discounts. $$$$$

🏠 **Citrus Waskaduwa** (150 rooms) Samanthara Rd, 700m south of Waskaduwa railway station; 📞 034 763 4634; e web@ citrusleisure.com; w citrusleisure.com/ waskaduwa. The monolithic concrete-&-glass architecture of this 4-storey hotel feels more suited to the city than the beach, but compensation comes in the form of the bold & stylish orange-themed décor, which creates a hip state-of-the-art feel. All rooms come with AC, TV, minibar, safe & balcony/terrace with sea view. There are 4 well-equipped disabled rooms. The 3ha gardens run down to the beach & incorporate a large modern swimming pool. Decent value. US$210/215 sgl/dbl B&B, plus US$20 pp FB, with low-season discounts. $$$$$

🏠 **Blue Water Hotel** (140 rooms) Upali Rd, 1.7km north of Wadduwa railway station; 📞 038 223 5067; e reservations@thebluewatersrilanka. com; w bluewatersrilanka.com. Designed by Geoffrey Bawa in keeping with the trend towards clean lines & minimalistic décor, this well-established hotel has a contemporary & airy but rather sombre feel underscored by the military formations of palm trees that shade the neatly cropped beachfront lawn & massive swimming pool. Large rooms are decorated with terracotta tiles, traditional fabrics, & pictures & engravings of old Sri Lanka, & come with AC, fan, minibar, TV, shower & tub, & sea-facing terrace or balcony. It's an above-average resort, a touch bland but very comfortable & reasonably priced. US$185/200 sgl/dbl B&B with low-season discounts. $$$$$

🏠 **Royal Palms Beach Hotel** (129 rooms) De Abrew Dr, 1km north of Kalutara North railway station; 📞 011 242 2518/9; e info@royalpalms. lk; w royalpalms.tangerinehotels.com. One of the busier & more happening places around Kalutara, this smart 3-storey hotel stays on the right side of the line that divides the stylish from the ostentatious, & a few old-fashioned touches betray its age (constructed 1996), but overall it comes across as a modern, well-maintained and enthusiastically managed set-up. Large rooms have teak-&-tile floors, vintage furniture, private balcony with sea or garden view, AC, TV, minibar & 4-poster bed with fitted net. The garden, complete with the usual large swimming pool, is shaded by

tall palms & borders a beach no less rough than its neighbours but with the distinction of being manned by a lifeguard. US$179/223 sgl/dbl B&B, with seasonal discounts. $$$$$

Moderate

🏠 **Villa Velmarie** (6 rooms) 39 Kudawa Rd, 400m southwest of Maggola railway station; m 0772 383690; e villavelmarie@gmail.com; w villavelmarie.com. This family-managed property comprises an old house constructed in the Dutch colonial era & fully renovated as a boutique lodge in 2014. Situated less than 5mins' walk from Maggola beach, it is set in a large natural garden with a swimming pool & newly built Ayurveda spa, while tasty home-cooked Western & Sri Lankan meals in the US$5–7 range can be taken on a wide sheltered balcony with black-&-white tiles & cane furniture. The crisply decorated rooms all have AC, TV & fridge. From US$88 dbl B&B; extended all-inclusive Ayurveda packages also available. $$$$

🏠 **Villa Ocean View** (150 rooms) Samanthara Rd, 1km south of Wadduwa railway station; 📞 038 429 9691; e villaocn@sltnet.lk; w villaoceanview. lk. Built in the 1980s but regularly renovated, this low-rise hotel is situated in 2.8ha tropical gardens set around a large swimming pool area that runs down to the beach. Small, uninspired & rather old-fashioned villa rooms are arranged in 4-unit blocks while larger & more modern superior rooms, all with tubs & pool-facing terrace or balcony, are in a newer 3-storey main block. All rooms have AC & TV. Great value assuming you pay the slight extra for a superior room & take advantage of the FB rate. US$70/75 sgl/dbl B&B villa room, US$75/80 sgl/dbl B&B superior room, plus US$10 pp FB. $$$

Budget

🏠 **Green Shadows Hotel** (20 rooms) Samanthara Rd, 1.5km south of Waskaduwa railway station; 📞 034 223 6233; m 0779 927214; e info@greensshadowsbeachhotel. com; w greensshadowsbeachhotel.com. Set in small palm-studded gardens that run directly to the beach, this unpretentious small hotel has comfortable but simple rooms with tiled or treated concrete floor, AC, fan, fridge & private balcony. Amenities include a swimming pool & decent restaurant. Very good value. US$35/40 sgl/dbl B&B. $$

WHAT TO SEE AND DO Although beaches and beach hotels abound in the vicinity of Kalutara, swimming is generally unsafe owing to the rough sea and steep incline, so be sure to ask local advice before you take the plunge. A well-known beauty spot is the suburban Calido public beach, which lies at the north end of the long, narrow sandy spit that separates the lagoon-like Kalu river mouth from the open sea, and offers access to both. It lies almost 1km from the main Colombo–Galle Road and can be reached by following Calido Beach Road as it branches southwest 100m north of the Kalu River Bridge.

Kalutara Bodhighara and Chaitya [map, page 164] (❀ *034 222 6483;* w *kalutarabodhiya.com*) Rededicated in 2015 following extensive renovations, Kalutara Bodhighara, set alongside the main road immediately south of the bridge across the River Kalu, protects one of the most venerable and revered Bo Trees in Sri Lanka. It is widely believed to be one of the 32 saplings sprouted from Anuradhapura's Jaya Sri Maha Bodhi during the 2nd-century BC reign of Devanampiya Tissa and planted countrywide by Indian monk Mahinda Thera. Others claim that the sacred tree at Kalutara was planted during the river mouth's 11th-century tenure as the capital of King Vikrama Pandu of Ruhuna. Either way, the ancient Bo Tree was the only part of the Kalutara Gangatilaka Temple to escape demolition by the Portuguese in 1622 to make way for a fort. Then, having thrived alongside a succession of colonial edifices for almost 350 years, the sacred tree was almost chopped down in 1880 to make way for the railway line to Galle, only to receive a last-minute reprieve following protests by local Buddhist leaders. The Bodhighara remains an important Buddhist pilgrimage site, and passing train passengers often toss coins out of the window in its direction to ward off bad luck during their journey.

Since 1951, Kalutara Bodhighara and the revived Kalutara Gangatilaka have fallen under the care of the Kalutara Temple Bodhi Trust (KBT), which was formed by prominent lawyer Sir Cyril de Zoysa. The KBT is responsible for the temple's most prominent feature: Kalutara Chaitya, a domed 3-storey dagoba constructed over 1964–76. This is reportedly the largest hollow dagoba in Sri Lanka, with a bright interior that incorporates a second smaller dagoba, a circular row of windows offering great views across the river and bridge, and a cartoon-like strip of 74 paintings depicting episodes in the Buddha's life. The dagoba has a lovely riverside setting and its handsome whitewashed exterior is most photogenic from the road bridge across the Kalu, or the car park on an island in the middle of it.

Richmond Castle [map, page 164] (*3km east of Kalutara;* ▮ *richmond.castle;* ⊕ *08.00–16.00; entrance US$1.50*) Set in lush 17ha grounds on the south bank of the River Kalu, this imposing 16-room castle was the home of Arthur de Silva Wijesinghe (1888–1949), a wealthy Mudaliyar who studied in the UK and was friends with the British royal family. The castle was built in 1910 to host the wedding of the Mudaliyar to Clarice Maude Sooriya Bandara, a grand ceremony, complete with fireworks, for which the social elite of Colombo and representatives of King George V were ferried to Kalutara South in a special royal train. Sadly, the marriage proved to be barren, a circumstance that frustrated the Mudaliyar's deep-felt wish to father a male heir, and led to the formal separation of the unhappy couple in 1940. Following the separation, Clarice moved back with her family, while Arthur relocated to Kandy's Queen's Hotel (where he lived until his death in 1949) and donated the custom-built mansion to the government to serve as a male-only children's home.

Currently undergoing renovations initiated in 2011, Richmond Castle still functions as a children's home today, albeit one with the surreal appearance of a misplaced English stately home in the heart of tropical Sri Lanka. The double-storey building's colonnaded and arched façade rises from a poorly tended but nonetheless attractive manicured garden. The interior is even more impressive: 2m-thick walls of imported Indian bricks, a magnificent Burmese teak stairwell, Italian marble floors and stained-glass windows, and an ornate dancing hall whose audience platform is reached by a wrought-iron spiral staircase shipped across from the UK. And yet a things-that-money-can't-buy sadness hangs over the estate. A first-floor gallery hosts a collection of photographs that show the mansion back in its heyday, many taken during the ill-fated wedding ceremony associated with its construction. More poignant still are the statues of women and children that dot the garden, with females all facing away from the house, while boys look towards it as a symbol of Arthur's unfulfilled desire to father a son.

BENTOTA AND SURROUNDS

Some 65km south of Colombo, Bentota – or, more accurately, the 10km stretch of coastline flanking the Bentota river mouth – traditionally constitutes the most developed beach resort on Sri Lanka's west coast (a status admittedly now challenged by Negombo and Hikkaduwa). The Bentota area incorporates four major population centres. Most northerly, only 13km south of Kalutara, is Beruwala, a historic fishing port often touted as a beach destination, though most of the resort action associated with its name actually happens a few kilometres further south, at Moragalla beach. South of Moragalla, the River Bentota (also known as Bentara) separates the large functional north-bank town of Aluthgama from the overgrown south-bank village of Bentota, which is the heart of the area's tourist industry. Altogether more modest is the village of Induruwa, which starts just 3km south of Bentota.

Traditionally, each of these four towns tends to be treated as a tourist destination in its own right. And we have to some extent followed suit by splitting coverage from north to south across five geographic headers, namely Beruwala, Moragalla, Aluthgama, Bentota and Induruwa. But nothing feels quite so clear-cut on the ground. On the contrary, the coast between Beruwala and Induruwa is cluttered with literally hundreds of package resorts, boutique hotels, budget guesthouses and seafood restaurants, to form an all-but-contiguous 10km band of tourist development wherein any beach, hotel, restaurant or sites of interest can easily be visited from any other. Note, too, that most sites of interest and activities covered on pages 187–195 are also easily visited as a day trip from Bentota and surrounds.

GETTING AROUND For local excursions, tuktuks are in abundant supply, at the usually negotiable rates, wherever there is a possibility of a hire, not just from tourists but from locals too. Cars, minibuses and their drivers are also readily available to the high proportion of hotel guests who book a two-week stay in or around Bentota, then decide to make a short day or overnight tour – 'round trip', as it's known locally – to Kandy or elsewhere in the interior. Rates are all over the place, but expect a ballpark figure of around US$50–80 per day, inclusive of fuel, depending on the quality of the car and how far afield you're going. Some enterprising drivers/guides will create (at a day's notice) an entire package for guests that includes transport and hotels and even admission charges. This is a good way to set your own itinerary instead of being confined to organised tours.

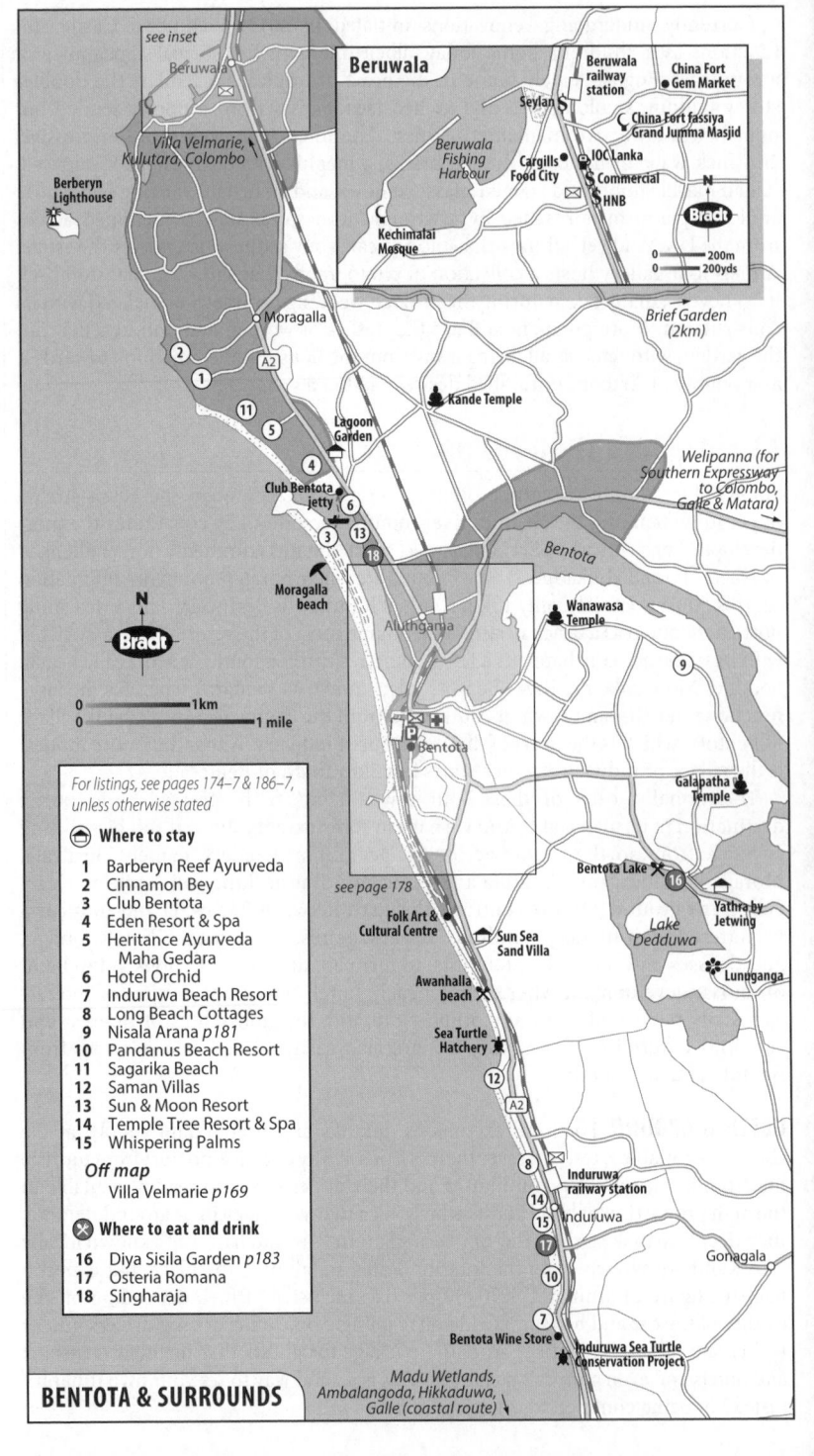

Beruwala

- Beruwala railway station
- China Fort Gem Market
- Seylan
- China Fort fassiya Grand Jumma Masjid
- IOC Lanka
- Cargills Food City
- Commercial
- HNB
- Beruwala Fishing Harbour
- Kechimalai Mosque

Bradt

| 0 | 200m |
| 0 | 200yds |

see inset

Beruwala

Villa Velmarie, Kulutara, Colombo

Berberyn Lighthouse

Moragalla

A2

Brief Garden (2km)

Kande Temple

Lagoon Garden

Club Bentota jetty

Moragalla beach

Welipanna (for Southern Expressway to Colombo, Galle & Matara)

Bentota

Wanawasa Temple

Aluthgama

Bradt

N

| 0 | 1km |
| 0 | 1 mile |

Galapatha Temple

Bentota

Bentota Lake

Lake Dedduwa

Yathra by Jetwing

Lunuganga

see page 178

Folk Art & Cultural Centre

Sun Sea Sand Villa

Awanhalla beach

Sea Turtle Hatchery

For listings, see pages 174–7 & 186–7, unless otherwise stated

Where to stay

1 Barberyn Reef Ayurveda
2 Cinnamon Bey
3 Club Bentota
4 Eden Resort & Spa
5 Heritance Ayurveda Maha Gedara
6 Hotel Orchid
7 Induruwa Beach Resort
8 Long Beach Cottages
9 Nisala Arana *p181*
10 Pandanus Beach Resort
11 Sagarika Beach
12 Saman Villas
13 Sun & Moon Resort
14 Temple Tree Resort & Spa
15 Whispering Palms

Off map
   Villa Velmarie *p169*

Where to eat and drink

16 Diya Sisila Garden *p183*
17 Osteria Romana
18 Singharaja

Induruwa railway station

Induruwa

Gonagala

Bentota Wine Store

Induruwa Sea Turtle Conservation Project

Madu Wetlands, Ambalangoda, Hikkaduwa, Galle (coastal route)

BENTOTA & SURROUNDS

BERUWALA Known to ancient mariners as Barberyn, Beruwala is possibly Sri Lanka's oldest Islamic port. Arab sailors first settled here between the 8th and 12th centuries AD, and its harbour looks across to a headland topped by the venerable Kechimalai Mosque. In the colonial era, Beruwala and its port thrived on the shipment of cinnamon grown in the hinterland. Beruwala today is a workaday town rather than a resort, with an estimated population of 35,000, and no swimming beach in the immediate vicinity. Most commercial activity is focused on the 500m stretch of the Colombo–Galle Road that runs through the town centre, as well as the renowned gem market in China Fort and the scenic fishing harbour. Those resort hotels that are nominally associated with Beruwala actually front on to the lovely and relatively calm Moragalla beach, which lies about 3km further south, halfway towards Aluthgama.

Getting there and away Beruwala stands about 58km south of Colombo along the main coastal road through Mount Lavinia and Panadura, and only 13km south of Kalutara. All buses heading south from Colombo to Aluthgama can drop you at the bus station in the town centre, and Beruwala railway station is stopped at by most southbound trains from Colombo. In practice, however, since there is no accommodation worth talking about in Beruwala itself, you would be most likely to visit as a day trip from Moragalla, Aluthgama or Bentota, in which case there are loads of buses, and a tuktuk shouldn't set you back more than about US$2 one way.

What to see and do Down-to-earth Beruwala makes an interesting goal for a day-excursion from nearby Moragalla, Aluthgama or Bentota.

China Fort Gem Market [map, opposite] Situated about 500m east of the main Galle Road, the predominantly Muslim suburb of China Fort reputedly acquired its intriguing name in the 17th century, when a coterie of Chinese traders settled here. Probably at around the same time, it became the site of what is now Sri Lanka's second-largest gem market, which is held every Wednesday and Saturday morning, when it extends over two blocks and attracts several thousand traders from Ratnapura and elsewhere. Even on other days, China Fort is studded with shops that trade in gems and jewels, or offer facilities for gem cutting, calibration and polishing.

Beruwala Fishing Harbour [map, opposite] The sheltered fishing harbour at Beruwala has been a centre of international trade for more than a thousand years but was more recently extended as an anchorage for deep-sea fishing boats, which motor in after several weeks at sea to unload deep-sea fish on the quayside for auction. Smaller boats, which go to sea in the evenings, return in dawn's early light with rockfish. Visitors can pay a nominal fee to enter the harbour and watch the open-air fish auction, which begins at dawn and is usually over by breakfast time. The harbour suffered terrible damage in the 2004 tsunami, when many boats and people were swept out to sea. A new 500m-long rock breakwater has been constructed to protect against future incidents. A nice view over the harbour can be obtained from Kechimalai Mosque.

Kechimalai Mosque [map, opposite] Also spelt Ketchimala, this picturesque glistening-white mosque stands on a rocky headland that hems in the east side of Beruwala fishing harbour some 1km out of town. It is reputedly the oldest mosque in Sri Lanka, having been established by a Yemeni sultan who settled at Beruwala, probably in the 12th century, and was buried at the site. The present-day building, constructed in 1911 by a wealthy Muslim businessman, is a handsome squarish construction with an ornate arched exterior, curvaceous Dutch-style gables and an unusual domed minaret topped by what looks like a birdcage. Its slight elevation on a headland means it was spared the destruction wrought by the tsunami on the harbour below. Regarded by many as the home of Islam in Sri Lanka, it is the focal point of a pilgrimage attracting many thousands of worshippers for two or three nights immediately before Ramadan.

Berberyn Lighthouse [map, page 172] Set on a lush palm-swathed 3ha island at the northern end of Berberyn Reef, this 34m-high lighthouse is one of the oldest in Sri Lanka, built by the British in 1889, and it boasts perhaps the loveliest setting of them all. The island upon which it stands is about 500m offshore, facing the small Maradana fishing harbour, which is contained by a 200m breakwater about 1.5km south of Kechimalai Mosque. Plenty of tuktuks are available in Beruwala and Aluthgama to take you to Maradana, from where the short crossing can be made by private arrangement with any boat.

Other practicalities Branches of all the main private banks, complete with ATMs, can be found on the main road through Beruwala, along with a branch of Cargills Food City.

MORAGALLA BEACH Often referred to as Beruwala beach, the gorgeous 1.5km stretch of palm-lined golden sand at Moragalla starts about 3km south of Beruwala and runs south to the mouth of the Bentota River at Aluthgama. It's a fun stretch of beach, lined with upmarket resorts that cater primarily to package tourists, but also home to a couple of highly rated health retreats in the form of the Heritance Ayurveda Maha Gedara and Barberyn Reef Ayurveda. Moragalla has a shallow incline and is hemmed in by an offshore coral reef that runs south from Berberyn Island, which means it is usually safe for swimming and also offers good conditions for snorkelling, which can be arranged through any of the beachfront hotels.

Getting there and away The resorts at Moragalla lie just over 60km from Colombo and a similar distance north of Galle, but only 3–5km south of central Beruwala and 2–4km north of central Aluthgama. Since they also lie some distance west of the nearest bus and railway station, the most straightforward option using public transport is to bus or train to Aluthgama, and catch a tuktuk from there.

Where to stay, eat and drink *Map, page 172*

Upmarket

☀ ⌂ **Cinnamon Bey Hotel** (200 rooms) Maradana Rd, 4km north of Aluthgama railway station; ☎034 229 7000; e bey@cinnamonhotels. com; w cinnamonhotels.com. This agreeably modern hotel is situated at the north end of Moragalla beach. The décor has a Turkish feel with colourful mosaic tiles breaking up expanses of light grey concrete walls & columns. Refreshingly chic & soothing, the spacious rooms come complete with AC, TV, work desk & sliding wooden lattice doors to the separate shower & toilet. A range of Asian-

fusion, Japanese, Arabic, grill & other cuisines are served at the 5 restaurants & 3 bars. *US$240 dbl B&B.* **$$$$$**

⌂ **Heritance Ayurveda Maha Gedara** (64 rooms) Colombo Rd, 2km north of Aluthgama railway station; ☎034 555 5000; e info.amg@heritancehotels.com; w heritancehotels.com. Built in the 1970s but more recently restyled as a specialist Ayurveda retreat, this 3-storey hotel on Moragalla beach has a colonial-meets-Mediterranean feel with its whitewashed exterior, red tile roof & spacious rooms with terracotta tiles, darkwood furniture, fitted nets & wide balcony facing the swimming pool. There's AC throughout, but in keeping with the Ayurveda ethic, no TV, tea, coffee, alcohol or red meat. The beautiful gardens, sense of isolation & enforced minimum stay of 4 days enhance the feeling this is a genuine retreat as opposed to a hotel with a sideline. *From US$203/317 sgl/dbl FB inc yoga & Ayurveda treatments.* **$$$$$+**

🏠 **Barberyn Reef Ayurveda** (75 rooms) 6th Ln, 3.5km north of Aluthgama railway station; ☎ 034 227 6037; **e** info@barberyn.lk; **w** barberynresorts.com. This dedicated Ayurveda resort with AC rooms is set in tranquil wooded gardens leading down to Moragalla beach & a small swimming area protected by a reef. It also incorporates a deep blue free-form pool enclosed by a jungle gallery. All food is vegetarian & no alcohol is served, making it the ideal place to detox & de-stress. *€135/195 sgl/dbl FB, plus €560/wk for a full Ayurveda package.* **$$$$$**

🏠 **Eden Resort & Spa** (158 rooms) Galle Rd, Aluthgama; ☎ 034 227 6075; **e** eden@ brownshotels.com; **w** brownshotels.com/eden.

Set at the south end of Moragalla beach where the Bentota River enters the ocean, this well-run set-up seems like the archetypal tropical beach resort with its large palm-shaded gardens set around a massive free-form swimming pool & popular herbal spa. There's a selection of 4 restaurants & 4 bars, & modern rooms come with AC, TV & private balcony, but no net or fan. Unexciting, but decent value. *From US$150 dbl B&B with substantial off-season discounts.* **$$$$**

Moderate

🏠 **Sagarika Beach Hotel** (7 rooms) 4th Ln, 3km north of Aluthgama railway station; **m** 0777 790580; **e** sagarikabeach@asia.com; **w** sagarikabeachhotel.webs.com. Set in a long narrow tranquil garden offering direct access to the lovely Moragalla beach, this old-fashioned & thoroughly pleasant hotel feels bit like an upmarket homestay, thanks to the warm hands-on family management. Rooms have AC, fan, net & tea/coffee, & most have a terrace facing the swimming pool. No TV. Good value. *US$80 dbl B&B with low-season & long-stay discounts.* **$$$**

ALUTHGAMA Built-up, bustling Aluthgama crowds a flat square-kilometre wedge of land hemmed in to the east, south and west by a U-shaped bend in the Bentota River as it approaches its lagoon-like mouth. Very much the functional modern entity suggested by its prosaic name (literally 'New Town'), Aluthgama seems surprisingly unaffected by tourism and is strong on amenities, including a good selection of supermarkets, banks and ATMs, a busy Monday market, a host of unpretentious local eateries, and other assorted small-town Sri Lankan staples. Aluthgama is also the main regional transport hub, serviced by the busiest railway and bus stations in the vicinity of Bentota. Several riverside watersport centres offer a range of aquatic activities including boat trips on the Bentota River.

Getting there and away

By road Aluthgama lies about 65km south of Colombo along the main coastal road through Mount Lavinia and Panadura. It's about 20km further using the Southern Expressway, exiting at Interchange 5 (Welipanna) then driving 10km west to meet the coast at Aluthgama. Its central bus station is connected to Colombo, Galle and most points in between by buses that depart in either direction every 10–15 minutes. Depending on traffic, allow 2 hours to/from Colombo and 90 minutes to/from Galle.

By rail Aluthgama has the busiest railway station [178 B1] in the vicinity, serviced by at least 15 trains daily from to/from Colombo and around a dozen to/from Galle. In both cases, the trip usually takes up to 2 hours.

🏠 **Where to stay** The hotels listed below are all situated to the north of the road and rail bridges across the Bentota River. A potential source of confusion is the inclusion of Club Bentota, which stands to the north of the bridges, but south of the river mouth, on the narrow spit of land separating the lagoon from the open sea, and is most usually reached by ferry crossing from Aluthgama.

Upmarket

🏠 **Club Bentota** [map, page 172] (146 rooms) Parking on Galle Rd, next to Hotel Orchid; 📞034 227 5167; e info@clubbentota.com; w clubbentota.com. Built in 1981 to resemble a school or similar institution, Club Bentota – accessible by ferry from Aluthgama only – has a prime 'tropical island' location on the peninsula separating the lagoon from the open sea. Due to reopen following renovations in May 2019. *US$210/325 sgl/dbl FB & drinks.* **$$$$$**

Moderate

🏠 **Hotel Orchid** [map, page 172] (8 rooms) Galle Rd, Aluthgama; 📞034 570 8070; m 0775 424149; e info@hotelorchidsrilanka.com; w hotelorchidsrilanka.com. Elevated from ordinariness by its beautiful & breezy riverside location facing Club Bentota, this unpretentious set-up has spacious & bright tiled rooms with AC, king-size bed, simple but colourful décor & balcony overlooking the river. A waterfront restaurant serves seafood & local dishes in the US$6–8 range. *US$52/62 sgl/dbl B&B.* **$$$**

🏠 **Sun & Moon Resort** [map, page 172] (8 rooms) Galle Rd, Aluthgama, 📞034 494 3454; m 0771 747123; e info@resortsunandmoon.com; w resortsunandmoon.com. This well-priced & central hotel stands in a small garden with a lovely riverside setting. Rooms are colourful & spacious, furnished with dark wood, & come with AC, fan, TV, fridge, tea/coffee, large bathroom & private balcony with river view. A licensed 1st-floor terrace restaurant serves a varied choice of mains in the US$5–8 range. *US$53/70 sgl/dbl B&B.* **$$$**

Budget

☀ 🏠 **Hemadan Hotel & Beer Garden** [178 B3] (10 rooms) River Av; 📞034 227 5320; e hemadan@sltnet.lk. This characterful & friendly hotel has a central location, clean dbl & twin rooms with terracotta tiles, fan, net & optional AC, & a shady terrace restaurant & bar overlooking a relaxed riverfront garden with summer houses. It is well positioned for watersports, & also offers guests a free boat transfer across the river to Bentota beach. *U$43/50 sgl/dbl with fan only, or US$62 dbl with AC; seasonal discounts available.* **$$$**

🏠 **Riverbank Bentota** [178 C2] (5 rooms) Welipanna Rd, Aluthgama; 📞034 227 0022; m 0773 934477; e info@riverbank.lk; 📘 riverbankbentota. Owned & managed by a helpful family who speak good English, this neat little guesthouse has a lovely setting in a small garden with swimming pool on the west bank of the river upstream of the bridge to Bentota. Comfortable rooms have AC, net, wooden furniture & balcony with river view. *US$44 dbl B&B with seasonal discounts up to 30%.* **$$**

🏠 **Thumbelina Apartments** [178 B3] (6 rooms) Welipanna Rd, Aluthgama; 📞034 327 0055; m 0777 899710; e nebula@dialogsl.net; w thumbelinaapartments.bookings.lk. Situated close to the riverfront above the more prominently signposted Nebula Supermarket, this central 3-storey apartment complex offers AC self-catering apartments with a well-equipped kitchenette, sitting/dining room with TV & furniture made from grained coconut timber, & broad balcony with river view. Housekeeping is included in the room rate, & communal amenities include a washing machine & ironing facilities. The excellent Pier 88 restaurant, under the same management, conveniently stands next door. Great value. *US$38 dbl.* **$$**

✕ Where to eat and drink

☀ ✕ **Pier 88** [178 C3] Welipanna Rd; 📞034 229 1799; w thumbelinaapartments.com. One of the nicest & best-priced tourist-oriented eateries close to Bentota, this waterfront café-bar-restaurant has a bright AC interior with Wi-Fi, as well as stilted terrace seating in colourful bougainvillaea-draped gardens on the Bentota River. Excellent cocktails & coffee are supplemented by the usual local beers & imported wines. The well-priced menu embraces salads, sandwiches, Sri Lankan curries & devilled dishes (all **$$**), as well as continental-style grilled seafood, meat & poultry. **$$$**

✖ Nero's Kitchen [178 B1] Galle Rd; m 0765 301313; 🅵 nerokitchen; ⏰ 11.30–15.00 & 17.30–22.00. This clean fast-food outlet with free Wi-Fi is best known for its pizzas, which come piping hot out of the wood-fired oven but only in the evening, but it also serves great burgers, filled pancakes & juices. No alcohol. $$

✖ BBQ Chicken Hut [178 B1] Galle Rd; m 0777 196836; ⏰ 08.00–22.00. Tastily spiced rotisserie chicken is the speciality at this friendly little hole-in-the-wall catering mainly to locals. No alcohol. Half-chicken with condiments. $$

✖ Happy Fish [178 B3] Galle Rd; m 0776 209942; ⏰ 10.30–23.00. This unpretentious floating restaurant stands on a pontoon moored next to Bentota Bridge but the owner will cruise further upriver for groups. The menu includes local curries & devilled dishes ($$), as well as pasta, seafood & steaks ($$$).

✖ Singharaja Restaurant [map, page 172] Galle Rd; 📞 034 227 4978; ⏰ 06.00–21.00. Superior local bakery & restaurant serving good-value lunchtime buffets & a range of cakes, bread, etc. Very affordable. $

Other practicalities

Banking Branches of all the main private banks, complete with ATMs, can be found on the main road through Aluthgama.

Shopping The tourist-oriented **Nebula Supermarket** [178 C3] (m *0777 899710; ⏰ 09.00–22.00*) next to Pier 88 stocks a good selection of local groceries and imported goods. There is also a branch of Cargills Food City [178 B1] on the main road. The **Barley Street Wine Shop** [178 B2] (*Galle Rd; ⏰ 09.00–21.00*) has the best liquor selection in Aluthgama, but several close-by hole-in-the-wall places are cheaper for beer and arrack. For high-quality crafts and antiques, try the self-explanatory **Traditional Mask Show Room** [178 C2] and **Aluthgama Wood Carving Centre** [178 B3], both in Aluthgama.

What to see and do Aluthgama doesn't boast any direct beach access but it has plenty of river frontage and the waterside roads afford attractive views to the opposite shore. Further afield, it's only about 1km south across the bridge to Bentota beach or 2km north to Moragalla beach. Aluthgama also hosts a large Monday market on the north bank of the Bentota River next to Pier 88 restaurant.

Watersports, snorkelling and boat trips Mostly clustered on the south side of River Avenue, a number of operators in Aluthgama offer waterskiing, jet-ski, windsurfing and other activities on the Bentota Lagoon, as well as snorkelling excursions on Berberyn Reef (off Moragalla beach) and mellow boat trips up the Bentota River to enjoy the scenery and search for crocodiles, water monitors and a rich variety of birds. The following companies are recommended:

Sunshine Watersports [178 B2] River Av; 📞 034 428 9379; m 0777 941857; e sunshinesrilanka@ gmail.com; w srilankawatersports.com. Owned by former national windsurfing champion Thusal Gunawardena, this respected & fully insured operation offers snorkelling trips (*US$125 for up to 4 people*), deep-sea fishing (*US$125 for up to 4 people*), canoe rental (*US$8/hr*), windsurfer rental (*US$15/hr*), jet-ski rental (*from US$30/ hr*), bodyboard rental (*US$5/hr*) and waterskiing excursions (*US$10*). It arranges river trips too, but is relatively pricey.

Diyakawa Watersports Centre [178 B2] River Av; 📞 034 454 5105; m 0779 165330. Situated just up the road from Sunshine Watersports, Diyakawa offers a similar range of activities at similar prices.

Riverbank Bentota [178 C2] Welipanna Rd; 📞 034 227 0022; m 0773 934477; 🅵 riverbankbentota. This budget lodge arranges 2hr boat trips up the Bentota River for around US$15 per group.

Lucky Boat Safaris [178 D2] Yathramulla Rd; 📞 034 227 0443; 🅵. Based at Lagoon Bentota

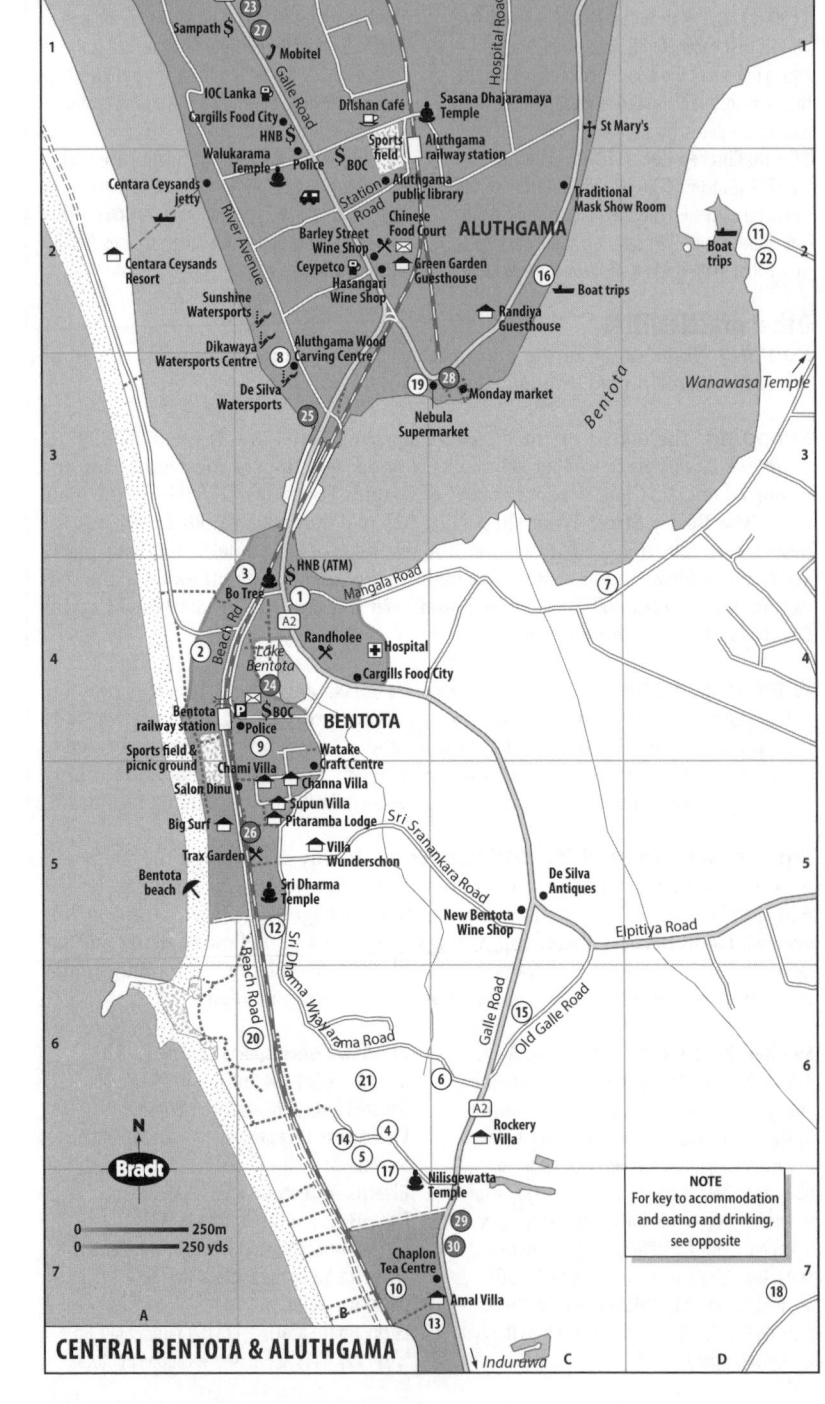

CENTRAL BENTOTA & ALUTHGAMA

(page 182) but able to pick up passengers in Aluthgama, this small owner-managed set-up

charges US$20 per party for a 3hr boat trip.

Kande Temple [map, page 172] Founded in the 18th century, this hilltop temple 1km from Aluthgama is best known for a massive 48m-high statue, constructed over 2002–07, of the Buddha seated in the Bhumisparsha mudra on a lipstick-pink lotus flower. The main temple incorporates a graphic mural of drowning people and a train and cars being swept out to sea in the 2004 tsunami. A second older image house behind the Bo Tree has an attractive ornate arched façade and contains a few rather faded Kandyan-era paintings. The temple can be reached by tuktuk or on foot by branching east on to the Kalawila Road opposite the car park for Club Bentota and following it inland for about 1km.

Brief Garden [map, page 172] (℡ *034 567 6298;* e *briefgarden@gmail.com;* ⊕ *08.00–17.00; entrance US$7*) Situated about 5km inland of Aluthgama as the crow flies, Brief is the former home of Major Bevis Bawa, a self-taught artist whose hedonistic lifestyle didn't prevent him from acting as aide-de-camp to four successive Governors of Ceylon during the late colonial era. Elder brother to architect Geoffrey Bawa, Bevis converted what was formerly his family's rubber estate into a quirky arboretum that manages to combine an elaborate European layout with a tropical wilderness feel. It can be explored on a rambling path that leads through a succession of tranquil landscaped gardens containing a total of 120-plus different tree species, as well as countless plants and bushes, but only a few flowers. (When asked by an eager journalist what was the plan of the garden, Bawa replied: 'No plan. It's just a happening.')

The footpath ends at Bawa's old house, which played host to several celebrity visitors including writer Agatha Christie and actors Lawrence Olivier and Vivien Leigh. It's a fascinating place, not just for the unexpected design, which leads visitors downstairs to a door out to the car park, but also for the objets d'art within. Pride of place is a weather-worn mural by Australian artist Donald Friend. It shows many local scenes and people, including an image of Bevis Bawa lying full length in a planter's chair directing some planting. 'You didn't do the garden,' Friend told him. 'Your gardeners did.' The house includes a gallery of photos of Bevis Bawa, who stood 6'7" tall and had a strong face that must have deterred dissent.

Brief Garden can be reached by branching east on to the Kalawila Road opposite the car park for Club Bentota and following it inland, passing Kande Temple to your right, for about 7km.

BENTOTA In the coaching days, Bentota – which lies on the south bank of the eponymous river opposite Aluthgama – was recognised as the halfway house along the 120km coastal road and railway line connecting Colombo to Galle. Back then, tourist development amounted to a modest government resthouse, which was famed for its succulent fresh oysters, and stood on the tamarind-shaded site of an old Portuguese and Dutch fort near the mouth of the crocodile-infested Bentota River. Today, by contrast, Bentota and its gorgeous beach – a swathe of broad palm-lined golden sand running south from the river mouth along a narrow spit – stand at the epicentre of what is arguably Sri Lanka's most developed coastal resort area. The government resthouse is long gone, replaced by the so-called National Holiday Resort, a rather soulless toytown-like square that dates to the 1970s and comes complete with bank, post office, police station, railway station and pond shaped like a map of Sri Lanka. Meanwhile, the long lagoon at the Bentota mouth is used for jet-skiing and banana raft rides, as well as being the launch for motorboat and outrigger canoe trips upriver. And further afield, the sprawling village hosts a selection of lodgings and eateries as diverse as any outside Colombo or Galle. Yet while tourists throng to the area in season (November–May, peaking over mid-December–mid-January), Bentota is surprisingly quiet, even rather forlorn, at other times of year, when rack rates drop dramatically and become highly negotiable to walk-ins.

Getting there and away

By road Bentota lies about 1km south of Aluthgama, which is connected to Colombo, Galle and most points in between by buses that depart in either direction every 10–15 minutes. Southbound buses also stop at Bentota but, unless you know exactly where you're going, there's a good case for disembarking at Aluthgama and catching a tuktuk from there.

By rail Slow trains stop at Bentota stations, but it would be more efficient to take an express train to Aluthgama and catch a tuktuk from there.

Where to stay Accommodation listed below lies to the south of the Bentota River, either along or close to the 1.5km of beach running south from the National Holiday Resort, or inland towards Lake Dedduwa. Seafront accommodation is dominated by mid-range to upmarket package resorts, most of which flank the railway line running parallel to, and a few hundred metres from, the beach. Immediately inland, a labyrinth of quiet, narrow alleys leads west from the main Galle Road through a jungle-like tangle of vegetation dotted with characterful boutique hotels (many converted from colonial-era villas) and more down-to-earth family-run budget guesthouses generally offering far better value than might be expected for Bentota. East of the main Galle Road, a growing number of boutique and budget hotels can be found on or close to the banks of the Bentota River or Lake Dedduwa.

Exclusive

✳ 🏠 **Paradise Road The Villa** [178 B6] (15 rooms) Nilisgewatta Temple Rd; ☎ 034 227 5311; e reservations@villabentota.com; w paradiseroadhotels.com. One of the most stunning boutique hotels anywhere in Sri Lanka, this sumptuous beachfront property, run through by the railway line, comprises an old walauwa (colonial villa) that was converted to a hotel by Geoffrey Bawa in the 1970s and taken over by Paradise Road in 2006. The main wow factor is the inspired décor, with all rooms being individually styled in grey, black & white & hung with contemporary artworks & antique traditionally crafted artefacts. Other selling points are the understatedly professional staff & the choice of two swimming pools, as well as a directly accessed beach & a charming restaurant with open kitchen.

Rates seem eminently reasonable compared with the infinitely less charming package hotels elsewhere in Bentota. *From US$235 dbl or US$310 suite, all B&B.* **$$$$$**

✳ 🏠 **Rock Villa** [178 B7] (7 rooms) Nilisgewatta Temple Rd; ☎ 011 234 0033; m 0777 966252; e info@taruvillas.com; w taruvillas.com. This superb classic-contemporary boutique hotel is set in a gracious mid-19th-century walauwa surrounded by a manicured 1ha bird-friendly garden, where neat rows of palms are hung with hammocks. Rooms & suites differ greatly in shape, size & cost, but all are decorated in period style & come with king-size bed, AC, fan, nets, TV & a good DVD selection. A path across the railway track leads to a clean semi-private beach. Other amenities include a large swimming pool, a gazebo spa & a top-notch terrace restaurant whose varied menu is dominated by, but not confined to, fresh seafood. *Rooms from US$140/195 standard/deluxe dbl, suites from US$550, all B&B, with low-season discounts.* Room **$$$$**, suite **$$$$$+**

🏠 **Nisala Arana** [map, page 172] (7 rooms) Circular Rd; m 0777 733313; e info@nisalaarana.com; w nisalaarana.com. Set 3km along the riverside road connecting Bentota to Galapatha Temple, this owner-managed boutique lodge exudes an aura of old-world charm & Arcadian tranquillity. It comprises 3 rooms in a restored 19th-century homestead complete with antique furniture, & 4 split between a pair of new purpose-built annexes decorated in the same vintage colonial style. High-ceilinged rooms come with AC, fan, TV, coffee machine & 4-poster bed with fitted net, & some have an open-air bathroom. Set behind long, grey wall & gates made from railway sleepers, the secluded 2ha garden is enclosed by forest & incorporates a temple for meditation, sparkling swimming pool & open-sided dining pavilion. Utterly idyllic, despite the distance from the beach & lack of river view. Good value. *US$200 dbl.* **$$$$$**

🏠 **Club Villa** [178 B6] (17 rooms) Nilisgewatta Temple Rd; ☎ 034 227 5312; e info@clubvillabentota.com; w club-villa.com. Situated next door to Paradise Road & sharing its lovely beachfront location, this place also has a similar back story, being an old colonial villa that was converted to an elegant hotel under the watch of Geoffrey Bawa. The large AC rooms are nice enough, with Dutch-era furniture throughout,

& the gardens are lovely too, making it a far better choice for discerning travellers than any of the upmarket package resorts listed below. That said, it doesn't quite attain the heights of its neighbour. *From US$250 dbl B&B.* **$$$$$**

Upmarket

🏠 **Avani Hotel** [178 A4] (75 rooms) Beach Rd; ☎ 034 494 7878; e bentota@avanihotels.com; w minorhotels.com. Designed by Geoffrey Bawa in the style of a Dutch colonial seaside village, the former Serendib Hotel, situated opposite the railway station, is the most low-rise and architecturally harmonious of Bentota's more package-oriented hotels. It also has a stunning location in large palm-studded grounds centred on a massive swimming pool running down to Bentota beach, where lifeguards are stationed to keep an eye on guests. Recently refurbished rooms come with AC, TV, minibar, tea/coffee & balcony or terrace with ocean view. *From US$205 dbl B&B, dropping by 40% out of season.* **$$$$$**

🏠 **Bentota Beach by Cinnamon** [178 B4] (133 rooms) Beach Rd; ☎ 034 227 5176; m 0715 344732; e info@cinnamonhotels.com; w cinnamonhotels.com. Dating from the 1970s but regularly renovated & still setting the standards for resort hospitality, this well-run package hotel stands in lovely 4ha gardens flanked by the beach to the west & lagoon to the east. Stylish modern rooms all have AC, TV, safe & minibar. A large swimming pool meanders through the garden & the complex also includes a spa, sports & live entertainment centre, & choice of buffet or à la carte restaurant. *US$220 dbl B&B.* **$$$$$**

🏠 **Aida Ayurveda & Holistic Health Resort** [178 B4] (28 rooms) Mangala Rd; ☎ 034 227 1137; e aida1@sltnet.lk; w aidaayurveda.com. A hotel with a difference in terms of design as well as character, Aida functions primarily as an Ayurveda, yoga & wellness centre, though the airy & modern hotel building is a delight with its garden vistas, 1st-floor swimming pool & riverside location. *US$165 dbl B&B.* **$$$$**

🏠 **Vivanta by Taj** [178 B6] (160 rooms) Beach Rd; ☎ 034 555 5555; e bookvivanta.bentota@tajhotels.com; w vivanta.tajhotels.com. Situated at the southern end of the road running parallel to the railway line & the beach, this 5-star resort hotel possesses an exaggerated grandeur that would arguably be better suited to the Bahamas, but it also has a great beachfront location & good amenities including several speciality restaurants, a large swimming pool, & a bar that doubles as a bingo hall on some nights. The AC rooms have all the facilities you'd expect of a hotel of this quality. *US$270/280 sgl/dbl B&B.* **$$$$$**

Moderate

✳ 🏠 **Shangri-Lanka Villa** [178 D7] (5 rooms) De Alwis Rd; 📞 034 227 1181; m 0777 234344; e info@shangrilankavilla.com; w shangrilankavilla.com; see ad, page 208. Owned & managed by a welcoming & helpful British–Sri Lankan couple, this perennially popular boutique guesthouse has an isolated jungle-like setting in leafy grounds with a large swimming pool about 1km inland of the beach & main drag through Bentota. The unusually large chalets are stylishly but informally decorated with darkwood furniture, bright fabrics & colourful local art on the walls, & come with AC, minibar, king-size bed, separate dressing area & a massive bathroom with standing tub & separate shower. Excellent seafood & other meals in the US$5–12 range can be served in the terrace restaurant or on your private veranda. *US$110/125 sgl/dbl B&B.* **$$$$**

✳ 🏠 **Waterside Bentota** [178 D2] (6 rooms) Yathramulla Rd; 📞 034 227 0080; e reservations@ bentotawaterside.com; w bentotawaterside.com. Boasting a fabulously lush waterfront location opposite Aluthgama & 1.5km east of Bentota, this difficult-to-fault small lodge comprises a 2-storey building with all rooms opening out to private terracotta-tiled balconies facing the swimming pool & wooded riverbank. Rooms come with AC, fan & TV, & are very light & spacious, with the 1st floor offering a better view & greater privacy than ground. Obliging & enthusiastic staff, good food in the fan-cooled open-sided restaurant, & free boat transfers downriver to the beach help seal a pretty good deal. *US$130 dbl B&B dropping to US$80/90 sgl/dbl out of season.* **$$$$**

🏠 **Hotel Wunderbar** [178 B7] (24 rooms) Galle Rd; 📞 034 227 5908; m 0777 908640; e wunderbar@sltnet.lk; w hotel-wunderbar.com. A superb & all-but-unimpeded location on the palm-lined beach (only the railway line stands in the way) & breezy stilted 1st-floor restaurant are the best features of this well-established hotel catering mainly to the German market. It also has

a good-sized swimming pool & large comfortable rooms with darkwood furniture, AC, fan, TV & private balcony. The architecture & layout feel a bit incohesive & cobbled together, but not to an extent that's off-putting, & overall it seems like a very friendly, well-run, solidly built & reasonably priced set-up. *From US$118 dbl B&B, with substantial low-season discounts.* **$$$$**

Budget

✳ 🏠 **Hotel Susantha Garden** [178 B4] (24 rooms) Station Access Rd; 📞 034 227 5324; e susanthas@sltnet.lk; w hotelsusanthagarden. com. This popular & central guesthouse adjoining the railway station has come up in the world since it started life as a batik factory in 1971, but it still retains an informal vibe, plenty of character & sensible prices. Only 100m from the beach (crossing the railway line), it stands in leafy tropical gardens that incorporate a swimming pool & an agreeable & well-priced terrace restaurant. Rooms in the colonial-style 2-storey building are on the small side, but come with 4-poster bed & fitted net, fan, fridge & private balcony. Deluxe rooms also have AC. *US$45/54 standard sgl/dbl or US$58/64, with slight premium for sea views.* **$$$**

🏠 **Lagoon Bentota** [178 D2] (8 rooms) Yathramulla Rd; 📞 034 227 0443; m 0714 207400; e lagoonbentota@gmail.com; w lagoonbentota. com. Standing right next door to Waterfront Bentota, this new owner-managed 2-storey lodge seems to be modelled on its neighbour but currently lacks the swimming pool (though you can swim in the river) & offers considerably cheaper rates. Spacious slate-tiled rooms all have AC, fan, TV & private balcony with river view, & it doubles as the base for Lucky Boat Safaris (page 177). Good value. *US$60 dbl B&B.* **$$$**

🏠 **Fuji Riverside Inn** [178 C4] (6 rooms) Yathramulla Rd; 📞 034 227 5303; m 0723 333734; e fujiguesthouse@sltnet.lk; w riversideinnfuji. com. Situated in pretty & tranquil riverfront gardens only 600m east of the main drag through Bentota, this likeable owner-managed lodge has neat & clean rooms with AC, fan, TV, fridge & river view. Fair value. *US$60/77 sgl/dbl with seasonal discounts.* **$$$**

🏠 **Palm Beach Inn** [178 C7] (14 rooms) Galle Rd; 📞 034 227 5352; m 0775 870114; e pbibentota@ymail.com; w pbibentota.com. Set only 200m back from the beach, this low-key family-run guesthouse offers accommodation in comfortable rooms or cabanas, all with queen-size bed, AC & fan. Newer & larger deluxe rooms also have TV & private balcony. A restaurant is attached. *US$60 dbl cabana, US$65/75 standard/deluxe dbl, all rates B&B, with 20% discount out of season.* **$$$**

🏠 **C-Lanka Family Guesthouse** [178 B6] (5 rooms) Nilisgewatta Temple Rd; m 0715 698512; e ariyarathnelenora@gmail.com; w bentotaguesthouse.com. This welcoming 2-storey guesthouse has a quiet location in leafy tropical gardens 300m inland of the beach. Small spotless rooms, some with AC, have 4-poster bed & fitted net, fan, large modern bathroom & balcony looking into the canopy. An open-sided ground-floor restaurant serves 3-course meals for US$10 (advance order only). It's smarter than anywhere listed under shoestring, but a notch below the other budget options, so might qualify as good value or feel a bit overpriced, depending on your perspective. *US$40 dbl with fan or US$50 with AC, all rates B&B.* **$$**

Shoestring
🏠 **Dimuthu Tour Inn** [178 C6] (4 rooms) Sri Dharma Wijayarama Rd; \034 227 0023; e thanuskajayasinghe@gmail.com; w dimuthu-tour-inn-lk.book.direct. Owned & managed by a former chef at Vivanta by Taj & his family, this friendly little guesthouse stands close to the main Galle Rd but just far enough down a leafy alley

to have a rustic feel & be free of traffic noise. The spotless rooms come with fan, net & hot water but no AC, & they serve tasty local b/fasts (*US$3*) & dinner (*US$6.50*) by request. *US$17 dbl.* **$**

🏠 **Okay Goldi Guesthouse** [178 B5] (10 rooms) Pitaramba Rd; m 0759 758643; e anuradha7418@gmail.com. Located on a quiet back road only 100m from Bentota beach, this owner-managed lodge comprise a slightly rundown 2-storey building set in a wild & leafy garden next to the railway line. Clean & comfortable high-ceilinged rooms come with fan, net, cold shower & optional AC. Lunch & dinner cost US$5 each. Good value. *US$17 dbl with fan only or US$22 with AC, all rates B&B.* **$**

🏠 **Wasana Inn** [178 B6] (2 rooms) Sri Dharma Wijayarama Rd; m 0727 111380. Set in a century-old house complete with original wooden roof, windows & frames, this no-frills homestay won't be for everyone, but the family who run it are very welcoming, the small rooms with fan & cold shower are adequately clean & cosy, & it adds up to a traditional villa experience at a backpacker's price. *US$17 dbl.* **$**

🏠 **Rivelco Holiday Inn** [178 C6] (3 rooms) Galle Rd; m 0726 122050, 0773 397973; e kaneshbananjaya@gmail.com. Although it's undeniably simple & set right alongside the noisy main road, this dead cheap owner-managed lodge has nice clean rooms with fan & wooden balcony, & an attached restaurant & juice bar serves local food at local prices. *US$10 dbl.* **$**

✗ Where to eat and drink
✗ **Diya Sisila Garden** [map, page 172] Elpitiya Rd; m 0777 402138; w diyasisila.com; ⊕ 10.00–22.00. Perched attractively on the shore of Lake Dedduwa 2.5km east of the Galle Rd, this owner-managed restaurant has terrace seating in the gardens, as well as floating & stilted summer houses above the lake. The seafood-dominated menu embraces Chinese, Indian, Sri Lankan & Western dishes. Wine & beer are served. **$$$**

✗ **Hotel Wunderbar** [178 B7] Galle Rd; \034 227 5908; w hotel-wunderbar.com; ⊕ 08.00–22.30. Boasting the best location of any restaurant in Bentota, this stilted wooden 1st-floor construction looks out across the railway line to the palm-lined beach & is usually wafted over by a cooling sea breeze. The menu embraces seafood, steaks, pasta, curries & devilled dishes, & it is all

very well priced, as are the beers, wine & cocktails. **$$$**

✗ **Hotel Susantha Garden** [178 B4] Station Access Rd; \034 227 5324; w hotelsusanthagarden.com. The licensed terrace restaurant at this characterful old central hotel serves good-value curries, sandwiches, seafood & grills in the fun setting of a busy tropical garden behind Bentota railway station platform. **$$**

✗ **Malli's Seafood Restaurant** [178 B5] Beach Rd; \034 454 5131; m 0778 514894; ■ MallisSeafoodRestaurant; ⊕ 09.00–23.00. This relatively classy 1st-floor restaurant offers the choice of seating in the AC interior or on a terrace overlooking the railway track. The specialities are fresh seafood & Asian fusion cuisine. Beer & wine are served. A touch pricey but good. **$$$$**

✕ Pradha Restaurant [178 C7] Galle Rd; m 0786 258667; ☺ 08.00–22.00. Tasty & inexpensive curries & seafood, all cooked by the amiable owner-manager-chef, which ensures quality is consistent but means service can be slow when it's busy. No alcohol. **$$**

✕ Prem Café [178 C7] Galle Rd; m 0776 239251; ☺ noon–21.00. Seafood is the main speciality at this unpretentious local restaurant, but it also has a good selection of Chinese & Sri Lankan curries. No alcohol. **$$–$$$**

✕ Golden Grill [178 B4] Station Access Rd; m 0778 566 7081; w goldengrill.lk; ☺ 11.00–21.30. Established in 1980, this relatively formal restaurant consists of a large AC interior reminiscent of a banquet hall & a terrace overlooking the pond in the National Tourist Resort. Service is excellent, with young bow-tied waiters, & the food, whether Western or Eastern, comes quickly. The lunchtime buffet is particularly recommended but it also has a long & varied à la carte menu & decent wine list. Good value. **$$$**

Other practicalities

Banking There's an HNB ATM [178 B4] immediately south of the bridge from Aluthgama. If it isn't working, cross the bridge and you'll find all the main banks represented in Aluthgama.

Shopping A branch of Cargills Food City [178 B4] stands on the main road just south of the bridge, but there are better shops in Aluthgama. For high-quality antiques, De Silva Antiques [178 C5] (✆ 034 227 5507), housed in a former village headman's house on the corner of the Galle and Elpitiya roads, is laid out like a museum with exhibits neatly grouped together, labelled with historical information and stored in glass showcases.

What to see and do The main attraction is Bentota beach, which follows the

coast south from the National Holiday Resort for about 2km. It is usually good for swimming in season, but if conditions are rough you could think about heading north to Maggola beach, which is protected by a reef. Watersports and boat trips along the Bentota River, as well as snorkelling excursions to Berberyn Reef, can be arranged through any of the more upmarket hotels or the watersports operators listed under Aluthgama on pages 177–9.

Galapatha Temple [map, page 172] Straddling a rocky hillock on the west bank of the Bentota River 2.5km inland of the beach, Galapatha is probably the most interesting Buddhist shrine in this part of Sri Lanka. A fenced-off rock inscription to the right of the main entrance states that it was established by royal decree during the 12th-century reign of King Parakramabahu I, but archaeological evidence suggests it might date back to the 3rd-century BC rule of King Devanampiya Tissa. Sadly, the Portuguese destroyed the original temple during their 16th-century occupation of Bentota, but a few stone relicts remain, most notably an exquisitely engraved door-frame adorned with 17 figures of dancing women and dwarves. There's also a large whitewashed dagoba, which some say was originally constructed by King Saddha Tissa in the 2nd century BC to hold the tooth relic of Maha Kassapa, a venerated disciple of the Buddha. The two main image houses date to the Kandyan period, when the temple was revived, and they both have ornate façades that protect lavishly painted interiors and large statues of the sleeping Buddha. The monks on site claim that some of the paintings are very old, but they look relatively modern, so it might well be that the Kandyan-era originals were extensively 'touched up' towards the end of the colonial era.

Coming from Bentota, turn east on to the Elpitiya Road, just past De Silva Antiques, but instead of turning right towards Elpitiya after 1.5km, keep straight and you will reach the signposted temple after another 1km. Buses from Aluthgama to Elpitiya can drop you at this junction, but it might be easier to charter a tuktuk. No entrance fee is charged but a donation is expected.

Lunuganga [map, page 172] (\ *034 428 7051;* m *0773 308602;* w *geoffreybawa. com;* ⊕ *09.30–16.30; entrance US$8*) A former rubber plantation situated on a 6ha peninsula that juts into the eastern shore of Lake Dedduwa, Lunuganga was the home of Geoffrey Bawa, who bought the estate in 1949, when his future prowess as an architect was unsuspected. Bawa renamed the estate Lunuganga (Salt River) and set about transforming the typically robust and characterless plantation house, and surrounding plantation and abandoned paddy fields, to become both an extension and a reflection of the surrounding countryside. He created not an ornamental garden but a fantasy of light and shade, of water and space, of green and brown, of dips and mounds, with vistas framed by doorways and arches and soaring views punctuated by the classic form of a perfect jar or a Grecian statue. To preserve the natural environment, and the view from his patio, he bought the Honduwa Island, in the middle of the lake, and dedicated it as a bird sanctuary. Bawa had his favourite walks and viewpoints that visitors can now enjoy, while they marvel at how he moulded nature to fashion the landscape he wanted. Curiously, although he became such a famous and much-imitated architect, the buildings in the garden have a rustic simplicity. Visitors can peep into his house where the atmosphere owes a lot to venerable and sometimes eccentric pieces of furniture, including kerosene-powered fans and religious statues from Europe.

Lunuganga is unsignposted and quite difficult to find. To get here, follow the Galle Road south from the Bentota–Aluthgama Bridge for 1km, then turn east on to the Elpitiya Road, just past De Silva Antiques. Turn right after another 1.5km, then continue south past the Diya Sisila Restaurant, crossing a long bridge over an inlet to Lake Dedduwa, for another 1.8km (if you see Dedduwa Gangarama Temple to your right, you've gone 200m too far) before turning right again. Lunuganga, protected by a tall gate, stands about 900m along this dirt road. Using public transport, buses from Aluthgama to Elpitiya can drop you at this last junction only 10 minutes' walk from the estate entrance.

INDURUWA Though it lies just 3km south of Bentota, the small fishing village of Induruwa has an altogether more organic and isolated feel. It stands on a long, palm-lined beach where stretches of white sand alternate with rocky outcrops and headlands that leave it more exposed, but also render it more scenically interesting, than some other beaches in the area. As with Kosgoda to the south, Induruwa is an important turtle-nesting beach, and the site of a couple of turtle hatcheries, notably the well-organised Induruwa Sea Turtle Conservation Project [map, page 172] (m *0776 690168, 0777 858679;* w *srilankaseaturtles.com; entrance US$7 pp*), which stands alongside the Galle Road 300m south of Induruwa Beach Resort. An interesting short excursion, 2km inland along the Kaikawala Road, is the Tuesday morning market at Gonagala (at the junction between the 67km and the 68km posts), which features a range of intriguing tropical fruits and vegetables.

Getting there and away Buses between Aluthgama or Colombo and Galle stop at Induruwa, as do slow trains on the Southern line. However, it might be more efficient to take an express train, hop off at Aluthgama, and catch a tuktuk from there.

8

🏠 Where to stay *Map, page 172*

Induruwa is considerably less resorty than neighbouring Bentota, and it supports a more limited and scattered selection of accommodation.

Exclusive

※ 🏠 **Saman Villas** (27 AC suites) Galle Rd, 1km north of Induruwa; 📞034 227 5435; e resv@samanvilla.com; w samanvilla.com. This classy all-suite lodge offers accommodation in 5 categories of villa spread widely across a tall rocky headland flanked by two long idyllic beaches of golden sand lined by curving palms. The genuinely spectacular location is complemented by a massive wedge-shaped infinity pool & the Kandyan-style architecture of the individual villas, whose bright & well-lit teak-dominated split-level interior incorporates AC, dressing room, well-equipped TV lounge with iPod dock & DVD player, semi-open bathroom with tub & shower, & terrace or balcony with bed & seats. The 10 swishest rooms also have plunge pools. *From US$576/589 sgl/dbl B&B, with seasonal discounts.* **$$$$$+**

Upmarket

🏠 **Whispering Palms** (15 rooms) Galle Rd; 📞034 227 5181; m 0711 908474; e bookings@whisperingpalmshotel.com; w whisperingpalmshotel.com. Small enough but too lacking in affectations to qualify as a boutique hotel, the well-equipped 3-storey property combines a perfect beachfront location with spacious tiled rooms that all come with queen-size bed, AC, fan, tea/coffee, dressing room, large modern bathroom & private balcony offering a great sea view. The British owner-manager lives on the property, which also incorporates a keyhole-shaped beachside swimming pool & breezy 2nd-storey restaurant/bar serving a varied selection of continental & Asian dishes in the US$7–10 range. *US$153/168 B&B standard/deluxe dbl, with hefty off-season discounts.* **$$$$**

🏠 **Temple Tree Resort & Spa** (48 rooms) Galle Rd; 📞034 227 0700; e info@templetreeresortandspa.com; w templetreeresortandspa.com. This pleasant beachfront property has an idyllic location on a quiet section of beach at the south end of the village. The main building has a warehouse-like feel, with its grey tiles & neat concrete walls, while the spacious rooms with AC & fan are decorated with abstract art & lead out through glass doors

hung with white linen blinds to a sea-facing balcony. An attractive feature is the long, narrow swimming pool & row of lush green vegetation that separates the main building & open-sided restaurant from the surf. The hotel celebrated its 10th anniversary in 2017 & is starting to look a little frayed at the seams, but it's still good value at the price. *US$90/120 sgl/dbl B&B.* **$$$$**

🏠 **Pandanus Beach Resort** (76 rooms) Galle Rd; 📞034 227 5363; e info@pandanusbeach.com; w pandanusbeach.com. Opened in 2014, this state-of-the-art hotel is set on a steep sandy incline running down to an arcing bay with a small rock peninsula a few hundred metres to the south. A long swimming pool stands right on the beach, & other amenities include a beachfront seafood restaurant, a stylish bar, a snooker room & a good spa. The rooms have a contemporary Asian feel & come with funky modern art on the walls & AC, TV, minibar, coffee/tea & safe. All rooms have a sea-facing terrace/balcony but those on the 1st floor feel more private than on the ground floor. *US$150/175 sgl/dbl B&B.* **$$$$**

🏠 **Induruwa Beach Resort** (93 rooms) 📞034 428 7124; e inbeachr@sltnet.lk; w induruwabeachresort.lk. This shabby & architecturally outmoded 4-storey monolith is partially redeemed by its fabulous location on a sandy beach flanked by a pair of rocky outcrops. A kidney-shaped swimming pool overlooks the beach, & other amenities include a gym, spa, bar & 2 restaurants. The large tiled rooms are old-fashioned & dominated by murky browns & yellows, but they're serviceable & come with AC, fan, minibar, TV & sea-facing balcony. Unless you subscribe religiously to the location, location, location school of thought, the official rack rate isn't worth considering, but budget travellers who scour the usual online booking agencies might pick up a room for well under half the price – at which point it becomes a pretty good deal. *US$110/130 sgl/dbl B&B.* **$$$$**

Shoestring

※ 🏠 **Long Beach Cottages** (5 rooms) Galle Rd; m 0716 398899; e hanjayas@yahoo.de. Established in 1982 by the same welcoming

English-speaking couple who still run it today, this beachfront lodge opposite Induruwa Post Office is set in sandy green gardens & offers accommodation in simple but spotless rooms with twin bed, fan, nets & private sea-facing balcony. Excellent value. *US$18 dbl, plus US$3 pp b/fast & US$4 pp lunch/dinner.* **$**

✕ Where to eat and drink *Map, page 172*

All the hotels listed above serve food and there is a good choice of restaurants 3km further north in Bentota.

✳ ✕ **Osteria Romana** Galle Rd; ☎ 034 229 1602/4; ⓕ osteriaromana.induruwa123; ⏰ 15.00–22.00 Tue–Sun. This exceptional Italian restaurant offers the choice of eating in the beachfront terrace garden or in a stylish interior adorned with vintage monochrome photos of movie stars and musicians. Pasta & pizza are the main specialities, but a good seafood & meat selection is also on offer, supplemented by a long wine list & scrumptious desert selection. **$$$$**

Other practicalities There are no banking facilities in Induruwa; you will need to head north to Aluthgama. A few local shops are dotted around the village, including the Bentota Wine Store immediately south of the Induruwa Beach Resort, but there is far more choice in Aluthgama.

THE COAST FROM KOSGODA TO AMBALANGODA AND MADU WETLANDS

KOSGODA, AHUNGALLA AND BALAPITIYA Situated along the 8km stretch of coast between the Kosgoda and Madu lagoons, the small villages of Kosgoda and Ahungalla and larger town of Balapitiya all have lovely palm-lined beaches that offer good swimming in season, but are far less developed and resort-like than their counterparts around Bentota and Hikkaduwa. The beaches at Kosgoda and Ahungalla in particular also form the island's most important breeding site for marine turtles. All five species known from Sri Lanka have been recorded here at some point, but green and olive ridley turtles are the most regular visitors during the main breeding season, which runs from November to July (peaking January–May). Several privately run turtle hatcheries operate in the area, including the pioneering and highly regarded Kosgoda Sea Turtle Conservation Project, which was established in 1988 and is still under the same management today. The area offers some good birdwatching, and provides access by boat or on foot to the ecologically important Madu Wetlands (pages 191–2).

Getting there and away Kosgoda, Ahungalla and Balapitiya respectively lie about 75km, 77km and 83km south of Colombo Fort following the coastal road through Aluthgama, or about 20km further along the faster Southern Expressway, exiting at Interchange 5 (Welipanna) for Kosgoda or Ahungalla, or Interchange 6 (Kurundugahahetekma) for Balapitiya. Allow roughly 3 hours in a private vehicle. Any bus heading between Colombo and Ambalangoda or Galle can drop you at Kosgoda, Ahungalla or Balapitiya, and all three towns are serviced by railway stations stopped at by non-express trains between Colombo and Galle.

⌂ Where to stay *Map, page 188*
Exclusive

✳ ⌂ **The River House** (5 rooms)
Uththumagnana Rd, Balapitiya; ☎ 091 225 6306; m 0777 748064; e theriverhouse@asialeisure.lk; w theriverhouse.lk. This tranquil retreat stands in lovely forested 3ha grounds running down to the

187

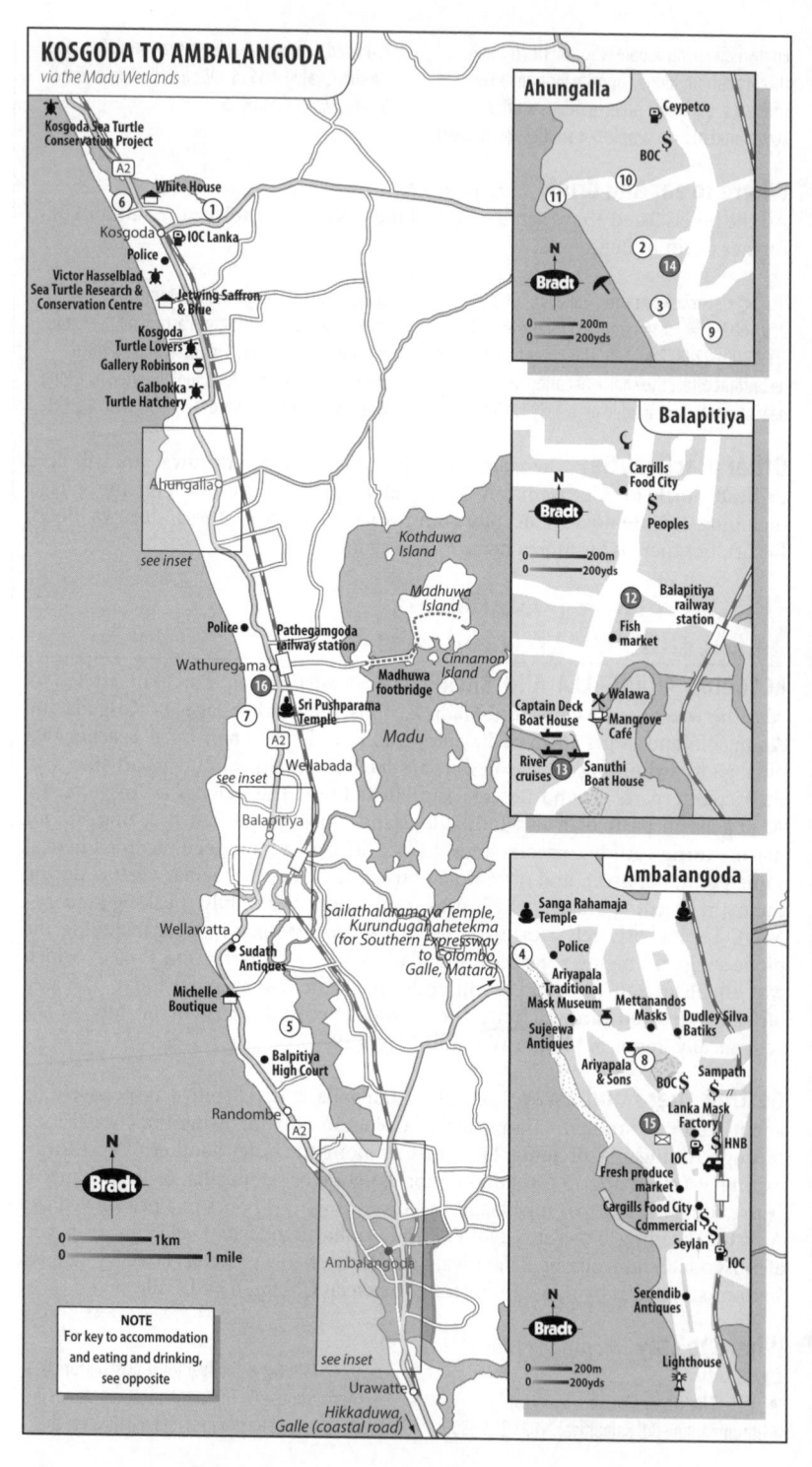

KOSGODA TO AMBALANGODA
via the Madu Wetlands

Kosgoda Sea Turtle
Conservation Project

A2

White House
1

6

Kosgoda
IOC Lanka

Police

Victor Hasselblad
Sea Turtle Research &
Conservation Centre

Jetwing Saffron
& Blue

Kosgoda
Turtle Lovers
Gallery Robinson
Galbokka
Turtle Hatchery

Ahungalla

see inset

Kothduwa
Island

Madhuwa
Island

Police

Pathegamgoda
railway station

Wathuregama
16

7
Sri Pushparama
Temple

A2

Wellabada

see inset

Balapitiya

Cinnamon
Island

Madhuwa
footbridge

Madu

Wellawatta

Sailathalaramaya Temple,
Kurundugahahetekma
(for Southern Expressway
to Colombo, Galle, Matara)

Sudath
Antiques

Michelle
Boutique

5

Balpitiya
High Court

Randombe

A2

N

Bradt

0 — 1km
0 — 1 mile

Ambalangoda

see inset

Urawatte

Hikkaduwa,
Galle (coastal road)

NOTE
For key to accommodation
and eating and drinking,
see opposite

Ahungalla

Ceypetco

BOC

11   10

2

14

N

Bradt

0 — 200m
0 — 200yds

3

9

Balapitiya

Cargills
Food City

Peoples

N

Bradt

12

Fish
market

Balapitiya
railway
station

Captain Deck
Boat House

Walawa
Mangrove
Café

River
cruises
13

Sanuthi
Boat House

0 — 200m
0 — 200yds

Ambalangoda

Sanga Rahamaja
Temple

4   Police

Ariyapala
Traditional
Mask Museum

Mettanandos
Masks

Dudley Silva
Batiks

Sujeewa
Antiques

Ariyapala
& Sons
8

BOC

Sampath

Lanka Mask
Factory

15

HNB

IOC

Fresh produce
market

Cargills Food City

Commercial

Seylan

IOC

Serendib
Antiques

N

Bradt

0 — 200m
0 — 200yds

Lighthouse

Madu River about 3km south of Balapitiya. Alive with monkeys & birds, it also offers paid motorboat excursions & free kayaking on the river, & has a swimming pool & lovely restaurant sprawling out on to a shady deck. Accommodation is in massive & earthily decorated suites with high ceiling, teak floor, stylish darkwood furniture, queen-size bed, AC, fan, TV, DVD player & library, tea/coffee & private walled garden with koi pond. A wonderful back-to-nature antidote to the large resorts that line the nearby coast. *From US$348 dbl B&B, with substantial low-season discounts, plus US$40/45 pp lunch/dinner.* $$$$$+

Upmarket

🏠 **Heritance Ahungalla** (152 rooms) Galle Rd, Ahungalla; 📞 091 555 5000; e gre. ahu@heritancehotels.com; w heritancehotels. com. Sri Lanka's first 5-star beach hotel, originally the Triton, has a magnificent approach through an avenue of palm trees set around a large pond, and a swimming pool visible from the open entrance terrace with the sea glistening beyond it. It has another swimming pool in its newer, northern wing. Despite its age, it has been revamped with glitz, glamour & a fine-dining restaurant commanding a dramatic view & serving some of the best fare on the coast. There is also a nightclub & a main dining room where most meals are buffets. Very good value. *US$125/132 sgl/dbl B&B, with low-season discounts.* $$$$

KOSGODA TO AMBALANGODA

via the Madu Wetlands
For listings, see pages 187–90 & 193

🛏 **Where to stay**

1	Happy Man Guesthouse
2	Heritance Ahungalla
3	Hotel Riu Sri Lanka
4	Juce
5	The River House
6	Sankarest Villa
7	Shinagawa Beach
8	Sumudu Guesthouse
9	Villa Ranmenika
10	Walauwa Villa
11	White Villa Resort

✖ **Where to eat and drink**

12	Asian
13	Bord'eau
14	Daniel's Pub
	Juce (see 4)
15	Seven Two Note
16	Walauwa Tea Room

🏠 **Shinagawa Beach** (26 rooms) Old Guru Niwasa Rd, Balapitiya; 📞 091 203 0444; e info@ shinagawabeach.com; w shinagawabeach.com. This stylish service-oriented Japanese-owned hotel 1km north of Balapitiya has a fabulous open reception area decorated with old boat hulls, a quality contemporary-looking restaurant heavy on glass, wood & metal, & spacious but rather mundane rooms with AC, TV, darkwood furniture & full-length windows offering a great sea view. The small garden has a swimming pool & attractive beach frontage scattered with deckchairs. Very nice, almost boutiquey, but feels a touch overpriced. *US$285/330 sgl/dbl B&B, seasonal discounts.* $$$$$+

🏠 **Hotel Riu Sri Lanka** (500 rooms) Galle Rd, Ahungalla; 📞 091 522 0000; w riu.com. Opened in mid-2016, this gleaming white 5-storey monolith is Sri Lanka's largest hotel, & supplements an idyllic location on Ahungalla beach with 3 swimming pools, a children's pool, gym, spa & several themed restaurants. Though very large & somewhat deficient in character, it offers good-value all-inclusive club-style packages & also arranges day & overnight trips further afield for more adventurous types. *From US$233/298 sgl/dbl FB inc drinks, with seasonal discounts of up to 25%.* $$$$$

Moderate

🏠 **White Villa Resort** (11 rooms) Thotawatha Rd, Ahungalla; 📞 091 226 5065; m 0773 372694; e bookingwhitevilla@gmail.com; w whitevillaresort.com. Sprawling across a small rocky headland flanked on either side by wide, sandy palm-lined beaches, this attractively located small hotel has modern tiled rooms with AC, fan, TV & solid wood furniture. Amenities include a swimming pool set on a seafront deck & a cleverly designed restaurant serving cocktails, beer, wine & a varied selection of seafood- & Italian-dominated mains ($$) while waves crash on the rocks below. *More than decent value at US$110 dbl B&B, & significantly better rates are available through the usual online booking agencies.* $$$$

🏠 **Villa Ranmenika** (14 rooms) Galle Rd, Ahungalla; 📞 091 226 4251; e ranmenika@sltnet. lk; w villaranmenika.com. Set on the landward side of the main road 200m from the beach, this characterful old villa stands in a large & delightful tropical garden whose huge & sparklingly clean swimming pool is hidden by a plethora of palms

8

& crotons. Rooms & suites with AC, fan & TV are spread across 2 floors, with some opening on to their own miniature garden. An agreeable & well-priced base from which to explore the west coast, or retreat from it. Meals & snacks are available on demand. *From US$87 dbl B&B.* **$$$$**

Budget

✳ 🏠 **Happy Man Guesthouse** (5 rooms) Uragaha Rd, Kosgoda; **m** 0777 198192; **e** sulalitha.kosgoda@yahoo.com; **w** su-tours. com. Set in sprawling jungle-like gardens 600m east of the Galle Rd, this eco-aware, family-run lodge is bordered to the north by a mangrove-lined creek that flows into the Kosgoda Lagoon & to the east by a 3ha patch of unspoilt forest. The 3 nicest rooms are set in a restored 19th-century villa decorated in Kandyan style, & come with fan, net & private terrace or balcony. The other 2 rooms, situated on the 1st floor of the more modern & less characterful house where the family lives, come with AC & a balcony offering great in-house birding. Amenities include kitchen access, a swimming pool, paddle boats to explore the lagoon or visit the beach 1.2km to the west, & home-cooked curry buffets for around US$8 pp.

The hands-on owner is a guide with 20 years' experience & bags of enthusiasm when it comes to helping guests locate birds & other wildlife. Rates include free pick-up from Kosgoda bus or railway station. A well-priced gem! *US$50 dbl B&B.* **$$$**

🏠 **Sankarest Villa** (4 rooms) 100m west of Galle Rd, Kosgoda; **m** 0771 879257; **w** sankarest. webs.com. Set in small neat gardens with swimming pool within earshot of the Galle Rd, this owner-managed villa has large, comfortable & attractively decorated rooms with AC, net & fridge. The garden restaurant serves good Sri Lankan food & stands only 200m from the beach just south of the Kosgoda lagoon mouth. *US$40–70 dbl B&B.* **$$–$$$**

Shoestring

🏠 **Walauwa Villa** (4 rooms) Thotawatha Rd, Ahungalla; ☎ 091 226 5015; **e** dinuka.dhananjana@gmail.com; **w** walauwavillaahungalla.com. Set in a small quiet tropical garden 400m west of the Galle Rd & a similar distance from Ahungalla beach, this pleasant family-run place offers the choice of older dbl rooms with fan or newer AC rooms with 4 beds. *From US$14 dbl.* **$**

✕ Where to eat and drink *Map, page 188*

All the hotels listed above have restaurants. Kosgoda and Ahungalla are not large enough to sustain the variety of tourist-oriented standalone restaurants associated with Bentota or Hikkaduwa, but there are a few adequate options in Balapitiya, catering mainly to tour parties before or after an excursion on the Madu Wetlands.

✕ **Bord'eau Restaurant** Galle Rd, Balapitiya; ☎ 091 225 4173; **m** 0777 566503; ⏲ 10.00–22.00. Situated about 100m south of the bridge across the River Madu, this relatively smart restaurant serves seafood, filled crêpes & local dishes in a palm-shaded riverside garden. **$$$**

✕ **Asian Restaurant** Galle Rd, Balapitiya; ☎ 091 309 5333; **m** 0777 867667; ❦ balapitiiya; ⏲ 10.00–22.00. The pick of a few eateries lining Balapitiya main road north of the bridge serves a varied selection of tasty Chinese & Sri Lankan dishes. No alcohol. **$$–$$$**

☕ **Walauwa Tea Room** Galle Rd; ⏲ 09.00–18.00. This cosy tearoom opposite the junction for Madhuwa Bridge is set in the quaint walauwa (colonial-era villa) for which it is named. No food, but a good variety of locally produced teas is served & sold.

🍷 **Daniel's Pub** Galle Rd, Ahungalla; **m** 0783 962705; ⏲ 11.00–14.00 & 17.00–23.00. A great place for escaping the resort hotels & associating with locals, this characterfully dingy pub has inexpensive draught on tap & a good choice of imported & local spirits. The limited selection of local dishes feels like a bit of an afterthought & is served evenings only. **$$**

Other practicalities There is a Cargills Food City in Balapitiya, but the only ATMs there don't accept foreign cards, so you need to head north to Aluthgama or south to Ambalangoda to draw money. For hunters of quirky souvenirs, the eclectically stocked Sudath Antiques, set in a rather dilapidated house just south of Balapitiya, might be worth a look.

What to see and do The most attractive of the string of soft sandy beaches running along the coast between the Kosgoda and Madu lagoons is Ahungalla, which stretches for 3km between the White Villa Resort and Shinagawa Beach, and is verged upon by the Heritance Ahungalla and Hotel Rui. The beaches here are all very unsheltered and unprotected, so rough waves and undercurrents make it unsafe to swim out of season, and the red flag often flies during the height of the season too.

Kosgoda Sea Turtle Conservation Project (KSTCP) [map, page 188] *(Galle Rd, between Induruwa & Kosgoda;* \ *091 226 4567;* m *0776 007302;* e *kosgodaseaturtle@hotmail.com;* w *kosgodaseaturtle.org;* ◷ *09.00–17.00; entrance US$3.50)* Established in 1988 by Dudley Perera, who still manages it today, the KSTCP is the longest-serving and most highly regarded of half a dozen independent turtle hatcheries run by local villagers in the vicinity of Kosgoda. Established at the urging of environmentalists, the hatcheries collect newly laid turtle eggs before they can be scooped up as food, then re-bury them until they hatch, giving the turtles a chance to grow in a protected environment until they can be released into the sea, usually at around 18.15, shortly after sunset, and often by tourists who pay a contribution for the privilege. During the breeding season, it also arranges night patrols, starting at 20.00, which serve the dual purpose of deterring poachers and offering visitors the thrilling – and rather humbling – opportunity to witness female turtles coming ashore to lay their eggs in the sand. A fee is charged and this helps support the turtle nest protection and awareness programme.

Victor Hasselblad Sea Turtle Research and Conservation Centre [map, page 188] *(School Ln, Kosgoda;* m *0722 248300;* ◷ *09.00–17.00; entrance US$3.50)* Another well-established and reputable hatchery offering similar experiences to the KSTCP.

MADU WETLAND SANCTUARY One of the most popular and rewarding excursions along the coast between Colombo and Galle is a motorised boat trip into the Madu (or Maduganga) Wetland, a beautiful estuarine ecosystem rich in wildlife, old temples and other sites of cultural significance. The main wetland is situated about 1.5km inland of Ahungalla but is more easily reached from Balapitiya, to which it is connected by a 2km stretch of the Madu River that flows south past town before emptying into the ocean. Extending over 915ha, the wetland is essentially an estuarine system associated with the Madu River and comprising 770ha of open water and as many as 64 islands, some of which are inhabited while others are entirely tidal. Noted for its biodiversity, the estuary gained international recognition in 2003 when it was listed as Sri Lanka's third Ramsar Site (of what are now six). The dominant vegetation type is mangrove forest, composed of around 14 specialised tree and shrub species that thrive in tidal saline waters. However, an IUCN (International Union for Conservation of Nature and Natural Resources) study undertaken in 2000 determined that the estuary actually incorporates 10 major wetland vegetation types, and a total of more than 300 plant, 250 vertebrate and 50 butterfly species.

Exploring the wetlands
By boat The starting point for boat trips is Balapitiya, which is easily reached by train, bus or tuktuk from anywhere along the nearby coast. The riverbank either

side of Balapitiya Bridge is lined with operators offering 1–3-hour boat trips into the wetland. Rates are typically around US$27 per party of up to six for the first hour, then US$7 for every additional 30 minutes. It is best to take a trip early in the morning, into the sunrise, when birds and the prawn fishermen (dropping nets into the reed baskets at the end of bamboo-fenced funnels) are busy. Recommended operators are as follows:

Captain Deck Boat House Galle Rd, north of Balapitiya Bridge; ☎ 091 225 7614; m 0777 641659; e gangabadaasiri@sltnet.lk; w gangabadaasiriya.com
Sanuthi Boat House Galle Rd, south of Balapitiya Bridge; ☎ 091 225 9771; m 0771

281615; e sudathreginold@gmail.com; f sudathreginold
Bord'eau Restaurant & River Cruises Galle Rd, south of Balapitiya Bridge; ☎ 091 225 4173; m 0777 566503

By road/on foot For those who don't fancy or feel like paying for a boat trip, the wetland's largest island, Madhuwa, can be reached from the western shore along a 700m foot/bicycle bridge that crosses the open water and extensive mangroves. To get here from Balapitiya, follow the Colombo road for 2km to Pathegamgoda, then take the small road running east opposite the Walauwa Tea Room, passing Pathegamgoda railway station to your left after about 100m, and follow it east for another 1.2km until you see the footbridge in front of you. Tuktuks can take you all the way to the bridge but not across it. Once on the island, allow up to an hour to walk around its circumference.

What to see and do
Wildlife is everywhere. Water monitors nudge along the banks, both species of crocodile lurk ominously in the shallows, and leaping purple-faced langurs with attractive black and grey markings are a common sight. A fish unique to this tidal habitat is the mudskipper – a strange amphibious creature that flip-flops along exposed mudbanks below the mangroves. Birdlife is diverse and conspicuous, with 115 species recorded, ranging from soaring white-bellied sea-eagles and various herons, egret and cormorants to a variety of pretty kingfishers and bee-eaters. An estimated 300 families live on the estuary's islands, deriving a meagre income from prawn farming, catching fish using traditional bamboo fences as traps, and stripping the bark off cinnamon branches to make aromatic quills.

Most tours incorporate a stop at Madhuwa (a truncation of Maha Duwa, meaning 'Large Island'), which is indeed the wetland's most extensive island at 36ha. Connected to mainland Pathegamgoda by a footbridge, Madhuwa supports around half the estuary's population, and is serviced by a primary school, a post office and two temples including one dedicated to the goddess Pattini. Another island worth seeing is tiny Kothduwa, site of Kothduwa Rajamaha Temple, which was reputedly founded in the 13th century by a minister of King Parakramabahu II, and briefly stored the Buddha tooth relic during the Portuguese era, though none of its buildings dates to before 1890.

AMBALANGODA A busy and substantial port town with a population of 60,000, Ambalangoda is in most respects remarkably unaffected by tourism, despite being ensconced as the region's main centre of wooden mask and puppet production. The bustling main road (which runs parallel to and west of the coastal highway) provides access to a large bustling market, as well as a picturesque fishing harbour protected by a solid rock 600m breakwater with a narrow entrance. The harbour is flanked by a stretch of coast that is undeveloped for tourism but offers considerable promise with its sandy beaches and shallow offshore waters punctuated with rocky reefs. For all that, most foreigners who pass through Ambalangoda are on their way somewhere else, stopping only to take a quick look at one of its thoroughly worthwhile mask museums, or possibly to divert 4km northeast to the less rewarding Sailathalaramaya Temple.

Getting there and away As the second-largest town on the coast between Colombo and Galle, Ambalangoda has good public transport connections in both directions. It lies 85km south of Colombo along the coastal road through Aluthgama, or 20km further along the faster Southern Expressway via Interchange 6 (Kurundugahahetekma). It is only 35km north of Galle along the coastal road through Hikkaduwa. Buses to/from Colombo, Aluthgama, Hikkaduwa and Galle depart every 15 minutes in either direction. Most trains between Colombo and Galle (about 10 daily) stop at Ambalangoda, whose central railway station reflects its 19th-century origins.

Where to stay *Map, page 188*

Accommodation options are limited by comparison with more resorty parts of the coast, but the places listed below stand out.

＊ ⌂ **Sumudu Guesthouse** (6 rooms) Main St; 📞091 225 8832; **e** sumuduguesthouse@gmail.com. A simple but very agreeable family-run set-up, this ornately gabled early 20th-century villa, centrally located in a pretty garden around the corner from the mask museums, has been welcoming budget travellers for more than 30 years. A restaurant is attached, all rooms have net & fan, & some have AC. Great value. *US$8/13 dbl with fan/AC.* **$**

⌂ **Juce** (21 rooms, 1 dorm) Galle Rd; 📞011 452 0130; **e** whatsup@jucehotels.com; **w** jucehotels.com. Situated next to the police station 600m north of the town centre, this unusual beachfront hotel is designed to attract a younger crowd, with its funky glass-sided rooftop bar & well-priced ground-floor restaurant (pizzas, burgers, curries & seafood in the **$$–$$$** range). Full marks for the beach setting & the swimming pool, but the boldly coloured rooms, complete with AC, fan, built-in TV & commanding sea view, are let down by cheap fittings & gimmicky features (such as an app to change light colours from red to green to blue as you like). Fair value. *US$120 dbl B&B, US$18 pp dorm bed.* **$$$$**

Where to eat and drink *Map, page 188*

The best restaurant is Juce, as listed under *Where to stay*. The usual motley collection of local eateries can be found along Main Street, but only one stands out.

✕ **Seven Two Note** Main St; **m** 0719 466729; **e** aselagodahewa@gmail.com; 🕐 06.00–21.00 Mon–Sat. Tasty Sri Lankan buffet lunches & South Indian & Chinese à la carte with prices aimed squarely at the local market. No alcohol, but good juice. **$**

Other practicalities All the major **banks** and associated 24-hour ATMs can be found on one of the two main north–south thoroughfares. There are two branches of **Cargills Food City** on the Galle Road, and a good **fresh produce market** stands on the west side of Main Street close to the fishing harbour. In addition to the mask museums and shops described below, **Sujeewa Antiques** at the north end of town and **Serendib Antiques** in the south can be interesting places to rustle around. **Dudley Silva Batiks** (📞 *091 225 9411;* **e** *dudleybatik@ sltnet.lk*) is regarded to be one of the finest practitioners of batik in the country, but it isn't cheap.

The average age at which women in Sri Lanka marry has risen to 26. There are advertisements in the Sunday newspapers seeking brides/grooms. This is not a lonely hearts column but part of the ancient tradition of arranged marriages which assures that couples are matched through horoscope, cultural identity and social status.

The central feature of a Sinhalese wedding is the *poruwa* ceremony. Foreigners who come on special wedding-package tours can also be married in this fashion. A registrar attends such a ceremony and issues a marriage certificate. The following description has been supplied by the **Bentota Beach Hotel**, a favourite venue for visitors who stay there, especially to get married in the local style.

The poruwa is a decorated marriage platform used for the bride and groom to stand upon until the traditional wedding ceremony is completed. In accordance with ancient Sinhalese rites and customs, the platform is covered with a clean white cloth, upon which are placed five kinds of medicinal herb, a coconut, rice, and a few coins to bring blessings and prosperity to the couple.

Four pots adorned with coconut flowers, upon which four oil lamps are placed, are kept on the four corners of the poruwa. The lamps are lit before the ceremony starts, to give protection and to invoke blessings upon the couple by the gods in charge of the four zones. The traditional marriage ceremony is officiated by a Gurunnanse, or Master of Ceremonies.

Traditionally, the groom is escorted to the right side of the poruwa and then the bride to the left. With the reciting of *ashtaka* (stanzas) the couple will get on to the poruwa together. The ashtaka are eulogies composed in Sanskrit calling upon the gods to invoke blessings and good wishes on the couple.

Once the couple are on the poruwa, they are given seven sheaves of betel leaves to drop on the dais of the poruwa. This act represents unity, friendship and co-operation. The offering of betel leaves to elders by the couple is considered a gesture of great respect and is done on special occasions.

The bride's right little finger and the groom's left one are tied together with a blessed thread and water is sprinkled on the hands, which denotes Oneness. At this stage, four girls dressed in traditional half-saris chant *Jayamangala Gatha*, a set of stanzas used only for special occasions, wishing the couple well in health, wealth, prosperity and happiness. Rings are exchanged.

During the chanting of stanzas blessing the couple, bride and groom are led off the poruwa, with both putting their right foot forward. Then the couple light the oil lamp together, depicting unity and for prosperity. The entire ceremony is accompanied by the beating of drums.

What to see and do   Mask- and puppet-making are the best-known crafts of the Ambalangoda area. Both have their roots in folk craft. The exorcism rituals of low-country folk-dancing demand grotesque and garishly painted demon-faced masks to scare away the devils. The masks are carved out of balsa-like Kaduru wood, so they are light enough to be worn throughout a night-long dance performance. Each mask is hand-carved and painted with symbols according to what demon it is supposed to frighten away. The town has two privately run mask and puppet museums, both run by active mask-makers who are also the sons of Ariyapala

Wijesooriya (1901–95), a master craftsman whose mask-making credentials can be traced back seven generations to Bioris de Silva Wijesooriya (1798–1868). Both museums are genuinely interesting, and are attached to shops selling masks, puppets and other items crafted on site.

Ariyapala & Sons [map, page 188] (*Main St;* \ *091 225 8373;* e *info@ masksariyapalasl.com;* w *masksariyapalasl.com;* ⊕ *08.30–17.30*) The better of the two mask museums, and the only one open on Sunday, this contains a fabulous collection of masks and puppets, some more than 200 years old, as well as an active workshop and a library of anthropological literature pertaining to Sri Lankan masked dances. Displays are well annotated and an articulate guide will show you around for free. The attached shop sells small keepsake masks for around US$12–15, while larger masks start at around US$50.

Ariyapala Traditional Mask Museum [map, page 188] (*Main St;* \ *091 225 4899;* ⊕ *09.00–18.00 Mon–Sat*) The museum here is more modest than its main rival, but since they stand right opposite each other, it's still worth a look for a few exceptional examples of vintage masks. The shops seems to be slightly cheaper on the whole.

Sailathalaramaya Temple [map, page 188] (\ *091 492 2884; entrance US$1.70*) Situated in a cinnamon plantation 4km from town and 1km off the main road to the Kurundugahahetekma Interchange, hilltop Sailathalaramaya is the most important temple in the vicinity of Ambalangoda. Its most famous feature is a 35m reclining Buddha, which is the longest sculpture of its type in Sri Lanka, and painted bright orange and yellow. The temple was reputedly founded about 200 years ago, but fell into disrepair until it was revived c2000 by a monk called Magala Somananda Thero. Plenty of other artworks and statues adorn the main image house, but it is all very modern and nothing seems particularly distinguished.

HIKKADUWA

Known for its excellent bathing since the 1930s, Hikkaduwa sprung to prominence in the 1970s when its popularity with young independent travellers sparked some initial low-key tourist development and earned it the nickname Hippy-kaduwa. Since then, it has grown from a charming little fishing village to a large modern town (population 100,000) whose 4km-long developed coastline has drawn slightly fanciful comparisons to Benidorm. The beach itself is undeniably one of Sri Lanka's finest, whether for swimming or snorkelling, thanks to a calming offshore reef protected in Hikkaduwa Marine National Park, though conditions are usually too rough for either activity during the off-season of May–November. And rather paradoxically, while built-up Hikkaduwa feels more resort-like than sprawling Bentota, it actually has fewer large resort hotels, with the focus being more on small boutique-style lodges and backpacker-oriented guesthouses. That said, the options for accommodation are practically limitless, with more than 200 lodgings of varying types competing for tourist traffic, and dozens upon dozens of restaurants, cafés, fast-food outlets and discos catering to all tastes and budgets.

The range of activities in Hikkaduwa isn't quite so daunting. Swimming and snorkelling aside, glass-bottomed boats are available for sedate viewing of the marine park's coral gardens, while the more southerly Wewala and Narigama beaches rank among the country's best spots for surf- and bodyboarding. A pair of

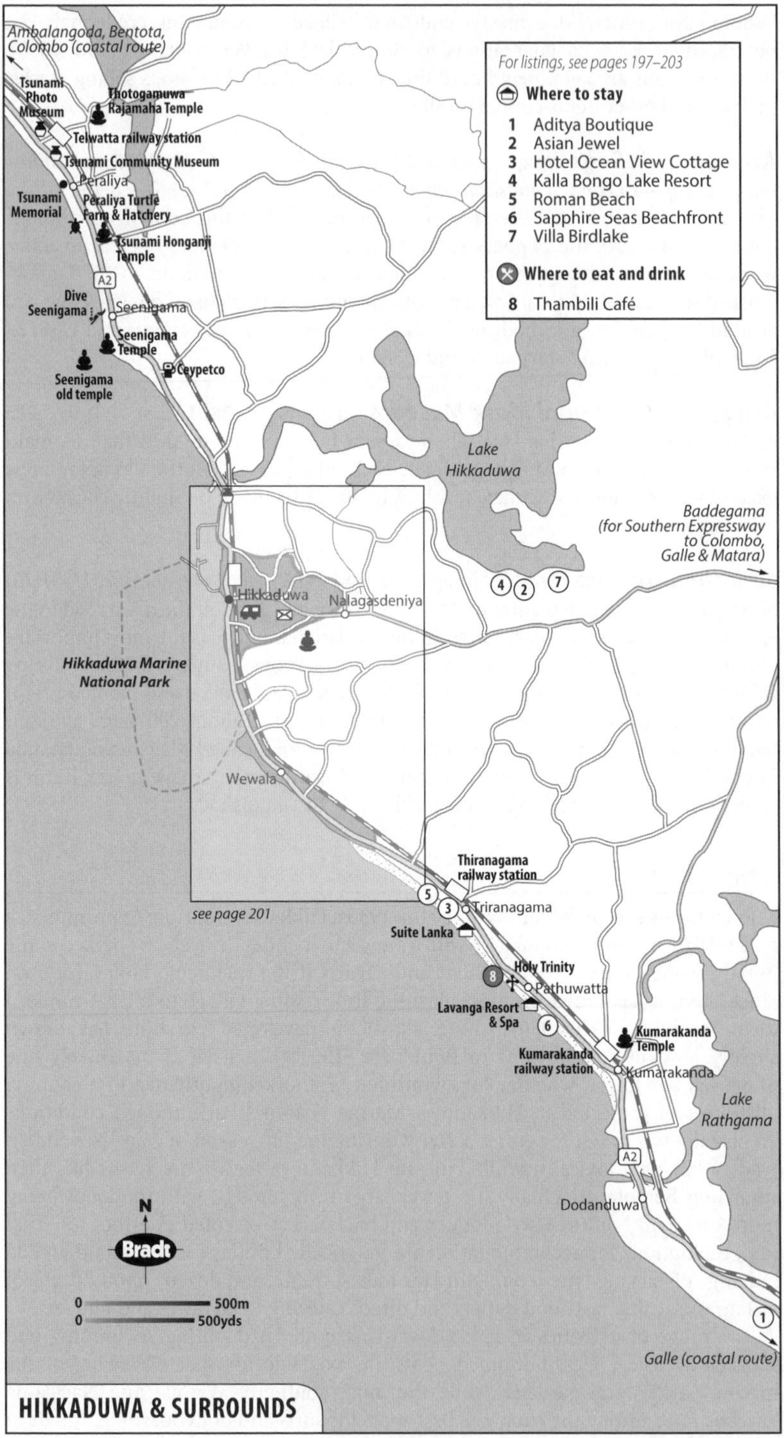

Ambalangoda, Bentota,
Colombo (coastal route)

Tsunami
Photo
Museum

Thotogamuwa
Rajamaha Temple

Telwatta railway station

Tsunami Community Museum

Peraliya

Tsunami
Memorial

Peraliya Turtle
Farm & Hatchery

Tsunami Honganji
Temple

A2

Dive
Seenigama

Seenigama

Seenigama
Temple

Ceypetco

Seenigama
old temple

Lake
Hikkaduwa

Baddegama
(for Southern Expressway
to Colombo,
Galle & Matara)

For listings, see pages 197–203

Where to stay

1 Aditya Boutique
2 Asian Jewel
3 Hotel Ocean View Cottage
4 Kalla Bongo Lake Resort
5 Roman Beach
6 Sapphire Seas Beachfront
7 Villa Birdlake

Where to eat and drink

8 Thambili Café

④ ② ⑦

Hikkaduwa

Nalagasdeniya

**Hikkaduwa Marine
National Park**

Wewala

see page 201

Thiranagama
railway station

⑤
③ Triranagama

Suite Lanka

Holy Trinity

⑧ Pathuwatta

Lavanga Resort
& Spa ⑥

Kumarakanda
Temple

Kumarakanda
railway station Kumarakanda

Lake
Rathgama

A2

Dodanduwa

N

0 ———— 500m
0 ———— 500yds

Galle (coastal route)

①

HIKKADUWA & SURROUNDS

habituated green turtles regularly hangs out on the beach in front of the Cinnamon Hikka Tranz, and the beach north of town is an important turtle breeding site tended by the Peraliya Turtle Farm and Hatchery. Fittingly for a town whose name probably derives from the Sinhala phrase Shilpaya Kaduwa (Sword of Knowledge), several venerable Buddhist shrines can be found in the vicinity, including the central Jananandharamaya Temple and island-bound Seenigama Temple. Hikkaduwa was one of the towns worst affected by the tsunami of 2004 and several memorials and museums commemorating this tragedy stand on the beach north of town.

GETTING THERE AND AWAY

By road Following the coastal road through Bentota and Ambalangoda, the distance from Colombo to Hikkaduwa is about 100km south. The route via the Southern Expressway, exiting at Interchange 7 (Baddegama), is 20km longer, but usually a lot quicker (plan on up to 3 hours allowing for traffic around Colombo). Coming from the southeast, Hikkaduwa is only 20km from Galle, a traffic-dependent 30–45-minute drive along the coastal road. Buses connecting Hikkaduwa to Colombo, Galle and most points in between leave every 15 minutes in either direction. The bus station [201 A2] is at the northern end of town, so you may need to catch a tuktuk on to your hotel.

By rail All trains between Colombo and Galle stop at Hikkaduwa. Express trains won't stop at the more southerly Thiranagama or Kumarakanda, so if your hotel is closer to one of these stations, you may need to disembark at Hikkaduwa and catch a tuktuk from there.

ORIENTATION AND GETTING AROUND
Tourist developments and sights associated with Hikkaduwa sprawl along some 10km of coastline. Peraliya, 3km north of the town centre, is home to the eponymous turtle hatchery and several temples and monuments commemorating the devastation wrought by the tsunami. The town centre itself houses the main bus and railway station, as well as several supermarkets, shops, fishing harbour and other amenities associated with a working town. Several older and relatively upmarket tourist hotels line the beach immediately west of the town centre, and the main reef protected in the marine national park lies about 200m offshore of it. About 1km south of the fishing harbour, the Cinnamon Hikka Tranz, set in isolation on a large peninsula, marks the divide between Hikkaduwa proper and the so-called tourist zone, which runs southeast along the coast for 3km through the suburbs of Wewala and Narigama (which are flanked by Hikkaduwa's main surfing beach) and Thiranagama and Kumarakanda as far as Kumarakanda railway station. Walking distances between the more southerly hotels and town centre are significant, but there are tuktuks on every corner to whisk you where you want.

WHERE TO STAY
Hikkaduwa has perhaps the widest range of accommodation of any comparably sized town in Sri Lanka. Upmarket hotels, boutique properties and budget guesthouses rub shoulders along the entire beachfront strip from Hikkaduwa to Kumarakanda, but the broad trend is for cheaper accommodation to predominate as you head further south. Out of season, there is little reason to book in advance, and so much choice you can cheerfully decline what you are first offered if it doesn't suit you. In season, booking is advisable.

Exclusive

✳ 🏠 **Aditya Boutique Hotel** [map, opposite] (16 rooms) Galle Rd, Devenigoda;

☏ 091 226 7708; m 0777 718588; e adityavilla@ sltnet.lk; w aditya-resort.com. The loveliest & most isolated lodge associated with Hikkaduwa, beachfront Aditya stands about 2.5km south of Kumarakanda & only 12km from Galle. It's a sublimely tasteful & beautiful set-up, from the high-ceilinged, open-sided reception & lounge adorned with antique Sri Lankan furniture & crafts to the spacious rooms whose stylish retro look is complemented by all the amenities you'd expect of a hotel in the price range. Other features include a beautiful beach, a large swimming pool, attentive staff, a gym & spa, & a stylish restaurant serving delicious fresh seafood at flexible mealtimes. Ranks high on the 'wow factor' scale. *From US$400 dbl B&B*. **$$$$$+**

🏠 **Roman Beach** [map, page 196] (6 rooms) Galle Rd, Thiranagama; m 0712 275831; e reservations@romanhotels.lk; w romanbeach. lk. The top-notch boutique hotel is centred on an open ground-floor dining area that leads out to a long swimming pool set in leafy gardens running down to the beach. The spacious high-ceilinged rooms have wooden floors, AC, TV, minibar, balcony with sea view & bathroom with shower or spa bathtub. Arguably the most stylish option in Hikkaduwa, & reasonably priced in that context. *From US$221 dbl B&B*. **$$$$$**

Upmarket

✳ 🏠 **Cinnamon Hikka Tranz** [201 B5] (150 rooms) Galle Rd, Hikkaduwa; 091 227 7188/8000; e info@cinnamonhotels.com; w cinnamonhotels.com/hikkatranzbycinnamon. Hikkaduwa's slickest hotel, the 5-storey Hikka Tranz caters largely to package tourists but has a more contemporary & lively feel than most generic seaside resorts, with architecture seemingly inspired by traditional Sri Lankan temple pagodas & walls covered in graffiti, murals & modern art. Dividing the town centre & offshore coral garden from the more southerly tourist zone & surfing beach, the hotel occupies a lovely grassy peninsula complete with idyllic beach, crashing waves & a beautiful free-form swimming pool. Its signature Crab Restaurant is often packed with non-residents, & there are 5 other restaurants & bars. Service is on the ball & the bright, spacious & colourfully decorated rooms all have AC, TV, broad sea-view balcony & neatly equipped bathrooms. *US$200 dbl*. **$$$$$**

🏠 **Sapphire Seas Beachfront Hotel** [map, page 196] (10 rooms) Galle Rd, Kumarakanda; 091 227 7047; e bookings@sapphireseassrilanka.

com; w sapphireseassrilanka.com. Set at the southern end of the hotel strip, far away from most of the hustle & bustle, the popular new joint Canadian-Sri Lankan venture currently spans 2 storeys but a 3rd is planned. It stands in small but well-tended palm-shaded gardens that are centred on a nice swimming pool & run right down to the beach. The modern rooms are variable in size but all come with AC, fan, TV, fridge, 4-poster bed & fitted net, & terrace or balcony seating. An open-side restaurant catches a good sea breeze & serves a varied selection of local & Western dishes in the **$$$** bracket. Morning yoga seasons are offered in season & the friendly hands-on management can help arrange transport & excursions. *US$95–140 dbl B&B, depending on room size & whether it has a sea view, with 20% low-season discount*. **$$$$**

🏠 **Kalla Bongo Lake Resort** [map, page 196] (15 rooms) Baddegama Rd, Nalagasdeniya; 091 494 6324; e info@kallabongo.com; w kallabongo. com. Situated in large green grounds that slope down to the south shore of Hikkaduwa Lagoon 3km east of town, this Dutch-owned resort has a lovely stilted wooden restaurant perched above the lake, a swimming pool & comfortable rooms with contemporary décor, queen-size or twin bed, AC, fan, tea/coffee & private balcony with lagoon view. You can swim in the brackish lake, or take out a kayak & enjoy the abundant birdlife. Very good value. *US$90/98 standard sgl/dbl, US$105/112 deluxe, all rates B&B*. **$$$$**

🏠 **Asian Jewel** [map, page 196] (5 rooms) Baddegama Rd, Nalagasdeniya; 091 493 1388; m 0774 029589; e info@asian-jewel.com; w asian-jewel.com. Occupying a unique niche that slots in somewhere between boutique hotel & upmarket homestay, this attractive property 3km east of the town centre stands in a leafy garden with swimming pool overlooking Hikkaduwa Lagoon. Very much an extension of its affable English owner-manager, it has public areas cluttered with vintage hand-carved furniture, old engravings & maps, & pool table, while the highly rated terrace restaurant serves a cosmopolitan menu that includes filled jacket potatoes, fish & chips, chile con carne & Thai & Indian curries (**$$$$**). The spacious 1st-floor rooms all come with vintage wood furniture including 4-poster bed with fitted net, plus AC, TV & private balcony, some with lagoon view. *US$115–130 dbl B&B, with seasonal discounts*. **$$$$**

🏠 **Citrus Hikkaduwa** [201 B5] (90 rooms) Galle Rd, Hikkaduwa; 📞091 556 0001/5; e web@citrusleisure.com; w citrusleisure.com/hikkaduwa. One of the less alluring properties in the reliable & dynamically managed Citrus chain, this architecturally bland 5-storey monolith nevertheless has a superb location in a compact grassy beachfront garden with a large free-form swimming pool, an attractive open-sided restaurant & spacious wooden-floor rooms with AC, sea-facing balcony & the chain's trademark orange fabrics. *US$140 dbl B&B, but bargain online specials are often available.* **$$$$**

🏠 **Coral Sands Hotel** [201 A4] (80 rooms) Galle Rd, central Hikkaduwa; 📞091 227 7436; e coralsands@sltnet.lk; w coralsandshotel.com. The décor isn't exactly state-of-the-art, but this unpretentious & well-run beachfront hotel boasts a prime location for sunbathing & snorkelling, an L-shaped swimming pool, a decent restaurant & well-appointed tiled rooms with AC, fan, TV, writing desk & balcony offering in-your-face sea views. *US$120/155 sgl/dbl B&B, dropping by 20% out of season.* **$$$$**

Moderate

☀ 🏠 **Mandala Beach** [201 B6] (5 rooms) Galle Rd, Wewala; m 0766 821074; e bookings@mandalabeach.lk; w mandalabeach.lk. This utterly idyllic boutique resort stands in a sandy palm-shaded beachfront compound close to Hikka's top surfing spot. Simply decorated in beach house-style whites & greys, the spacious rooms come with AC, fan & good natural ventilation, and full-length glass doors lead out to private balconies that open out on to the beach. A small but attractive beach bar serves cocktails & plays chilled music. Good value. *US$80/95 dbl B&B with fan/AC, dropping to US$75 dbl with AC out of season.* **$$$**

🏠 **Refresh Hotel** [201 B5] (12 rooms) Galle Rd, Hikkaduwa; 📞091 227 7332; e hotel@refreshsrilanka.com; w refreshhikkaduwa.com. The best feature of this newly built 5-storey hotel is the rooftop swimming pool & restaurant/bar, which catches a welcome sea breeze in the evening & offers lovely views towards the beach & over the surrounding palm plantations. Stylish & spacious rooms come with treated-concrete-&-wood floor, king-size bed, AC, fan & TV, & most have tub & shower. It stands opposite the Refresh Restaurant, falls under the same management, & serves the

same food. Good value. *US$110/130 dbl/apt B&B, dropping by almost 50% out of season.* **$$$$**

🏠 **Coral Rock by Bansei** [201 A4] (30 rooms) Galle Rd, central Hikkaduwa; 📞091 227 7021; e info@bansei-resorts.lk; w bansei-resorts.lk. Coral Rock has a superb seaside location on the main swimming & snorkelling beach, as well as a seafront deck with swimming pool, pool bar & stylish restaurant. Rooms are smallish but have a modern feel with treated cement floor & wooden furniture, & they all come with AC fan, TV & small but serviceable bathroom. Bizarrely, the bright sea-facing rooms with spacious balcony & sea view cost the same as the darker & noisier roadside rooms. A good & well-priced mid-range option assuming you're offered a sea view, but rather poor value if you are not. *US$100 dbl B&B, with significant seasonal discounts.* **$$$$**

🏠 **Hikkaduwa Beach Hotel** [201 A3] (50 rooms) Galle Rd, central Hikkaduwa; 📞091 227 7327; e reservations@hbeachhotel.com; w hikkaduwabeachhotels.com. This veteran hotel has a superb location on the main beach facing the marine national park, but the AC rooms have seen better days & it feels overpriced. *US$130 dbl B&B.* **$$$$**

Budget

☀ 🏠 **Camellia Dwellings** [201 B2] (5 rooms) Baddegama Rd; 📞091 227 7999; m 0712 277999; e info@camelliadwellings.com; w camelliadwellings.com. Set in large gardens alive with birdsong 200m east of the junction with the Galle Rd, this budget boutique hotel comprises a renovated 1950s villa using water from a well constructed in 1874. The individually decorated & named rooms all come with tall ceiling, AC, fan & darkwood furniture offset by colour-themed fabrics. Most rooms have direct garden access. Charming management too. Fantastic value. *US$35 dbl, plus US$2 pp b/fast.* **$$**

🏠 **Blue Ocean Villa** [201 B6] (8 rooms) Galle Rd, Wewala; 📞091 227 7566; e blueoceanvilla420@gmail.com; w blueoceaweb.blogspot.com. Set in a neat little compound with a fabulous beachfront location, this welcoming & long-serving family-run guesthouse has bright clean rooms with 4-poster bed, AC, fan, net, fridge & art on the walls. The couple who run it can prepare local-style meals, but guests can also self-cater using the communal kitchen. *US$43/50 B&B*

standard/sea-facing dbl, with 30–40% discounts out of season. **$$**

🏠 **Curry Bowl** [201 B5] (12 rooms) Galle Rd, Hikkaduwa; ☏091 227 7201; e currybowl@live. com. Set in small palm-shaded gardens running down to the beach, this lovely 19th-century villa has characterful terracotta-tiled rooms with access to a wide lazy balcony, fan, net & in some cases AC. The attached curry & seafood restaurant is good value. *A touch overpriced at US$50/65 dbl with fan/AC but excellent value out of season when prices drop by 50%.* **$$$**

🏠 **Villa Birdlake** [map, page 196] (8 rooms) Baddegama Rd, Nalagasdeniya; m 0775 019171; e villabirdlake@gmail.com; w villabirdlake. com. Set on a terraced peninsula jutting into Hikkaduwa Lagoon 3km east of the town centre, this quirky owner-managed lodge has large overgrown jungle-swathed grounds alive with birds, monkeys, lizards & other small wildlife. The spacious rooms are decorated in colonial style with king-size bed, fitted net, fan & private balcony but no AC. An open-sided restaurant with time-warped décor serves excellent curries & other local dishes. It's a little too rundown & individualistic to suit all tastes, but it will hold plenty of appeal to easy-going nature lovers seeking affordable & characterful non-beach accommodation. *US$46 dbl B&B.* **$$$**

🏠 **Tandem Guesthouse** [201 C6] (9 rooms) Galle Rd, Wewala; ☏091 227 7103; e wewala@ sltnet.lk; w lankaland.com/tandem. Set in a small leafy garden on the opposite side of the main road to the beach, this well-priced guesthouse has clean room with AC, fan, 4-poster bed with fitted net, fridge, plentiful wardrobe space & semi-private balcony. Front rooms can be quite noisy so ask for one at the back. *US$40 dbl B&B, dropping to a negotiable US$35 out of season.* **$$**

🏠 **Neela's Guesthouse** [201 D6] (8 rooms) Galle Rd, Narigama; ☏091 438 3166; m 0777 645365; e neelasbeach@gmail.com; w neelasbeach.com. Established as a homestay back in the 1970s & still managed by the eponymous owner, this popular & unpretentious beachfront property has comfortable rooms with AC, net & semi-private balcony & a great little beach restaurant serving great seafood (**$$$**) & local curries (**$$**). *US$45/50 sgl/dbl B&B.* **$$$**

🏠 **Hotel Blue Note** [201 B6] (9 rooms) Galle Rd, Wewala; ☏091 438 3052; e bluenotehotel@

gmail.com; w eureka.lk/bluenote. There's a no-nonsense feel to this beachfront property, which is owned & managed by a local couple who live on site. Accommodation is in two rows of small chalets set either side of a palm-shaded gravel path that runs down to a funky little beach bar 10m from the surf. All rooms come with AC, fan, fridge, balcony angled towards the beach, & décor that's colourful to a fault. Decent value. *US$60 dbl B&B, dropping to US$50 out of season.* **$$$**

🏠 **Hotel Ocean View Cottage** [map, page 196] (20 rooms) Galle Rd, Thiranagama; ☏091 227 7237; m 0777 608542; e oceanview@ sltnet.lk; w oceanviewcottage.net. The pleasant owner-managed lodge has a good beachfront location, comfortable & colourful rooms with AC, fan, fridge & private balcony, & a swimming pool & restaurant. Rates are all over the place, even by Hikkaduwa standards – online rates in season start at a pricey US$80 dbl B&B but low-season walk-in rates can be a bargain, dropping as low as US$23/37 dbl with inland/sea view. **$$$**

🏠 **Drifters Hotel** [201 D6] (20 rooms) Galle Rd, Narigama; ☏091 227 5692; m 0777 067091; e drifters.lanka@hotmail.com; w driftershotel. com. This popular hotel has a great beachfront location, a nice swimming pool, friendly young staff & a good beach restaurant, but the small, dark rooms are nothing special & the relatively high rack rates suggest it is trading on reputation. *From US$54 dbl fan-only to US$100 dbl with sea view & AC, up to 30% discount off season, plus US$5 pp b/fast; much lower rates are sometimes available through the usual online agencies.* **$$$–$$$$**

🏠 **Hotel Vibration** [201 C6] (18 rooms) Galle Rd, Wewala; ☏091 494 3857; m 0777 606361; e vibrationhotel@gmail.com; w vibrationhotel. com. This well-priced venue on the non-beach side of the main road has the look of a boutique hotel with its Japanese-influenced 2-storey open reception area overlooking a swimming pool, & stylish modern AC rooms with colourful art on the walls. But it is also a big party venue, especially on Fri nights (page 203) & best avoided unless you plan on joining in. *From US$45 dbl.* **$$**

Shoestring

✴ 🏠 **Harmony Guesthouse** [201 D7] (12 rooms) Galle Rd, Narigama; ☏091 227 7551; m 0776 135238, 0777 628682; e topsecret@ srilanka-holiday.info; w srilanka-holiday.info.

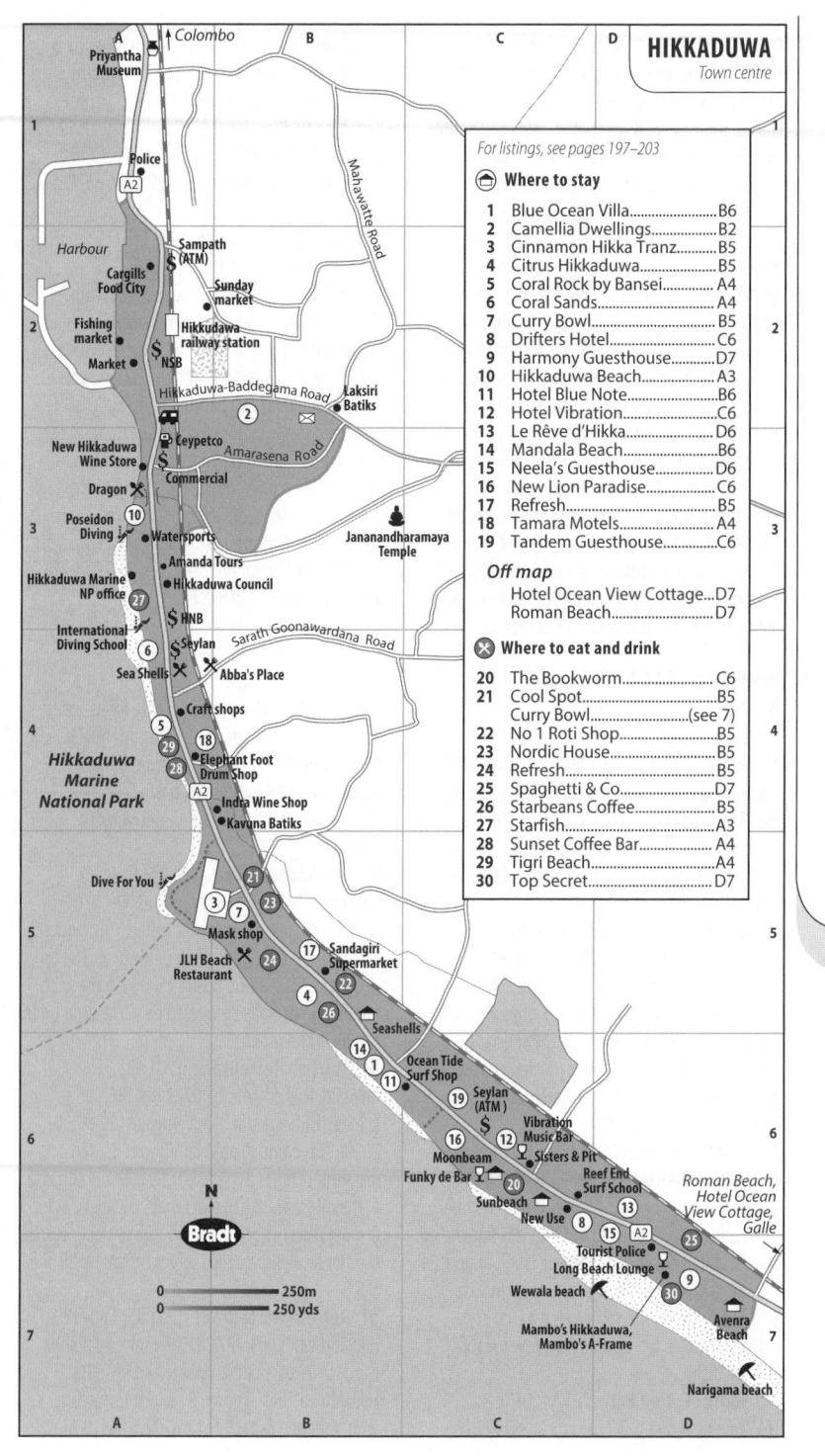

HIKKADUWA
Town centre

For listings, see pages 197–203

🏠 **Where to stay**

1	Blue Ocean Villa	B6
2	Camellia Dwellings	B2
3	Cinnamon Hikka Tranz	B5
4	Citrus Hikkaduwa	B5
5	Coral Rock by Bansei	A4
6	Coral Sands	A4
7	Curry Bowl	B5
8	Drifters Hotel	C6
9	Harmony Guesthouse	D7
10	Hikkaduwa Beach	A3
11	Hotel Blue Note	B6
12	Hotel Vibration	C6
13	Le Rêve d'Hikka	D6
14	Mandala Beach	B6
15	Neela's Guesthouse	D6
16	New Lion Paradise	C6
17	Refresh	B5
18	Tamara Motels	A4
19	Tandem Guesthouse	C6

Off map

	Hotel Ocean View Cottage	D7
	Roman Beach	D7

😋 **Where to eat and drink**

20	The Bookworm	C6
21	Cool Spot	B5
	Curry Bowl	(see 7)
22	No 1 Roti Shop	B5
23	Nordic House	B5
24	Refresh	B5
25	Spaghetti & Co	D7
26	Starbeans Coffee	B5
27	Starfish	A3
28	Sunset Coffee Bar	A4
29	Tigri Beach	A4
30	Top Secret	D7

The Western Resort Coast HIKKADUWA

8

Owned & managed by a hands-on Austrian-Sri Lankan couple, this extension of the popular Top Secret restaurant combines a great beach location, chilled atmosphere & great food with comfortable no-frills rooms with fitted net, fan & cold shower, but no AC or hot water. It is well positioned for surfers & has boards to rent. *Rack rates start at US$20 dbl, but drop significantly out of season.* **$**

⌂ **Le Rêve d'Hikka** [201 D6] (4 rooms) Galle Rd, Narigama; **m** 0778 438789; **e** lerevedhikka@gmail.com; **f** pg/lerevedhikka. A bright & stylish little guesthouse with red polished floors throughout, darkwood furniture & walls hung with colourful paintings & fabrics. Local-style meals start at US$3.50. There's no direct beach access & quite a bit of traffic noise, but otherwise it's great value. *€20/25 dbl with fan/AC.* **$**

⌂ **Tamara Motels** [201 A4] (7 rooms) Galle Rd, central Hikkaduwa; **m** 0723 564476, 0756 111064; **e** u.gunwardana@gmail.com. Only 100m from the beach down a quiet (except when trains roll past) cul-de-sac running inland from Galle Rd,

this clean & well-priced guesthouse is run by a friendly family who live on site. Clean rooms are pleasantly decorated in blue & white, & come with fan, net & optional AC. Snorkel hire US$2.50 per day. *US$27/30 dbl with fan/AC, dropping to US$20/23 out of season, plus US$2 pp for b/fast.* **$$**

⌂ **New Lion Paradise** [201 C6] (19 rooms) Galle Rd, Narigama; **** 091 227 6363; **w** newlionsparadise-hikkaduwa.jimdo.com. Established by its German owner-manager back in 1980, this quirky multistorey guesthouse, as garishly painted as it is rundown, comes across as the last fading relict of the Hippy-kaduwa era. The beachfront location is unbeatable & the atmosphere can be very sociable, but the main virtue of the scruffy rooms, which come with fan & net but no AC, is the knockdown rates. *From US$10 for a dingy ground-floor cell with twin beds to US$23 for a larger breeze-cooled 2nd-floor dbl, all very negotiable out of season.* **$**

✖ **WHERE TO EAT AND DRINK**
Medium to expensive

✖ **Spaghetti & Co** [201 D7] Galle Rd, Thiranagama; **m** 0776 698114; ⊕ 18.00–22.30. Hikkaduwa's top Italian restaurant, set in an old villa & large garden on the landward side of the main road, has a genuine wood-fired pizza oven & also serves good homemade ravioli, lasagne & other pasta dishes. **$$$**

✖ **Nordic House** [201 B5] Galle Rd, Hikkaduwa; **** 091 227 5970; **m** 0775 917176; **e** nordichousesrilanka@gmail.com; ⊕ 10.00–21.00. Superb gourmet burgers & chips with a variety of unusual toppings are the speciality at this brightly decorated Danish-owned café, which also serves good sandwiches, coffee, shakes & smoothies. No alcohol. **$$$**

✖ **Cool Spot** [201 B5] Galle Rd, Hikkaduwa; **m** 0772 334800; **e** coolspothikka@gmail.com; ⊕ 08.30–10.00 or later. Managed by the same family since it first opened in 1972, this fan-cooled central stalwart, set on a wooden 1st-floor deck offering a busy street view, focuses mainly on seafood, with the speciality being a Thai-style catch of the day, but also serves a few meat & chicken dishes. **$$$**

✖ **Sunset Coffee Bar** [201 A4] Galle Rd, Hikkaduwa; **** 091 227 7241; ⊕ 08.00–22.00.

Great little beachfront café notable for its breezy 1st-floor deck & quaffable budget-friendly Italian house wine. The menu ranges from burgers & sandwiches (**$$**) to curries, pasta & seafood (**$$$**), with prawns being something of a speciality.

✖ **Starbeans Coffee** [201 B5] Galle Rd, Narigama; **** 091 227 5797; ⊕ 08.00–19.00. In addition to Hikkaduwa's best coffee, this modern café serves a varied selection of Mexican, Italian (inc pizzas) & seafood dishes (**$$$**) in the AC interior or naturally ventilated beach seating under a palm-frond roof.

✖ **Starfish Restaurant** [201 A3] Galle Rd, Hikkaduwa; **m** 0777 820136; **f** StarfishRestaurantAndCampsite; ⊕ 06.30–20.30. This palm-shaded family-run garden restaurant comes as a pleasantly low-key surprise in the midst of Hikkaduwa's main cluster of older & more resorty hotels. Good-value seafood, curries & other local dishes. Also serves b/fast. No alcohol. **$$$**

✖ **Refresh Restaurant** [201 B5] Galle Rd, Hikkaduwa; **** 091 227 7810; **w** refreshsrilanka.com; ⊕ 09.00–23.00. Established in 1986, Hikkaduwa's best-known & largest restaurant, with a seating capacity of 250, also has its most voluminous menu, with plenty of fresh seafood options but also a long list of Chinese, Indian, Sri Lankan & Western dishes, including delicious chilli crab & oddities such as stuffed aubergine. The more formal dining area is close to the main road but a second one runs down to the beach. Fully licensed, it has a good cocktail menu & wine list, service & ambience are excellent, but it feels a touch overpriced. **$$$–$$$$**

Cheap to medium

✳ ✗ **Thambili Café** [map, page 196] Galle Rd, Thiranagama; m 0776 750864; f thambili; ⏲ 08.00–20.00. Hikkaduwa's most healthy, eco-conscious & vegetarian-friendly eatery has the chilled feel of a beach bar & prides itself on using organic ingredients sourced from local families wherever possible & minimising the use of plastic. A tempting menu includes juices, salads, seafood, sandwiches & the likes of falafel & hummus (**$$**) & it arranges beach BBQs by prior request. No alcohol, but you can bring your own, provided you have the receipt.

✳ ✗ **Top Secret** [201 D7] Galle Rd, Narigama; m 0777 629682; ⏲ 07.30–late. Sand underfoot, palm-frond roof overhead & conventional seating supplemented by matting & scatter cushions are the trademarks of this vibey beach bar & restaurant. The food is also very good & ranges from inexpensive vegetarian & meat curries (**$$**) to slightly pricier fresh seafood (**$$$**). Cocktails, beer & wine are served.

✳ ✗ **The Bookworm** [201 C6] Galle Rd, Thiranagama; m 0776 225039; ⏲ 08.00–22.00. Book in advance to enjoy a fabulous home-cooked 8-dish vegetarian rice-&-curry feast at this intimate rooftop restaurant on top of the eponymous lending library. Great value. **$$**

✗ **Tigri Beach Restaurant** [201 A4] Galle Rd, Hikkaduwa; m 0771 048202; ⏲ 08.00–22.30. Decorated with colourful local art & black-&-white stills of iconic musicians, this above-par beachfront terrace restaurant serves tasty b/fasts, salads, sandwiches & light snacks (**$$**), as well as a seafood-dominated selection of more substantial grills & curries (**$$$**). Inexpensive beers & cocktails, a good sound system & cooling sea breeze complete a most agreeable picture.

✗ **Curry Bowl** [201 B5] Galle Rd, Hikkaduwa; ☎ 091 227 7201; e currybowl@live.com; ⏲ 08.00–23.00. Attached to the hotel of the same name, this unpretentious but characterful restaurant serves tasty, filling & inexpensive local curries & biriani dishes (chicken, fish or vegetable) in the **$$** range, as well as a few seafood options (**$$$**). Casual diners are usually allowed to eat in the lovely beachfront garden when rooms aren't too full. No alcohol, but you can bring your own.

✗ **No 1 Roti Shop** [201 B5] Galle Rd, Narigama; m 0772 454177; f no1roti, ⏲ 08.30–22.00. This inexpensive eatery serves a huge variety of tasty filled savoury & sweet rotis, along with curries, juices & milkshakes. Vegetarians are well catered for. You might need 2 rotis to fill up, but even so it slots comfortably into the **$** category.

BARS AND NIGHTLIFE Most of the beach restaurants listed above, most notably perhaps Top Secret, provide a congenial atmosphere for a few drinks. Hikkaduwa is also one of the few beach resorts in Sri Lanka to host a nocturnal party scene, at least during the high season.

♀ **Vibration Music Bar** [201 C6] Galle Rd, Wewala; m 0777 606361; f Vibration. Hikkaduwa; ⏲ 24hrs. Hikkaduwa's top party venue since it opened in 2000, the club attached to the Vibration Hotel is open daily but most popular on Friday nights, when local and foreign DJs play electronic & dance music. Check the Facebook page for live music, drumming sessions & other events.

♀ **Funky de Bar** [201 C6] Galle Rd, Wewala; m 0777 521003; ⏲ 09.00–late. This chilled beachfront bar is ideal for a quiet sundowner & as the evening wears on it morphs into more of a

genuine nightlife venue, especially on Tue (karaoke night) and Thu (DJ night).

♀ **Mambo's Hikkaduwa** [201 D7] Galle Rd, Thiranagama; m 0777 822524; w mambos. lk; ⏲ 07.00–late. The lively relative of its A-Bay namesake has a dance floor that sees some action most nights but is busiest on Sat, when it hosts a pumping beach party.

♀ **Long Beach Lounge** [201 D7] Galle Rd, Wewala; m 0776 167519. Tranquil beachfront bar that transforms into a nightspot on Mon nights.

OTHER PRACTICALITIES

Banking Banks are concentrated at the north end of town close to the bus and railway stations. These include branches of Seylan [201 A4], Sampath [201 A2] and Commercial [201 A3] banks with ATMs. A standalone Seylan Bank ATM [201 C6] can be found in Wewala close to the Vibration Hotel.

Shopping For groceries, toiletries and imported goods, the well-stocked Sandagiri Supermarket [201 B5] (\ *091 227 5549;* w *sandagirilk.com;* ⊕ *08.00– 22.00*), which stands opposite the Citrus Hikkaduwa and incorporates a wine and liquor store, is the pick. There's also a reliable Cargills Food City [201 A2] (⊕ *08.00–22.00*) 100m north of the railway station. In Wewala, New Use [201 C6] (m *0771 3749059;* w *newuse.org;* ⊕ *09.30–20.00 Mon, Wed, Thu, Sat, 09.30– 13.00 Tue, noon–20.00 Sun*) is a charity shop dealing in used clothing and other items imported from Norway. About 100m further north, The Bookworm [201 C6] (m *0776 225039;* ⊕ *08.00–22.00*) is a well-stocked private lending library that charges US$2 to borrow a book, but also takes a small refundable deposit. Two souvenir and handicraft shops worth checking out are Laksiri Batiks (*Baddegama Rd;* \ *091 227 7255;* ◾ *LaksiriBatiks;* ⊕ *09.00–18.00*), which specialises in high-quality batiks, and the fabulous Elephant Foot Drum Shop [201 A4] (m *0766 137799;* w *elephantfootsrilanka.com*), which stocks music-related items such as traditional drums, CDs of Sri Lankan music, and beads, and keeps suitably whimsical opening hours.

WHAT TO SEE AND DO
Hikkaduwa is essentially a chill-out spot, with the main tourist focus being the long sandy beach that runs almost unbroken from the fishing harbour south past Kumarakanda, punctuated only by the peninsula that seats the Cinnamon Hikka Tranz. North of this landmark hotel, Hikkaduwa beach is hemmed in by an offshore reef that usually ensures safe swimming conditions from December to April, and also offers some fine snorkelling and diving opportunities. South of the Hikka Tranz, the less sheltered beaches at Wewala and Narigama form the pulse of the surfing scene for which Hikkaduwa is renowned. Away from the beach, several temples and other sites of interest merit a look.

Town centre Emanating for a couple of hundred metres north and south from the junction of the Galle and Baddegama roads, Hikkaduwa's small town centre is unexpectedly untouristy, even a little grungy, in feel. Its most interesting feature is the colourful fishing harbour [201 A2], which stands opposite the railway station and is protected by a substantial stone breakwater. The small fish market in the harbour and adjacent fruit and vegetable market are both of interest to self-caterers. There is also a larger and busier Sunday market [201 A2] next to the playing field on the opposite side of the tracks to the railway station.

Hikkaduwa Marine National Park [map, page 196] Proclaimed a wildlife sanctuary in 1979 and upgraded to its present status in 2002, the 1km² Hikkaduwa Marine National Park (HMNP) protects a 3km coral reef that runs parallel to Hikkaduwa beach from the fishing harbour south past the Cinnamon Hikka Tranz Hotel. An estimated 60 varieties of coral species occur in the park, along with 170-plus species of reef fish, and green and olive ridley turtle, while dugongs occasionally visit to feed on the abundant sea-grass. In recent decades, live coral cover has declined from almost 50% to less than 15%, largely due to natural causes, most notably a coral bleaching incident linked to unusually warm oceanic conditions caused by an El Niño event in 1998, but also as a result of commercial exploitation, irresponsible tourism and pollution. Recent indications are that the coral is recovering – very gradually – from its post-tsunami nadir, but it is still threatened by the same human factors that have played a part in its former decline.

The coral can easily be explored, at least over December–April, when the water is very calm. All visitors must first check in with the HMNP office [201 A3], which is centrally located next to the Starfish Restaurant, and levies a nominal visitation fee (*less than US$1*). The most popular way of exploring the reef is in a glass-bottomed boat, which can be arranged through the HMNP office and various private operators for around US$12 per party. A more engaging option, at least for reasonably confident swimmers in suitably calm conditions, is to swim out 200m from the beach to the reef and snorkel, taking great care not to stand on the coral or touch it with your flippers, both of which will contribute to its degradation. Snorkelling gear can be rented from the HMNP office and various hotels for around US$3 per hour. Finally, several outfits are licensed to teach PADI diving courses and to lead one-off dives out to more remote and deep-water sites such as Kiralagala, Godagala and Black Coral Point. Expect to pay around US$35–40 per dive for single or multiple sessions, including equipment and boat transfers. Multi-day courses start at around US$250.

Recommended **diving and snorkelling** operators include:

Dive For You [201 A5] (Aka Sunshine Watersports) Cinnamon Hikka Tranz Hotel; ⟍091 308 0400; m 0713 534628; e diveforyou@yahoo. com; w diveforyou.com

Dive Seenigama [map, page 196] Galle Rd, just north of Seenigama Temple; ⟍091 309 6545; m 0714 651418; e info@diveseenigamadivelanka. com; w diveseenigamadivelanka.com

International Diving School [201 A3] Coral Sands Hotel; m 0717 251024; e internationaldivingschool@hotmail.com; w theinternationaldivingschool.com

Poseidon Diving [201 A3] Galle Rd, 100m north of the HMNP office; ⟍091 227 7294; e info@divingsrilanka.com; w divingsrilanka.com

Surfing As with snorkelling and diving, the main surfing season runs from November to April, with activity peaking over February and March. The main surfing beaches at Wewala and Narigama are suited to beginners, but there also several other larger breaks – notably North Jetty and Benny's – that should only be attempted by confident and experienced surfers owing to the proximity to potentially lethal submerged rocks and corals. Boards can be hired at around US$2/hour or US$6/day from the following surf shops, which also offer lessons and sound local advice.

Mambo's A-Frame Surf Shop [201 D7] Galle Rd, Thiranagama; m 0777 822524; w mambos.lk

Reef End Surf School [201 C6] Galle Rd, Wewala; m 0777 043559/069525; e reefend@

yahoo.com; w reefendsurfschool.com

Ocean Tide Surf Shop [201 C6] Galle Rd, Wewala; m 0777 604620; e surftour@sltnet.lk; w srilankasurftour.com

Jananandharamaya Temple [201 B3] Situated off the Baddegama Road 600m inland of the bus station, this attractively laid-out and tranquil temple contains a couple of noteworthy buildings. The first, possibly dating to the late 19th century, is an unusual double-storey outbuilding whose wrap-around ground-floor balcony is enclosed by stilts supporting a wooden upper-storey set below a tall Kandyan-style roof. The other is the octagonal shrine set below the hollow dagoba to the right as you enter the main temple complex. With a layout reminiscent of the famous vatadage in Polonnaruwa, this shrine has four entrances, each of which looks towards one of four Buddha statues seated at right angles around an inner dagoba.

The provenance of this attractive and unusual building is unclear, but the strips of Kandyan art on the inside of the outer walls, now very faded in parts, suggest it might be at least 200 years old. Incidentally, one of the few pre-World War II recordings of Ceylonese pirith chants, released on an HMV 78 in 1939, was made at Jananandharamaya Temple (check out w *youtube.com/watch?v=NjHlGo408-4*).

Priyantha Museum [201 A1] (*Galle Rd, 500m north of the town centre;* m *0776 343234;* e *antiques@priyanthamuseum.com;* w *priyanthamuseum.com*) Technically more an antique shop than a museum, this owner-managed set-up welcomes casual browsers and displays a range of quality handicrafts and genuine antiques from old Ceylon, ranging from furniture and religious icons to animal statues from Jaffna, keys, bottles, puppets and brassware. Most items are for sale. There are also some fascinating old farming implements on display.

Peraliya The coastal village of Peraliya, 4km north of Hikkaduwa, was among the hardest hit by the 2004 tsunami. Struck by a giant wave at 09.26 on that tragic Boxing Day, Peraliya lost at least 249 residents in the flood according to government figures, though some sources suggest the figure might have been closer to 700. The Matara Express, which passed through Peraliya at the moment of impact, was swept from the tracks in what is listed as the world's largest ever rail disaster, with fatalities officially given as 1,270, though some estimates stand at above 1,700. Now a focal point for commemorating the tsunami, Peraliya hosts several permanent shrines and museums dedicated to the tragedy, as well as an annual religious ceremony held every 26 December and attended by the locomotive and two salvaged carriages that were rebuilt and resumed service in 2008. Peraliya is also the site of a turtle hatchery and two venerable temples: island-bound Seenigama and Thotogamuwa Rajamaha 500m inland. Any of the sites described below can be reached in a few minutes from Hikkaduwa by tuktuk.

Seenigama Temple [map, page 196] Set on a rocky island 200m offshore halfway between Hikkaduwa and Peraliya, the small temple at Seenigama is dedicated to Devol, one of 12 deities believed by Sinhala Buddhists to intervene in human affairs. It is a popular site with local pilgrims, who cross here to leave offerings to Devol, a deity associated with vengeance, as well as prosperity. The temple's reputation was enhanced by the tsunami, which it miraculously survived unscathed, despite the devastation wrought on the facing mainland. The island also supports an ancient freshwater well and is the site of an important week-long festival in late August and/ or early September. Boats wait at the Seenigama harbour on the opposite mainland to take passengers across; expect to pay around US$6–10 to charter a whole boat for the return crossing, or under US$1 to join a boat already crossing. The water is often choppy and the island is very rocky, so take up the offer of a life jacket.

Peraliya Turtle Farm and Hatchery [map, page 196] (m *0776 974521;* e *bknimal@yahoo.com;* w *srilankaseaturtle.com;* ⊕ *09.00–18.00; entrance US$3.50*) One of the oldest and most reputable turtle hatcheries in Sri Lanka, this place was founded in 2000 and destroyed four years later by the tsunami, which also claimed the life of its manager and six other family members. It reopened in 2006 under the direction of one of the manager's brothers, who was in Colombo at the time the tsunami struck. During the turtle nesting season (October–March), the farm buys turtle eggs from local villagers for a small fee, allows them to hatch on site, and then usually releases the youngsters into the sea the same evening. Up to 20,000 baby turtles are released annually, but a few are kept on site in tanks to attract tourists, whose entrance fees fund the operation.

Tsunami Memorial [map, page 196] Situated alongside the Peraliya Turtle Farm and Hatchery, this modest memorial was erected by the government in 2006 to commemorate the 1,270 train passengers and 249 villagers who officially lost their life in the tsunami. A graphic depiction of the train disaster is engraved behind the plaque.

Tsunami Honganji Temple [map, page 196] Built on a foundation laid on Boxing Day of 2006, this sombre and moving memorial to Sri Lanka's 35,000 tsunami victims consists of a giant Buddha statue set on a square concrete island in the middle of a small artificial lake. The central figure is an as-exact-as-possible replica of the taller of Afghanistan's Bamiyan Buddhas, a pair of statues that were carved into a cliff niche in the 6th century and destroyed by the Taliban in 2001. It was based on the earliest-known sketch of the 53m-tall statue, which dates to 1832, and shows that it had by then already been subjected to some mild defacement.

Tsunami Community Museum [map, page 196] (⊕ 08.00–20.00; donations accepted) This small community-run museum stands on the east side of the Colombo Road in Telwatta, 1km north of Peraliya. It is divided into three sections, one dedicated to educating visitors about tsunamis in general, one to the events of 26 December 2004, and one to the resilience demonstrated by the tight-knit community of Peraliya in the aftermath of the tragedy. The photographs taken during and after the tsunami are deeply sobering and almost intolerably heartbreaking, but parents of young children should be advised that few punches are pulled.

Tsunami Photo Museum [map, page 196] (✆ 091 390 0884; w tsunami-photo-museum-srilanka.blogspot.com; ⊕ 09.00–18.00; donations accepted) Also situated in Telwatta just 100m from the community museum, this Dutch-assisted museum opened in 2007 and documents the tsunami and its immediate aftermath in equally graphic detail. It's a shocking, distressing and profoundly humbling experience.

Thotogamuwa Rajamaha Temple [map, page 196] Situated 500m inland of Telwatta, this ancient temple houses some of the finest Kandyan art anywhere in Sri Lanka, yet it remains relatively unpublicised and little visited, despite its proximity to one of the country's main beach resorts. It was reputedly founded during the 3rd-century BC reign of Devanampiya Tissa, when it housed some 500 arhat bhikkhu monks, and was revived in the 14th century by King Parakramabahu IV, who reputedly planted the surrounding coconut groves, prior to being razed by the Portuguese in the early 16th century. Rediscovered in 1765, the temple was revived with support from the Kandyan monarchy, who funded the construction of two large image houses that stand to the left of the main path through the complex. No buildings from the temple's earliest incarnations survive, though the site is dotted with stone pillars and other small relics from the Anuradhapura era. The main point of interest is the first temple to the left, which was built in 1805 and painted at around the same time by the celebrated low country artist Siththara Muhundiram. The most famous figure in the (mostly well-preserved) interior is a rare depiction of Cupid, but there is also a large reclining Buddha protected by a cobra's hood and a fine assemblage of larger-than-life Hindu deities, dwarves and mythical beasties. A second temple behind this is even older, dating to 1777, and it reputedly also contains some fine Kandyan art, but it is currently closed for repair.

Further afield

Kumarakanda Temple [map, page 196] Situated around the corner from Kumarakanda railway station 5km southeast of central Hikkaduwa, this is another temple of ancient origins whose original incarnation was destroyed in the 16th century by the Portuguese. The present temple was revived in 1765 and is unusual in that several aspects of its architecture display a clear Dutch influence. This is most evident in the fortress-like outer walls, the ornate arched belfry, and the gabled exterior of the main image house, which dates to 1784 and incorporates a large reclining Buddha statue but still feels rather churchlike. Architecture aside, the temple contains no artworks of great note or antiquity.

Baddegama Christ Church Situated about 10km inland of Hikkaduwa at the junction with the Southern Expressway to Galle, Baddegama is the site of the island's first Anglican church, built on a hilltop overlooking the Gin River in 1818 and consecrated in 1825. Notable for its ironwood pillars and tall fortlike turret, the church now stands in the grounds of the Christ Church Girls' College, a pioneering educational institution founded c1870.

Part Three

THE CULTURAL TRIANGLE

Overview of Part Three

Extending over a relatively compact and low-lying swathe of the interior northeast of Colombo and Bandaranaike International Airport, the so-called Cultural Triangle is the first inland stop on most extended tours through Sri Lanka. As its name suggests, the region is primarily of interest for its collection of ancient monasteries, decorated cave temples, abandoned capitals, towering dagobas and other archaeological reserves whose collective history spans a period of more than 2,500 years. The Cultural Triangle houses no fewer than half of Sri Lanka's eight UNESCO World Heritage Sites: Dambulla Cave Temple, Sigiriya Rock Fortress and the ancient cities of Polonnaruwa and Anuradhapura. But these popular heavyweights are supplemented by literally dozens of lesser-known sites, many only marginally less rewarding, yet boasting a more tranquil and untrammelled feel. Unexpectedly, perhaps, the Cultural Triangle is also home to two excellent safari destinations: the popular cluster of 'elephant reserves' centred on Minneriya to the east of Dambulla, and the more neglected but arguably superior Wilpattu National Park near Anuradhapura.

The Cultural Triangle has three main pivots, namely Dambulla/Sigiriya, Polonnaruwa and Anuradhapura, each of which is accorded its own dedicated chapter in the section that follows. Logistically, Dambulla/Sigiriya is the most accessible starting point coming from or heading to Colombo or other southerly and westerly locations. It is also a conveniently central base from which to explore Polonnaruwa (about 90 minutes to the east) and/or Anuradhapura (a similar distance north) as day trips. For those with sufficient time, however, we would recommend allocating a couple of nights to each of the three pivots on the Cultural Triangle, allowing you to explore the primary ruins in the cooler, less crowded and more photogenic early morning or late afternoon hours.

HIGHLIGHTS

DAMBULLA CAVE TEMPLES (pages 217–20) Set in a tall granite outcrop overlooking the town, Dambulla's 'Caves of Infinite Buddhas' form the largest and best-preserved complex of its type in Sri Lanka, stuffed with a wealth of ancient rock statues and murals dating from the 15th century onwards.

SIGIRIYA (pages 226–30) For many the unqualified highlight of the Cultural Triangle, the 'Lion Rock' developed as a skyscraping 5th-century citadel by the ill-fated King Kasyapa is a towering volcano plug adorned with ancient ruins and the country's oldest and most iconic Buddhist paintings.

RITIGALA (pages 238–40) Perhaps the best preserved and the most expansive of Sri Lanka's ancient forest monasteries is protected within this little-visited 24ha archaeological reserve set at the jungle-swathed base of northern Sri Lanka's tallest mountain, Ritigala.

RESWEHARA AND AVUKANA BUDDHAS (pages 223–4) Set 10km apart in the countryside separating Dambulla from Anuradhapura, these two monumental Buddha statues were probably carved simultaneously – by a master sculptor and his pupil – during the 5th century. Avukana is the more artistically meritorious of the two, but Reswehara wins out when it comes to its spectacularly isolated setting.

MINNERIYA NATIONAL PARK (page 241) This popular safari destination close to Dambulla and Sigiriya is renowned for the Elephant Gatherings, often comprising several hundred individuals, that aggregate on its floodplains between June and October.

POLONNARUWA (pages 242–56) Though not as ancient as its predecessor Anuradhapura, this former Sinhala capital is if anything even more engaging, thanks to the immense architectural skills demonstrated in its diverse collection of ruined palaces, temples, dagobas and other structures.

DIMBULAGALA (pages 257–9) Highlights of this off-the-beaten-track myth-swathed mountain near Polonnaruwa are the atmospheric jungle-bound monastic ruins at Namal Pokuna and the exquisite 4th-century cave paintings at Pulligoda.

ANURADHAPURA (pages 261–75) The on-and-off Sinhala capital for more than 1,300 years, ancient Anuradhapura houses the country's oldest and most sacred Bo Tree, a treasury of ancient statues and engravings, and a trio of 2,000-year-old dagobas that form the only comparably ancient structures whose altitude approaches that of the tallest Egyptian pyramids.

MIHINTALE (pages 275–9) The cradle of Sri Lankan Buddhism is this mountainside monastery, whose extensive and fascinating ruins are almost eclipsed by the fabulous jungle setting and views from the pinnacle.

WILPATTU NATIONAL PARK (pages 281–4) Sri Lanka's largest national park feels very untrammelled by comparison with Yala, and a full-day safari comes with a good chance of spotting elephant, sloth bear and to a lesser extent leopard.

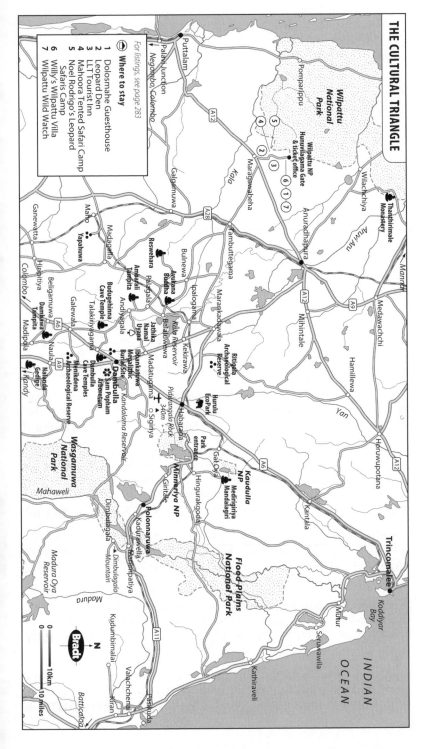

THE CULTURAL TRIANGLE

Dambulla, Sigiriya and Surrounds

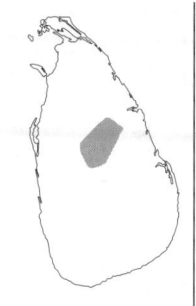

Situated midway between Anuradhapura and Polonnaruwa, and closer than either to both Colombo and Kandy, Dambulla is at once the main road gateway to the Cultural Triangle and an important route hub within it. It stands within easy striking distance of two exceptional UNESCO World Heritage Sites: the eponymous cave temple overlooking central Dambulla houses an incomparable collection of ancient Buddha statues and paintings, while the spectacular Sigiriya Rock, only 16km to the northeast, is renowned for its 5th-century ruins, frescoes and water gardens. Logistically, each of Dambulla, Sigiriya and the nearby crossroads town of Habarana is equipped with a plethora of hotels and guesthouses, and collectively the three form a cluster of interchangeable travel hubs that can be used not only to visit each other but also to explore the nearby Minneriya and Kaudulla National Parks, the more remote ancient capitals of Polonnaruwa and Anuradhapura, and as many as a dozen other low-key historical and archaeological sites situated within a 30km radius of Dambulla.

DAMBULLA

Dambulla is a pivotal crossroads town that sprawls for 5km along the road between Kandy and Jaffna. It has a modern built-up façade that flatters to deceive, since in reality its 20,000-odd inhabitants almost all reside within a narrow ribbon of urbanisation that gives way to farmland 100m either side of the main strip. The town is an important hub for agricultural distribution, with much of the action taking place in the Dambulla Dedicated Economic Centre, a custom-built fruit and vegetable produce market that incorporates more than 150 stalls and operates 24/7, except on poya days. Geographically, it is dominated by Dambulla Rock, a massive granite outcrop that houses the country's largest and best-preserved cave temple complex, founded in the 1st century BC by King Valagamba. Other historical and archaeological sites around Dambulla range from a suburban dagoba built by Valagamba to the pre-Buddhist megalithic burial site at Ibbankatuwa 5km south of town and a host of more far-flung temples and monasteries.

GETTING THERE AND AWAY
By air or rail There are no rail or air services to Dambulla but daily flights connect Colombo to Sigiriya Airport 15km to the northeast, and trains between Colombo and Trincomalee or Batticaloa stop at Habarana railway station 25km to the northeast.

By road Dambulla is a major route focus situated 150km (3½ hours) inland of Colombo via Kurunegala (60km/1½ hours), 75km (2 hours) north of

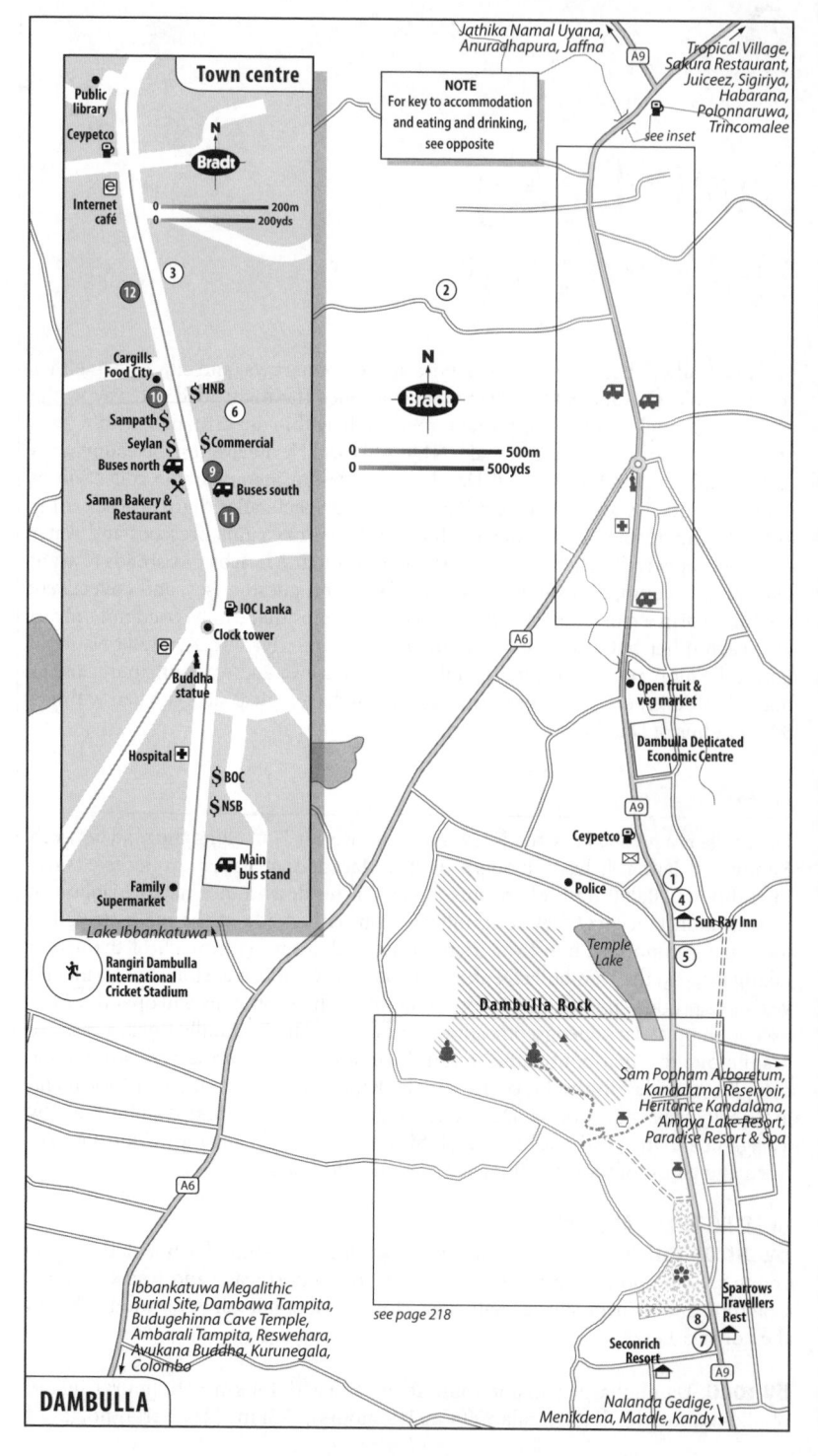

Town centre

Public library

Ceypetco

Internet café

Cargills Food City

HNB

Sampath

Seylan

Commercial

Buses north

Saman Bakery & Restaurant

Buses south

IOC Lanka

Clock tower

Buddha statue

Hospital

BOC

NSB

Main bus stand

Family Supermarket

Lake Ibbankatuwa

Rangiri Dambulla International Cricket Stadium

0   200m
0   200yds

NOTE
For key to accommodation and eating and drinking, see opposite

Jathika Namal Uyana, Anuradhapura, Jaffna

Tropical Village, Sakura Restaurant, Juiceez, Sigiriya, Habarana, Polonnaruwa, Trincomalee

see inset

A9

A9

A6

0   500m
0   500yds

Open fruit & veg market

Dambulla Dedicated Economic Centre

Ceypetco

Police

Sun Ray Inn

Temple Lake

Dambulla Rock

Sam Popham Arboretum, Kandalama Reservoir, Heritance Kandalama, Amaya Lake Resort, Paradise Resort & Spa

see page 218

Sparrows Travellers Rest

Seconrich Resort

A9

Ibbankatuwa Megalithic Burial Site, Dambawa Tampita, Budugehinna Cave Temple, Ambarali Tampita, Reswehara, Avukana Buddha, Kurunegala, Colombo

Nalanda Gedige, Menikdena, Matale, Kandy

DAMBULLA

Kandy via Matale (50km/1½ hours), 245km (4–5 hours) south of Jaffna via Vavuniya (105km/2 hours) and Anuradhapura (65km/1 hour), 105km (2 hours) southwest of Trincomalee via Habarana (20km/30 minutes) and 160km (3 hours) west of Batticaloa via Polonnaruwa (68km/1–1½ hours). Although some public transport originates in Dambulla, its crossroads location means that plenty more buses pass through, and it is usually easy enough to find a seat to wherever you are headed. Buses to Kandy (five to six per hour) and Colombo (five to six per hour, plus one air-conditioned bus every 45 minutes) can be picked up on the east side of the main road 100m south of the Commercial Bank. Buses to Polonnaruwa (three to four per hour), Anuradhapura (three to four per hour), Habarana (five to six per hour) and Sigiriya (every 30 minutes between 06.00 and 19.00) leave from the west side of the road directly opposite the Commercial Bank. Buses to Batticaloa, Trincomalee, Vavuniya and Jaffna also leave from this stop, but are less frequent.

DAMBULLA
For listings, see pages 215–17

🛏 **Where to stay**
1 Avinka Holiday Home
2 Dignity Villa
3 Gimanhala
4 Healy Tourist Inn
5 Heritage Dambulla
6 Rock Arch Dambulla
7 Saman's Guesthouse & Restaurant
8 Sunduras Resort

Off map
 Amaya Lake Resort
 Heritance Kandalama
 Paradise Resort & Spa

✖ **Where to eat and drink**
9 Bentota Bake House
 Heritage Dambulla (see 5)
10 Mango Mango
11 Man-J Restaurant & Bar
12 My Burger Family
 Saman's (see 7)

Off map
 Juiceez
 Tropical Village
 Sakura Restaurant

WHERE TO STAY *Map, opposite*

In addition to the hotels listed below, Sigiriya and Habarana are both commonly used as a base for visiting Dambulla.

Town centre
The town centre is well equipped with budget hotels & also has a few adequate mid-range options. For more upmarket accommodation, you'll need to head out of town or to Sigiriya or Habarana.

Moderate
🏠 **Gimanhala Hotel** (17 rooms) Main Rd, Dambulla; ☎ 066 228 4864; e gimanhala@ gmail.com; w gimanhala.com. Set in large green grounds with a swimming pool & decent restaurant, this pleasant & unpretentious central hotel has smart spacious rooms with AC, fan & TV. *US$54/58 sgl/dbl B&B.* **$$$**

🏠 **Heritage Dambulla** (4 rooms) Main Rd; ☎ 066 228 4799. This former government resthouse has characterful tall-ceilinged rooms with old-fashioned furniture, AC, fan, TV & adequate bathroom but little to insulate you from the ongoing street noise. The restaurant, complete with shady terrace, serves good spicy curries & other local & Western fare (**$$**) & has a licensed bar. *US$57 dbl B&B.* **$$$**

🏠 **Sunduras Resort** (17 rooms) Main Rd; ☎ 066 228 3317; m 0727 086000; e booking@ sundaras.com; w sundaras.com. About the smartest option in central Dambulla, & conveniently close to all the historic sites, this place has a free-form swimming pool set in a large green garden, a decent restaurant, & bright rooms with AC, fan & TV. A touch overpriced. *US$75 dbl B&B, dropping to US$50 out of season.* **$$$**

Budget
✱ 🏠 **Dignity Villa** (4 rooms) Yaya Rd; ☎ 066 493 5335; m 0775 180902; w thesimpletraveler. com. Set in a neat rustic garden only 700m west of the main road, this owner-managed gem has bright clean rooms with AC, fan, queen-size or twin bed with net. The owner is a great chef & a

fount of local travel info. He has a tuktuk for free transfers from the main road, & will take you to the cave temples for US$1 & to Sigiriya for around US$12 including waiting time. *US$27 dbl*. **$$**

🏠 **Rock Arch Dambulla** (2 rooms) Off Main Rd; ☎ 066 228 4443; **m** 0777 685400; **e** hello@ dambullarockarch.com; **w** dambullarockarch.com. Boasting a secluded suburban garden feel despite its location only 100m east of the main road, this agreeable little lodge is owned & managed by a charming semi-retired architect & his wife. Small but comfortable rooms have AC, net & TV. Rates inc b/fast & laundry. *US$40 dbl*. **$$**

Shoestring

☀ 🏠 **Saman's Guesthouse & Restaurant** (10 rooms) Main Rd; ☎ 066 228 4428; **m** 0774 353484; **e** samanrest@gmail. com; **w** samans-guesthouse-dambulla.com. The standout feature of this owner-managed lodge is a characterful fan-cooled restaurant with traditional décor matched by exceptional & rice-&-curry buffets nudging into the **$$$** category. The well-priced rooms, set back in the garden, are also pleasant & come with 4-poster beds with fitted net, fan & seating. A convenient location amid the historical sites clinches it as the pick in this range. *US$13/23 dbl with fan/AC*. **$**

🏠 **Avinka Holiday Home** (4 rooms) Main Rd; ☎ 066 360 8888; **m** 0727 901490; **e** dimuthuuresh@ yahoo.com. Set in a large but rather unkempt garden only 500m north of the temple car park, this family-run place has clean white-tiled rooms with net, fan, large bathroom & optional AC. Good value. *US$17/27 dbl with fan/AC*. **$**

🏠 **Healy Tourist Inn** (5 rooms) Main Rd; ☎ 066 228 4940. Simple, well-priced twin rooms with net & fan 500m north of the cave temple car park. *US$13/17 dbl/trpl occupancy*. **$**

Out of town
The properties below all slot into the upmarket category & have attractive jungle settings in the vicinity of Kandalama Reservoir to the west of Dambulla.

☀ 🏠 **Heritance Kandalama** (152 rooms) ☎ 066 555 5000; **e** hk.ebiz.lk@aitkenspence. lk; **w** heritancehotels.com/kandalama. Situated 12km from Dambulla on the fringe of a 20km² forest overlooking Kandalama Reservoir, this breathtaking 1994 Geoffrey Bawa creation, its 6-storeys & swimming pool locked to a cliff face overrun by jungle vegetation & monkeys, is a nature lover's delight & model of hotel development within an ecologically sensitive area. Reached via a labyrinth of passages & walkways, the well-equipped & stylish rooms have wooden floors, floor-to-ceiling windows looking into the forest, queen-size beds, AC, fan, TV, sofa, private balcony & well-lit, spacious bathrooms. Activities include jungle trekking, canoeing, safari by river, birdwatching & horse, pony & bullock cart rides. *From US$274/324 sgl/dbl B&B*. **$$$$$+**

🏠 **Amaya Lake Resort** (101 rooms) ☎ 066 446 1500, 011 476 7888; **e** reservations@ amayaresorts.com; **w** amayaresorts.com. Situated on the northwest shore of the Kandalama Reservoir 11km from Dambulla, this lovely hotel blends attractively into a wilderness setting alive with monkeys, birds & butterflies. The 16ha gardens conceal elegant AC cottages with all mod cons & a blue swimming pool, modelled on ancient baths at Mihintale. Activities include elephant safaris, canoe cruises & guided nature walks. There's a good Ayurveda spa & the buffet meals are laid out against a serene lakeside backdrop. Very good value. *From US$122 dbl B&B*. **$$$$**

🏠 **Paradise Resort & Spa** (67 rooms) ☎ 066 228 6300; **e** paradise@brownshotels. com; **w** brownshotels.com/paradise. This attractive complex of terraced deluxe chalets & semi-detached garden villa suites lies 14km from Dambulla in the wilderness north of Kandalama Reservoir halfway to Sigiriya. It has its own nature trail to a small lake, huge boulders to climb, a swimming pool, gym & spa, & an open-sided bar & dining pavilions. Chalets are grouped around a park & each room is creatively designed with AC, huge wardrobe, Italian fittings & birdsong chorus accompanying perfect peace. *From US$90 dbl B&B*. **$$$$**

✖ **WHERE TO EAT AND DRINK** *Map, page 214*

All the hotels listed above serve food. The standouts are Saman's, for its enthusiastic presentation and not-too-spicy (unless otherwise specified) curry buffet, and the Heritage Dambulla for the ambience of its wide street-facing veranda and licensed bar.

✗ Tropical Village Habarana Rd; ☎066 493 2288; ⏰ 11.30–15.30 & 19.00–21.00. The smartest eatery in town – actually 3km to the northeast – has an expansive lunchtime buffet but switches over to à la carte (local & Western dishes) in the evening. There's plenty to keep vegetarians interested. There's a pub upstairs. $$$

✗ Sakura Restaurant Habarana Rd; m 0775 202995; ⏰ 11.30–21.00. Situated 3km northeast of the town centre next to Tropical Village, this more modest owner-managed restaurant also attracts lots of tour groups to its lunch- & dinnertime rice-&-curry buffets. No alcohol. $$

✗ Mango Mango Main Rd; ☎066 228 5410; ⏰ 07.00–22.00. This modern restaurant has a fantastically varied menu, with everything from steak & spare rib to pasta & kottu roti, but the specialities are pizza & curry. Also serves fresh bread, juice & coffee. No alcohol. Prices from $ (local fare) to $$$ (Western mains).

✗ My Burger Family Restaurant Main Rd; ☎066 228 5099; ⏰ 11.00–23.00. Décor reminiscent of a 1970s Wimpy Bar, this agreeable & affordable restaurant serves decent burgers, as well as a varied selection of Indian, Arabian, Chinese & Sri Lankan mains. No alcohol. $$

✗ Bentota Bake House Main Rd; ⏰ 07.00–21.00. Popular with locals, this place serves cheap & tasty curries & other local fare. $

♉ Man-J Restaurant & Bar Main Rd; ⏰ 11.00–22.00. The food at this slightly seedy 2-storey pub isn't madly alluring, but the drinks are cheap & it's one of the few places in town where you can settle in for a few chilled beers.

♉ Juiceez Habarana Rd; ☎011 268 8200; ⏰ 08.00–19.00. Part of an agricultural centre situated more or less opposite Tropical Village, this modern juice bar serves superb juices – freshly pulped, thick & not overly sweetened. Plain juices cost around US$1.50 while 'medicinal' blends are closer to US$3.

OTHER PRACTICALITIES Dambulla is the best equipped of the three towns covered in this chapter when it comes to banks, with all the main chains represented, including a Commercial Bank with an ATM. The well-stocked Cargills Food City (⏰ 08.00–22.00) has a wine and beer shop on the first floor.

WHAT TO SEE AND DO The *raison d'être* for most visits to Dambulla is the eponymous cave temple complex excavated into the rocky outcrop that dominates the town's southern skyline. This can easily be visited in conjunction with a pair of museums and the Somawathi Temple at the rock base. For wildlife enthusiasts, the out-of-town Sam Popham Arboretum is highly recommend – early morning is best for birds but night walks come with a good chance of spotting the oddball slender loris. Dambulla is a viable base for day visits to all sites of interest described in this chapter, as well as to Anuradhapura and Polonnaruwa.

Dambulla Cave Temples [map, page 218] (✎ 066 228 3605; ⏰ 07.30–18.00; *entrance currently free; see note overleaf*) Set in the face of an isolated granite outcrop that stands 340m high and has a circumference of 1.6km, the quintet of cave temples of Dambulla – a UNESCO World Heritage Site since 1991 – ranks as the largest, most beautifully decorated and best-preserved complex of its type in Sri Lanka. Tradition associates the complex with King Valagamba, who took refuge in the area during his 14-year exile from Anuradhapura and returned to establish the first two cave temples after he regained the throne in 89BC. However, 2nd-century BC inscriptions above the largest cave temple's drip ledge suggest it might be older than tradition asserts. The complex was renovated under several monarchs, most notably Nissanka Malla and Kirti Sri Rajasinha. A colonnaded and whitewashed covered porch with arched entrances was added in the early 20th century.

The temples at Dambulla are neither wholly natural nor entirely artificial, but were excavated deeper into an existing cave then walled off at the front. Sometimes referred to as the 'Caves of Infinite Buddhas', the complex is notable for its elaborately decorated interiors, which incorporate 160-plus statues, many etched into the natural rock over a thousand years ago, and more than 2,000m² of ceiling and wall murals, most of which date from the 15th–18th centuries. For those with limited time or a reduced attention span, the cathedral-like Maharaja Cave Temple, second from the main entrance, should be your first port of call. For those with fewer constraints, there's much to be said for taking a few hours to look around on your own, then returning with an official guide who you can pummel with questions about individual paintings and statues.

Practicalities There are four foot ascents, all of which lead to a manned entrance gate where shoes and headgear must be removed. Most widely used but least interesting is the Modern Route, which follows a steep staircase uphill from the Golden Temple on the main road through Dambulla. The more tranquil Ancient Route starts opposite Rangiripaya Temple (900m west of the Kandy Road *en route* to Somawathi Dagoba) and leads up leaf-shaded time-worn granite steps inscribed with the name of King Kutakanna Tissa, their 1st-century BC sponsor. An equally peaceful – but shadeless – option, popular in the colonial era, is the Whaleback Route, which starts at the massive Bo Tree Shrine on the west side of the Kandy Road 300m south of the Golden Temple. Finally, the easiest ascent of all is a flattish stone path that runs north from a prominent gateway halfway between the Kandy Road and Rangiripaya Temple.

Note: Admission is currently free, but this is a temporary reprieve (the result of a territorial dispute between temple and government) and it seems inevitable that the old fee of US$10 will be reinstated and possibly upped to US$25 at some point. Should this happen, all visitors will need to visit the ticket office at the Golden Temple before they make the ascent.

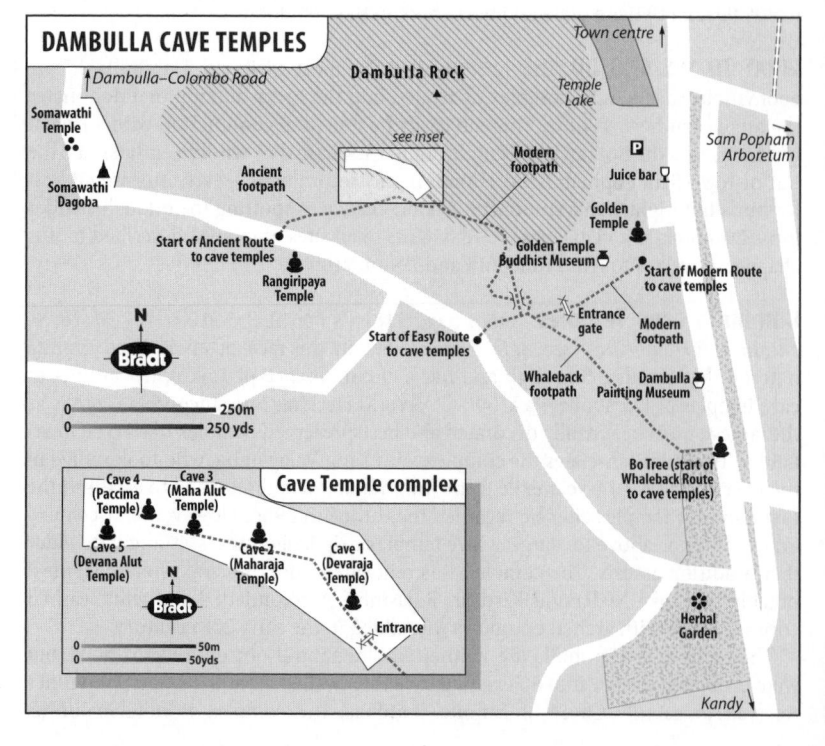

Devaraja Cave Temple The most easterly temple, and the closest to the entrance, is named after the 'Lord of the Gods', or Vishnu, to whom a separate external shrine is dedicated. The interior is dominated by a 14m-long rock-hewn reclining Buddha, posed in the parinirvana mudra, and attended by the smaller sculpted standing figure of Ananda. According to local tradition, this is the oldest of the Dambulla cave temples, and all six of its stone sculptures, the recumbent Buddha included, were carved under the direction of King Valagamba. There is also a wooden Vishnu statue that was brought to Dambulla after the Portuguese plundered its home temple in Matale in 1587. The main Buddha figure has been painted many times over the millennia, most recently in the early 20th century, but other murals are mostly faded or blackened as a result of incense and oil smoke.

Maharaja Cave Temple Some 52m long, 23m deep and up to 7m high, this largest, second oldest and most beautiful of the Dambulla cave temples is named after the 'Great King' Valagamba, who is represented within it by a painted wooden sculpture complete with *makuta* headdress. The cave also incorporates a wooden effigy thought to be the only surviving contemporary depiction of King Nissanka Malla, and a more recent statue of King Kirti Sri Rajasinha. Of the cave's other 50-plus statues, the majority depict the Buddha, with the most beautiful being the larger-than-life standing figure, carved in the abhaya mudra, below a striking engraved archway in front of the westernmost door. Stylistically, this statue might well date back to the Anuradhapura period, though it was probably renovated under Nissanka Malla, and it is very unusual in that it is flanked by the Avalokiteshvara and Maitreya Bodhisattvas, who are seldom depicted in the same place. The Maharaja Temple also incorporates a small dagoba encircled by eight seated Buddhas, two protected by cobra hoods. Even more striking than these statues, however, are the many thousands of paintings that clutter the walls and ceiling, among them a fabulous sequence depicting the conversion of Devanampiya Tissa to Buddhism at Mihintale and the arrival of the Bo Tree at Anuradhapura. The majority of the paintings date to the Kandyan era, but some have since been touched up, and others are quite possibly older.

Maha Alut Cave Temple The central 'New Great' Temple dates to the 18th century, when King Kirti Sri Rajasinha converted it from a storeroom to a shrine. The second largest of the Dambulla cave temples, it is almost square in shape, being about 25m deep and 27m wide, and the highest point in the ceiling is more than 10m above the floor. The sides are lined with gold and yellow Buddhas, the largest being a reclining figure carved directly into the natural rock. The ceiling is covered in hundreds of repetitive gold-on-red Buddha paintings.

Paccima Cave Temple Paccima literally means 'western', and this modestly proportioned shrine, possibly dating back to the reign of Valagamba, was indeed the complex's westernmost temple prior to the colonial era. Its central dagoba is traditionally said to have contained the jewellery of Valagamba's second wife, Soma Devi, prior to bring looted a few years back. Small but atmospheric, the temple is dominated by a row of seated golden Buddhas, with the largest and most central figure being posed in the dhyana mudra below an engraved arch.

Devana Alut Cave Temple The 'Second New' temple, now the complex's westernmost excavation, is a relatively small shrine converted from a storeroom sometime in the 19th century. It contains 11 Buddha statues, all created from brick and plaster. The paintings, which were touched up extensively in 1915 but possibly date back a few decades earlier, include striking depictions of Vishnu, Kataragama and a local deity Devata Bandara, who respectively represent time past, present and future.

Golden Temple Buddhist Museum [map, page 218] (⊕ *07.00–21.00; entrance US$1.30; photography permitted*) Situated in the Golden Temple compound at the base of Dambulla Rock, this two-storey museum doubles as the pedestal for what is claimed (with audacious inveracity) to be the world's largest Buddha statue, a prominent gold-plated seated figure that stands 30m high and is depicted in the dharma chakra mudra. Entered via a Disney-world pastiche of Sigiriya's famous lion gate, the museum is sparsely populated and poorly labelled, but does contain some quality reproductions of the paintings in the Dambulla Cave Temples, a few interesting ancient Buddhist manuscripts and icons, an array of Buddhist statues from around the world, and murals depicting the life of the Buddha from conception to the attainment of parinirvana (death). Diverting but inessential.

Dambulla Painting Museum [map, page 218] (☏ *066 228 4760; ⊕ 07.30–16.30; entrance US$2; photography permitted*) An essential stop for anybody with a more-than-passing interest in mural art, this small educational museum traces the history of painting in Sri Lanka from prehistoric to modern times. It includes faithful reproductions of some of the country's most iconic rock murals: from squiggly cave paintings of people hunting and riding animals executed in pre-Buddhist times by the hunter-gatherer Vedda, to some superb examples of Kandyan-era temple paintings in the central and low country traditions. And while visiting a museum isn't quite the same as seeing the actual paintings *in situ*, the lighting is superior to most temples, the displays are well labelled, and it would take weeks of dedicated travel to visit all the sites represented. Sadly, the museum gets so few visitors that it often powers down when quiet, so you may need to ask them to switch on all the lights and the air conditioning – without which it can feel very gloomy and stuffy. A good bookshop is attached.

Somawathi Temple and Dagoba [map, page 218] Set in a parklike stand of shady woodland below the southern face of Dambulla Rock, this atmospheric and surprisingly little-visited temple, now in ruins, was reputedly founded in the 1st century BC by Valagamba, though one nearby rock inscription suggests he expanded it from a dagoba built 50 years earlier by his father, Saddha Tissa. The temple is named after Valagamba's second wife, Soma Devi, who famously allowed herself to be captured during the Tamil invasion of 103BC in order to facilitate the escape of the king and his pregnant first wife and children, and was held in exile in India for 14 years prior to being repatriated and restored as queen after her husband recaptured Anuradhapura in 89BC. The ruins' central feature, reached via a unique curved stairwell, is a medium-sized brick dagoba, whose square base also supports a small block-like structure said to be Soma Devi's tomb. The site incorporates several other stone platforms, one of which has ornate moonstones on its northern, southern and western entrances, and supports 32 stumpy pillars that must once have supported a low roof. The overgrown slopes behind the ruins are studded with dozens of drip-ledged caves and other minor ruins, suggesting this must once have been a very large monastic complex indeed. Somawathi Temple stands 1km west of the main road through Dambulla. To get here, follow directions from the start of the Ancient Route to the Dambulla Cave Temples, and continue past Rangiripaya Temple for another 200m until you see the dagoba to your right.

Sam Popham Arboretum [map, page 212] (m *0777 267951;* w *sampophamarboretum.wordpress.com;* ☉ *06.00–18.00, night walks start 19.00; entrance US$7/10 day/night inc guide*) Situated 3km along the Kandalama Road and easily reached by tuktuk, Sri Lanka's oldest dry-zone arboretum was started in 1963 by the British naval-officer-turned-tea-planter for whom it is named. Originally 3ha in extent, but expanded by another 11ha in 1989, it consists of land savaged by slash-and-burn cultivation but now largely restored to the original cover of thorny scrub jungle by allowing it to rejuvenate with minimal human interference, a technique now dubbed the 'Popham Method'. In addition to 282 plant species belonging to 67 families, the arboretum is home to medium and small mammals such as spotted deer, spotted chevrotain, grizzled giant squirrel, pangolin, slender loris and rusty-spotted cat, more than 80 resident and migrant bird species, and 67 butterfly species. A good network of trails leads through the arboretum, and early morning walks (with optional guide included in the ticket price) are especially rewarding for birders, with a good chance of spotting Sri Lanka junglefowl, white-naped woodpecker, brown-headed barbet, Malabar hornbill, black-capped bulbul, white-rumped shama, Asian paradise-flycatcher and other woodland species. Guided night walks, starting at 19.00, must be booked in advance and come with a good chance of seeing slender loris and other nocturnal species. The visitor centre is a granite bungalow designed by Geoffrey Bawa, and two simple self-catering cottages (*US$25/30 sgl/dbl;* **$$**) are available for overnight stays.

HISTORIC SITES SOUTH AND WEST OF DAMBULLA

A number of exceptional archaeological sites and ancient temples can be found within a 30km radius of Dambulla. Best known and most popular (though not necessarily most rewarding) is the Avukana Buddha. Some 35km northwest of Dambulla off the main road to Anuradhapura, Avukana can easily be visited as a standalone trip from Dambulla (or, for that matter, from Sigiriya or Habarana) or as a longer day trip taking in some or all of the other four sites described under the heading *West of Dambulla*. None of the four sites described under *South of Dambulla* is anywhere like as popular as Avukana. Indeed, for adventurous travellers, half the charm of most of the attractions listed below is how refreshingly quiet and off the beaten track they feel by comparison with the four UNESCO World Heritage Sites that form the focal points of sightseeing in the Cultural Triangle. You can get to within easy striking distance of most of these sites using public transport, but with tuktuks being so inexpensive, you'll save a lot of hassle by chartering them to hop between sites of interest. No admission fees are charged unless otherwise stated.

WEST OF DAMBULLA Any of the sites described below makes for a worthwhile goal for a day trip in its own right. With sufficient energy and interest, you could fit all five into a longish day out of Dambulla, Sigiriya and Habarana. Were you to do this, we would recommend starting with Jathika Namal Uyana in the cool of the morning, then looping north from Andiyagala through Ambarali, Reswehara and Avukana, before returning to Dambulla through Andiyagala and Budugehinna, possibly even squeezing in a side trip to Ibbankatuwa (described under *South of Dambulla*) en route.

Jathika Namal Uyana [map, page 212] (☏ *066 228 3420;* w *jathikanamaluyana. com;* ☉ *07.30–17.00; entrance US$3.30*) Situated less then 10km west of Dambulla as the crow flies, this tranquil 10km² forest reserve is renowned for two unusual natural phenomena. Most impressive and unusual is an eponymous rose-quartz mountain whose pink-hued crystalline rocks were reputedly used as building material for India's Taj Mahal. The reserve also protects the island's largest forest of Ceylon ironwood (*Mesua ferrea*), which is the national tree of Sri Lanka, and comes into flower over April–June. A well-maintained footpath runs south from the ticket office through the shady forest, which can be rewarding for birdwatchers (look out for the lovely white-rumped shama and lesser minivet) and is also home to giant squirrel, grey langur and toque macaque. The footpath brings you to a forest clearing containing a modern gold-painted Buddha statue and a dappled 8th-century brick dagoba. From here, a rougher and less clear footpath runs eastward up the exposed and denuded rose-quartz slopes to a ridge-top white Buddha statue that offers great views over the lake-studded countryside. The best time to walk is first thing in the morning, when the soft sunlight enhances the quartz's natural hue.

The most direct route from Dambulla is to follow the Anuradhapura Road north out of town for 7km to Madatugama, then turn left on to the Andiyagala Road, which leads to the car park and ticket office after 6.5km. Alternatively, the car park is only 6.5km east of Andiyagala, a pivotal junction town on the road connecting Dambulla and Budugehinna to Ambarali, Reswehara and Avukana.

Budugehinna Cave Temple [map, page 212] Dubbed 'Punchi Dambulla' (Little Dambulla) on account of its resemblance to the larger cave temple 10km to its east, Budugehinna was first occupied by Buddhist monks in the 3rd century BC and, as with Dambulla, it is said that the original temple was established by King Valagamba. The dagoba is a modern construction, but it stands on the site of the Anuradhapura-era original and incorporates three flagstones from it, as well as an ancient Buddhapada. The main cave temple, protected from seepage by two parallel drip ledges, must be about 35m long and is dominated by a sleeping Buddha figure in an orange robe. It also contains a 5th-century granite Buddha statue, with a clay head added in the 19th century after the original broke off, and a collection of lively and colourful paintings that mostly look quite modern. The real gem, however, is a much smaller upper-level temple whose heavy wooden Kandyan-era doors are normally opened only on poya days, though the head monk might make an exception if you ask very nicely. The tiny interior of the cave temple is adorned with superb and well-preserved Kandyan-era paintings, including an unusual deception of a five-headed, ten-armed Hindu deity on elephant back, a man being eaten alive by a blue lion-like creature, and the Buddha enclosed by a cobra. Most bizarre perhaps is a row of three bare-breasted dancing women holding up their skirts like performers in a risqué 1930s revue.

Coming directly from Dambulla, the quickest route to Budugehinna entails following the Kurunegala Road south for 7km to Talakiriyagama, then turning right on to the Andiyagala Road and continuing for 10km until you see the cliffside temple to your left. Coming from Jathika Namal Uyana, drive west for 5.5km until you reach a T-junction at Andiyagala, where a left turn brings you to Budugehinna after almost 6km.

Ambarali Tampita [map, page 212] Ambarali, 10km north of Budugehinna, is perhaps the finest surviving Sri Lankan example of a tampita, a type of wood-and-clay temple built on wood or stone stilts to protect it from damp and termites. The tampita at Ambarali reputedly has the tallest base in the country, and although it was built in the Kandyan era, the upper storey is supported by about a dozen rock-hewn pillars similar to those found at more ancient monasteries, while the grounds

are scattered with engraved stones that appear to date back to the Anuradhapura era. It is a fascinating and charming construction, made entirely of organic materials without any nails, and the tiny interior contains an odd mix of faded 250-year-old Kandyan artworks and modern paintings in bright pop-art colours.

Ambarali Tampita stands 4km north of Andiyagala along the main road to Avukana. Coming from Dambulla, follow directions to Budugehinna, then continue north for another 5.5km to Andiyagala, and keep on straight ahead. Coming from Jathika Namal Uyana, drive west for 5.5km to Andiyagala, then turn right at the T-junction. Either way, once at Andiyagala, you need to continue north for another 3km then turn left into the 1km feeder road to Ambarali.

Reswehara [map, page 212] (m *0776 108057;* ☉ *07.00–18.00; entrance US$7*) One of Sri Lanka's most evocative and underrated off-the-beaten-track Buddhist sites, Reswehara (a corruption of Res Vihara, literally 'Temple of Light') is set around a striking rocky outcrop in what is now the thickly forested Kahalle-Pallekele Sanctuary, an important refuge for elephants and other wildlife. The temple was founded by Devanampiya Tissa in the 3rd century BC, and its Bo Tree is reputedly one of the 32 original saplings of the Sri Maha Bodhi in Anuradhapura. In its prime, the monastery extended over 6.5km², and incorporated 99 drip-ledged caves and 32 ponds, as well as a host of other buildings, less than 10% of which have been excavated. The main cave temple, adorned with a Brahmi inscription indicating it was excavated during the 1st-century BC reign of Valagamba, is dominated by an 11.5m-long reclining clay Buddha statue, which is unusual not only in that it is dressed in a genuine hand-spun cloth robe, but also in that it stands free from the wall and can be walked around in its entirety. Both this temple, and a second smaller cave behind it, contain some superb and very well-preserved Kandyan-era paintings similar in style to those at Dambulla.

Reswehara's most famous feature, reached via a steep stone staircase, is a masterful but not-quite-finished 12m standing Buddha carved into a rock face in the abhaya mudra. The mysterious relationship between this statue and the similarly proportioned (but otherwise quite different) Avukana Buddha 10km to the east is alluded to in Reswehara's alternative name, Sasseruwa, which probably derives from a Sinhala phrase meaning 'similar image'. Some say that Reswehara is synonymous with the 3rd-century AD Rehara Buddha mentioned in the *Mahavamsa* as being carved into a cliff face by King Mahasena, in which case it may well have been the prototype for the Avukana Buddha. Another legend states that the two statues were carved simultaneously by a competing master sculptor and his apprentice during the 5th-century reign of King Dhatusena, and that the pupil abandoned work at Reswehara when his mentor was adjudged the victor. It has been argued that the personage depicted at Reswehara is not in fact the Buddha, but King Mahasena.

Reswehara is the most remote site of interest described in this section, almost 45km from Dambulla by road. The easiest route here entails following the Kurunegala Road for 7km to Talakiriyagama, then turning right and continuing north for 22km (via Budugehinna, Andiyagala and Ambarali) to Palagala. At Palagala, fork left for Bulnewa rather than right for Avukana, and after another 10km you'll find the 6km feeder road to Reswehara signposted to the left. Coming from Avukana, it is only 15km to Reswehara via Negama.

Avukana Buddha [map, page 212] (m *0776 464890;* ☉ *24hrs; entrance US$7*) Also spelt Aukana, the Avukana Buddha is the best preserved and perhaps the most iconic of a half-dozen colossal granite statues and engravings of the standing Buddha dotted around Sri Lanka. Standing more than 11m tall, the statue is traditionally accredited to King Dhatusena, who ruled in the 5th century and also constructed the Kala Reservoir 2.5km to the east, but some experts believe it to be an 8th-century work, while others still attribute it to the 12th-century reign of Parakramabahu I of Polonnaruwa. Extruding forward from a golden granite face, the impassive Buddha, set on a separately carved double-petalled lotus platform, is depicted looking straight ahead in a variation of the abhaya pose known as the asiva mudra, with the right hand raised towards the shoulder and the palm facing left, while the other arm reaches down towards the immaculately pleated robe. The statue was originally situated in an image house, all that remains of which is the foundation and lower wall, and it is now protected from the elements by a distracting scaffolded roof. Another modern addition is the siraspata on the statue's head, which was placed there by a local administrative officer in 1870. A quintet of superb 9th-century bronzes depicting the Hindu deities Indra, Brahma, Kubera, Varuna and Yama was found in a chamber 2m below the statue and is now displayed in the Anuradhapura Museum. Budget-conscious visitors tend to feel the admission fee is rather steep just to see one statue, and certainly the site lacks the mystique and multiple dimensions of nearby Reswehara. Then again, Avukana, as suggested by its name (literally 'eat the sun'), can be spectacularly beautiful at dawn, when the first rays of sunlight burnish the Buddha's face.

There are several routes from Dambulla to Avukana. The most straightforward, especially if you are visiting in conjunction with other sites described above, is to follow directions to Reswehara but fork right at Palagala, from where it is about 8km to Avukana. Coming from Reswehara, it is only 15km to Avukana via Negama. Some trains between Colombo and Trincomalee, Polonnaruwa and Batticaloa stop at Avukana railway station, 1km from the Buddha statue.

SOUTH OF DAMBULLA

SOUTH OF DAMBULLA The four sites described below all lie to the south of Dambulla and could be visited individually or together over the course of a long but rewarding day. With the exception of Nalanda Gedige (a popular stop on the road between Dambulla and Kandy), these sites are seldom visited by domestic or international travellers, and you'll most likely have them to yourself. The best route if you want to visit all four would be to follow the Kurunegala Road through Ibbankatuwa to Dambawa, then to retrace your steps to Galawela Junction, cross to the Kandy Road via Menikdena, and then head south to Nalanda Gedige.

Ibbankatuwa Megalithic Burial Site

Ibbankatuwa Megalithic Burial Site [map, page 212] Little-known Ibbankatuwa, only 5km southwest of Dambulla, is Sri Lanka's most accessible pre-Buddhist burial ground. The main site consists of around ten exposed megalithic cist tombs, each comprising four horizontal stone slabs arranged in a rectangle with a fifth slab placed flat on top. Most of the graves were found to contain a terracotta pot that held the ashes of the deceased, together with valuables such as clay-bead jewellery, copper bracelets, pearls, and gems of Sri Lankan and Indian origin. A second group of 15-odd similar tombs was discovered during excavations in 2015, and it's thought that several other clusters might lie buried beneath the two. Dated to between 750 and 400BC, the graves would have been roughly contemporaneous with the earliest Iron Age settlement at Anuradhapura 60km to the north, but no link between the sites is evident and the identity of the megalithic culture at Ibbankatuwa is a matter of speculation.

No admission fee is currently charged. This might change, however, when plans to develop the site as an open-air museum, complete with explanatory panels and labelled displays of artefacts currently stowed away in Sigiriya Museum, come to fruition. To get here, follow the Kurunegala Road out of Dambulla, sailing past the potentially confusing junction for Ibbankatuwa Reservoir, until you see the prominent signpost for the burial site to your right. The site is less than 200m from the main road.

Menikdena Archaeological Reserve [map, page 212]

About 12km by road from Dambulla, this tranquil 16ha archaeological reserve on the south bank of the small Menikdena Reservoir protects one of the island's most atmospheric and well-preserved forest monasteries. According to an on-site slab inscription, the monastery was founded in the 9th century under the name Buthgama on a group of five paddies donated by the wife of a local dignitary. The ruins of five buildings are present: an old chapter house survived by an arrangement of unusually tall (3–4m) rock pillars, a restored dagoba and relic chamber with niches containing a Buddha statue adorning the four cardinal points, an image house protected by handsome engraved guardstones, a congregation hall, and a Bodhighara. The reserve doubles as an arboretum run though by a walking trail with several trees labelled in Sinhala and English (red labels indicate Sri Lankan endemics) and it looks very promising for birding.

To get to Menikdena, follow the Kandy Road south of Dambulla for 8km to Pannampatiya, then turn right and continue for another 2.2km to a small Bodhighara and Buddha shrine, where you need to fork to the left. After another 1km, the 700m feeder road to the archaeological site and car park is signposted to the left. Buses between Talakiriyagama and Pannampatiya can drop you at the road fork with the Bodhighara, from where you could walk to the site along the earth walls of the twin Menikdena Reservoir in around 15 minutes.

Nalanda Gedige [map, page 212]

Situated 26km south of Dambulla, Nalanda Gedige made headlines when it was the subject of an Aswan-style rescue mission to prevent it being submerged below the Bowatenna Reservoir, which was created in 1980 as part of a hydro-electric scheme along the Mahaweli River. A narrow but tall (almost 8.5m high) and rather mysterious stone building, it was completely dismantled by archaeologists, then reconstructed on higher ground just above the flood line. The gedige started life as a Hindu shrine, built in the Dravidian style of South India between the 8th and 10th centuries, but was later converted to a Buddhist temple, possibly in the 12th century, when Nalanda served as the military base of King Parakramabahu I. A weird and unique hybrid of Tamil and Sinhala influences, it has an ornately carved exterior that incorporates a row of tiny but exquisite cherub-like faces about 3m above the ground, as well as dwarves engraved in a squatting position or holding up the roof. An unusual feature of the temple, described with bland economy in the site museum as a 'carving depicting a couple', is in fact the only Sri Lankan example of a South Indian tantric motif depicting sexual intercourse between a lion and two people (it can be seen less than 1m from the ground and 2m along the wall to the right as you enter the clearing). The only known Sri Lankan carving of the deity Kubera, here shown seated on a lotus plinth, can be found at Nalanda.

Coming from Dambulla, Nalanda Gedige is reached by following the Kandy Road south for 25km until you see the 1km feeder road signposted to the left. Any bus running between Dambulla and Matale or Kandy can drop you at the junction, from where it's a 15-minute walk to the temple.

Dambawa Tampita [map, page 212]

Built in 1747 for King Kirti Sri Rajasinha, this tiny wooden tampita is an astonishing masterpiece in miniature, so small it feels crowded with more than two people inside, yet covered from floor to ceiling with some of the most exquisite and best-preserved surviving examples of Kandyan art of the Nilagama school. The most famous sequence of paintings at Dambawa depicts Sujata milking a cow then preparing the *madhupayasa* (rice and milk pudding) that became the emaciated Buddha's first meal after attaining enlightenment. Six of its finest panels were reproduced on a series of six stamps issued in 1976 to commemorate the 2,600th anniversary of the birth of the Gautama Buddha. The original wooden door, hinge and lock are still in place.

Dambawa Tampita lies about 26km from Dambulla by road. The most straightforward route entails following the Kurunegala Road south for 22km then, as you exit the small village of Beligamuwa, turning left on to the Madipola Road and following it for 3.5km, then turning left on to a small side road and continuing for another 800m until you see a modest and rather undistinguished temple to your right. The tampita stands within the same compound, to the right of the main temple.

SIGIRIYA

The most impressive of Sri Lanka's archaeological sites is centred on Sigiriya (Lion Rock), a spectacular golden-hued granite toadstool that protrudes 183m into the searing blue sky from the jungle- and paddy-swathed plains 16km northeast of Dambulla. A hermitage since the earliest Buddhist times, this near-impregnable natural citadel was domesticated over AD477–85 by the upstart King Kasyapa, who converted it into a skyscraping fortress-cum-palace at the heart of an ingeniously landscaped water garden. The palace was abandoned after Kasyapa's self-inflicted death in AD495, making it perhaps the most short-lived of all the ancient Sinhalese capitals, yet ironically this UNESCO World Heritage Site stands as probably the most singular and impactful of Sri Lanka's archaeological treasures, and is widely regarded to be the Cultural Triangle's one absolute 'must-see'.

The most convenient base for exploring Sri Lanka's most iconic archaeological site is the tiny village of Sigiriya, which stands a few hundred metres further southwest, and is flanked by an ever-multiplying sprawl of hotels, guesthouses and restaurants. Basing yourself here also allows you to explore several other local sites of interest, the most notable of which is the oft-overlooked Pidurangala, a similarly impressive natural granite citadel whose scramble-able summit provides a thrilling view across to Sigiriya Rock 1km to the south (and is sometimes favoured by budget-conscious travellers as a cheap alternative to the main attraction). Sigiriya and Pidurangala can also easily be visited as a day trip from Dambulla or Habarana. Conversely it is perfectly possible to use any of the lodges around Sigiriya as a base for visits to other parts of the Cultural Triangle as far afield as Anuradhapura and Polonnaruwa.

SIGIRIYA

For listings, see pages 228–30 unless otherwise stated

🛏 **Where to stay**

1	Elephant Corridor	B2
2	Flower Inn	C7
3	Fresco Water Villa	C2
4	Green Grass Homestay	C7
5	Hotel Eden Garden	A3
6	Hotel Sigiriya	D7
7	Hotel Wewa Addara	D2
8	Jetwing Vil Uyana	B3
9	Lakmini Lodge	B7
10	Lal Homestay	A7
11	New Sigiri Resort	B7
12	Nilmini Lodge	C7
13	Sigiri Lion Lodge	B7
14	Sigiriya Village	D7

Off map

Paradise Resort & Spa *p216* D3

❌ **Where to eat and drink**

15	Croissant Hut	C7
16	Gamagedara Village Food	B7
17	Lion Hut	C2
18	New Sigiri Café	C7
19	Pradeep	C7
20	RastaRant Sigiriya	C7
21	Restaurant Shenadi	C7
22	Sigiri Nirwana	B7

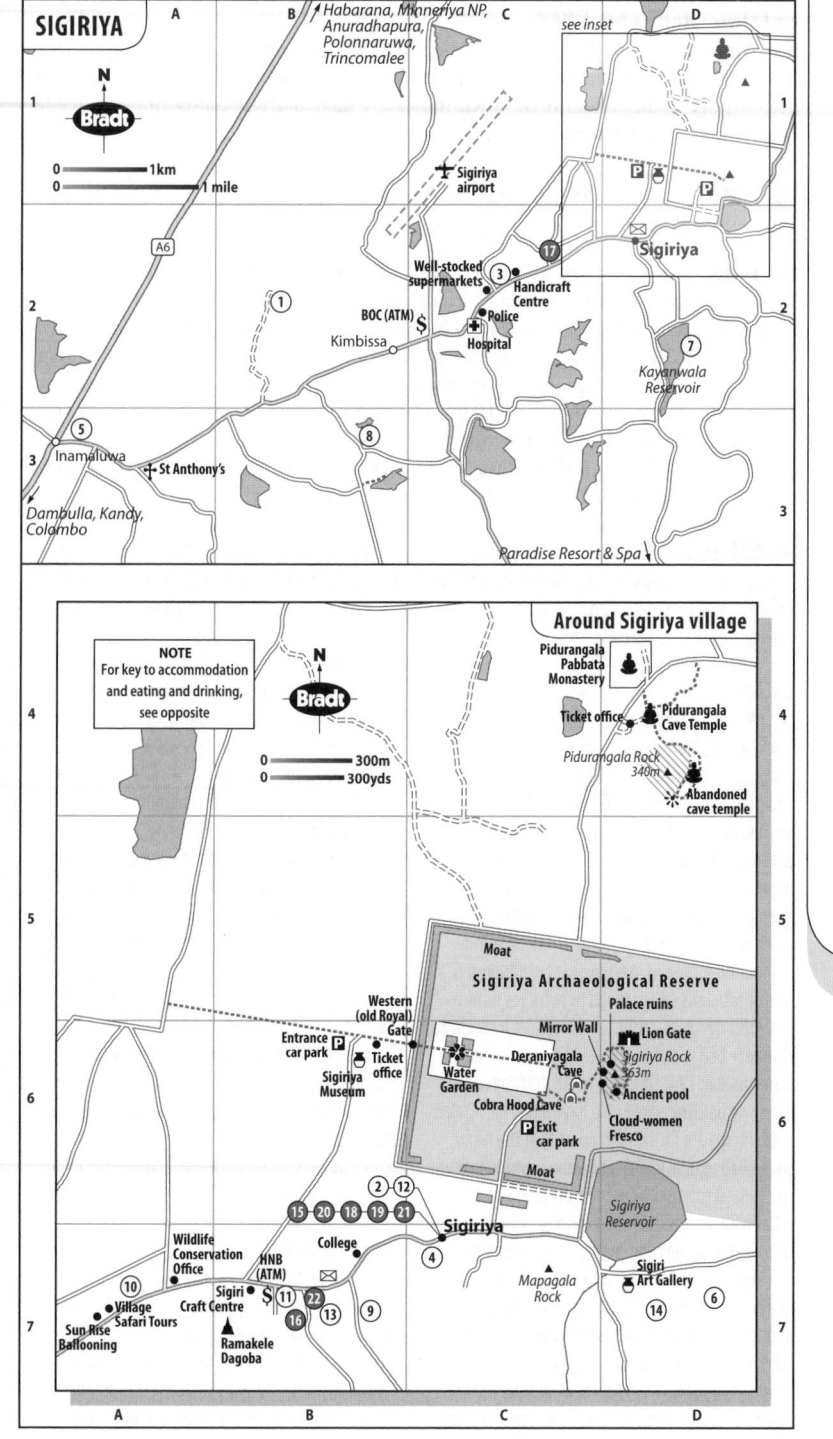

SIGIRIYA

N

Bradt

0 ___ 1km
0 ___ 1 mile

A6

Habarana, Minneriya NP,
Anuradhapura,
Polonnaruwa,
Trincomalee

see inset

Sigiriya
airport

Sigiriya

Well-stocked
supermarkets

Handicraft
Centre

BOC (ATM)

Police

Kimbissa

Hospital

Kayanwala
Reservoir

Inamaluwa

St Anthony's

Dambulla, Kandy,
Colombo

Paradise Resort & Spa

Around Sigiriya village

N

Bradt

NOTE
For key to accommodation
and eating and drinking,
see opposite

0 ___ 300m
0 ___ 300yds

Pidurangala
Pabbata
Monastery

Ticket office

Pidurangala
Cave Temple

Pidurangala Rock
340m

Abandoned
cave temple

Moat

Sigiriya Archaeological Reserve

Palace ruins

Western
(old Royal)
Gate

Mirror Wall

Lion Gate

Entrance
car park

Deraniyagala
Cave

Sigiriya Rock
563m

Ticket
office

Sigiriya
Museum

Water
Garden

Ancient pool

Cobra Hood Cave

Cloud-women
Fresco

Exit
car park

Moat

Sigiriya
Reservoir

Wildlife
Conservation
Office

College

Sigiriya

Sigiri
Art Gallery

HNB
(ATM)

Mapagala
Rock

Village
Safari Tours

Sigiri
Craft Centre

Sun Rise
Ballooning

Ramakele
Dagoba

GETTING THERE AND AWAY

By air Cinnamon Air (w *cinnamonair.com*) operates a daily flight from Bandaranaike International Airport (outside Colombo) to Sigiriya and Trincomalee. The airport stands 1km north of Kimbissa, a village halfway along the 9km feeder road from Inamaluwa to Sigiriya.

By rail The closest railway station is Habarana, 25km north of Sigiriya via Inamaluwa Junction.

By road Sigiriya is 16km from Dambulla by road. To get here, follow the Habarana Road north for 7km to Inamaluwa, where you need to turn right on to a 9km feeder road to Sigiriya via Kimbissa. Coming by public transport from Colombo, Kandy, Anuradhapura or elsewhere to the south or northwest, bus to Dambulla, then pick up one of the buses that run back and forth to Sigiriya every 30 minutes between 06.00 and 19.00, or catch a tuktuk (*US$5–6*). Coming from Habarana, Polonnaruwa, Trincomalee or other destinations to the northwest, catch a Dambulla-bound bus, hop off at Inamaluwa, where you can either catch a tuktuk to Sigiriya (*US$2–3*) or else wait for the next bus coming from Dambulla.

WHERE TO STAY There's plenty of accommodation in and around Sigiriya. Budget-conscious travellers are pointed to the large selection of affordable options in or within walking distance of Sigiriya village, which also hosts a great selection of budget eateries to help you keep down costs.

Exclusive

※ 🏠 **Jetwing Vil Uyana** [227 B3] (36 rooms) 📞066 492 3585/6; e viluyana@jetwinghotels. com; w jetwinghotels.com. Situated 1km along a back road that runs south from the Inamaluwa Road 4km west of Sigiriya, this nature-lover's paradise – the name means 'Garden of Ponds' – occupies a 28ha reclaimed wetland comprising open pools, grassy paddies, reedy marshes & patches of indigenous woodland. The luxurious accommodation is in massive, well-ventilated & utterly fabulous stilted wooden cottages whose tastefully decorated split-level interiors incorporate king-size bed with fitted net, AC, fan, minibar, coffee maker, TV & DVD player. All units have at least one balcony, some also have a plunge pool, & all are spaced far enough apart that the night air is filled with frog, insect & other natural noises. The central complex houses an underground cellar with a formidable selection of wines, an upstairs restaurant dominated by an 8m-high mural of temple legends, a cavernous bar with reproductions of the Sigiriya frescoes, a swimming pool & a viewing platform strewn with cushions. A knowledgeable & enthusiastic resident naturalist conducts night walks in search of slender loris & other nocturnal wildlife, as well as early morning bird walks that provide a great introduction to typical woodland & water birds. Exceptional. *From US$285/299 sgl/dbl B&B.* **$$$$$**

🏠 **Elephant Corridor** [227 B2] (20 rooms) 📞066 228 6950/5; e info@elephantcorridor.com; w elephantcorridor.com. Set in wild & secluded 81ha gardens 1.5km north of the road between Sigiriya and Inamaluwa Junction, this luxurious boutique lodge is centred on a glass-panelled dining & sitting area with a replica of the Cloud-women Fresco on the walls & breathtaking views across to Sigiriya Rock & the cupola of Kandalama hills. Accommodation is in lovely semi-suite bungalows with tall ceilings, stylish wood furnishings, king-size bed, AC, TV, easel & sketch pad, binoculars, dressing room & private balcony facing a lake. There's a great swimming pool & some units have a plunge pool. *From US$254 dbl B&B, with hefty seasonal discounts.* **$$$$$**

Upmarket

🏠 **Hotel Sigiriya** [227 D7] (79 rooms) 📞066 493 0500; e inquiries@serendibleisure. lk; w serendibleisure.com/hotelsigiriya. Though not exactly cutting edge on the décor front, this well-run 1970s stalwart can be recommended as an attractively priced wildlife-friendly hotel offering an unbeatable view of Sigiriya Rock poking above the canopy 600m to the north. An enthusiastic resident naturalist can offer advice about wildlife excursions & leads guided bird walks that frequently throw up 30–40 of the 100-plus bird species recorded in the wooded gardens. Amenities include a swimming pool, a bar serving award-winning cocktails & a restaurant serving decent buffet fare. Rooms are small but colourfully decorated & come with AC, fan, TV & fridge. *From US$148/160 sgl/dbl B&B, with substantial off-season discounts.* **$$$$**

🏠 **Sigiriya Village Hotel** [227 D7] (120 rooms) 📞 066 228 6803/6; e sigiriyavillage@ forthotels.com; w sigiriya-village.com. This pleasant but slightly timeworn 1980s hotel bordering Sigiriya village stands in lush tropical gardens with a swimming pool & large well-wooded artificial pond where kingfishers hawk from the branches & monkeys come to drink. Spacious tiled rooms with a rather garish colour scheme are arranged in circular clusters to emulate a village feel & come with AC, fan & TV. *From US$120/140 sgl/dbl B&B, with good seasonal discounts.* **$$$$**

🏠 **Fresco Water Villa** [227 C2] (48 rooms) 📞 066 228 6161; m 0777 999252; e oakrayreserv@sltnet.lk; w oakrayhotels.com/ fresco-water-villa-sigiriya. This modern 3-storey hotel has spacious & attractive rooms with AC & private balcony arranged around a large swimming pool & koi ponds. Décor is a bit stark & a location on the main road 1.5km west of Sigiriya doesn't bode well for a quiet night. *US$135/160 sgl/dbl HB, with hefty online & seasonal discounts.* **$$$$**

Moderate

🏠 **Hotel Eden Garden** [227 A3] (48 rooms) 📞 066 228 6635/6; e info@edengardenlk.com; w edengardenlk.com. Usefully located 150m east of Inamaluwa Junction, halfway between Dambulla and Sigiriya, this unexciting but functional hotel stands in well-wooded gardens with a swimming pool & restaurant serving a varied selection of Asian & Western mains in the **$$** range. Rooms are large, rather garish & come with AC, fan, TV & balcony. Difficult to fault at the price. *US$65/70 sgl/dbl B&B.* **$$$**

🏠 **Hotel Wewa Addara** [227 D2] (12 rooms) 📞 066 493 5745; e info@wewaaddara.com; w wewaaddara.com. Offering a view across the

small but lushly vegetated Kayanwala Reservoir to Sigiriya Rock 2km to the north, this peaceful not-quite-boutique 2-storey retreat has spacious modern rooms with AC, fan, queen-size bed, wall fresco of Sigiriya Rock & private terrace or balcony with lake view. Birdlife is prolific & elephants occasionally come to drink. There's a swimming pool & good open-sided restaurant that doesn't stock alcohol but allows guests to bring their own. *US$90/140 sgl/dbl HB, with seasonal & online discounts of up to 50%.* **$$$$**

Budget

☀ 🏠 **Sigiri Lion Lodge** [227 B7] (18 rooms) m 0714 793131; e sigirilionlodge@gmail.com; w sigirilionlodge.com. Owned & managed by a delightful & obliging husband-&-wife team, this recently expanded lodge offers the choice of ground-floor budget rooms with fan & net in the old wing or smarter AC rooms with balcony in a new 3-storey wing. Rates include an excellent local-style b/fast & there's also a self-catering kitchen & new rooftop restaurant. Tucked away on a short side road, it is only 5mins' walk from the village & 15mins from Sigiriya Rock. Bicycle hire & well-priced jeep safaris are on offer. *US$15/20 sgl/ dbl with fan, or US$20/33 with AC.* **$**

🏠 **Lakmini Lodge** [227 B7] (27 rooms) m 0717 098128, 0710 638959; e lakminilodge@ hotmail.com; w lakminilodge.com. This friendly & unpretentious owner-managed 3-storey guesthouse is only a 15min walk from Sigiriya Rock & offers superb views of it from the elevated b/ fast platform & rooftop sitting area. Large modern tiled rooms have AC, fan & semi-private balcony. *US$33/40 B&B dbl in old/new wing, or US$53 for a top-floor room with a view of Sigiriya Rock.* **$$**

🏠 **New Sigiri Resort** [227 B7] (10 rooms) 📞 066 228 6525; m 0778 666555; e info@ newsigiriresort.com; w newsigiriresort.com. The closest hotel to the Sigiriya ticket office is a functional modern 3-storey building whose rooms all have AC, fan, net & balcony with a view to the rock. A ground-floor restaurant/bar serves a good variety of dishes both local (**$$**) & Western (**$$$**). Good value. *US$35/40 B&B sgl/dbl.* **$$**

Shoestring

🏠 **Lal Homestay** [227 A7] (5 rooms) m 0777 045386; e lalhomestay@gmail.com. Set in a neat jungle-fringed garden 20mins' walk from Sigiriya

Rock, this friendly little place is named after its owner-manager, a former guide whose wife conjures up terrific curries & other local dishes. The clean rooms have a red polished floor, fan, net & terrace seating. Good value. *US$20 B&B dbl.* **$**

🏠 **Flower Inn** [227 C7] (12 rooms) **m** 0775 672197. Conveniently located in the heart of the village, this is the oldest private guesthouse in Sigiriya, founded by the parents of the present-day owner-managers in 1972. It's a friendly set-up, & aptly named, with a leafy garden supplemented by an abundance of pot plants, but looking a little worn at the edges, though this is reflected in the low prices. All rooms have net & fan, & some come with AC. *US$13/15 sgl/dbl with fan, or US$23 dbl with AC.* **$**

🏠 **Green Grass Homestay** [227 C7] (2 rooms) **m** 0777 941281, 0773 604810; **e** greengrasstay@ gmail.com. Situated just behind Croissant Hut, this friendly & super-central homestay has a small but pleasant garden & simple but clean rooms with fan & balcony. *US$10/13 sgl/dbl.* **$**

🏠 **Nilmini Lodge** [227 C7] (8 rooms, 1 dorm) 📞 066 228 6313; **e** nilminilodge@gmail.com. This friendly & long-serving family-run lodge in the centre of Sigiriya village stands in large green gardens that attract plenty of small wildlife & are hung with hammocks. Simple but clean rooms have fan, net & optional AC. There's also a 4-bed dorm with fan. *US$17/23 dbl with fan/AC, US$7 pp dorm bed.* **$**

✕ WHERE TO EAT AND DRINK
Sigiriya village
A cluster of decent & very well-priced restaurants is clustered along the 150m main road through Sigiriya village.

✕ **Pradeep Restaurant** [227 C7] **m** 0710 438733; 🕐 08.00–21.00. It may not look like much from the outside, but this busy family-run restaurant serves possibly the best curries in the village, as well as good kottu roti & other local dishes. Vegetarian friendly. Large portions. **$$**

✕ **Croissant Hut** [227 C7] 📞 066 228 6306; **m** 0773 877934; 🕐 08.00–21.30. This small & friendly owner-managed restaurant serves an interesting selection of pasta dishes & grills along with the usual Sri Lankan fare. Croissants cost US$1. **$$$**

✕ **RastaRant Sigiriya** [227 C7] **m** 0777 942095; 🇫 rastarant.sigiriya. An evening barbecue joint that keeps flexible hours, this garden restaurant sits alongside a stream at the entrance to the village. It serves grilled chicken, fish & salad, as well as good cocktails & beers, to a backdrop of insect noises & chilled (mostly reggae) music. **$$$**

✕ **New Sigiri Café** [227 C7] **m** 0778 666555; 🕐 07.30–21.00. This bright little café specialises in rotis with sweet & savoury fillings but also serves curries & sandwiches. **$$**

✕ **Restaurant Shenadi** [227 C7] **m** 0777 855690; 🕐 06.30–23.00. Keeping the longest hours in the village, this is a useful b/fast spot & it also serves a wide selection of tasty local dishes including curries, string hoppers & kottu roti. Good value. **$$**

Inamaluwa Road
Most of the hotels along the Inamaluwa Rd serve food, but if you need a change of scene try one of the following.

✕ **Sigiri Nirwana Restaurant** [227 B7] **m** 0711 336616; 🕐 08.00–22.00. Practically the house restaurant for the nearby Sigiri Lion Lodge, this low-key owner-managed place serves excellent & well-priced kottu roti, devilled stir-fries & 5-dish rice-&-curry spreads. Vegetarians are well catered for & you can bring your own booze. **$$**

✕ **Gamagedara Village Food** [227 B7] **m** 0717 003706; 🕐 09.30–21.00. Situated 10m south of the main road, this simple, family-run place is the culinary equivalent of a homestay, serving a seasonally influenced spread of 5–8 delicious vegetarian curries (chicken, too, by request) cooked in traditional clay pots. **$$**

✕ **Lion Hut** [227 C2] **m** 0715 301909; 🕐 10.00–21.00. Set alongside the Inamaluwa Rd 1.5km west of Sigiriya village, this place has outdoor seating on a wooden deck & a varied menu of local curries (**$$**) & Western-style grills (**$$$**). No alcohol.

OTHER PRACTICALITIES There is no bank but you can usually draw money from the HNB ATM [227 B7] next to the New Sigiri Resort, 1km west along the Inamaluwa Road. Failing that, there are plenty of banks and ATMs in Dambulla. A supermarket stocked with items aimed at a tourist clientele is attached to the New Sigiri Café, and a few more locally oriented supermarkets flank the Inamaluwa Road, but none compares with the Cargills Food City in Dambulla for variety. For curio shopping, try the Handicraft Centre [227 C2] (✆ 066 778 6065; ⏰ 08.00–20.00) next to Fresco Water Villa on the Inamaluwa Road, or the Sigiri Craft Centre [227 B7] attached to the New Sigiri Resort.

THE LION KING OF SIGIRIYA

More than any other comparable monument in Sri Lanka, Sigiriya is associated with a single ruler: the controversial King Kasyapa, whose 18-year reign in the late 5th century AD was bookended by bloodshed and high intrigue. Kasyapa was son of King Dhatusena of Anuradhapura, a popular and unifying figure who had come to power in AD455 following his defeat of a short-lived dynasty founded by Tamil invaders from South India. Kasyapa was Dhatusena's eldest son, but his mother was not from a royal bloodline, so he was overlooked as heir apparent in favour of his more pedigreed younger half-brother Moggallana. Disharmony in the royal family came to a head when a transgression by Dhatusena's son-in-law Magara led to the latter's mother bring stripped and burnt alive at the vengeful monarch's instruction. Magara and Kasyapa conspired to capture Dhatusena, and when the ageing king refused to hand over his wealth to his eldest son, or to endorse him as heir, was chained up naked in a cell and entombed alive.

Kasyapa became king in AD477, and appointed Magara as his military commander, but he was never popular with his subjects, who nicknamed him Pitru Ghataka (Father Killer), and also met with the disapproval of the Buddhist clergy. As a result, he abandoned the long-serving Sinhala capital at Anuradhapura in favour of Sigiriya Rock, and built himself a fortified palace at the summit of this superb natural citadel and watchtower. This he surrounded with a beautiful landscaped garden whose irrigated pools and fountains were enclosed within a network of protective ramparts and moats.

Even as Kasyapa consolidated his defences, however, his younger brother Moggallana, long exiled in South India, returned to Anuradhapura with a ragtag army to reclaim the throne. The bullish Kasyapa led his mighty army out of Sigiriya to meet Moggallana in battle, but before he could, Magara, having switched loyalties to the younger brother, contrived to abandon the king in a swamp with only a royal elephant for company. Rather than be captured alive, Kasyapa held his jewel-encrusted dagger to his throat, and took his own life. Moggallana was crowned in AD495 to widespread approval and returned the capital to its traditional seat at Anuradhapura. This means that the palatial complex at Sigiriya, for all its architectural ambition and aesthetic merit, acted as royal capital for a mere ten years after its completion. Sigiriya did, however, continue to function as a Buddhist monastery, hermetic retreat and – as attested to by the plethora of verses inscribed on the Mirror Wall – tourist attraction of note, attracting pilgrims and sightseers from far and wide. Sigiriya was abandoned to obscurity in the mid 12th century, only to be rediscovered by Major Jonathan Forbes of the 78th Highlanders in 1832.

WHAT TO SEE AND DO In addition to the sites listed below, Sigiriya is a useful base for day trips to Dambulla and most other attractions described in this chapter. Tuktuks are widely available to get you around cheaply, while jeep safaris to Minneriya and nearby reserves can be arranged for around US$27 per vehicle (inclusive of driver and fuel) through the Sigiri Lion Lodge and most other hotels, or you could bus through to Habarana and pick up a vehicle slightly more cheaply there.

Sigiriya Rock [227 C/D 5–6] (w *sigiriyatourism.com*; ⊕ *07.00–18.00 (ticket office closes 17.00); entrance US$30*) A prime candidate for Eighth Wonder of the Ancient World, Sigiriya Rock, a towering volcanic plug studded with 5th-century ruins and frescoes, forms the centrepiece of a fantastic 1km² archaeological site that also incorporates an ingeniously landscaped water garden hemmed in by protective ramparts and moats. The original rock staircase to the summit, though partially intact, is now supplemented by a series of narrow metal stairs and caged-in ladders. The ascent isn't physically demanding, assuming a moderate level of fitness, but more precarious stretches might be testing to acrophobics. A morning visit is recommended, aiming to be at the ticket office when it opens, in order to ascend the rock in the relative cool, before the post-breakfast masses descend. The next best time for a visit is late afternoon, starting at around 15.00, when the crowds start to thin out. If at all possible, Sigiriya is best avoided entirely over weekends, poya days and public holidays, when the site as a whole – and the stairs in particular – invariably becomes uncomfortably congested.

The ticket office is situated at the original Western Gate, which was probably reserved for royalty in Kasyapa's day. This stands 1km north of the Inamaluwa Road; the signposted junction, 700m before Sigiriya village, is more or less opposite the prominent Ramakele Dagoba. In addition to tickets, the office issues useful free site maps, and is a good place to pick up (non-mandatory) private guides at a negotiable rate. The admission fee includes entrance to the inessential but still worthwhile **Sigiriya Museum**, which stands alongside the ticket office, and includes some informative historical displays and a reproduction of the Cloud-women Fresco. If you visit in the morning, best save the museum until after you've summited. On an afternoon visit, by contrast, it makes a good first port of call before you explore the archaeological site proper.

Water Garden Softening the harsh outline of Sigiriya Rock, King Kasyapa's elaborate water garden extends in a rectangle in all directions from the towering eyrie. It was originally enclosed by three sets of ramparts and three moats, substantial relicts of which are still intact today, particularly on the complex's western side. It is regarded to be one of the world's oldest extant landscaped gardens, and the broad layout is still clearly discernible more than 1,500 years after its creator's death, as are several well-preserved individual features. It is named for an ingenious ancient network of ponds, channels, islets, pavilions, promenades and fountains – some of which still spout after rain, following a recent clean-up of the underground conduit! The water garden is ideal for a whimsical stroll, with Sigiriya Rock looming overhead to form a backdrop that is especially dramatic in the burnishing late-afternoon sun. There are also plenty of monkeys, giant squirrels and birds to keep you amused (look out overhead for the dashing shaheen falcon, *Falco peregrinus peregrinator*, a localised race of peregrine that breeds on the rock). Be sure to visit the so-called Cobra Hood Cave, which is named for its sinister shape, and includes a drip ledge and a 2nd-century BC inscription that indicates Sigiriya served as a Buddhist hermitage several centuries before Kasyapa showed up. Nearby Deraniyagala Cave contains faint traces of paintings similar to the Cloud-women Fresco on the main rock.

The ascent The first and most famous feature of the ascent, reached via a narrow metal spiral staircase, and protected from the elements by a deep rock overhang, is the **Cloud-women Fresco**. This astonishingly well-preserved and hauntingly beautiful 5th-century gallery comprises 21 naturalistic waist-upwards portraits of bejewelled, bare-breasted women whose strongly individualistic facial features suggest they were based on real-life models. The fresco is acknowledged as one of Sri Lanka's oldest and finest art treasures, but the exact nature of its intensely characterful and rather sombre-looking subjects is a matter of conjecture. For many years, it was assumed they were members of Kasyapa's royal harem, possibly depicted in mourning shortly after his death in AD495. These days, it is more widely believed that the women represent apsaras – shape-shifting angel-like Hindu and Buddhist cloud or water spirits – accompanied by female attendants carrying fruit and flower platters. Photography of the paintings, with or without flash, is now absolutely forbidden.

A unique feature of Sigiriya's staircase is the so-called **Mirror Wall**, a brick structure that Kasyapa had coated with an albumen, lime and honey plaster, and buffed until it showed his reflection as he walked past. After the site was abandoned and the wall's lustre faded, it was used as a kind of visitors' book, one inscribed with more than a thousand rhapsodic snippets of (mostly Sinhala) poetry and graffiti written by dazzled Medieval sightseers. Most of the graffiti was composed in the 7th and 8th centuries, but some snippets date to the 6th and others as late as the 14th century. Intriguingly, one ancient visitor wrote that the Cloud-women Fresco incorporated '500 damsels [to] arrest the progress of him who is going to heaven', in which case today's 21 stragglers must represent a mere fragment of a vast mural that once covered a 140m-long, 40m-high vertical slab on the western wall and would have been visible for miles around. This supports archaeologist John Still's contention, back in 1907, that 'the whole face of the hill appears to have been a gigantic picture gallery'.

The final ascent passes through what remains of the **Lion Gate**, a massive statue depicting the most important symbol of the Sinhala monarchy. All that is left of the original sculpture is the lion's hefty three-toed feet and bird-like claws, but even these give some idea of its imposing scale. Back in the day, the stone staircase that still runs between the paws continued uphill through the lion's mouth to the summit. Graffiti on the Mirror Wall suggests that the Lion Gate remained intact for around 400 years after its creation, but started to crumble away in the 9th century. The original stone steps to the summit have been replaced by a metal staircase that recalls a fire escape.

The summit Extending over 1.5ha, the summit of the volcanic plug is a broad tabletop whose descending terraces were hand-carved around the natural contours. The rock's highest point, approximately 360m above sea level, is marked by a now-ruined dagoba and the slab-like remains of what was probably a throne or royal meditation seat. All that remains of Kasyapa's surprisingly modest palace is the foundation of a single square 90m^2 room, which occupies the upper terrace, on the brink of the rock almost directly above the Lion Gate. Below this, the multi-terraced palace garden is dominated by a finely executed 560m^2 rock-hewn swimming pool (or possibly ornamental pond) fed by rainwater run-off supplemented by jugs of water carried up from the gardens below (or, as has been suggested, based on limited evidence, by a complicated windmill-powered hydraulic system). Perhaps the most memorable feature of the summit, however, is the sensational views that

Kasyapa would once have enjoyed, panning Sigiriya Reservoir, the manicured Water Gardens, Pidurangala Rock and a vast swathe of surrounding jungle.

Pidurangala Rock [227 D4] (m *0770 331068;* ⊕ *06.00–19.00; entrance US$3.30*) Situated exactly 1km north of Sigiriya as the falcon darts, Pidurangala (literally 'Straw-Gold Rock') is a burnished volcanic plug topped by a flattish heart-shaped 2.5ha boulder that rises to within about 1m of its slightly loftier and far more lauded neighbour. The hill has served as a hermetic retreat since the earliest days of Sri Lankan Buddhism, but its role as a monastery was probably formalised when King Kasyapa built his palace on Sigiriya Rock and relocated the Buddhist monks who had previously occupied that site to Pidurangala. The ascent of Pidurangala, on a steep but reasonably well-marked 1km trail, takes around 30 minutes in either direction. *En route*, you pass an abandoned cave temple dominated by a 6th-century reclining Buddha made of bricks and with some of its original limestone plaster still intact. The path terminates with a rather stiff scramble to the summit, which is uninhabited and empty of ruins, but offers absolutely fantastic views towards Sigiriya Rock (and its more distant counterpart at Dambulla) across a delightful landscape of tropical jungle, lush cultivation and sparkling reservoirs. As with Sigiriya, it is a good site for rock-nesting raptors, in particular the handsome shaheen falcon.

For energetic travellers, the ascent of Pidurangala Rock is an excellent addendum to a visit to Sigiriya, and many budget-conscious travellers now climb it in preference to Sigiriya in order to save on entrance fees. Better still, unlike Sigiriya, it is very uncrowded and you might well have it to yourself out of season. The climb starts at Pidurangala Temple, which stands about 2km north of the Sigiriya ticket office by road, and 3km from the junction on the Inamaluwa Road. If you don't feel like the flattish 30–45-minute walk, a tuktuk from Sigiriya village should cost around US$2. The view is particularly rewarding in the early morning, and it is permitted to climb it in time for sunrise, leaving at around 04.30 (ideally with a headlamp or torch) to summit in time for sunrise, then to pay the fee after you descend. It's worth dropping into the ancient Pidurangala Temple, a two-chambered built-up cave that incorporates a large recumbent Buddha, several seated and standing Buddhas, relatively modern murals that include a replica of Sigiriya's Cloud-women Fresco, and a Vishnu shrine that opens only on Wednesdays and Saturdays. Also worth a look, on the jungle-clad plains about 200m north of the ticket office, are the substantial and atmospheric ruins of Pidurangala Pabbata, an abandoned forest monastery that was once associated with the temple.

Ramakele Dagoba [227 B7] Situated in a large clearing on the south side of the Inamaluwa Road less than 1km west of Sigiriya village, this moss- and grass-covered brick dagoba is variously ascribed to King Kasyapa and his half-brother, rival and successor Moggallana. Its most interesting feature, a carved stone replica of the mythical mountain Mahameru Parwatha stowed away in its relict chamber, is now housed in the National Museum in Colombo. The dagoba was once the centrepiece of a sprawling forest monastery which is survived by a scattering of more than 120 ruins in the jungle that encloses the clearing. An easily missed footpath leads through the forest and ruins protected within the Ramakele Archaeological Site, but you need decent walking shoes to explore it, and should also be conscious of the possible presence of elephants, especially in the late afternoon. Birdlife is plentiful.

Hot-air ballooning Established in 2003, Sun Rise Ballooning (m *0770 215513, 0773 651227;* e *info@srilankaballooning.com;* w *srilankaballooning.com*) operates daily sunrise flights over Sigiriya and Kandalama Reservoir during the main tourist season of November–April. Flights last 1 hour and cost US$210 per adult, inclusive of lunch and hotel pick-up between 04.45 and 05.15.

Jetwing Vil Uyana guided walks The evening loris walks (*US$30 pp*) and morning and evening bird walks (*US$25 pp*) conducted by the resident naturalist at Jetwing Vil Uyana (page 228) are open to all, though the former is for a maximum of six people and preference is given to hotel guests. Sightings of the slender loris, an oddball nocturnal primate related to lemurs and bushbabies, are a near certainty on the former, while the 90-minute bird walks frequently yield up to 50 species, especially during the migrant season.

Kayanwala Reservoir [227 D2] This pretty lotus-covered lake about 1.5km south of Sigiriya village makes a great goal for a short afternoon or morning stroll. It supports an abundance of aquatic birds and the views back towards Sigiriya Rock are tremendous, especially towards dusk. To get here, turn south from the Inamaluwa Road 400m west of the village, at the junction signposted for Lakmini Lodge, then continue south past the lodge until you reach the bund (reservoir wall) after another 1km or so.

HABARANA

Though it lacks any significant dagobas or other historical monuments, the small crossroads town of Habarana is ideally positioned for those who want to explore the Cultural Triangle using one hotel as a base. It stands on the most direct route between Polonnaruwa and Anuradhapura, around 45km from the former and 60km from the latter, at the junction with the main road running south to Dambulla and Sigiriya (both around 20km distant). It is also the closest town to the ruins of Ritigala, and to the Minneriya-Kaudulla complex of national parks and their famous elephants. The most prominent feature of this attractive town is the jungle-bound Habarana Reservoir, which was excavated in the late 3rd century AD by King Mahasena. Though it is far smaller than Dambulla, Habarana is well equipped with hotels catering to all but shoestring budgets, plenty of buses trundle in and out in all directions, it hosts several jeep safari operators, and it also boasts the closest railway station to Dambulla and Sigiriya.

GETTING THERE AND AWAY
By rail Little more than a halt, Habarana railway station, set alongside the Trincomalee Road 2.5km north of the town centre, is also the closest train stop to Dambulla and Sigiriya. All trains between Colombo and Trincomalee or Batticaloa via Polonnaruwa stop here.

By road Habarana lies 20km north of Dambulla, so travel times to/from most destinations are broadly similar (add 30 minutes coming from the south and subtract it from other directions). Several buses hourly connect Habarana to Dambulla, Polonnaruwa, Anuradhapura and Trincomalee.

WHERE TO STAY *Map, page 236*
Upmarket
✳ 🏠 **Aliya Resort & Spa** (96 rooms) Dambulla Rd; ✆ 011 738 6386; e info@

aliyaresort.com; w theme-resorts.com/ aliyaresort. Offering a great view to Sigiriya Rock 4km to the southeast as the crow flies, this

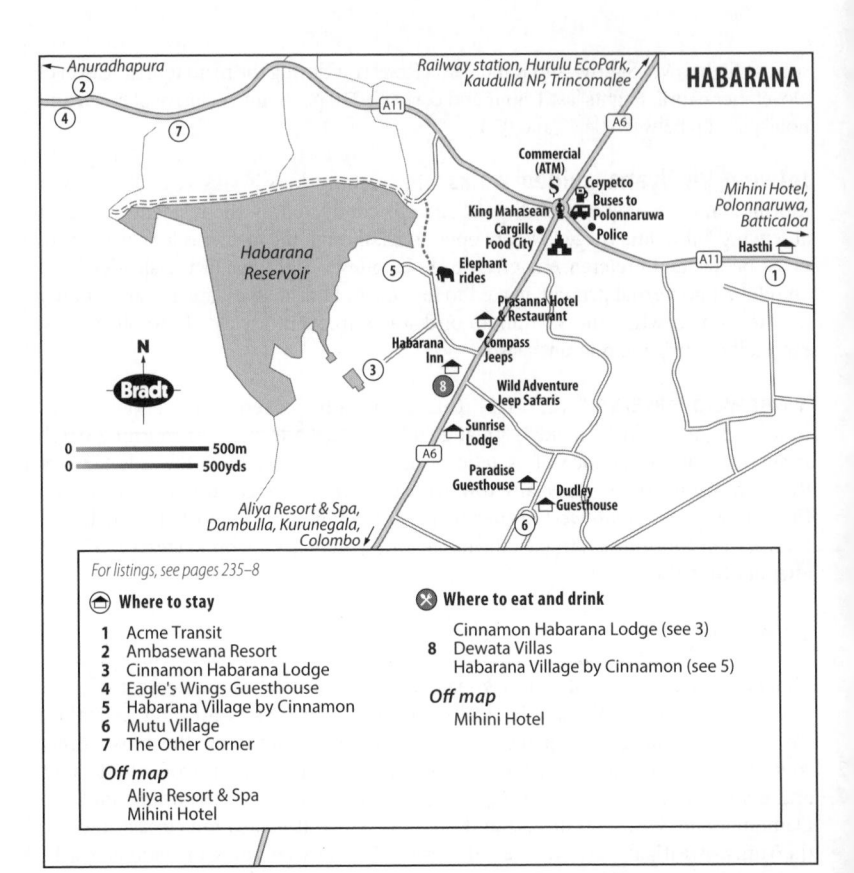

For listings, see pages 235–8

Where to stay

1 Acme Transit
2 Ambasewana Resort
3 Cinnamon Habarana Lodge
4 Eagle's Wings Guesthouse
5 Habarana Village by Cinnamon
6 Mutu Village
7 The Other Corner

Off map
Aliya Resort & Spa
Mihini Hotel

Where to eat and drink

Cinnamon Habarana Lodge (see 3)
8 Dewata Villas
Habarana Village by Cinnamon (see 5)

Off map
Mihini Hotel

modern resort 5km south of Habarana is also notable for its massive infinity pool, slick service & state-of-the-art minimalist décor. Bright rooms in the main 2-storey building have cane & wood furniture & soothing colour schemes. There are also stylish standing tents set on low stilted wooden platforms carved into the woodland. All accommodation has AC, fan, TV & private terrace or balcony. Excellent value. *From US$95 dbl.* **$$$$**

Cinnamon Habarana Lodge

(138 rooms) Off Dambulla Rd; ☏ 011 216 1161; e info@cinnamonhotels.com; w cinnamonhotels.com. This top-notch package hotel stands in attractively feral 4ha gardens bordering the Habarana Reservoir & shaded by tall indigenous trees & clumps of giant bamboo. Spacious semi-suites in the 2-storey wings have a stylish classic-colonial feel & come with terracotta tiles, cane-&-wood furniture, queen-size bed, AV, TV, granite-walled bathrooms & semi-private balcony. Plenty of birds, monkeys & other wildlife pass through the grounds, which also include a massive swimming pool. Meals can be taken à la carte or as buffets, & there's a good Ayurveda spa. *Walk-in rates are US$238/338 sgl/dbl B&B but direct online bookings start at US$120 dbl B&B!* **$$$$**

Habarana Village by

Cinnamon (106 rooms) Off Dambulla Rd; ☏ 011 216 1161; e info@cinnamonhotels.com; w cinnamonhotels.com. This oldest hotel in Habarana, opened in 1976, is now under the same management as the adjacent Cinnamon Habarana Lodge and shares a similar natural setting & attributes. Semi-detached AC rooms are grouped in single-storey clusters around central paths meandering through the vast tropical parkland. The triangular swimming pool, entered by 3 different level terraces of water & then tapering off into infinity, is irresistible. There are also tennis & badminton courts, a jungle gym & a jogging track. Rates are marginally cheaper than its neighbour. **$$$$**

Moderate

🏠 **The Other Corner** (9 rooms) Anuradhapura Rd; 📞 066 492 9892; **m** 0773 749904; **e** toc@starrongroup.com; **w** tocsrilanka.com. Set in jungle-like 4.5ha gardens 2km west of the town centre, this back-to-nature lodge is reached by a suspension bridge across a stream & is linked to Habarana Reservoir by a 200m footpath. The grounds incorporate an organic vegetable garden & small swimming pool, but are mostly dense with indigenous trees & there's a resident naturalist to show visitors the wildlife (among other things, more than 120 recorded bird species). The cottages & stilted tree-houses are built with natural materials (wood, thatch, adobe plaster) to create an organic down-to-earth feel & come with AC, fan, king-size bed, private terrace & tub or shower. A touch overpriced but highly recommended to nature lovers. *US$100/130 sgl/dbl B&B, plus US$20/30 pp for lunch/dinner.* **$$$$**

🏠 **Acme Transit Hotel** (27 rooms) Polonnaruwa Rd; 📞 066 227 0016; **m** 0777 229965; **e** acmetran@sltnet.lk; **w** acmehotelhabarana.com. This functional 2-storey hotel 1km east of the town centre is best known for the lunchtime buffets (**$$$**) served at its restaurant, which also has an à la carte menu (**$$**). Spacious tiled rooms are somewhat character-deficient but come with AC, TV, fridge, dressing table & private balcony overlooking palm-shaded garden & large swimming pool. *US$60/65 sgl/dbl B&B.* **$$$**

Budget

🏠 **Ambasewana Resort** (5 rooms) Anuradhapura Rd; 📞 066 585 1132; **m** 0723 076601; **e** ambasewanaresort@gmail. com. Boasting a rustic location 2km west of the town centre, this delightful homestay, run by a friendly husband-&-wife team, is set in pretty hammock-hung gardens & has a spa, children's playground & semi-open restaurant serving delicious homemade curries. The attractive & brightly decorated rooms all have AC, net & modern bathroom, & some have a private patio. *From US$35 dbl B&B.* **$$**

🏠 **Eagle's Wings Guesthouse** (8 rooms) **m** 0773 264090; **e** brianjyoung123@gmail. com; **w** eagleswingsguesthouse.bookings.lk. Set in a lushly wooded 2ha garden that's rattling with birds & regularly visited by other wildlife, this likeably quirky & rustic lodge 2km west of the town centre provides accommodation in a variety of tree-houses, wooden cabins & cottages, all with net & fan, & some with AC. *From US$30/35 dbl with fan/AC.* **$$**

🏠 **Mutu Village** (7 rooms) Kashyapagama Rd; **m** 0772 694579; **e** info@mutuvillage.com; **w** mutuvillage.com. This suburban owner-managed guesthouse offers the choice of spacious but slightly gloomy standard rooms in the main house, or lighter & more characterful stilted tree-houses, all with AC & fan. The adobe spa with palm-leaf roof is lovely, as is the compact but leafy garden complete with hammocks & a small pond. *From US$50 dbl B&B, with low-season discounts.* **$$$**

🏠 **Mihini Hotel** (6 rooms) Polonnaruwa Rd; **m** 0777 913289; **e** mihinihotel@gmail. com. Situated among the paddies 1.8km east of the town centre, this low-key owner-managed lodges is renowned for its excellent rice-&-curry buffet (**$$$**, by advance order only), but it also offers accommodation in spacious tiled rooms with AC & wooden bed, & has a pleasant garden setting. *US$50 dbl B&B, dropping to US$40 out of season.* **$$$**

🍴 **WHERE TO EAT AND DRINK** *Map, opposite*
All the hotels listed above serve food to guests. For walk-in clients, the Mihini Hotel is highly recommended, but you need to phone through in advance, while the two Cinnamon properties have good international-style restaurants with great lake views.

✘ Dewata Villas Dambulla Rd; m 0723 076611, 0767 161658; e lakmal6611@gmail. com; ☉ 06.30–22.00. This central owner-managed eatery is renowned for its superb rice-&-curry buffets ($$$), with all dishes cooked in traditional clay pots, as well as the evening chicken & seafood barbecue ($$$$), the latter for a minimum of 2 diners. Beers & cocktails are also served, & it has a winning garden setting, marred only by the aural intrusion of the nearby main road.

OTHER PRACTICALITIES There are no private banks in Habarana but a Commercial Bank ATM can be found on the northwest side of the main crossroads. A small branch of Cargills Food City stands 100m south of this.

WHAT TO SEE AND DO Habarana functions more as a base to visit attractions described elsewhere in this chapter (or indeed in the two chapters that follow) than as a place to explore in its own right. The one point of interest, 500m west of the Dambulla Road, is **Habarana Reservoir**, which supports a varied aquatic birdlife, often attracts thirsty elephants in the evening and can be circumnavigated on foot over a couple of hours, or viewed from above by scurrying up the dagoba-capped whaleback rock 150m south of the Anuradhapura Road. A popular but more controversial attraction are elephant rides, which leave from outside the Habarana Village by Cinnamon and cost US$25 organised through the hotel, but more like US$5–10 arranged directly with the mahout. For independent travellers, tuktuks are widely available to take you to the likes of Sigiriya, Dambulla, Anuradhapura and Polonnaruwa, and rates are negotiable, but expect to pay US$30–40 for a half-day excursion, including waiting time. Jeeps for safaris to Minneriya, Kaudulla or Hurulu cost around US$25 for up to nine people, inclusive of driver and fuel but exclusive of park fees, and can be arranged through any hotel or one of several local operators, including the well-regarded **Compass Jeeps** (*Dambulla Rd, just north of the junction for Cinnamon Habarana;* \ *066 227 0009;* m *0777 171600;* w *compassjeepsafari.blogspot.com*) and **Wild Adventure Jeep Safaris** (m *0712 760995*).

RITIGALA ARCHAEOLOGICAL RESERVE [map, page 212] (☉ *08.30–16.30; entrance US$2*) Towering above the low-lying plains 12km northwest of Habarana, Mount Ritigala is the tallest prominence in northern Sri Lanka, and its forested upper reaches and 765m-high peak are frequently shrouded with mist, just as its long and mysterious history is obscured by a fog of myth and legend (see box, opposite). The mountain's steep granite slopes are now protected within the Ritigala Strict Nature Reserve, whose dense tangle of dry-zone evergreen forest supports a rich faunal diversity including more than 20 mammal species (among them elephant, and possibly sloth bear and leopard) and a wide range of forest birds. Unauthorised visits to the 16km^2 nature reserve are forbidden, which means that Ritigala's lofty upper slopes are all but off limits to tourists. As compensation, however, the 24ha archaeological reserve at the eastern base of Ritigala protects a mysterious sprawl of jungle-bound ruins that constitutes probably the best preserved and the most expansive of Sri Lanka's many Medieval forest monasteries.

The provenance of Ritigala Monastery is obscure. Almost certainly, the remote caves of this gargantuan 'Rock of Safety' have provided sanctuary to reclusive monks since the earliest days of Buddhism in Sri Lanka. What survives today, however, is essentially the ruins of an elaborate 9th-century devotional complex built by King Sena I for monks of the ascetically minded Pansukulika (Rag-robe)

RITIGALA IN LEGEND AND HISTORY

The name Ritigala is an ancient one, thought to derive from a Pali phrase, Aritta Gala, meaning 'Safety Rock', a theory informed by the mountain's legendary status as a place of sanctuary for royal refugees in the early days of the Anuradhapura era. More prosaically, the mountain might simply be named after the *riti* or poison-arrow tree *Antiaris toxicaria*, a tall fast-growing fig whose fruit is eaten by many wild birds and mammals (as well as by people), while its sap was once harvested as a poison for arrows and blow-darts in several Asian cultures. Ritigala is the subject of two ancient legends pertaining to Hanuman, the monkey god and servant of King Rama who features prominently in the epic *Ramayana*. The first is that Ritigala was the base from where Hanuman propelled himself on a gigantic leap across to India, where he let Rama know the location his wife Sita was being held by the demon prince Ravana. The second is that the mountain and forest are a relict of the giant herb-bearing chunk of the Himalayas that Hanuman carried across from India to save Rama's wounded brother, Lakshmana. Even today, Ritigala is regarded to support a rare wealth of medicinal plants – indeed, its upper slopes were once regularly visited by traditional healers to harvest *sansevi*, a mysterious herb believed to cure all forms of pain and to greatly prolong life.

sect, whose lives were dedicated almost exclusively to meditation. The monastery was abandoned to the engulfing jungle in the 10th century, and stood there more or less forgotten until 1872, when it was rediscovered by a colonial government surveyor. The site was explored, mapped and partially restored by H C P Bell, the first Archaeological Commissioner of Ceylon, in 1893.

Ritigala is a fascinating place to explore. True, there are no giant dagobas, Buddha statues or ancient paintings to dazzle you, nor any of the other adornments associated with Sri Lanka's most famous archaeological sites. But the archaeological reserve does possess a compellingly haunted quality, one amplified not only by the scarcity of other visitors, but also by the litany of mysterious rustles and strange squawks and chirrups that emanates from the forest's depths. Starting at the car park, a well-preserved stone footpath climbs through the forest for about 1km, gaining about 80m in elevation as it runs past a succession of ancient platforms and circular gimanhalas (places of rest) and other structures. In the order you reach them, these include an amphitheatre-like ritual bathing pool known as the Banda Pokuna, a janthagara (sunken steam bath used for therapeutic purposes), several intriguing double terraces of a type almost unique to this site, and a sunken courtyard with two short engraved obelisks at its southern end.

To get to Ritigala from Habarana, follow the Anuradhapura Road west out of town for 11km, then turn right on to a road that runs north for 8km along the eastern base of the mountain to the Ritigala Information and Research Centre, from where it is another 2km passing through lush submontane forest teeming with birds and butterflies to the archaeological site car park. This road used to be very rough and accessible only by jeep, but it was recently surfaced for most of its length and can now be traversed in any car or tuktuk. No public transport runs further than the junction on the Anuradhapura Road, but a tuktuk from Habarana should only cost US$10–13 return, inclusive of waiting time.

THE ELEPHANT PARKS: MINNERIYA, KAUDULLA AND HURULU

Perhaps the best place to see elephants anywhere in Sri Lanka, this trio of protected areas north and west of Habarana is to some extent best treated as a single destination, since local jeep safari operators tend to switch between them seasonally depending on elephant activity. The largest of the three, and most important in ecological terms, Minneriya National Park is centred on the eponymous reservoir and renowned for its annual dry-season elephant 'gathering'. The smaller Kaudulla National Park, also centred on an eponymous reservoir, is another important dry-season gathering point for elephants, with numbers usually peaking later in the year. The newer Hurulu EcoPark was created as a rainy season alternative to the two nearby national parks, and it offers more reliable elephant viewing at that time of year. Elephants aside, Minneriya and to a slightly lesser extent Kaudulla also offer pretty good general game viewing (chances of leopard or sloth bear are slim, but monkeys and deer are common) and their scenic lakes are also excellent birdwatching sites. Hurulu lacks the scenic wetlands that enhance the two national parks and is more limited when it comes to general game viewing and birds.

GETTING THERE AND AWAY The most normal way to visit all three parks is as a jeep safari from Habarana (page 238) or elsewhere in the Cultural Triangle. Jeep rental rates start at around US$25 out of Habarana for up to six people, inclusive of driver and fuel, but you should pay less for Hurulu, as it is far closer to town than Minneriya or Kaudulla. Safaris out of Sigiriya or Dambulla will cost more, since they are further from the parks, but are not prohibitively pricier. Polonnaruwa (page 248) is also a good base for jeep safaris to Minneriya and to a lesser extent Kaudulla and Hurulu.

If you are driving yourself, the entrance to Minneriya stands alongside the Polonnaruwa Road 8km east of Habarana, the entrance to Hurulu is 2.5km northeast of Habarana on the road to Trincomalee, and Kaudulla is reached by following the Trincomalee Road out of Habarana for 15km to Gal Oya, then turning right on to the signposted 5km feeder road to the entrance gate.

WHAT TO SEE AND DO If you are deciding which park to visit, and elephants are your priority, then broadly speaking they start congregating on Minneriya National Park in June and numbers peak over August to October, when it is not unusual to see gatherings of 100-plus individuals on the floodplain. Numbers at Kaudulla usually peak later in the year, from October through to December, sometimes even January or February. Hurulu EcoPark offers more reliable elephant viewing in the rainy season, especially over March to May. Bear in mind, however, that elephant behaviour depends greatly on rainfall patterns, which can change from one year to the next. So do take on-the-spot local advice about which park to visit, bearing in mind that less scrupulous operators might push you towards Hurulu simply because it is a less fuel- and fee-heavy excursion, so potentially more profitable. For birdwatching and general (non-elephant) game viewing, Minneriya is probably your best bet throughout the year. Elephant viewing is almost invariably best in the afternoon, when they come to the lakes to drink, so the best time to start a half-day safari out is around 14.30. Birdwatching is inherently better in the early to mid morning, a time of day that also has the advantage of being far quieter in terms of jeep traffic.

Minneriya National Park [map, page 212] (⏰ *06.00–18.00; entrance US$15 pp, plus US$8 service charge per party, plus 12% tax*) Gazetted in 1997 but protected as a nature sanctuary since 1938, this 89km² national park is centred on the 30km² Minneriya Reservoir, which was constructed in the 3rd century AD by King Mahasena, who also built the Jetavana Dagoba at Anuradhapura. It is renowned for the spectacular annual Elephant Gathering, when the fertile grassland of the lake floodplain attracts the largest elephant aggregation known anywhere in modern Asia, ranging from around 150 to 400 individuals at its busiest. Elephant viewing at Minneriya is reliably good from June to October, but numbers usually peak in August and September, when you will also see plenty of social interaction. Other commonly seen wildlife includes water buffalo, spotted deer, sambar, toque macaque, purple-faced langur and wild boar. Leopard and sloth bear are present but seldom seen by comparison with Yala or Wilpattu. An alluring bird checklist of 160 species is strong on waterbirds, with flocks of several thousand little cormorant often recorded alongside the likes of cotton pygmy-goose, painted stork, woolly necked stork, spot-billed pelican and white-bellied sea eagle. Notable woodland species include Sri Lanka junglefowl, Malabar hornbill, blue-faced malkoha and crimson-fronted barbet.

Kaudulla National Park [map, page 212] (⏰ *06.00–18.00; entrance US$10 pp, plus US$8 service charge per party, plus 12% tax*) Created in 2002, this 33km² national park is almost entirely dominated by the Kaudulla Reservoir, which is also accredited to King Mahasena, and was renovated in the 1950s. Its limited terrestrial habitat is more densely wooded than Minneriya and it is usually only visited towards the end of the dry season, when a significant proportion of the elephants that comprise the Minneriya gathering migrate northward and settle around the lakeshore for a couple of months, only to disperse further afield when the rainy season kicks in properly. At this time of year, you might easily see 50–100 individual elephants in one afternoon. Other wildlife is similar to Minneriya, and the birdlife is excellent.

Hurulu Eco Park [map, page 212] (⏰ *14.00–18.30; entrance US$7 pp*) This small elephant sanctuary 2.5km north of Habarana is effectively an annex of the 25km² Hurulu Forest Reserve. Elephants are resident throughout the year but usually only seen in ones and twos, though larger herds are sometimes seen between March and May, when the population is boosted by regional migrants from Kaudulla and Minneriya. At other times of year, it is cheaper to visit than the two national parks, owing to the lower fees and closer proximity to Habarana, but generally a less satisfying all-round experience.

10

Polonnaruwa

In some respects the most engaging of the Cultural Triangle's main pivots, Medieval Polonnaruwa was neither as ancient as its predecessor Anuradhapura, nor anything like so long-lived, but the diversity of secular and sacred edifices built during its brief golden age (1152–96) arguably represents the very zenith of Sinhalese architectural fecundity. Still partially subdued by the jungle that engulfed it for six centuries prior to recent restoration work, the sprawling ruined city incorporates ostentatious palaces that tower above colonnaded council chambers and ornate bathing pools, along with sky-scraping Buddhist image houses, intricately carved Hindu shrines, colossal monolithic dagobas, and quirky one-offs such as Parakramabahu I's circular vatadage, and the wonky-pillared lotus platform built by his successor Nissanka Malla. Minutiae include the beautiful paintings at Tivanka, and a wealth of intricately carved statues, moonstones, guardstones and stuccos that tend to be better preserved than their older counterparts at Anuradhapura.

Organised tours tend either to omit Polonnaruwa or to incorporate it as a day trip out of Dambulla, Sigiriya or Habarana. This makes logistical sense on a fast-moving itinerary, especially as Polonnaruwa is undersupplied with quality upmarket accommodation, but independent travellers will get far more out of dedicating a night or two to the old town, and exploring the ruins in the early morning or late afternoon, before the crowds of day trippers arrive and the midday heat descends.

HISTORY

The earliest evidence of human occupation at Polonnaruwa is a 2nd-century BC inscription on one of the Gopala Pabatha monastic caves. It was possibly at around this time that Polonnaruwa was first developed as an outpost of Anuradhapura, thanks to its strategic command of the major crossings over the Mahaweli River and its location along the trade routes to the ports of Ruhuna and Gokanna (Trincomalee). It is unclear when Anuradhapura first maintained armies at Polonnaruwa, but we do know that the Topawewa Reservoir (a precursor of the Parakrama Samudra) dates back to the 4th-century reign of Upatissa I, and that Aggabodhi IV maintained a country residence here in the 7th century. Back then, the small lakeside outpost was known as Pulasthinagara (Pulasthi's Town), after a Hindu sage who played an important advisory and ceremonial role in the Sinhalese royal court (and who may well be the actual subject of the so-called Parakramabahu Sculpture near the Pothgul Vihara; page 256).

Polonnaruwa rose to prominence after the sacking of Anuradhapura by the Chola King Rajendra I in 1017, and the deportation of King Mahinda V to India. Rajendra relocated the capital to Pulasthinagara, renamed it Jananathamangalam, and established a Hindu dynasty that endured for 53 years. The Chola monarchy was driven out by Vijayabahu I, a member of the Sinhalese royal family who took control of Ruhuna in 1053, aged only 24, and went on to capture Polonnaruwa twice – first, briefly, in 1066, then again, with a more enduring outcome, in 1070. Despite being crowned at Anuradhapura, Vijayabahu retained Polonnaruwa as capital, renaming it Vijayarajapura, and proved to be a strong and unifying king who did much to revive the state of Buddhism following five decades of Hindu rule, and he also helped restore the island's war-battered infrastructure by rebuilding several dams, reviving the irrigation system, and opening new roads.

Vijayabahu I's death of natural causes in 1110 precipitated a series of secession battles and a period of devastating civil war that endured until the capture of Polonnaruwa by his grandson Parakramabahu I in 1153. Much of the credit for developing Polonnaruwa goes to Parakramabahu. He fortified the city with three concentric walls, commissioned many of its most impressive and beautiful monuments, and expanded Topawewa Reservoir to create the vast Parakrama Samudra. He was also one of the last Sinhala monarchs to unify the island's three provinces, and vigorously defended his sovereignty, going so far as to invade India c1169 to discourage further Chola raids. The religious and agricultural influence of this remarkable king – often dubbed Parakramabahu the Great – endures to this day. His restoration of the historic Mihintale Monastery near Anuradhapura helped revitalise Buddhism as did his unification of the island's three bickering monastic orders under one supreme code. A prescient conservationist, he once famously stated that 'not one drop of water must flow into the ocean without serving the purposes of man', and his considerable (though possibly exaggerated) hydrological legacy includes the construction or restoration of 163 major reservoirs countrywide, as well as 2,346 minor dams and 3,910 irrigation canals.

The death of Parakramabahu in 1186 marked the beginning of the end for Polonnaruwa. Parakramabahu's successor, Vijayabahu II, was murdered a year later by Mahinda VI, whose five-day reign was in turn terminated at the instruction of Nissanka Malla, a strict Buddhist who claimed descent from Vijaya, the first Sinhalese monarch. Nissanka Malla ruled for only nine years, but he appears to have been a popular monarch, thanks largely to his reduction of the hefty taxes that had been imposed by Parakramabahu. He also left behind a significant architectural and artistic legacy (it was he, for instance, who funded the gilding of the interior of Dambulla's main cave temple), but such works weighed heavily on the diminishing state coffers. Nissanka Malla was an enthusiastic commissioner of rock inscriptions recording his architectural and other achievements, and while many of these provide genuine insight into Medieval Sri Lanka, the veracity of others is undermined by his evident need to take credit for monuments commissioned by Parakramabahu.

Nissanka Malla died of unknown causes in 1196. His son and chosen successor, Virabahu I, was killed a few hours later by the army's commander-in-chief who regarded him to be unfit for the role. In the ensuing chaos, the near-bankrupt state crowned ten different monarchs in the space of 15 years, with one – Parakramabahu's wife, Lilavati, of royal descent herself – enjoying three separate queenly stints prior to being deposed by King Parakrama II of Pandy, who captured Polonnaruwa in 1211. Three years later, the weakened city was captured and looted by Kalinga Magha, a fanatical Hindu leader whose 25,000-strong private army and penchant for attacking Buddhist temples did much to entrench the island's ongoing northeast–southwest, Tamil–Sinhalese divide. The Indian invaders were ousted from Polonnaruwa in 1236 and the city enjoyed a low-key late 13th century under Parakramabahu III, but after his death the capital and the tooth relic were relocated to Kurunegala.

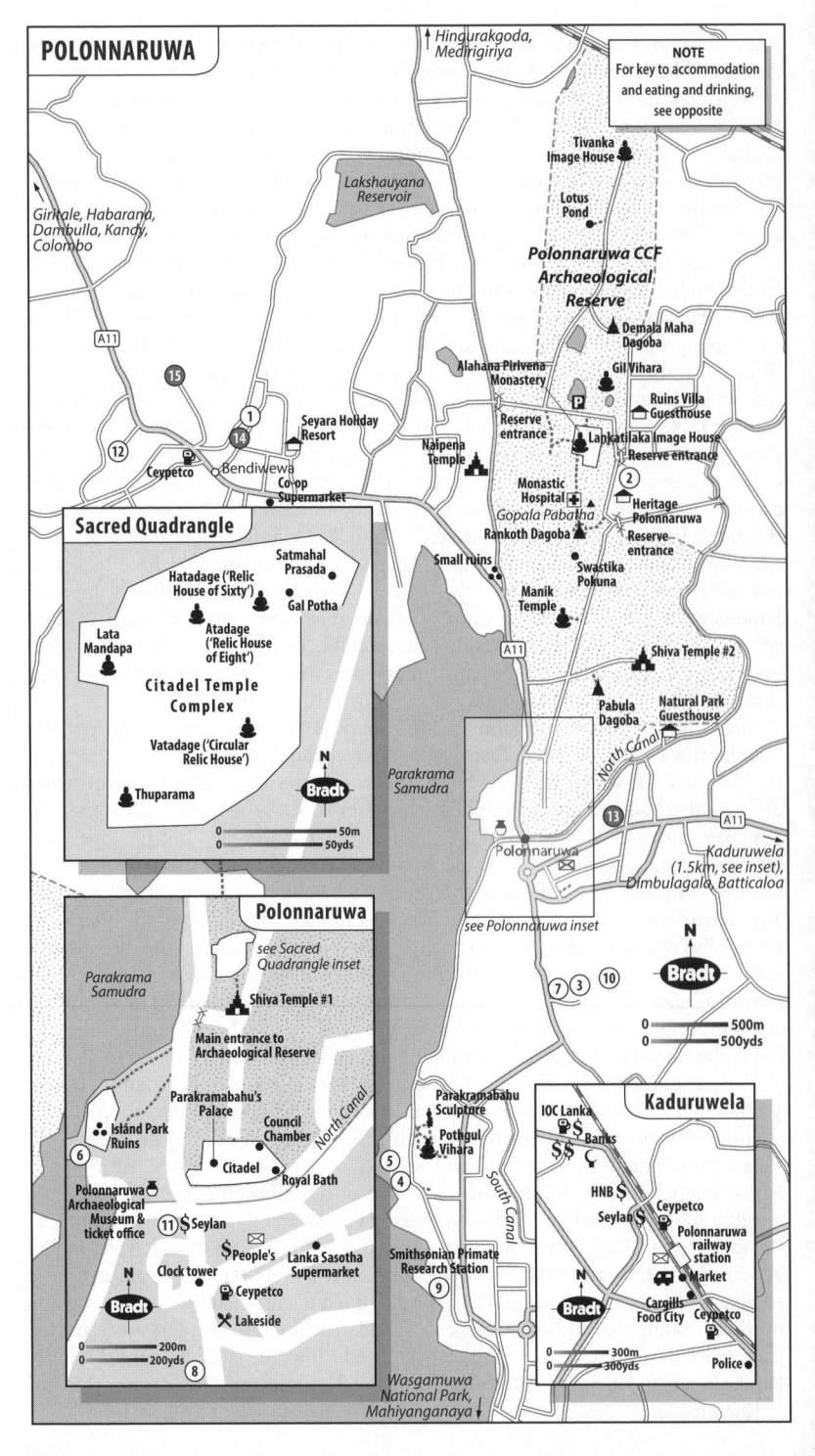

POLONNARUWA

↑ *Hingurakgoda, Medirigiriya*

NOTE
For key to accommodation
and eating and drinking,
see opposite

Lakshauyana Reservoir

Tivanka Image House

Lotus Pond

Polonnaruwa CCF Archaeological Reserve

← *Girikale, Habarana, Dambulla, Kandy, Colombo*

A11

Demala Maha Dagoba

Gil Vihara

Alahana Pirivena Monastery

Ruins Villa Guesthouse

Seyara Holiday Resort

Reserve entrance

Lankatilaka Image House

Reserve entrance

Naipena Temple

Ceypetco

Bendiwewa

Co-op Supermarket

Monastic Hospital

Gopala Pabatha

Rankoth Dagoba

Heritage Polonnaruwa

Reserve entrance

Sacred Quadrangle

Satmahal Prasada

Hatadage ('Relic House of Sixty')

Gal Potha

Lata Mandapa

Atadage ('Relic House of Eight')

Citadel Temple Complex

Vatadage ('Circular Relic House')

Thuparama

Small ruins

Manik Temple

Swastika Pokuna

Shiva Temple #2

Parakrama Samudra

A11

Pabula Dagoba

Natural Park Guesthouse

North Canal

0 — 50m
0 — 50yds

Polonnaruwa

Parakrama Samudra

see Sacred Quadrangle inset

Shiva Temple #1

Main entrance to Archaeological Reserve

Island Park Ruins

Parakramabahu's Palace

Council Chamber

Citadel

Royal Bath

North Canal

Polonnaruwa Archaeological Museum & ticket office

Seylan

People's

Clock tower

Lanka Sasotha Supermarket

Ceypetco

Lakeside

0 — 200m
0 — 200yds

Polonnaruwa

Kaduruwela (1.5km, see inset), Dimbulagala, Batticaloa

A11

see Polonnaruwa inset

0 — 500m
0 — 500yds

Parakramabahu Sculpture

Pothgul Vihara

IOC Lanka

Banks

Kaduruwela

HNB

Seylan

Ceypetco

Polonnaruwa railway station

Market

Smithsonian Primate Research Station

South Canal

Cargills Food City

Ceypetco

Police

0 — 300m
0 — 300yds

Wasgamuwa National Park, Mahiyanganaya ↓

The jungle took over and the city's large, brick buildings were lost underneath thick tropical forest. The Portuguese looted what they could in the 16th century, then the city remained undisturbed until the beginning of the 19th century, when the British rediscovered it. The first excavations, undertaken by H C P Bell in 1897, concentrated on Gil Vihara and Tivanka Image House. Several subsequent excavations have taken place, and many larger monuments have been restored, but it is estimated that as much as 80% of the old city still lies undisturbed. In 1982, the Ancient Cities of Polonnaruwa, Anuradhapura and Sigiriya were inscribed by UNESCO as Sri Lanka's first World Heritage Sites.

ORIENTATION

Spread out between the paddy fields, Polonnaruwa is a patchwork-like conglomeration that extends over an area far greater than population figures might lead you to expect. The main focal point is the so-called **Old Town**, which extends eastward from the Parakrama Samudra close to where it is exited by the North Canal. A major route crossroads, Old Town is also the site of the Archaeological Museum and the main entrance gate to the **Sacred City**, an uninhabited archaeological reserve that measures 5km from north to south and is fenced off in its entirety to form a significant navigational obstacle between any two sites lying either side of it. About 2km south of the Old Town, and much larger than it, the **New Town** is seldom visited by tourists, though a number of popular accommodation options run along lakeshore Bund Road to its immediate west. A more significant entity to travellers is **Kaduruwela**, which flanks the Batticaloa Road 4km southeast of Old Town, and is the site of the main railway and bus station serving Polonnaruwa, as well as a number of supermarkets, banks and other such amenities scarce in Polonnaruwa itself. Finally, the residential suburb of **Bendiwewa**, which flanks the Habarana Road 3–4km from the Old Town, is home to a number of popular budget hotels and local eateries.

GETTING THERE AND AWAY

Kaduruwela, the main public transport hub for Polonnaruwa, is connected to Old Town by regular buses. Kaduruwela is the site of the misleadingly named Polonnaruwa railway station, which stands practically opposite Kaduruwela bus station, the terminus for pretty much all inbound and outbound road transport. Note, however, that if you're arriving from the more westerly likes of Dambulla, Sigiriya, Kandy and Colombo, you can hop off in Polonnaruwa Old Town *en route*.

BY RAIL Polonnaruwa lies 260km from Colombo along on the Batticaloa line, via Kurunegala, Maho and Gal Oya Junction. In either direction, two trains between Colombo and Batticaloa stop daily at Polonnaruwa (actually Kaduruwela).

BY ROAD Polonnaruwa lies 220km (4½–5½ hours) from Colombo via Kurunegala (125km/3 hours), Dambulla (70km/1½ hours) and Habarana (45km/1 hour), 140km (3 hours) from Kandy via Dambulla and Habarana, 130km (2½ hours) from Trincomalee via Habarana, and 90km (2 hours) from Batticaloa via Valaichchenai/Pasikuda (60km/1½ hours). Bus connections are good in most directions, though it is generally easier to get a seat at Kaduruwela than Polonnaruwa itself. Between 05.00 and 18.00, at least two buses run hourly in either direction to/from Colombo and Kandy, and any of them will stop at Habarana, Sigiriya Junction or Dambulla. There is also at least one bus every hour to/from Batticaloa. If you can't find a direct bus to Anuradhapura, hop on to Habarana and change there.

⌂ WHERE TO STAY *Map, page 244*

Polonnaruwa was once a major overnight transit point for visitors driving to Pasikuda and Kalkudah, but the onset of the civil war in the early 1980s transformed it into something of a dead end in itinerary-planning terms, and most organised tours now visit as a day trip from Dambulla, Sigiriya or Habarana. As a result, Polonnaruwa lacks for genuinely upmarket options, the closest thing being a trio of slightly timeworn and lacklustre mid-range hotels on the shore of Parakrama Samudra. By contrast, budget travellers are spoilt for choice both in town and at Bendiwewa, 4km back along the Habarana Road.

UPMARKET

⌂ **The Lake House** (14 rooms) Off Bund Rd, Old Town; ✆027 222 2411; e reservations@ceylonhotels.net; w thelakehouse.lk. Formerly the Old Polonnaruwa Resthouse, this historic lakeshore property opposite the Archaeological Museum was established in 1870 & hosted Queen Elizabeth II on the royal visit of 1954. Spacious rooms, recently refurbished in classic contemporary style, come with queen-size or twin beds, AC, wooden writing desk & wardrobe, cable TV, & private balcony only 10m from the lake. The AC glass-sided restaurant, cantilevered above the lake, serves a variety of grills & local dishes in the US$6–11 range. Service isn't what it might be, but it's still undoubtedly the top address in town. *US$135/150 B&B sgl/dbl.* **$$$$**

MODERATE

⌂ **Hotel Sudu Araliya** (104 rooms) Bund Rd, New Town; ✆027 222 4849; m 0777 880115; e suduaraliya@sltnet.lk; w hotelsuduaraliya.com. Boasting a great lakeshore location 100m south of the Lake Hotel, this well-priced & relatively modern hotel has smart & functional carpeted rooms with AC, fan, cable TV, minibar & the choice of tub or shower. Ask for a room in the new wing. *US$85/95 B&B sgl/dbl.* **$$$$**

⌂ **The Lake Hotel** (40 rooms) Bund Rd, New Town; ✆027 222 2411; e reservations@ ceylonhotels.net; w thelakehotel.lk. This former government resthouse is so outmoded it might generously be described as retro, but it boasts an attractive location in 1.5ha of landscaped lakeshore gardens set around a swimming pool 2km south of the Old Town, & the slightly timeworn AC rooms, some with lake-facing private balcony, seem quite realistically priced. Renovations are planned. *From US$93/109 B&B sgl/dbl.* **$$$$**

⌂ **Siyanco Holiday Resort** (25 rooms) 1st Canal Rd, Old Town; ✆027 222 6868; e info@ siyancoholidayresort.com; w siyancoholidayresort. com. This relatively smart, sensibly priced, very central & somewhat characterless 3-storey hotel has modern AC rooms with cable TV & a well-maintained swimming pool. *US$63/70 B&B sgl/ dbl.* **$$**

BUDGET

✳ ⌂ **Primate Centre Lodge** (10 rooms) Bund Rd, New Town; ✆027 222 2552; m 0777 282700; e vatsalaw@gmail.com; w primates. lk. Set in a patch of dense lakeshore jungle 700m south of the Hotel Sudu Araliya, this unique facility forms part of the Smithsonian Primate Research Station, whose work formed the basis of the 2015 Disney film *Monkey Kingdom*. A likeable & unpretentious set-up, it feels more like a backpacker hostel than a hotel. Simple but comfortable rooms have nets & AC or fan, & there are several communal areas where you can enjoy the tasty rice-&-curry buffets, watch TV, or socialise with staff & guests. An ideal base for budget-conscious nature lovers, whether to enjoy the immediate environs or to partake in a programme of organised nature tours (page 248). *US$20/30 sgl/dbl fan only, US$40/50 with AC, B&B; other meals around US$7.50 pp.* **$$–$$$**

✳ 🏠 **Clay Hut Village** (4 rooms) Rankothwehere Rd; ☎ 027 205 6180; m 0777 470560; e clayhutvillage@gmail.com; w clayhutvillage.com. Owned & managed by a well-spoken former guide, this attractive outdoorsy lodge inhabits a bird-friendly 1ha property only 200m from the archaeological site's eastern entrance gate (or, more accurately, unless you already bought a CCF ticket, exit gate). As the name suggests, the spacious AC rooms have an earthy feel, with treated concrete floors & private balconies. Excellent home-cooked set menus (lower **$$$** range) are served on a wooden deck overlooking a small pond that sometimes attracts monkeys & deer. *US$31 sleeping up to 4 in 2 dbl beds.* **$$**

🏠 **Tishan Holiday Resort** (10 rooms) Bendiwewa; ☎ 027 222 4072; m 0779 329451; e tishanholiday@gmail.com; w tishanholidayresort. bookings.lk. This peaceful & friendly family-run guesthouse stands in a large garden surrounded by rice paddies, 150m south of the Habarana Rd and 4km from the Old Town centre. Attractively decorated rooms have fan, net, TV & optional AC. Amenities include a good restaurant, a swimming pool, Wi-Fi & free pick-up from the bus station. Ask for a 1st-floor room with balcony. Exceptional value. *US$17/20 B&B sgl/dbl with fan, plus US$3 for AC.* **$**

🏠 **Ariya Resthouse & Restaurant** (8 rooms) Bendiwewa; ☎ 027 222 2727; m 0773 586060, 0778 762528; e aariyaresthouse@yahoo.com; w ariyaresthouse.com. Renowned for its buffet lunches, this rustically located restaurant 400m north of the Habarana Rd is owned & managed by a welcoming live-in family. Neat clean rooms come with AC, fan, tent-style nets & cable TV. *US$20/24 B&B sgl/dbl.* **$**

🏠 **Samagi Villa** (5 rooms) Church Rd; m 0777 587327; e info@samagivillasafari. com; w samagivillasafari.com. Particularly well suited to small groups with private transport, this well-established property consists of comfortable 2-bedroom & 3-bedroom cottages with a quiet cul-de-sac location 500m east of the main road between the Old and New Town. Meals are provided by arrangement, & each cottage has a shared dining room, TV lounge & bathroom. *US$35 dbl B&B.* **$$**

🏠 **Manel Guesthouse** (17 rooms) New Town Rd; ☎ 027 222 2481; m 0717 132884; e manelguest@sltnet.lk; w manelguesthouse. com. Set far enough back from the main road to avoid the worst of the traffic noise, this offers the choice of slightly frayed but adequate shoestring rooms in the 2-storey old wing or smarter rooms with balconies overlooking the paddy fields in the 3-storey new wing. All rooms have AC, fan & net. An OK restaurant is attached. *US$18 dbl fan only, US$21/27 dbl with AC in the old/new wing.* **$**

SHOESTRING

🏠 **Leesha Tourist Home** (7 rooms) New Town Rd; m 0723 340591; e leeshatourist@hotmail. com; w leeshatouristhome.com. If you don't mind the traffic noise from the main road, this well-managed guesthouse 500m south of the Old Town is a real gem, with its brightly coloured dining area & neat, clean rooms with king-size or 2 x ¾ beds, net, fan, large bathroom & optional AC. It's also a good place to put together groups for budget safaris to Minneriya National Park. *US$12.50 dbl fan only, US$21 with AC.* **$**

🏠 **Devi Tourist Home** (5 rooms) Church Rd; ☎ 027 222 3181; m 0779 081250; e devitourishome@aol.com. This likeable homestay-type set-up has a quiet location 300m east of the main road between the Old and New Town & clean rooms with fan & optional AC. The friendly couple who own & manage prepare excellent local food & bicycles are available for rent. *US$17 dbl fan only, add US$5.50 for AC.* **$**

✗ **WHERE TO EAT AND DRINK** *Map, page 244*

The closest thing to fine dining in Polonnaruwa is Lake House's licensed restaurant, which serves erratic food but enjoys a central location and fabulous setting above the lake. Otherwise, the places listed below all serve good local fare, with the emphasis on buffet-style rice-and-curry dishes, but are alcohol free unless stated otherwise.

✗ **Ariya Restaurant** See page 247; ⊕ 11.30–21.30. Fabulous buffet-style rice-&-curry is the speciality. It also has a good à la carte menu & serves good fruit juice & beer. **$$**

✗ **Banana Leaf** Kaduruwela Rd, Old Town; m 0765 412629; ⊕ 10.30–22.30. The most appealing place to eat in the old town, this earthy mud-&-wood construction serves up a varied menu of grilled, pasta & devilled dishes on banana leaves. **$$–$$$**

✗ **Priyamali Gedara** Bendiwewa; m 0717 216480; ⊕ noon–15.00. Named after its hospitable owners, this rustic eatery tucked away 500m north of the Habarana Road is famed for its

inexpensive vegetarian buffet lunch. Dinner by prior arrangement only. **$**

✗ **Maha Kithula** Bendiwewa; m 0773 573344; ⊕ noon–15.00. Another popular stop for lunchtime buffets, this friendly little eatery is set in a lush out-of-town garden a couple of gates down from the Ariya Resthouse. The buffet includes around 10 chicken & vegetarian curries, plus dessert & tea/coffee. **$$**

✗ **Kamatha Restaurant (Samagi Villa)** See page 247. This extension of Samagi Villa serves good lunchtime rice-&-curry by prior arrangement in a rustic building overlooking the paddy fields. **$$**

OTHER PRACTICALITIES

There's a well-stocked Cargills Food City in Kaduruwela, an adequate Co-op Supermarket in Bendiwewa, and a few basic grocery shops scattered around Old Town. A Seylan Bank with ATM stands on Old Town's main crossroads. The Commercial Bank and ATM in Kaduruwela stand 1km from the railway station on the road to Polonnaruwa.

TOUR OPERATORS AND BICYCLE HIRE

The best way to explore the Sacred City is on a bicycle, which can be arranged through most hotels for around US$2 per day. Failing that, rent one directly through Samagi Villa.

Samagi Villa Safari m 0777 587327; e info@ samagivillasafari.com; w samagivillasafari.com. Established in 1990, this vastly experienced safari company is the main operator out of Polonnaruwa. It charges US$45 per jeep (up to five passengers) to nearby Minneriya or Kaudulla national parks (page 241), US$60 to Hurulu EcoPark, or US$120 to Wasgamuwa National Park. Rates include fuel and driver but exclude park entrance fees. It also has around 500 bicycles for hire at US$3 per day, including drop-off at your hotel or the main entrance to the Sacred City.

Smithsonian Primate Research Station \027 222 2552; m 0777 282700; e vatsalaw@gmail.

com; w primates.lk. This lakeshore research centre is well known for its behavioural research into the macaque and langur troops that inhabit the jungle-like Polonnaruwa Archaeological Reserve. Educational tours, led by experienced researchers, allow visitors to observe the habituated monkeys as they go about their daily routine, a fascinating outing that starts at US$25 per person (exc CCF entrance fee). Other activities include guided bird walks (*US$20 pp*), nocturnal loris walks (*US$25*) and boat trips to a bird colony (*US$25*). Longer packages and volunteer research programmes are also offered – it's all on the highly informative website!

WHAT TO SEE AND DO

The most popular activity in Polonnaruwa – indeed the *raison d'être* for most visits – is a tour around the 3.5km² Polonnaruwa Archaeological Reserve, a fenced-off tract of woodland that borders the Old Town and falls under the auspices of the Central Cultural Fund (CCF). The key sites within the reserve are scattered alongside about 5km of road, so visitors without access to a car generally rent a bike to get around.

There are four entrance gates to the CCF archaeological reserve. Most convenient is the main gate, which is in the Old Town 600m north of the Archaeological Museum, the only place that sells CCF entrance tickets (*US$25; available 07.30–17.00*). The other more remote gates – one on the western boundary 2km north of the main gate, two on the eastern boundary near the Rankoth Dagoba and Alahana Pirivena – are mainly used to exit the reserve, though holders of a valid CCF ticket are in theory allowed to enter through them.

The CCF entrance ticket is valid for the day of purchase only, and it allows for just one visit to the archaeological reserve. This restriction is designed to avoid tickets being re-used by different people, but it also frustrates genuine ticket holders who'd like to head out for lunch, then return in the afternoon. If you are in this situation, the gatekeepers should allow you to re-enter later the same day provided that you show them your passport when first you exit the gate, so they can copy the details on to your ticket.

The CCF ticket covers one visit to the Archaeological Museum only. It's difficult to say whether you're better off doing this before or after the archaeological reserve. Visit the museum first, and its scale models and other displays will be a great help in making sense of what you see on the ground. Logistically, however, there's a lot to be said being at the ruins as soon as possible after they open, before the crowds arrive and the heat of the day kicks in. Ideally, you'd slot in the museum over a midday break between morning and afternoon visits to the ruins, but that will depend on the gatekeepers agreeing to let you back into the archaeological reserve.

Several ruins stand outside the archaeological reserve's perimeter. Most important among these are the Island Park Ruins adjacent to the museum and the lakeshore Pothgul Vihara and Parakramabahu Sculpture 2km south of the Old Town. Neither compares in impact to the most important structures within the archaeological reserve, but entrance is theoretically free (though there seems to be some ambiguity) and they'd make perfect bookends to a half-hour stroll along the wall of the Parakrama Samudra.

Good interpretative plaques can be found at most individual ruins and other monuments in Polonnaruwa, but for more in-depth coverage, S C Fernando's excellent 60-page *Guide to Polonnaruwa* costs less than US$2 and is sold by local vendors, as well as at the Archaeological Museum.

POLONNARUWA ARCHAEOLOGICAL MUSEUM [map, page 244] (*Off Bund Rd;* 027 222 4850; 09.00–17.30; *entrance inc in the CCF ticket; photography forbidden*) This excellent museum warrants at least 30 minutes' exploration before, after or between visiting the actual ruins. It has eight well-lit sections linked by a long, straight corridor. Most instructive is the topographical model of the old city, which include semi-conjectural reconstructions of Parakramabahu's seven-storey palace and the circular vatadage, and helps to convey something of what the city must have looked like in its Medieval glory days. Artefacts unearthed at the site range from well-preserved guardstones to a 12th-century gold chalice of presumed Chinese origin. But in pure aesthetic terms, pride of place goes to the exquisitely crafted sculptures displayed in the backmost room. Look out for the unusually sensual bronze of a bare-breasted, wide-hipped Parvati, a meticulously detailed portrayal of one-tusked Ganesh seated on a lotus leaf, and a four-armed Shiva holding a snake as he dances on the back of a midget – quite exceptionally beautiful, these

12th-century icons also emphasise the extent to which Hinduism coexisted with Buddhism in the old city!

POLONNARUWA CCF ARCHAEOLOGICAL RESERVE [map, page 244] (🕐 *07.30–18.00; entrance US$25, ticket available at the Archaeological Museum ticket office 07.30–17.00*) Extending for 5km from north to south, the CCF reserve incorporates more than two dozen individual ruins, described below starting in the south, close to the main entrance gate and Old Town. It would take a full day to explore all the sites fully, but highlights, for those with limited time or energy, include Parakramabahu's Palace, the vatadage and other temples set within the Sacred Quadrangle, Lankatilaka Temple, the sculptures at Gal Vihara and the painted Tivanka Image House. The reserve's uninhabited woodland also protects plenty of wildlife, including spotted deer and the 'temple troop' of macaques that attained celebrity status following the release of the Disney film *Monkey Kingdom* in 2015.

Parakramabahu's Palace and Citadel Situated 400m south of the main entrance gate, the palace of Polonnaruwa's most celebrated king towered a full seven storeys above the ground in its 12th-century prime, and a contemporary chronicle claims it comprised a thousand chambers and rooms. The top four storeys, probably made of wood, have disintegrated, but the lower three floors – thick stone walls towering almost 10m into the air – give some idea of its enormity. It must also have been astonishingly beautiful, if the one surviving corner of original plaster, engraved with ornate line and curves, is any indication.

Back in Parakramabahu's time, the palace was the centrepiece of an 8ha Royal Citadel that included several other structures, two of which survive more or less intact 100m to the east. Parakramabahu's 3m-high **Council Chamber**, a three-tiered platform whose sides are engraved with dwarves, elephants and lions, is reached via a stone stairwell guarded by two leering lions and supports a forest of stone pillars that once held up the long-since eroded wooden roof. During council meetings, the king sat at the back of the chamber flanked by two chief advisers, while his ministers lined up along the two sides. The nearby sunken **Royal Bath**, a relict of Parakramabahu's amazing hydrological system, is a cruciform excavation fed from the Parakrama Samudra via a canal, a series of underground pipes, and the pair of crocodile-mouth spouts that flank the ancient steps.

Shiva Temple #1 The closest ruin to the main entrance, this Hindu shrine is also, rather intriguingly, the closest temple of any type to Parakramabahu's citadel. A 13th-century edifice made by South Indian refugees, it shows clear Pandyan architectural influences in its use of finely carved imported stone blocks held together without plaster. The domed stone roof has collapsed, but the walls are well preserved and are notable for their engraved lotus motifs. The original Shiva lingam is preserved inside. Several bronzes now on display in the Archaeological Museum were unearthed here.

The Sacred Quadrangle The spiritual centrepiece of the old city, the Sacred Quadrangle or Dalada Maluwa (Terrace of the Tooth) is an elevated 1ha platform studded with almost a dozen religious structures including a trio of temples that housed the tooth relic between the mid 11th century and late 12th century. The oldest of these is the **Atadage** (Relic House of Eight) built by King Vijayabahu I, reputedly over eight days, shortly after he recaptured Polonnaruwa from the Chola occupiers in 1070. The only extant structure attributed to Vijayabahu I, the Atadage is survived by one Buddha statue and 54 stone pillars (some adorned with detailed engravings), but nothing remains of the first-floor chamber where the tooth relic was stowed away. A Tamil inscription close to the Atadage provides its Velaikkara (Indian mercenary) guards with instructions for its protection.

To the left as you enter the Sacred Quadrangle, the spectacular **Vatadage** (Circular Relic House) was most likely constructed by Parakramabahu to replace the Atadage, though an inscription at the entrance attributes it to Nissanka Malla. A beautifully proportioned circular building centred on a stumpy dagoba, the temple is divided into four quarter segments, each of which has its own Buddha statue and is reached by a separate staircase. The roof – now collapsed – was supported by five concentric rows of pillars, and the guardstones and moonstones on the north and east of the building are among the oldest in Polonnaruwa. The Vatadage is thoroughly impressive even its ruinous state, but you need to compare it against the reconstructed model in the Archaeological Museum to appreciate it fully.

Opposite the Vatadage, the **Hatadage** (Relic House of Sixty), Polonnaruwa's last tooth relic temple, was commissioned by King Nissanka Malla and built over 60 days. Despite the large ground plan, it seems rather plain and unimaginative by comparison with its circular neighbour, and the upper floor is long collapsed, but it does contain three impressive granite Buddhas and a lively stucco procession of musicians and dancers. Next to the temple, the **Gal Potha** (Stone Book) is a massive stone slab dragged to Polonnaruwa from Mihintale by King Nissanka Malla, cut to resemble a palm-leaf manuscript, and decorated with a fine engraving of two elephants sprinkling water on the Hindu goddess Lakshmi. Its 8.2m upper face is covered with densely inscribed propaganda justifying Nissanka Malla's claim to the throne and providing details of his architectural and other achievements.

Several other unique structures can be found in the Sacred Quadrangle. The quirky but very beautiful **Lata Mandapa** (Lotus Pavilion), a raised stone platform where King Nissanka Malla would sit in the evening and listen to monks chanting Buddhist scriptures, is notable for its eight irregularly shaped 2.5m-tall granite pillars, each of which is curved in three places, engraved to resemble a flower stem, and capped by a carving of a lotus bud in blossom.

Set at the northeast end of the quadrangle, the mysterious **Satmahal Prasada** (Seven-storeyed Edifice) is an eye-catching seven-stepped pyramidal structure that towers to a height of almost 10m above all its neighbours. Absolutely unlike any other ancient structure in Sri Lanka, this brick-and-masonry oddity has drawn comparison to the pyramids of Egypt, the ziggurats of ancient Mesopotamia and the temples of Angkor Wat, but most likely it was built as a Buddhist temple by refugees or mercenaries from Thailand.

The second-tallest building in the Sacred Quadrangle is the so-called **Thuparama**, a massive vaulted brick image house generally attributed to Parakramabahu, though some say it was the work of Vijayabahu I. In its heyday, the Thuparama contained a large gemstone-embedded Buddha statue that lit up magnificently when the sunlight reflected on it through the windows. The temple is rather plainly decorated today, but its cathedral-like dimensions and aura of stillness and sanctity still impress, as does the fact that its semi-cylindrical roof still survives more or less intact, nine full centuries after it was constructed.

Pabula Dagoba and Shiva Temple #2

These two disparate monuments lie along a dirt path that runs east from the main road through the archaeological reserve some 300m north of the Sacred Quadrangle. A right turn about 50m along this path leads to Pabula Temple, whose dominant feature is a tall two-tier brick dagoba attributed to one of Parakramabahu's queens and surrounded by several ruined image houses. Veer back to the main path and follow it east for 400m to reach the more northerly of the ancient Polonnaruwa's two Shiva Temples. This little-visited temple is actually the oldest complete edifice in the archaeological reserve, pre-dating the birth of Parakramabahu by the best part of a century. Tamil inscriptions on the outer walls state that it was built in the early 11th century by Vanavan Madevi, the chief wife of King Rajendra I of Chola and mother of his successor, Rajadhiraja I. A tiny but perfectly formed and well-preserved structure, it stands about 10m high, has a small domed roof, and preserves an ancient lingam dedicated to Shiva.

Manik Temple On the west side of the road 500m north of the Sacred Quadrangle stands this isolated and rather mysterious monastic complex, parts of which date to the 8th century, though others were added later. The low dagoba, supported on an unusually tall platform, is thought to be the oldest in Polonnaruwa, and its relic chamber is open for viewing from the outside. Interesting adornments include a terracotta sequence of smirking forward-squatting lions on the dagoba's basal circle, and a rare and well-preserved example of a guardstone in a laughing posture.

Rankoth Dagoba Standing 33m high and with a base diameter of 170m, this magnificent dagoba is the fourth largest in Sri Lanka, outranked only by those at Anuradhapura. An inscription records that it was commissioned by King Nissanka Malla, who took a strong personal interest in its construction, but it may well have been started by Parakramabahu. Nissanka Malla modelled the gargantuan gold-pinnacled monument on Anuradhapura's Ruwanweli Dagoba, which – to place things in some historical scale – would already have been more than 1,300 years old during his 12th-century reign.

Two sites of particular note stand within a couple of minutes' walk of the dagoba. Surrounded by jungle only 100m further south, the little-visited **Swastika Pokuna** is a bathing pond for monks built during Parakramabahu's reign and excavated in 2013. As its name suggests, it takes the shape of a swastika, an ancient Buddhist symbol representing eternity. A similar distance to the north, shadowing a monastic hospital complex, the low rocky outcrop known as **Gopala Pabatha** (Cowherds' Hill) is dotted with monastic caves protected by drip ledges. A Brahmi wall inscription in one such shelter, recording that it was donated to Buddhist monks by a benefactor called Madala, has been dated to the 2nd century BC, providing strong evidence to suggest that Polonnaruwa was the site of a monastery back in the early Anuradhapura era.

Alahana Pirivena Monastery King Parakramabahu established the sprawling Alahana Pirivena (Cremation Monastery) on the site of a burial ground used for ritual Buddhist cremations before, during and after his reign. The exact boundaries of the vast monastic complex and education centre are open to conjecture, but it was focused on a collection of edifices situated on the left of the main road 2km north of the Sacred Quadrangle. The site is dotted with funerary dagobas, two of which are built alongside each other on the same platform, possibly over the ashes of a king and queen. Other notable features are a cruciform mandapa (drumming house) and a monastic chapter house that reputedly stood 12 storeys high, which would make it the tallest building of its type ever constructed in Sri Lanka.

Alahana Pirivena's most captivating structure, the cathedralesque **Lankatilaka Image House**, originally stood five storeys high and was topped by a magnificent domed roof that evidently succumbed to gravity's pull at some point in the past 800 years. Now only half its original height, it remains an imposing and satisfying architectural work, centred on a narrow hall that leads to a massive Buddha statue that would have stood almost 15m tall before it was decapitated, probably by looters in the process of removing the gems and jewels from its eyes. Relics of the original plasterwork can still be seen on the engraved exterior walls, and a few paintings adorn the arch above the side door in the right wall. Impressive though it is today, Lankatilaka must have been an absolutely stupendous sight back in its Medieval heyday.

Immediately next to the image house, the 25m-high **Kiri (Milk) Dagoba** dates to the reign of Parakramabahu and is associated with his consort Queen Subhadra, though accounts diverge as to whether it was commissioned by her or constructed in her memory. It is Polonnaruwa's second-largest dagoba, and the best preserved, with much of the original white lime plaster for which it is named still intact.

Gil Vihara

Originally known as the Uttararama (Northern Monastery), the spectacular Gil Vihara (Rock Temple) commissioned by Parakramabahu comprises a quartet of giant Buddha sculptures – two seated, one standing, one reclining – fashioned into a single rock face immediately north of the Alahana Pirivena These rank among the most beautiful sculptures in Sri Lanka, thanks to the serenity of the facial features and flowing lines of the bodies. Indeed, H C P Bell, who excavated Gil Vihara in 1907, eulogised it as 'the most impressive antiquity par excellence to be seen in the Island of Ceylon, and possibly not rivalled throughout the continent of India'. Deceptively, the statues now appear to form a cohesive panorama, one whose aesthetic attributes are enhanced by the granite's natural grain, and only slightly diminished by the tall corrugated-iron shelters that protect against weathering. Back in the day, by contrast, the statues would have been covered in plaster, and each of the four stood in gloomy candlelit isolation within an individual brick shrine (the foundations of which can still be discerned in front of the rock face).

The largest of the four sculptures is the 14m reclining Buddha on the right of the rock face. A serene figure with left foot drawn back slightly above the right, it is generally thought to depict the Buddha entering the state of parinirvana in his last moment of life, but some believe he is sleeping, a far more common subject in Sri Lanka. More controversial is the subject matter of the statue immediately to the left, a strikingly naturalistic and well-proportioned 7m-tall figure standing with eyes cast down and arms crossed over its chest. This was once thought to represent the grieving disciple Ananda, a theory based largely on the cross-armed mudra, which is very rare in statues of the Buddha, and would usually indicate a subject in mourning or paying homage to a higher being. Most of the statue's other features are consistent with it being Buddha, and the most likely explanation for the unusual gesture is that it depicts him venerating the Bodhi tree in the weeks after his enlightenment. The two seated Buddha statues on the left side of the rock face are less memorable but equally well realised, with the endmost figure, shown deep in meditation, being set below a fabulous ornamental arch engraved with all manner of mythical beasties.

The rock face between the seated and standing Buddha sculptures holds one of Sri Lanka's longest Medieval inscriptions. It describes in some detail Parakramabahu's successful bid to consolidate the island's three conflicting Buddhist sects into one unified order. A council called by Parakramabahu in 1165 led to the expulsion of many monks who had contravened the monastic code by fathering children, partaking in mystical rituals, or otherwise acting corruptly. The inscription at Gil Vihara also lays out in full a new code of monastic conduct drawn up in consultation with certain learned monks. Translated in its entirely, it provides a fascinating insight into the concerns of Medieval Polonnaruwa, no less so because it places the city's purest artworks in an ephemeral contemporary context of religious bickering and bureaucracy.

Demala Maha Dagoba Easily mistaken for a natural feature at first glance, this densely wooded brick mound 300m north of the Gil Vihara was the most ambitious architectural project undertaken by King Parakramabahu. With a circumference of roughly 650m, it has the broadest base of any dagoba in the world, and it would also have been the tallest Buddhist monument ever constructed had it ever attained its projected height of 185m. The name Demala refers to the Tamil prisoners of war from India that provided labour for the project, which was abandoned before it could be completed, for reasons that remain conjectural.

Lotus Pond The most beautiful of several bathing pools in the Sacred City, the sunken Nelum Pokuna (Lotus Pond) stands in isolation 150m west of the main road leading through the northern part of the sanctuary, almost 1.5km past the Gil Vihara. Few tourists visit it, on account of its remoteness, but it is worth a stop *en route* to the Tivanka Image House, 500m further to the north. Roughly circular in shape, the now-dry pool comprises six tiers, each of which contains eight seats shaped like the petals of a lotus flower. Several other pools of similar design have been discovered in the environs, but none has been excavated as yet.

Tivanka Image House The northernmost building in the archaeological reserve is also one of the most beautiful. The name Tivanka translates as 'thrice bent' and refers to the central Buddha statue, a tall brick figure with a trio of prominent curves – at the shoulders, waist and knees – that lend it a rather feminine appearance. The angular building's colonnaded exterior displays a clear South Indian influence – indeed, it might easily be mistaken for a Hindu temple at first glance – but look more closely and you'll see it has some splendid adornments, including some frolicking stucco lions and a row of boisterous dwarves.

The only paintings to have survived Polonnaruwa's centuries of abandonment are the riot of colourful and well-preserved frescoes that adorn the interior of Tivanka. Most date back to the 12th-century reign of Parakramabahu I, but some were restored or added a century later during a brief revival under Parakramabahu II. Considering that Tivinka's roof collapsed at some point in the interim, it is quite remarkable that these paintings constitute the best-surviving example of the so-called Early Medieval Style in Sri Lanka, which shows strong continuity with the classical style associated with the likes of Sigiriya, but is also influenced by the Pallava school associated with South India. Although most paintings depict scenes from the life of the Buddha, the classical links are epitomised by several portraits of women whose bare-breasted, narrow-waisted form and realistic individual faces recall the legendary cloud-borne apsaras of Sigiriya.

OTHER ARCHAEOLOGICAL SITES The scattered sites described below all lie outside the CCF Archaeological Reserve and are freely accessible without a site ticket, which means that you could plan on visiting them on a separate day to the main cluster of sites within the reserve.

Island Park Ruins [map, page 244] Spread over 1ha on the lakeshore immediately north of the Archaeological Museum car park, Island Park is a rough translation of

Hemmed in by a 13km-long and 10m-high dam immediately west of Polonnaruwa, the Parakrama Samudra – the largest of Sri Lanka's ancient reservoirs at 22.5km^2 – is not only the city's main source of water but also the fount of an eastward-flowing canal network that irrigates 73km^2 of paddy fields. The lake is named after King Parakramabahu, and is perhaps the most ambitious of the many hydrological projects he undertook during his 33-year rule. Despite the association with Parakramabahu, however, the lake started life almost 800 years before his reign, when King Upatissa I created the 5km^2 reservoir now known as Topawewa (Upper Lake) CAD386.

It was Parakramabahu who upgraded Topawewa to become the lynchpin of a larger and more complex network of five interconnected reservoirs, each with its own separate wall, a system designed to reduce water pressure on the main bund (the Sinhalese name for an earth dam). The lake took its more monolithic modern-day form as a result of restoration work undertaken in the British colonial era. Today, the ancient reservoir created by Upatissa I forms the northernmost and deepest part of Parakrama Samudra, stretching south from the suburb of Bendiwewa, past Polonnaruwa Old Town, to the vicinity of Pothgul Vihara. It is connected to the lake's more southerly reaches by a narrow 200m-long channel – a vestige of Parakramabahu's original vision – that flows past the peninsula that houses the Sudu Aliya and Lake hotels.

The easiest way to see something of Parakramabahu's Sea today is to walk or cycle along the 2km stretch of Bund Road that connects the Old Town to Pothgul Vihara and the Lake Hotel. From here, you could continue south along the Kalahagala Road, which runs along the southern bund for another 7km or so. Boat tours aimed mainly at birders can be arranged through the Smithsonian Primate Research Station (page 248).

Deepa Uyana, the name of an attractive complex of ponds and gardens created by King Parakramabahu and flanked by canals flowing out of the lake. This cool green garden was favoured by King Nissanka Malla, who built his own palatial complex alongside it. The inscription next to the Hatadage records that **Nissanka Malla's Palace**, like the one constructed by Parakramabahu four decades earlier, originally stood seven storeys high, but all that remains today are a few relatively unexciting ground-floor ruins – a reflection, perhaps, of the quality of workmanship implicit in the same inscription's claim the building was erected in a mere six weeks! Far more impressive is **Nissanka Malla's Council Chamber**, which incorporates 48 tall stone columns that originally supported the wooden roof, each one inscribed with the designation of the person who sat next to it, as well as a massive stone lion sculpture that formed part of the throne upon which the king would have presided over council meetings.

Southern ruins [map, page 244] The most interesting site outside the main CCF reserve is the misleadingly named **Pothgul Vihara** (Library Temple) on the east side of Bund Road just before the entrance to the Lake Hotel. This circular brick structure, still with some surviving plaster, was clearly never a library, yet the absence of anything that resembles a shrine or bodhighara makes it unlikely it was ever a temple. It might well be the circular mandala house built by Parakramabahu, according to an ancient chronicle 'for listening to the birth stories of the Great Sage being related to him by a teacher' – a theory supported by the excellent acoustics of the round room, despite the collapsed roof.

Impossible to miss, some 200m north of the Pothgul Vihara, the 3.5m-tall **Parakramabahu Sculpture** is carved three-quarters round on the side of a granite boulder. In welcome contrast to the many conventional Buddha statues to be seen elsewhere in the ruined city, this unusually realistic masterpiece depicts a strong and rather earnest-looking elderly man with a thick beard, long moustache and bare pot belly, wearing a cloth around the waist and tall conical cap, and holding an item variously identified as a palm leaf manuscript, a royal yoke of virtue, or a papaya. Suggestively overlooking the reservoir built by Parakramabahu, the statue is traditionally held to be the only surviving portrait of Polonnaruwa's greatest king, but the smarter money is on it representing an Indian sage, most likely the city's spiritual guardian Pulasthi.

Naipena Vihara [map, page 244] This important cluster of Hindu temple buildings lies just outside the archaeological reserve, about 2.5km north of the Old Town and 400m south of the northern exit gate. Its name translates as Cobra Shrine, in reference to the stucco cobra's hood that decorates the collapsed brick dome. The pillars of the main temple still stand intact, while other points of interest include a Shiva langur and some inscriptions on an outer pillar.

AROUND POLONNARUWA

The sites described below are all easily visited as day trips out of Polonnaruwa, though some are only accessible in a private vehicle, or might more realistically be visited as a side trip *en route* to/from Habarana or Batticaloa. Giritale, 15km to the northwest along the Habarana Road, is also the site of two good hotels that many tours prefer to staying in Polonnaruwa itself. Note, too, that Polonnaruwa is as good a base as Habarana, Dambulla or Sigiriya for safaris to look for elephants and other wildlife in Minneriya and Kaudulla national parks (page 241), and it also forms a possible springboard for safaris to Wasgamuwa National Park (pages 407–8); these can be arranged through most hotels or directly with Samagi Villa Safari (page 248).

GIRITALE The village of Giritale is named after the adjacent reservoir built by King Aggabodhi II in the early 7th century and later restored by Parakramabahu to become the country's deepest tank. A pretty spot encircled by tall green mountains, it is often visited by elephants during the dry season, and its eastern shore borders Minneriya National Park. The main point of interest is a pair of lake-facing hotels that form a popular alternative to staying overnight in nearby Polonnaruwa. The only formal tourist attraction is the **Giritale Wildlife Museum** (𝄞 027 224 6773/4; ⊕ 08.30–16.30; entrance US$1.50), which lies in the grounds of the National Wildlife Research and Training Centre and displays a collection of stuffed wildlife indigenous to Sri Lanka. Resist offers of a canoe ride on the lake; people have drowned when wind and waves turned boisterous.

Getting there and away Giritale lies 15km northwest of Polonnaruwa and 30km east of Habarana on the main road between these two towns. The two hotels listed below stand adjacent to each other on the Elahera Road, about 2km from the village and main road, and the wildlife museum is 1km further past them. Using public transport, any bus running between Polonnaruwa and Habarana can drop you at the junction, but you'll need to walk or charter a tuktuk for the last 2–3km to the hotels and museum.

Where to stay, eat and drink

🏠 **Deer Park Hotel** (80 rooms) 📞027 224 6272; e reservations@deerparksrilanka.com; w deerparksrilanka.com. Set in a former royal hunting ground, the manicured sloping garden of this well-established hotel is no longer roamed by the titular ungulates, but it does overlook the Giritale Reservoir & hosts plenty of birdlife. Despite this natural alliance, the single-storey cottages and duplexes (the latter with bedroom upstairs & bathroom downstairs) are city-slick & come with twin or queen-size bed, AC, fan & cable TV. Amenities include a tumbling 3-tiered swimming pool, gym & spa. The hotel was built in 1993 &,

despite recent modernisations, it feels slightly outmoded & overpriced for what it is. *From US$180 dbl B&B*. **$$$$$**

🏠 **Giritale Hotel** (42 rooms) 📞027 224 7311. The best thing about this 1980s relict is the stunning view across the canopy to the forested eastern shore and islands of Lake Giritale. The tiled rooms come with AC, cable TV & a sitting area, but the décor is old-fashioned & the bathroom very small. There's also a small swimming pool. Fair value at the price, but overdue some refurbishment. *US$95/110 sgl/dbl B&B*. **$$$$**

MEDIRIGIRIYA MANDALAGIRI [map, page 212] (⏰ *07.00–18.00; entrance US$5*) An abandoned temple complex containing four major shrines, Medirigiriya Mandalagiri was established in the 2nd century BC, according to an on-site Brahmi inscription, and is traditionally associated with King Kanittha Tissa. It was an active monastery for longer than a millennium before being abandoned at around the same time as Polonnaruwa. After that, the ruins – which include an image house with three tall standing Buddha statues, and a well-preserved bathing pool – were smothered by dense jungle for centuries prior to their rediscovery in 1897 by H C P Bell. Restoration was undertaken in the 1940s.

The crowning glory of Medirigiriya Mandalagiri, set on a four-tier base atop a low granite outcrop, is a magnificent 7th-century vatadage built around a central dagoba and divided into four equal segments, each containing a finely carved seated Buddha. This large round shrine is built to similar proportions to Parakramabahu's 12th-century vatadage at Polonnaruwa, and presumably formed the inspiration for it. The nature of its roof has long puzzled archaeologists, but the 68 octagonal pillars that once supported it are still in place, arranged in three concentric circles of which the tallest stands almost 5m high.

Little visited and often sublimely peaceful, Medirigiriya Mandalagiri lies about 32km north of Polonnaruwa via Hingurakgoda. To get here, head northward out of the Old Town, ignoring the left fork to Habarana, and continue for about 15km to Hingurakgoda. From Hingurakgoda, it's another 14km to the small town of Medirigiriya, then 3km northeast along a well-signposted but rather rough road to the ruined temple. If you're coming from the direction of Habarana, follow the A11 towards Polonnaruwa for 24km to Minneriya Junction, where a left turn will bring you to Hingurakgoda after 5.5km. Using public transport, buses between Polonnaruwa and Hingurakgoda leave every 30 minutes, but transport between Hingurakgoda and Medirigiriya is scarce, so you may need to charter a tuktuk. No public transport covers the last 3km to the ruins.

DIMBULAGALA MOUNTAIN [map, page 258] Rising to 545m above the Mahaweli floodplain southeast of Polonnaruwa, Dimbulagala is a fortress-like prominence known in colonial times as Gunner's Quoin, presumably because it resembles the eponymous island offshore of Mauritius. Steeped in history and legend, the wooded slopes and soaring cliffs of Dimbulagala are engraved with 100-plus ancient Brahmi cave inscriptions, and support a number of other archaeological sites, including what might well be the second-oldest Buddhist paintings anywhere in Sri Lanka. Yet despite its proximity to Polonnaruwa, this fascinating mountain is seldom visited by tourists, making it a great goal for an off-the-beaten track day excursion.

History It is difficult to separate history from myth where Dimbulagala is concerned. Legend holds that it was once the mountain stronghold of Kuveni, the Yaksha queen who had two children with Prince Vijaya in the 5th century BC. A century later, Prince Pandukabhaya, together with his wife Swarnapali, took refuge in the caves of Dimbulagala prior to his ascent to the Sinhalese throne and foundation of Anuradhapura as his capital. According to the same legend, Pandukabhaya's son and successor Mutasiva was born in one of these caves, and his grandson Devanampiya Tissa returned to Dimbulagala in the 3rd century BC to establish a Buddhist hermitage. While such legends are impossible to verify, a wealth of Brahmi inscriptions on Dimbulagala, some dating back to pre-Buddhist times, lend them some credibility. The presence of ancient monastic cave cells and paintings on the slopes of Dimbulagala certainly confirm that it was an important monastic site long before the 12th century, when it enjoyed the patronage of Parakramabahu I, housed around 5,000 Buddhist monks, and was regarded as a great centre of learning.

Getting there and away The springboard for exploring Dimbulagala is the junction town of Manampitiya, which straddles the Batticaloa Road 15km east of Polonnaruwa and 11km past Kaduruwela. Here, you need to turn right on to the Mahiyanganaya Road, forking right again after 3km at Dulakane. After 2.5km you'll pass the car park for the Namal Pokuna Ruins on the left side of the road. Another 2.5km past this, you reach the junction village of Dimbulagala, from where it is just 500m to the Dimbulagala Monastery, and another 3km, crossing the wall of the beautiful lily-covered Iddapichcha Reservoir, to the car park for the Pulligoda Cave Paintings.

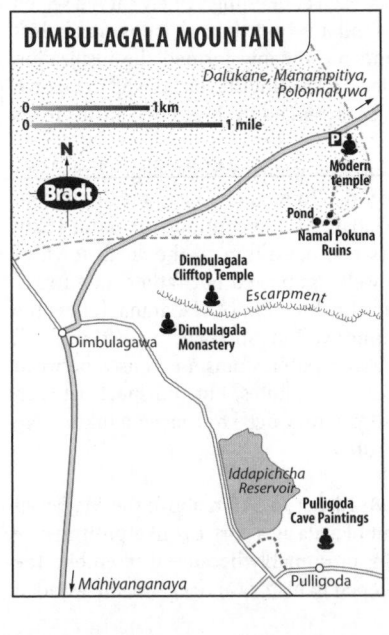

Using public transport, buses run almost non stop between Kaduruwela and Manampitiya, and more occasional buses to Mahiyanganaya stop at Dimbulagala village, passing Namal Pokuna *en route* and offering easy access to Dimbulagala Monastery. From here you could either walk to the Pulligoda Cave Paintings, or wait for one of the very occasional buses to Bimpokuna that run within 500m of the car park. It is also quite easy to get around using tuktuks.

What to see and do The three main attractions, in sequential order coming from Manampitiya, are the Namal Pokuna Ruins, the modern Dimbulagala Monastery, and the Pulligoda Cave Paintings.

Namal Pokuna Ruins This atmospheric ruined monastery, reached from the roadside car park via a steep but clearly marked 10-minute footpath through thick jungle, is named after the forest-fringed old pokuna (bathing pond) around whose curative waters it was built. The main temple complex, hemmed in by a quadrangle of stone walls, comprises a small brick dagoba set on a tall platform, two other platforms studded with pillars, and an image house whose decapitated Buddha statue is collapsed and broken into segments. Next to the dagoba is a water feature with four balancing water basins. A Brahmi rock inscription in the west wall mentions a donation made by a villager during the first year of the reign of Jetta Tissa II (AD332–41). A short footpath running west from here, across a small stone bridge, leads past a bathing pool to the right then curves uphill to a set of ancient monastic caves with drip ledges and in some cases more Brahmi inscriptions. Another 200m past this is the small but pretty Namal Pokuna for which the monastery is named. From here, you could continue further uphill to an old wattle-and-mud cave temple with ancient Brahmi inscriptions, but the path is quite indistinct.

Dimbulagala Monastery Reputedly founded in the 3rd century BC, Dimbulagala Hermitage was one of the country's most important monastic sites during the reign of Parakramabahu, when its main focal point was the ruined temple at Namal Pokuna. So far as we can ascertain, the temple at the modern monastery is of no historical interest, though the two-storey, 12-sided pagoda is decorated with some unusual wood sculptures made in the last 20 years. However, it's worth following the steep footpath that leads uphill from here to the spanking new white clifftop pagoda that offers superb views across the plains to the Mahaweli River.

Pulligoda Cave Paintings Set in a shallow granite overhang at the southern base of the Dimbulagala massif, this beautifully executed painting, now protected from vandalism by a metal cage, is reached via a well-signposted 200m footpath that leads uphill from the village of Pulligoda, 3km past Dimbulagala Monastery. A relict of a larger wall panel that almost certainly had the Buddha at its centre, the mural depicts five meditative male figures dressed in striped pantaloons, seated on lotus flowers, and with red halos behind their heads that suggest a state of serene saintliness. Back in the colonial era, various experts dated the mural to the 8th or 12th century AD. In 1990, however, archaeological commissioner Raja de Silva, citing the strong stylistic similarities with the famous panel of apsaras at Sigiriya, concluded it was executed in the 4th century AD, which would make it the second-oldest extant painting anywhere in Sri Lanka. Either way, the bizarre isolation of this exquisite artwork only adds to its enigmatic aura.

UPDATES WEBSITE

Go to w bradtupdates.com/srilanka for the latest on-the-ground travel news, trip reports and factual updates. Keep up to date with the latest posts by following Philip on Twitter (🐦 *@philipbriggs*) and via Facebook (📘 *fb.me/ pb.travel.updates*). And, if you have any comments, queries, grumbles, insights, news or other feedback, you're invited to post them directly on the website, or to email them to Philip (e *philip.briggs@bradtguides.com*) for inclusion.

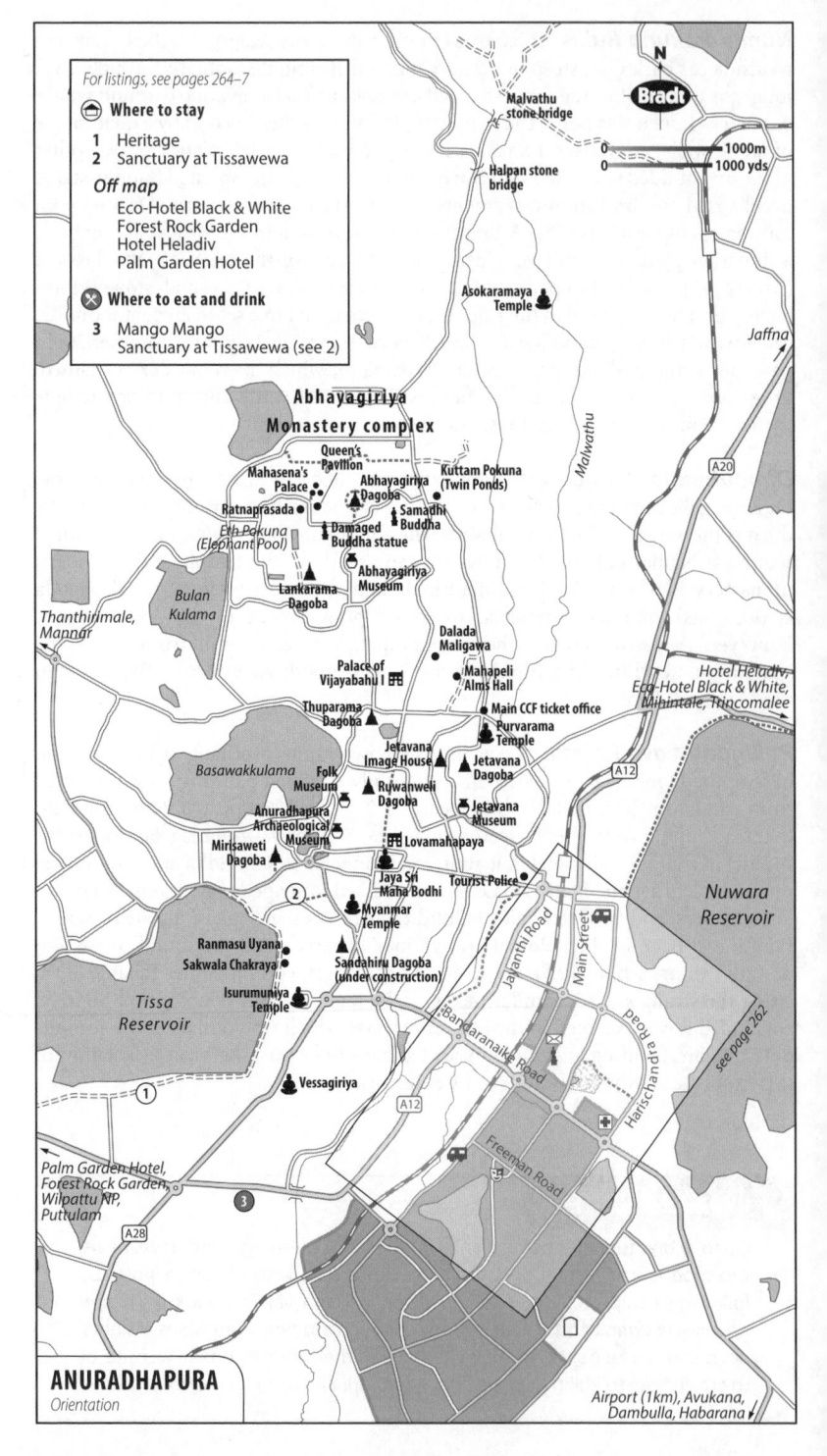

ANURADHAPURA
Orientation

For listings, see pages 264–7

🛏 **Where to stay**
1 Heritage
2 Sanctuary at Tissawewa
Off map
   Eco-Hotel Black & White
   Forest Rock Garden
   Hotel Heladiv
   Palm Garden Hotel

❌ **Where to eat and drink**
3 Mango Mango
   Sanctuary at Tissawewa (see 2)

N

Bradt

0 ___ 1000m
0 ___ 1000 yds

Malvathu stone bridge

Halpan stone bridge

Asokaramaya Temple

Jaffna

A20

Malwathu

Abhayagiriya
Monastery complex

Queen's Pavilion

Mahasena's Palace

Ratnaprasada

Eth Pokuna (Elephant Pool)

Abhayagiriya Dagoba

Kuttam Pokuna (Twin Ponds)

Samadhi Buddha

Damaged Buddha statue

Abhayagiriya Museum

Lankarama Dagoba

Bulan Kulama

Thanthirimale, Mannar

Dalada Maligawa

Palace of Vijayabahu I

Mahapeli Alms Hall

Thuparama Dagoba

Main CCF ticket office

Purvarama Temple

Basawakkulama

Folk Museum

Jetavana Image House

Jetavana Dagoba

Ruwanweli Dagoba

Jetavana Museum

Anuradhapura Archaeological Museum

Mirisaweti Dagoba

Lovamahapaya

Jaya Sri Maha Bodhi

Tourist Police

Hotel Heladiv, Eco-Hotel Black & White, Mihintale, Trincomalee

A12

Myanmar Temple

Ranmasu Uyana

Sakwala Chakraya

Sandahiru Dagoba (under construction)

Isurumuniya Temple

Tissa Reservoir

Nuwara Reservoir

Jalanthi Road

Main Street

Bandaranaike Road

Harischandra Road

see page 262

Vessagiriya

A12

Freeman Road

Palm Garden Hotel, Forest Rock Garden, Wilpattu NP, Puttulam

A28

Airport (1km), Avukana, Dambulla, Habarana

11

Anuradhapura and Surrounds

The birthplace of Sri Lanka's ancient Buddhist culture, Anuradhapura served as the Sinhala capital for an astonishing 1,400 years prior to being abandoned for Polonnaruwa. The Sacred City's spiritual heart is Jaya Sri Maha Bodhi, an iconic Bo Tree cultivated from a sapling of the original under which the Buddha became enlightened. Its rich architectural legacy includes the labyrinthine ruins of some of the country's earliest and most influential Buddhist monasteries, and a vast collection of statues, guardstones, moonstones and other ancient engravings. Crowning all this is a trio of gargantuan domed dagobas: Asiatic counterparts to the Gaza Pyramids erected more than 2,000 years ago, and the only comparably ancient structures to approach these Egyptian icons in terms of neck-craning height. As might be expected, Anuradhapura's architectural treasures tend to be more timeworn than their counterparts at Polonnaruwa, and the ancient capital also has a more scattered and unfocused feel than its Medieval successor. Nevertheless, the ongoing vitality of the ancient Bo Tree, the recent restoration of the age-old Ruwanweli Dagoba, and the importance of both as modern-day Buddhist pilgrimage sites creates a genuine spiritual link between ancient Anuradhapura and the contemporary UNESCO World Heritage Site inscribed in 1982.

Anuradhapura is often visited as a day trip from Dambulla, Sigiriya or Habarana. If at all possible, we advise against this, since it forces you to explore the ruins in the heat of the day (which might mean temperatures of 35°C) and leaves little time to visit outliers such as Mihintale and Thanthirimale. Note, too, that Anuradhapura tends to attract plenty of local tourism over poya (full moon) and other religious holidays, particularly when they coincide with weekends. This is a mixed blessing. Depending on your priorities, the influx of pilgrims lends colour and vibrancy to active shrines such as Jaya Sri Maha Bodhi and the various restored dagobas, but it is also the case that the crowds tend to detract from the more subdued atmosphere of the city's other ruins and temples.

HISTORY

The history of Anuradhapura between the 4th century BC and 10th century AD is difficult to disentangle from that of the island of which it was capital. Situated along the banks of the south-flowing Malvathu River, it was settled by iron-age farmers and pastoralists as early as the 10th century BC, and it supported a substantial trade settlement, extending over some 50ha, by the 7th century BC. The documented history of Anuradhapura dates back to 377BC, when its strategic location and fertile surrounds led to it being made the capital of King Pandukabhaya, who named it after the auspicious Saturn-ruled Hindu constellation Anuradha, and constructed the Basawakkulama Reservoir to irrigate the surrounding farmland.

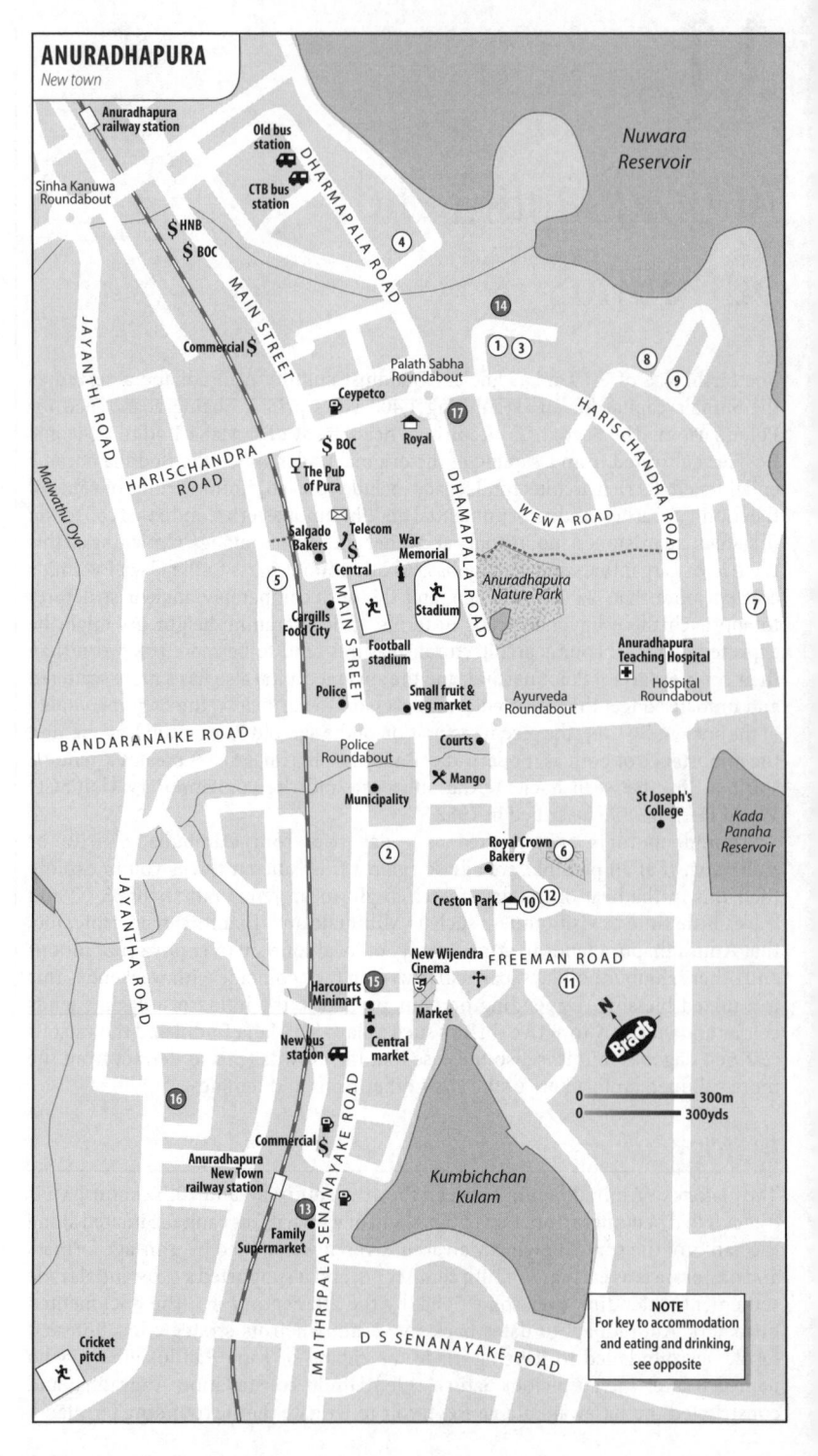

ANURADHAPURA
New town

Anuradhapura railway station
Sinha Kanuwa Roundabout
Old bus station
CTB bus station
DHARMAPALA ROAD
4
HNB
BOC
JAYANTHI ROAD
MAIN STREET
Commercial
Malwathu Oya
HARISCHANDRA ROAD
14
Palath Sabha Roundabout
1 3
8
9
Ceypetco
BOC
Royal
17
HARISCHANDRA ROAD
The Pub of Pura
WEWA ROAD
Salgado Bakers
Telecom
War Memorial
Central
5
Anuradhapura Nature Park
DHAMAPALA ROAD
Cargills Food City
Stadium
Football stadium
Anuradhapura Teaching Hospital
7
Police
Small fruit & veg market
Ayurveda Roundabout
Hospital Roundabout
BANDARANAIKE ROAD
Police Roundabout
Courts
Mango
St Joseph's College
Kada Panaha Reservoir
JAYANTHA ROAD
Municipality
2
Royal Crown Bakery
6
Creston Park
10 12
New Wijendra Cinema
FREEMAN ROAD
11
Harcourts Minimart
15
Market
Central market
New bus station
16
N
Bract
0   300m
0   300yds
Commercial
Anuradhapura New Town railway station
13
Family Supermarket
MAITHRIPALA SENANAYAKE ROAD
Kumbichchan Kulam
Cricket pitch
D S SENANAYAKE ROAD
Nuwara Reservoir

NOTE
For key to accommodation and eating and drinking, see opposite

Pandukabhaya was succeeded by his son Mutasiva, who ruled for six decades, overseeing an era of peace and prosperity during which Anuradhapura blossomed as a spacious, carefully laid-out and sanitary Hindu town whose fame extended as far away as the Mediterranean. Mutasiva was succeeded by his son Devanampiya Tissa, who converted to Buddhism at Mihintale in c260–255BC (pages 275–6), and planted the iconic Jaya Sri Maha Bodhi next to his palace at Anuradhapura.

The *Mahavamsa* cites ancient Anuradhapura as a model of hierarchical city planning. Precincts were set aside for huntsmen and scavengers, even for heretics and foreigners, so that members of the establishment were not disturbed. There were cemeteries for high and low castes, and also hospitals. The city's most glaring technological achievements include the giant dagobas constructed in the 3rd and 2nd centuries BC, and a sophisticated hydrological system incorporating the Basawakkulama, Tissa and Nuwara reservoirs as well as a network of canals, channels and bathing pools still largely operational today. A trade delegation from the capital presented its credentials to Claudius Caesar in Rome cAD50, and met Pliny the Elder. Within another three centuries, a connection had been established eastward with China. In AD412, the Chinese monk Faxian passed through Anuradhapura and penned one of the few surviving eyewitness descriptions of the ancient capital: 'The city is the residence of magistrates, grandees and many foreign merchants; the mansions beautiful and public buildings richly adorned, the streets and highways straight and level, and houses for preaching built at every thoroughfare.'

With a few brief interruptions, Anuradhapura remained the Sinhala capital into the 10th century, when its position was weakened by internecine struggles for royal succession. The final blow came in AD993 when King Raja-Raja I of Chola and his army crossed to the island from India, burned and looted Anuradhapura, deported King Mahinda V, and relocated the capital to Polonnaruwa. In 1070, the Chola interlopers were driven out of Sri Lanka by Vijayabahu I, who became the last Sinhala king to hold his coronation at Anuradhapura but retained Polonnaruwa as his capital. After this, the buildings slowly crumbled into ruin as the jungle closed in, though communities of dedicated Buddhists remained, many as guardians of the sacred Bo Tree planted by Devanampiya Tissa more than a thousand years earlier. Ironically, it was the island's British conquerors, intrigued by tales of the ruins of the ancient capital, who 'rediscovered' what John Davy described in 1821 as 'a small mean village, in the midst of a desert … [with] a large tank, numerous stone pillars, two or three immense tumuli [probably old dagobas] [and] still considered a sacred spot, and a place of pilgrimage'. Anuradhapura was designated capital of North Central Province in 1873, and the first excavations were undertaken here over 1884–86. In the 1950s, its role as provincial capital was entrenched by the creation of a new town on the southern outskirts of the ancient city.

GETTING THERE AND AWAY

BY RAIL This is best way to travel between Colombo and Anuradhapura. The 203km track via Polgawehala, Kurunegala and Maho is used by all trains heading to Northern Province, a total of eight services daily. The daily air-conditioned intercity express that leaves from Colombo at 05.45 and Anuradhapura at 16.30 takes only 4 hours, but other services take up to 7 hours. Good train connections also continue to Jaffna or Mannar, and it's possible to travel between Kandy and Anuradhapura by rail, changing at Polgawehala. All trains stop at Anuradhapura station, which was built in 1904 at the north end of the new town. Some also stop at Anuradhapura New Town station, which is more convenient for hotels at the south end of the town centre.

BY ROAD Anuradhapura lies 200km from Colombo via Kurunegala (110km) and Maho (65km). Several other routes are possible: it's only 210km from Colombo via Chilaw (130km), Puttalam (55km) and Wilpattu Junction (24km), or 225km via Kurunegala and Dambulla (70km). Coming from elsewhere, Anuradhapura is 200km from Jaffna via Vavuniya (60km), 85km from Mannar Island, 110km from Trincomalee, 135km from Kandy via Matale (110km) and Dambulla, and 105km from Polonnaruwa via Habarana (60km).

Buses are plentiful in all directions, with several leaving every hour to/from nearby Habarana and Dambulla. At least two buses an hour run to/from Colombo (6–7 hours), some routing via Dambulla and others via Puttalam, and there are also two per hour to Kandy (4–5 hours), one per hour to Jaffna (5–6 hours), Mannar (3 hours) and Polonnaruwa (3 hours), and at least two daily to Trincomalee (3 hours).

There are three bus stations. Southbound government buses (to the likes of Dambulla, Colombo and Kandy) leave from the **old bus station** at the north end of the new town centre 500m east of the old railway station. All private buses leave from the adjacent **CTB station**. Government buses to destinations north and east (for instance Jaffna, Trincomalee and Polonnaruwa) leave from the **new bus station** at the south end of the new town centre, 300m from the new town railway station.

⌂ WHERE TO STAY   *Map, page 262, unless otherwise stated*

There's no shortage of budget accommodation in Anuradhapura, with plenty of good deals to be had at the lower end of the price scale. Options in the mid-range and upmarket bracket are more limited and tend to be looking a little tired, presumably because most organised tours visit Anuradhapura as a day trip from Dambulla, Sigiriya or Habarana.

UPMARKET

⌂ **Palm Garden Hotel** [map, page 260] (65 rooms) Pandulagama, 5km along the Puttalam Rd; ☎ 025 222 3961; e pgvh@sltnet. lk; w palmgardenvillage.com. Set in lush & well-wooded (but oddly palm-deficient) 25ha gardens, this out-of-town hotel has much to offer wildlife enthusiasts, with monkeys & deer wandering through the woodland, plenty of

birdlife, & elephants making regular evening visits to the jungle-fringed watering hole at the back of the property. Mediterranean-style villas have AC, fan, cable TV, private balcony, 4-poster beds with fitted nets, darkwood furniture & quality fittings imported from Italy. There's a good spa, large swimming pool & stylish restaurant, but maintenance standards have declined in recent years. *From US$140/153 sgl/dbl B&B.* **$$$$**

Forest Rock Garden [map, page 260] (25 rooms) Andarawera, 12km along the Puttalam Rd; 025 203 3000; e reservations@forestrockgarden.lk; w forestrockgarden.lk. Set amid the boulders of the Andarawera Forest Reserve, this gorgeous eco-friendly boutique hotel/spa presents a 21st-century take on the architecture of ancient Anuradhapura. The luxurious rooms have 4-poster bed with fitted net, AC, cable TV, terracotta tiles, solid hardwood furniture & large modern bathrooms. There are also 6 suites with private swimming pools. Amenities include a lovely swimming pool, spa & meditation centre, & a stilted restaurant with views into the canopy. All meals are vegetarian. No alcohol. Pricey for Anuradhapura. *From US$270/310 sgl/dbl B&B.* **$$$$$+**

MID-RANGE

Lakeside at Nuwarawewa (70 rooms) Dharmapala Rd; 011 258 3133/5; m 0766 914880; e gmnuwarawewa@sltnet.lk; w nuwarawewa.com. Established as a government resthouse in 1957, this 3-storey hotel stands in well-wooded grounds with frolicking monkeys & a swimming pool on the western shore of Nuwara Reservoir, between the new town centre & ancient city. Reopened in 2014 following extensive refurbishments, it has large, agreeably decorated & well-equipped rooms with AC, cable TV & private balcony, & a good licensed restaurant with mains in the US$5–7 range. Nothing extraordinary but conveniently located & well priced. *US$86/105 sgl/dbl B&B.* **$$$$**

Sanctuary at Tissawewa [map, page 260] (21 rooms) Old Puttalam Rd; 011 258 3133/5; e hotels@tissawewa.com; w tissawewa.com. Established as the British Governor's residence in the late 19th century & converted to a hotel in 1907, this is the only accommodation set within the sacred precinct & the most characterful option anywhere in Anuradhapura thanks to its commanding colonial architecture & décor, & large well-wooded gardens where monkeys play & peacocks strut 5mins' walk from Tissa Reservoir. The spacious rooms are furnished in period style, with 4-poster bed, fitted nets, tall wooden ceiling, AC, fan, fridge & bathroom with old tiles & tub/shower. Food & service don't match up to expectations. No alcohol. *From US$112/118 sgl/dbl B&B.* **$$$$**

Rajarata Hotel (50 rooms) Rowing Club Rd; 025 203 0000; m 0772 030000; e reservations@rajaratahotel.lk; w www.rajaratahotel.lk. This well-managed, sensibly priced & unpretentious 2-storey hotel has comfortable & spacious modern rooms with AC, cable TV & private balcony or veranda facing the large courtyard swimming pool. There's a good licensed restaurant. *From US$63/83 sgl/dbl B&B.* **$$$**

Heritage Hotel [map, page 260] (42 rooms) Galwala Rd; 025 223 7806; e info@heritagehotel.lk; w heritagehotel.lk. A 3-storey block set in pleasant green gardens facing Tissa Wewa, this well-run & reasonably priced but uninspiring hotel has a swimming pool, bicycle rental service & brightly decorated AC rooms with king-size bed, cable TV, minibar, lake-facing balcony & decent bathroom. *US$100/110 sgl/dbl B&B.* **$$$$**

Miridiya Lake Resort (57 rooms) Rowing Club Rd; 025 222 4466; e info@miridiyahotel.lk; w miridiyahotel.lk. Set in green landscaped lakeside gardens centred on a large swimming pool, this slightly outmoded hotel has neat little AC rooms with wooden furniture & white tiles offset by colourful fabrics. A notch down from the places listed above, but priced accordingly. *From US$55/65 sgl/dbl B&B.* **$$$**

BUDGET

Little Paradise Guesthouse (6 rooms) Godage Rd; 025 223 5132; e sumane2@hotmail.com; w littleparadiseanuradhapura.com. Owned & managed by a very friendly & hands-on family, this 2-storey guesthouse has a tranquil suburban location in a small garden opposite a park & close to the town centre. The spacious rooms offset quality darkwood furniture & terracotta tiles with brightly coloured fabrics, & come with AC, fan, nets, cable TV & private balcony or terrace. Excellent home-cooked rice-&-curry too. *US$29/35 sgl/dbl B&B.* **$$**

Eco-Hotel Black & White [map, page 260] (8 rooms) Kannatiya, 10km along the Kandy Rd; 025 226 6159; m 0773 358333; e ecohotelblackandwhite@gmail.com; w ecohotelblackandwhite.com. Set in large green grounds with a neatly cropped lawn & swimming pool, this relaxed & peaceful owner-managed hotel lies in farmland 400m south of the main road, only 2km from Mihintale's railway station. Spacious, bright & airy rooms come with AC, fan & private balcony. An appealing open-sided restaurant serves local cuisine. Good value. *US$27/41 sgl/dbl B&B.* **$$**

🏠 **Hotel Heladiv** [map, page 260] (6 rooms) 4th Ln, 5km along the Kandy Rd; ☎ 025 205 6438; w hotelheladiv.com. Set in peaceful palm-shaded rural gardens 500m south of the main road between Anuradhapura & Mihintale, this small hotel has shared lounge, barbecue facilities & a restaurant serving great Sri Lankan cuisine. Spacious & stylish rooms all come with AC, cable TV & private terrace. Monkeys & birds frequent the garden & the surrounding area offers good cycling & fishing. Good value. *US$40 dbl.* **$$**

🏠 **Hotel Rovilta Garden** (4 rooms) Mihidu Rd; ☎ 025 222 6529; m 0718 308533; e hotelroviltagarden@gmail.com; w hotelroviltagarden.com. This little gem feels almost like a budget boutique hotel with its stylish bright décor. All rooms have AC, fan, net & cable TV. The location is quiet but central. *US$24/27 sgl/dbl.* **$$**

🏠 **Ceylan Lodge** (16 rooms) Mihidu Rd; ☎ 025 223 5114; m 0773 885533; e ceylanlodge@gmail.com; w ceylanlodge.lk. This smart & stylish 3-storey hotel, centred on a small courtyard swimming pool, has a pleasant restaurant serving mostly local fare. Brightly decorated rooms with tall ceilings have AC, fan, cable TV, private balcony & modern bathroom. *US$41/48 sgl/dbl B&B.* **$$$**

🏠 **Thilaka City Hotel** (11 rooms) Godage Rd; ☎ 025 223 5877. Get past the shocking yellow exterior & this family-run 3-storey hotel feels like a very pleasant & on-the-ball set-up. Good Chinese & Sri Lankan dishes (*US$3–4*) & Western fare (*US$7*) are served indoors or on a 1st-floor balcony shaded by mango trees. Well-tended modern rooms have AC, fan & cable TV. *US$25/31 sgl/dbl B&B.* **$$**

SHOESTRING

✳ 🏠 **Swiss Garden** (11 rooms) Freeman Rd; ☎ 025 205 5449; m 0777 866710; e swissgarden66@gmail.com; w swissgardensl. com. This clean & well-run 2-storey lodge has small but pleasant rooms with fan, Wi-Fi & in some cases balcony. A streetside beer garden serves grills, noodles & Chinese dishes in the **$$** range. *US$13.50 dbl, b/fast US$3 pp.* **$**

🏠 **Lievi's Tourist Accommodation** (7 rooms) Vidyala Rd; ☎ 025 222 2760; m 0773 206073; e lievisguesthouse@gmail.com; w lievistourist. com. Centrally located but with a pleasant garden setting, this homestay-like set-up has become very popular with budget travellers for its comfortable AC rooms, attractive prices, responsive management & great Sri Lankan cuisine. *From US$20 dbl.* **$**

🏠 **Milano Tourist Rest** (15 rooms) Jaya Rd; ☎ 025 222 2364; e milanotrest@yahoo.com; w milanotouristrest.com. Set in a neat suburban garden, this thoroughly likeable family-run guesthouse has neat little rooms with AC, fan, net, fridge & TV. A restaurant with indoor & outdoor seating at wrought-iron tables serves good local food. *US$20–7 dbl, depending on size, US$3 pp b/fast.* **$**

🏠 **Secret Sanctuary** (6 rooms) Godage Rd; ☎ 025 222 7548; m 0703 201202. Set in a small garden shaded by mango trees in a quiet part of the town centre, this owner-managed lodge has very well-priced rooms with AC & hot water. *US$20 dbl.* **$**

🏠 **French Garden Tourist Rest** (7 rooms) Maithreepala Senanayake Rd; m 0716 141590; e gardenfrench@yahoo.com; w frenchgardenanuradhapura.com. This comfortable & central little hotel has friendly & engaged staff & small but clean & cared-for rooms with AC, TV & fridge. *US$20 dbl.* **$**

✖ **WHERE TO EAT AND DRINK** *Map, page 262, unless otherwise stated*

Anuradhapura is lacking when it comes to bespoke restaurants. Of the larger hotels, the licensed Lakeside at Nuwarawewa is a reliable bet with a well-priced international menu, while the Sanctuary at Tissawewa ranks higher on setting and ambience, but the food isn't what it could be and there's no booze. The wallet-friendly beer garden at the Swiss Garden is a nice spot for an outdoor beer and meal. None of the places listed below serves alcohol.

✕ Seedevi Family Restaurant Jayantha Rd; ☏ 025 222 5508; m 0777 390306; w seedevirestaurant.com; ⊕ 06.00–22.30. Probably the best standalone restaurant in town, the family-managed Seedevi is renowned for its lunchtime buffets (*US$4 pp*) but it also has a globetrotting à la carte menu embracing Thai, Chinese, Indian, Sri Lankan & pasta dishes, along with steaks, burgers & sandwiches. Good choice of desserts too. **$$**

✕ Pizza Hut Main St; w pizzahut.lk; ⊕ 11.00–23.00. Offering some respite from the ubiquitous rice-&-curry, this clean & cheerful branch of the international chain, complete with blasting AC & beats, serves a varied selection of pizzas (including devilled chicken & Punjabi mutton, for those who want to keep it local) along with a few pasta & fried rice dishes. **$$**

✕ Mango Mango [map, page 260] Puttalam Rd; ☏ 025 222 7501; ⊕ 08.00–21.00. The local branch of this popular restaurant chain lies about 1km out of town along the Puttalam Rd. Blasting AC, Wi-Fi, cakes & decent North & South Indian cuisine. **$$**

✕ Walkers Harischandra Rd; m 0777 286297; ⊕ 07.00–22.00. This friendly & unpretentious eatery serves excellent fresh orange juice, along with a selection of sandwiches & local dishes. **$**

✕ Casserole Restaurant Main St; ☏ 025 222 4443; ⊕ 11.00–22.00. Busy central eatery with a menu dominated by Chinese & Thai dishes (**$$**) & plenty of vegetarian options (**$**). The downstairs bakery sells good cakes.

✕ Grand Heritance Mihidu Rd; ⊕ 09.00–21.00. Popular with tour groups as much as anything for the balcony seating with views across Nuwara Reservoir to a backdrop of mountains, this aspirant mid-range eatery serves a varied selection of local & Western dishes. **$$$**

OTHER PRACTICALITIES

Cargills Food City is situated on Main Road opposite the stadium, while further south along the road you'll find the well-stocked Family Supermarket and several wine shops selling beer and spirits. All the main banks are represented; the Commercial Bank has two branches, both with ATMs, at the north and south ends of Main Road.

WHAT TO SEE AND DO

There's enough to Anuradhapura to keep you interested for 1½ or even two full days. If you have that sort of time available, a factor in your planning is likely to be the split between sites included in the Central Cultural Fund (CCF) Sacred City ticket (which is valid for the date of issue only) and those that can be visited without it. Ideally, you'd want to dedicate a full day to the sites covered by that ticket (Ruwanweli Dagoba, Jetavana Monastery, Thuparama Vatadage, Abhayagiriya Monastery and associated site museums) and a separate day to the extralimital Jaya Sri Maha Bodhi, Isurumuniya Temple and Sakwala Chakraya, along with the out-of-town Mihintale and Thanthirimale. For those with tighter time restrictions, a good 'highlights' itinerary would start at Jaya Sri Maha Bodhi and take in the three giant dagobas (Ruwanweli, Jetavana and Abhayagiriya) and main archaeological museum before heading south to the lakeshore Isurumuniya Temple. Either way, unless you arrive in Anuradhapura with a vehicle and driver, the best way to get around is a pushbike, which can be rented through any hotel or guesthouse for around US$3 per day.

NEW TOWN Anuradhapura New Town, where most visitors end up staying, is high on bustle but short on sights, with the former quality being epitomised by the **central market**, near the new bus station. Opposite the central stadium, the unheralded **Anuradhapura Nature Park** (*entrance less than US$1*) protects 5ha of forest and aquatic habitats, and looks promising for birds and monkeys, though it seems to derive most of its custom from young courting couples. For a brisker leg stretch, a pretty dirt road follows the tall bund (wall) of the **Nuwara Reservoir** for 2.5km north of the Lakeside at Nuwarawewa Hotel.

JAYA SRI MAHA BODHI AND SURROUNDS [map, page 260] Anuradhapura's most venerated religious site, Jaya Sri Maha Bodhi is a sacred Bo Tree (*Ficus religiosa*) grown from the southern branch of the original under which the Buddha attained enlightenment at Buddha Gaya (India) in 528BC. According to legend, Princess Sangamitta Thera, the eldest daughter of Emperor Ashoka, sailed across from India with the sacred bough in 249BC, landed at Dambakola (page 313), and handed it over to the recently converted King Devanampiya Tissa, who transported the bough to Anuradhapura via Thanthirimale (page 279) and planted it outside his palace next to a channel that flowed out of Tissa Reservoir. The sacred tree formed the centrepiece of a Theravada monastery that dominated religious affairs in Anuradhapura for five centuries after its foundation. Traces of a 3rd-century rubble wall built around the shrine still survive, as does part of a stone terrace and latticed wall added by King Sirimeghavanna a century later. When Chinese explorer and monk Faxian visited Anuradhapura in AD413, he noted that, 'as the tree bent over to the southeast, the king feared it would fall, and therefore placed a prop to support it'.

Jaya Sri Maha Bodhi survived the Chola sacking of Anuradhapura in AD993, since this species of fig is also sacred to Hindus. Over subsequent centuries, even as the jungle returned to engulf the old capital, the tree's guardians still burnt fires around it at night to keep away wild animals. Since the late 18th century, Jaya Sri Maha Bodhi has been protected within a quadrangular Bodhighara whose 3m-high, 1.5m-thick wall was constructed under King Kirti Sri Rajasinha and supplemented by a gold-plated fence in the 1960s. Today, as in Faxian's time, several of the heavier boughs are propped up by scaffolding. Despite this, two branches broke off during separate storms in 1907 and 1911, and a third was hacked off by a human assailant who attempted to chop down the whole tree in 1929. Tragically, on 14 May 1985, Jaya Sri Maha Bodhi was the target of an LTTE attack in which 146 Sinhalese civilians were gunned down.

Surrounded by a copse of offshoots grown from its roots, Jaya Sri Maha Bodhi is the world's oldest-known artificially planted tree. Since the Indian original was chopped down in the 2nd century BC, it is also the most sacred individual plant in the Buddhist world, and the source of cuttings from which all other Bo Trees in Sri Lanka are grown. Given all the above, the ancient tree – only 10m high, heavier limbs supported by scaffolds – is surprisingly unimposing, and arguably less memorable in itself than for the vibrant scenes of human veneration it invokes. Particularly over weekends and around the full moon, many thousands of pilgrims and other worshippers congregate at Anuradhapura's tree of enlightenment to pay their respect. It's a stirring spectacle, all the more so because there are no formal or centralised services – instead, a free-for-all stream of individual worshippers, family groups and religious parties, often but not exclusively dressed in white, arrive as they please, to pray, chant, lay down lotus flowers, light candles, mill around or otherwise do their own thing, and then move on as and when they are ready.

The CCF site ticket is not required to enter the compound of Jaya Sri Maha Bodhi, and there's no entrance fee, but a small donation may be asked. A visit can easily be combined with a quick look at the **Lovamahapaya** (Brazen Palace), another relic of the original Maha Vihara (Grand Temple) founded at Anuradhapura by the Thera Mahinda. A chapter house built by King Devanampiya Tissa for the original monastic guardians of the Bo Tree situated 150m to its south, the building was expanded by King Dutugamunu to become a nine-storey, thousand-room palace topped by the copper-tiled roof for which it is named. In the central pavilion there was an ivory throne inlaid with a sun in gold, a moon in silver and stars in pearls. This wood-dominated edifice burnt down 15 years after it was built; all that remain are 1,600 pillars erected during 12th-century restoration work undertaken by Parakramabahu I, and a cluster of columns decorated with friezes of dwarves. The Lovamahapaya is closed to tourists, but you can see most of it through the perimeter fence. Its parklike environs are home to several habituated macaque and langur troops, which move photogenically through the trees and old stone pillars, but might become aggressive when approached too closely.

THE SOUTHWESTERN RUINS [map, page 260] Strung along the shore of the Tissa Reservoir 1km southwest of Jaya Sri Maha Bodhi is a cluster of relatively obscure ruins centred on an ancient rock temple called Isurumuniya. Because it is excluded from the CCF site ticket, Isurumuniya makes an ideal itinerary filler for those with a spare afternoon or morning in Anuradhapura, and it can be combined with forays to four nearby sites: Vessagiriya, Ranmasu Uyana, Sakwala Chakraya and the more mundane Sandahiru Dagoba (a modern monument, still under construction, to commemorate the end of the civil war). Isurumuniya is most appealing in the late afternoon, when you can hang on to watch the sun set over the lake, and best avoided in the heat of the day, when the bare stone is searing underfoot. A nominal entrance fee is levied at Isurumuniya Temple; access to the other sites listed below is free.

Isurumuniya Temple (*Entrance US$1.30*) Among the most venerable of Sri Lanka's Buddhist sites, Isurumuniya was established as a monastery to house 500 young high-caste *bhikkhus* during the reign of Devanampiya Tissa. It is reputedly where the sacred tooth relic was stowed when it first arrived at Anuradhapura from India CAD312, and has been renovated on several occasions, most famously by King Kasyapa I of Sigiriya. Points of interest include a small cave temple that leads to a small boulder-top dagoba offering views across to the lake, a modern stone temple containing a massive statue of the reclining Buddha, and a Bo Tree reputedly grown from one of the eight original saplings of Sri Maha Bodhi.

Isurumuniya's most celebrated feature, thought to date to the 7th century AD, is a pair of superficially different engravings etched into the rock face above the pond in front of the main temple. An exceptional carving of a seated man and horse head in a small niche above the pool is widely thought to represent the rain god Parjanya and his horse Agni, though the absence of the conical crown worn by such deities has led dissenters to suggest the seated figure is actually a military officer. Below this, an elegantly executed group of three elephants is depicted drinking from the pond, while another frolics with head and tusks raised above the water. This juxtaposition tends to support the association of the first carving with Parjanya, and has led to some speculation that Isurumuniya was once used to perform rain-making ceremonies.

The archaeological museum at Isurumuniya houses a couple of dozen stone carvings unearthed in the vicinity. A world-famous 6th-century tableau depicts a woman perched gracefully on the right thigh of a seated man, her left arm raised, possibly in defence, and face turned away coyly from her companion. Nicknamed 'The Lovers', it is said to represent Dutugamunu's son Prince Saliya seducing his beloved Ashokamala, the chandala (untouchable caste) sweetheart for whom he renounced his claim to the throne. Another fine engraving of similar vintage has been dubbed the 'Royal Family', though the conical crowns on the heads of its central male and female figures are consistent with deities more than royalty.

Vessagiriya Set among a group of massive boulders 600m south of Isurumuniya, Vessagiriya is a cluster of 20-odd monastic caves protected by drip ledges and engraved with 3rd-century BC Brahmi inscriptions naming their donors. One of the larger boulders is capped by the remains of a small dagoba, which can be reached by a rock-hewn staircase. These modest ruins might be a relict of the earliest incarnation of Isurumuniya, but more likely the site was a subsidiary place of meditation used by the same monks.

Ranmasu Uyana Only 300m north of Isurumuniya, the Ranmasu Uyana (Goldfish Pond) was a pleasure garden and bathing complex established in the 3rd century BC and enjoyed by a succession of Anuradhapura monarchs right through to the city's sacking in AD993. It stands close to the shore of Tissa Reservoir, to which it is linked by a sophisticated system of water hydraulics that funnels through the pools before being released into the surrounding agricultural land. A magnificent elephant herd engraved on to a boulder once lapped by the empty pool's water is so similar to its counterpart at Isurumuniya it seems reasonable to assume they are the work of the same artist. Many other engravings from Ranmasu Uyana are displayed in Isurumuniya's museum.

Sakwala Chakraya Etched on to an easily overlooked boulder between Ranmasu Uyana and Isurumuniya, this curious and controversial diagrammatic petroglyph has no obvious parallels in Sri Lanka, nor indeed anywhere else in the world. Roughly 2m in diameter, the Sakwala Chakraya (literally 'Wheel of the Universe') is broken up into three main parts. There are two concentric outer circles separated by a narrow band of fishes and other swimming creatures. These circles enclose an irregular grid of vertical and parallel lines interspersed with mysterious symbols – mostly crosses within circles, but also two umbrella-like shapes, and several other peculiar one-offs. At the very centre of the diagram is a dot enclosed by seven concentric circles, a pattern repeated on a slightly smaller scale in one of the top left grids.

Exactly what the Sakwala Chakraya is, or represents, is a matter of conjecture. In 1901, H C P Bell postulated that it might be an 'ancient "map of the world" – perhaps the oldest in existence' and noted that 'its presence here, within an eremite's cave at an out-of-the-way nook of ancient Anuradhapura, testifies to the antiquity of the astronomical lore still pursued in some of the Buddhist monasteries of Ceylon'. More recent commentators have suggested that the diagram was carved for the purpose of contemplation by meditating monks sitting in the facing stone seats, or more prosaically that it was simply a blueprint for an architectural development of some sort. A more left-field notion casts the Sakwala Chakraya – together with the Abu Ghurab Sun Temple in Egypt, and the Peruvian 'Gateway to the Gods' near Lake Titicaca – as one of several so-called stargates constructed by extraterrestrial visitors to the ancient world. None of these explanations is entirely satisfactory, and the longer you gaze at this weird and impossible-to-date petroglyph – widely assumed to be the handiwork of Anuradhapura-era Buddhists, but conceivably much older – the more enigmatic it feels.

THE SACRED CITY [map, page 260] With the exception of Jaya Sri Maha Bodhi and the southwestern sites clustered around Isurumuniya, the main sites associated with ancient Anuradhapura all fall within a loosely demarcated archaeological reserve (henceforth referred to as the Sacred City) that extends over 5km² northwest of the new town. Although several public roads run through the Sacred City, a Central Cultural Fund (CCF) ticket, costing US$25, and valid for the day of issue only, is required to explore all sites and museums that fall within it. Tickets are issued at the CCF ticket office 400m north of Jetavana Dagoba (⊕ *07.30–17.00*), as well as at the Archaeological or Abhayagiriya museums, and are regularly checked by site attendants. Sites within the Sacred City are described starting with Mirisaweti Dagoba in the southwest then following a roughly northeasterly direction to Abhayagiriya Monastery.

Mirisaweti Dagoba
The most southerly of Anuradhapura's mega-dagobas is the recently restored and whitewashed Mirisaweti, which stands close to the northern shore of Tissa Reservoir. Dating to the 2nd century BC, it marks the burial place of the sacred sceptre – complete with embedded Buddha relic – instrumental in King Dutugamunu's defeat of the Chola leader Elara. After the original 50m-tall dagoba collapsed, it was restored to a height of 36m by Parakramabahu I. Reduced to an overgrown heap of rubble by the 19th century, Mirisaweti was partially restored over 1888–96 with funds from the King of Siam. A more recent restoration effort ended in disaster when the dagoba collapsed in June 1987, destroying a Vahalkada front widely regarded to be the most beautiful artefact of its type in Anuradhapura. Restoration was finally completed in 1993.

Anuradhapura Archaeological Museum
(*Thuparama Rd;* ☏ *025 385 6564;* ⊕ *09.00–17.00; entrance inc in site ticket*) Closed for renovation for two years as of late 2017, the Cultural Triangle's oldest museum was established in the handsome colonial-era Kachcheri Building in 1947. It houses a varied collection of statues, inscriptions, drawings, coins, jewellery and other antiquities unearthed in Anuradhapura and elsewhere in Sri Lanka. Notable displays include a model reconstruction of the Thuparama Vatadage, and the relic chamber of the Kantaka Dagoba at nearby Mihintale. It will hopefully reopen in 2018, possibly rebranded as the National Museum of the Department of Archaeology.

Ruwanweli Dagoba
Dominating the southern skyline of Anuradhapura today as it did in ancient times, the magnificent whitewashed dome of Ruwanweli is topped by a tapering conical spire and gold-plated minaret whose pinnacle stands a neck-craning 103m above the ground below – the second-tallest dagoba ever constructed in the ancient world. Situated 500m north of Sri Maha Bodhi, Ruwanweli was commissioned in 144BC by King Dutugamunu to commemorate the recapture of Anuradhapura from the usurper Elara. Legend has it that the architect who won the competition to design the dagoba called for a golden bowl of water, scooped some of its contents into his hand, and let it fall back in to form the perfect bubble on which its shape is based.

The ancient *Mahavamsa* describes how Ruwanweli's foundation was laid:

> First the land was excavated to a depth of 6m, then filled with crushed stones that were stamped down by elephants whose feet were bound by leather. Butter clay was spread over the stones, bricks were laid over the clay, and a layer of rough cement and network of iron was placed above these. Finally, a sheet of copper and a sheet of silver were laid.

Construction work continued for at least two decades after the foundation was complete, and while Dutugamunu didn't live long enough to see it through, his successor Saddha Tissa did.

As lofty as a 35-storey skyscraper, Ruwanweli was the tallest building in Asia at the time of its original construction, hence the alternative name of Mahathupa (literally 'Great Dagoba'). Prior to the 12th century, it was restored several times by various kings, often resulting in subtle changes in shape, but its height remained more or less unchanged. Then followed centuries of neglect during which Ruwanweli fell into a ruinous and overgrown state. It was restored to its former glory, largely at the initiation of a monk called Naranvita Sumanasara, between 1893 and 1940. An active shrine of worship today, Ruwanweli is the most revered of Sri Lanka's ancient mega-dagobas, and it is also once again the tallest, despite having been eclipsed by its close neighbour at Jetavana for some centuries.

Jetavana Monastery and Dagoba Situated just 700m east of Ruwanweli, the most ambitious of Sri Lanka's ancient dagobas was the brainchild of King Mahasena, who initiated its construction CAD280, but died before it could be completed under the watch of his son and successor Sirimeghavanna I. Upon completion, Jetavana Dagoba stood 122m high, and would have been the third-tallest manmade structure anywhere on the planet, exceeded in loftiness only by the pyramids of Khufu and Khafre at Gaza. It is also the largest and most technologically challenging dagoba ever constructed: the main dome incorporates more than 93 million bricks (sufficient, calculated 19th-century colonial secretary James Emerson Tennent, to build 8,000 houses with a 6m frontage) and extends over 9,000m² above an 8m deep foundation.

Jetavana Dagoba presumably remained intact into the 12th century, when King Parakramabahu made superficial modifications to its square pavilion-like base. At some unknown point after that, the steeple and minaret collapsed, reducing it to its present height of 70m. Unlike Ruwanweli, Jetavana Dagoba has never been properly renovated; as a result, the rough red-brick exterior and truncated steeple make it feel more like an ancient ruin than an active site of worship. It also tends to be quieter than Ruwanweli, and less touristy. All the same, a straggle of locals can usually be seen lighting candles or laying lotus flowers at the small and attractively engraved shrines set within the quartet of Vahalkadas that project from the cardinal points.

Jetavana Dagoba was the centrepiece of a Mahayana monastery founded after King Mahasena's antipathy towards the Theravada school prompted the monks at the Maha Vihara to abandon the capital. Indeed, much of Jetavana was built from the rubble of its old Theravada counterpart. The dagoba reputedly marks the creation and burial place of Thera Mahinda, the monk who first brought Buddhism to Sri Lanka – a legend supported by recent excavations that revealed the inner terrace to incorporate the 3rd-century BC brick wall of a crypt-like structure containing ash and charcoal.

The extensive monastic ruins surrounding Jetavana Dagoba mostly date to the 9th and 10th centuries, shortly before Anuradhapura was overrun by the Chola invaders, and are generally of less interest than their older and more substantial counterparts at Abhayagiriya. One major exception, situated only 150m west of the dagoba, is a vaulted image house that forms a stylistic precursor of the tall narrow image houses associated with Polonnaruwa. The **Jetavana Museum**, 300m south of the dagoba, houses the so-called Jetavana Treasure, a diverse collection of homegrown and imported artefacts whose cosmopolitan provenance – from Rome and Arabia to India and China – underscores Anuradhapura's standing as a centre of international trade.

The Thuparama Built to enshrine the right collarbone of the Buddha, the Thuparama is the oldest dagoba in Anuradhapura, and one of the most revered, despite its relatively modest height of around 19m. It dates to the reign of King Devanampiya Tissa, though his original pioneering construction probably bore little resemblance to the present-day dagoba, a whitewashed bell-shaped product of restoration work completed in 1862. In the late 6th century, almost a thousand years after it was originally built, the Thuparama once again played a pioneering role in Sri Lankan architecture when King Aggabodhi II refurbished it as the gold- and silver-plated centrepiece of the country's first known vatadage, a type of circular image house that would reach its ultimate expression at the Medirigiriya Mandalagiri near Polonnaruwa. The gold and silver disappeared when the city was looted by the Chola army in AD993, but the stone pillars that supported the dome-shaped roof of the vatadage still remain, arranged in four concentric circles around the central dagoba. An excellent scale reconstruction of the vatadage can be seen in the archaeological museum.

Royal Citadel That so little survives of the palaces that once graced the moat-enclosed Royal Citadel north of the Thuparama is perhaps an indication of the destruction wrought by the Chola invaders in AD993. The most substantial secular building in the old citadel, the so-called **Palace of Vijayabahu I** is a temporary residence built for the coronation of its Polonnaruwa-based namesake in 1073. The ground plan of this multistoreyed building is still intact, its main entrance flanked by a pair of fine guardstones depicting Sankha and Padma, the attendants of Kubera, respectively wearing headdresses made of their trademark lotus flowers and conches. The most interesting feature of the **Mahapeli Alms Hall**, 400m further east, is a massive stone trough used as a receptacle for rice fed to the monks by the royal kitchen. The nearby **Dalada Maligawa**, according to an on-site inscription, is a former Temple of the Tooth; indeed, it might well be the original shrine built by King Sirimeghavanna in AD313 after Princess Hemamali smuggled the tooth relic to Sri Lanka.

Abhayagiriya Monastery Now an atmospheric sprawl of ruins carved into the jungle north of the royal citadel, Abhayagiriya – one of the highlights of Anuradhapura – was founded by King Valagamba when he recaptured Anuradhapura in 89BC. Fourteen years before that, Valagamba had been ousted from his capital by a Tamil invasion and, as he fled the city through its northern gate, he vowed that he would one day return to build a Buddhist monastery on the site, which then housed a Jain Temple built during the reign of King Pandukabhaya. Abhayagiriya originally shared a conservative Theravada code with the city's oldest Buddhist temple, but it developed stronger Mahayana leanings over the centuries, largely as a result of exposure to monks from mainland Asia. Doctrinal disputes came to a head under the 3rd-century reign of Mahayana-sympathising King Mahasena, leading Abhayagiriya to become the city's largest and most influential monastery. Indeed, when Faxian visited Anuradhapura in the 5th century, Abhayagiriya had grown into a cosmopolitan centre of Buddhist scholarship that housed almost 5,000 monks and maintained links with its peers in China, Indonesia and northern India. Abhayagiriya fell into decline after the 10th century sacking of Anuradhapura, and was abandoned in the late 12th century following attempted revivals by Vijayabahu I and Parakramabahu I.

11

Coming from the royal citadel, the small **Abhayagiriya Museum** (⊕ *09.00–17.00*), tucked away 250m north of the main road, is as good a place as any to start your exploration of the ruined monastery. It houses a wealth of artefacts unearthed during excavations, ranging from a superbly crafted bronze bowl and Buddha miniature to locally minted coins, limestone Samadhi statues with bejewelled eyes, and a restored crystalline limestone statue of a Naga Raja adorned with five cobra hoods.

On the right (north) side of the road, 300m past the path to the museum, the whitewashed **Lankarama Dagoba** was the first and smallest of two such edifices built by King Valagamba. Little is known about the size and shape of the 1st-century BC original, but the concentric circles of tall stone pillars that surround its modest modern counterpart suggest that it was at some point converted to a vatadage. A 250m footpath runs northward from the left side of the Lankarama to the **Eth Pokuna** (Elephant Pool), whose name refers to its status as the largest ancient manmade pond in Sri Lanka. Built in the 3rd century as a bathing place for the monks of Abhayagiriya, this stone pond – still full with water – is three times as long as an Olympic-size swimming pool at 159m, while a width of 53m and depth of 9.5m give it a total holding capacity of almost 80,000m^3.

The monastery's centrepiece is the **Abhayagiriya Dagoba**, which was built by Valagamba in the 1st century BC, enlarged by King Gajabahu I in the 2nd century AD, and renovated a thousand years later by Parakramabahu I. With a diameter of 106m and damaged spire that attains a height of 75m, this is generally regarded to be the third-tallest dagoba ever constructed in Sri Lanka, though some sources speculate it would have been second to Jetavana prior to the spire's collapse. Handsome vahalkadas flanked by engraved stone pillars project from the four cardinal points, and a pond designed to catch any rain off-flow stands outside each of the four entrances. The least visited of Anuradhapura's mega-dagobas, Abhayagiriya is also perhaps the most impressive, or at least the one with the greatest sense of place, thanks to the jungle-like surrounds and rough unpainted exterior, which somehow accentuate the antiquated feel.

The ruins of several substantial buildings lie on opposite sides of the road about 200m west of Abhayagiriya Dagoba. **Mahasena's Palace** is named after the 3rd-century king that founded the Jetavana Monastery but is more likely to be a 7th- or 8th-century monastic residence. Its beautifully executed and remarkably well-preserved moonstone is adorned with a carved menagerie of elephants, swans, lions and other animals. A guardstone of comparable quality stands at the entrance to the equally misleadingly named **Queen's Pavilion** 100m to the south, and both buildings have some richly detailed dwarves engraved into their staircases. Opposite this, what a plaque describes as 'the most artistic Guardstone in Sri Lanka', depicting two embracing lovers and a lion as they emerge from (or are swallowed by) the mouth of a dragon-like beast above the shoulder of an anthropomorphic Naga Raja, stands sentinel at the entrance to the **Ratnaprasada**, a chapter house that stood five storeys high in its 8th-century prime.

About 200m east of the dagoba, the **Samadhi Buddha** is an exquisitely carved open-air dolomite statue that shows its seated subject in a state of deep meditation after he attained enlightenment. It has been dated to the 4th century AD, though some experts believe it to be older. Examine the head closely from both sides, and you might notice that the Buddha looks earnest on one side but has the hint of smile on the other. It is said that Jawaharlal Nehru, later to become the first prime minister of India, gained solace by contemplating a photograph of this statue while jailed for civil disobedience over 1940–41. Fittingly, the shelter that protects the statue from rain damage was donated by the government of India.

Another 500m past this, the most easterly site of note in Abhayagiriya is the **Kuttam Pokuna** (Twin Ponds), a pair of dressed-stone bathing pools attributed to the 6th-century King Aggabodhi I and still fully functional today. Separated by a narrow passage, these sunken stone pools both measure 17m across, have a combined length of 75m, and were used as a bathing place by members of one of the monastery's four fellowships. Look out for the five-headed cobra statue at the far end of the second pond.

ASOKARAMAYA TEMPLE AND THE STONE BRIDGES [map, page 260] These little-visited sites stand 1.5km apart along the Malvathu River about 4km north of town. Asokaramaya, sometimes referred to as Pankuliya after a nearby village, consists of a 2m-high 9th-century dolomite Samadhi Buddha, regarded to be the equal of its more accessible counterpart in Abhayagiriya, and set within the ruins of a narrow stone building watched over by a pair of fine guardstones. Also dating to the 9th century, possibly earlier, a pair of partially restored stone bridges, similar to but less impressive than the Maha Kanadarawa Stone Bridge near Mihintale (page 279), span the rivers Halpan and Malvathu along what was presumably an important ancient trade route running north out of Anuradhapura.

The easiest way to reach these sites is through Abhayagiriya Monastery. From Kuttam Pokuna, head north along Sangamitta Road for 2km, then turn right and follow a path through the paddies for 700m to reach Asokaramaya Temple. To reach the stone bridges, return to Sangamitta Road and after 1km you'll cross the Halpan, where the first stone bridge is about 50m to your right. The partial stone bridge across the larger Malvathu River is another 500m further ahead. Although access to these sites is free, it would be difficult to reach them without passing through the Abhayagiriya Monastery, where foreigners will almost certainly be asked to produce their CCF ticket.

MIHINTALE MONASTERY

Celebrated as the cradle of Sri Lankan Buddhism, mountainous Mihintale sprawls across a thickly wooded four-pinnacled ridge that rises to 332m some 10km east of Anuradhapura. Tradition holds that this ancient monastery is one of the 16 sacred Solosmasthana visited by the Buddha during his lifetime, but more singularly that it is where a proselytising Indian monk called Mahinda converted King Devanampiya Tissa to Buddhism in the 3rd century BC. The significance of this epochal encounter – commemorated in the hill's name, a derivative of 'Mahinda Thale' (Mahinda's Plateau) – has made it a popular pilgrimage site over the June poya, when tens of thousands of devotees converge on its hilltop dagobas. But even at other times, Mihintale forms a rewarding goal for a half-day excursion out of nearby Anuradhapura, one that lacks the architectural grandeur of the ancient capital, but is no less engaging thanks to the intimate forest setting, tranquil atmosphere, and grand views offered from the pinnacles.

HISTORY Even before a monastery was established here, Mihintale – then known as Missaka – and the surrounding forests were preserved as a royal hunting ground for the Anuradhapura monarchy. It was on one such deer-hunting excursion, on a fateful June poya c260–255BC, that Devanampiya Tissa was hailed by Thera Mahinda, who was the eldest son of the devout Emperor Ashoka of Maurya (India), but had chosen a monastic life over a political career. According to the *Mahavamsa*,

Mahinda rattled off a series of riddles at Devanampiya Tissa to assess his shrewdness, then started preaching the pacifist teachings of the Buddha, converting both the king and his sizeable entourage on the spot. With royal blessing, Mahinda established Anuradhapura's two first Buddhist monasteries: Maha Vihara in the capital and Chetiyagiri at Mihintale. The latter was a favourite retreat of Mahinda, who died there at the age of 80. Devanampiya Tissa's brother and successor Uttiya organised a state funeral for Mahinda at Mihintale, and built a dagoba there to house relics belonging to the revered monk. The monastery remained an important centre of Theravada Buddhism for almost two millennia, supporting more than 2,000 monks in its prime. And although it suffered several dips in fortune after the 10th-century sacking of Anuradhapura, it enjoyed a major revival in the 12th century under King Parakramabahu, then again in the 17th century under Kirti Sri Rajasinha of Kandy. Finally abandoned in the 18th century, Mihintale fell into ruins and was consumed by the jungle prior to its rediscovery in 1886 by R W Ivers, the colonial government agent who undertook pioneering excavations at the site.

PRACTICALITIES Mihintale Monastery stands on the southern outskirts of the eponymous small town, 12km from Anuradhapura along the Trincomalee Road. The drive shouldn't take longer than 20 minutes, and buses ply back and forth throughout the day. The monastery is open 24 hours and admission costs US$3.50, but the archaeological museum is only open ⊕ 08.00–16.30. The forested nature of the monastery makes it cooler than more exposed sites, but with 1,840 stone steps to navigate, it can be quite taxing to explore.

If you come by public transport, the archaeological museum and ruins associated with the lower terrace stand about 400m south of Mihintale's main traffic circle and bus stop. On foot, it's a 500m climb from the archaeological museum and lower terrace to the middle terrace, but the legwork can be reduced significantly by driving or catching a tuktuk along the more circuitous 1.5km road to the car park and entrance gate at the middle terrace. Either way, the 300m climb from the middle to the upper terrace can be covered on foot only.

WHAT TO SEE AND DO [map, opposite] The extensive ruins at Mihintale divide into three main parts: a lower, middle and upper terrace split from each other by a long flight of steep stone steps as old as the monastery itself. For those with limited time or energy, the key sites are the archaeological museum on the lower terrace, the Kantaka Dagoba and Sangha Pokuna near the middle terrace car park, and the Sela Cetiya and views from the Maha Dagoba on the upper terrace. Those with sufficient time could continue to the Kaludiya Pokuna in the separate western ruins, or divert 8km north to the unique Maha Kanadarawa Stone Bridge.

Lower Terrace The **archaeological museum** (⊕ 08.00–16.30), on the left side of the car park at the lower entrance gate, is an obvious place to start. A 1:1,000 relief model provides a good overview of the monastic site, while artefacts on show include the relic chamber of Giribhanda Dagoba (decorated with 7th-century line drawings of the Buddha and other figures), a 9th-century gold-plated manuscript, and various imported and homegrown earthenware, statues and clay figurines, some dating back to the 1st century BC. About 150m west of the museum stands **Mihintale hospital**, complete with a hollowed-out stone bath, a therapeutic janthagara (hot water) pool and central Buddha shrines. One of the world's oldest hospitals, it was founded several centuries before the current ruinous building was constructed during the 9th-century reign of King Sena II.

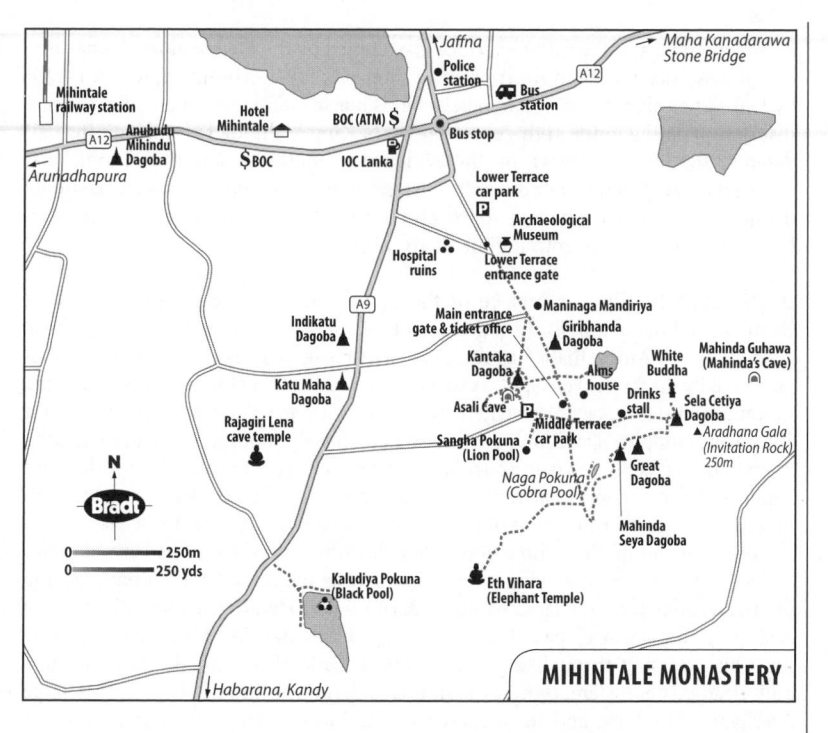

MIHINTALE MONASTERY

From the lower entrance gate, a 500m footpath leads to an ancient flight of 320 stone steps that lead uphill to the middle terrace and main entrance gate. Most visitors skip this steep footpath in favour of driving to the middle terrace car park, but it's a lovely walk. *En route*, the **Maninaga Mandiriya** is an intriguing temple whose quincunx floor plan comprises four square corner cells arranged symmetrically around a larger central image house. About 100m further, also to the left, stands **Giribhanda Dagoba**, whose relic house is reproduced in the archaeological museum.

Middle terrace Standing on a small peak 150m west of the main middle terrace, **Kantaka Dagoba** is the oldest such construction at Mihintale, possibly anywhere in Sri Lanka. It dates back to the reign of Devanampiya Tissa, who also opened up around 80 monastic cells in the surrounding caves. Standing 21m tall and with a circumference of 130m, the dagoba was reputedly built to house a collar-bone relic from the Buddha, transported to Anuradhapura by the monk Mahinda, and each of its four cardinal points is marked with a well-preserved vahalkada decorated with the country's oldest Buddhist engravings, depicting various animals, lotus flowers and dwarves, as well as the sagacious elephant-headed Ganesh. The dagoba can be reached on a short footpath running west from the steps between the lower and middle terrace, or along an even shorter path leading uphill from the middle terrace car park.

Another relict of Devanampiya Tissa's reign, accessible along a short footpath running south from close to the car park, the **Sangha Pokuna** (Lion Pool) was reputedly built as part of the royal garden prior to the king's fateful encounter with Mahinda. Embellished from natural rock curves on three sides, it is named for a 2m-high standing lion statue whose mouth once spouted water into a second pool below the outer wall. Though the main lion figure is badly damaged, several smaller but better-preserved ancient carvings can be seen above its head.

The main part of the middle terrace is occupied by the **Medamaluwa Monastery**, which was once the main focal point of monastic life at Mihintale. It is survived by two rather plain buildings: a massive **alms house** mentioned in an adjacent slab inscription dating to the 10th-century reign of King Mahinda IV, and a **dining hall** dated to the 5th century AD on the evidence of another inscription. From here, it's another steep 300m uphill climb on stone steps to the upper terrace, passing a drinks stall to your left as you approach the top, then a stand where you need to leave your shoes before entering the main ruins.

Upper terrace The centrepiece of the upper terrace is **Sela Cetiya**, a modest palm-shaded dagoba built during the 2nd-century BC reign of King Lanja Tissa. Also known as Ambasthala Dagoba, Sela Cetiya is of dual significance insofar as it purportedly marks the very spot chosen by the Buddha to meditate on his visit to the mountain, and the exact place where monk Mahinda struck up a conversation with King Devanampiya Tissa four centuries later. Heavily modified by King Kanittha Tissa in the 1st century AD, the dagoba was later converted to a vatadage with a roof supported by two concentric rows of pillars. The statue of a bearded, helmeted man in the stone courtyard in front of the dagoba may depict Devanampiya Tissa.

Four short footpaths – three uphill, one downhill – lead from the central upper terrace to other sites of varying interest. Least essential is the 50m footpath leading up a bare stone face to a large white **modern Buddha statue**. The footpath running east from the terrace, past the modern monks' quarters, meanders downhill for 300m, passing through a peaceful jungle glade alive with the calls of birds and cicadas, before emerging at **Mahinda Guhawa** (Mahinda's Cave). This large overhang, the oldest and most sacred of Mihintale's many meditation caves, is formed by a massive balancing boulder perched on a flat rock whose floor is carved with a 2.3m-long rectangle, where the monastery's founder, Mahinda, reputedly once meditated and slept. Also running east from the main upper terrace, a very short but equally steep flight of rock-hewn steps allows you to ascend precariously to the **Aradhana Gala** (Invitation Rock), a spectacularly sited pinnacle from where Mahinda reputedly spoke his first words after reaching Sri Lanka.

From afar, the most prominent feature at Mihintale is King Mahadathika Mahanaga's **Great Dagoba**, built to hold a sacred eyebrow relic of the Buddha. Standing 14m high, this recently restored, whitewashed dagoba is reached along a steep uphill footpath on a rock face to the west of the upper terrace. The smaller brick dagoba behind this is thought to be where King Uttiya enshrined the relics of Mahinda. These two shrines are set on a small hilltop plateau that offers spectacular views towards Anuradhapura, whose great dagobas protrude like massive domed and spired hillocks above the surrounding jungle and lakes. West of the plateau, a 100m footpath leads downhill to the **Naga Pokuna** (Cobra Pool), a long, oval bathing pool constructed by Devanampiya Tissa for Mahinda, and named for the striking five-headed cobra sculpture on the rock above it. A rather obscure 500m path leads west from the Naga Pokuna to the clifftop Eth Vihara (Elephant Temple), a smallish layered brick dagoba that offers views over the whole Mihintale complex.

Western ruins A scattering of relatively little-visited ruins lie alongside the Kandy Road below the western base of Mihintale. These include the small and rather undistinguished **Indikatu** and **Katu Maha dagobas**, set 100m apart on the west side of the Kandy Road as you drive between the archaeological museum and the middle terrace car park, as well as the isolated cave temple at **Rajagiri Lena** about 500m further east. A more worthwhile diversion is the **Kaludiya Pokuna**

(Black Pool), which lies on the east side of the Kandy Road about 500m further south. The largest and most beautiful of several artificial pools at Mihintale, it forms an important component in the advanced hydrological system that once served the monastery. Kaludiya has been identified with the 'Porodini Pokuna' mentioned in the tablet inscribed King Mahinda IV on the middle terrace, but most likely it was originally constructed by King Saddha Tissa a thousand years before that. The most interesting building associated with the pond is a cave shrine with a colonnaded built-up exterior set in the rocks 50m uphill of the eastern shore. Other notable features include an island pavilion on the northeast shore, and a small dagoba overlooking the northwestern corner.

Maha Kanadarawa Stone Bridge [map, page 212] The best-preserved *gal palama* (stone bridge) of a type that once formed a vital conduit in Anuradhapura's far-reaching trade network spans the Kanadarawa River 500m east of the Maha Kanadarawa reservoir and 8km north of Mihintale. Roughly 25m long and 3m wide, the bridge was probably constructed at least 2,000 years ago as part of a road linking Anuradhapura to Gokanna (Trincomalee). It was built in three stages. First, about a dozen groups of three stone pillars were erected at regular intervals on the riverbed. After that, a horizontal stone slab was laid across each trio of upright pillars. Then finally each of the width-wise struts was connected to the next by spanning them length-wise with six horizontal stone slabs.

To get here from Mihintale, follow the Trincomalee Road for 1.3km east of the central traffic circle, then turn left on to the dirt road to Kudagama. The road reaches the west shore of the Maha Kanadarawa Reservoir after 3.5km and follows it for another 2.5km before veering sharply to the west and then again to the north. From here, you need to walk the last 200m west to the stone bridge.

THANTHIRIMALE TEMPLE

The remote hamlet of Thanthirimale, 40km northwest of Anuradhapura, shares its name with an ancient, ruggedly picturesque monastery that sprawls along a ridge of outsized granite boulders interspersed with pretty lotus ponds rising from a wild jungle setting outside the northeast boundary of Wilpattu National Park. Few traces of the old monastic buildings remain, but the site is home to Sri Lanka's second-oldest Bo Tree, as well as a pair of fine, centuries-old rock-hewn Buddha statues, a rare example of pre-Buddhist rock art dating back 4,000 years, and a small but worthwhile museum. Though little visited, Thanthirimale is also a very atmospheric spot, with a tranquillity far removed from the touristy bustle of Anuradhapura.

HISTORY Thanthirimale has been identified as the 'village of the Brahman Thivakka' where, according to the *Mahavamsa*, a procession led by King Devanampiya Tissa and Sangamitta Thera stopped overnight with the sacred Bo Tree *en route* from Dambakola to Anuradhapura. The account states that Brahmana Thivakka joined the royal procession in order to participate in the Bo planting ceremony at Anuradhapura, where he was given custody of one of its Ashtapalaruha saplings. He took it back to its village and planted it in the same high spot where the pot holding the original tree had been placed on its overnight sojourn. Shortly afterwards, the whole village converted to Buddhism, leading to the foundation of a monastery on the rocky site. Eighty years later, Prince Saliya and his low-caste wife Ashokamala (the 'lovers' depicted in the engraving at Isurumuniya Temple) were banished to the village for several years prior to being pardoned by King Dutugamunu and

11

presented with a gold necklace shaped like a butterfly (*thantiri*), which led to the place being renamed Thanthirimale (also spelt Tantrimalai). The monastery and temple of Thanthirimale thrived until the 10th century AD, when they were abandoned in the wake of the Chola invasion of Anuradhapura. The ruined monastery was rediscovered in the early 20th century by British archaeologists. The temple was revived in 1960, and a new dagoba was constructed on a rock close to the ancient Bo Tree in 1976.

PRACTICALITIES Thanthirimale can easily be visited as a day trip out of Anuradhapura, or *en route* to Mannar. With a private vehicle, just follow the surfaced Thanthirimale Road north out of Anuradhapura for about 40km. Using public transport, two buses hourly connect Anuradhapura and Thanthirimale, taking about 1 hour either way, and stopping alongside the monastery. Coming from Mannar, Thanthirimale is accessible along a 12km dirt road leading south from the A14 at Gajasinghaputa, 20km west of Madawachchi.

The monastery is open 24 hours daily, while opening hours for the site museum are ⊕ 08.00–16.30. Thanthirimale is best avoided in the midday heat, when the rocks can be intolerably hot underfoot (though foreigners seem to be permitted to wear shoes). It is most captivating towards dusk, when the antiquities are artificially lit. There's no entrance fee.

WHAT TO SEE AND DO [map, right] Start at the **site museum**, which contains a useful relief map of the site and some antiquities unearthed during excavations. From here, a 200m climb on the bare rocks leads to the

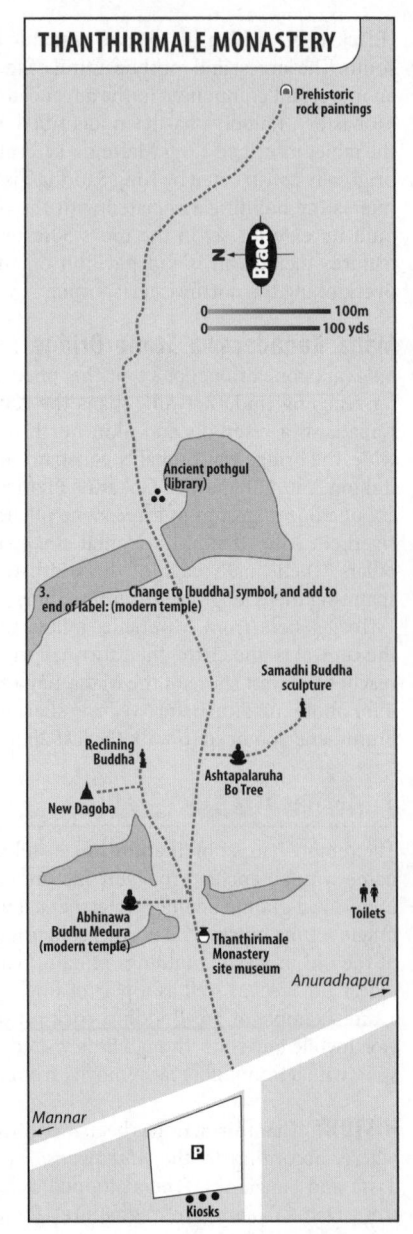

THANTHIRIMALE MONASTERY

Prehistoric rock paintings

N

Bradt

0   100m
0   100 yds

Ancient pothgul (library)

3. Change to [buddha] symbol, and add to end of label: (modern temple)

Samadhi Buddha sculpture

Reclining Buddha

Ashtapalaruha Bo Tree

New Dagoba

Toilets

Abhinawa Budhu Medura (modern temple)

Thanthirimale Monastery site museum

Anuradhapura

Mannar

P

Kiosks

Ashtapalaruha Bo Tree, which is venerated as having grown from the original sapling planted by Brahmana Thivakka all those centuries ago. Protected within an ancient Bodhighara that was restored in the 1960s, the ancient *Ficus* seems to be thriving despite its exposed boulder-top location, though the lack of water and salty soil might explain its unusually small leaves.

The bare granite faces of Thanthirimale are adorned with two superb **rock-hewn Buddha statues** executed sometime between the 8th and 12th centuries. About 50m north of the ancient Bo Tree, hidden in the base of the wooded gully that separates it from a boulder-top whitewashed dagoba constructed in 1976, is a 15m-long reclining Buddha set in a wide niche that originally formed the back wall of an image house. Sadly, this sculpture was defaced at the hands of treasure hunters, and cannot be properly restored, despite the recent efforts of the Department of Archaeology. Smaller but of greater aesthetic merit is the 2m-high Samadhi Buddha carved into an enclave 50m south of the Bo Tree. The niche, which also once formed part of an image house, is beautifully decorated with a dragon supported by two lions, and a pair of human attendants holding fly-whisks. Two unfinished Buddha statues have been carved into smaller and plainer niches on the same rock face. The incomplete nature of the rock-hewn Buddhas at Thanthirimale, together with their stylistic similarity to their counterparts at Polonnaruwa's Gil Vihara, has led to some speculation they are precursors to that more famous site, but were left incomplete after the Chola invasion that led to the original monastery being abandoned.

The main lotus pond to the east of these impressive sculptures is worth a stop to look for **wildlife**: crocodiles are resident, kingfishers hawk above the water, and the surrounding forest is home to monkeys and a good place to look for the endemic Ceylon grey hornbill. A rocky path across the pond leads to an expanded cave that once served as a **Pothgul** (library) to store palm-leaf manuscripts and important ritual objects. Scattered around the cave are a dozen old padhanaghara meditation platforms and monastic cells engraved with Brahmi characters dated to the 1st century BC. Continue east for another 500m, and you come to a pair of caves decorated with **prehistoric rock paintings** thought to be at least 4,000 years old. Monochrome and very faded, the paintings are attributed to the predecessors of the Vedda and are thought by some to be stylised depictions of celestial bodies and wild animals, and by others to be a form of pictographic writing.

WILPATTU NATIONAL PARK

[map, page 212] (025 385 5691; w *dwc.gov.lk*; ⊕ *06.00–18.00; entrance US$15 pp, plus US$8 service charge per party, plus 12% tax*) Sri Lanka's largest national park, and one of its oldest, Wilpattu extends over 520km² of low-lying dry-zone woodland running inland from the coast north of the main road between Colombo and Anuradhapura. Proclaimed in 1938, this vast national park has its roots in a pair of separately administered game sanctuaries established in 1905, and its name (literally 'Land of Lakes') refers to the many shallow seasonal sand-rimmed pans (villus or wilas) scattered across its wooded interior. The park was extended eastward in 1969, and attained its present-day size in 1973, following the addition of 220km² of territory stretching west towards what is now a 50km seafront. Wilpattu closed to tourism after May 1985, when 24 park employees were slaughtered by the same terrorists responsible for the bombing of Jaya Sri Maha Bodhi in Anuradhapura. It reopened in 2003, though it has only been properly functional since 2010. The national park recently attained international recognition as the core of the 1,638km² Wilpattu Wetland Cluster, which incorporates an astonishing 208 water bodies, most of them natural, and was listed as Sri Lanka's sixth Ramsar site in 2013.

Serviced by a well-maintained network of sandy roads and a cluster of camps and hotels situated outside the entrance gate, Wilpattu now forms an excellent goal for a safari in its own right, as well as offering a refreshing change of scene from the ruined monasteries and other antiquities associated with the Cultural Triangle. It is the most productive park in Sri Lanka for sloth bear sightings, though these are far from guaranteed, and it also supports significant numbers of elephant and

11

leopard, though neither is observed as regularly as in Yala National Park. When it comes to smaller mammals and birds, however, it seems to be a lot more productive than Yala, though the biggest difference between the two is Wilpattu's much lower volume of tourist traffic and relatively untrammelled wilderness feel.

FLORA AND FAUNA More than 70% of Wilpattu, including the area covered by the main game-viewing circuit, is dominated by dense evergreen woodland and scrub where some of the more conspicuous tall trees include the black-wooded Ceylon ebony (*Diospyros ebenum*), East Indian satinwood (*Chloroxylon swietenia*), peacock chaste tree (*Vitex altissima*) and pallu (*Manilkara hexandra*), whose slightly alcoholic fruit frequently attracts sloth bears over June and July. The shallow lakes for which the park is named – an important source of sustenance in the dry season, though many dry out during extended periods of drought – usually support a belt of littoral grass fringed by patches of jungle-like riparian forest.

At least 30 mammal species are present, including the country's largest and most conspicuous population of sloth bears, which are quite often seen lumbering along the roads towards dusk, but are most visible over June–July, chilling out tipsily on the branches of fruiting pallu trees. An estimated 50–100 leopards inhabit the park, and while they tend to be more secretive than their counterparts in Yala, sightings do increase in number towards the end of the dry season (July and August) and preoccupied mating pairs are quite often encountered over January–March. Allowing for some seasonal flux, Wilpattu supports around 300 elephants whose tendency to be above average size is attributed to the nutrient-rich grass growing around the villus. Other mammals regularly seen on game drives include Eurasian jackal, wild boar, water buffalo, grey langur, toque macaque, and spotted, sambar and barking deer.

Almost 200 bird species have been recorded, including Sri Lanka junglefowl (noisy and conspicuous in the morning but more elusive in the afternoon) and other actual and proposed endemics such as Sri Lanka green pigeon, Sri Lanka grey hornbill, crimson-fronted barbet, greater flameback, common wood-shrike and black-crested bulbul. Among the more striking and common woodland birds are Indian peafowl, Malabar pied hornbill, white-throated kingfisher, little green bee-eater, Asian paradise flycatcher and white-rumped shama. The lakes support a wonderful profusion of waterbirds throughout the year, and are particularly important as a stronghold for the localised lesser adjutant stork, but numbers peak over November–March, when the park hosts large flocks of winter migrants.

GETTING THERE AND AWAY Wilpattu is readily accessible on public transport from Anuradhapura or Colombo, and jeep safaris can be arranged on the spot. The main Hunuvilagama entrance gate stands 8km north of Maragawaheha (also known as Wilpattu Junction) on the main road between Anuradhapura 30km to the east and Puttalam 40km to the southwest. Coming directly from Colombo, it's about 180km by road to the entrance gate, a drive of around 4 hours depending on traffic, and any bus heading from Colombo to Anuradhapura can stop at Maragawaheha. A more popular and attractive option is to travel by train to Anuradhapura, then bus the last 30km to Maragawaheha. Alternatively, you could also catch one of three daily trains from Colombo to Puttalam, and bus the 40km to Maragawaheha from there. Maragawaheha is also easily reached from the Kalpitiya Peninsula via Puttalam, whether in a private vehicle or by bus (though most likely you'll need to change bus at Puttalam). Once at Maragawaheha, tuktuks are available for the 8km trip to Hunuvilagama.

For those who prefer not to make their way independently, all-inclusive safaris to Wilpattu can be arranged at a premium through any hotel in Anuradhapura or Kalpitiya, or indeed directly out of Colombo. Most organised safaris out of Kalpitiya travel by road through Puttalam, as described below, but an increasingly popular option is to boat across via Puttalam Lagoon to a recently opened southwestern gate.

WHERE TO STAY *Map, page 212*
Upmarket

☀ 🏠 **Noel Rodrigo's Leopard Safaris Camp** (4 tents) m 0713 314024; e reservations@leopardsafaris.com; w leopardsafaris.com. This eco-friendly tented camp, set in a patch of pristine woodland about 6km outside the park entrance, offers a wonderful all-inclusive bush experience that incorporates expertly & enthusiastically guided jeep safaris into the park, superb & innovative Sri Lankan cuisine, & a well-stocked bar with chilled drinks. The modern South African 2-compartment tents are tall enough to stand in & come with proper beds & private outdoor shower & toilet. *US$555/990 sgl/dbl inc meals, drinks & activities; low-season discounts available.* **$$$$$+**

🏠 **Mahoora Tented Safari Camp** (19 tents) ✆ 011 583 0833; m 0710 662224; e info@mahoora.com; w mahoora.com. Sri Lanka's longest-serving safari operator now runs a permanent 'glamping' camp in a thick patch of jungle overlooking a pretty natural lake about 6km south of the park entrance. The tented units with net & fan (but no AC), en-suite shower/toilet & outdoor sitting area are no more than adequate at the price, but the exceptionally high standard of guiding compensates, as does the excellent food & drink. Guided night walks & camp offer the chance of spotting secretive nocturnal creatures such as slender loris & various reptiles & birds. *From US$380 pp inc all meals, drinks, park fees, safaris, game drives & other activities.* **$$$$$+**

Budget

🏠 **Willy's Wilpattu Villa** (3 rooms) Hunuvilagama; ✆ 011 309 1786; e willyssh@sltnet.lk; w willyssafari.com. Set in a green forest-fringed garden 200m southeast of the entrance gate, this is a pleasant little set-up offering simple but spacious rooms with AC & fan, meals by arrangement on a shaded balcony, & well-priced safaris into the park. *US$35/41 dbl/trpl.* **$$**

🏠 **Leopard Den** (10 rooms) Maragawaheha; ✆ 025 325 9128; m 0767 959485; e reservations@leoparddenwilpattu.com; w leoparddenwilpattu.com. Conveniently located alongside the main Puttalam–Anuradhapura road right next to the junction for the park entrance, this place isn't quite as nice as it looks from the outside, but it offers the choice of clean & spacious AC rooms with cold shower, or smaller & stuffier rooms with fan only. A busy restaurant serves mains in the US$4–6 range. It offers attractively priced guided safaris in its own well-maintained jeeps. *US$24/31 trpl without/with AC.* **$$**

🏠 **LLT Tourist Inn** (7 rooms) Maragawaheha–Hunuvilagama Rd; ✆ 025 325 3838; m 0714 187083; e safarillt@gmail.com; w lltsafariwilpattu.com. This agreeable guesthouse lies 250km east of Maragawaheha Rd some 4km south of the entrance gate. The clean & spacious rooms feel rather non-cohesively furnished but all come with AC & fan. It has a pleasant outdoor restaurant & a reputation for reliable safaris. *US$35 dbl.* **$$**

🏠 **Wilpattu Wild Watch** (5 rooms) Hunuvilagama; m 0777 959583. Overlooking forest-fringed paddy fields alongside the main road 300m south of the entrance gate, this smartish house has a lounge & dining room with cable TV & meals to order, & neat rooms with AC & fan. It can arrange guided safaris into Wilpattu. *US$35 twin/dbl, US$50 family room sleeping 5.* **$$**

Shoestring

☀ 🏠 **Dolosmahe Guesthouse** (10 rooms) Hunuvilagama; m 0713 903504, 0729 988664. This unpretentious & friendly 4-storey lodge on the main road 300m south of the entrance gate has clean AC rooms & a decent restaurant. *US$24 dbl.* **$**

WHAT TO SEE AND DO The main activity is half- or full-day jeep safaris. Plenty of jeeps are available in Maragawaheha and Hunuvilagama, or you can make arrangements through any hotel in the vicinity. Either way, a party of up to five can expect to pay around US$35/55 per half-/full-day for the jeep, inclusive of driver and fuel, but exclusive of park fees. Half-day safaris start at Hunuvilagama entrance gate and usually follow a 20km road northwest, through thick forest interspersed with a few small natural ponds, before emerging at the main game-viewing circuit, which weaves between a dozen lakes, of which the largest is the 1km-wide Kokkare Villu. The road from Hunuvilagama to the lakes circuit takes 45–60 minutes to cover in either direction, so allow at least 4 hours, better five, for a half-day safari. If you are restricted to a half-day, mornings are more productive for birds, but afternoons are better for the so-called 'Big Three' of elephant, leopard and sloth bear, since the latter two tend to be most active after 17.00. Odds of encountering elephants are greatly increased on a full-day drive, which allows you to head deeper into the southwest at a time of day when they most often come to drink.

Part Four

NORTHERN AND EASTERN PROVINCES

Overview of Part Four

Differing greatly from the rest of Sri Lanka both in their ethnic make-up and religious affiliations, Northern and Eastern Provinces – merged as one administrative unit, called North Eastern Province, between 1988 and 2007 – are dominated by Hindu Tamils, but also host sizeable Christian Tamil (north) and Moorish Muslim (east) minorities. During the civil war, Northern Province in particular was the main stronghold of the LTTE, whose activities rendered the entire region off limits to tourism. Since the war ended, Eastern Province has staged a remarkable recovery, particularly along the coast, where the backpacker-friendly Arugam Bay, resorty Pasikuda and more urbanised ports of Trincomalee and Batticaloa and have emerged as popular beach destinations whose peak seasons coincide with the wettest months on the better-established southwest coast. Northern Province has lagged behind somewhat in terms of tourist development, partly because of its remoteness from the capital, but the recent reopening of a train service to the provincial capital Jaffna has helped open this intriguing and most untouristy part of Sri Lanka to adventurous and inquisitive travellers.

HIGHLIGHTS

MANNAR (pages 289–98) Ideal for off-the-beaten-track junkies and highly alluring to birdwatchers, sleepy Mannar is a flat and narrow not-quite-of-this-world island that terminates at Adam's Bridge, the partially submerged isthmus that once linked Sri Lanka to India.

JAFFNA (pages 299–309) Sri Lanka's most overtly Tamil and Hindu city, the energetic and emphatically untouristy capital of Northern Province is studded with historic sites, ranging from a historic fort and several temples to the mysterious field of miniature dagobas at Kantharodai.

VELANAI ISLAND (pages 309–10) The second-largest island in the Jaffna Archipelago, linked to the city centre by a 4km causeway, is worth exploring in its own right or as a springboard to the historic temples on Nainativu (pages 310–11) and more far-flung Delft (page 311).

CHUNDIKULAM NATIONAL PARK (pages 316–17) Probably the best birding site in a region known for its avian wealth, Chundikulam protects an estuarine wetland that might host flocks of up to 10,000 flamingo at any time, and also attracts a wide variety of migrants between November and April.

TRINCOMALEE (pages 321–32) Often neglected by tourists, the sprawling capital of Eastern Province is a likeable jack-of-all-trades offering great seasonal whale watching and snorkelling, fine beaches, and some fascinating historic sites rooted in pre-Buddhist times.

PASIKUDA (pages 332–5) The most overtly resort-like destination on the east coast is serviced by several well-priced new package hotels on a delightful swimming beach lapped by calm aquamarine waters.

BATTICALOA (pages 335–44) This low-key island-bound port town, studded with unpretentious homestays, is steeped in history and lends itself to unstructured exploration.

GAL OYA NATIONAL PARK (pages 347–51) Among the least publicised of Sri Lanka's terrestrial national parks, Gal Oya is relatively accessible to backpackers, for whom boat safaris on Senanayake Reservoir offer a good chance of close-up elephant sightings.

ARUGAM BAY (pages 351–8) Renowned as Sri Lanka's top surfing destination, staggeringly beautiful Arugam Bay is a superb chill-out destination whose popularity with backpackers makes it Sri Lanka's answer to Goa.

KUMANA NATIONAL PARK (page 361) An extension of the better-publicised and far busier Yala National Park, Kumana supports plentiful elephants and leopards, and is regularly visited on jeep safaris out of Arugam Bay, stopping *en route* at Kudumbigala's mysterious monastic ruins.

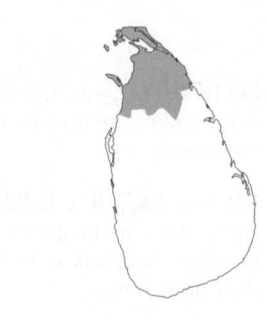

12

Northern Province

Only recently emerged from the ravages of civil war, Northern Province is still finding its feet as a tourist destination, though things have already improved greatly since the dark days of 1983–2009, when travel was at best foolhardy and at worst outlawed. As of 2014, Jaffna, the region's most important population hub and tourist centre, is once again linked to Colombo and the rest of the country by a good asphalt road and active railway track, as is the less well-known island of Mannar to its south. Hotels are also growing rapidly both in number and quality, while sites of interest once regarded as impossibly off the beaten track are once again

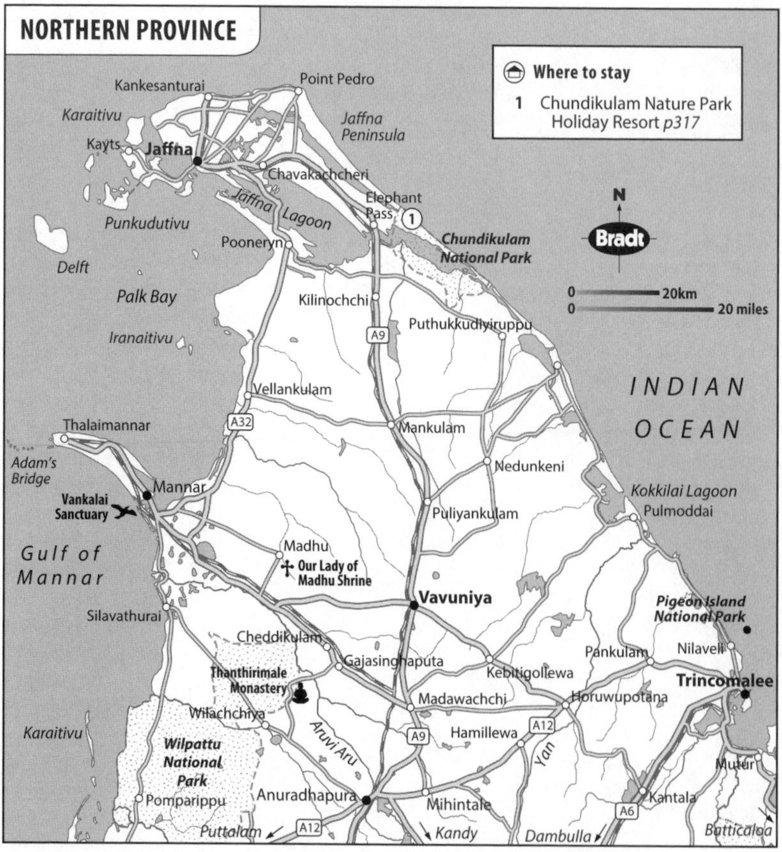

NORTHERN PROVINCE

Where to stay

1 Chundikulam Nature Park
   Holiday Resort *p317*

Kankesanturai

Point Pedro

Karaitivu

Jaffna
Peninsula

Kayts **Jaffna**

Chavakachcheri

Jaffna Lagoon

Elephant
Pass 1

*Chundikulam
National Park*

Punkudutivu

Pooneryn

N

Bradt

Delft

Palk Bay

Kilinochchi

0   20km
0   20 miles

Iranaitivu

Puthukkudiyiruppu

A9

Vellankulam

*INDIAN
OCEAN*

Thalaimannar

A32

Mankulam

*Adam's
Bridge*

**Vankalai
Sanctuary** Mannar

Nedunkeni

Kokkilai Lagoon
Pulmoddai

*Gulf of
Mannar*

Puliyankulam

Madhu

✝ **Our Lady of
Madhu Shrine**

Vavuniya

Silavathurai

*Pigeon Island
National Park*

Cheddikulam

Gajasinghaputa

Pankulam   Nilaveli

**Thanthirimale
Monastery**

Kebitigollewa

Trincomalee

Wilachchiya

Madawachchi

Horuwupotana

Karaitivu

Aruvi Aru

A9

Hamillewa

A12

Van

**Wilpattu
National
Park**

Pomparippu

Anuradhapura

Mihintale

Kantala

Mutur

A6

Batticaloa

Puttalam

Kandy

Dambulla

functional and readily accessible, whether by private car, tuktuk or bus. For all that, it has to be said that the north lacks for the obvious travel highlights that abound in more southerly parts of Sri Lanka. True enough, there are beaches aplenty, but none that compares with the established resorts of the south. Likewise, though Jaffna and Mannar are dotted with venerable temples and other archaeological sites, there is nothing to compare with Sigiriya or Dambulla. And unless you are a dedicated birder, it would be hard to make a case for the likes of the Vankalai Sanctuary or Chundikulam National Park being some sort of northern counterpart to Yala, Wilpattu or Gal Oya. Add to that a climate that is hot and sweaty even by Sri Lankan standards, and it is clear that the north has a long way to go before it rivals the south and central districts as a hub of mass tourism. All of which is to say, perversely, that Northern Province is tailor-made for those independent-minded travellers who habitually scour guidebooks in search of uncrowded and unaffected off-the-beaten-track destinations that can still be experienced more or less for what they are, rather than as the backdrop to an organised tourist industry.

MANNAR ISLAND

Protruding like a beckoning finger into Palk Strait, Mannar is a flat, dry, sandy 50km^2 island separated from the rest of Sri Lanka by a narrow channel of tidal shallows and shape-shifting sandbars whose rich marine birdlife is conserved in the Vankalai Sanctuary. Mannar is the closest part of Sri Lanka to India, terminating less than 30km from the Asian mainland, to which it is linked by Adam's Bridge, a chain of sandy islets, limestone reefs and shallow shoals that incorporates the world's shortest international land border. Although it is something of backwater today, Mannar was renowned for millennia as the world's largest supplier of pearls, and it served as the terminus of the only ferry service between Sri Lanka and India between 1914 and the outbreak of the 1983–2008 civil war, when the island was occupied by the LTTE. Perfectly accessible today whether by rail or by road, Mannar still boasts little in the way of bespoke tourist development, but low-key attractions include the characterful old town of Mannar and its timeworn 17th-century fort, a couple of excellent bird sanctuaries, the attractive coastal scenery around Thalaimannar and Adam's Bridge, and – above all perhaps – the sensation, increasingly rare in Sri Lanka, of being completely removed from any beaten tourist track.

HISTORY Mannar's long and chequered history is strongly influenced by its close proximity to India. According to the *Ramayana*, it was here that the Rama first arrived in Sri Lanka, crossing from the Asian mainland on Adam's Bridge. In ancient times, the most important port in the vicinity was Manthai (also known as Manthota), where the King Vijaya made his first Sri Lankan landfall in the 6th century BC on the mainland opposite present-day Mannar Town. Manthai thrived as a centre of international trade for at least 2,000 years prior to the arrival of the Portuguese, but whatever remains of the old port now lies buried beneath the coastal sands around Ketheeswaram Temple.

Manthai and Mannar formed part of the Rajarata Kingdom from the 5th century BC until the early 13th century AD. Back then, Manthai served as the gateway to the world's most productive pearl fishery. A series of 50-odd individually named pearl banks stand in the shallows stretching south from Mannar Island to Chilaw, and these have been exploited for at least 2,500 years by Tamil divers trained to hold their breath for several minutes as they descend to depths of up to 20m to pluck the pearl-producing *Pinctada radiata* and *Pinctada fucata* oysters. Pearls from Mannar were coveted by the Ancient Greeks and Romans, and were praised as the world's finest by the Greek explorer Megasthenes in the 4th century BC, as well as in the 1st-century AD writings of Pliny the Elder.

In the 13th century, Mannar was incorporated into the Jaffna Kingdom. In the 1530s, the island fell under the informal influence of the Portuguese, who attempted to wrest control of the pearl trade by installing several hundred recently converted Catholic Paravar divers from the Indian mainland. This Portuguese incursion was deeply resented by King Cankili I of Jaffna, who ordered the massacre of 600 Paravar settlers in 1544. The Portuguese captured the island in 1560, built a fort there, and attempted to convert the local Tamils to Catholicism by destroying rival shrines such as the ancient Shiva Temple at Ketheeswaram. Mannar Fort fell to the Dutch in 1658, and then to the British in 1795. Pearl harvesting remained the mainstay of the local economy throughout the British colonial era, when the industry was centred out of Arippu and Silavatturai, 25km south of Mannar Island. Traditional pearl harvesting still continues to this day, but on a far smaller scale, thanks largely to the monopoly of artificially cultured pearls since the first commercial crop was produced in 1928.

FLORA AND FAUNA Mannar has a rather dry climate, which coupled with the infertile sandy soil makes it less than conducive to agriculture. The dominant tree is the Asian palmyrah, but Mannar also supports several coconut palm plantations, and a scattering of a few dozen baobab trees, squattened African implants introduced by Arabian mariners prior to the 16th century. A rather less welcome

BRIDGE OF THE GODS

Adam's Bridge is a unique and rather enigmatic geological phenomenon. Its name derives from an Islamic belief that Adam, following his expulsion from the Garden of Eden, fell to earth in the central highlands of Sri Lanka, then crossed to India using the islets as stepping stones (according to this legend, Adam was around 30m tall). Even more pervasive is the belief that the formation is synonymous with the Rama Sethu (Rama's Bridge), an artificial floating bridge built, according to the *Ramayana*, by Hanuman and an army of monkeys in order to allow the Rama to cross from India to Sri Lanka and rescue his wife, Sita, from the clutches of Ravana. The association with Rama has led to ongoing speculation that the islets of Adam's Bridge are relics of a manmade construction, one built by layering coral and sandstone boulders on to a shallow bed of submarine sand, most likely between 3,500 and 6,000 years ago. This type of speculation reached its fantastic apex in 2007, when India's Bharatiya Janata Party, citing fresh NASA satellite images and carbon-dating results, pronounced not only that the Rama Sethu was manmade, but that it was constructed a full 1.7 million years ago – about 1.65 million years before the first humans arrived on Sri Lanka. In reality, however, Adam's Bridge is almost certainly a natural geological formation, effectively a giant tombolo that started to form when the two landmasses first drifted apart some 15–20 million years ago, and then kept growing to its unprecedented modern length of almost 30km. Nevertheless, the ancient legends might well have a factual foundation, as some geologists believe that Adam's Bridge did indeed form a complete and possibly walkable land link tying Sri Lanka to India until it was partially submerged by a landscape-altering cyclone in AD1480.

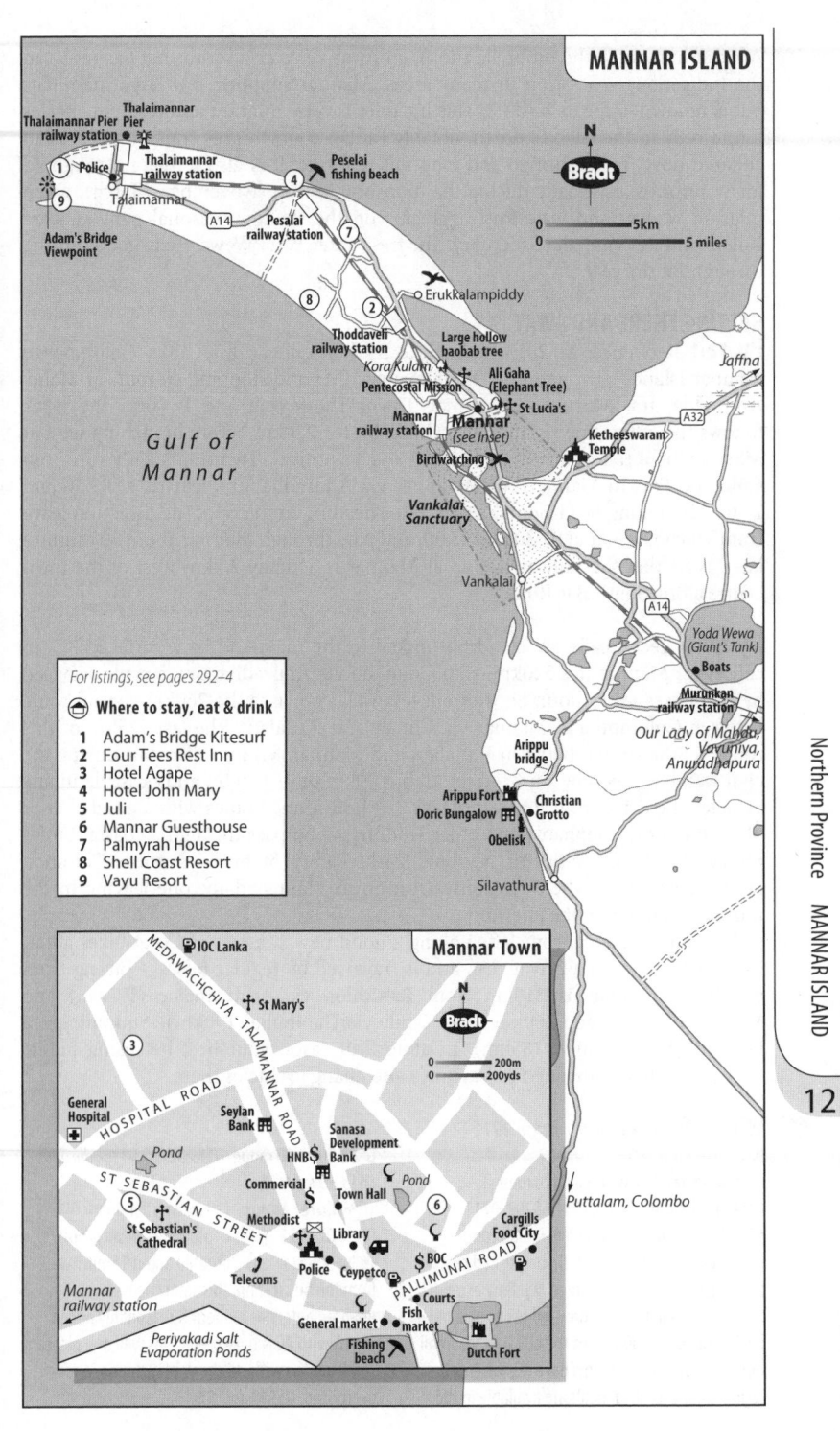

MANNAR ISLAND

N

Bradt

0 —————— 5km
0 —————— 5 miles

Thalaimannar Pier
railway station
Thalaimannar Pier
Police
Thalaimannar
railway station
Talaimannar
Adam's Bridge
Viewpoint
A14
Pesalai
fishing beach
Pesalai
railway station
Erukkalampiddy
Thoddaveli
railway station
Large hollow
baobab tree
Kora Kulam
Pentecostal Mission
Ali Gaha
(Elephant Tree)
Mannar
railway station
Mannar
(see inset)
St Lucia's
Birdwatching
Ketheeswaram
Temple
Jaffna
A32

*Gulf of
Mannar*

*Vankalai
Sanctuary*

Vankalai

A14

*Yoda Wewa
(Giant's Tank)*
Boats
Murunkan
railway station
*Our Lady of Madhu,
Vavuniya,
Anuradhapura*

Arippu
bridge
Arippu Fort
Doric Bungalow
Christian
Grotto
Obelisk
Silavathurai

For listings, see pages 292–4

Where to stay, eat & drink

1   Adam's Bridge Kitesurf
2   Four Tees Rest Inn
3   Hotel Agape
4   Hotel John Mary
5   Juli
6   Mannar Guesthouse
7   Palmyrah House
8   Shell Coast Resort
9   Vayu Resort

Mannar Town

N

Bradt

0 —————— 200m
0 —————— 200yds

IOC Lanka
St Mary's
MEDAWACHCHIYA - TALAIMANNAR ROAD
General
Hospital
HOSPITAL ROAD
Seylan
Bank
Sanasa
Development
Bank
Pond
HNB
Commercial
Town Hall
Pond
ST SEBASTIAN STREET
Methodist
Library
Mannar
railway station
St Sebastian's
Cathedral
Telecoms
Police
Ceypetco
BOC
PALLIMUNAI ROAD
Cargills
Food City
Puttalam, Colombo
Courts
Fish
market
General market
Fishing
beach
Dutch Fort
*Periyakadi Salt
Evaporation Ponds*

African implant is the umbrella thorn, an invasive Acacia scrub that has replaced the indigenous vegetation in many areas. Mannar supports few large mammals but is renowned for its birdlife. This includes several migrant and resident species found only in the island's north, notably Indian courser, grey francolin, Eurasian collared dove, black drongo and long-tailed shrike. It is also a major stronghold for waterbirds, especially during the monsoon season (November–March), when migrant waders and waterfowl aggregate on the shallow seasonal pans at Kora Kulam and the Vankalai Sanctuary. The freshwater Yoda Wewa offers good birding throughout the year.

GETTING THERE AND AWAY

By rail Reopened in 2013, a historic 335km railway line links Colombo to Mannar Island, terminating at Thalaimannar Pier and stopping *en route* at Maho, Anuradhapura, Murunkan, Mannar Town, Thoddaveli and Pesalai. The track follows the Jaffna line north out of Colombo for 230km before branching west at Madawachchi (between Anuradhapura and Vavuniya). Two trains daily run from Colombo Fort to Mannar/Thalaimannar via Anuradhapura, leaving at 08.50 and 19.00, and taking 8–11 hours, while trains heading in the opposite direction leave from Thalaimannar at 07.30 and 21.30, and pass through Mannar about 30 minutes later. Note that the railway station at Mannar is actually 2.5km west of the town centre along South Bar Road.

By road Technically an island but linked to the mainland by a surfaced 3.5km causeway, Mannar lies 320km from Colombo via Anuradhapura, a route serviced by two buses every hour. Shorter but less well known is the 260km coastal route between Colombo and Mannar via Chilaw and Puttalam. The last 125km of this route, ie: the stretch between Puttalam and Mannar, fell into disrepair during the civil war, but it is now surfaced for all but 30km of its length, and passable in any vehicle. The drive from Puttalam takes 2–3 hours, and comes with a good chance of encountering elephants and other wildlife as you pass through a coastal buffer reserve bordering Wilpattu National Park. Plenty of buses connect Colombo to Puttalam, from where two buses run on to Mannar daily, one leaving in the morning and one in the afternoon.

Mannar is 125km from Jaffna along a good new coastal road that takes about 2 hours to cover in a private car, and is traversed by regular buses. Coming from elsewhere, Mannar is 310km from Batticaloa via Trincomalee (175km) and Vavuniya (85km), and 260km from Kandy via Dambulla (190km), Anuradhapura (140km) and Vavuniya (85km). In almost all cases, your best bet using public transport is to bus through to Vavuniya and change vehicles there.

⌂ WHERE TO STAY *Map, page 291*
Mannar Town

⌂ **Mannar Guesthouse** (20 rooms)
Off Ayan Theatre Rd; m 0773 168202, 0711 527100; e mannarguesthouse@gmail.com; w mannarguesthouse.com. Distinguished by its fabulously garish purple, green & yellow exterior, this owner-managed 3-storey lodge lies on a quiet back road about 500m from the bus station. Small but adequately clean rooms have AC, fan & net, & good home-cooked meals are available in the

US$2.50–3.50 range. *US13.50/20.50 sgl/dbl, plus US$3.50 for AC.* **$**

⌂ **Hotel Agape** (10 rooms) Seminary Rd; ☏ 023 225 1678; e info@lovethestay.com; w lovethestay.com. Situated about 15mins' walk from the bus station, this smart new service-oriented hotel has modern & reasonably priced rooms with AC & flatscreen TV, as well as a pleasant small garden with children's playground. A touch overpriced. *US$40 dbl.* **$$**

The construction of a railway bridge connecting Mannar to its Indian counterpart, Dhanushkodi, was first mooted by the colonial authorities back in 1894. It would be another 20 years, however, before the railway reached Thalaimannar, on the northwest coast of Mannar, and in the end the Indo-Lanka Railway service opted to install a ferry service to Dhanushkodi rather than a bridge. For half a century thereafter, Thalaimannar thrived as the most important – indeed, only non-aerial – goods and passenger conduit between Sri Lanka and the continental mainland. Disaster struck in December 1964 in the form of a cyclone that transformed the flourishing Indian tourist resort of Dhanushkodi into a ghost town, swept a train into the sea, and claimed 1,800 lives in total. A reduced passenger ferry service resumed in 1967, but operations ceased entirely in 1984 when Mannar was captured by the LTTE, though the boat would remain in service for another ten years as a vessel for repatriating Indian citizens affected by the war. The railway also fell into disuse during the civil war, but a new branch line from Madawachchi reached Mannar Town in 2013 and Thalaimannar Pier in March 2015. Months later, the Indian Transport Minister submitted a proposal to the Asian Development Bank to build a 23km road bridge across the Palk Strait between Thalaimannar and Dhanushkodi. This proposal has reputedly been rejected by the Sri Lankan Minister of Highways, but even if it doesn't go ahead, it seems likely a ferry service will resume in the foreseeable future.

🏠 **Juli Hotel & Restaurant** (9 rooms) St Sebastian St; ☎ 023 225 1515; m 0767 605710; e info@julireception.com; w julireception.com. This 4-storey hotel opposite the church has modern rooms with TV, AC, writing desk & uninhibited use of purple paint. The restaurant serves the usual Sri Lankan dishes in the US$2–3 range. *US$20.50/27 sgl/dbl.* **$$**

Mannar Peninsula
Moderate

✳🏠 **Palmyrah House** (6 rooms, more under construction) Thalaimannar Rd, between Thoddaveli & Pesalai; ☎ 011 259 2363; m 0777 776065; e info@palmyrahhouse.com; w palmyrahhouse.com. This superb boutique hotel has a slightly uninspiring location in the countryside 12km northwest of Mannar Town, but compensation comes in the form of the spacious AC semi-suites with quality fittings & stylish furnishings, exceptional & imaginative Sri Lankan cuisine prepared in consultation with the guests, attractive 1st-floor balcony & large infinity pool. The lovely photographs that adorn the rooms & common areas reflect the owner's passion for birds, & there's an on-site naturalist to help visitors make the most of the many birding opportunities in & around Mannar. The enthusiastic management is also clued up on local historical sites. Good value. *From US$115/140 sgl/dbl FB.* **$$$$**

🏠 **Shell Coast Resort** (11 rooms) South Coast; m 0771 449062; e management@shellcoastresort.com; w shellcoastresort.com. The island's closest approximation to a resort has an isolated location among sandy dunes set a few hundred metres back from a rather scruffy beach about 18km from Mannar Town & 6.5km drive south of the Thalaimannar Rd. Accommodation is in stilted wood cabanas with AC, fan, net & wide wooden balconies, while amenities include a restaurant & well-kept but unattractive elevated swimming pool. Overall it's a pleasant enough set-up but could do with a greater management presence & a little TLC. *From US$45/50 sgl/dbl; add US$4 pp for b/fast & US$7 pp for other meals.* **$$$**

Moderate

🏠 **Vayu Resort** (10 rooms) Opposite Adam's Bridge; m 0773 686235; e vayu@kitesurfingmannar.com; w kitesurfingmannar.com. Scheduled to open in Jun 2017, this new lodge by the Kitesurfing Lanka team at Kalpitiya is named after a Sanskrit word meaning 'wind' & is aimed mainly at kitesurfers, though it also offers good birding, paddling, kayaking, cycling, yoga, massage & a great view across Adam's Bridge. The attractively rustic & naturally ventilated bungalows have nets & private veranda with ocean view. *€75/120 sgl/dbl inc all meals & use of kayaks & bicycles.* **$$$$**

🏠 **Adam's Bridge Kitesurf** Urumale beach; m 0777 461261, 0766 596959; e adamsbridgeresort@yahoo.com; w abkitesurf. com; ⏰ Jun–Sep only. This seasonal camp near Thalaimannar is aimed primarily at kitesurfers, who can expect ideal conditions over Jun–Sep, with steady 20–30-knot winds & waist-deep water up to a kilometre offshore in the islets at the east end of Adam's Bridge. Accommodation is in simple but comfortable wooden beach cabanas, & it also offers equipment hire & lessons. It lies about 3km from Thalaimannar along a side road running west from Thalaimannar police station. *From US$39pp FB.* **$$$**

Budget

🏠 **Four Tees Rest Inn** (12 rooms) Thoddaveli; ✆ 023 323 0008. Situated directly opposite Thoddaveli railway station & only 600m south of a bus stop at the junction with Thalaimannar Rd, this simple & friendly guesthouse stands in an agreeably overgrown garden roamed by pet guinea fowl. Spacious rooms come with fan & shower but no AC or hot water. Meals are by arrangement. *US$13.50 dbl.* **$**

🏠 **Hotel John Mary** (10 rooms) Pesalai Main St; ✆ 023 205 0160; m 0777 286610; e hoteljohnmary@gmail.com; w hotelmannarjm.com. The island's most westerly non-seasonal accommodation is this small hotel set on the south side of the Thalaimannar Rd, close to a bus stop, only 500m from Pesalai railway station & a similar distance from its fishing beach. AC rooms with nets are adequate but nothing to write home about, but the food – mains in the US$2–3 range, when available – is pretty good. *US$20.50 dbl.* **$**

✕ **WHERE TO EAT AND DRINK** *Map, page 291*
Aside from a few basic local eateries around the market area, the only options for eating out are the hotels listed above, with the Juli Hotel & Restaurant being the pick of the central options. There's also a Cargills Food City Supermarket on the Pallimunai Road about 500m east of the main intersection.

OTHER PRACTICALITIES All the hotels listed for Mannar town centre have free Wi-Fi. Several banks lie along the main road through Mannar Town, including a Commercial Bank with an ATM. There are branches of the Bank of Ceylon in Pesalai and Thalaimannar, but neither can be relied upon to draw money with a foreign card.

WHAT TO SEE AND DO Note that none of the sites described below charges an entrance fee, nor do they have meaningful opening hours. The area offers ideal kitesurfing conditions between June and September, and two lodges near Thalaimannar (pages 293–4) now cater specifically to this activity.

Mannar Town [map, page 291] The district's principal town, also called Mannar, supports a predominantly Tamil population of 35,000 at the island's southeastern extremity, where it is linked directly to the mainland by a rail bridge and causeway. Steeped in history, Mannar retains a rather isolated and sleepy character, with bicycles still outnumbering cars on the trunk roads, and donkeys – rare elsewhere in Sri Lanka – meandering slowly through the alleys. Mannar is also one of Sri Lanka's most Christian-dominated towns, as evidenced by several historic Catholic churches, but Muslims, Hindus and Buddhists are well represented too.

Mannar's oldest and most imposing building is the so-called **Dutch Fort**, a four-bastioned hulk enclosed by a moat on the waterfront only 100m east of the causeway. The fort in its present form is indeed a Dutch construction, dating to 1696, but it was expanded from a Portuguese fortification built in 1560, and was surrendered to the British in 1795. It is now a substantial ruin, but you can walk up to the ramparts for a view over the channel, and explore a number of roofless ground-floor rooms including what appears to be an old chapel adorned with 17th–19th-century memorial stones.

Other buildings of historical interest include: **St Mary's Church**, which dates to the 1860s and stands alongside the Thalaimannar Road 1.5km north of the fort; the larger, newer and more central **St Sebastian's Cathedral**, which now serves as the seat of the Catholic Diocese of Mannar; and the striking century-old Indian building that houses the **Sanasa Development Bank**. Other points of interest include the fish market, general market and fishing harbour, all of which lie to the immediate west of the causeway. About 500m further west, South Bar Road – which terminates at the railway station – leads for 2km past the **Periyakadi Salt Evaporation Ponds**, whose artificial shallows often attract an interesting selection of wading birds.

About 1km east of the fort, the suburb of **Pallimunai** (Place of the Church) is named after St Lucia's, a handsome Catholic house of worship built by the British in the early 20th century, but with altar and walls that incorporate parts of a much older Dutch edifice. Pallimunai's principal site of interest, now maintained by the church, is the ancient **Ali Gaha** (Elephant Tree), a 7m-high baobab whose evocative name refers to the gnarled grey bark's resemblance to a pachydermal hide. Thought to be more than 500 years old, this fantastical multi-limbed goblin warren also ranks as the girthiest tree in Sri Lanka, with a circumference of almost 20m.

Around Mannar Island [map, page 291] Two worthwhile birding sites lie on the southeast of the island close to Mannar Town. **Kora Kulam**, a shallow tidal and seasonal reservoir flanking the west side of the Thalaimannar Road 3.5km north of the causeway, frequently hosts large numbers of migrant ducks and waders, including greater flamingo, black-tailed godwit, grey plover and various sandpipers, between November and April. The other is the small town of **Erukkalampiddy**, which is flanked by an open lagoon and wide tidal flats, and lies 1.5km from the Thalaimannar Road along an unsignposted track running north at Thoddaveli. Further northwest, about 18km from Mannar Town, the Thalaimannar Road runs through the small town of **Pesalai**, known for its large Catholic church and long lively fishing beach, which tends to be busiest between 06.00 and 09.00.

Mannar Island's western railhead since the track here reopened in 2015, **Thalaimannar Pier** has an attractive seaside location dominated by the ruined ferry terminal and the long wooden pier from which boats to India used to – and may once again soon – depart. A major landmark on the sandy beach below the pier is **Thalaimannar Lighthouse**, which dates back to 1915.

About 4km southwest of Thalaimannar as the crow flies, Urumale beach marks the rather indistinct spot where Mannar Island gives way to islets and sandbars that comprise **Adam's Bridge** (see box, page 290). The navy base at Thalaimannar can arrange boat trips to Adam's Bridge but, at the time of writing, the service is offered only to Sri Lanka residents. During the kitesurfing season (June–September) it can also be accessed from Adam's Bridge Kitesurf (see opposite). Otherwise, the best view of the island chain is obtained from a chunk of undeveloped private land owned by the same people as Palmyrah House. To get there, follow the Thalaimannar Road as far as Thalaimannar police station, where you need to turn left on to a motorable track, then left again after 2.5km, from where it's another 1.5km to the beach. Best to drop in at Palmyrah House to obtain permission before heading this way.

Getting around the island is straightforward. In addition to the twice-daily train service between Mannar and Thalaimannar, two or three buses hourly run back and forth in either direction, stopping at Thoddaveli and Pesalai, or indeed at any other landmark *en route*. The island is small enough that exploring by tuktuk wouldn't be prohibitively expensive.

Ketheeswaram Temple [map, page 291] Situated on the mainland coast

at Manthai, less than 5km from Mannar as the crow flies, Ketheeswaram (or Ketisvaram) is one of Sri Lanka's five oldest and most important Shiva Temples, pre-dating the arrival of Buddhism 2,400 years ago. In 1575, the original temple was destroyed by the Portuguese, who then shipped its component stones across the channel to be used in the construction of Mannar Fort. The shrine at Ketheeswaram lay dormant from then until 1894, when its ancient lingam was rediscovered and incorporated into a new temple built in 1903. Despite the site's antiquity and significance to local Hindus, the modern temple – which underwent major renovations in 2016 – is of limited architectural interest, though it does incorporate several impressively tall gopurams decorated in typically ornate style. To get to Ketheeswaram from Mannar, cross the causeway to the mainland, then follow the northern coastal road towards Jaffna for 4.3km until you see the temple signposted to the left. It's about 1.2km from this junction to the temple.

Vankalai Sanctuary [map, page 291] Gazetted in 2008 and listed as a Ramsar

wetland two years later, the Vankalai Sanctuary protects 48km^2 of tidal flats, seasonal salt pans, thorny scrub and other coastal habitats flanking the open waters of the shallow channel that separates Mannar from the Sri Lankan mainland. It is an important natural fishery, but was mainly set aside for its prolific birdlife, which numbers around 150 different species. Vankalai is a far more seasonal site than the freshwater Yoda Wewa (see opposite), and it protects a somewhat different assemblage of bird species, with migrant waders and marine specialists generally more abundant than waterfowl. Bird activity peaks during the wet season (October–April), when it hosts up to 50,000 greater flamingos, along with large numbers of migrant waders such as black-tailed godwit, pied avocet, crab plover, Pacific golden plover, Eurasian oystercatcher and lesser sandplover. Large flocks of overwintering Eurasian widgeon and Northern pintail are also sometimes present when conditions are suitable. Marine species commonly seen in the reserve include lesser crested, great crested, little and Caspian tern. Away from the water, the Vankalai Sanctuary is also a good place to look for non-aquatic 'northern specials' such as grey francolin, black drongo and long-tailed shrike.

The best way to explore the wetland from Mannar Town – whether by car, tuktuk, bike or on foot – is to take the causeway across to the mainland, then after about 1km turn right on to the Puttalam Road and follow it southeast through the sanctuary for about 5km until you reach the coastal village of Vankalai. Here, you can turn left on to another quiet road that runs northeast through the sanctuary to connect with the Mannar–Vavuniya Road about 6km east of the causeway. Using public transport, the buses that travel between Mannar and Arippu every 30 minutes could drop or pick you up pretty much anywhere along the 5km road between the causeway and Vankalai.

The two roads described above are flanked by wetlands and usually offer superb birding during the wet season. Birding is rather indifferent during the dry season, when the wetlands recede, but it might still be worth stopping at the designated 'birdwatching facility' on the Mannar Causeway to scan the island-strewn channel and see what's around. Either way, binoculars are all but essential and a scope will be useful to help identify more distant waders.

The Doric Bungalow and Arippu Fort [map, page 291] Perched on a low coastal cliff on the mainland 30km south of Mannar, the Doric Bungalow was built in 1804 as a residence from where Governor North could monitor the lucrative pearl-diving industry that then sustained this part of the coast. Reverend James Gardiner, who visited the double-storey house three years after its construction, described it as 'undoubtedly the most beautiful building on the island, and the only one planned according to the order of architecture'. Certainly, it was unique among colonial buildings of that vintage, with a marble-like exterior of lime plaster made from burnt oyster shells, and an upper floor supported by columns that mimic the Doric architectural style of ancient Greece. Nothing remains of the columns or upper floor today, but the ground floor plan remains reasonably clear, though the exposed location means it is only a matter of time before it too will crumble to the ground.

Two other structures stand close to the Doric Bungalow. On the opposite side of the road is a stone grotto built by Catholic Tamils housed in a refugee camp here over 2008–13. Only 100m further south stands a tall concrete clifftop obelisk whose antiquity and purpose are open to conjecture; some say it is a 19th-century lighthouse, but more likely perhaps that it's another relic of the Tamil refugee camp.

About 1.5km north of the Doric Bungalow, the overgrown ruins of the two-bastion Arippu Fort can still be seen in the village of the same name. Originally built by the Portuguese, Arippu Fort was captured by the Dutch in 1658, and during the British colonial era it served as a bungalow for officers supervising the local pearl-diving industry before being converted to a resthouse. The fort's main claim to historical fame is that it is where Robert Knox – the sailor whose remarkable *An Historical Relation of the Island Ceylon* not only is a unique document of Kandyan-era Sri Lanka, but also inspired Daniel Defoe's novel *Robinson Crusoe* – arrived at the coast in 1679, having walked here via Anuradhapura after escaping from 19 years in captivity under King Rajasinha II of Kandy.

In a private car, allow 45 minutes to drive from Mannar to Arippu and the Doric Bungalow, crossing the causeway then following the main road to Puttalam south through Vankalai. Both sites are well signposted. Using public transport, buses run between Mannar and the village of Arippu every 30 minutes. Arippu Fort is only 2 minutes' walk west of the main road through the village, while the Doric Bungalow lies about 15 minutes' walk further south.

Yoda Wewa (Giant's Tank) [map, page 291] Abutting the small town of Murunkan 20km east of Mannar, Yoda Wewa (also known as Giant's Tank, and by the Tamil name Kattukarai Kulam) is a large irrigation reservoir constructed in the 5th century by King Dhatusena, rebuilt in the 12th century by King Parakramabahu I, and most recently restored under the colonial administration over 1888–1902. Centrepiece of the 45km^2 Giant's Tank Bird Sanctuary, the roughly circular Yoda Wewa, its surface punctuated by reed beds, semi-submerged trees and drifting islands of floating vegetation, supports a remarkable diversity and density of aquatic birds. At any time of year, a brief scan across the lake with binoculars might yield a couple of dozen species, among them purple swamphen, pheasant-tailed jacana, white-bellied sea-eagle, white-winged tern and spot-billed pelican. Between November and April, the lake is also a magnet for migrant waterfowl such as Indian spot-billed duck, garganey, Eurasian widgeon and northern pintail.

The characteristic tree of northern Sri Lanka, the Asian palmyrah (*Borassus flabellifer*) is a robust fan-crowned palm that takes up to 20 years to reach maturity, attains maximum height of around 30m, and can live for longer than a century. Literally millions of palmyrahs are cultivated throughout Jaffna and Mannar districts, thriving on the parched sandy soil where most other trees would wilt. Known as *tal gaha* in Sinhala or *panay* in Tamil, the palmyrah is venerated locally as the Tree of Life and dedicated to the elephant-headed deity Ganesh. The palm's most commercially important product is its sap, which is obtained between January and August by tapping the tip of the flower head. The sap can be served fresh as a sweetish non-alcoholic drink called sweet toddy, but it is also sometimes subjected to an evaporative process to create jaggery (a sugar-like block eaten with unsweetened tea), or fermented to make a strong spirit known locally as *raa*. No part of the tree is wasted. The timber, unusually hard for a palm, and resistant to termite infestations, is good for house construction. The average tree produces around 300 fruits annually: large red- or black-husked coconut lookalikes that protect a trio of socket-like compartments whose tasty contents – a translucent jelly-textured flesh called nongu or ice-apple – finger-scoop neatly into the mouth. The leathery fan-like leaves make for excellent roofing, and are also used to weave mats and baskets. In bygone times, the palmyrah even provided the main material for manuscripts in many parts of India and Sri Lanka, where the mature leaves would be boiled in water and turmeric, then sun-dried and cut to size, before they were inscribed upon with a stylus.

Murunkan is about 30 minutes' drive from Mannar. Any bus heading between Mannar and Vavuniya Road can drop you, and there's also a railway station. Coming from Mannar, the reservoir runs practically alongside the main road and railway line for 3km as you approach Murunkan, hidden from view by its tall grassy bund; if in doubt, hop out at the Irrigation Department office on its southeastern shore and walk along the bund from there. If you want to head out on to the water for a couple of hours, negotiate a fee with one of the fishermen whose boats line the bund about 1km west of the Irrigation Department.

Our Lady of Madhu Shrine [map, page 288] Graced by a visit from Pope Francis in January 2015, Madhu is Sri Lanka's oldest and holiest Catholic shrine, established in 1670 by 20 Catholic Tamil families who fled inland from Manthai (opposite Mannar) to escape persecution by the Protestant Dutch. The refugees carried with them a small Madonna-and-Child statue revered for its powerful healing powers, and this became the focal point of a shrine at their new home in Madhu. The current church was built in the 1870s and consecrated in 1944, when the original wood altar was reworked in marble. During the civil war, Madhu was designated as a UNHCR demilitarised zone that housed to up to 15,000 refugees, most of them displaced Catholic Tamils. In November 1999, an LTTE mortar attack on Madhu killed 40 refugees and injured another 60.

Madhu can be reached along a surfaced 12km feeder road that branches north from the Vavuniya Road about 35km inland of the Mannar Causeway. The most interesting time to visit is on major Catholic holidays, particularly Assumption Day (15 August), when up to 500,000 Catholic pilgrims gather here to commemorate Mary's ascent to heaven.

The capital of Northern Province, Jaffna is the main historic focal point of Sri Lanka's Tamil population, and the country's ninth-largest city, supporting a predominantly Hindu population of around 90,000. Historically, politically and culturally, this most northerly outlier of Sri Lanka is something of a land apart, owing in part to its location on the Jaffna Peninsula, a 1,000km² not-quite-island connected to the rest of the country by two road causeways, one entirely artificial while the other crosses a narrow natural isthmus called the Elephant Pass. Jaffna's isolation was all but total between 1986 and 1995, when it was the main stronghold of the secessionist LTTE. The physical destruction and social disruption wrought over two decades of civil war should not be underestimated but, following the defeat of the LTTE in 2009, the once-beleaguered city has recovered with admirable speed and tenacity, thanks partly to investment associated with a reversal of the Tamil diaspora to wealthier countries in Europe, North America and elsewhere.

Unlike most Sri Lankan towns with a comparable population, Jaffna has the bustling, built-up feel of a proper city. Lined with medium-rise buildings, the claustrophobic grid of narrow roads that cuts through the compact commercial centre spills over with chaotic activity: horn-blasting cars and tuktuks, weaving bicycles and dilly-dallying pedestrians all mingle with a bouquet of spicy aromas and blasting Bollywood tunes, which – together with the proliferation of Hindu temples, and occasional traffic-defying cow on urban walkabout – underscore Jaffna's cultural affiliation with the Indian state of Tamil Nadu, only 50km distant on the opposite side of the Palk Strait. Furthermore, for all the hardships it has endured, central Jaffna today feels adamantly alive and very friendly, modestly prosperous even, while the leafy avenues that extend eastward to the historic suburbs of Nallur and Chandikuli exude an aura of unexpected gentility. For obvious reasons, Jaffna was off-limits to foreign travel throughout the civil war, and while amenities and access have improved greatly over the intervening years (not least with the resumption of train services from Colombo in 2014), it still feels like a destination suited primarily to inquisitive and adaptable travellers. That said, the city and surrounding peninsula are dotted with venerable temples and other attention-worthy historical sites, while the readily accessible islands of the nearby Jaffna Archipelago offer an opportunity for some genuinely off-the-beaten-track exploration.

HISTORY Archaeological excavations undertaken at Kantharodai and elsewhere suggest that Jaffna supported several ports with international trade connections as early as 2000BC. Little is known about the inhabitants of the peninsula at that time, but the epic *Mahavamsa* indicates it was home to the cobra-worshipping Naga people. Several Hindu shrines dotted around the peninsula reputedly date to around this time, most notably the pre-Buddhist Shiva temple at Naguleswaram. The Jaffna Peninsula probably fell into the realm of Anuradhapura for much of the period between the 4th century BC and 11th century AD, but at other times it evidently supported short-lived self-governing Tamil polities. Hindu appears to have remained the dominant religion throughout, but Jaffna was evidently the conduit through which Buddhism – and the sacred Bo Tree – arrived in Sri Lanka in the mid 3rd century BC.

The post-Anuradhapura history of Jaffna is informed by its relative proximity to India and the much larger distance that divides it from the likes of Polonnaruwa, Kandy and Colombo. In the early 13th century, the Aryacakravarti Dynasty, an offshoot of the Pandyan Empire of South India, established the independent

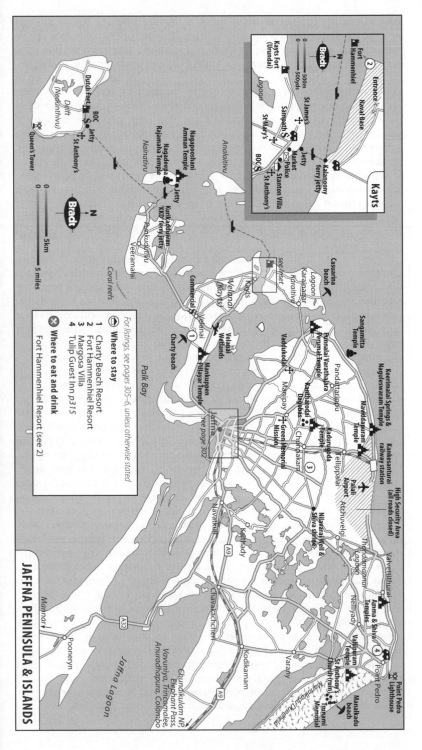

kingdom of Yalpanam-Puttanam (a Tamil name later bastardised to Jaffnapatnam). Based out of their capital at Nallur (now a suburb of Jaffna), a succession of Aryacakravarti kings held sway over northern Sri Lanka for more than three centuries, a period during which many new Hindu temples were built on the peninsula, and international trade flourished, as did the arts and literature.

The first portent of change occurred in 1560, when Portugal launched a naval attack on Jaffna. The motivation for the attack was ostensibly religious, but its primary result was the annexation of Mannar and its legendarily productive pearl gardens to Portugal's existing Asian territories. Having secured Mannar, Portugal then sought to take control of Jaffna and its lucrative export trade in elephants. In 1591, the Portuguese executed the King of Jaffna and installed a client monarch in his place. Then, in 1619, two years after the death of the chosen monarch by natural causes, the Portuguese dispatched a 5,000-strong land force to Jaffna, captured the city, and shipped the youthful king and all other male members of the royal family to Goa, where the former was executed, and the remainder were spared on condition they took a vow of celibacy to became Catholic monks.

The Portuguese immediately started work on the construction of Jaffna Fort, which enabled them to protect their new acquisition from a succession of raids launched by Tamil leaders from South India. A religious purge led to the destruction of the peninsula's most venerable Hindu temples, including Nallur and Naguleswaram, while Portuguese merchants took over the elephant trade, which flowed through the island-bound port of Kayts. The Portuguese occupation ended in 1658, following a three-month siege by the Dutch VOC, who rebuilt and expanded the battle-scarred fort. The Protestant Dutch proved to be more tolerant than their Catholic predecessors: Hindu temples were rebuilt, local involvement in trade was encouraged, and the surrounding countryside thrived as a centre of agriculture for export. The British took over in 1796, and over the course of the next century the city took its modern shape, as missionaries extended their activities by providing a good selection of schools, as well as opening up land communications. By 1891, when the first national census was taken, Jaffna was the second-largest town on the island, with a population of 43,000. The Jaffna Peninsula assumed the status of a northern gateway to the country following the arrival of the railway line from Colombo in 1905.

Jaffna stood at the forefront of the post-independence Tamil nationalist movement. Mounting Tamil–Sinhalese tension led to the LTTE assassination of the city's mayor, Alfred Duraiappah, in 1975, and the razing of Jaffna Public Library and its collection of almost 100,000 (predominantly Tamil) manuscripts by a Sinhalese mob in 1981. When war was formally declared in 1983, the Sri Lankan military were practically confined to Jaffna Fort, while the LTTE held sway over the rest of the city. Three years later, the military was forced to withdraw from Jaffna completely. In 1987, an Indian Peace Keeping Force attempted to wrest control of the city, but succeeded only in killing hundreds of civilians before they too were forced to withdraw. Only in 1995 was the LTTE ousted from Jaffna, following a 50-day siege involving 10,000 government troops. Although this decisive victory marked the beginning of Jaffna's post-war recovery, the battle-scarred city remained tense and isolated until the final defeat of the LTTE in 2009.

GETTING THERE AND AWAY

By air Helitours (w *helitours.lk*) flies thrice-weekly between Colombo (Ratmalana), Trincomalee and Palali (also spelt Palaly) airport in the eponymous naval base 15km north of central Jaffna. Flights are on Monday, Wednesday and Friday, and cost around US$100 one way coming from Colombo or US$55 from

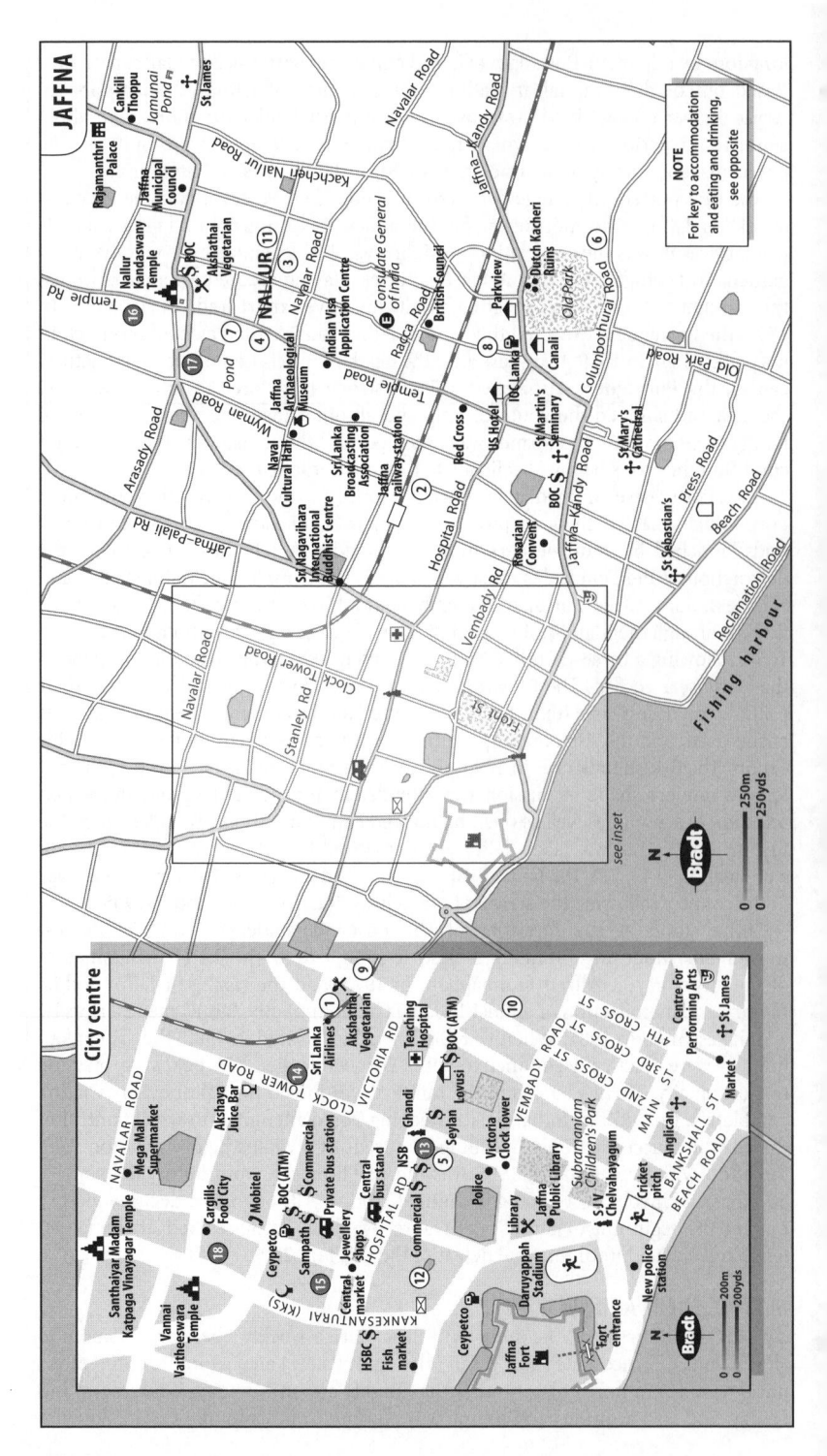

JAFFNA

Cankili Thoppu
Jamunai Pond
St James
Rajamanthri Palace
Jaffna Municipal Council
Nallur Kandaswamy Temple
Temple Rd
BOC
Akshathai Vegetarian
NALLUR (11)
Kachcheri Nallur Road
Navalar Road
16
17
Wyman Road
Nallur Pond
4
1
7
Jaffna Archaeological Museum
Navalar Road
Indian Visa Application Centre
3
Consulate General of India
Radca Road
British Council
Parkview
Dutch Kacheri Ruins
6
Old Park
Arasady Road
Jaffna–Palali Rd
Sri Nagavihara International Buddhist Centre
Naval Cultural Hall
Sri Lanka Broadcasting Association
Jaffna railway station
2
Temple Road
Red Cross
US Hotel
8
IO Lanka
Canali
Columbothurai Road
Old Park Road
Hospital Road
Rosarian Convent
BOC
St Martin's Seminary
PIO Road
St Mary's Cathedral
Navalar Road
Stanley Rd
Clock Tower Road
Vembady Rd
Front St
Jaffna–Kandy Road
St Sebastian's
Press Road
Beach Road
Reclamation Road
f i s h i n g   h a r b o u r
see inset
N
Bradt
0   250m
0   250yds

NOTE
For key to accommodation and eating and drinking, see opposite.

City centre

Santhaiyar Madam Katpaga Vinayagar Temple
NAVALAR ROAD
Mega Mall Supermarket
18
Cargills Food City
Akshaya Juice Bar
Alshaya
Mobitel
CLOCK TOWER ROAD
Sri Lanka Airlines
1
9
Akshathai Vegetarian
Teaching Hospital
Vannai Vaitheeswara Temple
Ceypetco
BOC (ATM)
Commercial
Sampath
14
VICTORIA RD
BOC (ATM)
Jewellery shops
Central bus station
Private bus station
Ghandi
5
B
Seylan
Lovusi
10
HSBC
Central market
Fish market
KANKESANTURAI (KKS)
HOSPITAL RD
NSB
Commercial
12
Victoria Clock Tower
Police
Library
Jaffna Public Library
Subramaniam Children's Park
VEMBADY ROAD
3RD CROSS ST
4TH CROSS ST
2ND CROSS ST
MAIN ST
Anglican
SJV Chelvahayagum
BANKSHALL ST
Centre For Performing Arts
St James
Market
Ceypetco
Daruyappah Stadium
Jaffna Fort
Fort entrance
New police station
Cricket pitch
BEACH ROAD
N
Bradt
0   200m
0   200yds

302

Trincomalee. The airline operates a free shuttle bus between the airport and central Jaffna.

By rail The 400km railway line from Colombo Fort to Jaffna, via Maho, Anuradhapura and Madawachchi (for Mannar Island), originally opened in 1902, closed in 1990 due to the war, and resumed operations in 2014. Far and away the most pleasant way to travel to Jaffna, the track is now serviced by four trains daily, the most popular being the nippy air-conditioned intercity express that takes around 7 hours in either direction, leaving Colombo Fort at 05.45 or Jaffna at 06.10. This and all other trains between Colombo and Jaffna stop at Anuradhapura to pick up and drop passengers. Jaffna railway station is conveniently located on the northeastern verge of the city centre, but trains stop there only for a few minutes, as the terminus for the line is actually Kankesanturai (KKS) station on the coast 15km to the north.

By road Allow 8–10 hours to drive between Colombo and Jaffna, whether you use the 365km coastal road through Chilaw (320km), Puttalam (250km) and Mannar (120km), or the 400km inland route through Kurunegala (305km), Anuradhapura (200km) and Vavuniya (145km). The inland route, though longer, is generally quicker as the roads are in better shape. However, the less-used coastal road is also now in good condition, with the exception of a short stretch of dirt between Puttalam and Mannar, and can be covered in any vehicle. Coming from elsewhere, Jaffna lies 320km north of Kandy via Dambulla (250km), Anuradhapura and Vavuniya, and 360km from Batticaloa via Trincomalee (230km) and Vavuniya.

Using public transport, around a dozen private coaches cover this route daily, as do a similar number of air-conditioned private buses, which generally run overnight and leave Colombo from Galle Road near Wellawaya Market, and from Jaffna on the south side of Hospital Road, more or less opposite the private bus station. Recommended operators include PPT Express (☎ *011 236 4999;* m *0775 755175;* e *info@ppttravel.com;* w *ppttravel.com*) and Avro (m *0774 541341*). At least ten buses daily connect Jaffna directly to each of Mannar, Vavuniya, Trincomalee and Kandy, and there's even one early morning bus to Batticaloa. If you can't find direct transport to your destination of choice, then catch the next bus heading to or passing through Vavuniya and change over there.

A good network of buses connects Jaffna to Point Pedro, Keerimalai and most other places of interest on the peninsula, as well as to the islands of Velani (Kayts), Punkudutivu and Karaitivu, all of which are linked to the mainland by a causeway. On most of these routes, buses leave every 15–20 minutes.

WHERE TO STAY *Map, opposite, unless otherwise stated*
Accommodation is generally disappointing by comparison with other parts of Sri Lanka, but the situation is improving as the war recedes deeper into history. The

12

one standout is the spanking new Jetwing Jaffna, which offers reasonably priced upmarket accommodation in the heart of the city centre. Most other places listed are rather hit and miss and would be borderline inclusions were they situated elsewhere in the country. Those with a generous budget and private transport might want to consider a pair of more individualistic out-of-town options: stylish Margosa Villa and historic Fort Hammenhiel Resort.

Jaffna city
Upmarket

✻ 🏠 **Jetwing Jaffna** (55 rooms) Mahatma Gandhi Rd; 📞 021 221 5571; e resv.jaffna@jetwinghotels.com; w jetwinghotels.com. Opened in 2016, this central high-rise is by far the smartest hotel in Jaffna, with a classy 2nd-floor restaurant serving a cosmopolitan selection of Western & Asian dishes (including Jaffna crab curry) & 8th-floor bar offering great views over the city centre & ocean. The airy & attractive rooms are characterised by crisp contemporary lines, an oriental touch to the décor & quality furnishings & fittings. All rooms come with AC, king-size bed, large cable TV, coffee-/tea-making facilities, fridge, safe, free Wi-Fi, large modern bathrooms & glass door opening out to a private balcony. Ask for a room with a fort view. The helpful front desk can arrange tours around the Jaffna Peninsula. *From US$137 dbl B&B.* **$$$$**

Moderate

🏠 **Taprospa Palm Leaves** (7 rooms) 2nd Cross St; 📞 011 438 0707; m 0773 095516; e info@taprospa.com; w taprospapalmleaves.bookings.lk. Probably the pick in this range, not so much because it's inherently superior to anything below, but because it represents better value, this villa-like hotel is set around a courtyard swimming pool & has attractive rooms with AC, fan, cable TV, fridge, wooden floors & queen-size bed. A little frayed at the edges but fine at the price. *US$45/50 sgl/dbl B&B.* **$$$**

🏠 **Jaffna Heritage Hotel** (17 rooms) Temple Rd; 📞 021 222 2424; m 0772 514986; e gmstpholdingsleisure@gmail.com; w jaffnaheritage.com/jaffnahotel. Set in a small palm-shaded garden a short walk south of Nallur Temple, this place has pleasant & quite stylish rooms with AC, fan, cable TV, treated concrete floor, darkwood furniture & colourful batik hangings. A good unlicensed South Indian vegetarian restaurant is attached. The swimming pool, though small, is welcome in this climate. *US$68/89 sgl/dbl, plus US$7 pp b/fast, other meals cost around US$10.* **$$$$**

🏠 **Tilko Jaffna City Hotel** (39 rooms) KKS Rd; 📞 021 222 5969; m 0702 502505; e info@cityhoteljaffna.com; w cityhoteljaffna.com. This pioneering central high-rise, set in an unexpectedly luxuriant garden close to the fort & market, was the first proper hotel built in the city centre after the war. The semi-suites with AC & fan are looking a little timeworn & the rather garish décor doesn't help. It has a reasonably priced bar & rather institutional restaurant serving Chinese, Indian & Western dishes in the US$3–5 range. Acceptable value. *US$58/72/82 sgl/dbl/trpl B&B.* **$$$**

Budget

🏠 **Hotel Lux Etoiles** (24 rooms) Chetty Ln; 📞 021 222 3966; e reserve.luxetoiles@yahoo.com. This modern hotel with enthusiastic staff feels more on the ball than most in Jaffna, which isn't saying a lot. Amenities include a large but ugly 2m-deep swimming pool & a licensed restaurant serving good seafood, pizzas & traditional Jaffna cuisine in the US$5–7 range. The comfortable rooms all come with AC, cable TV, Wi-Fi & combined tub/shower. A new wing with luxury rooms & apartments is under construction. *US$28/43 standard/superior dbl, US$4 pp b/fast.* **$$**

🏠 **Kais Guesthouse** (3 rooms) Colombothurai Rd; 📞 021 222 7229/7897; m 0773 024234; w kaisguesthouse.com. If you don't mind the suburban location 2km east of the city centre, this homestay-type set-up is one of the town's most appealing budget options. The comfortable rooms have AC, nets & good Wi-Fi, the excellent home-cooked Jaffna cuisine is served on a small breezy rooftop, & other communal areas include a lounge with TV & small leafy garden. *US$27 dbl.* **$$**

🏠 **Station Garden Motel** (10 rooms) Station Rd; 📞 021 221 7770; m 0772 561990; e stationgardenmotel@gmail.com. Boasting a conveniently central location close to the railway station, this new & modern-looking hotel isn't exactly brimming with character, but it's possibly the only budget option in Jaffna where standards of cleanliness border on the clinical. The tall-ceilinged rooms come with AC, fan, cable TV, tea-/coffee-making facilities & fridge. The AC restaurant is OK but service is slow. *US$31–8 dbl.* **$$**

🏠 **Morgan's Guesthouse** (4 rooms) Temple Rd; 📞 021 222 3666; m 0776 351719. Set in a characterful villa with a neat garden & chilled-out balcony space near Nallur Temple, this high-profile backpackers' haunt (a former UN Guesthouse) absolutely looks the part, but the actuality is more hit & miss, depending largely on the mood of the omnipresent management. Simple rooms with AC & fan are clean & have fitted nets. Local meals & chilled beers & juices are served. Overpriced but negotiable. *US$27/35 sgl/dbl, plus US$3 pp b/fast.* **$$**

🏠 **Green Grass Hotel** (52 rooms) Aseervatham Ln, off Hospital Rd; 📞 021 222 4385; e greengrassjaffna@gmail.com; w jaffnagreengrass.com. Greatly expanded since it opened in 2009, this warren-like hotel adjacent to the railway station makes few concessions to aesthetics, but the functional AC rooms are reasonably priced, amenities include a swimming pool & decent garden restaurant & bar, & the location is usefully central. *US$20/23 sgl/dbl in old wing, US$27/30 in the (far superior) new wing.* **$–$$**

Shoestring

🏠 **Thinakkural Rest House** (13 rooms) Chetty Ln; 📞 021 222 6476. Set in a quiet suburban garden a couple of doors down from Lux Etoiles, this standout cheapie has spacious clean rooms with TV & net. *US$15 fan-only dbl using communal showers, US$22 en-suite dbl with AC & large bathroom.* **$**

🏠 **Sarras Guesthouse** (6 rooms) Somasundaram Av; 📞 021 567 4040; m 0772 377463, 0777 756904; e jaffnasarras@gmail.com; w jaffnasarras.lk. Set in a fabulously rambling & rundown double-storey villa of some antiquity, this family-managed lodge has a peaceful setting in a lovely garden 2km east of the city centre. Rooms are shabby but spacious & clean, & come with AC, fans & nets. Decent value. *US$17 dbl, plus US$3.50 for AC.* **$**

🏠 **Cosy Hotel** (8 rooms) Stanley Rd; 📞 021 222 7100. Better known for its ground-floor restaurant, this small hotel around the corner from the railway station charges rock-bottom prices for smallish & slightly musty rooms with fan, Wi-Fi & optional AC. *US$11/18 sgl/dbl, plus US$3.50 for AC.* **$**

Out of town
Upmarket

🏠 **Margosa Villa** [map, page 300] (6 rooms) Chunnakam, 12km north of city centre; m 0773 788795; e fitsmargosa@fitsair.com; 📘 FitsMargosaJaffna. The only true boutique hotel in the vicinity of Jaffna is this restored 19th-century villa set in a large garden, ideally situated for those with private transport to explore the peninsula. Lovingly decorated AC rooms have brushed cement floors & cement-block beds, & some come with open-roofed bathrooms. Delicious traditional Sri Lankan cuisine (not too spicy for tourists unless requested) is served on the shady courtyard balcony. No alcohol is served but you can bring your own. Well priced. *US$110/123 sgl/dbl B&B.* **$$$$**

🏠 **Fort Hammenhiel Resort** [map, page 300] (4 rooms) Karaitivu Island; 📞 011 381 8215/6; e forthammenhielresort@gmail.com; w forthammenhielresort.lk. Possibly Sri Lanka's most unusual hotel, this Navy-owned resort occupies the eponymous 335-year-old fort, which stands on a tiny island in the narrow channel that divides Karaitivu and Velanai (Kayts) islands. Luxury suites have AC, cable TV, minibar & 24hr room service & the sense of exclusivity is underscored by the restriction on day visitors to the resort crossing over to the actual fort. Overnight guests are ferried across by motorboat from the Fort Hammenhiel Naval Base, which stands on the southern end of Karaitivu Island, 21km from Jaffna by road & causeway. An inexpensive & scenically located licensed restaurant is attached. *US$132 dbl B&B.* **$$$$**

Budget

🏠 **Charty Beach Resort** [map, page 300] (10 rooms) Charty beach, Velanai Island; 📞 021 222 5969; m 0702 502505; e info@cityhoteljaffna. com. The only beach resort near Jaffna, this doesn't quite hold together. Set in palm-shaded grounds opposite the breach, the spacious bungalows come with AC, fan, cable TV & leather seating, but the bathrooms are grotty & it lacks for any winning decorative touches. An undistinguished restaurant is attached. No alcohol. *Overpriced at US$40 dbl.* **$$**

In the town centre, aside from the standalone restaurants listed below, standout hotel restaurants include the Lux Etoiles for its excellent pizzas and Jaffna cuisine, the second-floor restaurant at the Jetwing Jaffna for its stylish interior and sophisticated cosmopolitan menu, and the Green Grass for its outdoor seating, cheap beers and down-to-earth vibe.

Town centre

Medium to expensive

✳ 🍴 **Cosy Restaurant** Stanley Rd; ☎ 021 222 7100; ⏰ 11.00–23.00. The fan-cooled courtyard restaurant at the otherwise indifferent Cosy Hotel is about the only central budget eatery to serve inexpensive beer. Most dishes (Indian, Sri Lankan & Chinese) are in the $$ range, but the deliciously spiced tandoor chicken (evenings only) is $$$.

🍴 **Cargills Square Food Court** Mahatma Ghandi Rd; ⏰ 08.00–22.00. Jaffna's most Westernised place to eat is this slick 2nd-floor food court complete with the city's only KFC, a branch of Lux Etoiles with a pizza-dominated menu & a branch of Rio Ice-Cream. $$–$$$

Cheap to medium

✳🍴 **Malayan Café** Ponnampalam Rd; ☎ 021 222 2373; ⏰ 07.00–21.30. The oldest & most characterful eatery in central Jaffna was established as the Ceylon Café back in 1951. It retains a gloriously time-warped feel with its wood-panelled walls, marble tables & memorabilia. Eaten without cutlery off a banana leaf, the vegetarian cuisine – more South Indian than Malayan – seldom disappoints & nothing costs much more than US$1. Specialities include filled thosai pancakes, dumpling-like deep-fried vadai, & kottu made not from roti but from string hoppers. $

🍴 **Mangos** Off Temple Rd; ☎ 021 222 8924; m 0777 661083; ⏰ 08.30–22.00. This popular South Indian vegetarian restaurant a short distance north of Nallur Temple is renowned for its lunchtime thalis & birianis, but serves a varied

selection of other mains. The wooden seating below a palm-leaf roof has a nice outdoor feel, & it's also good for juices & shakes. $

🍴 **Vishnu Bhavan** KKS Rd; m 0777 404089; ⏰ 07.00–22.00. Busy fan-cooled vegetarian restaurant specialising in pothu kottu. $

Ice cream parlours

🍴 **Lingam Ice-Cream** Clock Tower Rd; ☎ 021 222 7327; ⏰ 08.30–21.30. This Jaffna institution was founded in 1971 &, though best known for its delicious sundaes, also serves good coffee, great juice & a selection of cakes & savoury snacks. Most items cost US$1 or under. $

🍴 **Rio Ice-Cream** Point Pedro Rd; ☎ 021 222 7224; ⏰ 08.30–22.30. Situated next to a lily-covered pond opposite the Nallur Temple, this well-known landmark is widely regarded to serve the best sundaes in Jaffna (*around US$1.50*) & it offers the choice of sitting on the balcony or in the fan-cooled interior. $

Out of town

✳🍴 **Fort Hammenhiel Resort** [map, page 300] *See Where to stay;* ⏰ 08.30–22.00. The 335-year-old fort itself is off limits to day visitors, but not so the associated restaurant, which has a lagoonside location in the Naval Base on Karaitivu Island. Difficult to better as a relaxed lunch stop, it has a lengthy & cosmopolitan menu with most mains in the US$3–4 range, a licensed bar serving chilled beers & spirits, & the choice of dining in the AC interior or on a shady balcony offering views across the channel to Fort Hammenhiel & Kayts Island. $$

OTHER PRACTICALITIES There's a large and well-stocked branch of Cargills Food City (⏰ *08.00–22.00*) in Cargills Square on the junction of Hospital and Mahatma Ghandi roads. Cargills Square is also home to the Majestic Cinema (w *ceylontheatres.lk*), which shows recent Bollywood and Hollywood fare. A second smaller branch of Cargills Food City (⏰ *08.00–21.00*) can be found on Kanathiddy Road. Plenty of other small supermarkets and groceries are dotted around the city centre, and (worth knowing in a town dominated by dry restaurants) a couple of wine shops selling liquor and cold beer can be found on Kankesanturai (KKS) Road south of the junction with Hospital Road.

TOUR OPERATORS The Jetwing Jaffna has an in-house operator that arranges guided city and peninsula tours, as well as excursions further afield to the likes of Delft Island and the Chundikulam Bird Sanctuary. The Tilko Jaffna City Hotel also operates local day tours

WHAT TO SEE AND DO
Central Jaffna [map, page 302] Although it lacks for major historical sites, Jaffna's compact commercial centre is a fun place to follow your nose. The **central market** on the west end of Hospital Road is alive and buzzing with mercantile activity, with Jaffna products such as hand-woven palmyrah baskets, sweet blocks of jaggery and juicy tropical fruit being of particular interest. There's also a small **fish market** down the south end of KKS Road, and no shortage of cheerful little eateries selling fruit juices and all manner of colourful homemade sweets and confectioneries. Half a dozen Hindu temples are packed into the city centre, and visitors are welcome, though cameras are best left in your bag during puja services. The oldest and most attractive, **Vannai Vaitheeswara Temple** is an ancient Shiva shrine whose current incarnation, complete with a prominent five-tier gopuram, was built in 1790, and whose broodingly atmospheric stone-and-wood interior is free of the flamboyant flourishes associated with more modern temples. It is busiest during the 20-day Shiva Festival and ten-day Ambal Devi Festival, which respectively climax on the full moon of March and July.

The obvious place to start a more directed exploration of the city is **Jaffna Fort** (⊕ *08.00–18.00*), a hulking 7ha pentagon that dominates the waterfront immediately south of the commercial centre. Protected by five tall granite buttresses and enclosed by a moat along its four landward sides, the fort as it stands is essentially a Dutch edifice constructed between 1658 and 1680, but it was expanded from the original four-sided Fortress of Our Lady of Miracles of Jafanapatão built by the Portuguese over 1619–25. Ironically, following the three-month Dutch siege of 1658, the fort went untested for more than three centuries prior to the outbreak of the civil war, when it served as the Jaffna stronghold of the Sri Lankan military until they evacuated the city in 1986. Although the stone buttresses and ramparts were badly damaged during the LTTE bombardments, they have since been patched back together with concrete. By contrast, the old Dutch Groote Kerk (Big Church) and other interior buildings were mostly flattened beyond superficial repair, though several historic artefacts protected within the fort were rescued from the rubble, and placed in the archaeological museum. There's not much here in the way of interpretative material, but adventurous travellers might find their appetite for exploration whet by the photographs of some of Northern Province's more obscure archaeological sites displayed in the rooms flanking the main entrance.

Set in manicured green gardens 200m east of the fort, the **Jaffna Public Library** (☏ *021 222 6028;* ⊕ *working hrs 09.00–19.00 exc Tue; visiting hrs 16.30–18.00*) started life in 1933 as a small private book collection. By 1959, the collection had expanded sufficiently to be relocated to a handsome multi-domed three-storey Indo-Saracenic building commissioned for the purpose by Alfred Duraiappah, then the city's deputy mayor. The library grew to become one of the largest and most valuable in Asia, housing some 97,000 books and other documents, including many historic and unique Tamil palm-leaf and other manuscripts. In June 1981, the entire collection went up in smoke when the library was burnt down by Sinhalese rioters, an act of mob violence perceived by aggrieved Tamils to be an indirect government attack not only on their academic traditions but on their very place in modern Sri Lanka. The partially restored building was set on fire again in 1985, this time by LTTE soldiers, after which it stood as a burnt-out shell for almost two decades prior to being restored to its former architectural glory and reopening in 2004. The library's irreplaceable contents are lost forever, but more than US$1 million has been spent on assembling a new collection of mostly Tamil literature.

Two other sites of modest interest are close to the library. Standing tall and white against the skyline, the domed **Victoria Clock Tower**, on the junction with Mahatma Ghandi Road 150m to the north, was built in 1882 to commemorate a visit to Ceylon by the Prince of Wales (the future King Edward VII) seven years earlier. A similar distance south of the library, the **S J V Chelvahayagum Garden** and its peculiar top-heavy central monument opened in 1998 to commemorate the centenary of the birth of its namesake, a revered Tamil separatist committed to the attainment of his goals using non-violent Gandhian tactics.

Follow the waterfront east of the fort for 700m, and you'll arrive at **Jaffna Fishing Harbour**, which runs along Reclamation Road for more than 1km. With hundreds of colourfully painted wooden fishing boats bobbing offshore, the friendly harbour forms a surprisingly rustic appendage to central Jaffna, and it's very photogenic too, especially towards dusk with the sun setting in the background over the Velanai Causeway. Inland of the harbour, Bankshall and Main streets run east from the city centre through leafy residential suburbs that must have been rather posh in the colonial era and are still studded with a few churches dating to those days. These include the grand **St James Church**, an Anglican edifice built in 1861 and notable for its twin domes and grand Italian-influenced façade, and **St Martin's Seminary**, whose characterful French-founded church, set in a palm-shaded tropical garden, dates to the early 1880s. Nearby **St Mary's Cathedral**, head of the Jaffna Catholic diocese, is a massive but rather plain building whose foundation stone was laid in 1938, but on the site of an eponymous late 18th-century cathedral itself constructed to replace a modest wood-and-clay Portuguese-era Catholic church.

Nallur [map, page 302]

The built-up suburb of Nallur served as the capital of Jaffna for several centuries prior to the arrival of the Portuguese and relocation of the administration to the modern city centre 2km to the southwest. Its principal site, **Nallur Kandaswany Temple** (*Temple Rd;* ⊕ *04.30–19.90; indoor photography forbidden*) is the city's most important and spectacular Hindu shrine, dedicated to Skanda (Kataragama). The original temple, which possibly stood 1km east of its modern counterpart, was founded CAD948 and destroyed by the Portuguese in the 1620s. The present-day structure started life in the mid 18th century as a small stone shrine with a palm-leaf roof, and has undergone several expansions over the centuries, most recently with the unveiling of two new nine-storey gopurams – reputedly the tallest and second-tallest in Sri Lanka – in 2011 and 2015. The most interesting time to visit is during the one of the daily pujas (held at 05.00, 10.00, 16.00, 17.00 and 18.45); all the better should your time in Jaffna coincide with the latter part of the 25-day annual Nallur Festival, which ends on the last poya weekend in late August or early September (see w nalluran.com for details). In addition to removing their shoes, male visitors are required to take off their shirt.

Nallur is dotted with less publicised sites associated with its tenure as Jaffna's capital. On the east side of the Point Pedro Road 1km past the temple, the striking **Cankili Toppu** is an isolated ornamental stone arch claimed by some to have been the entrance to the palace of King Cankili (1519–65), though others assert, perhaps more credibly, that it was part of the 17th-century home of Poothathamby Mudaliyar, a Tamil administrator executed by the Dutch for treason. On the opposite side of the road, only 150m further north, the abandoned **Rajamanthri Palace**, also known as Mandrimanai, has a Dutch-era façade, but the main body dates to the 16th century and is claimed variously to have been the palace of Cankili's successor, Puviraja Pandaram, or the home of the minister of one of these two kings. On Chemmani Road, 300m east of the junction with the Point Pedro Road, **St James Church** – not to be confused with its more central namesake – is an appealing tall-spired Anglican edifice built in 1828 from the shell of a dilapidated Dutch church that reputedly stood on the original site of Nallur Temple. Follow a winding back road north of the church for 150m, and you'll reach **Jamunai Pond**, a sunken stone pool that was reputedly the favourite bathing spot of King Cankili's wife.

Hidden away behind the Navalar Cultural Hall 1km south of Nallur Temple, the **Jaffna Archaeological Museum** (*Navalar Rd;* \ *021 222 4574;* ⊕ *08.00–16.45 exc Tue; free entrance but donation requested; no photography*) might initially come across as musty and disorganised, but an eclectic selection of displays justifies the effort of locating it. Of particular interest is a superb collection of Medieval brass statues and granite carvings excavated at the ancient Hindu temple sites of Nallur and Keerimalai, an intricately carved 17th-century wood temple door-frame, a good example of an old palmyrah-leaf manuscript, also dating to the 17th century, and – more macabrely – kavadi skewers, spiked wooden sandals and other items associated with Hindu self-mutilation rituals. Items that found their way here from Jaffna Fort include a Dutch gravestone complete with skull-and-crossbones, a brass sundial, and a war-scarred 1853 portrait of a 34-year-old Queen Victoria said, rather fancifully, to smile at the viewer at certain angles. The museum reputedly once housed several 2,000-plus-year-old items unearthed during early 20th-century excavations at Kantharodai (page 312), but these no longer seem to be on display.

Velanai and the southern Jaffna Archipelago

Probably the most straightforward goal for a short trip out of Jaffna, the island of Velanai – sometimes called Kayts after its largest town, or by the old Dutch name of Leiden – is connected directly to the city centre by a 4km road causeway and regular buses. Another road causeway connects Velanai to Punkudutivu Island, where the end-of-the-road village of Kurikadduwan – also accessible by bus – serves as the springboard not only for the short ferry hop across to Nainativu Island and its pair of historic temples, but also for a day trip to the more far-flung island of Delft.

Velanai (Kayts) Island [map, page 300] The second largest of the eight main islands that comprise the Jaffna Archipelago, Velanai is a 35km^2 expanse of flat sandy soil, dotted with seasonal pans and palmyrah plantations and separated from the mainland by a gorgeous shallow lagoon. The island is thinly populated by comparison with the built-up Jaffna Peninsula, and far more rustic in feel, though this is partly an aftermath of the civil war, which left the countryside scarred with ruined and abandoned homesteads.

Situated on Velanai's northern shore, the intriguing and unexpectedly substantial town of **Kayts** (pronounced 'Kites') is separated from Karaitivu Island by a 500m-wide channel serviced by regular ferries. Decidedly backwaterish today, Kayts was an important port during the Portuguese occupation of Jaffna (1619–58) thanks to its good and easily defended harbour and strategic location in terms of maritime access to the mainland peninsula. It was then that it acquired the name Kayts (a derivative of Caes dos Elefantes, meaning 'Elephants' Quay', in reference to the main item of export) and that a pair of Portuguese forts were built to guard the channel entrance 1km to its west. Kayts retained its strategic significance into the 19th century, when the original St Anthony's church and adjacent Stanton Villa – both now atmospherically overgrown ruins – were constructed alongside the main road. Older than either of these, St James's Church, about 250m west of the ferry jetty, was established in 1718, rebuilt in 1815, badly damaged during the civil war, and reopened in 2015 following extensive renovations. About 1km west of the town centre, reached along a bumpy road opposite St Mary's Church, stands the ruined Kayts Fort (also known by the Tamil name Urundai, meaning 'round', on account of its horseshoe shape), which was built by the Portuguese in 1629, abandoned in 1651, and unlike the facing Fort Hammenhiel offshore of Karaitivu, never rebuilt by the Dutch. Kayts town is 20km by road from Jaffna, and regular buses run back and forth all day. Once you're done, instead of returning to Jaffna the way you came, you could catch a ferry to Kalanoony, only 500m across the water on Karaitivu Island (and 30 minutes' walk from the Fort Hammenhiel Naval Base and its ideally located restaurant; page 306) and bus to Jaffna from there.

Running along a sheltered bay on Velanai's southern shore 12km from Jaffna, **Charty beach** doesn't compare to the resorts of the southwest coast, but an attractive combination of white sands and calm water – complete with lifeguards, surprisingly enough – makes it the most popular swimming destination in the vicinity. Charty's only resort hotel isn't up to much (page 305), but if you feel like getting out on to the water, it does arrange snorkelling trips to a nearby reef (*US$45–50 per party, inc gear*) and has a few jet-skis for rent (*US$13/15mins*). To get to Charty beach from Jaffna, either charter a tuktuk, or else catch a bus to Kayts or Punkudutivu Island, then hop off halfway at the Mankuppen Pillayar Temple (visible from afar thanks to its tall gopuram) and take a left turn to walk the last 2.5km.

The island's other main point of interest, albeit primarily to birders, is the expansive and partly seasonal **Velanai Wetlands**, where resident flocks of black-headed ibis, spot-billed pelican, painted stork and various egrets and herons are augmented by large numbers of migrant waders between November and March. The Velanai Wetlands start about 12km from Jaffna and are centred on the junction of the roads to Kayts and Punkudutivu, so a bus to either of these places could deposit you there.

Nainativu Island [map, page 300] Only 4.5km^2 in extent and with a population estimated at 2,500, Nainativu is remarkable for housing active shrines to all four of Sri Lanka's major religions. Among these are two ancient pilgrimage sites – a Hindu temple at Nagapooshani and its Buddhist counterpart at Nagadeepa – notable among other things for their close similarity to Nagadibois, the name applied to Jaffna by the 1st-century geographer Ptolemy, in reference to the shape-shifting, snake-worshipping Naga deities who, according to the *Mahavamsa*, ruled the area between the 6th and 3rd centuries BC. Access to Nainativu is by passenger ferry from the village of Kurikadduwan (often abbreviated to KKD), which stands on the west shore of Punkudutivu Island, 30km from central Jaffna along a surfaced road crossed from Velanai Island via a 3.5km causeway. Regular buses run between Jaffna and KKD, while ferries to Nainativu, which cost next to nothing, cross the 2km channel in either direction every 30 minutes between 07.30 and 16.30.

When you hop off the ferry from KKD, you'll be hard pushed to miss the looming **Nagapooshani Amman Temple** and its spectacular quartet of gopurams, the tallest of which stands 33m high. Dedicated to Parvati, this Hindu temple was legendarily founded by Indra during a period of self-exile on Nainativu. According to the *Mahabharata*, this occurred after Indra disguised himself as the Gautama Maharishi in order to seduce his wife Ahalya, and was punished with a curse that caused his body to be blemished with a thousand individual marks, each resembling a vagina. Disgraced and humiliated, Indra fled to Nainativu and dedicated himself to the goddess Bhuvaneswari Amman, who was so impressed by his remorse and dedication that she eventually transformed the marks of infidelity into eyes. The temple was destroyed by the Portuguese in 1620, but an original statue of a Naga was incorporated into the structure when it was rebuilt in 1788. The relatively modest eastern gopuram also dates to this time, but the other three gopurams are modern, built between 1971 and 2012, which is also when most of the temple's estimated 10,000 statues and sculptures were added. The side entrance is flanked by an inscribed stone dating to the 12th-century reign of Parakramabahu I, and an equally ancient anchor stone as used by ships from Arabia. Despite its remote location, Nagapooshani Temple's six daily pujas regularly attract up to a thousand pilgrims. It is busiest during the annual Mahostavam festival, which falls over late June and early July.

On the east shore of Nainativu 750m south of Nagapooshani, **Nagadeepa Rajamaha Temple** (w *nagadeepaviharaya.lk*) has been identified as one of the 16 Solosmasthana but it was abandoned for centuries prior to being rediscovered in 1931 and is of limited archaeological interest. That said, the modest dagoba – restored in the 1930s and again after the civil war – was reputedly constructed by a pair of warring Naga kings to enshrine a gem-studded throne over which they had engaged in a long, violent dispute prior to the Buddha's mediation.

Delft Island [map, page 300] The largest and most easterly component in the Jaffna archipelago, Delft (or Nedunthivu) is a byword for remoteness. Stark, flat and sparsely populated, the 50km² near-rhomboid island is best known for its 500-strong population of wild horses, progeny of a domestic herd abandoned by the Dutch when they vacated the island more than 200 years ago, but possibly first introduced by the Portuguese. Only one daily ferry services Delft, leaving from Punkudutivu's Kurikadduwan Pier at 09.30, taking an hour to complete the crossing, then starting the return journey at 14.30. This leaves a relatively short time window for exploration, and most visitors hire one of the tuktuks that wait at the ferry jetty and charge around US$10 to scoot between a few low-key highlights. You're almost certain to see the wild horses, which are unusually small of stature, and favour the southern part of the island. The most interesting Dutch-era relicts are the ruined fort, stables and hospital, not to mention an unusual and well-preserved chimney-like lighthouse known as the Queen's Tower. Other points of interest include several ancient dagoba bases, a stone-and-concrete dovecote built during the early colonial era to house carrier pigeons, and a magnificent centuries-old baobab tree whose hollow trunk is large enough to fit three or four people. Before you visit Delft, be warned that the ferry offers no shade, and there are no life jackets on board, so bring a hat, and check the weather forecast a day ahead in case of stormy weather.

The western peninsula and Karaitivu Island [map, page 300] The mainland

sites described below all lie to the west of the Jaffna–Kankesanturai (KKS) Road and the Palali military zone (which effectively splits the north coast in two). The odd man out is Karaitivu Island, which forms part of the same archipelago as Velanai, Nainativu and Delft, but is linked to the western peninsula by a road causeway, and feels like an extension of it from a logistical perspective. With a private vehicle, you could easily loop through all the sites below in a day, possibly lunching at the Fort Hammenhiel Resort. Using public transport, it should be noted that the hourly passenger ferry service between Kayts and Kalanoony (both of which are linked to Jaffna by regular buses) would allow you to loop through the islands of Velanai and Karaitivu as a long but rewarding day trip out of the city.

Kantharodai Dagobas [map, page 300] (⊕ *24hrs*) Perhaps the most intriguing archaeological site in Jaffna despite a frustrating dearth of interpretative material, Kantharodai (also known as Kadurugoda) comprises 60 dwarf dagobas clustered tightly in a palm-shaded field 10km north of the town centre. Each of these domed brick constructions is set on a round base divided into at least four step-like bands and topped by a grooved conical spire. Of the 20 that are fully intact, none stands taller than 3m, but several of the damaged ones have larger bases. The age and purpose of the dagobas is highly conjectural. Locals believe that they mark the graves of 60 Buddhist monks who were served a poisoned mushroom curry at the instruction of King Cankili I in the mid 16th century. Other accounts suggest that the monks died of old age, or as a result of famine. There is also good reason to think the Kantharodai dagobas are far older than any tradition holds. Excavations undertaken shortly after the dagobas were rediscovered in 1917 unearthed a trove of ancient artefacts – Indian and Roman coins minted in the 5th–6th centuries BC, Tamil Brahmi manuscripts from the 3rd century BC, and black-and-red potsherds of a Vedic style prevalent prior to the 9th century BC – that indicate Kantharodai has been an important centre of trade since pre-Buddhist times.

Given its enigmatic history, Kantharodai is appropriately difficult to find, tucked away in a maze of back roads north of Uduvil. To get here from Jaffna, follow the Kankesanturai (KKS) road north for 10km to Chunnakam crossroads, then turn left on to the Sandilipay Road and follow it for 2km, turning left again at the signpost for Kadurugoda Hindu Temple. From here it is 1.5km to the dagoba field, turning right after 400m, then left just after you pass the Hindu temple. Plenty of buses run up the KKS road between Jaffna and Chunnakam, from where you could either charter a tuktuk for the last 3.5km, or walk.

Keerimalai Springs [map, page 300] (⊕ *06.00–18.00; no entrance fee but a nominal charge to swim*) Revered for its curative powers since time immemorial, Keerimalai is a natural freshwater spring overlooking a pretty coral-rag beach on the north coast of the Jaffna Peninsula, where it feeds two artificial pools, one set aside exclusively for men and the other for women, before flowing into the sea. The pools stand adjacent to the Naguleswaram Temple, which is reputedly one of the five Shiva shrines founded in Sri Lanka in pre-Buddhist times. The names Keerimalai and Naguleswaram respectively derive from the Tamil and Sanskrit words for mongoose; both refer to the legend that a wizened old sage called Nagula Muni established the shrine at Naguleswaram in gratitude after his repellent mongoose-like features were cured by bathing at Keerimalai. Echoing this is another legend that the ancient Maviddapuram Temple, 3km southeast of Naguleswaram, was renovated, expanded and given its present name by an 8th-century King of Madurai after a swim at Keerimalai cured his daughter, Princess Jamathakiri, of a chronic intestinal disorder and transformed her dowdy horse-like visage to one of radiant beauty (Maviddapuram translates as 'where the horse left').

Keerimalai and Naguleswaram have suffered mixed fortunes of late. After the Portuguese destroyed the temple in the early 17th century, the site fell into disuse for more than 250 years prior to being revived in late 19th century under the guidance of Hindu reformer Arumuka Navalar. The new temple was destroyed by fire in 1918, rebuilt shortly afterwards, then razed once again in 1990 in a Sri Lankan Air Force aerial bombardment. The latest incarnation of Naguleswaram was formally opened in 2012, since when Keerimalai has resumed its status as an important popular pilgrimage site with Sri Lankan Hindus.

Keerimalai lies 20km north of Jaffna along the Kankesanturai (KKS) Road, and the two are connected by regular buses, which branch to the left at Maviddapuram to avoid the military zone around Palali. The large temple area is unusually attractive and the atmosphere can be compelling, especially over the fortnight leading up to the Maha Shivaratri (Festival of Shiva), which occurs over the new moon in late February or early March. That said, while the bathing pools at Keerimalai are popular with local revellers, the murky green water is unlikely to tempt many foreign visitors into putting its curative powers to the test. There's no entrance fee, but nominal amounts are charged to park outside the temple, or to bathe in the pool. Nearby Maviddapuram Temple, which falls within a military area studded with bombed-out buildings, is still disused, but its striking five-tiered gopuram, covered in dozens of unpainted sculptures, looms on the roadside as you approach Keerimalai from Jaffna.

Sangamitta Buddhist Temple [map, page 300] (⊕ *24hrs*) This temple is situated at Dambakola (also known as Jambukola), a site of immense historical significance to Sri Lankan Buddhists, since it is where Princess Sangamitta Thera came ashore in 249BC bearing the sapling that was planted in Anuradhapura to become the sacred Jaya Sri Maha Bodhi. Despite this ancient claim to prosperity, Sangamitta Temple is a thoroughly modern construction, built by the navy over two months in 2009 on the site of a Bo Tree planted by the same institution in 1998. The construction of such a temple in the heart of Tamil/Hindu country so soon after the civil war's end undoubtedly had a political agenda, but it's a tranquil spot, overlooking a pretty sandy beach, and marked by a large modern dagoba, with panels depicting the full history of the Bo Tree's passage from Bodh Gaya (India) to Anuradhapura. Already emerging as a popular Sri Buddhist pilgrimage site, the temple is likely to be busiest on the December poya (full moon), which is commemorated as Sangamitta Day and said to mark the arrival of the Bo Tree in Sri Lanka. Set alongside a partial dirt road that follows the peninsula's little-known northwest coast, the temple lies about 9km west of Keerimalai and 6km northeast of Karaitivu Causeway. No buses head here so far as we are aware, but you could catch a tuktuk from Keerimalai.

Vaddukodai Church [map, page 300] Jaffna's oldest functional Christian shrine, Vaddukodai is often referred to as a Portuguese church on account of it being founded by them in 1626, but the present-day building dates to the Dutch occupation, at least according to a foundation stone to the left of the altar dated 1670, and an inscription above the ornate main door stating it was built in 1678 under Commander Laurens Pyl. An unpretentious but characterful old building large enough to seat several hundred worshippers, it was taken over by the American Mission in the early 19th century, and has been under the Church of South India since 1947. The churchyard contains about two dozen 17th-century Dutch tombstones relocated from Jaffna Fort for safekeeping during the civil war, while the interior incorporates several 19th-century plaques commemorating parishioners. The historic Jaffna College opposite was founded in 1823 as Batticotta

Seminary (Batticotta being a Europeanisation of Vaddukodai) and incorporates several 19th-century structures. The church lies 100m north of the main crossroads in Vaddukodai, about 9km west of Jaffna Town along the main road to Karaitivu Causeway, and connected to it by regular buses.

Karaitivu Island [map, page 300] The most northerly island in the Jaffna Archipelago, 20km² Karaitivu is also the only one aside from Velanai linked directly to the mainland by road, thanks to a 3.5km causeway – flanked by fish traps, mangroves and shallows hosting marine birds – that crosses Jaffna Lagoon about 13km north of the city centre. The island has two main attractions. Close to the northeastern tip, the Navy-run **Casuarina beach** (⊕ *07.00–18.00; nominal entrance fee*), lined with the whispering fir-like trees for which it is named, is washed by calm shallow water that usually offers ideal conditions for swimming, though you are advised to check first, especially as it also has a reputation for occasional influxes of stinging jellyfish. Only 500m from the beach is a large lagoon that supports a varied aquatic birdlife.

At the opposite end of Karaitivu, octagonal **Fort Hammenhiel**, constructed by the Dutch in 1680, occupies a tiny offshore island, whose name alludes to its purported resemblance to a heel of ham (this is also how the Dutch viewed Sri Lanka when it was mapped, as was often the case back then, with north orientated to the left). Post independence, the fort was used as a gaol to detain political prisoners and Navy men accused of misdemeanours, but more recently it has been converted to a small Navy-run upmarket hotel (page 305). Unfortunately, the fort is off limits to day visitors, but the well-sited modern restaurant complex in the Fort Hammenhiel Naval Base is open to all comers, and makes for a lovely lunch stop (page 306).

Karaitivu is easy to explore using public transport. Regular buses cover the 25km road between central Jaffna and Kalanoony (the jetty at the southern end of the island) via Vaddukodai, Karaitivu causeway and the island's principal town, Karainagar. Most follow the more direct eastern road between Karainagar and Kalanoony, but others take the slightly longer western loop that runs right past the signposted junction for Casuarina beach and the difficult-to-miss entrance to Fort Hammenhiel Naval Base. Casuarina beach lies about 2km north of Karainagar, and if you don't fancy the walk, you could charter a tuktuk. It is also easy enough to pick up a tuktuk to Fort Hammenhiel Naval Base at Kalanoony. If you want to vary your return route, note that an hourly passenger ferry service connects Kalanoony to Kayts (the largest town on Velanai), from where plenty of buses run on to Jaffna.

Point Pedro and surrounds Connected to Jaffna by a 32km road and regular buses, Point Pedro is an attractive small port town set on the north coast of the peninsula and easily visited as day trip from the city centre. Sites of interest *en route* from Jaffna include the low-key Nilavarai Well and port of Valvettithurai, while Point Pedro itself is the springboard for visits to the striking Manalkadu Dunefield and nearby Vallipuram Temple.

Nilavarai Well [map, page 300] Clearly signposted on the left side of the Valvettithurai Road about 14km northeast of central Jaffna, this freshwater well, enclosed in a square concrete tank, can easily be visited *en route* to or from Point Pedro. Essentially a sinkhole created by the ancient collapse of a limestone cavern, the natural well is claimed locally to be bottomless, to become more saline as the water gets deeper, and to be the source of a subterranean passage that feeds the springs at Keerimalai. The nearby ruins of a 10th-century dagoba and discovery of a roughly contemporaneous limestone Buddha statue indicate Nilavarai once hosted an important Buddhist temple. Today, the well is overlooked by a small Shiva shrine, and most interesting to visit during the Maha Shivaratri, over the new moon in late February or early March, when it is customary for local devotees to dive into the murky green water.

Valvettithurai [map, page 300] An ancient harbour town that once rivalled Jaffna in significance, Valvettithurai (or VVT) now has a reputation as something of a smuggling entrepôt thanks to its proximity to the Indian port of Kodikkarai, which lies a mere 60km distant across the Palk Strait. Predominantly Tamil, it supports a population of 18,000 and stands on the peninsula's north shore some 30km northeast of Jaffna by road, and 8km west of Point Pedro. Valvettithurai is best known today as the birthplace and home of LTTE founder and leader Velupillai Prabhakaran. Largely due to this association, Valvettithurai was the site of two civilian massacres during the early years of the civil war. In 1985, 70 townspeople were rounded up into the library, which was then blown up, allegedly by the Sri Lankan army. Four years later, Indian Peace Keeping Forces executed at least 60 people in punitive killings following an LTTE ambush on their ranks in Valvettithurai market. The childhood home of Velupillai Prabhakaran was a popular curiosity with domestic tourists until it was destroyed in 2010, reputedly by the army, but the Shiva temple used by his family can still be visited. War association aside, VVT's main point of interest is the bird-rich Thondamannar Lagoon, which is crossed by the Jaffna Road about 3km to the west of town.

Point Pedro [map, page 300] The northernmost town in Sri Lanka, Point Pedro, a characterful fishing port with a population of 33,000, was formerly an important centre of cotton production and export to India, and it is still sometimes referred to by its old Tamil name, Paruthithurai, which means 'Cotton Harbour'. Oddly, the identity of the Pedro alluded to in its present name is a mystery, though some say it was the first Portuguese navigator to identify it as the island's northernmost extremity. Point Pedro today supports the usual scattering of Hindu temples and Catholic churches, but it lacks for any truly compelling tourist attractions, not unless you count the 32m-high British-built Point Pedro Lighthouse, which stands at its eastern end 500m before the main road curves south towards Vallipuram, and celebrated its centenary in 2016. Nevertheless, it is an unexpectedly picturesque small town, one whose relaxed end-of-the-island charm belies the hardships it experienced during the civil war and in the aftermath of the tsunami. Coming from Valvettithurai, the winding main road follows the curves of the coast for a full 10km, offering pretty views across a narrow sandy beach where stone breakwaters shelter bobbing flotillas of colourful fishing boats. There's no shortage of seaside activity to engage promenading visitors: off-duty fishermen mend their nets on the beach, brightly dressed raven-haired Tamil girls weave past on bicycles, screeching gulls soar overhead, scavenging crows bustle on the sand, heat-weary dogs wallow in the shallows, and the pungent smell of sun-drying fish infuses the salty air.

A steady stream of buses runs along the 32km road from Jaffna to Point Pedro, so it is easy enough to visit as a day trip. Should you fancy staying overnight, the pick of a few simple lodges, set on Vinayaga Mudaliyar Veethy Road 800m from the bus station, is the **Tulip Guest Inn** [map, page 300] (*5 rooms;* ✆ *021 226 0186;* m *0775 835037;* e *info@tulipguestinn.com;* w *tulipguestinn.com; US$13/20 sgl/dbl, plus US$7 for AC;* $).

Vallipuram Temple [map, page 300] Dedicated to Vishnu, Vallipuram (literally 'Sandy Town', in reference to the bordering dunes of Manalkadu) is the second-largest temple in Northern Province, and one of the oldest, with a recorded history that dates back to the 2nd century BC. Archaeological excavations undertaken at Vallipuram in 1936 yielded Sri Lanka's oldest-known inscribed gold plate, a 1,900-year-old artefact that namechecks King Vasabha of Anuradhapura and the Buddhist Temple at Nagadeepa. According to the inscription, Vallipuram was then a Buddhist temple called Badakara-Atana, as confirmed by the discovery of an ancient Buddha statue buried below the modern Hindu edifice. The extant Hindu temple probably dates to the 13th century, and is notable for its well-maintained seven-tier gopuram, and the riot of colourful and ornate carvings that adorn it. The roadside temple is easily visited *en route* between Point Pedro and Manalkadu, and is particularly worth a diversion during the annual Vishnu festival held over late September and/or early October.

Manalkadu Dunefield [map, page 300] Running southeast along the coast from Point Pedro towards the Chundikulam Lagoon mouth, the 75km² dunefield known as Manalkadu (a Tamil name meaning 'Sand Forest'), though frequently dubbed a desert, might less fancifully be described as an overgrown beach that extends up to 3.5km inland at its widest. Nestled among the dunes, the village of Manalkadu can be reached along a signposted 3km feeder that branches east from the main coastal road 4km south of Vallipuram Temple. Shortly before you reach the village, the original St Anthony's Church, reputedly built by the Dutch in the 18th century, now stands in an evocatively ruined and roofless state, half-buried below a golden dune that presumably engulfed it c1935, when a newer and larger namesake was built a few hundred metres to the northeast. About 500m past the new St Anthony's, the long, palm-lined and potentially idyllic Manalkadu beach is strewn with litter washed ashore from mainland Asia, as well as rubble from the tsunami, whose destructive impact is testified to by a row of skeletal and abandoned seaside homesteads. A Tsunami Memorial stands in front of the new St Anthony's Church, and many of the victims are buried in a simple cemetery on the dune behind the old church.

The Vavuniya Road
The sites described below all lie alongside or close to the A9, which is the main road connecting Jaffna to the important junction town of Vavuniya, 145km to the south. Most are of passing interest and are more likely to be visited briefly *en route* to or from Jaffna than as a day trip from it. The exception is the Chundikulam National Park, which is well worth an overnight stay, especially if you've a strong interest in birds and other wildlife.

Chundikulam National Park Set aside as a bird sanctuary in 1938 and upgraded to national park status in 2015, Chundikulam protects a 200km² tract of dry forest, coastal scrub, undulating dunes, seasonal flats and perennial pools boasting around 25km of Indian Ocean frontage. Situated 65km southeast of Jaffna Town by road, it was one of the country's most popular birdwatching sites prior to the outbreak of the civil war, when it was occupied by the LTTE and then declared a military zone after being recaptured by the army in 1995. The park is named after its dominant feature, the Chundikulam Lagoon, a vast estuarine wetland that divides the Jaffna Peninsula from the rest of Sri Lanka. Although many small and medium-sized mammal species are present, along with both species of crocodile, the main attraction is the rich and varied avifauna which justifies a visit throughout the year, with up to 10,000 greater flamingos potentially present at any time, alongside resident species such as painted stork, spot-billed pelican, white-bellied sea-eagle and greater thick-knee, and non-aquatic northern specials such as grey francolin and back drongo. Birding can be absolutely sensational between November and April, when Chundikulam attracts large numbers of migrant waterfowl and waders.

Getting there and away The main junction for Chundikulam National Park is Iyakachchi, which lies on the surfaced A9 to Vavuniya 50km from Jaffna town and 5km north of the Elephant Pass causeway. It's a 15km drive from Iyakachchi to Chundikulam Nature Park Holiday Resort, following a reasonable and well-signposted dirt road that passes through Kaddaikadu Junction about halfway. There is no public transport to Chundikulam, but any bus heading between Jaffna and Vavuniya can drop you at Iyakachchi Junction, where tuktuks are available for charter.

Where to stay *Map, page 288*

Chundikulam Nature Park Holiday Resort (8 rooms) 021 321 6254; e nphr.cdk@ gmail.com; w thalsevanaresort.com/naturepark. Attractively located on the north bank of a 20ha pool only 500m south of the sandy beach, this army-run resort offers a choice of en-suite accommodation, including lovely tree-house cottages with AC, & it also has a restaurant, boats for exploring the wetlands, a walkway & summer hut above the water, & a restaurant. *US$27 4-bed room with fan, US$35 dbl with AC.* **$$**

Elephant Pass The narrow isthmus that ensures Jaffna is a peninsula rather than an island, the Elephant Pass, 55km southeast of Jaffna town, is also now traversed by an artificial road causeway on the A9 to Vavuniya. The pass's name derives from the days when the main item of export from Jaffna was elephants, which were herded across the natural causeway from more southerly regions. The Elephant Pass has long been recognised for its strategic significance, and until recently it was overlooked by a twin-bastioned Dutch fort built c1760 and destroyed during the civil war, when three major battles were fought over the local Sri Lankan army base. In 1991, the LTTE suffered more than a thousand casualties in an attack foiled partly by the heroics of Corporal Gamini Kularatne, who climbed on to a reinforced rebel bulldozer tank as it powered towards the base, and hurled two live grenades inside, a fatal act of gallantry for which he posthumously became the first recipient of the Parama Weera Vibhushanaya (the Sri Lankan equivalent of the Victoria Cross). A more successful assault on the Elephant Pass in April 2000 led to the LTTE controlling it for almost nine years prior to it being recaptured by the army in January 2009.

The north side of the Elephant Pass is flanked by two commemorative sites. Set atop a grassy mound on the east side of the road, the formal Elephant Pass War Memorial, comprising a massive outline of Sri Lanka supported by four hands on a plinth guarded by a quartet of lotus flowers and lions, celebrates the government victory of 2009. To the west, the contorted tank destroyed by Corporal Kularatne, stood where it was stopped in its tracks, provides a sobering reminder of the human cost of that victory. As you take the causeway across the pass, you cross the same lagoon protected within Chundikulam National Park, and might well want to scan the flat shallow water for flamingos and other wading birds. Look out too for the soon-to-be-revived evaporation pools that made Elephant Pass the country's most productive source of household salt, with an annual yield of 80,000 tons, prior to the civil war.

Kilinochchi Probably the largest town along the A9 between Jaffna and Vavuniya, Kilinochchi also stands at the junction of the slightly shorter but less historically significant alternative route to/from Jaffna via the artificial road causeway running north from Pooneryn. Purpose-built in 1936 to ease overpopulation and unemployment in Jaffna, the small town was hard hit by the civil war, thanks to its proximity to the Elephant Pass. Indeed, it served as the main administrative centre of the LTTE from 1990 until 2009, bar a two-year period over 1996–98 when it was recaptured by the army. The most obvious relict of the war, 500m north of the railway station on the east side of the A9, is a massive water tank that stands collapsed where it was felled by the LTTE in order to starve the town of fresh water when they evacuated it in 2009.

Vavuniya The most important route focus in northern Sri Lanka, Vavuniya is a substantial town (population 70,000) that straddles the A9 and main north–south railway line 145km southeast of Jaffna, at the crossroads of trunk roads running east to Trincomalee, west to Mannar, and south to Kandy and Colombo via Anuradhapura. Travellers exploring the north on public transport may well end up changing buses in Vavuniya, but they are unlikely to need, or want, to spend longer here than it takes to navigate the bus station. The main central point of interest, set in green gardens immediately south of the main traffic circle, is the **Vavuniya Archaeological Museum** (🖉 021 222 4574; ⏰ 08.30–17.00 exc Tue; photography forbidden), which houses an interesting and reasonably well-labelled collection of statues and other antiquities, most notably an unusually vivid guardstone-like engraving of a Naga figure sat on a bull's head, and several detailed terracotta miniatures. Situated just 3km out of town on the north side of the main road to Trincomalee, Madukanda Temple – now a sprawling ruins notable for some well-preserved Anuradhapura-period guardstones – is reputedly where King Sirimeghavanna received the tooth relic shortly after it was transported to Trincomalee in the early 4th century. Should you need to stay overnight, the pick of a few adequate lodgings with air conditioning are the very central Vanni Inn (*2nd Cross St;* 🖉 *024 222 2074;* 🅵; *US$15 dbl;* **$**) and smarter out-of-town Thampa Inn (*1st Ln, Sinaputhukulam, 2km along the Trincomalee Rd;* 🖉 *024 222 0598;* m *0777 153963;* e *info@thampahotel.com;* w *thampahotel.com; US$26/35 sgl/dbl B&B;* **$$**).

13

Eastern Province

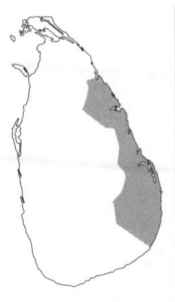

The 9,996km² Eastern Province, Sri Lanka's second largest in area but sixth in terms of population, is dominated by a lovely coastline that stretches for more than 300km south from the small town of Pulmoddai to the border between Kumana and Yala National Parks. Culturally, it is Sri Lanka's most multifaceted and demographically balanced province, with roughly 40% of the population listed as Tamil, 37% as Moorish and 23% as Sinhalese, while religious affiliations work out at 37% Hindu, 35% Muslim, 23% Buddhist and 5% Christian. During the civil war, much of Eastern Province fell under LTTE control, which led to serious cultural schisms in certain areas, though the region suffered less destruction than Northern Province. The 2004 tsunami inflicted further damage on what little remained of the province's tourist infrastructure after the long years of war and economic isolation.

The fractiousness of the recent past notwithstanding, Eastern Province has bounced back vigorously since 2007. Trunk roads have been resurfaced, rail links are fully restored, the economy is visibly thriving, and the coastline, with its wide sandy swimming beaches and shimmering blue lagoons, is rapidly emerging as a tourist hub to rival its more established western counterpart. Furthermore, as beach destinations go, Eastern Province really does have something for everybody. The provincial capital, Trincomalee, and more southerly Batticaloa, both ranked among the country's ten largest towns, are characterful ports whose lively multi-ethnic urban bustle is offset by a genuinely beautiful lagoonside location. Situated between these two towns, Pasikuda is a custom-designed resort village whose picture-perfect beach, its becalmed waters hemmed in by a shallow offshore reef, is lined with a row of sumptuous new upmarket hotels. Further south, there's happy-go-lucky Arugam Bay, a legendary surfer and backpacker hang-out serviced by dozens of small hotels, down-to-earth homestays and family-run seafood restaurants. And while beach tourism dominates, the national parks of Eastern Province have much to offer natural history enthusiasts, whether it's snorkelling offshore at Pigeon Island, or taking a boat safari into Gal Oya or jeep into Kumana in search of elephants and birds, while the countryside is dotted with little-visited Hindu and Buddhist temples dating back more than 2,000 years.

WHEN TO VISIT

An important feature of the east coast is that seasonal rainfall patterns are the exact opposite of those experienced at the more established west- and south-coast resorts. The high season, and best time to visit climatically, is June–September, when monthly rainfall is typically below 50mm. Conditions are also quite dry from March to May, but this falls outside the high season, so most hotels charge heavily discounted rates (officially up to 50% lower, and often negotiable for longer stays). December–February, the wettest months, are best avoided if hanging out on the beach is your main priority, but fine for more general travel.

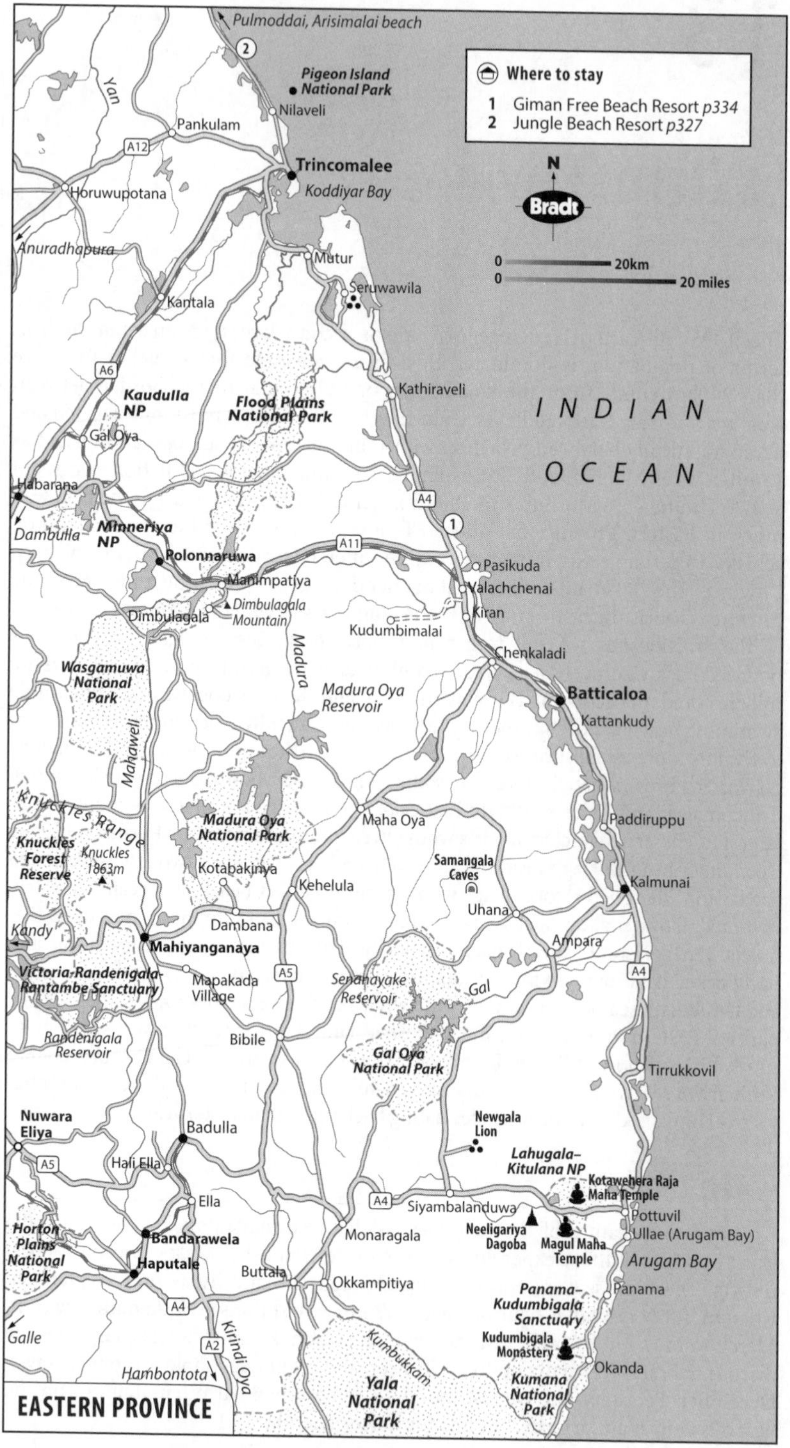

Pulmoddai, Arisimalai beach

Where to stay
1 Giman Free Beach Resort *p334*
2 Jungle Beach Resort *p327*

N

Bradt

0 ——— 20km
0 ——— 20 miles

Pigeon Island National Park

Nilaveli

Pankulam

Yan

A12

Trincomalee
Koddiyar Bay

Horuwupotana

Anuradhapura

Mutur

Kantala

Seruwawila

A6

Kathiraveli

Kaudulla NP

Flood Plains National Park

Gal Oya

INDIAN

OCEAN

Habarana

Minneriya NP

Dambulla

Polonnaruwa

Manimpatiya

A11

A4
1

Pasikuda

Valachchenai

Kiran

Dimbulagala

▲ *Dimbulagala Mountain*

Kudumbimalai

Chenkaladi

Madura

Wasgamuwa National Park

Mahaweli

Madura Oya Reservoir

Batticaloa

Kattankudy

Knuckles Range

Knuckles Forest Reserve

Knuckles 1863m ▲

Madura Oya National Park

Maha Oya

Paddiruppu

Kotabakinya

Kehelula

Samangala Caves

Uhana

Kalmunai

Kandy

Dambana

Mahiyanganaya

A5

Mapakada Village

Senanayake Reservoir

Gal

Ampara

A4

Victoria–Randenigala–Rantambe Sanctuary

Randenigala Reservoir

Bibile

Gal Oya National Park

Tirrukkovil

Nuwara Eliya

A5

Badulla

Hali Ella

Newgala Lion

Lahugala–Kitulana NP

Kotawehera Raja Maha Temple

Ella

A4

Siyambalanduwa

Neeligariya Dagoba ▲

Magul Maha Temple

Pottuvil
Ullae (Arugam Bay)

Horton Plains National Park

Bandarawela

Monaragala

Arugam Bay

Haputale

Buttala

Okkampitiya

Panama

Galle

A4

A2

Kirindi Oya

Panama–Kudumbigala Sanctuary

Kudumbigala Monastery ▲

Hambontota

Kumbukkan

Yala National Park

Kumana National Park

Okanda

EASTERN PROVINCE

FURTHER INFORMATION

The highly informative website w easternsrilanka.natgeotourism.com, put together by the Eastern Sri Lanka Geotourism Forum in collaboration with National Geographic, includes an interactive map allowing you click on sites of interest throughout the region for further information.

TRINCOMALEE

Sri Lanka's seventh-largest town and the administrative capital of Eastern Province, Trincomalee – often shortened to Trinco – is an ancient centre of maritime trade whose predominantly Tamil population stood at an estimated 110,000 in 2017. The agreeably time-worn town centre straddles a narrow peninsula that hems in the northeastern shore of Koddiyar Bay, a deep natural harbour whose southern shore is flowed into by the island's longest river, the Mahaweli. It's an attractive location, flanked to the east by the open sea, and to the west by the flatter waters and enclosing green hills of the harbour described by Admiral Lord Nelson as 'the finest in the world'. Historical landmarks include several low-key colonial-era buildings, as well as Fort Frederick and a clutch of ancient Hindu temple sites set atop the tall cliffs of Swami Rock, an imposing promontory that juts into the Indian Ocean immediately northeast of the town centre. Standard seaside activities aside, Trinco is a seasonally good base for whale watching, while Pigeon Island National Park, 2km offshore of Nilaveli, is one of the country's top snorkelling sites.

There are three main tourist bases around Trinco: the town centre, and the more northerly resort villages of Uppuveli and Nilaveli. Each has its own appeal. The town centre offers some worthwhile urban sightseeing, an adequate swimming beach, and several appealing harbour-front walks, while a good selection of budget hotels and eateries means it scores highly on the wallet-friendliness front. A more focused centre of tourist activity, only 4km from the town centre, Uppuveli's oddly named Alles Garden comprises a 500m strip of bumpy road lined with at least a dozen hotels (mostly in the mid-range to upmarket bracket) and as many seafood restaurants, all leading down to a lovely white beach lined with coconut palms and overlooked by the shapely Swami Rock. Another 10km north of Uppuveli, the less focused resort village of Nilaveli supports a scattering of more upmarket resorts along a pretty beach facing Pigeon Island.

HISTORY Trincomalee is one of Asia's oldest seaports. Traditions associate a cleft in the cliffs of Swami Rock with the prehistoric King Ravana, while the fine natural harbour on the Mahaweli mouth has attracted regular mercantile traffic from the Bay of Bengal mainland since the 6th century BC, possibly earlier. Originally known as Gokanna, Trincomalee is also where Prince Panduvasudeva, founder of the pre-Anuradhapura kingdom of Upatissa Nuwara, legendarily made his epochal landfall on Sri Lankan soil c504BC. The earliest incarnation of the Koneswaram Shiva Temple was constructed on the pinnacle of Swami Rock at around the same time. Throughout the Anuradhapura and Polonnaruwa periods, Gokanna was Sri Lanka's busiest trade port, and its hilltop temple become one of the holiest pilgrimage sites in the Hindu world. Indeed, Constantino de Sá de Noronha, the sixth Portuguese Governor of Ceylon, was so impressed by Koneswaram when he set anchor here in April 1622 that he dubbed it the 'Temple of a Thousand Pillars' – before instructing his pillaging troops to topple it over the cliffs into the sea and to kill any worshippers who didn't flee the scene.

13

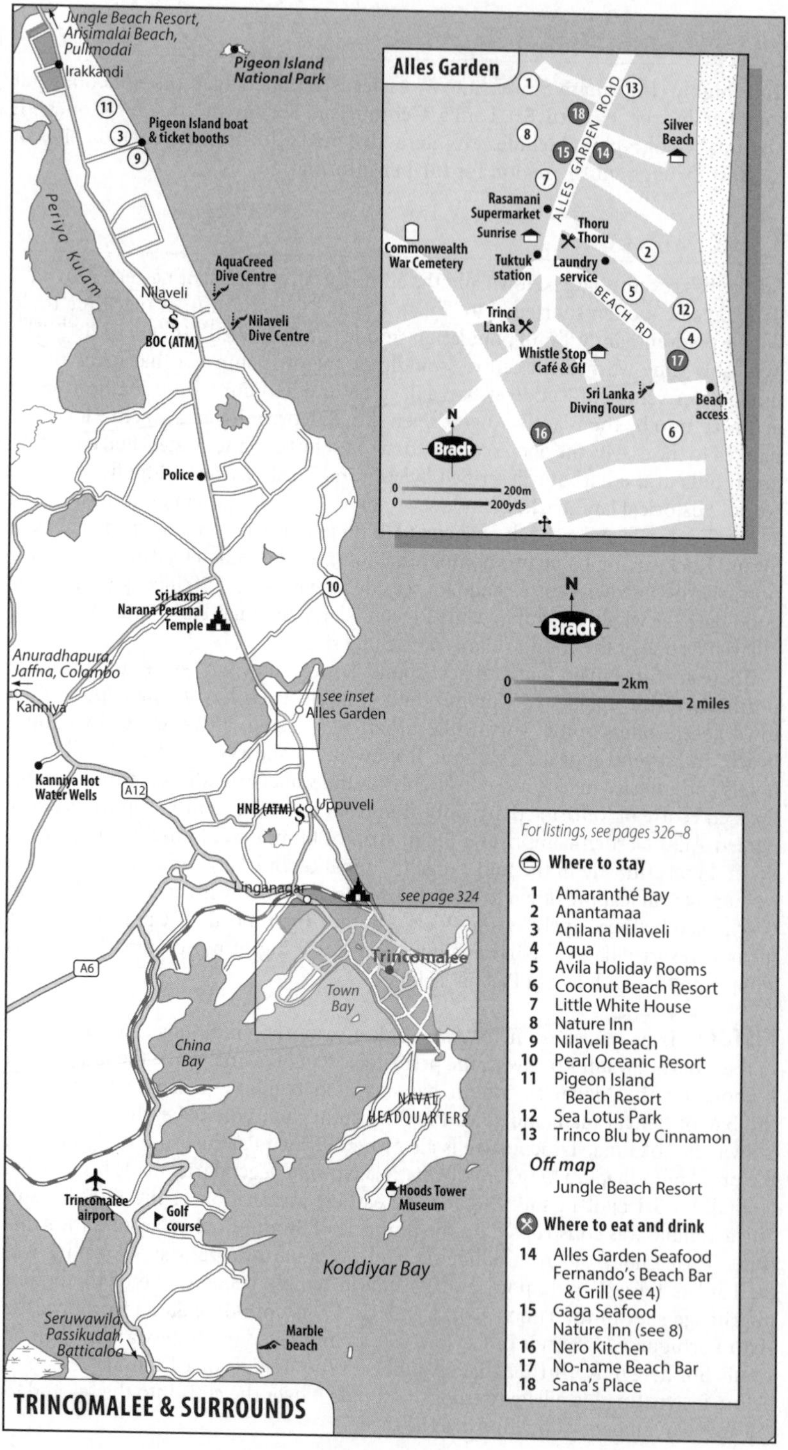

Alles Garden

Silver Beach

Rasamani Supermarket

Sunrise

Thoru Thoru

Commonwealth War Cemetery

Tuktuk station

Laundry service

ALLES GARDEN ROAD

BEACH RD

Trinci Lanka

Whistle Stop Café & GH

Sri Lanka Diving Tours

Beach access

N

Bradt

| 0 | | 200m |
| 0 | | 200yds |

Jungle Beach Resort, Arisimalai Beach, Pullmodai

Irakkandi

Pigeon Island National Park

Pigeon Island boat & ticket booths

periya Kulam

AquaCreed Dive Centre

Nilaveli

Nilaveli Dive Centre

BOC (ATM)

Police

Sri Laxmi Narana Perumal Temple

Anuradhapura, Jaffna, Colombo

Kanniya

Kanniya Hot Water Wells

A12

HNB (ATM)

Uppuveli

see inset Alles Garden

Linganagar

see page 324

Trincomalee

Town Bay

A6

China Bay

NAVAL HEADQUARTERS

Hoods Tower Museum

Trincomalee airport

Golf course

Koddiyar Bay

Seruwawila, Passikudah, Batticaloa

Marble beach

N

Bradt

| 0 | | 2km |
| 0 | | 2 miles |

For listings, see pages 326–8

Where to stay

1 Amaranthé Bay
2 Anantamaa
3 Anilana Nilaveli
4 Aqua
5 Avila Holiday Rooms
6 Coconut Beach Resort
7 Little White House
8 Nature Inn
9 Nilaveli Beach
10 Pearl Oceanic Resort
11 Pigeon Island
   Beach Resort
12 Sea Lotus Park
13 Trinco Blu by Cinnamon

Off map
Jungle Beach Resort

Where to eat and drink

14 Alles Garden Seafood
   Fernando's Beach Bar
   & Grill (see 4)
15 Gaga Seafood
   Nature Inn (see 8)
16 Nero Kitchen
17 No-name Beach Bar
18 Sana's Place

TRINCOMALEE & SURROUNDS

In 1623, the Portuguese built a fort close to the site of the demolished temple, incorporating what rubble remained into the new structure. They named the fort Triquillimale, a bastardisation of Tiru Kona Malai (literally 'Holy Lord's Hill'), the local name for the peninsula, and the root of the name Trincomalee. The Portuguese fortification was captured by the Dutch in 1639, who reconstructed it in 1665, and renamed it Fort Fredrick. Thereafter, Trinco was often used as a back door for foreign missions to the King of Kandy, and it changed hands half a dozen times before the British took occupation in 1795 and Anglicised the fort's name to Frederick. During the Portuguese and Dutch tenures, Trinco diminished in significance in favour of Colombo and Galle, which were situated closer to the main production areas for cinnamon, then the island's most coveted export crop. In the 19th century, the British considered relocating their administration to Trincomalee – indeed, one-time colonial secretary Sir James Tennent wrote that

on comparing this magnificent bay with the open and unsheltered roadstead of Colombo, and the dangerous and incommodious harbour of Galle, it excites an emotion of surprise and regret that any other [port] should ever have been selected as the seat of government and the commercial capital of Ceylon.

Trincomalee served as the home base for the combined East Asian fleets of the Allied Powers during World War II. On 9 April 1942, the naval base was attacked by the Japanese air force, who lost five bombers and six fighters in the course a kamikaze attack that left the navy's giant fuel tanks ablaze for almost a week. HMS *Hermes*, the world's first purpose-built aircraft carrier, launched in 1919, was berthed in Trincomalee harbour when early warning of the raid was received, and immediately set sail for the Maldives, only to be spotted by a Japanese plane in the waters off Batticaloa. The *Hermes* was sunk in the ensuing Japanese air bombardment, taking down 307 men with it. Despite this tragic loss, Japan's failure to capture Ceylon averted what the British prime minister Winston Churchill would later refer to as 'the most dangerous moment of the war, and the one which caused me the greatest alarm'.

Trincomalee also suffered greatly during the 1983–2009 civil war, when it formed part of the eastern territory claimed (and briefly occupied c2006–07) by the LTTE. The town and its environs experienced several bombardments, petrol bombings, riots and influxes and outpourings of refugees, as well as partial economic isolation linked to a deterioration in transport links to the rest of the country. The post-2009 recovery of Trincomalee has been remarkable, not least when it comes to a tourist boom centred on the nearby resort village of Uppuveli. Despite this, Trinco is still under-utilised as a commercial port, though it remains an important naval base, and Fort Frederick is still in military use.

GETTING THERE AND AWAY An important transport hub, Trinco is readily accessible by rail, bus or air. Heading on to Uppuveli or Nilaveli, catch one of the regular buses (every 30 minutes) that run from the central bus stand to Pulmoddai, and pass within 300m of the railway station *en route*. Alternatively, a tuktuk to Uppuveli shouldn't cost more than US$2.50 one way.

By rail Trincomalee is the terminus of a 295km line running northeast from Colombo via Kurunegala, Maho and Gal Oya Junction. At present, the line is serviced by just one daily 9-hour overnight train (second and third class only) in either direction. This leaves from Colombo Fort at 21.30, and from Trincomalee

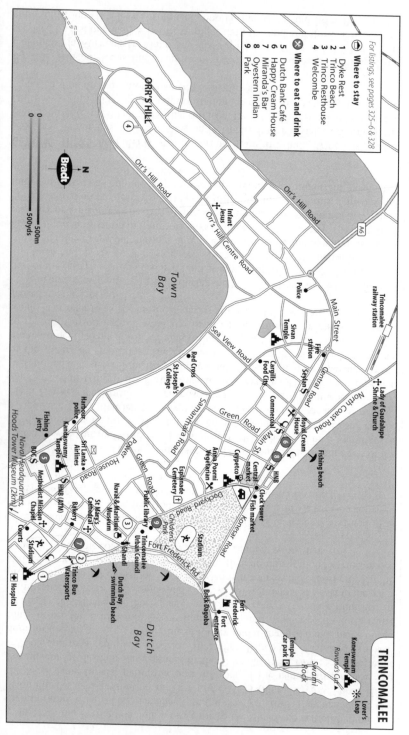

TRINCOMALEE

For listings, see pages 325–6 & 328

Where to stay
1 Dyke Rest
2 Trinco Beach
3 Trinco Resthouse
4 Welcombe

Where to eat and drink
5 Dutch Bank Café
6 Happy Cream House
7 Miranda's Bar
8 Oyestern Indian
9 Park

at 19.00. Trinco's railway station is at the north end of the town centre, only 300m from the main road to Uppuveli and Nilaveli.

By road Trinco lies about 265km from Colombo via Kurunegala and Dambulla. Buses run back and forth in either direction every 30–45 minutes, taking 7–8 hours one way, and stopping at Kurunegala, Dambulla, Sigiriya Junction and Habarana. A few air-conditioned buses leave in the evening. Regular intercity buses also run to/from Kandy (hourly, 5–6 hours, stopping at Matale, Dambulla, Sigiriya Junction and Habarana), Batticaloa (every 30 minutes, 3–4 hours) and Jaffna (hourly, 7 hours, stopping at Vavuniya). Heading to or from Mannar or Anuradhapura, direct buses are few and far between, so best to take the first bus to Vavuniya and change there. Direct buses to Polonnaruwa are also infrequent, but you can always catch a Colombo- or Kandy-bound bus as far as Habarana, and change there.

By air Helitours (w *helitours.lk*) operates thrice-weekly return flights between Colombo and Trinco at a very reasonable fare of around US$70 one way. Cinnamon Air (w *cinnamonair.com*) also flies between Colombo and Trinco at least three times weekly, more often in season, but it's a more costly option at anything upwards of US$165 one way. Both have online booking services. The airport is at China Bay, 5km west of Trinco across the bay, but twice that distance by road. Tuktuks meet all flights.

WHERE TO STAY   *Map, page 322, unless otherwise stated*

Accommodation in the town centre mostly slots into the shoestring and budget categories, while the resorts at Uppuveli and Nilaveli tend to be more upmarket.

Town centre
Map, opposite

Beachfront Dyke St is lined with perhaps a dozen cheap guesthouses & homestays. Our 2 favourites are listed below, but the others are perfectly acceptable if these are full. The town's smartest hotel is the not-quite-central but appealingly quirky Welcombe Hotel.

Moderate

🏠 **Welcombe Hotel** (20 rooms) Lower Orr's Hill Rd; ✆ 026 222 3885/6; e welcombe@sltnet. lk; w welcombehotel.com. Built in 1937, this once fashionable hotel is preserved in jungle-like hillside gardens on a promontory 2km southwest of the town centre. Slightly past its prime, it retains a faded colonial charm, epitomised by the saloon with wall panels & curved bar counter made of Burma teak. Amenities include a huge bean-shaped swimming pool & restaurant serving 3-course meals for US$8.50. Rather old-fashioned but large & comfortable rooms come with wood shutters, queen-size or twin bed, AC, cable TV, safe & Wi-Fi. 1st-floor rooms offer tremendous views

across the treetops to the harbour. Fair value. *US$50/55/60 sgl/dbl/trpl.* **$$$**

Budget

🏠 **Trinco Beach Hotel** (21 rooms) Dyke St; ✆ 026 205 6464; e trincobeach1@gmail.com. The largest & perhaps the smartest of the budget hotels lining Dyke St, this modern medium-rise has pleasant rooms with AC & nets, & a patio restaurant leading right out to the beach. *US$40 dbl. Low-season discount.* **$$**

🏠 **Trinco Resthouse** (14 rooms) Dockyard Rd; ✆ 026 222 4440. Set in leafy gardens only 150m from the beach, this refurbished government resthouse has spacious modern rooms with a treated concrete floor, wood furniture, 2 ¾ beds, AC, cable TV & fridge. An attached restaurant serves Chinese & Sri Lankan mains for around US$4. *US$38/48 sgl/dbl.* **$$$**

Shoestring

✳ 🏠 **Dyke Rest** (8 rooms) Dyke St; ✆ 026 222 5313; m 0771 230802; e dykerest@gmail. com. An ideal beachfront location, obliging owner-managers & decent inexpensive food are the hallmarks of this excellent homestay. Rooms are spotless & comfortable but on the small side. Great value. *US$14 dbl with fan, or US$30 with AC.* **$**

Uppuveli

Most of the hotels listed below lie within 100m of the Alles Garden Rd. The exception is the Pearl Oceanic, which has an isolated location 4km further north by road.

Upmarket

✴ 🏠 **Amaranthé Bay** (30 rooms) Alles Garden Rd; ☎026 205 0200; e reservations@ amaranthebay.com; w amaranthebay.com. Perched on the bank of the pretty Pillaikulam Lagoon, 5mins from the beach at neighbouring Trinco Blu, this exclusive new resort is centred on a lovely infinity pool ideally sited to watch the sun set over the palms. The clean architectural lines & contemporary décor ensure that the spacious rooms are the most attractive on offer in the Trinco area, none more so than the immense split-level top-floor suites with jacuzzi. All rooms have fan, AC & large flatscreen TV. *From US$163/210 B&B sgl/ dbl Jul–Sep, dropping by about 20% out of season.* **$$$$$**

✴ 🏠 **Anantamaa** (28 rooms) Alles Garden Rd; ☎026 205 0250; e info@anantamaa.com; w anantamaa.com. Though it isn't on the beach, this boutique-style hotel stands in secluded & neatly manicured gardens set around a swimming pool & restaurant with an unusually cosmopolitan menu. Stylish rooms decorated with contemporary wooden furniture & boldly coloured fabrics & wall hangings come with fan, AC, TV, queen-size beds & plenty of cupboard space. Great value, especially out of season when substantial discounts are offered. *US$75/95/120 sgl/dbl/trpl.* **$$$$**

🏠 **Trinco Blu by Cinnamon** (81 rooms) Alles Garden Rd; ☎026 222 2307; e reservations@ cinnamonhotels.com; w cinnamonhotels.com. Set on a perfect palm-lined beach at the north end of Alles Garden, this long-serving hotel under new management has undergone extensive modernisation of the lobby & restaurant, which are adorned with neutral tiles, brightly coloured fabrics & patterned mosaics. The AC rooms with TV & fan are on the small side but have been made over in retro beach-house style & come with a balcony facing the beach &/or swimming pool.

From US$228 dbl B&B, with significant low-season discounts online. **$$$$$**

Moderate

✴ 🏠 **Pearl Oceanic Resort** (8 rooms) Sampalthivu beach, 2.5km northeast of the Nilaveli Rd along a side road signposted 1.5km past Alles Garden; ☎026 205 1111; m 0779 949909; e bookings@pearloceanicresort.com; w pearloceanicresort.com. This low-key family-run retreat has an isolated location in large palm-shaded beachfront gardens 2km north of the Pillaikulam Lagoon mouth. The airy & uncluttered rooms, split between 4 cottages, have treated concrete floors, darkwood furniture, AC, fan, TV, fridge & private balconies only 10 paces from the beach. Amenities include a swimming pool, restaurant & Wi-Fi. Not for those seeking a bustling beach resort scene, but ideal for getting away from it all. Excellent value. *US$60 dbl B&B.* **$$$**

🏠 **Sea Lotus Park Hotel** (51 rooms) Alles Garden Rd; ☎026 222 5327/8; e info@ sealotuspark.com; w sealotuspark.com. Cup-half-fullers will draw attention to this beachfront hotel's fabulous location & lotus-shaped swimming pool; the half-empty brigade might focus on the timeworn look of the seafront old wing or soulless architecture of the viewless 3-storey new wing. Both would probably concede that the rooms, all with AC, fan, cable TV & tea/coffee, represent decent value for money. *From US$38/48 sgl/dbl B&B.* **$$$**

Budget

🏠 **Little White House** (3 rooms) Alles Garden Rd; m 0715 213701. Set in secluded gardens backed by a coconut plantation & only 400m walk from the beach, this aptly named house has just 3 bedrooms with fan but no AC, a common lounge & a small balcony hung with hammocks. *US$25 dbl.* **$$**

🏠 **Coconut Beach Resort** (8 rooms) Off Alles Garden Rd; m 0773 044750; e coconutbeachlodge@gmail.com. This small family-run lodge has a fabulous beachfront location a few hundred metres south of the main beach activity at Alles Garden. The spacious & attractively decorated budget rooms with fan are good value, those with AC less so. Excellent home-cooked 5-dish rice-&-curry (**$$**). *US$20 with fan or US$45 with AC.* **$**

Shoestring

✳ 🏠 **Nature Inn** (4 rooms) Alles Garden Rd; 📞026 370 4583; m 0773 174692; e arumbugal. batti.org@gmail.com. Tucked away behind a coconut plantation 100m from the main road, this new lagoonside lodge is centred on a cute green 2-storey 2-bedroom house with a kitchen, dining room, shady balcony & fans but no AC. Though best known for its vegetarian food, the comfortable rooms are also good value. Another 2 huts with AC are under construction. All proceeds go towards the Arumbugal Foundation, which supports local disabled people & sells handicrafts made by them in a small on-site shop. *US$17 dbl with fan, US$34 with AC*. **$**

🏠 **Aqua Hotel** (20 rooms, 18 backpacker caves) Off Alles Garden Rd; 📞026 205 0202; m 0778 546139; e aquainns@gmail.com; w aquahotel-trincomalee.com. A bit of a mixed bag, the Aqua Hotel is the closest thing in Trinco to a bona fide backpackers' hang-out, thanks largely to the great beachfront location of the popular Fernando's Bar & Grill & the rock bottom prices of its beach-facing 'backpacker caves' (customised lengths of concrete drainage pipe that sleep 2, so long as they're skinny & not prone to claustrophobia). Other pluses are the manicured gardens, small swimming pool, dive centre, spa & yoga centre. Rooms in the main block are fine but nothing special & feel a touch overpriced. *US$31 dbl with fan, from US$45 dbl with AC & TV, US$7/ unit backpacker cave.* **$–$$**

🏠 **Avila Holiday Rooms** (4 rooms) Off Alles Garden Rd; 📞026 454 5263; m 0776 048256. Simple & well-priced homestay-type set-up where clean & basic rooms come with nets & fan. *US$8 dbl.* **$**

Nilaveli & further north

The hotels & resorts at Nilaveli are less densely clustered & typically more upmarket than their counterparts at Uppuveli. Jungle Beach Resort, 10km further north, must rank as the premier property anywhere in the vicinity of Trinco. Rooms at all hotels listed below come with AC, fan, cable TV & Wi-Fi access.

Upmarket

✳ 🏠 **Jungle Beach Resort** (48 rooms) Kuchchaveli beach, about 10km north of Nilaveli; 📞026 567 1000; e reservations@ugaescapes. com; w ugaescapes.com. This luxurious retreat lies in lushly vegetated 6ha grounds flanked to the east by a wild & untrammelled sandy beach & to the west by a shallow lagoon lined by salt extraction pools. Spacious & attractively decorated cabins with a 50m² floor area, king-size bed, indoor & outdoor shower, & all mod cons are all constructed from natural material & carved unobtrusively into the forest, which supports plenty of birds. Amenities include a fabulous forest-fringed swimming pool, spa, gym & open-air restaurant. Rates vary depending on whether you want a jungle, ocean or lagoon view. *From US$335/394 sgl/dbl B&B, with low-season discounts.* **$$$$$+**

🏠 **Anilana Nilaveli** (54 rooms) 📞011 203 0900; m 0779 925222; e reservations@anilana. com; w anilana.com. This slick & supremely stylish new hotel is set in a narrow near-treeless property dominated by two long, skinny swimming pools running down to an idyllic beach lined with reclining deckchairs. The clean lines, liberal use of whites & sparse décor give the rooms a contemporary-bordering-on-clinical feel, an effect softened by the use of bold-coloured fabrics & sepia-toned reproductions of old maps on the walls. All rooms have a large modern bathroom, king-size bed & private balcony. *From US$220 B&B, with low-season discounts.* **$$$$$**

🏠 **Nilaveli Beach Hotel** (45 rooms) 📞026 222 6294; e nilaveli@sltnet.lk; w nilaveli. tangerinehotels.com. Sharing a sumptuous beach with neighbouring Anilana, the landmark NBH, built in 1974 but extensively renovated after the tsunami, is set in rambling wooded grounds alive with monkeys & birds, & serviced by an attractive swimming pool area. Rooms are a bit old-fashioned but well maintained & dominated by warm terracotta & wood textures, & all come with a private balcony. Unpretentious & sensibly priced. *US$140/150 sgl/dbl B&B.* **$$$$**

🏠 **Pigeon Island Beach Resort** (43 rooms) 📞011 268 3383; e info@pigeonislandresort.com; w pigeonislandresort.com. This long-serving resort has many strong assets – a superb beach location, 2m-deep swimming pool, good in-house dive centre, artily attractive stone, wood & terracotta lobby/dining area set around koi ponds – but the rooms, though well-equipped, feel a little outmoded & tattered at the edges. Acceptable value. *US$120/140 sgl/dbl B&B.* **$$$$**

✕ WHERE TO EAT AND DRINK Map, page 322, unless otherwise stated

Eateries in the town centre typically cater to a local clientele, and are priced accordingly, the one notable exception being Dutch Bank Café. Alles Garden in Uppuveli is lined with tourist-oriented restaurants, many specialising in seafood. Nilaveli lacks for standalone restaurants so most people staying there eat at their hotel.

Town centre

❋ ✕ **Dutch Bank Café** [map, page 324] Inner Harbour Rd; ☏ 026 222 2377; m 0772 690000; e dutchbankcafe@gmail.com; w grandthalassic. com; ⏱ 08.30–22.00. Situated a few hundred metres southwest of the town centre in a grand 19th-century building that once housed the Bank of Ceylon, this European-style café serves a combination of Western fare (burgers, pizzas, pasta) or Thai & Chinese. Beer is served, but no other liquor. Eat in the stylish AC interior or enjoy terrace seating with views across the inner harbour. **$$–$$$**

✕ **Oyestern Indian Restaurant** [map, page 324] Central Rd; ☏ 026 222 0883; ⏱ 11.00–23.00. The top restaurant in the town centre serves a good selection of Indian-style meat & vegetarian curries, along with burgers & a few other more Western dishes. No alcohol. **$$**

✕ **Park Restaurant** [map, page 324] Dockyard Rd; ☏ 026 720 0102; ⏱ 11.30–22.00. Set next to the central park, this informal eatery serves burgers & Sri Lankan staples (**$$**), but the speciality is pizzas (**$$$$**). No alcohol.

✕ **Happy Cream House** [map, page 324] Central Rd; m 0776 170810. Inexpensive freshly blended ice creams, as well as a good array of homemade sweets, mostly under US$1. **$**

♀ **Miranda's Bar** [map, page 324] Dockyard Rd. Inexpensive beers in a converted 19th-century merchant warehouse barely 50m from the north end of Dyke St.

Uppuveli

❋ ✕ **Nature Inn** See page 327. A must for fans of Sri Lankan rice-&-curry, this family-run gem serves generous & tasty vegetarian spreads, which must be ordered a few hours in advance. No alcohol. Great value. **$$**

❋ ✕ **Fernando's Beach Bar & Grill** Aqua Hotel (page 327). Wafted over by a welcome sea breeze & contemporary beats, the Aqua Hotel's beachfront eatery is Uppuveli's liveliest & most cosmopolitan, serving a tempting array of wraps, grills, pizzas, pasta dishes & seafood. The bar is well stocked but pricey. **$$$**

✕ **Alles Garden Seafood Restaurant** Alles Garden Rd; m 0773 281596; e allesgardenseafoodrestaurant@gmail.com; ⏱ 08.00–22.00. Friendly & unpretentious eatery serving delicious devilled dishes & curries in the **$$** range along with pricier seafood (**$$$**).

✕ **Nero Kitchen** Trinco–Nilaveli Rd, 200m south of the Alles Garden junction; m 0765 301318; ⏱ 11.30–22.00. Despite the unpromising exterior, this friendly little eatery with a wood-fired oven serves the best pizzas in the Trinco area (**$$$**) along with a tempting selection of filled pancakes (**$**) & good juices & shakes. No alcohol.

✕ **Sana's Place** Alles Garden Rd; m 0777 004047. This characterful & friendly 2-storey wooden construction serves a good selection of curry, pasta & devilled dishes, with crab curry something of a speciality (**$$**), & superb freshly caught & grilled seafood (**$$$**).

✕ **Gaga Seafood** Alles Garden Rd; m 0716 692471; e gaga25tm@gmail.com; ⏱ 08.00–22.00. Currently the most popular eatery on the Alles Garden strip, this serves a good selection of fresh seafood, though service can be slow & portions aren't especially generous. No alcohol. **$$$**

♀ **No-name Beach Bar** Situated outside the Aqua Hotel & operating under the same license, this tree-shaded bar wouldn't win any awards for décor or ambience, but the beers are significantly the cheapest in Uppuveli.

TOUR OPERATORS Most hotels and guesthouses in Trincomalee, Uppuveli and Nilaveli can arrange the various boat, diving and snorkelling trips mentioned below. In addition, several specialist diving and watersport operators are either based in Trincomalee or have offices there. The following are recommended:

ı⁄ **AquaCreed Dive Centre** Nilaveli beach;
m 0766 981885; e dive@aquacreedscuba.com;
w aquacreedscuba.com

ı⁄ **International Diving School** Pigeon
Island Beach Hotel, Nilaveli; m 0717 251024;
e internationaldivingschool@hotmail.com;
w theinternationaldivingschool.com

ı⁄ **Nilaveli Dive Centre** Nilaveli beach;
m 0774 436173; e info@nilavelidiving.com;
w nilavelidiving.com

ı⁄ **Sri Lanka Diving Tours** Alles Garden,
Uppuveli; m 0778 762085; e sashaanfernando@
yahoo.com; w srilanka-divingtours.com

ı⁄ **Trinco Blue Watersports** Dyke
St, Trinco town centre; ☏ 026 222 2455;
m 0767 078040; e seelan1973@yahoo.com;
w trincobluewatersports.com

OTHER PRACTICALITIES There's a well-stocked Cargills Food City on Samanthara Road. Most of the banks, including a Commercial with ATM, are on Central Road, but there are also some on North Coast Road. There are no banks or ATMs in Uppuveli but there is a Bank of Ceylon ATM on the main road through Nilaveli.

WHAT TO SEE AND DO

Around town Trinco is an engaging and attractive town to explore on foot, though rather enervating in the midday heat. The commercial centre is focused along three roughly parallel thoroughfares (North Coast Road, Central Road and Main Street) lined with small shops and eateries whose complexion reflects the town's dominant Tamil and to a lesser extent Muslim influences. The central market and fish market, both situated near the clock tower at the southeast end of Central Road, are busiest in the morning; rather unusually, they seem to be home to a few habituated spotted deer that subsist on vegetable waste. Less than 100m from North Coast Road, the main fishing beach, lapped by the Indian Ocean and lined with colourful small boats, runs west from the base of Swami Rock, and can easily be reached by wandering up one of several short alleys leading north between the clock tower and railway station. South of the commercial centre, a maze of small roads leads through residential and former administrative suburbs dotted with colonial-era relicts. These include a plain 1821 Methodist Mission Chapel on Dockyard Road, the ornately gabled blue-and-white 1852 St Mary's Cathedral tucked away on Cathedral Road, and the 19th-century Esplanade Cemetery where Rear-admiral Charles Austen (brother of novelist Jane) was buried following his death from cholera in 1852. Other key points of interest are described below.

Swami Rock, Fort Frederick and Koneswaram Temple [map, page 324] (⊕ *24hrs; photography permitted exc inside Koneswaram Temple*) Swami Rock, the roughly triangular 30ha peninsula whose rocky cliffs tower above the Indian Ocean immediately east of the town centre, is the most historically important site in Trincomalee. It is accessed via Fort Frederick, whose imposing outer granite buttresses are entered via a gateway emblazoned with the British coat of arms and a Dutch inscription dated 1675. The fort itself isn't of much architectural note, and the southern end of the peninsula now hosts a military camp, but it does provide refuge to a few herds of spotted deer, and its northern summit, hemmed in by 120m-high cliffs, is truly spectacular (and, seasonally, a good place to look out for blue whales).

The northern cliffs of Swami Rock are renowned as the site of Koneswaram, a Shiva temple founded in or around the 6th century BC (though it may have started life as a cave temple more than a thousand years earlier) and ranked among the island's largest Hindu shrines prior to being destroyed by the Portuguese in 1622. The 20th-century temple that now graces Koneswaram remains an important pilgrimage site, but – built to modest proportions, with a façade dominated by a massive cartoon-like Shiva wearing his trademark cobra necklace – it conveys little of its illustrious predecessor's pedigree. Fortunately, two interesting relics of the original temple are also on display. On the right side of the courtyard outside the main temple is an 11th-century sculpture of Shiva's humpbacked bull Nandi unearthed during renovations in 2013. Pride of place, however, goes to the Swayambhu Lingam, a metre-high circular stone obelisk salvaged in 1962 by divers exploring the submerged ruins of the original temple, and associated by legend with King Ravana, who reputedly brought it here from the Tibetan Mount Kailash.

The wave-battered cliffs that hem in Koneswaram Temple are punctuated by two well-known landmarks. The gaping Ravana Cleft, overlooked by a modern statue of its quick-tempered namesake, is said to have been carved in anger by the king's blade when Shiva challenged him to relocate the temple to his ailing mother's home in Tibet. At the northern tip of the peninsula, the precipitous Lover's Leap is named in memory of Francina van Rheede, a young Dutch woman who reputedly flung herself from the rocks to a watery death in April 1687 after having been abandoned by her fiancé (a legend contradicted by contemporary church records indicating that Francina was sufficiently recovered to marry one Anthony van Panhuys in 1694).

Dutch Bay beach [map, page 324] A fine stretch of white sand arcing for 1.2km along the bay bounded by Swami Rock in the north and a smaller rocky peninsula at the south end of Dyke Street, Trinco's main urban beach is usually safe for swimming in calm conditions, and hundreds of locals often take to its shallows over weekends.

Naval and Maritime Museum [map, page 324] (*Lavender Ln;* \ *011 242 1151;* NavalAndMaritimeMuseum; 08.30–16.30 *exc Tue; photography forbidden*) Situated 100m from Dutch Bay beach, this museum opened in 2013 in leafy gardens often frequented by troops of grey langurs. Displays range from black-and-white footage of the attack on HMS *Hermes* to ancient ceramics, coins and other artefacts unearthed around Trinco. It also details the rehabilitation of the handsome two-storey building that houses the museum – a former Dutch Navy Commissioner's Residence built in 1602 and enclosed by a handsome wrap-around colonnaded balcony on both levels.

Inner Harbour Walk Assuming you don't find the heat too sapping, it's possible to follow the shore of the hill-ringed Inner Harbour for about 5km starting at High Court at the south end of Inner Harbour Road, then heading north for about 2km before turning west to circumnavigate the wooded Orr's Hill Peninsular. The walk is particularly attractive towards dusk, when the sun sets over the harbour and the surrounding slopes light up. Do the walk in reverse, possibly starting by catching a tuktuk to the Welcombe Hotel or any other landmark on Orr's Hill, and you'll end up at Dutch Bank Café on time for a cold sundowner and snack!

Hoods Tower Museum [map, page 322] (*Naval Dockyard;* 14.00–17.00; *entrance US$16*) Assuming you aren't deterred by the eyebrow-raising entrance fee (and requirement to show your passport), this small naval museum set in the Naval Dockyard about 2km south of town displays an interesting selection of artillery ranging from colonial-era cannons to modern guns captured from the LTTE. The fire control tower and observation post for which it is named, built by Sir Samuel Hood in the early 19th century, stands on the site of the defunct Dutch Fort Ostenberg, and offers fine views over Koddiyar Bay.

Further afield

Trincomalee War Cemetery [map, page 322] (*Nilaveli Rd, 5km from Trincomalee & 200m north of Alles Garden junction; w cwgc.org; ⊕ 09.00–17.00*) The well-tended Commonwealth war cemetery in Uppuveli contains the graves of 303 World War II casualties, including RAF pilots and HMS *Hermes* crewmen killed in the Japanese attack of April 1942. Several of the graves were transferred from the more central cemeteries of St Mary's and St Stephen's after the war. Among the neat rows of white headstones separated by flowering shrubs are 60 graves of post-war Admiralty servicemen, civilian employees and their dependants.

Pigeon Island National Park [map, page 320] (*2km offshore of Nilaveli beach; ⊕ 06.00–18.00 (closed Nov–May); entrance US$10/party plus US$11/person*) Used as a military shooting range prior to being set aside as a marine sanctuary in 1963, this 500m-long island, named after the rock pigeons that breed here, is now the centrepiece of a 4.7km² marine national park designated in 2003. Incorporating several rocky islets and shallow reefs, the national park is one of Sri Lanka's top snorkelling and diving sites, supporting a wide variety of soft and hard corals and 100-plus species of reef fish, and also known for sightings of black-tipped shark and green turtle. How long this will remain the case is uncertain, given that the extent of live coral has decreased by 80% since the park was created, though it is unclear to what extent this is linked to tourism or simply the natural result of a post-tsunami current change that exposes more of the reef at low tide.

All visitors must stop at the national park kiosk, on the beach between Anilana and Nilaveli Beach Hotel, to pay fees and obtain a permit. Boats can be rented here at around US$13 per party of up to seven, inclusive of snorkelling gear. Snorkelling or diving excursions to Pigeon Island can be arranged with any of the diving companies listed on page 329, or through most hotels in Trinco, Uppuveli or Nilaveli, inclusive of transport to the beach. The park tends to be busiest over weekends, so try to visit on a weekday. Some boat operators offer snorkelling trips to the base of Swami Rock as a budget alternative to Pigeon Island; there's isn't any coral here, and fish are fewer, but no national park fees apply.

Whale watching Although Swami Rock provides a superb vantage point for land-based whale watching, a more certain option, at least between April and September, when the area's resident blue whales are joined by migrant pods of sperm whales from the south coast, is a dedicated boat trip to the deeper waters about 15km out to sea. In season, a highly regarded Colombo-based company, Sail Lanka Charters (**m** 0714 405000; **e** contact@sail-lanka-charter.com; **w** sail-lanka-charter.com) keeps a boat docked in Trinco and runs public whale-watching trips daily for US$50 per person. Trips can also be arranged through many hotels and dive companies at around US$40 per person, usually with a minimum group size of two or three.

Arisimalai beach [map, page 288] Situated on a wild and rocky headland on the southern outskirts of Pulmoddai about 30km north of Nilaveli, Arisimalai literally means 'pile of rice', a name that refers to the freakishly large grains of sand that characterise the beach. It lies about 1km east of the main road, and you need to pass through a (friendly) military checkpoint to get here. Using public transport, all buses running north from Trinco to Nilaveli continue to Pulmoddai, from where it's about 2.5km on foot or by tuktuk to the beach.

Kanniya Hot Water Wells [map, page 322] (🕐 *24hrs; entrance Rs50*) This cluster of seven hot springs, situated on the south side of the Anuradhapura road 5km west of Uppuveli, was legendarily created by the grief-stricken King Ravana when he struck the earth with his sword seven times while performing the last rites for his mother Kaikesi. Protected in a cluster of small rectangular stone pools, the springs have been regarded as therapeutic since the Anuradhapura era and are sacred to both Hindus and Buddhists, who still visit in their droves at weekends. Some tours include the site on their itinerary, but it is all rather underwhelming and there's very little to see.

Marble beach [map, page 322] (📞 *026 302 1000;* w *marblebeach.lk;* 🕐 *08.00–18.00; entrance Rs50*) This fine white-sanded swimming beach, named after the marble-floor effect created by the sun reflecting off the shallow water, lies on an all but unspoilt wooded peninsular cove on the west side of Koddiyar Bay, 6km southwest of Trincomalee town centre as the crow flies, but more like 18km by road. It lies on military property and is serviced by a small air-force-managed resort offering affordable meals and rather pricey accommodation. To get here from Trinco, follow the Anuradhapura Road out of town for about 6km then turn left on to the Batticaloa Road and follow it south along the west coast of Koddiyar Bay for another 10km until you see the signposted turn-off to your left just before it crosses Kinniya Bridge. It's 2km from the turn-off to the beach. Using public transport, you could bus to Kinniya town (immediately south of the bridge) and catch a tuktuk from there.

Seruwawila Archaeological Reserve [map, page 320] (🕐 *24hrs*) Claimed to be the 17th Solosmasthana (a group of 16 sacred places reputedly visited by the Buddha over the course of his three visits to Sri Lanka), Seruwawila, some 40km south of Trinco by road, is the site of an ancient monastery focused on a massive dagoba whose relic chamber reputedly enshrines the forehead bone of the Buddha. Built in the 2nd century BC by King Kavan Tissa, the ancient dagoba had fallen into disuse for several centuries prior to being rediscovered in 1922 by the Buddhist monk Dambagasare Sri Sumedhankara Thero, who then restored it with the assistance of the Department of Archaeology. The site also incorporates the ruins of an image house, bathing pool, chapter house, bodhighara and various engravings. It lies about 5km southeast of the Batticaloa Road along a junction signposted just past the village of Palatoppu.

PASIKUDA

In the process of reclaiming its 1970s mantle as the east coast's top tourist hotspot, Pasikuda (sometimes spelt Passikudah) is renowned for its beautiful golden beach, calm warm aquamarine waters, and an offshore incline so gradual you could wade out for 50m and still have a dry waist. Despite its natural assets, however, Pasikuda and neighbouring Kalkudah managed to vanish from Sri Lanka's tourist map for the best part of three decades, the result of a 1978 cyclone, whose devastating aftermath was prolonged by a series of LTTE attacks during the civil war, and finally by the 2004 tsunami. Then, in 2012, some 75ha of land alongside this picture-perfect family-friendly beach was designated as the Pasikuda Tourist Zone, and earmarked for the construction of 14 new upmarket hotels with a total of 930 rooms. Since then, Pasikuda beach has undergone a remarkably rapid and thorough transformation to a contemporary beach resort ideally located – though still slightly under-utilised – to be an overnight diversion *en route* between the Cultural Triangle and Kandy over

April to September. For independent travellers, Pasikuda does support a scattering of decent budget hotels but, without the urban context of nearby Trincomalee or Batticaloa, it inevitably feels slightly contrived, which might – or might not – be exactly what you are looking for!

GETTING THERE AND AWAY The urban gateway to Pasikuda is Valaichchenai, a smallish but well-equipped town whose main junction lies about 7km from the various beach resorts by road. A tuktuk from Valaichchenai railway station or junction to Pasikuda won't cost more than US$2.

By air The closest airport is at Batticaloa, 20km to the south. It is serviced by Sri Lanka Airlines and Cinnamon Air, both of which fly there from Colombo.

By rail The 06.05 and 19.00 trains from Colombo Fort to Batticaloa via Polonnaruwa stop at Valaichchenai. Heading in the opposite direction, trains from Batticaloa to Colombo Fort stop briefly at Valaichchenai at 06.58 and 21.00. The trip to/from Colombo takes about 8 hours.

By road Pasikuda lies 100km south of Trincomalee by road, about 300km from Colombo via Dambulla (135km), Habarana (115km), and Polonnaruwa (70km), and 190km from Kandy via Mahiyanganaya (110km) and Batticaloa (30km). The main local transport hub is Valaichchenai Junction, which is passed through by buses between Batticaloa and Trincomalee every 30 minutes, as well as equally regular between Batticaloa and Polonnaruwa, Dambulla and other destinations along the Colombo Road.

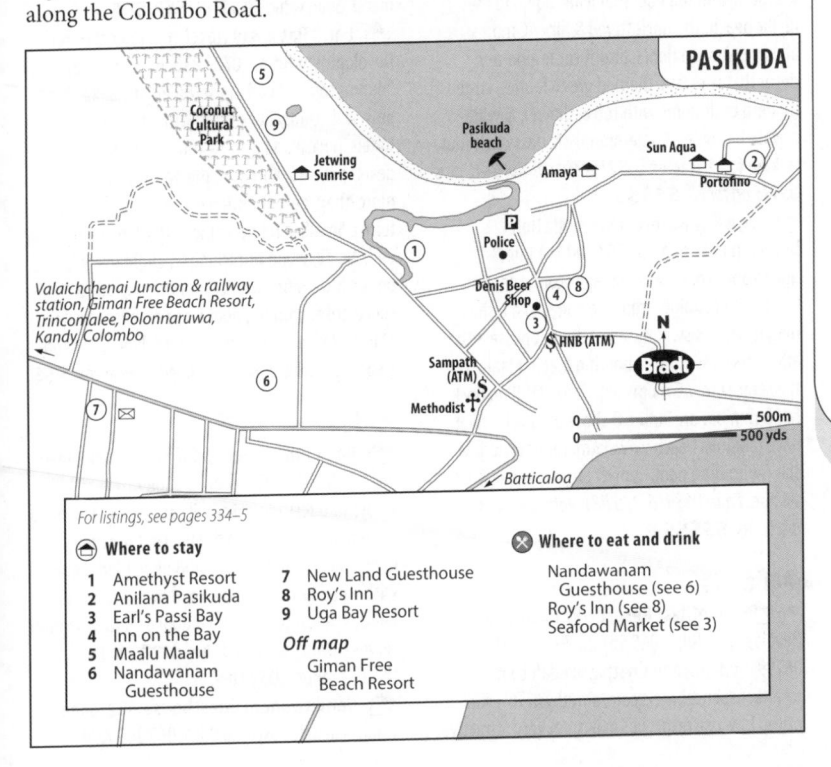

For listings, see pages 334–5

Where to stay

1 Amethyst Resort
2 Anilana Pasikuda
3 Earl's Passi Bay
4 Inn on the Bay
5 Maalu Maalu
6 Nandawanam Guesthouse
7 New Land Guesthouse
8 Roy's Inn
9 Uga Bay Resort

Off map
Giman Free Beach Resort

Where to eat and drink

Nandawanam Guesthouse (see 6)
Roy's Inn (see 8)
Seafood Market (see 3)

WHERE TO STAY *Map, page 333*

Upmarket

Anilana Pasikuda (25 rooms) Hotel Development Rd; 065 203 0900; e info@anilana.com; w anilana.com. This stylish new resort is the most easterly development on Pasikuda beach, with a high-ceilinged lobby & restaurant hung with modern art & monochrome photos, & a massive swimming pool set right on the beach. Large, modern & subtly lit & decorated AC rooms have king-size bed, semi-abstract watercolours of rural Sri Lankan scenes on the wall, large flatscreen TV, sofa, private balcony with pool or ocean view, & super-modern bathroom with slate-tile & treated concrete floor. *Well-priced at US$185 dbl B&B, plus US$55 pp for FB.* **$$$$$**

Maalu Maalu (40 rooms) Hotel Development Rd; 065 738 8388; e info@themeresorts.com; w maalumaalu.com. Pasikuda's pioneering post-war resort, opened in 2011 & named after the fish vendor's cry of '*maalu maalu*', is designed like an upmarket variation on a fishing village, with 2 rows of elegantly simple 2-storey wood-clad thatched cottages flanking a large swimming pool that leads down to the idyllic beach. The uncluttered & airy AC rooms all have wooden floors, bright contemporary décor that uses fish-themed green fabrics, large modern bathrooms with tub & shower, & wide private balconies. Contemporary & classy, without lacking for character. *US$216/254 sgl/dbl B&B, plus US$45 pp for FB.* **$$$$$**

Uga Bay Resort (48 rooms) Hotel Development Rd; 065 567 1000; e info@ugaescapes.com; w ugaescapes.com. Seemingly transported straight from the pages of a fashion magazine, this swanky resort doesn't possess the effortless class of neighbouring Maalu Maalu, but the semi-suite AC rooms with large TV, iPod dock, fan & minibar are larger, & those on the 1st floor have fabulous beach views. Amenities include a spa, swimming pool, gym, & bicycle, canoe & jet-ski hire. *From US$316/370 B&B with low-season discounts.* **$$$$$+**

Moderate

✳ Amethyst Resort (97 rooms) Hotel Development Rd; 065 567 2005/7; m 0771 062995; e fom@amethystpassikudah.com; w aitkenspencehotels.com/amethyst. This well-priced low-rise resort lies in large & very attractive grounds bisected by a river teeming with fish, birds & crocodiles, & runs down to a large swimming pool set on a wooden deck, & a particularly wide stretch of beach with hammocks hanging from the palms. Unpretentious but spacious, comfortable & agreeably furnished rooms have a high wooden ceiling, grey tile floor, roomy bathroom, AC, fan, darkwood furniture & balcony with beach or river view. Very good value at *US$101/109 sgl/dbl B&B*, rather less so at *US$175/206 FB*, so the cost-conscious might think about taking lunch & dinner elsewhere. **$$$$**

Giman Free Beach Resort (14 rooms) About 1km east of the Trincomalee Rd 13km north of Valaichchenai Junction; 065 364 9977/99; e info@gimanfree.com; w gimanfree.com. This small & down-to-earth resort has a wonderfully isolated location on a shallow & pristine beach north of Pasikuda & is popular with divers thanks to its excellent in-house dive centre (⊕ *May–Sep*). The comfortable AC chalets are built using organic materials, while other facilities include a swimming pool & good restaurant with a seafood-dominated menu. Good value. *US$88 dbl B&B.* **$$$$**

Earl's Passi Bay Hotel (35 rooms) Hotel Development Rd; m 0777 836468; e a-1768@lakpura.com; w earls-passikudah-sri-lanka.en.ww.lk. Oddly out of step with other tourist hotels in Pasikuda, this 5-storey mid-range development 200m from the beach seems like a more-than-decent option taken on its own bland terms. Smallish rooms come with twin or king-size bed, AC, TV, wood furnishings & slight overkill on the blue-fabric front. Amenities include a courtyard swimming pool & the excellent Seafood Market Restaurant on the ground floor. *US$53 dbl B&B; negotiable discounts offered to walk-ins.* **$$$**

Budget

Roy's Inn (5 rooms) Off Hotel Development Rd; 065 205 0223; m 0775 036696; e roysinnguesthouse@gmail.com. Set in a wooded garden only 400m from the beach, this small guesthouse has spacious standalone tiled rooms with wood furniture, walk-in nets, fan & private balcony. A restaurant with indoor & garden seating serves curries, devilled dishes & pasta in the US$2–4 range. *US$24 dbl.* **$**

Nandawanam Guesthouse (12 rooms) Valaichchenai–Pasikuda Rd; 065 225 7258;

m 0719 714799; e nandawanam@live.com; w nandawanam.blogspot.com. Situated 1.5km from the beach, this well-established local favourite comprises a modern 2-storey building with terrace restaurant (mains in the US$3–5 range) set in attractive & well-tended gardens. Rooms are spacious, with AC, Wi-Fi, flatscreen TV, wooden writing desk & wardrobe, & most have a balcony. *US$27/30 sgl/dbl.* **$$**

Shoestring

🏠 **New Land Guesthouse** (8 rooms) Valaichchenai–Pasikuda Rd; ☏ 065 568 0440.

Situated on a palm-shaded sandy plot almost 2km from the beach, this pleasant homestay-style lodge has small but neat rooms with net. *US$7 dbl with fan, or US$20.50 with AC.* **$**

🏠 **Inn on the Bay** (7 rooms) Hotel Development Rd; ☏ 065 225 7484; m 0776 327842. This rustic set-up 200m from the beach proudly proclaims itself to be Pasikuda's oldest hotel, & once you've resisted the urge to point out that it shows, the wood & banana-leaf huts with net, fan, nice outdoor shower & private balcony come across as decent value. *US$13.50 dbl with fan; trpl rooms with AC also available at US$31.* **$**

✖ WHERE TO EAT AND DRINK *Map, page 333*

Most people eat at their hotel. Roy's Inn and the Nandawanam Guesthouse stand out for decent local-style curries and devilled dishes in the **$$** range.

✖ **Seafood Market Restaurant** Earl's Passi Bay Hotel (opposite); ☏ 065 205 0203; ⏱ 07.00–22.00. This unexpectedly stylish AC restaurant has clinical white interiors brightened up by abstract art on the walls, & a cosmopolitan menu of seafood & meat dishes in the US$6–10 range. **$$$**

OTHER PRACTICALITIES There are no banks in Pasikuda, but HNB maintains an ATM next to Earl's Passi Bay Hotel, and Sampath Bank has one on the main junction next to the Methodist church. There are also a few banks on the main street through Valaichchenai.

WHAT TO SEE AND DO Activities in Pasikuda are dominated by the child-friendly beach, which really is a stunner, admittedly in a rather becalmed way. Easy to wade out to, the offshore reef that protects the beach is too shallow for diving, but it offers some rewarding snorkelling, and gear is available at most of the beach resorts. Back on terra firma, the only formal tourist attraction, flanking the south side of Hotel Development Road, is the Coconut Cultural Park (⏱ 08.00–17.00; *entrance US$9*), which comprises an 11ha plantation owned by the Coconut Cultivation Board, and offers informative guided tours showing most stages in the traditional production of coconuts, as well as several other fruits, herbs and spices. Otherwise, if lounging around the beach and hotel swimming pool start to pall, you could always head out for a day trip to Batticaloa, which is only 20km to the south and serviced by regular buses from Valaichchenai.

BATTICALOA

Situated near the mouth of the eponymous 115km² estuarine lagoon, Batticaloa – plain Batti, once you're sufficiently familiar – is the eighth-largest town in Sri Lanka, supporting a predominantly Tamil population estimated at around 100,000. It was effectively off limits to tourism during the civil war, and was hit worse than most by the 2004 tsunami, but now that the strife is settled and the NGOs have moved on, it is starting to emerge as an engaging travel destination, albeit one that's first and foremost a working town. Batti's recognised attractions tend towards the low-key – a few minor historical landmarks, a serviceable beach at Kallady, and

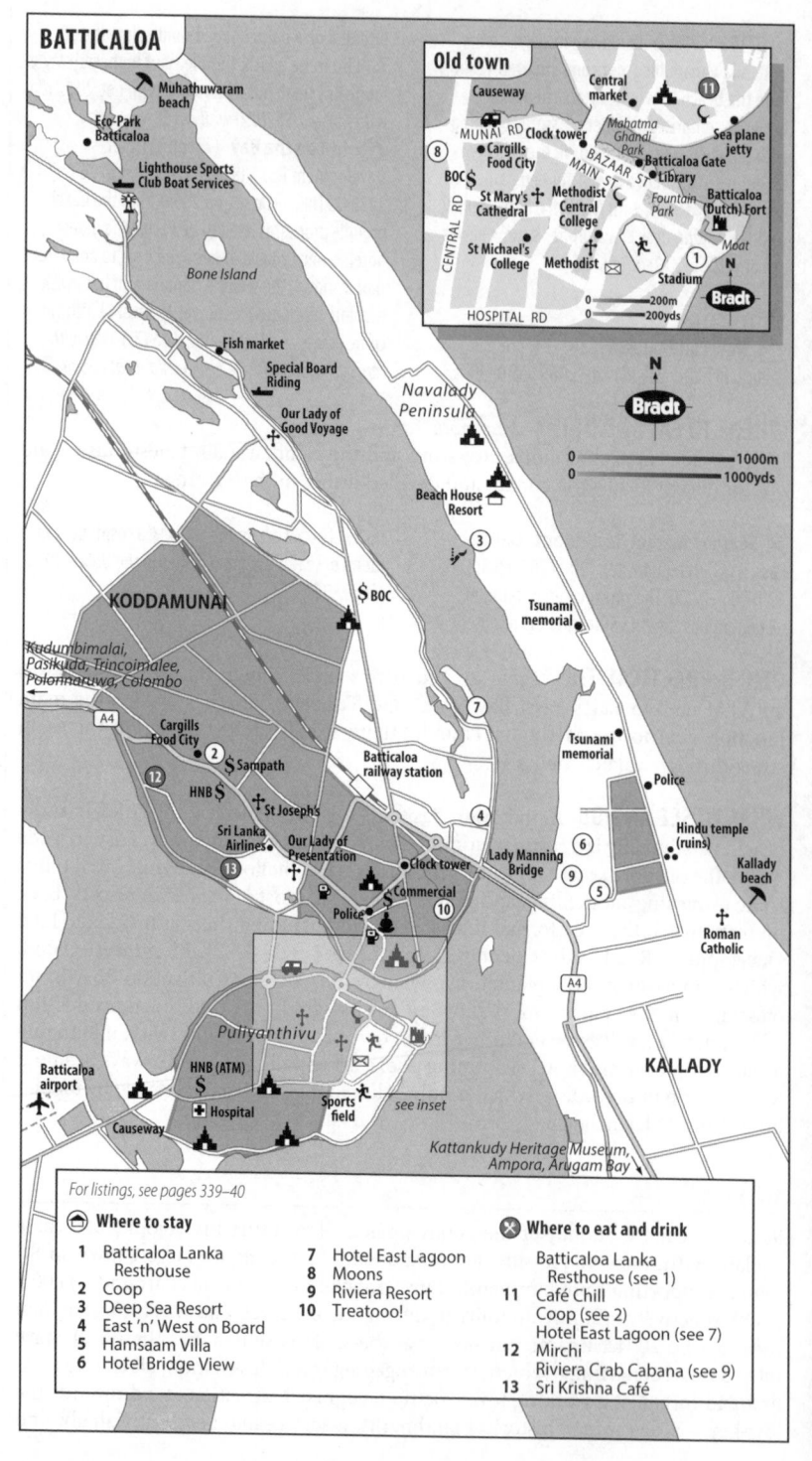

BATTICALOA

Old town

Central market
Causeway
Clock tower
MUNAI RD
Mahatma Ghandi Park
Sea plane jetty
Cargills Food City
Batticaloa Gate
BAZAAR ST
Library
MAIN ST
BOC
Batticaloa (Dutch) Fort
St Mary's Cathedral
Methodist Central College
Fountain Park
CENTRAL RD
Moat
St Michael's College
Methodist
Stadium
N
HOSPITAL RD

0   200m
0   200yds

Muhathuwaram beach
Eco-Park Batticaloa
Lighthouse Sports Club Boat Services

Bone Island

Fish market
Special Board Riding
Our Lady of Good Voyage

Navalady Peninsula

Beach House Resort
3

KODDAMUNAI

Kudumbimalai, Pasikuda, Trincoimalee, Polonnaruwa, Colombo
A4

$ BOC

Tsunami memorial

7

Cargills Food City
2
$ Sampath
HNB $
St Joseph's
Sri Lanka Airlines
13
Our Lady of Presentation

Batticaloa railway station
4

Tsunami memorial
Police

Hindu temple (ruins)
6
Kallady beach

Clock tower
Lady Manning Bridge
9
5
Commercial
10
Police

Roman Catholic

A4

KALLADY

Puliyanthivu
HNB (ATM) $
Batticaloa airport
Hospital
Causeway
Sports field
see inset

Kattankudy Heritage Museum, Ampora, Arugam Bay

N
0   1000m
0   1000yds

For listings, see pages 339–40

🛏 Where to stay

1 Batticaloa Lanka Resthouse
2 Coop
3 Deep Sea Resort
4 East 'n' West on Board
5 Hamsaam Villa
6 Hotel Bridge View
7 Hotel East Lagoon
8 Moons
9 Riviera Resort
10 Treatooo!

✴ Where to eat and drink

Batticaloa Lanka Resthouse (see 1)
11 Café Chill
Coop (see 2)
Hotel East Lagoon (see 7)
12 Mirchi
Riviera Crab Cabana (see 9)
13 Sri Krishna Café

a lagoon easily explored by boat or along the roads that hug its banks – but it's a likeably unaffected town and feels like more than the sum of its landmarks; in the right frame of mind, one might easily settle in here for a few cheap days and explore at leisure.

Batticaloa's most elusive residents are the 'singing fishes' that legendarily inhabit the vast lagoon. Theirs is by all accounts an eerie call: 'like the gentle thrills of a musical chord, or the faint vibrations of a wine glass when its rim is rubbed by a wet finger,' wrote James Tennent in 1848, but possessed of a 'weirdness [that] almost placed sleep out of the question,' according to J Penry Lewis in the 1920s. Tennent suggested that the creature responsible might be 'Mollusca, not fish', a theory supported by the local Tamil name *Oorie Coolooroo Cradoo* (Crying Shells). The truth is nobody knows for sure. In practice, you'd need to mount a small expedition to stand much chance of hearing the sound *in situ*: it's most likely to be heard by taking a boat out on to the lagoon at full moon, lowering an oar into the water, and placing your ear at the other end. Failing that, it's worth tuning in to a recent 30-minute BBC documentary about the phenomenon, available online at w bbc. co.uk/programmes/b04bn086.

Batticaloa comprises three distinct divisions, isolated from the others by the calm waters of the lagoon. Most interesting, contained on the 1.4km^2 Puliyanthivu Island, is Old Batticaloa, whose scattering of colonial relicts includes Sri Lanka's oldest Dutch fort. A little surprisingly, the island-bound old town also houses Batti's main bus station, but the railway station, as well as most banks and other modern amenities, can be found opposite Puliyanthivu in the new town centre, called Koddamunai or Arasuda. Altogether more low-rise, the residential suburb of Kallady stands on the narrow Navalady Peninsula on the east side of the lagoon, and houses several popular budget hotels and homestays. Three roads connect Old Batticaloa to the mainland. These are the 120m-long bridge and 350m causeway linking the north shore of Puliyanthivu Island to the new town centre, and a 200m causeway to the southern mainland and the airport. Kallady has no direct road link to Old Batticaloa, but it is connected to the new town by the modern Lady Manning Bridge, which also forms part of the main road running south to Ampara and Arugam Bay.

HISTORY Medieval Batticaloa was known to its predominantly Tamil inhabitants as Mattakallappu (Flat or Muddy Lagoon), the Sinhalese equivalent of which is Madakalapuwa. A mythologised version of its early history is documented in the anonymous manuscript *Mattakallappu Manmiyam*, which was compiled at the start of the Dutch colonial era but probably contains some much older elements. According to this manuscript, the first migrants to Batticaloa were the Mukkuvar: Tamil fishermen who sailed cross from southern India, and established seven villages in the area under one King Pandia. The timing of this migration is unknown, but archaeological evidence in the form of several South Indian-style megalithic burial sites suggests it might have been between the 2nd century BC and 2nd century AD. According to the *Mattakallappu Manmiyam*, the name Puliyanthivu (the island housing Batticaloa old town) is ancient indeed, referring as it does to a Vedda chief called Puliya, who occupied it prior to the Mukkuvar migration; other sources indicate it might just mean 'Island of Tamarinds'.

Batticaloa was largely unaffected by the 16th-century Portuguese occupation, which focused mainly on Colombo and the west coast. It was, however, the first Dutch landfall on the island. In 1602, a fleet of three Dutch boats landed at Batticaloa, and Admiral Joris van Spilbergen travelled overland from here to Kandy, hoping to persuade its king to enter into a trade treaty. In 1628, the growing Dutch influence on the Ceylonese cinnamon trade prompted the Portuguese to build a fort in Batticaloa. The Dutch captured the fort in 1638, but demolished it a year later and handed control of Batticaloa – 'a vile, stinking place' – to the Sinhalese. The Dutch once again occupied Batticaloa in 1665, when the fort was reconstructed. Batticaloa and its fort were captured by the British in 1796.

Batticaloa was one of the Sri Lankan districts most isolated and damaged by the recent civil war. All train services here were discontinued in 1995 for fear of terrorist bombings, and while the town remained under government rule, much of the surrounding countryside fell under LTTE control, as did Kokkaddicholai, a substantial town only 10km to the south. By the turn of the millennium, Batticaloa, writes Nirupama Subramanian in *Sri Lanka, Voices from a War Zone*, 'was answerable to the Sri Lanka army brigade … by day [but] by night the town took orders from the Tigers'. The district's woes were compounded by the 2004 tsunami, which practically submerged the Kallady Peninsula as the water swelled to almost 5m above sea level within 90 minutes of the beginning of the earthquake that triggered the disaster. At least 13,000 people died in Batticaloa and neighbouring Ampara districts, accounting for more than 40% of the national tsunami death toll. Meanwhile, the stand-off with the LTTE came to a head in early 2007, after the Italian, German and US ambassadors were injured in a rebel artillery attack on two helicopters transporting them to Batticaloa. This incident prompted the Sri Lankan army to launch what would prove to be a decisive attack on the LTTE's mountain stronghold at Kudumbimalai (Thoppigala) Rock, 35km inland of Batticaloa. Around three-quarters of the 1,000-strong LTTE force at Kudumbimalai was killed in the attack, allowing the government to reclaim full control over Batticaloa District.

GETTING THERE AND AWAY Whether you arrive by bus or by rail, you'll be greeted by plenty of tuktuks to take you to your hotel. Expect to pay up to US$1 within the town centre and more like US$2 to cross over to Kallady.

By air Batticaloa Airport, set on a thinly inhabited mainland peninsula only 1km from Batticaloa Island and linked to it by a causeway, is serviced by Sri Lanka Airlines (w *srilankan.com*), Cinnamon Air (w *cinnamonair.com*) and the far more affordable Helitours (w *helitours.lk*), all of which fly there from Colombo several times weekly.

By rail Batticaloa is connected to Colombo by a 348km railway track lain in 1928 as an extension to the railway to the more strategically important harbour of Trincomalee. Two train services cover the route daily, leaving from Colombo Fort at 06.05 and 19.00, from Batticaloa at 07.15 and 20.15, taking up to 9 hours one way, and stopping at Maho, Gal Oya Junction, Polonnaruwa and Valaichchenai (for Pasikuda). Batticaloa railway station, situated off Bar Road at the north end of the new town centre, is graced by an extraordinary Rococo fountain crowned by a mermaid strumming a guitar made out of a plaster fish.

By road Batticaloa lies 120km south of Trincomalee by road, about 320km from Colombo via Dambulla (155km), Habarana (135km), Polonnaruwa (90km) and Valaichchenai (for Pasikuda, 20km), and 185km from Kandy via Mahiyanganaya (105km). All buses arrive and leave from the adjacent public and private bus terminals on the old town's Munai Road, which runs along the north shore of Batticaloa Island between the bridge and the causeway to the new town. Services to and from Trincomalee via Valaichchenai run every 30 minutes, and there's at least one departure every hour to Colombo via Polonnaruwa and Dambulla, taking around 7 hours. The pick of the private buses to/from Colombo is Surena Travels (*Munai Rd;* ☎ *065 222 6152;* m *0771 075670;* e *surenatravels@gmail.com;* w *surenatravels.lk*), which operates three coaches in either direction daily, including an overnight air-conditioned service leaving at 21.00 in either direction. Note that there is only one direct bus to/from Kandy daily (departing from Batticaloa at 05.15 and from Kandy at 14.15). Heading to/from Arugam Bay, an early start is recommended, as there is plenty of transport between Batticaloa and Kalmunai, but rather less between Kalmunai and Arugam Bay (indeed, you may need to divert inland to Siyambalanduwa to get through more quickly).

WHERE TO STAY *Map, page 336*

Batticaloa is only recently re-emerging as a tourist destination after a hiatus of several decades, and although budget accommodation is plentiful, more commodious options are limited to the mid-range Hotel East Lagoon, while those seeking a more resort-like retreat would be better off in Pasikuda 20km to the north.

Moderate

✳ 🏠 **Hotel East Lagoon** (45 rooms) Uppodai Lake Rd; ☎ 065 222 9222; e info@hoteleastlagoon. lk; w hoteleastlagoon.lk. By far the most attractive hotel in Batticaloa, the 4-storey East Lagoon boasts a superb location on a peninsula that juts into the calm lagoon about 1km north of Kallady Bridge. Spacious rooms with imported fittings & furniture all have AC, fan, fridge, flatscreen TV & balcony with lagoon view. Amenities include a sparkling swimming pool, waterside seating, well-stocked bar & restaurant serving a selection of tasty Western, Indian & Sri Lankan dishes in the US$5–9 range. Very reasonably priced for a hotel of this standard. *US$45/52 sgl/dbl, b/fast US$7 pp extra.* **$$$**

Budget

✳ 🏠 **East 'n' West on Board** Uppodai Lake Rd; ☎ 065 222 6079; m 0725 615980; e eastnwestonboard@yahoo.com; w eastnwestonboard.com. Not a hotel as such, but a commendable & responsive joint French & Sri Lankan-run venture that arranges homestays with 11 different local families, all of which are checked regularly by management, & come with good beds, nets, fans & purified drinking water. Most of the homestays are located in Kallady but others are further afield. Clients can be met at the bus or railway station by request. *Rates range from US$17 dbl for a simple beach hut to up to US$40 for an AC bungalow.* **$–$$**

🏠 **Riviera Resort** (26 rooms) New Dutch Bar Rd, Kallady; ☎ 065 222 2164/5; e bookings@ riviera-online.com; w riviera-online.com. Batti's most established backpacker haunt possesses an agreeably dishevelled feel that evokes the sort of place where travellers used to congregate in the days before bespoke backpacker hostels existed. A steady stream of travellers and volunteers are attracted by the large wooded lagoonside grounds, shady & well-priced licensed restaurant, sociable feel, & good facilities (Wi-Fi, book swap, swimming pool & kayaks for hire). For all that, the rooms are quite shabby & feel rather overpriced by local standards, so you might prefer to sleep elsewhere & just head here for the occasional meal. *US$25 dbl with fan, US$40 dbl with AC.* **$$**

🏠 **Batticaloa Lanka Resthouse** (7 rooms) Fort Rd; ☎ 065 222 7882; m 0777 633449. Set in a large breezy seafront garden right opposite the old Dutch Fort, this timeworn government resthouse also has a licensed restaurant serving chilled beers and decent Chinese & local cuisine in the US$3–4 range. Rooms are a bit rundown & rather close to the bar, but decent value given that they come with AC & fan. *US$20.50 dbl.* **$**

🏠 **Treatooo!** (9 rooms) Lady Manning Dr; ☎ 065 222 7600; m 0766 710050; e info@ treatooo.com; w treatooo.com. Set alongside the lagoon 300m south of Lady Manning Bridge, this pleasant but unremarkable lodge has clean rooms with TV & a restaurant serving good seafood & Indian dishes in the US$4–5 range. Decent value. *US$16 dbl with fan, US$21/27 dbl/twin with AC.* **$**

🏠 **Deep Sea Resort** (6 rooms) Navalady Peninsula; m 0777 648459; e felicianfernando@ hotmail.com; w srilanka-divingtours.com. Aimed mainly at divers, this simple resort has a very isolated location on the Navalady Peninsula, west of the lagoon, about 3km north of Lady Manning Bridge. Simple en-suite rooms have AC, & there's a small swimming pool. *US$31 dbl.* **$$**

Shoestring

✻ 🏠 **Hamsaam Villa** (3 rooms) New Dutch Bar Rd, Kallady; 📞065 222 8060; m 0775 803845; e anandahrajah@gmail.com. This super little homestay, tucked away on a side road behind the Riviera, has very well-priced bright-blue rooms with fan, Wi-Fi & TV, & home-cooked meals can be supplied by request. *US$12.50/13.50 sgl/dbl with fan, US$20.50/22 with AC.* **$**

🏠 **Coop Hotel** (9 rooms) Trincomalee Hwy; 📞068 222 8613. Deceptively smart from the outside, this central multistorey hotel next to Cargills Food City supermarket is one of Batti's better shoestring options. The slightly rundown but clean rooms have fan, TV & optional AC, & there's also a breezy rooftop bar & cheap ground-floor restaurant. *US$13.50 dbl, plus US$5 for AC.* **$**

🏠 **Moons Hotel** (10 rooms) Covington Rd; 📞065 222 9123; m 0774 089788. En-suite rooms here are on the gloomy side, but they're very reasonably priced & as central as it gets, situated in the old town only 100m from the bus station. *US$10 dbl with fan, US$17 with AC.* **$**

🏠 **Hotel Bridge View** (20 ooms) New Dutch Bar Rd; 📞065 222 3723; m 0774 846414. This prominently & promisingly signposted (yet oddly difficult to find) hotel behind the Riviera has no view worth talking about, bridge or otherwise, and its moribund exterior is the very definition of 'past the sell-by date'. Rooms are better than might be expected & the ones with AC are actually quite good value. *US$11/15 sgl/dbl with fan, US$22/30 with AC.* **$**

✗ WHERE TO EAT AND DRINK   *Map, page 336*

Aside from the ever-popular Riviera (listed below), most eateries and hotels in Batti don't serve alcohol. Noteworthy exceptions are the rooftop bar at the Coop Hotel (🕐 *18.00–22.00*) and the open-all-hours bar at the lagoonside Batticaloa Lanka Resthouse. Also worth a shout, despite its rather non-central location, is the altogether less disreputable Hotel East Lagoon, which has a good Western-style restaurant, a licensed bar and well-appointed waterfront seating.

✻ ✗ **Riviera Crab Cabana Restaurant** Riviera Resort; 🕐 07.00–22.00. Shady outdoor seating below whirring fans, a well-stocked bar, & a varied menu of affordable Sri Lankan & Western mains have made this a long-serving favourite with budget travellers. Full marks for food & ambience, but be warned that service tends to be slow, orders are often mixed up (so spell out what you want carefully) & the excellent local dishes tend to be searingly hot unless you specify otherwise. **$$**

✗ **Café Chill** Pioneer Rd; m 0777 779598; 🕐 09.30–21.00. Batti's hippest eatery offers free Wi-Fi, outdoor seating with wooden tables shaded by palm-frond roofs, good coffee & milkshakes, & a selection of tasty burgers, sandwiches & other light meals. **$**

✗ **Sri Krishna Café** Slaughterhouse Lake Rd; 🕐 06.00–22.00. Good vegetarian restaurant whose ambience deficiency is compensated for by the lagoonside location & very low prices (*US$1–1.50*). **$**

✗ **Mirchi Restaurant** Slaughterhouse Lake Rd; 📞065 205 7777; 🕐 07.00–22.00. This quirky new restaurant set in a rickety wooden 2-storey construction overlooking the lagoon specialises in South Indian cuisine. Vegetarian dishes **$**, fish & meat dishes **$$**

OTHER PRACTICALITIES The top shopping area is the old town's Bazaar Street, which hosts all manner of small local shops. There are two Cargills Food City Supermarkets, one on Munai Road in the old town opposite the bus station, and the other on Trincomalee Highway next to the Coop Hotel. There's a Commercial Bank with ATM on Bar Road in the new town centre, and plenty of other banks and ATMs scattered around the town centre. Kallady is short on amenities so if you are staying there, best do any banking or shopping before you head across the bridge.

TOUR OPERATORS AND INFORMATION

East 'n' West on Board Uppodai Lake Rd; \065 222 6079; m 0725 615980; e eastnwestonboard@ yahoo.com; w eastnwestonboard.com. This excellent centrally located joint French & Sri Lankan operation doesn't only specialise in arranging homestays, it also maintains a very useful website (w *welcometobatticaloa.com*), and offers visitors a free fold-out tourist map, reliable city & mountain bike rental (*US$3.50/day*), and can put you in touch with reliable taxi drivers for both local hops and longer hauls. A selection of customised tours in and around Batticaloa can incorporate visits to most established & many lesser-known sites of interest within a day-tripping distance of town, & optionally incorporate activities such as cooking lessons, birdwatching, fishing, village visits & the like. It also offers snorkelling excursions to the reefs off Pasikuda. Rates depend on what you do & group size but typically work out at around US$30 pp for a full-day outing.

Sri Lanka Diving Tours m 0777 648459; e felicianfernando@hotmail.com; w srilanka-divingtours.com. This Negombo-based operator sets itself up at Batticaloa seasonally between May & Sep, using **Deep Sea Resort** (page 339) as its base. It offers wreck dives to HMS *Hermes*, which sunk offshore of Batticaloa during World War II, as well as to other local dive sites.

WHAT TO SEE AND DO

Batticaloa Fort [map, page 336] (⊕ *07.00–17.00*) Dominating the northeast corner of Puliyanthivu Island, Batticaloa's oldest building is generally referred to as the Dutch Fort, though in fact it started life in the 1620s under the Portuguese. A contemporaneous description of the original Portuguese fortification, dating to 1628, details 'a square structure with four bastions of ancient design, armed with a dozen iron cannons, and [a] garrison … of a captain and 50 soldiers, with a gunner, 20 inhabitants, a chaplain, a church and a magazine of stores and ammunition'. Ten years later, the Dutch captured and destroyed the Portuguese fort, but they returned in 1665 to rebuild it in the same place with a similar four-bastioned footprint. Further renovations were undertaken in the 1680s, and again after the British occupation of Batticaloa in 1796. When Tennent visited Batticaloa, he described its fort as 'a grim little quadrangular stronghold … surrounded by a ditch swarming with crocodiles', but was impressed by the healthy and sizeable coconuts grown there, which he attributed to 'a soil sandy and pervious, a profusion of water from the fresh lake on the one side and the sea on the other, a warm and genial sun, and timely rains'. The fort was in active use throughout the colonial period, and today – surrounded by the lagoon on two sides and the remains of a moat on the third – it houses various administrative buildings. The old Dutch VOC inscription can still be seen on the main entrance, built into the eastern wall, and from here you can turn left then left again up a stone staircase to the stone ramparts, which can be walked around in their entirety and offer some good views over the lagoon. A small museum housing various colonial artefacts and some ancient palm-leaf manuscripts (including a *Mattakallappu Manmiyam*) opened inside the fort in 1999, but we found no trace of it in 2016. Plans do exist, however, to relocate the government offices elsewhere and convert the fort to a regional museum.

Puliyanthivu and the old town [map, page 336] After visiting the fort, consider dedicating a couple of hours to exploring island-bound Old Batticaloa, which – lapped on all sides by the normally calm waters of the lagoon – retains a laid-back tropical ambience redolent of a river port. The neatly paved waterfront Mahatma Ghandi Park, adorned with a golden statue of its namesake, is a popular local evening and weekend promenade, offering good views across the narrow lagoon to the Koddamunai mainland. Set within the park, the three-arched Batticaloa

13

Gate (and remains of an old hand-winch) marks the island's main boat landing and loading site prior to the construction of the trio of modern bridges and causeways linking it to the mainland. Next to it is a statue of the Reverend William Ault, the influential Methodist missionary who established eight schools in Batticaloa between landing here in July 1814 and dying of an unknown tropical illness nine months later. Running parallel to the waterfront park, and only 50m further inland, Bazaar Street, lined with jewellers, clothing outlets and sweet shops, is the closest the old town gets to exuding a real urban bustle. Further south, an organic maze of curving roads meanders through the island's sleepy residential suburbs, leading past several Hindu temples and old colonial homesteads and offices set in leafy gardens inhabited by squawking parakeets and preening peacocks. Important colonial-era landmarks include St Mary's Catholic Cathedral (built 1808), the Methodist Central College founded by Reverend Ault in 1814, the adjacent Methodist church (1838) and St Michael's College (1873). And if you're up for a good leg stretch, Esplanade and Lake roads run around the fish-shaped island's entire 5.5km circumference, offering lovely views across the lagoon to the mainland.

The northern lagoon, lighthouse and Eco-Park Batticaloa [map, page 336]

Back on the mainland, the quiet, scenic and eminently walkable (or cycleable) 5km Uppodai Lake Road follows the west bank of the lagoon north from Lady Manning Bridge to Batticaloa Lighthouse, and offers some great birding possibilities *en route*, as well as an opportunity to watch local fishing boats in action or to get out on to the water yourself. Just over halfway between the bridge and the lighthouse, Special Board Riding (m *0779 919403*) operates 90-minute motorboat trips around the lagoon for US$35 per party (up to nine), and it also rents out one-person kayaks and two-berth swan-shaped paddle boats at US$1.60 an hour (to see birds and possibly other wildlife, paddle along the west bank for another 50m, then turn left, under a bridge, into a lovely small lagoon enclosed by mangroves). The 28m-high Batticaloa Lighthouse, built in 1913, is nothing to get excited about, especially now that entrance is forbidden so visitors can't enjoy the sterling views across the lagoon to the open sea. Below it, the Lighthouse Sports Club Boat Services (LSCBS) runs motorboat trips all around the lagoon, incorporating stops at Bone Island and Batticaloa Gate (around US$24 per party of up to eight).

A partially wooded dune opposite the lighthouse is the site of Eco-Park Batticaloa (❜ *065 222 9144*; m *0771 117535*; e *lagoon.environmental@yahoo.com*; ⊕ *08.30–17.00*), which is run by the Lagoon Environmental Learning Centre (LELC) primarily as an educational facility, but also welcomes tourists. The park incorporates a 15m-high bird-viewing tower, a souvenir shop selling handicrafts made by unemployed young locals, and a short access path to Muhathuwaram beach, a lovely stretch of golden sand with a magnificent location at the lagoon mouth 200m to the north. The easiest way to reach the Eco-Park is a short motorboat transfer with the LSCBS, which costs around US$2.50 per party return. If you are headed to the beach, you might want to bring swimming gear, but do check conditions before you take the plunge, as currents around the lagoon mouth can be strong.

Kallady beach [map, page 336]

Running for several kilometres along the east side of the Navalady Peninsula, this casuarina-lined fishing beach lies about 500m from the main residential part of Kallady and is easily accessed from any of its hotels or homestays. It is emphatically not a resort beach: a steep incline and propensity for dangerous riptides make it unsafe for swimming, dress codes should be in line with the sensibilities of the predominantly Hindu and Muslim local population, and its recreational value is further undermined by a quite remarkable volume of litter carried across from the Asian mainland. Still, it's a pleasant place for a seaside walk, and quite engaging to watch the various activities of the local fishermen. Follow the beach (or parallel road) north for a few kilometres, and you'll come across several reminders of the tragedy that befell Kallady on 26 December 2004: partially ruined temples, Hindu and Christian tsunami memorials, foundations of buildings swept away by the waves, and the distinctive two-storey tsunami houses built by foreign NGOs to house the survivors.

Kattankudy Heritage Museum (*Kattankudy Main Rd;* \ *065 224 8311, 097 286 1312;* ⊕ *09.00–18.00 exc Fri; entrance US$1.60)* Kattankudy, straddling the main coastal road 5km south of Kallady, is Sri Lanka's most Islamic town (99.75% of its 40,000 inhabitants describe themselves as Muslim) and also quite possibly its oldest Arab settlement. A credible local tradition has it that the area around Poonochchimunai Mosque, halfway between Kallady and Kattankudy, was settled by shipwrecked Arabs back in the 5th century (around a hundred years before the birth of the Prophet Muhammad) and that they were joined by Muslim traders from Arabia in the 8th century. As such, Kattankudy is an appropriate setting for this exceptional new museum dedicated to the history and culture of Sri Lanka's Islamic community, whose influence on national affairs peaked between the early Polonnaruwa period and the persecutory Portuguese and Dutch colonial regimes. A thoroughly modern installation that warrants at least an hour's exploration, the four-storey museum incorporates a varied selection of artefacts – metal oil lamps, clay water holders and bound Korans going back to the 18th century, ornately decorated swords, and the 18 different saris worn by local women on different occasions – as well some informative wall displays recounting the history of Islam in Sri Lanka. An entire floor is given over to a recreation of the traditional Muslim bazaar, while another is dominated by a 200-year-old traditional fishing boat from Mannar. Coming from Batticaloa or Kallady, the museum stands in a striking tall building on the right side of the main road about 300m south of the bus station. Buses between Batticaloa and Kalmunai run right past the museum every 30 minutes or so.

Kudumbimalai Mountain [map, page 320] Rising to an altitude of 534m about 35km inland of Batticaloa as the crow flies, Kudumbimalai is an isolated granite outcrop whose striking appearance is alluded to both in its British colonial name Baron's Cap, the Sinhalese Thoppigala (a type of hat) and the local Tamil name meaning 'hair-knot'. Kudumbimalai served as an LTTE stronghold in the civil war and the assault on it by the Sri Lankan army in July 2007 was pivotal in returning full control of Batticaloa District to the government. The mountain is also the centrepiece of a 70km² forest reserve whose thick woodland and scattering of lakes are inhabited by elephants, monkeys and a wide variety of birds. In 2013, it also became the site of the Thoppigala Heritage Centre, a joint effort by the Sri Lankan Army's 232 Brigade and the Dilmah Foundation (w *dilmahconservation.org*) to open the area to ecotourism and preserve its biodiversity, among other things through a reforestation programme that involved the planting of 20,000 indigenous species within the reserve. A monument and informative (though arguably rather one-sided) museum detailing the battle now stand at the mountain's base, and the hike to its magnificent peak, accompanied by a military guide, usually takes 30–45 minutes.

Kudumbimalai lies about 55km (up to 2 hours) from Batticaloa by road. To get here, head north towards Valaichchenai (Pasikuda) for about 25km to Kiran

13

Junction, then turn left on to a 30km dirt road that starts to deteriorate badly (requiring a high-clearance vehicle at all times, and 4x4 during the rains) as you approach the mountain's base. Two government buses run from Batticaloa to Kudumbimalai daily, or you could catch any Valaichchenai-bound bus as far as Kiran and rent a tuktuk from there. However, independent foreign travellers are still a rare sight, and the strong military presence can make for an edgy atmosphere, so it might be advisable to visit as a day trip with East 'n' West on Board (page 341), which visits the site regularly.

AMPARA AND GAL OYA NATIONAL PARK

The most significant town in the interior of Eastern Province, Ampara lies about 20km inland of the historic but little-visited seaport of Kalmunai, roughly halfway between Batticaloa and Arugam Bay. Despite being the eponymous capital of the largest and most southerly of the three districts that comprise Eastern Province, Ampara is a rather humdrum and forgettable town, of interest primarily as the gateway to the underrated Gal Oya National Park, an important elephant refuge unique in Sri Lanka insofar as most wildlife viewing is done by boat. A few ancient religious and archaeological sites also lie in the vicinity of Ampara, but none that really warrants a special trip.

AMPARA A modern town by Sri Lankan standards, Ampara was established in 1949 as a worker's village to service the construction of Gal Oya Dam 18km to the southwest. It grew in stature after 1961 as the administrative capital of a new district created from what was formerly the southern two-thirds of Batticaloa District. Unlike most other towns in Eastern Province, it is predominantly Sinhalese, and more than 90% of its population of 45,000 is Buddhist. Rice production is big business, with more than 30% of Ampara District being under paddies, accounting for around 15% of the national yield. Although Ampara is mainly of interest as a springboard for trips into Gal Oya National Park, a few local sites of interest – a clutch of minor temples and archaeological sites, as well as the Japanese Peace Pagoda on Ampara Tank – are worth checking out.

Getting there and away Ampara lies 310km east of Colombo via Kandy (190km) and Bibile (80km); 185km from Nuwara Eliya via Bibile; 200km from Trincomalee via Batticaloa (70km) and Kalmunai (25km); 195km from Dambulla via Polonnaruwa (135km); and 175km from Tissamaharama via Buttala (110km) and Siyambalanduwa (60km). Buses leave every hour to/from Kandy and Colombo (private air-conditioned services are available) and there is also plenty of transport to Batticaloa, though you might need to change vehicles at Kalmunai. Buses to Nuwara Eliya and Polonnaruwa are more occasional, so best to check current timings a day ahead. In a private vehicle, Ampara is only 65km from Pottuvil (for Arugam Bay), but travellers using public transport might need to use a longer (75km) coastal route changing minibuses at Akkaraipattu, or even longer (100km) inland route changing buses at Siyambalanduwa. The bus station is 50m south of the central clock tower.

Where to stay, eat and drink *Map, opposite*
The hotels listed on page 346 all serve decent food. Of a handful of bespoke local eateries along the main road, the oddly named Samurai Family Restaurant near the clock tower looks the most promising.

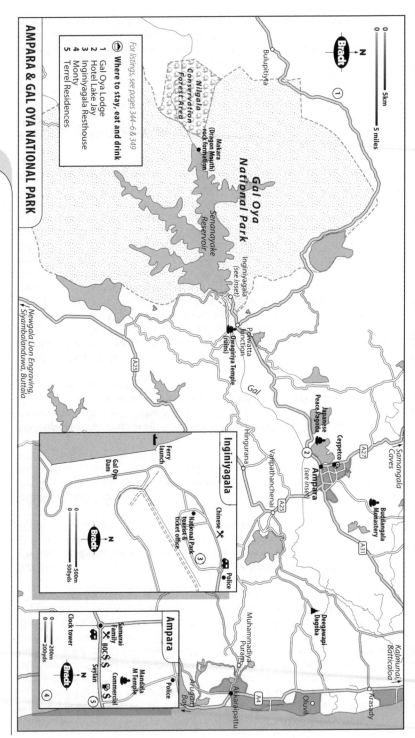

AMPARA & GAL OYA NATIONAL PARK

Where to stay, eat and drink

For listings, see pages 344–8 & 349

1 Gal Oya Lodge
2 Hotel Lake Jay
3 Inginiyagala Resthouse
4 Monty
5 Terrel Residences

Inginiyagala

- Gal Oya Dam
- Ferry launch
- Chinese
- National Park tourist & Ticket office
- Police

Ampara

- Clock tower
- Samurai Family
- BOC
- Sejian
- Mandala M Temple
- Commercial
- Police

Gal Oya National Park

- Nilgala Conservation Forest Area
- Makara (Dragon Mouth) rock formation
- Senanayake Reservoir
- Inginiyagala *(see inset)*
- Owagiriya Temple (ruins)
- Porwatta Junction
- Bulupitiya
- Newgala Lion Engraving,
  Siyambalanduwa, Buttala
- Hingurana
- Vampathanchenai
- Japanese Peace Pagoda
- Ceypetco
- Ampara *(see inset)*
- Samangala Caves
- Budhangala Monastery
- Deegwapi Dagoba
- Muhammadiyapuram
- Kalmunai/Batticaloa
- Arugam Bay
- Akkaraipattu
- Oluvil
- Arasady

Moderate

🏠 **Monty Hotel** (40 rooms) 1st Av; ✆063 222 2169; m 0777 129129; e julinmonty@yahoo. com. This unexpectedly smart medium-rise on the town's wooded southern outskirts has comfortable modern rooms with cable TV & AC, as well as pokier rooms with fan only. A decent restaurant serves Western & Sri Lankan meals in the US$3–5 range. *US$36/42 sgl/dbl with AC, US$25/32 fan only; all rates B&B.* **$$**

Budget

🏠 **Terrel Residences** (11 rooms) Stores Rd; m 0775 384915; e terrelb@gmail.com; w hotelterrel.lk. This good all-round budget hotel has small but brightly decorated rooms with AC, fan & fridge, a popular courtyard Chinese restaurant with mains for around US$4, & a tour desk with several years' experience arranging safaris to Gal Oya National Park. Good value. *US$13.50 dbl with fan only, US$19/22 sgl/dbl with AC* **$**

🏠 **Hotel Lake Jay** (9 rooms) Inginiyagala Rd; ✆063 222 3106; m 0773 754825; e info@ hotellakejay.com; 📘. Situated opposite Ampara Tank 2km west of the clock tower, this isolated 3-storey hotel has comfortable & sensibly priced rooms with AC, fan, cable TV channels & views of the surrounding paddy fields. *US$24/25 sgl/dbl B&B.* **$$**

Other practicalities

Banks All the main banks are represented in Ampara, including the Commercial Bank, which operates a bank and ATM on the main road around the corner from Terrel Residences.

Tour operators There are no tour operators in Ampara but Terrel Residences can arrange jeep safaris to Gal Oya National Park for around US$55 per party, inclusive of driver, fuel and a game drive on the eastern side of the park, but excluding boat trip and park entrance fees.

What to see and do

Japanese Peace Pagoda [map, page 345] (*Inginiyagala Rd, 3km west of Ampara Clock Tower;* ⊕ *24hrs*) Perched on the western shore of Ampara Tank, the Ampara Peace Pagoda is one of about 80 similar temples built worldwide by the Nipponzan-Myohoji, a Buddhist order founded by Nichidatsu Fujii, a Japanese monk who dedicated his life to promoting non-violence after meeting Mahatma Gandhi in 1931. Officially opened in 1988, this massive Japanese-style construction resembles a squatter version of a typical Sri Lankan dagoba, enclosed by a wide balcony supported by arches and pillars and adorned with two sizeable golden Buddha statues, one each in the Sri Lankan and Japanese styles. It's a pleasant goal for a short stroll out of Ampara, and there's plenty of avian action – pelicans, herons, egrets, kingfishers and such – to divert birdwatchers. Set on an ancient elephant path, the pagoda also used to be a reliable site to look for elephants between 17.00 and dusk, but sightings are more infrequent following the erection of an electric fence to block their access to town.

Buddangala Monastery [map, page 345] (*6km northeast of Ampara;* ⊕ *24hrs*) Prominently signposted from the town centre, and easily reached by tuktuk, this ancient monastery stands in vast jungle-like grounds punctuated by massive granite outcrops and small artificial pools. Although the monastery's original name is forgotten, ancient Brahmi rock inscriptions state that a temple was built here in the 2nd century BC by Princess Chitra of Anuradhapura, but some sources suggest it was founded 200 years earlier during the reign of Prince Dighayu, founder of the Digamadulla Kingdom. It had been abandoned for several centuries prior to 1964, when a young monk called Kalutara Dhammananda stumbled across the ruined dagoba in the jungle and revived the monastery, eventually to become its high priest. Prominent features include a modern boulder-top golden Buddha statue, and a recently added rock-hewn replica of the Gal Vihara at Polonnaruwa. The restored and whitewashed dagoba, unveiled by President Gopallawa in 1974, is surrounded by stone relicts of the unexcavated original temple. Of greater interest than any of the above, the small site museum, set in a rock overhang close to the car park, houses a number of human and animal bones including a massive elephant skull. Pride of place, however, goes to a tiny gold casket, more than 2,000 years old and engraved with three golden lotus flowers and inscription.

Samangala Caves [map, page 320] (*23km north of Ampara; ⌚ 07.00–18.00*) A recently revived mountain hermitage established during the 2nd-century BC reign of King Saddha Tissa, mysterious jungle-swathed Samangala is best known for the inscriptions and engravings that adorn some of its 50-odd drip-ledged cave shelters, though the remains of an ancient dagoba and other monastic shrines have also been discerned at the unexcavated site. The most important engraving at Samangala is believed to depict the Great Dagoba at Sanchi (the oldest stone structure of comparable dimensions in India, built in the 3rd century BC for the influential Emperor Ashoka), while more recent Vedda-style cave paintings indicate that the hermitage was occupied by these hunter-gatherers after the monks abandoned it. To get here from Ampara, follow the main road running north from the clock tower for 17km to Werankatagoda, then when you reach '28 Junction', turn left on to a rough 6km dirt road that leads to the base of the mountain through a dense jungle interspersed by feral orchards denoting the site of homesteads evacuated during the civil war. From the car park, it's about 100m on foot to the first cave, but another 700m or so along a gradually steepening footpath to the main cave, set below a granite outcrop overlooking the pretty Samangala Tank.

Deegawapi Dagoba [map, page 345] (*16km southeast of Ampara; ⌚ 24hrs*) Also spelt Dighavapi, this most sacred temple and archaeological site is centred on a ruined brick dagoba attributed (like nearby Samangala) to King Saddha Tissa. Deegawapi is renowned as one of the 16 Solosmasthana visited by the Buddha during his lifetime. Indeed, the central dagoba, which stood more than 100m tall in its prime, reputedly stands at the exact spot where the Buddha sat to meditate, and its relic chamber is said to hold one of his toenails. As with so many Buddhist sites in this part of Sri Lanka, the original monastery was abandoned many centuries ago, only to be reinstated as a temple some years after the rediscovery of the overgrown dagoba in 1916. Deegawapi required military protection after the LTTE hacked 13 villagers to death here in 1988, and it only reopened to outsiders after the end of the civil war, which is when its large modern temple was built. Despite its significance to Sri Lankan Buddhists, Deegawapi has little to show for its antiquity other than the massive overgrown dagoba, though this might change once proper excavations take place. Coming from Ampara in a private vehicle, the temple is prominently signposted, and it can easily be visited *en route* to Arugam Bay, since it stands less than 1km from a surfaced road connecting with the main coastal highway at Oluvil.

GAL OYA NATIONAL PARK Extending over 260km^2 of undulating terrain focused on the vast multiple-armed Senanayake Reservoir, Gal Oya is unique among Sri Lanka's non-marine national parks in that it can be explored on boat safaris, which frequently yield excellent sightings of elephants at thrillingly close quarters.

The park came into being as a postscript to Sri Lanka's first major post-independence development project: the construction of a hydro-electric dam on the Gal Oya River at Inginiyagala over 1949–53, and resultant creation of the 90km² Senanayake Reservoir. This is the largest freshwater body in Sri Lanka, named after Prime Minister Senanayake, who initiated the hydro-electric project and whose statue overlooks the dam wall. One unplanned-for side effect of the flooding was the displacement of thousands of large mammals into the reservoir's mountainous catchment area, an exodus that prompted the establishment of a national park in 1954 to protect the wildlife from hunters. A proposal to develop Gal Oya for tourism was put forward in 1973 but it has never been enacted, partly due to the civil war. Despite this, the national park is accessible to independent travellers, with its main attraction being relatively affordable boat safaris on the island-studded Senanayake Reservoir (also sometimes referred to as Lake Gal Oya or Inginiyagala). Generally, jeep safaris are less rewarding, the exception being from December to February, when the water level is at its highest and elephants are more likely to be seen from the limited road network. For serious birders, jeep safaris also offer the best chance of seeing those woodland and forest species regarded as Gal Oya specials.

Flora and fauna Terrestrial habitats are split more or less evenly between savannah grassland and evergreen forest transitional to the dry and moist zones, while the varied topography – spanning altitudes of 30–900m – includes several prominent mountains. More than 30 mammal species have been recorded, the most visible being elephant, but spotted deer, wild boar, grey langur and toque macaque are also quite common, and predators such as leopard and sloth bear are far more secretive than in Yala or Wilpattu. A bird checklist of more than 150 species represents about one-third of the national total. Aquatic birds are to the fore on the boat trip, but wooded habitats are an important stronghold for certain more localised species, notably painted francolin, jungle bush-quail, yellow-footed green pigeon, Layard's parakeet, sirkeer malkoha, streak-throated woodpecker, Marshall's iora and grey-breasted prinia. Many of these species also occur in the 26km² Nilgala Conservation Forest Area, which abuts the national park and is passed through *en route* to the Nilgala Gate on its western boundary.

Getting there and away The park headquarters and office at Inginiyagala lie 20km west of Ampara along a good surfaced road via Polwatta Junction. Using public transport, buses between Ampara and Inginiyagala run every 30 minutes or so, stopping at the main traffic circle about 250m from the Inginiyagala Resthouse and less than 1km from the park office. Coming from further south, buses heading to Ampara from Monaragala (on the main road between Buttala and Arugam Bay) can drop you at Polwatta, which is only 3km from Inginiyagala and stopped at by all buses headed there from Ampara. Organised half-day safaris from Ampara can be arranged with Terrel Residences (page 346).

Travellers headed to Gal Oya Lodge should note that it is situated alongside the village of Ratugula, which straddles the Bibile Road outside the northern park boundary 30km northwest of Inginiyagala. To get there from Ampara, turn right on to the Bibile Road at Polwatta, then continue for 28km to Ratugula, where (assuming you're expected) a lodge vehicle will be waiting at the junction for the 700m feeder road. Ratugula is well positioned for game drives in the national park's little-used Nilgala sector, but boat trips can only be undertaken from Inginiyagala, so coming to/from Ampara, you might want to slot yours in *en route*, rather than doing it as an excursion out of the lodge.

Where to stay, eat and drink *Map, page 345*

Gal Oya Lodge (8 rooms) Ratugula, 30km from Inginiyagala; **m** 0768 424612; **e** info@ galoyalodge.com; **w** galoyalodge.com. Set in a patch of jungle outside the park boundary, this stylish but well-priced upmarket bush lodge has a magnificent setting at the base of the 600m-high 'Monkey Mountain'. The 75m^2 wood-and-thatch bungalows have king-size beds with walk-in nets, separate sitting area, treated concrete floors, ethnic-style décor, a large outdoor shower & toilet, & glass doors leading out to a private balcony. In keeping with the rustic eco-friendly ethos, there is no TV or AC in the rooms, but temperatures are maintained by fans & good natural ventilation, & there's also solar-powered hot water. The attractive open-sided thatch restaurant overlooks the swimming pool & serves a good 3-course dinner catering both to those who enjoy Sri Lankan food and to blander palates. Free activities include a trek to the top of Monkey Mountain, which offers fabulous views to Gal Oya Dam, as well as guided birding walks to a nearby dam where 30-odd species might be seen in the space of an hour. Additional activities include jeep safaris into the nearby Nilgala sector of the park (*US$55 pp*), boat trips from Inginiyagala (*US$150/party of up to 4*), visits to a local Vedda community (*US$50 pp*) & night safaris (*US$50 pp*). All activities are accompanied by one of the lodge's knowledgeable guides. *From US$120/155 sgl/dbl B&B.* **$$$$**

Inginiyagala Resthouse (5 rooms, 21 more under construction) Inginiyagala village, 250m from the main traffic circle; \063 224 7121. An unexpected gem, this well-run government resthouse stands in jungle-fringed gardens about 10mins' walk from the national park booking office. A restaurant & bar with indoor & terrace seating serves b/fast for US$1.50 & other meals for around US$2.50. The existing rooms are simple but have a fan & net, while newer rooms are likely to be smarter & might have AC. *US$10/17 sgl/dbl.* **$**

Tourist information

National Park Tourist Office Inginiyagala Park Headquarters; \063 224 4002; ⊕ 06.00–18.00. Situated about 750m past Inginiyagala traffic circle in the direction of the dam wall, this well-signposted information & booking office is where all boat trips must be arranged & entrance fees paid.

What to see and do Boat trips on Senanayake Reservoir are a must-do, but game drives into the park can also be undertaken, and it's well worth popping into the (free) Owagiriya Ruins just outside Polwatta.

Boat trips One of Sri Lanka's most exciting wildlife experiences, boat trips on Senanayake Reservoir run twice daily from the park headquarters at Inginiyagala. The scenery alone is spectacular, with the (often choppy) lake waters being punctuated by small rocky islands, lined with lush jungle, and encircled by jagged mountains. Elephants are frequently seen foraging on the shore or swimming between the islands, and it is usually possible to approach them within clear photographic range, with sightings peaking during the height of the dry season (July–early September), when the water level is lowest. Several islands close to the launch support large numbers of cormorants, egrets, herons and other communal roosters, while the wooded shore is a good place to see the relatively localised lesser adjutant stork, white-bellied sea-eagle, grey-headed fish-eagle, great thick-knee and stork-billed kingfisher. Elephants aside, large mammals are quite scarce, though you might be lucky enough to see spotted deer, wild boar and a few monkeys, and the lake is known for its impressively proportioned crocodiles and water monitors.

Boat trips leave at 06.00 and 15.00, and last for around 3 hours. Afternoon trips generally offer the best elephant viewing in numeric terms, and the light can be sensational towards sunset, but the water tends to be calmer in the early morning, which is also when you are most likely to see elephants swimming. There are only two boats, so it might be a good idea to book ahead, especially at weekends, though in practice the excursions can be arranged at short notice, assuming vessels are available. If the boats have been booked up, it is permitted for walk-ins to join a pre-booked group, provided that they agree to it (which they may well do, in order to cut the cost per person).

The pricing structure is rather complicated. Foreigners pay US$7 per person and locals pay US$4.50, with the minimum group size being five, and unused seats being charged as locals. A service fee of US$3 is also charged, along with 15% VAT on the whole transaction. In total, then, you're looking at US$32/36/39/42/45 per party of one/two/three/four/five people, then an extra US$8 for each additional person after the first five. This means that it makes sense for cost-conscious single travellers and couples to try to cut costs by grouping together. The good news is *no* park entrance fees are charged for boat trips, so if you can put together a group of five, the total cost of the excursion will work out at less than US$10 per person.

Game drives   There are two short roads available for jeep safaris, one leading west into the park from Inginiyagala Gate (on the Siyambalanduwa Road about 7km south of the park headquarters) and the other running southeast from Bulupitiya (on the Bibile Road about 10km southwest of the Ratugula and Gal Oya Lodge) via the Nilgala Forest Reserve and Nilgala Gate to the north bank of the Gal Oya River. Neither road is much more than 10km long, both require you to return the way you came, and game viewing tends to be patchy except between December and February, when elephants are more likely to be seen from a jeep than on a boat safari. The Nilgala Road is also of particular interest to birders, as it offers a pretty good chance of seeing some of the more localised forest birds associated with Gal Oya and Nilgala, in particular yellow-footed green pigeon and Layard's parakeet. It also leads to some pleasant swimming pools and the Makara (Dragon Mouth) rock formation where the Gal Oya River funnels into the reservoir.

All game drives attract a park entrance fee of US$10 per person, plus a service fee of US$8 per party and 15% VAT. This can be paid at the tourist office in Inginiyagala or at the Nilgala Gate. Unless you are staying at Gal Oya Lodge, jeeps are not available for hire locally; the nearest possibility is Terrel Residences in Ampara town.

Owagiriya Temple [map, page 345] (*300m south of Polwatta Junction;* ◷ *07.00–18.00*) Although it's less well known than the contemporaneous likes of Deegawapi and Buddangala, this mysterious but readily accessible ruin on the outskirts of Polwatta is more likely to engage the casual visitor. Exposed during the construction of the Gal Oya Dam and excavated over 2004–08, the ruin probably dates to the time of King Saddha Tissa. Its name Owagiriya (which roughly translates as 'Rock of Advice') suggests its monks had a reputation for sagacity. The centrepiece is a partially restored image house whose engraved stairwells lead to a platform dominated by a 3.5m-tall Buddha statue. The medium-sized brick dagoba is unusual for Sri Lanka in that its base is square as opposed to circular. Several other pillars and building stones are scattered around the site, which is set in a tangle of jungle alive with monitor lizards, monkeys and birds.

Newgala Lion Engraving [map, page 320] Among the more unusual archaeological sites in this part of Sri Lanka, this cartoon-like metre-long engraving of a catlike creature stands in strange isolation on a boulder next to a pool on the outskirts of the village of Newgala, only 6km east of the Siyambalanduwa Road. Stylistically dissimilar to other engravings in Sri Lanka, its age and provenance is anybody's guess, and while it is generally assumed to depict a lion, it could as easily represent any other felid. The engraving isn't worth a major diversion, but it can quite easily be visited *en route* between Gal Oya and Siyambalanduwa. Coming from Inginiyagala or Ampara, the two roads connect at Wadinagala, from where it is another 18km south to the junction for Newgala. Coming from Siyambalanduwa, you'll reach the junction after driving north for 10km.

ARUGAM BAY

Sri Lanka's top surfing destination and one of its most popular backpacker chill-out venues, the great curving coastline of Arugam Bay is fringed by a wide sweep of surf-kissed palm-lined white sand that runs south from Pottuvil Point. Yet despite its iconic status today, Arugam's rise to prominence has been anything but smooth. The bay first attracted the attention of travellers in the 1970s, and while some of these pioneering visitors would ride out lazily on tyre tubes, they didn't surf as such, but were attracted by the beach's solitude and undiscovered feel. By the early 1980s, the near-perfect waves of A-Bay – as it's known to aficionados – were attracting more serious surfers, and the legend grew during the late 1980s and 1990s, when LTTE activity rendered the east coast unsafe for visitors. By the turn of the millennium, Arugam Bay had started to attract a steady trickle of adventurous surf enthusiasts, prompting a second wave of low-key tourist development, but this was curtailed by the tsunami, which flattened most of the beach resorts and claimed an untold number of lives. Since then, tourist amenities have developed at quite an astonishing pace. Indeed, with its chilled atmosphere, tropical seaside setting, and plethora of backpacker-friendly mom-and-pop restaurants and lodges, A-Bay today feels like an embryonic Sri Lankan counterpart to Goa or Phuket.

So far as most tourists are concerned, Arugam Bay is all but synonymous with Ullae, the smaller and more southerly of its two discrete and rather contrasting settlements. An overgrown village whose mixed Tamil, Muslim and Sinhalese population totals no more than a couple of thousand, Ullae is the sort of place whose every last resident seems to dabble in tourist-related services, be it a homestay, a restaurant, a taxi service, a surf shop, or whatever. Yet despite Ullae's almost bewildering choice of lodgings and eateries, the village retains a genuinely welcoming, relaxed and down-to-earth feel. By contrast, Pottuvil, at the northern end of the bay, is a substantial town whose 35,000-odd predominantly Islamic inhabitants seem to carry on with their lives largely aloof from the hubbub of tourist activity barely a kilometre to the south. Despite this, Pottuvil is better equipped than Ullae when it comes to amenities such as banks, buses and supermarkets, and it also offers access to two worthwhile attractions in the form of the wildlife-rich Pottuvil Lagoon and ancient temple of Muhudu Maha. Halfway down the bay, the Arugam Lagoon divides Ullae from Pottuvil, and helps reinforce their separate identifies, despite being spanned by a modern motor bridge that opened in 2008 to replace an older one destroyed by the tsunami.

Arugam Bay is a highly seasonal destination, with the main traveller influx falling from June to September, when accommodation fills up quickly and prices skyrocket. High season broadly coincides with the driest weather (April–September) and best surfing conditions (May–August), but the village is a lot more peaceful out of season. Surfing and other seaside activities aside, A-Bay is the base for a number of popular excursions, ranging from boat trips on the Pottuvil Lagoon and jeep safaris to Kumana National Park (an extension of the renowned Yala National Park) to visits to a number of ruined temples and monasteries.

GETTING THERE AND AWAY

By road Coming from elsewhere in Sri Lanka, Pottuvil is the only road funnel to Arugam Bay. It lies about 340km from Colombo via two practically equidistant road routes that converge at Monaragala 65km to the west. These are the northern route via Kandy (210km) and Mahiyanganaya (145km) and the southern route via Ratnapura (245km) and Wellawaya (105km). Government buses between Colombo and Pottuvil depart from Pettah bus station every hour, but most make lots of stops *en route*, so you are best off using the quicker private bus that leaves Colombo from the Central Bus Stand (opposite Pettah) at 22.15 and from Pottuvil, in front of the Sampath Bank, at 19.45. There is also a pricier (US$10) luxury air-conditioned bus that leaves Colombo from the Zahira College Car Park (opposite Maradana railway station) at 20.00 and from Pottuvil at 21.00. In all cases, the trip takes 8–10 hours, so there's something to be said for using a train some of the way.

Pottuvil lies 110km south of Batticaloa and the two are connected by a good road and plenty of public transport, though you may need to change vehicles at Kalmunai or divert inland to Siyambalanduwa, so an early start is recommended. Coming from most places further north, you'd funnel though Batticaloa anyway. Coming from Ella, 135km to the west of Pottuvil, catch a bus to Monaragala (these pass through Ella every 15–30 minutes) and change vehicles there.

Some buses to Pottuvil continue south to Ullae and Panama, but others terminate at Pottuvil bus station [354 B2], 2–3km north of the main cluster of accommodation in Ullae. Tuktuks between Pottuvil and Ullae cost US$1–2.

By rail Although there are no train services to Arugam Bay, it lies only 110km south of the railhead at Batticaloa, and 135km from Ella railway station, so coming from most parts of Sri Lanka it is possible to catch a train to either of these towns and bus through from there.

⌂ WHERE TO STAY

When it comes to accommodation, Arugam Bay – or more specifically Ullae – can feel like the backpacker equivalent of a tourist trap. More than a hundred hotels, guesthouses and homestays are packed into the confines of what is essentially an overgrown village, and it's fair to say that a significant proportion of these establishments come across as a bit grotty, or overpriced, or both. That said, there are a few establishments that stand out in terms of quality or value for money, and the listings below concentrate on these options. Note, however, that while we have attempted to give high-season prices (typically applicable June–September), and to indicate to what extent they are discounted in the low season, room rates here tend to fluctuate from one week to the next, depending on tourist volumes and managerial whim, so nothing is set in stone. Fortunately, the accommodation in Ullae is so tightly packed together that if your first-choice option doesn't work out, there will be plenty of other choices within a couple of minutes' walk.

Upmarket

✳ ⌂ **Hideaway Resort** [354 A4] (14 rooms) Ullae Main Rd; 063 224 8259; m 0774 596670; e info@hideawayarugambay.com; w hideawayarugambay.com. This is Ullae's closest approximation of a boutique hotel, comprising a characterful main building & smart chalets spaced out in large & beautifully laid-out gardens that retain something of a jungle feel but lack direct beach access. The stylish rooms all come with queen-size bed, hand-crafted wood furniture & balcony or veranda. The classy restaurant & cocktail bar – arguably the best in A-Bay when it comes to quality – serve a changeable feast of Asian fusion dishes using home-grown ingredients where possible, with mains costing around US$6–8 at lunch or US$12–15 at dinner. Fair value. *US$60/68 sgl/dbl B&B with fan only, US$99/145 with AC.* **$$$–$$$$**

⌂ Jetwing Kottukal Beach House [354 D1] (4 rooms) Pottuvil Point; ✆ 011 470 9400; m 0775 348807; e resv.kottukal@jetwinghotels. com; w jetwinghotels.com. The only genuinely upmarket accommodation at A-Bay, this classy boutique-style beach villa has an isolated location in stunning palm-shaded beachfront gardens at the southern base of the sandy spit that divides the open sea from Pottuvil Lagoon, about 4km north of Ullae. Bedrooms are individually styled but all come with 4-poster bed & walk-in net, wood furniture, outdoor & indoor shower, & there is also a communal lounge & TV room with DVD player. *US$216/235 sgl/dbl B&B, dropping by around 35% out of season.* **$$$$$**

Moderate

✷ ⌂ Bay Vista Hotel [354 B3] (25 rooms) Ullae Main Rd; ✆ 063 224 8577; m 0771 850328; e info@bayvistahotel.com; w bayvistahotel.com. This owner-managed 4-storey hotel combines a prime beach location with comfortable accommodation in smallish but attractive rooms with wood laminate floor, colourful fabrics, modern fittings, AC, fan & private balcony. A good ground-floor restaurant (no alcohol) leads out to a beachfront garden with deckchairs, while the shaded rooftop runs daily yoga sessions & houses a funky café with the best view in A-Bay, tasty filled bruschettas & other snacks including vegan options (*around US$5*). *US$85/95 dbl B&B with land/sea view; 50% discount offered out of season.* **$$$**

✷ ⌂ Stardust Beach Hotel [354 A1] (20 rooms) 100m east of Ullae Main Rd; ✆ 063 224 8191; m 0779 067841; e stardust@ arugambay.com; w arugambay.com. The longest-serving beach hotel in A-Bay, this Danish-owned & -managed establishment lies almost immediately south of the lagoon that separates Ullae from Pottuvil. Three room types are available, all with fan, good natural ventilation, nets, minibar & veranda/balcony. Cosy beachfront wooden cabanas have an organic feel, outdoor shower & cold water only. Spotless, spacious & brightly decorated standard rooms are set at the back of the property in a 2-storey building with sea views. There are also larger rooms with AC in a 2-storey self-catering villa on a separate plot adjacent to the main lodge. Amenities include an excellent (but quite pricey)

seafood restaurant & bar, a well-stocked library & a yoga hall, but Stardust's single best feature is its large, shady & well-maintained beachfront gardens, which stand in idyllic contrast to the cramped compounds occupied by most other A-Bay lodges. *US$35/43 sgl/dbl cabana, US$70/80 std dbl on ground/1st floor, villa rooms from US$95 dbl; rates exc b/fast.* **$$–$$$$**

✷ ⌂ Sandy Beach Hotel [354 A2] (14 rooms) Ullae beach; ✆ 063 224 8403; m 0773 242764; e reservations@arugambayhotel.net; w arugambay-hotel.com. Set in small but well-maintained beachfront gardens scattered with palm-shaded lounger-chairs, this unpretentious low-rise hotel has comfortable modern rooms with net, AC &/or fan & private balcony. A decent restaurant is attached. *From US$35 dbl with fan, or US$55–80 with AC; prices drop by 50% or more out of season.* **$$–$$$**

✷ ⌂ Galaxy Lounge [354 A1] (13 rooms) Ullae beach; ✆ 063 224 8415; m 0773 109920; e info@galaxysrilanka.com; w galaxysrilanka. com. Set in spacious & well-wooded beachfront gardens, this delightfully relaxed lodge comprises a variety of cabanas ranging from quaint naturally ventilated stilted wooden tree-houses with fan to solid brick cottages with AC. All units have simple but attractive décor, balcony, net & private bathroom. One of A-Bay's top eateries, its cosmopolitan menu includes snacks & filled subs for around US$4 & more substantial seafood & other mains for around US$6–8. *From US$31 dbl with fan or US$48 dbl with AC; rates drop by up to 50% out of season.* **$$–$$$**

⌂ Arugam Bay Surf Resort [354 B4] (15 rooms) Ullae Main Rd; ✆ 063 224 8189; m 0777 804272; e abaysurfresort@gmail.com; w arugambay.lk. More hotel than resort, this friendly & down-to-earth set-up has a great beachfront location right in the heart of Ullae, attractively furnished rooms with fan &/or AC, queen-size bed, a licensed beach restaurant serving Mexican dishes, seafood & pizzas in the US$3–7 range, & a reputable on-site surf shop. *Maybe a touch overpriced at US$60/70 for a dbl with fan/AC, but good value out of season, when rates drop by almost 50%.* **$$$**

⌂ The Danish Villa [354 A3] (7 rooms) Ullae Main Rd; m 0776 957936; e info@ thedanishvilla.com; w thedanishvilla.dk. Set in large but rather scruffy gardens on the landward

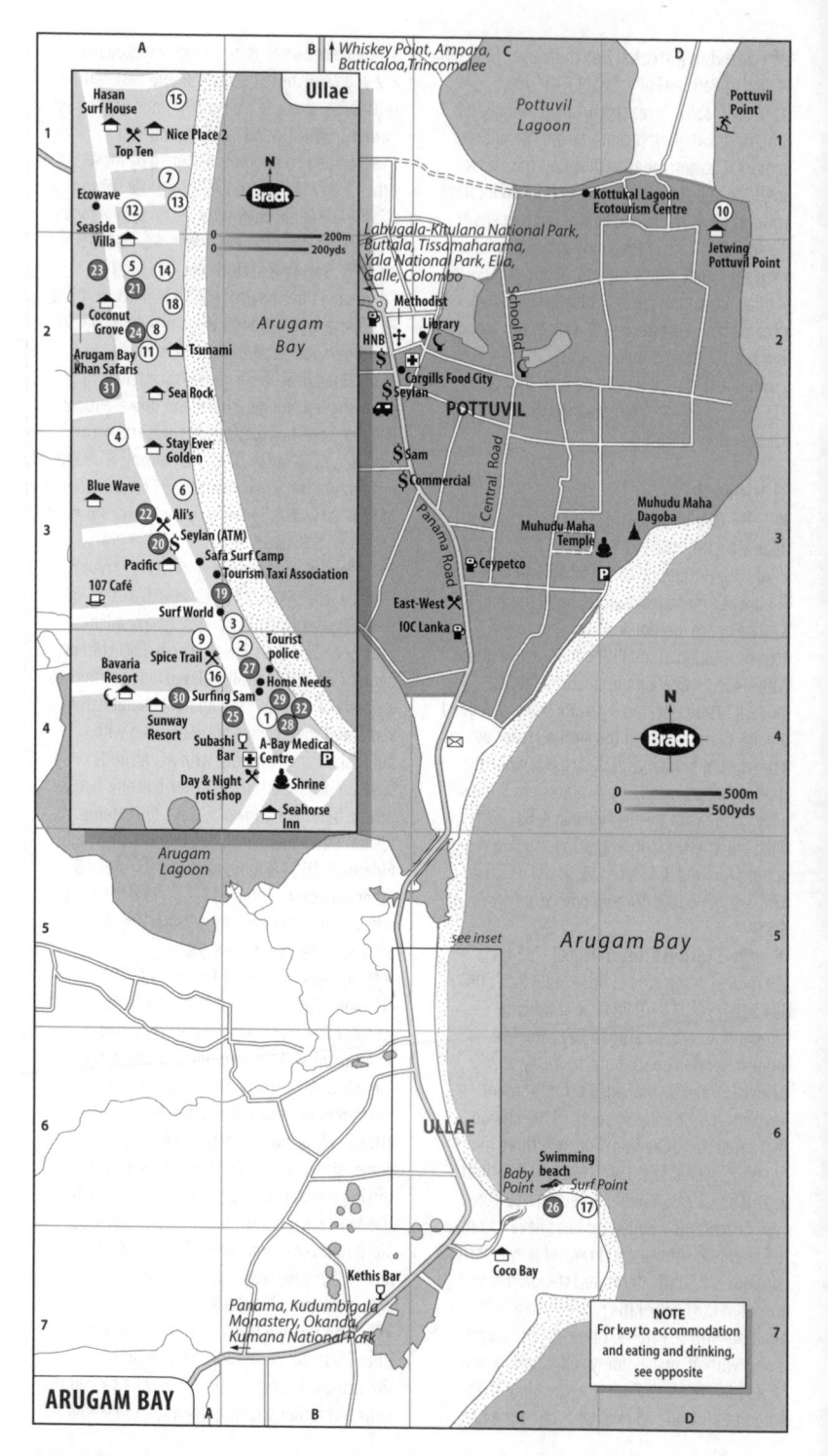

ARUGAM BAY

Inset: **Ullae**

Map labels:
- Whiskey Point, Ampara, Batticaloa, Trincomalee
- Pottuvil Lagoon
- Pottuvil Point
- Kottukal Lagoon Ecotourism Centre
- Jetwing Pottuvil Point
- Labugala-Kitulana National Park, Buttala, Tissamaharama, Yala National Park, Ella, Galle, Colombo
- Methodist
- Library
- HNB
- Cargills Food City
- Seylan
- **POTTUVIL**
- Sam
- Commercial
- Muhudu Maha Dagoba
- Muhudu Maha Temple
- Ceypetco
- School Rd
- Central Road
- Panama Road
- East-West
- IOC Lanka
- **Arugam Bay**
- **N**
- **Bradt**
- 0 500m
- 0 500yds

Inset labels:
- Hasan Surf House
- Nice Place 2
- Top Ten
- Ecowave
- Seaside Villa
- Coconut Grove
- Arugam Bay Khan Safaris
- Tsunami
- Sea Rock
- Stay Ever Golden
- Blue Wave
- Ali's
- Seylan (ATM)
- Pacific
- 107 Café
- Safa Surf Camp
- Tourism Taxi Association
- Surf World
- Spice Trail
- Bavaria Resort
- Surfing Sam
- Sunway Resort
- Subashi Bar
- Tourist police
- Home Needs
- A-Bay Medical Centre
- Day & Night roti shop
- Shrine
- Seahorse Inn
- Arugam Lagoon
- **Arugam Bay**
- **N**
- **Bradt**
- 0 200m
- 0 200yds

Circled numbers: 15, 7, 13, 12, 23, 5, 14, 21, 18, 24, 8, 11, 31, 4, 6, 22, 20, 19, 3, 9, 2, 27, 16, 30, 25, 1, 29, 32, 28

- see inset
- **ULLAE**
- Baby Point
- Swimming beach
- Surf Point
- 26, 17
- Kethis Bar
- Coco Bay
- Panama, Kudumbigala Monastery, Okanda, Kumana National Park

NOTE
For key to accommodation and eating and drinking, see opposite

354

ARUGAM BAY

For listings, see pages 352–7

side of the main road, this popular Danish-owned set-up consists of a main house & garden cottage whose simple but stylishly modern rooms have ceiling fans &/or AC, treated concrete floors & darkwood furniture including wardrobe, writing desk & dbl bed with fitted net. *US$30 dbl with fan, US$49–65 dbl with AC; small out-of-season discounts.* **$$–$$$**

⌂ Upali Beach Resort [354 C6] (9 rooms) **m** 0771 128866; **e** upalibeach@gmail.com; **w** upali-beach.com. This low-key family-owned resort, accessible only by walking along the beach south of Ullae for 5mins, is a firm favourite with surfers thanks to its idyllic location sandwiched between forested dunes & A-Bay's most popular surfing beach. The beach accommodation, all with dbl bed & net, is in simple breeze-cooled kiosks using common showers, or smarter en-suite 'glam cabanas' with fan. *US$35 dbl kiosk, US$80 dbl cabana; low-season discounts of around 15%.* **$$–$$$**

Budget

❋ ⌂ Surf 'n' Sun [354 A4] (11 rooms) Ullae Main Rd; **m** 0776 065099; **e** surfsaman@yahoo. in; **w** thesurfnsun.com. Accommodation at this attractive & well-priced lodge consists of wood or concrete cabanas strung out alongside long & well-tended gardens on the opposite side of Main Rd to the beach. All cabanas have nets, fan & private balcony, & the attached restaurant/bar serves seafood-dominated mains in the US$7–10 range, as well as good cocktails. *US$30/40 wood/cement dbl cabana, villas from US$70.* **$$–$$$**

❋ ⌂ Water Music [354 A2] (8 rooms) Ullae beach; **m** 0775 395818; **e** info@watermusicarugambay.com; **w** watermusicarugambay.com. This idyllic & super-chilled beach lodge, all sand underfoot & palms overhead, has 5 well-ventilated en-suite beach huts with net, fan & private balcony, as well as 3 rooms in the main house with similar facilities but using a shared bathroom. A beach restaurant serves inexpensive daily specials for lunch & dinner. *US$33–40 dbl, dropping by 50% out of season.* **$–$$**

⌂ East Beach Surf Resort [354 A2] (12 rooms) Ullae Main Rd; **☏** 063 224 8394; **m** 0776 618534; **e** eastbeachsurfresort@gmail. com. The friendly staff & sensible prices make this small 2-storey lodge one of A-Bay's most attractive budget options. All rooms are en suite with AC &/or fan, nets, seating area, tea/coffee & fridge, & there's also a communal lounge & garden with barbecue facilities. *US$20 dbl with fan, US$35 with AC, dropping by around 40% out of season.* **$–$$**

⌂ Etnico Surf Resort [354 A3] (6 rooms) Ullae Main Rd; **m** 0767 795780; **e** etnicosurfresort@gmail.com. Decent owner-managed lodge with a beachfront setting, good Italian restaurant (*mains around US$5*) & comfortable rooms with net & AC. *A touch overpriced at US$50 dbl B&B Jun–Sep, but great value out of season at US$17 dbl.* **$–$$$**

Shoestring

❋ ⌂ Ranga's Beach Hut [354 A1] (22 rooms) 100m east of Ullae Main Rd; **☏** 063 224 8202; **m** 0771 606203; **e** arugambaybeachhut@ gmail.com; **w** arugambaybeachhut.com. Spread across 2 plots set 100m apart at the north end of Ullae beach, this backpackers' stalwart offers the winning combination of comfortable & sensibly priced accommodation in well-ventilated wooden beach huts, excellent vegetarian buffet dinners for US$2.50 pp & a welcoming vibe generated by the dynamic owner-manager, who can also help put together groups for jeep safaris to Kumana & Lahugala-Kitulana national parks. *US$4–6 pp using shared bathroom, depending on season, US$13.50 en-suite dbl.* **$**

☀ 🏠 **Nice Place** [354 A2] (5 rooms) Tsunami Hotel Rd; **m** 063 224 8193; **m** 0773 412240; **e** rifainiceplace@gmail.com; **w** niceplaceguesthousesrilanka.weebly.com. This aptly named homestay occupies compact green gardens only a few paces from the beach & offers surfboards to rent & a well-priced tuktuk service. The smallish but attractively decorated rooms come with fan, net & private balcony. Very good value. *US$24 dbl, dropping to US$17 out of season.* **$**

🏠 **Happy Panda Homestay** [354 A2] (3 rooms) Tsunami Hotel Rd; **m** 0772 990779; **e** karikh@gmail.com; **w** happypandahotel.com. This cosy Russian-owned & -managed homestay consists of a tiny garden clumped with bamboo stands, a brightly coloured balcony café hung with hammocks (& panda mascot), & 3 comfortable en-suite rooms with net & fan. The vegetarian café serves great smoothies, affordable b/fasts (the speciality being Russian-style oladushki pancakes) & a home-cooked dinner of the day. *US$15 dbl.* **$**

🏠 **Arugam Bay Hostel** [354 B4] (4 dorms) Ullae Main Rd; **m** 0777 267887; **e** arugamdallas@gmail.com; 🅕 ArugamHostel. The former YMCA, set in the building below Siam View, now offers accommodation in clean, bright & freshly renovated 4–8-bed dorms, all with their own bathroom & all-but-direct access to the beach. *US$12 pp B&B, dropping to US$10 pp out of season.* **$**

✖ **WHERE TO EAT AND DRINK** In addition to the standalone eateries listed below, most hotels listed above have a restaurant of sorts. Of these, the Hideaway, with its fusion menu and selection of cocktails, is the closest thing on offer to fine dining, while Galaxy Lounge stands out for its varied menu and beachfront location, and the rooftop café at the Bay Vista is a great place for a coffee or snack with a view.

Medium to expensive

☀ ✖ **Zephyr Restaurant & Bar** [354 B4] Ullae beach; **m** 0777 333474; ⏰ 11.00–23.00. Reached via a side alley next to the Siam View, this friendly & popular restaurant ticks all the right boxes: fabulous beachfront location, great cocktails, sensibly priced beers & a varied selection of seafood, burgers & curries. **$$–$$$**

☀ ✖ **Siam View** [354 B4] Ullae Main Rd; **m** 0777 267887; 🅕 SiamViewArugam; ⏰ 24hrs. This A-Bay landmark boasts a breezy rooftop location shaded by cashew boughs, quirkily attractive décor, large-screen TVs to broadcast international football, DJ at w/ends, adventurous Thai-influenced menu & well-stocked bar with draught beer & wine by the glass. Service can be slow when it's busy & drinks are on the pricey side, but overall it stands out as perhaps the most chilled eatery & nightspot in town. **$$$**

✖ **Maleena Italian Restaurant Ullae** [354 B4] Main Rd; **m** 0777 970709; 🅕 maleenaarugambay; ⏰ 09.00–23.00. Boasting an Italian-trained chef & genuine wood-fired oven, this is A-Bay's top pizza & pasta venue. It also has a good selection of salads. Prices are a little steep, but portions are correspondingly generous. No licence but you can bring your own beer or wine. **$$$–$$$$**

✖ **Tandoori Hut** [354 A4] Mafaza Mosque Rd; **m** 063 224 8580; **w** dragonflyarugambay. com; ⏰ 11.00–14.00 & 18.00–23.00. Not to be confused with a recently opened main road namesake trying to cash in on its popularity, the original Tandoori Hut is perched on a stilted wooden platform in the gardens of the Dragonfly Inn about 150m west of the main road through Ullae. It specialises in lunchtime thalis, & evening curries & seafood, with prawn curry being something of a signature dish. No alcohol. **$$$**

✖ **Mambo's** [354 C6] Ullae beach; **m** 0777 822524; **e** surfmambo50@hotmail.com; **w** mambos.lk. Accessible by foot only, this popular resort runs down to A-Bay's main swimming beach & it also serves a varied international menu embracing burgers, salads & local dishes. It's also probably A-Bay's hottest nightspot, with a licensed bar, contemporary music & beach parties complete with DJ every Sat night May–Oct. **$$**

The Green Room Ullae [354 A3] Main Rd; f thegreenroom.arugambay; ⏰ 07.00–23.00. This funky fan-cooled wood-&-palm-leaf eatery is one of the longest serving in A-Bay, owned & managed by 2 brothers who are also talented chefs. It serves excellent Sri Lankan curries & kotti roti, supplemented by other Asian dishes & plenty of vegetarian options including salads, as well as good juices & lassis. No alcohol. Most mains $$$, seafood $$$

Sub Bay Snack Bar [354 B4] Ullae Main Rd; m 0779 000666; ⏰ 10.00–22.00. Despite the rather misleading name & logo, there are no subs on offer at this modern & friendly diner lookalike, but it does serve good chicken tandoor & tikka masala, grilled steak & fish, & a selection of burgers & kebabs. No alcohol. $$$

Point View Restaurant [354 B4] Ullae Main Rd; m 0779 584308; ⏰ noon–22.00. Good Indian & seafood restaurant whose best feature is the evening barbecue, which cooks up good-value whole fish or chicken tikka with chips. $$–$$$

Why Not? [354 A2] Ullae Main Rd; m 0750 739452; ⏰ 07.00–23.00. Good seafood, pasta, salads, curries, kotti roti & devilled dishes. No alcohol. $$

Cheap to medium

In addition to the sit-down eateries listed below, a cluster of impermanent-looking roti restaurants stands at the south end of Ullae Main Rd close to the Buddha shrine. You'll get 3 rotis for US$1 by day,

while the evening speciality is kotti roti for around US$1 (slightly more if you want chicken or meat). None of the places listed below serves alcohol.

✳ **The Lemon Tree** [354 A2] Ullae Main Rd; m 0778 151583; ⏰ 07.30–21.30. A great b/fast spot, this unpretentious owner-managed eatery serves omelettes & filled rotis & pancakes ($), while an imaginative selection of more substantial mains ($$) includes chicken kebabs & prawn-&-mango curry.

✳ **Fly Moon** [354 A2] Ullae Main Rd; m 0770 454848; ⏰ 08.00–20.00. This unpretentious little place serves great local-style vegetable or chicken rice-&-curry. Great value. $

Hello Burger [354 A2] Ullae Main Rd; m 0771 927667; ⏰ 08.30–23.30. Arguably the best burgers in A-Bay, together with a good pasta selection, make this family-run establishment a great option when you're ready for a break from seafood & curries. $$

Baba's Roti Shop [354 A3] Ullae Main Rd; m 0772 600475; ⏰ 08.30–23.00. A strong Rasta vibe & stack of hookah pipes distinguish this agreeable local eatery, which serves curries, fried rice & filled rotis. $

Danny's Soul Kitchen [354 A3] Ullae Main Rd; m 0773 242185; e soulkitchen.arugam@gmail.com. Renowned for its delicious meat & vegetarian curries, this chilled garden eatery also does good local b/fasts & offers Sri Lankan cooking lessons. $$

OTHER PRACTICALITIES

Shopping There's a well-stocked Cargills Food City Supermarket [354 B2] (⏰ 08.00–22.00) in Pottuvil and a couple of more tourist-oriented supermarkets in Ullae, the pick being Home Needs [354 B4] (⏰ 07.30–22.30) towards the south end of the main street. There are no liquor shops in Pottuvil or central Ullae, but the Kethis Bar [354 B7], about 600m south of the main strip through Ullae, sells takeaway beer and other booze at about half the price of those restaurants that serve it.

The main strip in Ullae is also lined with several surf shops and trendy clothing boutiques. The shop at Ecowave (page 358) is an excellent place to buy local basketwork and textiles, along with locally sourced organic spices and other lightweight foodstuffs, and an innovative range of bags and other items made with recycled plastic and cloths.

Medical Aimed mainly at tourists, A-Bay Medical Centre [354 B4] (m 0773 133170; ⏰ 06.00–08.00 & 16.00–20.00) on the main street through Ullae doubles as a consultation and dispensary.

Banking There no banks in Ullae, but the HNB has an ATM outside the Arugam Bay Surf Hotel [354 B4], and there's also a Seylan Bank ATM [354 A3] on the main road about 200m north of this. If neither of these give you joy, the Commercial Bank [354 C3], HNB [354 B2] and Seylan Bank [354 C2] all have branches with an ATM on the main road through Pottuvil.

TOURIST INFORMATION AND OPERATORS There is no formal tourist information office, but the following websites are worth browsing: w arugam.info, w arugambay. com and w arugam.com. Another good source of travel information is Ecowave [354 A1] (m 063 373 0404; e info@ecowave.lk; w ecowave.lk), which operates an office and shop on Ullae Main Road.

Safaris Jeep safaris to Kumana and Lahugala-Kitulana national parks can be arranged through the Arugam Bay Tourism Taxi Association [354 A3] (m *0769 191784;* w *arugamtours.com*) or Arugam Bay Khan Safaris [354 A2] (m *0774 285716;* e *akhansafari@gmail.com*). A five- or six-berth jeep to Kumana, inclusive of driver/guide and fuel but excluding entrance fees, should cost around US$60/105 per party for a half-/full day. You'll pay US$25–30 per half-day for similar transport to Lahugala-Kitulana, which is closer to Arugam Bay but tends to offer inferior game viewing. Budget-conscious travellers hoping to put together a group to split the cost should talk to the helpful owner of Ranga's Beach Hut (pages 355–6).

Surfing At least a dozen surf shops offering board and other equipment rental, as well as lessons catering to all levels of expertise, are scattered around Ullae. The surf shops at the Arugam Bay Surf Resort [354 B4], Surf 'n' Sun [354 A4] and Upali Beach Resort [354 C6] are particularly recommended. Other good options are as follows:

Safa Surf Camp [354 A3] 063 454 5158; m 0779 552268; w safaarugambay.com
Surf World [354 A3] m 0777 113685; e surfworld2016@gmail.com

Surfing Sam [354 B4] m 0776 956160; e surfingsam@ymail.com

WHAT TO SEE AND DO Tourist activity in A-Bay is dominated by the beach, which stretches for 6km south from Pottuvil Point to Pasarichenai, interrupted only by the mouth of the Arugam Lagoon between the townships of Pottuvil and Ullae. Ironically, though, while this stretch of coast offers superb surfing, the water is generally too rough to be safe for swimming without a flotation device, the main exception being the sheltered shallow stretch of beach in front of Mambo's (at the south end of Ullae), where local holidaymakers frequently congregate to take a dip. Further afield, there are plenty of opportunities for day excursions. For wildlife lovers and birders, highlights are a boat trip on the Pottuvil Lagoon or jeep safari into Kumana or Lahugala-Kitulana National Park, while archaeological sites of note include Muhudu Maha Temple, set right on the bay, and the more remote ruined monasteries of Kudumbigala and Magul Maha.

Around Arugam Bay
Surfing The top surfing spot at Arugam Bay is the southern headland between Mambo's and the Upali Beach Resort. The best swell magnet of all the points in the region, this is where the long right-hand reef breaks to create waves in the 0.6–2m range, and – on a good day – a clean wall that barrels in the sections and gives the surfer a 400m ride right through to the inside. Close to this, between Mambo's and the tourist police station, Baby Point is ideal for beginners, also a right-hand break but with waves seldom reaching more than 1m high.

Other excellent surfing sites further afield include Pottuvil Point, whose right-hand break, best from August to November, is suited to more experienced surfers; and the more northerly Whiskey Point, which has good metre-high waves all year round. Several other good surfing spots line the coast south towards Kumana National Park. The scenic Elephant Rock beach 4km south of Ullae and Peanut Farm beach another 1.5km south of that are both good for beginner to intermediate surfers. Panama beach, close to the small town of the same name, typically has 1–1.5m-high waves suited to intermediate surfers, while Okanda beach, near the entrance to Kumana National Park, is a scenic and remote spot whose 2m waves should be attempted only by experienced surfers.

Muhudu Maha Temple [354 D3] (*Pottuvil beach, about 1km east of the main road*) Predominantly Muslim since the early 17th century, Pottuvil is nevertheless the site of an active beachfront Buddhist temple founded by King Kavan Tissa in the 2nd century BC. Now greatly reduced in area, Muhudu Maha Viharaya reputedly extended over more than 100ha in its ancient prime, and presumably many of the original buildings have been engulfed by the surrounding tall dunes. According to certain traditions, it was at Muhudu Maha rather than Kirinda that Princess Viharamahadevi came ashore and met her future husband Kavan Tissa. Today, the most obvious relict of the original monastery is an Anuradhapura-period image house complete with the original 3.5m-high rock-hewn pillars, and a badly damaged statue of the Buddha with two minutely hewn and well-preserved Bodhisattva figures looking back at it. The prominent white dome-top dagoba, by contrast, is a modern addition, unveiled by President Sirisena in 2015. The temple is 15 minutes' walk and signposted from just north of the bridge over Arugam Lagoon; a tuktuk from Ullae should cost around US$1–2.

Pottuvil Lagoon [354 C1] Extending over 2km² immediately north of Pottuvil town, this mangrove-lined estuarine lagoon supports a rich marine birdlife, and it is also a good place to see large crocodiles, water monitors and more occasionally elephants. Two-hour return boat trips to the lagoon mouth are run by the Kottukal Lagoon Ecotourism Centre (m *0778 619959*; ⊕ *06.00–10.00 & 15.00–17.30*) from an office and jetty on the northern outskirts of Pottuvil. The excursion can be done first thing in the morning, when the birdlife is most conspicuous, or in the late afternoon, when the odds of coming across an elephant are highest. The boat trip costs US$13.50 per person, irrespective of group size, while a return tuktuk from Ullae should set you back around US$5–6. You might well get a better price by booking the whole excursion, inclusive of transport, though Ranga's Beach Hut or Ecowave in Ullae.

South of Arugam Bay The most popular half-day trip out of Arugam Bay is a jeep safari to Kumana National Park, which is renowned for its elephants and birdlife. The road to Kumana passes through Panama and the Panama-Kudumbigala Sanctuary, and safaris there usually include a diversion to the atmospheric Kudumbigala Monastery. Other than Kumana National Park, however, the sites below could easily and more cheaply be visited by tuktuk, and there is even public transport as far as Panama.

Panama Heading south from Arugam Bay, an 18km drive through paddy fields and scrubland leads to Panama, a one-street town of sufficient antiquity to be depicted on early Portuguese and Dutch maps of Sri Lanka. A left turn at Panama's main intersection leads past the Bank of Ceylon, a pretty lagoon and a small windswept graveyard to the crest of a tall arcing dune that shelves deep into the sea at Panama beach. This wild, isolated and very beautiful beach is ideal for long barefoot walks, but while the tall waves that crash into the shore make it attractive to experienced surfers, swimming would be reckless indeed. About 1km from town on the Okanda Road, crocodiles are often seen at a small lake identified by the sign reading *Be Alert: Area Where Crocodiles Common*. Several buses daily run between Pottuvil and Panama via Ullae, but it is also cheap and easy to get there by tuktuk.

Panama-Kudumbigala Sanctuary [map, page 320] The more northerly component in a 190km² Ramsar site that was proclaimed in 2010 and also incorporates parts of Kumana National Park, the Panama-Kudumbigala Sanctuary protects a mosaic of wetlands and near-pristine woodland running along the coast south of Panama for about 10km. Bisected by the main road between Panama and Kudumbigala Monastery, it is readily accessible by car but, unlike the bordering national park, no entrance fees are charged. *En route* from Panama to the park entrance, the main road skirts a trio of lagoons that frequently host impressive numbers of aquatic birds, especially in the European winter when resident species are supplemented by large flocks of migrants. Mugger crocodiles are also common, while elephants are quite often seen from the road in the late afternoon. The sanctuary's beaches form an important breeding site for marine turtles and the localised fishing cat is also present but very seldom seen.

Kudumbigala Monastery [map, page 320] Rediscovered in 1942 after languishing forgotten in its remote jungle setting for several centuries, the hermitage at Kudumbigala is one of the oldest in Sri Lanka, having been established under King Devanampiya Tissa shortly after his conversion to Buddhism. Despite this, the site is arguably of less interest for its antiquities than for its spectacular setting amid 250ha of tangled jungle and giant granite ridges, whose peaks offer stirring views across the canopy. The complex houses some 200 caves and rock shelters, many with drip ledges, once used as kutis by the resident monks. The most important of these, 5 minutes' walk from the car park, is Sudharshana Cave, where ancient Brahmi inscriptions dating to the reign of King Dutugamunu can be seen alongside an engraving of the triple gem. Forking left from here, a steepish 10-minute walk uphill through dense jungle leads to the Madhya Mandalaya (Plain of Ruins), a large rocky outcrop whose most important feature is the Sagari Bulumgala, a small domed brick dagoba of a design only known elsewhere from India. A few metres away from this is a small hall built since the hermitage was re-established following the end of the civil war. Return to Sudharshana Cave, take the right fork, and an even steeper climb leads you to a modern boulder-top dagoba whose limited architectural interest is offset by stunning views over the coastal plain to the beach.

To get to Kudumbigala, follow the Okanda/Kumana Road south of Panama for about 12km, then turn right at a signposted intersection that leads to the car park after about 1.5km. No public transport runs south of Panama, but the monastery is easy enough to reach in a normal car or tuktuk, and is also commonly visited as a side trip on jeep safaris to Kumana National Park. Our understanding is that the hermitage technically lies within the national park, but no entrance fee is charged.

Okanda (w *okanda.org*; ◷ *24hrs*) Also known as Ukantha, this tiny seaside village 500m east of the entrance gate to Kumana National Park is celebrated as the site of an ancient shrine dedicated to the Murugan/Kataragama. The main shrine forms part of a temple complex at the base of a rocky hill dotted with 32 sacred natural pools and topped by a secondary shrine dedicated to Murugan's consort Valli. Legend has it that Murugan rested over at Okanda on his journey to Koneswaram (Trincomalee) and some say it is where the deity first sailed into Sri Lanka on his golden boat. Every year, on a changeable date in July, thousands of Hindu worshippers gather at Okanda to embark on the last and most arduous stretch of the Pada Yathra (foot pilgrimage) from Jaffna to Kataragama, a 60km barefoot hike through the wilds of Kumana and Yala National Park.

Kumana National Park [map, page 320] A popular goal for a half-day safari out of Arugam Bay, the 187km² Kumana National Park is effectively a northeastern extension of the better-known and more heavily traversed Yala National Park (pages 508–15), with which it shares a 20km border along the Kumbukkan River. Although the park's predominant vegetation type is moist evergreen forest, the road circuit focuses on the narrow coastal strip, which supports a cover of thorny scrubland and grassland punctuated by more than 20 shallow lagoons and lakes. Kumana supports a similar range of large mammals to neighbouring Yala, with elephant, water buffalo, wild boar and spotted deer all likely to be encountered in the course of any given game drive, and while it is less reliable for leopard sightings, this is compensated for by the relatively low tourist traffic and untrammelled feel. The national park is renowned for its birdlife, with more than 250 species recorded, and was first set aside as a smaller bird sanctuary – centred on Kumana Marsh near the Kumbukkan mouth – back in 1938. It was expanded to its present size and upgraded to national park status in 1970 under the name Yala East, but renamed Kumana in 2006.

Kumana is serviced by 50km of roads and tracks, all of which require high clearance and ideally 4x4 vehicles. Most popular is the 20km coastal road that runs southwest from the entrance gate to the Kumbukkan mouth, veering up to 2km inland as it skirts a succession of about eight lagoons. The two most southerly lagoons, Yakkala and Kumana, are generally the most rewarding in terms of birds, particularly between November and April, when resident populations are boosted by large numbers of migrant waders and waterfowl. However, birding is rewarding throughout the year, especially as these two lagoons are the most reliable site for spotting Sri Lanka's last half-dozen breeding pairs of the localised black-necked stork. A handful of roads run inland from the main coastal drag, but these exist mainly to provide access to some of the park's many archaeological sites. The most interesting of these, about 10km inland of the coastal road, is Bambaras Thalawa Temple, which was established in the 1st century BC and incorporates about ten ruined dagobas, several ancient rock inscriptions, and a hilltop cave temple adorned with a very old statue of a reclining Buddha.

The entrance gate to Kumana (✆ 063 363 5867) is 28km southeast of Arugam Bay via Panama. Most people explore the park on a jeep safari, which costs US$60/105 for a half-/full day per party with one of the Arugam Bay operators listed on page 358. This rate is usually inclusive of a side trip to Kudumbigala Monastery, but it excludes park entrance fees (US$10 per party for vehicle and service fees, plus US$10 per person, plus 15% VAT). If you can find your own way to the entrance gate (regular public transport only heads as far as Panama, but occasional vehicles continue to Okanda), you should be able to hire a jeep more cheaply on the spot (around US$35 per party). Overnight safaris, though far more rewarding, are prohibitively expensive owing to the park fees, which sound reasonable enough at US$15 per person plus VAT until you realise it is charged at a minimum group size of ten.

13

Lahugala and surrounds A number of worthwhile attractions are clustered around the village of Lahugala, which straddles the Monaragala Road about 15km inland of Pottuvil. These include Lahugala-Kitulana National Park, one of the country's top elephant-viewing spots, and a trio of 2,000-plus-year-old ruins of which the most significant is Magul Maha Temple. Several operators in Arugam Bay offer jeep safaris to Lahugala-Kitulana, which could be extended to include a couple of the ruins, but it would also be easy enough to catch a Monaragala-bound bus from Pottuvil to Lahugala, and explore the ruins on foot or by tuktuk.

Lahugala-Kitulana National Park [map, page 320] One of Sri Lanka's smallest national parks, the 51km² Lahugala-Kitulana is renowned for its dense population of elephants, which frequently come to drink at the four reservoirs set within its boundaries. The park was proclaimed in 1980 as a corridor reserve between the larger Yala–Kumana complex of reserves and Gal Oya National Park, and it protects a habitat of moist forest and tall grass bounded by the Monaragala Road and Hada River in the south, and the Koranda River in the north. Its dominant features are the massive Lahugala (or Maha), Kitulana, Sengamuwa and Yalpotta tanks, which together with the abundant grass make it an ideal habitat for elephants, especially over July–August, when the dry season kicks in and the small resident population is joined by migrants from further afield to boost the numbers to around 150 individuals. Leopards and sloth bears are present but seldom seen, while other reasonably common large mammals include spotted deer, wild boar, toque macaque and grey langur. Birdlife includes a good selection of aquatic species, as well as the endemic Sri Lanka junglefowl and red-faced malkoha.

The entrance gate and ticket office for Lahugala-Kitulana lie on the north side of the Monaragala Road about 15km west of Pottuvil, just after you pass Lahugala post office. The easiest way to explore the park is on a jeep safari from Arugam Bay, which should set you back around US$25 per party, exclusive of national park fees (US$10 per party for vehicle and service fees, plus US$10 per person, plus 15% VAT). The park's internal road network is currently limited to around 15km cut in 2010 to connect the entrance gate to the shores of Lahugala and Kitulana tanks, both of which are prime elephant territory, especially in the afternoon, but plans are in place to extend this by another 35–40km. Even if you don't enter the park proper, you can walk to the bund of Kitulana across 150m of paddy fields from the main road immediately west of Lahugala Hospital, and the road offers direct views on to Lake Lahugala about 3km further west. The Sengamuwa and Yalpotta can be viewed more distantly from Kotawehera Raja Maha Temple.

Kotawehera Raja Maha Temple [map, page 320] This minor but readily accessible archaeological site stands on a small hilltop only 250m north of the Monaragala Road about 12km from Pottuvil and 3.5km east of the Lahugala-Kitulana ticket office. Comprising the ruins of a temple most likely founded in the 1st century BC, it is reached via rock-hewn steps and incorporates the base of a large brick dagoba, a rock-hewn pillar, several engraved paving stones, and a small bathing pool with carved rock steps. The views over the jungle of Lahugala-Kitulana go as far as Kitulana and Sengamuwa tanks, which lie within the national park and are regularly visited by elephants, so if you have binoculars, bring them.

Magul Maha Temple [map, page 320] Architecturally the most impressive ruin in the vicinity of Arugam Bay and graced with unusually informative interpretive panels, the ancient temple of Magul Maha is reputedly where Kavan Tissa married

Princess Viharamahadevi in the 2nd century BC. The main ruin is reached along a 300m footpath flanked by two ancient bathing pools, and a small modern temple stands outside the chest-height stone perimeter wall. Magul Maha's single most impressive feature, fenced off outside the Chapter House immediately left of the northern entrance, is a well-preserved and beautifully engraved moonstone unique in Sri Lanka in that it depicts an elephant being ridden by a mahout. Elsewhere, an Anuradhapura-era image house incorporates several intact guardstones and a headless Buddha statue, while the dagoba stands on a platform reached via a carved stairwell guarded by sculpted lions. Magul Maha Temple stands about 1km south of the Pottuvil–Monaragala road, 10–15 minutes' walk along a feeder road signposted 2km west of Kotawehera and 1.5km east of the Lahugala-Kitulana ticket office.

Neeligariya Dagoba [map, page 320] The largest dagoba in Eastern Province, Neeligariya has a circumference of 180m and its three-tiered base currently stands about 22m high. According to a recently discovered inscription, it was constructed as part of a large monastery around 2,000 years ago, during the reign of Kutakanna Tissa or his successor Bhatikabhaya Abhaya. Although the site is scattered with rock-hewn pillars and column bases, there isn't much to see apart from the central dagoba, though that may change once ongoing renovations are complete. Neeligariya has an isolated location in the dense Lahugala Forest Reserve west of Pottuvil, from where it can be reached by following the Monaragala Road for 700m past the Lahugala-Kitulana ticket office, then turning left on to a 4km side road that enters the forest after crossing the Hada River.

UPDATES WEBSITE

Go to w bradtupdates.com/srilanka for the latest on-the-ground travel news, trip reports and factual updates. Keep up to date with the latest posts by following Philip on Twitter (🐦 @philipbriggs) and via Facebook (f fb.me/pb.travel.updates). And, if you have any comments, queries, grumbles, insights, news or other feedback, you're invited to post them directly on the website, or to email them to Philip (e philip.briggs@bradtguides.com) for inclusion.

SEND US YOUR SNAPS!

We'd love to follow your adventures using our *Sri Lanka* guide – why not send us your photos and stories via Twitter (@BradtGuides) and Instagram (@bradtguides) using the hashtag #srilanka? Alternatively, you can upload your photos directly to the gallery on the Sri Lanka destination page via our website (w bradtguides.com/srilanka).

Part Five

KANDY AND THE HILL COUNTRY

Overview of Part Five

Sri Lanka's famous Hill Country, a loosely defined part of the southern interior set between altitudes of 300m and 2,524m, is usually visited *en route* between the sweltering plains of the Cultural Triangle and the sparkling beaches and national parks of the Deep South. Geographically, Hill Country divides into three broad regions, all of which share a relatively cool and moist climate that supports a mosaic of natural forest, montane grassland and subsistence agriculture, as well as the tea plantations that have become an indelible feature of the sloping highlands since they were first planted at Loolecondera in 1867. The most northerly part of the Hill Country, and main gateway to the region coming from the Cultural Triangle or Colombo, focuses on the mid-altitude city of Kandy, whose venerated Temple of the Tooth is a fixture on almost all tours through Sri Lanka. Further south, the High Hill Country, much of it set at altitudes of greater than 1,500m, is almost as popular as Kandy, and renowned for its refreshing climate and wealth of walking opportunities through lovely highland landscapes dominated by babbling waterfalls, quaint colonial towns and neat tea estates. Further southwest, the relatively little-visited and ill-defined Low Hill Country, most of which lies below 1,000m, is dominated by the Sinharaja massif and supports a relict cover of wet-zone rainforest whose unique biodiversity and wealth of endemics is a magnet for birdwatchers, wildlife enthusiasts and hikers.

HIGHLIGHTS

KANDY (pages 369–95) The last capital of the Sinhala monarchy, this delightful UNESCO World Heritage Site is at once a pretty modern town enclosed by verdant slopes and a sacred Buddhist shrine dominated by the striking Dalada Maligawa (Temple of the Tooth).

GAMPOLA TEMPLES (pages 400–2) Constructed during Gampola's 14th-century stint as Sinhala capital, a trio of stunning and very different Buddhist temples at Embekke, Lankatilaka and Gadaladeniya are clustered together within easy day-tripping distance of Kandy.

ADAM'S PEAK (pages 413–17) Sri Lanka's holiest summit, this tall pyramidal peak, reached via more than 5,000 steps, is the subject of a multi-denominational nocturnal pilgrimage attracting up to 20,000 Buddhist and other worshippers daily between the December and May poyas.

NUWARA ELIYA (pages 417–28) Situated at the base of the country's tallest peak, Nuwara Eliya is not only Sri Lanka's highest and coldest town, but also perhaps its most quirky, thanks to a pervasive colonial influence reflected in the nickname Little England.

HORTON PLAINS NATIONAL PARK (pages 430–5) Best known for the walking trail to the spectacular World's End Viewpoint, Sri Lanka's most ecologically important highland reserve supports misty moorland, pockets of elfin cloudforest, and a wealth of endemic wildlife.

LIPTON'S SEAT (page 440) Often treated as a poor man's answer to World's End, this 1,920m-high viewpoint – a favourite of the 19th-century tea magnate Sir Thomas Lipton – offers fantastic views across the southern lowlands.

ELLA (pages 443–52) A favoured highland base with backpackers, this quaint green village boasts a fabulous escarpment location, plenty of walking opportunities, and a high street brimming with budget-friendly restaurants and bars.

RAKKHITHTHA KANDA (page 456) The most impressive Buddhist shrine near Ella, this obscure cave temple incorporates some fine Kandyan paintings and is also the springboard for guided hikes up vertiginous Kurullangala to the country's oldest rock art site.

KITULGALA (pages 457–64) Long famed as the country's premier white-water rafting destination, jungle-bound Kitulgala now offers an alluring bouquet of outdoor activities, from canyoning, abseiling and zip-lining to mountain biking and birding.

SINHARAJA FOREST RESERVE (pages 471–82) Sri Lanka's most important biodiversity hotspot, this UNESCO World Heritage Site is criss-crossed with walking tails offering access to the magnificent rainforest interior and the opportunity to see more than 30 endemic bird species.

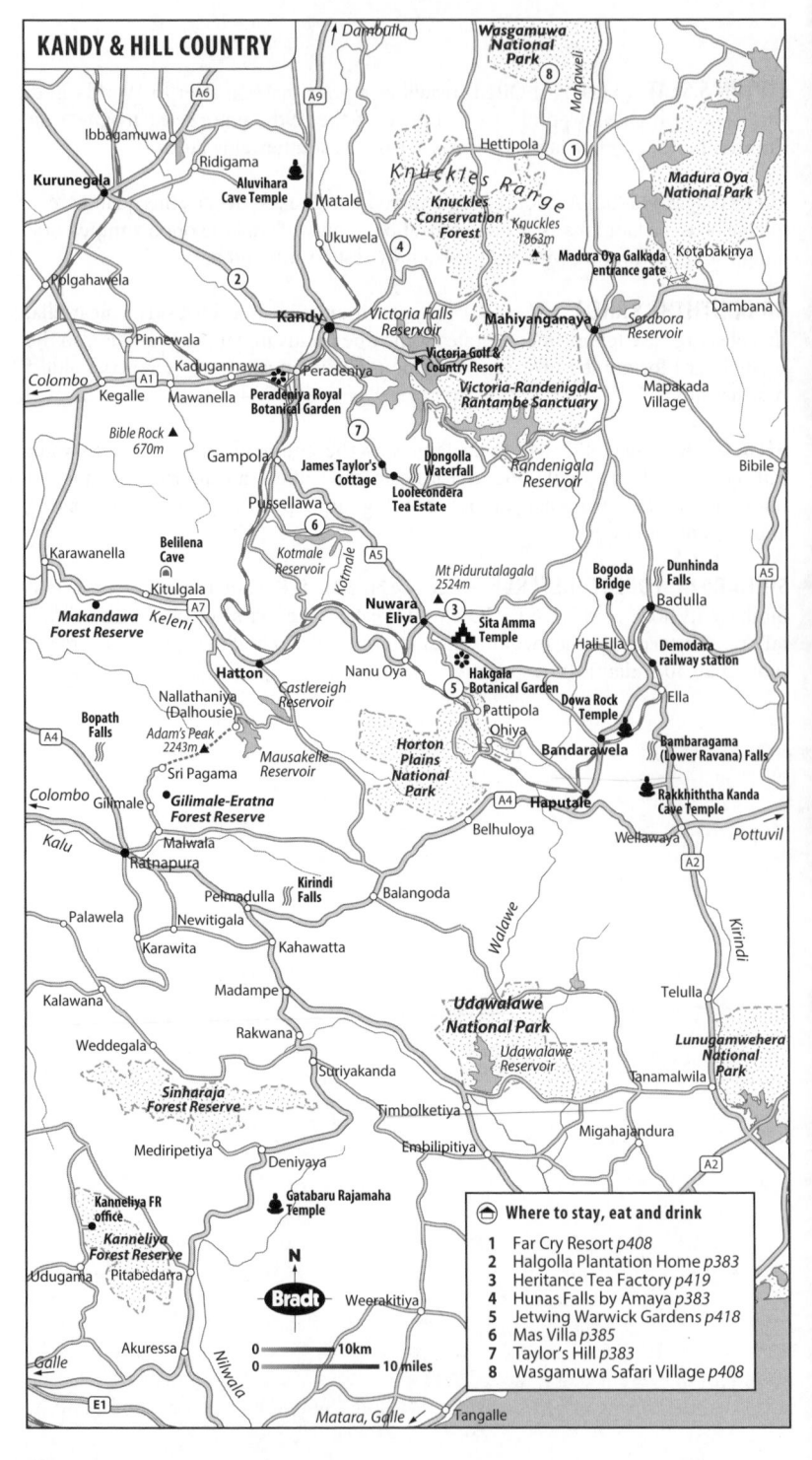

KANDY & HILL COUNTRY

↑ *Dambulla*

Wasgamuwa National Park ⑧

Ibbagamuwa

Ⓐ6 Ⓐ9 *Mahaweli*

Ridigama

Kurunegala

Aluvihara Cave Temple Matale

Hettipola ①

Knuckles Range

Madura Oya National Park

Ukuwela ④ **Knuckles Conservation Forest** *Knuckles 1863m* ▲

Polgahawela

Ⓐ2 Kandy

Madura Oya Galkada entrance gate Kotabakinya

Pinnewala Kadugannawa Peradeniya

Victoria Falls Reservoir

Dambana

Colombo Ⓐ1 Kegalle Mawanella

Mahiyanganaya *Serabora Reservoir*

Peradeniya Royal Botanical Garden **Victoria Golf & Country Resort**

Victoria-Randenigala-Rantambe Sanctuary Mapakada Village

Bible Rock ▲ 670m Gampola

James Taylor's Cottage **Dongolla Waterfall** *Randenigala Reservoir* Bibile

Loolecondera Tea Estate ⑦

Pussellawa ⑥

Karawanella **Belilena Cave** *Kotmale Reservoir*

Mt Pidurutalagala 2524m ▲ **Bogoda Bridge** **Dunhinda Falls** Ⓐ5

Kitulgala Ⓐ7 *Keleni* Ⓐ5

Nuwara Eliya ③ Sita Amma Temple Hali Ela Badulla

Makandawa Forest Reserve

Nanu Oya Hakgala **Demodara railway station**

Hatton *Castlereigh Reservoir* ⑤ Botanical Garden **Dowa Rock Temple** Ella

Nallathaniya (Dalhousie) Pattipola Ohiya

Bopath Falls Ⓐ4 *Adam's Peak 2243m* ▲ *Mausakelle Reservoir*

Bandarawela **Bambaragama (Lower Ravana) Falls**

Sri Pagama **Horton Plains National Park**

Colombo Gilimale **Gilimale-Eratna Forest Reserve** Ⓐ4 **Haputale** **Rakkhiththa Kanda Cave Temple**

Kalu Malwala Belhuloya Wellawaya *Pottuvil*

Ratnapura Ⓐ2

Palawela Pelmadulla **Kirindi Falls** Balangoda *Walawe* *Kirindi*

Newitigala

Karawita Kahawatta

Kalawana Madampe Telulla

Rakwana **Udawalawe National Park** **Lunugamwehera National Park**

Weddegala Suriyakanda *Udawalawe Reservoir* Tanamalwila

Sinharaja Forest Reserve Timbolketiya Migahajandura

Mediripetiya Embilipitiya Ⓐ2

Deniyaya

Kanneliya FR office Gatabaru Rajamaha Temple

Kanneliya Forest Reserve

Udugama Pitabedara

N

Bradt

Weerakitiya

0 ___ 10km
0 ___ 10 miles

Galle *Nilwala*

Akuressa

Ⓔ1 *Matara, Galle* ↙ Tangalle

Where to stay, eat and drink

1 Far Cry Resort *p408*
2 Halgolla Plantation Home *p383*
3 Heritance Tea Factory *p419*
4 Hunas Falls by Amaya *p383*
5 Jetwing Warwick Gardens *p418*
6 Mas Villa *p385*
7 Taylor's Hill *p383*
8 Wasgamuwa Safari Village *p408*

14

Kandy and Surrounds

As sweet and ripe for exploration as its irresistible name suggests, Kandy finds its way on to the itinerary of pretty much every visitor to Sri Lanka, and it seldom disappoints. Also known as the Maha Nuwara (literally 'Great City') or by the ancient name Senkandagala, Kandy served as the last capital of the Sinhala monarchy from the 1590s until it was signed over to Britain in 1815. It remains the capital of Central Province, and a population of 130,000 makes it the island's largest city outside the urban conglomeration centred upon Colombo and Negombo. The sacred old city – lapped by the ornamental Lake Kandy, and overlooked by the verdant slopes of the Udawatte Kele Sanctuary – is a UNESCO World Heritage Site, whose spiritual focal point Dalada Maligawa (Temple of the Tooth) ranks high among the world's most venerated Buddhist shrines. Enclosed on three sides by the jungle-fringed Mahaweli River, the greater city is studded with other historic landmarks, ranging from a quartet of ancient shrines dedicated to the city's four guardian deities, to imperious colonial edifices such as the Hotel Suisse and Queen's Hotel, to the vast and well-maintained Peradeniya Botanical Garden, which celebrates its bicentennial in 2021.

Logistically and climatically, Kandy is a convenient and agreeably temperate mid-altitude halfway point between the sweltering coast and northern lowlands, and the misty cool highlands to the immediate south. Indeed, the majority of organised tours incorporate Kandy as a one- or two-night stop *en route* from the ancient cities of the Cultural Triangle to the High Hill Country around Nuwara Eliya. But for those with limited time, or who have pre-booked a beach holiday on the southwest coast, Kandy can also be visited as a day or overnight trip by train or express bus from Colombo, or – more ambitiously – with a chartered car and driver from the likes of Bentota and Galle. By contrast, for those with sufficient time, it wouldn't be difficult to spend an enjoyable week exploring this delightful town and more far-flung rural attractions such as the magnificent 14th-century temples built by the Gampola monarchy, the bird-rich dwarf cloudforest of the Knuckles Range, or the hunter-gatherer Vedda communities of the lowlands around Mahiyanganaya.

HISTORY

In ancient times, the Hill Country around the south of Kandy formed part of the Buddhist kingdom ruled from Anuradhapura and later Polonnaruwa, and it frequently served as a place of refuge for Sinhala royalty during periods of internecine strife or occupation by outsiders. It became the island's main power base in the 1340s, when King Bhuvanaikabahu IV relocated his capital to Gampola, 25km to the south of present-day Kandy. Bhuvanaikabahu IV's son Vikramabahu III, who ascended the throne in 1357, was the first king to build a palace at Kandy, and he

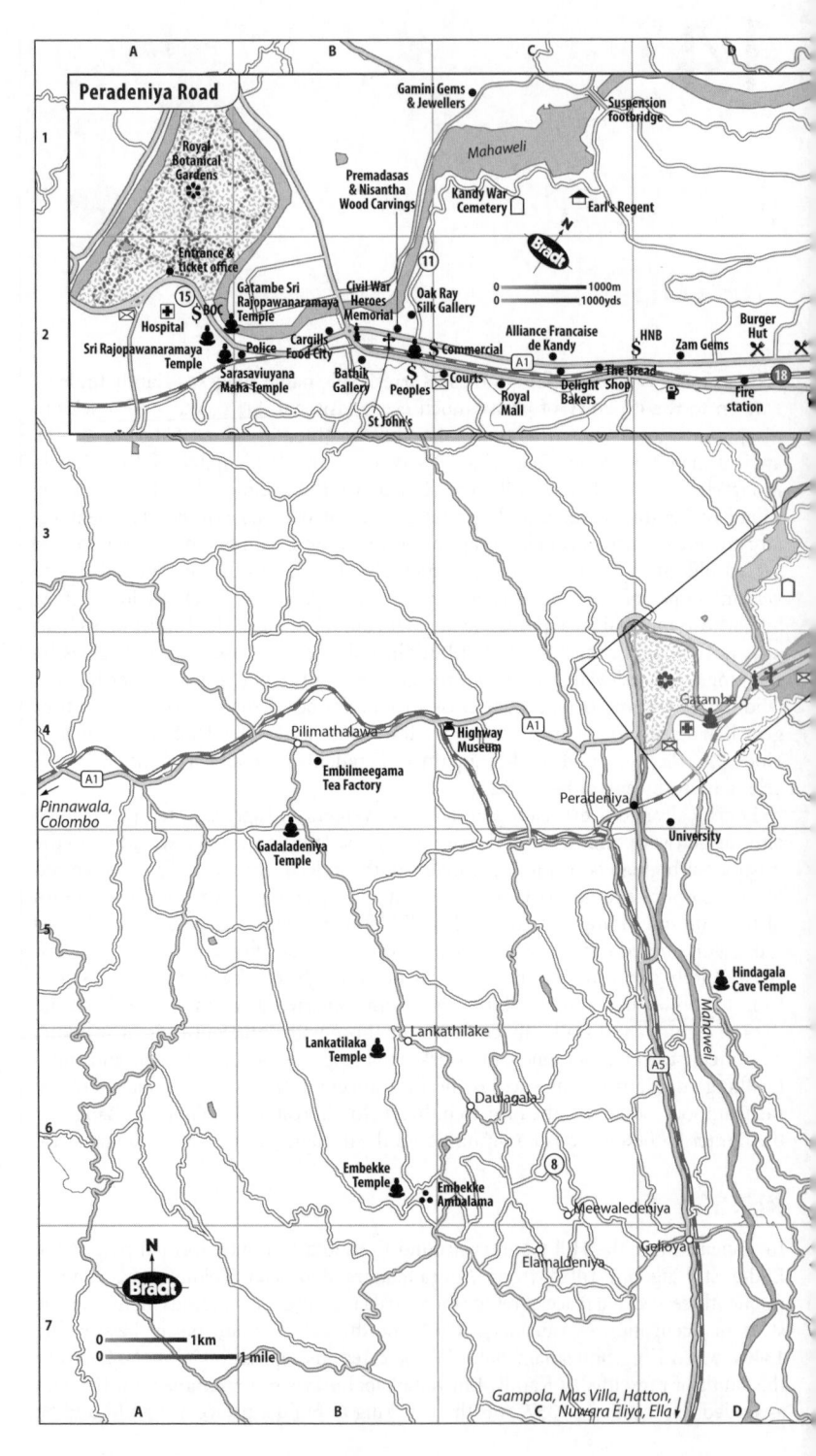

Peradeniya Road

A B C D

1

Royal Botanical Gardens

Gamini Gems & Jewellers

Mahaweli

Suspension footbridge

Premadasas & Nisantha Wood Carvings

Kandy War Cemetery

Earl's Regent

Entrance & Ticket office

N

0 ——————— 1000m
0 ——————— 1000yds

2

Gatambe Sri Rajopawanaramaya Temple

Civil War Heroes Memorial

Oak Ray Silk Gallery

Hospital

BOC

Alliance Francaise de Kandy

HNB

Zam Gems

Burger Hut

Sri Rajopawanaramaya Temple

Police

Cargills Food City

Commercial

A1

18

Sarasaviuyana Maha Temple

Bathik Gallery

Peoples

Courts

Royal Mall

Delight Bakers

The Bread Shop

Fire station

St John's

3

Gatambe

4

Pilimathalawa

Highway Museum

A1

Embilmeegama Tea Factory

Peradeniya

Pinnawala, Colombo

A1

University

Gadaladeniya Temple

5

Hindagala Cave Temple

Mahaweli

Lankatilaka Temple

Lankathilake

A5

Daulagala

6

Embekke Temple

Embekke Ambalama

8

Meewaledeniya

Gelioya

Elamaldeniya

N

Bradt

7

0 ——————— 1km
0 ——————— 1 mile

Gampola, Mas Villa, Hatton, Nuwara Eliya, Ella

A B C D

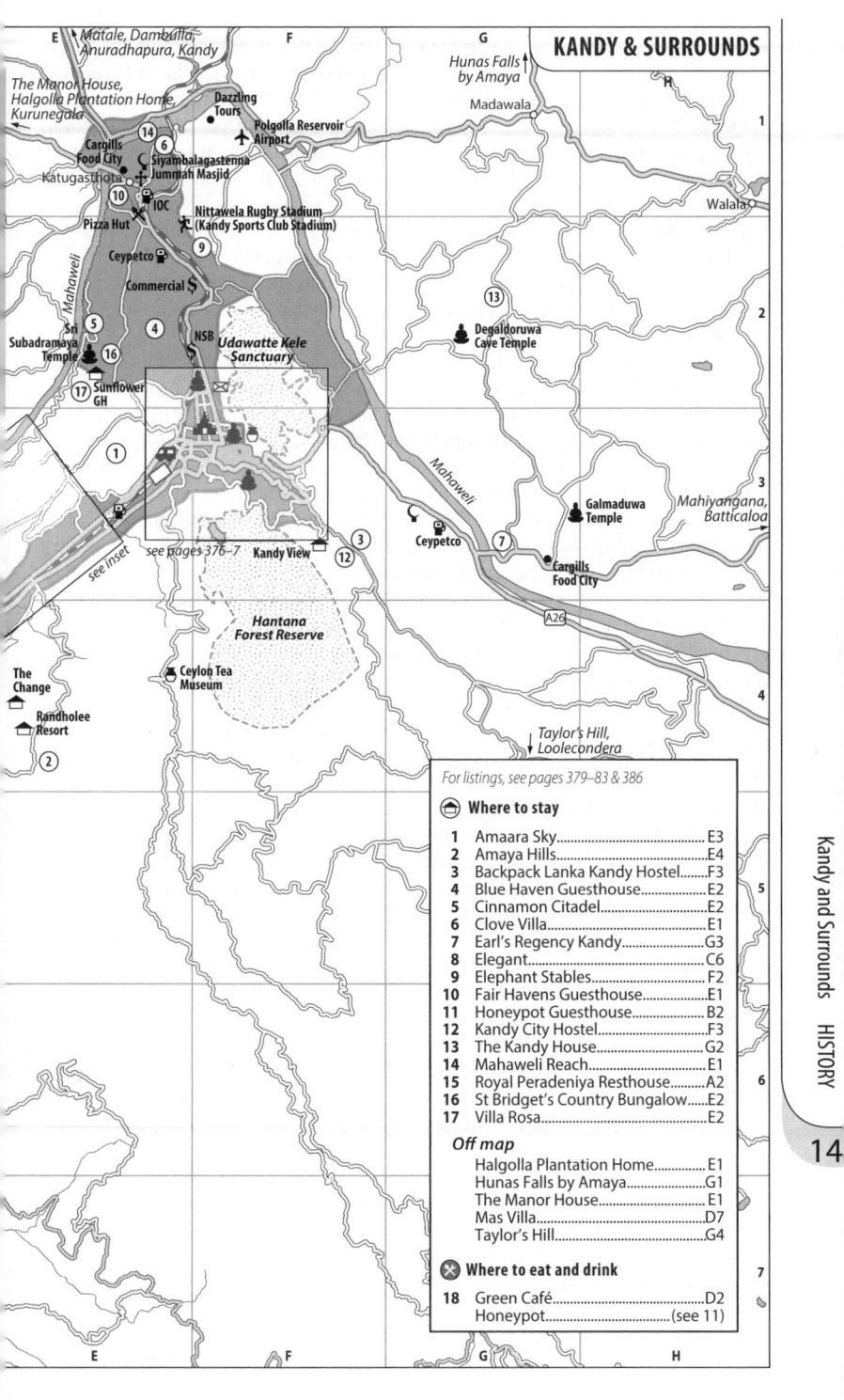

E · Matale, Dambulla, Anuradhapura, Kandy   F   G   H

The Manor House,
Halgolla Plantation Home,
Kurunegala

Hunas Falls
by Amaya

Madawala

Dazzling
Tours

Polgolla Reservoir
Airport

Cargills
Food City   14   6

Siyambalagastenna
Jummah Masjid

Katugastota   10   IOC

Pizza Hut

Ceypetco

Commercial $

Walala

Nittawela Rugby Stadium
(Kandy Sports Club Stadium)   9

13

Sri
Subadramaya
Temple   5   4   NSB   Udawatte Kele
Sanctuary

16

17   Sunflower
GH

Degaldoruwa
Cave Temple

2

Mahaweli

1

see inset

see pages 376–7   Kandy View   12   3   Ceypetco   7   Galmaduwa
Temple

Mahaweli

Cargills
Food City

Mahiyangana,
Batticaloa

3

Hantana
Forest Reserve

A26

The
Change

Ceylon Tea
Museum

Randholee
Resort   2

Taylor's Hill,
Loolecondera

For listings, see pages 379–83 & 386

Where to stay

1	Amaara Sky	E3
2	Amaya Hills	E4
3	Backpack Lanka Kandy Hostel	F3
4	Blue Haven Guesthouse	E2
5	Cinnamon Citadel	E2
6	Clove Villa	E1
7	Earl's Regency Kandy	G3
8	Elegant	C6
9	Elephant Stables	F2
10	Fair Havens Guesthouse	E1
11	Honeypot Guesthouse	B2
12	Kandy City Hostel	F3
13	The Kandy House	G2
14	Mahaweli Reach	E1
15	Royal Peradeniya Resthouse	A2
16	St Bridget's Country Bungalow	E2
17	Villa Rosa	E2

Off map

Halgolla Plantation Home	E1
Hunas Falls by Amaya	G1
The Manor House	E1
Mas Villa	D7
Taylor's Hill	G4

Where to eat and drink

18	Green Café	D2
	Honeypot	(see 11)

Kandy and Surrounds   HISTORY

14

is also accredited as having constructed the city's oldest extant building, the Natha Devale opposite the more modern Sri Dalada Maligawa. Vikramabahu III named his capital Senkandagalapura (City of Senkanda's Rock) after he was inspired to settle there by an oracular hermit called Senkanda, who reported witnessing a cobra chasing off a predatory mongoose (or, in some variations, a rabbit turning to pursue its human hunters) outside his cave dwelling in what is now the suburban Udawatte Kele Sanctuary, an unusual sight which the king regarded to be auspicious. The royal capital evidently relocated back to Gampola after Vikramabahu III's death in 1374, then – after a period of instability that saw a turnover of six different kings within the space of 12 years – even further afield, to Kotte (aka Sri Jayawardenepura Kotte), close to present-day Colombo, following the ascent of Parakramabahu VI in c1415.

Kandy was revived as a vassal kingdom of Kotte under King Sena Sammatha Wickramabahu in 1473. Though subsidiary to Kotte, it proved to be a very stable political entity, ruled by just three long-reigning kings from then until the death of Karaliyadde Bandara in 1581, by which time Kotte had more or less collapsed under the twin assault of the Portuguese at Colombo and the rival Kingdom of Sitawaka. The Portuguese tried to intervene in Kandyan affairs by installing the puppet Queen Dona Catherina, aka Kusmasana Devi, a teenage daughter of Karaliyadde Bandara who had been taken hostage by them as a child and raised as a Catholic. Within months of taking the throne, Dona Catherina was deposed by Rajasinha I (son of King Mayadunne of Sitawaka), who was in turn defeated in battle and evicted from the throne by King Vimaladharmasuriya I in 1592.

Though he ruled for just 12 years, Vimaladharmasuriya I has as great a claim as any to be the founder of the latter-day Kandyan Kingdom. One of his first actions as king was to relocate the sacred tooth relic to a purpose-built two-tiered Dalada Maligawa (Temple of the Tooth) in Kandy, confirming the highland city – protected within a wide horseshoe bend on the Mahaweli River, and separated from the distant Portuguese-controlled littoral by a series of readily defensible mountain passes – as the true Sinhala capital. Two years later, he married Dona Catherina, furthering his popular hold on the throne. Furthermore, his reign was also bookended by crushing defeats of two Portuguese offensives into Kandy, the Campaign of Danture in 1594 and the Battle of Balana in 1602. It was at around this time that Kandy acquired the Sinhala name Maha Nuwara (literally 'Big Town'), still in wide use today. (The name Kandy, first used by the Dutch, derives via the Portuguese *candea* from the Sinhala *kanda* (hill), an abbreviation of Kanda Uda Pasrata (Five Countries of the Hills), a name that dated back to Medieval times and covered much of the medium-altitude territory running south from Dambulla to Gampola.)

In 1604, Vimaladharmasuriya was succeeded by his brother or cousin King Senarat, who legitimised a tenuous claim to the throne by marrying the widowed Dona Catherina and her two daughters. Senarat's lengthy reign was characterised by frequent rebellions and Portuguese incursions into Kandyan territory. He did, however, record one famous victory over the Portuguese at the Battle of Randeniwela in August 1630, when a Kandyan army led by his son, the future Rajasinha II, repulsed an attempt to breach the southern escarpment near Wellawaya. In 1638, three years after his coronation, King Rajasinha II signed a treaty with the Dutch, who agreed to help expel the Portuguese from the island in exchange for certain economic privileges over the other European powers eyeing the island's lucrative trade in cinnamon, oysters and other goods. The first Portuguese ports (Batticaloa and Trincomalee) fell in 1639, but by the time the last one was captured – Jaffna, in 1658 – it had become abundantly clear to

Rajasinha II that the Dutch had no intention of returning the littoral to Kandy but instead intended to occupy their ports as bases from which to monopolise the island's export trade. For a century and a half, starting in the mid 1640s, the two powers coexisted uneasily alongside each other – the Dutch along a coastline interspersed with thick-buttressed forts, the Kandyans in the near-impregnable hills – with Rajasinha II and his successors engaging in regular trade and sporadic warfare with ports such as Colombo and Galle.

Rajasinha II was succeeded by his son Vimaladharmasuriya II (r1687–1707) and teenage grandson Vira Narendra Sinha (r1707–39), devout Buddhists both who dedicated their reigns to literary and religious pursuits and took little notice of their Dutch neighbours. Vira Narendra Sinha turned out to be the last Sinhalese King of Kandy: he died without eligible issue (his only son had a lower-caste mother) precipitating a succession crisis that led to the coronation of Sri Vijaya Rajasinha, the aristocratic Tamil brother of his senior wife, a princess from the Madurai Nayak dynasty of southern India. Sri Vijaya Rajasinha (r1739–47) was succeeded by his brother-in-law Kirti Sri Rajasinha, who built the present-day inner sanctum of the Sri Dalada Maligawa and several noteworthy temples east of the city centre during his influential 35-year reign. Hostilities with the Dutch were resumed in 1761, when Kirti Sri Rajasinha's army attacked and captured Matara Fort, and 'put every European to the sword except two officers who are now prisoners of the country' according to John Pybus. The Dutch recaptured Matara in 1762 and started amassing troops along the coast in order to enact a plan to capture Kandy by attacking it from six different directions. Echoing events a century earlier, Kirti Sri Rajasinha invited the intervention of the British, whose own agenda in terms of monopolising the coastal trade barely needs pointing out, but in the end no treaty was signed. A new Dutch–Kandyan treaty was hammered out in 1765, and by the time of Kirti Sri Rajasinha's death in 1782, the mood of tense coexistence between the two powers had been restored. Kirti Sri Rajasinha was succeeded by his brother Sri Rajadhi Rajasinha.

John Pybus, who visited 'Candia' in 1762 on behalf of the British East India Company in the hope of securing a trade alliance with the king, left behind a detailed description of the royal capital:

> Built in a kind of valley formed by hills, [it had] two principal streets [that] run north and south [of which the longer] is near a mile long, but the houses are not so well or uniformly built at the extreme ends as those towards the centre, which are most of them tiled…. The palace stands in a manner detached from the rest of the houses … and is a large, lofty, spacious building, containing a large number of apartments and seemingly well constructed…. Most of the houses are built near the declivity of the hills which surround the town, and are six or seven feet [about 2m] from the streets, which are spacious and clean, from whence you go up to them by a long flight of brick or stone steps…. The town is tolerably well inhabited, and they have plenty of good wells.

In 1796, the Dutch were forced to hand over all their Sri Lanka possessions to the British. Two years later, Sri Rajadhi Rajasinha died, to be succeeded by his teenage nephew Sri Vikrama Rajasinha, the last King of Kandy. In February 1803, two British columns, led by a defected Kandyan minister called Pilimatalawe, marched on the city, set up a garrison, and installed a puppet king called Muttusami in place of Sri Vikrama Rajasinha, who had evacuated his palace in order to conduct a guerrilla war from the surrounding hills. The occupying forces were ravaged by disease and offered little resistance to a Kandyan counter-attack a month later that left only one

14

British survivor. Sri Vikrama Rajasinha retaliated with an unsuccessful attack on the British garrison at Hanwella in 1804 and the occupation of Katuwana in 1805, when the appointment of General Thomas Maitland as Governor of Ceylon led to a cessation of hostilities. Back in Kandy, however, Sri Vikrama Rajasinha became an increasingly volatile, paranoid and autocratic presence, focusing his energy on vainglorious projects such as the construction of Lake Kandy, which was completed in 1807, and ordering cruel and gruesome public executions to dispose of enemies, both real and imaginary. The matter came to a head in 1814, when the unpopular king ordered the execution of the entire family of his senior adigar (minister) Ehelepola, drowning his children and wife in his newly built lake. Disillusioned and afraid for their own lives, Ehelepola and other senior ministers and chiefs willingly signed the Kandyan Convention of 1815, which ceded control of Kandy – and, effectively, the rest of Sri Lanka – to the British, and stripped all powers from Sri Vikrama Rajasinha, who was exiled to India and died there in 1832.

Kandy remained an important city throughout the colonial era, among other things serving as the headquarters of the South East Asia Command from 1944 until the end of World War II. Its relatively high elevation and cool climate, at least by comparison with Colombo and the coast, contributed to its popularity with colonial agents and settlers, as did the coffee and later tea industry that thrived on the surrounding hills (see box, page 8). Today, it is the largest town in the Sri Lankan interior, and an important hub of transport between north, west, south and to a lesser extent east. The Dalada Maligawa (Temple of the Tooth) built by Kirti Sri Rajasinha is one of the country's most sacred Buddhist sites and the centrepiece of the Sacred City of Kandy UNESCO World Heritage Site inscribed in 1988.

GETTING THERE AND AWAY

Kandy lies 115km inland of Colombo, a trip that takes less than 3 hours by train and only slightly longer by road. As you whizz between the two, you might contemplate the fact that the same journey took six weeks, following jungle trails in single file, prior to the British construction of a road between Colombo and Kandy, which commenced in 1820. The opening of the road in 1825 reduced the journey to ten days by bullock cart, and it was only after the opening of a passenger train service in 1867 that the journey between Colombo and Kandy was reduced to less than a day.

BY AIR Cinnamon Air (w *cinnamonair.com*) seaplanes fly daily between Kandy and Colombo, Batticaloa, Bentota and Dickwella, though in most cases the short distances, high fares and more complex logistics associated with flying arguably make a train trip or road transfer more inviting. The planes land at Polgolla Reservoir Airport, on the Mahaweli River about 5km north of the town centre.

BY RAIL The most agreeable way to travel between Colombo and Kandy is by train, with up to ten services daily each typically taking 2½–3 hours one way. Travelling from Colombo to Kandy, try to get a seat on the right-hand side of the train, facing the engine, for the best views. Kandy railway station stands alongside the main road to Peradeniya (and Colombo). Most Colombo–Kandy trains continue on to Badulla, stopping *en route* at Hatton (for Adam's Peak), Nanu Oya (for Nuwara Eliya), Pattipola and Ohiya (both for Horton Plains National Park), Haputale, Bandarawela and Ella. A secondary line running north from Kandy to Matale is serviced by half a dozen trains daily and takes up to 1½ hours. The most comfortable carriages between Colombo and Kandy are those operated by

Rajadhani Express (w *rajadhani.lk*) and ExpoRail (w *exporail.lk*). ExpoRail also continues on to Badulla, stopping at all major stations in between. However, both services were suspended, hopefully on a temporary basis, in late 2017. For contact details, see the general section on train travel on pages 47–50.

BY ROAD The scenic 115km road trip from Colombo to Kandy typically takes around 3 hours, depending greatly on where exactly you start, the time of day, and the volume of traffic on the city outskirts. Possible stops along this road are covered in the chapter *Inland of Colombo* (pages 144–63). Intercity buses between Colombo and Kandy leave every 15 minutes throughout the day. Coming from elsewhere in Sri Lanka, Kandy lies 220km (6–7 hours) from Galle via Bentota (180km) and the outskirts of Colombo; 320km (8–9 hours) from Jaffna via Anuradhapura (135km/3–4 hours), Dambulla (75km/2 hours) and Matale (25km/30 minutes); 220km (5 hours) from Trincomalee via Habarana (95km/2½ hours), Sigiriya Junction, Dambulla and Matale; 140km (3–4 hours) from Polonnaruwa via Habarana, Sigiriya Junction, Dambulla and Matale; 185km (4–5 hours) from Batticaloa via Mahiyanganaya (75km/2 hours); 215km from Arugam Bay via Bibile; 225km (5–6 hours) from Tissamaharama via Ella (140km/3–4 hours) and Badulla (115km/2½–3 hours); 75km from Nuwara Eliya and 70km from Hatton. At least one direct bus per hour runs in either direction to/from Anuradhapura, Dambulla, Matale, Badulla (where you can change buses for Ella), Nuwara Eliya, Hatton and Polonnaruwa, and there are also a few buses daily to/from Jaffna and Trincomalee. The main bus station is immediately north of the railway station, but some local services leave from the more central clock tower station, and express services to Colombo leave from a smaller stand on Keppetipola Road about halfway between the two.

WHERE TO STAY

There are several clear advantages to staying in the town centre, north of Lake Kandy, primarily that it allows you to explore its old buildings and the royal temple complex on foot, while placing you within walking distance of a good selection of restaurants, cafés and bars. Unfortunately, however, the choice of central accommodation is surprisingly limited, though a few good options exist and should probably be the first choice of travellers who want to immerse themselves in old Kandy rather than just flit in for a day visit. Far more lodges, most aimed at budget travellers, can be found south of Lake Kandy, which does lie within walking distance of the old town centre, though it is more of a hike. Most hotels in the moderate to exclusive ranges are dotted around the suburbs or further afield. Accommodation rates in and around Kandy are less seasonal than in some parts of Sri Lanka, though most places charge inflated prices over the Perahera, as well as around Christmas and New Year.

TOWN CENTRE
Upmarket

Queen's Hotel [384 D3] (81 rooms) Dalada St; \ 081 223 3026; e queenshotel1938@gmail. com; w queenshotel.lk. Built in 1844, Kandy's longest-serving hotel has a prestigious location overlooking Lake Kandy on the west side of the garden in front of the Temple of the Tooth. Its antiquity is reflected in the palatial façade,

castellated roof complete with corner bell tower & lobby graced with marble floor, ornate tall ceiling & creaking 1930s-style lift. The rooms combine a period feel (wooden floor, antique furniture) with modern amenities (AC, fan, TV) but are a little frayed at the edges & have small bathrooms. Facilities include a banquet hall of a restaurant (*lunch & dinner buffets cost US$11*) & an interior secret garden with swimming pool.

14

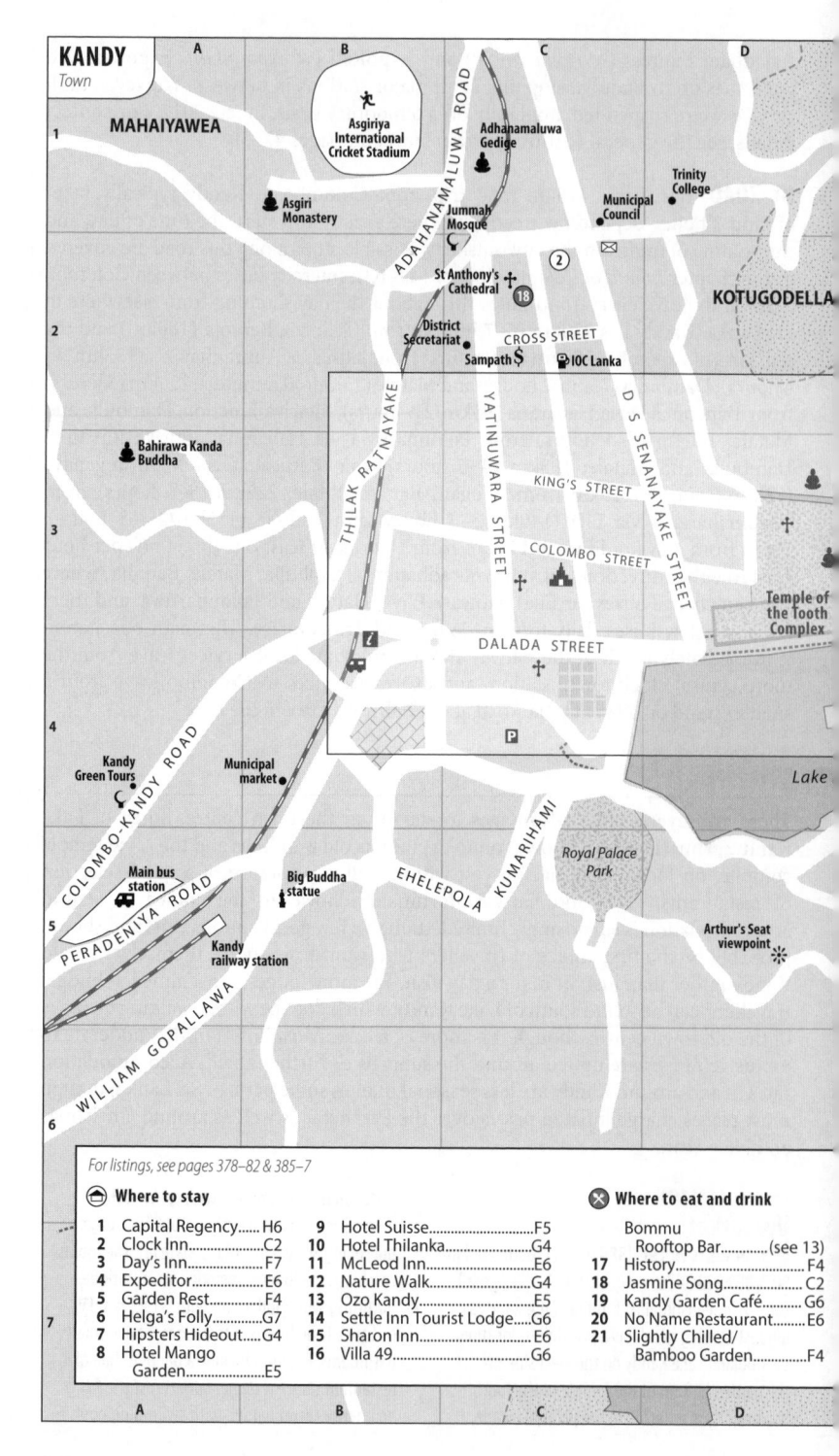

KANDY
Town

MAHAIYAWEA

Asgiriya International Cricket Stadium

Asgiri Monastery

Adhanamaluwa Gedige

Jummah Mosque

Municipal Council

Trinity College

St Anthony's Cathedral

KOTUGODELLA

District Secretariat

CROSS STREET

Sampath

IOC Lanka

Bahirawa Kanda Buddha

THILAK RATNAYAKE

YATINUWARA STREET

KING'S STREET

COLOMBO STREET

D S SENANAYAKE STREET

Temple of the Tooth Complex

DALADA STREET

Kandy Green Tours

COLOMBO-KANDY ROAD

Municipal market

Lake

Main bus station

PERADENIYA ROAD

Big Buddha statue

EHELEPOLA KUMARIHAMI

Royal Palace Park

Arthur's Seat viewpoint

Kandy railway station

WILLIAM GOPALLAWA

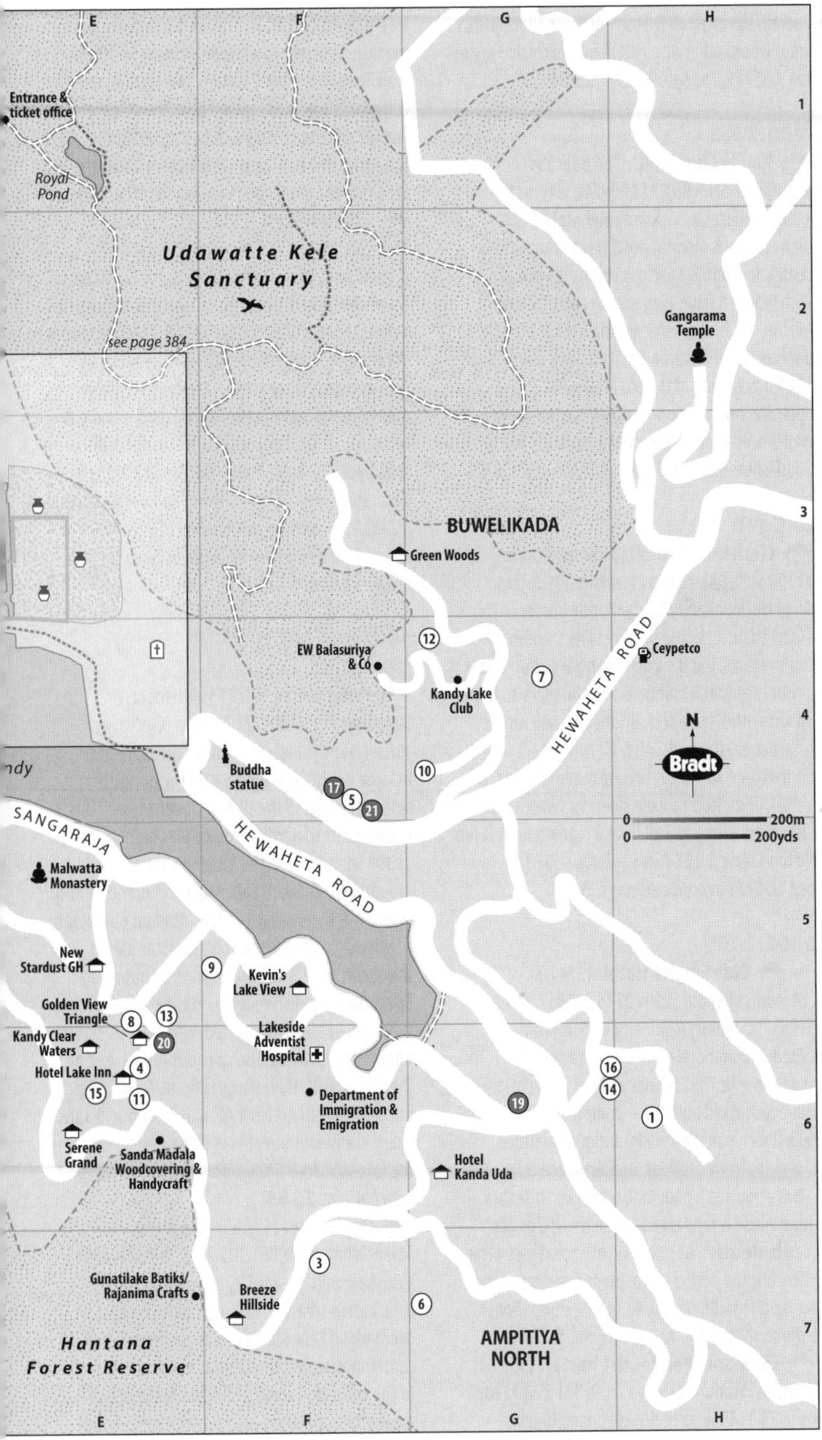

E

Entrance &
ticket office

Royal
Pond

Udawatte Kele
Sanctuary

see page 384

F

G

H

1

2

**Gangarama
Temple**

3

BUWELIKADA

🏠 Green Woods

EW Balasuriya
& Co ●

(12)

(7)

HEWAHETA ROAD

🛒 Ceypetco

Kandy Lake
Club ●

4

N

0   200m
0   200yds

andy

🧍 Buddha
statue

(17) (5)
(21)

(10)

SANGARAJA

HEWAHETA ROAD

🧍 Malwatta
Monastery

5

New
Stardust GH 🏠

(9)

Kevin's
Lake View 🏠

Golden View
Triangle

(8)

(13)

Kandy Clear
Waters 🏠

(20)

Lakeside
Adventist
Hospital ✚

(16)

(14)

Hotel Lake Inn 🏠

(4)

(1)

(15)

(11)

● Department of
Immigration &
Emigration

(19)

6

Serene
Grand 🏠

● Sanda Madala
Woodcovering &
Handycraft

Hotel
🏠 Kanda Uda

Gunatilake Batiks/
Rajanima Crafts ●

Breeze
Hillside 🏠

(3)

(6)

**AMPITIYA
NORTH**

7

Hantana
Forest Reserve

E

F

G

H

Overall, the location & ambience just about justify what would otherwise feel like an excessive price tag. *US$149/155 sgl/dbl B&B*. **$$$$**

Moderate

🏠 **Kandy City Hotel** [384 B3] (25 rooms) Yatinuwara St; ☎ 081 222 0002/4; e fom@ kandycityhotel.lk; w kandycityhotel.lk. This unpretentious modern hotel has a wonderfully central location & spacious comfortable rooms with wooden floor, king-size or twin ¾ beds, AC, fan, TV, fridge, safe, writing desk & blandly unobjectionable décor. Pricier deluxe rooms have a balcony & view of the old Methodist church opposite, but are more exposed to street noise. The well-priced ground-floor restaurant/bar is a bonus. Good value. *US$80/93 standard/deluxe dbl*. **$$$**

Budget

🏠 **Clock Inn** [376 C2] (8 rooms, 4 dorms) 11 Hill St; ☎ 081 223 5311; e kandy@clockinn. lk; w clockinnkandy.lk. The Kandy outlier of this hostel chain lacks the pizzazz of its Colombo counterparts, but it's a good central option & the bright communal lounge is a useful place to hook up with other travellers. Bright en-suite rooms have queen-size beds, AC & TV, while 6- & 8-bed dorms come with AC & private reading lights, & a stack of rooftop 'capsule sleepers' (which look rather like wine vats) all have a reading light & fan. No food served. *US$40/45 sgl/dbl, US$12 pp dorm bed, US$11 pp capsule sleepers*. **$$**

Shoestring

✳ 🏠 **Olde Empire Hotel** [384 D3] (14 rooms) Temple St; m 0776 321867, 0777 619637; e inquiry@oldeempirehotel.com; w oldeempirehotel.com. Built as a coffee warehouse in 1857 & later used as a tavern, this characterful old building – complete with original teak floors, panelled walls, antique furniture & wide balcony overlooking the palace & lake – has served as a popular backpacker-oriented guesthouse & rendezvous since the 1970s. It's seen better days, as might be expected given the price, but the period atmosphere & central location are hard to fault. *US$10/13 sgl/dbl using shared bathrooms, US$15–22 en-suite dbl*. **$**

🏠 **Elephant Shed Tourist Hostel** [384 A3] (2 dorms) Wadugodapitiya Ln; ☎ 081 222 1220; m 0773 134558; e hello@elephantshed.lk;

w elephantshed.lk. This relaxed & sociable owner-managed hostel has a handy location 5–10mins' walk from the railway station, bus station, temple complex & a host of popular bars & restaurants. The 6-bed female-only & 8-bed mixed dorms are a little cramped but come with lockers under the bed & private reading lights. Good value. *US$8.50 pp*. **$**

🏠 **Charlton Rest** [384 C2] (17 rooms) King's St; ☎ 081 753 8352; m 0755 939300; e charltonkandyrest@gmail.com. This very central & sensibly priced owner-managed guesthouse has a pleasant courtyard restaurant (**$$**) & it arranges informative & affordable full-day city tours, as well as trips further afield. Standard 1st-floor rooms using common shower are a bit gloomy & compartmental, but come with fan, net & dbl or twin bed. Superior ground-floor rooms are brightly decorated, with TV, en-suite hot shower & optional AC. Walk-in rates are negotiable. *US$15 standard dbl, US$25/30 superior dbl with fan/AC, plus US$4–5 b/fast*. **$**

SOUTH OF LAKE KANDY
Upmarket

🏠 **Hotel Suisse** [377 F5] (90 rooms) Sangaraja Rd; ☎ 081 223 3024; e reservations. suisse@kandyhotels.lk; w hotelsuisse.lk. Set in large landscaped gardens on the opposite side of the lake to the sibling Queen's Hotel, this magnificent Edwardian edifice was built in the 1930s and served as the headquarters of Lord Mountbatten's South East Asian Command during World War II. Its name refers to Madam Burdayron, a Swiss woman who started a guesthouse on the site in 1867. The hotel retains an imposing Edwardian façade, while the marble-floored lobby & banquet hall are decorated with black-&-white photos of Old Kandy. The spacious rooms reek of the 1950s, with their parquet floors & tall ceilings, but are refurbished with AC, fan, TV, fridge & safe. There is a swimming pool in its garden overlooking the lake. *US$164/170 sgl/dbl B&B, US$204/210 with balcony*. **$$$$**

🏠 **Ozo Kandy** [377 E5] (122 rooms) Saranankara Rd; ☎ 081 203 0700; e reservations. srilanka@onyx-hospitality.com; w ozohotels. com/kandy-srilanka. This slick high-rise upstart overlooking Lake Kandy has an uncomplicated contemporary feel that stands in direct contrast to the cultivated colonial chic characteristic of most other upmarket accommodation in Kandy.

Rooms have a pale wood-laminate floor, bright décor, writing desk, TV, AC & tall windows offering a panoramic view over the city or mountain behind. A killer feature is the rooftop bar & swimming pool, which has the finest view in town. *From US$163 dbl, plus US$16 pp b/fast.* **$$$$**

🏠 **Helga's Folly** [377 G7] (20 rooms) 32 Frederick de Silva Rd; ☎081 223 4571; e helga@ helgasfolly.com; w helgasfolly.com. The inspiration behind the Stereophonics' 2003 hit single 'Madame Helga', this self-proclaimed anti-hotel comes across as a psychedelic Addams Family mansion rubbing outrageous colour schemes against a whimsical mismatch of artefacts antique, poppy & kitsch. Even the swimming pool, surrounded by jungle & guarded over by some sort of pixie-gargoyle hybrid, has an air of magic & enchantment. Individually styled rooms have 4-poster beds with fitted net, AC & fan, while amenities include a private cinema. It isn't for everyone – the eclecticism of its antique-shop clutter could quickly become exhausting & service is patchy – but it's fun for a night or 2 & makes a welcome break from package hotel conformity. *From US$160/170 sgl/dbl B&B, with significant off-season discounts & even better deals often available through the usual online agencies.* **$$$$**

Moderate

🏠 **Villa 49** [377 G6] (6 rooms) Louis Peiris Rd; ☎081 224 1142; m 0714 460911; e diludu49@ gmail.com; w villa49.weebly.com. This tightly managed sub-boutique guesthouse occupies a converted family house with a lovely common lounge decorated in traditional Sri Lankan style. Spacious individually styled rooms are colourfully decorated with winning attention to detail & come with AC & safe, the only negative being the rather cramped bathrooms. The dynamic owner-manager is usually on site & can arrange great home-cooked local food. The rooftop terrace has a great view. *From US$80 dbl B&B, dropping by 25% out of season.* **$$$**

Budget

✳ 🏠 **McLeod Inn** [377 E6] (10 rooms) Rajapihilla Rd; ☎081 222 2832; m 0716 820914, 0777 460065; e mcleod@sltnet.lk; w mcleodinnkandy.com. Owned & managed by the same hands-on family for 20-plus years, this well-kept ridge-top lodge offers stunning views

over the lake to Udawatte Kele from the lounge & simple but brightly decorated rooms with terracotta tiles, AC, fan & TV. Home-cooked local meals are available (**$$$**). *US$27/33 dbl without/ with lake view, plus US$3.30 pp b/fast.* **$$**

🏠 **Settle Inn Tourist Lodge** [377 G6] (9 rooms) Louis Peiris Rd; ☎081 222 2421; m 0714 344966; e udithaekanayeka@yahoo.com; w settleinnkandy.com. This rather stylish owner-managed guesthouse stands in well-maintained gardens with a shady courtyard at the back. Compact but attractive dbl & twin rooms have terracotta floor, paintings on the wall, AC, fan, TV, fridge & tea/coffee. *US$50 dbl B&B, dropping to US$37 out of season.* **$$$**

🏠 **Sharon Inn** [377 E6] (12 rooms) Saranankara Rd; ☎081 222 2418; m 0777 804900; e sharon@sltnet.lk. Set in a neat & quiet little garden at the summit of this long sloping road, this narrow 6-storey building offers fabulous views to the lake & is renowned for the vegetarian curry buffets (**$$$**) served at its rooftop restaurant every evening: Rooms are unremarkable but clean & attractively decorated with polished floor, wood furniture, AC, net, TV & private balcony. *US$43 dbl B&B, with off-season discounts.* **$$**

🏠 **Day's Inn** [377 F7] (6 rooms) Rajapihilla Rd; m 0718 376679, 0715 775094; e info@ daysinn-kandy.com; w daysinn-kandy.com. This above-par budget hotel has a small leafy garden, swimming pool, abundant art on the walls & comfortable, brightly coloured rooms with AC, fan, net, wooden furniture & private balcony. *US$39 dbl B&B.* **$$**

🏠 **Capital Regency** [377 H6] (15 rooms) Louis Peiris Rd; ☎081 224 1117; m 0770 474473; e info@capitalregency.com; w capitalregency. com. Formerly the Cool Inn, this comfortable & quiet lodge has bright & spacious rooms with AC, fan & wooden furniture. Deluxe rooms have private balconies. Amenities include a restaurant & a garden with a new 50m-long swimming pool. *US$37/50 standard/deluxe dbl B&B; very negotiable out of season.* **$$**

Shoestring

🏠 **Kandy City Hostel** [371 F3] (1 room, 3 dorms) Ampitiya Rd; ☎081 742 9890; m 0774 449182; e getmeabed@kandycityhostel.com; w kandycityhostel.com. Kandy's most chilled hostel, situated about 1km south of Lake Kandy, has small but clean 6-bed dorms with nets, mini-fans & lockers, as well as a dbl room with AC & balcony. Amenities include a self-catering kitchen, free tea & coffee, laundry, bike rental & a pleasant rooftop space with table tennis & big screen for regular movie nights. *US$13 pp dorm bed, US$40 dbl, all B&B.* **$–$$**

🏠 **Garden Rest** [377 F4] (6 rooms) Vihara Rd; 📞 081 388 5696; **m** 0775 569756; **e** gardenrestkandy1@gmail.com; 🄵 gardenrestkandy. Tucked way behind the popular Slightly Chilled Restaurant, within easy walking distance of the town centre, this friendly little place is particularly suited to small groups, since all the simple but clean rooms have 4 beds, net, fan & hot shower. Great value. *US$13 for up to 4.* **$**

🏠 **Hotel Mango Garden** [377 E5] (17 rooms) Saranankara Rd; 📞 081 223 5135/6; **e** mangogarden32@hotmail.com; **w** mangogarden.lk. Situated opposite the Ozo Kandy, which blocks the once-fine view from the wooden deck, this friendly owner-managed lodge is something of a backpacker's one-stop shop. Clean bright accommodation ranges from simple dbls with fan & outside bathroom to larger en-suite rooms with AC. It also has a well-priced local restaurant (**$$**), offers scooter & car rental, & arranges day & overnight tours to Dambulla, Sigiriya & Anuradhapura. *US$17 dbl using shared bathroom, US$23/47 en-suite dbl with fan/AC.* **$**

🏠 **Expeditor Hotel** [377 E6] (12 rooms) Saranankara Rd; 📞 081 223 8316; **m** 0772 606069; **e** expeditorkandy@hotmail.com; **w** expeditorkandy.com. Owned & managed by the same traveller-savvy family as Sri Lanka Trekking Expeditor, this clean & friendly hotel has a selection of rooms to suit most backpacker budgets, from dbls using common bathrooms to en-suite rooms with AC. Rates are negotiable, especially for walk-in clients out of season. Management can be a bit pushy about its tours. *From US$15/18 fan-only dbl with common/en-suite shower to US$43 dbl with AC.* **$**

🏠 **Backpack Lanka Kandy Hostel** [371 F3] (9 rooms, 2 dorms) Ampitiya Rd; **m** 0770 300900; **e** admin@backpacklanka.com; **w** backpacklanka.com. This popular backpacker-oriented set-up opposite Kandy City Hostel has a small green garden, swimming pool, 2 rooftop terraces,

self-catering kitchen & a large swimming pool. Rooms & 6-bed dorms with lockers all have AC & use of shared hot showers. *US$32 dbl, US$18 pp dorm bed, all B&B.* **$$**

SUBURBAN KANDY
Exclusive

☀ 🏠 **The Kandy House** [371 G2] (9 rooms) Amunugama Rd; 📞 081 492 1394; **e** info@ thekandyhouse.com; **w** thekandyhouse.com; see ad, 2nd colour section. Set in lush suburban gardens about 5km east of the town centre, this converted walauwa was originally built in 1804 as the home of the last chief minister to the last king of Kandy. Its low, clay-tiled roof, entrance arches & deep wrap-around verandas conceal an astonishing transformation to what is now arguably Kandy's finest boutique hotel. The main doors open on to a hall & formal dining area with a long table, & on to a courtyard where suites are spread over 2 floors. The upper rooms have the original wooden floorboards & all bedrooms have polished titanium cement bathrooms as a contrast to the traditional furnishings & fittings. There are chairs & tables throughout the verandas & the patio garden has mirrored walls that give it a delightful depth & brightness. Beyond the trees at the garden's edge is an infinity swimming pool. The table d'hôte meals are as memorable as the hotel's design. *From US$290 B&B dbl, with significant low-season discounts.* **$$$$$**

🏠 **Elephant Stables** [371 F2] (7 rooms) Nittawela Rd; 📞 011 282 1515; **m** 0778 623900; **e** reservations@elephantstables.com; **w** elephantstables.com. Set on a quiet back road near the rugby stadium, this wonderful ridge-top boutique hotel is set in a lovely palm-shaded garden with lit swimming pool offering a view over town to the hillside Bahirawa Kanda Buddha statue. The playfully stylish décor of the plentiful common rooms is dominated by dark woods & floral fabrics, & feels very Sri Lankan but also eclectically cosmopolitan. Large individually styled guest rooms have AC, fitted nets & private balconies. *From US$355 dbl B&B.* **$$$$$+**

Upmarket

☀ 🏠 **Villa Rosa** [371 E2] (8 rooms) Dodanwela Passage; 📞 081 221 5556; **m** 0773 260360; **e** info@villarosa-kandy.com; **w** villarosa-kandy.com. Set on a tall ridge 2km west of the town centre, this stunning 3-storey boutique hotel offers sensational views to the forested banks of the Mahaweli River & green hills behind it. Set behind a Tuscan façade, large & stylishly retro rooms have 4-poster beds with fitted nets, old Ceylon tourist posters on the walls, fan, & private terrace or balcony. The food is excellent, with the choice of a set 6-dish Sri Lankan curry or continental à la carte. An excellent & sensibly priced set-up – but poorly signposted & difficult to find, so get your driver to call ahead for directions. *From US$95/160 sgl/dbl B&B.* **$$$$**

Cinnamon Citadel [371 E2] (119 rooms) 124 Srimath Kuda Ratwatte Rd; 081 223 4365; e reservations@cinnamonhotels.com; w cinnamonhotels.com. Surrounded by paddy fields & perched on the bank of the Mahaweli River, this lovely hotel feels more 'jungle' than 'city', despite being a mere 2km crow's flap west of the town centre. A stylish & breezy open-plan lobby leads through the bar to a riverside swimming pool & a highly regarded restaurant. Set below Kandyan-style tiled roofs, the unusually large rooms come with terracotta tiled floor, warm fabrics, quality wooden furniture, AC, fan, TV & unexpectedly small bathroom. Insist on a room with a river view (most do). *Rack rates are US$178 dbl B&B, but discounts of up to 50% are frequently offered through online booking sites.* **$$$$**

Amaara Sky Hotel [371 E3] (14 rooms) A B Damunupola Rd; 081 223 9888; e res@ amaarasky.com; w amaarasky.com. Soaring skyward from a hilltop 1km west of central Kandy, this service-oriented boutique property offers fine views over the town & incorporates a cosmopolitan restaurant with long terrace for alfresco dining & a sky spa with experienced Ayurveda therapists. The contemporary feel is enhanced by the 80-plus paintings by local artists that adorn the public areas & stylish bedrooms, which come with AC, TV & bright furniture. *From US$145 dbl B&B.* **$$$$**

Mahaweli Reach Hotel [371 E1] (112 rooms) 35 P B A Weerakoon Rd; 081 247 2727; e sales@mahaweli.com; w mahaweli.com. Set on the south bank of the Mahaweli River 3.5km north of the town centre, this privately owned & operated 5-storey hotel was founded in the 1970s & has something of a colonial feel, though the classiness aimed for by the marble-floored lobby is undermined somewhat by the cheesy muzak. Rooms are unusually large & come with king-size

beds, wooden floor, walls adorned with etchings of old Ceylon, writing desk, AC, fan & private balcony. The attractive wooded gardens have a massive swimming pool, tennis court & launch for riverboat cruises, while other amenities include a spa, snooker table & table tennis. A likeable set-up & pretty good value. *US$130/140 sgl/dbl B&B.* **$$$$**

Earl's Regency Kandy [371 G3] (134 rooms) Mahiyanganaya Rd; 081 242 2122; e res@earlsregency.lk; w aitkenspencehotels. com/earlsregency. Situated 5km southeast of the town centre, this stylish chain hotel stands in sprawling boulder-studded tropical gardens on the east bank of the Mahaweli River across Tennekumbura Bridge. Its central edifice, designed with a high-pitched roof of deep eaves in the Kandyan style, rises several storeys, but the interior has the spacious feel of an atrium, with a gallery bar, restaurant & coffee shop on the upper floor leading from it. Rooms have private balcony, wooden furniture & all the accoutrements expected of a 5-star property. The manicured yet romantically rustic gardens incorporate a tennis court, swimming pool, cliffside gym & Ayurveda centre. *From US$275 dbl B&B, but it's worth scouring online booking agencies for (often significant) discounts.* **$$$$$**

Hotel Thilanka [377 G4] (92 rooms) Sangamitta Rd; 081 447 5200; e thilankah@ sltnet.lk; w thilankahotel.com. Expanded from a 150-year-old mansion (now the reception lobby, complete with original ceramic floor tiles) on the slopes below Udawatte Kele, this hotel has been operating since 1983 but extensive renovations undertaken in 2012 ensure it has a classy contemporary veneer. Spacious tiled rooms with AC, fan, TV & private balcony are simply decorated with local fabrics, while the corridors are hung with modern art & the kidney-shaped swimming pool offers a great view across Lake Kandy to the surrounding hills. *US$125/146 B&B sgl/dbl.* **$$$$**

Clove Villa [371 E1] (7 rooms) P B A Weerakoon Rd; 081 221 2998/9; e info@ clovevilla.com; clovevilla.com. This popular boutique hotel opposite Mahaweli Reach has spacious & artily decorated, individually styled modern rooms with all the amenities you'd expect, as well as an excellent restaurant, billiard table & small swimming pool. It bills itself as offering unpretentious luxury, & is stronger on the latter

14

than the former – the décor actually is rather ostentatious – but is still a refreshing alternative to the large-chain hotels that dominate this price category. *Overpriced in season at US$200 dbl B&B, but good value at other times when rates drop by 50%.* **$$$$**

Moderate

🏠 **The Manor House** [371 E1] (10 rooms) Kurunegala Rd; 📞081 563 8062; e bdesilva@ srimal.com; w manorhousekandy.com. This restored twin-towered 19th-century mansion somehow managed to survive while around it the monstrous cement box houses of the Kandyan suburb of Nugawela were being built. Built by a Kandyan aristocrat & restored by a Sri Lankan living in the USA, it has comfortable traditionally decorated AC rooms & grandly chintzy public areas including a lobby with a restored copper ceiling. Amenities include a spa, restaurant, billiard hall & garden swimming pool. *From US$85 B&B dbl.* **$$$**

Budget

🏠 **Fair Havens Guesthouse** [371 E1] (5 rooms) Sri Kuda Ratwatte Rd; 📞081 222 3555; m 0715 743477. This characterful old lodge comprises a converted 19th-century villa with wide wrap-around balcony set in large green gardens 4km north of the town centre & only 50m from the Mahaweli River. Large tall-ceilinged trpl rooms have fan & net but rather poky bathrooms. The helpful owner-manager also cooks excellent local meals. A well-priced gem. *US$37 trpl, plus US$7 pp b/fast.* **$$**

🏠 **Royal Peradeniya Resthouse** [370 A2] (22 rooms) Kandy Rd; 📞081 238 8299/494 0861; w royalgrouplk.com. This former government resthouse in Peradeniya, 5km southwest of central Kandy, is perfectly sited for visits to the botanical garden & also stands alongside a main trunk road to the city. It was constructed in the early 19th century as a circuit bungalow for the British road engineer Captain W F Dawson, & retains a strong period character – check the 1844 Aga cooker in the reception lobby – though hints of Art Deco indicate it has been remodelled on more than one occasion. The tiled rooms are a little old-fashioned but have AC, fridge, TV & private balcony, with deluxe rooms being considerably larger. Amenities include a well-priced restaurant, coffee shop & bar & a large swimming pool. It can be a bit noisy

when weddings are held in one of the reception halls. Nothing fancy but ideal for the budget-conscious who place a high premium on character. *US$40/42 standard/deluxe dbl.* **$$**

🏠 **Honeypot Guesthouse** [370 B2] (4 rooms) Sri Kuda Ratwatte Rd; 📞081 238 4082; e thehoneypotbear@yahoo.com; 🅵. Attached to the popular restaurant of the same name, this low-key riverside lodge 500m north of Peradeniya offers a killer view over a set of babbling rapids to the forested west bank of the Mahaweli. The rooms are small but attractively decorated & come with net, fan, balcony & tall French windows looking on to the rapids. Great value. *US$25/32 sgl/dbl B&B.* **$$**

🏠 **Nature Walk** [377 G4] (17 rooms) Sangamitta Rd; 📞081 222 4337; m 0777 717482; e info@naturewalkhr.net; w naturewalkhr. net. Set on the slopes south of the Udawatte Kele Sanctuary 1km east of the town centre, this low-key owner-managed lodge has attractive tiled dbl or twin rooms with AC, fan, net & private balcony. The wrap-around 2nd-floor balcony offers great views over the surrounding green hills & an open-sided rooftop restaurant (regularly visited by thieving monkeys) serves pasta & local dishes (**$$**), as well as pricier grills (**$$$**). *US$50 dbl, plus US$5 pp b/fast; negotiable out of season.* **$$$**

Shoestring

✳ 🏠 **St Bridget's Country Bungalow** [371 E2] (8 rooms) Sri Sumangala Rd; 📞081 221 5806/37; e stbridge@sltnet.lk; w stbridgets-kandy.com. This delightful lodge 2km northwest of the town centre stands in calm lushly forested gardens alive with birds & regularly visited by monkeys. The charming couple who own & manage it live on site & can provide reliable local travel information & arrange affordable day & overnight tours. Small but spotless rooms come with net & fan, & tasty local meals are served in a lovely dining room with tall windows looking into the forest. Excellent value for money, with the only real negative being the distance from town. *US$20/22 dbl without/with balcony.* **$**

🏠 **Hipsters Hideout** [377 G4] (18 rooms, 2 dorms) Anagarika Dharmapala Rd; m 0773 134558; e backpackersvibe.kandy@gmail.com; 🅵 thehostelkandy. This relaxed backpacker-friendly lodge incorporates a thatch-shaded terrace bar with wooden seating, hammocks, contemporary music, cold beers, cocktails, shisha pipes, light meals & welcoming dog. The staff can arrange day trips in & around Kandy. There's an 8-bed mixed dorm & 4-bed female-only dorm, as well as dbl & twin rooms most using common showers. Very good value. *From US$14/18 dbl/twin or US$6 pp dorm bed, plus US$3 pp b/fast.* **$**

🏠 **Blue Haven Guesthouse** [371 E2] (15 rooms, 1 dorm) Poorna Ln; 🖀 081 222 9617; m 0777 372066; e bluehavtravels@gmail.com; w bluehaventours.com. Tucked away in the hills 1.5km northwest of the town centre, this long-serving guesthouse has a swimming pool, restaurant & the choice of staying in an 8-bed dorm, budget rooms with fan & common shower, or en-suite deluxe rooms with AC. It's a reliable shoestring option & the affiliated Blue Haven Tours can arrange inexpensive transport here from its office on D S Senanayake St. *US$20/23 standard sgl/dbl, US$30/33 deluxe sgl/dbl, US$7 pp dorm bed.* **$**

OUT OF TOWN
Exclusive
🏠 **Taylor's Hill** [map, page 368] (5 rooms) Deltota; 🖀 081 720 1115; e info@taylorshillkandy.com; w taylorshillkandy.com; see ad, 2nd colour section. This 5-star boutique property comprises a restored 2-storey stone-walled planter's bungalow set in lovely wooded grounds complete with tennis court, croquet lawn & swimming pool. The tasteful use of bright colours & understated modern fittings creates a winning contemporary-colonial chic enhanced by tall windows that let in plenty of light to chase away the musty gloom one sometimes associates with old colonial properties. Amenities include a TV room & library, large billiard room, terrace & indoor dining, & spacious individually styled rooms with 4-poster beds, fitted nets, fans, funky wallpaper & large bathrooms. It is a great base for rambling through sloping tea estates & also offers tours of the Loolecondera Tea Factory, constructed in 1923 on Sri Lanka's oldest tea estate (page 402). All in all, it is a lovely set-up, but situated around 90mins' drive from Kandy, it is better considered as a retreat in its own right than a base for exploring the town. *From US$265 dbl HB.* **$$$$$**

Upmarket
🏠 **Amaya Hills** [371 E4] (100 rooms) Heerassagala; 🖀 081 447 4022; e reservations@ amayaresorts.com; w amayaresorts.com. Situated 10km southwest of the town centre & 3km uphill from the Botanical Gardens, this is a breezy hilltop hotel constructed to imitate a Kandyan palace, with similarly themed décor & staff uniforms & engraved wooden pillars mimicking those at the iconic Embekke Shrine. Spacious clean rooms have AC & balcony but only deluxe rooms give a view of the hills. Other features include a massive 2.5m-deep swimming pool, squash court, gym, herbal spa & residents-only underground disco. *From US$190/200 sgl/dbl B&B, but usually a lot cheaper through online booking agencies.* **$$$$$**

🏠 **Hunas Falls by Amaya** [map, page 368] (31 suites) Elkaduwa; 🖀 081 247 0041; e reservations@amayaresorts.com; w amayaresorts.com. Set at an elevation of 1,100m among the jungle & tea plantations east of the Matale Rd, this hilltop boutique hotel 30km from Kandy is popular with honeymooners but also has a scenic jogging trail running above the lip of the waterfall, as well as a heated swimming pool, health spa, snooker table, 6-hole golf course, pony riding, mountain biking, fishing & boating. Despite its austere exterior, the hotel is pervaded by a gentle tranquillity encapsulated by a library with deep-wing chairs for dozing over a book after a good lunch. The rooms all have AC, TV, minibar, balcony or terrace, & a gorgeous bathroom fit for a Hollywood star. There is also a Japanese-themed Katsura Suite & more eclectic Highlander Suite. *From US$191/201 sgl/dbl B&B.* **$$$$$**

Moderate
☀ 🏠 **Elegant Hotel** [370 C6] (5 rooms) Miwaladeniya; 🖀 081 231 5830; m 0729 039630; e elegantguest@sltnet.lk; w eleganthotel.lk. About 15km southwest of Kandy & 1.5km from Gelioya, this ridge-top boutique guesthouse is well positioned for exploring the temples around Gampola. It is set in lush wooded gardens with a swimming pool, & offers a great view to the surrounding hills, with Adam's Peak sometimes visible on clear days. The beautifully decorated interior makes tasteful use of traditional fabrics to create a modern but down-to-earth feel, & the spacious rooms all come with AC, fan & TV. A resident chef conjures up great local & international cuisine. *From US$95 dbl B&B.* **$$$$**

🏠 **Halgolla Plantation Home** [map, page 368] (3 rooms) Galagedera; m 0722 849770,

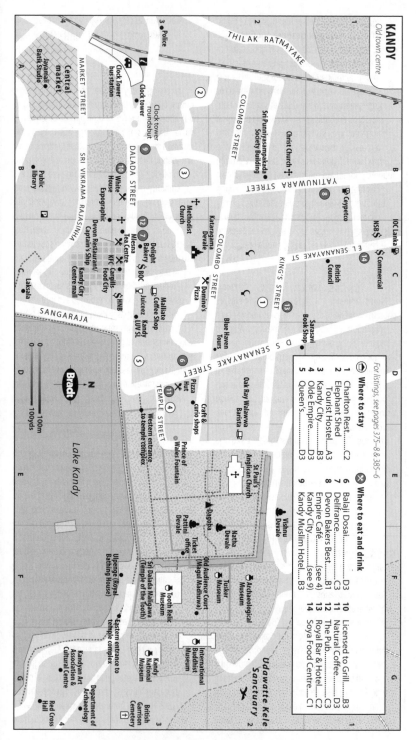

0773 470702; e emil@halgollaplantationhome.com; halgollaplantationhome.com. Owned & managed by a third-generation Sri Lankan who lives on the property, this restored 19th-century bungalow stands in a 20ha plantation about 18km out of town on the Kurunegala Rd. A portrait of the owner's ancestor hangs proudly on the wall, & the building incorporates a handmade stained-glass window that was installed in 1890 & shines light on old bookcases & rural antique furniture. Delicious & fragrant lunches & dinners as well as b/fast can be provided. It is a super base for contemplative travellers & trekkers, reflecting the heart & soul of Sri Lanka in congeniality, scenery & tranquillity. *From US$70 dbl B&B.* **$$$**

🏠 **Mas Villa** [map, page 368] (5 rooms) Kotmale; m 0777 715747; e resv@masvilla.com; w masvilla.com. This reproduction Kandyan mansion boasts an isolated & peaceful location of paddy fields & woods on the banks of the Kotmale reservoir about an hour's drive south of town. Reached by a private road, the entrance leads into a central courtyard of wooden columns & a gallery giving access to modern & well-equipped bedrooms. There is an outdoor swimming pool, spa & mini gym. *From US$120 dbl B&B.* **$$$$**

✖ WHERE TO EAT AND DRINK

In direct contrast to accommodation, most of Kandy's bespoke eateries are in the old town centre, and the majority of these (including several passable places not listed below) stand along or within a block or two of Dalada Street. Less central options are limited, though almost all the hotels listed above serve meals to overnight guests. No alcohol is served anywhere in Kandy between 14.00 and 17.00.

OLD TOWN CENTRE
Medium to expensive
✳ ✖ **Empire Café** [384 D3] Temple St; ☎ 081 223 9870; w empirecafekandy.com; ⏰ 07.30–20.30; see ad, 2nd colour section. Occupying the ground floor of the venerable Olde Empire Hotel around the corner from the temple complex, this classy tall-ceilinged café has terrace & fan-cooled indoor seating, brightly coloured walls adorned with retro posters & an imaginative cosmopolitan menu of all-day b/fasts, wraps, burgers, local-style curries & other light meals. Good juices, tea & coffee. No alcohol. More affordable than you'd expect. **$$–$$$**

✖ **The Pub** [384 C3] Dalada St; ☎ 081 223 4341; ⏰ 11.00–23.00. With its darts room, pool tables & time-warped atmosphere evoking a 1970s English pub, this 1st-floor bar & eatery is especially popular in the evenings. It has a broad gallery overlooking the street, an extensive menu of unpretentious pub grub & grills (**$$$**), draught beer & a good selection of cocktails, wine, whisky & liqueurs.

✖ **Jasmine Song** [376 C2] E L Senanayake St; ☎ 081 223 2888; w jasminesong.com; ⏰ 11.30–22.30. This clean & bright 1st-floor Chinese is short on atmosphere but the blasting AC is welcome on hot days & the long menu, with plenty of vegetarian options, is good value. No alcohol served but you can bring your own. **$$$**

✖ **Kandy City Hotel** [384 B3] Yatinuwara St; ☎ 081 222 0002; ⏰ 07.00–22.30. The ground-floor restaurant at this mid-range hotel has a separate street entrance & modern interior with a well-priced bar & limited courtyard seating. The varied menu is strong on Thai, Chinese & Sri Lankan dishes (**$$**) but also includes pricier steaks, burgers & the like (**$$$**). Good value.

🍷 **Royal Bar & Hotel** [384 C2] King's St; ☎ 081 222 4449; w royalbarandhotelkandy.com; ⏰ 11.00–22.30. Kandy's most historic bar started life in the early 19th century as a 1-storey prince's palace, & was used as an extension of the Queen's Hotel from 1844, prior to reopening as a licensed tavern frequented by British settlers & officers in 1860. Now fully renovated & decorated in retro style, complete with vintage posters & piano, it is a great spot for a few drinks, but the food (**$$$**) is nothing special & overpriced.

Cheap to medium
None of the places in this range serves alcohol or encourages diners to bring their own bottle.

✳ ✖ **Balaji Dosai** [384 D3] D S Senanayake St; ☎ 081 563 7704; f ⏰ 07.30–21.30. This popular vegetarian eatery has a bright modern interior & serves a varied selection of inexpensive Tamil &

Sinhala dishes including filled thosai 'pancakes', rice-&-curry, & thalis. Excellent value. $

✳ ✘ **Delifrance** [384 C3] Dalada St; ☎ 081 750 0896; ⊕ 07.00–21.00. This bright, classy & spotlessly European-style café specialises in tasty fresh filled baguettes but also does other toasted sandwiches & light meals in the $$ range. Early opening hours & a good selection of croissants, pastries & coffees make it an ideal b/fast spot.

✘ **Licensed to Grill** [384 B3] Dalada St; m 0778 550639; w licensed2grill.blogspot.com; ⊕ 17.00–midnight exc Mon. Set on the edge of G E de Silva Park, this vibey mobile street stall serves excellent & freshly grilled burgers, ribs, chicken & seafood, as well as wraps & salads. Good value. $$

✘ **Kandy Muslim Hotel** [384 B3] Dalada St; ☎ 081 222 9129; ⊕ 06.00–21.00. Well known for its kottu roti, this downmarket halal restaurant also does tasty roti wraps, chicken biriani & other Tamil dishes spiced to please local palates. Portions are generous, prices cheap & it is housed in an interesting old building. Good value. $

✘ **Soya Food Centre** [384 C1] YMCA Bldg, E L Senanayake St; ☎ 081 220 2016; ⓕ TheSoyaCentre; ⊕ 08.00–18.30. Best known for its delicious soya ice cream, this vegan eatery, founded in 1986, also serves up a great selection of inexpensive savoury tofu- & soya-based snacks such as Chinese rolls & filled rotis. $

✘ **Natural Coffee** [384 D3] Temple St; ☎ 081 222 5734; w naturalcoffee.lk; ⊕ 08.30–19.15. Situated just outside the temple complex, this cosy 2-storey café serves fair-trade coffee, revived from strains first planted around Kandy in the 1860s, in a cafetière, together with a sand hourglass that measures the optimum moment to hit the plunger. Also on the menu are waffles, toasted sandwiches, cakes & shakes. $$

✘ **Devon Bakers Best** [384 B1] Yatinuwara St; ☎ 081 223 5164; ⊕ 08.00–21.00. Aimed squarely at the local market, this wallet-friendly restaurant & bakery serves a varied range of sweet & savoury snacks (mini pizzas, samosas, cakes, etc), as well as lunchtime curries. $

FURTHER AFIELD

✘ **Kandy Garden Café** [377 G6] Sangaraja Rd; ☎ 081 222 0355; ⊕ 07.00–23.00. Situated 100m southeast of Lake Kandy, this place is convenient for those staying at any of the many hotels in the vicinity. An extensive local menu of curries, thosai, fried rice, biriani, kottu roti & devilled dishes ($–$$) is supplemented by a counter selling donuts, cakes & eclairs.

✘ **No Name Restaurant** [377 E6] Saranankara Rd; ☎ 081 220 0952; ⊕ 07.00–22.00. Ideally situated for the many travellers who end up staying along Saranankara Rd, this friendly local eatery serves good rice-&-curry, as well as other local dishes. $

✘ **Bommu Rooftop Bar** [377 E5] Saranankara Rd; ☎ 081 203 0700. Visit the funky, ultra-modern rooftop bar, shisha lounge, café & swimming pool atop the Ozo Kandy Hotel to admire the finest view in town over a happy-hour sundowner (*18.00–19.30*). The varied & surprisingly wallet-friendly à la carte menu cusps the $$–$$$ ranges.

✘ **Slightly Chilled/Bamboo Garden** [377 F4] Anagarika Dharmapala Rd; m 0778 037308; w slightly-chilled.com; ⊕ 11.00–23.00. This 2-in-1 rooftop Chinese restaurant & cocktail lounge has open sides offering staggering views of the lake & the sprawl of Kandy town, but it does indeed get slightly chilly in the evenings Oct–Jan. It's a great spot for a relaxed drink at sunset, when large flocks of fruit bats & birds fly past to a backdrop of chilled contemporary music. The restaurant serves a fairly broad selection of Chinese, Mexican & Western dishes, mostly in the $$$ range, as well as cocktails, beer & wine.

✘ **Green Café** [370 D2] Peradeniya Rd; m 0779 944808; ⊕ 07.00–22.00. This clean, affordable & prominently signposted local eatery, halfway along the main road between Kandy & Peradeniya, serves great lunchtime rice-&-curry along with a host of other local meat & vegetarian dishes. $

✘ **Honeypot Restaurant** [370 B2] Sri Kuda Ratwatte Rd; ☎ 081 238 4082; ⓕ; ⊕ noon–21.00. Boasting a fabulous location overlooking a set of rapids on the forest-fringed Mahaweli River 500m north of Peradeniya, this likeable restaurant offers the choice of eating in the fan-cooled interior or on a riverside terrace. It serves a varied selection of Sri Lankan, Chinese, Italian & Western-style grills, as well as beer & wine but no spirits. $$$

✘ **History Restaurant** [377 F4] Anagarika Dharmapala Rd; ☎ 081 447 0642; ⊕ 11.00–22.00.

Claiming rather fancifully to be Sri Lanka's only theme restaurant, this place does indeed host an interesting selection of black-&-white photos of old Ceylon, but there's nothing obviously historical, or typically Sri Lankan, about the not-quite-fusion menu, which includes items such as sesame-coated fried fish & Yakitori. Beer & wine are served. **$$$**

OTHER PRACTICALITIES

FESTIVALS The most important festival is the Kandy Esala Perahera, which is held over the days leading up to the Esala (July) or Nikini (August) Poya and focuses on the Temple of the Tooth. Seats are sold at strategic points for the public to watch. See page 58 for further details, or check out **w** sridaladamaligawa.lk for exact dates.

SHOPPING Kandy has plenty of places for shopping in a leisurely fashion. There are alleys with small shops selling clothes, and an occasional glimpse of old craftsmen at work, either cleaning silver or pedalling a contraption with a bicycle wheel to turn a grinding stone to sharpen knives. The central Kandy City Centre [384 C4] (*KCC, Dalada St;* \ *081 220 2844;* **w** *kandycitycentre.lk*) is a large modern shopping mall that hosts several banks, fashionable boutiques and other shops. The best-stocked supermarket is the central Cargills Food City [384 C3] (*Dalada St;* ⊕ *08.00–22.00*), which also has an attached liquor outlet selling beer, wine and spirits.

Bookshops
Expographic [384 C4] Dalada St; \ 081 220 9115; ⊕ 09.00–18.30 exc Sun. Stocks a decent selection of books about Sri Lanka.
Sarasavi Book Shop [384 D2] D S Senanayake St; ⊕ 09.00–18.00. Has an English-language section on the 5th floor.

Jewellery, crafts & curios
E W Balasuriya & Co [377 F4] Sangamitta Rd; \ 081 223 4369; **m** 0777 810717; **w** www. ewbjewel.com; ⊕ 08.30–17.30. This massive jewellery & gemstone outlet incorporates an interesting free museum detailing the history of mining & gemstones in Sri Lanka, & it's the site of the Kandy Lake Club's excellent evening cultural performances.
Gunatilake Batiks/Rajanima Crafts [377 E7] Rajapihilla Rd; \ 081 222 3815. Batik sarongs & shirts with innovative designs, as well as a good selection of wood carvings.
Jayamali Batik Studio [384 A4] 1st Fl, Central Market; \ 081 224 0568; **m** 0777 833938;

w jayamalibatiks.com; ⊕ 10.00–18.00. Founded in 1979, Jayamali is widely regarded to produce the best handmade batiks in Kandy, & it is also very reasonably priced.
Kandy LUV SL [384 C3] Queen's Hotel Bldg, Dalada St; \ 081 220 5388; **w** odel.lk/odel-kandylovesl; ⊕ 09.00–20.00. Colourful Sri Lanka-branded modern souvenirs ranging from T-shirts & caps to mugs, fridge magnets & toiletries.
Laksala [384 C4] Sangaraja Rd; \ 081 222 2087; **w** laksala.gov.lk; ⊕ 09.00–21.00. Central government-run souvenir shop selling a varied selection of well-priced handicrafts, tea, spices, gems & jewellery. A second branch stands at the entrance of the Peradeniya Botanical Garden.
Nishantha Wood Carvings [370 B2] Peradeniya Rd; \ 081 739 0390; ⊕ 08.00–18.00. Well-stocked outlet for wood carvings in Peradeniya.
Premadasas [370 B2] Peradeniya Rd; \ 081 238 4318; ⊕ 09.00–18.00 exc Sun. Reputable jewellery & gemstone outlet in Peradeniya.

BANKS All the main banks are represented by several branches and ATMs are easy to find. The most central Commercial Bank [384 C1] is at the north end of E L Senanayake Street but there is also a standalone ATM on Dalada Street near the Cargills Food City [384 C3]. Otherwise, try Kandy City Centre.

GOLF

Victoria Golf & Country Resort [map, page 368] ☏ 081 237 6376; e reservations@victoriagolf. lk; w golfsrilanka.com. This spectacular 18-hole, par-73 golf course stands on undulating & well-wooded 209ha grounds on the north bank of the Victoria Reservoir some 23km east of Kandy, branching south from the Mahiyanganaya Rd at the junction village of Digana. Its grounds look across 1km of water to Victoria Dam, which was built between 1977 & 1985 to harness the waters of the Mahaweli, the country's longest river, to power a 210MW hydro-electric plant & store up to 730 million cubic metres of water to provide irrigation for dry-zone cultivations. The reservoir is also the centrepiece of the vast but little-visited 420km^2 Victoria-Randenigala-Rantambe Sanctuary, which provides an important refuge to elephants, water-associated birds & raptors. A full round costs US$60 pp for non-members. Clubs, shoes, caddies & ball spotters can be hired. The site also incorporates birdwatching & nature trails, bike riding, horseriding, canoeing, croquet, paddle tennis & boules. Visitors are welcome to play.

TOURIST INFORMATION The official tourist information office is next to the Clock Tower bus station on Dalada Street [384 A3] (☏ 081 312 2143; ⊕ 08.30–19.00).

TOUR OPERATORS Most sites of interest in and around Kandy can be visited independently, but several operators are available to arrange sightseeing trips for those who prefer to do things that way, or to explore less readily accessible destinations such as the Knuckles Range.

Blue Haven Tours [384 D2] D S Senanayake St; ☏ 081 222 9617; m 0777 372066; e bluehavtravels@gmail.com; w bluehaventours. com. This experienced operator, under the same management since the 1980s, arranges day trips around Kandy based out of the eponymous guesthouse, as well as full countrywide tours.

Dazzling Tours [371 F1] m 0777 379752; e bookings@dazzlingtours.com; w dazzlingtours. com. Small owner-managed operator specialised in Kandy city tours but also offering day & overnight excursions to attractions throughout Hill Country & the Cultural Triangle.

Kandy Green Tours [376 A4] Peradeniya Rd; m 0712 686972, 0778 899326; e kandygreentours@gmail.com; w kandygreentours.com. This eco-friendly company with young & enthusiastic guides specialises in hiking, birdwatching & camping tours of the Knuckles Range, but also offers safaris to Wasgamuwa National Park & day trips to Gadaladeniya, Lankatilaka & Embekke temples.

Trekking Expeditor [377 E6] Saranankara Rd; ☏ 081 490 1628; m 0717 204722; e smnbandara@ yahoo.com; w trekkingexpeditor.com. Day & overnight (up to 6-day) trekking trips to the Knuckles Range & visits to remote Vedda communities are the speciality of this vastly experienced operator based in the Expeditor Hotel, but it is also a good contact for arranging hiking excursions to Horton Plains & Adam's Peak, & a day walk between Gadaladeniya, Lankatilaka & Embekke temples.

WHAT TO SEE AND DO

Many organised tours literally just overnight in Kandy *en route* between the Cultural Triangle and the High Hill Country or South Coast, in which case the done thing is to take in a late afternoon cultural (dancing and drumming) show, then to move on to the vaunted Sri Dalada Maligawa (Temple of the Tooth) for the evening puja. With more time, however, Kandy offers no shortage of other worthwhile sightseeing opportunities. For keen ramblers and outdoors enthusiasts, there's the choice of the beautifully manicured Royal Botanical Gardens at Peradeniya, or the wilder and more ecologically significant Udawatte Kele Sanctuary verging the town centre, while those who prefer an urban stroll could focus on lovely Lake Kandy and bordering sites of interest. The hills around Kandy are liberally scattered with ancient temples,

Cascading dramatically into a forest-fringed pool, Dunhinda Falls is especially beautiful after heavy rains
pages 454–6

above According to legend, the cave temple of Ridi Vihara dates to the 2nd century BC, and was built by King Dutugamunu around the silver mine that funded the construction of Anuradhapura's Ruwanweli Dagoba page 159

left Built on the site of its 6th-century BC predecessor, the modern Koneswaram Temple in Trincomalee is an important Hindu pilgrimage site pages 329–30

below Archaeological excavations around the dagobas at Kantharodai, and elsewhere, indicate Jaffna's importance as an international trading port since pre-Buddhist times pages 299–301 and 312

above   The second-tallest dagoba ever constructed in the ancient world, the imposing whitewashed dome of Ruwanweli dominates Anuradhapura's southern skyline still today pages 271–2

right   The vivid murals inside Pidurangala Temple make for a worthwhile side-trip from nearby Sigiriya page 234

below left   The spectacular Vatadage is one of many highlights of a visit to Polonnaruwa pages 248–56

below right   Breathtaking centrepiece of Sri Lanka's most impressive archaeological site, Sigiriya ('Lion Rock') is an absolute 'must-see' pages 232–4

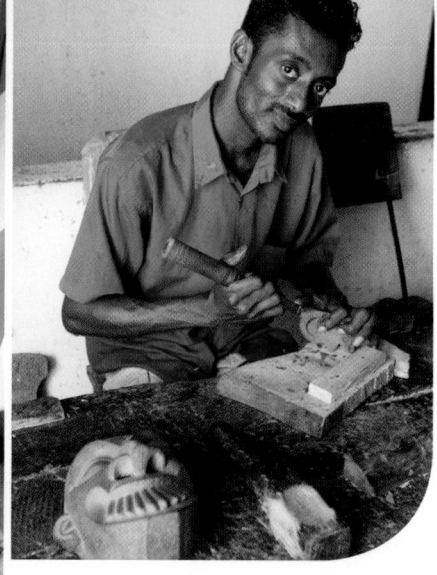

above   Ambalangoda has a long tradition of mask-making, linked to the area's strong folk culture pages 194–5

left   The final poya of the rainy season, the Ill (or Full Moon) Poya is celebrated in November with traditional music, drumming and dancing page 58

below   *Beeralu* lace-making was introduced by the Portuguese in the 16th century page 59

above   It is said that the first migrants to Batticaloa were Tamil fishermen from southern India – a heritage that continues today pages 335–44

right   Buddhism, still preserved in its purest Theravada form in Sri Lanka, is followed by the majority of the population page 10

below   The second most popular religion in Sri Lanka, Hinduism is practised mostly among the Tamils of the north and east pages 10–11

above   Lush tea plantations swathe the hills around Dambatenne, one of Sri Lanka's oldest tea factories, established in 1890 page 440

left   Hiyare Reservoir is one of hundreds of man-made lakes that dot the Sri Lankan landscape, known locally as tanks or *wewas* page 578

below   The greater and lesser St Clair's Falls, near Hatton in High Hill Country, plummet 80m and 50m respectively page 413

above Originally created as a source of drinking water, Lake Gregory has long been used for recreational purposes page 427

right Rising majestically above the surrounding hills, Adam's Peak — Sri Lanka's holiest mountain — attracts hundreds of thousands of pilgrims each year who, along with foreign visitors, climb to its summit pages 413–17

below Explore Gal Oya National Park by boat safari for up-close sightings of elephant and other wildlife pages 347–51

none more atmospheric than the architecturally divergent Gampola-era trio of Embekke, Lankatilaka and Gadaladeniya southwest of the town centre. For the museum-minded, highlights – or perhaps more accurately middlelights – include the central Archaeological, International Buddhist and (soon to reopen) National museums, as well as the out-of-town Ceylon Tea Museum. Further afield, there's some superb highland hiking on offer in the untrammelled Knuckles Conservation Forest, the renowned Aluvihara Monastery alongside the main road running north to Dambulla and Sigiriya, and the opportunity to explore Vedda culture or take a safari into the little-visited Wasgamuwa National Park near remote Mahiyanganaya.

KANDYAN CULTURAL SHOWS One of the most popular activities in Kandy is the late afternoon cultural show staged daily at several venues around the city. The shows include displays of typical Kandyan dances by men and women, in which the participants wear elaborate costumes with an extravagance of silver ornaments on ears and chests, as well as a juggling performance involving intricate twirling of lacquered wooden plates, some energetic somersaulting, daredevil displays of fire-eating and fire-walking, and a mask dance representative of low-country dancing. The authenticity, if these things bother you, is open to question, but there is no denying that the frenetically percussive music – provided by a dervish-style drum troupe whose polyrhythms are adorned with occasional horn- and flute-like melodic flourishes – is utterly compelling. All the shows cost around US$7 per person, start at 17.00 and last for about 1 hour, an arrangement that allows audience members to move on to Sri Dalada Maligawa in time for the 18.30 puja. For those on foot, the shows put on at the Kandyan Art Association and Cultural Centre [384 G4] (*Sangaraja Rd;* 081 222 3100; *KandyanArtAssociation*) and neighbouring Red Cross Hall [384 G4] (*Sangaraja Rd;* 081 222 2100) are particularly convenient as they stand opposite the Department of Archaeology only 100m from Sri Dalada Maligawa. If you have a vehicle, or don't plan to head on to Sri Dalada Maligawa, the more suburban Kandy Lake Club [377 G4] (*Sangamitta Rd;* m 0773 670763; *kandylakeclub*) tends to be less crowded and the dynamic performers are generally regarded to be the best in town.

SACRED CITY OF KANDY Inscribed as a UNESCO World Heritage Site in 1988, the Sacred City of Kandy is focused on the old town centre and Sri Dalada Maligawa (Temple of the Tooth) complex, both of which extend northward from the shore of the artificial Lake Kandy. Of more than 400 historic structures designated as World Heritage buildings by UNESCO, 162 have also been gazetted and signposted by the Department of Archaeology as Sites of National Importance. Far and away the most important of these landmarks, both in architectural and cultural terms, is Sri Dalada Maligawa, a magnificent temple surrounded by an impressive complex of lesser Buddhist shrines and secular buildings associated with the defunct Kandyan monarchy. Other protected buildings, most of them concentrated in the block or three immediately west of the Dalada Maligawa, include a Hindu temple dedicated to Kataragama, several mansions built by members of the Kandyan monarchy, and various churches, residences and other edifices dating to the British colonial era.

Security around the Dalada Maligawa has been tight since February 1998, when a destructive LTTE suicide bombing claimed 17 lives (including those of the attackers) and damaged several buildings within a radius of 5km. The temple is now enclosed by a tall fence with two entrance points, the main gate opposite the Queen's Hotel and a second one next to the National Museum, where all visitors are subjected to a body search, and may also be refused entry if their knees or shoulders are uncovered. The admission fee to Dalada Maligawa (also incorporating the Tooth Relic Museum, Tusker Museum, International Buddhist Museum and Old Audience Court) is paid 200m inside the main gate, at a kiosk immediately in front of the temple. The ticket allows for a single entry only, which effectively means you need to visit all incorporated sites at the same time unless you are willing to pay a second entrance fee. No entrance fee is charged to visit the Archaeological Museum or Natha, Vishnu and Pattini shrines, so although these lie alongside the Dalada Maligawa compound, they can be visited separately to the main temple, or at least after a coffee or meal break.

Sri Dalada Maligawa (Temple of the Tooth) [384 F3] (*Dalada St;* \ *081 223 4226;* w *sridaladamaligawa.lk;* ☉ *05.30–20.00; entrance US$13 pp (single entry); photography permitted*) Sri Lanka's holiest Buddhist shrine, the Dalada Maligawa houses the venerated top right canine of the Buddha, which was smuggled to Sri Lanka in the hair of a princess from Orissa in the 4th century AD, and secured as a symbol of nationhood in a succession of custom-built temples countrywide until it came to rest in Kandy in 1592. The original two-storey temple completed in 1595 by King Vimaladharmasuriya I now forms the core of an inner temple enclosed in a grander and more expansive three-storey structure built a century later by King Vimaladharmasuriya II and further expanded under King Kirti Sri Rajasinha, while the moat and other adornments were added by King Vikrama Rajasinha, the last Kandyan monarch. The tall golden canopy that shades the central relic chamber was donated by President Premadasa in the 1980s, and extensive restoration work had to be undertaken in the aftermath of the 1998 bombing.

The temple's plain but attractive white façade, set below layered Kandyan tiled roofs, is seen to best advantage from a distance (try the sloping Royal Palace Park or one of several viewpoints along Rajapihilla Road), with Lake Kandy in the foreground and a verdant backdrop provided by Udawatte Kele. Up close, the most prominent frontal feature is the Pittirippuva, an extruding octagonal belvedere that was originally built as an audience platform by King Vikrama Rajasinha and now houses a library in its base. The main entrance leads across the moat and up a flight of stairs into the surprisingly small drumming courtyard, which is dominated by the inner shrine. Standing two storeys high, this handsome small building, the oldest part of the temple, is supported by engraved wooden pillars and its walls are adorned with a fantastically chaotic melange of intricate paintings and engravings (those at the rear are easier to inspect closely than the ones at the front). The inner temple is opened only during the thrice-daily pujas, when drummers and trumpeters perform sinuously in an ornate entrance terrace guarded by an avenue of massive elephant tusks. Even then, entrance is forbidden except to the monks charged with performing the puja, which takes place behind all-but-closed doors, though you can go upstairs to join the throng filing past a small window that offers a brief glimpse of the outermost of the seven gem-encrusted gold caskets that enclose the tooth relic like dagoba-shaped Russian dolls. One thing you won't see is the actual tooth relic, which has been kept under almost permanent lock-and-key for security reasons since 1998, and is no longer even hauled out for the Esala Perahera.

The most rewarding time to visit Dalada Maligawa is during one of the lively daily pujas, which start at 05.30, 09.30 and 18.30, and last for an hour and a bit. Bear in mind, however, that almost all tour groups and local worshippers time their visit to coincide with a puja, so the confined interior can get very crowded during these times, claustrophobically so during high tourist seasons and on poya days. From this point of view, assuming you're up for an early start, best to aim for the 05.30

puja, when most foreign visitors will still be tucked up in their hotel bed. Failing that, the 09.30 puja offers the best photographic light, while the 18.30 puja tends to be more atmospheric and also ties in neatly with the drumming and dancing shows held at the nearby Kandyan Art Association and Cultural Centre. For those who want to absorb the temple's architecture and art when things are less crowded, you could aim to visit mid afternoon, between the two busier pujas, or pitch up at around 08.30 and poke around for an hour before the mid-morning puja. If you visit Kandy for the Esala Perahera, which takes place over ten days leading up to the Esala (July) or Nikini (August) Poya (page 58), Sri Dalada Maligawa is the focal point of these festivities, which honour the sacred tooth relic, so it will be strong on atmosphere but also very hectic!

Around the Dalada Maligawa compound Situated within the same compound as the Temple of the Tooth, the excellent Tooth Relic Museum and rather less compelling Tusker Museum and Old Audience Court are included in the single-entry admission ticket to the main temple. The International Buddhist Museum has a separate entrance outside the main compound, but admission is also included in the main ticket. The Archaeological Museum, bordering the compound, can be entered from next to the Audience Court, as well as from the main road outside the compound.

Tooth Relic Museum [384 F3] (⏰ 07.30–18.00) This worthwhile museum sprawls across the upper two floors of the Alut Maligawa, a three-storey building constructed at the back end of the drumming courtyard to commemorate the 2,500th anniversary of the Buddha's death in 1956. One set of exhibits details the long and storied journey made by the tooth relic between its removal from the Buddha's cremated ashes in 543BC and its arrival in Kandy two millennia later. Another displays some of the improbable miscellany of artefacts that have been left at the temple to honour the tooth relic, highlights of which include a magnificent gold Buddhapada gifted by the King of Siam during the reign of Kirti Sri Rajasinha, carved elephant tusks and ancient illuminated manuscripts. There is also a set of photographs detailing the damage done to the temple by the 1998 bombing, and a collection of royal artefacts that includes the golden pingo used to carry the tooth relic during the Esala Perahera back in King Kirti Sri Rajasinha's day.

Tusker Museum [384 F2] (⏰ 08.30–14.00) This single-chambered museum on the north flank of Dalada Maligawa gives new meaning to the expression 'elephant in the room'. The elephant in question, preserved in a lifelike stance in a massive glass cabinet, is Raja, a magnificent and much beloved tusker who participated in the Esala Perahera for more than 50 successive years prior to his death (aged approximately 75) in July 1988, and was charged with carrying the sacred casket bearing the tooth relic for the last 37 of these.

Magul Madhuwa [384 F3] This open-sided audience court behind the Tusker Museum was begun in 1784 by King Rajadhi Rajasinha but not completed until 1820. It is here that the Kandyan Convention, ceding the territories of the kingdom to the British, was signed on 2 March 1815. Its most striking feature is the carved wooden pillars whose characteristically Kandyan designs echo those at the superiorly crafted Embekke Temple.

International Buddhist Museum [384 G3] (*Off Anagarika Dharmapala Rd;* \ *081 223 4226;* w *ibm.sridaladamaligawa.lk;* ⏰ *08.00–19.00; entrance US$3.50* *but free with a valid ticket for Sri Dalada Maligawa; no photography*) Established in 2011, this modern installation, immediately east of the Sri Dalada Maligawa compound, occupies the imposing Victorian-era High Court building constructed by the British on the site of the former palace of King Vimaladharmasuriya II. It lacks the wealth of historic artefacts displayed in the National or Archaeological museums, but makes far better use of its limited resources, and qualifies as a must-visit for anybody with a strong interest in Buddhism or world religions. It traces the history of Buddhism in Sri Lanka and also contains rooms dedicated to each of 16 other countries with strong Buddhist traditions, from India and Afghanistan, where it is now practised by a tiny minority, to modern strongholds such as Cambodia, Thailand and Japan.

Archaeological Museum [384 F2] (⏲ *08.00–16.30 exc Tue; entrance by donation; photography forbidden*) This underwhelming museum is housed in the remains of the long, narrow single-storey palace built by King Vimaladharmasuriya I alongside the original Tooth Temple he constructed in 1595. It contains a rather arbitrary and disjointed – not to say poorly labelled – collection of ancient artefacts excavated at various sites in and around Kandy. Highlights include some well-preserved Kandyan wooden pillars and a few superb 18th-century engravings of stick dancers.

Hatara Devale and Temple Square
Revered by Buddhist and Hindu residents alike, the Hatara Devale (four shrines) are each dedicated to one of Kandy's four guardian deities, namely Natha, Pattini, Vishnu and Kataragama. Three of the shrines stand clustered close together in Temple Square, the large leafy block immediately west of Sri Dalada Maligawa. The fourth, dedicated to Kataragama Shrine, stands two blocks further west, at the southern end of Kotugodella Street. Entrance to all four shrines is free.

Natha Devale [384 F2] Directly facing Sri Dalada Maligawa, Natha Devale was reputedly constructed by King Vikramabahu III of Gampola in the 14th century, making it the oldest-known extant structure in Kandy. Unlike the other three guardian deities, Natha is more or less a purely Buddhist figure, yet paradoxically his shrine shows the most overt Hindu architectural influence of any in Kandy, with a vaulted roof topped by a brick dome, and a general appearance that recalls the Nalanda Gedige and Hindu temples of Polonnaruwa. The Natha Devale is where the Kings of Kandy were invested with their royal names back in the day, when it was also used as a preparation site for herbal medicines.

Pattini Devale [384 E3] Kandy's most popular shrine is dedicated to a female deity associated with both chastity and fertility. Little is known about the shrine's age, except that it is named in the writings of Robert Knox, an English sailor held captive in Kandy over 1660–79. The temple has a large open-sided drumming courtyard supported by varnished and engraved wooden pillars of obvious antiquity. Some well-preserved old paintings flank the entrance to the tiny indoor shrine, which is said to hold Pattini's golden anklet.

Vishnu Devale [384 E2] Dedicated to Vishnu but also commonly referred to as the Maha (Grand) Devale, this relatively large shrine at the north end of Temple Square comprises three buildings, the longest of which has a two-storey sanctum topped by a Kandyan roof that probably replaced an original dome. As with the

Pattini Devale, it was probably established at least 400 years ago and may be considerably older. It used to be the coronation site of the Kings of Kandy, and its main hall still houses the palanquin used in the Esala Perahera.

St Paul's Church [384 E2] (w *stpaulschurchkandy.lk*) Something of an odd-shrine-out, situated on the northwest side of Temple Square, this massive Anglican edifice, originally known as the Garrison Church but later dedicated to St Paul, was built over 1843–48 and enlarged in 1878 and again in 1928. Cruciform in design, it has a neo-Gothic brickface façade topped by a square clock tower, whose tall castellated roof rather cheekily has the altitudinal advantage over nearby Sri Dalada Maligawa. The interior is typically Victorian, with its wooden ceiling, sombre stained-glass windows and walls inset with memorial plaques dating back to the 19th century.

Prince of Wales Fountain [384 E3] Another colonial incongruity situated in the shadow of Sri Dalada Maligawa, this extravagant Glasgow-made cast-iron memorial was erected by the 'Coffee Planters of Ceylon' to commemorate the Prince of Wales's visit to Kandy in 1875. Misplaced though it feels alongside the Pattini Devale, the fountain is a wonderful example of the Victorian foundry-man's art, adorned liberally with cherubs, while crocodiles spurt water from their mouths, at least on the rare occasions when it's working.

Kataragama Devale [384 C3] Tucked away discreetly two blocks west of Temple Square, this shrine dedicated to Kataragama, the guardian deity of Sri Lanka, is also set apart from the other Hatara Devale in that is officiated over by Hindu Brahmi priests. The painted arched entrance, topped by an unusual two-tiered Kandyan tiled roof, leads to a painted inner sanctum, an image house where the priests perform their rites, and the drummers' quarters. Its age is unknown but, as with the Vishnu and Pattini shrines, it is most likely at least 400 years old.

Kandy National Museum [384 G3] (*Anagarika Dharmapala Rd;* \ *081 222 3867;* w *museum.gov.lk;* ⊕ *09.00–17.00 exc Sun & Mon; entrance US$4*) Closed for renovation since the end of 2014, Kandy's National Museum, which stands immediately east of the Dalada Maligawa compound, finally reopened to the public in April 2017. It is housed in the Palle Vahala (Lower Palace) built in the late 18th century as a royal harem (or, if you prefer, Queens' Palace) for the consorts of King Sri Vikrama Rajasinha. A museum since 1942, it contains more than 5,000 artefacts relating to the Kandyan period, including the original Kandyan Convention signed by the British and the Chiefs of the Kandy on 10 March 1815.

British Garrison Cemetery [384 G3] (*Anagarika Dharmapala Rd;* ⊕ *08.00–13.00 & 14.00–18.00 exc Sun; donations requested*) Situated behind the Department of Archaeology 150m east of Sri Dalada Maligawa, this cemetery was established in 1817 after the British capture of Kandy and it officially closed in 1873, though occasional burials took place until as recently as 1951. It is crowded with 163 graves of British pioneers and settlers, most of whom succumbed young to malaria and other tropical diseases, though others were killed by sunstroke, wild animals, and in one case a collapsed house. Most notable among those who rest in peace here is Sir John D'Oyly (page 598). The affable and articulate caretaker is a fount of interesting anecdotes and makes an excellent guide. Monkeys from neighbouring Udawatte Kele often make an appearance and can be aggressive towards visitors carrying food.

14

Asgiri Monastery [376 B1] Founded during the 14th-century reign of King Parakramabahu IV of Kurunegala, this historic and influential Buddhist monastery once extended all the way from the hills west of the town centre to the more easterly site of present-day Trinity College. The core monastery now stands about 5 minutes' walk west of the town centre and incorporates several small temples with painted interiors. During the Kandyan era, Asgiri served as a royal crematorium and burial ground, a tradition that started in the late 14th century when Queen Chandravati, the mother of King Sena Sammatha Vikramabahu, was cremated and buried here. The old royal burial ground and its funerary dagobas were cleared to make way for the construction of the railway line to Matale in 1880. However, the monastery's most intriguing structure, tucked away in a leafy compound 100m north of Hill Street, is the beautiful Adhanamaluwa Gedige, which reputedly stands on the exact spot where Queen Chandravati was cremated and was built as a memorial by her son c1500. This robust and intricately carved stone temple, set below a striking two-tiered Kandyan tiled roof, is almost certainly Kandy's second-oldest building and, as with the older Natha Devale, its architecture displays a strong Hindu influence.

Lake Kandy [map, pages 376–7] It might come as a surprise to learn that the tranquil ornamental lake so integral to the modern-day Kandyan landscape was in fact completed in controversial and bloody circumstances a mere three years before the city's Sinhalese monarchy was evicted by the British. Also known as Lake Bogambara or Kiri Muhuda (Sea of Milk), it was constructed over 1810–12 at the command of King Sri Vikrama Rajasinha, who used slave labour to dam the marshes and paddy fields that skirted his capital, and was delighted when they filled up not only with water but with fish, which he fed with boiled rice from a small island (reputedly connected to the palace by a subterranean tunnel so secret its existence has yet to be corroborated). The reservoir's construction was undertaken against the counsel of several royal advisers, many of whom were impaled on its wall in punishment, and the enterprise was widely perceived to be emblematic of endemic royal self-indulgence at a time when the Kandyan kingdom was under threat from the British, who eventually captured it in 1815 with the backing of certain disgruntled noblemen. Today, the tadpole-shaped lake extends over 19ha and can be circumnavigated on foot along a shady 3.5km footpath. You'll pass several impressive Indian flying-fox roosts, and should also look out for waterbirds such as spot-billed pelican, Indian pond heron, black-crowned night heron, white-breasted waterhen and various cormorants and egrets. The walk could be extended with diversions to the Royal Palace Park, Malwatta Monastery and historic Hotel Suisse, all on the south side of the lake. Unfortunately, the handsome colonnaded Ulpenge (royal bathing house) built for the wives of King Sri Vikrama Rajasinha, on a platform immediately south of the Dalada Maligawa, is now a police checkpoint and closed to the public.

Royal Palace Park [376 C5] (⏰ *09.00–18.00; entrance Rs100*) Busier with courting teenagers than with tourists, this 2ha park slopes upward from the southwest lakeshore to offer splendid views across the water to the old town centre and Dalada Maligawa. Its official name refers to it having been the site of a palace built for King Vimaladharmasuriya I, who famously repelled two attempted Portuguese invasions of Kandy during a 12-year reign that started in 1592. Later a lakeside terrace built by King Sri Vikrama Rajasinha, it was remodelled as a park in 1880 under the acting Colonial Secretary Herbert Wace, and is still sometimes referred to as Wace Park (or, rather confusingly, as Wales Park, reputedly also its official name for a period, in honour of the Prince of Wales). Today, pride of place goes to a Japanese artillery gun captured in Burma during World War II and now housed under a small Kandyan-style pagoda.

Malwatta Monastery [376 E5] Older than Lake Kandy, whose southern shore it overlooks, this attractive monastery was established in 1753 by Sri Sarankara Sangaraja and it contains two separate temples embellished with 18th-century architectural features, as well as a venerable Chapter House and tall octagonal library. A small museum exhibits several artefacts owned by the temple's founder or dating back to that time.

SUBURBAN KANDY
Bahirawa Kanda Buddha [376 A3] (*Bahirawa Kanda Rd;* m *0718 381367;* ⊕ *06.00–18.00; entrance US$1.35*) This 25m-high white Buddha has dominated the western skyline of Kandy since the early 1990s, when it was constructed at the command of President Premadasa, partly to assuage the demon for which Bahirawa Kanda (Bahirawa's Hill) is named. The association between the hill and the demonic deity Bahirawa goes back to the 14th-century reign of King Parakramabahu IV, who constructed the Asgiri Monastery below it. Legend has it that Bahirawa possesses an insatiable hunger for human flesh, and in times past the people of Kandy avoided the mountain, though it was traditional for the King of Kandy to order the annual sacrifice of a virgin of noble birth, who was tied to a stake in a clearing, and left overnight to be devoured by the demon. According to one legend, the last such attempted sacrifice, ordered by Sri Vikrama Rajasinha in the dark dying years of his reign, failed when the selected virgin was rescued by her suitor.

The Bahirawa Kanda Buddha stands 1.5km from the town centre, a steep but straightforward walk, a journey that the less energetic might prefer to undertake by tuktuk. The magnificent view over Lake Kandy and Dalada Maligawa will be of greater interest to most than the actual statue, and while the entrance fee is nominal, the caretakers have a reputation for pressuring foreigners into making further, more substantial, donations.

Udawatte Kele Sanctuary [377 F2] (*Sri Dalada Thapowana Rd;* ℡ *081 223 2873;* ⊕ *06.00–18.00; entrance US$4.30*) Extending across a tall forested ridge to the north of Lake Kandy, this tranquil 1km² enclave of suburban tropical jungle supports a wealth of birds, monkeys and other wildlife on the edge of the town centre. The forest was actively conserved by the Kandyan monarchy, who reserved it for their exclusive use as a recreational park and bathing place, as well as a source of firewood for the royal palace and fodder for the temple elephants at Sri Dalada Maligawa. Back then, it was formally known as Uda Wasala Watte, meaning 'Garden above the Palace', but commoners more often referred to it as Thahasi Kele, the 'Forbidden Forest'. Following the British occupation of Kandy in 1815, parts of the original forest were cut down to make way for administrative buildings, coffee plantations and the garrison cemetery, but what remained was declared a reserved forest in 1865, and accorded sanctuary status in 1938.

Udawatte Kele provides refuge to varied indigenous flora and fauna, despite the introduction of invasive trees such as the South American *Myroxylon balsamum* and *Swietenia macrophylla* and the devil's ivy creeper *Epipremnum aureum*. A checklist of more than 450 indigenous plant species includes leafy tree ferns, creeping rattan palms and at least a dozen species of flowering orchids. The sanctuary's most impressive single plant is a giant 250-year-old *Entada puseatha*

14

liana that extends over more than a hectare and has 1.5m long pods. The most conspicuous mammals are common palm squirrel and toque macaque, the latter sometimes moving in troops of 50-plus individuals. Other less commonly observed mammals include red muntjac, yellow-striped chevrotain, porcupine, wild boar and various mostly nocturnal small predators, including the rare fishing cat, which is very occasionally seen at the Royal Pond near the main entrance (also home to monitor lizards and terrapins). Butterflies are conspicuous, with 32 species recorded.

Udawatte Kele is an important birdwatching site, with more than 80 species recorded, including 11 endemics, namely Sri Lanka junglefowl, Sri Lanka green pigeon, Sri Lanka wood pigeon, Sri Lanka hanging parrot, Layard's parakeet, Sri Lanka grey hornbill, yellow-fronted barbet, crimson-fronted barbet, crimson-backed goldenback, brown-capped babbler, and Sri Lanka scimitar babbler. Other localised species associated with the sanctuary are brown fish owl and oriental dwarf kingfisher, both of which might be seen at the Royal Pond, and the striking white-rumped shama and secretive velvet-fronted nuthatch. The best times for birdwatching are 06.00–08.30 and 16.30–17.30.

Several cultural sites lie within the sanctuary. The fern-draped Royal Pond [377 E1], accessed from the Lovers' Walk footpath running to the right of the entrance gate, was once a royal bathing place, and its murky green waters supposedly hide a golden pot guarded by a serpent with glowing red eyes. Senkanda's Cave, at the far south end of Lovers' Walk, was the home of the Brahman hermit later immortalised in the name Senkandagala, as Kandy was known back in the time of King Vikramabahu III. Kodimale, the highest point within the sanctuary, is where the royal flag was flown during the Kandyan era.

The entrance to Udawatte Kele lies 500m east of D S Senanayake Street, turning on to Sri Dalada Thapowana Road immediately north of the post office. The sanctuary is easily explored on an extensive network of walking trails named after colonial administrators and/or their spouses, the oldest being Lady Horton's Drive, which was cut by Governor Horton in 1838 in remembrance of his wife. Allow 3 hours to cover the full trail network, which is reasonably well marked so no local guide is required, though it is worth picking up a map at the gate. Knowledgeable bird guides are also sometimes available at the gate. Very occasional robberies have been reported, so best avoid carrying unnecessary valuables. More likely nuisances are the monkeys, which can become quite aggressive towards people carrying food, and the leeches that proliferate in moist areas after rain.

Peradeniya and surrounds Flanking the Colombo Road 6km southeast of Kandy, the suburb of Peradeniya is the site of the country's second-oldest university, founded in 1942, and the renowned Royal Botanical Gardens, which are probably the city's most popular attraction after the Dalada Maligawa. Its only other attractions are the Commonwealth War Cemetery, which is often visited in conjunction with the botanical garden, and the more obscure Hindagala Cave Temple.

Royal Botanical Gardens [map, opposite] (*Peradeniya Rd;* ✆ *081 238 8088;* ⏲ *07.30–17.00; entrance US$10, golf cart hire US$7/hr*) No visit to Kandy is complete without a stop at Sri Lanka's largest and most historic botanical garden, which is bordered to the south by the main Colombo Road as it runs through Peradeniya, and on the other three sides by a horseshoe bend in the Mahaweli River. This is reputedly the same site that King Vikramabahu III chose as his temporary capital in 1371, and it also served as a royal residence and park under King Kirti Sri

Rajasinha. It formally became a botanical garden in 1821 and it is where Ceylon's first tea seedlings were planted in 1824, at the behest of Governor Barnes.

The gardens consist of nearly 60ha dedicated primarily to the flora of Sri Lanka, with a total of 4,000 indigenous and exotic plant species represented, including almost 600 endemics, some of which are extinct in the wild. Highlights include a beautifully landscaped fernery, a lake lined with papyrus and covered in water lilies, three palm avenues (look out for the remarkable Seychellois double coconut palm flanking Monument Road 100m from the entrance), an otherworldly bamboo garden with specimens towering up to 40m high, and a vast arboretum studded

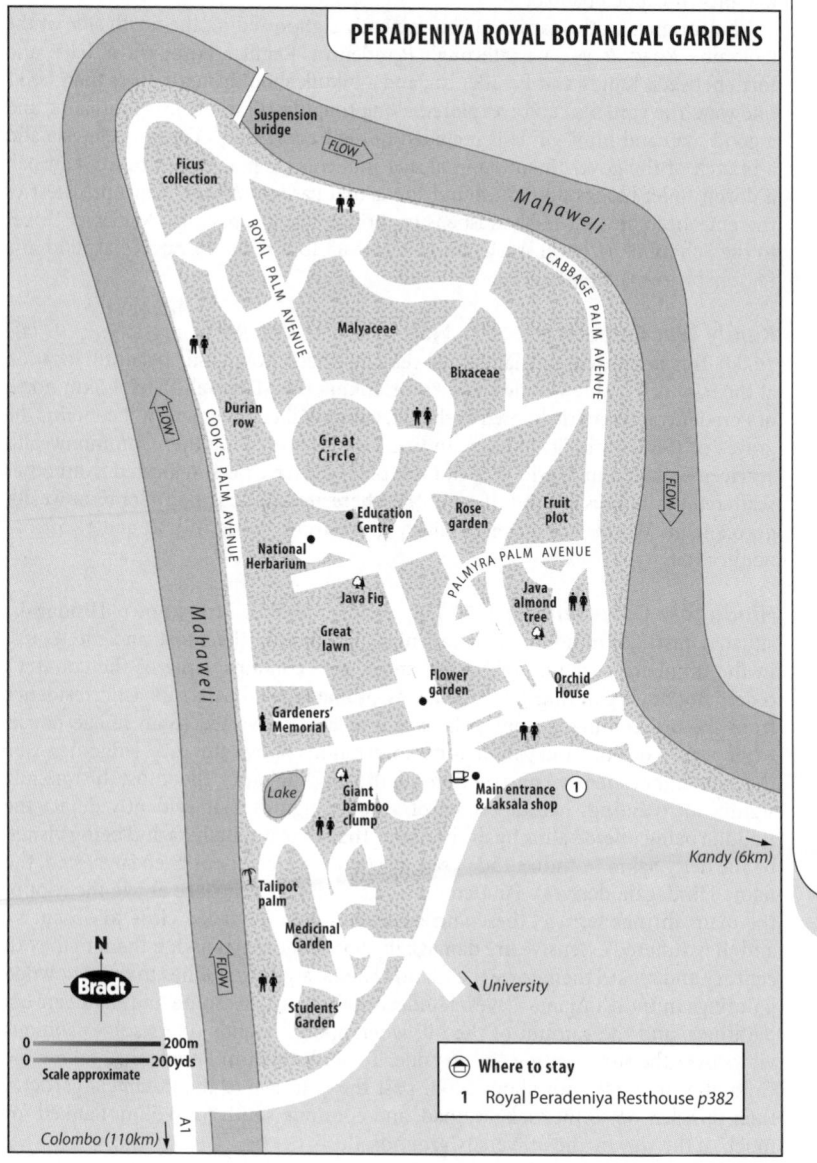

PERADENIYA ROYAL BOTANICAL GARDENS

Suspension bridge
FLOW
Ficus collection
Mahaweli
ROYAL PALM AVENUE
CABBAGE PALM AVENUE
Malyaceae
Bixaceae
Durian row
COOK'S PALM AVENUE
Great Circle
Education Centre
Rose garden
Fruit plot
FLOW
National Herbarium
PALMYRA PALM AVENUE
Java Fig
Java almond tree
Great lawn
Flower garden
Orchid House
Mahaweli
Gardeners' Memorial
Lake
Giant bamboo clump
Main entrance & Laksala shop ①
Kandy (6km)
Talipot palm
N
Bradt
Medicinal Garden
FLOW
0 ——— 200m
0 ——— 200yds
Scale approximate
Students' Garden
University
A1
Colombo (110km) ↓

⊖ **Where to stay**
1 Royal Peradeniya Resthouse *p382*

with century-old mahoganies, satinwoods and other slow-growing hardwood trees. Indoor features include a delightful orchid house, whose collection of 300 species includes a specimen of the gigantic epiphytic tiger orchid *Grammatophyllum speciosum*, and a herbarium containing more than 200,000 dried and preserved specimens collected during the two centuries the gardens have been in existence. In the medicinal herb garden grow some of the herbs used in Ayurveda medicine. An impressive arboreal colony of tens of thousands of Indian flying foxes stands in the north of the gardens, and the varied birdlife includes forest-fringe species such as the endemic Layard's parakeet, Sri Lanka hanging parrot, yellow-fronted barbet and brown-capped babbler.

The entrance to the gardens is prominently signposted on the north side of the Colombo Road as you pass through Peradeniya. Regular buses travel back and forth between Kandy and Peradeniya, and a tuktuk shouldn't cost more than US$2 one way. The gardens can be explored along roughly 10km of clear footpaths, and a good map and mini-guide is included in the ticket price. There's a cafeteria and a branch of the government-run Laksala souvenir shop at the entrance, and half a dozen toilet blocks dotted around the actual garden. About 1km northwest of the entrance gate, a wobbly suspension bridge leads across the Mahaweli River to the School of Tropical Agriculture. Allow up to 4 hours to ramble around at a reasonably relaxed pace.

Kandy War Cemetery [370 C1] (*Sri Kuda Ratwatte Rd;* w *cwgc.org;* ⊕ *09.00–16.00*) This immaculately maintained cemetery has a poignantly beautiful location at the base of a lushly wooded slope overlooking the Mahaweli River 1.5km north of Peradeniya. Formerly known as the Pitakande Military Cemetery, it contains the graves of 196 British, Sri Lankan, Indian, East African and other Commonwealth servicemen killed in World War II, most of which have been relocated from other scattered burial sites around the country. There are also four non-Commonwealth graves from World War II, one solitary grave from World War I, and two from neither war.

Hindagala Cave Temple [370 D5] Picturesque but little-known Hindagala, situated just 3.5km south of Peradeniya, is possibly the most ancient temple in the immediate vicinity of Kandy, and it also contains some of the country's oldest Buddhist paintings. The cave was probably used as a monastic residence from the 3rd century BC onwards, and was later converted to an image house, while a pair of 6th- and 7th-century inscriptions above the drip ledge describe the contemporaneous construction of the Bodhighara. The most historically significant paintings here are a set of a dozen figures that evidently depict the Buddha being offered alms by the brothers Thapassu and Balluka and being visited by the deity Sakra in India's Indalasa Cave (from which, it has been suggested, the name Hindagala derives). Painted on to a sloping rock surface above the roof of the main shrine's terrace, these ancient figures are now faded close to obscurity, and they suffered extensive fire damage in 1965, but experts assign them to the 6th century and regard them to be the island's closest stylistic siblings to the renowned paintings in India's Ajanta Caves. Hindagala also contains some fine Kandyan-era paintings, and the summit of the hill whereupon it stands offers some fabulous views over the surrounding countryside. To get here from Peradeniya, follow the Colombo Road west for about 200m past the entrance to the botanical gardens, then turn left on to the Galaha Road, and continue south for 3.5km, flanked for much of the way by the university grounds.

Eastern temples Situated between 2km and 5km east of the city centre is a trio of interesting temples built over 1752–71 by the devout King Kirti Sri Rajasinha and his younger brother, the future King Sri Rajadhi Rajasinha. Although these relatively modern edifices don't match up to their Gampola counterparts in terms of antiquity or architectural variety, all three retain some engaging Kandyan paintings or architectural features, and have a more off-the-beaten-track feel. None of these temples charges an entrance fee; indeed, outside of puja hours, you'll be lucky to find anyone around to open the temple doors.

Gangarama [377 H2] The attractive Gangarama (River Temple) built by King Kirti Sri Rajasinha in 1752 stands on a high slope adjacent to Lewella Road less than 2km east of the town centre and only 500m from (but out of sight of) the Mahaweli. It is dominated by a handsome two-storey image house built in the traditional Kandyan style but as an extension of a natural rock shelter, into which has been carved an exceptional 8.5m-tall standing Buddha. The inside walls are covered in hundreds of paintings executed at the time of its construction, as is the creaky old wooden door and frame.

Degaldoruwa [371 G2] This three-chambered cave temple, renowned for its exceptionally fine 18th-century Kandyan paintings, was reputedly excavated by the future King Sri Rajadhi Rajasinha from 1771 onwards, to be completed shortly after he ascended the throne in 1782. Cloistered behind the original heavy wooden door and monstrous metal key, the interior is adorned with a wealth of original 1770s paintings, most of them unusually well preserved though some have suffered from severe water damage. The interior is quite gloomy, so a torch will be useful. In the inner sanctum, look out for a famous ceiling painting depicting the Buddha resisting the seductions of the evil demon Mara, and a striking portrait of the earth goddess Mahi Kantawa. The outer sanctum wall is dominated by a cartoon-like series of murals that relates the Vessantara Jataka in finely detailed lines set against a bold red background. Degaldoruwa lies about 4km from central Kandy, and 2.5km east of Gangarama, along the Yakgahapitiya Road. Buses from Kandy to Yakgahapitiya or Amunugama can drop you a few metres from the entrance.

Galmaduwa [371 G3] J P Lewis, an amateur historian active in the early 20th century, described Galmaduwa (literally 'Stone Pavilion') as 'the most Hindu-looking Buddhist temple in existence'. It is certainly the most remote and unusual of the eastern temples. The lower terrace is a large, square and rather austere two-storey construction, with the forbidding look of a prison or similar institution, and a wide elevated wrap-around veranda hemmed in by stone arches. This encloses a much smaller inner shrine whose tapering multi-tiered roof protrudes several storeys high in a manner reminiscent of a Hindu temple's gopuram. Local tradition attributes the construction of this quirky building to King Kirti Sri Rajasinha, who evidently abandoned it in favour of Degaldoruwa shortly before its completion. Galmaduwa remained unused until a small peripheral image house was added in the 1960s. To get here, follow the Mahiyanganaya Road out of town across the Tennekumbura Bridge, passing the Earl's Regency to your left, and continue for about 1km to Kalapura. Here, a left turn immediately after Cargills Food City leads to the temple after about 700m. Regular buses connect Kandy to Kalapura, but you need to walk from there.

Ceylon Tea Museum [371 E4] (*Hantana Rd;* ☎*081 380 3204;* **w** *ceylonteamuseum. com;* ⏱ *08.30–16.30 Tue–Sat, 08.30–15.30 Sun; entrance US$3.40; guided tours on* *demand*) This converted four-storey tea factory stands about 4km uphill of the town centre along the winding Hantana Road. The ground floor is dedicated to the 19th-century machinery used to operate a pulley-powered factory, while the first floor displays a selection of items associated with James Taylor (page 603) and a library of old books about tea, the second floor is dominated by shops selling tea, and the top floor has a unique high-flying catwalk from which supervisors could view the factory operations. A tuktuk out should cost around US$1.50 one way.

FURTHER AFIELD

Gampola temples Now a modest highland junction town with a population of 30,000, Gampola served as Sinhala capital for a 70-year period starting in the mid 1340s, when King Bhuvanaikabahu IV relocated here from Kurunegala. The town retains few traces of its prestigious past, but the surrounding countryside is scattered with ancient temples associated with Bhuvanaikabahu IV, his co-ruler and eventual successor Parakramabahu V, and the latter's successor, Vikramabahu III. These include a trio of incredible shrines called Embekke, Lankatilaka and Gadaladeniya, which stand around 10km southeast of Kandy and are all very different from each other. Two lesser but still noteworthy temples from the same period are Niyamgampaya and Vallahagoda, both of which stand in Gampola itself. Despite being almost 700 years old, these temples all remain active shrines, and this human dimension makes them in some respects more rewarding and engaging than the far older abandoned temples of the Cultural Triangle.

Embekke, Lankatilaka and Gadaladeniya stand within 5km of each other on the so-called Three Temples Loop, a back road that connects Gelioya (on the Kandy–Gampola Road) to Pilimathawala (on the Kandy–Colombo Road). Coming from Kandy, the loop can be explored over the course of a morning or afternoon by tuktuk (expect to pay around US$10–15 to visit any one temple and US$20 for all three, including waiting time) or on an organised day tour with any operator. Another option would be to catch one of the twice-hourly buses that run from Kandy to Embekke village, from where you could walk or tuktuk-hop the 7km north to Pilimathawala via the Three Temples, then pick up a bus heading east along the Colombo road back to Kandy. To visit Niyamgampaya and Vallahagoda, just catch a bus or train from Kandy to Gampola, and walk or tuktuk-hop from there.

Embekke [370 B6] (⏀ *06.00–18.00; entrance US$2*) One of the most beautiful temples in all Sri Lanka, Embekke is a combined Buddhist and Hindu shrine dedicated to the guardian deity Kataragama, and renowned for its forest of pillars adorned with what is undoubtedly the island's finest collection of old woodcarvings. Reputedly founded in 1371 by Vikramabahu III, Embekke originally stood three storeys high, but it now comprises just one storey dominated by an open-sided drumming pavilion with 32 ironwood pillars topped by fine floral brackets. The woodcarvings that adorn the pillars' four sides depict everything from wrestlers, horsemen, dancing ladies and musicians to a lion devouring an elephant, and a menagerie of mythical creatures such as a dragon, *kinnara* (bird woman), *herunda* (two-headed bird) and *gajasinha* (elephant-lion). Locals claim that the drumming pavilion started life as a royal audience hall, and that the pillars date to the Gampola period, but it is more likely they date to the Kandyan era, a timeline supported by the presence of a carving of what appears to be a Portuguese soldier. The temple is also notable for the original Kandyan paintings in the inner sanctum, an ingeniously engineered roof that holds together 26 angled wooden struts under one heavy kingpin, and the incorporation of the 14th-century Gampola Palace's original jackwood door, complete with heavy brass bolts and lock. Outbuildings include an ancient *vee bissa* (paddy barn) built on stilts to deter rats, termites and other vermin, and a covered entrance gate supported by another ten engraved wooden pillars including one that depicts a breastfeeding mother. Only 200m from the temple, the abandoned Embekke Ambalama, built up to three decades earlier by Bhuvanaikabahu IV, is survived by 16 engraved stone pillars with a similar design to their wooden counterparts in the drumming hall.

Lankatilaka [370 B6] (⏱ *06.00–18.00; entrance US$2*) The most imposing surviving relic of the Gampola period, the Lankatilaka stands atop the granite pinnacle of a forested hill called Panhalgala and is reached via a case of rock-hewn steps offering splendid views over the surrounding jungle and paddy fields. A three-storey brick monolith topped with a flourish of red-tiled hipped roofs, it is somewhat reminiscent of its ruinous namesake in Polonnaruwa, but the ornate Rococo-like architecture also incorporates Dravidian and Chinese influences. The building was almost certainly commissioned in the 1340s by Bhuvanaikabahu IV, but the presence of a few very weathered Anuradhapura-style rock carvings might indicate that an older temple once existed at the same site. The interior is dominated by a massive seated Buddha statue, flanked by two standing Buddhas and stucco sculptures of various Hindu gods, but its outstanding aesthetic feature is a rare treasury of pre-Kandyan paintings from the Gampola period, including a fine Hansa Puttuwa (swans conjoined as a symbol of unity and prosperity) in a circle above the main roof arch. Priceless 14th-century artefacts protected at Lankatilaka include the ivory casket that held the sacred tooth relic during its tenure at nearby Niyamgampaya, a metal statue of Bhuvanaikabahu IV, a miniature Buddha made of blue sapphire, and a copperplate book detailing the temple's history.

Gadaladeniya [370 B5] (⏱ *06.00–18.00; entrance US$2*) Perched on a low flat-topped rocky hill only 1km south of the main Colombo Road, Gadaladeniya is – for those with limited time – perhaps the most missable of the Three Temples, but it is still emphatically worth a visit. Reputedly built in 1344 by Bhuvanaikabahu IV, the massive main image house, currently being renovated and under scaffolding, is the largest granite temple anywhere in Sri Lanka, with a design strongly influenced by the Pallava architectural school from South India. It is entered via a stone stairwell flanked by a pair of large gajasinha sculptures with broken trunks, and set below an ornate dragon's arch incorporating engravings of Shiva and Krishna. The solid jackwood door, complete with a 2kg brass-and-iron key, is adorned by well-preserved red-and-gold stylised Gampola-period paintings of a *narilatha* (half woman, half flower) and peacock-like kinnara. The sombre interior is dominated by an unusually stern-looking gold-plated seated Buddha statue, as well as a wooden Kandyan cupboard and gold-plated dagoba-shaped casket similar to the one that holds the sacred tooth relic at the Dalada Maligawa. A separate building, set below a roof added in the Kandyan period, contains a 12m-high dagoba accredited to King Parakramabahu V, and is divided into four equal chambers, each containing its own Buddha figure and adorned with some superb art whose extremely faded condition lends some credence to the claim it harks from the Gampola period.

Niyamgampaya The most significant antiquity within the town limits of Gampola, situated alongside the main road 1.5km south of the railway station, Niyamgampaya, though far less impressive than Embekke, Lankatilaka or Gadaladeniya, is an intriguing and readily accessible small temple that still remains refreshingly off the established tourist track and still doesn't charge an entrance fee. It was founded in the Anuradhapura era and then revived in the mid 13th century by King Vijayabahu IV during a pilgrimage from his capital in Dambadeniya to Adam's Peak. Reputedly seven storeys high in its prime, the temple housed the sacred tooth relic during the mid-14th-century reign of Parakramabahu V and his successor Vikramabahu II. The present-day single-storey building, dating to the reign of Sri Vikrama Rajasinha, is a peculiar era-spanning hybrid. The actual temple, set below a pagoda-style roof, is a typical late Kandyan edifice, wooden door and interior complete with what appear to be original 18th-century paintings. Yet the stone door-frame, engraved with swans, snakes and festoons, probably dates to the Gampola era, while the layered stone plinth, adorned with several dozen engravings of contorted dwarves and animals, is most likely a relic of the Anuradhapura-era original. A small museum houses a betel stand that once belonged to King Sri Vikrama Rajasinha, as well as some old Kandyan clothes and jewellery, and artefacts from the periods of Portuguese, Dutch and British rule.

Vallahagoda Also known as Valvasgoda, this attractive hillside temple 1km west of Gampola reputedly started life c1350 when King Bhuvanaikabahu IV constructed a Kataragama shrine in front of what was then his palace. The main temple is notable for its finely worked wood-and-tile Kandyan roof and beautifully painted door and frame (original but touched up in 2010), while the smaller Kataragama shrine to its right has a lovely carved door. The ancient stone pillars and column bases scattered in the grounds are presumably relics of the original 14th-century shrine but could be older. The temple stands right opposite the small Wallahagoda railway station, so could be reached by train from Kandy, but easier perhaps to bus to Gampola then walk out through the paddy fields or catch a tuktuk – the junction is on the opposite side of the main road to Niyamgampaya and less than 100m south of it. No entrance fee is charged and on non-poya days you may well find it is locked outside of puja hours.

Loolecondera Tea Estate [map, page 368] The roots of Sri Lanka's tea industry are to be found at Loolecondera, 35km south of Kandy, where in 1867 Scotsman James Taylor planted the first 8ha of tea seedlings on the coffee estate he had acquired 15 years earlier as a 16-year-old just weeks after he landed in Ceylon. The estate can still be visited as a scenic day trip out of Kandy, following the Deltota Road south out of town past Taylor's Hill (page 383) then continuing south for another 5km until you see the tea factory to your right. Another 1km past this, just before a hairpin bend in the main road, turn right on to a rough 4km road that twists and turns to the foundations and remains of the brick chimney of Taylor's old log cabin, set at an altitude of around 1,250m in the middle of his pioneering tea field. From here it's another few hundred metres to Taylor's Seat, a natural granite bench offering spectacular views to the Victoria Reservoir and Knuckles Range.

Muthumari Amman Temple (*Entrance US$1.60*) Situated in the centre of Matale, a medium-sized town straddling the Dambulla Road 25km north of Kandy, this landmark Hindu temple was established in 1850 and has since grown from a single tree-shaded statue to a massive complex whose 12-storey main gopuram is covered with hundreds of small statues of Hindu deities. For those who've not spend time in Hindu parts of Sri Lanka, its very flamboyance makes for a refreshing change from the more sombre Buddhist temples that dominate

in Kandy and the Cultural Triangle. At Tamil New Year, Muthumari Amman is the focal point of a famous and colourful street festival complete with fire-walking sessions. Matale is easily reached from Kandy, whether by train (five to six services daily) or by a regular bus service.

Aluvihara Cave Temple [map, page 368] (*Entrance US$1.60*) One of Sri Lanka's oldest and most revered Buddhist sites, Aluvihara (Temple of Light) was founded during the 3rd-century BC rule of King Devanampiya Tissa, who reputedly built its first dagoba and planted the original Bo sapling. Situated just 2km north of present-day Matale, its network of caverns is famously where the *Tripitaka* was first committed to writing by 500 scholarly monks in the 1st century BC. Incredibly, these ancient palm-leaf manuscripts survived in the temple's library for almost two millennia, only to be destroyed – along with much of the original monastery – during a British retaliatory raid in the wake of an anti-colonial rebellion in Matale in 1848. Today, Aluvihara, situated at the base of a jungle-swathed boulder-strewn maintain, is most memorable for its atmospheric 'lost temple' setting, which is seen to best advantage from the prominent yellow-and-gold Buddha statue situated a 1km walk uphill from the main cave temples. Remarkable in an altogether more disturbing way is the caverns' graphic, almost gleeful, series of life-size tableaux and paintings depicting crews of long-fanged demons dismembering, skewering, crucifying, hacking the genitals off or otherwise torturing souls whose bad karma led to their reincarnation into one of the hell-like subterranean Narakas layered below our terrestrial world. Following on from this, it's a relief to step into the stuffy old International Buddhist Library and Museum, whose scattershot collection of historic images and artefacts incorporates nothing significantly more grisly than a newspaper clipping reporting how, during the 1954 royal visit to Ceylon, the Duke of Edinburgh slipped on the stairs at Aluvihara, but 'escaped a nasty fall' thanks to the swift reaction of an alert police superintendent.

Knuckles Conservation Forest [map, page 368] Rising to an altitude of 1,893m some 20km northeast of Kandy, the Knuckles Range, the country's sixth highest, is named for the resemblance of its five main peaks, from certain angles, to a clenched fist. The upper slopes have been protected in a 155km² forest reserve since 1873, and the area above the 1,000m contour was inscribed as part of the Central Highlands of Sri Lanka UNESCO World Heritage Site in 2010. As reflected in its original Sinhala name, Kanda Dumbara (Mist-covered Hills), the Knuckles Range receives a high precipitation (up to 5,000m per annum) and is an important watershed in the Mahaweli catchment area. The most interesting component in its diverse mosaic of grassy and wooded highland habitats is dwarf cloudforest, whose stunted trees are typically no more than 1.5m high and are covered with lichens, mosses and epiphytic orchids.

Large wildlife includes sambar deer, purple-faced langur, the ubiquitous toque macaque, the dark montane highlands race of giant squirrel, and a seldom-seen population of leopard. A bird checklist of around 120 species includes 18 national endemics, namely Sri Lanka junglefowl, Sri Lanka spurfowl, Sri Lanka wood pigeon, Sri Lanka hanging parrot, Layard's parakeet, Sri Lanka grey hornbill, yellow-fronted barbet, yellow-eared bulbul, brown-capped babbler, orange-billed babbler, ashy-headed laughing thrush, spot-winged thrush, Sri Lanka whistling thrush, Sri Lanka blue magpie, Sri Lanka hill myna, dull-blue flycatcher, Legge's flowerpecker and Sri Lanka white-eye. The mountains are also home to several other endemic small vertebrates, including three fish, two lizard and one frog species whose range is restricted to this one massif.

A popular starting point for hikes into the Knuckles Range is Corbet's Gap, a spectacular viewpoint named after the surveyor who mapped the area in late 19th century. To get here, follow the Mahiyanganaya Road east out of Kandy for roughly 40km until you reach Hunnasgiriya, then turn left and continue north for another 18km. Beyond this viewpoint, independent exploration is difficult, but affordable day and overnight hikes (up to six days' duration) can be arranged through the experienced and well-regarded Kandy Green Tours and Trekking Expeditor (page 388). The main road running east from Hunnasgiriya also offers lovely views over the paddy fields and jungle around Mahiyanganaya as it descends through a series of 18 hairpin bends.

MAHIYANGANAYA AND SURROUNDS

Situated at an altitude of 100m some 75km east of Kandy, historic Mahiyanganaya is renowned as the site of an eponymous temple and associated dagoba claimed to be the oldest in Sri Lanka, founded shortly after the Buddha's first visit to the island a mere nine months after his enlightenment. Though little visited by tourists, this low-rise, modestly proportioned and resolutely off-the-beaten-track town sprawls attractively along the east bank of the Mahaweli River below the forested peaks of the Knuckles Range. If you overnight here, it is also worth wandering or driving 2.5km north to the vast and ancient Sorabora Reservoir, which was reputedly constructed in the 2nd century BC by King Dutugamunu and is often visited by elephants at dusk and dawn. Mahiyanganaya is also the springboard for visits to the traditional Vedda communities that inhabit Dambana 18km to the east, and for safaris into the little-visited Wasgamuwa National Park.

GETTING THERE AND AWAY Coming to or from Kandy, the scenic 75km drive across the Knuckles Range takes up to 2 hours, traversing a thrilling sequence of 18 hairpin bends as it descends to the plains. If you are travelling as a round trip from Kandy, you could make things more interesting by returning along the slightly longer but very scenic road through Mediyaya and Rantambe, which skirts the southern boundary of the Victoria-Randenigala-Rantambe Sanctuary and offers good views over the associated reservoirs as well as a fair chance of encountering elephants. Coming to or from elsewhere, Mahiyanganaya stands 160km (3–4 hours) from Anuradhapura via Dambulla (100km/2½ hours), 200km (4–5 hours) from Trincomalee via Polonnaruwa (90km/2 hours), 105km (2½ hours) from Batticaloa, 110km (2½ hours) from Ampara, 140km (3 hours) from Arugam Bay, and 60km (1½ hours) from Badulla. Regular buses connect it to Kandy, Polonnaruwa (where you can change for Trincomalee), Dambulla (change for Anuradhapura), Batticaloa, Ampara and Badulla.

🏠 **WHERE TO STAY** *Map, opposite*
Budget
✳ 🏠 **Mapakada Village** (6 rooms)
Bibile Rd; 📞 055 493 6937; m 0772
209977; e mapakadavillage@gmail.com;
w mapakadavillage.lk. Set bordering the forest-
fringed Mapakada Reservoir 10km south of town,
this friendly owner-managed resort stands in
large lawns with an infinity pool & shaded terrace

restaurant serving local & Western cuisine. The
large modern rooms have AC, TV & balcony. Bikes
& scooters are available to rent & there's a boat
for pottering around the lake. *US$34/56 sgl/dbl
B&B.* **$$$**
🏠 **Sorabora Gedara Guesthouse** (10 rooms)
Sorabora Lake Rd; 📞 055 225 8307; m 0777
403940; e info@soraboragedara.com;

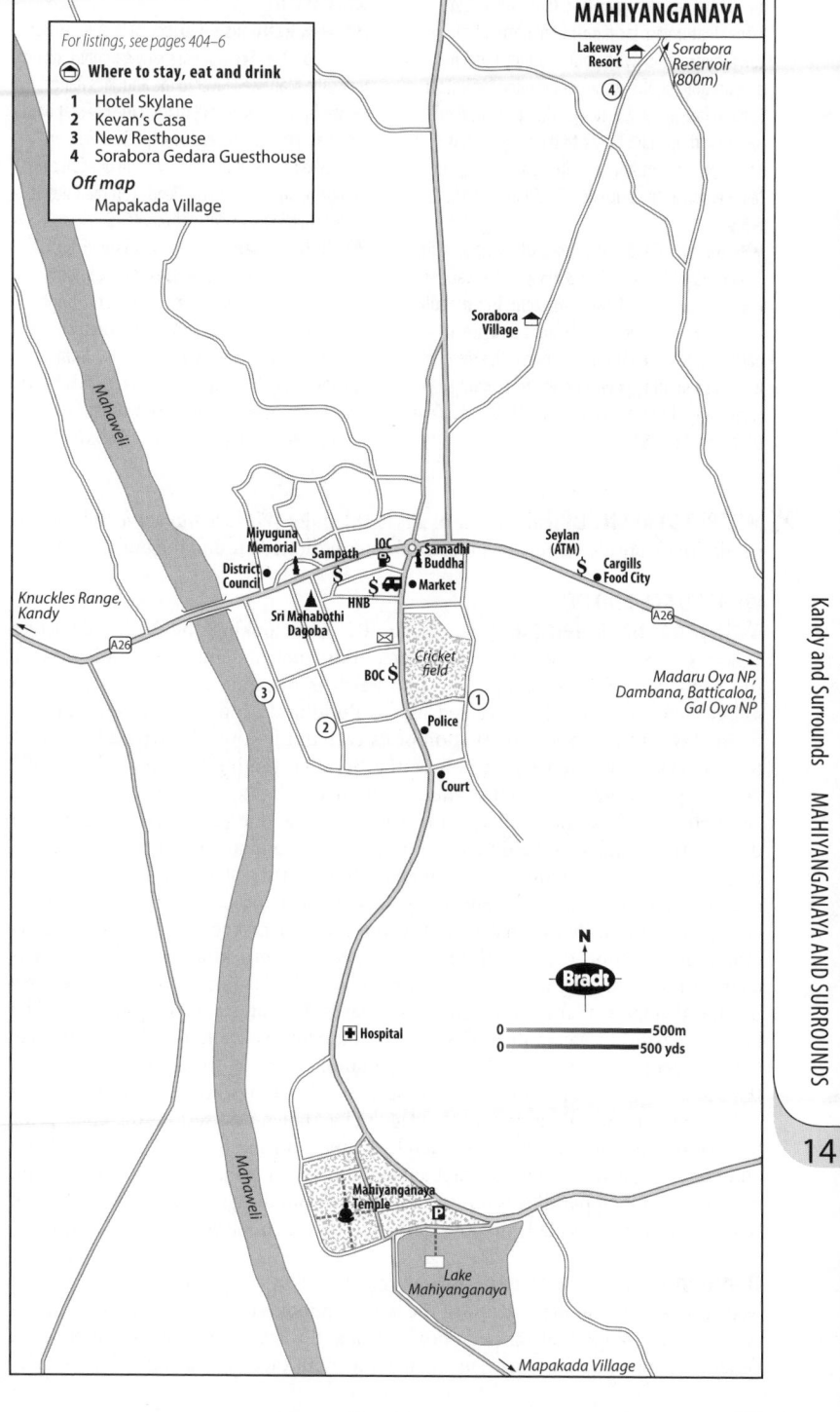

MAHIYANGANAYA

Lakeway Resort
Sorabora Reservoir (800m)
④

For listings, see pages 404–6

🍴 Where to stay, eat and drink
1 Hotel Skylane
2 Kevan's Casa
3 New Resthouse
4 Sorabora Gedara Guesthouse

Off map
   Mapakada Village

Sorabora Village

Mahaweli

Miyuguna Memorial
Sampath
IOC
Samadhi Buddha
Seylan (ATM)
Cargills Food City

District Council
Sri Mahabothi Dagoba
HNB
Market

Knuckles Range, Kandy
A26
A26

BOC
Cricket field
①
Madaru Oya NP, Dambana, Batticaloa, Gal Oya NP

③
②
Police

Court

N
Bradt

0 ——————— 500m
0 ——————— 500 yds

✚ Hospital

Mahaweli

Mahaweli

Mahiyanganaya Temple
P
Lake Mahiyanganaya

Mapakada Village

14

w soraboragedara.com. Boasting a rustic but rather featureless location 1.8km north of the town centre, this swish double-storey hotel has a swimming pool & restaurant serving typical Sri Lankan fare in the $$ range. The spacious tiled rooms with AC, fan, TV, writing desk & smallish bathroom are nothing to write home about, but fair enough at the price. *US$37/50 sgl/dbl B&B.* $$$

🏠 **Kevan's Casa** (16 rooms) Off Resthouse Rd; ☏055 225 8120; m 0777 935985; e reservation@kevanscasa.com; w kevanscasa.com. This friendly new owner-managed hotel stands on a green back road between the bus station & the river. It has a swimming pool, a decent restaurant & smart brightly decorated rooms with AC & TV. *From US$65 dbl B&B.* $$$

🏠 **New Resthouse** (10 rooms) Resthouse Rd; ☏055 225 7304. Set in small shady gardens looking across the Mahaweli River to the Knuckles Range, this well-priced set-up 600m from the bus station has a bar, a restaurant, & clean, spacious & recently refurbished rooms with balcony & fan or AC. It can arrange budget visits to the Vedda communities at Dambana. *US$17/23 dbl with fan/AC.* $

🏠 **Hotel Skylane** (12 rooms) Samagi Rd; ☏055 255 7256; e hotelskylanea@gmail.com; w hotelskylane.weebly.com. Get past the bright purple cave-themed décor & this is a pretty decent shoestring option, situated about 500m from the bus station on the opposite side of the cricket field. Clean rooms have fitted nets, TV, writing desk & fan or AC, & a restaurant is attached. *US$10/20 dbl with fan/AC.* $

✖ **WHERE TO EAT AND DRINK**   All the places listed under *Where to stay* serve well-priced meals. There are also plenty of small local eateries dotted around the bus station.

WHAT TO SEE AND DO
Mahiyanganaya Temple [map, page 405] Overlooking the Mahaweli River 1.5km south of the modern town centre, this ancient temple is dominated by the 37m-high Mahiyanganaya Dagoba, which is not only one of Sri Lanka's 16 sacred Solosmasthana (sites visited by the Buddha during his lifetime), but also often cited as the oldest construction of its type in the country. Legend has it that the dagoba marks the very site where the Buddha, visiting Sri Lanka during the January poya only nine months after he attained enlightenment, preached to and converted a Yakka chief called Saman, who is now one of the island's guardian deities. The Buddha left behind a curl of hair, which Saman enshrined in a 3m-tall dagoba. After the Buddha was cremated, one of his collarbones was recovered and brought to Saman to be enshrined within the same dagoba, which was then enlarged to twice its original height. Over subsequent centuries, Mahiyangana's crossroads location between the northern and southern kingdoms and the east-coast ports meant that it was regularly visited by Sinhala kings. In the 3rd century BC, the dagoba was further extended skywards, to stand almost 15m tall, at the behest of King Devanampiya Tissa of Anuradhapura. It attained its present-day height a century later under King Dutugamunu. Over the centuries, renovation of the sacred dagoba was undertaken by several other kings, most recently Kirti Sri Rajasinha of Kandy. Despite this, the dagoba had fallen into serious disrepair prior to a reconstruction project undertaken by Prime Minister Senanayake in 1953 and completed eight years later. The bell-shaped modern dagoba is an impressive sight, reached via a long parklike walkway, and the surrounding temple is often a hive of religious activity, especially on poya days, but the site contains few other antiquities.

Dambana [map, page 368] Situated on the Batticaloa Road 17km east of Mahiyanganaya, Dambana is one of the last strongholds of the Vedda or Wanniyala-Aetto (Forest People) recognised both by oral and written tradition and by modern genetic testing to be the oldest surviving indigenous race in Sri Lanka. Traditionally the Vedda are animist hunter-gatherers who spoke a unique language, controversially classified as a Sinhala-based creole, and would have inhabited most of the island a few thousand years ago. But Vedda numbers and territory have both diminished steadily over the centuries, partly due to deforestation and competition with agriculturists, but also as a result of active persecution, which attained genocidal proportions under the British colonial administration in 1818 and 1848. Today, the moribund Vedda language, spoken only by a few village elders living around Dambana, has been all but abandoned in favour of Sinhala or Tamil, while the surviving population of a few thousand individual Veddas has abandoned the no-longer-sustainable hunter-gatherer lifestyle and has also tended to gravitate towards Hinduism and Buddhism.

The focal point of tourist activity in the vicinity is Kotabakinya, a traditional village of around ten Vedda families set at the end of a clearly signposted 3km side road running north from Dambana Junction, just within the borders of the obscure Madura Oya National Park. Here, set behind an inauspicious and unassuming adobe exterior, the Adivasi Jana Urumu Kendra Tribal Heritage Museum (*entrance US$3.30; photography forbidden*), opened in 2006, turns out to be a modern multimedia installation that does an unexpectedly good job of educating foreigners (and, importantly, other Sri Lankans) about the lifestyle, beliefs and history of the island's oldest cultural group. There are reproductions of prehistoric Vedda rock art, lively displays about hunting methods and spiritual beliefs, informative panels detailing the many changes undergone by this ancient culture in recent times, well-labelled collections of traditional artefacts, and fascinating recordings of centuries-old lullabies and other songs.

Just hanging around Kotabakinya, you'll see plenty of Vedda men milling around with their trademark shock of wild hair, full beard, waist-high robe and axe habitually slung over shoulder. Interaction is a little trickier, but it's easy enough to get chatting to the small stall-owners that sell traditional crafts to visitors, and there's no hassle or huge pressure to buy. If you want to see traditional dancing, drumming and other activities, the village offers a full-hour cultural programme, charging around US$70 for groups (up to three people) and US$200 for full bus parties. These can be arranged on the spot or by calling ahead (m *0722 985571*).

Wasgamuwa National Park [map, page 368] (⊕ *06.00–18.00; entrance US$15 plus VAT*) Hemmed in by the Mahaweli River to the east and by various smaller tributaries to the north and west, the little-visited 370km² Wasgamuwa National Park started life as a wildlife sanctuary in the 1940s and was upgraded to its present status in 1984, primarily to provide refuge to animals displaced by the Mahaweli Development Project. The park incorporates the remains of three reservoirs built in the 12th century by King Parakramabahu I, but it contains little standing water today, the exception being a cluster of small lakes near the entrance gate. Its name derives from the Sinhala phrase 'Walas Gamuwa' (Sloth Bear Forest), but while these large carnivores are present, as are leopards, neither is easily seen. Wasgamuwa is better known for a seasonal population of 150 elephants, which are most easily located over January–April, but evacuate the park to participate in the legendary Minneriya 'gathering' over July–September. The dry-zone evergreen forest of Wasgamuwa also supports a sizeable population of water buffalo and spotted and sambar deer, while a checklist of 140-plus bird species includes eight national endemics.

Getting there and away Wasgamuwa is somewhat remote from the major tourist centre. True, its northern tip extends to within 5km of Polonnaruwa, but the entrance gate, in the southeast of the park, is a full 100km from Polonnaruwa by road. The gate stands 15km north of Hettipola, a small junction town only 30km north of Mahiyanganaya. Reaching Wasgamuwa on public transport isn't realistic.

Where to stay *Map, page 368*

Far Cry Resort (6 rooms) 011 282 4500; m 0773 899498; e res@lsrhotels.com; w farcry. lk. The most upmarket option in the vicinity of Wasgamuwa, the rustically stylish resort is set in 6ha gardens with a restaurant & swimming pool fronting the Mahaweli River 800m north of the so-called Nippon Bridge, 8km east of Hettipola, & about 1hr's drive from the park entrance gate. Rooms all have AC, king-size bed, cable TV, safe & tea-/coffee-making facilities. *US$260 dbl B&B.* **$$$$$**

Wasgamuwa Safari Village Hotel (12 cottages) 011 259 1728; e kinjoulanka@sltnet.lk; w safarivillagehotels. com. Set on the shore of Lake Dunuwila in the shadow of the Knuckles Range, this pleasant mid-range lodge 10mins' drive from the entrance gate offers accommodation in thatched cottages with fan, bathroom, lake-facing balconies & 2 rooms that sleep up to 5 people. The restaurant serves Sri Lankan & Chinese cuisine. *US$36/42 sgl/dbl.* **$$**

15

High Hill Country:
Adam's Peak,
Nuwara Eliya and Ella

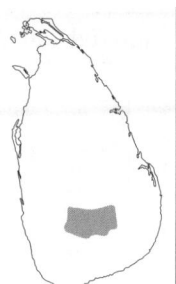

There is a touch of romance and adventure in the phrase Hill Country. It sounds like a different world. And in Sri Lanka, as in India, the chilly mist-swathed towns and villages of the highlands – sometimes referred to as hill stations – have traditionally doubled as holiday resorts to domestic tourists seeking refuge from the relentless heat of the plains and coast. And while this agreeably temperate climate might not sound like much of a selling point to international sun-seekers, it is still well worth building a Hill Country sojourn into any Sri Lankan itinerary, ideally *en route* between the old city of Kandy and the sultry south coast. Scenically, the high Hill Country of south-central Sri Lanka is simply exquisite: all steep verdant slopes adorned with tangled indigenous forests, high grassy meadows, orderly tea plantations, tall tumbling waterfalls and blissfully panoramic viewpoints. And while perceptions of Hill Country culture are dominated by its conspicuous colonial legacy, sometimes to an uncomfortable degree, its quirky little towns and villages actually support a rich mixed Sinhala and Tamil heritage, along with several ancient Buddhist and Hindu shrines.

The acme of Hill Country – in terms of altitude, mood and tourist development – is Nuwara Eliya, a self-styled 'Little England' set in a pretty valley at the base of Sri Lanka's highest mountain. Renowned for its wealth of restored colonial hotels, Nuwara Eliya is an excellent base for day trips into the surrounding hills, most notably the scenic Horton Plains, which are protected in the country's highest-altitude national park. Elsewhere, the towering summit of Adam's Peak, sacred to Buddhist, Hindu, Muslim and Christian alike, is a popular goal for hikers, especially during the busy pilgrimage season. Then there's Ella, a stunningly located village that has also emerged as the Hill Country's trendiest backpacker hang-out, while providing an excellent base for day walks, temple visits and other outings. And for those who want to avoid the crowds, there are also the less-fancied towns of Haputale and Bandarawela, both of which provide useful and emphatically down-to-earth bases for exploring this lovely part of Sri Lanka.

HATTON

The rail springboard and main road funnel for Adam's Peak, Hatton, named after an obscure Scottish village, is a medium-sized town (population 15,000) that started life as a British colonial hill station perched at an altitude of 1,250m in the western highlands 120km inland of Colombo. The town came into its own during in the 1870s, after the nearby Bogawantalawa Valley became one of the first parts of the highlands where tea was planted to replace coffee, and today the surrounding plantations, many also

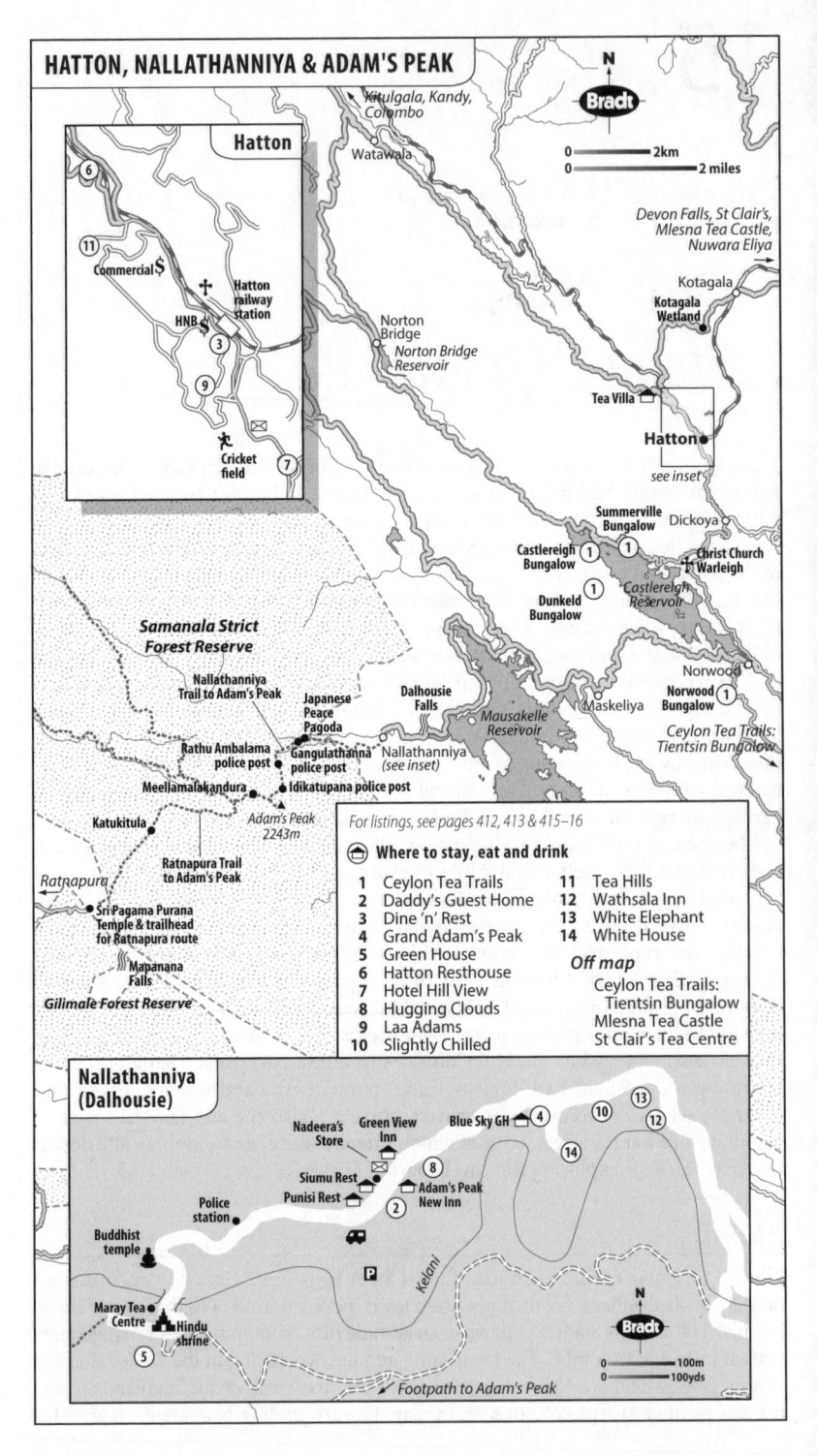

HATTON, NALLATHANNIYA & ADAM'S PEAK

Hatton

Kitulgala, Kandy, Colombo

Watawala

Devon Falls, St Clair's, Mlesna Tea Castle, Nuwara Eliya

Kotagala
Kotagala Wetland

6

11
Commercial $

HNB

3

9

Hatton railway station

Norton Bridge
Norton Bridge Reservoir

Cricket field

7

Tea Villa

Hatton
see inset

Summerville Bungalow   Dickoya

Castlereigh Bungalow   1   1

Christ Church Warleigh

Dunkeld Bungalow   1

Castlereigh Reservoir

Samanala Strict Forest Reserve

Nallathanniya Trail to Adam's Peak

Japanese Peace Pagoda

Dalhousie Falls

Mausakelle Reservoir

Norwood

Norwood Bungalow   1

Maskeliya

Ceylon Tea Trails: Tientsin Bungalow

Rathu Ambalama police post   Gangulathanna police post

Meellamalakandura

Nallathanniya *(see inset)*

Katukitula

Idikatupana police post

Adam's Peak 2243m

Ratnapura

Ratnapura Trail to Adam's Peak

Sri Pagama Purana Temple & trailhead for Ratnapura route

Mapanana Falls

Gilimale Forest Reserve

For listings, see pages 412, 413 & 415–16

⌂ Where to stay, eat and drink

1	Ceylon Tea Trails
2	Daddy's Guest Home
3	Dine 'n' Rest
4	Grand Adam's Peak
5	Green House
6	Hatton Resthouse
7	Hotel Hill View
8	Hugging Clouds
9	Laa Adams
10	Slightly Chilled

11	Tea Hills
12	Wathsala Inn
13	White Elephant
14	White House

Off map

Ceylon Tea Trails:
   Tientsin Bungalow
Mlesna Tea Castle
St Clair's Tea Centre

Nallathanniya (Dalhousie)

Nadeera's Store   Green View Inn   Blue Sky GH   4   10   13

Siumu Rest   8   12

Punisi Rest   Adam's Peak New Inn   14

Police station   2

Kelani

Buddhist temple

Maray Tea Centre   Hindu shrine

5

P

Footpath to Adam's Peak

The four-times-daily train service connecting Colombo to Badulla via Kandy is the most pleasant way to travel through Hill Country, not only because rail is a more inherently relaxed mode of transport than road, but also because it offers some splendid views over otherwise inaccessible or difficult-to-reach vistas. The track distance from Colombo to Badulla is 290km, a 10–12-hour journey that passes through 44 tunnels (the longest being the 560m Poolbank Tunnel between Hatton and Nanu Oya). In practice, however, few travellers would cover it all in one go, and fewer still would travel all the way to Badulla, a town whose appeal to tourists is relatively limited (though the short leg between Ella and Badulla does allow rail buffs to experience the Demodara Loop described on page 453). More normal would be to travel the 118km from Colombo to Kandy, stop in the latter for a couple of days, then continue by rail to one (or more) other hill stations. In order to facilitate trip planning, this chapter is sequenced to follow the railway as it winds southeast from Kandy to Badulla via Hatton (for Adam's Peak), Nanu Oya (for Nuwara Eliya), Pattipola and Ohiya (both for Horton Plains National Park), Haputale, Bandarawela and Ella. If you do only one leg by train, make sure it includes the stretch between Nanu Oya and Bandarawela, which wends through vegetation so lush and scenery so dramatic it ranks as one of the world's great little train trips. This leg incorporates the railway's highest point (1,911m above sea level) 1km past Pattipola, while the 17km track between Ohiya and Haputale passes through more than a dozen tunnels, climaxing at the incredibly sited Idalgashinna station.

named after Scottish villages, produce some of the world's finest tea (see box, page 8). Another well-known export is the Hatton National Bank (HNB), which was founded here in 1888 to service the tea plantations and their workers, and now has over 250 branches countrywide. Considering its relatively small size, Hatton is a surprisingly energetic and colourful small town, which packs plenty of character and mercantile activity into its predominantly Hindu and Tamil centre. The town also has good amenities, including several banks and ATMs, a Cargills Food City, a busy market and a scattering of hotels; but most travellers simply pass through *en route* to the surrounding tea estates (serviced by several small colonial-style upmarket lodges) or the village of Nallathanniya (Dalhousie) at the base of Adam's Peak. Other out-of-town sites of interest include the Devon and St Clair falls on the road running east to Nuwara Eliya.

GETTING THERE AND AWAY

By road Hatton lies just south of the busy main road connecting Colombo to Nuwara Eliya via Avissawella and Kitulgala. It's a 125km/2½-hour drive from Colombo, 75km/1½ hours from Kitulgala, and 40km/1 hour from Kitulgala. Coming from Kandy, most people use the train, but the 70km drive via Gampola and Ginigathena can be covered in 90 minutes.

By rail Up to five trains daily run between Colombo and Hatton via Kandy, continuing east to Badulla via Nuwara Eliya and Ella. Extra trains run during the pilgrimage season for Adam's Peak (January–April). The train journey from Colombo or Kandy takes around 6 and 3 hours respectively, and it's another 5 hours from Hatton to Badulla.

High Hill Country   HATTON

15

WHERE TO STAY, EAT AND DRINK *Map, page 410*

Exclusive

✱ 🏠 **Ceylon Tea Trails** (30 rooms) 📞 011
774 5700; e reservations@resplendentceylon.
com; w resplendentceylon.com. Not some hare-
&-hounds paper chase, but Sri Lanka's first Relais
& Châteaux resort, Ceylon Tea Trails comprises 5
standalone bungalows, each individually managed
and with 4–6 guest bedrooms, scattered amid the
tea plantations of the lovely Bogawantalawa Valley
around 3km south of Hatton. Transformed from old
plantation managers' houses, the bungalows date
to the period 1890–1939, and all but 2 overlook
the lovely Castlereigh (also spelt Castlereagh)
Reservoir, a fabulous setting for canoeing, rambling,
birdwatching or just idling around the infinity pool
in tranquil highland surrounds, as well as being
a possible base for the ascent of Adam's Peak.
Though the bungalows are all different in character,
the rooms all epitomise designer luxury with
their comfortable net-draped beds & expansive
bathrooms equipped with tubs, period tiles & neo-
colonial fittings. Rates include delicious table d'hôte
b/fast, lunch & dinner, as well as afternoon tea & all
drinks, which can be taken in the luxuriant dining
room or wide terrace. *From around US$615 all-
inclusive dbl, with low-season discounts.* **$$$$$+**

Moderate

🏠 **Tea Hills Hotel** (11 rooms) 📞 051 222 3460;
m 0772 027766; e sales@teahillsbungalow.com;
w teahillsbungalow.com. Situated on a steep
hillside overlooking the town centre, this converted
planter's bungalow offers great views over the
valley & pleasant rooms decorated in period style
with 4-poster bed, fitted net, fan, TV, & bathroom
with tub & shower. The communal sitting room has
a log fire & a fine wooden floor. The traditional Sri
Lankan curries, made with ingredients grown on

site, are exceptional. Climbs of Adam's Peak can be
arranged. *US$110 dbl B&B.* **$$$$**

🏠 **Laa Adams Hotel** (18 rooms) 📞 051 222
3666; e reservations@laaadams.net; w laaadams.
com. Not quite so swanky as it would like to be, this
modern high-rise is nonetheless the smartest option
in the town centre, and its well-priced ground-floor
Indian restaurant (**$$**) scores full marks for décor &
a lengthy menu with plenty of options for carnivores
& vegetarians alike. The small but comfortable
carpeted rooms are equipped with AC, fan, TV, safe
& fridge, but feel a touch overpriced. *US$75/90 sgl/
dbl B&B.* **$$$$**

Shoestring

🏠 **Hatton Resthouse** (7 rooms) 📞 051 222
2751. This hillside resthouse on the Colombo Road
500m from the town centre has spacious twin
rooms with fan, a small sitting room, a dining hall
(where rice-&-curry appears quickly at lunchtime)
& a dispensary-style bar. It's a 15/25min walk from
the railway/bus station. *US$15/18 sgl/dbl.* **$**

🏠 **Hotel Hill View** (15 rooms) 📞 051 222
3456; e hotelhillviewhatton@gmail.com. Situated
alongside the Dickoya Road 400m past the bus
station, the well-run budget hotel has clean rooms
with fan & TV, so-called luxury rooms with AC, & a
restaurant with a nice view over the hills. OK at the
price. *US$20/27 sgl/dbl, US$40 luxury dbl.* **$$**

🏠 **Dine 'n' Rest** (5 rooms) 📞 051 222 2524;
m 0777 594506. Conveniently located above
Cargills Food City practically opposite the railway
station, this place seems stronger on the dine front
than the rest front. The wallet-friendly restaurant
(**$**) has a long menu of Western, Sri Lankan &
Chinese dishes, but the spacious rooms with fan
are a little tatty. *US$17 dbl.* **$**

WHAT TO SEE AND DO Hatton is well positioned for overnight ascents of Adam's
Peak, which stands about 30km to the southwest, and for rafting, birdwatching and
other excursions at Kitulgala, a similar distance back along the Colombo Road. The
area is a potential base for day visits to Horton Plains National Park, 60km away by
road, but it's somewhat less convenient than Nuwara Eliya or Haputale, especially
if you plan on a morning walk. The scenic tea estates out of town offer plenty of
opportunities for unstructured rambling.

Christ Church Warleigh [map, page 410] This stone church was built in 1878
by the British tea planter William Scott on a hilltop 3km south of Hatton. Still
maintained in perfect condition by its last few Anglican parishioners, it still contains

the original Bible donated by Scott, along with an old pipe organ, precious 19th-century stained-glass windows, and two aisles of worn timber pews. A well-tended cemetery pays testimony to the many planters and their families who were felled by malaria and other tropical diseases. Even if quaint old churches aren't your thing, it's worth stopping for the wonderful view over Castlereigh Reservoir, a narrow 12km-long lake created in 1965 to feed a 50MW hydro-electric plant.

Along the Nuwara Eliya Road A small lake at the village of Kotagala, 5km along the road to Nuwara Eliya, is the centrepiece of a proposed wetland reserve that might be of interest to birdwatchers. Another 6km towards Nuwara Eliya, the 97m-high three-stage Devon Falls, formed by a tributary of the Kotmale River, can be viewed from a well-signposted lay-by. From the viewpoint, a 1km walk downhill through the tea plantation takes you to the falls. There are two good places to freshen up and grab a bite (**$**) near the waterfall. Mlesna Tea Castle (**** *051 222 2561;* **w** *mlesnateas. com;* ⊕ *08.00–18.00*), a modern extravaganza built as a replica castle with an emporium showcasing Sri Lanka's best teas for purchase in artistically designed containers, serves one of the best rice-and-curry lunches in Sri Lanka, with rare ingredients such as plantain blossoms and bitter gourd. About 600m further, the quaint Devon Cottage, built in 1923, has been converted to the St Clair's Tea Centre (⊕ *08.00–17.30*), which serves a selection of teas from the St Clair's Estate, as well as inexpensive cakes and snacks. Another 6km past this, a newly built viewpoint, complete with café and museum, overlooks the greater and lesser St Clair's Falls, which stand close to the road and fall 80m and 50m respectively.

ADAM'S PEAK AND NALLATHANNIYA

A monumental granite prominence that rises in pyramidal isolation above the surrounding hills, Adam's Peak is quantitatively only the fifth-highest summit in Sri Lanka, but few would question its status as the country's most imposing natural feature. As suggested by its Sinhala name Sri Pada (Sacred Footprint), the 2,243m peak is also the island's holiest summit, attracting hundreds of thousands of Buddhist pilgrims between the Unduvap (December) and Vesak (May) poyas, supplemented throughout the year by a relative trickle of fit and energetic tourists. By far the most popular of the four foot trails to Adam's Peak starts at Nallathanniya (also known as Dalhousie, pronounced Dell House), a pretty village set at an altitude of 1,250m above the Kelani River 30km by road from Hatton. Be warned, however, that even this most undemanding ascent route gains almost 1,000m over the course of 7km, and incorporates around 5,200 stone steps, making for a rather challenging workout, particularly as you close in on the mountaintop shrine. The climb is normally undertaken at night, in order to summit before dusk, when the cloud cover is most likely to lift, offering a fabulous sunrise and long views in all directions, with the mountain casting an unerringly perfect triangular shadow to its west. Ecologically, the countryside around Nallathanniya and Adam's Peak, for all its verdant veneer, is now dominated almost entirely by tea, eucalyptus and other non-indigenous plantations, making for a bleak contrast to the more pristine likes of Horton Plains or Sinharaja. That said, during the pilgrimage season, when any given night might see up to 20,000 local worshippers ascending this Buddhist Mecca, foreign hikers will find themselves swept up into a colourful cultural experience as absorbing and inclusive as it is unique.

BACKGROUND AND HISTORY Adam's Peak is a contender for the world's most broadly revered mountain. Indeed, all four of Sri Lanka's main religions regard its summit not only as sacred, but also as an important pilgrimage site. Some of its mystique can be attributed to the striking triangular outline that led certain older Tamil works to dub it Svargarohanam (Ascent to Heaven). But the mountain's most sacred feature is the large Buddhapada (footprint-shaped indentation) set in a boulder at the rocky pinnacle. Buddhists believe that this footprint was made by no lesser personage than the Buddha, who is said to have paused here on one of his visits to Sri Lanka. Hindus, meanwhile, have long claimed that the footprint is a relic of a dance performed here by the deity Shiva, and refer to the mountain as Shiva Padam (Shiva's Footprint). Muslims consider the indented pinnacle to be where Adam, a 10m-tall giant, made his first early footfall after he was cast out from the Garden of Eden. This Islamic belief was later adopted by the Portuguese, who knew the mountain as Pico de Adão, a name subsequently Anglicised to Adam's Peak. Another widespread belief, reflected in the alternative name Samanela Kanda (Saman's Mountain) is that the summit is home to Saman, one of the island's four ancient guardian deities.

Whatever the belief, Sri Lanka's holiest mountain has been a point of pilgrimage and worship for millennia. Tradition has it that the first of many Sinhala monarchs to visit the Buddhapada was King Valagamba. The summit has also attracted global travellers since ancient times. In AD412, the Chinese Buddhist monk Faxian undertook the first documented foreign ascent. He was followed in 1298 by Marco Polo and in 1344 by Ibn Battuta, who referred to the mountain as Serendib and described it as going 'up in the air like a pillar of smoke'. Though open to all faiths, the peak has been under Buddhist custodianship for most of the past two millennia, the one exception being a short period in the late 16th century when King Rajasinha I, having recently converted to Hinduism, ordered the massacre of the mountaintop shrine's Buddhist guardians, and handed it over to priests of the Shiva-worshipping Shaivite persuasion.

GETTING THERE AND AWAY

By road Coming directly from Colombo, the most direct route to Nallathanniya is the 140km/3-hour drive via Avissawella and Kitulgala, branching south from the main road to Nuwara Eliya just before Watawala. Slightly longer but in a better state of repair is the 155km route through Hatton and Dickoya. Nallathanniya lies about 100km/2 hours south of Kandy via Gampola and Hatton, or 130km/2½ hours from Ella via Nuwara Eliya (70km), 235km from Galle (following the Southern Expressway almost as far as Colombo). The only long-haul buses servicing Nallathanniya all year through are the twice-daily 5-hour service to/from Colombo (leaving at 04.30 and 07.30) and the once-daily 10-hour service to Tissamaharama via Nuwara Eliya and Ella (leaving at 07.30). There may also be direct buses from Kandy and Nuwara Eliya in pilgrimage season. Failing that, first make your way to Hatton, which is serviced by plenty of buses in all directions, then bus or tuktuk the final 30km to Nallathanniya. During the pilgrimage season, the road from Hatton is covered by one or two buses an hour between 08.00 and 18.00, but you may need to change vehicles at Maskeliya, 10km before Nallathanniya. Outside the season, buses are slightly less regular and you'll almost certainly have to change at Maskeliya. Alternatively, a one-way tuktuk from Hatton to Nallathanniya shouldn't cost more than US$8 (though overcharging is commonplace), while the taxi fare is around US$15–20.

By rail There's no railway station at Nallathanniya, but many travellers bound for Adam's Peak catch a train to Hatton, which lies on the scenic main line between Colombo and Badulla via Kandy, Nuwara Eliya and Ella, then continue by bus or tuktuk to Nallathanniya.

WHERE TO STAY, EAT AND DRINK *Map, page 410*

A straggle of small hotels backs on to the south side of the main road through Nallathanniya, most with public areas facing the Kelani River and plantation-covered hills below Adam's Peak. Overpriced mediocrity is very much the order of the day in Nallathanniya, and while most of the hotels listed below should prove acceptable to readers who routinely stay in lodgings in the budget or shoestring categories, those used to smarter accommodation are unlikely to be too impressed. All the hotels listed below serve decent and well-priced meals.

Moderate

🏠 **Slightly Chilled** (15 rooms) 📞 052 205 5502; m 0719 098710; e slightlychilled@outlook. com; w slightlychilledhotel.com. Barely nudging above the budget category, this relaxed family-run multistorey lodge is Nallathanniya's smartest. Tiled rooms are a little old-fashioned but brightly decorated with a private balcony offering views across the river to Adam's Peak. The colourful restaurant serves tasty & filling Sri Lankan buffets. *US$60 dbl HB, with off-season discounts.* **$$$**

Budget

❊ 🏠 **Hugging Clouds** (5 rooms) m 0721 826333; e huggingclouds@yahoo.com; 🔘 Huggingguest. In the mould of its young & energetic owner-manager, this standout new lodge has cute rooms with treated concrete floor, private balcony & colourful fabrics & batiks, but no net or fan, which shouldn't be a huge issue in this relatively cool climate. The funky industrial-style restaurant with open kitchen & wooden benches & tables should be fully operational by the time you read this. *US$20/25 sgl/dbl, plus US$5 pp b/fast.* **$**

🏠 **White House** (25 rooms) 📞 052 205 5520; m 0777 912009; e ynimal@yahoo. com; w adamspeakwhitehouse.com. Boasting a peaceful forested riverbank location 100m downhill from the main road, this agreeable place is owned & managed by a dynamic guide who has climbed Adam's Peak more than 1,000 times & can also arrange rafting trips to Kitulgala. Small budget log cabins come with queen-size beds, nets & private balcony, while so-called deluxe rooms in the peculiar oblong 3-storey main building have TV & views of Adam's Peak. Amenities include a natural swimming pool & a well-appointed terrace restaurant. HB rates are especially good value. *US$20/30 B&B budget/deluxe dbl, plus US$3.50 HB.* **$**

🏠 **Daddy's Guest Home** (9 rooms) m 0712 017300; e hello@daddysguest.com. The bright,

clean, tiled rooms with private balcony at this friendly family-managed guesthouse are among the better options in town. A terrace restaurant, soon to relocate to the roof, serves curry & kotti roti dishes in the **$$** range. *US$30/35 dbl without/ with TV.* **$$**

🏠 **Wathsala Inn** (20 rooms) 📞 052 205 5505; m 0777 861456; e wathsalainn@yahoo. com; w adamspeakhotels.com. Offering perhaps the best view in Nallathanniya, this time-warped hotel stands above a wide bend in the river & offers good views towards Adam's Peak from the 1st-floor restaurant & all rooms. Though strong on character, the spacious rooms would benefit from maintenance & seem a bit overpriced. *US$40/47 B&B standard/deluxe dbl.* **$$**

🏠 **White Elephant Hotel** (18 rooms) 📞 052 205 5511; m 0777 171395; e hotelwhiteelephant@gmail.com; w hotelwhiteelephant.com. This adequate but characterless multistorey hotel has spacious modern rooms with net & fan. A 1st-floor restaurant serves good affordable meals (**$$**) & offers great views towards Adam's Peak. *US$40/56 twin/dbl B&B, or US$48/62 HB, with substantial off-season discounts.* **$$**

Shoestring

🏠 **Green House** (12 rooms) 📞 051 222 3956; m 0766 662101; e greenhouse.adamspeak@ gmail.com; 🔘 greenhouse.adamspeak. This popular cheapie has a personable manager & stands in terraced flowering gardens close to the start of the footpath up Adam's Peak. *US$10/18 sgl/dbl with common shower or US$15/20 en suite, with 50% off-season discount.* **$**

🏠 **Grand Adam's Peak** (32 rooms) 📞 052 353 0377; m 0716 058485; e achinikainn97@ sltnet.lk; w adamspeakholidayinn.com. Formerly the Achinika Holiday Inn, this place is something of a curate's egg, even by Nallathanniya's standards. The simple but clean budget rooms with shared bathroom are the cheapest in town, and the en-suite standard rooms are also pretty good value, but other rooms are pricey for what you get. A terrace restaurant with a view serves a varied selection of local dishes (**$$**), as well as slightly pricier sandwiches, pizzas & filled rotis. A swimming pool is scheduled for 2017. *US$7 budget dbl, US$23 standard dbl, dropping to US$17 out of season; other rooms start at US$60.* **$**

OTHER PRACTICALITIES The closest banks and ATMs are in Hatton 30km to the north. In lieu of a proper supermarket, the central Nadeera's Store stocks a fair selection of imported and other goods aimed at tourists, as well as sweatshirts, balaclavas and the like for under-clothed nocturnal hikers to chilly Adam's Peak.

CLIMBING ADAM'S PEAK In theory, four different trails lead to the summit, but only two are now in regular use: the popular modern Nallathanniya Trail and to a lesser extent the ancient and tougher Ratnapura Trail. Whichever route you use, and whatever time of year, a nocturnal ascent is recommended, with the aim of summiting shortly before sunrise. Walking shoes with a good tread, or better still hiking boots, are recommended, and older or less fit travellers might also find a walking stick useful. The mountain's windswept upper slopes can be surprisingly chilly at night, so bring plenty of warm clothing. And bear in mind that traipsing up and down 5,000-plus steps will put some strain on the leg muscles and knees of all but the fittest walkers, so plan on a couple of days' rest after the climb.

Most popular today is the **Nallathanniya Trail**, which was pioneered in the 19th century following the creation of a road infrastructure around Hatton, and is now the choice of most local pilgrims and practically all tourists. Starting in Nallathanniya, this is the shortest route up Adam's Peak at 7km, and it starts at a higher altitude than any of the alternatives, meaning the total altitude gain is slightly under 1,000m. It is also the best-maintained route, paved almost in its entirety, and punctuated by police posts at 1.5–2km intervals, namely Gangulathanna, Rathu Ambalama and Idikatupana. The toughest part of the trail is the final 1km ascent from Idikatupana, which comprises an outrageously steep flight of rock steps, hemmed in by steel bars and known as the Mahagiri Damba (literally 'Great Rock Climb').

For those primarily interested in the cultural experience, the best time to climb Adam's Peak is during the five-month **pilgrimage season**, which runs from the December poya to the May poya. The path of uneven steps is illuminated at night throughout the season so there is no need for a guide, and there are plenty of small food stalls and tea shops to refresh hungry and thirsty travellers. The downside of climbing in season is that progress tends to be slowed by the sheer volume of pedestrian traffic, which can get a bit claustrophobic, and means you need to allow at least 4 hours for the nocturnal ascent, setting off from Nallathanniya by 01.30–02.00. Unless you've an insatiable appetite for crowds, try to avoid climbing on poya nights or over weekends in late December or March and April, when the procession frequently slows from a dawdle to a standstill. Things tend to be quieter and more manageable in January and February, especially on non-poya and weekday nights.

Advantages of climbing Adam's Peak **outside the pilgrimage season** are that the scenery tends to be greener, the mountain is cleaner, you can be more confident of ascending at your own pace (rather than one dictated by the crowds) and will not need to battle through the summited throng to have a good view of the sunrise. The path will be unlit, so you will need a local guide, which costs around US$20 per party and can be arranged at any hotel in Nallathanniya. Other out-of-season essentials are a torch, enough food and water to last around 6 hours, and – given that it is also the rainy season – a waterproof windbreaker. The unimpeded ascent usually takes up to 3 hours, so you could set off from Nallathanniya an hour later than you would in season.

Prior to the 19th century, the main pilgrimage route up Adam's Peak, traversing sections of stone stairs set in place more than a thousand years ago, was the **Ratnapura Trail**, which actually starts 20km from Ratnapura at the village of Sri Pagama (altitude 250m). Some pilgrims still use this most ancient route today, believing that, as the toughest ascent, climbing around 2,000m over the course of 11km, it is also the most spiritually meritorious. It is also open to foreign travellers who want to follow in the footsteps of Marco Polo, Ibn Battuta and dozens of ancient Sinhala kings, at least during the pilgrimage season, when regular buses run from Ratnapura to the trail head at Sri Pagama, and the whole route is lit up at night. Be warned, however, that this is a genuinely demanding ascent that takes at least 8 hours, and as such it can be recommended only to hardcore hikers.

NUWARA ELIYA

Sri Lanka's highest, coldest and quirkiest town, Nuwara Eliya stands at an altitude of 1,950m at the southern base of Pidurutalagala, the country's tallest peak. Affectionately dubbed 'Little England', it started life as a sanatorium and retreat for overheated colonial administrators, and almost two centuries later its fresh highland climate and quaintly misplaced olde worlde architecture evoke a through-the-looking-glass variation on small-town Blighty. The compact town centre and winding suburban lanes are lined by a miscellany of Victorian, Edwardian, mock-Tudor and faux-colonial adobes whose whitewashed walls, colonnaded balconies and creaky teak floors are protected by corrugated iron roofs, many still painted red in line with an edict issued by some long-forgotten governor in c1900. Some of the larger mansions have been upgraded to become world-class hotels; others are maintained as quietly charming holiday villas; others still have devolved into tatty guesthouses that exude the mustily time-worn aura of a 1950s boarding house.

Yet there is more to Nuwara Eliya than might be suggested by its strong-brewed English tea-plantation architectural legacy and the stiff-upper-lip affectations of its swankier hotels. Indeed, the town today possesses an emphatically Sri Lankan cultural pulse. The population of 45,000 is split more or less evenly between Sinhala Buddhists and Tamil Hindus, supplemented by a sizeable Muslim and smaller Christian minority, though dress codes – sweatshirts, gloves and knitted beanies are understandably de rigueur – require some adjustment coming from the lowlands. So, too, does a chilly but otherwise changeable highland climate that might see swathes of mist giving way to squalls of rain then intervals of sparkling sunshine, all within the space of an hour. And while this may not sound madly appealing to freshly arrived European sun-seekers, the damp and lingering cool can come as a genuine relief after a while in Sri Lanka. And if nothing else, Nuwara Eliya is a strikingly green town. A curvaceous road plan accommodates tea-swathed slopes, several well-wooded parks, a sprawling golf course and the pretty Lake Gregory, while the northern skyline is dominated by the forested slopes of Pidurutalagala, and it is the most normal base for day trips to the lovely Horton Plains National Park.

HISTORY Inhabited at least since the 10th century, Nuwara Eliya first came to prominence in c1610, when the Kandyan monarchy retreated here to escape the attention of the warmongering Portuguese. The town's name (literally 'Royal City of Light') also probably dates to this time. The first British visitor was Dr John Davy, who led a hunting party to the area in 1818, and described it as 'beautiful … possessing a fine climate (certainly a cool climate) … quite deserted by man [and] the domain entirely of wild animals', but noted signs of an ancient irrigation system. Impressed by Davy's description, Governor Edward Barnes built a holiday bungalow (now the iconic Grand Hotel) at Nuwara Eliya in the 1820s and hosted regular parties whose 'riotous folly' did much to attract the colonial elite, and ordered the construction of a road connecting it to Kandy. In 1847, the fledgling settlement was joined by the 26-year-old Samuel Baker, who founded an influential market-gardening community based on the English model (Baker abandoned Ceylon in 1855 following the death of his first wife, Henrietta, but went on to play a major role in the exploration of the Sudanese Nile, accompanied by his second wife, Florence, a feat for which he was knighted in 1866). Important factors in the town's development over the late 19th and early 20th centuries included the emergence of a lucrative tea industry in the surrounding hill country, and the arrival in 1885 of the railway from Colombo at nearby Nanu Oya (between 1905 and 1948, a narrow-gauge track also covered the 6km from Nanu Oya to Nuwara Eliya). The town also thrived as Ceylon's premier tourist resort – a popular 'hill station' providing a cool and healthy retreat to heat-sated residents of Colombo and other coastal towns. So it was that tea planters, estate managers, senior public servants and other wealthy settlers congregated on Nuwara Eliya to build permanent homes or holiday bungalows (as late as 1910, only two Sri Lankans owned houses here). This European-heavy demographic led to the creation of an infrastructure that provided the town not only with the usual civil amenities, but also with such luxuries as racetracks, golf courses, cricket pitches, polo fields, *et al*. Today, tourism, both domestic and international, remains big business in Nuwara Eliya, while tea production remains the main local industry, but the region's fertile soils and precipitative climate ensure it still yields the varied agricultural produce envisaged years ago by Baker.

GETTING THERE AND AWAY

By rail All trains on the Hill Country line connecting Colombo and Kandy to Hatton, Ella and Badulla stop at Nanu Oya, 6km from Nuwara Eliya. Local buses meet the trains at Nanu Oya station and minibus taxis and tuktuks can be hired in the station forecourt for the short drive.

By road Nuwara Eliya lies 165km/3½ hours inland of Colombo via Kitulgala (70km/1½ hours) and Hatton (40km/1 hour); 75km/1½ hours south of Kandy, 255km from Galle via Colombo, 144km/3 hours from Tissamaharama via from Ella (56km/1½ hours) and Bandarawela (45km/1 hour), 50km from Badulla, and 190km from Arugam Bay via Ella. The central bus station is connected to Colombo, Kandy and Badulla by at least one bus every hour, and there are also regular buses to Ella, Bandarawela and Hatton.

WHERE TO STAY
Nuwara Eliya is dedicated to holidaying so there is no shortage of places to stay. In fact the whole town seems to consist of bungalow-style guesthouses of varying quality, though budget accommodation usually costs more than in less popular hill stations such as Haputale and Bandarawela. The listings below are highly selective and exclude several adequate but unexceptional and overpriced colonial-style set-ups in the vicinity of Haddon Hill Road. Nuwara Eliya is often cold at night, so few hotels have air conditioning and many have log fires.

Exclusive

Jetwing Warwick Gardens [map, page 368] (5 rooms) Ambewela, 17km south of the town centre; \011 470 9400, 052 353 2284; e resv. andrews@jetwinghotels.com; w jetwinghotels. com. Set along a rough feeder road *en route* to

Horton Plains, this restored 2-storey granite mansion was constructed in 1880 & stands in a 12ha highland tea estate that offers breathtaking views & utter tranquillity where the only sound is that of birdsong. The individualised rooms are decorated & furnished in period style, while common areas include a library, TV lounge, drawing room with piano, formal dining room with chandelier, b/fast room & flagstone terrace. A butler is on hand, experienced cooks operate in the open kitchen & the manager acts as host & guide for eco-, cultural & agricultural excursions. *From US$339 dbl B&B.* **$$$$$+**

Upmarket

🏠 **Ferncliff** [421 H5] (4 rooms) Wedderburn Rd; **m** 0722 519443; **e** reservations@ferncliff.lk; **w** ferncliff.lk. Set in a large & lushly wooded garden complete with croquet lawn behind Victoria Park, this lovingly restored bungalow was reputedly constructed in 1831 by Governor Edward Barnes, which would make it the oldest substantially unchanged building anywhere in town. There are teak floors throughout, but while the lounge with log fire & other common areas are decorated in period style, the massive guest rooms have a more classic-contemporary feel & come with TV & DVD player. Excellent home-cooked meals & butler service are offered. A fabulous boutique alternative to the larger & more impersonal hotels listed below. *From US$185 dbl B&B.* **$$$$$**

🏠 **Jetwing St Andrew's** [420 A1] (56 rooms) St Andrew's Dr; **** 011 470 9400, 052 222 3031; **e** resv.andrews@jetwinghotels.com; **w** jetwinghotels.com. Built as a British coffee-planter's mansion in 1875, this magnificent mock-Tudor building later served as the Scots Club prior to being converted to a hotel a few years before the outbreak of World War I, when it closed following the arrest of its German owner-manager. It reopened as the St Andrew's Hotel in 1919, was incorporated into the Jetwing group in 1986, & now ranks as the most appealing of Nuwara Eliya's larger colonial-era hotels. Relicts of the original building include the restaurant with its tall copperplate ceiling & terracotta tiled floor, and the old music room (complete with billiard table imported from Calcutta in the 1890s), but the spacious rooms have a classic-contemporary feel, with parquet floor, fireplace & darkwood furniture offset by bright modern fabrics. Rooms in the old wing also have a balcony. The large well-wooded

gardens overlooking the golf course support a good variety of highland birds. *US$180/200 B&B sgl/dbl, or US$255/275 suite.* **$$$$$**

🏠 **Heritance Tea Factory** [map, page 368] (57 rooms) **** 052 555 5000; **e** htf.ebiz.lk@ aitkenspence.lk; **w** heritancehotels.com/teafactory. Resembling a gigantic & thrilling Meccano construction, this unique hotel has been converted from an abandoned tea factory near Kandapola, which stands at an altitude of 2,200m some 16km northeast of Nuwara Eliya. The unchanged factory-like exterior of silver-painted corrugated iron is punctuated with hundreds of tall wooden casement windows. The interior is unconventional. The reception hall, once the drying room, incorporates a steel-latticed atrium, while guest rooms, carved from the old tea-withering lofts, are dominated by woody textures but have carpets to dull the sound of footfalls on the original pine-wood floors. All rooms have a built-in dressing table with wrap-around mirror, bathroom with tub & shower, & expansive view of tea-lined slopes in front of distant hamlets, hills & forest. A fine-dining restaurant serving 7-course meals has been created out of a railway carriage. *From US$249 dbl B&B.* **$$$$$**

🏠 **Grand Hotel** [421 F7] (154 rooms) Grand Hotel Rd; **** 052 222 2881/7; **e** reservations@ grandhotel.lk; **w** grandhotel.tangerinehotels.com. Expanded repeatedly from the holiday bungalow built by Sir Edward Barnes in the 1820s, Nuwara Eliya's oldest hotel has served in that role since 1891 & is now a 3-storey building with two wings & a handsome Tudor façade set in neat flowering gardens opposite the golf course. The bungalow-like entrance of teak & stained-glass panels is probably part of the original Barnes Hall, while a grand staircase, which could have been built for a leading lady to make an impressive entrance, leads upstairs to the spacious guest rooms. Stylish in a rather old-fashioned way, these all have wooden or red-carpeted floors, king-size or twin bed, electric fireplace, dressing table, antique furniture & period décor including black-&-white photos from the colonial era. Because it was built at different times, the hotel is an unplanned warren of rambling corridors that lead to unexpected delights such as an octagonal lounge with mirrored ceilings, walls & coffee tables. Amenities include a health centre & sauna, 3 exceptional restaurants & a billiard room with 3 championship tables. *From US$229/242 sgl/dbl B&B.* **$$$$$**

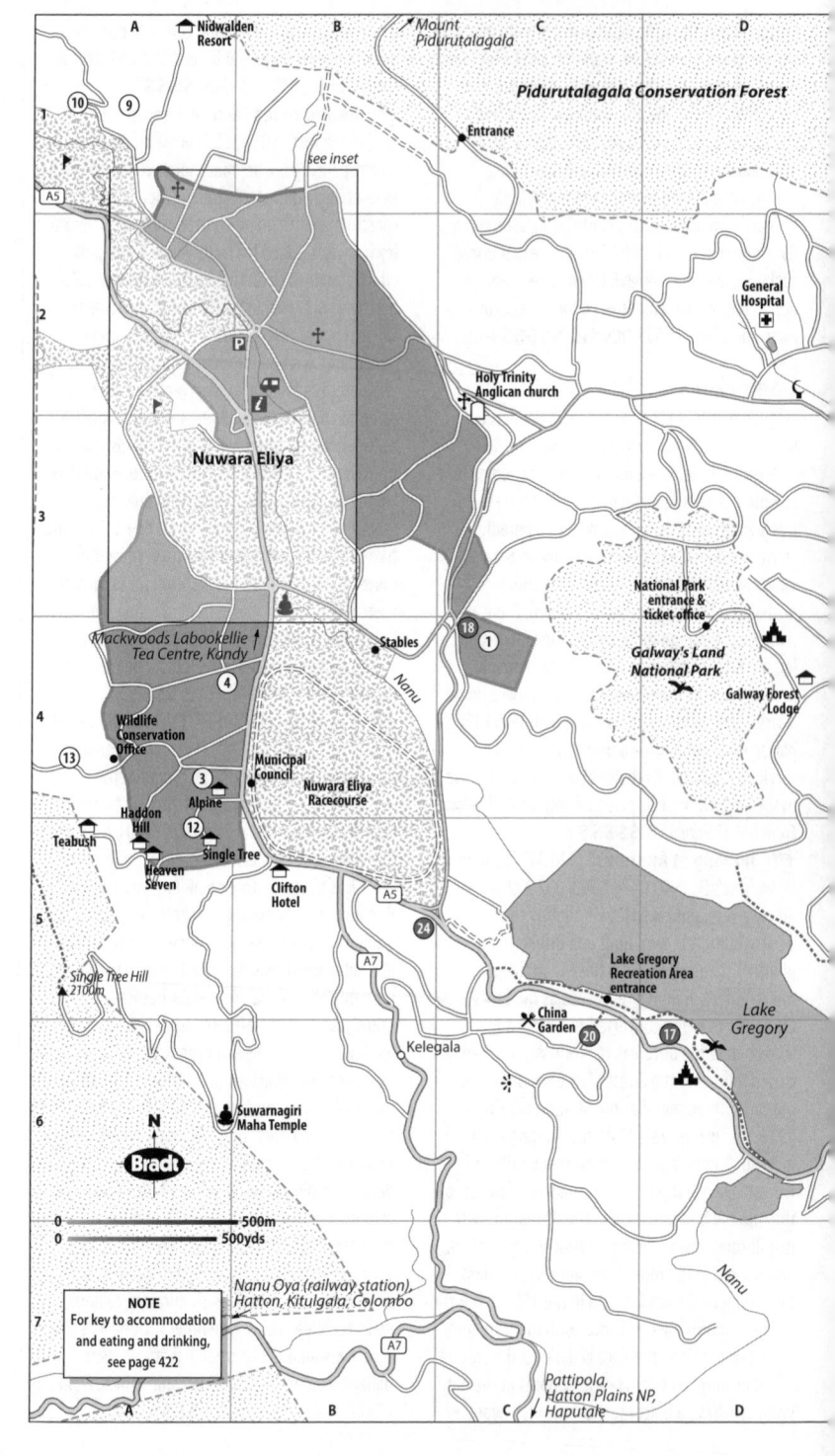

A
B
C
D

Nidwalden Resort

Mount Pidurutalagala

Pidurutalagala Conservation Forest

10 9

1

Entrance

A5

General Hospital

2

Holy Trinity Anglican church

P

i

Nuwara Eliya

3

National Park entrance & ticket office

Mackwoods Labookellie Tea Centre, Kandy

4

Stables

18 1

Galway's Land National Park

Galway Forest Lodge

Wildlife Conservation Office

13

Nanu

Municipal Council

3

Alpine

Nuwara Eliya Racecourse

Haddon Hill

12

Teabush

Single Tree

Heaven Seven

Clifton Hotel

A5

5

24

Lake Gregory Recreation Area entrance

Lake Gregory

Single Tree Hill 2100m

A7

China Garden

20

17

Kelegala

N

Bradt

Suwarnagiri Maha Temple

6

0   500m
0   500yds

7

NOTE
For key to accommodation and eating and drinking, see page 422

Nanu Oya (railway station), Hatton, Kitulgala, Colombo

A7

Nanu

Pattipola, Hatton Plains NP, Haputale

A
B
C
D

420

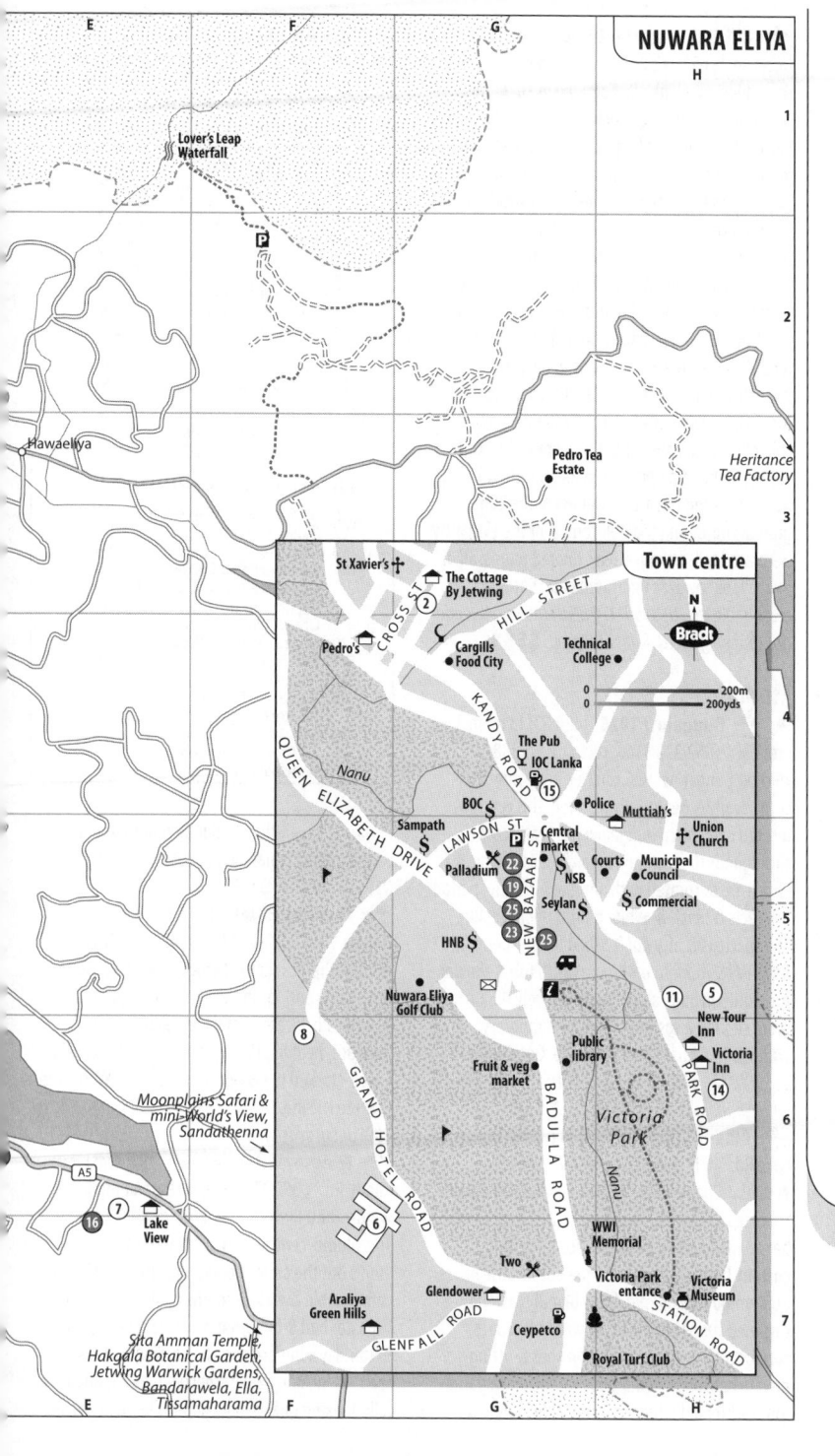

NUWARA ELIYA

Lover's Leap
Waterfall

Hawaeliya

Pedro Tea
Estate

Heritance
Tea Factory

Town centre

St Xavier's
The Cottage
By Jetwing
Pedro's
Cargills
Food City
Technical
College

0   200m
0   200yds

Nanu

The Pub
IOC Lanka
(15)

BOC
Police
Muttiah's
Union
Church

Sampath
Central
market
Courts
Municipal
Council
Palladium
(22)
NSB
Commercial
(19)
Seylan
(25)
(23) (25)

HNB

Nuwara Eliya
Golf Club

(11) (5)
New Tour
Inn
(8)
Public
library
Victoria
Inn
(14)

Moonplains Safari &
mini-World's View,
Sandathenna

Fruit & veg
market

Victoria
Park

Nanu

(16) (7)
Lake
View

(6)

WWI
Memorial

Two
Victoria Park
entrance
Victoria
Museum

Araliya
Green Hills
Glendower
Ceypetco

Sita Amman Temple,
Hakgala Botanical Garden,
Jetwing Warwick Gardens,
Bandarawela, Ella,
Tissamaharama

Royal Turf Club

High Hill Country   NUWARA ELIYA

15

Hill Club [421 F6] (40 rooms) Grand Hotel Rd; ☎052 222 2653; e hillclub@sltnet. lk; w hillclubsrilanka.lk. Founded in 1876, this Gothic neighbour to the Grand takes the Nuwara Eliya hotel industry's English-colonial fixation to dementedly haughty extremes, with its country-club members/foreigners-only policy, after-19.00 tie-&-jacket dress code, hushed library stacked with ageing tomes, old-style wooden-floored & -ceilinged banquet hall, & fabulously gloomy billiards room adorned with a menagerie of trophy heads & cue holder made from a genuine elephant foot. Despite a few concessions to modernity (wenches can now raise a glass in what was formerly a male-only bar, the TV lounge has a DVD collection), it all feels slightly creepy or brilliantly surreal, depending on your mood, but there's no questioning the attractiveness of the 10ha grounds bordering the golf course, or the elegantly decorated tall-ceilinged teak-floored rooms, all of which look towards Pidurutalagala. Rates are very reasonable too. *US$150/170 B&B standard/superior dbl, dropping by 10% out of season.* **$$$$**

Moderate

✱ **Bungalow 1926** [420 G3] (3 rooms) Cross St; ☎052 222 3168; m 0773 572288; e info@bungalow1926.com; w bungalow1926. com. Newly & beautifully restored, this centrally located Edwardian bungalow has teak floors throughout the common areas & guest rooms, which are decorated with antique furniture, period artefacts & black-&-white photos of old Ceylon. The spacious & airy dbl & 5-bed family rooms all have TVs & modern bathrooms with tub & shower. Amenities include a pool room & lovely dining room serving a cosmopolitan contemporary menu with most mains in the **$$** range. Good value. *US$100/175 dbl/family room, or US$350 for the whole bungalow sleeping up to 12.* **$$$**

Albany Villas [420 C4] (4 rooms) Upper Lake Rd; ☎011 451 6364; m 0777 586434; e sales@albany.villas; w albany.villas. Expanded from an old colonial house on a quiet back road between Victoria Park & the race track, this custom-built 3-storey boutique guesthouse offers accommodation in massive & blandly tasteful carpeted suites with loads of wardrobe space, comfortable seating, quality finishes & fittings, & private balconies. Common areas include a games room with pool table, a comfortable lounge &

library, & a teak-floored dining room serving a varied international menu in the **$$$** range. *US$150 dbl B&B.* **$$$$**

The Rock Hotel [420 A4] (10 rooms) Unique View Rd; ☎052 567 9002; m 0713 230290; e info@therock.lk; w therock.lk. Among the best-value options in this range, this quite smart & scenically located hotel has modern rooms with fireplace, heaters, TV, DVD & tea/coffee, as well as a well-stocked bar & restaurant serving Western & Chinese cuisine. *US$61/72 sgl/dbl B&B, dropping by 10% out of season.* **$$$**

Windsor Hotel [421 G4] (49 rooms) Kandy Rd; ☎052 222 2554; e reservations@ windsorhotellk.com; w windsorhotellk.com. This plumb-central stalwart was founded in the 1950s but the current building dates to 1981. The comfortable & well-lit rooms with parquet floor, 4-poster bed & bay windows have seen slightly better days, but are priced accordingly. Other features include a skylit courtyard rock garden, the jolly-looking guests-only Rogue Elephant Bar, &

a licensed restaurant serving a varied selection of local & international snacks (**$$**) & mains (**$$$**). *US$62/84 sgl/dbl B&B, with hefty discounts offered to walk-ins, assuming availability.* **$$$**

⌂ **Ceybank Rest** [420 A4] (19 rooms) Badulla Rd; ☎ 052 222 3855; e ceybank_ne@sltnet. lk; w ceybankholidayhomes.com. Formerly the Heritage Hotel, this handsome 2-storey Victorian mansion opposite the race track, now operated by the Bank of Ceylon, is a good option for travellers seeking a colonial-themed experience at moderate prices. The spacious wood-floored rooms & suites, though a little frayed at the edges, reflect the stylish solid décor of the Edwardian era, & the charm & willingness of the staff create a personalised atmosphere. *US$83 dbl B&B, dropping to US$70 out of season.* **$$$**

Budget

✴ ⌂ **King Fern Cottage** [420 A1] (10 rooms) St Andrews Dr; ☎ 052 490 0503; m 0773 586284; e kingferncottage@yahoo.com; w kingferncottage. com. Set on the edge of the golf course, this magical owner-managed boutique guesthouse is entered via a beautiful wood- & glass-dominated lounge & dining area that makes the most of the lush surrounds & serves a varied selection of pasta dishes, curries & other mains in the **$$** range. From here a labyrinthine warren of paths & babbling stream lead through a veritable zen-garden of giant ferns & pot plants to the bright & artsy rooms, which have wooden floors, boldly painted walls, comfortable queen-size beds & modern bathrooms. Bikes & scooters available to rent. Call in advance to arrange a free pick-up from the bus station. Top value. *US$20/30 sgl/dbl, plus US$3–4 pp b/fast.* **$$**

✴ ⌂ **Trevene Hotel** [421 H6] (10 rooms) Park Rd; ☎ 052 222 2767; m 0722 304220; e nisa264@gmail.com; w hoteltrevenenuwaraeliya.com. Overlooking Victoria Park 300m south of the town centre, this characterful colonial bungalow, built as a governor's residence in 1834, is set in manicured flowering gardens so large & steep there's a hairpin bend in the driveway. Restored & decorated in period style, the house still boasts its original teak floors, marble fireplaces & wood-panelled walls, & the large comfortable rooms have tall wood ceilings & bathrooms with tub or shower. The live-in owner-managers speak good English & French, & offer local & international cuisine in

the **$$–$$$** range on the sunny glassed-in veranda. Free pick-up from anywhere in town. Very reasonably priced. *US$30/37 B&B sgl/dbl, dropping to US$20/30 in low season.* **$$**

✴ ⌂ **Heidi's Home** [421 E6] (5 rooms) Off Badulla Rd; ☎ 052 454 5013; m 0777 699042; e heidihome1@gmail.com; w heidishomestay.com. In refreshing contrast to the stuffy colonial aesthetic typical of Nuwara Eliya, this family homestay near the southeast tip of Lake Gregory evokes late-60s Marrakesh, with an eclectic décor of colourful scatter cushions, luxuriant pot plants & antique furniture that shouldn't really work as well as it does. The warm & friendly live-in owner-managers speak excellent English & are a great source of local travel leads. A small but pretty garden offers views to the lake & they can also arrange yoga lessons & home-cooked Chinese or Sri Lankan meals. Neat rooms vary in size but are all well tended & comfortable. The only negative of this otherwise charming set-up is the non-central location 2km from the town centre. *US$35–47 B&B dbl.* **$$–$$$**

⌂ **Richmond Inn** [420 A5] (11 rooms) Haddon Hill Rd; ☎ 052 222 3304; m 0712 087578; f HaddonHillInn. Rooms in this restored colonial building are variable in size & comfort but all come with wood panel flooring, period furniture & a large TV. Decent value. *US$40–50 dbl B&B, depending on size.* **$$–$$$**

Shoestring

⌂ **Park View Guesthouse** [421 H5] (6 rooms) Park Rd; ☎ 052 222 2767; m 0773 456345; e guesthouseparkview@gmail.com; w parkviewnuwaraeliya.com. The standout option in this range, this converted 2-storey house stands in large well-tended gardens & offers great views of Victoria Park from the common upstairs balcony. There's a common TV lounge & garden seating, & the management can arrange day tours to most local sites of interest. The large, clean & comfortable rooms feel a little damp & old-fashioned, but they are still good value at the price. *US$17 dbl, dropping to US$13 out of season.* **$**

⌂ **Carnation Rest** [420 A4] (10 rooms) Unique View Rd; ☎ 052 222 3630; m 0777 175452; e carnationrest.nuwaraeliya@gmail.com. This clean, friendly & comfortable guesthouse has small but brightly decorated rooms with modern bathrooms & TV. Good value for Nuwara Eliya. *US$23 dbl, dropping slightly out of season.* **$**

✖ WHERE TO EAT AND DRINK
Town centre
New Bazaar Street is lined with half a dozen small & inexpensive unlicensed eateries that cater primarily to locals but are regularly frequented by tourists. All are quite basic, with interiors designed to evoke the heebie-jeebies in fussier or more hygiene-obsessed travellers, but the food is generally tasty & prices are very low. If the places listed below are too down to earth for your tastes, or you fancy washing down a more Westernised meal with some beer or wine, then the best — make that only — central option is the terraced restaurant at the Windsor Hotel. Part of the same hotel, the gloomy but cheaper basement Lion Bar has a separate street entrance & caters to a more local clientele.

✳ ✖ **Sri Ambaal's Vegetarian Restaurant** [421 G5] New Bazaar St; ⊕ 07.00–20.30. 2 restaurants of this name stand more or less opposite each other on the main street, both under the same Hindu ownership & serving similar menus to a predominantly Tamil clientele that wouldn't all fit into one or the other. The lunchtime buffet is strongly recommended, but it's also a great place to try string hoppers, filled rotis, thosai 'pancakes' & other Indian-influenced specialities. $

✖ **Remarko Bakery & Restaurant** [421 G5] New Bazaar St; ☎052 223 5490; ⊕ 06.00–21.30. The main attraction here is the excellent & very inexpensive lunchtime rice-&-curry buffet (vegetarian, chicken or fish) but it also has an à la carte selection, a display cabinet laden with filled buns, burgers, pizzas slices & such, as well as juices & cakes. $

✖ **De Silva Food Centre** [421 G5] New Bazaar St; ☎052 222 3833; ⊕ 08.15–21.30. This long-serving & affordable main-street eatery has bright modern décor & is well known for its burgers & fries, but it also serves a good selection of local dishes such as kottu roti, devilled dishes, curries & fried rice. $

✖ **Milano Restaurant** [421 G5] New Bazaar St; ☎052 222 2763; ⊕ 07.30–22.00. This central restaurant has a snack-oriented ground floor serving a varied selection of filled rolls, cakes & juices, while the upstairs specialises in Chinese, Sri Lankan & Western mains. Nothing special but good value. No alcohol. $

South of the town centre
Standalone restaurants are few in suburban Nuwara Eliya, & most of what does exist is on the patchy side. There are plenty of hotel restaurants, most notably the excellent & very well-priced trio affiliated to the Grand Hotel which are listed below. Restaurants at the Jetwing St Andrew's & Hill Club are also good but pricier.

✳ ✖ **Salmiya** [420 B5] Badulla Rd; m 0779 135263; ⊕ 11.00–21.00. It doesn't look much from the outside, but this modest hut (currently opposite the race track, but likely to relocate soon) serves delicious pizzas with a thin crusty base ($$$), as well as great pasta & burgers ($$). Seating is limited to a handful of plastic tables, & all meals are prepared by the friendly owner-manager, so speed of service depends on how busy it is. No alcohol.

✳ ✖ **Grand Indian** [421 F7] Grand Hotel Rd; ☎052 222 2881; ⊕ noon–15.30 & 18.30–22.00. Probably the most popular tourist restaurant in town, this well-priced & perpetually busy annex to the Grand Hotel has indoor & outdoor seating, a full bar, & a varied selection of vegetarian, mutton, chicken & seafood curries, birianis & other North Indian dishes. $$$

✖ **Grand Thai** [421 F7] Grand Hotel; ☎052 222 2881; ⊕ noon–15.30 & 19.00–22.30. Set inside the Grand Hotel, this excellent Thai restaurant has plenty of ambience & it's more affordable than you'd have any reason to expect. Signature dishes include stir-fried chicken with cashew, seafood fried rice & pineapple fried rice. Fully licensed. $$$

✖ **Grand Coffee Bar** [421 F7] Grand Hotel Rd; ☎052 222 2881; ⊕ 07.00–19.00. Situated next to the Grand Indian, Nuwara Eliya's best coffee shop also serves iced drinks, juices & a mouthwatering array of cakes, savoury pastries, mini-pizzas & the like. $

✖ **Indian Summer Restaurant** [421 E6] Badulla Rd; ☎052 222 4411; w indiansummerlk. com; ⊕ 11.00–22.00. Opened in 2016, this branch of its well-established Colombo namesake overlooks Lake Gregory about 2km southeast of the town centre & has a varied pan-Asian menu specialising in North Indian & fusion cuisine. The food is excellent but portions are small & it's pricey for Nuwara Eliya. No alcohol. $$$$

✖ **Hansa Coffee Store** [420 C6] Fife Rd; ☎052 223 4370; w srilankacoffee.com; ⊕ 09.00–17.00. This outlet for Sri Lanka's only gourmet coffee producer serves (& sells) its own blends of black coffee & espresso (*around US$1*) at this little shop overlooking Lake Gregory, as well as inexpensive cakes, sandwiches & paninis. No alcohol. **$**

✕ Adma Agro Strawberries [421 E7] Badulla Rd; **m** 0777 293299; ⏱ 07.00–19.00. Offering a view over Lake Gregory, this unusual eatery specialises in strawberries grown on site & served fresh or coated in chocolate, blended into a milkshake or smoothie, or as the primary ingredient in a filled pancake or, um, 'strawberry spaghetti cake'. No alcohol. **$**

✕ Calamander Restaurant [420 D6] Badulla Rd; 052 223 4967; ⏱ 07.00–21.30. On paper this place has everything going for it: an attractive location on the shore of Lake Gregory, bright contemporary décor, choice of indoor or outdoor seating & cosmopolitan menu of filled baguettes, salads, devilled dishes, pizzas & Asian fusion specialities in the **$$$** range. Unfortunately, the standard of food is very erratic, though even on an off-day it offers the opportunity to enjoy a chilled beer or glass of wine alongside the pretty lake.

⛾ Club Trout [420 C4] Upper Lake Rd; **m** 0778 831777; **f**; ⏱ 08.00–late. This sporadically lively wood-panelled pool bar west of Victoria Park is a pleasant enough spot for a drink, & there's even occasional live music, but the selection of food is limited to non-existent.

OTHER PRACTICALITIES Most of the main nationwide banks are represented in the town centre, including branches of the Commercial [421 H5], Sampath [421 G5] and HNB [421 G5] with ATMs. For grocery shopping, the historic Cargills Food City [421 G4] (⏱ *08.00–21.00*) is well stocked and there's a wine shop attached. Fresh produce can also be bought at the busy little market [421 G6] on New Bazaar Street.

WHAT TO SEE AND DO

In and around town The attractions described below lie either within the city limits or – in the case of Single Tree Hill – within realistic walking distance of the town centre.

Old Town Centre The most important of the triangle of roads at the core of the commercial town centre, New Bazaar Street runs south from the Windsor Hotel to the bus station, and is lined with lively local eateries and small shops. At its north end, the covered central market complex [421 G5] (⏱ *09.00–19.30*), tucked away between the shops and entered through a passageway, is a fascinating little warren, whose chatty stallholders sell meat and fish, as well as vegetables. The area is studded with colonial buildings dating to the late 19th and early 20th centuries. Opposite the bus station, on the junction with Queen Elizabeth Drive, stands the striking Victorian post office [421 G5], a bright pink mock-Tudor building that was constructed in 1894 and comprises two storeys topped by a prominent clock spire. Another prominent Victorian landmark, the Cargills Food City [421 G4] on St Andrew's Street, 300m north of the Windsor Hotel, is housed in the original building acquired by its namesake when it bought out James McLaren & Co in 1898. A pair of bronze signs outside the heavy wooden doors advertise everything an Edwardian shopper might need – Smoker's Requisites, Fishing Tackle, Fancy Goods and the like – while the warehouse-like wood-floored interior still incorporates a 'Chemists & Druggists', as well as what appears to be the town's only liquor store. The oldest place of worship in the town centre is the austere St Xavier's Church [421 G3], which was built on Cross Street over 1838–48. There is also an attractive old Buddhist temple at the south end of New Bazaar Street.

Nuwara Eliya Golf Club [421 G5] (\ *052 222 2835*; **e** *negolf@sltnet.lk*; **w** *nuwaraeliyagolfclub.com*) Established in 1889, this is one of the oldest golf clubs in Asia and the centrepiece of a lovely par-71 18-hole golf course that extends over

40ha immediately west of the old town centre. Golfers of all ages and abilities are welcome to play a round, which costs around US$50 per person inclusive of caddy fees and club rental. Non-golfers might be willing to pay the temporary membership fee of US$3.50 just to soak up the ambience of the 19th-century clubhouse, which incorporates a wood-panelled bar, decent little restaurant, badminton hall and billiards room. The grounds also house the neglected remains of the original British cemetery, which formed the burial place of Major T W Rogers, an empire-builder who claimed to have shot dead more than 1,300 elephants before he was killed by a lightning strike at a resthouse near Haputale in 1845.

Holy Trinity Church [420 C2] (*Church Rd;* \ *052 222 2344;* ☉ *09.00–noon & 15.00–18.00; communion 08.00 Sun*) Initiated in 1845, consecrated in 1852 and enlarged in the 1890s, this imposing white Gothic church stands in large wooded hillside grounds about 300m east of the town centre. The sombre and timeworn interior has an impressive arched roof and old timber floor, and it incorporates a 19th-century pipe-organ that was restored in 2001, several old memorial plaques, and a stained-glass window commemorating the 1954 service attended by Queen Elizabeth II and the Duke of Edinburgh. The overgrown cemetery, shaded by fir trees and seasonally coloured by blooming poppies, evokes an English village graveyard below the cloudy skies not untypical of Nuwara Eliya. It is the last resting place of a couple of hundred colonial-era settlers, including members of Samuel Baker's family, Lady Olive Mary Caldecott (wife of Sir Andrew Caldecott, the last Governor of Ceylon) and Lindsay Wright, who started a mail-coach service at Nuwara Eliya in the 1860s, and later owned St Andrew's Hotel and served as managing director of the Grand Hotel.

Victoria Park [421 H6] (*Udupussellawa Rd;* m *0777 354648;* ☉ *07.00–18.00; entrance US$2*) Initially established as a research field centre for Hakgala Botanical Garden, this 11ha park was renamed in honour of Queen Victoria and opened to the public to commemorate her diamond jubilee in 1897. It is flowed through by the Nanu River, a babbling stream that's diverted into a succession of pretty lily-covered ponds, and supports a riot of colourful flowers that bloom most profusely over March–May and August–September, with the best displays usually occurring in April. The small museum (☉ *closed Sun*) at the southern gate displays old black-and-white photos of Nuwara Eliya in its colonial prime. Victoria Park can also be a rewarding site for birdwatchers. The endemic yellow-eared bulbul, Sri Lanka white-eye and dull-blue flycatcher are resident and likely be seen at any time of year, along with the uncommon and localised grey-headed canary flycatcher and velvet-fronted nuthatch, while noteworthy migrants regularly encountered between November and March include Indian pitta, pied thrush, Indian blue robin, Kashmir flycatcher and forest wagtail. Whether you're into birds or just want to enjoy the park at its most tranquil, avoid weekends and try to be here as soon as possible after it opens, before the crowds descend to blithely ignore signposts requesting them to 'drop garbage in kept bins' while being admirably behoving of instructions to 'behave decently'.

Nuwara Eliya Racecourse [420 B4] (*Badulla Rd;* \ *011 302 4524;* w *royalturfclub. com*). Sri Lanka's last remaining horse-racing venue was laid out in its present form, with a 1,800m circumference and 333m straight, in 1900, but it has its roots in a training course that was established in the 1840s by John Baker, the brother of Samuel, and later formalised as a Gymkhana Club that held its inaugural race meeting in 1875. The course fell into disuse between 1956, when horse racing was banned countrywide, but it reopened in 1981 when the activity was legalised. The most prestigious race held here today is the Governor's Cup, which was first contested at the now defunct Colombo Racecourse in 1833 and takes place on or around 14 April (Sinhala and Tamil New Year). Other races also take place in February, April, August and December and ticket prices start at US$1.50; see the website above for pending fixtures. In front of the race track, the Municipal Council compound is the site of a tree planted in 1937 to commemorate the coronation of King George VI.

Lake Gregory [420 D5–6] Extending over 90ha southeast of the racecourse, this pretty reservoir was constructed in 1873 by damming a small river that rises on Mount Pidurutalagala, and named after the then-Governor of Ceylon. The lake was originally created as a source of drinking water, but has also long been used for recreational purposes – it was first stocked with trout back in 1881 – and in 1913 its outflow was diverted to a hydro-electric plant that still powers the town to this day. Lake Gregory also now forms the centrepiece of a grassy park (*entrance US$1.50*) where activities such as horseriding, jet-skiing and paddle-boating are offered to domestic tourists for round US$7 a pop, and motorboat trips cost around US$15, but foreigners tend to be asked monumentally inflated (and very downwardly negotiable) rates. Alternatively, the lakeside Calamander Restaurant (page 425) is perfectly positioned to enjoy the fun and games over a coffee, beer or light meal.

Galway's Land National Park [420 D4] (*Havelock Rd; ⏰ 06.00–17.00; entrance US$10 pp plus VAT*) Set aside as a forest reserve in 1938 and upgraded to national park status in 2007, this 30ha stand of pristine suburban forest was acquired in the late 19th century by Colonel Galway, who protected it as a private conservation area for several decades prior to donating it to the colonial government on condition it would continue to be conserved 'for the sake of unknown generations of the Ceylonese'. It is home to a small population of secretive red muntjac deer (listen out for their distinctive bark), as well as wild boar and giant squirrel – but oddly no monkeys or flying squirrels – as well as an interesting selection of highland butterflies and lizards. The main point of interest, however, is the birdlife, which includes ten endemic species, most conspicuously Sri Lanka junglefowl, yellow-eared bulbul, dull-blue flycatcher and Sri Lanka white-eye, but also Sri Lanka wood pigeon, Sri Lanka bush warbler, Sri Lanka hill myna, Sri Lanka whistling thrush, spot-winged thrush and Sri Lanka scaly thrush. Other birds commonly seen here include grey-headed canary flycatcher and (between November and March) same Himalayan migrants listed for Victoria Park. Amenities are limited to a 1km walking trail, which is best taken slowly, and very quietly, as soon as possible after it opens in the morning. You are unlikely to see much without binoculars, and the low level of wildlife activity makes it less than ideal for children.

The national park lies 2.5km from the town centre by road. The most direct route coming from the Badulla Road entails following the Udupussellawa Road east past Victoria Park for about 500m to a rather confusing five-way junction overlooked by Club Trout. Here, you need to veer northeast along Havelock Road, which leads into the forest after about 600m and reaches the ticket office after another 400m. An alternative and better-known route entails turning south on to Upper Lake Road at the five-way junction, but this road circles south and east of the forest for 2.5km before it brings you to the ticket office.

Single Tree Hill [420 A5] Although the namesake tree has given way to a fenced-off copse of satellite towers and antennae, this 2,100m peak, reputedly the ninth tallest in Sri Lanka, offers fabulous views over Nuwara Eliya and Lake Gregory to forest-swathed Mount Pidurutalagala, as well as distant glimpses of Adam's Peak 30km to the southwest on clear days. Only 1.5km southwest of the town centre as the crow flies, the summit is roughly twice as far away on foot, making it a perfect goal for a brisk but undemanding morning or afternoon leg stretch (allow up to 90 minutes in either direction from the town centre). To get here, follow Badulla Road south from Victoria Park for about 750m, with the racecourse to your left, then turn right on to Scur State Road immediately before the Clifton Hotel. From here, the road switchbacks uphill through tea plantations for 2.5km to the summit, passing the Suwarnagiri Maha Temple about halfway up. A guide isn't necessary but female travellers are advised against walking up alone. The ascent road is quite rough and narrow in parts but perfectly doable by tuktuk.

Further afield The places listed below all make for worthwhile half-day excursions out of Nuwara Eliya, and can be reached on public transport and/or by tuktuk. Another popular goal for a day excursion, covered separately later in the chapter, is Horton Plains National Park (pages 430–5).

Mount Pidurutalagala [map, page 368] The tallest mountain in Sri Lanka, Pidurutalagala rises to a 2,524m summit immediately north of Nuwara Eliya, where its upper slopes are protected in an eponymous forest reserve. Anglicised to Mount Pedro in colonial times, Pidurutalagala is a Sinhala name that means 'straw-covered rock', a reference to the yellow-brown hue attained by the flat grassy summit towards the end of the dry season, though a more notable feature of the slopes above Nuwara Eliya is the extensive cover of more or less pristine montane rainforest. Wildlife includes a few secretive leopards, some more conspicuous troops of purple-faced langurs, a variety of squirrels, and a wide range of highland forest birds, including all the endemics and other species associated with Galway's Land. A 7km footpath to the top of Mount Pedro was pioneered back in 1897, after which it became a popular goal for a hike or horseback excursion, though ladies were often borne up on a sedan chair supported by two bamboo poles and carried by four bearers.

The summit of Pidurutalagala is now the site of a military communications centre and high-altitude training camp, and as such the whole mountain was off limits to the public for many years. It recently reopened and entrance is free, but you need to show your passport at the entrance gate, and the sealed road to the summit may not be tackled on foot or by bicycle or tuktuk, only in a closed vehicle (ostensibly owing to the danger posed by leopards, though military security seems a more likely reason). This restriction reduces the likelihood of seeing shy forest birds and other wildlife, but even so it's a truly lovely ascent, as the road switchbacks through a lush tangle of gnarled evergreen trees draped in old man's beard lichen, giant tree ferns and flowering rhododendrons, a-swirl with atmospheric mist or offering fabulous views back towards town, depending on the weather. Unless you're a fan of military architecture or satellite towers, the summit itself is likely to prove anticlimactic, while peak-baggers will be frustrated to learn that the tallest peak – indeed, the geographic highpoint of all Sri Lanka – is guarded by a no-entry sign. Fortunately, the views compensate.

To get to Pidurutalagala from the town centre, follow Sri Jayathilaka Road north from the main circle, turning sharply to the right after 500m, then left after another 500m at the signpost for Pidurutalagala Base Complex, until you reach the entrance gate (signposted Pidurutalagala Conservation Forest), which is where you need to show your passport. From here it is another 5.5km to the summit. A taxi from the town centre should ask around US$15–20 for the round trip, including waiting time at the summit. The mountain is clearest in the early morning, so visit as soon as possible after the entrance gate opens (theoretically 07.00, but often only 07.30).

Pedro Tea Estate [421 G3] (📞 042 222 2016; ⏰ 08.00–17.00) Flanking the Udupussellawa Road 3km out of town, Sri Lanka's highest tea estate was reputedly established in 1886 by James Taylor, the Scotsman who planted the island's first commercial tea crop near Kandy 20 years earlier. Guided factory tours take 30 minutes and cost US$1.35 per person (photography forbidden), while the Lover's Leap Ethical Tea Boutique sells a selection of the estate's teas, which it claims to be the cleanest in the world. Most people charter a tuktuk to the estate, which costs US$2–3 including waiting time, but you could also board a Kandapola bus out of Nuwara Eliya, hop off at the junction, and walk the last 500m.

Lover's Leap Waterfall [421 F1] Whether visited in isolation or together with the nearby Pedro Tea Estate, this narrow 30m waterfall, set in a wooded gorge on the southern slopes of Pidurutalagala, is one of the prettiest in the vicinity of Nuwara Eliya and it also offers great views back towards town. Its name dates back to ancient times when, according to legend, a young prince was forbidden from marrying the beautiful peasant girl he loved, and the two leaped to their death from the top. To get here, follow the Udupussellawa Road out of town for 3km, turn left opposite Pedro Tea Estate, and follow the signposts for another 1.5km to the flat grassy area that passes for a car park, only 5 minutes' walk from the waterfall's base. As with Pedro Tea Estate, you can bus to the junction and walk from there, or just catch a tuktuk directly from town (*around US$4*). If you opt for the former, ignore the tuktuk drivers who lurk around the junction claiming it's 5km to the waterfall and ask wildly inflated prices (*up to US$10*) to take people there.

Mackwoods Labookellie Tea Centre [map, page 368] (📞 052 223 6306; e *tea@mackwoodstea.com*; w *mackwoodstea.com*; ⏰ 08.30–18.30) Flanking the Kandy road 15km northwest of Nuwara Eliya, Mackwoods's venerable Labookellie Estate conducts free tea-factory tours throughout the day and you can have a nice cup of tea (just pay for the chocolate cake) in the tea café and garden. The different grades of High Grown tea are displayed in a glass case on the counter, and Labookellie single-estate tea can be bought from the sales centre.

Sita Amma Temple [map, page 368] Situated alongside the Badulla Road 8km southeast of Nuwara Eliya, this burnished Hindu temple stands at Sita Eliya (Light of Sita), which is said to be where Sita, the wife of Prince Rama, was held captive by the demonic Ravana for several years prior to her rescue by the monkey-god Hanuman. Reputedly the only temple in the world dedicated to Sita, it is a modern building adorned with several brightly painted statues of Hanuman and other Hindu deities. The temple's most sacred feature, carved into the rocky stream below the temple, is a quartet of natural pot-holes, supposedly arranged in the shape of a gigantic monkey's paw print, and claimed to have been made by Hanuman when he rescued Sita. Any Badulla- or Welimada-bound bus can drop you at Sita Eliya, and the temple can also be visited *en route* to Hakgala.

Hakgala Botanical Garden [map, page 368] (📞 052 222 2182; ⏰ 07.30–17.00; *entrance US$10 pp*) Legend associates this lovely botanical garden with Ashok Vatika, the beautiful pleasure garden that the demon-king Ravana crafted for Sita when he held her captive at nearby Sita Eliya. In its modern incarnation, Hakgala was established in 1861 to test-grow *Cinchona succirubra*, a South American tree whose bark is a source of anti-malarial quinine, and then remodelled as a 28ha botanical garden specialising in montane flora in 1884. It has a fabulous location below Hakgala (Jaw Rock), a 2,200m-high mountaintop formation that legendarily formed part of the Himalayan rock carried to Sri Lanka by Hanuman and dropped at various sites around the island. This hillside location means that the garden is landscaped on several different levels. Features include a fernery dominated by 10m-high tree ferns, a Japanese rock garden constructed in 1921 around a natural spring, an arboretum with labelled trees from all around the world, a superb wild orchid collection, and several ponds fed by a trio of mountain streams running through the property. It is also an exceptional birdwatching site, thanks in part to the large tract of natural forest protected in the contiguous Hakgala Strict Nature Reserve. All the key endemics and migrants associated with Galway's Land and Victoria Park occur here, along with the endemic Sri Lanka blue magpie, brown-capped babbler and orange-billed babbler, and localised Legge's hawk-eagle and rufous-bellied eagle. The relatively broken vegetation makes it quite easy to observe forest fringe birds, while other visible wildlife includes purple-faced langur, toque macaque and giant squirrel. Floral displays are most rewarding over March–May, peaking in April, while birdlife is most prolific over November–March.

Hakgala Botanical Garden stands on the south side of the Badulla Road 9.5km southeast of central Nuwara Eliya. Any bus headed to Welimada or Badulla can drop you at the entrance, or you could charter a tuktuk. Several kilometres of footpaths lead to all corners of the botanical garden, which takes several hours to explore in full. Motorised golf carts are also available at the entrance to take you around.

Moon Plains [421 F6] (**m** *0776 349141;* ◻ ◷ *07.00–17.00*). Also known by the local name Sandathenna or more hyperbolically as the mini-World's View, this panoramic viewpoint 9km southeast of central Nuwara Eliya provides a view of Sri Lanka's three highest peaks on a clear day. Now a municipal reserve, it is touted with some veracity as a quick-fix scenic alternative to World's View at Horton Plains National Park, and more exaggeratedly as a safari experience offering potential sightings of leopard, buffalo, Sambar deer and 100-plus bird species including 16 endemics. In practice, the brusque 3km jeep ride between ticket office and viewpoint, though pleasant enough in itself, provides limited opportunities for wildlife viewing or birdwatching, and seems like poor value at the inflated foreigners' rate of US$3.50 per person entrance plus US$35 per party. To get here from the town centre, follow the Badulla Road to the southern end of Lake Gregory, then turn left at Magastota Junction, then right after 300m into Upper Lake Road, and right again after another 600m into to an unnamed road that leads to the ticket office after 1km.

HORTON PLAINS NATIONAL PARK

[map, opposite] (◻ *011 288 8585;* ◷ *06.00–18.00 (ticket office closes 16.00); entrance US$15 pp, plus US$8 service charge per party, plus 12% tax*) Gazetted in 1988, the 31.6km² Horton Plains National Park protects a biodiverse watershed of montane grassland and dwarf forest perched at elevations of greater than 2,100m above the southern escarpment. Its best-known geographic feature is the sheer World's End Viewpoint, which offers a spectacular vista over hills and valleys to the distant south coast, and forms the focal point of a popular 9km walking trail. A UNESCO World Heritage Site since 2010, the national park also incorporates the island's second- and third-highest peaks in the form of the 2,395m Kirigalpotha and 2,357m Thotupola, both of which are accessible to hikers, though neither is as prominent as Adam's Peak 30km to the west. The evocative highland scenery is very different from anywhere else in Sri Lanka: the undulating windswept plains possess a haunting melancholy air reminiscent of Scotland's grouse moors, while interspersing pockets of elfin cloudforest, all gnarled boughs encrusted with old-man's-beard lichen, have the enchanted quality of a fairy-tale setting. Biodiversity is high, with shaggy-coated sambar deer being the most conspicuous large mammal, but the park also supports a large number of endemic birds and other wildlife, most quite difficult to see on a short visit. The national park receives an average annual precipitation of around 5,000mm, with rain falling throughout the year, though October–April are usually the driest months and the best time to visit. Overnight frost is a common occurrence in December and January, the coldest months.

HISTORY AND CONSERVATION The oldest-known evidence of cereal cultivation in Sri Lanka comes in the form of 16,000–17,500-year-old oat and barley pollen discovered at Horton Plains. It is believed that the ancient culture responsible for

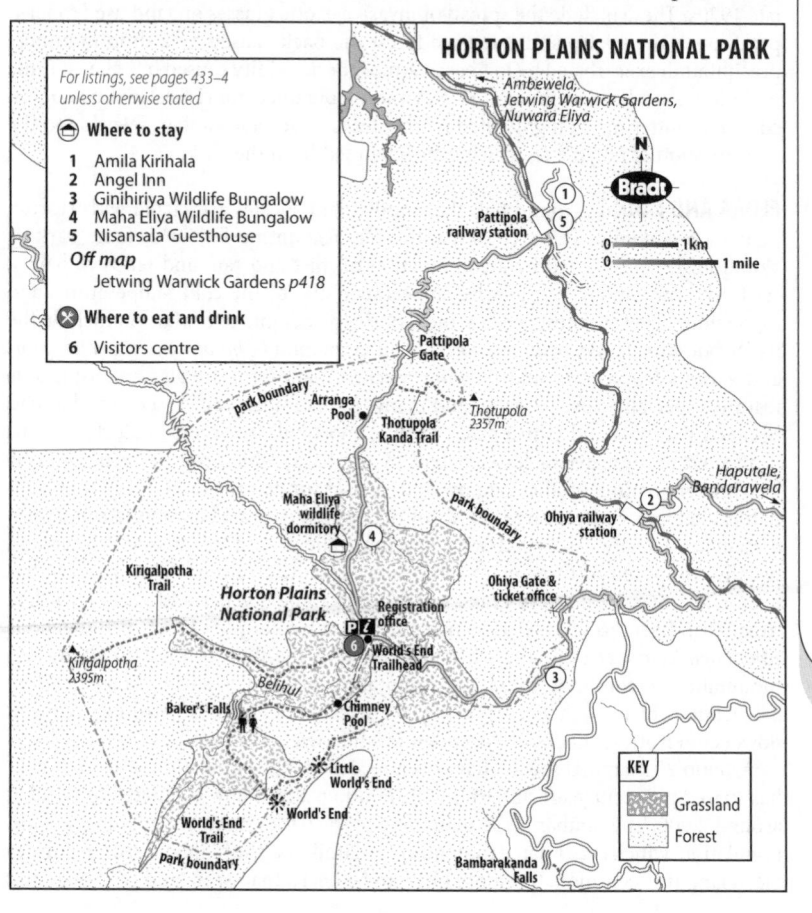

HORTON PLAINS NATIONAL PARK

For listings, see pages 433–4 unless otherwise stated

Where to stay
1 Amila Kirihala
2 Angel Inn
3 Ginihiriya Wildlife Bungalow
4 Maha Eliya Wildlife Bungalow
5 Nisansala Guesthouse

Off map
Jetwing Warwick Gardens *p418*

Where to eat and drink
6 Visitors centre

KEY
Grassland
Forest

this cultivation migrated to the lowlands around 7,000 years ago during a period of widespread drought in the highlands. In more recent historical times, the area was known by the Sinhala name Maha Eliya Thenna, which roughly translates as 'Great Open Plain'. The first documented European visitor was British coffee planter Thomas Farr, who arrived in 1836 and named the plains after Sir Robert Wilmot Horton, the incumbent British governor (1831–37). Another early visitor was Sir Samuel Baker, who popularised it as a hunting ground for elephant, deer and other large mammals over 1847–55, when he lived in nearby Nuwara Eliya. At around this time, a hunting lodge accessible only by foot was built by Thomas Farr. This later became a resthouse known as Farr Inn, but the old bungalow was transformed into the present-day information centre in 1999.

The wooded parts of Horton Plains were accorded official protection as early as 1873, when the colonial government passed an edict that all forests above the 5,000ft (1,524m) contour must be left undisturbed. Horton Plains was made a wildlife sanctuary in 1969 and upgraded to a national park in 1988. It is also the centrepiece of the UNESCO 'Central Highlands of Sri Lanka' World Heritage Site, which was inscribed in 2010 and also incorporates the less accessible Peak Wilderness Protected Area and Knuckles Conservation Forest. Despite this high level of protection, the park has experienced several ecological setbacks since the late 1970s. These include the spread of invasive exotic grasses on land used to farm potatoes in the 1960s, and extensive forest die-back caused by a drop in annual precipitation exacerbated by increased atmospheric acidity caused by exhaust fume pollution elsewhere in the country. A more contained tourist-related ecological concern is littering, as highlighted by the death of several sambar deer due to the consumption of polythene, which is now banned from the park.

FLORA AND FAUNA Around half the woody plant species associated with Horton Plains are endemic. The predominant cover, accounting for 70% of the park, is cloudforest, which is fed by a combination of mist and rain and tends to have a relatively low canopy and gnarled appearance due to the cold temperatures and high winds. Typical forest species, most of them endemic to Sri Lanka, include the hardwood kina (*Calophyllum walker*), wild cinnamon (*Cinnamomum ovalifolium*) and various *Elaeocarpus* and *Syzgium* species. Giant ferns are also a conspicuous feature, especially close to water, and many fine examples can be seen on the road between Pattipola and Ohiya gates. Sadly, almost half the forest in Horton Plains is affected to a greater or lesser extent by die-back, which can be recognised by the broken nature of the canopy and denser undergrowth. Other important natural habitats include large stands of the endemic dwarf bamboo (*Arundinaria densifolia*), usually associated with swampy valleys, and tall tussocky grassland usually composed of three main indigenous species. Around 2% of the park has been taken over by invasive grass, which tends to be greener and more lawn-like than its indigenous counterpart. Also present are a large number of indigenous *Rhododendron* species, many with affinities with the flora of the Himalayas and mountains of southern India, most notably the Asoka shrub *Rhododendron arboreum*, which often occurs alongside streams, and whose striking crimson flowers often attract flocks of the endemic white-eye.

Around 20 mammal species have been recorded. The population of sambar deer has soared in recent years, litter notwithstanding, and is now estimated to stand at around 2,000. The sambar is the main prey of the park's small but growing leopard population, which is estimated to stand at 15–20 adults. The highland race of purple-faced langur is common, but more likely to be heard than seen, and wild boar and the highland races of the grizzled Indian squirrel are also present. The endangered Horton Plains slender loris (*Loris tardigradus nycticeboides*) is a secretive nocturnal primate known only from this one locality. Other mammals include the rusty-spotted cat, fishing cat, muntjac, mouse deer, stripe-necked mongoose and otter. All but one of the six reptile and one of the 14 amphibian species recorded at Horton Plains are endemic to Sri Lanka, and several are thought to be restricted to this one site. Most likely to be seen by casual visitors are two endemic tree-dwelling agamid species: the brown and yellow pygmy lizard (*Cophotis ceylanica*) and unmistakable rhino-horned lizard (*Ceratophora stoddartii*).

Horton Plains is an important site for highland birds. The checklist of 60-odd species includes 13 national endemics. This includes five key species more or less confined to highland forests, namely Sri Lanka wood pigeon, yellow-eared bulbul, Sri Lanka bush warbler, Sri Lanka whistling thrush and dull-blue flycatcher, as well as the more widespread Sri Lanka junglefowl (often uttering its familiar call), Sri Lanka spurfowl, Sri Lanka blue magpie, brown-capped babbler, Sri Lanka scimitar babbler, orange-billed babbler, spot-winged thrush and Sri Lanka white-eye. Possibly the commonest passerine along the World's View Trail is the pied bush chat, a drab but very localised montane species most often seen in pairs. Other montane birds include the migrant Indian blue robin, the resident grey-headed canary flycatcher (whose canary-like call involves a series of rapid notes fired off like a machine gun), black bulbul, bar-winged flycatcher-shrike and black eagle.

GETTING THERE AND AWAY There are two entrance gates to Horton Plains, connected by an 11km road that runs through the national park, passing by the visitor centre roughly halfway along its length. The northerly Pattipola Gate lies 25km southeast of Nuwara Eliya via Pattipola village, while the southerly Ohiya Gate stands a similar distance northwest of Haputale via Ohiya village. The World's End Trail head starts at the visitor centre, some 5–6km from either gate. The trail head for Thotupola Mountain is only 500m inside Pattipola Gate.

No public transport runs to either gate, let alone to the visitor centre, so almost all independent visitors charter a vehicle in Nuwara Eliya or Haputale, which can be arranged through any hotel and should work out at US$25–35 for a small party, inclusive of driver, fuel and a few hours' waiting time. The driver and/or renting agency will assume you want to head straight to the visitor centre, hike the World's End Trail, and head back as soon as you are finished. Should you have different or more elaborate plans, best you clear that with them upfront – and be prepared to pay slightly extra if it increases the mileage or waiting time.

If you're determined to use public transport, trains between Nuwara Eliya and Hatton stop at the villages of Pattipola and Ohiya, and a few buses run between Nuwara Eliya and Pattipola daily. The villages (and railway stations) respectively lie 6km and 4km from their namesake gates, distances that are theoretically walkable provided you're prepared for a seriously steep climb, but are more realistically conquered by tuktuk (readily available in both villages; but bear in mind when you negotiate a fare that the visitor centre and World's End Trail head are 5–6km from either gate, and you need to allow 3–4 hours' waiting time).

WHERE TO STAY *Map, page 431*
Most people visit as a day trip from Nuwara Eliya or Haputale. If you want to spend longer, the only option within the park is a couple of government-run self-catering bungalows – **Ginihiriya Wildlife Bungalow** and **Maha Eliya Wildlife Bungalow** – that are aimed at large local parties, charge heavily inflated rates to foreigners and must

be booked in advance through the head office in Colombo or, if you can get it to work, online (📞 *011 288 8585;* w *dwc.lankagate.gov.lk; around US$80 dbl;* **$$$**). More affordable options in the shoestring category are the family-run **Nisansala Guesthouse** (*4 rooms;* 📞 *052 490 0110; US$10 dbl;* **$**) and **Amila Kirihala** (*5 rooms;* m *0777 451354; US$17 dbl;* **$**) in Pattipola village and **Angel Inn** (*3 rooms;* m *0729 126926; US$28 dbl B&B;* **$$**) in Ohiya village. All these places can provide inexpensive local meals and can arrange tuktuks to the national park, making them ideal bases for budget travellers who arrive by train or bus.

✖ WHERE TO EAT AND DRINK *Map, page 431*

A small canteen in the visitor centre serves tea, coffee, soft drinks and snacks, and also stocks a limited selection of biscuits and other packaged goods, but don't rely on it for meals.

WHAT TO SEE AND DO Most visitors restrict their exploration of Horton Plains to World's End Trail, setting off at dawn or as soon as possible thereafter, since this provides the best chance of reaching the viewpoints in clear weather. This approach makes perfect sense in itself, but it does mean that the trail tends to be uncomfortably busy – and downright crowded in season – between 06.00 and 11.00. For this reason, hikers who place a high premium on peace and quiet, or whose main interest is the immediate environment or birds and other wildlife, might consider bucking the trend and setting off in the afternoon, which increases the odds that rain or mist will envelop the main viewpoints, but also means they'll likely as not have the trail to themselves. Alternatively, consider taking the less popular Kirigalpotha or Thotupola Kanda Trail, or hiking along the Pattipola–Ohiya Road, neither of which are as busy as the World's End Trail, and which tend to be better for forest birds and wildlife. Whenever and wherever you hike, you ideally want to be wearing solid walking shoes, and to carry some warm waterproof clothing in case of rain.

World's End Trail Roughly 10km in length, the circular World's End Trail sticks mainly to the tussocky grassland of the open plateau for which the park is named, but it also passes through patches of dwarf forest and traverses marshy areas dominated by dwarf bamboo. It is normally hiked in a clockwise direction, branching left at the junction about 500m past the visitor centre, a point that also offers a good view west across to Kirigalpotha, the highest point in the range. From here, the trail runs to Little World's End, then on through a dense epiphyte-rich forest stand to World's End, an 880m drop set at the head of Sri Lanka's largest ravine. Both viewpoints stand at around 2,100m and offer spectacular views southward over layers of rolling hills to the Udawalawe Reservoir and, on a very clear day, the Indian Ocean. The return leg from 'Big' World's End follows the Belihul River and its tributary streams, which feed a number of pretty montane pools. The most significant features along this stretch are the forest-fringed 20m-high Baker's Falls (named after Sir Samuel) and the Chimney Pool, a small manmade reservoir passed about 500m before you climb back to the junction where the circular trail starts. The trail is quite flat and well marked throughout, so there is no real risk of getting lost, except perhaps in extreme misty conditions, but some parts are heavily eroded and can be slippy after rain, so tread carefully. Timing will depend on your fitness and how often you stop to admire the views or wildlife, but 3–4 hours is normal.

Kirigalpotha Trail About 6km in either direction, the least popular of the park's three trails runs directly west from the visitor centre to Sri Lanka's second-highest peak, Kirigalpotha (literally 'Milky Rock Face', in reference to its reflective white northern slope). It is a rougher and slightly steeper trail than World's End, gaining some 300m in altitude, and less well marked, but the absence of other tourists gives it a genuinely off-the-beaten-track feel and means it provides a better chance of spotting wildlife and birds. Ecologically, the first half of the trail passes through tussocky grassland with the Belihul River and associated bogland a few hundred metres to the south, while the second half climbs through increasingly dense forest cover, before reaching the open rock face at the summit. The view from the top isn't quite so dramatic as World's End, but it provides an impressively panoramic view over the national park and environs. Allow 5–6 hours for the walk there and back.

Thotupola Kanda Trail Only 1.5km in either direction, this short but relatively steep trail leads uphill from the main road 500m south of Pattipola entrance gate to the 2,357m Thotupola Peak. It passes through dense montane forest where observant visitors might well see the pygmy and rhino-horned lizards, as well as several of the endemic and highland forest birds associated with the park. As you approach the peak, the trail runs through a peculiar pygmy forest whose species composition is similar to the park's other montane forest, but with most trees coming in a kind of natural bonsai form, typically no more than 2m high. The summit offers a good view to the lower-lying country to the east. The trail for the short climb is in generally good condition, but may be slippery in parts. Allow 1½ hours for the return trip.

The Pattipola–Ohiya Road The 11km road that connects the two gates is possibly more rewarding for wildlife than any of the walking trails, passing as it does through the full gamut of the park's habitats, but offering better visibility particularly into the forested areas. The section between Pattipola Gate and the visitor centre tends to be quite busy with traffic between 06.00 and 08.00, when day trippers arrive from Nuwara Eliya, and again from 10.30 to midday, when most of them leave. The section between Ohiya Gate and the visitor centre carries very little traffic. There is nothing preventing you from walking any stretch of this road, nor from driving along it and using the car as a mobile photographic hide, provided you don't walk or drive off-road. Sambar deer are particularly common and often quite relaxed around vehicles in the open country between Ohiya Gate and the visitor centre. The road between Pattipola Gate and the visitor centre supports a higher proportion of forest; the Arranga Pool about 1km south of Pattipola Gate is a particularly rewarding spot for birdwatchers hoping to glimpse the rare and elusive Sri Lanka whistling thrush.

Ambewela Farm Shop Boasting a pastoral setting on a crossroads near Ambewela village *en route* between Nuwara Eliya and Pattipola, this shop selling balls of cheese, jars of strawberry jam, goat's milk, bottles of ghee and other homemade dairy products is a popular stop on the return trip from Horton Plains.

HAPUTALE

The sole Sri Lankan inclusion on CNN's 2010 list of Asia's 25 most overlooked destinations, Haputale is a precipitous hill station that meanders for a couple of kilometres along a 1,450m-high ridge offering spectacular clear-weather views all the way to the coast. It was established in the c1860s to service the then-booming

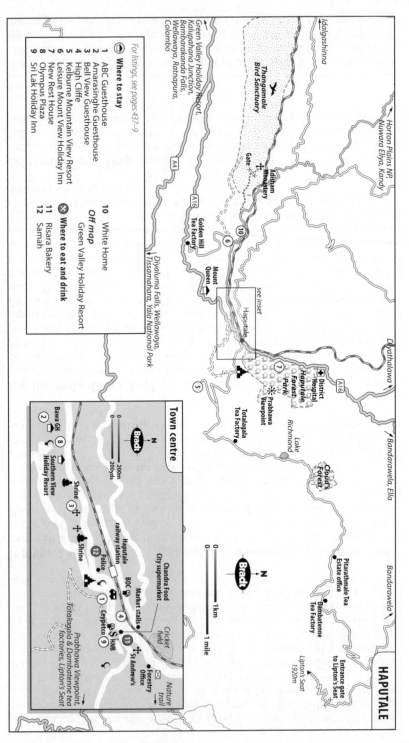

HAPUTALE

Horton Plains NP,
Nuwara Eliya, Kandy

Idalgashinna

Thangamale
Bird Sanctuary

Green Valley Holiday Resort,
Kalupahana Junction,
Bambarakanda Falls,
Wellawaya, Ratnapura,
Colombo

Adisham
Monastery

Gate

Golden Hill
Tea Factory

Diyaluma Falls, Wellawaya,
Tissamahara, Yala National Park

Mount
Queen

Haputale

Diyathalawa

Bandarawela, Ella

Bandarawela

For listings see pages 437–9

🛏 **Where to stay**
1 ABC Guesthouse
2 Amarasinghe Guesthouse
3 Bell View Guesthouse
4 High Cliffe
5 Kelburne Mountain View Guesthouse
6 Leisure Mount View Holiday Inn
7 New Rest House
8 Olympus Plaza
9 Sri Lak Holiday Inn
10 White Home

Off map
Green Valley Holiday Resort

✗ **Where to eat and drink**
11 Risara Bakery
12 Samah

District
Hospital

Haputale
Forest
Park

✳ Prabhawa
Viewpoint

Totalagala
Tea Factory

Lake
Richmond

Cloud's
Forest

Pitarathmale Tea
Estate office

Dambatenne
Tea Factory

Entrance gate
to Lipton's Seat

Lipton's Seat
1920m

Town centre

see inset

Bawa GH

Southern View
Holiday Resort

Shrine

Shrine

Police

Haputale railway station

Chandra Food
City supermarket

Market stalls

BOC

Cepgeto

HNB

St Andrew's

Cricket
field

Nature
trail

Forestry
Office

Prabhawa Viewpoint,
Totalagala & Dambatenne tea
factories, Lipton's Seat

N Bradt

0   200m
0   200yds

N Bradt

0   1km
0   1 mile

local coffee industry, but tea has been its economic mainstay since the 1890s, when Thomas Lipton bought several struggling old estates around Haputale, and reversed their fortunes by pursuing a more professional approach not only to cultivation but also to marketing his eponymously branded Ceylon tea. Today the town supports a Tamil-dominated population of 6,000, and has an irregular layout dictated by the steep contours, focused on a compact but energetic centre that houses the bus and railway stations along with a scattering of quirky little shops. One of the chilliest towns in Sri Lanka, and often swathed in mist, Haputale vies with the even nippier Nuwara Eliya as the best springboard for day trips to Horton Plains, while more budget-friendly local attractions include the peri-urban Haputale Forest Park, the stunning Lipton's Seat viewpoint, and Sri Lanka's tallest waterfall, Bambarakanda. Despite this, tourist development remains low-key. Indeed, while disappointment awaits those who arrive in Haputale expecting a plethora of Nuwara Eliya-style colonial-era lodges, or a cluster of trendy cafés and boutique hotels à la Ella, this unheralded small town does rather excel when it comes to well-priced and down-to-earth budget hotels and homestays.

GETTING THERE AND AWAY
By road Haputale is roughly 175km from Colombo via Ratnapura. Twice-hourly buses from Colombo to Badulla all stop here. More locally, at least two buses an hour connect Haputale to Bandarawela, Nuwara Eliya and Ella.

By rail All trains on the upcountry line connecting Colombo, Kandy, Nuwara Eliya to Bandarawela, Ella and Badulla stop at the central station in Haputale.

WHERE TO STAY *Map, opposite*
Haputale is particularly well served when it comes to small, family-run hotels in the budget and shoestring range, especially by comparison with Nuwara Eliya. For somewhere smarter, the only central option is the more-than-adequate Olympus Plaza.

Upmarket
Kelburne Mountain View Resort (3 bungalows) Haputale; 057 226 8029, 011 257 3382; e mountainview@sltnet.lk; w kelburnemountainview.com. Situated on the Lipton-owned Pitaratmalie Estate about 1.5km southeast of town, this resort comprises a trio of chintzy 2- or 3-bedroom colonial-style cottages, each nestled in its own flower garden at the very edge of a 1,300m escarpment overlooking the stippled quilt of hills & hazy plains stretching 40km to the south coast. Hearty meals – think British planters' fare with a spicy tropical touch – are served in the dining room of each bungalow, or in the central pavilion, by a barefoot steward in tunic & sarong. Staff also includes a personal chef, butler & room boy. *From US$190 dbl.* $$$$$

Moderate
Olympus Plaza Hotel (42 rooms) Welimada Rd; 057 226 8544; e olympusplaza@ gmail.com; w olympusplazahotel.com. Haputale's smartest hotel has a hillside location offering good views 500m west of the train station. The bottom 4 floors are below the roadside reception area, which also houses a good restaurant (local & Chinese dishes in the $$ range), while the 6th floor stands above it, ensuring that all the stylish contemporary rooms have a balcony & fine view. *US$55/75 sgl/ dbl B&B.* $$$

Budget
✳ **Sri Lak Holiday Inn** (24 rooms) Arthur Sirisena Rd; 057 226 8125; m 0772 440082; e info@srilakviewholidayinn.com; w srilakviewholidayinn.com. Scenically perched on the green slopes 200m southeast of the bus station, this top-notch cheapie offers the choice of small but cosy ground-floor rooms in the old wing or new teak-floored rooms with modern furniture & a private balcony in the new wing. A decent restaurant with glass windows & fabulous

15

views serves Sri Lankan mains in the **$$** range. *US$10/23 dbl in old/new wing.* **$**

✳ 🏠 **Leisure Mount View Holiday Inn** (10 rooms) Off Welimada Rd; ☎ 057 226 8327; m 0725 914529; e leisuremvinn@yahoo.com. This popular out-of-town medium-rise is run by a friendly & obliging family & offers great views over the surrounding tea estates. Spacious & light rooms are brightly furnished with modern bathrooms & some have a private balcony. The top-floor restaurant serves excellent homemade rice-&-curry in the **$$$** range. Also arranges car rental for Horton Plains. *US$17/30 dbl without/ with balcony.* **$**

🏠 **Green Valley Holiday Resort** (13 cottages) Haldummulla; ☎ 057 579 4324; m 0779 975051; e greenvalleycottage123@ gmail.com; w greenvalleycottage.com. Situated alongside the Colombo Rd 6km from Haputale, this attractively rustic property sprawls across wooded 8ha hillside gardens where birds & butterflies hover, monkeys gambol, & a cool mountain stream feeds a freshwater rock pool. Rather tired-looking but well-priced accommodation ranges from self-catering cottages to 4-bed mixed dormitories. Good wholesome food is freshly prepared on order. *US$20/30 budget/deluxe dbl, US$8 pp dorm bed*; all rates B&B. **$**

🏠 **Amarasinghe Guesthouse** (8 rooms) Thambapillai Av; ☎ 057 226 8175; m 0777 763397; e agh777@sltnet.lk. Reached via a 200m footpath leading downhill from Welimada Rd, this newly renovated but rather characterless guesthouse stands on the 1st floor above the family home of the helpful owner-managers. Clean & pleasant rooms have parquet floor & a balcony with a green view. Home-cooked b/fast, lunch & dinner in the **$** range. *US$17/20 sgl/dbl B&B.* **$**

🏠 **New Rest House** (7 rooms) ☎ 057 226 8099. Sandwiched between the Bandarawela Rd & Haputale Forest Park 600m north of the town centre, this government resthouse isn't quite so spruce-looking as its name suggests, but it has a scenic location & seems decent value at the price.

Spacious rooms have red polished floors, wooden furniture & fan. A restaurant & bar are attached. *US$23 dbl.* **$**

Shoestring

🏠 **White Home** (6 rooms) Welimada Rd; ☎ 057 226 8449; e whitehouse123@gmail.com. This unpretentious homestay has small clean rooms with TV & net. Tiled ground-floor rooms are better than their 1st-floor counterparts with faded linoleum. A common lounge faces the surrounding hills & the restaurant serves delicious homemade curries (**$$**). Very good value. *US$10 dbl, plus US$2 pp b/fast.* **$**

🏠 **ABC Guesthouse** (12 rooms) Sherwood Rd; ☎ 057 276 8630; m 0771 012113; e abcguestinn. haputale@gmail.com; w abcguestinn.blogspot. com. Scenically located on the slopes immediately south of the town centre, this tall & narrow 4-storey hotel is owned & managed by the friendly family that lives on the ground floor. Good home cooking in the **$$** range is complemented by small but clean rooms with a view & in some cases a balcony. Very good value. *US$6/8 sgl/dbl.* **$**

🏠 **Bell View Guesthouse** (10 rooms) Welimada Rd; ☎ 051 226 8213; m 0717 108830; f belviewhaputale. Next to an old church, this is a friendly homestay where meals (**$–$$**) are cooked by the owner-manager's mother & the garden offers good views to the lowlands. Rooms all have nets but twins use a shared bathroom while dbls are en suite. *US$6/9 twin/dbl.* **$**

🏠 **High Cliffe Hotel** (9 rooms) Station Rd; ☎ 057 226 8096; e highcliffe.hotel@gmail.com. Something of a hippy hang-out in the 1970s, this prominent 4-storey building 150m from the railway station betrays its age with an angular reddish façade reminiscent of a converted cinema. Access is via a sleazy 1st-floor & brighter restaurant whose varied menu includes curries, prawns & steaks (**$$**). Spacious & brightly painted rooms have wood-panelled walls & nets. Decent value, though the bar clientele might make things uncomfortable for unattached women. *US$10–13 dbl depending on season.* **$**

✕ **WHERE TO EAT AND DRINK** *Map, page 436*

Bespoke restaurants are limited to a few decent local eateries. For Western fare or something more ceremonious, your best bet is the smart Olympus Plaza or more low-key Sri Lak, both of which have restaurants with a view. The High Cliffe has a lively little bar.

✖ Samah Restaurant Welimada Rd. Not for the faint of palate, this place serves superb but very spicy lunchtime curries. $

✖ Risara Bakery Off the Bandarawela Rd. In addition to a good ground-floor bakery, this popular central joint has a 1st-floor restaurant serving curries & other typical Sri Lankan fare. $

OTHER PRACTICALITIES The only private bank with an ATM that accepts foreign cards is the HNB behind the Ceypetco filling station. If that doesn't work, there are plenty of banks in nearby Bandarawela (pages 442–3). The best supermarket is Chandra Food City, but there are also several stalls selling fresh produce past the level crossing at the east end of Station Road.

WHAT TO SEE AND DO In addition to the sites described below, Haputale rivals Nuwara Eliya as the best base for visits to Horton Plains National Park, using the southerly Ohiya entrance gate. Transport to the park can be arranged through any hotel in Haputale and should cost around US$30–35 per party inclusive of fuel, driver and waiting time. Cash-strapped travellers might note that Lipton's Seat and the Prabhawa Viewpoint afford views comparable to Horton Plains's renowned Word's End Viewpoint, while the pedestrian-friendly Haputale Forest Park and Thangamale Bird Sanctuary protect a similar range of forest wildlife. That said, none of these sites possesses the expansive wilderness character or ecological diversity of the national park.

St Andrew's Church (*Bandarawela Rd;* ☎ *057 222 2294*) The oldest building in Haputale, pre-dating the Lipton-engineered tea boom by a quarter of a century, this modest Anglican church opened for worship on a small bluff above the town centre in 1869. British residents spanning many generations from 1870 onwards are buried in the well-tended cemetery, among them the Reverend W S Senior (1876–1938), a highly regarded British scholar who served for ten years as Vice Principal of Kandy's Trinity College, but is better known for penning several poems and hymns dedicated to his adopted homeland. The gravestone of the so-called Bard of Ceylon, third to the right as you enter, is inscribed with the opening lines of one of his poems, and the simple assertion 'He Loved Ceylon'.

Haputale Forest Park (*Bandarawela Rd;* ☎ *057 226 8078; office* ⊕ *08.00–16.00 Mon–Fri*) This underpublicised and readily accessible sanctuary protects a 1km² stand of indigenous montane forest that rises to the crest of a 1,600m-high ridge immediately northeast of the town centre. Little information is available about the park's wildlife, but we would expect it to harbour a broadly similar forest fauna (including a dozen endemic bird species) to Thangamale Bird Sanctuary, which protects a near-identical habitat only 2.5km to the west. The reserve is traversed by a circular 3.5km nature trail, which can be hiked unguided and starts at the forestry office between St Andrew's Church and the Post Office. In theory, foreigners pay an entrance fee of US$1.35, but this is seldom enforced even when the ticket office is open.

Prabhawa Viewpoint This rocky vantage point, perched at around 1,750m atop the same ridge whose western slope is protected in Haputale Forest Park, offers a superb view over the southern lowlands but requires a bit more effort to reach than the better-known Lipton's Seat. Accessible on foot only, and from the east, it is best reached by walking or bussing along the Dambatenne Road for 3.5km until you reach the Totalagala Tea Factory, where you can take your pick of a few footpaths that run up the tea-swathed mountain to the left. Allow about 90 minutes in either direction from here. Prabhawa is also the site of a Hindu and Buddhist shrine, respectively called Surangamuni and Aakasha Samagi, names that are likely to mean more than Prabhawa to anybody of whom you ask directions.

Cloud's Forest Nature Trail Extending over about 18ha, this relict montane forest is bisected by the Dambatenne Road about 5km out of Haputale, shortly after you pass the reed-encircled Lake Richmond to your left. Less than 1km east of Haputale Forest Park as the crow flies, it is the only surviving patch of natural forest on the Lipton Estates, and home to at least 70 bird species and around ten endemic types of reptile. Access from the road is limited but permission to walk in the forest can be obtained from the Pitaratmalie Tea Estate office 2km further towards Dambatenne.

Dambatenne Tea Factory (\057 567 7978; ⊕ 08.00–18.00; guided tours US$1.50; photography forbidden) Situated 9km from Haputale along a scenic back road that reconnects to Bandarawela town after another 13km, the massive tea factory at Dambatenne is one of Sri Lanka's oldest, established in 1890 by Sir Thomas Lipton. From a travel perspective, the factory is arguably of less interest of itself than as a break en route to/from Lipton's Seat, some 6km distant by road. Inexpensive but rather cursory 15-minute factory tours theoretically end with a tea-tasting session, but this seems to be a matter of whim.

Lipton's Seat The most popular goal for a day trip out of Haputale, the 1,920m-high Lipton's Seat is a stunning escarpment-edge promontory flanked by precipitous cliffs on three sides and offering views across the southern lowlands that bear comparison to the Horton Plains's legendary World's End Viewpoint. Back in the day, the viewpoint was a favourite of Sir Thomas Lipton, whose cast bronze likeness has now taken permanent occupation of a rock next to the car park. A 50m climb leads from the main viewpoint to a slightly higher one, and there is a simple tea shop on the site. It is best visited as early as possible in the morning, before the mist sets in for the day.

Operated by the Lipton Estate, the viewpoint is accessible by road, via an entrance gate that levies an entrance fee of US$0.70 per car and US$0.35 per 'soul' – a phrasing whose new-age pseudery is exposed by the recognition that Sri Lankan 'souls' pay a much lower fee than their foreign counterparts. No less eyebrow-raising is the need to harangue visitors with a succession of sanctimonious roadside signs whose eco-friendly and socialist sentiments seem at odds with reality on an estate where almost every last tract of natural vegetation has made way for tea plantations, and whose management has shown no indication of carving the whole thing up into allotments and handing them over to its ragged and poorly paid tea pickers.

Lipton's Seat stands 15km from Haputale via Dambatenne along an atrocious road that takes at least 30 minutes and possibly up to an hour in a private vehicle. A return tuktuk will cost around US$10 including waiting time. Using public transport, you could bus as far as Dambatenne, then walk the last 6km to the viewpoint, or charter a tuktuk, which will cost US$5–6 return. It is equally possible to visit Lipton's Seat from Bandarawela, a 14km trip that also takes 30-plus minutes by car. A return tuktuk will cost around US$10, or you could hop on one of the regular minibuses that ply from Bandarawela to Haputale via Dambatenne, hop off 3km before the tea factory at the signposted junction for Lipton's Seat, and walk the last 3km.

Adisham Monastery (057 226 8030; e info@adisham.org; w adisham.org; ⊕ 09.00–noon & 13.30–16.30 Sat, Sun, public holidays & school holidays; entrance US$1) Now a training centre for Benedictine monks, this neo-Gothic stone mansion 3km west of Haputale was built in 1931 as the home of Sir Thomas Villiers, a wealthy English tea planter (and grandson of a former British prime minister) who had first arrived in Ceylon back in 1887, aged 18 and with just US$10 in his pocket. Named after the rectory where Villiers was born, Adisham is a grey brooding pile of granite blocks and teak-framed turret windows patterned on Tudor lines, and modelled on Leeds Castle in Kent. Its very solidity seems rather anomalous in its equatorial setting of lushly wooded valleys, acres of tea bushes and cloud-shrouded mountains. Day visitors can tour the lower part of the house, which includes Villiers' fine library, on weekends, public holidays and school holidays only. A shop sells delicious jam, chutney, cordial and other preservative-free produce made at the monastery.

Thangamale Bird Sanctuary Created in 1938 at the behest of Sir Thomas Villiers, this sanctuary protects a 1km² relict patch of indigenous montane forest running along the same ridge whereupon Adisham was built. Small though it is, Thangamale (literally 'Golden Hill') protects a surprisingly diverse fauna. Purple-faced langur, toque macaque, muntjac deer, wild boar and grizzled giant squirrel are the most conspicuous mammals, but the sanctuary is particularly renowned for its birdlife, which includes at least a dozen endemics. Most common are Sri Lanka hill myna, yellow-eared bulbul, dull-blue flycatcher and Sri Lanka white-eye, but Sri Lanka junglefowl, Sri Lanka spurfowl, Sri Lanka wood pigeon, yellow-fronted barbet, Sri Lanka hanging parrot, brown-capped babbler, Sri Lanka grey hornbill and reputedly even Sri Lanka blue magpie are also present. For dedicated birdwatchers, it is worth getting here as early as possible, and walking slowly up and down the last 500m of the approach road to Adisham Monastery, which bisects the forest and offers quite good visibility into the canopy. It is also worth exploring the short footpath into the forest that starts on the right side of the road about 150m before the monastery gates. For a more energetic leg stretch, a lovely and easy-to-follow 4.5km footpath runs west from Thangamale to the pretty railway village of Idalgashinna. The footpath starts to the left of the monastery gates, then runs through a mosaic of indigenous and plantation forest for about 2.5km, offering occasional views of the Glananore Estate to the north, before descending to the railway line and following the tracks into Idalgashinna. Allow 90 minutes to 2 hours for the walk, depending on how often you stop, and try to time it so that you arrive in Idalgashinna in time to pick up the 11.26 train back to Haputale. Failing that, a tuktuk back to Haputale will cost around US$4.

Bambarakanda Falls [map, page 431] (*Entrance US$1*) Sri Lanka's tallest waterfall, single-drop Bambarakanda is formed by the Kuda River, a tributary of the Walawe, as it plunges 263m over the escarpment through steep rocks and a forest of pines between the Welihena and the Bambarakanda mountains. Tall as it is, the waterfall is very narrow, and while it tends to be quite spectacular after rain, especially between October and January, it wilts to an underwhelming trickle towards the end of the dry season. To get here from Haputale, follow the Colombo Road west out of town for 15km to Kalupahana Junction, then turn right on to a rougher dirt road that leads to the base of the waterfall after 5km. No shortage of buses runs along the main road between Haputale and Kalupahana Junction, where you will find a few tuktuks ready and waiting to ferry you to and from the waterfall for around US$4 including waiting time. A well-built 500m footpath leads to the base of the waterfall and chilly natural rock pool where swimming is permitted. It is also possible to hike to the top of the falls, but it's quite a tough ascent and requires good walking shoes, especially after rain when the rocks can be slippery.

BANDARAWELA

Set at an elevation of 1,225m in a wooded valley halfway along the 25km road between Haputale and Ella, Bandarawela is a much larger town than either of these neighbours, with a population estimated at 70,000. In colonial times, it was considered second only to Nuwara Eliya as a hill station, thanks to a restorative mid-altitude climate that still makes it popular with domestic holidaymakers. For international travellers, it is now largely overshadowed by nearby Ella and its burgeoning backpacker scene, and it also lacks Haputale's immense setting and relative proximity to several worthwhile attractions including Horton Plains. That said, Bandarawela remains a useful base for exploring the surrounding highlands, and it retains the unpretentious bustling feel of a functional upcountry town whose economy is fuelled not by tourism but by the needs of its hard-working inhabitants and the plantation workers and farmers who live in the vicinity. The closest thing the town centre has to a tourist attraction is the Mlesna Tea Centre (✆ 057 223 1663; ⊕ 08.00–17.00), where you can taste and buy the fine tea produced by the eponymous estate while exploring some interesting tea-related displays and paraphernalia. About 2km out of town and reachable on foot or by tuktuk via Kinigama Junction, Porawagala is a 1,330m-high rocky outcrop that offers a fine view over the town centre nestled into its green valley.

GETTING THERE AND AWAY

By road Bandarawela is roughly 190km from Colombo via Ratnapura and Haputale. Twice-hourly buses from Colombo to Badulla all stop in Bandarawela. More locally, at least two buses an hour connect Bandarawela to Haputale, Nuwara Eliya (changing at Welimada) and Wellawaya via Ella. The stand for Colombo and Haputale is next to the railway station, for Ella and Wellawaya opposite the HNB, and for Welimada and Nuwara Eliya around the corner from Cargills Food City.

By rail All trains on the upcountry line connecting Colombo, Kandy, Nuwara Eliya and Haputale to Ella and Badulla stop at the central station in Bandarawela.

⌂ WHERE TO STAY *Map, opposite*
Moderate
⌂ **Bandarawela Hotel** (33 rooms) Welimada Rd; ✆ 057 222 2501; e gm@ bandarawalahotel.lk; w aitkenspencehotels. com. Dating back to 1893, this charming & well-managed hilltop hotel remains locked in a pre-WWII time warp, with its sanatorium-style brass-knobbed beds, dark lounge heavy with chesterfields & blazing log fire, dining room complete with silver dinner services & starched-uniformed waiters, & public bar with wood-panelled walls, heavy wooden shelves & teak

bar-stools. A little renovation wouldn't go amiss, but it's a fun & characterful set-up, evoking a time when tea not tourism ruled the hills. Good value. *US$88/103 sgl/dbl B&B.* **$$$$**
⌂ **Orient Hotel** (50 rooms) Dharmapala Rd; ✆ 057 222 2407; m 0776 475694; e orient-bwela@eureka.lk; w orienthotelsl.com. This sprawling 1960s-built hotel stands on well-tended 1.2ha sloping gardens that incorporate a spa, beer garden & 24hr café-with-a-view serving local & Western fare in the **$$$** range. Indoor public areas look effortlessly retro &

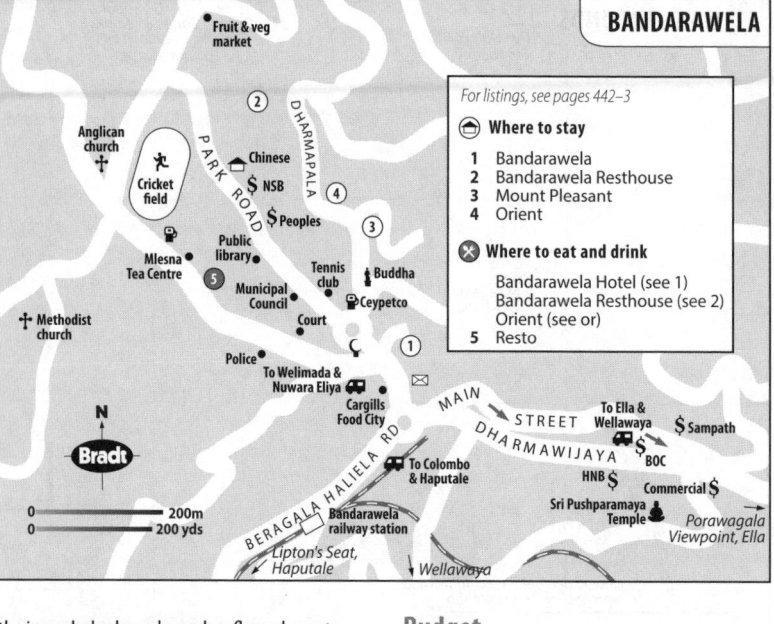

For listings, see pages 442–3

BANDARAWELA

🛏 **Where to stay**
1   Bandarawela
2   Bandarawela Resthouse
3   Mount Pleasant
4   Orient

❌ **Where to eat and drink**
    Bandarawela Hotel (see 1)
    Bandarawela Resthouse (see 2)
    Orient (see or)
5   Resto

the irregularly shaped wooden-floored guest rooms all have fan, TV & combined tub/shower. Convenient & well-priced. *US$75/93 sgl/dbl B&B*. **$$$$**

🛏 **Mount Pleasant Hotel** (4 rooms) Mount Pleasant Rd; 057 222 2646. Centrally located in peaceful gardens, this likeable bungalow has a boutique feel with its spacious & stylish rooms, all with TV & large bathroom, & dining room (specialising in local curries) & common lounge (with piano) decorated in classic contemporary style. Good value. *US$40–65 dbl depending on room size.* **$$$**

Budget

🛏 **Bandarawela Resthouse** (9 rooms) Vishaka Rd; 057 222 2299; m 0778 116686. Set in well-maintained flowering gardens offering a view over a playing field to the surrounding hills, this agreeable resthouse is time-warped in a somewhat more downmarket way than its namesake hotel, but the well-priced rooms all come with queen-size bed, net, TV & private balcony (some in better shape than others, so look before you commit). An inexpensive restaurant serves sandwiches, curries & other local dishes (**$**) & there's a bar with garden seating. *US$17/23 sgl/dbl.* **$**

❌ **WHERE TO EAT AND DRINK**   *Map, above*
The hotels listed above all have restaurants, with the Orient (**$$$**) winning out on location, the Bandarawela Hotel (**$$$**) on colonial ambience, and the Bandarawela Resthouse (**$**) on affordability. All three are licensed too.

❌ **Resto** Welimada Rd; 057 223 3999; ⏰ 11.00–16.00 & 18.00–23.00. The former Kamuko Restaurant is conveniently located next door to the Mlesna Tea Centre & serves a decent selection of Chinese cuisine & seafood with plenty of options for vegetarians. **$$**

ELLA

An attractive green village set at a temperate elevation of 1,050m, tiny Ella occupies a breach in the Hill Country's southeast escarpment overlooking a lush riverine valley known as the Ella Gap and offering fantastic views across the inselbergs and

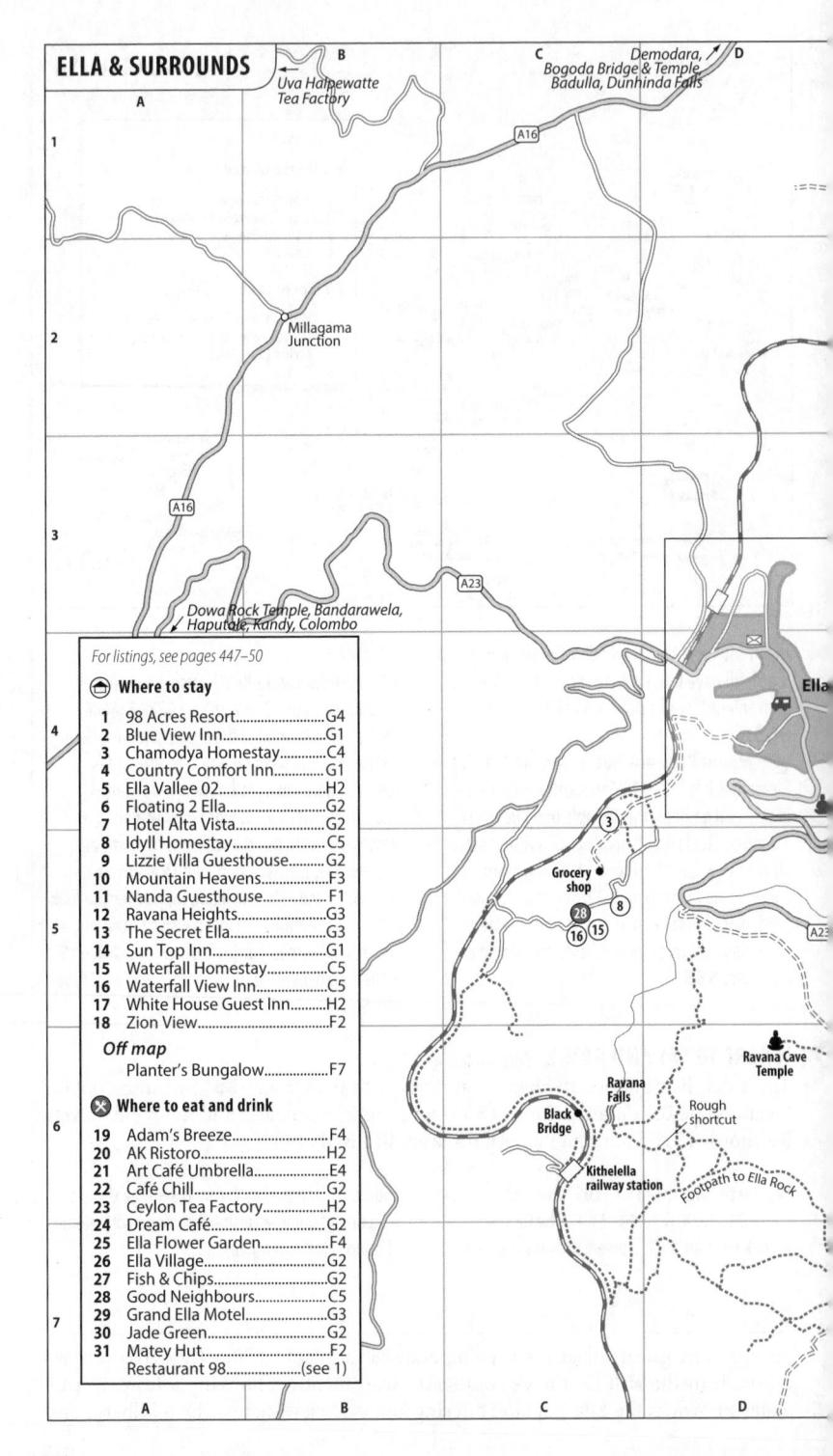

ELLA & SURROUNDS

Uva Halpewatte Tea Factory

Demodara,
Bogoda Bridge & Temple,
Badulla, Dunhinda Falls

Millagama Junction

Dowa Rock Temple, Bandarawela,
Haputale, Kandy, Colombo

Ella

Grocery shop

Ravana Cave Temple

Ravana Falls

Rough shortcut

Black Bridge

Kithelella railway station

Footpath to Ella Rock

For listings, see pages 447–50

🏠 Where to stay

1	98 Acres Resort	G4
2	Blue View Inn	G1
3	Chamodya Homestay	C4
4	Country Comfort Inn	G1
5	Ella Vallee 02	H2
6	Floating 2 Ella	G2
7	Hotel Alta Vista	G2
8	Idyll Homestay	C5
9	Lizzie Villa Guesthouse	G2
10	Mountain Heavens	F3
11	Nanda Guesthouse	F1
12	Ravana Heights	G3
13	The Secret Ella	G3
14	Sun Top Inn	G1
15	Waterfall Homestay	C5
16	Waterfall View Inn	C5
17	White House Guest Inn	H2
18	Zion View	F2

Off map
Planter's Bungalow................F7

🍴 Where to eat and drink

19	Adam's Breeze	F4
20	AK Ristoro	H2
21	Art Café Umbrella	E4
22	Café Chill	G2
23	Ceylon Tea Factory	H2
24	Dream Café	G2
25	Ella Flower Garden	F4
26	Ella Village	G2
27	Fish & Chips	G2
28	Good Neighbours	C5
29	Grand Ella Motel	G3
30	Jade Green	G2
31	Matey Hut	F2
	Restaurant 98	(see 1)

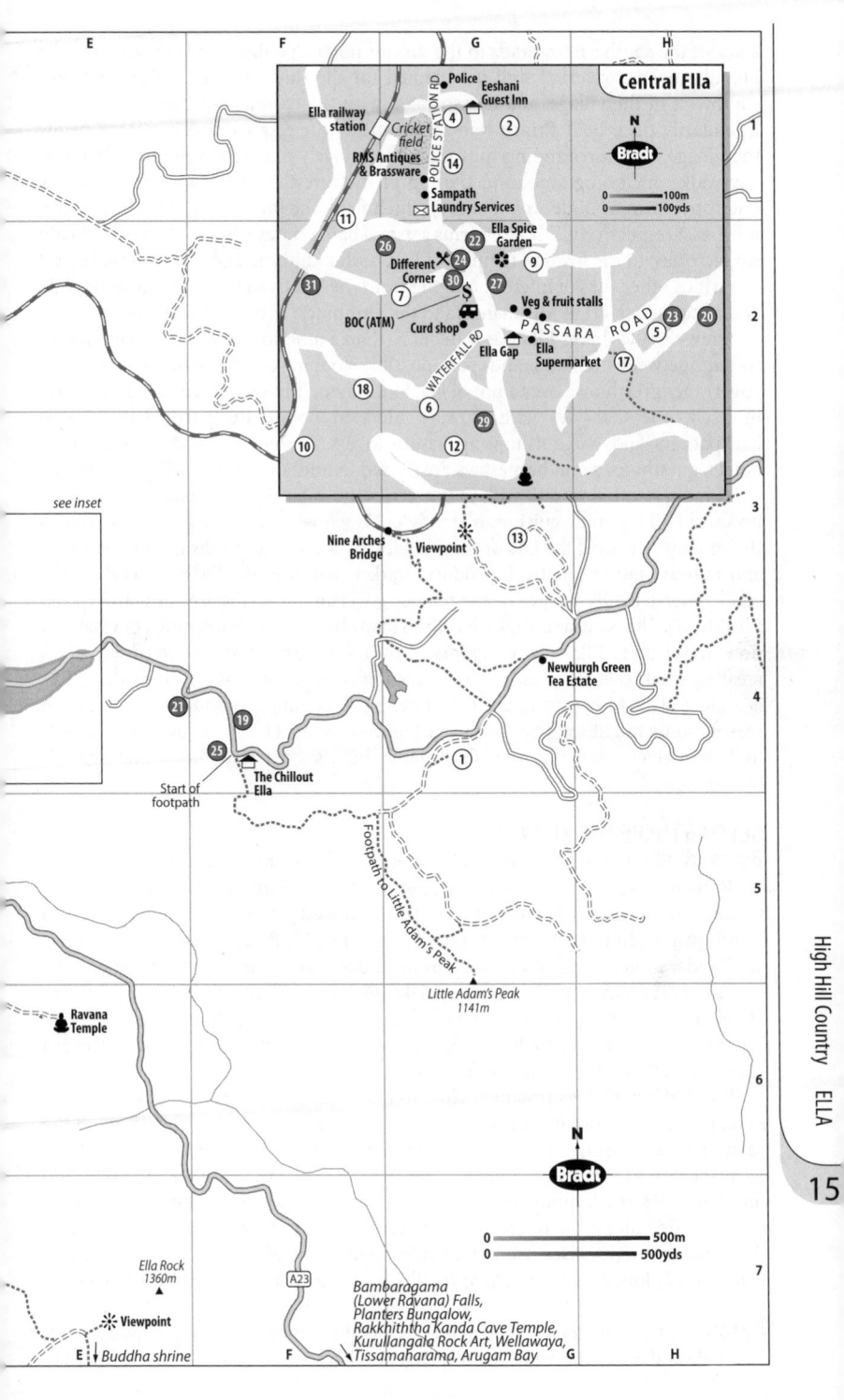

Central Ella

Police
Eeshani Guest Inn
Ella railway station
Cricket field
RMS Antiques & Brassware
Sampath Laundry Services
Ella Spice Garden
Different Corner
BOC (ATM)
Curd shop
Veg & fruit stalls
Ella Gap
Ella Supermarket

N

0   100m
0   100yds

POLICE STATION RD
WATERFALL RD
PASSARA   ROAD

see inset

Nine Arches Bridge
Viewpoint

Newburgh Green Tea Estate

The Chillout Ella
Start of footpath

Ravana Temple

Footpath to Little Adam's Peak

Little Adam's Peak
1141m

N

Ella Rock
1360m
Viewpoint
Buddha shrine

Bambaragama
(Lower Ravana) Falls,
Planters Bungalow,
Rakkhiththa Kanda Cave Temple,
Kurullangala Rock Art, Wellawaya,
Tissamaharama, Arugam Bay

0   500m
0   500yds

lakes of the southern lowlands to the distant nocturnal lights of Hambantota. Ella literally means 'waterfall' and it is named for the Ravana Falls, which lie 1.5km southwest of the village, and is associated with the eponymous demon-king who legendarily once held Prince Rama's beautiful wife Sita captive in a cave below the village. The surrounding hills offer some lovely and relatively unchallenging day walks, including ambles to the top of the forested Ella Rock and the rocky outcrop known as Little Adam's Peak, which flank the breach to the southwest and northeast respectively. Ella also forms a useful base for day excursions to several old tea factories, to the historic temples of Dowa, Rakkhiththa and Buduruvagala, and to various other sites of interest, ranging from the Kandyan wood bridge at Bogoda and ancient rock art at Kurullangala to the Dunhinda and Diyaluma Falls.

A few decades back, Ella was little more than a junction village to drive through *en route* between highlands and coast, possibly stopping to admire the view from the government resthouse over a pot of tea. Since then, it has emerged as a destination in itself, one that vies with Nuwara Eliya in popularity, particularly among backpackers and bargain-hunting nature lovers. Dozens upon dozens of small hotels, guesthouses and homestays are dotted in and around the village, while the short main street is vibrant with jolly eateries, from family-run restaurants serving up tasty Hill Country cuisine to trendy cafés whose décor is as cosmopolitan as their menu. Traces of the Ella of yore remain, be it the quaint Edwardian post office and railway station, the fresh-produce market that lines the Passara Road, or the sundowner-friendly terrace of the former government resthouse (now the Grand Ella Motel). That said, as is the case with so many backpacker hubs, much of what first drew travellers to Ella is now sublimated by a self-perpetuating Westernised scene, creating what feels like a rather dilute version of Sri Lanka. Make no mistake, Ella is a great place to hang out, but with foreigners seemingly outnumbering locals in season, some might feel that the village has become a victim of its own success, and find themselves gravitating towards the larger but less contrived likes of Bandarawela or Haputale.

GETTING THERE AND AWAY

By road Ella is roughly 210km (5–7 hours in a private vehicle) from Colombo via Ratnapura (115km/3–4 hours), Haputale (25km, 45 minutes) and Bandarawela (12km, 30 minutes). Coming from the northwest, it is 140km/4 hours from Kandy via Badulla (20km/45 minutes), or 55km/1½ hours from Nuwara Eliya via Bandarawela. The gateway to/from most destinations further south or east, be it Galle (215km/5 hours), Matara (165km/4 hours), Tangalle (140km/3 hours), Hambantota (105km/2 hours), Tissamaharama (90km/2 hours), Kataragama (90km/2 hours) or Arugam Bay (135km/3 hours), is the junction town of Wellawaya 28km (45–60 minutes) to the south.

Plenty of buses pass through or close to Ella in all directions, but none originates here, which can mean it is easier to get here by bus than it is to get away, as all the seats on most passing buses will be taken. Note, too, that while buses coming from or headed on to Wellawaya and other destinations further south and east will stop on Ella's main road, immediately north of the crossroads with the Passara Road, buses headed along the main road between Bandarawela and Badulla (including the twice-hourly service from Colombo) will stop 3km northwest of Ella at Kumbalwela Junction, from where you'll need to catch a tuktuk into the village.

By rail All trains on the upcountry line connecting Colombo, Kandy, Nuwara Eliya, Haputale and Bandarawela to Badulla stop at Ella's central railway station [445 F1].

WHERE TO STAY There's no shortage of accommodation in and around Ella, but while places in the moderate and upmarket categories tend to have competitive rates, budget accommodation is pricey by Sri Lankan standards, and there are very few places that would qualify as shoestring on a price basis anywhere else in the country. Budget-conscious travellers who don't mind being based away from the action are pointed to the cluster of likeable and (for Ella) reasonably priced homestays in leafy Kithelella 1–2km out of town along Waterfall Road.

Exclusive

✳ 🏠 **The Secret Ella** [445 G3] (5 rooms) Passara Rd; ☎057 222 6333; m 0775 995999; e info@thesecrethotels.com; w thesecrethotels.com/ella. Situated 3km east of the town centre, this gorgeous property comprises a restored & refurnished 1850s planter's bungalow with original high ceilings, treated concrete floors, traditional central courtyard, old black-&-white photos on the walls, open kitchen & a lovely green garden that's regularly visited by muntjac deer & various highland birds, and incorporates a viewpoint over the surrounding tea plantation to Nine Arch Bridge. Spacious individually styled rooms are brightened up with colourful ethnic fabrics & come with fan, fridge, tea-/coffee-maker, TV & large bathroom with tub & shower. *From US$195/230 sgl/dbl B&B, plus US$35 pp FB.* **$$$$$**

Upmarket

🏠 **98 Acres Resort** [445 G4] (30 rooms) Passara Rd; ☎057 205 0050; e info@resort98acres.com; w resort98acres.com. Situated on a tea estate 2km east of the town centre, this attractive resort offers accommodation in standalone stone chalets with thatched roofs, treated concrete floors, wide balconies offering a view towards Little Adam's Peak & cheerful interiors with furniture made from old railway sleepers. The restaurant is one of the best in Ella & other amenities include a spa & swimming pool. Older & unfit travellers be warned that the property sprawls extensively across steep slopes so there are lots of stairs. *From US$185/195 sgl/dbl B&B.* **$$$$$**

🏠 **Mountain Heavens** [445 F3] (8 rooms) Waterfall Rd; ☎057 222 8800; e mountainheavens@gmail.com; w mountainheavensella.com. Situated 600m along the road to Kithelella, this quiet & unpretentious owner-managed hotel affords the most sensational imaginable views over the Ella Gap, framed by Ella Rock & Little Adam's Peak, with the Ravana Falls in the foreground. Massive modern rooms with an attractive colour scheme all come with fan, TV, and private balcony led to by tall French windows that make the most of the setting. A good restaurant, also with a view, serves well-priced local & international cuisine, plus beer & wine. *US$160 dbl B&B.* **$$$$**

Moderate

✳ 🏠 **Planter's Bungalow** [445 F7] (6 rooms) Wellawaya Rd; ☎057 492 5902; m 0771 540737; e plantersbungalow@aol.com; w plantersbungalow.com. An imaginative contemporary take on the colonial style typical of Hill Country, this restored planter's bungalow is set in lush tropical birdsong-filled gardens in the Ella Gap 11km south of town. Offering stylish accommodation in individually decorated colour-themed rooms, it's ideal for those who want to retreat to nature with every comfort & good food (the owners once ran a Michelin-star inn in Britain). *US$94 dbl, US$144 for a 2-room unit sleeping 4; all rates B&B.* **$$$$**

🏠 **Zion View** [445 F2] (14 rooms) Waterfall Rd; m 0773 810313, 0727 855713; e zionviewella@gmail.com; w ella-guesthouse-srilanka.com. Boasting a stylish terrace restaurant/bar that makes the most of a fine view over the Ella Gap, this owner-managed hotel 300m east of the town centre has something of a boutique feel, & the brightly decorated dbl or twin rooms with nets, safe & private balcony are among the most attractive & best sited in town. It's very child-friendly, with several family rooms & a playground, which might not be a selling point to travellers without children. *From US$90 dbl B&B.* **$$$$**

🏠 **Ravana Heights** [445 G3] (6 rooms) Wellawaya Rd; ☎057 222 8888; m 0777 309542; e senadhi@slt.lk; w ravanaheights.com. Boasting a magnificent location 300m downhill from the town centre, this long-serving owner-managed hotel underwent a complete overhaul in late 2016 & the small tiled rooms are

15

now all stylishly decorated with colourful fabrics, wood furniture, fan, TV, fridge & private balcony overlooking the Ella Gap & facing Ella Rock. Nice but feels a bit overpriced. *From US$121 dbl B&B.* **$$$$**

Budget

✴ 🏠 **Waterfall Homestay** [444 C5] (4 rooms) Kithelella; \057 567 6933; m 0776 957496; e waterfallshomestay@gmail.com; w waterfalls-guesthouse-ella.com. Arty, individualistic & eclectic are the adjectives that spring to mind in relation to this Australian-owned & -managed lodge facing the Ravana Falls 1.5km southwest of the town centre, but it also has a great jungly setting alive with birds & monkeys, while homesick pet-owners will enjoy the opportunity to bond with the cats & dogs. Rooms are decorated with flair & colour, & meals other than b/fast can be taken at the close-by & affiliated Good Neighbours Restaurant. *US$40/47 sgl/dbl B&B.* **$$$**

✴ 🏠 **White House Guest Inn** [445 H2] (5 rooms) Passara Rd; \057 205 0294; m 0772 290803; e khmwhitehouse@gmail. com. One of Ella's newer guesthouses, this little gem is owned & managed by a friendly & efficient family who live on the property, which has a quiet corner location 300m east of the town centre. The open & airy modern 3-storey building has the feel of an architect-designed family home, thanks to the great use of space, & an outstanding feature is the breezy rooftop dining area where b/fasts & dinners are served. Rooms have tall ceilings, treated concrete floors, darkwood furniture offset by colourful fabrics, fan, TV & small but modern bathrooms. It also offers taxi services locally & all over Sri Lanka. Excellent value. *US$33/43 sgl/dbl B&B, dropping to US$23/30 out of season.* **$$**

🏠 **Hotel Alta Vista** [445 G2] (14 rooms) Main St; \057 567 5014; e altavistasrilanka@ gmail.com; w hotel-alta-vista-ella-sri-lanka. en.ww.lk. This modern high-rise has an elevated location in the heart of the village but set back far enough from the main road that traffic noise isn't an issue. Spacious rooms have wooden floor, fan, TV, & balcony with a view. Furniture & fabrics are quite fuddy-duddy but not offensively so. Decent value. *US$51/US$70 dbl B&B with fan/ AC.* **$$$**

🏠 **Lizzie Villa Guesthouse** [445 G2] (13 rooms) \057 222 8643/205 1799. Named after its friendly owner-manager, Ella's oldest private guesthouse in Ella opened under the same management back in 1978 & retains a quiet location next to Ella Spice Garden only 250m from the main road. The original 7-room villa is old-fashioned in the nicest possible way, with a shared lounge & wide shady terrace looking out to a pretty flowering garden. The more modern-looking new wing spans 2 storeys & offers great views to Ella Rock. All rooms have net & those in the new wing also have balconies. *US$35/40 sgl/dbl in old wing, or US$40/50 in new wing, with significant discounts to walk-ins & out of season; all rates B&B.* **$$**

🏠 **Floating 2 Ella** [445 G2] (3 rooms) Waterfall Rd; m 0715 228750; e info@ floating2ella.com; w floating2ella.com. Set in a tall narrow building only 150m west of the town centre, the colourfully decorated rooms here offer sensational views to Ella Rock & come with fan, net, balcony, & cheap-looking but serviceable furniture. Good value, taking into account the view. *US$43 dbl B&B.* **$$**

🏠 **Ella Vallee 02** [445 H2] (9 rooms) Passara Rd; \057 222 6280; m 0778 438811; e info@ vallee02.com; w vallee02.com. This new 3-storey hotel is set on a quiet back road 400m from the town centre & close to several good restaurants. Small neat rooms have treated concrete floors, fan, TV & a modern bathroom. Decent value. *US$37/40 sgl/dbl B&B.* **$$**

🏠 **Sun Top Inn** [445 G1] (7 rooms) Police Station Rd; \057 222 8673; m 0773 999552; e suntopinn@yahoo.com; 📘 suntopella. This family-run 2-storey lodge around the corner from the railway station has a pleasant 1st-floor restaurant & lounge, a large garden with wooden tables & chairs, & small but clean modern rooms with net, fan & somewhat confrontational orange floor tiles. Fair value. *US$30/37 sgl/dbl, dropping by 25% out of season.* **$$**

🏠 **Country Comfort Inn** [445 G1] (12 rooms) Police Station Rd; \057 222 8532; m 0777 378754; e info@hotelcountrycomfort. lk; w hotelcountrycomfort.lk. A new building constructed in the colonial style, this place is less characterful than the façade would have you believe, but the location is quiet & convenient, & the large rooms with queen-size bed seem like decent enough value. *US$37 dbl.* **$$**

Shoestring

🏠 **Chamodya Homestay** [444 C4] (4 rooms) Kithelella; ☎ 057 357 5432; e chamodyahomestay@hotmail.com. Named after the likeable host couple's young daughter, this excellent homestay 1km west of the town centre offers great views to Ella Rock & the top of the Ravana Falls, & the rooms all come with fan, net, wood or tile floor, spotless modern bathroom & balcony. The 2 top rooms have more privacy & the best views. *US$27 dbl B&B.* **$$**

🏠 **Idyll Homestay** [444 C5] (4 rooms) ☎ 057 205 0834; m 0719 113701; e idyella788@gmail. com; w idyllhomestay.strikingly.com. Offering a great view of Ella Rock, this simple homestay 1.2km from the town centre has comfortable rooms with modern black-&-white décor, net, clean bathroom & balcony. The owner-managers are very friendly & professional, & speak good English. *US$27 dbl B&B.* **$$**

🏠 **Waterfall View Inn** [444 C5] (4 rooms) Kithelella; m 0779 961971; e waterfallview@ gmail.com. The most westerly lodge in Kithelella, this family-owned & -managed lodge has cool

& comfortable but tackily decorated rooms with net & a close-up view of the Ravana Falls. Good Sri Lankan meals are served by request. *US$30 B&B.* **$$**

🏠 **Nanda Guesthouse** [445 F1] (5 rooms) Station Rd; ☎ 057 222 8768. The closest guesthouse to the railway station & possibly the cheapest anywhere in town, this has small but adequate rooms with net & fan. The proximity to the main road makes it a bit noisy, but that's a small quibble at this price. The ground-floor restaurant is well priced too. *US$14/20 dbl with shared/en-suite bathroom, dropping to US$7/14 out of season.* **$**

🏠 **Blue View Inn** [445 G1] (3 rooms) Police Station Rd; m 0776 954243. This agreeable homestay has a quiet back-road location only 300m from the railway station & 400m from the main road, though the rustic surrounds are being replaced by a spate of new constructions. Clean rooms have fan, nets & optional AC. Excellent local b/fasts & other meals are offered by request. *US$20/30 dbl with fan/AC.* **$**

✗ WHERE TO EAT AND DRINK
Moderate to expensive

✗ **AK Ristoro** [445 H2] Passara Rd; ☎ 057 205 0676; ⏰ 11.00–22.00. Situated 500m east of the town centre, this classy cement, brickface & darkwood restaurant has an open kitchen, sensibly priced & well-stocked bar, & contemporary music playing in the background. It's strong on pasta, but also serves curries, salads, tapas & a fusion menu, with plenty of choice in the **$$** range. A pleasant place to settle in for the evening, with a more subdued vibe than comparable places on Main St.

✗ **Restaurant 98** [445 G4] Passara Rd; ☎ 057 205 0050; w resort98acres.com; ⏰ 07.30–22.00. Set in the 98 Acres resort, this hilltop stone-&-thatch construction has an organic feel enhanced by the deck made from old railway sleepers & lovely view of the surrounding tea estates. Choose between a Sri Lanka set menu or an international à la carte menu of salads, sandwiches, pasta & other mains. It has a full bar & serves great coffee. Book ahead for dinner as space is limited & preference is given to resort guests. **$$$**

✗ **Dream Café** [445 G2] Main St; ☎ 057 222 8950; w dreamcafe-ella.com; ⏰ 07.30–21.30.

This licensed split-level restaurant has the urban feel of an open-sided warehouse & serves an appropriately contemporary Western menu, with thin-crust pizzas being the acknowledged speciality, though a good variety of wraps, burgers & grills is also served, along with a few local dishes. **$$–$$$**

✗ **Café Chill** [445 G2] Main St; m 0771 804020; ⓕ cafechillnescoffeeshop; kitchen ⏰ 10.00–22.00. Bold colour schemes offset by lush greenery visible through its open sides give this funky 2-storey cocktail bar/restaurant a contemporary tropical feel. Specialities include curries & lamprais, but the menu also extends to salads, burgers, steaks, pizzas & one-offs such as Greek grilled fish & chicken schnitzel. Always busy at night, the bar usually stays open long after the kitchen switches off. **$$$**

✗ **Ceylon Tea Factory** [445 H2] Passara Rd; m 0749 339430; ⓕ pg/ceylonteafactoryella. The brainchild of the management of Uva Halpewatte Tea Factory, this stylish new addition to Ella's burgeoning culinary scene claims to be the world's first tea factory-themed restaurant. The exterior does indeed look like a miniature tea factory, while the retro interior incorporates a small museum about tea production, & the licensed bar serves tea-infused cocktails & mocktails along with the usual beer, wine & spirits. The menu is cosmopolitan & the food generally good, but it is quite pricey by Ella standards. $$$–$$$$

♀ **Grand Ella Motel** [445 G3] Wellawaya Rd; ☎057 567 0711; w chcresthouses.com. A minute's walk downhill from the town centre, the reincarnated & renamed Ella Resthouse is the village's oldest hostelry & the licensed restaurant & garden pavilion offer an unbeatable view to the lowlands through the Ella Gap. The food is nothing special but it's ideal for a sundowner cocktail or beer with a view.

Cheap to moderate

✕ **Matey Hut** [445 F2] Main St; m 0772 583450; ⊕ 08.00–21.00. As cheerful & unpretentious as its name suggests, this small owner-managed eatery next to the railway bridge serves a good selection of super-affordable curries, rotis & sandwiches, as well as cakes & coffee. No alcohol. $

✕ **Ella Village Restaurant** [445 G2] Main St; ☎057 222 8685; m 0726 727890; ⊕ 07.30–10.00 & 13.00–late. This small owner-managed country-style restaurant has a lovely deck decorated with wooden furniture & lush pot plants. It specialises in curries, string hoppers & other Sri Lankan fare, cooked mild by default to cater to foreign palates, but spiced up by request. The traditional b/fast is particularly good. No alcohol. $$

✕ **Adam's Breeze** [445 F4] Passara Rd; m 0775 066560; ⊕ 07.30–late. Situated opposite the start of the walking trail to Little Adam's Peak, this place doesn't have much of a view but the owner-manager/chef is very friendly & the food is tasty & good value. Round off your hike with a Western or local b/fast, sweet

or savoury filled roti, or filling curry. No alcohol. $$

✕ **Art Café Umbrella** [445 E4] Passara Rd; m 0728 149595; **f**; ⊕ 09.00–21.00. This quirkily colourful 2-storey café, 750m east of the town centre, has a limited but interesting menu including the likes of muesli & fruit with curd, pumpkin & shiitake mushroom soup, kottu roti & chop suey ($$). It also has a good dessert & coffee menu. The 1st-floor terrace looks into a pine plantation. No alcohol.

✕ **Fish & Chips Restaurant** [445 G2] Main St; m 0719 466700; ⊕ 08.00–20.00. This cosy & colourful local eatery with indoor & terrace seating is strong on seafood, as might be expected, but it also serves kebabs, kottu roti, devilled dishes, curries & a selection of shakes, lassis & juices. No alcohol. $$

✕ **Good Neighbours Restaurant** [444 C5] Kithelella; m 0784 718145, 0775 144699; w ellagoodneighbours.com; ⊕ dinner served 19.30. This rustic locally owned restaurant serves the cluster of homestays in Kithelella 1.5km southwest of the town centre. Expect a varied rice-&-curry buffet dominated by vegetarian dishes but with 1 protein dish. It costs US$6 pp including desserts. Booking is essential. No alcohol but you can bring your own. $$$

✕ **Jade Green Restaurant** [445 G2] Main St; ☎057 222 8786; ⊕ 09.00–21.00. Despite its inauspicious setting above the Bank of Ceylon, this family-run restaurant serves one of the best rice-&-curry spreads in Ella, with plenty on offer for vegetarians. $$

✕ **Ella Flower Garden** [445 F4] Passara Rd; ☎057 205 0480; w ellaresort.com; ⊕ 06.00–22.00. Offering a great view at the junction for the walking trail to Little Adam's Peak, this garden restaurant serves a varied selection of international & local dishes in the $$ range. It doubles as a nursery & breeding centre for caged birds, & also has (overpriced) accommodation.

OTHER PRACTICALITIES There is no bank in Ella and the only ATM, operated by the Bank of Ceylon, cannot be relied upon to accept foreign cards. If you run short of cash, head to Bandarawela and Badulla, where all the usual banks are represented. For packaged hiking snacks, you'll find the well-stocked Ella Supermarket [445 G2] (⊕ 08.00–19.30) on Passara Road a few metres east of the junction with Main Street. Police Station Road, just north of the post office, is home to two useful enterprises: the efficient and inexpensive Sampath Laundry Services [445 G1] and the eclectic, quirky and fun RMS Antiques & Brassware [445 G1] (m 0779 297811).

WHAT TO SEE AND DO An attractive village in its own right, Ella is well positioned for day trips to the places described below. Further afield, Buduruvagala Temple and Dialyuma Falls near Wellawaya (pages 495 and 496) are perfectly feasible goals for a day trip out of Ella, as are most sites of interest listed under Haputale (pages 439–42), the one obvious exception being Horton Plains National Park, at least if you want to be there in the early morning, before the mist descends.

Around the village The sites of interest described below are all easily (or most normally) reached from central Ella on foot.

Ella Spice Garden [445 G2] (m *0752 363636;* e *ellaspicegarden@gmail.com;* f *ella.spicegarden*) Set back 250m from Main Street, this lush family-run garden contains 15 types of spice, including cinnamon, and also runs popular cooking lesson for groups of two to eight people. Cooking lessons run between 17.00 and 20.00, cost US$17 per person, and culminate in a delicious curry spread. A simple tour of the garden and its various spices costs US$0.70.

Ravana Cave and Temple [445 D5] (*Entrance US$1*) A natural fissure in the craggy cliffs below Ella, this small cave is reputedly where the demon-king Ravana imprisoned Sita before relocating her to the Ashok Vatika pleasure garden outside Nuwara Eliya. Another legend claims that it forms the entrance to an 11km subterranean tunnel that connects it to Dowa and Bogoda temples. On a more certain footing, recent excavations undertaken by the Department of Archaeology suggest the cave supported human habitation some 25,000 years ago. The cave's impressive pedigree notwithstanding, there isn't a great deal to see here, though the views are impressive and an associated temple, established by King Valagamba in the 1st century BC, incorporates some well-preserved Kandyan-era paintings and architectural features. To get here, follow the Wellawaya Road south out of town for 1.5km, then turn right on to a rough but clearly signposted feeder road that leads to the temple after 1km. A short but steep climb incorporating 500 steps leads to the cave.

Ravana Falls [444 D6] This 25m-high waterfall 1.5km southwest of the town centre, like the eponymous cave, is traditionally associated with King Ravana and his captive Sita, who reputedly used to bathe in the pool at its base. Surrounded by lush forest, it is quite an impressive sight in the rains but is often reduced to a trickle in the dry season. It is sometimes referred to as the Upper or Little Ravana Falls to distinguish it from the Bambaragama Falls, which is also often (but incorrectly) referred to as the Ravana Falls. Good views of the waterfall can be obtained by walking south along Waterfall Road to the cluster of homestays at Kithelella. The footpath to Ella Rock also crosses the slope above the waterfall and provides access to a viewpoint of it.

Ella Rock [445 E7] The most enjoyable hike in the vicinity of Ella is the ascent of Ella Rock, which rises to an elevation of 1,360m on the escarpment south of the town centre, and offers sensational views over the Ella Gap and lowlands to its south. Starting at Ella railway station or the main crossroads in the town centre, it's 4–5km in either direction, depending on which route you use, and it usually takes at least 2 hours out and 90 minutes back, so allow up to 5 hours with pauses. The best time to hike is early morning, when the risk of mist and cloud is lowest. It's easy enough to do the walk unguided, but a guide can be arranged at any guesthouse in town for around US$10. If you decide to go it alone, be wary of any local who offers you unsolicited (mis)directions or tries to latch on to you in hope of a payment. Since much of the path follows the railway line, you also need to keep eye and ear open for trains, which move slowly enough to allow plenty of time to get out of the way.

Two routes lead out of town towards Ella Rock. The most popular and straightforward entails following the railway track southwest out of Ella railway station for 2.5km to the so-called Black Bridge [444 C6]. A more scenic alternative, only 500m longer, involves following Waterfall Road for 2km, passing Mountain Heavens and Waterfalls Homestay to your left, and offering views across to the Ravana Falls, until it intersects with the railway, then turning left on to the line and continuing for 1km to the Black Bridge. From the bridge, follow the railway line for another 600m, passing through Kithelella railway station after 200m, before taking a clear footpath to the left and them almost immediately crossing a small bridge where you need to fork left. From here, the footpath curves back uphill through tea fields and a rubber plantation to reach the summit after another 1.5km. Having reached the summit, you can extend the walk by following a 200m footpath south to a small Buddhist shrine. On the return leg, once you have your bearings, look out for the steeper and more overgrown shortcut that skirts the cliff above Ravana Falls before emerging on the railway track between Kithelella station and the Black Bridge.

Little Adam's Peak [445 G5] Named for its rather tenuous resemblance to Adam's Peak, this 1,141m summit stands sentry above the east side of the Ella Gap, and offers views almost as spectacular as those from Ella Rock, its taller southwestern counterpart. To get here, follow the Passara Road out of town for 1km until you reach Ella Flower Garden Resort, then turn right through a gateway on to a well-marked footpath that leads to the peak after 1.8km, culminating in a series of around 250 steps. Allow 90 minutes from the town centre for the round trip. No guide is required.

Newburgh Green Tea Estate [445 G4] Now part of the Finlay's Group and specialised in green tea, the Newburgh Estate was established in 1884 and its factory opened on the Passara Road 2.5km east of Ella in 1903. Cursory 15-minute tours of the factory include a green cuppa but seem rather overpriced at US$3.30 per person.

Nine Arches Bridge [445 G3] Built between Ella and Demodara in 1921, this iconic 92m-long, 25m-high rock-and-cement viaduct is the longest and tallest railway bridge in Sri Lanka. Its rather evocative Sinhala name Ahas Namaye Palama means 'Nine Skies Bridge' and refers to the way the sky is framed by each of the nine arches when viewed from below. It can be reached either by following the railway track northeast out of Ella for 2.5km (keeping an ear open for oncoming trains) or else by walking or driving along the Passara Road for 2.5km then turning left just past Newburgh Green Teas Estate to a great viewpoint from where you can scramble down on foot to the valley it spans.

West and north of Ella The attractions described below are all accessed from the main road that runs between Bandarawela and Badulla to the northwest of Ella.

Uva Halpewatte Tea Factory [444 B1] (*057 222 8599*; w *halpetea.com/halpe-tea-factory*; ⊕ *07.30–17.00*) Perched at an altitude of 1,350m some 4km northwest of Ella, this iconic tea factory was built in 1940 and changed very little in the interim, despite having changed ownership in 1971 and now ranking as the largest tea producer in Uva Province, with a staggering average monthly production of 150,000kg. Entertaining and informative 30-minute factory tours cost US$2 per person and culminate with a tea-tasting session and opportunity to buy some of Halpewatte's produce. The factory lies about 1.7km off the Bandarawela–Badulla Road and is most easily reached by tuktuk, which should cost US$3–4 return, inclusive of waiting time.

Dowa Rock Temple [map, page 368] Sandwiched between a babbling brook and the Bandarawela Road 6km from Ella, Dowa reputedly provided sanctuary to King Valagamba – who is also associated with the foundation of Abhayagiriya Monastery and the oldest cave temple at Dambulla – at some point during his 14-year exile from Anuradhapura in the 1st century BC. The temple's best-known feature is an 11.5m-high engraved Buddha with a finely executed head and torso but unfinished lower body. Set in a tall granite rock face, the incomplete engraving is traditionally attributed to King Valagamba, who abandoned work on it when his enemies discovered his whereabouts. Scholarly sources date it to the 3rd or 4th century AD, while its similarity to the more impressive sequence of engravings at nearby Buduruvagala has led to speculation that it was a near-contemporaneous prototype for this 10th-century Mahayana masterpiece. Also of interest, the main five-chambered cave temple has an engraved 10th-century stone door-frame and is flanked by paintings of the fang-toothed Hindu guardian deities Kubera and Bhairava, the latter with two arms and an elephant in his mouth, the former eight-armed with a grazing cow below his teeth. The temple's first three chambers contain some superb Kandyan paintings, among them the timeworn red 17th-century images on the lower walls of the first chamber. Plenty of more mundane modern paintings adorn all five chambers. Look out too for the entrance to the Ravana Tunnel, which is guarded by a sculpted clay king cobra, and reputedly runs underground for 11 km, connecting Dowa both to Ella's Ravana Temple and to the more northerly Bogoda Temple. No admission fee is charged but a nominal donation might be asked to enter the cave temple. Any bus running along the busy road between Ella or Badulla and Bandarawela can drop you at Dowa. A tuktuk from Ella will cost US$3–4 return, inclusive of waiting time.

Demodara railway station [map, page 368] The first of three stations punctuating the 14km track that runs north from Ella to Badulla, Demodara is renowned among train buffs for its innovative 900m-long spiral loop, which forces the train to turn kittenish and chase its tail into a 320m-long tunnel directly below the station. Known as the Demodara Loop, the track was laid in 1921 and designed to conform to a colonial government ruling imposing a maximum incline of 1 in 44. D J Wimalasurendra, the Sri Lankan engineer responsible for the innovation, was reputedly inspired by the sight of a Sikh supervisor on a local tea estate wrapping a turban around his head. To see the loop in action, head out to Demodara station (1.5km off the Badulla Road, just past the eponymous tea factory) in time to catch a passing train (Ella railway station will have the schedule). Alternatively, to experience the Demodara Loop (and Nine Arches Bridge) for yourself, hop on a Badulla-bound train at Ella, and take it at least as far as Udurawa, which is the first station after Demodara.

Bogoda Bridge and Temple [map, page 368] Constructed in c1700, the unique timber bridge at Bogoda spans a small stone gorge flowed through by the Gallanda River on an ancient trade route connecting Kandy to Badulla. The 15m-long bridge is reputedly the oldest surviving construction of its type in Sri Lanka, providing a unique example of early Kandyan architecture and engineering held together without nails. It comprises a 1.5m-wide timber deck enclosed by wooden balustrades, supported by three gigantic tree trunks on a rock base, and buttressed

15

in the middle by two strong timber uprights. A series of carved pillars, once lacquered in black, red and yellow, supports a roof of flat tiles. Next to the bridge, the much older Bogoda Temple stands alongside an inscription declaring it was established in the 1st century BC by King Valagamba, and the interior incorporates some striking Kandyan paintings. In theory, entrance to the site costs US$1.35, but there's seldom anybody around to collect the money.

Bogoda lies 10km along a side road that branches northwest from the main road between Ella and Badulla at the junction village of Hali Ella. To get here on public transport, catch a bus or train between Ella and Badulla and ask to be dropped at Hali Ella, then catch another bus to Jangulla, from where a 2.5km dirt road branches left to take you to the top of the steep 200m staircase leading down to the temple and bridge. If you don't fancy the walk from Jangulla, pick up a tuktuk in Hali Ella.

Badulla Situated only 20km north of Ella, the provincial capital of Uva stands at an altitude of 680m below the nine peaks of the 2,036m-high Namunukula range. A thriving town with a population of 50,000, Badulla is also an important road transport hub, not to mention the eastern terminus of the 290km upcountry railway track that runs inland from Colombo. From a tourist perspective, however, Badulla sees very little action compared with nearby Ella, and what little traffic does pass through is usually headed straight for the pretty Dunhinda Falls 3km further north. The town's most important historical site, the central Muthiyangana Temple was reputedly built in the 3rd century BC by King Devanampiya Tissa, and its bell-shaped dagoba is said to contain a collarbone relic of Lord Buddha, but there is little else about its architecture that indicates any great antiquity, partly because the original was razed during the Portuguese occupation. Also of interest is the ornately carved Kandyan-era Kataragama Shrine on Devale Street, which comes complete with a pair of ivory tusks donated by a 19th-century chieftain, and the British-built St Mark's Church, an Anglican edifice that contains a plaque commemorating the life of the empire-builder and serial elephant-killer Major T W Rogers, whose grave can be seen in Nuwara Eliya's golf course. In the unlikely event you end up overnighting in Badulla (see map, opposite), the pick of the cheapies is the Dunhinda Falls Inn (*Bandaranayake Rd;* \ *055 222 3038;* m *0777 378727; US$10/17 sgl/dbl with fan only, or US$17/20 with AC;* $), which has clean but old-fashioned rooms with net and TV. A slightly sleeker option is the four-storey Hotel Onix (*Bandaranayake Rd;* \ *055 222 2080; US$30/33 dbl with fan/AC;* $$), which has a small courtyard swimming pool and spacious tiled rooms with fridge, TV and private balcony.

Dunhinda Falls [map, page 368] (*Entrance US$1.35 pp*) The biggest tourist attraction in the immediate vicinity of Badulla, the relatively torrentous Dunhinda Falls is reached along a 1.25km footpath leading east from the Mahiyanganaya Road about 5km north of the town centre. A classic bridal-veil waterfall, it is created by the Badulu River, a tributary of the Mahaweli, as it plunges over a 64m cliff into a near-circular forest-fringed pool, generating considerable spray – the 'evaporating smoke' alluded to in its Sinhala name – after heavy rains. For newcomers to Sri Lanka, the rocky path to the waterfall, intermittently lined with stalls selling everything from tea and popcorn to children's toys and garish sun hats, provides something of a when-in-Rome education. Between the stalls, patches of riverine forest are home to pretty butterflies, cute squirrels, endemic birds such as Sri Lanka hill myna, and some notoriously quarrelsome macaque monkeys. The footpath leads to a perfectly sited viewpoint opposite the main falls. From here, steady-footed travellers can make their way cautiously to the base of the waterfall.

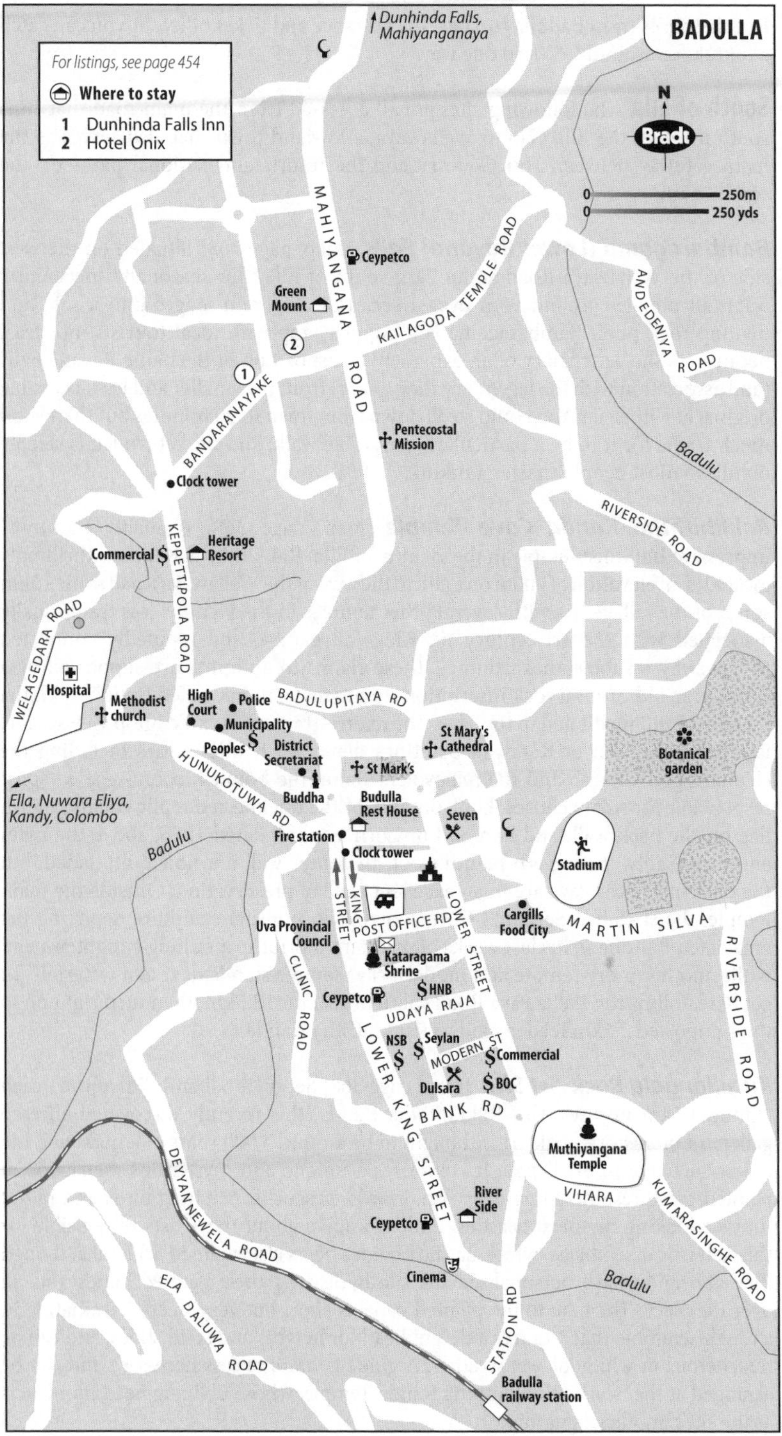

BADULLA

N

↑ Dunhinda Falls,
Mahiyanganaya

For listings, see page 454

🏠 **Where to stay**
1 Dunhinda Falls Inn
2 Hotel Onix

0 ——— 250m
0 ——— 250 yds

Ceypetco

Green Mount

KAILAGODA TEMPLE ROAD

MAHIYANGANA ROAD

BANDARANAYAKE

Pentecostal Mission

ANDEDENIYA ROAD

Badulu

RIVERSIDE ROAD

Clock tower

KEPPETTIPOLA ROAD

Heritage Resort

Commercial $

WELAGEDARA ROAD

Hospital

Methodist church

High Court
Police
Municipality
Peoples $
District Secretariat
Buddha

BADULUPITAYA RD

HUNUKOTUWA RD

Badulu

Ella, Nuwara Eliya,
Kandy, Colombo

St Mary's Cathedral

St Mark's

Budulla Rest House

Seven ✕

Fire station

Clock tower

Botanical garden

Stadium

MARTIN SILVA

RIVERSIDE ROAD

KING STREET

Uva Provincial Council

POST OFFICE RD

Kataragama Shrine

LOWER STREET

Cargills Food City

CLINIC ROAD

Ceypetco

UDAYA RAJA

$ HNB

NSB $
$ Seylan

MODERN ST
$ Commercial

Dulsara ✕
$ BOC

LOWER KING STREET

BANK RD

Muthiyangana Temple

VIHARA

KUMARASINGHE ROAD

DEYYAN NEWELA ROAD

River Side

Ceypetco

Cinema

ELA DALUWA ROAD

STATION RD

Badulu

Badulla railway station

High Hill Country ELLA

15

Regular buses from Badulla run past the entrance and ticket office, or you can catch a tuktuk for around US$1.50 one way.

South of Ella The following sites are all accessed from the main road that runs south through the Ella Gap to Wellawaya, a lowland town that also serves as the main gateway between Hill Country and the resorts and national parks on the south coast.

Bambaragama (Lower Ravana) Falls [map, page 368] Situated on the west side of the Wellawaya Road about 7km south of Ella, this seasonally spectacular waterfall plunges around 90m over a series of cliffs and ledges into a safe and inviting rock pool. Bambaragama is a popular stop with local tourists, not least because it's the beneficiary of an expedient transposition of the name Ravana Falls (and association with the legendary *Ramayana*) from the smaller and less accessible original at Kithelella. You could stroll down from town in 90 minutes but there's too much traffic for it to be a particularly enjoyable walk, and the return leg is steeply uphill, so most people charter a tuktuk.

Rakkhiththa Kanda Cave Temple [map, page 368] Arguably the most impressive Buddhist temple in the vicinity of Ella, Rakkhiththa Kanda is thrillingly located at an elevation of 700m on a cliff to the west of the Wellawaya Road some 15km south of the village. As with several other temples in the vicinity, it is traditionally associated with the 1st-century BC King Valagamba, and reputedly connected to Dowa by a subterranean tunnel. These claims to antiquity are supported by a 2,200-year-old Brahmi rock inscription stating that a monk called Buddharakkitha then lived and meditated in the cave. The main attraction today, clifftop views aside, is a fine collection of Kandyan paintings depicting Hindu deities including the elephant-god Ganesh and the malevolent Rahu, the bodiless cobra-headed spirit responsible for solar eclipses. Look out too for the unexpected replica of an English flag on the back wall, and lion and unicorn symbol, dated 1886, above the main entrance. Sadly, the superb paintings on the outer wall are now quite faded, but the ones inside the cave are in an excellent state of preservation. Outside the main temple, the so-called Serpent's Cave contains an unusual sculpture depicting the emaciated Buddha in his last weeks of meditation prior to attaining enlightenment, while another more remote and modern cave temple stands next to a waterfall. To get here, follow the Wellawaya Road south of Ella for 12.5km, then turn right on to the signposted 2.5km feeder road to Rakkhiththa Kanda.

Kurullangala Rock Art Site [map, page 368] Set on a tall and difficult-to-reach clifftop 1.5km northwest of Rakkhiththa Kanda, this recently discovered alfresco gallery of prehistoric rock art is thought to be around 5,000 years old, making it the oldest such site in Sri Lanka. It comprises a unique and mysterious menagerie of painted creatures, including deer, fish, lizards, peacocks, perching birds and rather Jurassic-looking mythical beasties. Little is known about the artists responsible for this fantastic assemblage, which has no obvious peers elsewhere in Sri Lanka, though they appear to have personalised the site by leaving their painted handprints all over the place. The hike to the painted panel is short but very steep, terminating in a tough scramble that requires a decent head for heights and solid shoes, and can be treacherous in windy or wet weather. A guide is more or less necessary and can be arranged at the nearby Rakkhiththa Kanda Temple, whose obliging head monk acts as the site's unofficial guardian.

Low Hill Country: Kitulgala, Ratnapura and Sinharaja

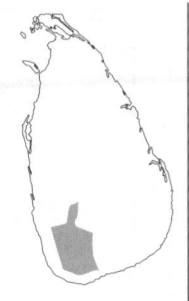

Sandwiched between the beach resorts of the southwest coast and the tall mountainous highlands around Adam's Peak and Horton Plains, the Low Hill Country of southwest Sri Lanka is a rather nebulous but very exciting region of sloping terrain characterised by a high year-round rainfall pattern and a natural cover of lush jungle. Renowned for its biodiversity, the region has two established and one nascent tourist focal point, all of which are of particular interest to adventurous travellers and dedicated birdwatchers. First up is Kitulgala, which has emerged in recent years as a hub of adrenaline and other outdoor activities, ranging from white-water rafting on the Kelani River to canyoning, abseiling, zip-lining and mountain biking. The other established attraction of the Low Hill Country is Sinharaja Forest Reserve, a UNESCO World Heritage Site whose dense rainforests offer great hiking opportunities and the country's most alluring spread of endemic and other localised forest birds. Less well known but almost as rich in terms of forest biodiversity is the Kanneliya Forest Reserve, which lies only 40km inland of Galle, making it far more accessible than Sinharaja as a day trip from the southwest coast. Altogether different is Ratnapura, a refreshing untouristy provincial capital situated on the Kalu River between Kitulgala and Sinharaja, where it has served as the pivot of Sri Lanka's lucrative gem trade for millennia.

KITULGALA

Picturesque Kitulgala (often spelt Kithulgala) stands at an altitude of 175m in a lushly forested valley on the north bank of the Kelani River, 6km downstream of its confluence with the Maskeliya. Straddling the A7 some 85km east of Colombo, it is a convenient place to break the journey from the capital to the higher Hill Country around Hatton and Nuwara Eliya, whether it be for a quick lunch or rafting trip, or an overnight stay. The village takes its name from the locally profuse kitul palm (*Caryota urens*), whose effervescent cloud-coloured sap can be drunk neat as toddy, thickened to become treacle, or boiled down to make jaggery, a fudge-like confectionery that rural folk like to nibble with black tea. Kitulgala is renowned as the location for the Oscar-winning 1957 war epic *Bridge on the River Kwai*, and while this association now probably means little to most under-40s, it retains a fabulously cinematic setting, dominated by the country's fourth-longest river as it flows fast and furious between widely spaced banks lined with a tangle of luxuriant jungle.

Since the 1990s, Kitulgala and the adjacent stretch of the Kelani have emerged as the focal point of Sri Lanka's white-water rafting industry. Several dozen rafting

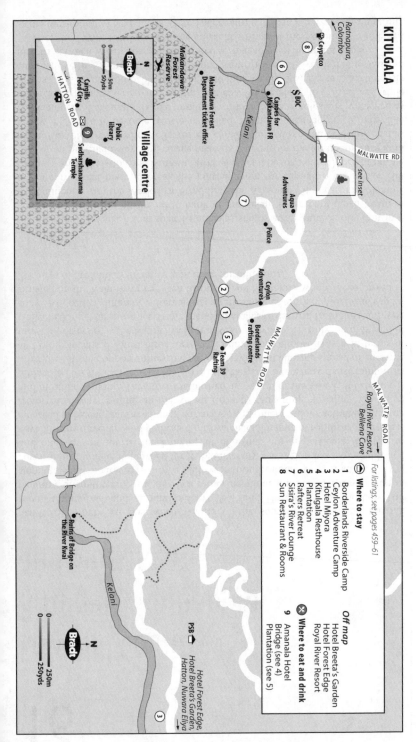

KITULGALA

Ratnapura, Colombo

⚑ Leypeto ⑧

⑥ ④

$ BOC

Village centre

Mandandawa Forest Reserve

● Makandawa Forest Department ticket office

● Canoes for Makandawa FR

N · Bradt

0 ____ 50m
0 ____ 50yds

Cargills Food City ●

HATTON ROAD

⑨ ✉ Public library

● Sudharshanarama Temple

Kelani

see inset

MALWATTE RD

🏠 🏕

● Aqua Adventures

⑦

● Police

● Ceylon Adventures

② ①

● Borderlands rafting centre ⑤

● Team 39 Rafting

MALWATTE ROAD

MALWATTE ROAD

Royal River Resort, Belilena Cave

● Ruins of Bridge on the River Kwai

Kelani

PSB 🏠

Hotel Forest Edge, Hotel Breeta's Garden, Hatton, Nuwara Eliya

③

N · Bradt

0 ____ 250m
0 ____ 250yds

For listings, see pages 459–61

ⓘ Where to stay

1 Borderlands Riverside Camp
2 Ceylon Adventure Camp
3 Hotel Miyora
4 Kitulgala Resthouse
5 Plantation
6 Rafters Retreat
7 Sisira's River Lounge
8 Sun Restaurant & Rooms

Off map

Hotel Breeta's Garden
Hotel Forest Edge
Royal River Resort

✖ Where to eat and drink

9 Amanala Hotel
Bridge (see 4)
Plantation (see 5)

companies now operate along a series of scenic grade 2–3 rapids upstream of the village, though sadly the future of this activity has been threatened by the construction of two dams associated with the Broadlands Hydropower Project on the Maskeliya and Kehelgamu rivers a short distance upstream of their respective confluences. Fortunately, rafting aside, Kitulgala now offers a veritable bouquet of adrenaline and other outdoor activities such as canyoning, abseiling, zip-lining and mountain biking. For wildlife enthusiasts, the Makandawa Forest Reserve, a readily accessible tract of lowland rainforest on the south bank of river opposite Kitulgala, is home to a wealth of localised wildlife, including 26 of the 33 bird species endemic to Sri Lanka. Another local site of interest is the Belilena Cave, which has thrown up some of the earliest evidence of human habitation anywhere is Sri Lanka.

GETTING THERE AND AWAY   Kitulgala lies 85km east of Colombo via Avissawella. Most buses from Colombo to Hatton (33km further southeast) and Nuwara Eliya (72km to the east) pass through Kitulgala and can drop or pick up passengers at the stage 50m east of the bridge. Kitulgala isn't on the rail network, but you could take the Kelani Valley Line to Avissawella and catch a bus from there.

WHERE TO STAY   *Map, opposite*
Plenty of accommodation is scattered along the riverbank and hillsides around Kitulgala, but while there are a few really good and well-priced boutique hotels and mid-range river camps, quality budget options are not so much thin on the ground as absent entirely.

Upmarket
✳ 🏠 **Borderlands Riverside Camp** (13 rooms) 📞 011 441 0110; **m** 0777 588370; **e** journeys@discoverborderlands.com; **w** discoverborderlands.com. By no means a conventional upmarket property, this wonderful & perennially popular eco-lodge sprawls across the sloping & thickly wooded riverbank alongside the Hatton Rd 1.5km east of the village centre. Combining a genuine bush atmosphere with funky & eclectic 21st-century furnishing, it is aimed at those who want to rough it in style, offering accommodation in a variety of wood & canvas units, most of which have a river view, though cheaper rooms use common bathrooms. Borderlands is very highly rated when it comes to rafting & other adventure activities, most of which are run by guides with international experience & training, & it offers reasonably priced packages inclusive of activities. *From US$60 pp HB.* **$$$$**

🏠 **Royal River Resort** (4 rooms) 📞 036 492 0790; **e** plantation.gh@gmail.com; **w** plantationgrouphotels.com. Situated about 7km north of the A7 along the same rough road that leads to Belilena Cave, this extraordinary wilderness retreat has an isolated forest setting around a swimming pool fed by a cascading mountain stream. The 4 rooms are split between 2 separate blocks, one by the river with French windows opening on to the bracingly cool pool, the other atop the kitchen with river view. The AC rooms are bright with sunlight bursting through windowed walls, but furnishings & bathrooms are basic & there's a touch of eccentricity in the décor. Meals are refreshingly neither fancy nor expensive, & are prepared in a galleried kitchen where guests in the pool can look up & see the chefs at work. *US$80/95 sgl/dbl B&B.* **$$$$**

Moderate
✳ 🏠 **Hotel Forest Edge** (4 rooms) 📞 051 492 4733; **e** plantation.gh@gmail.com; **w** plantationgrouphotels.com. Situated at a relatively crisp altitude of 520m off the Hatton Rd 10km east of the village centre, this is the pick of the Plantation Group's trio of stylish boutique properties near Kitulgala. Though the lodge isn't on the main river, a waterfall babbles soothingly past & the view from the balcony across the surrounding hills is spectacular. The large & attractively decorated rooms have paintings of endemic birds on the walls, & come with AC, cable TV, modern fittings, teak floor & skate-tiled bathrooms. Rafting & other excursions can be

16

arranged through reception. The short but steep feeder road can be very slippery after rain & may be problematic without a 4x4. *US$65/75 sgl/dbl B&B.* **$$$**

🏠 **Hotel Breeta's Garden** (7 rooms) ☏ 051 224 2020; **e** info@breetasgarden.com; **w** breetasgarden.com. Easily the best-value set-up near Kitulgala, this modest hilltop hotel surrounded by tea plantations 7km east of the village has a lovely garden setting, a kidney-shaped swimming pool with a view & a licensed restaurant serving tasty local & international dishes in the US$4–6 range. The spacious tiled rooms have wooden furniture, fan & cable TV. There's no AC but the higher altitude & exposed location keeps things relatively cool & breezy. The hands-on management can arrange rafting & other activities. *US$40/45 sgl/dbl B&B.* **$$**

🏠 **Plantation Hotel** (11 rooms) ☏ 036 228 7575; **e** plantation.gh@gmail.com; **w** plantationgrouphotels.com. This attractive & well-priced boutique hotel has a sumptuous riverside location on the Hatton Rd 1.5km east of the village centre. Stylish rooms have wrought metal & antique wood furnishing, AC, fan & cable TV, but it's definitely worth splashing out on the modest premium for one of the 3 larger super-deluxe units (rooms 9–11) with private balcony & river view. A licensed restaurant (⏱ 06.30–23.30) set amid clumps of bamboo overlooks a flat stretch of river, & serves local & international dishes in the US$4.50–6.50 range. It's a good place to arrange rafting trips & there's an on-site Rolls-Royce Museum. *US$61/66 sgl/dbl B&B, US$68/75 super-deluxe.* **$$$**

🏠 **Rafters Retreat** (10 rooms) ☏ 036 228 7598; **m** 0777 421455; **e** channape@sltnet.lk; **w** raftersretreat.com. Established in the 1990s & still under the same bush-savvy management, this pioneering rafting enterprise has a prime riverside location overlooking a set of gushing rapids on the western fringe of the village. The property's centrepiece, still lived in by the owner's family, is a fabulous colonial mansion complete with deep veranda, wooden shutters & hints of a bygone era. Guest accommodation is in stilted log cabins that are the antithesis of everything 5-star, with open fronts facing the roaring river & nothing but a net to fend off the mosquitoes & other bugs – not for the squeamish, but an ideal all-consuming jungle

experience for poetic &/or athletic travellers wanting to get back to nature. Excellent Sri Lankan food is served in an open-sided 2-storey restaurant overlooking the river. *US$95 dbl HB, but check in advance about package deals inc rafting & other activities.* **$$$$**

🏠 **Ceylon Adventure Camp** (15 rooms, 12 tents) ☏ 036 567 7871; **m** 0773 603723; **e** info@ceylonadventure.com; **w** ceylonadventure.com. Another place aimed at adventurous travellers with some tolerance for rough-&-ready conditions, this lovely riverside camp – reached along a 200m jungle footpath leading south from the Hatton Rd about 1km east of the village – offers the choice of an open-fronted stilted wood cabin with a private balcony overlooking the river, or a standard tent with mattress. It offers the widest range of adventure activities of any camp in Kitulgala & the enthusiastic guides are also very knowledgeable about birds & other wildlife. The restaurant serves Western & local food in the US$6–8 range. *US$70/83 sgl/dbl B&B, US$39 pp tent.* **$$$**

🏠 **Kitulgala Resthouse** (20 rooms) ☏ 036 228 7528; **m** 0766 836561; **e** kithulgala@ chcresthouses.com; **w** chcresthouses.com. This agreeably time-worn resthouse has a very central & equally spectacular setting on a forested rise overlooking the river. The justifiably popular Bridge Restaurant (⏱ 07.00–22.00), with its terracotta floor & wood ceiling, combines period character & a fine view with a good selection of local dishes & international grills in the US$5–11 range. Rooms are quaintly old fashioned, with plenty of cupboard space & fan but no nets, so it is worth paying extra for AC to keep the mosquitoes at bay. *Overpriced at the tourist rate of US$84/91 sgl/dbl B&B, plus US$10 for AC, but walk-ins could ask about the more realistic local rate.* **$$$$**

Budget
🏠 **Hotel Miyora** (25 rooms) ☏ 051 492 4744, 036 228 7007; **e** hotelmiyora@gmail.com; **w** hotelmiyora.com. Set alongside the Hatton Rd 4km east of the village centre, this bland & slightly rundown riverside hotel would be undistinguished in most other contexts, but in Kitulgala it stands out as perhaps the best-value & least-dire option in the budget range. Adequate rooms all come with AC & TV, & amenities include a swimming pool & restaurant, though sadly the river frontage

is hogged by a wedding reception hall that blocks the view even from the 5 so-called riverside rooms. *From US$31 dbl*. **$$**

🏠 Sisira's River Lounge (3 rooms)
✆ 036 226 7793; **m** 0778 558825; **e** info@sisirariverlounge.com. Situated about 1km southeast of the village along the same side road as the police station, this place has a fabulous riverside setting close to the main canoe crossing point for Makandawa Forest Reserve, & the surrounding riparian woodland offers excellent birding. The musty cabins have seen better days but all come with a riverfront view, fan & net. Meals cost around US$3/head. Adequate at the

asking price but could really do with a facelift. *From US$20–30 dbl*. **$**

Shoestring
🏠 Sun Restaurant & Rooms (6 rooms)
✆ 011 491 2787; **m** 0722 133584. Boasting a central location only 150m west of the Kitulgala Resthouse, this small owner-managed guesthouse seems to be the only genuine shoestring option in the vicinity. No-frills rooms are pleasantly cool & come with fans, but are quite dingy & scruffy. A restaurant is attached & the owner arranges very cheap rafting excursions with his own boats. *From US$8 dbl*. **$**

✗ WHERE TO EAT AND DRINK The unfocused nature of accommodation around Kitulgala, combined with the lack of bespoke restaurants, means that most overnight visitors tend to eat at their camp or hotel. For passing traffic, the best choice for a relaxed post-rafting lunch falls between the Plantation Hotel and the Bridge Restaurant (in the Kitulgala Resthouse). For instant lunchtime gratification, the Amanala Hotel (✆ *036 490 4010*) next to the post office serves up a tasty plate of rice-and-curry for US$1–2, and also a limited selection of pastries, rolls and the like.

OTHER PRACTICALITIES Despite being a major tourist focus, Kitulgala is a very small village with few amenities. A Bank of Ceylon can be found close to the Kitulgala Resthouse, but don't rely on being able to draw money here. Internet access and shops are also limited.

WHAT TO SEE AND DO
White-water rafting The Kelani River upstream of Kitulgala is the most popular white-water destination in Sri Lanka, serviced by several dozen rafting companies, and attracting around 50,000 tourists – mostly domestic day-trippers from Colombo – annually. Most companies set off in guided 6–12-berth rafts 5km upstream of Kitulgala and then follow the river through a series of grade 2–3 rapids back to the village, a 30–60-minute voyage depending on how high and fast the water is moving. The rafting here is considered to be very safe, as none of the rapids is dangerously large, and all are followed by a stretch of flat water where involuntary evacuees can catch their breath and climb back on board. However, when the water is too high, rafting may be suspended for a few days, and some concerned parties fear that the completion of the Broadlands Hydropower Project in 2017/18 might result in water levels being too low for the rafting to be offered on a regular basis. Some companies also offer an advanced rafting trip immediately upstream that incorporates a few grade 4 rapids, subject to the suitability and experience of the client. Excursions can leave at short notice at any time between 07.00 and 17.00, which means that it is perfectly possible to stop off in Kitulgala for a couple of hours to go rafting *en route* between Colombo and Hatton or Nuwara Eliya, even if you are travelling by bus. Most companies theoretically require a minimum of two clients, but most will accept solo travellers when they are not busy.

Dozens of rafting operations line the Hatton Road for several kilometres east out of Kitulgala. These range from a few large and well-established operations with professionally trained guides, permanent river camps, quality equipment and full insurance, to a proliferation of more ropey one-man-and-his-boat set-ups that generally offer cheaper rates but fewer guarantees when it comes to experience and quality. Top of the range is Borderlands (w *discoverborderlands.com*; page 459), an international organisation that charges US$43 per person for a standard rafting excursion. Rafters Retreat (w *raftersretreat.com*; page 460) and Ceylon Adventure (w *ceylonadventure.com*; page 460) are highly reputable companies with a long and impeccable track record but more affordable rates in the US$20–30 range. Of the smaller operations, Team 39 Rafting (❨ *036 474 7747;* m *0773 559945;* e *info@ raftingteam39.com;* w *raftingteam39.com*) has a good reputation and might well offer walk-in rates below US$20 per person when they are not busy. All these operations – and many others – are signposted prominently along the Hatton Road east of Kitulgala, and arrange a host of activities other than rafting.

Other adventure activities The companies listed above have responded to the potential threat to Kitulgala's rafting industry by developing a range of other activities aimed at thrill-seeking travellers. These include canyoning aimed at beginners and more experienced participants, zip-lining, rappelling, abseiling and climbing – most notably perhaps waterfall abseiling the 32m-high Sandun River Falls. More sedate activities include flat-water kayaking downstream of Kitulgala, mountain biking and forest walks. Expect to pay around US$20–30 per person per activity with most companies.

Rolls-Royce Museum Set in the grounds of the Plantation Hotel, this private museum displays about 15 vintage cars, all in running condition, including three Rolls-Royces, an MG and a Mini. No fee is charged and outsiders are welcome to pop in for a look.

Bridge on the River Kwai [map, page 458] Prior to the establishment of the rafting industry, Kitulgala's main claim to fame was as the location of *The Bridge on the River Kwai*, a David Lean film that starred William Holden, Jack Hawkins and Alec Guinness, and netted an impressive seven Oscars in 1958, among them Best Picture, Best Director and Best Actor. The namesake bridge, blown up during the film's climactic scene, spanned the Kelani River about 3km upstream of Kitulgala, a location passed by all rafting expeditions. It can also be reached on terra firma by following the Hatton Road east out of the village for 2.5km, then taking a footpath signposted to the right. After less than 50m, the path crosses a small footbridge and comes to a T-junction in front of a small house where you need to turn left then keep arcing around a hill for 500m until you reach the riverbank. All that remains of the bridge is a concrete support block, but the scene will be immediately familiar to anybody who has seen the film. The house at the T-junction, incidentally, is the home of Samuel Perera, who played a minor character called Jungle Boy in the film, and customarily stops any passing tourist to show them memorabilia – and ask for money!

Makandawa Forest Reserve [map, page 458] Running south from the Kelani River opposite Kitulgala, this 195ha reserve was set aside in 1903 to protect a tract of lowland rainforest that subsequently suffered from extensive logging, mostly in the 1950s and 1960s, but still supports an exceptionally high level of biodiversity. Streams running through the forest support 44 fish species, of which 20 are endemic to Sri Lanka, among them the very localised Ashoka barb and combtail paradise fish. In addition, checklists of 36 amphibian and 71 reptile species respectively include 27 and 35 endemics. More than 70 butterfly species have been identified, as have 30 mammals, most visibly wild boar, porcupine, purple-faced langur, toque macaque and giant flying squirrel.

Makandawa is best known for its birdlife. A checklist of 154 species includes 26 of the 33 national endemics, many of which are otherwise likely to be seen only in Sinharaja Forest (see box, pages 32–3). Among the more localised and conspicuous endemics reasonably likely to be encountered by day visitors are Sri Lanka spurfowl, green-billed coucal, Sri Lanka blue magpie, spot-winged thrush, Sri Lanka scimitar babbler and brown-capped babbler. The rivers that run through the reserve are known as a good site for the elusive oriental dwarf kingfisher and red-faced malkoha. Stick around until early evening, and you might even glimpse the endangered Serendib scops owl, which is the most recently discovered Sri Lankan endemic, originally located in 1995 when ornithologist Deepal Warakagoda heard an unfamiliar two-note *whoo-oh* call in Makandawa.

The easiest way to get to Makandawa is to take one of the canoes that ferry passengers across the Kelani River (*US$1.35 per person*) from the north bank just below the Kitulgala Resthouse. It's then a 500m walk to the forest department ticket office, where you must pay an admission fee equivalent to US$4.50 per person. From here, a network of signposted footpaths and nature trails runs south through the forest reserve, bypassing two significant waterfalls, on the Makul and Lenthiri rivers. There is no restriction on exploring the forest under your own steam, but you'll be more likely to see a good selection of forest birds on a guided trip with a reputable company such as Ceylon Adventure (*US$25 per person*), Rafters Retreat or Borderlands (*US$43 per person*).

Birdwatching north of the river Although dedicated birders will most certainly want to cross the river to visit the Makandawa Forest Reserve, the riparian woodland on the north bank also offers some rewarding birding and is easily explored on foot from any of the riverside camps and hotels. Endemic and other localised species that might be encountered here include Sri Lanka green pigeon, green-billed coucal, Sri Lanka hanging parrot, Malabar trogon, Sri Lanka grey hornbill, Malabar pied hornbill, yellow-fronted barbet and spot-winged thrush, the latter notable for its lovely song. Chestnut-backed owlet is resident in the grounds of Ceylon Adventures Camp. Generally, you'll see more birds in riverine woodland that stands next to flat water, as the rapids tend to drown out all other sounds including birdsong.

Belilena Cave [map, page 368] This massive open-sided cave stands at an altitude of 500m in the forested escarpment about 3km east of Kitulgala as the crow flies. Excavated over 1978–83, it has yielded some of the most important relics of prehistoric human activity yet uncovered in Sri Lanka. These include the fossilised skeletal remains of *Homo sapiens balangodensis* (commonly dubbed Balangoda man), which date back around 16,000 years. Rubble foundations of a similar vintage constitute the earliest evidence of manmade structures in South Asia. More ancient still is a cache of geometric microlithic stone tools and bone tools, which – together with evidence of the fire usage – suggest the cave sheltered a stone-age culture at least 30,000 years ago. Although these finds have been removed to the archaeological museum in Colombo, the cave is an attractive and atmospheric spot, all the more so thanks to the waterfall that plunges down in front of the entrance.

Belilena Cave lies about 6km from Kitulgala by road. To get here, follow the Hatton Road east out of the village for 1km, then turn left on to a signposted dirt road, then

With Royston Ellis

Boasting the world's highest density of gem deposits compared to landmass, Sri Lanka was known in times past as Ratnadipa, meaning 'Island of Gems'. A great ruby given to the Queen of Sheba by King Solomon is said to have come from the island. A gem adorning the Ruwanweli Dagoba at Anuradhapura was described in 1293 by Marco Polo as 'a flawless ruby a span long and quite as thick as a man's arm'. The British crown contains a 400-carat sapphire known as 'Blue Belle' mined in what was then Ceylon. Also from Ratnapura, but wrongly named the 'Star of India', is the 563-carat blue sapphire on display at the Museum of Natural History in New York.

Sri Lanka today ranks among the world's top five gem producers, containing deposits of more than 50 types of precious stone. Most popular is a form of blue sapphire known as Ceylon sapphire and famed for its unique clarity and lustre. The island also produces the world's finest chrysoberyl, a very hard yellow-green stone that includes the devastatingly attractive cymophane (also known as cat's eye) and alexandrite. Other gems commonly found on Sri Lanka include ruby, sapphire, spinel, topaz, tourmaline, quartz, peridot, moonstone, garnet and zircon. No emeralds or diamonds (except the Matara diamond, another name for zircon) are found, although imported diamonds are cut and polished for export. Because the cutting and polishing of stones was almost entirely in the hands of Muslims, the Medieval Chinese called gems from the island 'Mohammedan stones'.

Most sacred in Sri Lanka, and other Hindu and Buddhist cultures, are the precious stones known collectively as the Navaratna (literally 'Nine Gems'). Each of these gems represents a specific celestial body, and helps to protect the wearer from its negative powers. They are the ruby (associated with the sun), pearl (moon), emerald (Mercury), diamond (Venus), red coral of the *Corallium* genus

left again where the road switchbacks after about 600m, and continue for about 4km to a car park from where it's a few hundred metres' walk to the cave entrance. The road out is in terrible condition and there is no public transport, but any operator in Kitulgala can arrange a day trip, or you could rent a mountain bike for the outing.

RATNAPURA

The bustling capital of Sabaragamuva Province, Ratnapura – a Sanskrit name translating as 'City of Gems' – stands at an elevation of 130m on the north bank of the Kalu River 100km southeast of Colombo. Situated in a well-watered valley separating the Sinharaja massif from Adam's Peak, the town is regarded to be the wettest in Sri Lanka, receiving an average annual rainfall of around 3,500mm, and the surrounding countryside supports plentiful forests and a rich tropical agriculture. As its name suggests, however, Ratnapura is best known as the long-serving hub of Sri Lanka's lucrative gemstone industry, renowned for the wealth of rubies, sapphires and other precious stones mined in the vicinity. Unsurprisingly, these prodigious gems have long attracted foreign interest: Muslim merchants based at Kalutara (on the Kalu mouth) used to sail upriver to Ratnapura in Medieval times, while the Portuguese and Dutch captured the town and constructed fortresses here in 1620 and 1658 respectively, and it served as a district administrative centre during the British colonial era. Today, Ratnapura supports a population of around 60,000, and its chequered past means that all the country's main religious groups – Buddhist, Hindu, Muslim and Christian – are significantly represented. Never a major tourist

(Mars), yellow sapphire (Jupiter), blue sapphire (Saturn), hessonite (Rahu, the head of the demon that swallows the sun during eclipses) and cat's eye (Ketu, the headless torso of the same demon). The powerful Navaratna setting is a traditional arrangement featuring all of the nine sacred gems, with the ruby (sun) in the centre, and the other eight arranged around it in a specific sequence.

The ancient Precambrian rocks that underlie Ratnapura contain Sri Lanka's richest gem deposits, and the surrounding countryside is dotted with thatched awnings that mark the location of an active mine. These excavations might look quite crude, but they follow a traditional design that enables the near-naked miners at the bottom to pass up gem-bearing gravel to the top. Known as 'illam', this gravel is washed in shallow reed baskets that allow the mud and water to fall away, then sifted through thoroughly for gemstones. Small ones are sold directly to dealers, while larger ones are auctioned.

The auctions are almost silent affairs as the bidding is done by a complicated system of handholding and finger-tapping. Proceeds are shared according to a traditional formula with 20% going to the owner of the land where the mine is located, 20% to the owner of the pump that keeps the mine workable and 10% to the holder of the licence to mine. The workers involved share the balance, and also share half their income with their own backers. Dozens if not hundreds of small gem retailers line the streets of Ratnapura, selling locally sourced stones on to national and international dealers, but unless you really know your stuff, you should authenticate any planned purchase with the National Gem and Jewellery Authority (based in the Old Dutch Fort), or save your jewellery shopping for a reputable outlet in Galle or Colombo.

focus, Ratnapura used to be the closest base for exploring northern Sinharaja (there are now more convenient options at Kudawa) and it is also the starting point of the little-used long pilgrimage route up Adam's Peak (less than 20km northeast as the crow flies). Busy and agreeable though rather lacking in excitement, the town itself boasts a decent national museum, at least one temple of significant historical and aesthetic interest, and plenty of action for those of a gemological bent.

GETTING THERE AND AWAY
By road Ratnapura is 100km from Colombo along the A4 through Avissawella, a drive that typically takes up to 3 hours, depending on traffic, and is serviced by up to four buses hourly. Several direct buses run daily between Ratnapura and Deniyaya (100km/3 hours), Kandy (120km/3–4 hours), Bandarawela (100km/3 hours, with onward transport to Ella and Nuwara Eliya) and Matara (170km/4–5 hours). Travelling between Galle and Ratnapura, you'll most likely need to change buses at Akuressa.

By rail Although there is no rail service to Ratnapura, train enthusiasts might consider catching the Kelani Valley service from Colombo to its terminus at Avissawella, only 40km away, and catching one of the regular buses from there.

WHERE TO STAY *Map, page 466*
Accommodation is unusually thin on the ground, and costs and standards are both on the low side, but a few places stand out.

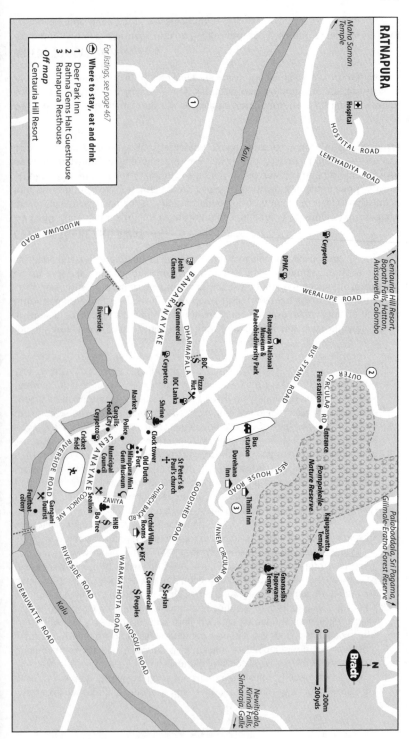

RATNAPURA

Maha Saman Temple

HOSPITAL ROAD
LENTHADIYA ROAD
Hospital

Kalu

MUDDUWA ROAD

Centauria Hill Resort, Bopath Falls, Hatton, Avissawella, Colombo

Ceypetto
DPMC
WERALUPE ROAD

Riverside

Jothi Cinema
BANDARANAYAKE
$ Commercial
DHARMAPALA
Ceypetto
IOC Lanka
Shrine
BOC
Pizza Hut
Ratnapura National Museum & Palaeobiodiversity Park

BUS STAND ROAD

OUTER CIRCULAR RD
Fire station
Entrance
Pompokelle Nature Reserve
Kahugaswatta Temple

Market
Cargills Food City
Police
Ceypetto
SENANAYAKE
Municipal Council
Clock tower
Old Dutch Fort
Minipura Mini Gem Museum
St Peter's & Paul's church

Cricket field

RIVERSIDE ROAD

Bus station
Dorehana Inn
REST HOUSE ROAD
Thilini Inn
INNER CIRCULAR RD
GOODSHED ROAD

Gnanasiha Tapovana Temple

RIVERSIDE ROAD
COUNCIL AVE
Gangani Tourist
Fruitbat colony

ZAVIYA
HNB
Bo Tree
Orchid Villa Rooms
KFC
$ Commercial
$ Peoples
$ Seylan

WARAKATHOTA ROAD
MOSQUE ROAD

DEMUWATTE ROAD

Kalu

Palabaddala, Sri Pagama, Gillmale-Eratna Forest Reserve

N
Bradt
0   200m
0   200yds

Newitigala, Kirindi Falls, Sinharaja, Galle

For listings, see page 467

Where to stay, eat and drink
1 Deer Park Inn
2 Rathna Gems Halt Guesthouse
3 Ratnapura Resthouse

Off map
Centauria Hill Resort

Moderate

🏠 **Centauria Hill Resort** (12 rooms) Colombo Rd; 📞 045 222 2704; **w** centauriahotel.com/hill. Situated in the suburb of Veralupa about 3km north of the town centre, Ratnapura's smartest hotel has large functional rooms with AC, TV, minibar & tub, as well as a swimming pool & restaurant. *From US$100 dbl.* **$$$$**

Budget

🏠 **Ratnapura Resthouse** (12 rooms) Resthouse Rd; 📞 045 222 2299. Bursting with character, this charming government resthouse comprises a lovely old British colonial building, credibly claimed to be 200 years old, set in leafy hilltop gardens inhabited by the likes of Asian paradise-flycatcher & imperial green pigeon, & offering a view over the town centre about 300m to the south. Standard rooms in the main building retain a real period feel, while deluxe rooms are in a newer annex, but all come with AC & fan. A licensed restaurant/bar with parquet floor & terrace seating serves decent local & Western fare (**$$$**). *US$33/41 B&B standard/ deluxe dbl.* **$$**

🏠 **Deer Park Inn** (5 rooms) Sri Khemananda Rd; 📞 045 223 1403; **m** 0773 646457; **e** deerparkratnapura@gmail.com; **w** deerparkratnapura.com. This superior homestay-type run by a friendly elderly couple has a rustic setting about 3km out of town in Muwagama, south of the Kalu River. The comfortable rooms have AC, but use a shared bathroom. There is also a common TV lounge with DVD player & a selection of movies. Local-style meals (**$$**) are served by request, or you can self-cater in the well-equipped kitchen. *From US$27 dbl.* **$$**

Shoestring

🏠 **Rathna Gems Halt Guesthouse** (9 rooms) Outer Circular Rd; 📞 045 222 3745; **m** 0716 955959; **e** rathnagemshalt@gmail.com; **w** ratnapura-online.com. This unusually constructed 4-storey hotel 1km north & uphill of the bus station has a range of bright clean rooms with fan &/or AC & views over the surrounding marshes & hills. A small restaurant serves local vegetarian (**$**) or meat (**$$**) dishes. *US$10/15 dbl with fan/AC.* **$**

✖ **WHERE TO EAT AND DRINK** *Map, opposite*
All the hotels listed above serve food, with Ratnapura Resthouse being the standout for ambience and location. The town centre is scattered with the usual collection of cheap local eateries, and if you're seeking a break from curries and the like, there's a Pizza Hut on the main road close to the bus station and a KFC 500m further east along the same road.

OTHER PRACTICALITIES There are two branches of the Commercial Bank, both with ATMs, and all the other private banks are represented. The Cargills Food City supermarket is on Senanayake Road opposite the police station.

WHAT TO SEE AND DO Dominated by the gem industry, Ratnapura's compact and busy centre is easily explored on foot, and the Pompakelle Nature Reserve and National Museum also stand within walking distance. Further afield, you'll probably want to catch a tuktuk to the Maha Saman Temple, 2.5km west of the town centre, and to the various waterfalls in the surrounding hills. Ratnapura is sometimes cited as a useful base for exploring Sinharaja Forest Reserve and Udawalawe National Park, but in both cases there are plenty of more convenient and attractive options. For serious hikers, Ratnapura is, however, the best starting point for the little-used long hike up Adam's Peak (pages 413–17).

Town centre Ratnapura's old town is focused on the twin traffic circles running northeast from the market to Cathedral Road. Immediately south of this, the Old Dutch Fort, despite being declared an archaeological monument in 2005, has been substantially demolished to make way for an office block that houses the National

Gem & Jewellery Authority and private Minipura Mini Gem Museum (see below). The most obvious relict of the fort is a tall arched entrance inscribed 1817, the year Ratnapura fell to the British, suggesting it was constructed or heavily modified shortly after the Dutch were ousted. Within the old fort premises, the police station, public library and former district secretariat building all date to the early to mid 19th century. About 100m north of this, the handsome St Peter and Paul's Cathedral was constructed in c1880 and has served as the head of the Catholic Diocese of Ratnapura since it was established in 1995.

The hub of the gem industry is on the east side of the town centre, 300m from the Old Dutch Fort. Here, Zaviya Road hosts a gem market every morning, while Council Avenue is lined with numerous small dealerships and cutting shops, which run down past Riverside Road towards the Kalu River footbridge (which, incidentally, provides a great platform for viewing an impressive colony of Indian flying fox in the fringing trees). As you wander around this district, expect to be beckoned at, or sidled up to by, the occasional shifty-looking character offering to sell you gems at a bargain price – harmless enough, unless you're daft enough to enter into a transaction, in which case you'll almost certainly come off second best.

Minipura Mini Gem Museum (*Old Dutch Fort;* ☏ *045 223 1949;* m *0714 070849;* e *info@minipuraminimuseum.com;* f *minipurammgems;* ⏰ *08.00–18.00*) This worthwhile private museum houses an amazing collection of raw and processed gemstones, as well as a few large crystalline rocks, including a branching pipe of purple amethyst quartz and a sponge-like crystal calcite formation salvaged from under the sea. It also contains information about and has examples of the nine so-called Navaratna Gems (see box, pages 464–5) most valued in Hindu mythology. Of course, like other gem museums in Sri Lanka, Minipura doubles as a platform to draw visitors into an attached shop selling gems and other souvenirs, but it's still an excellent collection, with friendly staff, and the pressure to buy is minimal.

Pompakelle Nature Reserve (*Pompakelle Rd;* ⏰ *08.00–16.00; entrance US$1.50*) Proclaimed in 1886 and site of a small municipal reservoir since 1931, this 14ha urban reserve protects a forested hill just north of the bus station and government resthouse. It received IUCN protection in 2008 on account of being one of only two sites known to host the Sri Lankan relict ant, a living fossil that dates back to the time of dinosaurs and whose unique features have led it to being placed in a monotypic subfamily, *Aneuretus*. The first invertebrate to be IUCN listed as 'Critically endangered', the relict ant forms colonies of up to a hundred individuals that nest in rotting logs at the edge of forest clearings, and a survey undertaken in 2001 discovered it to be quite numerous in suitable habitat in Pompakelle. Ants aside, the small reserve is home to macaque, wild boar, porcupine and giant squirrel, and it also looks promising for wet-zone birds. Amenities include at least 1km of footpaths and a 'natural swimming pool' with the muddy look of a buffalo wallow. To get here from the bus station, follow Bus Stand Road west for about 100m, then fork right and uphill on to Outer Circular Road, passing the fire station after 100m and reaching the entrance (signposted 'Pomakalae') after another 200m.

Ratnapura National Museum and Palaeobiodiversity Park (*Colombo Rd;* ☏ *045 222 2451;* ⏰ *09.00–17.00 Tue–Sat; entrance US$2; photography US$2*) Set in parklike surrounds 500m northwest of the town centre, Ratnapura's modest museum was founded in 1946 but relocated in 1988 to the Ehelepola Walauwa,

The beautiful and well-preserved walauwa (mansion) that now houses the Ratnapura National Museum was built in the early 19th century as the official residence of Ehelepola Nilame, an aristocratic Kandyan courtier who hailed from the village of Ehelepola, near Matale. In 1811, Ehelepola was appointed maha adigar (a role similar to prime minister) of King Sri Vikrama Rajasinha, and also acted as the royal district agent in Ratnapura, but the two fell out in 1814 owing to the former's supposed mishandling of a rebellion in Sabaragamuva Province. Afraid for his life, Ehelepola fled from Ratnapura to the British-occupied port of Kalutara to avoid capture by the Kandyan army. The king retaliated by drowning the adigar's wife and children in Lake Kandy, and executing 47 prominent leaders from Sabaragamuva, brutal acts of repression that left the rest of the Kandyan court disenchanted and fearful, and paved the way for the signing of the Kandy Convention of March 1815. Ehelepola played an important role in the British administration – effectively serving as the stand-in king – until he fell out of favour with the colonists in the wake of the Uva rebellion of 1817–18. He was placed under house arrest in the Ehelepola Walauwa from 1818 to 1825, then exiled to Mauritius, where he died in 1829.

a Dutch-influenced villa built over 1811–14 for its namesake Ehelepola Nilame (see box, above). The museum doesn't quite live up to its grand setting, but it displays some genuinely interesting Kandyan art and artefacts dating from the 16th to 18th centuries. Well-labelled but less engaging displays cover the wealth of prehistoric human remains unearthed in Sabaragamuva, and provide the inevitable introduction to Ratnapura's gem industry. The less said the better when it comes to the embarrassing collection of stuffed creatures that passes for the natural history section. By contrast, the loftily named Palaeobiodiversity Park – a menagerie of life-size animal statues that frolic in suspended animation in the walauwa's sprawling tropical gardens – does possess a certain surreal charm.

Maha Saman Temple Set in tranquil and graciously laid-out grounds overlooking a bend in the Kalu River, this large temple west of the town centre is easily the most significant and historic Buddhist shrine in the vicinity of Ratnapura. Its foundation is associated with the 2nd-century BC King Dutugamunu, while a 15th-century inscription to the left of the main temple indicates it underwent extensive renovations during the reign of Parakramabahu IV. In 1620, the temple was captured and razed by the Portuguese, who built a fortress and church on the site before relocating to the present-day town centre. The shrine was revived during the mid-18th-century reign of King Kirti Sri Rajasinha of Kandy, who is believed to have built the current temple, whose striking façade and tall stairwell flanked by colonnaded verandas are possibly modelled on Kandy's famous Temple of the Tooth.

Today the temple is reached via a long shady avenue through a well-tended park. The main entrance has a handsome engraved granite frame that evidently dates to pre-Portuguese times, while the inner wall behind it is adorned with exceptional but rather faded Kandyan-era paintings. Also close to the entrance is an inscribed Portuguese engraving that depicts a general named as Simão Pinnao trampling a Sinhalese soldier while he brandishes his sword. The main three-storey temple, complete with Kandyan-style wrap-around balconies, is dedicated to Saman, one of the island's four guardian deities. It is regarded to be the most important such shrine in Sri Lanka, due to its proximity to the deity's home on Adam's Peak (one name for this lofty mountain is Samanalakanda, meaning 'Saman's mountain', and it was he who is said to have invited the Buddha to visit its summit). Flanking this, to the left and right respectively, is a rather plain Pattini shrine notable for its Kandyan-era door, and a Buddha shrine sporting some striking dragon sculptures and an atmospheric interior rich with beautiful incense-darkened Kandyan paintings. Behind the Pattini shrine, an old brick dagoba looks to be of pre-Portuguese vintage, but it is surrounded by pillars constructed in the Kandyan era to support a long-gone roof.

Maha Saman lies 3km west of the town centre along the Panadura Road. A tuktuk shouldn't cost more than US$1 one way, but any bus headed to Panadura can drop you at the entrance. No fee is charged but, unusually for a Buddhist temple, photography is forbidden. A spectacular carnival-like Esala Perahera (procession) is held here over the first two weeks of September.

Bopath Falls [map, page 368] Situated on the Kuru River (a tributary of the Kalu) 16km north of Ratnapura, the attractive Bopath (literally 'Bo Leaf') Falls is a 30m-high, 100m-long cascade associated with the deity Saman and reputedly favoured as a bathing spot by the ancient rulers of Anuradhapura when they visited the area. As its name suggests, the cascade is revered locally on account of its resemblance to the leaf of the sacred Bo Tree. To get here, drive or bus along the Colombo Road out of Ratnapura for 13km to Kuruwita, where you need to turn right on to a rough feeder road just after the police station and continue for 3km until you see the Bopath Falls Rock Chalets to your right.

Newitigala [map, page 368] Sometimes spelt Nivithigala, this junction town 15km south of Ratnapura, and connected to it by regular buses, is the site of the country's most important raw gem market, attracting hundreds of local miners and dealers, as well as savvy traders from all over the world. Weather permitting, the market usually opens at 09.00 and starts to wind down before midday. Trade is centred entirely on uncut stones, often brought straight from the mine where they were discovered, rather than the cut gems you'll find on sale at dealerships in Ratnapura. It's an interesting place, but if you are thinking of buying, be warned that tourists will be seen as a soft target by any chancer trying to offload glass or other synthetic fakes.

Kirindi Falls [map, page 368] Situated at an altitude of 940m roughly 25km east of Ratnapura, this seasonally spectacular 116m-high waterfall is created by the Kirindi River, a tributary of the Kalu, as it tumbles down a rock wall on the slopes of jungle-swathed Mount Kuttapitiya. It can be reached by following the A4 to Bandarawela east out of Ratnapura for about 19km to the substantial town of Pelmadulla, then turning left on to a rougher 6km road that leads to the Kuttapitiya Tea Estate. Here, a good roadside viewpoint faces the top of the waterfall, and you can also descend down a series of around 400 steps to the base, site of a small pool where, according to legend, the 2nd-century BC King Valagamba hid his treasures during his period of exile from Anuradhapura, and never returned to retrieve them. Kirindi Falls is at its most sensational after heavy rain, when a succession of sheets of white water spray down the not-quite-vertical rock face, but it sometimes dries up entirely during prolonged dry spells. Using public transport, you'll have no problem picking up a bus to Pelmadulla, but you'll need to walk or catch a tuktuk from there.

Gilimale-Eratna Forest Reserve [map, page 368] Divided into several blocks with a combined extent of almost 50km², this little-known but richly biodiverse forest reserve is set on the lower slopes of the Adam's Peak massif northeast of Ratnapura. Bisected by the Kalu River and several of its tributaries, it hosts several impressive waterfalls, most notably Mapanana, Sri Lanka's fourth highest, comprising three separate cascades with a combined fall of 141m. Gilimale-Eratna protects one of the country's few remaining stands of wet-zone rainforest, and is rather similar to Sinharaja in broad ecological terms, but smaller, less pristine and more disjunct. The forest and its fringes are of particular interest to birders for the presence of localised endemics such as Sri Lanka hanging parrot, Layard's parakeet, Serendib scops owl, red-faced malkoha, yellow-fronted barbet, Sri Lanka blue magpie, ashy-headed laughing thrush and Sri Lanka drongo. Other wildlife ranges from purple-faced langur and palm civet to Ranwella's spined tree frog (an endemic first discovered in 2000) and the critically endangered Sri Lanka relict ant only otherwise known from Pompakelle Nature Reserve.

Several roads in the vicinity skirt the forest, but the most popular point of access, 25km from Ratnapura, is Mapanana Falls, which can be truly spectacular after rains, when its roar is audible from several kilometres away. The better of two routes here involves following the Galabada Road out of Ratnapura for 7km to Malwala, then turning left on to a road that passes through Gilimale village after 7km, then arrives at Sri Pagama after another 7km. From Sri Pagama (sometimes spelt Siripagama, and also the starting point for the long route up Adam's Peak; page 417), it's 3km along a rougher road to the Mapanana Estate, where a flattish 100m footpath – through wet grass inhabited by leeches – leads to the base of the waterfall.

SINHARAJA FOREST RESERVE

Sri Lanka's most important biodiversity hotspot and number-one birdwatching destination is the 88km² Sinharaja Forest Reserve, which protects the largest remaining tract of rainforest in the island's southwestern wet zone. An important watershed, it swathes a rugged mountain range that extends for 21km from east to west, but is classified as lowland rainforest owing to its relatively modest altitudes, which rise from below 100m to 1,171m at the summit of Hiti Pitigala. Sinharaja has a hot and sweaty climate typical of tropical rainforests, with temperatures ranging from 19°C to 34°C, high humidity, and an average annual precipitation in the ballpark of 4,500mm. Unlike most other parts of Sri Lanka, rain falls prodigiously throughout the year, even during the relatively dry period from January to March, when the monthly average still exceeds 200mm. In zoological terms, Sinharaja's most remarkable feature is a quite extraordinary level of endemism, which embraces at least 830 plant and animal species unique to Sri Lanka, and more than a dozen plant genera whose range is confined to this one forest. The forest reserve is of particular interest to birdwatchers, since all but two of the 33 species endemic to Sri Lanka have been recorded here, and it is the easiest place to see many of them.

For all its biodiversity, Sinharaja ranks as one of Sri Lanka's most undersubscribed major attractions. In part, this can be attributed to the relatively basic nature of accommodation in the area, and to it lying on something of a limb off the country's main tourist circuits. Equally, it seems fair to say that a ramble through Sinharaja wouldn't conform to everyone's idea of a fun day out. The lush rainforest interior can realistically be explored only by keen walkers prepared to brave an army of creepy-crawlies (not only leeches – see box page 475 – but also fist-sized spiders, evil-eyed snakes, and much else besides), and the likelihood of being drenched in

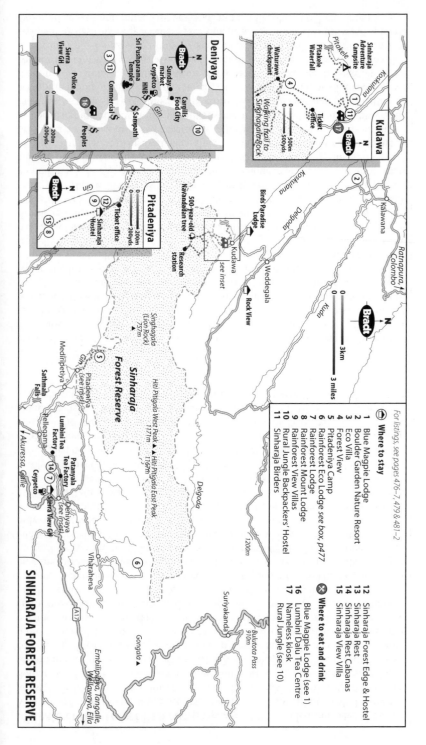

SINHARAJA FOREST RESERVE

For listings, see pages 476–7, 479 & 481–2

Where to stay

1 Blue Magpie Lodge
2 Boulder Garden Nature Resort
3 Eco Villa
4 Forest View
5 Pitadeniya Camp
6 Rainforest Eco Lodge see box, p477
7 Rainforest Lodge
8 Rainforest Mount Lodge
9 Rainforest View Villas
10 Rural Jungle Backpackers' Hostel
11 Sinharaja Birders

12 Sinharaja Forest Edge & Hostel
13 Sinharaja Rest
14 Sinharaja Rest Cabanas
15 Sinharaja View Villa

Where to eat and drink

16 Blue Magpie Lodge (see 1)
Lumbini Dalu Tea Centre
17 Nameless kiosk
Rural Jungle (see 10)

one of the all-but-daily tropical downpours. Of course, especially in the company of a (mandatory) guide, Sinharaja is actually a very safe place – far more so, it has to be said, than the country's recklessly driven roads – and rough-'n'-ready travellers seeking a little outdoor adventure are likely to look back on a rainforest hike as a highlight of their time in Sri Lanka.

ORIENTATION Sinharaja can be explored from separate accommodation clusters: Kudawa on the northern side of the forested range, and Deniyaya and Pitadeniya on the south. Each of the three is covered in greater detail in the sections that follow, but an overview of their pros and cons might be useful. Rustic Kudawa is the most established option and the easiest to reach from Colombo, as well as being the best spot for birdwatching, but its one drawback being that accommodation is relatively poor value for money. More popular with backpackers, the small but well-equipped town of Deniyaya is the most accessible base using public transport, and it boasts several excellent budget lodges that arrange reliable day forest hikes (starting from nearby Pitadeniya), but it is also the most urbanised of the three clusters, and feels quite removed from the forest. A good compromise between these two extremes, Pitadeniya itself boasts a genuine forest-fringe setting, and is more accessible and better value than Kudawa, but it does tend to be less rewarding to birders. Finally, the isolated Rainforest Eco Lodge (see box, page 477), set in a tea estate bordering the forest reserve, offers the closest thing to a genuinely upmarket Sinharaja rainforest experience.

HISTORY The forest at Sinharaja is a partial relict of ancient Gondwanaland, containing several elements that pre-date the split of the Deccan tectonic plate from Africa around 140 million years ago. Many colourful traditions are associated with its evocative name, which literally means 'Lion King' and relates to a fearsome creature that reputedly inhabited the heart-shaped Singhagala (Lion Rock) and impregnated a princess to sire the Sinhala race. Sinharaja was initially gazetted as a 27km² forest reserve in 1875, and expanded to roughly its present size in 1920. The rugged terrain of Sinharaja ensured it was spared from significant logging activity in the colonial era, and while some areas were subjected to a selective felling programme in the 1970s, this was terminated in 1978 when the forest was designated a World Biosphere Reserve in 1978. It was inscribed as a UNESCO World Heritage Site in 1988.

FLORA More than 330 woody tree and liana species have been identified in the lowland and submontane evergreen rainforest of Sinharaja, a list that includes 192 endemics. The closed upper canopy stands some 30–45m above the ground, and it shades a subcanopy at 15–30m, an understorey of small trees at 5–15m, and a shrub-like ground layer. Standing tall above the congested canopy is a scattering of emergent trees, which stand up to 50m high, and mostly comprise endemic species of the genera *Dipterocarpus* (on the lower slopes) and *Shorea* (at higher altitudes). The forest interior at Sinharaja supports a wonderfully varied collection of tangled lianas, bark-hugging epiphytes and beautiful ferns. It hosts Sri Lanka's most varied collection of wild orchids, with 32 endemics among the 80-odd species recorded, most famously the Vesak orchid (*Dendrobium maccarthiae*), a wet-zone epiphyte named after the month (May) when it flowers. Perhaps the most sensational plant in Sinharaja, commonly seen on the forest edge, is the bandura or pitcher plant (*Nepenthes distillatoria*), a carnivorous creeper named for its elongated cup-like sac, which is filled with a sweet liquid that lures, traps and then digests flies and other insects, allowing it to thrive on nitrogen-poor soils.

BIRDLIFE Sinharaja is quite simply the most alluring destination in Sri Lanka for dedicated birdwatchers, as well as providing the single most important refuge for many, if not most, of the island's endemic avifauna. More than 140 bird species have been recorded, a list that includes dozens of rainforest and/or wet-zone specialists unlikely to be seen anywhere else readily accessible to tourists. The star attraction is a near full house of birds endemic to Sri Lanka: indeed, of the 33 endemic species listed in the box on pages 32–3, only Sri Lanka bush-warbler and Sri Lanka wood-shrike are wholly absent from Sinharaja. Among the more easily observed of these endemics are Sri Lanka junglefowl, Sri Lanka grey hornbill, Sri Lanka hanging parrot, Layard's parakeet, yellow-fronted barbet, orange-billed babbler and Sri Lanka hill myna, many of which are quite common in forest fringe habitats bordering the reserve. Other forest-interior endemics likely to be seen with a bit of searching and a good local guide include Sri Lanka spurfowl, crimson-fronted barbet, red-faced malkoha, Sri Lanka drongo, green-billed coucal, black-capped bulbul, yellow-eared bulbul, Sri Lanka scimitar babbler, brown-capped babbler, ashy-headed laughing thrush, dull-blue flycatcher and Legge's flowerpecker. The most challenging endemics include a trio of secretive ground-hugging thrushes, the nocturnal chestnut-backed owlet and Serendib scops owl (though some guides may know where to locate their daytime roosts), and the iconic but frustratingly elusive Sri Lanka blue magpie, which is most noisy and conspicuous at dawn and dusk. Note also that a few highland endemics, though listed for Sinharaja, are irregular visitors or restricted to higher slopes seldom visited by travellers, and are far more common in the likes of Hakgala or Horton Plains National Park.

In addition to these recognised endemics, Sinharaja is home to several endemic races that are sometimes listed as full species or regarded as potential 'splits', among them (Sri Lanka) black bulbul and (crimson-backed) greater flameback. It is also the best place in Sri Lanka to see several other Indian subcontinental endemics, notably the lovely Malabar trogon and bizarre Sri Lanka frogmouth. A host of other forest birds include green imperial pigeon, common tailorbird, scarlet minivet, Indian swiftlet, Indian pitta, blue-naped monarch, black-headed cuckooshrike, velvet-fronted nuthatch and yellow-browed bulbul. Forest-associated raptors include crested goshawk, black eagle and besra.

Although these forest birds are generally resident throughout Sinharaja, they are most easily seen in and around Kudawa, which tends to have a more open understorey than Pitadeniya as a result of logging, and also provides better opportunities for forest-fringe birding outside the reserve boundaries. Within the interior of Sinharaja, the avian jackpot every birder hopes to hit is one of its renowned mixed bird parties, which move in noisy chaotic flocks that might comprise more than a dozen alluring species. In forest-fringe habitats, look out for fruiting trees, which often attract a steady stream of barbets, parakeets, dove and other frugivores.

OTHER FAUNA Although birds hog the limelight, Sinharaja supports a varied fauna that includes about 40 mammal species (seven endemic), 71 reptiles (33 endemic), 19 amphibians (eight endemic), ten fish (seven endemic), and innumerable invertebrates including 65 butterflies (21 endemic). Among the larger mammals, leopards and elephants are present but very secretive and seldom seen, except by a lucky few. Rather more conspicuous are the purple-faced langur, toque macaque and black highland race of the grizzled giant squirrel. More secretive species include the golden palm civet, Travancore flying squirrel, fishing cat and rusty-spotted cat. Reptiles include the endangered rough-nosed horned lizard and conspicuous green forest lizard, a striking spined agamid with a chameleon-like ability to change

Distantly related to earthworms but with a more caterpillar-like locomotive style, leeches are black segmented annelids associated with moist habitats and best known for that subgroup of species which feeds on the blood of humans and other vertebrates. Though they get something of a bad rap, leeches were once valued for their supposed curative properties (bloodletting was all the rage in ancient and Medieval medical circles, from India and Sri Lanka to Greece and Britain), and at worst they are a harmless nuisance rather than presenting any real threat to health and safety.

All the same, Sinharaja is justifiably known for its prolific leeches, and most travellers would prefer to avoid being latched on to by these inveterate bloodsuckers. Fortunately, this is more easily achieved than might be expected. For one, most footpaths through Sinharaja are wide and clear, so provided you stick to the trail, opportunities for leeches to take hold are quite limited. The risk can be further reduced by wearing knee-height 'leech socks', which can be bought or rented locally for US$2–3, and are most effective when tucked around long trousers, and sprinkled with salt or a strong insect repellent. Assuming you do this, even if you walk through thick grass or other dodgy areas, you'll have a minute or two to spot and flick off any unwanted hitchhikers. At the other extreme, you could follow the practice of most local visitors of walking around in shorts and flip-flops, being acutely alert to the tell-tale tickling or itching of a leech crawling up an uncovered leg, and brushing off any offender before it takes hold. (If you're undecided, it might be worth noting that most local guides seem to prefer leech socks to the bare-legged approach.)

If a leech does take hold, don't fret. The bite is totally painless, thanks to the injection of an anaesthetic anti-coagulant fluid, and it isn't known to transmit disease. In fact, the biggest danger is if you try to yank off the leech, but fail to remove the sucker-like mouth, causing the wound to go septic. Rather sprinkle the leech with salt or alcohol, or place a cigarette lighter flame close to it. You can also try spraying the leech with a DEET-based insect repellent. Failing that, if you aren't too squeamish, it only takes 15–20 minutes for a leech to fill up with blood, after which it will drop off of its own accord, though it often takes longer for the bleeding to stop.

colour. Threatened freshwater fish include combtail, smooth-breasted snakehead, black ruby carp, cherry barb and red-tail goby. Invertebrates are everywhere, and diverse beyond comprehension, but do look out for the gigantic (and harmless) golden orb spiders that weave their massive webs alongside forest footpaths, and the black-and-yellow Sri Lankan birdwing, which is the country's largest butterfly, boasting a 15cm wingspan.

KUDAWA AND THE NORTHERN TRAIL CIRCUIT The most established gateway to Sinharaja, Kudawa is a blink-and-you'll-miss-it village situated only 800m from the eponymous ticket office and trail head on the northern boundary of the forest reserve. The village has a lovely setting, surrounded by a mosaic of indigenous forest and cultivation, and it is flowed through by the babbling Koskulana River, whose surprisingly chilly waters rise in the mountains above. Coming from the south coast, as many travellers do, Kudawa is slightly less accessible than Deniyaya, but it also has a wilder feel, and is indisputably the best base in Sinharaja for those whose main interest is birds and other wildlife.

Getting there and away Kudawa lies about 50km south of Ratnapura via Kalawana and Weddegala (also spelt Vedegala), a winding drive that can take up to 2 hours. Self-drivers coming directly from Colombo can bypass Ratnapura in favour of the shorter and quicker route following the Southern Expressway to Bandaragama then travelling inland and southeast via Molkowa and Kalawana. Coming by bus, you must first get yourself to whichever is most convenient of Ratnapura, Kalawana or Rakwana (a junction town 40km east of Kudawa on the main road connecting Ratnapura to Deniyaya and the south coast). Regular buses run between Ratnapura and Kalawana, from where there is an hourly bus to Kudawa via Weddegala. Regular buses from Rakwana run through Weddegala, where you can either wait for the hourly bus from Kalawana, or grab a tuktuk to cover the last 5km to Kudawa.

☖ Where to stay *Map, page 472*
A few decent places to stay are dotted around Kudawa, but while the location is supreme, particularly for birders, nothing matches the best options in Deniyaya and Pitadeniya when it comes to value for money.

Moderate
☖ **Boulder Garden Nature Resort** (10 rooms) \045 225 5812; e info@ bouldergarden.com; w bouldergarden.com. Situated alongside the Ratnapura Rd in Kalawana 10km north of Kudawa, this rustic lodge stands in a forested 4ha estate strewn with giant boulders & alive with birds & other wildlife. The architecturally innovative thatched stone suites with private terraces utilise the natural contours of the rocks. Amenities include a bar in a natural cave, a restaurant under a rock, a swimming pool & excursions to Sinharaja. Tranquil & well run, but pricey. *US$200 dbl B&B.* **$$$$$**

Budget
☖ **Sinharaja Birders** (14 rooms) \045 347 1414; m 0777 609000; e info@ sinharajabirderslodge.lk; w sinharajabirderslodge. lk. Situated on the forested bank of the Koskulana about 1km from the ticket office, this unpretentious lodge offers good birding in the grounds (several endemics pass through regularly) & there's a fabulous natural swimming pool in the chilly clear river. Rooms are simple but clean & come with fan & hot water, & excellent curry buffets (**$$$**) are

served on a relaxing wrap-around veranda. It also offers attractive multi-day packages inclusive of forest walks, mountain biking & other activities. *US$60/77 sgl/dbl B&B.* **$$$**

☖ **Blue Magpie Lodge** (19 rooms) \011 243 1872; m 0727 446776; e info@bluemagpie. lk; w bluemagpie.lk. Situated on 9a wooded slope about 1.5km from the ticket office, this pleasant lodge opposite the Koskulana River has modern rooms with AC, twin or king-size bed & private balcony. A licensed open-air restaurant serves buffet lunches & dinners in the **$$$** range. A touch overpriced. *From US$89/98 sgl/dbl b&b.* **$$$$**

☖ **Forest View** (4 rooms) \045 568 1864. Run by a knowledgeable former guide, Forest View has to be the single most rewarding base in Sinharaja for dedicated birders, thanks to its location deep in the rainforest, a short walk from the visitor centre. Judged on any other terms, however, the basic & rundown accommodation feels madly overpriced. Be warned too that the 2km road from Kudawa is too rough for ordinary vehicles, so you must either walk or pay a hefty US$25 for a 4x4 transfer. *US$55 dbl B&B, plus US$3.50 pp lunch or dinner.* **$$$**

✕ Where to eat and drink *Map, page 472*
All the lodges listed above prepare food, though usually only for their own guests or by advance order. For quick cheap eats, the nameless kiosk at the junction for

In keeping with a destination known among other things for its rain, mud and leeches, Sinharaja caters to a reasonably rough-'n'-ready clientele, and accommodation tends to slot into the budget category. The one notable exception, perched in glorious isolation at the lush rainforest edge, is **Rainforest Ecolodge** [map, page 472] (*16 rooms;* m *0766 900900/919233;* e *sales@rainforest-ecolodge.org;* w *rainforest-ecolodge.com; US$189/285 sgl/ dbl HB;* $$$$$), which stands at a relatively cool altitude of 900m on the Ensalwatta Tea Estate 15km northeast of Deniyaya. Accommodation here is in spacious chalets that are built almost entirely with recycled or organic material (disused shipping containers, rejected railway sleepers and bamboo panelling), and have a sitting area, deck offering views over the tea estate and solar-heated water. Forest walks on a private trail network are guided by experienced naturalists, and cater to special interests as required. The 11km track up to the lodge, branching northeast from the surfaced Viharahena Road 4km out of Deniyaya, is very rough, steep and winding, and takes up to 1 hour, ideally in a 4x4. In another context, it might feel slightly overpriced, but the lack of competition still makes it the most suitable option for those seeking an upmarket base in Sinharaja.

Sinharaja Birders and Blue Magpie Lodge sells simple packages of rice and dhal curry for less than US$1, as well as a limited selection of bread, biscuits, cold drinks and the like.

Other practicalities Amenities are minimal. There are no banks or ATMs, only a couple of small shops, and it is one of the few places in Sri Lanka where both landlines and mobile reception (and as a result Wi-Fi) are non-existent.

What to see and do Forest hikes start at the ticket office about 800m south of Kudawa. Here you must pay an entrance fee equivalent to US$4.50 and (if you don't have one already) arrange a mandatory guide for US$7. One wide and well-maintained footpath leads into the forest from here, passing the Waturawe checkpoint, where you need to show your ticket, after 1.5km, then running southeast for 2.5km to the research station, and continuing for another 8km to Singhagala Rock (where it meets up with the trail from Pitadeniya to Singhagala, though we've never heard of anybody traversing through). Unless you are madly energetic and/or have little interest in birds and wildlife, aim to turn back at the research station, a distance that allows you to get deep into the forest, but at a pace geared towards looking for wildlife rather than merely covering ground. It's well worth diverting to the 500-year-old Navandadan tree, which is a good example of a tall emergent *Shorea stipularis*, and keep your eyes open for pitcher plants and flowering orchids. Birders should ask their guide about possible day roosts used by the nocturnal Serendib scops owl and Sri Lanka frogmouth, and listen out for the mixed bird parties whose presence is often signalled by the raucous chatter of the aptly named ashy-headed laughing thrush or orange-billed babbler.

The dirt roads around Kudawa also offer some great walking, and the opportunity for birders to familiarise themselves with more common species before they enter the more challenging forest interior. A very pleasant short walk, only 2km in either direction, is the so-called waterfall trail along a dirt road running southwest from directly opposite Sinharaja Birders Lodge. The road leads to a pretty waterfall on the Pitakele River (culminating in a steep and gravelly descent running to your right), and also passes several small forest patches and seasonally fruiting trees attractive to birds. Another great walk, leading through proper forest for much of its length, is the 4x4 trail running south to Forest View. For more open views into riparian woodland inhabited by kingfishers and the like, a quiet 3km road follows the south bank of the Koskulana River as it runs northeast of Blue Magpie Lodge.

DENIYAYA Perched at an altitude of 450m in the southern Sinharaja foothills, the sprawling and steeply contoured town of Deniyaya was established alongside the Gin River in 1904 to service the surrounding tea estates and now supports a mixed Tamil–Sinhalese population estimated at 15,000. It's a pretty little town, with the forested upper slopes of Sinharaja and the more southerly Mount Gatabaru providing an appealingly feral backdrop to a relatively domesticated environment of marshy valleys planted with rice, steep terraced slopes swathed in neat rows of tea bushes, small plantations of eucalyptus and other exotics, and the occasional relict patch of indigenous forest. Tea remains the main economic impetus in Deniyaya, but it has also emerged as the most developed, accessible and popular base for exploring Sinharaja, thanks to a good selection of budget hotels offering reliable day hikes along the southern trail circuit which starts at Pitadeniya 15km to the northeast. It should be noted that, while this makes Deniyaya a great base for travellers who want to take a quick look at the forest on an organised excursion, both the town and its lodges lack the forest-fringe atmosphere – and rich potential for casual wildlife-viewing and birdwatching – offered by their counterparts at Kudawa or Pitadeniya.

Getting there and away Deniyaya, more than any comparably popular tourist destination in Sri Lanka, doesn't slot clearly into any specific circuit, and as such it might be visited *en route* to or from almost anywhere south of Kandy.

Coming directly from Colombo in a private vehicle, it's about 165km (4 hours) to Deniyaya, following the Southern Expressway then exiting at interchange 5 (Welipanna) to weave southwest through Moragalla, Neluwa and Morawaka. Driving from elsewhere, Deniyaya lies about 105km (2½ hours) from Aluthgama/ Bentota or Hikkaduwa, 85km (2 hours) from Galle via Akuressa, 70km (1½ hours) from Weligama, Mirissa or Matara, 60km (1½ hours) from Tangalle, 60km (1½ hours) from Udawalawe National Park via Embilipitiya, 105km (3 hours) from Tissamaharama via Embilipitiya, 220km (5½ hours) from Arugam Bay via Wellawaya, 145km (4 hours) from Ella via Wellawaya, 180km (5 hours) from Nuwara Eliya via Haputale and Embilipitiya, 170km (6 hours) from Nallathanniya (Adam's Peak) via Balangoda and Embilipitiya, 240km (6½ hours) from Kandy via Ratnapura, 190km (5 hours) from Kitulgala via Ratnapura, 120km (3½ hours) from Ratnapura and 95km (3½ hours) from Kudawa.

Using public transport, one direct bus runs to/from Galle every hour, but for most other destinations south and/or west you'll be best off changing buses at Akuressa, which lies 45km south along the Galle Road and is connected to Deniyaya by four buses an hour. Akuressa also has good bus connections to Galle, Weligama, Mirissa, Matara and Tangalle. Coming to/from Colombo, Aluthgama/Bentota or Hikkaduwa, there are no direct buses, so you will need to change at Galle. Coming to/from Ratnapura, there are six direct buses daily, with the last one leaving at 14.00. Coming to/from Kandy or Kitulgala, you need to change buses at Ratnapura. Coming to/from Ella or Nuwara Eliya, change buses at Ratnapura or Embilipitiya.

Where to stay *Map, page 472*

Deniyaya has the biggest choice of accommodation in the vicinity of Sinharaja, most of it in the budget and shoestring category.

Moderate

🏠 **Rainforest Lodge** (11 rooms, more under construction) Temple Rd; 📞 041 492 0444; m 0777 068128; e rainforestlodge@ymail.com; w rainforestlodge-srilanka.de. Set amid broken forest & tea fields 2km west of the town centre, this agreeably disjointed & multi-decked German-owned hotel is the smartest place to stay in Deniyaya, & the most rustic, with plenty of birdlife & attractive views. All rooms have net & fan, but the new rooms are much larger & feel more modern than the older ones. €39/44 old/new dbl B&B. **$$$**

🏠 **Sinharaja Rest Cabanas** (2 chalets) Temple Rd; contact details as for Sinharaja Rest. Perched atop a forested hillock 3km west of Deniyaya, this secluded annex of Sinharaja Rest comprises a 1-bedroom family unit sleeping 4 & a smaller dbl chalet. There's a stilted viewing platform, good on-site birding & a shared kitchen. US$100/140 for 2/4 people. **$$$$**

Budget

☀ 🏠 **Sinharaja Rest** (6 rooms) Temple Rd; 📞 041 227 3368; m 0773 419061; e info@ sinharajarest.com; w sinharajarest.com. Set in small jungly gardens 200m west of the town centre, this relaxed guesthouse was established in 1994 by a knowledgeable & articulate owner-manager who is also a vastly experienced guide & still runs daily guided hikes into Sinharaja. Small but comfortable rooms, some using common

showers, all have net & fan. A sociable terrace restaurant serves tasty & inexpensive communal meals. US$25/40 dbl using common/en-suite showers. **$$**

🏠 **Eco Villa** (7 rooms) Temple Rd; 📞 041 227 3367; m 0723 448512; e ecovilladeniyaya@gmail. com; w ecovillasinharaja.com. Situated alongside Sinharaja Rest, this renovated old villa has pleasant & clean tiled rooms with fan & net, & serves tasty local meals using organic ingredients & homemade spices where possible. The owner-manager, a trained biologist, is the brother & former business partner of his counterpart at Sinharaja Rest, & also runs daily guided hikes into the forest. US$30/40 old/new dbl B&B. **$$**

Shoestring

☀ 🏠 **Rural Jungle Backpackers' Hostel** (6 rooms, 1 dorm) Main Rd; 📞 041 227 3099; e deniyaya@hotmail.com; w deniyayanationalmotel.weebly.com; 🟦 deniyayahostel. Formerly called Deniyaya National Motel, this down-to-earth lodge sloping downhill from the main road 1km north of the bus station has simple but clean & airy rooms with mud finish, leafy garden setting, en-suite bathroom, nets & good ventilation, but no fan. A likeable & well-priced local restaurant is attached & it offers day hikes into Sinharaja, as well as tuktuk, scooter & cycle hire. Excellent value. US$12–18 dbl, US$5 pp dorm bed. **$**

✗ Where to eat and drink *Map, page 472*

All the lodges listed above serve meals but the only one that functions as a proper restaurant is Rural Jungle, whose earthy street-side restaurant-cum-bakery (🕐 08.00–19.00) serves inexpensive breakfasts, curries and cakes (**$**). Next to the bus station, the smart new Lumbini Dalu Tea Centre (m 0703 600900; 🕐 08.30–18.30 Mon–Sat) is a pleasant spot for a (pricey) pot of tea and cake in an air-conditioned environment with Wi-Fi.

Other practicalities Most of the main banks are represented including a Commercial Bank with an ATM 150m north of the bus station. There's a well-stocked Cargills Food City on the Pitadeniya Road only 50m west of the main road. A bustling market can be found alongside it on Sunday.

What to see and do The most popular activity out of Deniyaya, and main reason most people visit, is to undertake a full-day rainforest hike in the Pitadeniya sector of Sinharaja, usually as an organised activity by one of the town's specialised hotels and guesthouses. It is also perfectly possible to make your way to Pitadeniya independently, but this only makes sense if you intend to overnight there, in which case flip ahead to *Pitadeniya and the southern trail circuit* (see opposite).

Rainforest hike Deniyaya's most experienced hiking operations, Sinharaja Rest and Eco Villa, are owned and managed by two brothers whose guiding experience stretches back to the 1990s. The day packages offered by the two are very similar and include road transport to/from Mediripetiya (11km from Deniyaya and 2km from Pitadeniya), as well as packed lunch and all entrance and guiding fees. The programme entails walking from Mediripetiya to Pitadeniya, then entering the forest to do one of the hikes described on pages 477–8. A longer variation, recommended only to experienced hikers or second-time visitors, leads deeper into the mountains to the 757m Singhagala (Lion Rock). The all-inclusive fee for groups of two or more is US$27 per person, but solo hikers who travel on a day when there are no other takers might need to pay slightly more to cover fixed transport costs.

Rural Jungle also arranges day hikes for groups of two or more at US$17–20 per person, depending on duration and group size, inclusive of guide, transport to Mediripetiya and entrance fees, but exclusive of lunch, which costs US$2 per person.

Lumbini Tea Factory [map, page 472] (*Pitadeniya Rd;* ☎ *041 227 3277;* w *lumbinitea.com;* ⊕ *08.00–17.30*) Situated about 3km west of the town centre, the largest and best-equipped tea factory in the vicinity of Deniyaya offers free 40-minute guided tours throughout the day, while the attached Tea World is an attractive modern facility where you can taste and buy its range of home-grown pesticide-free teas while enjoying a lovely view over the slopes lined with tea plantations and forest.

Sathmala Falls [map, page 472] Also known as Hathmala, this pretty 45m-high, 150m-long waterfall lies on a well-wooded stretch of the Gin River 10km west of Deniyaya. It cascades over seven stages into a natural pool that's safe for swimming, and the road here passes several patches of riparian woodland that look promising for wet-zone forest-fringe birds and other wildlife. To get here from Deniyaya, follow the Pitadeniya Road for 6km to Pellegama, but instead of turning right towards Pitadeniya, continue straight ahead on the main road towards Belliatakumbura. After another 2km, the road crosses a bridge spanning the river. Take the side road to your right just before this bridge, and follow it for another 2.5km, with the river to your left the whole way, until you reach the waterfall. If you don't fancy walking all the way, buses run between Deniyaya and Belliatakumbura every 30 minutes or so, and can drop you at the bridge 2.5km from the falls.

Gatabaru Rajamaha Temple [map, page 368] This historic temple 11km south of Deniyaya stands at an altitude of 500m on the eastern slopes of Gatabaru Mountain, a large and lushly forested massif named after and legendarily inhabited by a deity who represents the dark side of the island's guardian-in-chief Kataragama. The main cave temple reputedly dates to the 1st-century BC reign of King Valagamba, though there are no inscriptions to confirm this and it had been abandoned for centuries prior to being rediscovered by a loyal hunter in 1834. It houses a well-preserved 8m-long reclining Buddha and relict murals thought to date to the Anuradhapura period, and is flanked by a statue of the local deity Rajjuru Bandara and shrines to Vishnu and Kataragama. Another attraction of the temple is that it stands a few hundred metres inside a 15km² block of indigenous forest that protects many of the wet-zone birds and other species associated with Sinharaja. The closest town to Gatabaru Rajamaha is Kotapola, which flanks the Akuressa (Galle) Road 10km south of Deniyaya, and is linked to it by regular buses. Branching west from the main road through Kotapola 500m south of the post office, a dramatic 2km dirt road switchbacks uphill through lushly vegetated slopes to the temple.

Casual walks Sinharaja aside, the verdant countryside around Deniyaya offers plenty of opportunities for unguided rambling, and the birdlife, though not comparable to the forest interior in terms of mega-rarities, includes plenty of wet-zone forest-fringe specials, as well as more widespread woodland and wetland species. One pleasant walk, with the Gin River flowing past to the north and several footpaths leading south to the base of the forested Gatabaru massif, leads west out of town along Temple Road past Rainforest Lodge to where the road ends a few hundred metres past Sinharaja Rest Cabanas. The Pellegama Road running west from Deniyaya and Viharahena Road climbing to the north also have plenty of rambling potential.

PITADENIYA AND THE SOUTHERN TRAIL CIRCUIT
The starting point for practically all hikes arranged in Deniyaya, pretty Pitadeniya amounts to little more than a ticket office and scattering of local homesteads nestled at an altitude of 330m between the reserve boundary and the Gin River. Despite this, it now rivals Deniyaya as a useful overnight base for exploring the forest, serviced as it is by a cluster of inexpensive rustic lodges catering mostly to budget-conscious travellers. Logistically, making your own way to sleep over in Pitadeniya is slightly more hassle than just bussing into Deniyaya and booking a guided walk from there. But – assuming you're not put out by a little creepy-crawly activity – the effort will be rewarded by an altogether more integrated forest experience, especially at night when the air reverberates with clicks, croaks, rustles, rattles and other mysterious animal noises. By day, Pitadeniya also offers greater opportunities than Deniyaya when it comes to leisurely wildlife viewing, with giant squirrels, purple-faced langurs and a variety of forest-fringe birds, lizards and frogs all jostling for attention.

Getting there and away It's about 13km from Deniyaya to Pitadeniya. In a private vehicle, head west out of town for 6km to Pellegama, then turn right on to a dirt road that starts to deteriorate as it climbs for 5km to Mediripetiya, where the proper road ends, leaving you to walk or charter a waiting tuktuk for the last 2km to Pitadeniya. Using public transport, buses between Deniyaya and Mediripetiya run every 30–45 minutes, while a tuktuk from Deniyaya to the forest edge at Pitadeniya should cost around US$6–7 one way. Alternatively, if you stay overnight in Deniyaya, most hotels there arrange all-inclusive day hikes from Pitadeniya.

Where to stay, eat and drink
Map, page 472

Budget

✻ 🏠 Sinharaja Forest Edge & Hostel (9 rooms, 2 dorms) 041 341 4444; m 0772 978233; e exploresinharaja@gmail.com; w sinharajaforestedge.com. Fringing the forest & a swampy pool 100m from Pitadeniya Entrance Gate, this attractive owner-managed lodge comprises a row of 7 airy modern rooms with slate tile floors, wrought-iron décor, optional AC, fan, modern bathroom & shared balcony with view, as well as a separate hostel containing 2 smaller budget rooms without balcony & a 6-bed mixed & 4-bed female-only dorm. The home of Explore Sinharaja (see overleaf), it organises good guided forest hikes

& there's often good in-house wildlife viewing. A restaurant serves local & Western dishes in the $$$–$$$$range. All rates include a free pick-up from Mediripetiya. Very good value. *US$30/35 standard sgl/dbl B&B, or US$20/25 budget sgl/dbl, plus US$10 per room for AC (it also offers packages inc guided activities, meals & soft drinks for US$130/150 sgl/dbl).* **$$**

🏠 **Rainforest View Villas** (5 rooms) 📞041 491 8651; **m** 0718 010700; **e** rainforestview@gmail.com; **w** rainforestviewvillas.com. Only 200m from Pitadeniya entrance gate, this lodge is attractively perched on a rise overlooking the Gin River & large swathes of gallery forest. Make sure you are booked into 1 of the 3 spacious & attractive wood cabins with net, fan, fridge, tea/coffee & private balcony with a view, as the 2 smaller cabins at the back are far less appealing. *US$43/51 sgl/dbl B&B, with low-season discounts, plus US$12/15 pp lunch/dinner.* **$$$**

Shoestring

🏠 **Sinharaja View Villa** (2 rooms) 📞041 578 5097; **e** samanguid99@gmail.com. Run by a friendly & enthusiastic local guide, this modest villa has small & clean but rather dark rooms with fan, net & shared hot shower, but 4 new cabins on a site with a great view are planned. A terrace restaurant serves curries & devilled dishes etc in the **$$–$$$** range. *US$17 dbl, plus US$5 pp b/fast.* **$**

🏠 **Rainforest Mount Lodge** (3 rooms) 📞041 490 5017; **m** 0712 001635; **e** rushan0713@gmail.com. Practically opposite Sinharaja View Villa & similar in standard but pricier, this agreeable family-run set-up has simple but clean rooms with fan & net, & a terrace facing a tea plantation rather than the forest. *US$22 dbl.* **$**

🏠 **Pitadeniya Camp** (1 x 5-bed bungalow, 2 x 16-bed dorms) 📞011 286 6631/2 (Colombo), 041 223 2957 (Matara); **w** forestdept.gov.lk. Set in the heart of the forest 2km on foot from Pitadeniya, this inexpensive forestry-managed camp is the ideal base for serious wildlife enthusiasts wanting the full Sinharaja immersion experience. Bookings must be made in advance through the forest department head office in Colombo or district office in Matara. A cook is provided but you'll need to bring provisions. *From US$5 pp.* **$**

What to see and do The main activity is guided forest hikes, which can be arranged through any lodge listed above, or the private guides who hang around the bus and tuktuk station in Mediripetiya. An entrance fee equivalent to US$4 per person must be paid at the ticket office, and the fixed fee for a mandatory guide is US$5 per person for one or two people, then US$3.50 per person for additional hikers. Bearing the above in mind, there's much to be said for arranging a no-hassle hike with the well-regarded Explore Sinharaja (**w** *exploresinharaja.com; US$25 pp inc naturalist/guide, entrance fee, leech socks, water & lunch*), which is based at Sinharaja Forest Edge and has the same contact details. Cheaper still is Sinharaja View Villa, which only charges standard guiding fees but has less-qualified guides and doesn't include the extras.

Although people may tell you otherwise, route options within the forest are quite limited, and the best choice depends on how fit and energetic you feel. The shortest trail (5km/4 hours) takes in Pathan Oya and Kakuna Falls. A longer variation (8km/6½ hours) also passes Malmora Falls, and the longest route takes in two further falls (13km/10 hours). Most of this hiking takes place on good paths at altitudes of 400–600m, so walking times are conservative, allowing for stops to look at wildlife and swims below the waterfalls. Generally, the best time to walk is the early morning, when wildlife is most active, but the eagerly sought and elusive blue magpie is sometimes seen at Kakuna Falls towards dusk.

KANNELIYA FOREST RESERVE

Sprawling across 51.3km² of some 42km inland of Galle, the Kanneliya Forest Reserve is the largest and most accessible component in the Kanneliya-Dediyagala-Nakiyadeniya Biosphere Reserve, which protects Sri Lanka's second-largest tract of wet-zone rainforest. Nurtured by an average annual rainfall of 4,000mm, the low hills and ridges of Kanneliya rise to a maximum altitude of 425m and form an important watershed of the Gin and Nilwala river catchments. Though it is less well publicised than the larger Sinharaja, Kanneliya is almost its equal when it comes to biodiversity. Some 301 floral species have been identified, more than half of which are endemic to Sri Lanka, while 5% are listed as globally threatened. The vertebrate fauna of at least 220 species and 40 endemics includes large mammals such as leopard and sambar deer, as well as the more common grizzled giant squirrel and purple-faced langur. Kanneliya is one of the most important birding destinations in Sri Lanka, with a checklist of 120 species incorporating at least 20 of the 33 national endemics including the eagerly sought chestnut-backed owlet, red-faced malkoha, green-billed coucal, Sri Lanka scimitar babbler, Sri Lanka blue magpie and most other species listed for Sinharaja, the main exceptions being those associated with higher altitudes. Kanneliya was only recently developed for tourism and in most respects it is still overshadowed by Sinharaja, but it also has several points in its favour, namely that the two day hikes into the forest get far less busy in season, that it forms a realistic goal for a day trip out of Galle or Unawatuna, and that it offers a relatively inexpensive and easy do-it-yourself alternative to Sinharaja to those on a tight budget

GETTING THERE AND AWAY The gateway town to Kanneliya is Udugama, which lies on a bend in the Gin River 38km north of Galle, passing *en route* through Kottawa Arboretum. From Udugama, continue north along the Neluwa Road for 4km to Kanneliya Junction, from where it is about 1.6km to the car park outside the reserve's entrance gate and ticket office. Using public transport, two buses an hour plough back and forth between Galle and Udugama, from where you can either charter a tuktuk for the last 5.5km to the entrance gate, or catch a bus to Neluwa or Dellawa, hop off at Kanneliya Junction, and walk from there.

WHERE TO STAY, EAT AND DRINK A few simple guesthouses line the 1.6km feeder road between Kanneliya Junction and the reserve, and the forest department also runs a dormitory-only camp inside the gate. Those seeking more upmarket accommodation will need to visit as a day trip from Galle or Unawatuna.

Kanneliya Forest Resort (7 rooms) m 0777 747818, 0778 416560. Situated about 800m before the entrance gate, this pleasant family-run lodge is reached via a bamboo tunnel and set in lush riparian forest fringing the fast-flowing Nannikitta River. Stilted wooden huts with terracotta floor, net & fan but no AC look into the canopy, and an alcohol-free restaurant serves simple Sri Lankan meals in the **$$** range. *US$23/30 sgl/dbl.* **$$**

Forest Department Camp (6 dorms) \011 286 6631/2 (Colombo), 091 223 2994/4306 (Galle); w forestdept.gov.lk. Boasting a convenient & attractive location just inside the main entrance gate, this clean & welcoming guesthouse has 6 dorms, each with between 5 & 15 beds, all with nets & en-suite shower.

It's seldom full so odds are you'll have a room to yourself. A restaurant serves simple & inexpensive local fare. Beds must be booked in advance through the forest department in Colombo (*Parliament Rd*) or Galle (*Lower Dickson Rd;* \091 223 2994/4306) during office hours (⏲ *08.30–16.15 Mon–Fri*). *US$4.50 pp dorm bed.* **$**

Kanneliya Mount Resort (4 rooms) m 0772 090457; e mountresortkanneliya@gmail. com; w kanneliyamountresort.lk. Set on the north side of the feeder road 500m before the entrance gate, this colourful but somewhat rundown guesthouse has adequate rooms with fan but no net or AC, & serves simple local meals. *US$14/17 dbl/trpl.* **$**

16

WHAT TO SEE AND DO The main attractions are a lovely jungle-fringed natural swimming pool on the Nannikitta River 200m from the entrance gate and ticket office, and the two day hiking trails that lead deeper into the reserve. The more popular and straightforward of the trails follows a old logging track along the south bank of the fast-flowing Nannikitta River, a tributary of the Gin, via a large bat cave (1.6km from the start) and Anagimale Falls (2.3km) to its source at the Narangas Falls (5.2km). It takes about 5 hours to hike to Narangas Falls and back, but less energetic travellers, or wildlife and bird enthusiasts who want to take it slowly, can turn back at Anagimale Falls. A more demanding hike, taking around 6 hours in total, is the gradual 4.8km ascent to the 425m-high Kabbale Peak, where a simple resting hut offers a panoramic view over the surrounding forest-swathed slopes. In addition to the entrance fee, hikers are obliged to take a guide, which costs US$5.50 per party to go as far as Anagimale Falls, or US$11 to Narangas Falls or Kabbale Peak.

The old logging track to Narangas Falls is wide and relatively well maintained, but the short footpaths to the two waterfalls alongside it are quite rough and steep. The trail to Kabbale Peak is narrower and steeper. Leeches are present along both routes, so take the same precautions you would in Sinharaja (see box, page 475). Guides are less experienced and knowledgeable than their counterparts at Sinharaja, so while they should be able to show you some interesting plants, lizards and possibly monkeys, you'd be fortunate indeed to see more than a couple of the avian endemics. Birding is far easier in the vicinity of the forest-fringed entrance and camp, where the likes of Sri Lanka junglefowl, Sri Lanka grey hornbill, yellow-fronted barbet and Sri Lanka hanging parrot are common, as well as the walk to the nearby swimming pool, both of which can be explored without a guide.

Part Six

GALLE AND THE DEEP SOUTH

Overview of Part Six

The coastal hinterland east of Galle was dubbed the Deep South back in the days when Sri Lanka's shoddy road and rail infrastructure made the region seem further removed from Colombo and Bandaranaike International Airport than it does today. All the same, the towns, beaches and national parks of the Deep South do retain an appealingly untamed and non-institutional quality, at least in comparison with the more established but rather one-dimensional coastal resorts between Colombo and Galle. For the purposes of this book, the Deep South splits neatly into three chapters. The first covers the far southeast – the Deepest South, if you like – a region whose main attractions are not so much beaches as a cluster of jungle-bound ruins and national parks (most famously Yala and Udawalawe) serviced by the historic towns of Kataragama, Tissamaharama and Hambantota. The next chapter covers the Southern Resort Coast, which is bookended by Hambantota and Galle, and liberally punctuated with ports and resorts such as Tangalle, Matara, Mirissa and Weligama. The third and final chapter covers the not-so-deep city of Galle and the suburban coast running a short distance east through Unawatuna to Koggala. Logistically, almost anywhere along the coast west of Hambantota could easily be visited as a standalone holiday destination from the capital, which meant there was a strong case for placing this coverage closer to the section on Colombo and environs. In practice, however, the Deep South tends to be tagged on to the end of tours and independent visits to Sri Lanka, with people typically arriving here from Hill Country (or in some cases the east coast) to do a safari in Yala or Udawalawe, then travelling west through Tangalle and Matara to end their trip at Galle or one of the resorts between there and Colombo.

HIGHLIGHTS

UDAWALAWE NATIONAL PARK (pages 490–4) Among the most readily accessible of Sri Lanka's national parks, Udawalawe, centred around the reservoir of the same name, offers the county's most reliable year-round elephant viewing.

BUDURUVAGALA TEMPLE (page 496) Complemented by a wild jungle setting, this open-air frieze of seven larger-than-life rock-hewn figures, though surprisingly little-visited, is perhaps the most aesthetically pleasing Buddhist site in the Deep South.

KATARAGAMA (pages 498–502) Named after Sri Lanka's most prominent guardian deity, this Hindu-dominated small town abuts a diverse sprawl of temples whose multi-denominationalism encapsulates the island's syncretic religious character.

TISSAMAHARAMA (pages 502–7) Best known as a gateway to Yala National Park, the former capital of the Ruhuna Kingdom is studded with giant dagobas and lush reservoirs constructed back in its 3rd- and 2nd-century BC heyday.

YALA NATIONAL PARK (pages 508–15) Sri Lanka's most popular and rewarding safari destination is renowned for its dense populations of elephant, leopard and other wildlife, and it also hosts more than 200 bird species.

HIRIKETIYA AND TALALLA BEACHES (pages 533–4) It's hard to decide which of these two idyllic beaches on the coast east of Matara is the more gorgeous; both are characterised by low-key, budget-friendly and unobtrusive tourist developments.

MATARA (pages 535–45) Largely overlooked by the tourist industry, this historic port town, with its ancient fort and marketplace, is enjoyable to explore on foot, while the abutting Polhena and Madiha beaches are hemmed in by a coral reef that offers good conditions for swimming and snorkelling.

WELIGAMA BAY (pages 545–58) The Deep South's most developed stretch of coastline, incorporating the small towns of Mirissa, Weligama and Midigama, is renowned for its lovely beaches, superb surfing, seasonal whale watching and varied collection of hotels, guesthouses and other amenities.

GALLE FORT (pages 572–8) Protected by ramparts dating back to the Dutch and Portuguese eras, this atmospheric old-world UNESCO World Heritage Site is studded with timeworn colonial architecture, informative museums, and restored restaurants and boutique hotels bristling with period character.

UNAWATUNA BAY (pages 579–84) Only 5km east of Galle yet generally treated as a destination in its own right, this well-developed kilometre-long beach offers year-round bathing at the base of the forested Rumassala Peninsula.

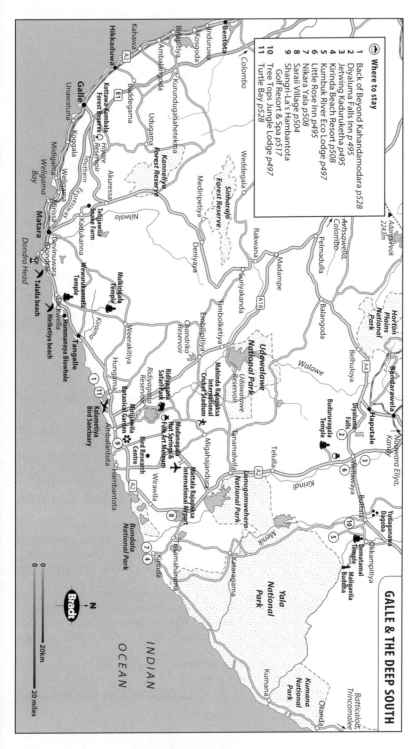

GALLE & THE DEEP SOUTH

17

Tissamaharama and the Southern Safari Circuit

By comparison with the resort-studded south and west coasts, or the relatively urbanised east coast, the far southeast of Sri Lanka possesses a decidedly wild and untrammelled feel. Indeed, most of the 160km coastline that separates the popular resorts of Tangalle and Arugam Bay is protected within one or another national park or wildlife sanctuary, and the region's only substantial seaside settlement is Hambantota, a port town that could scarcely be less touristy if it tried. The main regional travel focus, incorporating roughly 50km of pristine coastline, Yala National Park supports the country's densest leopard population and is also its most popular safari destination. Other worthwhile wildlife destinations include Udawalawe and Bandula national parks, famed respectively for their abundant elephants and rich birdlife, while cultural highlights include the massive 2,200-year-old dagobas that grace Tissamaharama town, the fascinating multi-denominational Kataragama Temple in the town of the same name, the jungle-bound Maligawa Buddha statue, and the beautiful rock engravings at Buduruvagala Temple.

EMBILIPITIYA

The fast-growing crossroads town of Embilipitiya, set on the northwest shore of Chandrika Reservoir, is the gateway to the Deep South coming from Sinharaja or Ratnapura. Of little inherent interest to travellers, it is only 25km by road from the main entrance gate to Udawalawe National Park, but its role as a potential safari springboard has been negated by the recent rash of tourist development around Udawalawe village.

GETTING THERE AND AWAY Embilipitiya is an important transport hub located 75km southeast of Ratnapura, 45km east of Deniyaya (for Sinharaja), 65km northeast of Matara, 40km north of Tangalle, 50km northwest of Hambantota, 65km northwest of Tissamaharama and 75km southwest of Wellawaya (the junction for most destinations in the High Hill Country). Hourly buses connect it to all the destinations listed above, so while many travellers pass through *en route* between Low Hill Country and the Deep South, few stay any longer than is required to change vehicles at the busy bus station. At least one bus an hour connects Embilipitiya to Udawalawe village, the springboard for safaris into the eponymous national park.

WHERE TO STAY, EAT AND DRINK

🏠 **Centauria Lake Hotel** (72 rooms) Concrete Yard Rd; \047 223 0514; e centauria@ sltnet.lk; w centauriahotel.com/lake. The one hotel in Embilipitiya regularly used as a base for Udawalawe, the labyrinthine Centauria is set in well-wooded 2ha gardens lapped by Chandrika

Reservoir. Spacious rooms have wood laminate floors, AC, TV & balcony with lake view. Amenities include a swimming pool, boat rides & lake fishing trips. The setting & sensible prices compensate for overblown & outmoded décor. *From US$93 dbl B&B.* **$$$$**

🏠 **Hotel Ravindu Palace** (16 rooms) Udagama Rd; ✆ 047 226 2566. The pick of a few cheapies scattered around town, this has comfortable rooms with fan & TV, a decent restaurant/bar, & free bicycles for the use of guests. *US$29 dbl B&B.* **$$**

UDAWALAWE NATIONAL PARK

[map, opposite] (✆ *047 347 5892;* **w** *dwc.gov.lk;* ⊕ *06.00–18.00; entrance US$15 pp, plus US$8 service charge per party, plus 12% tax*) The 308km² Udawalawe (or Uda Walawe) National Park offers the most reliable year-round elephant viewing in Sri Lanka, as well as some exceptional birdwatching. Established in 1972, it encloses the Udawalawe Reservoir, which was created in 1969 following the construction of a 3.9km-long dam and 6MW hydro-electric plant on the Walawe River as it flows out of what is now the southern park boundary. Udawalawe stands below the hilly backdrop of the Horton Plains escarpment 20km to the north, but it is essentially a lowland reserve, protecting a mosaic of dry-zone grassland, wooded scrub, abandoned teak plantations, open water and ribbons of riverine gallery forest. A popular day or overnight excursion from the south coast, Udawalawe is serviced by a couple of dozen lodges and guesthouses, most of which are set just outside its southern boundary close to the main entrance gate. The main focal point of tourist development, 10km west of the entrance gate, is the village of Udawalawe, which is also the site of a centre for orphaned and injured pachyderms called Elephant Transit Home. While Udawalawe usually comes up trumps for elephant sightings, the general game viewing and scenery aren't quite up there with Yala National Park, and predator sightings are relatively uncommon.

FLORA AND FAUNA The area closest to the park entrance gate is dominated by abandoned teak plantations interspersed with grassland created by past slash-and-burn cultivation. The spread of two species of invasive evergreen shrub, *Lantana camara* and to a lesser extent *Phyllanthus polyphyllus*, is an ecological concern in open areas that once experienced overgrazing by livestock. Elsewhere, the predominant ecosystem is dense woodland and grassy or scrubby savannah where common hardwood species include Ceylon satinwood (*Chloroxylon swietenia*), Ceylon ebony (*Diospyros ebenum*) and halmilla (*Berrya cordifolia*). River margins are characterised by the water-loving kumbuk (*Terminalia arjuna*), which is easily identified by its pale trunk.

The park supports an estimated 500 elephants. Some individuals move in and out of the park seasonally, but most are resident and stay within its boundaries all year through, which means that elephant sightings are a near certainty whenever you visit. Other mammals likely to be seen include buffalo, spotted deer, sambar, toque macaque, grey langur, wild boar, black-napped hare and ruddy mongoose. More secretive species include stripe-necked mongoose, muntjac, pangolin, jungle cat, porcupine, slender loris and golden palm civet. Leopard and sloth bear are also both present in fair numbers, but sightings, though not absolutely out of the question, are very infrequent.

A striking feature of Udawalawe is the abundant birdlife. The checklist includes around 160 resident and 45 migrant species, and a single game drive can yield up to a hundred species when migrants are in. Five national endemics are present, most visibly (and audibly) Sri Lanka junglefowl but also Sri Lanka spurfowl, Sri

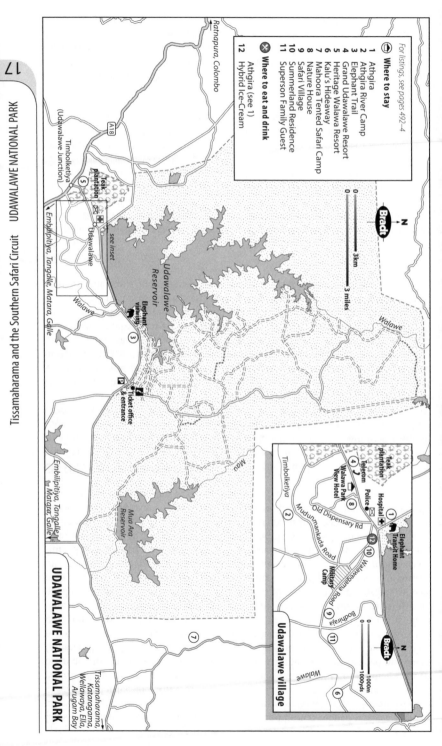

Ratnapura, Colombo

Bradt

N

0   3km
0   3 miles

Timbolketiya
(Udawalawe Junction)

A18

Teak plantation

see inset

Udawalawe

Walawe

Embilipitiya, Tangalle, Matara, Galle

Elephant viewing

P

Ticket office & entrance

Udawalawe Reservoir

Walawe

Mau

Mua Ara Reservoir

Embilipitiya, Tangalle & Matara, Galle

UDAWALAWE NATIONAL PARK

Udawalawe village

Bradt

N

0   1000m
0   1000yds

Teak plantation

Telecom

Walawa Park View Hotel

Hospital

Police

Timbolketiya

Old Dispensary Rd

Mudunmankada Road

Walawegama Road

Military Camp

Bodhiraja

Elephant Transit Home

Tissamaharama, Kataragama, Wellawaya, Ella, Arugam Bay

Walawe

Lanka hanging parrot, Sri Lanka grey hornbill and brown-capped warbler. Raptors are well represented, and good views can often be obtained of black-winged kite, grey-headed fish eagle, white-bellied sea eagle, crested serpent eagle, crested hawk eagle, shikra and (especially over the reservoir) Brahminy kite. Adding a touch of colour to woodland and savannah habitats are the chestnut-headed bee-eater, Indian roller and Asian paradise-flycatcher, supplemented seasonally by blue-tailed bee-eater and Indian pitta. The spectacular peacock might be seen fanning its tail in a courtship ritual, while the related but far smaller jungle bush-quail is often observed scarpering across the tracks, and the scarcer but more beautiful king quail is also present. Interesting forest birds include Malabar pied hornbill, sirkeer malkoha and blue-faced malkoha. The reservoir is a good place to look out for the internationally endangered lesser adjutant, as well as painted stork, woolly-necked stork, black-headed ibis, stork-billed kingfisher and various egrets and herons. Udawalawe is often touted as *the* place to see black-capped kingfisher, a scarce migrant to Sri Lanka, but so far as we can ascertain this reputation rests on the repeat appearance of one (presumably long-dead) individual at the same waterhole for eight successive seasons a couple of decades back

GETTING THERE AND AWAY The entrance gate stands on the southern park boundary 13km along the surfaced Tanamalwila Road as it runs east from the small town of Timbolketiya (aka Udawalawe Junction) on the main road running southeast from Colombo to Hambantota, 65km past Ratnapura and 10km before Embilipitiya. For those in a private vehicle, a jeep park stands right outside the park entrance, but it is generally cheaper and easier to arrange a game drive in the village of Udawalawe, which stands just outside the park's southwestern boundary 3km east of Timbolketiya and 10km west of the entrance gate. Travellers heading to Udawalawe from Colombo or Ratnapura could catch one of the buses to Monaragala that follow the Timbolketiya–Tanamalwila Road through Udawalawe and past the entrance gate. Alternatively, catch an Embilipitiya-bound bus from Colombo or Ratnapura, hop off at Timbolketiya, and then tuktuk the last 3km to the village (*US$1*). Coming from elsewhere, it is usually easiest to get yourself to Embilipitiya first, and then pick up one of the buses that run to Udawalawe village every 30–60 minutes.

WHERE TO STAY *Map, page 491*

Exclusive

Mahoora Tented Safari Camp (18 tents) 011 583 0833; **m** 0710 662224; **e** info@ mahoora.com; **w** mahoora.com. This well-established bush camp is set in a large private property situated right on the park's eastern boundary, some 30mins' drive from the entrance gate. The tented units with net & fan (but no AC), en-suite shower/toilet & outdoor sitting area are adequate at the price, the standard of guiding is exceptional, & food & drink are very good. Because of its proximity to the national park, elephants are often heard at night, & the birdlife is excellent, with wild peacocks being a particularly colourful & noisy presence. *From US$380 pp inc all meals, drinks, park fees, safaris, game drives & other activities.* **$$$$$+**

Upmarket

Kalu's Hideaway (14 rooms) Walawegama Rd; 4km from Udawalawe village; 047 492 9930; **e** info@kalushideaway.com; **w** kalushideaway. com. Owned by the former test wicketkeeper/ batsman Romesh Kaluwitharana (nickname Kalu), this attractive retreat, studded with wildlife photographs & cricketing memorabilia, stands in large wooded riverside grounds far enough from the main road to give it a genuine bush feel. All rooms are spacious, stylish & come with AC, fan & TV, but standard rooms in the main block are a bit gloomy compared with the lighter & more modern deluxe rooms. Amenities include an infinity pool, riverside spa & highly rated restaurant. Jeeps are available for game drives. *US$100/150 B&B standard/deluxe dbl.* **$$$$**

🏠 **Grand Udawalawe Resort** (79 rooms) Tanamalwila Rd; 📞 047 223 2000; **m** 0777 998282; **e** info@grandudawalawe.com; **w** grandudawalawe.com. The largest & most conventionally upmarket accommodation servicing Udawalawe is this enthusiastically staffed hotel set in large jungle-like grounds run through by a river on the western edge of the village. The architecture feels slightly outmoded but rooms are spacious & modern, & come with treated concrete floor, king-size bed, AC, fan & private balcony. Amenities include a swimming pool, gym, movie theatre & attractive restaurant/bar. *From US$120/140 sgl/dbl B&B, plus US$36 pp FB.* **$$$$**

Moderate

☀ 🏠 **Athgira River Camp** (20 rooms) Mudunmankada Rd; **m** 0770 375857; **e** info@ athgirarivercamp.com; **w** athgirarivercamp.com. Situated along a forested riverbank 2km south of Udawalawe village, this neat little bush camp, affiliated to Niluka Safari, has plenty of birds & other wildlife (including giant squirrel) rustling around the gardens. Simple but comfortable tents have canvas sides & thatch roofs & come with wood furniture, fan (but no AC), nets & private balcony with seating. Ask for 1 of the 11 riverside tents. Other amenities include a swimming pool, 2-storey open-sided restaurant, lamplit riverside dinners on clear nights & guided walks to a village on the opposite bank. *US$83 dbl HB.* **$$$**

🏠 **Elephant Trail** (14 rooms) 📞 047 493 7494; **m** 0773 167602; **e** info@elephanttrail.lk; **w** elephanttrail.lk. Set on the south side of the Timbolketiya only 3km west of the park entrance, this modern 3-storey hotel affiliated to Niluka Safari is notable for its innovative architecture & has comfortable & pleasant rooms with bright wall fabrics, wood furniture, white linen blinds, AC, fan, TV & quality finishes. There's a swimming pool & cosmopolitan restaurant. Stylish & good value but lacking any semblance of a bush aesthetic. *US$63/77 sgl/dbl B&B.* **$$$**

Budget

🏠 **Nature House** (4 rooms) Tanamalwila Rd; 📞 047 223 3482; **m** 0777 043482; **e** thilak. dineth@gmail.com; **w** nature-house-guest-house-udawalawe.bedspro.com. Situated along a quiet lane 150m south of the main road through

Udawalawe village, this family-run lodge has a friendly & responsive owner who speaks good English & German. Small but very neat rooms have bright fabrics & paintings on the walls, king-size or twin bed, fan, net, optional AC & private terrace or balcony with hammocks, seating & a view into leafy woodland rattling with birds. Good local meals (**$$**) are available on request. *US$30/50 B&B dbl with fan/AC.* **$$**

🏠 **Athgira Hotel** (20 rooms) C P de Silva Rd; 📞 047 223 2275; **m** 0773 167602; **e** info@ hotelathgira.com; **w** hotelathgira.com. Situated opposite the Elephant Transit Home, this well-run affiliate of Niluka Safari has a swimming pool, a popular restaurant, & bright modern rooms with AC, fan, TV & modern bathrooms, plus deluxe rooms with private balcony. Good value. *US$45/60 B&B standard/deluxe dbl, with off-season discounts.* **$$**

🏠 **Safari Village** (19 rooms) Walawegama Rd, 2km from Udawalawe village; 📞 047 492 0982; **e** kinjoulanka@sltnet.lk; **w** safarivillagehotels. com. Founded in 1993, this is the oldest hotel in Udawalawe & rather shows its age, though the unkempt wooded garden looks promising for birding & it has a swimming pool & a decent but architecturally quirky restaurant. Agreeably old-fashioned rooms have fan, net & private balcony. *US$30/35 B&B sgl/dbl, plus US$8 for AC.* **$$**

Shoestring

☀ 🏠 **Superson Family Guest** (5 rooms) Walawegama Rd, 2.5km from Udawalawe village; 📞 047 347 5172; **m** 0712 872901; **e** supersonfg@ gmail.com. Expanded from a family house set in a large & peaceful palm-shaded garden, this agreeable homestay-like guesthouse has clean spacious rooms with fan & net, as well as a super cottage with private balcony & optional AC. It serves up delicious curry buffets (**$$**) & can arrange affordable safaris. *US$17 dbl, US$20/27 cottage without/with AC.* **$**

🏠 **Summerland Residence** (4 rooms) Dakunu Ala Rd; 📞 047 560 1176; **m** 0777 151092; **e** summerlandresidence1122@gmail.com. Friendly family-run set-up offering the choice of 2 smallish rooms in the main 2-storey house using shared bathrooms, or 2 larger en-suite rooms with AC & shared TV lounge in a separate cottage alongside the main road. *US$17/25 dbl with shared/en-suite bath.* **$**

17

🏠 **Heritage Walawa Resort** (5 rooms) Tanamalwila Rd; ☎ 047 223 2022; m 0718 216059; e info@heritagewalawa.com; w heritagewalawa. com. Situated about 1km west of the village this converted house, set in a leafy garden, has decent budget rooms with fan or AC, & a good restaurant with a predominantly Sri Lankan menu. *US$15/23 dbl with fan/AC.* **$**

✖ **WHERE TO EAT AND DRINK** *Map, page 491*

All the hotels listed above serve food. The lunchtime buffet (**$$$**) at the Athgira Hotel is recommended for those seeking a quick and tasty lunch opposite the Elephant Transit Home. Hybrid Ice-Cream (m *0718 938386;* **$**). is a superior local-style roadside eatery serving good rice-and-curry as well as ice cream and juices.

WHAT TO SEE AND DO

Game drives Almost all visitors do at least one game drive into the park. These typically last for up to 3 hours and stick to the well-trodden circuit of tracks between the entrance gate and the northeast shore of the Udawalawe Reservoir, an area where elephants are quite easily seen and most wildlife tends to be habituated to vehicles. Afternoon drives, starting at around 15.00 and ending at sunset, are usually regarded to offer your best chance of spotting elephants and predators. Early morning is better for birds and, especially if you are there when gates open, tourist traffic tends to be far lower than in the afternoon. The going rate for a 3-hour game drive out of Udawalawe village is around US$25 for up to four passengers, inclusive of driver and fuel but exclusive of park entrance fees. The pick of the village's operators is well-priced Niluka Safari (☎ *047 223 2275;* m *0773 167602;* e *info@nilukasafari.com;* w *nilukasafari.com*), whose fleet of 30 well-maintained jeeps is based at the Athgira Hotel. Counterintuitively, you'll most likely be asked a significantly higher rate (around US$35, presumably negotiable) at the jeep park outside the park entrance. A jeep safari out of Embilipitiya also costs about US$35; you'll usually find a few willing vehicles outside the Centauria Lake Hotel.

Elephant Transit Home [map, page 491] (*C P de Silva Rd;* ☎ *047 223 2147;* w *bornfree.org.uk (search 'Elephant Transit Home');* ⊕ *08.30–09.30, 11.30–12.30, 14.30–15.30 & 17.30–18.30; entrance US$3.30*) Situated in Udawalawe village but bordering the national park, this admirable facility was established by the Department of Wildlife Conservation back in 1995 to raise orphaned elephant calves, and rehabilitate injured individuals, for release into the wild. Supported by the Born Free Foundation since 2002, it typically hosts around 40 young elephants and has now successfully introduced more than a hundred hand-reared individuals into Udawalawe National Park and other protected areas. The release programme usually starts when the calf reaches the age of four, and the elephant will be collared for several years until researchers are satisfied it has made a successful transition to the wild. The home opens to the public four times daily to coincide with feeding hours (*09.00, noon, 15.00 & 18.00*), when you can watch from a raised viewing platform as the enthusiastic calves are fed. The complex also incorporates an interesting museum.

WELLAWAYA

Humdrum Wellawaya, located at the base of the escarpment 30km south of Ella and 45km southeast of Haputale, is the main gateway town to the Deep South coming from most parts of the High Hill Country. Logistically, it feels like an eastern counterpart to Embilipitiya, the sort of workaday market town that many travellers transit through but few dwell in for longer than is required to change bus or snatch a pit stop. Even if you do no more than pass through Wellawaya, the surrounding countryside is dotted with worthwhile diversions, notably the Buduruvagala Rock Carvings and the country's second-highest waterfall at Diyaluma – both also feasibly day trips from Ella or Tissamaharama.

GETTING THERE AND AWAY An important route crossroads, Wellawaya straddles the Colombo–Batticaloa Highway at the intersection of the main roads running north to Ella and Nuwara Eliya and south to Tissamaharama and Hambantota. It lies 215km (4–5 hours) east of Colombo via Ratnapura (120km/2–4 hours) and Haputale (1 hour), 80km (2 hours) south of Nuwara Eliya via Ella (30km/1 hour), 80km (1½ hours) from Hambantota via Tissamaharama (65km/1 hour), 60km (1–1½ hours from Kataragama via Buttala (18km/20–30 mins), 180km/4 hours from Batticaloa via Buttala, and 110km (2½ hours) from Arugam Bay via Buttala. At least one bus an hour runs back and forth to/from Ella and Haputale (both connected by regular buses and trains to Nuwara Eliya, Hatton, Kandy or Colombo), as well as Embilipitiya, Buttala, Hambantota and Tissamaharama.

WHERE TO STAY *Map, pages 510–11, unless otherwise stated*

Upmarket

🏠 **Jetwing Kaduruketha** (25 rooms) ✆055 471 0710; e resv.kaduruketha@jetwinghotels.com; w jetwinghotels.com. Overlooking a sprawl of paddy fields 6km north of town, this tranquil new hotel offers accommodation in lovely minimalist chalets, inspired by traditional Sri Lankan rural architecture (though arguably more Japanese in feel), with pagoda-style roof, outdoor bathroom & bamboo sides designed to optimise natural ventilation but screened to keep out insects. Amenities include an infinity pool & a superbly sited restaurant specialising in fusion & traditional Sri Lankan fare. The wooded garden supports plenty of birds & all chalets are allocated 3 bicycles for exploring the surrounding countryside. Day trips to Buduruvagala, Diyaluma Falls & Udawalawe are available. *From US$219/239 B&B sgl/dbl; check the website for major discounts.* **$$$$$**

Shoestring

✳ 🏠 **Little Rose Inn** (15 rooms) ✆055 567 8360; m 0776 573647; e littlerose.inn@gmail.com; w littlerosewellawaya.com. Situated among the paddies 1km south of town along the Hambantota Rd, this friendly owner-managed lodge offers the choice of small scruffy old rooms with fan & net, or larger & cleaner new rooms with AC, fan, TV & private balcony. The owner can arrange budget tuktuk excursions to Buduruvagala, Diyaluma Falls & Udawalawe. Excellent curries. *US$10/13 sgl/dbl with fan, US$20/27 sgl/dbl with AC.* **$–$$**

🏠 **Diyaluma Falls Inn** [map, page 488] (8 rooms) m 0777 874830. This slightly timeworn hotel stands in a wonderful 3ha property at the base of Diyaluma Falls 10km west of Wellawaya. There's a restaurant with a view, a natural swimming pool in the river as it runs through the property, & plenty of birds & other wildlife in the fringing woodland. The basic rooms are likely to be refurbished during the lifespan of this edition. *US$17 dbl, but expect that to rise to US$50 as & when renovations are complete.* **$**

WHAT TO SEE AND DO

Diyaluma Falls [map, page 488] Sri Lanka's second-tallest waterfall, Diyaluma – derived from the Sinhala 'Diya Haluma', meaning 'Gushing Water' – is formed by the Punagala River as it plunges 209m over a sheer escarpment 12km from Wellawaya alongside the main road to Haputale via Koslanda. The seasonally spectacular waterfall is easily observed from a viewing point on the main road just below its base. It is also possible to hike up a steep path to the top of the main waterfall to view a couple of smaller cataracts. Any bus headed between Wellawaya and Haputale or Bandarawela via Koslanda can drop you at the viewpoint.

Pahala Uva Archaeological Museum [map, pages 510–11] (☎ 055 355 3617; ⊕ 08.30–16.30 exc Tue) Closed for renovation at the time of writing, this small but prominently signposted museum stands 5km south of Wellawaya at the junction for Buduruvagala. It houses a collection of statues and other artefacts from Maligavila, Buduruvagala and various less well-known archaeological sites in the lowlands of Uva Province.

Buduruvagala Temple [map, pages 510–11] (*Entrance US$2*) As suggested by its modern Sinhalese name (literally 'Buddha image of stone'), Buduruvagala is an open-air frieze comprising seven larger-than-life Buddhist figures carved into a tall rock face southwest of Wellawaya. Among the most impressive and aesthetically satisfying of Sri Lanka's ancient Buddhist monuments, it also possesses an aura of tranquillity enhanced by a wild jungle setting and paucity of visitors relative to the better-known sites of the Cultural Triangle. In many respects, Buduruvagala is a rather mysterious site, one whose original name and provenance goes undocumented, though it was most likely carved between the 8th and 10th centuries, when the Mahayana school enjoyed its greatest influence in Sri Lanka. The dominant figure, the solemn 13m-high Buddha at the frieze's centre, is the island's largest Mahayana carving and depicts its subject in the abhaya (fearless) mudra. It is flanked by two Bodhisattva images carved in the kataka hasta mudra – Avalokiteshvara to the left and Maitreya to the right – both around half the height of the central Buddha, and flanked in turn by a pair of slightly shorter figures. The Avalokiteshvara engraving still retains an original layer of white plaster, complete with a halo-like multitude of orange rays, giving some idea of how the whole frieze would have looked in its heyday. Avalokiteshvara is flanked to the right by a rare female figure, carved in a tivanka position with bare breasts and a tall headdress, and thought to represent Tara, the mother of his son Prince Sudana, who stands to his father's left, completing the happy family snapshot.

As recently as the turn of the millennium, Buduruvagala stood deep in the jungle and could be reached only by following a rough footpath from the eponymous reservoir. Since then a new temple opened some 200m from the rock frieze, which is now easily reached along a short flat path from the car park. To get here, follow the Hambantota Road south out of Wellawaya for 5km, then turn west at the signposted junction next to the Pahala Uva Museum. Buduruvagala lies another 4km along this cul-de-sac, which climbs through a stand of dense natural forest past the hill-ringed lotus-covered Buduruvagala Reservoir, a crumbling dagoba and other mysterious ruins. Elephants often pass through in the afternoon, and birds and butterflies are everywhere. Using public transport, any bus running between Wellawaya and Hambantota Road can drop you at Buduruvagala Junction, from where you could either catch a tuktuk or walk. Alternatively, a direct tuktuk from Wellawaya should only cost around US$4 inclusive of waiting time.

BUTTALA

Derived from the phrase *Bath hala* (rice store), Buttala was reputedly named back in the 2nd century BC, when it served as a military outpost under Prince Dutugamunu of Ruhuna, who went on to reunify the island by ousting King Elara from Anuradhapura in c161BC. The surrounding area, though still an important centre of rice production, is now the site of the island's largest sugar mill, which was established at Pelwatte 5km east of Buttala in 1981. For travellers coming from Arugam Bay and elsewhere along the east coast, Buttala is the gateway town to the Deep South, though as with Wellawaya 15km to the west, a steady stream of passing tourist traffic has yet to translate into many overnight stays. Despite this, Buttala stands close to a trio of intriguing old Buddhist shrines, most notably Maligavila but also Yudaganawa and Dematamal. Also of interest are a couple of small eco-lodges set close to the northern boundary of Yala National Park and well placed for game drives into little-visited Block III and Block V.

WHERE TO STAY, EAT AND DRINK *Map, pages 510–11*

Tree Tops Jungle Lodge (3 units) **m** 0777 036554, 0775 768079; **e** treetopsjunglelodge@gmail.com; **w** treetopsjunglelodge.com. This wonderful low-impact glamping-style eco-lodge comprises an atmospheric adobe dining room (serving excellent vegetarian-dominated local curries) & recreation area & accommodation in 3 spacious standing tents with 4-poster beds, fitted nets, shaded front balcony with seating & en-suite bathroom at the back. Danish-owned & -managed, but staffed entirely by local villagers, it stands in a forest reserve close to the border of Yala National Park & forms a useful base for game drives in the untrammelled Blocks III & V. Elephants pass through regularly, often coming to drink at a nearby reservoir in the evening, & guided nature walks are great for birding, as well as for seeing other smaller creatures. Ideal for those seeking a genuine internet- & electricity-free back-to-nature experience, with a recommended minimum stay of 3 days. *From US$150 pp for the first night, dropping in price with each subsequent night, inc meals, soft drinks, camp services & transfer from Buttala.* **$$$$$+**

Kumbuk River Eco-lodge (4 units) **** 011 552 3140; **m** 0770 455494; **e** info@kumbukriver. com; **w** kumbukriver.com. Situated in wild 6.5ha grounds close to the northern border of Yala National Park & bounded by the Kumbuk River, this 1-of-a-kind lodge features a 13m-high 10-bed thatched & open-sided eco-villa built in the shape of an elephant, while other units (both with AC) include a 2-storey 4-person tree-house whose floor-to-ceiling glass walls offer mesmerising views over the river, & a decommissioned converted vintage Morris BMC sleeping 2. This is a good place for groups intent on having a fun adventure rather than for those seeking traditional comfort. *US$140/160 dbl B&B without/with AC.* **$$$$**

Kottawatta Holiday Resort (10 rooms) Kataragama Rd; **** 055 227 0177. The pick of a few simple lodgings in Buttala town, this place has attractive gardens & adequate but slightly scruffy rooms with net, fan & optional AC. A restaurant is attached. *US$30/37 dbl with fan/AC.* **$$**

WHAT TO SEE AND DO

Yudaganawa Yudaganawa, 3km northwest of Buttala, is reputedly where the future King Dutugamunu of Anuradhapura defeated his brother Saddha Tissa in the secession battle that followed the death of their father, King Kavan Tissa. Peace between the rival brothers was later brokered by their mother, Viharamahadevi, an event commemorated by the construction of a massive dagoba on the former battle site. All that survives of this ancient construction is a tall circular brick base whose 317m circumference exceeds that of any other dagoba in Sri Lanka, suggesting the structure itself might once have been the country's largest. Today, the base supports a relatively modest grassy hillock, topped unceremoniously by a pair of water tanks. Two other more recent historical structures can be seen at Yudaganawa. The atmospheric Kandyan-era temple right in front of the dagoba retains its original wooden ceiling and some fabulous old wall paintings and sculptures depicting the Buddha shaded by a cobra hood alongside the likes of Shiva and Ganesh. The starker Chulangani Temple, situated in a roadside forest glade just before the car park, comprises an abandoned 12th-century dagoba and an image house whose weathered Buddha statue dates to the 6th or 7th century. To reach Yudaganawa, follow the Wellawaya Road west out of Buttala for about 1km, then turn north on to a side road that leads to the carpark after 2km.

Dematamal Situated about 6km east of Buttala on the road to Okkampitiya and Maligavila, the ancient Dematamal Temple is reputedly where Saddha Tissa took refuge after his defeat at Yudaganawa. Its most prominent feature, rising high about the surrounding paddies, is a relatively modest (19m tall) unplastered brick dagoba built by Saddha Tissa almost 2,200 years ago, and extensively restored on several subsequent occasions. Still an active modern temple, Dematamal is studded with intriguing relicts of earlier incarnations, most notably a weathered 5th-century guardstone that depicts a Naga Raja embracing his queen in front of a fan-like arrangement of hooded cobra heads – an image sufficiently striking and unusual that it was reproduced on a Rs15 postage stamp issued in 2012.

Maligavila Buddha The tallest free-standing Buddha sculpted in ancient Sri Lanka, the exquisite 14.5m-high Maligavila Buddha lay toppled and forgotten in the jungle southeast of Buttala for many centuries prior to its rediscovery in 1951. Thought to have formed part of the Pathma Temple built by King Aggabodhi IV in the 7th century, it was originally enshrined within a 20m-high, 20m-long image house. Following an unsuccessful restoration effort in 1974, this crystalline limestone statue was eventually pieced together by an engineering team appointed under President Premadasa in 1980, and re-erected on the base of the ancient image house, which is still protected by the original guardstones. About 600m further east, perched atop a four-terraced hillock, the Dambegoda Bodhisattva is a 10m-tall limestone statue accredited to Aggabodhi IV's elder brother Dappula I. Discovered lying face-down but intact in the 1950s before being dynamited into segments by treasure hunters, this depiction of Avalokiteshvara or possibly Maitreya was reconstructed and re-erected in 1990; despite its rather patched-together appearance it is the more imposing and ornately carved of the two statues.

Maligavila lies 17km southeast of Buttala along a surfaced road through Dematamal and Okkampitiya. Coming from the east, it would be quicker to use the 26km route from Monaragala, branching south from the main Colombo Road at Kumbukkana Junction and then connecting with the route from Buttala at Okkampitiya. At least one bus an hour runs to Maligavila from both Buttala and Monaragala. Alternatively you could take a tuktuk and arrange to stop at Dematamal on the way. Once there, follow the main road south for about 100m past the parking lot in front of the modern and relatively uninteresting Maligavila Temple, then turn left into the entrance to the archaeological site. From here, a footpath leads through lush leafy jungle for 600m to a T-junction from where the Maligavila Buddha stands 350m to the left and the Dambegoda Bodhisattva 250m to the right.

KATARAGAMA

If any one place in Sri Lanka encapsulates and embodies the enigmatic syncretism that underpins the island's religious character, it is Kataragama. The ancient town shares its name with the island's most prominent guardian deity, a cultish figure revered not only by the Buddhist majority, but also by the Hindu minority (under the name Skanda or Murugan), and by Vedda animists (as a powerful ancestral spirit). More than this, Kataragama rivals Adam's Peak as the island's most important pilgrimage site, being particularly popular with Hindus, but also attracting Buddhists, Veddas and even Muslims. Geographically, it is a town of two distinct halves, separated by the forest-fringed Menik River. The secular town centre, a triangular grid of roads that runs southwest from the river towards the pretty Detagamuwa Reservoir, possesses little to distinguish it from any other similarly modest Sri Lankan market town. By contrast, the parklike Sacred Precinct north of the Menik is a multi-denominational sprawl of ancient shrines, dominated, inevitably, by the revered Kataragama Temple, but tailored to all religious persuasions. The town attracts a steady pilgrim traffic throughout the year, but arrivals peak during the Kataragama Perahera, a predominantly Hindu festival that coincides with Kandy's annual Esala Perahera, and is renowned for its displays of fire-walking and more gruesome acts of purgative self-mutilation.

HISTORY A former capital of Ruhuna, Kataragama is synonymous with Kajjaragama, a town name-checked in the 5th-century *Mahavamsa* as one of the eight sites where saplings from the original Bo Tree were planted during the 3rd-century BC reign of Devanampiya Tissa. This shrine evolved into the present-day Kataragama Temple, which was reputedly dedicated to the island's guardian deity by King Dutugamunu following his victory over Elara. According to Vedda tradition, the temple marks the site where Kataragama proposed to and married Valli, the daughter of a Vedda chief. Kataragama has been the island's most important Hindu pilgrimage site since the 15th century, possibly earlier, though it was set deep in the jungle and notoriously difficult to access prior to the construction of a motorable track from Tissamaharama in 1950. Today, though most pilgrims travel by bus, around 30,000 participate in the annual Kataragama Pada Yatra, a rigorous 45-day foot journey that starts at Jaffna then follows the east coast south to Okanda before culminating in a hazardous trek through the wilds of Yala National Park to arrive at the Sacred Precinct in time for the Kataragama Perahera.

GETTING THERE AND AWAY Kataragama stands 280km (5 hours) southeast of Colombo following the Southern Expressway past Galle (165km/3½ hours) and Matara (125km/2½ hours), then passing through Tangalle (88km/2 hours), Hambantota (45km/1 hour) and Tissamaharama (18km/30 minutes). Twice-hourly buses leave to and from Colombo, but not all use the expressway. If in doubt, hop off at Tangalle or Matara and pick up an express bus there. More locally, Kataragama is connected by regular buses to Tissamaharama (at least two an hour), as well as to the regional gateway towns of Wellawaya and Buttala.

WHERE TO STAY, EAT AND DRINK *Map, page 500*
The main street and Buttala Road are chock-full of budget guesthouses aimed mainly at pilgrims but open to all. Local eateries are plentiful too. Tourist-orientated options tend to be further out from the Sacred Precinct, where a ban on drinking alcohol is applied.

Moderate

✴ 🏠 **Tamarind Lake Hotel** (25 rooms) Kandasuridugama Raja Rd; 📞 047 223 6377; m 0776 074455; e info@tamarindlake. lk; w tamarindlake.lk. Opened in 2015, this stylish 3-storey hotel stands in massive wooded

grounds that run down to the northwest shore of Detagamuwa Reservoir (plenty of birding potential) & incorporate a large swimming-pool deck studded with sun chairs. The tall-ceilinged rooms are very spacious & come with king-size or twin bed, AC, fan, TV, modern bathroom & balcony

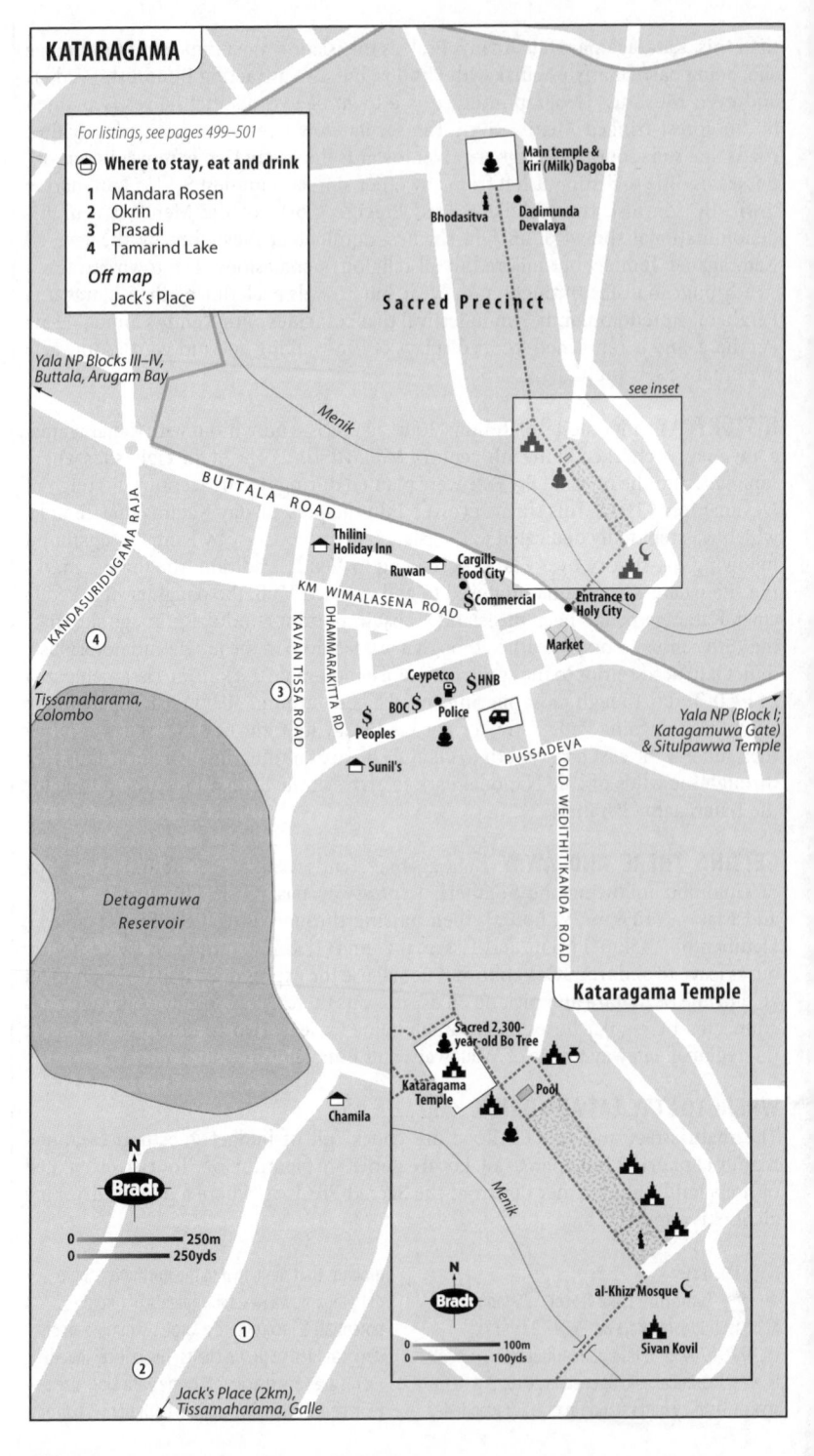

KATARAGAMA

For listings, see pages 499–501

⌂ **Where to stay, eat and drink**
1 Mandara Rosen
2 Okrin
3 Prasadi
4 Tamarind Lake

Off map
Jack's Place

Main temple &
Kiri (Milk) Dagoba

Bhodasitva

Dadimunda
Devalaya

Sacred Precinct

Yala NP Blocks III–IV,
Buttala, Arugam Bay

Menik

see inset

BUTTALA ROAD

KANDASURIDUGAMA RAJA

Thilini
Holiday Inn

Ruwan

Cargills
Food City

Commercial

Entrance to
Holy City

KM WIMALASENA ROAD

KAVAN TISSA ROAD

DHAMMARAKITTA RD

Market

Tissamaharama,
Colombo

Ceypetco $ HNB

BOC $

Peoples

$

Police

Sunil's

PUSSADEVA

Yala NP (Block I;
Katagamuwa Gate)
& Situlpawwa Temple

OLD WEDITHITIKANDA ROAD

*Detagamuwa
Reservoir*

Chamila

N

Bradt

0 ———— 250m
0 ———— 250yds

Kataragama Temple

Sacred 2,300-
year-old Bo Tree

Kataragama
Temple

Pool

Menik

al-Khizr Mosque

Sivan Kovil

N

Bradt

0 ———— 100m
0 ———— 100yds

①

②

Jack's Place (2km),
Tissamaharama, Galle

with seating facing the lake. A restaurant serves great seafood & Sri Lankan cuisine. Guided safaris to Yala are available. Good value. *US$79/89 sgl/dbl B&B*. **$$$**

🏠 **Okrin Hotel** (16 rooms) Tissamaharama Rd; 047 223 5032; e info@hotelokrin.com; w hotelokrin.com. This smart little hotel 2km south of town has an AC restaurant, a swimming pool, & spacious & comfortable rooms with queen-size bed, AC, TV & modern tiled bathroom. Rooms 110–12 & 201–3 have private balcony overlooking the pool. Rooms are good value if you skip the pricey b/fast. *US$50 dbl, or US$65/75 sgl/dbl B&B*. **$$$**

🏠 **Mandara Rosen** (58 rooms) Tissamaharama Rd; 047 223 6030; e rosenr@ sltnet.lk; w mandararosen.com. Set behind a sturdy granite wall & high, wrought-iron gates 1.5km south of town, this well-established but relatively pricey 2-storey hotel features a large courtyard swimming pool & glass-walled restaurant leading out to a garden terrace. Rooms have 2 dbl beds, AC, TV, minibar, safe & the

ambience of a city hotel. *US$110/135 sgl/dbl, plus US$10 pp b/fast*. **$$$$**

Shoestring

🏠 **Jack's Place** (8 rooms) Tissamaharama Rd; 047 223 5500; m 0724 088123; e udayade@ yahoo.com; w jacksplacekataragama.com. Situated alongside Jayasumanaramaya Temple 4km south of town, this popular little guesthouse has clean twin rooms with net, fan & optional AC, as well as a good open-sided garden restaurant serving local dishes in the **$$** range. The friendly owner-manager can arrange affordable Yala safaris. *US$17/33 dbl with fan/AC*. **$**

🏠 **Prasadi Hotel** (18 rooms) Kavan Tissa Rd; 047 223 5297. The pick of a few indifferent central cheapies is this colonial-style building set in large gardens facing the wall of the Detagamuwa Reservoir 500m west of the bus station. Rooms with polished floors & wood ceilings come with 2 beds, fan, net & optional AC. *US$15/25 dbl with fan/AC*. **$**

WHAT TO SEE AND DO Reached from the town centre via a footbridge across the Menik (literally 'Gem') River, Kataragama's **Sacred Precinct** is most spectacular over the festival period, but worth visiting at any time of year. Try to be here for the evening puja, which starts at around 18.00 daily, and usually attracts many hundreds of Buddhist and Hindu pilgrims seeking the blessing of Kataragama/Skanda. The custom is to take a ritual bath in the Menik's cleansing waters, then to don clean (usually white) clothes and walk to the temple to leave a fruit basket and/or smash a coconut as a sacrifice to the deity, usually to a stirring accompaniment of feral drumming and trumpeting.

The Kataragama Temple is reached along either of two parallel 250m-long avenues that enclose a leafy park and ornamental pool. Perhaps a dozen other places of worship flank the twin avenues. Most are colourful small shrines dedicated to various Hindu deities, among them Valli, the Vedda consort of Kataragama. There is also a large riverside Buddhist temple. More unexpected is the ancient al-Khizr Mosque, which is revered by the island's Muslims for harbouring the spirit of a mysterious pre-Koranic prophet or saint known as the 'Green One'. Nestled between these shrines, the one-storey Kataragama Museum (⏰ 08.00–16.30 exc Mon; entrance US$5), houses a surprisingly meagre and poorly labelled collection of items unearthed in and around the Sacred Precinct.

The centrepiece of the complex is Kataragama Temple (formally known as Ruhunu Maha Kataragama), a simple quadrangular white building with carved wooden doors at the east-facing entrance, walls coated with the accumulated soot of centuries of oil lamps and candles, and a courtyard housing what is said to be the original Bo Tree planted at Kataragama in the 3rd century BC. A unique aspect of the temple is that it is presided over by a hereditary line of priests known as Kapurala and who credibly claim Vedda descent. Rising 29m into the sky some 600m further north, the Kiri (Milk) Dagoba is a prominent whitewashed edifice attributed to King Mahasena, who also built the Jetavana Dagoba. Extensively

17

renovated in 1912, this dagoba is said to mark one of the 16 Solosmasthana visited by the Buddha during his three journeys to Sri Lanka, and to enshrine the sword he used to cut off his hair at the time of his renunciation.

TISSAMAHARAMA

The main gate urban gateway to nearby Yala and Bandula national parks, ancient Tissamaharama – familiarly known as 'Tissa' – also stands as a worthwhile destination its own right. It is an attractive small town, but strangely unfocused, comprising a seemingly random scattering of low-rise urban enclaves interspersed with green rice paddies, expansive reservoirs teeming with birdlife, and a quartet of giant dagobas dating back to its 3rd- and 2nd-century BC heyday as capital of Ruhuna. For budget travellers, Tissamaharama has a good selection of accommodation, and a plethora of jeeps for day safaris to Yala and Bandara.

HISTORY Archaeological evidence suggests that Tissamaharama was settled by immigrants from Cambodia or India during or before the 5th century BC. Known as Mahagama, it later became the capital of Ruhuna, an offshoot Sinhala Kingdom founded in the early 3rd century BC by Prince Mahanaga after he fell out with his brother Devanampiya Tissa of Anuradhapura. Mahanaga and his son and successor Yatala Tissa were reputedly responsible for the construction of a trio of massive dagobas at Tissamaharama as well as a sophisticated irrigation network centred on the Tissa and Yoda reservoirs. Ruhuna thrived as an independent sometime-rival, sometime-ally of Anuradhapura for roughly a century prior to the reamalgamation of the two polities under King Dutugamunu in c161BC. Over subsequent centuries, Ruhuna would offer refuge to many a Sinhalese prince forced to flee Anuradhapura, or later Polonnaruwa, to regroup their forces. The most renowned of these refugees was Vijayabahu I, who grew up in exile at a time when the north was controlled by Chola usurpers, but went on to lead a 17-year military campaign that resulted in the recapture of Polonnaruwa and his coronation in Anuradhapura in 1072. Tissamaharama itself was evidently abandoned in the 8th or 9th century, but its dagobas were restored during the tenure of Vijayabahu I. The reservoirs created by the ancient Ruhuna kings were restored by the British in the 1870s and still irrigate the town's abundant paddies to this day.

GETTING THERE AND AWAY
By air Cinnamon Air (w *cinnamonair.com*) and Helitours (w *helitours.lk*) both fly from Colombo to Mattala Rajapaksa International Airport, only 30km west of Tissamaharama by tuktuk or other road transport.

By road Tissamaharama lies 260km (5 hours) southeast of Colombo following the Southern Expressway. Twice-hourly buses between Colombo and Kataragama all stop at Tissamaharama, and are also your best bet for Galle (145km/3 hours). Buses run every 30–45 minutes between Tissamaharama and Matara (105km/2 hours) via Weligama (120km/2½ hours) and Tangalle (70km/1½ hours). For Arugam Bay (150km/3.5km), Ella (90km/2 hours), Nuwara Eliya (145km/4 hours) and other destinations in Hill Country, either catch an hourly bus to Wellawaya (60km/1½ hours) and change there, or catch a tuktuk to Wirawila Junction 8km west of Tissamaharama, and pick up a bus coming from Matara or Galle. For Kandy, head to Nuwara Eliya and change there. More locally, plenty of transport runs along the 18km road to Kataragama, the 10km road to Kirinda and the 27km road to Hambantota.

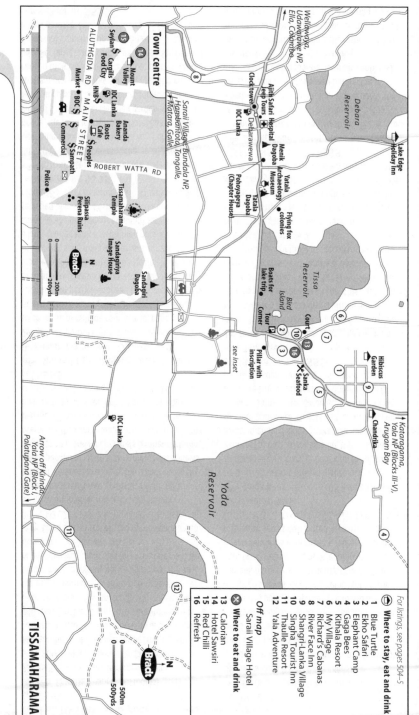

Town centre

Wellawaya,
Udawalawe NP,
Ella, Colombo

ALUTHGIDA RD

15 Seylan $
14 Mount Valley
Cargills Food City
IOC Lanka

Clocktower
Jeep Tours
Ajith Safari
Debarawewa
IOC Lanka

Ananda Bakery
BOC $
Roots Café
HNB $
Peoples $
Market
Commercial
Sampath $

M A I N   S T R E E T

ROBERT WATTA RD

Police

Saraii Village, Bundala NP,
Hapabantota, Tangalle,
Matara, Galle

Tissamaharama Temple

Silpassa Perena Ruins

Sandagiriya Image House

Sandagiri Dagoba

N

Bradt

0   200m
0   200yds

Menik Dagoba
Hospital
Yatala Archaeology Museum
Flying fox colonies
Yatala Dagoba
Pohoyageya (Chapter House)

Debara Reservoir

Lake Edge Holiday Inn

Tissa Reservoir

Bird Island

Boats for lake trip
Tour Corner
Pillar with inscription

see inset

Sanka Seafood

2
10
3
13
16
Court

6
7
1
5

Hibiscus Garden

9

Chandrika

4

Katargama,
Yala NP (Blocks III–VI),
Arugam Bay

Yoda Reservoir

IOC Lanka

11

12

Saraii Village, Bundala NP,
Arrow off Kirinda,
Yala NP (Block I),
Palatupana Gate)

N

Bradt

0   500m
0   500yds

TISSAMAHARAMA

For listings, see pages 504–5

Where to stay, eat and drink

1   Blue Turtle
2   Ekho Safari
3   Elephant Camp
4   Gaga Bees
5   Kithala Resort
6   My Village
7   Richard's Cabanas
8   River Face Inn
9   Shangri-Lanka Village
10 Singha Tourist Inn
11 Thaulle Resort
12 Yala Adventure

Off map
Saraii Village Hotel

Where to eat and drink

13 Calorian
14 Hotel Sawsiri
15 Red Chilli
16 Refresh

Upmarket

Thaulle Resort (28 rooms) 047 223 7900; e info@thaulle.com; w thaulle.com. Set on the southern shore of Yoda Reservoir 4km southeast of the town centre, this stylish German-owned boutique hotel has large rooms with wooden floor & hardwood furniture offset by bright fabrics, AC, fan, fridge, TV, safe, modern bathrooms with quality fittings, & wide slate-tiled terrace or balcony with a lake view. The airy open-sided restaurant also faces the reservoir. Well priced. *US$125 B&B dbl.* **$$$$**

Ekho Safari Hotel (50 rooms) Kataragama Rd; 047 223 7299; e fom@safari-tissa.net; w thesafarihotel.lk. This upgraded former government resthouse, perfectly positioned on the east shore of Tissa Reservoir, stands in a well-developed garden with a swimming pool & views across to an island where egrets & other birds roost overnight. The comfortable rooms have queen-size bed, AC, TV, minibar, safe & armchairs. There's a good restaurant, it couldn't be more central, & safaris are easily arranged. *US$100/110 B&B sgl/ dbl.* **$$$$**

Shangri-Lanka Village Hotel (3 rooms) Off Kataragama Rd; 047 223 8006; m 0773 298206; e info@shangrilankavillage.com; w shangrilankavillage.com; see ad, page 520. Affiliated to its namesake in Bentota, this attractive suburban property comprises 3 massive & brightly decorated cottages with terracotta tile floors, tall wooden ceiling, queen-size bed, sofa, AC, fan, TV, DVD player, safe, minibar & private terrace. There's a large garden with a swimming pool, free bicycle usage, & an open-sided restaurant serving a varied selection of local & Western dishes in the $$$ range. *US$100/115 sgl/dbl B&B, with walk-in & off-season discounts.* **$$$$**

Kithala Resort (40 rooms) Kataragama Rd; 047 223 7206; e info@theme-resorts.com; w theme-resorts.com. Tucked away behind a hedge, the former Priyankara Hotel boasts a pretty view of paddy fields, a lawned garden with pond & infinity pool, & a stylish lobby adorned with contemporary artworks reflecting traditional Sri Lankan themes. Simple but well-appointed rooms have AC, fan, TV, tea/coffee, garden-facing balcony & unusually small bathrooms. Smoothly managed & decent value. *US$102/120 sgl/dbl B&B, with off-season discounts.* **$$$$**

Moderate

Blue Turtle Hotel (16 rooms) Off Kataragama Rd; m 0775 486836; e blueturtlehotel@gmail.com; w blueturtlehotel. com. This modern owner-managed hotel stands in a large leafy property that attracts plenty of woodland birds & incorporates a large swimming pool. The spacious AC rooms are split across 2-storey blocks of 4 & come with classic-contemporary décor, wooden queen-size bed with fitted net, writing desk, quality fittings & private balconies with seating. A breezy 1st-floor restaurant serves well-priced 3-course meals ($$$). *US$72/83 sgl/dbl B&B, with 40% discount in low season.* **$$$**

Gaga Bees (9 rooms) Off Kataragama Rd; m 0716 205343; e info@gagabeesyala.com; w gagabeesyala.com. Overlooking the paddies 2km east of the Kataragama Rd, this isolated owner-managed lodge accommodates guests in spacious adobe eco-chalets with palm-frond roof, colourful ethnic-style décor, AC, fan, net, fridge & private balcony. There's a swimming pool & plentiful birdlife including free-ranging peacocks. *US$50/60 sgl/dbl B&B.* **$$$**

Yala Adventure (7 rooms) 011 245 4454; m 0773 906666; e info@theyalaholidays. lk; w theyalaholidays.lk. Boasting an isolated bush location on a peninsula jutting into the eastern shore of Yoda Reservoir, this aptly named lodge offers village visits, kayaking, abseiling, cycling & jeep safaris to Yala & Bandula. The large fruit & vegetable garden attracts plenty of birds & butterflies. A range of comfortable tents & bungalows, all with lake or garden view, AC, fan & private terrace, are complemented by an open-sided restaurant with a stilted lobby. *Rooms are good value, starting at US$80 dbl B&B, but the tired-looking tents seem overpriced at US$175 dbl B&B.* **$$$–$$$$**

Saraii Village Hotel [map, page 488] (9 rooms) m 0768 216363, 0710 377772; e info@ saraiivillage.com; w saraiivillage.com. Set in a teak & mahogany plantation 1.5km north of Wirawila Junction, this quirky but fun lodge offers a choice of elaborate naturally ventilated 2-storey tree-houses & more compact fan-cooled adobe huts. The romantic rusticity should appeal to adventurous glamping enthusiasts but might prove off-putting to those seeking more conventional accommodation. Amenities include a swimming pool & it offers yoga retreats, safaris & a wide range of day excursions. *From US$99 dbl B&B.* **$$$$**

Budget

✳ 🏠 **My Village** (7 rooms) Court Rd; **m** 0773 500090, 0711 560200; **e** info@myvillagelk.com; **w** myvillagelk.com. Offering a boutique hotel feel at near-budget prices, this stylish little lodge is set in leafy gardens close to the east shore of Tissa Reservoir 2km north of the town centre. Rooms have AC, tall wooden ceilings & treated concrete floor, while public areas include a shaded garden terrace & open-plan kitchen & restaurant. The friendly owner-manager lives on site & offers free pick-ups from the bus station & bicycle usage, as well as organising reliable safaris to Yala & Bundala. *US$40/50 sgl/dbl.* **$$$**

🏠 **River Face Inn** (7 rooms) Gangasiribura Rd; **** 047 348 6277; **m** 0773 890229; **e** info@ yalariverfaceinn.com; **w** yalariverfaceinn.com. Set in jungle-like bamboo-clumped grounds hung with hammocks & verging the Kirindi River, this family-run retreat has the choice of neat standard rooms in the main building, riverside rooms or a small but sumptuous elevated wooden tree-house. All rooms have fan & net. Affordable Yala safaris are offered. *US$28/38 dbl with fan/AC, riverside units from US$60.* **$$**

🏠 **Elephant Camp** (5 rooms) Kataragama Rd; **** 047 223 7231. This pleasant family-owned & -managed guesthouse stands in a tropical garden close to the reservoir & several restaurants about 1.5km north of the town centre. Clean rooms with fan & optional AC, superb homemade curries & reliable Yala safaris. *US$28/40 dbl with fan/AC.* **$$**

🏠 **Richard's Cabanas** (3 rooms) Galmadawwa Rd; **** 047 223 9193; **m** 0779 650306; **e** amila0215@gmail.com. Set in a pretty green garden opposite a babbling waterfall 400m north of the Kataragama Rd, this secluded & individualistic owner-managed lodge accommodates guests in spacious, brightly decorated, tall-ceilinged villas with AC, net, fan & a small balcony facing a riverine tangle of vegetation. The pool opposite the entrance hosts some interesting birds including a breeding pair of black-capped night heron. *US$48 dbl or twin.* **$$$**

Shoestring

🏠 **Singha Tourist Inn** (10 rooms) Off Kataragama Rd; **** 047 223 7090; **m** 0770 648088. For budget-conscious travellers, the attractive prices & pretty lakeshore location conveniently close to the town centre & several restaurants should compensate for the slightly rundown state of what are basically clean & pleasant rooms with fan & optional AC. *US$10/20 dbl with fan/AC.* **$**

✕ WHERE TO EAT AND DRINK *Map, page 503*

✕ **Calorian Restaurant** Kataragama Rd; **** 047 223 8808; **e** calorianrestaurant@gmail.com; ⏰ 05.00–21.30. Popular with tour groups, this reliable but unexciting restaurant serves a wide variety of Italian, Sri Lankan & seafood dishes, including pizzas & good kottu roti. **$$$**

✕ **Refresh Restaurant** Kataragama Rd; **** 047 233 7357; ⏰ 05.00–20.00. The 20-dish lunchtime curry buffet (⏰ 11.30–15.30) is the main attraction of this large modern restaurant with garden seating, but it also serves tasty seafood, steaks, Italian, Chinese & pizzas. **$$$**

✕ **Red Chilli Restaurant** Main St; **m** 0710 674363; ⏰ 08.00–22.00. Clean central eatery serving tasty Mongolian fare in small (**$**) or large (**$$**) portions.

✕ **Hotel Sawsiri** Main St; **m** 0773 883398; ⏰ 08.00–21.00. Good central spot for a lunchtime rice-&-curry buffet. Indoor & outdoor seating. **$**

OTHER PRACTICALITIES The main street through the compact town centre 1km south of Tissa Reservoir is serviced by branches of the Commercial, Seylan, HNB and various other banks, all with ATMs. There is also a Cargills Food City on Main Street and a large market between it and the bus station.

SAFARI OPERATORS Safaris are big business in Tissa, and assuming you are looking for a standard 5-hour trip to Yala National Park's popular Block I, the best place to organise it will more often than not be your hotel. Alternatively, you

17

could contact one of the two well-regarded companies listed below, or try your luck at the off-puttingly nicknamed Tout Corner, a jeep park situated alongside the Kataragama Road immediately south of the Ekho Safari Hotel. The standard rate for a 5-hour budget safari to Yala or Bandara is US$30–40 per jeep for up to 6 passengers, inclusive of driver/guide, fuel and vehicle entrance fees, but exclusive of meals, drinks or individual park entrance fees. Jeep rental to the more remote Udawalawe works out at around US$50. Other companies offer all-inclusive packages starting at around US$35/70 per person for a shared/private half-day tour.

Ajith Safari Jeep Tours ☏047 223 7557; m 0777 905532; e info@yalawild.com; w yalawild.com. Established in 1987, this well-regarded operator offers relatively pricey private safaris to Yala, Bandara, Udawalawe & the lesser-known Lunugamwehera.

Ceylon Safari m 0771 996796; e ceylonsafari@gmail.com; w ceylonsafari.com. Reliable &

affordable safaris run by a pair of dynamic & responsive brothers.

Daya Safaris ☏047 781 30444; m 0776 190873; e dayasafari@gmail.com; w dayasafari.com. Jeep hire & all-inclusive safaris at competitive rates.

Rathnayaka Safaris ☏047 561 6789; m 0779 161613. Well-priced jeep hire to Yala, Bandara & Udawalawe.

WHAT TO SEE AND DO The main attractions in the vicinity of Tissamaharama are Yala and Bandula national parks, both of which are easily visited on half- or full-day jeep safaris out of town. In addition, four ancient dagobas, one adjoined by an unexpectedly good museum, lie within easy walking (or even easier tuktuk) distance of the town centre, while the five lakes bordering the town offer some fine birdwatching. Tissamaharama is also well positioned for day trips to most other sites of interest covered in this chapter, with the nearby Kataragama Temple, Kirindi and Hambantota all set within easy bussing or tuktuk distance, and to the more remote Buduruvagala Rock Carvings and Maligavila Buddha statue equally feasible with private transport and an early start.

Sandagiri Dagoba Thought to be the oldest of Tissamaharama's quartet of ancient dagobas, Sandagiri is a plain domed brick structure that rises above the paddies 600m northeast of the modern town centre. Dating to the 3rd century BC, it is credited to Prince Mahanaga, and stands 55m tall, despite the absence of the minaret-like harmika that presumably once capped it. Legend has it that several gifts sent by Emperor Asoka to Mahanaga's brother Devanampiya Tissa are enshrined within Sandagiri, along with a Buddha forehead relic deposited there by King Kavan Tissa a century later. The substantial ruins of an 8th-century image house stand 200m further south.

Tissamaharama Temple Also reputedly founded by Mahanaga, this ancient temple a couple of hundred metres west of Sandagiri is the setting of Tissamaharama Dagoba, a prominent whitewashed landmark originally constructed by King Kavan Tissa, expanded during the 1st-century AD reign of King Ilanaga of Anuradhapura, and most recently renovated over 1858–1900. A bubble-shaped dome topped by an unusually squattened harmika, it is the largest dagoba in southern Sri Lanka, standing 47.5m high, with a circumference of 166m. According to legend it is one of the 16 Solosmasthana, having been visited by the Buddha, together with 500 followers, on his third visit to the island. A pillar inscription recently discovered in Kirinda indicates that it holds, or once held, the left tooth relic of the Buddha. Other ancient relics around the dagoba include a stone water trough, several Buddha statues, and a scattering of columns and bases.

Yatala Dagoba and environs Situated alongside the Wirawila Road 500m west of Tissa Reservoir's wall, the 37m-high bubble-shaped Yatala Dagoba is the most interesting construction of its type in Tissamaharama, not least because of the unassuming but illuminating museum that adjoins it. Centrepiece of a long-abandoned monastery, the dagoba marks the birthplace of Mahanaga's son and successor Yatala, though it's unclear which of the two kings actually built it. It stands on a brick platform adorned with ancient elephant carvings (the oldest such 'elephant wall' on the island), dotted with ornate stairwells and pillars, and enclosed by a lotus-covered moat. The only site in Tissa to have received more than cursory archaeological attention, the dagoba underwent extensive restoration and excavation between 1886 and 1987, and it's the main source of the relics housed in the adjoining Yatala Archaeology Museum (☉ *08.00–17.00; no photography*). These include some superb engraved guardstones dated to the 2nd and 3rd centuries BC, a large lotus-shaped 3rd-century Buddhapada, an 8th-century limestone Bodhisattva in the Ahavana mudra, and several ancient sculpted granite benches and urinals. Look out too for a striking robed Buddha statue thought to have been the blueprint for the almost identical but larger Avukana Buddha between Dambulla and Anuradhapura. Two other ancient sites, both associated with the same monastery as Yatala, stand a few hundred metres west along the Wirawila Road. The first is a 2nd-century BC Pohoyageya (Chapter House) whose 12 x 6 rows of 5m-tall standing pillars possess the uniform appearance of a petrified plantation forest. Past this, the smallish Menik Dagoba, restored in the 1890s, was reputedly built by King Dutugamunu alongside the still-standing pillar where he tethered his famous royal elephant, Kadol Etha.

The Five Lakes The quintet of ancient reservoirs that surround Tissamaharama forms part of an elaborate irrigation network formulated by Kings Mahanaga and Yatala. The centrepiece is Tissa Reservoir, which the British engineers who restored it in the 1870s recognised to be hemmed in by the world's oldest oblique dam wall, a technology pioneered in Sri Lanka almost 2,000 years before it was first used in Europe. Today, four of the reservoirs, namely Tissa, Wirawila, Debara and Pannegamuwa, stand within the informally protected Wirawila-Tissa Sanctuary, which extends for 50km² northwest of central Tissa. The fifth and largest, Yoda, stands a couple of kilometres further southeast. All the lakes are well vegetated and protect an interesting birdlife, particularly during the northern winter, when resident populations of painted stork, spot-billed pelican, pheasant-tailed jacana, purple swamphen and various bitterns, herons and kingfishers, are supplemented by migrant waterfowl, waders and aquatic warblers. The most accessible of the lakes on foot is Tissa, since it borders the town centre and its western shore – also home to some impressive fruitbat colonies – is readily explored along a road that leads after some 2km to the eastern shore of Debara, a lovely lily-covered lake, much of which is encircled by a dirt road. Boat trips on to Tissa from a jetty halfway along the reservoir wall (*US$15–20 per party*) offer a possibility of crocodiles, as well as plentiful birds and bats. Lakes further afield can easily be accessed by tuktuk, or you could think about arranging a half-day bird-oriented 'Five Lakes' jeep tour with Rathnayaka Safaris or indeed any other jeep operator (*around US$25 per group*).

KIRINDA

Known as Dovera in ancient times, the modest coastal village of Kirinda holds a special place in Sri Lankan legend as the place where Viharamahadevi, the daughter of King Kelani Tissa of Kelaniya, washed ashore after having been cast adrift in a golden boat to atone for a grievous sin committed by her father, whose kingdom stood close to present-day Colombo. The castaway princess was taken as queen by King Kavan Tissa of Ruhuna, whose capital Mahagama (Tissamaharama) stood only 10km to the north, and became the mother of King Dutugamunu, who recaptured Anuradhapura in 161 BC, and his younger brother and successor Saddha Tissa. The attractive Kirinda Temple, its boulder-top dagoba stood next to a large, modern and unusually effeminate white Buddha statue and affording lovely views over the village and beach, reputedly dates back to Viharamahadevi's day, but has little to show for it. A more compelling reason to visit Kirinda is its lovely beach, which can be safe for swimming over December–April, but is treacherously rough at other times.

GETTING THERE AND AWAY Kirinda stands about 12km south of Tissamaharama and the two are connected by a good tar road and regular buses. Jeeps to Yala National Park can be arranged through any hotel in Kirinda, but unless you plan on staying overnight, you'd be better off arranging a safari out of Tissamaharama.

WHERE TO STAY *Map, page 488*

A few low-key resort hotels in Kirinda double as a useful base for safaris to Yala National Park, the main gate of which stands just 12km to the northeast. Hotels listed under *Around Palatupana Gate* (page 513) for Yala National Park also lie very close to Kirinda.

Nikara Yala (7 rooms) Nidangalawella Beach Rd; ☏ 047 560 0848; m 0726 921169; e info@ nikarayala.com; w nikarayala.com. This attractive boutique hotel is set in landscaped tropical gardens, with lawns cropped rather oddly to resemble a giant chessboard, that run down to a wildly beautiful beach. Stylish modern rooms have laminate wood floors, wood ceiling, queen-size bed, AC, tea/coffee & minibar. The 3 upstairs rooms also have balconies with beach views, while some ground-floor rooms have private plunge pools. Jeeps are available for safaris at a rate of US$33 excluding entrance fees. *From US$150–175 standard dbl, US$200–300 villa with plunge pool; all rates B&B.* **$$$$**

Kirinda Beach Resort (23 rooms) Nidangalawella Beach Rd; ☏ 047 362 0500; m 0770 200897; e kirindabeachresort@yahoo. com; w kirindabeachresort.com. Set in thicketed sandy grounds running down to an unspoilt boulder-strewn beach, this quirky beach lodge has an unusual rooftop infinity pool, a spa, a restaurant serving good local buffets, & safari jeeps for Yala available at US$37 excluding entrance fee. The cool wooden cabins have a down-to-earth feel but good amenities including AC, fitted nets, fridge, fan, TV & sound system. *US$85/90 sgl/dbl B&B, dropping by around 30% out of season.* **$$$$**

YALA NATIONAL PARK

[map, pages 510–11] (☏ 047 348 9297 *(Palatupana Gate), 047 3628477 (Galge ticket office);* w dwc.gov.lk; ⊕ 06.00–18.00, *usually closed 1 Sep–16 Oct; entrance US$15 pp, plus US$8 service charge per party, plus 12% tax)* Sri Lanka's best and most popular safari destination, Yala National Park protects a vast tract of low-lying dry-zone wilderness which once formed part of the Ruhuna Kingdom, but was populated only by a thin spread of nomadic Vedda hunter-gatherers for centuries prior to being accorded official protection in 1900. Today, the park is renowned for its dense populations of elephant, leopard, water buffalo and to a lesser extent sloth bear, and it also hosts an exceptionally varied avifauna comprising more than 200 bird species. Divided into five blocks, the 978km² national park, though smaller than Wilpattu, forms the centrepiece of the island's largest conglomeration of protected areas, a

1,750km² tract of wilderness that also includes the contiguous Kumana National Park (accessible only from the northeast via Arugam Bay; page 361), the Yala Strict Nature Reserve (off limits to the public), Lunugamwehera National Park (gazetted in 1995 and accessible through Yala Block V) and three small buffer sanctuaries. Tourist activity is focused almost entirely on the southwesterly Block I (sometimes known as Ruhuna National Park), which extends over 141km² close to Tissamaharama and Kataragama, and was the first part of Yala to be gazetted as a national park, back in 1938. The rest of the present-day park, though annexed between 1954 and 1973, was practically closed to tourism until as recently as 2016, when the Galge ticket office and a pair of entrance gates opened at the three-way junction of Blocks II, IV and V. Game viewing is undoubtedly best in Block I, not least because the wildlife is more habituated than elsewhere; but this sector also tends to be overcrowded, especially in the high season, when a dozen or more jeeps are routinely found congregated around a bemused leopard or elephant. For this reason, there's a lot to be said for supplementing a safari to Block I with a visit to one of the lesser-known blocks, which are less reliable for big game but retain more of a wilderness feel.

FLORA AND FAUNA Yala National Park supports a varied mosaic of forest, woodland, grassland and wetland habitats, with a total of 700 flowering plant species recorded. Block I, the area most commonly visited by tourists, is dominated by dense evergreen thorn-scrub, which comprises more than 50% of its cover, with weera (*Drypetes sepiaria*), palu (*Manilkara hexandra*), wood-apple (*Limonia acidissima*), yellow bell-orchid (*Bauhinia tomentosa*) and droopy-leaf (*Aglaia elaeagnoidea*) being among the most common species. The scrub is interspersed with taller patches of closed-canopy forest, mostly in the vicinity of the Menik River (which runs along the eastern boundary with Block II), as well as tracts of open pitiya grassland (an important habitat for grazing wildlife) and coastal habitats such as sand dune and mangrove forest. The other blocks tend to be more densely forested, to an extent that can make wildlife viewing difficult, except in Block V, which has a parklike feel.

More than 40 mammal species have been recorded, with the biggest draws being elephant, leopard and sloth bear. The total elephant herd stands at 300-plus individuals, and sightings are very likely on any given game drive in Block I, though with the population spread over such a larger area, you seldom see the large breeding herds associated with the likes of Udawalawe. Yala reputedly hosts the world's densest concentration of leopards, with a population of 65 in Block I extrapolated to around 200 for the whole park. There's a strong hit-and-miss element to leopard sightings – on a lucky game drive you might see three or four individuals, but equally you might go three or four game drives without locating a single one. However, the general consensus among the cognoscenti is that leopards tend to be most conspicuous in the dry season, when the vegetation is thinner, and that diurnal encounters are most frequent around the new moon, when the lack of moonlight makes it difficult to hunt at night. Sloth bears, though scarcer, are most frequently observed in Pallu season (April–May), when they feed voraciously on the mildly inebriating berry of the Ceylon ironwood tree. Other commonly observed mammals include water buffalo, wild boar, spotted deer, red muntjac, sambar, grey langur, toque macaque, black-naped hare, stripe-necked mongoose, ruddy mongoose and jackal.

Yala is an exceptional birdwatching destination, with 215 species recorded, and there's a real chance of notching up to a hundred on a full-day game drive that includes a visit to the Menik River, especially during migrant season. Endemics are relatively

17

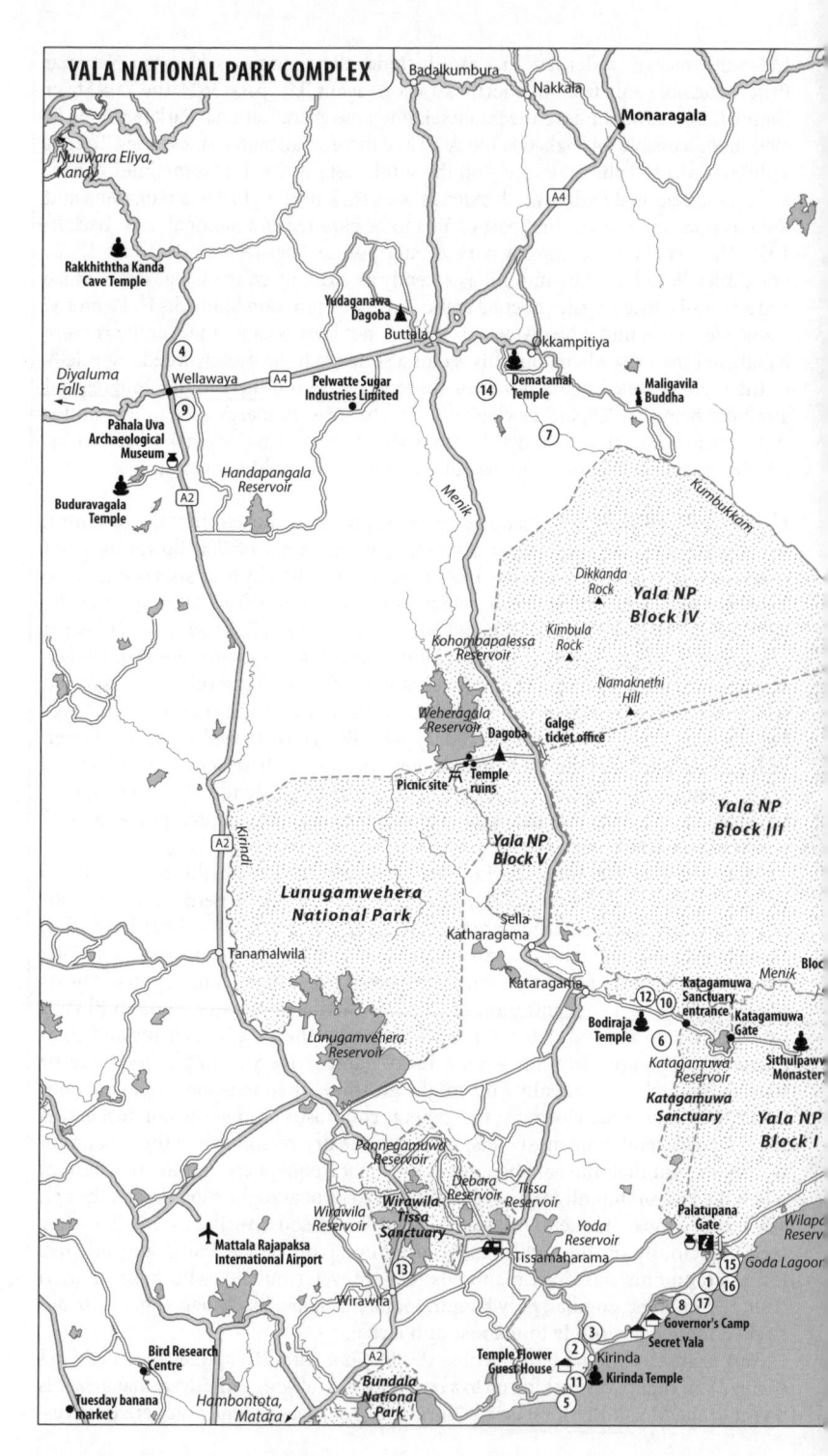

YALA NATIONAL PARK COMPLEX

Badalkumbura
Nakkala
Monaragala

A4

Nuuwara Eliya, Kandy

Rakkhiththa Kanda
Cave Temple

Yudaganawa
Dagoba
Buttala

Okkampitiya

Diyaluma Falls

④ Wellawaya A4

Pelwatte Sugar
Industries Limited

⑭ Dematamal
Temple

Maligavila
Buddha

⑨

⑦

Pahala Uva
Archaeological
Museum

Handapangala Reservoir

A2

Buduruvagala
Temple

Menik

Kumbukkam

Dikkanda Rock

**Yala NP
Block IV**

Kimbula Rock

Kohombapalessa Reservoir

Namaknethi Hill

Weheragala Reservoir

Dagoba Galge
ticket office

Picnic site ✠ Temple
ruins

**Yala NP
Block V**

**Yala NP
Block III**

Kirindi

**Lunugamwehera
National Park**

Sella
Katharagama

Tanamalwila

Kataragama

Menik **Bloc**

⑫ ⑩ Katagamuwa
Sanctuary
entrance

Katagamuwa
Gate

Bodiraja
Temple

⑥

Katagamuwa Reservoir

Sithulpaw
Monaster

*Lunugamwehera
Reservoir*

*Katagamuwa
Sanctuary*

**Yala NP
Block I**

Pannegamuwa Reservoir

Debara Reservoir

Tissa Reservoir

Wirawila Reservoir

**Wirawila-
Tissa
Sanctuary**

Yoda Reservoir

Palatupana
Gate

*Wilapo
Reserv*

✈ Mattala Rajapaksa
International Airport

⑬

Tissamaharama

⑮ Goda Lagoor

① ⑯

Wirawila

⑧ ⑰

Governor's Camp
Secret Yala

Bird Research
Centre

A2

*Bundala
National
Park*

Temple Flower
Guest House

② ③

⑪

Kirinda

Kirinda Temple

Tuesday banana
market

*Hambontota,
Matara*

⑤

510

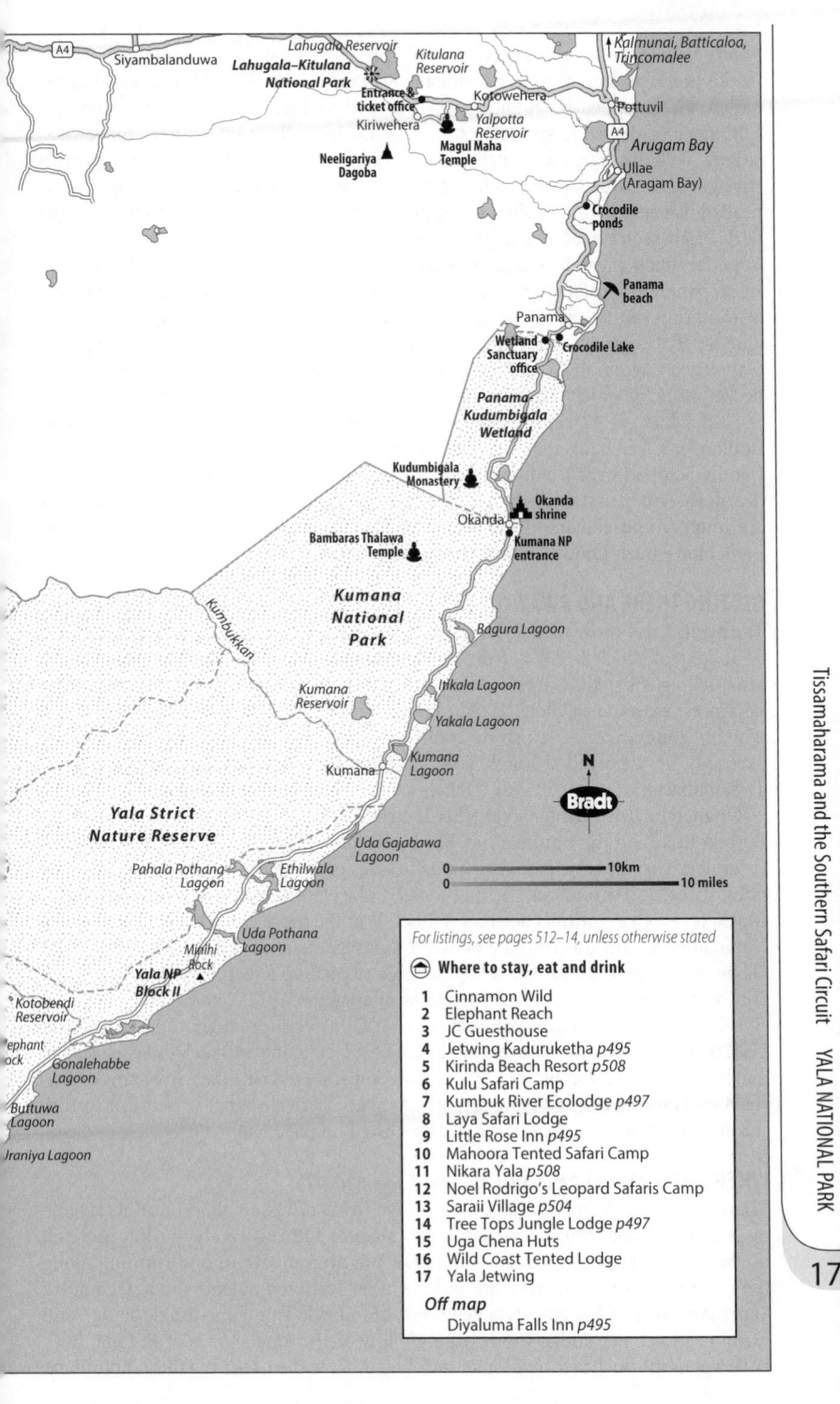

A4
Siyambalanduwa

Lahugala Reservoir
Kitulana
Reservoir

*Lahugala–Kitulana
National Park*
Entrance &
ticket office
Kiriwehera

Kalmunai, Batticaloa,
Trincomalee

Kotowehera

Yalpotta
Reservoir

Pottuvil

A4

Arugam Bay

**Magul Maha
Temple**

Ullae
(Aragam Bay)

**Neeligariya
Dagoba**

Crocodile
ponds

Panama
beach

Panama

**Wetland
Sanctuary
office**

Crocodile Lake

*Panama–
Kudumbigala
Wetland*

**Kudumbigala
Monastery**

Okanda
shrine

Okanda

**Bambaras Thalawa
Temple**

Kumana NP
entrance

*Kumana
National
Park*

Bagura Lagoon

Kumana
Reservoir

Itikala Lagoon

Yakala Lagoon

Kumbukkan

Kumana

Kumana
Lagoon

N

Bradt

*Yala Strict
Nature Reserve*

Uda Gajabawa
Lagoon

0 ——————10km

0 ——————————10 miles

Pahala Pothana
Lagoon

Ethilwala
Lagoon

Uda Pothana
Lagoon

Minihi
Block

*Yala NP
Block II*

Kotobendi
Reservoir

Elephant
Block

Gonalehabbe
Lagoon

Buttuwa
Lagoon

Uraniya Lagoon

For listings, see pages 512–14, unless otherwise stated

🍽 **Where to stay, eat and drink**

1   Cinnamon Wild
2   Elephant Reach
3   JC Guesthouse
4   Jetwing Kaduruketha *p495*
5   Kirinda Beach Resort *p508*
6   Kulu Safari Camp
7   Kumbuk River Ecolodge *p497*
8   Laya Safari Lodge
9   Little Rose Inn *p495*
10   Mahoora Tented Safari Camp
11   Nikara Yala *p508*
12   Noel Rodrigo's Leopard Safaris Camp
13   Saraii Village *p504*
14   Tree Tops Jungle Lodge *p497*
15   Uga Chena Huts
16   Wild Coast Tented Lodge
17   Yala Jetwing

Off map
Diyaluma Falls Inn *p495*

poorly represented, with just seven species present, namely Sri Lanka junglefowl, Sri Lanka green pigeon, red-faced malkoha, Sri Lanka grey hornbill, crimson-fronted barbet, black-capped bulbul and brown-capped babbler. The park is also good for a number of dry-zone specialities such as Eurasian thick-knee, great thick-knee, sirkeer malkoha, blue-faced malkoha and Malabar pied hornbill, and an important stronghold for large raptors such as crested serpent-eagle, crested hawk-eagle, grey-headed fish eagle, white-bellied sea eagle, oriental honey-buzzard and shikra. Other fairly easily seen birds include painted stork, yellow-wattled lapwing, emerald dove, imperial green pigeon, orange-breasted green pigeon, chestnut-headed bee-eater, Asian paradise-flycatcher and white-browed fantail. The park has a fine complement of wintering shorebirds as well as other attractive migrants including the common blue-tailed bee-eater and less common Brahminy myna and rosy starling. The Gonalabba Lagoon in Yala's Block I is the best place in Sri Lanka to see the black-necked stork, of which fewer than ten individuals are resident in the country.

A checklist of 47 reptiles includes three endemic snakes (Sri Lankan krait, Boulenger's keelback, Sri Lankan flying snake) and three endemic lizards (painted-lipped lizard, brown-patched kangaroo lizard and Bahir's fan-throated lizard, the latter first described in 2015). More likely to be seen by casual visitors are mugger and estuarine crocodile. All five marine turtles associated with Sri Lanka have been known to visit the park's lengthy coastline.

GETTING THERE AND AWAY There are three ticket offices and four entrance gates. The busiest and most southerly gate is Palatupana, which stands on the southwest boundary of Block I, 20km from Tissamaharama via Kirinda. Less popular but also well established, Katagamuwa Gate stands 12km east of Kataragama at the northwest extreme of Block I. No public transport runs to either of these gates, which – unless you have private transport – means that game drives in Block I can only be arranged through your hotel or one of many operators based in Tissamaharama (pages 505–6). Tickets can be purchased at both gates.

Opened in 2016, Galge ticket office is strategically located on the east side of the Buttala Road, on the boundary of Blocks III and IV, 18km north of Kataragama. It services two separate gates on opposite sides of the main road. The eastern gate offers direct access to Block III and Block IV. The western gate offers direct access to Block V, as well as indirect access via Block V to the more easterly Lunugamwehera National Park. Any bus running between Kataragama and Buttala can drop you at Galge ticket office, and it is usually possible to pick up a jeep on the spot, though you could as easily (and affordably) make arrangements in Kataragama.

Wherever you organise your safari, a straight jeep rental should work out at US$30–40 for up to 6 passengers, inclusive of driver/guide and fuel, but exclusive of meals, drinks and park entrance fees. Some companies offer all-inclusive game drives, starting at around US$35/70 per person for a shared/private half-day tour. For further recommendations, see the safari operators listed on page 506.

WHERE TO STAY, EAT AND DRINK *Map, pages 510–11*
Many people visit Yala National Park as a day trip out of Tissamaharama, Kataragama or one of the other towns covered in this chapter. Otherwise, the park is serviced by two main clusters of (mostly upmarket) accommodation, one running along the coast west of Palatupana Gate and the other scattered outside the Katagamuwa Sanctuary west of Katagamuwa Gate. Further afield, Tree Tops Jungle Lodge and Kumbuk River Eco-lodge (both page 497), near the small town of Buttala, both have a genuine bush setting despite standing outside the park's northern boundary.

Around Palatupana Gate

The largest cluster of accommodation, most of it falling in the upmarket or exclusive category, stands along the road connecting Kirinda to Palatupana Gate. These lodges have a great coastal location & are all well-positioned for game drives in the far southwest of Block I, which is the most productive part of the park for game-viewing but also the most congested in terms of tourist traffic.

Exclusive

Wild Coast Tented Lodge (28 rooms) \ 011 774 5700; e reservations@ resplendentceylon.com; w resplendentceylon. com. Scheduled to open as we went to print (Nov 2017), this luxurious all-suite camp, laid out in the shape of a leopard's claw, has a stunning beachfront location 1km west of the park boundary, a large freeform swimming pool, & offers accommodation in spacious & imaginatively designed cocoon tents with AC & all mod cons. *US$586/616 B&B with seasonal discounts & all-inclusive packages also offered.* **$$$$$+**

✳ **Uga Chena Huts** (14 rooms) \ 047 226 7100; e reservations@ugaescapes.com; w ugaescapes.com. Opened in 2015, this 5-star boutique lodge – comparable in feel & standard to the finest African bush lodges – stands in wooded 3ha beachfront gardens bordering the national park immediately outside Palatupana Gate. Accommodation is in stunning domed chalets with teak & mahogany floor & furnishings, private dining area, AC, fan, TV, stylish bathroom with tub & 2 showers, plus a balcony with outdoor shower & plunge pool, with a choice of sea or jungle view. There's also an AC glass-sided restaurant, free-form swimming pool & spa, & rates include game drive guided to the highest standard. *US$1,400 all-inclusive.* **$$$$$+**

Upmarket

Yala Jetwing (90 rooms) \ 047 471 0710; e resv.yala@jetwinghotels.com; w jetwinghotels.com. Set on magnificent beachfront grounds cropped by semi-habituated boars 3km west of the gate, this large & stylish 2-storey lodge is designed so that all rooms face the beach. Amenities include a remarkably long swimming pool, a gym & spa, 2 restaurants & a bar. The spacious rooms have a darkwood floor, understated colour scheme, king-size bed, AC, TV, sofa, minibar & wonderful private balcony with lounger chairs & a view of note. Good value. *From US$190/210 B&B sgl/dbl.* **$$$$**

Laya Safari Lodge (22 rooms) \ 047 223 9851; e inquiries@layahotels.lk; w layahotels.lk. Situated right on the beach a short stroll east of Jetwing Yala, this is a really nice little lodge with a beachfront infinity pool & restaurant serving excellent buffets. The well-lit split-level rooms have a king-size bed, colourful sofas, TV & a great wooden balcony overlooking the beach. *US$205 b&b dbl, with significant low-season discounts.* **$$$$**

Cinnamon Wild (68 rooms) \ 047 223 9449; m 0714 566561; e fom.wild@ cinnamonhotels.com; w cinnamonhotels.com. Situated just 2.5km west of the entrance gate, this unpretentious lodge overlooks a waterhole often visited by elephants. Spacious chalets are carved into the bush & have an earthy feel, with terracotta floor, queen-size bed with fitted net, writing desk, AC, fan, minibar & private balcony. Amenities include a swimming pool & a rooftop bar with great views to the sea & a rocky outcrop where leopards sometimes rest up. Good but overpriced by comparison with its closest competitors. *US$300 dbl HB, with seasonal discounts.* **$$$$$+**

Moderate

Elephant Reach (35 rooms) \ 047 721 2640; m 0772 075696; e frontoffice@ elephantreachyala.com; w elephantreach.com. Situated at Yala Junction, near Kirinda, about halfway between Tissamaharama & Palatupana Gate, this comfortable, well-managed & sensibly priced hotel has bright & crisply furnished rooms & chalets with AC, TV, minibar, safe & private balcony, & there's an AC restaurant, a Tree Tops bar, swimming pool & safari jeeps with trackers on hand. *From US$88/92 sgl/dbl B&B.* **$$$$**

Shoestring

J C Guesthouse (8 rooms) m 0772 737136; e jcguestyalakirinda@gmail.com; w jcguesthouseblog.wordpress.com. Owned & managed by a friendly live-in family that prepares great curry spreads, this agreeable & unpretentious guesthouse is situated in a tropical garden at Yala Junction, near Kirinda, & has comfortable rooms with fan, net & balcony. *From US$20 dbl B&B.* **$**

17

Outside Katagamuwa Sanctuary

The camps listed below are scattered outside the Katagamuwa Sanctuary, a protected buffer zone to the west of Katagamuwa Gate, & offer an all-inclusive glamping-type bush experience in standing tents. The meeting point for these camps is the car park opposite Bodiraja Temple on the Katagamuwa Rd 4km southeast of Kataragama town. All these camps are well positioned for game drives in Blocks III–V as well as in Block I.

✻ 🏠 **Noel Rodrigo's Leopard Safaris Camp** (10 tents) m 0713 314024; e reservations@leopardsafaris.com; w leopardsafaris.com. This superior eco-friendly tented camp stands on private land bordering Block III & only 10mins' drive from Katagamuwa Gate. Centred on a comfortable & shady open-sided fan-cooled lounge, bar & library, it offers a wonderful all-inclusive bush experience that incorporates enthusiastically guided jeep safaris into Blocks I or V. The innovative Sri Lankan cuisine is served at various different spots around camp & a bar is stocked with chilled drinks. The modern South African 2-compartment tents are tall enough to stand in & come with proper beds, a sitting area at the front, & private outdoor shower & toilet. There's also a new luxury AC tent set on a wooden platform. *US$555/990 sgl/dbl inc meals, drinks & activities; low-season discounts available.* **$$$$$+**

🏠 **Mahoora Tented Safari Camp** (20 tents) ☎011 583 0833; m 0710 662224; e info@mahoora.com; w mahoora.com. Yala's oldest bush camp stands in a peaceful tract of woodland bordering the Katagamuwa Sanctuary, just 10mins' drive from the entrance gate. The standing tents come with net & fan (but no AC), en-suite shower/toilet & semi-outdoor sitting area & the surrounding woodland offers exceptional birding. Rates include excellent meals, all drinks & expertly guided game drives & bird walks. *From US$380 pp all-inclusive.* **$$$$$+**

🏠 **Kulu Safari Camp** (6 tents) m 0715 338230, 0710 333634; e safari@kulusafari.com; w kulusafaris.com. Situated close to the boundary of the Katagamuwa Sanctuary, this attractive bush camp offers accommodation in spacious South African-made tents with king-size beds & solar-powered bathroom at the back, set on a stilted platform with private balcony overlooking the wooded grounds & Katagamuwa Reservoir. Rates include meals, selected drinks & game drives. *From US$800 pp all-inclusive.* **$$$$$+**

Camping

✻ 🏠 **Tuskers Camping** [not mapped] m 0724 737333, 0768 806830; e tuskerscamping@gmail.com; w tuskerscamping.com. This dynamic Tissamaharama-based company specialises in camping safaris within the park, an option that allows you to experience the sounds of the bush at night & also to enjoy early-morning & late-afternoon drives far from the gates & other vehicles. It sets up temporary camp at 1 of 3 sites alongside the Menik River on the eastern boundary in Block I. Tents are spacious enough to stand in & have proper beds. Rates include game drives, meals & drinks. *From US$500 dbl all-inclusive.* **$$$$$+**

WHAT TO SEE AND DO

Game drives The main activity in and around Yala is game drives, which can be arranged through any hotel or lodge in the area, as well as through a plethora of safari operators and one-man-and-his-jeep operations in Tissamaharama (pages 505–6). Morning drives tend to be most rewarding for birds but afternoon drives come with a better chance of spotting an elusive leopard or sloth bear. If your budget (and tolerance of the sticky climate) runs to it, best to opt for an all-day drive, taking a packed breakfast and lunch, since elephants are most often seen at watering holes in the heat of the day. A full-day drive in Block I also gives you time to explore the relatively untrammelled area around the Menik River, and ensures you will be out and about when most safari-goers are lunching outside the park. Almost all safaris take place in Block I, which supports high densities of game and a generous scattering of natural waterholes and artificial reservoirs, some originally constructed by the ancient kings of Ruhuna.

For those seeking a more off-the-beaten track experience, Block V, though relatively small at 26km², is highly recommended for scenery, waterbirds and relatively regular leopard sightings. Block V could easily be visited in conjunction with the contiguous and even less-visited Lunugamwehera National Park, a 245km^2 tract of disturbed woodland centred on the eponymous reservoir and known for its seasonal concentrations of elephants and varied birdlife (185 species, with aquatic species particularly well represented). Blocks III and IV are also now open to the public but the dense vegetation makes for challenging animal spotting (conversely, it is excellent for woodland and forest birds, and you'll most likely not see another jeep). Back with Block I, it is also possible to obtain advance permission to take the bridge across the Menik River into the little-visited Block II, whose 35km-long Indian Ocean shoreline is studded with streams, lagoons and restored Ruhuna-era reservoirs.

Palatupana Museum Attached to the ticket office at Palatupana Gate is an interesting museum showing the development of the national park, as well as models and skeletons of animals found there.

Sithulpawwa Monastery Enclaved within the northwest of Block I, this ancient and extensive Buddhist monastery – goal of an annual pilgrimage of tens of thousands of worshippers on the Poson (June) Poya – consists of more than a hundred caves with drip ledges centred on a massive whaleback outcrop surrounded by jungle and topped by a modern dagoba. It was founded in the 2nd century BC by Kavan Tissa, and legend holds that it housed more than 10,000 Arahant monks in its heyday, when it was surrounded by a productive agricultural area irrigated by a system of reservoirs. This system gradually deteriorated over the centuries and the monastery and surrounding land were abandoned around 700 years ago following a prolonged and devastating drought that caused many of the monks to starve to death. A few very faded Anuradhapura-era paintings are preserved in one of the caves, and the views from the hilltop to the ocean are spectacular. The monastery is about 5km and signposted from Katagamuwa Gate, and the ascent of the taller hill takes about 15 minutes in foot. Although it is surrounded by the national park, it stands outside and no entrance fee need be paid to visit.

BUNDALA NATIONAL PARK

(☎ 047 348 9070; w dwc.gov.lk; ⊕ 06.00–18.00; entrance US$10 pp, plus US$8 service charge per party, plus 12% tax) Less popular than nearby Yala and Udawalawe, the comparatively obscure Bundala National Park protects a scenic 37km^2 tract of coastal wetlands, intertidal habitats and dry thorn-scrub known for its abundant birdlife and conspicuous elephant population. In addition, the relative lack of tourist traffic lends it an untrammelled feel, even at the height of the tourist season. Designated as Sri Lanka's first Ramsar wetland in 1971, Bundala was gazetted as a 62km^2 national park in 1993 but reduced to its present size in 2004; it is also listed as an Important Bird Area, with 197 species recorded, and forms part of a UNESCO Biosphere Reserve. Its most significant geographic feature is a quintet of shallow brackish lagoons, three of which incorporate salt pans. Running from east to west, these are the 5km^2 Bundala, 4km^2 Embilikala, 6.5km^2 Malala, 4km^2 Koholankala and 2.5km^2 Mahalewaya lagoons, with the last two now given over almost totally to salt extraction pans. The park is criss-crossed by a 30km road network that can technically be covered in about 2 hours, though dedicated birdwatchers could easily spend a half- or even full day exploring them slowly. Aside from the lakes, all of which offer rewarding birding, individual sites of interest include a tower

17

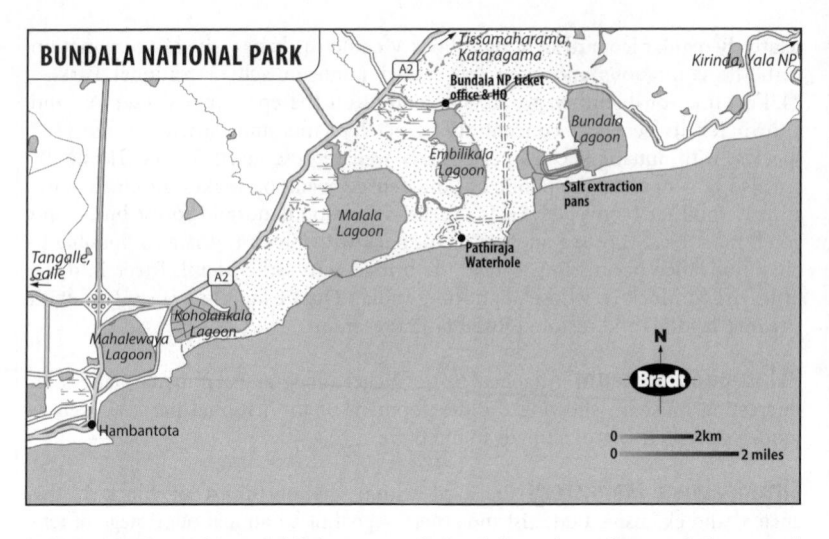

BUNDALA NATIONAL PARK

hide overlooking the Embilikala Lagoon behind the ticket office, and the coastal Pathiraja Waterhole, south of Malala Lagoon, where it is permitted to stretch your legs and enjoy a packed lunch.

FAUNA The most important mammalian draw is elephants, which are quite easily seen but seldom in big herds, since the resident population of around 15 individuals only comprises solitary males, though breeding herds do pass through from time to time. The moist habitat is unsuited to sloth bears, and although leopards are included on the park checklist, our understanding is that none has been observed since the turn of the millennium. Other common large mammals include jackal, buffalo, spotted deer, muntjac, toque macaque, grey langur and wild boar. The park also has a reputation as one of the better places to look for the localised fishing cat, though sightings are very common. Unlikely to be seen by visitors because of their nocturnal habits are civet, rusty-spotted cat, slender loris, porcupine and pangolin. Conspicuous among 50 reptile species are water monitor and both species of crocodile. Olive ridley and leatherback turtles are regular nocturnal beach visitors, whereas hawksbill and green turtles are rare. The endemic Athukoralei's toad is one of 15 amphibian species found in the park.

Birds are abundant and a successful game drive might easily yield upwards of 50 species. Spot-billed pelican, Eurasian spoonbill, pheasant-tailed jacana, grey-headed fish eagle and white-bellied sea eagle inhabit the lagoons, along with most of the more widespread heron, egret, stork, ibis and rallid species, and the more secretive likes of black bittern and yellow bittern. During the northern winter, seasonal aggregations of 15,000-plus shorebirds include an influx of migrants: golden plover, large sandplover, lesser sandplover, Kentish plover, curlew, greenshank, marsh sandpiper, little stint and curlew sandpiper. Bundala used to be the best place in Sri Lanka to see large seasonal concentrations of greater flamingo, but sightings have been few and far between in recent years, largely due to a drop in salinity and decrease in larvae levels associated with the 2004 tsunami and the construction of the Lunugamwehera Dam north of Tissamaharama. Non-aquatic birds are well represented too: the endemic Sri Lanka junglefowl and brown-capped babbler are both common along with the colourful likes of peacock, green bee-eater, blue-tailed bee-eater, Indian roller, baya weaver and various kingfishers.

GETTING THERE AND AWAY The well-signposted main entrance gate and ticket office lies 2km along a turn-off that runs south from the 27km main road between Tissamaharama and Hambantota roughly halfway between the two towns. No jeeps are available at the gate, so it is best to make arrangements in Tissa, where a straight half-day rental including driver/guide and fuel but excluding entrance fees should cost in the ballpark of US$30–35. Jeeps can also be hired in Hambantota but there is less choice there and rates tend to be higher. Afternoon game drives tend to be most productive for elephants and other large mammals, while mornings are best for birds.

HAMBANTOTA

Perhaps the least resort-like coastal town in southern Sri Lanka, Hambantota was the main gateway of international maritime trade out of ancient Ruhuna, and its name – originally applied to Godavaya Bay 3km west of the modern harbour – derives from the phrase 'Sampan Tota', meaning 'Port of Sampans' (a type of Chinese boat). The administrative centre of an eponymous district since the British colonial era, the historic port town slipped into backwater status after independence, a process hastened by the destructive 2004 tsunami, then reversed under the locally born President Rajapaksa, who earmarked Hambantota for development as the country's largest urban hub after Colombo. Developments completed under Rajapaksa include a 35,000-seat sports stadium that first saw action in the 2011 Cricket World Cup, the country's second-largest port 2km west of central Hambantota, a cluster of somewhat contrived tourist attractions a short distance inland, and possibly the world's least busy international airport. Funded largely by loans from China, these developments have by and large proved to be costly debt traps, and the announcement of plans to sign a 99-year lease of the port and associated industrial zone to a company with 80% Chinese ownership led to widespread protests in early 2017. Such controversies notwithstanding, Hambantota is a refreshingly down-to-earth port town, whose bustling commercial centre, overlooked by an unexpectedly well-preserved old colonial administrative quarter, could scarcely be further removed from any tourist treadmill.

GETTING THERE AND AWAY
By air The new but little-used Mattala Rajapaksa International Airport stands less than 30 minutes' drive north of Hambantota. Cinnamon Air and Helitours both fly here from Colombo.

By road Hambantota is about 230km from Colombo via Galle and Matara. Buses between Colombo and Kataragama can drop you here. There are also plenty of buses connecting Hambantota to nearby towns such as Tissamaharama, Wellawaya, Embilipitiya, Tangalle and Matara.

WHERE TO STAY, EAT AND DRINK *Map, page 518, unless otherwise stated*
Few tourists stay overnight in Hambantota and the options are limited, but it is a useful enough base for exploring the likes of Bandula National Park and the Kalametiya Bird Sanctuary. The old government resthouse stands out for its characterful accommodation, fine location and good food.

Shangri-La's Hambantota Golf Resort & Spa [map, page 488] (300 rooms) \ +94 47 788 8888; e slht@shangri-la.com; w shangri-la. com/hambantota/shangrila. Sandwiched between a lagoon & a lovely beach, this recently opened luxury resort & golf course stands in an old coconut

17

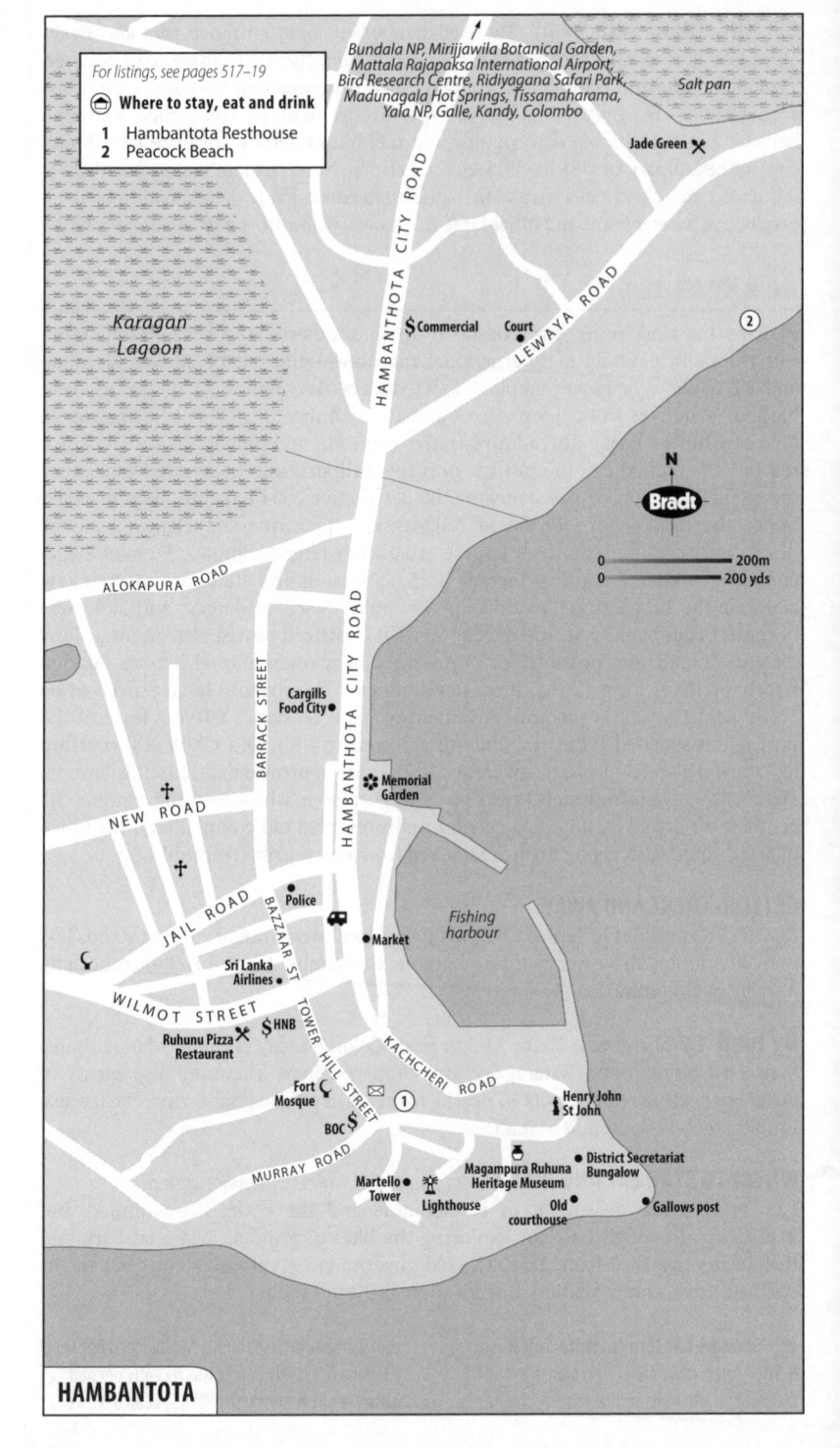

For listings, see pages 517–19

Where to stay, eat and drink
1 Hambantota Resthouse
2 Peacock Beach

Bundala NP, Mirijjawila Botanical Garden,
Mattala Rajapaksa International Airport,
Bird Research Centre, Ridiyagana Safari Park,
Madunagala Hot Springs, Tissamaharama,
Yala NP, Galle, Kandy, Colombo

Salt pan

Jade Green

Karagan
Lagoon

Commercial

Court

LEWAYA ROAD

HAMBANTHOTA CITY ROAD

N

Bradt

0   200m
0   200 yds

ALOKAPURA ROAD

BARRACK STREET

Cargills
Food City

HAMBANTHOTA CITY ROAD

Memorial
Garden

NEW ROAD

Fishing
harbour

JAIL ROAD

BAZZAAR ST

Police

Market

Sri Lanka
Airlines

WILMOT STREET

KACHCHERI ROAD

Ruhunu Pizza
Restaurant

HNB

TOWER HILL STREET

Fort
Mosque

1

Henry John
St John

BOC

MURRAY ROAD

Martello
Tower

Lighthouse

Magampura Ruhuna
Heritage Museum

Old
courthouse

District Secretariat
Bungalow

Gallows post

HAMBANTOTA

plantation on Godavaya Bay, about 5km west of Hambantota as the crow flies, & 10km distant by road. *From US$293 dbl.* **$$$$$**

🏠 **Peacock Beach Hotel** (94 rooms) Lewaya Rd; 📞047 567 1000; **e** sales@peacockbeachonline.com; **w** peacockbeachonline.com. This pleasant but slightly rundown resort hotel is set in large gardens abutting a rocky stretch of beach about 1km northeast of the town centre & harbour. Large & unexpectedly modish rooms have parquet floors, AC, fan & private balcony. Amenities include a decent restaurant, beachside swimming pool & excursions desk. *US$113/123 sgl/dbl B&B, but check for online discounts.* **$$$$**

🏠 **Hambantota Resthouse** (15 rooms) Kachcheri Rd; 📞047 222 0299; **m** 0777 182013; **e** donald.sisira@gmail.com; **f** Hambnthota. Located in the sloping colonial administrative quarter, this renovated former government resthouse offers fine views over the harbour & retains the original wing with its vintage Art Deco design. Massive rooms with tall ceilings & white tiled floors have AC, fan, net, TV & a nice big bathroom. The restaurant with licensed bar & terrace seating is the place to eat in Hambantota, with prices (**$$**) aimed at the local market (as is the fieriness of the rice-&-curry). Advance booking recommended. *US$44 dbl.* **$$**

WHAT TO SEE AND DO Hambantota is sandwiched between Bandula National Park and Kalametiya Bird Sanctuary, and could be used as a base for day visits to either, though generally they are easier and cheaper to reach from Tissamaharama and Tangalle respectively.

Around town The old administrative quarter, set on a sloping promontory immediately south of the harbour, contains a few restored relics of the British colonial era. The **Martello Tower**, built on the site of an older earthen Dutch fort in 1803, is a circular two-storey fortification that stands about 13m tall and offers rooftop views over the old and new harbour to the hills around Kataragama and Yala. Next to it, the 14m-high **Hambantota Lighthouse**, built in 1903 and operational into the 1970s, is a rather squattened round masonry tower painted in alternating spirals of black and white. The **District Secretariat Bungalow** lived in by Leonard Woolf during his stint as District Administrator of Hambantota is still standing, as is the **old courthouse** and a **memorial to Henry John St John**, a civil servant who died of fever in 1821, aged only 23. The rocky headland 100m south of the District Secretariat Bungalow is the site of an isolated **gallows post** that was erected to hang the leaders of the Uva Rebellion of 1817–18 and remained in use at least until the time of Leonard Woolf, who oversaw half a dozen hangings during his tenure.

Magampura Ruhuna Heritage Museum [map, opposite] (*Kachcheri Rd;* 📞*011 316 7739;* **w** *museum.gov.lk;* ⏰ *09.00–17.00 exc Sun & Mon; entrance US$3.30; no photography*) Opened in 2015, this small but well-presented museum occupies the former British Secretariat Building, a wide-balconied Dutch-era villa situated opposite the old courthouse. Displays cover the history of the Ruhuna Kingdom and key archaeological and historic sites such as Buduruvagala and Maligavila. It houses several Buddha and other statues dating back as far as the 8th century AD, and some excellent reproductions of murals and paintings from the Anuradhapura to the Kandyan era.

Inland of Hambantota [map, page 488] In an attempt to boost tourism to Hambantota following the opening of the nearby Mattala Rajapaksa International Airport, a number of rather contrived (and, for international visitors, dramatically overpriced) outdoor attractions have been developed in the immediate hinterland and are marketed to unsuspecting tourists. So, if only so you know what you might be letting yourself in for … Least like a theme park is the 1.2km² **Mirijjawila Botanical Garden** (*10km west of Hambantota near Mirijjawila Interchange;* 📞*047*

742 9975; ⏲ 07.30–17.00; entrance US$10; golf cart hire US$7/hr), which opened in 2013 to highlight the flora of the dry zone and remains something of a work in progress, though it does support sufficient free-ranging wildlife (monkeys, crocodiles, monitor lizards and birds) to justify a visit. The misleadingly named **Bird Research Centre** (*Nagarawewa, 14km north of Hambantota;* ☎ *047 493 7111;* 📱 *0771 111123;* ⏲ *06.00–18.00;* w *birdsibr.com; admission US$13*) is essentially an avian zoo dedicated to non-indigenous species such as toucans, cockatoos and ostriches. Opened in 2016, the 2km² **Ridiyagana Safari Park** (*north of Ridiyagana Reservoir, 35km northwest of Hambantota;* ☎ *047 362 0410;* w *nationalzoo.gov.lk/zoo/safari-park;* ⏲ *08.30–17.00; entrance US$17*) is another work in progress and offers visitors a 1-hour bus ride past open enclosures/cages, most of which hold exotic beasties such as lion, tiger and African buffalo. Only 1.5km further north, the unexciting **Madunagala Hot Springs** (⏲ *08.00–18.00; entrance US$1.30*) flow into a squarish pool where you can wash but not bathe; you could also take a peek at the adjoining **Ruhuna Folk Art Museum** (⏲ *08.00–11.30 & 14.00–18.00; entrance inc*) assuming you can find somebody to open it.

The Southern Resort Coast: Tangalle, Matara and Weligama Bay

Although it shares many physical attributes with the beaches of the west coast, the more remote Southern Resort Coast – or so-called Deep South – east of Galle has traditionally seen far less tourist development than the likes of Negombo, Bentota, Hikkaduwa and other resorts closer to Colombo. This has changed in recent years, partly due to the end of the civil war, partly due to an improved transport infrastructure (in particular the advent of the Katunayake and Southern expressways). Even so, tourist development on the south coast is dominated not by large bland glitzy resorts but by a mosaic of individualistic boutique hotels, guesthouses, backpacker hostels and homestays.

The region has three main tourist foci. Most remote, situated some 75km east of Galle, is Tangalle, which is flanked by half a dozen decent beaches of which Goyambokka and Marakolliya stand out. Around 30km further west, Matara is a historic seaport and major transport hub whose main tourist magnet is the swim-, snorkel- and surfer-friendly beach at Polhena and Madiha on its western outskirts. Most westerly is Weligama Bay, which lies only 30km from Galle and is renowned for its surfing and whale-watching opportunities. Several other minor resorts line the coast, the most notable being the gorgeous and largely undeveloped Talalla and Hiriketiya beaches between Tangalle and Matara.

Beaches dominate but there are other sightseeing possibilities too. Matara is well endowed with colonial-era historical sites, including the Dutch-built Star Fort (now a museum), while important religious shrines include the venerable cave temple complex at Mulkirigala, the island's largest seated Buddha statue at Weherahena, the lovely Kandyan-era blue temple at Devinuwara, and the mysterious statue of Kusta Raja Galla in the heart of Weligama. Elsewhere, Dondra Head Lighthouse stands facing Antarctica at the island's most southerly tip, the dramatic Hummanaya Blowhole erupts from the rocky coastline at Kudawella, and the Kalametiya Bird Sanctuary offers some of the most rewarding wetland birding in the country. It is probably worth noting that, despite its length, this chapter covers a relatively small area (around 50km of coastline in total) and that most attractions listed under any given town could be explored as a day trip from any other one.

TANGALLE

Once a rather quaint seaside village, now a scruffy but energetic town of 75,000 residents, Tangalle is the urban centrepiece of a gorgeous 10km stretch of coastline that lies around 45km west of Hambantota and 30km east of Matara. Set on the

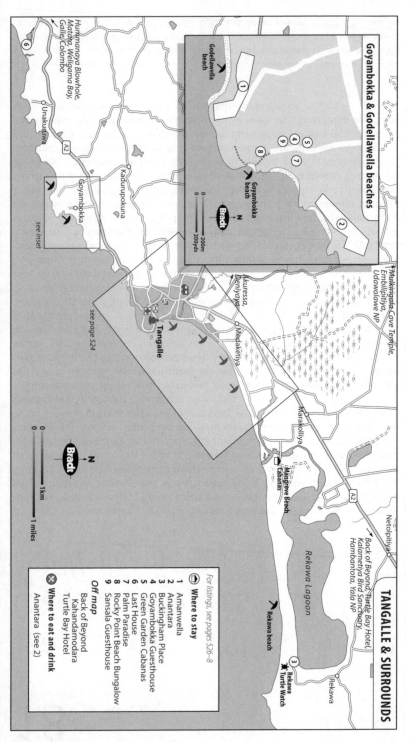

TANGALLE & SURROUNDS

Goyambokka & Godellawella beaches

Godellawella beach

Goyambokka beach

N Bradt

0   200m
0   200yds

Thulkirigala Cave Temple,
Embilipitiya,
Udawalawe NP

Akuressa,
Deniyaya

Medaketiya

Hummanaya Blowhole,
Matara, Weligama Bay,
Galle/Colombo

Unakuruwa

Goyambokka

Kadurupokuna

see inset

Tangalle

see page 524

N Bradt

0   1km
0   1 miles

Marakolliya

Mangrove Beach
Cabanas

Rekawa beach

Netolpitiya

Rekawa Lagoon

Rekawa

Back of Beyond, Turtle Bay Hotel,
Kalametiya Bird Sanctuary,
Hambantota, Yala NP

Rekawa
Turtle Watch

For listings, see pages 526–8

Where to stay

1 Amanwella
2 Anantara
3 Buckingham Place
4 Goyambokka Guesthouse
5 Green Garden Cabanas
6 Last House
7 Palm Paradise
8 Rocky Point Beach Bungalow
9 Sansala Guesthouse

Off map
Back of Beyond
Kahandamodara
Turtle Bay Hotel

Where to eat and drink
Anantara (see 2)

mouth of the River Kirama, the town runs inland from a pretty fishing harbour that has never matched Matara or Galle as a commercial port, but whose trade pedigree nonetheless stretches back several centuries, as evidenced by a scattering of time-warped Dutch-era buildings. Today, Tangalle is mainly of interest for the many fine beaches that flank it, from the westerly Godellawella to the easterly Marakolliya. Attractions further afield include turtle watches at Rekewa beach, the ancient cave temple of Mulkirigala, and the little-visited Kalametiya Bird Sanctuary. Tangalle is also a potential base for day safaris to Udawalawe and Yala national parks.

GETTING THERE AND AWAY Tangalle lies 190km from Colombo, a drive that takes 3–4 hours along the Southern Expressway, but significantly longer along the old coastal road. It is about 70km (90 minutes) from Tissamaharama (for Yala National Park) via Hambantota (45km), 45km (1 hour) from Embilipitiya (for Udawalawe National Park), 195km (5–6 hours) from Nuwara Eliya via Ella (145km), 80km (2 hours) from Galle via Mirissa (50km) and Weligama (35km), and 60km (90 minutes) from Deniyaya (for Sinharaja). These routes are all covered by regular buses (at least one an hour, generally more), though coming to/from Deniyaya you may need to divert through Embilipitiya and change buses there. Rail aficionados coming from Colombo could catch a train to Matara and travel on to Tangalle by bus or tuktuk. Domestic flights connect Colombo to Mattala Rajapaksa International Airport, which stands to the north of Hambantota, about an hour's drive from Tangalle.

WHERE TO STAY
Tangalle and Medaketiya beach The town centre boasts the only noteworthy place to stay in the form of the timeworn Dutch-era government resthouse, but Medaketiya beach, immediately to its northeast, is the site of Tangalle's busiest cluster of accommodation. With a few exceptions, most of the lodgings at Medaketiya feel a bit grotty and overpriced compared with what's on offer further east and west, and this is also one of the few places in the country plagued by overt touting. In its favour, Medaketiya has a very attractive beach, a quite lively feel at night, and it stands within easy walking distance of the bus station and town centre.

Budget
✳ 🏠 **Starfish Café** [524 E2] (4 rooms) ☏047 224 1005; m 0776 178785; e starfishtangalle@gmail.com. This owner-managed gem has a fantastic beachfront location only 15mins' walk from the town centre but just far enough along the beach to escape the crowds. Simple but spacious rooms have fan, net & balcony looking across the pretty hammock-slung garden to the beach. A terrace restaurant specialises in sweet & savoury filled rotis, curries & seafood (**$$**) & there's also a beach bar. *US$27 dbl, dropping by 50% out of season.* **$$**

🏠 **Frangipani Beach Villa** [524 C2] (15 rooms) m 0773 148889; e frangipanibeachvilla@gmail.com; w frangipanitangalle.com. The best of the budget hotels huddled along the main beach strip southwest of Starfish, friendly Frangipani is an owner-managed set-up decorated with colourful contemporary graffiti-style art. The breezy licensed beach restaurant caters to most tastes & budgets with a varied menu of curries (**$$**) & seafood, pizza & pasta (**$$$**). Deluxe rooms come with AC, fan, TV & balcony access, while smaller budget rooms have fan & net only. *US$30/40 budget dbl with fan/AC, US$90 deluxe dbl; significant seasonal discounts; all rates B&B.* **$$–$$$**

🏠 **Gayana Guesthouse** [524 D2] (21 rooms) ☏047 224 0477; m 0777 358606; gayana.gh@gmail.com. This quaintly old-fashioned 3-storey beachfront hotel is one of Tangalle's largest & longest-serving. Spacious clean rooms mostly come with AC, fan, net, TV & private balcony with sea view, but a few smaller budget rooms are available. *From US$23/30 budget dbl with fan/AC to US$73 3rd-floor dbl with balcony & sea view.* **$–$$$**

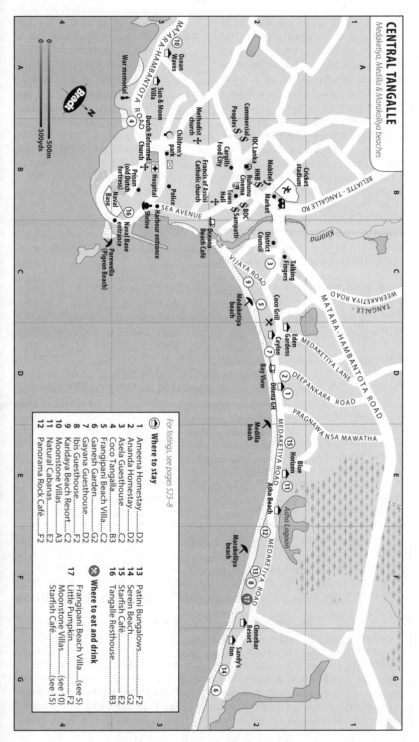

CENTRAL TANGALLE
Medaketiya, Medilla & Marakolliya beaches

0 500m
0 500yds

MATARA-HAMBANTOTA ROAD

Ocean Waves ⑩

War memorial

Sun & Moon Villa

Methodist church

Dutch Reformed Church

Children's park

Commercial $
Peoples $

Cargills Food City

Francis of Assisi Catholic church

IOC Lanka $

Mobitel $
Market

HNB $

Ruhunu Cinema
Town Hall

Sampath $ BOC

Prison (old Dutch fortress)

Hospital

Police

Naval Base

Harbour entrance

Shrine

Naval Base entrance

SEA AVENUE

Oceana Beach Café

Parewella (Pigeon Beach)

Cricket stadium

District Council

Kirama

BELIATTE - TANGALLE RD

Talking Fingers ③

VIJAYA ROAD ⑨

Medaketiya beach

Coco Grill ⑤

Ceylon ⑦

Eden Gardens

MEDAKETIYA LANE

TANGALLE - WEERAKETIYA ROAD

MATARA-HAMBANTOTA ROAD

Bay View

Ditena GH ①

②

DEEPANKARA ROAD

PRAGNAWANSA MAWATHA

Medilla beach

Blue Horizon ⑮

MEDAKETIYA ROAD

Asha Beach ⑪

Asha Lagoon

Marakolliya beach

⑫

Cinnebar Resort ⑰

⑧ ⑬

Sandy's Inn

⑥ ⑭

For listings, see pages 523–8

Where to stay

1 Ameena Homestay	D2
2 Ananda Homestay	D2
3 Asela Guesthouse	C2
4 Coco Tangalla	B3
5 Frangipani Beach Villa	C2
6 Ganesh Garden	G2
7 Gayana Guesthouse	D2
8 Ibis Guesthouse	F2
9 Karidaya Beach Resort	C2
10 Moonstone Villas	A3
11 Natural Cabanas	E2
12 Panorama Rock Café	F2

13 Patini Bungalows	F2
14 Serein Beach	G2
15 Starfish Café	E2
16 Tangalle Resthouse	B3

Where to eat and drink

Frangipani Beach Villa	(see 5)
17 Little Pumpkin	F2
Moonstone Villas	(see 10)
Starfish Café	(see 15)

Shoestring

🏠 **Tangalle Resthouse** [524 B3] (22 rooms)
📞 047 224 0299. The most characterful and central accommodation in Tangalle is this converted Dutch administrator's residence set in leafy gardens on a slope overlooking the fishing harbour & Pigeon beach 800m from the bus station. Complete with original gable stone giving the year of construction as 1774, the building incorporates a wide terrace & creaky arched & colonnaded bar/restaurant known for its good curries. A bit rundown & often fully booked, rooms are furnished in period style, come with fan or AC, & seem like more than adequate value at the asking rate. *US$15/24 dbl with fan/ AC.* **$**

🏠 **Ameena Homestay** [524 D2] (2 rooms)
m 0775 842748. Only 50m from the beach, this wallet-friendly homestay comprises 2 clean en-suite rooms with net & fan sharing a 1st-floor apt above the friendly owner-manager's house. *US$17 dbl.* **$**

🏠 **Ananda Homestay** [524 D2]
(4 rooms) 📞 047 224 0987; m 0719 776492; e anandahomestaytangalle@gmail.com. This friendly family-run place opposite Ameena's is famed for its home-cooked Sri Lankan food & cooking lessons. The clean rooms have nets & both standing & roof fans. *US$30 dbl, dropping to US$20 in low season.* **$$**

🏠 **Asela Guesthouse** [524 C2] (8 rooms)
📞 047 224 0356; m 0714 408336;
e n.desilva6379@yahoo.com. This agreeable owner-managed cheapie is set in a garden with shaded seating 200m from the beach along the main road to the town centre. The clean rooms have fans & optional AC. *US$12/17 dbl with fan/AC.* **$**

🏠 **Karidaya Beach Resort** [524 C2]
(5 rooms) 📞 047 224 0566; m 0714 383849;
w thekaradiyabeachresort.bookings.lk. The closest beachfront hotel to the bus station (about 600m) is set in a pretty garden with hammocks swinging from the palms & waves lapping the sand. Rooms are a bit shabby but come with AC & net, & seem fair value give the hard-to-fault location. *US$20 dbl B&B.* **$**

Medilla and Marakolliya beaches

Stretching along the coast for about 1.5km between Medaketiya and Rekawa, this pair of contiguous beaches lies on a narrow spit of terra firma bounded to the north by a labyrinthine wetland whose mangrove-lined creeks and lagoons support a wealth of birds and other small wildlife. The beaches at Medilla and Marakolliya are interspersed with tranquil, low-key and relatively tasteful lodges which aren't necessarily cheaper than their counterparts closer to town, but do tend to represent far better value. The area as a whole has a more mellow, rustic and hassle-free vibe than suburban Medaketiya, though it lacks the latter's bustle and party scene. The lodges listed below stand 2–3km from the bus station, so you will most likely want to catch a tuktuk out, though it might also be worth considering asking your hotel to arrange scooter or bicycle hire for the duration of your stay.

Moderate

✳ 🏠 **Serein Beach** [524 G2] (10 rooms)
📞 047 224 0005; m 0775 360708; e info@ sereinbeach.com; w sereinbeach.com. This contemporary not-quite-boutique hotel spans 3 storeys & stands in green beachfront gardens & is built with special sand bricks that allegedly keep the interiors cool. The attractive rooms have fan but no AC, nets, bright fabrics & wall art, & sea-view balcony. A good restaurant is attached. *From US$45/65 sgl/dbl B&B.* **$$$**

Budget

✳ 🏠 **Patini Bungalows** [524 F2] (5 rooms)
m 0775 402679, 0777 402038; e info@ patinibungalows.com; w patinibungalows.com. This truly paradisiacal & welcoming Swiss-Sri Lankan venture is set in a large tree-shaded seaside property & offers accommodation in spacious & attractive chalets with terracotta tiled floor, 4-poster bed with fitted net, fan but no AC, & large private balconies. No food is served but plenty of other eateries stand within easy walking distance. *From US$37 dbl, with discounts of around 20% out of season.* **$$**

🏠 **Ganesh Garden** [524 G2] (18 rooms)
📞 047 224 2529; m 0777 612181;
e ganeshgarden@yahoo.com; w ganeshgarden. com. Occupying a 150m-wide sliver of land that separates the ocean from a narrow mangrove-

lined lagoon, this is the most remote and isolated lodge at Marakolliya, with lovely landscaped palm-dominated gardens running down to a breathtaking beach. The superior accommodation consists of handsome stilted wooden bungalows with fan, 4-poster bed with fitted net & private balcony, but cheaper mud cabanas with fan & net are also available on the lagoon side of the property. The location & rooms are great, but overall it would benefit from a more visible & engaged management. *US$35–75 dbl, depending on cabana type & location.* **$$–$$$**

⌂ **Ibis Guesthouse** [524 F2] (12 rooms) ☎ 047 567 4439; **e** ibisguesthouse@yahoo.com; **w** guesthouse-ibis.de. Set in a dense seaside stand of palms slung with hammocks & interspersed with beach beds, this idyllically located German-Sri Lankan guesthouse offers accommodation in spacious rooms or cabins, all with fan & 4-poster bed with fitted nets, most with sea view, & some with AC. Nice enough, but the high-season rates seem a touch overpriced. *US$40 dbl room with fan,*

US$47/67 dbl cabin with fan/AC, dropping by 25% out of season. **$$–$$$**

⌂ **Panorama Rock Café** [524 F2] (9 rooms) **m** 0777 620092. This mellow lodge is set in small lush tropical gardens that incorporate a seaside restaurant overlooking a semi-private beach. Smart tiled rooms come with fan & net but no AC. The staff wouldn't win any awards for efficiency, but if that doesn't worry you, it's well above average in terms of value for money. *US$30 dbl B&B, dropping to US$20 out of season.* **$$**

⌂ **Natural Cabanas** [524 E2] (5 rooms) ☎ 047 790 1664; **m** 0779 936454; **e** naturalcabanas@ gmail.com; **w** naturalcabanas.com. Boasting a peaceful hammock-slung tropical garden 100m from Medilla beach & a similar distance from a small lagoon, this rustic family-run lodge offers accommodation in basic huts with fans, net & private terrace. Home-cooked curries & seafood are available. *US$20 dbl.* **$**

Western beaches

An excellent selection of beach accommodation can be found along the coast running 5km west of Tangalle, ranging from exclusive boutique lodges to unpretentious family-run guesthouse-cum-homestays. Of particular interest to cost-conscious travellers is a cluster of well-priced budget and moderate lodges at Goyambokka, whose calm and scenic beach, flanked by rocky extrusions, lies about 3km out of town. Most of the accommodation listed below flanks the main road between Tangalle and Matara, so any bus heading between the two can drop you at the entrance, but the Goyambokka lodges lie up to 500m along a signposted side road to the south, so you must either walk the last bit or else catch a tuktuk from Tangalle.

⌂ **Coco Tangalla** [524 B3] (6 rooms) Pallikkudawa beach; ☎ 081 720 1115; **e** info@ cocotangalla.com; **w** cocotangalla.com; see ad, 2nd colour section. This stylish boutique hotel 200m west of the town centre comprises a seaside villa with a wide balcony & infinity pool set in large wooded gardens sloping down to the beach. The sumptuous tall-ceilinged rooms are individually decorated with brightly coloured silks & other fabrics, & come with AC, fan, 4-poster bed with fitted net & private sea-facing balcony. Exceptional value in its range. *From US$220 dbl B&B, dropping by around 25% out of season.* **$$$$$**

⌂ **Anantara** [map, page 522] (152 rooms) Goyambokka beach; ☎ 047 767 0700; **e** tangalle@ anantara.com; **w** tangalle.anantara.com.

Welcoming visitors with a boisterous tattoo performed by a trio of traditionally attired female raban drummers, the largest resort in the vicinity of Tangalle, opened in 2016, stands in vast sloping landscaped gardens that dominate the eastern half of Goyambokka beach & offer superb views over the bay. Despite its size, the resort has a decidedly exclusive air, with an airy modern feel throughout & large stylish & well-equipped rooms that come with AC, TV, modern bathroom with tub & shower, wide balcony with daybed & garden or sea view. Excellent amenities include an Olympic-length pool, free shuttles to other beaches, spa, gym, library, business centre, surf shop, excursions desk, 3 restaurants & mega wine cellar, & squash, tennis & badminton courts. *Rack rates start at US$350 dbl B&B, but check the website for variable daily prices.* **$$$$$+**

The Last House [map, page 522] (6 rooms) Nakulugamuwa beach; 5km west of Tangalle; 081 720 1115; e info@thelasthouse. com; w thelasthouse.com; see ad, 2nd colour section. Although it's the most westerly property listed under Tangalle, the Last House is so named because it was the final work designed by Geoffrey Bawa before his death in 2003. A chic beach house converted to a boutique hotel, it has a thrillingly isolated location sandwiched between the ocean & a small palm-fringed lagoon 500m south of the Matara Rd. Individually styled & colourfully decorated rooms have AC, net, sea view & wide balcony. The lush gardens incorporate a large swimming pool & attract plenty of monkeys & birds. *From US$330 dbl B&B, with around 20% off-season discount.* **$$$$$+**

Amanwella [map, page 522] (30 rooms) Godellawella beach, 3km west of Tangalle; 047 224 1333; e amanwella@amanresorts.com; w amanresorts.com. Offering near-exclusive access to a sweeping horseshoe of palm-lined golden sand, this astonishing modern resort shows the influence of Geoffrey Bawa in its common areas, whose clean lines, tall ceilings & soft grey & brown hues are simple to the point of austerity, & offer a breathtaking view over the rectangular 45m² infinity pool poised above the beach. The spacious AC villas all have a private courtyard with rectangular plunge pool & a contemporary feel epitomised by the lattice-screened glass sides, dark-grained palm wood furniture, wooden-board ceilings under ancient clay tiles & large bathroom with tub & shower. Truly stunning & priced accordingly. *From US$950 dbl FB, with low-season discounts.* **$$$$$+**

Moderate

✳ ⌂ Goyambokka Guesthouse [map, page 522] (10 rooms) Goyambokka beach; 047 224 0838; m 0777 903091; e goyambokkaguesthouse@yahoo.com; w goyambokkaguesthouse.com. Set in well-tended gardens with a swimming pool & open-sided thatched restaurant 200m from Goyambokka beach, this neat 2-storey guesthouse offers two types of room: larger villas with modern décor, AC, fan, net, large bathroom & private balcony, or slightly smaller standard rooms without AC. Both represent exceptional value for money. *US$33/53 B&B dbl standard/villa, with significant seasonal discounts.* **$$–$$$**

Palm Paradise [map, page 522] (22 rooms) Goyambokka beach; 047 224 0338; e reservepalmparadise@gmail.com; w beach.lk. This aptly named complex of stilted & balconied wooden dbl villas & family cabanas is set in large tree-shaded gardens populated by monkeys & offering ample beach frontage. All rooms have good natural ventilation & are equipped with fans & nets, but there's no AC. *US$55/77 sgl/dbl villa, from US$138 cabana; all rates HB.* **$$$**

Moonstone Villas [524 A3] (10 rooms) Matara Rd, 500m west of Tangalle; m 0776 758656; e info@moonstonevillas.com; w moonstonevillas.com. Set on the landward side of the busy Matara Rd, this popular Canadian-owned & -managed lodge stands in small but well-cared-for gardens with a swimming pool & beach view. Bright, spacious & stylish rooms in 2-storey blocks come with twin ¾ beds under fitted nets, AC, fan & original artworks on the wall. The licensed restaurant (⏲ 07.00–22.00) ranks among the best in Tangalle & serves a cosmopolitan selection of wraps, burgers, pizzas, salads & daily meat, fish & vegetarian specials in the **$$$** range. *US$103 dbl B&B.* **$$$$**

Budget

Rocky Point Beach Bungalow [map, page 522] (10 rooms) Goyambokka beach; 047 224 0834; m 0779 067670; e samanthalanka@ gmail.com. The outstanding feature of this unpretentious guesthouse is the gobsmacking location in wooded gardens that slope sharply down to a small semi-private beach in a rocky cove at the west end of Goyambokka beach. It also has friendly live-in owner-managers, slightly rundown but clean & spacious rooms/bungalows with net, fan & private sea-facing balcony, a restaurant serving curries & seafood in the **$$$** range, & kayak & snorkel hire for US$3.50/item/day. *US$30/34 B&B dbl room/bungalow, with 10% off-season discounts.* **$$**

Green Garden Cabanas [map, page 522] (20 rooms) Goyambokka beach; m 0776 247628; e lankatangalla@yahoo.com; w greengardencabanas.com. This friendly & unpretentious owner-managed lodge has sprawling gardens with plenty of birdlife & a swimming pool only 20m from the beach, & choice of standard rooms with net & fan or AC in the main 2-storey building, or larger naturally ventilated

18

stone or wood cabanas with fan only, all with a private balcony. *US$30/50 dbl room with fan/AC, US$60 dbl cabana.* **$$–$$$**

🏠 **Sansala Guesthouse** [map, page 522] (3 rooms) Goyambokka beach; 📞 047 224 4212; **m** 0776 011693; **e** surangalanka@gmail.com. Lacking the singular location of next-door Rocky

Point but beating it on the maintenance front, this is another guesthouse with welcoming live-in owner-managers & easy access to Goyambokka beach. Rooms all come with fan, net & wide balcony overlooking a fruiting garden. *US$34 dbl B&B, dropping by 30% out of season.* **$$**

Rekawa and Kahandamodara beaches

All of the moderate to upmarket properties listed below boast an isolated location close to Rekawa or Kahandamodara beaches between 8km and 20km east of Tangalle *en route* to/from Hambantota.

Upmarket

🏠 **Turtle Bay Hotel** [map, page 488] (7 rooms) 📞 047 788 7853; **e** info@turtlebay. lk; **w** turtlebay.lk. Run by a young & flexible Sri Lankan team, this lovely boutique hotel stands on a bluff at the otherwise deserted eastern end of Kahandamodara beach, close to Kalametiya Bird Sanctuary & 4km south of the Tangalle–Hambantota highway (turn off near the 214km post). There's a Bawa-like austerity to the thicket of white square columns in the ground-floor restaurant, but this is relieved by colourful mosaic tiles & thoughtful décor. Large suites have AC, oversized luxurious bed (no nets), big bathroom, wooden floors & tea/coffee maker. Turtles often lay eggs on the beach by moonlight. Amenities include a large swimming pool & Ayurveda spa. Good value. *US$135/155 B&B sgl/dbl, with off-season discounts.* **$$$$**

🏠 **Buckingham Place** [map, page 522] (16 rooms) 📞 047 348 9447; **e** info@ buckinghamplace.lk; **w** buckinghamplace.lk. Named after its British owner-manager, Nick Buckingham, this informal & joyously addictive lodge has brightly decorated AC suites & bedrooms tucked away in woodlands sandwiched between

the rugged Rekawa beach & large eponymous lagoon. Bicycles & canoes for village & lagoon exploration are available. There's a large beachfront swimming pool, & refined fusion cuisine & wine are served in a central pavilion that lends itself to socialising with other guests. *From US$239 dbl B&B with long-stay & off-season discounts.* **$$$$$**

Moderate

🏠 **Back of Beyond Kahandamodara** [map, page 488] (9 rooms) **m** 0773 951527; **e** info@ backofbeyond.lk; **w** backofbeyond.lk. Set in a 5ha tract of woodland some 15mins' walk from Kahandamodara beach, this aptly named bush lodge has a remote & isolated location verging a wide lagoon about 15km east of Tangalle. Ideal for keen walkers & genuine wildlife enthusiasts, the property supports an abundant birdlife (the lovely Indian pitta is seasonally conspicuous) & you might well also encounter lizards, bats, frogs & the like. Boat trips & kayaking are available on the lagoon. Accommodation is in attractive modern 2- to 4-bedroom cottages with fans & common lounges. The choice of food is limited but the standard is good, but best to bring any drinks other than water with you. *US$70 dbl B&B.* **$$$**

✖ WHERE TO EAT AND DRINK

Most hotels listed above serve food and many have genuinely excellent restaurants. At the upper end of the price range, the trio of fine restaurants at Anantara stand out, while good medium-priced choices include Moonstone Villas and Frangipani Beach Villa, and the pick of the budget options is the Starfish Café. For those staying at Medilla or Marakolliya, the pick of the eateries in this area is the beachfront Little Pumpkin [524 F2] (**m** *0727 876539;* ⊕ *08.00–21.00*), which serves great seafood ($$$), as well as tasty local curries and pasta dishes ($$).

OTHER PRACTICALITIES Tangalle has a well-equipped town centre with several banks, including a Commercial Bank with ATM [524 B2], and a well-stocked Cargills Food City [524 B2] with wine store attached. Talking Fingers [524 C2], on the short road connecting the town centre to Medaketiya beach, is an Ayurveda spa and massage centre whose therapists are all visually impaired.

WHAT TO SEE AND DO Tourist activity tends to focus on the town centre and even more so the flanking beaches. Two minor but worthwhile attractions further afield are Mulkirigala Temple and Kalametiya Bird Sanctuary. For those who haven't scheduled a safari into their itinerary, Tangalle is also a viable base for day excursions to Udawalawe and Yala national parks, which respectively lie 70km to the north and 90km to the east. These typically cost around US$100–150 all-inclusive for two people, and can be arranged through most hotels.

Central Tangalle It's worth getting up early (around 06.00) to witness dozens of boats unloading the previous night's catch at the quayside in Tangalle's pretty fishing harbour [524 B3]. Fish are auctioned, gutted and cut up on the dock to be carried by pedal cycle and motorbike to eager customers in inland villages. Sandwiched between the harbour and an off-limits naval base is Parewella (Pigeon beach) [524 C4] and its natural saltwater pool. A trio of several centuries-old colonial structures scatter the town centre. The oldest and least adulterated is probably the Dutch Reformed Church [524 B3], a handsome gabled building constructed in 1755 on the site of an older Portuguese convent. There is also a modest Dutch fortress [524 B3], though this has served as a prison since the British colonial era, and the interior is still off limits to casual visitors. Altogether more accessible is the Tangalle Resthouse [524 B3], which started life in 1774 as a Dutch administrator's residence, and remains a fine place to enjoy an affordable drink or curry in view of the harbour.

Beaches The most central and reliable swimming beach in the vicinity of Tangalle, though far from being the most scenic, is Parewella [524 C4], which has a natural swimming pool that offers safe swimming pretty much all year through. Almost as central, Medaketiya [524 C2], immediately northeast of the town centre, is a lovely stretch of golden sand and far less developed than its counterparts at Mirissa and Unawatuna, but swimming conditions are variable, and it is also one of the few places in Sri Lanka with any sort of hassle factor. Far more chilled out and beautiful, though less conducive to swimming owing to rocky areas and unpredictable currents, the contiguous Medilla [524 E2] and Marakolliya [524 F2] beaches can be reached on foot by strolling east towards the Rekawa Lagoon for 15–30 minutes. More beautiful still are the sumptuously sleepy beaches at Goyambokka and Godellawella [map, page 522], which lie around 3km west of Tangalle and are most easily reached by tuktuk.

Rekawa Turtle Watch [map, page 522] (m *0766 857380;* e *turtlewatch.rekawa@ gmail.com;* w *turtlewatchrekawa.org*) Founded under a different name in 1993, Rekawa Turtle Watch is the semi-official guardian organisation of Rekawa beach, an important nesting site for green and olive ridley turtles (and more occasionally used by loggerhead, hawksbill and leatherback) 7km east of Tangalle. A community-run project, it attempts to provide a safe and secure nesting environment for turtles by employing former poachers to patrol the beach close to any known nests 24 hours a day to deter natural and human predators. It also operates nightly turtle watches, starting at around 20.30 and continuing until the first nesting turtle is observed, or the guide decides to call it a night (usually at around 23.30).

Nesting activity is highest between April and July, when an average of ten females lay eggs on the beach every night, and there is a secondary season between October and January, when one or two turtles might come ashore nightly, most usually on and around the full moon. A donation of US$7 per person (children pay half price) is levied, and the standard return tuktuk fee from Tangalle is US$10 per vehicle, inclusive of waiting time. An average of 60 tourists visit nightly in season, and many visitors find that the numbers detract from the experience and have some potential to disturb the nesting turtle. This is arguably counterbalanced by the reality that tourist donations both fund and motivate the turtle programme, and a policy that no more than one female should be visited on any given night.

Kalametiya Bird Sanctuary [map, page 488]

Kalametiya Bird Sanctuary [map, page 488] Created in 1984, the Kalametiya Bird Sanctuary protects around 10km² of lagoons, mangrove and other wetlands running inland from the 4km stretch of beach immediately east of Kahandamodara. Around 150 bird species have been recorded in the sanctuary, around one-third of which are migrants that congregate in the area between November and March. Among the more common birds are the endemic Sri Lanka junglefowl, Indian peahen, Eurasian spoonbill, black bittern, slaty-breasted crake, pheasant-tailed jacana, watercock, and various kingfishers, cormorants and herons. Migrant specialities include glossy Ibis, western reef heron, black-capped kingfisher, garganey, pintail duck, black-tailed godwit and various other waders. Other conspicuous wildlife includes langur monkeys and various types of mongoose, but 20 mammal, 38 reptile and 41 freshwater fish species have been recorded in total.

Access to Kalametiya is from the village of Hungama, which straddles the Hambantota Road about 20km east of Tangalle. From here, the sanctuary is most easily explored by boat, a 3–4-hour cruise that will delight birdwatchers and is pretty enjoyable just for the tranquil setting and lovely scenery. Recommended guides, best called a day in advance, are Gayan (m *0777 060920*) and Ranga (m *0716 789932*; f *kalametiyabirdwatching*), both of whom are knowledgeable and enthusiastic about the birdlife, and carry field guides and binoculars. Expect to pay around US$20 per boat for up to four people. No entrance fee is levied

Mulkirigala Temple [map, page 488]

Mulkirigala Temple [map, page 488] Nicknamed 'Little Sigiriya', Mulkirigala (also known as Giriba and Mulgirigala), 17km inland of Tangalle, is a spectacular gaunt-grey granite monolith that soars from the jungly vegetation to an elevation of 205m. Mulkirigala is also the site of one of southern Sri Lanka's most intriguing Buddhist shrines, an ancient complex of seven cave temples associated by some traditions with Devanampiya Tissa, who reputedly planted one of the original 32 shoots of the Jaya Sri Maha Bodhi there in the 3rd century BC. The temple was evidently abandoned in the 13th century following the fall of Polonnaruwa, only to be rediscovered intact but overgrown in 1747, and revived shortly afterwards under Kirti Sri Rajasinha of Kandy.

The temple complex is split across five terraces connected by a total of 533 steps. Coming from the ticket office, the first of the two lower-terrace cave temples is dominated by a long yellow sleeping Buddha but also contains a trio of near-life-size early 19th-century paintings depicting the multi-armed Vishnu, the blue-fanged Vibhishana, and the guardian deity Kataragama. The neighbouring cave is flanked by a pair of fabulous oil lamps that stand almost 3m tall and incorporate four tiers of sculpted figures: elephants at the base, then midgets, then some mythical tail-swallowing (or thick-tongued?) beasties, all topped by a row of crouched human figures with long hair and generous busts. The interior contains another sleeping Buddha, a small dagoba, and some superb Kandyan-era paintings depicting scenes from the Buddha's life, including sinners being devoured by vampiric-looking demons. A Brahmi inscription on the outer wall indicates that these caves were excavated in the 1st or 2nd century BC by the mysterious King Cuda Tissa.

From behind the ticket office, stone stairs lead uphill to the second and third terraces, which respectively house an ancient Bo Tree and a relatively mundane cave temple. The fourth terrace incorporates a rectangular rock pool and four more cave shrines, including the tiny but ornate Naga Temple, named after the fearsome painting of a striking snake on its inner door. The largest and presumably oldest fourth-terrace shrine, the Parana Rajamaha (Old Royal) Temple has an unremarkable interior dominated by the usual reclining Buddha. By contrast, its Kandyan-era wooden vestibule is adorned with a few beautifully executed (albeit rather faded) 19th-century paintings, some well-preserved pillars carved with mythical beasties (a centaur-like figure and a unicorn with elephantine trunk), and an engraved stone door-frame possibly salvaged from a pre-Kandyan incarnation. The ancient wooden wardrobe that stands unceremoniously in the middle of the vestibule has an important place in Sri Lankan history: it was here, in 1826, that the Ceylon-born British scholar George Turnour discovered the ancient parchment that enabled him to decipher the secrets of the *Mahavamsa* historical chronicle.

From the fourth terrace, a zigzag stairwell – so steep you can use the steps above as handholds – leads to the hill's summit. There are no temples here, but the large upper terrace is adorned by a tall whitewashed dagoba originally constructed in the 5th century by King Dhatusena, and renovated under King Kirti Sri Rajasinha. The views, though potentially spectacular, are blocked in most directions by thick foliage, but you might well see raptors soaring overhead.

Entrance to Mulkirigala costs US$3.30 and includes access to an informative site museum (☉ 07.30–16.30 Mon–Fri) next to the entrance gate. The museum contains a fascinating clutter of artefacts unearthed at the temple, from ancient palm-leaf manuscripts and Ayurvedic prescriptions to pots, fabrics, ceramics and kitchen utensils. All artefacts are labelled from the 18th century, but this presumably refers to when they were discovered, as some clearly date back to the Polonnaruwa era. It seems to be customary to visit the museum after touring the temples, but we recommend you stop in first, as it will help to make sense of the actual site. Avoid visiting Mulkirigala on weekends, when the museum is closed.

To get to Mulkirigala from Tangalle, drive 8km northwest to Belliata, then turn right on to the Weeraketiya Road and follow it for 9km until you see the temple signposted to your left. Using public transport, you could bus to Belliata, then catch another bus to Middeniya via Weeraketiya and asked to be dropped at the entrance. Alternatively, a return tuktuk shouldn't cost significantly more than US$10 including waiting time. An interesting onward option from Mulkirigala would entail continuing 4km north to Weeraketiya, where the pretty lotus-covered Lake Udakiriwila often hosts a wide variety of water-associated birds.

TOWARDS MATARA

Only 35km in length, the coastal road connecting Tangalle to Matara packs in some of the most worthwhile sightseeing in this part of Sri Lanka. It incorporates the island's most southerly headland at Dondra Lighthouse, as well as the intermittently spectacular Hummanaya Blowhole, a pair of idyllic and relatively undeveloped beaches at Talalla and Hiriketiya, and an assortment of temples ranging from ancient Devinuwara to modern Wewurukannala and its outsized 1970s Buddha statue. All the sites described below can be visited with ease using public transport, whether you come from Tangalle or Matara, but many younger travellers, and surfers in particular, prefer to base themselves at Talalla or Hiriketiya beach.

HUMMANAYA BLOWHOLE [map, page 488] A Sinhala name that supposedly imitates the sound of exploding water when spoken slowly, Hummanaya is a curious and at times breathtaking natural phenomenon created by waves gushing through a fissure in an overhanging cliff until sufficient pressure builds up, then shooting geyser-like into the air. Rather inconsiderately from a touristic perspective, the blowhole insists on being at its most gushingly spectacular during the monsoon season (May–August), when it might explode every 2 or 3 minutes and shoot more than 25m into the air. During the dry season, it erupts less frequently, perhaps once every 10–15 minutes, and seldom attains a height of much more than 5m (though it tends to be more impressive at high tide and/or in rough weather).

To get here, first head to Kudawella, a substantial village with a large fishing harbour and ice-cooler plant 5km east of Dickwella and 10km west of Tangalle. In a private vehicle, you can drive down to the harbour and park next to the signposted footpath to the blowhole. Using public transport, you'll need to hop on a Matara–Tangalle bus and hop off at Kudawella Junction, then walk or catch a tuktuk for the last 2km. Either way, it's about 300m on foot to the ticket office (⊕ 06.00–19.00; *entrance US$1.70*), which incorporates a small museum, then another 100m to the fenced-off blowhole itself.

DICKWELLA This medium-sized town (population 55,000) midway along the main road between Matara and Tangalle (and stopped at by all buses between them) is the site of a couple of formulaic beach hotels catering to a predominately Italian clientele, as well as a bustling Saturday market that warrants a look should you happen to pass through on the right day. For travellers staying at Talalla or Hiriketiya, it offers the closest opportunity to draw money from an ATM (Sampath and HNB are both represented) and it also has a Cargills Food City supermarket. The main local attractions are the Dickwella Lace Centre, Wewurukannala Temple and lovely Hiriketiya beach.

Dickwella Lace Centre (✆ 041 225 5896; e *dickwellalace@yahoo.com;* ⊕ 09.00–17.00) Situated roughly opposite the prominent Dickwella Resort & Spa, this admirable woman's co-operative was founded in 2007 to revive the dying craft of beeralu lacemaking and to provide a livelihood for local women affected by the 2004 tsunami. Comprising a production unit, an interesting beeralu lace museum and a retail outlet for handmade products, the project now helps generate an income for more than a hundred families around Dickwella.

Wewurukannala Temple [map, page 488] (*Entrance US$1.35*) Situated alongside the road to Beliatta 1.8km inland of Dickwella, Wewurukannala is renowned for housing the island's tallest seated Buddha statue, a 50m colossus whose flamboyance might reflect its construction during the psychedelic late 1960s (it was completed in 1970). Behind this, a somewhat drabber multistorey building allows visitors to climb eight flights to look into the Buddha's head. The main image house incorporates a gruesome house-of-horrors *tableau vivant* of an afterlife wherein a workmanlike crew of long-fanged devils impales, boils, saws apart and otherwise inflicts agonising tortures on earthly sinners – a subject seldom touched upon in Sri Lankan Buddhist temple art, but depicted with graphic relish when it is. A much smaller shrine dating to the mid 18th century contains a few less memorable but more historically significant Kandyan murals. Buses between Dickwella and Beliatta run past the temple.

Hiriketiya beach [map, page 488] Set in a small horseshoe-shaped cove less than 2km east of Dickwella and most easily reached from it by tuktuk, this sensational but largely undeveloped beach is growing in popularity with surfers and backpackers for its relaxed and down-to-earth off-grid atmosphere. The main attraction is a peeling left break, which holds up to 2m high and gives a 300m ride, making it ideal for beginner and intermediate surfers all year through. With the usual provisos, swimming is also safe, thanks to the bay's sheltered nature and lack of undercurrent, and marine turtles are frequently seen swimming in the shallows. Surfboard and other gear can be rented through Beach House Hiriketiya and most other lodges in the area. For a change of scene, head out to the pretty Nilwala fishing harbour, which is protected by a long breakwater 1.5km further west.

Where to stay, eat and drink

✳ 🏠 **Salt House** (6 rooms) ✆ 041 225 6819; m 0766 176969; e info@salthousesrilanka.com; w salthousesrilanka.net. This stylish boutique guesthouse stands 100m inland of Hiriketiya beach. The shaded rooftop restaurant, offering a coconut's-eye view into the canopies of the surrounding palms, is the best place to eat in Hiriketiya, with an open kitchen serving seafood, wraps, quiches, pasta and the like (**$$$**), as well as good coffee, shakes & smoothies. Ground-floor rooms have AC & semi-outdoor bathrooms, while open-sided 1st-floor rooms have good natural ventilation supplemented by fans only. *US$85 dbl B&B.* **$$$**

🏠 **Beach House Hiriketiya** (4 rooms) m 0766 176969; w beachhousehiriketiya.com. Affiliated to Talalla Retreat but very different

in feel, this pleasant villa stands on a small beachfront plot & offers accommodation in stylish rooms decorated in beach-house style & equipped with net, fan & open-air bathroom. A relaxed beach restaurant specialises in pizzas from a wood-fired oven (**$$$**) but also serves light meals & salads (**$$**), & tends to fill up during the day with surfers from Talalla Retreat. *US$80 dbl.* **$$$**

🏠 **Dot's Bay House** (4 rooms, 18 more under construction) m 0777 935593; e nawodh@gmail.com; 🇫. Situated alongside a mangrove-lined inlet a few metres from Hiriketiya beach, this chilled surfers' haunt has comfortable rooms with nets & a funky restaurant/bar that hosts occasional live music. *US$70 dbl B&B, dropping to US$50 Mar–Nov.* **$$$**

TALALLA BEACH [map, page 488] A contender for the accolade of Sri Lanka's most idyllic beach, Talalla is a kilometre-long arc of golden sand, lined with swaying palms and tangled jungle, set in a sheltered bay 11km east of Matara. Still actively used by local fishermen, the beach has seen very little tourist development, and most of what does exist is low-rise and low-key, so it feels unusually natural and not at all resorty. Talalla beach is widely touted as offering safe swimming all year around, and certainly this seems to be the case most of the time, but currents can be unpredictable, especially out of season. Conditions are too calm for surfers, who are better off heading 12km east to Hiriketiya (surfers staying at Talalla Retreat are ferried there and back daily for free).

Getting there and away The accommodation listed below is clustered at the west end of the beach about 500m along a signposted junction from the Matara–Tangalle Road 1km east of Talalla post office. Coming by public transport, you need to catch a bus from Matara to Tangalle and should either hop off in Talalla village (close to the post office) and charter a tuktuk, or ask to be dropped at the junction and walk.

🏠 Where to stay

Moderate

✳ 🏠 **Talalla Sunshine Beach** (4 rooms)
m 0775 141533; **e** nisansalalakmali7@gmail.com;
w talalla-sunshine-beach.com. Set in a 3-storey
building 20m from the beach, this gem of a lodge
has smart trpl rooms (1 dbl & 1 ¾ bed) with AC,
fan, net, fridge, spotless bathroom & private
balcony. The hands-on live-in owner-manager is
super helpful, & the small & well-priced restaurant
serves excellent b/fasts (**$$**) & homemade curries
& Western-style grills (**$$$**). *US$85 trpl B&B,
dropping to US$40/50 without/with AC out of
season.* **$$$**

🏠 **Talalla Retreat** (73 rooms & dorms) 📞 041
225 9171; **m** 0779 039515; **e** info@talallaretreat.
com; **w** talallaretreat.com. Sprawling across large
green grounds that run down to the east end of
Talalla beach, this lovely low-rise resort has an
unplugged feel & doubles as a yoga and surf camp
(ferrying surfers daily to nearby Hiriketiya beach),
attracting a relatively young outdoorsy crowd. A
large dining hall serves buffet-style meals & there's
a huge swimming pool. The organic rooms vary
in cost, style and quality but most have open-air
bathrooms, good natural ventilation, nets &
fans, but no AC. Justifiably popular but you'd be
pushed to call it good value. *US$38 pp dorm bed,
rooms from US$49/55 sgl/dbl (shared bathroom) or*
*US$67/83 (en suite); all rates B&B; add US$12 pp for
dinner & US$8 pp for lunch.* **$$$**

Budget

🏠 **Freedom Resort** (6 rooms) **m** 0717
199873, 0786 902922; **e** thalallafreedom@gmail.
com; **w** talallafreedomresort.com. Perched on a
steep rise overlooking the east end of the beach,
this unpretentious family-run lodge has the
best location in Talalla & neat well-ventilated
bungalows with net, standing fan & private
balcony with beach view. A perfectly sited
restaurant serves seafood mains in the **$$$**
range. *US$50 dbl B&B, with significant low-season
& walk-in discounts.* **$$$**

🏠 **Jasmine Resort** (7 rooms) **m** 0773
549621; **e** jasmineresortthalalla@gmail.com;
w jasmineresortthalalla.com. A pretty villa set
in lush tropical gardens 200m from the beach,
this has small but neat rooms with fan but no AC,
& friendly owners. Good value. *US$27 dbl plus
US$3 pp b/fast.* **$$**

🏠 **Swiss Lanka** (4 rooms) 📞 041 225 8393;
m 0713 082271; **e** milan.harsha8@gmail.com.
This holiday villa 300m from the beach has 4 well-
ventilated bedrooms with net, fan, private balcony
& shared bathroom. Good b/fast. *US$48 dbl B&B.*
$$$

✗ Where to eat and drink
The food at the Talalla Sunshine Beach is widely
regarded to be the best in Talalla, though the views are trumped by the Freedom
Resort. A couple of modest beach shacks also serve OK food.

✗ **Lal's Seafood Restaurant** **m** 0713 318466;
e laljayaweda@gmail.com. Though it lacks beach
frontage, this friendly owner-managed garden
eatery is about the best standalone option in
Talalla, serving a varied menu of sweet & savoury
roti, kottu & salads (**$**), as well as curries & noodles
(**$$**) & seafood & other grills (**$$$**).

DEVINUWARA (DONDRA) Also answering to the Anglicised name Dondra,
Devinuwara (literally 'City of Gods') was reputedly the site of one of the five ancient
Vishnu temples built and founded in Sri Lanka in pre-Buddhist times. It emerged as an
important seaport and Buddhist pilgrimage site after the Devinuwara Upulvan Temple
was established here in the 7th century AD. In 1344, Ibn Battuta visited Devinuwara (or,
as he called it, Dinawar) *en route* from Adam's Peak to Galle. In 1588, the Portuguese,
with characteristic crusading zeal, attacked and demolished the temple, which they
regarded to be most celebrated manmade pilgrimage goal anywhere on the island.
The temple was eventually revived in the 17th century under the patronage of King
Rajasinha II of Kandy, though a relict of the original still survives in the form of the
mysterious Galgane Shrine. In 1887, Dondra Head, 1km south of Devinuwara, was
chosen as the site of a British-built lighthouse which still stands there today.

Devinuwara Upulvan Temple [map, page 536] Dominating the small town centre, the reconstructed Upulvan Temple at Devinuwara stands in a 3ha compound that incorporates a smooth concrete replica of the Avukana Buddha, several stone pillars and other minor relicts of the original temple destroyed by the Portuguese in 1588, an ancient stone gateway carved in the Pallava style, and a large white dagoba. Its most striking building is the so-called Blue Temple, a handsome balconied three-storey Kandyan building whose construction is accredited to Rajasinha II. The temple's exterior is painted in honour of the guardian deity Upulvan. A pair of elephants lives in the temple grounds, which are the site of a popular festival at the time of the Esala (July) Poya.

Galgane Shrine [map, page 536] Situated in odd isolation on a slope 500m north of the town centre, this mysterious rectangular building made entirely with finely hewn granite blocks is reminiscent more of certain Hindu temples than of any other Buddhist shrine in Sri Lanka. One local legend holds that the Galgane marks the spot where the demon-king Ravana was slain by Rama, a claim supported by a scholarly hypothesis that this unique building might be the island's oldest stone construction, while the east-facing main door might indicate that it was some sort of sun temple. More probably it was part of the original Upulvan Temple at Devinuwara, which would mean it dates to the 7th century AD or earlier. Despite the high standard of stone-masonry, it has an unusually plain exterior, though a few etchings can be seen around the door-frames.

Dondra Lighthouse [map, page 536] About 1km south of Devinuwara, Sri Lanka's tallest lighthouse, comprising seven storeys and standing 49m high, was built between 1887 and 1890 to warn ships off the rocky headland that forms the island's southernmost tip. It is not permitted to climb the 196 steps to the top of the lighthouse, but the immaculate exterior, painted off-white, with wooden windows a Tuscan yellow, inspires a shiver of wonder at its survival. Beyond it, in a cleft in the coastline, bright blue fishing boats bob in a surreally turquoise sea, while boys with rods fish off huge sea-battered boulders. Astonishing to think, as you look south, that some 10,000km of open sea separates this lush tropical landfall from Antarctica!

MATARA AND SURROUNDS

An ancient seaport that's evolved into a prosperous 21st-century university town, Matara stands at the mouth of the River Nilwala, which cuts its historic centre into two discrete sectors linked by the six-lane Mahanama Bridge. It is Sri Lanka's southernmost major town, situated only 5km from the extremity of Dondra Headland, and an important transport hub, the terminus not only of a coastal railway line originally laid in Victorian times, but also of the spanking new Southern Expressway. Compared with the likes of Weligama and Mirissa, Matara is very much a working town as opposed to a tourist destination, yet it exudes a feistiness that hints at something more interesting. Indeed, the old town's understated riverside location is enhanced by a kilometre-long promenaded seafront and liberal scattering of time-warped architectural relicts, including two Dutch forts. About 3km to the west, separated from the town centre by the Nilwala mouth, the contiguous Polhena and Madiha beaches are relatively undiscovered suburban gems that offer safe swimming, good snorkelling and year-round surfing. Further afield, Matara is also the obvious springboard for day

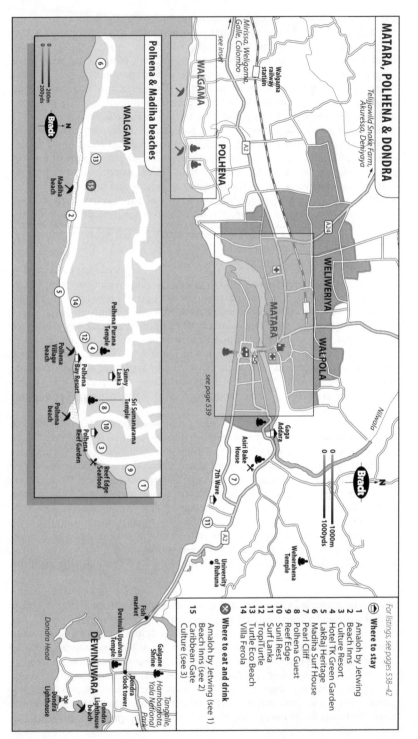

MATARA, POLHENA & DONDRA

*Telijjawila Snake Farm,
Akuressa, Deniyaya*

*Mirissa, Weligama,
Galle, Colombo*

Walgama
railway
station

WALGAMA

POLHENA

WALGAMA

MATARA

WELIWERIYA

WALPOLA

Niwala

Polhena & Madiha beaches

WALGAMA

Madiha
beach

Polhena Purana
Temple

Sunny
Lanka

Polhena
Bay Resort

Sri Sumanarama
Temple

Polhena
Village
beach

Polhena
beach

Polhena
Reef Garden

Reef Edge
Seafood

see page 539

see inset

Gaga
Addara

Asiri Bake
House

7th Wave

Weherahena
Temple

University
of Ruhuna

Fish
market

Devinula Uputhan
Temple

Galgane
Shrine

Dondra
clock tower

DEWINUWARA

*Tangalle,
Hambantota,
Yala National
Park*

Dondra Head

Dondra
Lighthouse

Dondra
Lighthouse
beach

0   200m
0   200yds

0   1000m
0   1000yds

Bradt

N

Bradt

N

trips or longer stays at a succession of low-key historical sites and breathtaking beaches described under *Towards Matara* (pages 531–5).

HISTORY Matara was an important maritime gateway to the ancient Ruhuna Kingdom, as evidenced by the recent discovery here of a hoard of Roman coins dating to the 5th-century reign of Emperor Theodosius II. Little is known about its early days, but the *Paravi Sandeshaya*, written in 1435 by the eminent Buddhist scholar Thotagamuwe Sri Rahula Thera, states that it was founded as the capital of an otherwise undocumented monarch called Weerabamapanam. Medieval trade out of Matara was dominated by spices, gems and elephants, the latter captured in a wild state and corralled into stockades on the banks of the Nilwala to be tamed. The busy ferry that crossed the Nilwala at the site of the present-day Mahanama Bridge is alluded to both in the town's Medieval name, Mahatota, a Sanskrit phrase meaning 'Great Ferry', and in its modern name, which was coined by the Portuguese and most likely derives from the Tamil *thurai* (ferry).

In 1560, Matara fell to the Portuguese, who razed several local Buddhist temples and developed it as a centre of export for cinnamon, citronella, cardamom and other spices. It was the Portuguese who first fortified the spit of land south and east of the Nilwala in c1595, but their original fortifications were greatly expanded and strengthened by the Dutch, who captured it in 1658. During the Dutch era, a quartet of stables capable of holding up to 80 elephants was constructed within the fort, immediately behind the present-day Matara Resthouse. The vulnerability of the Dutch fort was exposed during a local rebellion that erupted in 1760 in response to an attempt to dispossess peasants who couldn't prove title to their land. In March 1761, the fort was surrounded by Kandyan forces, who fired cannonballs right over the bastions, effecting an aerial bombardment that forced its occupants to flee to two waiting ships. The Dutch easily recaptured Matara in February 1762, after which they set about strengthening its defences with the construction of a second fort 150m north of the Nilwala.

In 1796, Matara was handed over to the British, who demolished the southern ramparts of the old fort to open the waterfront up for civilian buildings. Matara became capital of an eponymous administrative district in 1833 and its future importance was sealed in 1895 when it became the southeastern terminus of the coastal railway from Colombo. An important export item during this period was a colourless zircon gemstone known as the Matara diamond. The 2004 tsunami struck hard: more than a thousand deaths were recorded in Matara District, many waterfront constructions were destroyed, and the original Mahanama Bridge was swept away (its replacement, built with South Korean aid money, reopened in 2007). Now a city of 80,000 predominantly Sinhalese inhabitants, Matara remains one of just three district capitals in Southern Province, and it became its only university town in 1978.

GETTING THERE AND AWAY Matara is the main rail and bus terminus on the south coast between Galle and Hambantota, and details below concentrate mainly on long-haul travel. More locally, suffice to say that buses run back and forth to the likes of Tangalle, Mirissa and Weligama every 10–15 minutes, and travellers bound for these destinations from Colombo or other more remote locations might well consider catching an express bus or train to Matara and using it as a springboard for the last short leg.

By air The Mattala Rajapaksa International Airport near Hambantota is serviced by domestic flights from Colombo and is sometimes billed as a potential air gateway to Matara, but the reality is the two are 110km apart by road, only 50km less than the direct road route from Colombo to Matara.

By road Matara lies 160km (2 hours) from Colombo and 45km (1 hour) from Galle along the excellent multi-lane Southern Expressway. Distances are roughly the same along the coastal road through Bentota, Hikkaduwa and Mirissa, but driving times are far slower. Coming from elsewhere, Matara is around 250km (4–5 hours) from Kandy skirting Colombo and using the Southern Expressway, 220km (6 hours) from Nuwara Eliya via Ella (170km/4.5 hours) and Embilipitiya (80km/1.5 hours), 170km (5–6 hours) from Ratnapura via Deniyaya (75km/2 hours) and Akuressa (24km/45 minutes) and 110km/2½ hours from Tissamaharama via Hambantota (84km/2 hours) and Tangalle (38km/1 hour).

Matara is serviced by an extensive network of buses, all of which leave from the main terminus [539 E3] in the old town just south of the bridge and around the corner from the Matara Resthouse. Express buses to Colombo following the Southern Expressway leave every 15 minutes and take up to 2½ hours, while stopping buses along the coastal road leave at similar intervals but take twice as long. There are also regular buses (at least two an hour, usually more) to Akuressa (for Deniyaya), Embilipitiya (for Udawalawe National Park), Galle (via all coastal stops in between) and Tissamaharama (for Yala National Park and Kataragama). Less frequent buses (typically between one and three daily) connect Matara to Ratnapura, Ella, Nuwara Eliya, Kandy and other large towns in the Hill Country.

By rail Half a dozen trains run daily between Colombo and Matara via Galle, typically taking around 3–4 hours, though this depends greatly on the service and number of stops.

WHERE TO STAY   *Map, page 536, unless otherwise stated*
Town centre
Accommodation options in & around the town centre are unusually limited & all fall in the budget range, but do include two little gems in the form of the central Matara Resthouse & more remote beachside Surf Lanka.

* ⌂ **Matara Resthouse** [539 D3] (8 rooms) \041 222 2299; e resthousemh@sltnet.lk; w resthousematara.com. Dutch-built in 1780 and renovated several times since (most recently after the tsunami), this gracious old colonial building with wide wrap-around terrace has an agreeable seafront location in the old fort, walls hung with black-&-white photos of old Matara & restaurant/bar known for its good-value (*US$6.50*) buffet lunches. The spacious & well-maintained rooms have darkwood furniture including 4-poster bed with fitted net, AC, fan & private balcony. Rooms 801–5 are the pick as they all face the sea. *US$31 dbl.* **$$**

⌂ **Hotel Nawathana** [539 D3] (8 rooms) \041 493 6230. This very pleasant seafront

hotel lies in the Fort District 100m west of the Matara Resthouse. It lacks its neighbour's pedigree and historic character, but has the benefit of a swimming pool & genuine beach setting. A restaurant is attached & all rooms have AC, TV & private terrace. *US$35 dbl B&B, but check online vendors for hefty last-minute discounts.* **$$**

⌂ **Surf Lanka** (11 rooms) \041 222 8190; m 0773 877109; e info@surf-lanka.com; w surf-lanka.com. Situated on the excellent but little-known surfing beach at Meddawatta 2.5km east of the town centre, this laid-back family-owned guesthouse has brightly decorated rooms with AC, TV, tub & private terrace or balcony with sea view. Good food too. *US$42 dbl B&B.* **$$**

⌂ **Pearl Cliff Hotel** (10 rooms) \041 222 0222; e pearlcliff@gmail.com; w pearlcliff.com. Perched on the wooded Brown's Hill overlooking the sea about 1km east of the town centre, this idiosyncratic set-up has adequate accommodation in cabanas with tall wooden ceilings, fan, optional AC, TV & private balcony with a view. Not great, but

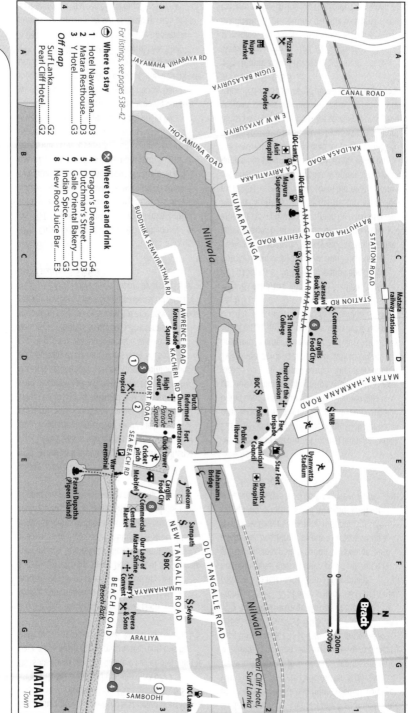

MATARA
Town

Where to stay

For listings, see pages 538–42

1   Hotel Nawathana..............D3
2   Matara Resthouse............D3
3   Y Hotel..............................G3

Off map
    Surf Lanka........................G2
    Pearl Cliff Hotel................G2

Where to eat and drink

4   Dragon's Dream................G4
5   Dutchman's Street............D3
6   Galle Oriental Bakery........D1
7   Indian Spice.....................G3
8   New Roots Juice Bar..........E3

fair at the price, & a licensed restaurant is attached. *US$43/50 sgl/dbl B&B, plus US$3.50 for AC.* **$$$**

🏠 **Y Hotel** [539 G3] (8 rooms) m 0775 085800. About the best of a few basic hotels on the back roads north of the central seafront, this has basic but neat rooms with AC & fan. *US$27 dbl.* **$$**

Polhena & Madiha beaches

Most accommodation associated with Matara actually lies along these 2 fine beaches, which together stretch for about 3km west of the Nilwala river mouth. Upmarket options are limited but there are some great-value budget & shoestring establishments. Polhena is the closer beach to the town centre, but both are easily reached from the central bus or railway station by tuktuk.

Upmarket

🏠 **Amaloh by Jetwing** (18 rooms) Polhena; ☎ 011 470 9400; e resv.amaloh@jetwinghotels. com; w jetwinghotels.com. Easily the top property in the vicinity of Matara, this converted villa is set in large manicured seaside gardens with swimming pool & sea kayaks to explore the ocean & neighbouring creek. Large, comfortable & colourfully decorated rooms have AC, separate dressing room, outdoor shower & wide terrace/ balcony surveying the grounds. The terrace bar/ restaurant majors in seafood but also serves a good selection of Sri Lankan & international cuisine. *From US$219/239 sgl/dbl B&B, dropping by around 25% out of season.* **$$$$$**

Moderate

🏠 **Culture Resort** (6 rooms) Polhena; m 0770 059841; e cultureresortsrilanka@gmail. com; w cultureresort.com. This smart 3-storey hotel – complete, unusually, with lift & indoor swimming pool – stands opposite the beach & has a fabulous rooftop restaurant with stylish décor, impeccable view & good seafood & curries in the **$$$** range. Modern rooms with AC, fan & net have treated concrete floors offset by colourful fabrics & linen curtains leading out to a wooden balcony with sea view. Friendly hands-on management, snorkelling gear for hire, free bicycle use & sensible rates. *US$90 dbl B&B.* **$$$$**

🏠 **Turtle Eco Beach** (18 rooms) Madiha; ☎ 041 222 3377; m 0716 846666; e booking@ duneecogroup.com; w duneecogroup.com. Set in a large tropical garden at the quiet western end of

Madiha beach, this comfortable & secluded lodge offers accommodation in bright modern cottages with treated concrete floor, AC, fan & private terrace. Amenities include a restaurant, saltwater swimming pool, spa, yoga sessions, gym & bicycle hire. Good value. *US$100 dbl B&B, dropping to US$63 out of season.* **$$$$**

🏠 **LakRaj Heritage Hotel** (12 rooms) Polhena; ☎ 041 223 8600; e info@lakrajheritage. com; w lakrajheritage.com. This aspirant boutique hotel doesn't quite pull it off, but it is still a pleasant enough option in its range, with a fabulous beachfront location incorporating a terrace restaurant & natural rock pool for safe swimming, & rather small AC rooms with some stylish decorative touches & sea view. *From US$120/125 sgl/dbl B&B.* **$$$$**

Budget

✳ 🏠 **Villa Ferola** (4 rooms) Polhena; ☎ 041 223 6060; m 0777 229565; e info@villaferola. com; w villaferola.com. Set on the landward side of the beach road, this Estonian-owned villa is a curiously suburban apparition with its brickface façade & neatly tended garden. There's a common TV lounge, garden seating, Sri Lankan cuisine prepared to order & a lovely beach just 50m away. Small but bright rooms come with net & fan or AC. Outstanding value. *US$25/35 B&B dbl with fan/ AC.* **$$**

🏠 **Beach Inns** (38 rooms) Madiha; ☎ 041 222 6356; m 0776 199413; e indikapg2006@ hotmail.com; w beach-inns.com. This family-owned & -managed 2-storey block is set in a neat palm-shaded beachfront garden overlooking what amounts to a private swimming beach protected by a reef & often visited by marine turtles. Budget rooms in the old wing are small but neat & come with net, private balcony, fan & optional AC, while large deluxe rooms in a new 3-storey wing on the landward side of the road all come with AC & should soon also be serviced by a swimming pool. A restaurant/bar with terrace seating serves good seafood, curries & Chinese in the **$$$** range. Great value. *US$23/38 standard dbl with fan/AC, US$54 deluxe dbl.* **$–$$$**

🏠 **Madiha Surf House** (6 rooms) Madiha; m 0766 718159, 0772 266566; e madihasurfhouse@gmail.com; 📷 pg/ madihasurfhouse. Situated at the western extreme of Beachside Rd, this chilled guesthouse has a pretty garden running down to the beach 5mins' walk from the best surfing spot, a terrace restaurant serving local curries & snacks (**$$**) & pleasant rooms with 4-poster bed, fitted net & fan. *US$23 dbl B&B.* **$**

🏠 **Hotel TK Green Garden** (16 rooms) Polhena; ☎ 041 222 2603; e hoteltk@sltnet.lk. Set in large, fussily manicured gardens less than 100m from the beach, this place offers the choice of 3 room types. Cheapest are the quiet & spotless ground-floor rooms with tiled floor, net, fan, writing desk, cold water & semi-private balcony. Best are the more spacious AC rooms whose semi-private balcony has a decent sea view. In-between rooms have AC but are not as nice as the other two types. *US$19 dbl with fan, US$23/37 lesser/superior dbl with AC.* **$–$$**

Shoestring

🏠 **TropiTurtle** (4 rooms, 1 dorm) Polhena; ☎ 041 223 8111; m 0775 883107; e info@ tropiturtle.com; w tropiturtle.com. Split across 2 houses, this friendly lodge is justifiably popular with backpackers, though standards tend to drop when the hands-on owner-manager is away. All rooms have net & fan, and the upstairs rooms also offer a sea view. A restaurant serves typical Sri Lankan fare & guests can also use the kitchen to self-cater. It rents out affordable snorkelling gear,

surfboards, bicycles & scooters, & can also arrange tours to Sinharaja & elsewhere. *US$12/14 dbl without/with sea view, US$5.50 pp dorm bed.* **$**

🏠 **Reef Edge** (4 rooms) Polhena; m 0772 978233, 0779 762456; e reefedge@gmail.com; w reefedge.lk. Set in a walled compound close to the beach, this stylish 2-storey villa has bright clean rooms with fan, net, private balcony & optional AC, as well as a large ground-floor dining & sitting area looking out to a lush tropical garden hung with hammocks. An eponymous seafood restaurant, under the same management, stands on a seafront terrace 100m to the south. *US$13 dbl without AC, US$17/22 ground-/1st-floor dbl with AC.* **$**

🏠 **Sunil Rest** (6 rooms) ☎ 041 223 2164; m 0777 101363; e sunilrestpolhena@yahoo.com. Situated at the end of a 100m dirt road running north from the beach, this long-standing & well-organised owner-managed lodge has adequately clean rooms with net & fan, & can also provide meals in the **$$** bracket & arrange a variety of excursions. *US$14 dbl.* **$**

🏠 **Polhena Guest** (4 rooms) Polhena; m 0776 154468, 0777 972795. This homestay-like set-up, more or less opposite Sunil Rest, has clean, neat & spacious rooms with fan & net. *US$10/17 dbl/twin.* **$**

✖ WHERE TO EAT AND DRINK
Town centre

☀ ✖ **Dutchman's Street** [539 D3] Court Rd; ☎ 041 223 6555; w thedutchmansstreet.com; ⏰ 09.00–22.00. This new restaurant in Fort District has quickly gained a reputation as Matara's finest. The attractively quirky interior sports an eclectic mix of treated concrete, painted wood & colourful fabrics, & there's also garden seating & a backdrop of contemporary music. Sri Lankan specialities (a signature dish being baked crab) are supplemented by a globetrotting Italian, Arabic, Caribbean & mainland Asian selection. It's all freshly prepared, so service can be on the slow side when busy. **$$$**

✖ **Galle Oriental Bakery** [539 D1] Anagarika Dharmapala Rd; ⏰ 08.00–21.00. Set in an old manor building whose eaves are laced with so much fretwork it looks like a gingerbread house, this Matara institution is arguably of greater historical than culinary note, but it's still worth dropping in for an inexpensive pastry, coffee or snack. **$**

✖ **Dragon's Dream** [539 G4] Beach Rd; m 0770 855586; ⏰ 08.30–22.00. Popular with Chinese residents, this slightly shabby family-run restaurant serves authentic & inexpensive Chinese fare to eat in or take away. **$$**

✖ **Indian Spice** [539 G3] Beach Rd; ⏰ 07.00–22.00. Despite a bizarre all-eyes-forward seating arrangement reminiscent of a lecture hall, this sea-facing restaurant serves unexceptional but adequate & filling Indian & Chinese staples (**$$**) & a selection of cheap cakes & pastries (**$**).

✖ **New Roots Juice Bar** [539 E3] Central market; m 0772 942578; ⏰ 09.00–21.00. Fresh fruit juice at US$1/glass, made in front of your eyes, with or without sugar as you prefer.

Polhena & Madiha beaches

Most of the accommodation listed above serves food, though budget places cater mostly to their own guests. Standouts are the rooftop restaurant at the Culture Resort, the terrace at the Beach Inns, & the more upmarket & somewhat pricier Amaloh by Jetwing. Only 1 standalone restaurant justifies a listing.

✗ Caribbean Gate [map, page 536] Madiha beach; m 0718 952475; f; ⊕ 11.00–22.30.

This likeably rickety wood & thatch structure opposite the beach might lack a view (there's a fence in the way) but the sea breeze & sand give it a genuine seaside feel. Local curries, devilled dishes & fried rice (**$$**) are supplemented by seafood & other grills (**$$$**) & it also serves beers & cocktails.

OTHER PRACTICALITIES Matara is a large well-equipped town with at least one branch of all the banks, including Commercial Banks with ATMs opposite the central bus station [539 E3] and 200m south of the railway station [539 D1]. There are no useful banks in the vicinity of Polhena and Madiha beaches, but it is a short tuktuk ride from these into the town centre. For grocery shopping, branches of Cargills Food City [539 E3] can be found on the New Tangalle Road just north of the bus station, and next to the Galle Oriental Bakery [539 D1]. There's a bustling central market [539 E3] opposite the bus station.

WHAT TO SEE AND DO The main centre of activity are the beaches at Polhena and Madiha, but Matara's old town and its many old buildings also warrant a few hours' relaxed exploration. Matara is also the obvious base from which to explore Dondra and other sites described under *Towards Matara* (pages 531–5), and it is close enough to Mirissa, Weligama, Galle and Tangalle to contemplate a day trip to any of these towns, assuming you have no plan to overnight at them.

Matara town The oldest part of Matara occupies a 2km-long, 300m-wide westward-orientated spit bounded to the north and west by the River Nilwala, to the south by the Indian Ocean, and to the east by the wooded slope of Brown's Hill. The western half of this spit comprises the old Fort District, which is still dominated by administrative and other government buildings, many dating back to the Dutch or British eras. A large cricket pitch [539 E3] below the ramparts divides the fort from the more easterly commercial and residential district emanating from Beach Road, which incorporates the central bus station and market, and the kilometre-long Beach Park. North of the Nilwala, the modern commercial centre also includes several historic buildings, notably the 18th-century Star Fort and Nupe Market, and the Victorian railway station. Sites below are described following the above sequence. No entrance fee is charged unless otherwise stated.

Fort District Unlike its counterpart in Galle, Matara's Fort District survives primarily in nominal form. The only remaining bastion of the fortifications built by the Portuguese in 1595 and expanded by the Dutch 50 years later is the 240m-long, 5m-high eastern rampart, a solid rock structure entered at the north via a lorry-height arched tunnel inscribed with the date 1780. Immediately inside the eastern bastion stands a clock tower [539 E3] erected by the British in 1883, the old parade ground [539 E3] and the Dutch Reformed Church (see opposite). From here, the roughly parallel Lawrence, Kachcheri and Court roads run west past an architectural melange of colonial administrative buildings and palatial walauwas (mansions) in various states of (dis)repair. Notable among these, overlooking Kotuwa Kade Square [539 D3], is the ornate but dilapidated Court View Hotel, a three-storey Dutch-era building (with several British enhancements) that once ranked as the tallest construction in the fort, and served until recent times as lawyers' chambers. About 1km from the Dutch Reformed Church, the spit's leafy western extremity is a picturesque spot overlooking the small but deep estuarine fishing harbour that forms the fort's *raison d'être*, as well as the sandy river mouth, and a small forested island midstream.

Dutch Reformed Church [539 D3] The oldest building within the fort, overlooking the parade ground, the yellow-washed Dutch Reformed Church has a plain gabled façade, tile roof and colonnaded side balcony. The year 1767 inscribed above the main doorway refers to reconstruction work effected in the aftermath of the Kandyan bombardment six years earlier. A less legible inscription indicates that this austere church was consecrated in 1706, but it may be even older, given that one of the many gravestones set into the floor dates to 1686. The church suffered minor damage in the 2004 tsunami and was used as a food distribution centre in its aftermath. Major restoration work undertaken in 2006 included renovation of the antique pump organ, pulpit and pew.

Paravi Dupatha [539 E4] The rocky wave-swept outcrop known as Paravi Dupatha (Pigeon Island) is the site of a modern Buddhist temple that is arguably of less interest for itself than for its tranquil setting and the stirring oceanic view from the *seema malaka* (ordainment hall), though it does incorporate a replica of the Buddhapada on Adam's Peak. It is linked to the mainland by a 100m-long suspension bridge, built in 2008 to replace the tsunami-damaged original, at the west end of Beach Park.

Beach Park [539 F4] Possibly as a result of tsunami damage, Matara's main seafront has a slightly down-at-heel aura, and there's not much happening tourist-wise bar a few seedy-looking hotels and adequate but unexceptional restaurants. Its main feature is Beach Park, a narrow and rather barren-looking promenade that stretches almost 1.5km east from the Matara Resthouse. At its west end stands a small war memorial [539 E3] and the bridge to Paravi Dupatha. Wander east along the seawall and you'll find it punctuated with couples sitting snugly beneath umbrellas or walking hand in hand. Oddly, however, the calm sandy beach below seems not to attract swimmers, presumably due to a combination of urban pollution and riptides.

Our Lady of Matara Shrine [539 F3] (w *ourladyofmatara.lk*; ⊕ *07.00–19.00*) Situated on the north side of Beach Road, this Catholic church was constructed in 1907 but is named after a 400-year-old Madonna and Child statue housed within its niche. Shrouded in legend and mystery, this solid ash-wood statue of Portuguese provenance was reputedly recovered from a large wooden crate hauled out of the sea at Weligama in the early 17th century, and taken to Matara to be placed in the care of what was then the Portuguese Church of St Mary (which may or may not have stood on the same site as its modern successor). The statue was secreted away by local Catholics who feared persecution under the Dutch, but mysteriously reappeared several years later to end a cholera epidemic that had claimed hundreds of lives in the district. Credited with supernatural powers ever since, it has disappeared and returned to Matara on two subsequent occasions. In 1911, having undergone restoration work in Belgium, the statue was listed as lost in transit when the ship assigned to return it home scuppered all its cargo in a storm, but it later transpired that it had actually been loaded on to a different ship as excess luggage. In 2004, when the tsunami flooded the church during mass, killing 24 worshippers, the statue was swept out to sea and presumed lost, only to be washed ashore three days later, with minimal damage, a mere 400m away. The church attracts hordes of pilgrims over a feast held over the second weekend in September, when the iconic statue is paraded around the streets.

Star Fort [539 E2] (w *archaeology.gov.lk;* ⏲ *08.00–16.30 Wed–Mo*n) Situated in the new town centre 150m north of the Nilwala River that bisects Matara, this six-pronged construction is the smallest fort in Sri Lanka, almost concealed by the surrounds of tall trees and buildings and daily commerce, but also one of the best preserved and most architecturally interesting. As the inscription and VOC symbol (complete with lolling-tongued lions) above its picturesque entrance gate indicate, it was built in 1763 under Governor Redoute Van Eck, largely to beef up the security in the wake of the Matara rebellion two years earlier. Functional in design, it had thick coral walls with elevated ramparts, a watchtower and several cells, and it was surrounded by a moat and drawbridge that once housed a crew of hungry crocodiles but is now home to a few less intimidating terrapins. The fort's effectiveness was never tested, since it was ceded to the British in 1796 by treaty. Having served as an administrative office from 1796 to 1914, the fort was restored to its original plan in 1986 under the Department of Archaeology. In 2006, it opened as a small museum whose well-labelled displays cover several historical sites close to Matara and Dondra, and include a collection of ancient pots, parts of Kandyan paintings, and the original well, which is now full of fish.

Nupe Market [539 A2] An odd public building constructed by the Dutch in 1763, Nupe Market is situated in the new town 1.5km west of the Star Fort, a surprisingly remote location, which presumably provides some indication of how widely Matara sprawled at the time. It was built, as its name suggests, to house a market, with a T-shaped floor plan whose stem was probably for the sale of textile and household items, while one wing would have housed vegetable stalls, and the other meat and fish. At first glance, the old building looks like something from Medieval England, thanks to its tiled pitched roof with three tiny conical towers and gabled entrance. The elaborate wooden frame supporting the roof is edged with lavish latticework and supported by massive white stone pillars typical of the British period when the imperial stamp was impressed on public buildings. An old well lies in the garden and the site houses a small bookshop selling Department of Archaeology publications.

Further afield
Polhena and Madiha beaches [map, page 536] Serviced by a row of (mostly low-key) hotels, these two suburban beaches stretch for about 3km past the Nilwala river mouth on the western outskirts of Matara. Closer-to-town Polhena and much of Madiha are hemmed in by an offshore coral reef that helps protect swimmers while being ideal for snorkelling, with a good chance of encountering marine turtles along with schools of colourful reef fish. Further west, just past Madiha Surf House, the reef breaks up to form a trio of fine surfing points whose consistent year-round swell can be harnessed by intermediate and advanced surfers for rides of up to 300m. Note that the two public beaches – Polhena opposite the Sri Sumanarama Temple, and to a lesser extent Madiha opposite Caribbean Gate – can get crowded and the closest coral is badly damaged, so better to head to one of the beach hotels between the two, and settle in there with a drink or meal. Snorkelling gear can be rented at Sunil Rest, TropiTurtle and other hotels in the vicinity for around US$2–3 a day.

Weherahena Temple [map, page 536] Situated in the village of the same name 3km east of Matara, this modern temple is of no historical interest, but it does claim to host the island's largest Samadhi Buddha, a 39m-high Disney-esque colossus painted bright yellow and red and seated on a gummy-pink lotus flower. Completed in 1976, the temple also claims to incorporate the world's longest subterranean Buddhist shrine, a 200m-long tunnel adorned with some 7,000 – or so we're told – cartoon-like frames depicting the life of the Buddha. A donation of US$1.50–2 might be requested.

University of Ruhuna [map, page 536] The only university in Southern Province was established as a college by presidential decree in 1978 and upgraded to university status in 1984. The attractively hilly 30ha campus is in Wellamadama on the eastern outskirts of town, and its red-roofed central buildings were designed by Geoffrey Bawa.

MIRISSA, WELIGAMA AND MIDIGAMA

Dotted around the 4km-wide near-oval Weligama Bay 30km east of Galle and 150km southeast of Colombo, Mirissa is renowned for its attractive swimming beach and as the focal point of the south coast's burgeoning whale-watching industry, and nearby Weligama and Midigama offer some of the best surfing in Sri Lanka. The coast running west from Weligama to Galle is also famed for its iconic stilt fishermen, who perch upon sticks in the shallows, dangling bamboo rods in the water, angling either for small fish, or (more likely, these days) for tourists willing to pay a few dollars to photograph them.

In addition to their physical proximity, Mirissa, Weligama and Midigama share the unaffected and down-to-earth feel of resorts that developed largely at their own pace and on their own terms. The imminent opening of a 200-room Marriott at Weligama might perhaps be a sign of things to come, but for now the area is notable for its paucity of Bentota-esque package resorts and multitude of smaller and more intimate properties, ranging from classy boutique hotels to easy-going no-frills guesthouses that evolved from homestays and are still owned and managed by local families who live on site.

Despite this, each of the three settlements has a distinct character and tends to cater to a different clientele. Jungle-fringed Mirissa, which flanks the bay's rocky eastern headland, boasts the area's finest beach, and a good selection of accommodation geared mainly to non-surfing budget travellers. The resort of Weligama, on the west shore of the eponymous bay, is particularly suited to beginner surfers and supports a healthy mix of boutique properties and budget guesthouses. Semi-rural Midigama, about 2km west of Weligama Bay, is dominated by small owner-managed lodges aimed at dedicated surfers. It should be noted, whichever of the three you stay at, that they are somewhat interchangeable in terms of activities – the surf at Weligama and Midigama is only a short tuktuk ride from Mirissa, and whale-watching excursions from Mirissa Harbour can be booked through any hotel in the vicinity.

MIRISSA A relatively modest (population 5,000) seaside town sprawling eastward from Weligama Bay, Mirissa has emerged in recent years as a popular and down-to-earth beach resort with amenities aimed mainly at youngish budget-conscious travellers and a reputation for offering excellent offshore whale watching. Though it sprawls for some way along the beach, it is an easy town to get around, amounting

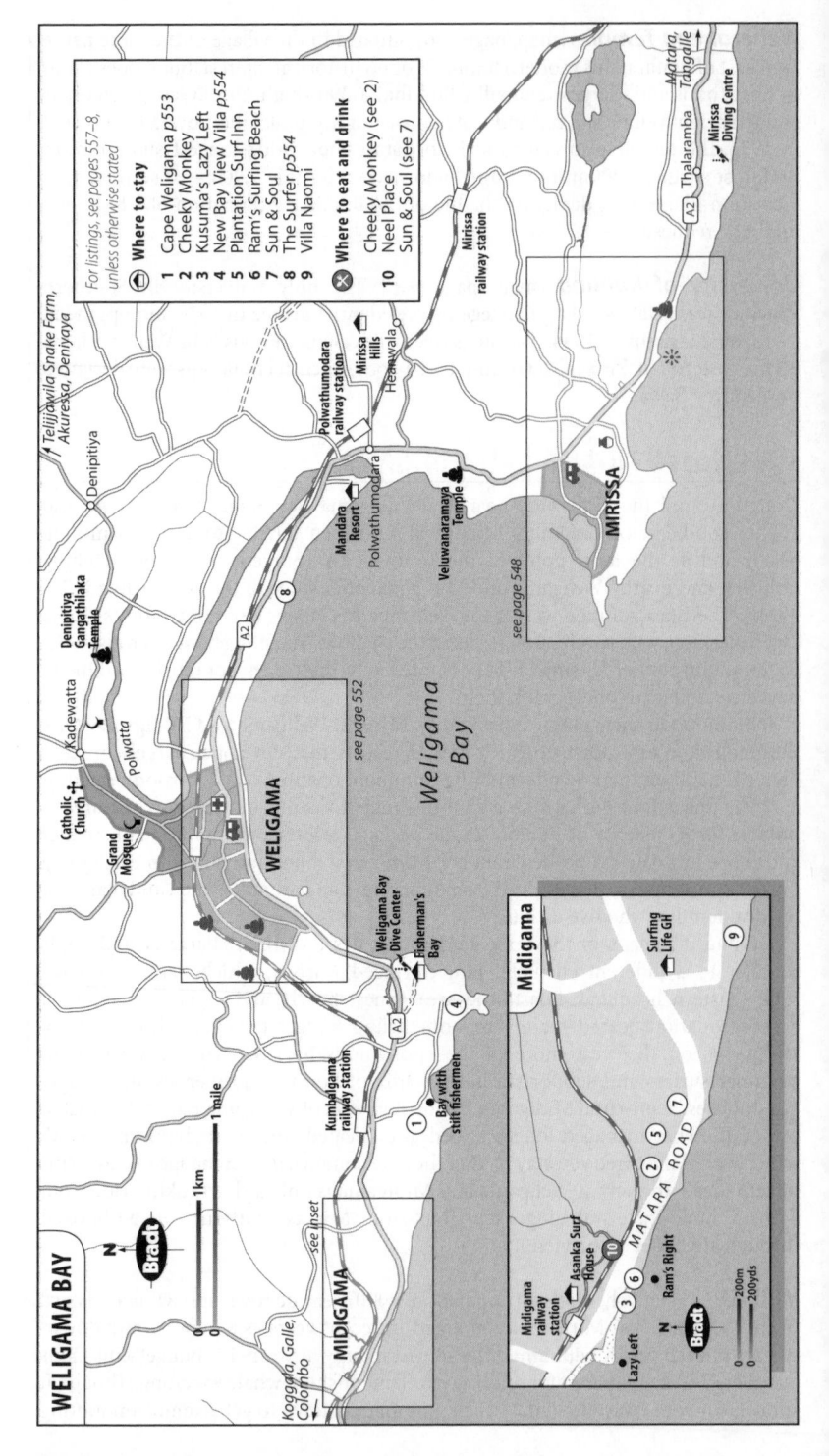

WELIGAMA BAY

For listings, see pages 557–8,
unless otherwise stated

Where to stay
1 Cape Weligama *p553*
2 Cheeky Monkey
3 Kusuma's Lazy Left
4 New Bay View Villa *p554*
5 Plantation Surf Inn
6 Ram's Surfing Beach
7 Sun & Soul
8 The Surfer *p554*
9 Villa Naomi

Where to eat and drink
10 Cheeky Monkey (see 2)
   Neel Place
   Sun & Soul (see 7)

to little more than a coastal strip of hotels and other such amenities backed by a lush inland backdrop of palm trees, paddy fields and jungle. An attractive feature of the town is the rocky forest-swathed headland that towers above the western end of the beach, and separates it from Weligama Bay and the colourful protected fishing harbour that now serves as the launch for most whale-watching cruises.

Getting there and away Mirissa straddles the main coastal road about 11km west of Matara, 5km east of Weligama and 32km east of Galle. Regular buses along the coastal road between Galle and Matara stop in the town centre. Stopping trains between Colombo/Galle and Matara (around five daily in either direction) stop at Mirissa railway station, about 2km inland of the town centre.

Where to stay Mirissa has good accommodation to suit all budgets but it is particularly strong on shoestring options, which are represented by two excellent hostels and innumerable quaint family-run homestay set-ups. Except where otherwise stated, places listed below flank the Colombo–Matara Road or lie along one of several short nameless side roads running to its north.

Exclusive

🏠 **Number One Mirissa** [548 D3] (8 rooms) Beachside Rd; `041 225 4884`; e info@ numberonemirissa.com; w numberonemirissa. com. Difficult to argue with the name of what is also Mirissa's only beachfront boutique property, a delightful owner-managed lodge set on the rocky headland that rises at the west end of the main beach. The light rooms have AC, fan, TV, king-size bed, fitted net, darkwood floors, antique furnishings & quality fittings, & extend on to private balconies with hammock & seating. Shaded by large trees, the sprawling garden incorporates a saltwater swimming pool & offers great views along the beach at sunrise. *US$200 dbl B&B, dropping to US$125 out of season.* **$$$$$**

Moderate

☀ 🏠 **The Spice House** [548 G3] (11 rooms) m 0773 510147; e thespicehousemirissa@gmail. com; w thespicehousemirissa.com. Owned & managed by a friendly British-Sri Lankan couple, this well-priced traditionally built boutique guesthouse stands in delightful green gardens that attract plenty of wildlife (monkeys, squirrels, birds) & has a dining terrace & infinity pool facing a forested hill at the back. Individually styled rooms named after local spices are decorated in classic-contemporary style with 4-poster bed, fitted net, AC & fan, & most have private terraces/balconies. Exceptional food, especially b/fast. *From US$58/86 sgl/dbl B&B (with 1 non-AC room at US$75 dbl), dropping by around 20% out of season.* **$$$$**

🏠 **Palace Mirissa** [548 C3] (17 rooms) Beachside Rd; `041 225 1303`; m 0777 352306; e admin@palacemirissa.com; w palacemirissa. com. Sloping across feral 2ha grounds on the tall headland at the west end of Mirissa beach, this hotel is notable for its remote feel, fine views & plentiful birdlife. The hexagonal chalets are widely scattered for privacy & come with AC, fan, 4-poster bed with fitted net, fridge, TV & private terrace, while other amenities include a kidney-shaped swimming pool & restaurant with a view. Though the immense potential is undermined by the disengaged staff & a faint but distinct whiff of neglect, it remains OK value at the price, especially for nature lovers seeking a tranquil retreat from Mirissa's seaside resort milieu. *US$120 dbl HB, dropping to US$100 out of season.* **$$$$**

Budget

☀ 🏠 **Secret Guesthouse** [548 F2] (4 rooms, 3 villas) m 0773 294332; e secret_root@yahoo. com; w thesecretguesthouse.com. This lovely & very reasonably priced boutique lodge has a quiet & leafy location 200m inland of the beach in a well-tended garden regularly visited by wild monkeys & peacocks. Individually decorated rooms all have tall ceilings, 4-poster bed with fitted net, stylish décor, fridge, terrace seating & fan, & most rooms also have AC. *From US$40/60 B&B dbl with fan/AC, dropping slightly out of season.* **$$**

🏠 **Palm Villa** [548 F3] (15 rooms) `041 225 0022`; e palmvillamirissa@yahoo.com;

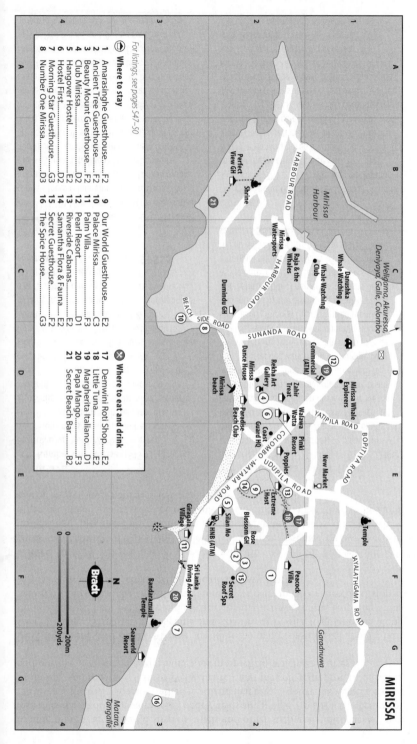

For listings, see pages 547–50

Where to stay

1 Amarasinghe Guesthouse............F2
2 Ancient Tree Guesthouse............F2
3 Beauty Mount Guesthouse..........F2
4 Club Mirissa............................D2
5 Hangover Hostel.......................E2
6 Hostel First..............................D2
7 Morning Star Guesthouse...........G3
8 Number One Mirissa..................D3

9   Our World Guesthouse.............E2
10 Palace Mirissa........................C3
11 Palm Villa..............................F3
12 Pearl Resort...........................D1
13 Riverside Cabanas...................D1
14 Samantha Flora & Fauna..........E2
15 Secret Guesthouse..................F2
16 The Spice House.....................G3

Where to eat and drink

17 Denwini Roti Shop....................E2
18 Little Tuna.............................E2
19 Margherita Italiano..................D1
20 Papa Mango...........................F3
21 Secret Beach Bar....................B2

MIRISSA

w palmvillamirissa.com. This laid-back & down-to-earth family-run guesthouse comprises a renovated & expanded colonial villa set in sprawling & well-wooded gardens that run on to a lovely stretch of beach. Spacious rooms with fan or AC all have nets & private terrace, while the restaurant – affiliated to nearby Papa Mango – serves seafood & curries in the $$$ range. *US$75/86 B&B dbl with fan/AC, dropping by US$8 out of season.* $$$$

🏠 **Riverside Cabanas** [548 E2] (8 rooms) Udupila Rd; ✆ 041 225 4771; m 0777 557060; e riversidecabanas@gmail.com. This above-average budget lodge, set in compact but attractive creekside gardens 250m from the beach, has smart, stylish & well-priced rooms with treated concrete floor, darkwood furniture, queen-size bed, AC, fan & private balcony. TV & reasonably priced meals are available in the garden pavilion restaurant. *US$55 dbl B&B, dropping to US$35 out of season.* $$$

🏠 **Samantha Flora & Fauna** [548 E2] (16 rooms) m 0776 355068; e samanthahewawaduge@yahoo.com; w samanthaflorafauna.yolasite.com. Set in a densely wooded garden bordering a mangrove-lined creek & visited by plenty of monkeys, birds & other wildlife, this unique owner-managed lodge offers the choice of modern rooms with AC, fan, net & private balcony in a 3-storey block with a bit of a sea view & plenty of traffic noise, or more rustic & quieter stilted wooden huts with fan & net but no AC & a balcony looking into the canopy. Right opposite the beach & good value. *US$35/40 dbl with fan/AC, dropping to US$25/30 out of season.* $$

🏠 **Morning Star Guesthouse** [548 G3] (9 rooms) ✆ 041 225 4445; m 0774 582594; e anurasamarasooriya@gmail.com; w morningstarmirissa.com. Situated on the landward side of the main road, this family-run lodge has 4 standard rooms in the main building & 5 more stylish superior rooms set at the back of the property out of traffic earshot. The spacious rooms all have 4-poster bed with fitted net, AC, balcony/terrace, fridge & access to a shared TV lounge & sparkling swimming pool. A most agreeable set-up but a touch overpriced given its non-seafront location. *US$72/140 standard/ superior dbl B&B, dropping by around 20% out of season.* $$$

Shoestring

✳ 🏠 **Our World Guesthouse** [548 E2] (6 rooms) ✆ 041 490 6342; m 0717 685034; e mirissaourworld@gmail.com; w our-world-sri-lanka.de.tl. This super little family guesthouse, set in large compound next to a mangrove-lined creek just back from the main road, has been welcoming travellers to Mirissa since 1997. Simple but perfectly pleasant rooms have net, fan, small en-suite bathroom & private balcony with seating. It also does great juices & all-you-can-eat curry buffets. Fabulous value. *US$13/17 dbl/family room, dropping by 50% out of season.* $

✳ 🏠 **Hangover Hostel** [548 E2] (3 rooms, 6 dorms) m 0777 917916; e get-in-touch@hangoverhostels.com; w hangoverhostels.com. Friendly & sociable backpackers with 4-berth AC dorms made from converted shipping containers & equipped with private locker & light for each bed, as well as small dbl rooms with AC & fan. The lively ground-floor Hangover Café plays contemporary music & serves tasty burgers, salads, sandwiches & similar fare in the $$ range, while the chilled rooftop with ocean view is used for yoga classes by day & hosts regular movie nights. *US$50 dbl, US$13/16 pp bed in mixed/female-only dorm.* $$

🏠 **Ancient Tree Guesthouse** [548 F2] (6 rooms) m 0778 595501; e ancient.tree.mirissa@gmail.com; w ancienttreemirissa.wordpress.com. Set on a quiet green back road less than 5mins from the beach, this homestay-like set-up is operated by a friendly family who speak good English & serve delicious home-cooked curries. Simple rooms with net, fan, adequate bathroom & private balcony all have 1 dbl & 1 ¾ bed. Good value! *US$20–27 twin or dbl B&B, dropping to US$10–17 out of season.* $

🏠 **Amarasinghe Guesthouse** [548 F2] (10 rooms) ✆ 041 225 1204; m 0716 899787; e info@amarasingheguesthouse.com; w amarasingheguesthouse.com. Situated 500m inland of the beach, this family-run lodge stands in sprawling green grounds with labelled trees, an organic fruit & vegetable garden, & plenty of bird & monkey activity. The rooms are simple but clean & comfortable, & a fan-cooled terrace restaurant serves delicious curries, rotis & devilled dishes ($$), as well as good grilled seafood ($$$–$$$$). Good value. *US$14/22 dbl with fan/AC.* $

Beauty Mount Guesthouse [548 F2] (3 rooms) **m** 0778 548240; **e** mangalika.kalua@yahoo.com; **w** beautymountmirissa.com. The super-friendly & informal owner-managed guesthouse has neat rooms with fan, net & shared terrace set in a green family back-road compound. Delicious home-cooked curries by request. *US$30 dbl B&B, dropping to US$25 out of season.* **$$**

Hostel First [548 D2] (5 rooms, 3 dorms) Beachside Rd; **m** 0767 986788; **e** mirissa@hostelfirst.com; **w** hostelfirst.com. A joint Russian-Sri Lankan venture, this friendly backpackers has clean & spacious dbl or twin rooms with optional AC, as well as mixed & female-only 4-bed dorms, all with net & fan. The main common area is a large room with beanbags scattered around the floor. No formal meals, but there's a self-catering kitchen & barbecues most nights. *US$12 pp dorm*

bed, US$35 dbl (plus US$5 for AC), with off-season discounts of around 15%. **$$**

Pearl Resort [548 D1] (4 rooms) Sunanda Rd; **m** 0767 034970; **e** pearlresort@gmail.com. Situated in the town centre about 500m inland of the beach, this good-value family-run guesthouse has simple but clean rooms with fan, net, optional AC & balcony with seating. *US$13 dbl, plus US$7 for AC.* **$**

Club Mirissa [548 D2] (12 rooms) Beachside Rd; **m** 0767 677467. Set in large overgrown palm-studded gardens on the landward side of the beach road, this anachronistic guesthouse comprises a slightly rundown Dutch-style villa with a wide shady terrace restaurant. En-suite rooms all have fan, & cabanas have AC. Strong on character but unsuited to fussy travellers. *From US$20 dbl.* **$**

✕ Where to eat and drink

✳ ✕ **Secret Beach Bar** [548 B2] **m** 0716 430898; ⊕ 08.00–19.00. One of the loveliest beaches in Sri Lanka is the private domain of this aptly named restaurant/bar set on a secluded bay on the rocky headland that divides Mirissa's beach from the harbour. Set below massive large-leafed trees, the small beach incorporates a natural rock pool that offers safe swimming, & there's also good snorkelling offshore (*gear rental US$3.35/2hrs*). The location rather than the food is the main attraction, but it can rustle up a varied menu of pizzas, fresh seafood, pasta & devilled dishes in the **$$$** range, & also serves cold beers & cocktails to a backdrop of contemporary music. It lies 2km from the town centre & 1km from the harbour following a narrow track running south from next to Mirissa Watersports. If you don't feel like walking, tuktuks can get to within about 100m of it.

✳ ✕ **Little Tuna** [548 E2] **m** 0772 806877, 0779 018051; **f** littletunamirissa; ⊕ 11.00–22.30. Fabulous little restaurant in hammock-draped garden with seating on scatter cushions in 2 zen fan-cooled pavilions whose walls are hung with black-&-white photos of local street scenes & temples. Sushi (fish or vegetarian) is the speciality,

with prices for 6 pieces nudging into the **$$$** range, & it also serves salads, wine, beer, coffee & homemade cakes.

✕ **Demwini Roti Shop** [548 E2] **m** 0715 162604; **w** dewminirotishop.wordpress.com; ⊕ 08.30–22.00. This family-run terrace restaurant has become something of a Mirissa institution since it opened in 2009, & the sweet & savoury rotis on which it built its reputation stand out for the generous & tasty fillings. Also on the menu are rice dishes & kottu roti. Great value. **$**

✕ **Margherita Italiano** [548 D1] **m** 0728 017274; **f**; ⊕ 10.00–23.00. This stylish little Italian eatery with foreign-trained chef, AC interior & terrace seating serves excellent & sensibly priced pizza, pasta, risotto, grilled seafood & chicken dishes. Shame about the uninspiring high-street location 500m from the nearest beach. **$$$**

✕ **Papa Mango** [548 F3] **m** 0777 726546; **f** papamangomirissasl; ⊕ 09.00–23.00. Laid-back beach bar & restaurant, all sand underfoot & palms swaying overhead, serving seafood-dominated & vegetarian mains (**$$$**) & tapas (**$$**). Also has a full bar, chilled music, & occasional DJ nights.

Other practicalities There is no bank but a Commercial Bank ATM [548 D1] stands on the main road next to Margherita Italiano. For grocery and liquor shops, or full banking facilities, catch a tuktuk to Weligama. The widely praised Secret

Roof Spa [548 F2] (m *0773 294332;* w *secretrootspa.com*) 200m inland of and well signposted from the main road, is a lovely family-run set-up offering massages and Ayuverdic treatments for around US$20.

What to see and do Whale watching aside, Mirissa's main attraction is its glorious 1.5km-long beach, which is usually cited as being safe for swimming due to its gradual shelf, though rip tides can be genuinely dangerous at times, so if in any doubt, ask local advice before wading beyond waist depth. For a change of scene and some fine offshore snorkelling, take a stroll out to the isolated Secret Beach Bar (page 550), which has a stunning intimate beach location and snorkelling gear to rent. Very different but also worth checking out is the Mirissa Dance House [548 D2] (m *0702 713734;* ; *entrance US$10 pp*), which puts on a performance of traditional devil dancing every Monday at 21.00.

Whale-watching trips Mirissa is one of the best places in the world to see the blue whale, the world's largest living creature, thanks to the larger number of it and other cetaceans that inhabit or migrate along the deep plankton-rich waters a few kilometres offshore. At least a dozen operators now run daily whale-watching cruises leaving at 06.00–07.00 from Mirissa's fishing harbour, which lies on the east side of Weligama Bay at the base of the headland dividing it from Mirissa beach. Rates with the better operators start at around US$40–50, but there are also several cheaper and less reputable operators offering trips from half that price. Some operators use small boats, others larger two-storey ships, and counter-intuitively perhaps the latter is generally the better option, as the additional altitude allows for better views of semi-submerged creatures. Although blue whales are the main attraction, you might well see several other species of cetacean, from massive fin whales to acrobatic spinner dolphins, as well as marine turtle and spectacular flying fish. Be aware that whale watching, like much wildlife viewing, can be a hit-and-miss thing. This is dependent to some extent on season – the best months are November–April, with sightings peaking over December–January and April, while the worst are May and June – but also on weather, and plain old luck of the draw. Some days a return outing of 3–4 hours will yield several good sightings, while other days you might be out until late afternoon without hitting the jackpot. We've had mixed feedback about the environmental impact of the activity in Mirissa, and certainly it seems like many operators pay scant regard to international criteria for responsible whale watching, as set by the Whale and Dolphin Conservation Society (w *uk.whales.org*), or for that matter to standard maritime safety guidelines, with boats being crammed to tipping point, and chasing or approaching whales too closely. The companies listed below are the pick of a mixed bunch.

Mirissa Watersports [548 C2] m 0773 597731; e whalewatching@mirissawatersports.lk; w mirissawatersports.lk
Raja and the Whales [548 C2] m 0713 331811, 0776 953452; e rajaandthewhales@gmail.com; w rajaandthewhales.com

Whale Watching Club [548 C1] m 0771 287100; e whalewatchingclubmirissa@gmail.com; w whalewatchingclub.com

WELIGAMA Fringing the beautiful northwest shore of the eponymous bay, Weligama (population 72,000) amply lives up to its name (literally 'Sand Village'), even if its long golden beach is a more reliable venue for surfing than for swimming. Its most prominent marine feature, tiny Taprobane Island, now a luxury boutique hotel, is

18

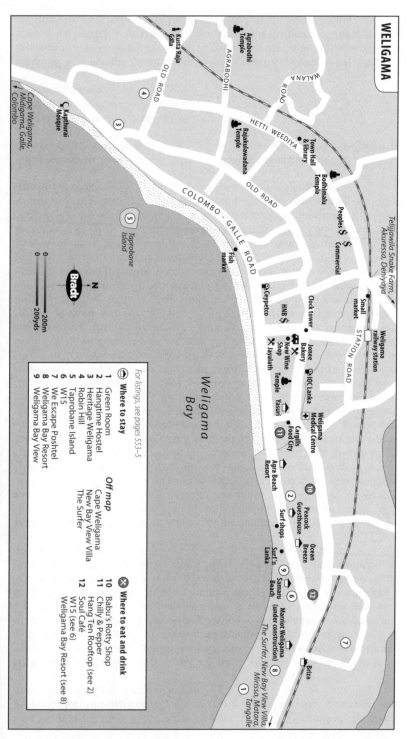

WELIGAMA

Weligama Bay

Bradt

N

0 ————— 200m
0 ————— 200yds

Cape Weligama,
Midigama, Galle,
Colombo

Kapthurai
Mosque

Kusta Raja
Gala

Agrabodhi
Temple

Bodhimalu
Temple

Town Hall
& library

Rajakulawadana
Temple

Peoples $
Commercial $

Fish
market

Taprobane
Island

COLOMBO - GALLE ROAD

AGRABODHI ROAD

OLD ROAD

HETTI WEEDIYA

WALANA ROAD

OLD ROAD

Telijjawila Snake Farm,
Akuressa, Deniyaya

Weligama
railway station

STATION ROAD

Small
market

Clock tower

Jonee
Bakery

IOC Lanka

HNB $

Geppetto

New Wine
Shop

Temple

Yasuri

Jayalath

Cargills
Food City

Weligama
Medical Centre

Agra Beach
Resort

Peacock
Guesthouse

Ocean
Breeze

Surf shops

Surf'n
Lanka

Samaru
Beach

Mariot Weligama
(under construction)

Briza

The Surfer, New Bay Villa,
Mirissa, Matara,
Tangalle

For listings, see pages 553–5

Where to stay
1 Green Room
2 Hangtime Hostel
3 Heritage Weligama
4 Robin Hill
5 Taprobane Island
6 W15
7 We Escape Poshtel
8 Weligama Bay Resort
9 Weligama Bay View

Off map
Cape Weligama
New Bay View Villa
The Surfer

Where to eat and drink
10 Babu's Rotty Shop
11 Chilly & Pepper
12 Hang Ten Rooftop (see 2)
Soul Café
W15 (see 6)
Weligama Bay Resort (see 8)

hotel, is flanked by a stretch of beach where local fishing vessels are pulled ashore between working excursions. Only 500m inland, carved into an isolated boulder, Kusta Raja Galla is a finely executed 3m-high engraved human figure of mysterious but ancient progeny. But the town's main tourist attraction is its beach, which offers ideal conditions for beginner surfers and is lined with operators offering surfing lessons, board hire and the like. A block or two inland, the town centre – hemmed in to the north by the last U-bend in the Polwatta River before it pours into the bay's northeast shore – is larger and more workaday than the leisure-oriented beachfront might lead you to expect. Weligama is known as a centre of beeralu lacemaking.

Getting there and away
Weligama lies on the main coastal road to Matara about 5km west of Mirissa and 27km east of Galle. Regular buses connect Galle, Mirissa, Matara and other coastal towns to Weligama, whose bus station has a bang central location next to the clock tower. All trains between Colombo/Galle and Matara (around ten daily in either direction) stop at Weligama, whose railway station is centrally located about 400m inland of the beach.

Where to stay
Map, opposite, unless otherwise stated

Weligama is serviced by some fine boutique properties in the middle to upper price ranges. There are also a couple of good budget and shoestring options, but fewer than in Midigama or Mirissa.

Exclusive

Cape Weligama [map, page 546] (40 rooms) 011 774 5730; e reservations@resplendentceylon.com; w resplendentceylon.com/capeweligama. One of the country's most sumptuous & prestigious properties, this resort sprawls across 5ha of indigenous vegetation & manicured gardens on a dramatic headland 2km southwest of Weligama. The apartment-like villas rank among the largest rooms in Sri Lanka with wood & soft fabric furnishings, flatscreen TV in both sitting & bed rooms, unobtrusive AC, large private balcony & massive bathrooms with tub & shower. Set below the cliffs are 2 semi-private beaches that usually offer safe swimming & a sport & dive centre that arranges everything from surfing & snorkelling in the immediate vicinity to whale-watching & diving trips further afield. There are also 2 public swimming pools, notably the 60m-long crescent-shaped infinity 'moon pool' affording a 270° view, while another 12 are split between the villa clusters. The seafood in particular is outstanding, as is the wine list. Unadulterated luxury, lots of privacy, making it ideal for a last few days of R&R on a tour of Sri Lanka. *From US$666 dbl FB inc drinks from the minibar & 1 activity daily.* **$$$$$+**

Taprobane Island (5 rooms) 091 438 0275; e info@thesunhouse.com; w taprobaneisland.com. This scrub-covered islet opposite the Heritage Weligama houses an open-sided 5-bedroom colonial villa once lived in by American writer Paul Bowles. It is rented out in its entirety. *US$1,000–2,200 depending on season, inc private chef & 4 other staff.* **$$$$$+**

Upmarket

Weligama Bay Resort (24 rooms) 041 225 3920; m 0773 814940; e info@weligamabayresort.com; w weligamabayresort.com. This attractive boutique resort has well-maintained gardens with swimming pool, spa & cosmopolitan seafood & curry-dominated restaurant (**$$$$**) in a beachfront location whose inherent perfection in marred only by its close proximity to the soon-to-open Marriott. Spacious rooms & suites have wooden floor & shutters, earthy geometric wall hangings & fabrics, AC, fan, TV, minibar, safe & sea-facing terrace. Check the website for special offers. *From US$284 dbl B&B, dropping by 30% out of season.* **$$$$$**

W15 (10 rooms) 041 225 4422; e reservations@w15.lk; w w15.lk. All clean architectural lines & bold red fabrics offset by green lawns running down to a surf-washed beach, this imaginatively designed new resort combines a great location with a young feel. The trendy music, funky beach restaurant & open-to-all infinity pool is dominated over w/ends by local day trippers in numbers that undermine the exclusivity one might expect of a self-proclaimed '10-room luxury boutique hotel'. Cheerfully decorated rooms all have king-size bed, AC, fan, TV, minibar, tea/coffee, safe & balcony/terrace, not all with ocean view. *From US$235/315 B&B dbl without/with ocean view.* **$$$$**

Moderate

✳ 🏠 **Robin Hill** (3 suites) **m** 0714 174714; **e** info@robinhill.lk; **w** robinhill.lk. Set in a century-old villa whose original Dutch-style features have been well preserved, this charming set-up is a welter of wooden furniture & tall classical columns offset by frivolous touches such as busts sprouting plants. It is famed for its flavourful curries, which are made from home-grown organic ingredients & slow-cooked on an open cinnamon-wood fire. The well-wooded garden is also a treat. Advance reservation essential. *US$125 dbl HB, dropping by 40% out of season.* **$$$$**

🏠 **Heritage Weligama** (10 rooms) 🞁 041 521 0013; **m** 0766 802922; **e** heritage.weligama@ chcresthouses.com; **w** chcresthouses.com/ weligama. Situated right opposite the main beach & Taprobane Island, this former government resthouse comprises a grand & agreeably old-fashioned colonnaded colonial building set in large gardens fringed to the back by a wall of jungle. The massive rooms have tiled floors, pastel orange walls hung with black-&-white photos, AC, TV, minibar & tall glass windows to let in the light, while a licensed terrace restaurant serves well-priced local meals. Decent value in its uncontrived retro way. *US$59/70 sgl/dbl B&B, with slight low-season discounts.* **$$$**

🏠 **We Escape Poshtel** (5 rooms, 6 dorms) 🞁 041 493 8520; **m** 0773 510147; **e** info@ mosvold.lk; **w** mosvoldhotels.com/weescape. Neither chalk nor cheese, or both perhaps depending on your viewpoint, this luxury hostel is set in a gracious mid-19th-century colonial villa decorated with retro posters & period furniture, & surrounded by lovely lush gardens on the landward side of the railway track at the east end of Weligama. The AC private rooms look like refugees from a boutique hotel & the 6- & 8-bed dorms are almost as swanky, coming with AC, net, modern bathroom & 1 cupboard per bed. A colourful

restaurant with TV & contemporary music serves full meals mostly using ingredients grown on the property. It also has a decent-sized swimming pool & offers yoga classes & surfing lessons. It'd be a stretch to call it good value, but it's an appealing set-up & might be a perfect fit for sociable single travellers seeking like-minded company but not a party atmosphere. *US$100–150 dbl depending on size & facilities, US$35 pp dorm bed, plus US$7.50 b/fast & US$10/15 lunch/dinner.* **$$$$**

Budget

✳ 🏠 **The Surfer** [map, page 546] (12 rooms) **m** 0773 926614; **e** info@thesurferweligama. com; 📘 pg/Thesurferweligama. Situated less than 100m from the beach off the Mirissa Rd 1km east of central Weligama, this glistening-white 4-storey surfer-oriented lodge has a small garden dominated by a deep swimming pool & it also offers surfboard hire, surfing lessons & yoga packages. Bright clean rooms have fan, net & optional AC, while the lively rooftop restaurant/bar offers the winning combination of affordable Western & local meals (**$$$**), friendly staff, pleasing décor & a fabulous view over the beach. Good value, especially as there's no seasonal price hike. *US$35/50 dbl B&B with fan/AC.* **$$**

🏠 **Weligama Bay View** (26 rooms) 🞁 041 225 1199; **e** info@bayviewlk.com; **w** bayviewlk.com. This unpretentious hotel stands in small but shady beachfront gardens with a terrace restaurant & plenty of seating. Smallish tiled rooms come with twin or queen-size bed with fitted net, AC, fan & balcony with part or full sea view. Good value, especially out of season. *US$52/60 sgl/dbl B&B, dropping by 50% out of season.* **$$$**

🏠 **New Bay View Villa** [map, page 546] (9 rooms) 🞁 041 521 0372; **m** 0776 405978; **e** sureshkumara2005@yahoo.com; **w** newbayviewvilla.com. Perched on the southwest corner of Weligama Bay, this isolated owner-managed seafront hotel has clean & comfortable rooms with fan, net, fridge, optional AC & balcony, some with sea view. Not a bargain but sensibly priced given the stunning clifftop location overlooking a sandy beach. *US$50/75 dbl with fan/AC, dropping by 20% out of season.* **$$$**

🏠 **Green Room** (5 rooms) **m** 0771 119896; **e** thegreenroomsinfo@gmail.com; **w** thegreenroomssrilanka.com. Chilled British-run surfers' hang-out with a strong environmental

& community ethos offering highly regarded & reasonably priced surfing & yoga packages inclusive of accommodation. Taken in isolation, the cosy stilted wood cabins with fan, balcony but no AC or hot water seem quite pricey in season but good value at other times. *GB£57.50 dbl B&B Sep–Apr, dropping by 50% May–Aug.* **$$$**

Shoestring
* 🏠 **Hangtime Hostel** (4 rooms, 4 dorms) m 0765 258933/573396; e hangtimehostel@ gmail.com; w hangtimehostel.com. This justifiably popular new Australian-owned 3-storey hostel has brightly painted ground-floor en-suite rooms with ¾ or dbl beds made out of old fishing boats, net, fan, private balcony with hammock & optional AC, as well as 6-bed dorms with individual fan & reading light, net & locker, all capped by the amiable Hang Ten Rooftop (see below). *US$30/37 dbl with fan/AC, US$10/12 pp dorm bed in a mixed/female dorm.* **$$**

✖ Where to eat and drink   *Map, page 552*

There are surprisingly few standalone restaurants in Weligama but most of the hotels serve food, with W15 and Weligama Bay Resort being the obvious standouts for something close to fine dining.

✖ **Hang Ten Rooftop**   m 0765 258933; w hangtimehostel.com; kitchen ⏰ 07.30–11.00 & 12.30–15.00 daily & 18.00–21.00 exc Mon. Perched atop the Hangtime Hostel, this friendly backpackers' & surfers' haunt offers a fine view to the beach & an imaginative continent-hopping menu (lower **$$$** range). Mon is open-mic night & Fri pizza night. It's unlicensed but you're welcome to bring your own booze.
✖ **Soul Café**   m 0775 294965; 🇫 soulcafeweligama; ⏰ 09.00–22.00. Run by a young Russian couple, this hip new café dishes up great b/fasts, filled pittas & stews (**$$**) & does the best evening seafood barbecue (**$$$**) in town. Good music & plenty of options for vegetarian & health-conscious travellers.
✖ **Babu's Rotty Shop**   m 0772 600475; ⏰ 08.00–23.30. An unwavering diet of reggae music accompanies the more varied selection of curries & sweet or savoury filled rotis (**$$**) & seafood grills (**$$$**) on offer at this relaxed local eatery with shady terrace seating.
✖ **Chilly & Pepper**   ⏰ 06.00–midnight. Good coffee, b/fasts, seafood & curries in a fan-cooled modern interior or pavement terrace. Good value. **$$**

Other practicalities   The most useful ATM is at the Commercial Bank, which is tucked away in the old town centre 300m inland of the beach and 400m west of the railway station. For groceries, there's a well-stocked Cargills Food City a block inland and 300m east of the bus station. The best-stocked liquor outlet is the New Wine Shop adjacent to the bus station.

What to see and do

Surfing and diving   The main beach activity is surfing, which can be undertaken all year through, though conditions tend to be best between November and February. Weligama is particularly well suited to beginners, as no dangerous underwater rocks lurk in the sandy-bottomed bay. There are three main breaks, all within short paddling distance of each other, and waves generally reach a height of around 1.5m, though they can be double that at times. More experienced surfers will find more challenging conditions at Midigama. At least half a dozen surf schools are clustered along the breach between W15 and Hangtime Hostel, all of them offering full courses, one-off lessons (*around US$14*) and board rental (*from US$2/hr*). Surf'n Lanka (m *0776 056196*; e *manjubandarage@yahoo.com*; w *surfnlanka.com*) has a good reputation and offers full packages including accommodation, as does The Surfer 1km out of town (see opposite). Diving excursions to the superb Yala Rock, 20 minutes offshore, and several other sites close to Weligama Bay can be arranged through Weligama Bay Dive Centre [map, page 546] (✆ *041 225 0799;* **m** *0777 850372;* **e** *chamindakh@sltnet.lk;* **w** *scubadivingweligama.com*), 1km out of town off the Midigama Road.

Taprobane Island [map, page 552] Formerly known as Gal Duwa (Rock Island), the small (0.4ha) rocky outcrop that dominates the west side of Weligama Bay is also more intriguingly named Yakinige Duwa (She-Devil's Island), presumably in reference to its former role as a dumping ground for dangerous cobras. The island was bought in 1925 by the Count de Mauny Talvande, a self-titled French eccentric who renamed it Taprobane (the ancient Greek name for Sri Lanka) and built a villa that later served as the home of US writer Paul Bowles and is now a boutique villa rentable by the night. Despite being a prominent landmark situated within wading distance of the shore opposite the Heritage Weligama, the island is closed to casual visitors.

Kusta Raja Galla [map, page 552] Situated 500m along a road running inland from next to the Heritage Weligama, the Kusta Raja Galla (literally 'Leper King Rock') is a 3m-tall statue of the Bodhisattva Avalokiteshvara engraved into a free-standing granite boulder. Right hand posed in the abhaya mudra (symbolising fearlessness), the bodhisattva is draped in an elegant robe and adorned with an unusually elaborate headdress in what is regarded as one of the finest sculptures dating to the period between the 7th and 9th centuries, when Mahayana Buddhism had its strongest hold on Sri Lanka. The progeny of this isolated masterpiece is a mystery. Its name alludes to a local tradition that it was built by a king whose long-standing leprosy-like condition was cured by a regime of coconut pulp and water prescribed by a foreign Mahayana monk or physician. More likely perhaps it is a finely hewn relict of the original Agrabodhi Temple, which was founded by Devanampiya Tissa, who planted one of the first offshoots of Jaya Sri Maha Bodhi here, then destroyed by the Portuguese in the 16th century, and revived – only 250m to the sculpture's north – under King Rajadhi Rajasinha of Kandy.

Telijjawila Snake Farm [map, page 488] (✆ *041 341 1876;* **m** *0777 401752;* ⏱ *06.00–17.00; entrance US$5.50 pp*) Menacing Indian cobras in all their hooded and masked glory, the endemic Sri Lanka krait and the massive rock python are highlights of this unusual farm, which lies 15km north of Weligama and has been in the same family of Ayuverdic physicians and snake-handlers for a century. The snakes are caged or boxed in the owner's garage but can be brought out into the open for visitors to view, photograph and (in the case of non-venomous specimens) handle. Our understanding is that most inmates were problem snakes rescued from local houses and farms, and are only retained for a month or two as a source of life-saving antivenins before being released at a suitably wild location. Certainly, the individuals we saw seemed to be in good health, despite being confined to boxes and cages, and to be handled with sensitivity by a genuine enthusiast. To get here, drive northeast out of Weligama for 10km to Telijjawila (the junction village with the main road from Matara to Akuressa) then continue towards Akuressa for another 1km before turning left on to the Henegama Road. The signposted snake farm stands on the right about 3km down this road. A return tuktuk from Weligama or Mirissa should cost around US$8.

MIDIGAMA Reputedly named after a vineyard that once grew in the area, Midigama (literally 'Grape Village') is the best spot around Weligama Bay for intermediate and experienced surfers. Most of its breaks are rideable all year through, but the best conditions are during the high season, from December to March, when the surf tends to be quieter than it is at Weligama. The well-known Ram's Right, situated in front of the eponymous guesthouse, is a fast right break that offers intermediate to advanced surfers a 400m ride on waves that rise up to 2m in season above a shallow reef. About 300m to its west, Lazy Left is a long left with an easy paddle out making it well suited to beginners. Other good lesser-known breaks are Plantations and Coconuts, about 500m to the east, and Kabalana at Ahungama 5km back towards Galle.

Getting there and away Midigama straddles the main coastal road to Matara 22km east of Galle and 5km west of Weligama. Any bus headed along the coastal road between Galle and Weligama can drop you here. It also has its own railway station, which is serviced by around five stopping trains daily in either direction between Colombo/Galle and Matara.

Where to stay *Map, page 546*
Accommodation in Midigama tends to be aimed at budget-conscious surfers, and is generally good value. For something more commodious, head to Weligama or Mirissa.

Moderate
⌂ **Villa Naomi** (5 rooms) m 0779 054142; e chameera@dream.com; w villanaomibeach. com. Boasting a lovely quiet beachfront location 400m south of the main road, this elegant villa has a wide colonnaded terrace overlooking the palm-shaded grounds, a wooden deck closer to the surf & a grand interior decorated with vintage furniture. The 4 upstairs rooms have AC, fan, 4-poster bed & private balcony with a sea view. There's a more basic ground-floor room with fan only. *US$40/80 B&B dbl with fan/AC.* **$$$**

Budget
✳ ⌂ **Cheeky Monkey** (12 rooms) m 0719 248686; e cheekymonkeymidi@gmail.com. Situated on the landward side of the main road directly opposite the main surfing beach, this popular backpacker-oriented lodge is moulded in the cast of its dynamic & helpful owner-manager. It incorporates Midigama's best surf shop, a breezy rooftop restaurant serving burgers, pasta & other simple fare (**$$**), & spacious, brightly decorated rooms with fan, AC & balcony. *US$40/45 B&B dbl with fan/AC, dropping by 50% out of season.* **$$**
⌂ **Sun & Soul** (4 rooms) m 0771 689104; e sun.soul.midi@gmail.com; w sunandsoulsl. com. Set back from the main road in a grassy garden opposite the beach, this funky Czech-owned & -managed place has attractive

warehouse-style AC rooms with treated concrete floors & walls, 4-poster bed with fitted net, minibar, private balcony & modern bathrooms. The attached garden café serves tasty & well-priced salads, filled pancakes, paninis & b/fasts (**$$**), but it's a bit of a 1-person show, so service slackens when it's busy. Good value. *US$45–55 dbl depending on room size & whether it has garden or ocean view.* **$$**
⌂ **Plantation Surf Inn** (5 rooms) m 0776 438912; w plantationsurfinn.com. This clean & friendly family-run guesthouse only 100m from the beach stands in lush tropical gardens regularly visited by monkeys. Well-ventilated & brightly painted rooms have a fan & fitted nets but no AC. An excellent garden restaurant is attached. Great value. *US$16/24 sgl/dbl with outside bathroom, US$20/30 en suite, with 15% low-season discount; all rates B&B.* **$$**

Shoestring
⌂ **Kusuma's Lazy Left** (5 rooms) m 0776 891215; e sugi.rest@yahoo.com. Set in a fenced beachfront compound overlooking the surf break for which it is named, this friendly owner-managed cheapie has clean rooms with fitted net, fan but no AC, shared balcony & garden with hammocks. Good seafood too. *US$27 dbl, dropping by 40% out of season.* **$$**
⌂ **Ram's Surfing Beach** (15 rooms) ☎041 225 2639; e ramssurfingbeach@gmail.com.

18

This Midigama institution boasts an unbeatable location in sleepy palm-shaded beachfront grounds hung with hammocks & close to all the main surfing breaks. It's a perennially popular surfers' hang-out but the rooms with fitted net & fan are starting to look a bit rundown. *US$27 dbl with 50% discount out of season.* **$$**

✶ Where to eat and drink *Map, page 546*

The standout eateries are the garden café at Sun & Soul and the rooftop restaurant at Cheeky Monkey. For tasty local fare, Neel Place opposite Ram's Surfing Beach serves delicious curries (**$**) and doubles as the village's best grocery store.

Other practicalities For banks and most shopping requirements, you'll need to catch a tuktuk through to Weligama. The well-run Baba's Surfing Shop, on the ground floor of Cheeky Monkey, has more than 150 surfboards of all sizes available to rent at US$7 a day.

Galle and Surrounds

The port of Galle, on the far southwest coast of Sri Lanka, has been a dominant force in the international cinnamon trade since ancient times. Now a metropolis of 100,000 inhabitants, it doubles as the administrative capital of Southern Province and as a thriving economic hub buoyed by a booming tourist industry and active modern port. The city centre stands on the northwest shore of a heart-shaped bay flanked to the east by the wooded Rumassala Cliffs and to the west by a partially reclaimed peninsula that houses the city's historic showpiece. This is Galle Fort, a UNESCO World Heritage Site founded by the Portuguese in the 16th century and expanded to cover 36ha under the Dutch and British. The best-preserved colonial sea fortress in all of Asia, Galle Fort encloses a timeworn colonial town centre whose compact grid of streets is lined with historic churches and museums, old government buildings and warehouses, and an ever-growing number of charming colonial homesteads restored as period-style boutique hotels and trendy modern bistros.

Galle Fort, the focal point of this chapter, is a fascinating and enjoyable place to explore, whether you base yourself here for a couple of nights, or just visit as a day trip (easily done by tuktuk or as a formal excursion from any beach resort on the coast between Bentota and Matara). But the chapter also covers a number of nearby attractions that are easily visited as a day trip from Galle, or could in some cases be used as an alternative base for exploring it. On the east coast, there is the legendary Jungle Beach on the suburban Rumassala Peninsula, the vibey satellite beach resort of Unawatuna, and a string of low-key beach resorts running along the Matara Road to Koggala, site of an attractive eponymous lake, a worthwhile sea turtle project, and the unexpectedly rewarding Martin Wickramasinghe Folk Museum. More far-flung inland attractions covered in this chapter include the Yatagala Temple, Handunugoda Tea Museum, Kottawa Arboretum and Hiyare Reservoir.

HISTORY

Galle harbour has been an international trade entrepôt for millennia. Indeed, it may well have become entrenched as an export centre as early as 2000bc, when cinnamon, a crop that originates from Sri Lanka, was first imported to ancient Egypt. Some scholars also believe Galle to be synonymous with the Old Testament port of Tarshish, a great Eastern emporium from where merchant ships from Tyre, Phoenicia and King Solomon's Jerusalem returned home laden with precious metals, spices and peacocks, as well as being the refuge to where Jonah was bound before his ship capsized in a storm and he was swallowed by a giant fish. In 1344, Galle was visited by Ibn Battuta, who referred to it as Qali and observed Moorish vessels in the harbour. Another renowned Medieval visitor to Galle was Zheng He, who arrived here in 1409 and erected a trilingual stone tablet (inscribed in Chinese, Tamil and Persian) that was rediscovered in 1911 and is now housed in the National Museum in Colombo.

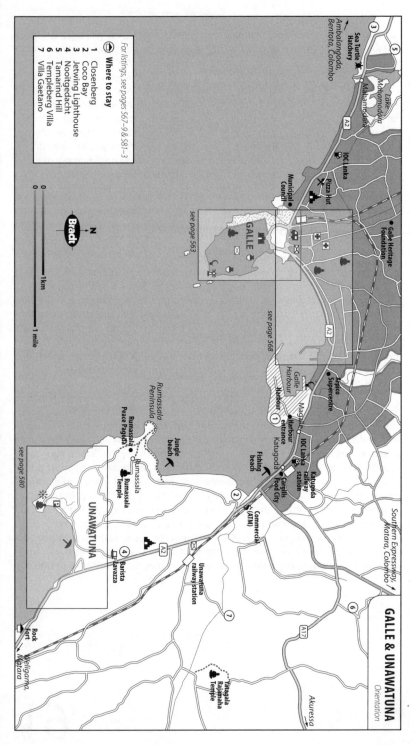

see page 563

see page 568

see page 580

For listings, see pages 567–9 & 581–3

Where to stay
1 Closenberg
2 Coco Bay
3 Jetwing Lighthouse
4 Nooitgedacht
5 Tamarind Hill
6 Templeberg Villa
7 Villa Gaetano

N

Bradt

0 ————————— 1km
0 ————————— 1 mile

Sea Turtle
Hatchery

Ambalangoda,
Bentota, Colombo

Lake
Mahamodara

Mahamodara

IOC Lanka

Municipal
Council

Pizza Hut

Galle Heritage
Foundation

GALLE

Galle
Harbour

Harbour
entrance

Katugoda

Magalle

IOC Lanka

Harbour
entrance

Alpico
Supercentre

Katugoda
railway
station

Cargills
Food City

Fishing
beach

Rumassala
Peninsula

Rumassala
Peace Pagoda

Rumassala
Temple

Jungle
beach

UNAWATUNA

Commercial
(ATM)

Barista
Lavazza

Unawatuna
railway station

Rock
Fort

Weligama,
Matara

Yatagala
Rajamaha
Temple

Akuressa

Southern Expressway,
Matara, Colombo

GALLE & UNAWATUNA
Orientation

A2
A2
A17

3
5
6
7
2
1
4

Medieval Galle was an entrenched settlement in the lowland territory of the Sinhalese kings and it would remain so for most of the 16th century, despite an accidental Portuguese landing in 1505 after one of their ships was blown off course *en route* to the 'money islands' of the Maldives. The modern rise of Galle started in 1588 when the Portuguese relocated there following an attack on their Colombo fort by King Rajasinha I of Sitawaka. The new arrivals constructed the small Fortress of Santa Cruz de Galle out of palm trees and mud on the western promontory of the bay, later extending it with a wall and watchtowers, three bastions, and a fortalice to guard the harbour. From here, the Portuguese spread their influence in the southern littoral and throughout the island by destroying many Buddhist temples and imposing Christianity on the locals. Common Sri Lankan family names such as Silva, Pereira and Fernando are a legacy of this era.

By the 1630s, Galle Fort held command over 280-plus villages in the fertile cinnamon lands of the southwest. The desire to break this Portuguese monopoly led to the Dutch–Kandyan alliance of 1638. Galle fell in March 1640, following a four-day naval bombardment and prolonged land assault from Rumassala Hill that claimed 70 Portuguese and hundreds of Dutch lives. The Dutch consolidated their presence in Galle by extending the original Portuguese fort to its present dimensions, adding ramparts and more bastions around the edges, and churches, houses and streets within the walls, together with a complex network of underground channels which enabled the sea to flush away the sewage. Under the Dutch, Galle remained the main centre of maritime trade out of the southwest. Today, many Dutch-era buildings still stand in and around Galle, while other relics of the era include a style of formal furniture adapted to tropical living, and the term 'burgher' to refer to the offspring of miscegenation.

Galle flourished for some years after the Dutch conceded it to the British in 1796, but fell into decline over the course of the 19th century. Ironically, this descent into relative obscurity protected the roads and timeworn buildings of Galle Fort from the attention of 20th-century developers, allowing it to retain the historic flavour that led not only to its inscription by UNESCO in 1988, but also to its recent emergence as a shabby-chic tourist destination steeped in colonial history.

GETTING THERE AND AWAY

BY ROAD Galle lies 115km from Colombo along the coastal road through Bentota and Hikkaduwa, but these days most self-drivers and many direct buses use the

Southern Expressway, a multi-lane toll road that opened in 2012 and is about 15km longer but might take half as long to drive (at a push, 1 hour to Galle from the northern entrance to the highway, at Kottawa, but there from the centre of Colombo can take another hour). The Southern Expressway also connects to the multi-lane Colombo–Katunayake Expressway, meaning that you can now travel between Galle and Bandaranaike International Airport, 30km north of central Colombo, in around 2 hours.

Public transport is plentiful, with frequent intercity air-conditioned buses to Galle leaving Maharagama station in southern Colombo every 15–20 minutes. There are also plenty of buses along the coastal route if you are coming from Aluthgama, Bentota, Hikkaduwa or elsewhere between Colombo and Galle. Galle lies 80km (2 hours) from Tangalle via Mirissa (36km/45 minutes) and Matara (45km/1 hour) along a coastal road or expressway covered by plenty of buses. It's about 85km (2 hours) from Deniyaya, the most popular base for exploring Sinharaja, though you may need to change buses at Akuressa. Further afield, heading to Kandy or most destinations further north, you'd be best off travelling through Colombo.

BY RAIL Ten express and commuter trains connect Colombo to Galle daily, typically taking up to 3 hours and in most cases continuing on to Matara, the terminus of the southern railway. The line is popular with visitors since it runs south along the western coast, beside the Indian Ocean, and serves all the main beach resorts between Colombo and Matara. For greater comfort, Rajadhani Express (w *rajadhani.lk*) and ExpoRail (w *exporail.lk*) also operate daily services in either direction between Colombo and Galle. However, both services were suspended, hopefully on a temporary basis, in late 2017. For contact details, see the general section on train travel on pages 47–50.

GETTING AROUND

Galle Fort is only 10 minutes' walk from the railway and bus stations, and is easy to explore on foot. However, tuktuks are available at the railway and bus stations – and pretty much anywhere else in and around the city – for driving to the hotels or for out-of-town excursions to the likes of Unawatuna.

GALLE Fort
For listings, see pages 564–6 & 569–71

⌂ **Where to stay**

1	62 Pedlar Guesthouse	C5	7	Fort Bliss	C6
2	Albert Fort Boutique	C6	8	Fort Dew Guesthouse	B5
3	Amangalla	C4	9	Fort Inn	C5
4	Beach Haven	C6	10	Fort Printers	C5
5	Deco on 44	B5	11	Galle Fort Hostel	C6
6	Fort Bazaar	C5	12	Galle Fort Hotel	C5

13	Mango House	C5
14	Pedlars Inn Hostel	C6
15	Seagreen Guesthouse	B4
16	Sunset Fort	B4
17	Taru Villa Rampart St	B4
18	Villa Razi	B5

✖ **Where to eat and drink**

19	The Blockhouse	C6	28	Mama's Galle Fort	C6
20	Café Punto	C5	29	Mansion Café	D5
21	Chambers	C5	30	National Tea Room	B3
22	Crêpe-ology	D5	31	Original Mama's Rooftop	D6
23	Elita	B4	32	Original Rocket Burger	D5
24	Fortaleza	C5	33	Pedlars Corner Café	B5
25	Heritage Café	C5	34	Pedlars Inn Café	B5
26	Indian Hut	C6	35	Poonie's Kitchen	B5
27	Lucky Fort	B5			

36	Rampart	B6
37	Serendipity Arts Café	D6
38	*in Old Dutch Hospital:*	
	Cannon Bar & Grill	D5
	Hammock Café	D5
	A Minute by Tuktuk	D5

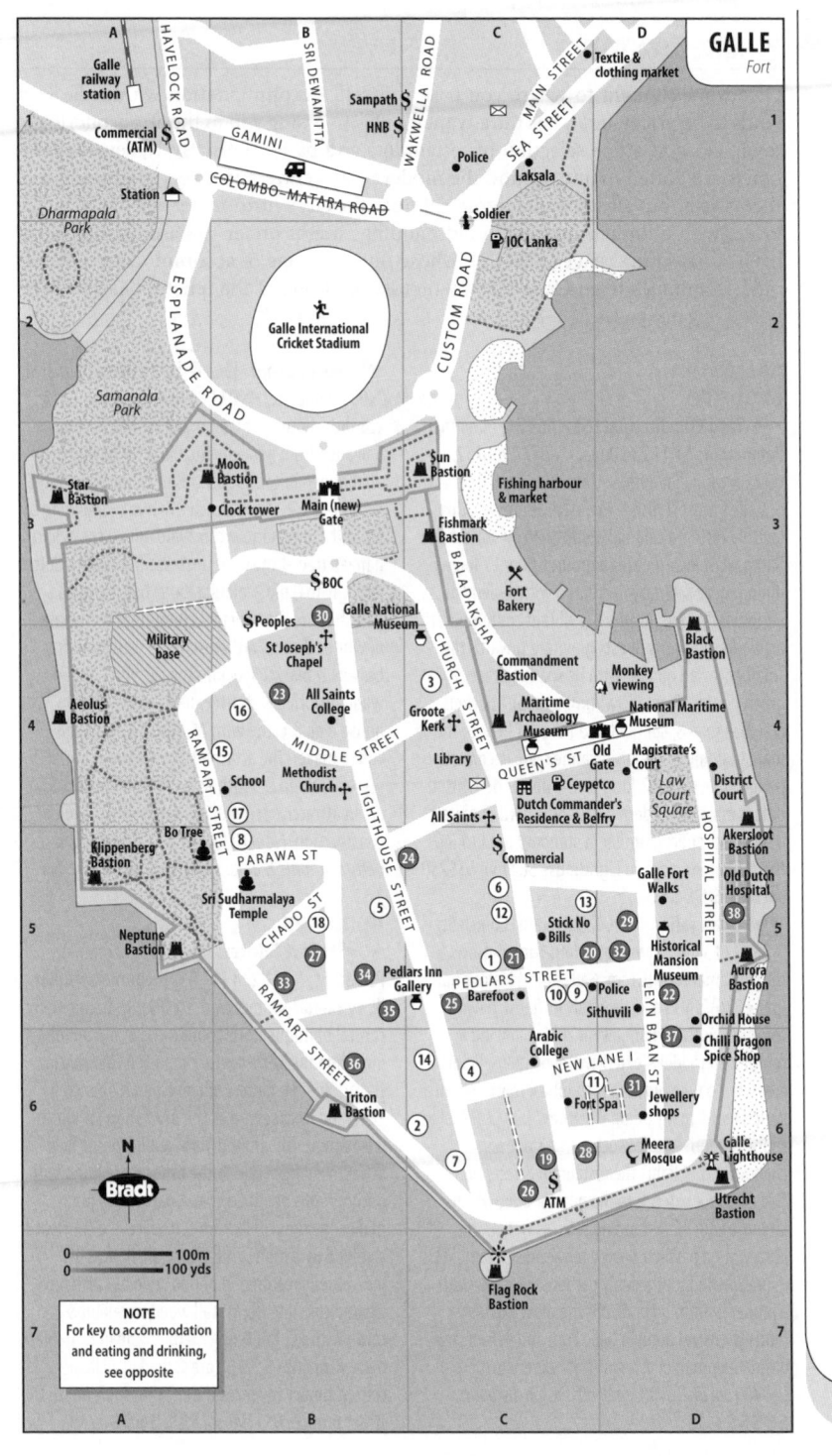

Galle railway station

Commercial (ATM) $

HAVELOCK ROAD

SRI DEWAMITTA

Station

Dharmapala Park

GAMINI

COLOMBO–MATARA ROAD

Galle International Cricket Stadium

Samanala Park

ESPLANADE ROAD

Sampath $

HNB $

WAKWELLA ROAD

MAIN STREET

SEA STREET

Police

Textile & clothing market

Laksala

Soldier

IOC Lanka

CUSTOM ROAD

Star Bastion

Moon Bastion

Clock tower

Main (new) Gate

Sun Bastion

Fishmark Bastion

Fishing harbour & market

Aeolus Bastion

Military base

BOC $

Peoples $

St Joseph's Chapel

30

Galle National Museum

All Saints College

23

16

Groote Kerk

Library

Methodist Church

School

15

17

8

Bo Tree

Klippenberg Bastion

PARAWA ST

Sri Sudharmalaya Temple

CHADO ST

18

27

Neptune Bastion

RAMPART STREET

MIDDLE STREET

LIGHTHOUSE STREET

CHURCH STREET

BALADAKSHA

Fort Bakery

Fort

Commandment Bastion

Monkey viewing

Maritime Archaeology Museum

National Maritime Museum

Black Bastion

QUEEN'S ST

Old Gate

Magistrate's Court

Ceypetco

Dutch Commander's Residence & Belfry

Law Court Square

District Court

Akersloot Bastion

Old Dutch Hospital

HOSPITAL STREET

All Saints

Commercial $

24

6

12

5

Stick No Bills

13

29

Galle Fort Walks

Historical Mansion Museum

38

Aurora Bastion

33

34

25

35

Pedlars Inn Gallery

Barefoot

1

21

PEDLARS STREET

10

9

20

32

Police

Sithuvili

22

37

Orchid House

Chilli Dragon Spice Shop

LEYN BAAN ST

36

14

4

Arabic College

NEW LANE I

11

31

Jewellery shops

Triton Bastion

2

7

Fort Spa

19

28

26

ATM $

Meera Mosque

Galle Lighthouse

Utrecht Bastion

N

Bradt

0   100m
0   100 yds

NOTE
For key to accommodation and eating and drinking, see opposite

Flag Rock Bastion

Give some thought to where you base yourself. Accommodation within the Fort tends to be pricey, but it has the advantage of immersing you in the atmospheric old town, close to a fine selection of restaurants and bars. Alternatively, several good hotels are dotted in and around the modern city centre, most very characterful of themselves, but all somewhat removed from the city's historic heart. Finally, beach lovers with a limited interest in old buildings might prefer to base themselves at lively Unawatuna (pages 579–83), whose diverse range of accommodation stands only 15 minutes from Galle Fort by tuktuk, or at one of the quieter beach resorts near Koggala (pages 586–8).

GALLE FORT
Exclusive

⌂ **Taru Villa Rampart St** [563 B4] (4 rooms) Rampart St; ☎011 234 0033; m 0777 966252; e info@taruvillas.com; w taruvillas.com. One of Galle's most stylish & exclusive addresses, this lavishly restored colonial homestead on waterfront Rampart St incorporates a ground-floor TV lounge, dining room & library decorated with a blend of period darkwood furniture & vibrant contemporary artworks, but most guests gravitate towards the small enclosed garden with its shady terrace, green borders & small swimming pool. Spacious & stylish rooms, split between the 1st floor of the main building & a poolside annex, are decorated in period style with AC, king-size 4-poster bed, fitted nets & massive modern bathrooms. Taru operates a second property, similar in standard but lacking the swimming pool, in Lighthouse St. *From US$250 dbl B&B.* **$$$$$**

⌂ **Amangalla** [563 C4] (28 rooms) Church St; ☎091 223 3388; e amangallafom@amanresorts.com; w amanresorts.com. Galle's most historic hotel (page 576) is also now arguably its finest, having reopened as the Amangalla in 2003 following a complete remodel & extensive renovations. Public areas, hung with old maps & nautical charts, retain a period feel & many original features, but also display subtle modern touches such as the stainless steel chandelier that lights the restaurant & reception. This elegance extends to the guest rooms, which all come with AC & standing tubs, as well as the library, yoga pavilion & wide terrace restaurant. Set in unexpectedly large leafy gardens complete with a proper swimming pool, it is the most expansive (and expensive) hotel in Galle Fort, and delivers the ultimate upmarket colonial-style experience. *From US$400 dbl B&B, with small off-season discounts.* **$$$$$+**

⌂ **Fort Bazaar** [563 C5] (18 rooms) Church St; ☎091 224 2822; m 0773 638381; e enquiries@teardrop-hotels.com; w teardrop-hotels.com. Salvaged from near-dereliction after having been abandoned in the 1950s, this new boutique hotel comprises a 2-storey Dutch-era market building set around a long narrow courtyard with a sprawling banyan tree at the rear. The restoration work defers strongly to Galle's colonial roots, but it also has a fresh contemporary feel epitomised by the use of whites & greys rather than the usual sombre browns & blacks. Spacious rooms with painted wood furniture & shutters have an airy beach-house feel, & come with AC, fan, TV, minibar & coffee maker. The attached Church Street Social serves Arabian & South Asian fusion fare (**$$$$**) on an attractive terrace. Swimming pool is under construction. *From US$320 dbl B&B, with good hefty discounts & online special offers.* **$$$$$+**

Upmarket

✱ ⌂ **Fort Printers** [563 C5] (13 rooms) Pedlars St; ☎091 224 7977; e theprinters@sltnet.lk; w thefortprinters.com. This classy & supremely central boutique hotel spans a trio of old buildings including the 18th-century mansion that housed the original Mahinda College when it opened in 1892 and later served as the print shop for which it is named. The ground-floor public rooms flow attractively from one to the other & are hung with photographs of old Ceylon. A narrow lap pool makes the most of the limited space in a courtyard shielded by a high sandstone wall. Rooms are individually restored in period style but all have treated concrete floors, tall wooden ceiling & come with AC, fan & net. Mediterranean & Arabian meze & mains (**$$$$**) are served in a classic-contemporary foyer restaurant that spills out to the street terrace. *US$190 dbl B&B.* **$$$$**

✳ 🏠 **Deco on 44** [563 B5] (7 rooms) Lighthouse St; ☎091 222 5773/4; e info@decoon44.com; w decoon44.com. A refreshing change from the Victorian sobriety that dominates Galle's hotel scene, this converted Art Deco mansion was built in 1936 for a wealthy gem merchant and has been furnished in period style with abundant gold paint & fabrics, & old *Vogue* & *New Yorker* posters on the wall. Individually styled rooms named after the fort's 7 bastions are decorated with flair & come with AC, TV, writing desk, plenty of wardrobe space & comfortable armchairs. Other facilities include a spa, one of the largest swimming pools in Galle Fort, & a top-notch terrace restaurant (**$$$$**) with 1930s décor & a cosmopolitan fusion menu. *From US$225 dbl B&B, with slight seasonal discounts.* **$$$$$**

🏠 **Galle Fort Hotel** [563 C5] (13 rooms) Church St; ☎091 223 2870; e info@galleforthotel.com; w galleforthotel.com. Opened in 2005 & recipient of a prestigious UNESCO Heritage Award 2 years later, the Galle Fort Hotel was converted from an abandoned Dutch mansion dating from 1695. Public areas are beautifully restored with opulent finishes. Rooms are individually & attractively decorated in period style, & come with AC & king-size beds. *From US$275 dbl B&B.* **$$$$$**

Moderate

✳ 🏠 **Mango House** [563 C5] (7 rooms) Leyn Baan Cross St; ☎091 224 7212; e info@mangohouse.lk; w mangohouse.lk. This gorgeous boutique hotel comprises a restored colonial homestead set in a shady green garden on a quiet side road only 2mins' walk from busy Pedlars St. Airy & comfortable rooms with rough terracotta tile floors all have 4-poster queen-size bed with fitted net, modern bathroom, AC, fan & TV. Contemporary 'world' music plays at a relaxed volume in the skylit public areas, which are scattered with colourful cushions & tall pot plants to generate a warm funky feel. *US$145 dbl B&B, rising seasonally over late Dec–end Jan.* **$$$$**

🏠 **Albert Fort Boutique Hotel** [563 C6] (9 rooms) Rampart St; ☎091 224 2813; m 0774 593343; e info@albertfort.com; w albertfort.com. This modern & efficiently staffed 2-storey hotel is conveniently located with an attractive 1st-floor restaurant serenaded by waves crashing below the southern ramparts. Simple but appealing

rooms are decorated in pastel shades & have wood ceiling & furniture, AC, fan, modern bathroom & direct balcony access. Good value. *US$90 dbl B&B, dropping to US$80 out of season.* **$$$$**

🏠 **Villa Razi** [563 B5] (4 rooms) Parawa St; m 0772 961944; e villarazifort@gmail.com; w villarazi.com. This newly restored 17th-century villa, complete with original plan hanging in the lobby, offers accommodation in small but attractively decorated rooms with AC, fan & 4-poster king-size bed with fitted net. There's a communal TV room & plenty of good eateries within close easy distance. A touch overpriced. *From US$100 dbl.* **$$$$**

Budget

🏠 **Fort Dew Guesthouse** [563 B5] (5 rooms) Rampart St; ☎091 222 4365; m 0727 526260; e fortdew@yahoo.com; w fortdew.com. This pleasant family-owned guesthouse, set in a characterful 3-storey building with wooden balconies, has comfortable AC rooms with treated concrete floors & vintage furniture including wood 4-poster beds with fitted nets. It's topped by the licensed Rooftop Café, which serves good b/fasts & a diverse seafood-dominated dinner menu (**$$**) with views across the green & ramparts to the ocean. Good value for Fort. *US$70 dbl, dropping to US$50 out of season.* **$$$**

🏠 **Fort Bliss** [563 C6] (4 rooms) Lighthouse St; ☎091 224 8168; m 0776 514632; e info@fortblissgalle.com; w fortblissgalle.com. Set in an elegant Dutch-era villa with a colonnaded street balcony & small back garden, this friendly family-run boutique guesthouse is so close to the ramparts that guests are lulled to sleep by the sound of the ocean. Attractive clean rooms with tall ceiling have AC, fan, 4-poster bed with fitted nets. Excellent b/fast inc. *US$85 dbl B&B.* **$$$$**

🏠 **Sunset Fort** [563 B4] (8 rooms) Middle St; m 0713 544806, 0777 938333; e sunsetfort23@gmail.com; w sunsetfort.com. This 2-storey guesthouse has an attractive terrace restaurant & characterless but comfortable rooms with AC, fan & a modern bathroom. Deluxe rooms have a balcony positioned to catch the sunset. *US$50/75 standard/deluxe dbl, with significant low season discounts.* **$$$**

🏠 **Seagreen Guesthouse** [563 B4] (6 rooms) Rampart St; ☎091 224 2754; m 0777 626571; e seagreen_tours@yahoo.

com; w seagreen-guesthouse.com. This well-established family-run guesthouse has comfortable spacious rooms with AC, net & balcony positioned to catch a sea breeze & maximise the view over the green & ramparts. The rooftop terrace is great for b/fast or a relaxed sundowner. *US$64 dbl, plus US$6 pp b/fast.* **$$$**

🏠 **62 Pedlar Guesthouse** [563 C5] (4 rooms) Pedlars St; m 0773 182389; e pedlar62@yahoo. com; w pedlar62.com. Set in an old Dutch building in the busiest part of the old town, this likeable little lodge has spacious 1st-floor rooms with AC, fan, 4-poster wooden bed with fitted net & access to a common lounge, street-facing balcony with seating, & nice rooftop terrace. The family that owns it lives on the ground floor. *US$75 dbl.* **$$$**

🏠 **Fort Inn** [563 C5] (4 rooms) Pedlars St; 📞 091 224 8094; m 0777 394820; e rasikafortinn@yahoo.com. This well-priced 2-storey inn has a central location, friendly & engaged management, & cosy but slightly cluttered & frayed rooms with 4-poster bed, fitted net, AC & TV. 1st-floor rooms have a private balcony. *US$50 dbl B&B, dropping to US$40 out of season.* **$$$**

Shoestring

✱ 🏠 **Pedlars Inn Hostel** [563 C6] (2 rooms, 1 dorm) Lighthouse St; 📞 091 222 7443; e hostel@ pedlarsinn.com; w pedlarsinn.com. This affordable gem in the heart of the old town has a sociable ground-floor café with beach house white-&-blue décor, a 4-bed dorm with fan, net & lockers, & 2 comfortable AC rooms, 1 with balcony. Excellent value but limited space, so book ahead. *US$20/27 dbl without/with balcony, US$12 pp dorm bed.* **$**

🏠 **Beach Haven** [563 C6] (10 rooms) Lighthouse St; 📞 091 223 4663; e 65beachhaven@ sltnet.lk; w beachhaven-galle.com. Managed by the same family since it opened in 1968, this friendly & central guesthouse has a variety of rooms, most en suite & some with AC, as well as a common lounge with balcony, kitchen & fridge. Inexpensive home-cooked Sri Lankan meals are served by request. *US$20/33 dbl with fan/AC.* **$**

🏠 **Galle Fort Hostel** [563 C6] (2 dorms) New Ln1; m 0777 389903; ⨎. Set in a 19th-century house with wooden floors, this functional & friendly backpacker-oriented hostel has 2 smallish mixed dorms, each with 4 bunk-beds & fan, & a common lounge & bathrooms. *US$15pp.* **$**

DICKSON ROAD

All the accommodation listed below stands within 500m of the modern city centre, either on Upper Dickson or Lower Dickson Rd, which make a parallel ascent of a leafy suburban hill dotted with fine old colonial mansions. The location lacks the immersive quality of staying in Galle Fort, but you're only 15–20mins from the northern ramparts on foot, & it's quicker still by tuktuk.

Exclusive

✱ 🏠 **The Dutch House** [568 C1] (4 rooms) Upper Dickson Rd; 📞 091 438 0275; m 0773 695004; e info@thesunhouse.com; w thedutchhouse.com. Winner of several Conde Nast awards, this 1-of-a-kind property comprises the restored 1712-built Doornberg (Thorn Hill), a Dutch villa with an appropriately antiquated-looking outside wall & entrance veranda. A wide wrap-around balcony with columned cloisters surrounds a ¾ courtyard leading out to a large tropical garden, where heavy-boughed trees shade a croquet lawn & a long narrow infinity pool offers elevated views over Galle Fort. The tall-ceilinged AC semi-suites are decorated with colonial-period furniture including Edwardian-style bathtubs. Pricey, but if your budget can absorb it, justifiably so. *US$500 dbl B&B, dropping to US$400 out of season.* **$$$$$+**

🏠 **The Sun House** [568 C1] (8 rooms) Upper Dickson Rd; 📞 091 438 0275; e info@thesunhouse. com; w thesunhouse.com. Jointly managed with the neighbouring Dutch House, this boutique hotel is also set in a restored villa, albeit one built on a somewhat less grand scale in the 19th century. A small terraced garden contains shady trees & a swimming pool, while public areas are decorated with antique wood & modern wrought-iron furniture to create a classic contemporary feel. Individually decorated rooms have wood ceilings, vintage 4-poster beds, AC & fan. Food, prepared to guests' wishes with supplies bought fresh that day in the fish & vegetable markets, is exquisite. *US$246 standard dbl B&B, rising by 25% 15 Dec–31 Jan.* **$$$$$**

Moderate

🏠 **Kikili House** [568 C1] (5 rooms) Lower Dickson Rd; 📞 091 223 4181; m 0777 300175; e info@kikilienterprises.com; w kikilihouse.com. Owned by the dynamic British former manager of

Sun/Dutch House & her Sri Lankan husband, this self-styled '5-star Boutique Bed & Breakfast' stands out for the relaxed enthusiasm of the management (a great source of local travel information), the flamboyant, colourful & eclectic décor throughout, & the cosy communal lounge with laden bookshelves. Small but comfortable rooms all have AC & fan. An exceptional b/fast is included in the room rate & other meals can be prepared by request. Good value. *US$125 dbl B&B.* **$$$$**

🏠 **Lady Hill Hotel** [568 C1] (12 rooms) Upper Dickson Rd; ✆091 224 4322/545 0950; e ladyhill@sltnet.lk; w ladyhillsl.com. Although the reception building dates to the 18th century, the core of this hotel is a modern 4-storey block topped by a licensed open-sided restaurant serving a varied selection of well-priced mains (seafood, steaks & local curries with a good vegetarian selection; **$$$**) & offering fine views in all directions from what is effectively the highest point in Galle. The bright white modern rooms feel a little clinical but have good amenities (AC, TV, minibar, tea/coffee, safe) & private balconies with a view. Amenities include a heart-shaped pool & walk-in aviary under construction. There's no lift so guests with mobility issues should request a 1st-floor room. *US$160 dbl B&B.* **$$$$**

FURTHER AFIELD
The mid-range to upmarket hotels listed below are all scattered within 5km of the city centre & fall outside normal walking distance of Galle Fort, but boast an interesting seaside or inland location & are of some architectural interest.

Upmarket
🏠 **Jetwing Lighthouse Hotel** [map, page 560] (63 rooms) Old Colombo Rd; ✆091 222 3744; e resv.lighthouse@jetwinghotels.com; w jetwinghotels.com. Designed by Geoffrey Bawa in 1997 to resemble a large ship, this iconic hotel – Galle's largest – stands above a dramatically rocky stretch of coast 2.5km from Fort, which is distantly visible to the southeast. First impressions are foreboding, as the stern granite-walled dungeon-like entrance leads up a spiral stairway adorned with a ghoulish life-size scrap-metal tableau of the Portuguese army in combat. Other public areas are somewhat more cheerful & include a fabulously positioned main restaurant & terrace at the building's prow. The spacious & attractive

teak-floored rooms all have a sea-facing balcony or terrace & come with king-size or twin bed, AC, huge TV, minibar, tea/coffee & large bathroom with tub & shower. Other amenities include a 2nd (very good) gourmet restaurant, swimming pool, spa, gym & tennis court. *From US$256 dbl B&B.* **$$$$$**

🏠 **Tamarind Hill** [map, page 560] (12 rooms) Old Colombo Rd; ✆091 222 6568; m 0773 011040; e tamarindhill@asialeisure.lk; w tamarindhill.lk. Set on a wooded hilltop 2.5km northwest of Galle Fort, this renovated mansion, complete with green courtyard & arched wrap-around veranda, is a particularly fine example of mid-18th-century colonial architecture. It was built for Sri Lankan aristocrat Don Johannes Amarasiri & later served as the official residence of the Admiral of famed British P&O Line. The massive semi-suites have tall wooden ceilings, treated concrete floors, darkwood furniture including fitted wardrobe/desk & 4-poster king-size bed with fitted net, & AC, TV, minibar, tea/coffee & safe. There's an infinity pool at the back of the property, a spa & massage facility, & fabulous terrace restaurant with a surprisingly modern decorative touch. Excellent value, assuming you don't mind the inland location. *US$146 dbl B&B.* **$$$$**

Moderate
🏠 **Templeberg Villa** [map, page 560] (5 rooms) Babaragoda Rd; m 0777 108477; e contact@templeberg.com; w templeberg.com. Situated on a 2ha coconut plantation off the eastern link road to the Southern Expressway, this former plantation bungalow was built in 1864 & has been converted to a 3-bedroom guesthouse with a detached 2-bedroom cottage. Far removed from Galle in feel, the lush garden is great for monkey spotting & birdwatching, & offers blissful solitude for relaxing or creative pursuits. There's a 30m jungle-edge infinity pool, while an abandoned lotus pond has been converted into a water-filled space with boulders as seats for chilling out as the sun sets. Meals prepared with locally sourced ingredients are taken in the semi-open parlour. Rooms vary in size & configuration but all have fan, Dutch antique furniture, & 4-poster bed with fitted net. *From US$80/100 sgl/dbl B&B.* **$$$$**

🏠 **Closenberg Hotel** [map, page 560] (16 rooms) Closenberg Rd; ✆091 222 4313; e closenberghtl@sltnet.lk; w closenberghotel.

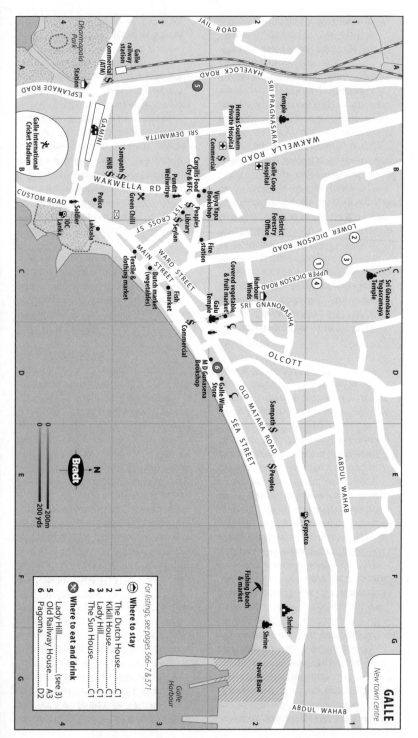

GALLE

New town centre

JAIL ROAD

Dharmapala Park

Galle railway station

Commercial (ATM)

Station

ESPLANADE ROAD

Galle International Cricket Stadium

GAMINI

HAVELOCK ROAD

SRI PRAGNASARA

Temple

WAKWELLA ROAD

SRI DEWAMITTA

Hemas Southern Private Hospital

Galle Coop Hospital

Commercial

Cargills Food City & KFC

Vijiya Yapa Bookshop

Pundit Weliwitiye

District Forestry Office

LOWER DICKSON ROAD

Sri Ghanobasa Yogasramaya Temple

UPPER DICKSON ROAD

SRI GNANOBASHA

Harbour Winds

OLCOTT

Sampath

HNB

Police

1ST CROSS ST

Peoples Seylan

Library

Fire station

Green Chilli

WAKWELLA RD

CUSTOM ROAD

Soldier

IOC Lanka

Laksala

MAIN STREET

WARD STREET

Textile & clothing market

Dutch market (vegetables)

Fish market

Galu Temple

Covered vegetable & fruit market

Commercial

M D Gunasena Bookshop

Galle Wine Store

OLD MATARA ROAD

SEA STREET

Sampath

Peoples

Peoples

ABDUL WAHAB

Ceypetco

Fishing beach & market

Shrine

Shrine

Naval Base

Galle Harbour

ABDUL WAHAB

N

Bradt

0   200m
0   200 yds

For listings, see pages 566–7 & 571

Where to stay

1 The Dutch House......C1
2 Kikili House.............C1
3 Lady Hill..................C1
4 The Sun House..........C1

Where to eat and drink

5 Lady Hill............(see 3)
5 Old Railway House....A3
6 Pagoma...................D2

com. Situated at the harbour entrance 2.5km east of Galle Fort, this architectural gem has a superb location on a rocky rise with waves crashing below & views across to forested Rumassala Hill. The main building was constructed in 1858 by P&O agent Captain Frances Bayley (on what was then Klossenberg Island, site of an abandoned fortalice that guarded the bay in Dutch times) & sold in 1889 to the Perera Abeyewaredene family, which stills owns it today. The AC rooms are magnificent: dark terracotta tiles, tall wood ceilings & French windows with reed blinds leading out to a private balcony with a splendid sea view. The bar & restaurant, with indoor & terrace seating, also ooze period character. Overdue a little slickening up, but still very likeable. *US$150 dbl B&B, dropping to US$125 out of season.* **$$$$**

✂ WHERE TO EAT AND DRINK

In addition to the places listed below, the plentiful eateries dotted in and around Unawatuna, and along the road towards Koggala, make for a good outing from Galle, and are easily reached in 15–20 minutes by tuktuk. Galle offers little in the way of nightlife or pubs, many restaurants are unlicensed, and most close quite early. Your best option for a night out would be one of the larger hotels or the cluster of restaurant-cum-bars in the Old Dutch Hospital Building.

GALLE FORT
Most of the hotels listed under Galle Fort above have restaurants. At the upper end of the price scale, these include Church Street Social at the Fort Bazaar & the terrace restaurants at Deco on 44 & Fort Printers, while a good budget option is the Rooftop Café at Fort Dew Guesthouse.

Medium to expensive
✳ ✂ **Pedlars Inn Café** [563 B5] Pedlars St; 091 222 5333; ⏰ 08.30–22.00. Billing itself as the oldest coffee shop in Galle Fort, Pedlar's Inn is more importantly one of its most appealing eateries, set in a 250-year-old Dutch house that offers the choice of dining in a stylish formal restaurant with AC, a café-like TV lounge, an open courtyard or a street terrace. The globetrotting menu includes Asian, Middle Eastern & Italian dishes, as well as sandwiches, burgers & pizza. Good value. No alcohol. **$$$**

✂ **Elita Restaurant** [563 B4] Middle St; m 0770 747295; f elita.restaurant; ⏰ 10.00–22.00. Owned by a Belgian-trained chef, this unpretentious & warmly decorated restaurant is set in an old colonial building with seating spilling out from the terrace to the street. The focus is on fresh seafood & to a lesser extent local curries (**$$$**) with a few pricier daily specials (**$$$$**). Limited beer & wine selection. Standards tend to drop when it's busy.

✂ **Pedlars Corner Café** [563 B5] Rampart St; 091 224 5131; ⏰ 08.00–21.30. This new corner restaurant has seating for more than 100 spread across 2 AC floors with simple but bold décor & a breezy roof terrace with sea view. The main menu of burgers, sandwiches & curries is supplemented by a more imaginative selection of daily specials. Excellent coffee, as well as juices, smoothies & wine by the bottle. No beer or spirits. **$$$**

✂ **Fortaleza** [563 C5] Church Cross St; m 0773 393397; w fortaleza.lk; ⏰ 08.30–22.00. Set in an old Dutch spice warehouse, this pleasant courtyard restaurant, decorated in contemporary Mediterranean style, has a welcome breeze created by industrial fans & a varied menu notable for seafood, fajitas & an excellent meze platter. Good wine list & cocktail menu too. **$$$$**

✂ **Cannon Bar & Grill** [563 D5] 1st Fl, Old Dutch Hospital; 091 222 2238; ⏰ 10.00–22.00. This fully licensed Western-style restaurant has something of a sports-bar feel & serves a varied selection of (mostly meat-based) continental, Mexican & Indian dishes, as well as pizza & pasta, in the slick modern interior or on a balcony offering great sea views. **$$$**

Medium
✳ ✂ **Poonie's Kitchen** [563 B5] Pedlars St; 091 222 6349; ⏰ 10.00–17.30. Delightfully quaint tree-shaded courtyard café complete with aged wood tables & khoi pond. Brunch- & lunch-oriented, a relatively health-conscious menu includes the likes of granola & yoghurt, sandwiches on multigrain toast & Thai curries, with

plenty of choice for vegetarians. Try the inventive juice of the day &/or carrot cake. No alcohol. $$$

✳ ✖ **A Minute by Tuktuk** [563 D5] 1st Fl, Old Dutch Hospital; ✆091 494 5000; ⨍; ⊕ 08.00–23.00. Boasting the best setting in the Old Dutch Hospital, with terrace seating offering a fine view to Galle Harbour & Rumassala Peninsula, this licensed eatery dresses as funkily as its name suggests, with an eclectic menu ranging from Chinese chilli pot & prawn curry to beef, tuna & tandoori chicken burgers, all at the bottom end of the $$$ range. Fun & good value.

✖ **Chambers Restaurant** [563 C5] Church St; ✆091 224 4320; ⊕ 09.30–21.30. Set in what was formerly a lawyer's chambers, this stylish Middle Eastern & Mediterranean restaurant, owned & managed by a chef with 20 years' work experience in Italy, serves the likes of shish kebabs & chicken-&-prune tagine, as well as pasta dishes, & hot & cold meze. No alcohol. $$$

✖ **Crêpe-ology** [563 D5] Leyn Baan St; ✆091 223 4777; w crepe-ology.lk; ⊕ 11.30–21.00. As its name suggests, this funky rooftop café & shisha bar specialises in sweet & savoury filled pancakes, the latter served with chips & salad. Also known for its coffee & smoothies. No alcohol. Low end of the $$$ range.

✖ **The Heritage Café** [563 C5] Pedlars St; ✆091 224 6668; ⨍; ⊕ 08.00–22.00. Set in a former bakery complete with 200-year-old wood oven that once produced 1,000 loaves daily, the attractive café is set around a shady fan-cooled courtyard & majors in seafood & South Asian dishes, supplemented by a varied selection of salads, wraps, sandwiches, pasta & other light meals. $$$

✖ **Original Rocket Burger** [563 D5] Pedlars St; m 0778 545395; w theoriginalrocketburger. com; ⊕ 11.00–21.30. Regarded to serve the best burgers in Galle Fort, this colourful, modern & enthusiastically staffed 2-storey diner also serves decent fish & chips, peri-peri chicken & a few vegetarian options. Suited to a quick bite more than a leisurely meal. No alcohol. $$$

✖ **Mansion Café** [563 D5] Leyn Baan St; ✆091 193 6126; ⊕ 08.00–20.30. Situated opposite the Historical Mansion Museum & under the same management, this attractive terrace restaurant is a pleasant place to stop for b/fast, a coffee or juice, or a light lunch of pastas, salads, burgers & pizzas. $$$

✖ **Rampart Hotel** [563 B6] Rampart St; m 0779 822430; ⊕ 08.00–21.00. Possibly the most characterful & attractively positioned restaurant in Galle Fort occupies a 2-storey 18th-century Dutch building whose darkwood staircase, hung with 19th-century photographs of the old town, leads to a large wooden balcony offering splendid views over the ramparts to the sea. Busiest at lunch when it is popular with group tours, it has a long & varied seafood, Chinese, Sri Lankan & continental menu & is also fully licensed. Prices are all over the shop but generally quite reasonable; quality & service are erratic. If nothing else, difficult to beat as a sundowner venue. $$$

✖ **Hammock Café** [563 D5] 1st Fl, Old Dutch Hospital; m 0771 910109; ⨍ hammoccafeandpub; ⊕ 10.00–23.30. Named for its novelty 'mini hammock' seating (supplemented by conventional wooden benches on the sea-facing veranda), this otherwise pub-like venue has a well-priced menu of kottu roti, tortilla wraps, burgers & curries. There's a lengthy cocktail & wine list for those planning to make an evening of it. Erratic food & indifferent service. $$$

Cheap

✳ ✖ **Indian Hut** [563 C6] Rampart St; ✆091 222 7442; ⊕ 10.30–22.30. This 1st-floor budget eatery serves generous portions of tasty & inexpensive North Indian vegetarian ($) & mutton/chicken ($$) dishes. The views to the ramparts & speedy, no-nonsense service are bonuses. Good lassis & milkshakes. No alcohol.

✳ ✖ **Lucky Fort Restaurant** [563 B5] Parawa St; ✆091 224 2922; ⊕ noon–22.00. This always-busy family-run restaurant serves delicious homemade rice-&-curry spreads (chicken & 9 different vegetable dishes) sufficient to feed 2 for a bargain US$6.50 on a small leafy terrace. Good juices & lassis. No alcohol. $$

✖ **Original Mama's Rooftop Restaurant** [563 D6] Leyn Baan St; ✆091 222 6415; ⊕ 06.30–22.00. Reached via a creaky wooden staircase, this fabulously informal rooftop restaurant serves traditional & Western b/fasts & a varied choice of Sri Lankan, Thai, Indian & Chinese mains. No alcohol but OK to bring your own. Good value & a lovely setting at sunset. $$–$$$

✖ **Mama's Galle Fort** [563 C6] Church St; ✆091 273 5214; ⊕ 11.00–21.00. Run, confusingly, by the original owner of the Original Mama's but at a new location, this Galle institution serves tasty & affordable homemade curries on a lovely rooftop. Great value. Bring your own alcohol. **$$**

✖ **The Blockhouse** [563 C6] Church St; m 0772 700300; ⊕ 11.00–21.00. Bright little fan-cooled eatery serving tasty & affordable vegetarian (**$**) & chicken or seafood (**$$**) kottu roti & curries. No alcohol. Good juices & shakes. **$–$$**

✖ **Café Punto** [563 C5] Pedlars St; m 0777 599994; ⊕ 08.30–21.00. Run by a friendly husband-&-wife team, this bright fan-cooled hole-in-the-wall serves good value curries, teriyaki, fried rice & noodle dishes. Outstanding lime juice. No alcohol. **$$**

✖ **Serendipity Arts Café** [563 D6] Leyn Baan St; m 0779 383340; ⊕ 07.30–21.30. Lively little café with terrace seating & a bright interior walls are hung with modern artworks. Wraps & sandwiches served with salads & chips (**$$**), as well as a more sophisticated pan-Asian selection (**$$$**).

✖ **National Tea Room** [563 B3] Lighthouse St; m 0727 100222; ⊕ 08.00–19.00. Established in 1932, the oldest (& possibly tiniest) café in Galle Fort is an unpretentious & welcoming mom-&-pop

set-up serving great local b/fasts, curries & rotis, as well as fresh juices, tea & cakes. **$**

OUTSIDE GALLE FORT

Options outside the fort are mostly limited to hotels, with the rooftop restaurant at the Lady Hill Hotel being a well-priced mid-range option offering excellent views in all directions.

✖ **Pagoma Restaurant** [568 D2] Marine Walk; 📞 091 222 6977; w pagomagalle.com; ⊕ 11.00–21.30. Catering mainly to the local market, this well-established 1st-floor restaurant (with take-away below) serves curries, wraps & other local dishes (**$**), as well as fresh seafood (**$$**), in a clean AC interior offering a view over the waterfront & bay. Great value.

✖ **Old Railway House** [568 A3] Havelock Rd; m 0778 809990; ⊕ 10.00–18.00 Mon–Sat. Situated on the 1st floor of an old arched railway building, the city centre's funkiest café has a blackboard menu of imaginative focaccias, burgers, tarts & wraps at the lower end of the **$$$** range. Good coffee or juice. A ground-floor shop sells handicrafts & fabrics.

OTHER PRACTICALITIES

BANKS The Commercial Bank has branches with ATMs on Church Street [563 C5] in Galle Fort and on Wakwella Road [568 B2] and Marine Walk [568 C3] in the city centre. There are also standalone Commercial Bank ATMs outside the railway station [563 A1] and on the Matara Road opposite the turn-off for the Rumassala Peninsula. All the other main banks are represented in Galle too.

MEDICAL The **Hemas Southern Private Hospital** [568 B2] (*Wakwella Rd;* 📞 *091 464 0640;* w *hemashospitals.com*) is a highly regarded private hospital in the centre of the town with modern facilities and a cadre of specialist doctors serving private patients from the west and south coasts.

TOURIST INFORMATION There is no tourist information office in Galle but the website w gallefort.lk is a useful source of up-to-date information.

SHOPPING Grocery and liquor shopping options are limited in Galle Fort, but there's a good Cargills Food City [568 B3] (⊕ *08.00–22.00*) opposite the traffic circle at the south end of Wakwella Road, while the well-stocked Galle Wine Store [568 D2] stands on Main Street. For crafts, souvenirs and such, try the following:

Barefoot [563 C5] Pedlars St; 📞 091 222 6299; e gallefort@barefoot.lk; w barefootceylon.com; ⊕ 09.00–20.00 Mon–Sat, 10.00–18.00 Sun. Set

in a beautifully restored Dutch building, this top-notch craft & fabric shop sells a similar selection of items to its elder sibling in Colombo (page 97)

19

& also has Galle's most extensive range of books about Sri Lanka.

Laksala [568 C4] Sea St; 📞091 222 2783; w laksala.gov.lk; ⊕ 09.00–18.30. The local branch of the state souvenir shop is situated less than 500m outside Galle Fort.

Orchid House [563 D5] Hospital St; 📞091 742 9090; w orchid-house.net; ⊕ 08.30–19.30. Well-stocked & friendly jewellers & craft store with a good selection of teas & books about Sri Lanka.

Sithuvili [563 D5] Leyn Baan St; m 0777 914277; 📘 sithuviligallery; ⊕ 09.00–18.00. This superb gallery is the place to head for quality reproductions of Kandyan masks & temple paintings, as well as genuine antiques.

Stick No Bills [563 C5] Church St; 📞091 224 2504; w sticknobillsonline.com; ⊕ 08.00–20.00. Situated in a handsome old building known as the Dutch Gallery, this shop sells a wonderful range of vintage postcards (*around US$2.50 each*) & retro posters pertaining to Sri Lanka.

WHAT TO SEE AND DO

The main point of interest is Galle Fort, an old-world architectural enclave that warrants at least half a day's exploration, though you'll get far more from the experience by spending a night or two within its atmospheric confines. The new town centre, immediately outside the fort, provides a very different – and far more vibrant – take on contemporary Sri Lankan life. Further afield, both Unawatuna and the Rumassala Peninsula (and its exquisite Jungle beach) are emphatically worth the slight effort required to reach them, as to a lesser extent are the Yatagala Temple, Handunugoda Tea Museum and other attractions described later in this chapter. For keen hikers, birdwatchers and wildlife enthusiasts, Kanneliya Forest Reserve (pages 482–4), protecting a similar flora and fauna to the better-known but more distant Sinharaja, forms an excellent but underpublicised goal for a day, or better overnight, trip out of Galle.

GALLE FORT The history of Galle is spun around the sombre grey walls of its historic fort. These brooding hulks of stone – shipped to Sri Lanka as ballast and hauled into place by slaves from Africa – dominate this coastal city, looming gaunt against the blue sky to guard the harbour and wall off a small peninsula less than 10 minutes' walk from the modern railway and bus stations. For four centuries the fort has stood here; the thin end of the wedge driven by European invaders to open up their conquest of the island. Generations of Portuguese, Dutch and British traders – following the sea lanes of Arab merchants – lived and died in the fort. The Dutch forbade their pilots ever to leave its walls in retirement, in case they divulged the secrets of the maritime approaches to enemies. Even today, when the battlements are brightly lit at night, there hovers a sense of foreboding, as though ghosts of soldiers past are waiting only for the light to dim so they may march again along its ramparts. As dusk gathers, its narrowed streets and cloistered inner courtyards of shuttered mansions echo softly with the murmurings of bygone evenings. The fort is steeped in history; you will sense it from afar and feel its spell from the moment you pass through its gates.

In Dutch times, the peninsula on which Galle Fort now stands was effectively an island, separated from the mainland by a moat and accessible only by drawbridge. The tall stone walls, complete with 14 bastions, are riddled with a warren of cells and punctuated by turrets that protrude like pepper pots above half-moons in the grass marking the foundations of gun emplacements. These ramparts, some more than 400 years old, are still more or less intact, but the moat was filled in by the British administration as part of a 19th-century land reclamation project that created a 500m-wide esplanade between the fortified peninsula and new town centre. Today, this area of landfill houses the test-match-class Galle International

Cricket Stadium (you get a superb view of play from anywhere along the northern ramparts) and provides road access into the fort via the original gate close to the Black Bastion, and a newer gate cut through the northern embankment between the Sun and Moon bastions in 1873.

Within the fort's 36ha confines, a grid of narrow roads is lined with Dutch and British colonial houses adapted to tropical living with colonnaded verandas and ornate gables. There are 473 houses in total, all catalogued by the Department of Archaeology, whose vigorous campaign to restore and preserve has ensured the old town retains the architectural integrity and cohesion that led to its inscription as a UNESCO World Heritage Site. Despite this, the fort's buildings have a diverse pedigree spanning almost 300 years. An estimated 50 pre-date the British occupation of 1796, and a further 104 were constructed before 1850. Also represented are Art Deco homes from the 1930s, earlier Art Nouveau styles (with peculiarly Sri Lankan touches), and even a few brash modern houses built before planning regulations were enforced. In recent years, a great many properties have been restored to serve as guesthouses, restaurants, swanky boutique shops or other tourist-related businesses, leading the seedy charm that once characterised Galle Fort to be superseded by a more gentrified feel. Even so, it is these timeworn buildings, with their proud façades and mysteriously shaded interiors, that give the fort much of its intriguing character, while their down-to-earth inhabitants provide its soul.

Extending over 800m from north to south and nowhere more than 600m wide, Galle Fort is easily and best explored on foot, and it is generally more fun to follow your nose than stick to a prescribed route. That said, the site descriptions below do follow a roughly 3.5km anticlockwise route around the old ramparts, starting at the Old Gate and Black Bastion, travelling west along Queen's Street and north along Church Street to the Main (new) Gate, then running along the northern and western ramparts to Sri Sudharmalaya Temple. From the temple, the route runs inland southeast along Parawa Street and east along Pedlars Street to the Historical Mansion Museum, then south along Leyn Baan Street to the southern ramparts and Galle Lighthouse, then north along Hospital Street via the Old Dutch Hospital back to the starting point at the Old Gate. Several shorter variations are possible.

Guided 90-minute walking tours of the Fort cost around US$25 per person. The most reliable contact is Galle Fort Walks (*25 Leyn Baan St;* m *0772 283001;* e *shanjei@gmail.com;* w *gallefortwalks.com*), which also offers extended tours and night-time 'ghost hunting' excursions for US$45 per person, and special cooking and children's packages.

Except where noted, no entrance fees are charged to visit the sites described below.

The Old Gate and Black Bastion

The Old Gate and Black Bastion The last remaining vestige of Portugal's original Fortaleza Santa Cruz is the northeastern protuberance known as Zwart (Black) Bastion [563 D3] due to its sooty appearance – it stood above the Portuguese gun smithery – when the Dutch captured Galle. Built using coral-rag and lime in c1620, the Black Bastion originally supported eight harbour-facing cannons, and it reputedly incorporates a secret tunnel that has yet to be excavated. The ramparts on Queen's Street immediately to the west of the Black Bastion are cut through by the Old Gate [563 C4], which possibly also dates back to Portuguese times and served as the only entrance until 1873. The outer wall above the gate is adorned with a Dutch VOC crest dated 1669, and an emblem of the cock for which Galle is supposedly named. The British coat of arms can be seen on the inside.

While the Old Gate is readily accessible, the Black Bastion stands within the Deputy Inspector General's office (junction of Queen's and Hospital streets), and access is technically forbidden without permission from the Galle Heritage Foundation [map, page 560] (*Wakwella Rd;* ☎ *091 224 6784;* w *galleheritage.gov. lk*), though you could try walking up to the compound entrance and asking to look around. Alternatively, the sandy fishing harbour [563 C3] 200m north of the Old Gate – site of a bustling daily fish market from around 06.00 to 09.00 – offers decent views of the timeworn northern protrusion's western wall. Look out, too, for the purple-faced langurs that frequent the trees between the Old Gate and fishing harbour. Rather more missable, despite having an entrance set into the Old Gate, the **National Maritime Museum** [563 D4] (☎ *091 224 2261;* w *museum.gov.lk;* ⊕ *09.00– 17.00 Tue–Sat; entrance US$2 pp, plus US$1.50 camera fee*) and its dull displays of traditional boats and local marine animals routinely disappoint those who confuse it with the superior Maritime Archaeology Museum around the corner.

Law Court Square [563 D4] Less than half a hectare in extent, Law Court Square is the second-largest public green space in the Fort, now paved over, but still shaded by century-old banyan trees. As its name suggests, the square is flanked by the Magistrate's Court to the west and District Court to the east; crowds sometimes gather on weekdays to watch cases in progress through the former's huge Dutch windows, while lawyers in ill-fitting black suits might be seen sauntering to and from the ancient book-lined chambers that line the square's south side. The Galle Pola (Flea Market) is held in Law Court Square over 10.00–16.00 on the first Sunday of the month.

Old Dutch Hospital [563 D5] At the south end of Law Court Square, the Old Dutch Hospital stands on the east side of Hospital Street, where it is flanked by Akersloot Bastion to the north and Aurora Bastion to the south. This two-storey Dutch building was constructed on the site of a former Portuguese mint in the early 17th century, and while it originally served as a hospital and smallpox research centre, it was converted to a barracks and then an administrative building during the British colonial era, and it housed the Galle Municipal Council from 1967 to 2003. Supported by colonnaded arched balconies on both sides, it is one of the Fort's oldest and most aesthetically pleasing buildings, and – like its counterpart in Colombo – it has recently been restored as a small modern mall dominated by upmarket restaurants, jewellers and boutique shops. The more interesting of the two bastions that flank it is Akersloot [563 D4], which is named after the birthplace of Governor Willem Coster, who led the victorious Dutch siege on the fort in 1640, and carries a worn inscription *Aker Sloot 1759*. Cannons point out to sea in the garden, and the island's oldest breadfruit tree grows behind it.

Maritime Archaeology Museum [563 C4] (*Queen's St;* ☎ *091 224 5254;* ⊕ *08.00– 17.00; entrance US$5; photography permitted*) Opened under the auspices of the Department of Archaeology in 2010, this worthwhile museum inhabits the longest Dutch building in Southeast Asia, a 130m-long spice warehouse built in 1672 as an extension of the northwest wall flanking the Old Gate. Befitting a museum dedicated to the inherently hit-and-miss discipline of maritime archaeology, it's a mixed bag, with highlights mostly constituting artefacts salvaged during 20th-century engineering work on the harbour and roads around Galle, or in the wake of the 2004 tsunami. These include ancient clay amphorae used to transport olive oil and wine from the Mediterranean, a 15th-century sandstone tablet inscribed in Persian, Chinese and Tamil, a 2,000-year-old Han-dynasty ceramic lion-dog, a 9th-century Vishnu bronze, and two beautiful wooden Buddhas of indeterminate antiquity and probable Thai and Indonesian origin. Also of interest are a few replicas of Kandyan paintings from Koggala's Kataluwa Purwarama Temple, and a life-size replica of the mysterious Sakwala Chakraya (Wheel of the Universe) carving at Anuradhapura (page 270). All in all, the well-labelled displays more than justify the entrance fee. A basement shop stocks a decent selection of books about Sri Lanka.

Dutch Commander's Residence and Belfry

[563 D4] These two relicts of the Dutch occupation stand opposite each other on the corner of Queen's and Church streets. Also known as Queen's House, the modest Dutch Commander's Residence, its doorway topped by a cockerel symbol dated 1683, served as the residence of its namesake and later his British counterpart prior to being auctioned to a private company in 1972. The small belfry tower, originally built in 1701, still has its original bell, which tolled hourly in the 18th century, timed by an hourglass.

All Saints Church

[563 C4] (*Church St;* w *allsaintsgalle.org;* ⊕ *07.00–18.00*) Consecrated in 1871 and newly renovated in 2016, this handsome stone Anglican church was designed in Gothic Revival style following a cruciform basilica plan by J G Smither, a well-known Victorian architect whose other works include the Old Town Hall and National Museum in Colombo. Legend has it that it was built on the site of an 18th-century courthouse whose gallows stood exactly where the altar does today. Interesting features of the imposing interior include several beautifully carved arches supported by stone columns, two rows of heavy teak pews engraved with the Star of David, and the original stained-glass windows.

Post Office

[563 C4] (*Church St;* \ *091 223 2050*) Situated next to All Saints Church, the attractive Dutch building that has housed the post office since the British colonial era started life in the 1760s, when it served as the VOC Trade Office, a workplace for 16 clerks and bookkeepers. Today, with its wide colonnaded veranda, antiquated wooden door and fabulously time-warped interior, the building looks ripe for restoration, or at least a little TLC.

Galle Library

[563 C4] (*Church St;* ⊕ *09.00–17.00 Mon–Fri; temporary membership US$7*) Sri Lanka's oldest public library, this handsome bungalow, with its arched entrance and Kandyan-style roof, was established as a reading room for the Ceylon Rifles Regiment in 1832, and converted to a public library in 1871. A bibliophile's delight, the library contains many old volumes donated back in the 1830s, including one of the last extant first editions of Captain Robert Percival's *Account of the Island of Ceylon* (published 1803) and an important collection of Sinhalese literature established in 1935.

Groote Kerk

[563 C4] (*Church St*) Situated at the highest point in the Fort on the site of a former Capuchin Franciscan Convent, the Groote Kerk (Big Church) is a handsome Dutch Reformed edifice constructed in a cruciform Doric style reminiscent of Colombo's Wolvendaal Church. Although its foundations were laid in 1682, the bulk of the construction work took place after 1752, funded by Casparus de Jong, then the Commander of Galle, in gratitude for the birth of his daughter. The church was dedicated in 1755 and the church register shows that the baptism of de Jong's daughter was postponed to 14 August of that year. Striking features of the cavernous interior include the tall sky-blue wooden ceiling, arched door and window frames, heavy wooden door, faded original stained-glass windows and honeycomb floor design. The original and rather unusual 18th-century canopied calamander-wood pulpit is still intact, as is a secondhand organ brought from Colombo in 1760. Several Dutch gravestones and family crests are laid into the floor, some pre-dating the church's dedication in 1755, and there are also many English-language memorial stones dating from the early decades of British rule, since the Groote Kerk was used by Anglican worshippers prior to the construction of nearby All Saints Church.

Amangalla Hotel [563 C4] Built in 1683 as a living quarter for VOC officers and later converted to a three-storey military garrison, Galle's most historic hostelry opened in 1864 as the Oriental Hotel, primarily to accommodate passengers from P&O and other steamers when they landed at Galle harbour. In 1899, it was bought by Albert Richard Ephraums, who rebranded it as the New Oriental Hotel (NOH) and for much of the 20th century its identity was intertwined with that of Ephraums' granddaughter Nesta Brohier (1905–95), the 'grand old lady of Galle Fort', who was born in room 25, went on to manage the hotel for 35 years, and lived there until her death in 1995. Famous guests during this period included American writer Paul Theroux, lawyer Proctor Bawa (father of Geoffrey Bawa), and future president J R Jayawardene. Now remodelled as the upmarket Amangalla Hotel (page 564), the former NOH retains many original features, most notably the tall ceilings, shuttered veranda and timber, terracotta and ceramic-tile floor of the grand Dutch-era Groote Zaal (Great Hall), which forms its reception area and restaurant, and is open to the public.

Galle National Museum [563 C4] (*Church St;* ✆ *091 223 2051;* w *museum.gov. lk;* ⊕ *09.00–17.00 Tue–Sat; entrance US$2 pp, plus US$1.50 camera fee*) The most notable feature of this modest museum is its location in the Fort's oldest Dutch building, a colonnaded bungalow reputedly constructed in 1656 as the VOC shop and converted to the billiards room of the adjacent NOH in the late 19th century. Renovated and opened as a museum in 1986, it houses moderately interesting displays of traditional masks, turtle-shell ornaments, beeralu lacework items, and Dutch-era armaments.

Northern ramparts and Main Gate [563 A3–C3] Measuring about 400m across, the imposing northern ramparts incorporate a trio of hulking bastions that started life in c1620 when the Portuguese extended the landward fortifications of their Fortaleza Santa Cruz, and is breached by the Main Gate, a relatively recent addition. Starting in the west, these large bastions were originally named after São Antonio (St Anthony), Conceycão (Immaculate Conception) and São Iago (St James), but they have been known as the Star, Moon and Sun bastions since Dutch times. Main Gate [563 B3], which pierces the northern embankment between Sun and Moon bastions at the north end of Lighthouse Street, was excavated by the British in 1873, and is flanked by ramps to the top of the ramparts. The gate also stands in front of a clock tower commemorating Dr P D Anthonisz (1822–1903), who was the inaugural president of the Ceylon branch of the British Medical Association, and a vociferous leader of a successful campaign to block a colonial proposal to raze the ramparts in 1889.

Western ramparts [563 A3–A5] From Star Bastion, you can walk south along the long western ramparts, which are separated from the old town by a 2.5ha patch of largely shadeless grass that forms the Fort's largest green space, a popular venue for informal cricket games and, in the late afternoon, promenades to enjoy the spellbinding sunsets over the ocean. A large L-shaped dungeon embedded into the ramparts just south of Star Bastion is said variously to have served as a prison cell or a powder magazine. Four full- or half-bastions once stood along the western wall, but most are now in poor repair and barely recognisable.

Sri Sudharmalaya Temple [563 B5] The only Buddhist temple in Galle Fort dates to 1889 and stands at the junction of Rampart and Parawa streets opposite a conspicuous Bo Tree. It has a large white dagoba but otherwise looks rather churchlike, thanks presumably to the Dutch and British architectural influence on its builders, though it could also be that it's a conversion of an older colonial building. The interior contains a reclining Buddha statue and a quaint diorama of the first Buddhist monks in Sri Lanka.

Parawa and Pedlars streets Curving inland from the temple, Parawa Street is reputedly named after the 'Parrua' community of fishermen of South Indian descent who once lived in this part of the city. Its southern end forms a T-junction with Pedlars Street, where those following the walking tour outlined on page 573 would want to turn left. The only inland artery that links the western and eastern ramparts, Pedlars Street (formerly known as the Street of Moorish Traders) is lined – appropriately enough, given its name – with restaurants, cafés, jewellers, hotels, clothing boutiques and other commercial outlets, and it is noticeably busier than any neighbouring roads.

Historical Mansion Museum [563 D5] (*Leyn Baan St, 20m north of junction with Pedlars St;* \ *091 193 6126;* m *0777 902200;* ⊕ *09.00–18.00*) More an elaborately cluttered gallery-cum-shop than a proper museum, this well-established private enterprise is nevertheless fun to look around. It is housed in an old residential building with 10m-high, 1m-thick clay-and-coral rock walls, a section of which has been left unplastered to show how it looked prior to its 1992 restoration from a near-ruinous state, and an ancient well set in the garden courtyard. Management claims it is the oldest building in the Fort, dating back to Portuguese times, but this strikes us as wishful thinking – a mid-18th-century construction date seems more likely. Either way, the museum incorporates a diverse collection of antiques, jewellery, pottery, coins, porcelain and old weapons collected over a 35-year period by the owner. There are also demonstrations of traditional hand-cutting and polishing of gemstones, and of the beeralu lacemaking for which Galle is famed. The front of the house is devoted to rooms selling gems, jewellery, brass and copper knick-knacks and handicrafts, as well as antique items, but the atmosphere is relaxed and there's no pressure to buy.

Galle Lighthouse and the southern ramparts From the junction with Pedlars Street, Leyn Baan Street leads down to the tall southern ramparts, flanked to the east and west respectively by Utrecht and Flag Rock bastions. A small sandy beach is tucked away below Utrecht Bastion, while Flag Rock is famed for its 'fort jumpers', a group of freestyle divers who, for a few dollars, will leap with suicidal abandon from the lookout into a narrow rocky channel 13m below (a trick not to be emulated unless you're willing to accept the high risk of broken limbs or worse). Galle Lighthouse, which stands 28m above the ocean waves, was constructed on Utrecht Bastion [563 D6] in 1940 to replace the original structure built in 1848 on Flag Rock [563 C7], at the south end of Lighthouse Street. Tourists are forbidden from entering the lighthouse but, if you catch the caretaker in the right mood, it offers a splendid view across red-tiled roofs and purple bougainvillaea bursting from the concealed gardens of hidden courtyards. Next to the lighthouse, a

19

stone-roofed Dutch powder magazine, inscribed with the year 1789, once stored gunpowder for the cannons that capped the southern bastions. Opposite the lighthouse, the gleaming white Meera Mosque [563 C6] dates to 1909, but old maps indicate a 'Moorish temple' has stood on the site at least since 1790.

OUTSIDE GALLE FORT
New town centre Coming from the rarified and sedated atmosphere that characterises Galle Fort, the new town centre only a few hundred metres to its north is at once rather refreshing and slightly overwhelming, serving to underscore how removed the historic old town has become from the 21st-century main stream. The roads of the new town, lined with quaint stalls and modern shops, positively surge with traffic and pedestrians, creating a genuine developing-world buzz that admittedly dissipates when you walk out a few hundred metres in any given direction. Main points of urban interest include the fish and vegetable markets [568 C3] flanking the junction of Dickson and Sea streets, the more low-key markets clustered off Main Street near Galu Temple [568 C2], and an urbane collection of banks, shops and such lining Wakwella Road. For a more relaxed promenade, follow Sea Street as it curves for about 1.5km eastward between the Old Gate to the Fort and the main harbour, offering lovely views across Galle Bay *en route*, as well as the opportunity to explore the sandy fishing beaches and fish markets at its two extremes.

Biking and boat trips An excellent option for a half-day out (or, if you prefer, overnight excursion) is the guided cycling tours offered by **Idle Bikes** (m *0777 906156; info@idlebikes.com; w idlebikes.com*), which is based at Wijaya beach about 5km east of Galle (page 588). Half-day trips span 12–40km in duration and US$20–35 in price, while overnight trips that involve upwards of 80km of peddling over two days start at US$180 all-inclusive. Its sister company **Idle Boats** (m *0778 034703; w idletours.com*) runs 1–2-hour tours on the Gin River starting at Tamarind Hill (page 567). These cost US$30 per person and are best in the early morning or late afternoon.

Hiyare Reservoir [map, page 488] (✆ *091 562 4227; m 0783 634438, 0763 137934; e info@wildlife.lk; w wildlife.lk; entrance US$1.35*) The 27ha Hiyare Reservoir, constructed in 1911 as a water source for Galle 15km to the southwest, is surrounded by 240ha of lowland forest set on former crown land that was donated to Galle Municipal Council in the late colonial era and now forms a disjunct extension of the 1,800ha Kottawa-Kombala Forest Reserve. A small part of the forest close to the reservoir wall is managed by the Wildlife Conservation Society of Galle (WCSG) as a research station and animal rescue centre. Biodiversity is very high and includes 60 reptile, fish, amphibian and invertebrate species whose known range is restricted to this one isolated forest patch. Mammals include sambar deer, giant squirrel, purple-faced langur and various more secretive species, while an impressive bird checklist includes 17 national endemics, as well as the localised blue-eared kingfisher. Unguided walking is forbidden but the WCSG can arrange combined boating and walking excursions guided by one of their knowledgeable staff for around US$14 per person, inclusive of the entrance fee. These should ideally be arranged at least a week in advance through the contacts given above. For keen and fit cyclists, Idle Bikes (see above) offers a 4-hour, 41km guided cycle tour that includes the challenging ascent to Hiyare Reservoir.

Kottawa Arboretum [map, page 488] (☏ *091 223 4306; ⊕ 08.30–17.00; entrance US$4.50 pp*) This 15ha arboretum 14km northeast of Galle, a northern extension of the Kottawa-Kombala Forest Reserve, is known to harbour 170 indigenous tree species, most endemic to Sri Lanka, and many labelled with their scientific name. Wildlife includes purple-faced langur, toque macaque, giant squirrel, a varied selection of forest butterflies, and around 70 bird species including endemics such as Sri Lankan spurfowl, Sri Lanka grey hornbill, yellow-fronted barbet, brown-capped babbler and spot-winged thrush. Unfortunately, the sole walking trail, which starts about 3km from the ticket office, is less than 3km long and never diverges far enough from the main road to allow you to hear much birdsong over the traffic, which makes for a rather unsatisfying experience compared with the more northerly Kanneliya Forest Reserve (pages 482–4). On the plus side, Kottawa is easy to reach on public transport – any bus headed from Galle to Udugama, 22km further north, can drop you at the ticket office – and if the wildlife disappoints, you could think about taking a dip in the murky forest-fringed swimming pool that lies about 200m from the main road 1.5km past the ticket office.

UNAWATUNA AND THE RUMASSALA PENINSULA

Unawatuna Bay, situated only 5km east of Galle Fort, has been acclaimed as one of the world's ten best beaches, and it's certainly one of the few in Sri Lanka suitable for year-round bathing. It's also a very beautiful spot, a kilometre-long arc of golden sand set below the eastern slopes of the lushly forested Rumassala Peninsula, which rises to a relatively giddy altitude of 60m between Galle and Unawatuna bays. The name Unawatuna reputedly derives from a Sinhala phrase meaning 'fell down', a reference to an ancient legend identifying the Rumassala Peninsula as part of the chunk of the Himalayas dropped accidentally by Hanuman after he carried it to Sri Lanka in the hope it contained the herb required to save the life of Rama's wounded younger brother, Lakshmana.

Once something of a well-kept secret, Unawatuna has gradually developed, almost without anyone noticing, from a homestay-oriented retreat favoured by independent budget travellers to a more conventional beach destination dominated not by large corporate resorts but by small locally owned budget and mid-range lodges. As such, it seems to have retained the laid-back sun-and-fun atmosphere of a lazy-days tropical haven, serviced by some fine beachfront restaurants, as well as several snorkelling and diving operators offering undersea excursions to the coral gardens and wreck sites that lie a short distance offshore. As the closest beach resort to Galle Fort, Unawatuna is well positioned for day excursions to this historic UNESCO World Heritage Site, while the 2km walk across the lovely Rumassala Peninsula to Jungle beach is a must-do for energetic travellers.

GETTING THERE AND AWAY The simplest way to get to Unawatuna is to catch a bus or train to Galle and then charter a tuktuk for the last 5km to the beach. There is also a railway station on the main road through Unawatuna, but it is almost 2km from there to the beach area.

WHERE TO STAY Unawatuna has a good selection of accommodation, most of it either set along the beach or in the forest just inland of it. Moderate hotels here tend to be better value than their counterparts in Galle, especially out of season when most offer hefty discounts. Pickings are thinner in the budget and shoestring ranges.

19

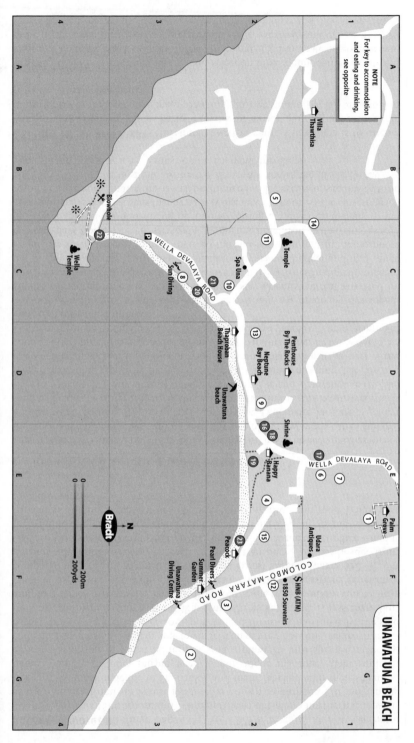

UNAWATUNA BEACH

NOTE
For key to accommodation
and eating and drinking,
see opposite

Villa
Thawthisa

Blowhole

Wella
Temple

22

WELLA DEVALAYA ROAD

P

Sun Diving

8   20   21

Spa Una

10

Temple

11

14

5

Thaproban
Beach House

13

Penthouse
By The Rocks

Neptune
Bay Beach

Unawatuna
beach

9

16   18

Shrine

19

Happy
Banana

4

WELLA DEVALAYA ROAD

17

6   7

Palm
Grove

1

Udara
Antiques

15

Peacock

23

Pearl Divers

Summer
Garden

Unawatuna
Diving Centre

3

COLOMBO–MATARA ROAD

HNB (ATM)

12

1850 Souvenirs

2

N

Bradt

0   200yds
0   200m

⌂ **Where to stay**

1	Bedspace Guesthouse	E1
2	Black Beauty Guesthouse	G3
3	Blue Eyes Inn	F2
4	Calamander Beach Resort	E2
5	French Lotus Guesthouse	B2
6	Gloria Grand	E1
7	Hotel Dunes	E1
8	Kingfisher	C3
9	Pink Elephant Hostel	D2
10	Prime Time	C2
11	Saadhana Bird House	C2
12	Sam's Guesthouse	F2
13	Secret Garden	D2
14	Thambapanni Retreat	C1
15	Unawatuna Beach Bungalow	F2

✖ **Where to eat and drink**

	Bedspace Guesthouse	(see 1)
16	Happy Spice	E2
17	Jina's Vegetarian	E1
	Kingfisher	(see 8)
18	Koha Surf Lounge	E2
19	Lucky Tuna Beach Resort	E2
20	One Love	C3
	Pink Elephant	(see 9)
21	Sunil Garden Coffee Bar	C2
22	Sunrise Seafood	C4
23	Surf City Black & White	F2

Upmarket

⌂ **Coco Bay** [map, page 560] (16 rooms) Rumassala Rd; ✆091 225 0560; e info@ cocobayunawatuna.com; w cocobayunawatuna. com. Situated at the base of the Rumassala Peninsula halfway between Galle & Unawatuna, this modern hotel possesses an almost Caribbean holiday ambience, combining bold décor with a superb beach location on a sheltered semi-private bay looking west to where the sun sets behind Galle Fort. A good licensed restaurant serving seafood ($$$$) & curries ($$$) offers terrace seating facing the beach & swimming pool. Well-appointed rooms come with AC, fan, minibar, jacuzzi & sea-facing private balcony. Deluxe rooms have a plunge pool. *From US$270 dbl HB, with low-season discount.* $$$$$

⌂ **Calamander Beach Resort** [580 E2] (83 rooms) ✆091 438 4545; e fom@ubr.com. lk; w unawatunabeachresort.com. The largest, slickest & most resorty hotel in Unawatuna proper has a full 135m of beach frontage and a great complex of 4 restaurants & swimming areas (including what they claim, thrillingly, to be the world's only vermillion-coloured swimming pool). The large modern rooms are colourfully decorated & come with AC, TV, private terrace & bathroom

with tub & shower. Good value. *US$140/190 dbl/ suite B&B, with modest low-season discounts.* $$$$

Moderate

☀ ⌂ **Thambapanni Retreat** [580 C1] (22 rooms) Unawatuna; ✆091 223 4588; m 0777 901559; info@thambapannileisure.com; w thambapannileisure.com. This stylish boutique hotel & Ayurveda spa stands in a secluded tropical garden dominated by a meandering bamboo-shaded swimming pool 300m from the beach. The timber-floored rooms have AC, fan, 4-poster bed with fitted net, hammock-slung balconies with sea view, & delightful bathrooms of coloured cut-&-polished cement with peacock-blue bathtub. A fully licensed terrace restaurant adorned with Kandyan-style art serves seafood, Italian & South Asian dishes ($$$). *US$75/105 standard/deluxe dbl B&B, dropping by 20% out of season.* $$$

☀ ⌂ **French Lotus Guesthouse** [580 B2] (6 rooms) m 0771 522867; e contact@ frenchlotus-unawatuna.com; w frenchlotus-unawatuna.com. Owned & managed by a friendly & obliging young French couple who live on site, this tranquil retreat is set in pretty manicured forest-edge gardens 300m from the beach. Individually styled rooms have tasteful finishes & décor, 4-poster bed with fitted nets, private terrace, fan &, with 1 exception, AC. Above-average b/fast. Great value. *US$61–85 dbl B&B, dropping by up to 40% out of season.* $$$

⌂ **Secret Garden** [580 D2] (4 rooms) ✆091 224 1857; m 0777 878416; e info@secretgardenunawatuna.com; w secretgardenunawatuna.com. This aptly named boutique guesthouse comprises a 19th-century 2-suite villa & 2 custom-built bungalows engulfed in wonderful jungle-like gardens on the landward side of the main beach road. The large rooms are individually decorated in period style & come with AC, fan, fitted net & in some cases outdoor shower. A good spa is attached & a garden dome is designed for yoga workouts. *US$66/82 sgl/ dbl bungalow, US$145 dbl suites, with seasonal discounts; plus US$6 pp b/fast.* $$$

⌂ **Nooitgedacht** [map, page 560] (37 rooms) ✆091 222 3449/494 6129; e nooitgedheritage@ gmail.com; w nooitgedachtheritage.com. Offering a very different experience from anything else in Unawatuna, Nooitgedacht (Never Thought)

19

comprises a former Dutch Governor's House built by the VOC in 1735 (the dated foundation slab stands at the entrance) in sprawling green gardens set around a freshwater spring at the base of Rumassala Hill 1km from the closest beach. The rooms don't quite live up to expectations created by the gardens, swimming pool and main building's impressive façade, but they seem quite reasonably priced for a genuine heritage property, and all come with AC, fan & twin or dbl bed. *US$40 dbl for a potentially musty budget room, US$80/100 for a much nicer standard/superior dbl, dropping by around 40% out of season; all rates B&B.* $$–$$$

🏠 **Hotel Dunes** [580 E1] (10 rooms) **m** 0777 423636; **e** dunesuna@gmail.com; **f** dunesuna. This eco-friendly owner-managed 2-storey hotel, built with recycled timber including window & door-frames from an old tea factory, is set 300m from the beach in leafy grounds dominated by a vegetated pond that attracts plenty of woodland birds & butterflies, as well as monkeys, mongooses, porcupines, palm civets & monitor lizards. Top-floor rooms are the nicest & come with fan, safe & tea/coffee but no AC, though the traditional asbestos-free clay-tiled roof keeps them cool. Ground-floor rooms are smaller but have AC. Not for everybody, but wildlife enthusiasts will love it. *US$50–100 dbl B&B.* $$$

🏠 **Gloria Grand Hotel** [580 E1] (20 rooms) **** 091 225 0557; **m** 0776 378608; **e** reservations@gloriagrandunawatuna.com; **w** gloriagrandunawatuna.com. This medium-rise hotel 200m from the beach might be a bit lacking in character but the rooms have a modern & well-maintained feel & come with king-size darkwood bed, modern art on the walls, AC, fan, minibar, tea/coffee, safe & TV. *Below-par value Dec–Mar at US$100 dbl B&B, but a bargain out of season when rates drop by a full 50%.* $$$$

🏠 **Kingfisher Hotel & Restaurant** [580 C3] (4 rooms) **** 091 225 0301/2; **m** 0773 408405; **e** info@kingfisherunawatuna.com; **w** kingfisherunawatuna.com. Having started life as an inauspicious beach hut several years ago, the Kingfisher is now a fine boutique hotel whose smart 1st-floor rooms all have AC, fan, TV, safe, minibar, modern bathroom & sea-facing balcony. A perennially popular beach restaurant ($$$) specialises in seafood supplemented by a selection of pita wraps, filled rotis, burgers & pasta dishes. Good value. *US$140 dbl, dropping to US$100 out of season.* $$$$

Budget

🏠 **Bedspace Guesthouse** [580 E1] (6 rooms) **** 091 225 0156; **m** 0716 119561; **e** info@ bedspaceuna.com; **w** bedspaceuna.com. Situated in leafy hammock-scattered gardens along a quiet narrow alley 500m walk from the beach, this chilled-out owner-managed lodge has comfortable AC rooms & great amenities including a library, free use of push bikes, guest-only TV/ movie room, honesty bar, kitchen & a great little garden restaurant. *From US$65 dbl B&B, dropping by 30% out of season.* $$$

🏠 **Unawatuna Beach Bungalow** [580 F2] (12 rooms) **** 091 222 4327; **m** 0779 140188; **e** unawatunabeachbungalow@yahoo.com; **w** unawatunabeachbungalow.com. Literally a pebble's throw from the beach, this modern family-run 2-storey hotel mightn't sound anything special on paper, but the clean & comfortable tiled rooms with AC, fan, net, fridge & balcony are exceptional value given its location. There's also an airy terrace restaurant. *US$50/55 sgl/dbl, dropping by 10% out of season.* $$$

🏠 **Prime Time Hotel** [580 C2] (11 rooms) **** 091 225 0275; **e** info@primetimehotelsrilanka. com; **w** primetimehotelsrilanka.com. Established in the 1980s & now under Scandinavian management, this well-maintained modern-looking hotel has a leafy ground-floor restaurant & spacious rooms with AC, fan, TV, fridge, king-size 4-poster bed, fitted net, modern bathroom & access to a shared balcony with plenty of seating. It's not on the beach but only a minute's walk away. Good value. *From US$59 standard dbl to US$77 suite with balcony & sea view, dropping by 20% out of season; all rates B&B.* $$$

🏠 **Saadhana Bird House** [580 C2] (9 rooms) **** 091 222 4953; **m** 0776 951227; **e** birdhouse_unawatuna@hotmail.com; **w** birdhouseunawatuna.bookings.lk. Set in lushly forested gardens 200m from the beach, this family-owned & -managed guesthouse has a welcoming feel & arranges a good selection of excursions including overnight birding trips into Sinharaja Forest. Large & light superior rooms are appealingly decorated with treated concrete floor, French window leading out to a private balcony, AC, fan, fridge & modern bathroom. A few older & smaller rooms also have AC. *US$40/65 standard/ superior dbl, dropping by 25–30% out of season & negotiable for longer stays.* $$$

Black Beauty Guesthouse [580 G3]
(8 rooms) ✆091 438 4978; m 0776 582909;
e mail@black-beauty-sri-lanka.com; w black-
beauty-sri-lanka.com. Situated about 200m from
the Colombo–Matara Rd, this pleasant family-
oriented guesthouse has a friendly live-in owner-
manager & spacious Lego-coloured garden cottages
with AC, fan, net & terrace seating. The floral bird-
friendly gardens include a small swimming pool &
it's just 2mins' walk from the beach. *US$45–75 dbl
depending on room size & season.* **$$$**

Blue Eyes Inn [580 F2] (12 rooms) ✆091
438 0445; m 0779 425669; e info@blueeyesinn.
com; w blueeyesinn.com. Situated on the
landward side of the Colombo–Matara Rd directly
opposite the beach, this 3-storey hotel suffers
slightly from traffic noise, but the smart & newly
renovated rooms are clean & comfortable, &
equipped with AC, fan, 4-poster bed, fitted net &
modern bathrooms. *Decent value, US$60 dbl B&B
dropping by 25% out of season.* **$$$**

Shoestring

✳ **Pink Elephant Hostel** [580
D2] (4 rooms, 1 dorm) m 0727 790793;
e unapinkelephant@gmail.com. This lively hostel
on the landward side of the main beach road has a
friendly hands-on owner-manager & funky terrace
restaurant/bar that plays contemporary music &
serves sensibly priced cocktails, snacks (**$$**) &
seafood mains (**$$$**). There's a spacious 13-bed
dorm with lockers, nets, fans & balcony, 2 dbl rooms
at the back with fan & shared forest-facing balcony,
& 2 at the front with AC & shared sea-facing balcony.
US$17/30 dbl with fan/AC or US$7 pp dorm bed. **$**

Villa Gaetano [map, page 560] (4 rooms)
m 0773 408047; e melani8921@yahoo.com;
w villagaetano.com. This creekside homestay 1.5km
inland of Unawatuna railway station is operated by a
welcoming young Sri Lankan couple with Ayurveda
training & set in an acre of papaya & banana orchards
with a swimming pool & even a fishing pond, as well
as opportunities for jogging & hiking. Great outdoorsy
vibe & equally good value. *From US$30 dbl B&B.* **$$**

Sam's Guesthouse [580 F2]
(8 rooms) ✆091 222 5467; m 0777 803686;
e samguesthouseunawatuna@gmail.com. This
3-storey block on the main Colombo–Matara Rd
suffers from its noisy location, but if that doesn't
phase you, the neat, clean & spacious rooms with
fan, net & optional AC are very good value, the
family who own & manage it are exceptionally
friendly & live on the ground floor, & it's closer to
the beach – about 150m – than you might think.
*From US$30/34 dbl with fan/AC, plus US$4 pp for a
good local b/fast.* **$$**

✂ **WHERE TO EAT AND DRINK** Unawatuna beach is lined with decent restaurants
and bars, and most of the hotels listed above also serve food, the standouts being
the Kingfisher Hotel & Restaurant, Pink Elephant and Bedspace. Standards are
generally high and prices are far lower than in Galle.

✳ ✂ **Sunil Garden Coffee Bar** [580 C2]
✆091 222 6654; w sunilgardenguesthouse.com;
🕐 08.00–20.00. Set in a thoughtfully laid-out
garden of shady trees, gravel paths & babbling
water features, this zen bistro opposite the main
beach serves an imaginative selection of salads,
filled wraps & paninis using organic ingredients
where possible, as well as coffee, tea, juices &
smoothies, & yummy cakes. **$$$**

✳ ✂ **One Love Restaurant** [580 C3] m 0777
069727; 🕐 09.00–midnight. Owned & managed
by a friendly Sri Lankan couple, this affordable
beach eatery & bar is renowned for its curries, but
also does good lemongrass seafood & offers plenty
of choice to vegetarians. Great value. **$$**

✳ ✂ **Jina's Vegetarian Restaurant** [580
E1] ✆091 438 0366; 🕐 08.00–16.00 & 18.00–
23.00. Set in a lovely old building with terrace &
garden seating, this excellent owner-managed
restaurant has a long menu of vegetarian &
vegan soups, salads & dips with health-bread
(**$**), as well as more substantial thalis, chapati
wraps, Mexican & pasta dishes (**$$**). It's also a
pleasant place to drop in for tea, coffee, juice or
cakes.

✂ **Happy Spice Restaurant** [580 E2] m 0771
113572; 🕐 08.00–10.30. This friendly family-run
local eatery mightn't look anything social from the
outside but it serves a varied selection of good-
value filled white or wholewheat rotis (**$**), noodles
& curries (**$$**) & seafood (**$$$**). Cooking lessons
are also offered.

✂ **Surf City Black & White** [580 F2] m 0771
136677; 🕐 07.30–22.00. Grilled fish & other

seafood ($$$) is the speciality at this attractive restaurant at the east end of the beach, but it is also strong on b/fasts, salads & local curries ($$). Added attractions are the shaded beach seating & full beer & cocktail menu.

✗ **Lucky Tuna Beach Resort** [580 E2] m 0777 566978; e luckytuna@hotmail.com; ⊕ 09.00–midnight. This well-designed 2-floored open-sided restaurant spills out on to the sandy beach & has a longstanding reputation for quality seafood & pasta, as well as burgers & curries in the lower $$$ range. The constant sea breeze, contemporary music selection & full alcoholic & non-alcoholic drinks menu invite you to make a night of it.

✗ **Sunrise Seafood** [580 C4] m 0777 931472; ⊕ 08.00–22.00. This modest & well-priced beach restaurant has a lovely location next to the mangrove-lined creek below Wella Devalaya & serves tasty pasta, curries & filled pancakes ($$), as well as good seafood ($$$). No alcohol.

✗ **Koha Surf Lounge** [580 E2] m 0778 966042; ⨍; ⊕ 07.00–23.30. This colourful backpackers' hang-out has seating on wooden benches & scatter cushions, a varied contemporary playlist & a drinks menu embracing cocktails, beer, lassis & juices. Mainly a drinking & chill-out venue, it also serves wraps, burgers & kebabs in the lower $$$ range.

WHAT TO SEE AND DO Unawatuna is usually safe for swimming all year round, though this does depend on weather and sea conditions on the day, and many visitors are content to while away their days relaxing on the beach, interrupted by an occasional dip and meal. It would be a shame to miss out on a day excursion to Galle Fort, which lies only 5km to the west (pages 572–8), or the relaxed stroll across the forested Rumassala Peninsula to the Peace Pagoda and lovely Jungle beach. Unawatuna also offers some very good diving opportunities, while the most significant Buddhist shrines in the vicinity are the Wella Temple at the northeast end of the beach, and the more remote Yatagala Temple. Cycling and boating trips can also be arranged though Idle Bikes/Boats (page 578).

Diving, snorkelling and other marine activities More than a dozen recognised dive sites lie a few kilometres offshore of Unawatuna and Galle. These include five shipwrecks, including the *Lord Nelson*, which sank to a depth of 15m in Unawatuna Bay in 2000, and the 60m-long SS *Rangoon*, which sank offshore of Galle Fort in 1872 to settle on a sandy plain 32m below the surface. Both sites host a profusion of reef fish and good visibility. Coral gardens include the reef off Jungle beach, a calm and shallow (but badly bleached) site where you can rent snorkelling gear cheaply on the spot, and the larger, deeper and more spectacular Talpe Reef and Navy Kupatha, both of which lie a few kilometres east of Unawatuna. For non-divers and nervous swimmers, glass-bottomed boats are available at Unawatuna beach to take you out to the shallower reefs. The reputable diving companies listed below all offer single dives and courses, as well as arranging other more remote marine excursions, for instance whale-watching trips in Mirissa.

Ⓢ **Pearl Divers** [580 F2] ☎ 091 224 2015; m 0727 903430; e info@pearldivers.lk; w pearldivers.lk.

Ⓢ **Sun Diving** [580 C3] m 0774 606008; e sundivingcentre@gmail.com; w sundivingsrilanka.com.

Ⓢ **Unawatuna Diving Centre** [580 F3] ☎ 091 224 4693; m 0774 436173; e info@ unawatunadiving.com; w unawatunadiving.com.

Rumassala Peninsula and Jungle beach [map, page 560] Flanked by Galle Bay to the west and Unawatuna to the east, the 60m tall Rumassala Peninsula supports a cover of lush forest renowned for its wealth of medicinal herbs. Now protected as a 1.7km² wildlife sanctuary, it is also home to several troops of toque macaque, a varied selection of woodland birds, and an offshore coral garden alive with reef fish. The peninsula retains the scenic qualities alluded to in its colonial-era name Buono Vista, a corruption of the Spanish *buena vista* (good view), while its most conspicuous architectural landmark – a tall white dagoba rising prominently from the cliffs as you look across the bay from Galle Fort – is the Rumassala Peace Pagoda, built in 2005 by Nipponzan-Myohoji Buddhists from Japan, and one of four such constructions in Sri Lanka.

Rumassala's main recreational draw is the legendary Jungle beach, a small, secluded and very beautiful sandy cove offering lovely views across the bay to Galle harbour and Fort. Set between two rocky outcrops, the beach stands at the base of the peninsula's lushly wooded western slopes, and can only be reached on foot, following a steep 300m footpath that requires some steadiness on your feet. The sheltered beach is usually safe for swimming (though do check conditions first) and there is also good snorkelling in the offshore coral gardens. A couple of chilled beach restaurants serve beers, cocktails and soft drinks, and adequate but predictably overpriced seafood meals (**$$$$**), and rent out snorkelling gear for around US$3.50 per 90 minutes.

Rumassala is accessible on foot from Unawatuna beach, following the road that climbs northwest past Saadhana Bird House for about 1km, then continuing along a well-marked footpath through a small valley with the Peace Pagoda rising prominently to your right. Coming from Galle, Rumassala stands less than 2km east of the fort as the seagull soars, but landlubbers will need to follow the Matara Road out of the new town centre for 3.5km, then turn right at a signposted junction from where it's 1km to the start if the footpath to Jungle beach, and another 500m to the Peace Pagoda. The easiest way to get here is by tuktuk, but you could also hop on a bus bound for Unawatuna, then hop off at the junction and walk from there.

Wella Temple [580 C4]

Founded at least 700 years ago, this small shrine on the rocky slopes at the southwest verge of Unawatuna beach is dedicated, like Seenigama near Hikkaduwa, to the vengeful guardian deity Devol. The extant temple is of no great architectural or historic interest, but the Saama Dagoba, perched on an elevated rock at the southern tip of the Rumassala Peninsula, offers excellent views back across the beach, and is primed to catch the sun setting over the ocean.

Yatagala Rajamaha Temple [map, page 560]

Nestled into a boulder-strewn hillside 2km east of Unawatuna railway station, Yatagala is a 2,300-year-old cave temple founded during the reign of Devanampiya Tissa and later patronised by Parakramabahu II and Sri Vikrama Rajasinha. It is renowned for its ancient Bo Tree, which started life as one of the first batch of saplings from the Jaya Sri Maha Bodhi tree in Anuradhapura, and whose heavy boughs are now supported by scaffolding. The main cave temple, built up from a large overhang and several other boulders, is dominated by a reclining Buddha sculpted during the 13th century at the command of Parakramabahu II. It also incorporates some faded Kandyan-era paintings, and ceramic floor tiles donated by Japanese benefactors in the 1940s. Though Yatagala is generally very tranquil, its antiquity and proximity to Galle ensures that it comes alive with colourful worshippers on poya days. To get here, branch east from the main road between Galle and Unawatuna beach at the junction immediately south of Unawatuna post office, passing the railway station after 200m, then continuing eastward for another 1.5km to Yatagala Junction, where you need to turn left. Buses do head out this way but it is probably easier to charter a tuktuk or cycle out.

19

Although it could be seen as an extension of Unawatuna or arguably even Galle, the 10km stretch of the old Matara Road running east towards Koggala is far less densely developed in tourist terms, strung as it is with a succession of exclusive villas and boutique hotels running down to the beaches at Dalawella, Mihiripenna, Talpe and of course Koggala itself. The largest settlement in the region, Koggala is named after the 6km² freshwater lake that borders it to the north and served as the launch for Asia's largest Allied flying-boat base during World War II. Indeed, it was shortly after taking off from Koggala that Air Commodore Birchall made what Sir Winston Churchill regarded to be 'one of the most important single contributions to victory' when he spotted planes from Japan heading towards Sri Lanka, and sounded the alarm that spoilt their planned surprise attack on the island. Koggala remains an important air force base today, thanks to the kilometre-long runway built there after the war. The small town's other main claim to fame is as the birthplace of eminent author Martin Wickramasinghe, whose family property now houses the unexpectedly illuminating folk museum that bears his name. Other points of interest are the boat trips on Lake Koggala, the most westerly bay regularly used by the south coast's so-called stilt fishermen, the lakeside Kataluwa Temple, and the more remote Handunugoda Tea Museum.

GETTING THERE AND AWAY Koggala straddles the main coastal road to Matara only 10km east of Unawatuna and 15km from Galle. Buses between Galle and Matara can drop you here – or indeed at any of the beaches in between – as can stopping trains between Galle and Matara. Tuktuks are also available.

WHERE TO STAY *Map, opposite*

Several exclusive beach villas and boutique hotels line the coast between Unawatuna and Koggala. Options for budget travellers are limited.

Exclusive

✳ ⌂ Apa Villa (7 rooms) Old Matara Rd, Mihiripenna; ☎ 091 228 3320; e booking@apavilla. com; w apavilla.com. This stylish boutique hotel stands in a tranquil palm-shaded garden with 25m-long swimming pool, hammocks strung between the trees & direct frontage on to Mihiripenna's idyllic sandy beach. Airy modern suites with AC, fan & fitted net are spread between 3 different villas that spill out on to ocean-facing terraces. The kitchen prepares exceptional Western or Sri Lankan b/fasts & candlelit 3-course dinners. The best value in this range. *From US$233 dbl B&B, dropping by around 30% out of season.* **$$$$$**

⌂ Frangipani Tree (9 rooms) Old Matara Rd, Mihiripenna; ☎ 091 228 3711; m 0770 406060; e reservations@edwards-collection. com; w edwards-collection.com/the-frangipani-tree. Set in beautiful wooded gardens between Mihiripenna & Thalpe, this chic little hotel has a villa-like feel, long swimming pool, tennis court

& direct access to a rocky beach. The tall-ceilinged wood-shuttered rooms are spacious & uncluttered, & come with AC, king-size 4-poster bed with fitted net, modern bathroom with tub & shower, outdoor bath & private sea-facing terrace. *US$360 dbl B&B, dropping to US$300 out of season.* **$$$$$+**

⌂ The Fortress (53 rooms) Old Matara Rd, Koggala; ☎ 091 438 9400; e info@thefortress.lk; w thefortressresortandspa.com. Designed like a fortress enclosing a 2-storey Dutch villa, Koggala's most luxurious beachfront hotel is entered through massive wooden doors reminiscent of those that used to guard Galle Fort, while the vast garden courtyard is lined with stout columns & cloisters, & incorporates a long swimming pool. Spacious & stylish teak-floored rooms with huge beds & open-plan bathroom have all the comforts you'd expect, as well as Bose speakers & a pre-programmed iPod, & standalone jacuzzi bathtub. Ground-floor rooms give access to the beach while 1st-floor rooms have a balcony. Despite its grandeur, the atmosphere is

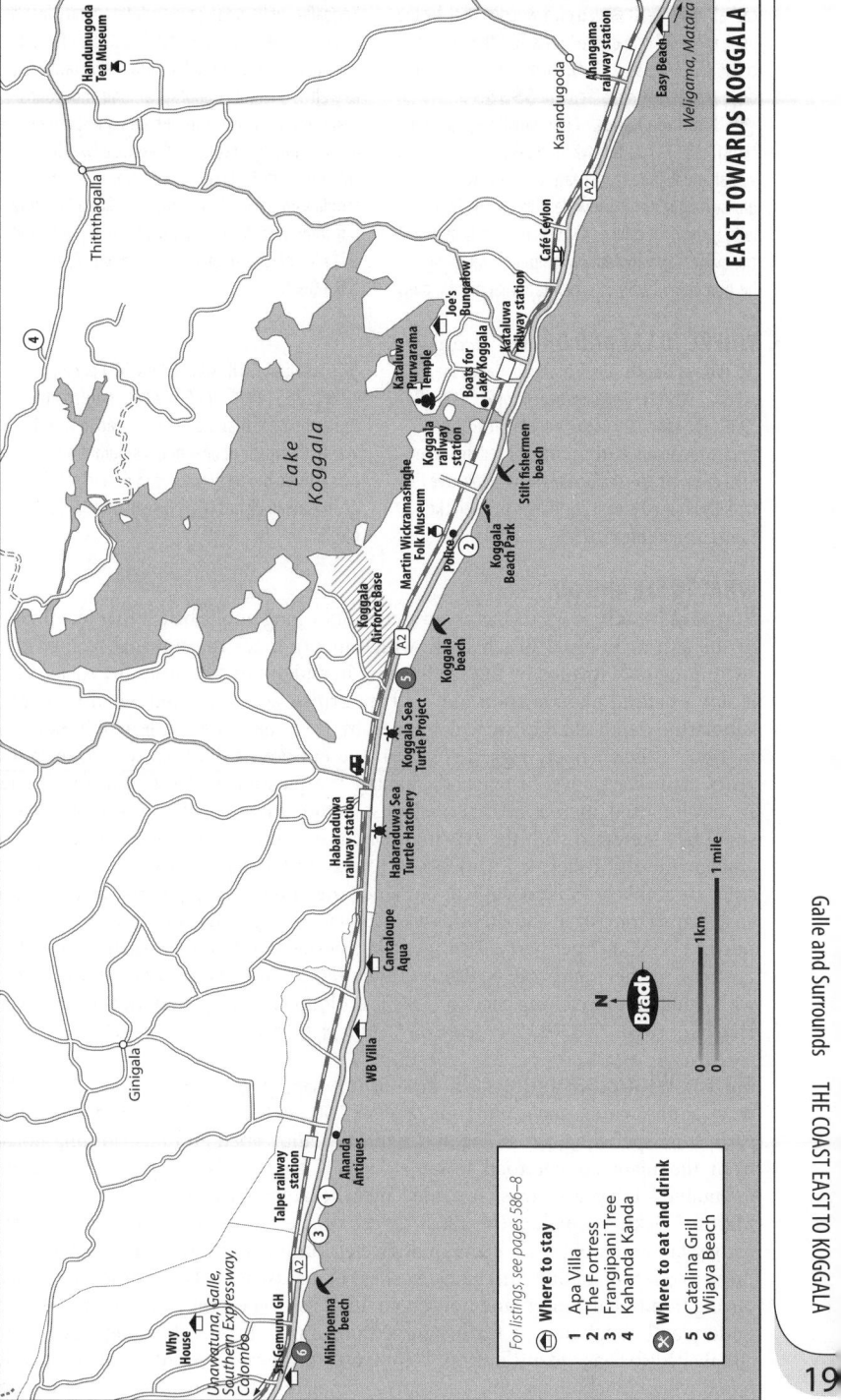

Handunugoda Tea Museum

Thiththagalla

④

Lake Koggala

Karandugoda

Café Ceylon

A2

Ahangama railway station

Easy Beach

Weligama, Matara

Joe's Bungalow

Kataluwa Purvarama Temple

Boats for Lake Koggala

Kataluwa railway station

Koggala railway station

Martin Wickramasinghe Folk Museum

Stilt fishermen beach

Koggala Airforce Base

Police ●

② **Koggala Beach Park**

Koggala beach

A2

⑤ **Koggala Sea Turtle Project**

Ginigala

Habaraduwa railway station

Habaraduwa Sea Turtle Hatchery

Cantaloupe Aqua

WB Villa

Ananda Antiques

Talpe railway station

① ③

Why House

Unawatuna, Galle, Southern Expressway, Colombo

Sri Gemunu GH ⑥

Mihiripenna beach

N

Bradt

0 ____ 1km
0 ____ 1 mile

For listings, see pages 586–8

🛏 **Where to stay**

1   Apa Villa
2   The Fortress
3   Frangipani Tree
4   Kahanda Kanda

✕ **Where to eat and drink**

5   Catalina Grill
6   Wijaya Beach

casual, with meals served on a wooden deck by the pool, in the AC café or the Surf & Turf themed wine cellar. *US$370/585 B&B dbl without/with sea view, dropping by 20% out of season.* **$$$$$+**

🏠 **Kahanda Kanda** (10 rooms) Angulugaha; 🔌 091 228 6717; e info@kahandakanda.com; w kahandakanda.com. Featured with awe in glossy magazines worldwide, this unique hilltop lodge, known locally as KK, was originally built as the owner's private fantasy residence following his purchase of a 5ha tea plantation 8km inland of Koggala. Public areas have a contemporary feel & include a stylish pavilion restaurant/bar offering splendid views over the forest to the distant ocean, as well as an infinity pool set among khoi ponds & ancient trees. Spacious but dark guest rooms are individually decorated & exude Edwardian sobriety, with 18th-century portraits of settler families on the walls & a clutter of floral furniture, but come with AC, fan, net & private terrace. *From US$410 dbl B&B, dropping by 20% out of season.* **$$$$$+**

✕ WHERE TO EAT AND DRINK *Map, page 587*

✕ **Wijaya Beach** Old Matara Rd, Dalawella; m 0777 903431; w wijayabeach.com; ⊕ 08.00–22.00. The speciality of this popular beachfront terrace restaurant is crisp pizzas cooked in a wood-fired oven, but the seafood menu is innovative too. It's fully licensed & well positioned to catch the sunset over the ocean. **$$$**

✕ **Catalina Grill** Old Matara Rd, Koggala; 🔌 091 228 3144; ⊕ 11.00–23.00. Named after the aeroplanes that buzzed overhead in World War II, this rustic open-sided restaurant is set in a beachside property & serves a decent selection of Sri Lankan dishes (**$$**) & seafood (**$$$**). No alcohol.

WHAT TO SEE AND DO

Koggala beach Koggala has an attractive 3km-long public beach that terminates in the east at Koggala Beach Park, which incorporates the unusual facility of a swimming pool formed by the sea flushing in and out of a basin in the rocks. This is not a natural phenomenon but another British legacy created when two anti-submarine depth charges were detonated by RAF members stationed at Koggala in 1947. This left many jagged edges on the bottom of the hole which, over the years, have been covered by sand, making it a pleasant and safe place to bathe. A few hundred metres further east, just before the Koggala river mouth, is a small bay skewered with the crucifix-like constructions used by the south coast's emblematic stilt fishermen. Unless you're here in the early morning, the wooden stilts are unlikely to be occupied, but since they now exist primarily as props for snap-happy tourists, it should be easy enough to arrange a few models for the going rate of US$3.50–7 per party. Two turtle hatcheries stand on the beach west of The Fortress; neither appears to be licensed and both get mixed feedback, but the better, with a pedigree stretching back to 1986, is undoubtedly the Habaraduwa Sea Turtle Hatchery (m *0777 836115*; w *seaturtlefarm.org; entrance US$3.50 pp*).

Martin Wickramasinghe Folk Museum [map, page 587] (📞 *011 286 5543*; w *martinwickramasinghe.info*; ⊕ *09.00–17.00; entrance US$1.50; photography permitted*) Sprawling across 3ha of delightfully landscaped grounds running north from the main coastal road towards Lake Koggala, this exceptional museum, maintained by a private trust, is named after the father of modern Sinhala literature, Martin Wickramasinghe. The main thrust of the museum is not, however, the namesake writer, but Sri Lanka's multifaceted rural culture, represented here by a diverse collection of Buddhist icons, a gallery of masks, puppets and other attire used during traditional dances, and household items associated with agriculture, fishing, pottery and metal craft. A further walk along a path lined with indigenous trees, all labelled for easy identification, brings you to the restored 200-year-old family home where Wickramasinghe was born, complete with Dutch-influenced façade, whitewashed walls, clay-brick floor and tubular red-clay roof tiles – and the author's bedroom with his spectacles on the bedside table and clothes in the cupboard.

Lake Koggala [map, page 587] This attractive 6km^2 lake is formed by the eponymous river before it drains into the ocean on the east side of Koggala town. Although it lies less than 1km from the open sea, it is very different in character, a calm and tranquil freshwater paradise studded with small islands and fringed by verdant palm-dominated forests. Two-hour boat tours can be arranged with private operators at the river mouth (behind the South Lake Resort) and cost a negotiable US$10–15 for up to six passengers. Most tours stop at two islands, one hosting a hilltop Buddhist monastery and the other a small family-run cinnamon plantation, as well as a 'fish feeling' facility (stick your feet in the water and let the fish nibble away at them) for a small fee. Wildlife wise, you should see plenty of aquatic birdlife, and might even luck a water monitor or (rare) crocodile sighting.

Kataluwa Purwarama Temple [map, page 587] Situated 1km inland of Koggala on a sloping peninsula jutting into the lake's eastern shore, the little-visited Kataluwa Temple reputedly dates back to the 13th century but the present-day buildings are all from the 19th century and display several unique features. Constructed in 1841, the Nawamuni Seya (Nine Dagobas) is an unusual monument comprising one large central dagoba surrounded by eight smaller ones. The main shrine, set on an elevated octagonal platform, contains a wealth of well-preserved 19th-century Kandyan-style paintings, which incorporate several figures wearing European clothing, among them a group of British soldiers participating in a Buddhist procession. Unusually, a British coat of arms dated 1886 is depicted above one of the doors; more unexpected still is a portrait of Queen Victoria that expresses gratitude for her role in allowing free expression of Buddhism under the Kandyan Convention of 1815. The temple also hosts the press used in 1860 to print the first Sinhalese newspaper, the twice-monthly *Lankalokaya* – how and when this historic artefact ended up at Kataluwa is unclear, but the head monk has thus far resisted all government attempts to relocate it to a museum in Colombo, despite it having been damaged in fire in 2012.

Handunugoda Tea Museum [map, page 587] (m *091 228 6364*; w *hermanteas. com*; ⊕ *08.00–17.00*) This family-run estate 6km inland of Koggala has attracted considerable interest since its 2009 launch of its super-expensive 'virgin white tea', a flagship brand that goes untouched by human hands, and untainted by natural body oils, prior to being packed (pickers wear gloves and use nail scissors), and reputedly has the highest antioxidant content (11%) of any tea. Specialising in artisanal black teas made with 150-year-old equipment salvaged from other factories, it produces the unique Sapphire Oolong (a low-caffeine strain intermediate between green and black teas), award-winning Ceylon Souchong, and 25 other specialist or innovative blends. Free guided tours include tea and cake at the proprietor's bungalow, a visit to the small but historic factory, optional tea tasting (and purchase) in a ground-floor sales outlet, and the opportunity to nose around a small first-floor tea museum dominated by photographs of the 'ancient Nuwara Eliya Golf Club' in its monochrome prime. It's a pleasant goal for an outing, and horse rides are also available at US$25/40 per 30/60 minutes.

Appendix 1

LANGUAGE

Three languages are spoken in Sri Lanka: Tamil mainly in the north, east and plantation interior; Sinhala mainly in the west, south and centre; and English island-wide. Since English is widely spoken and understood – most Sri Lankans delight in trying out their English on tourists – the list of useful words and phrases featured below is short but it should serve the needs of travellers when and where English is not understood.

Tamil and Sinhala each has its own alphabet, and for correct pronunciation and conversation the language enthusiast should purchase phrasebooks produced in Sri Lanka; they are available everywhere, even in village bookshops. The phrases below have been transliterated from Sinhala and Tamil in an effort to arrive at an approximation of how the words are pronounced. Other sources may give other spellings.

USEFUL WORDS AND PHRASES

	Sinhala	Tamil
Yes	*o-u*	*ama*
No	*naha*	*illai*
Please	*karunakarala*	*thayavu seithu*
Thank you	*istuti*	*naandri*
Sorry	*mata samavenna*	*mannikkanum*
What is your name?	*oyage nama mokadde?*	*ungada peyar enna?*
My name is	*mage nama*	*en peyar*
Where do you live?	*oba koheda innay?*	*neenga enga irukinga?*
Where are you from?	*oba kohendha?*	*nienga varrienga?*
I'm from …	*mama … ven*	*naan … irundhu varean*
I don't understand	*mata therenney naha*	*ennakku vilanga illai*
Do you speak English?	*oba ingreesi kathaa karanavadha?*	*neenga English pesuviengala?*
I'm lost	*mama ataarmang wella*	*enakku vazhi theriyala*
How much is it?	*keeyada?*	*evvalavu?*
Enjoy (for meals)	*vinoden kanna*	*nanraaga saappidunka*
doctor	*dostara*	*waithiyan*
hospital	*rohala*	*aspithri*
bank	*bankuwa*	*vangi*
post office	*thapal kantoruwa*	*anjal aluvelaham*
closed	*vahala*	*mudapatulladhu*
open	*arala*	*thranduladhu*
far	*aathah*	*tuuram*
near	*langa*	*arukkil*
right	*dakuna*	*valathu*
left	*vama*	*idathu*

GREETINGS

The Sinhala greeting *ayubowan* derives from three words: *ayu* (long life), *bo* (much) and *wan* (let it be) and means: 'may you live long'. It is used as a greeting, accompanied by palms held together at chest height on formal occasions. A more common greeting, the equivalent of 'hi' or 'hello', is *kohomada*. It is said in the manner of 'how are you?' and an answer is not expected, although it may bring the response: *ohe innava* or *varadak nee*, meaning 'fine'.

	Sinhala	Tamil
Traditional greeting	*ayubowan*	*vanakkam*
Hi/How are you?	*kohomada?*	*eppadi sugam?*
Good morning	*subha udhasanak*	*kaalai vanakkam*
Good evening	*subha sandhavak*	*maalai vanakkam*
Goodnight	*subha rahthryak*	*nal iravu*
Goodbye	*gihilla ennam*	*poittu varen*
Welcome	*sadarayen piligannawa*	*nalvaravu*
Nice to meet you	*oba dhanagana labema sathutak*	*ungalai santhithathil magalchi*

Numbers

	Sinhala	Tamil
one	*eka*	*onnu*
two	*deka*	*rendu*
three	*tuna*	*moonu*
four	*hatara*	*naalu*
five	*paha*	*indhu*
six	*haya*	*aaru*
seven	*hata*	*ealu*
eight	*ata*	*ettu*
nine	*namaya*	*onbadhu*
ten	*dahaya*	*patthu*

SEND US YOUR SNAPS!

We'd love to follow your adventures using our *Sri Lanka* guide – why not send us your photos and stories via Twitter (*@BradtGuides*) and Instagram (*@bradtguides*) using the hashtag #srilanka? Alternatively, you can upload your photos directly to the gallery on the Sri Lanka destination page via our website (**w** *bradtguides.com/srilanka*).

Appendix 2

GENERAL GLOSSARY

abhaya	fearless (also a commonly depicted mudra)
adigar	minister and royal adviser to the king of Kandy
ambalama	a wayside pilgrims' shelter
Anuradhapura era	period during which Anuradhapura was the main capital of Sri Lanka (4th century BC–10th century AD)
apsara	nymph-like cloud- or water-spirit recognised in both Hindu and Buddhist mythology
arahant (arhat)	Theravada term for a monk who has attained nirvana. In other Buddhist traditions it denotes someone well advanced on the path of enlightenment but not quite there yet.
arrack	Sri Lanka's whisky; an alcoholic drink distilled from toddy (the sap from a coconut tree)
Ayurveda	traditional herbal treatment
banyan	type of strangler fig (often *Ficus benghalensis*) that starts life as a epiphyte but gradually smothers and kills its host with a mesh of roots, and can grow over several centuries to cover more than a hectare
beeralu	lacemaking craft introduced by the Portuguese in the 16th century
bhikkhus	Buddhist monks
bhumisparsha	'ground-touching' mudra
Bo Tree	*Ficus religiosa*; a tree with spreading branches worshipped by Buddhists and found at all their temples
bodhighara	'house' or shrine containing a Bo Tree
bodhisattva	elusive concept embodying the highest Buddhist ideal in both the Theravada and Mahayana traditions and often portrayed in temple art; put very simply, a person capable of attaining nirvana but who delays it out of compassion for his fellow beings; may also refer to the Gautama Buddha pre-enlightenment or in a previous life
Buddha	The Enlightened One. See also *Gautama Buddha* (page 599)
Buddhapada	footprint of the Gautama Buddha or artificial representation thereof, the most famous being the 'natural' one atop Adam's Peak. These were seen as particularly important in the early days of Buddhism when statues and other representations of the Enlightened One were outlawed.
bund	bank of a reservoir (tank)
burgher	Sri Lankan citizen of Dutch ancestry

cadjan	a fence or wall or roof of plaited palm leaves
Cargills	well-known and widespread supermarket chain established in the 19th century
Ceylon	colonial-era name for Sri Lanka
chaitya	a Buddhist shrine with a dagoba at one end
Chola	long-ruling South Indian dynasty that captured Anuradhapura on several occasions and was responsible for its eventual downfall
coir	fibre spun from coconut husks
Culavamsa	sequel to the *Mahavamsa* covering the island's royal history from the 4th century AD to 1815
curd	buffalo-milk yoghurt
dagoba	dome-shaped Buddhist relic shrine, often tens of metres or even 100-plus metres high
Dalada Maligawa	temple built to house the sacred tooth relic. The current one was established in Kandy in 1592 but several others have existed over the millennia.
Dambadeniya	centred on present-day Kurunegala c1220–1345, the most island's important Sinhala kingdom between the fall of Polonnaruwa and rise of Kotte
deva	Buddhist and/or Hindu deity
devalaya	see *devale*
devale	Buddhist shrine to a deva (often dedicated to a Hindu deity)
devi	female equivalent to deva (Hindu only)
devilled	very spicy stir-fried stew
devol	Buddhist deity associated with vengeance and prosperity
dharma	elusive philosophical concept relating to the laws, duties and teachings of the Buddha or (for Hindus) the broader cosmic order
dharmapala	wrathful Buddhist deity
duwa	island
ella	waterfall
endemic	animal or plant with a range restricted to one specific place or country (in the context of this book, generally to Sri Lanka)
fox, flying	massive communal-roosting fruitbat
gala	rock (common component of Sinhalese place names)
gama	village (common component of Sinhalese place names)
ganga	river
gopuram	ornate multi-tiered tower associated with Hindu temples
HMS Hermes	aircraft carrier sunk off Batticaloa in World War II
hopper	steamed or fried pancake-like accompaniment
illam	gem-bearing gravel
image house	temple building or cave shrine housing statues and/or paintings of the Buddha and sometimes other figures and deities
indigenous	native to a place
Jaffna	Hindu Tamil kingdom centred on Nallur (now a suburb of Jaffna town) from its foundation in 1215 until its capture by the Portuguese in 1619. It was the dominant power in Sri Lanka for a few decades prior to being defeated by Kotte in 1650.

jaggery	palm sap sugar, like fudge
Jataka	the substantial part of the Pali canon detailing the previous human and animal incarnations of the Gautama Buddha in fable-like episodes that each demonstrate a virtue and/or moral. The Jataka tales are frequently related in Sri Lankan temple art.
Jaya Sri Maha Bodhi	ancient Bo Tree grown at Anuradhapura from a sapling of the original
kachcheri	local government secretariat
Kandyan era	period during which the Kingdom of Kandy was the island's dominant indigenous polity (roughly 1469–1815).
Kotte	Sinhala kingdom founded in the late 14th century, centred on Sri Jayawardenepura Kotte (bounding present-day Colombo) and dominant over much of Sri Lanka in the 15th century
kottu	chopped-up roti stir-fried with vegetables and usually meat
kovil	a Hindu temple
kuti	meditation hut or cave
langur	type of monkey
lingam	phallus-like icon worshipped by Hindus as a symbol of Shiva
LKR	Sri Lankan rupee
loris	small nocturnal primate
LTTE	Liberation Tigers of Tamil Eelam, a militant Tamil secessionist organisation and the main protagonist of the 1983–2009 civil war
macaque	type of monkey
maha	great
maha vihara(ya)	Great Temple
Mahabharata	along with the *Ramayana*, which has greater bearing on Sri Lankan history, the second of the two major ancient Indian Sanskrit epics
maharaja	great king
Mahavamsa	literally 'Great Chronicle', an epic Pali poem detailing the history of Sri Lanka from the 6th century BC to the 3rd century AD and arrival of Buddhism on the island
Mahayana	literally 'Great Vehicle', the world's largest school of Buddhism, now subservient to Theravada in Sri Lanka, but dominant school at certain periods in the island's history
malai	hill (common component of Sinhalese place names)
Mattakallappu Manmiyam	Tamil history of Batticaloa compiled in 1962 from anonymous ancient palm-leaf manuscripts
mawatha	road
Moor	well-established Islamic Sri Lankan community, largely of Arab origin
mudra	symbolic gesture, mainly involving the hands and fingers, depicted on Buddha, bodhisattva and other statues
muntjac	type of small deer (also known as barking deer)
naga	snake, specifically cobra
Naga Raja	Snake King
nirvana	state of enlightenment, and liberation from the samsara cycle, to which every Buddhist aspires

nuwara	town
ola	dried palm leaf used for writing with a stylus
oruva	a wooden dugout canoe with outrigger
oya	a stream or small river
paddy	unhusked rice; the rice plant
Pali canon	oldest collection of scriptures based on Gautama Buddha's teaching, transmitted orally until it was first transcribed at Aluvihara Cave north of Kandy in 29BC
palmyrah	type of fruiting palm cultivated widely in the north of Sri Lanka
pandal	a decorated illuminated hoarding
Pandy	an influential Tamil empire centred on the southern Indian mainland
Pandyan	relating to Pandy
pansala	Buddhist temple
parinirvana	final state of nirvana reached when someone who attained nirvana during their lifetime dies
perahera	grand procession
pirith	Buddhist chant
pirivena	a teaching monastery where young monks receive monastic training
pitiya	place or village (common component of Sinhalese place names)
plus-plus	price to which taxes and service charge must be added
pokuna	pool or pond
pol	coconut tree (common component of Sinhalese place names)
Polonnaruwa era	period during which Polonnaruwa was the main capital of Sri Lanka (roughly AD1056–1236).
pothgul	library
poya	full moon, an auspicious day to Buddhists and public holiday in Sri Lanka
puja	Hindu prayer ritual and/or religious offering
raja	king
Ramayana	ancient Indian epic poem whose namesake protagonist Prince Rama rescued his wife Sita from the clutches of the demon-king Ravana when she was imprisoned on the island of Lanka
roti	unleavened bread
Ruhuna	ancient kingdom encompassing much of southeast Sri Lanka, sometimes a rival to and at other times an ally of Anuradhapura, ruled in its 2nd-century BC prime from Tissamaharama
SAARC	South Asian Association for Regional Cooperation (comprising Afghanistan, Bangladesh, Bhutan, India, Maldives, Nepal, Pakistan and Sri Lanka)
sambar	largest deer found on Sri Lanka
samsara	eternal cycle of birth, existence (or suffering), death and reincarnation from which, according to Buddhist belief, only those who attain parinirvana are liberated
samudra	inland sea or large tank

sangha	monks
sinha	lion
Sinhala	majority ethnic group and language of Sri Lanka
siraspata	flame-shaped ornament depicted above the head of the Buddha
Sitawaka	kingdom that emerged from the division of the Kotte in 1521 and dominated the southwest of the island in the late 16th century
SLFP	Sri Lankan Freedom Party, founded in 1951 and the main rival to the more conservative UNP since it first came to power in 1956.
Solosmasthana	the 16 sites reputedly visited by the Gautama Buddha on his three visits to Sri Lanka
Sri	honorific prefix denoting a sacred or respected person or place
stage	bus stop
string hopper	tangled light-textured noodles
stupa	Sanskrit synonym for dagoba
sutra	Buddhist scripture expressing a rule or adage
Tamil	ethnic group and language associated with southern India and northeast Sri Lanka
Tamil Tigers	nickname of LTTE
tampita	small temple raised on wood or stone stilts
tank	a manmade reservoir
Temple of the Tooth	synonymous with Dalada Maligawa
thambili	a golden-hued (king) coconut containing liquid
Theravada	literally 'school of the elder monks', the most ancient form of Buddhism, and main one practised in Sri Lanka, based on the Pali canon
three-wheeler	synonymous with tuktuk
Tissa	king
toddy	fermented coconut sap
tooth relic	tooth of the Gautama Buddha, preserved after his cremation, and smuggled to Sri Lanka in the 4th century AD
tota	harbour (common component of Sinhalese place names)
Trimurti	trinity of supreme Hindu divinities, ie: Brahma, Vishnu and Shiva
Tripitaka	standard collection of Theravada Buddhist scriptures that comprise the Pali canon
tsunami, 2004	massive tidal wave that struck the Sri Lankan coast on 26 December 2004, claiming at least 35,000 lives and destroying 90,000 buildings
tuktuk	a three-wheeler taxi, trishaw, auto-rickshaw
UNP	United National Party, founded in 1946 and still a dominant force in post-independence politics
vatadage	Buddhist shrine or image house built to a circular design
Vedas (adj. Vedic)	the oldest Sanskrit scriptures and literary works, regarded by Hindus to be apauruseya (of supernatural, non-human origin)
Vedda	Sri Lanka's oldest surviving indigenous race and last hunter-gatherers
vihara(ya)	Buddhist temple or image house

VOC	Verenigde Oostindische Compagnie, or Dutch East India Company, chartered company that oversaw Dutch trade interests in Ceylon (and elsewhere in the Indies and Africa)
walauwa	ancestral mansion
Wanniyala-Aetto	literally 'Forest People', the name by which the Vedda identify themselves
wattalapam	dessert similar to crème caramel
wewa	manmade reservoir (or tank)
Yaksha	Hindu or Buddhist subterranean sprite or nature-spirits, usually seen to be benevolent, but occasionally malicious or sexually predatory

ANNOTATED GLOSSARY OF KEY HISTORICAL, LEGENDARY AND MYTHICAL FIGURES

Aggabodhi II	Sinhala king (r?AD598–608 from Anuradhapura), accredited with constructing Sri Lanka's first vatadage as well as Giritale Reservoir between Habarana and Polonnaruwa
Aggabodhi IV	Sinhala king (rAD673–89 from Anuradhapura), known to have had a temporary residence near Polonnaruwa
Ananda	first cousin of Gautama Buddha and one of his ten principal disciples, accredited with memorising most of the sutras later transcribed as part of the Pali canon
Ashoka, Emperor	Mauryan King (r?282–236BC), from mainland India, instrumental in adoption of Buddhism on Sri Lanka
Avalokiteshvara	Bodhisattva venerated by the Mahayana school as an embodiment of Buddhist compassion. One sutra assigns a creator-like role to Avalokiteshvara, stating the sun and moon were born from his eyes, Shiva and Brahma from his brow and shoulders, and the wind, earth and sky from his mouth, feet and stomach respectively
Baker, Sir Samuel	b1821, d1893. British explorer, best known for his exploits on the Sudanese Nile, but spent eight formative years in Nuwara Eliya starting in 1847
Barnes, Lt-Gen Edward	influential British governor of Ceylon (1820–22 and 1824–31)
Bawa, Geoffrey	b1919, d2003. Renowned architect, whose works include the Parliament Buildings at Sri Jayawardene Kotte and many of Sri Lanka's most iconic hotels
Bawa, Major Bevis	b1909, d1992. Artist, brother of Geoffrey Bawa, and aide-de-camp to four colonial governors
Bell, H C P	b1851, d1937. British archaeologist who undertook several pioneering excavations for the Archaeological Survey Department over 1890–1912 before retiring to the Maldives
Bhairava	fearsome manifestation of Shiva represented in 64 forms, the most important of which guard the cardinal points. All Hindu temples are protected by a Bhairava idol, and he is also depicted in some Buddhist temple paintings.

Bhatikabhaya Abhaya	Sinhala king (r20BC–AD9 from Anuradhapura), of posthumous note for being incumbent at the time of Christ's birth
Bhuvanaikabahu I	Sinhala king (r1271–83), best known as the architect of the spectacular Yapahuwa citadel
Bhuvanaikabahu II	Sinhala king (r1310–35), relocated capital from Polonnaruwa to Kurunegala
Bhuvanaikabahu IV	Sinhala king (r?1344–53), relocated capital to Gampola south of Kandy
Bhuvanaikabahu VII	Sinhala king (r1521–51 from Kotte), had extensive dealings with the Portuguese at Colombo
Brahma	Hindu creator and four-faced deity, part of the Trimurti (divine trinity)
Cankili I, King	King of Jaffna (r1619–61)
Dappula I	Sinhala king (rAD661–64 from Anuradhapura)
Davy, John	b1790, d1868. British chemist whose pioneering early 19th-century travels are documented in the book *An Account of the Interior of Ceylon and of Its Inhabitants*
Devanampiya Tissa	Sinhala king (r?307–267BC), first Sri Lankan monarch to adopt Buddhism, planted Jaya Sri Maha Bodhi at Anuradhapura
Devata Bandara	Buddhist deity representing the future; often portrayed alongside Vishnu (past) and Kataragama (present)
Dhatusena	Sinhala king (r?455–75BC from Anuradhapura), founder of the Moriyan dynasty, whose achievements include the construction of 18 reservoirs, the ingenious irrigation canal between Anuradhapura's Kala and Tissa reservoirs and possibly the Avukana Buddha
Dona Catherina	teenage daughter of Karaliyadde Bandara who served briefly in her own right as Queen of Kandy under Portuguese patronage in 1581. Later the queen of King Vimaladharmasuriya I and King Senarat
D'Oyly, Sir John	b1774, d1824. British administrator, known for his reclusive nature and command of the Sinhala language, and for drafting the Kandy Convention of 1815, which placed all of Sri Lanka under colonial rule
Dutugamunu	Sinhala king (r?161–137BC from Anuradhapura), renowned as the fearless prince from Ruhuna who restored Sinhala sovereignty by defeating the usurper Elara, and built many famous monuments including the Ruwanweli Dagoba
Ehelepola Nilame	b1773, d1829. Kandyan aristocrat and senior adigar under Vikrama Rajasinha (1811–14), who played a key role in the Kandy Convention of 1815 and served as stand-in king from 1815 to 1818. Later exiled to Mauritius, where he died.
Elara	usurping Chola King of Anuradhapura (r?205–161BC), defeated by Dutugamunu of Ruhuna
Faxian	aka Fa Hien. Chinese monk who made a pilgrimage to Adam's Peak in AD412
Gajabahu I	Sinhala king (r?136–114BC from Anuradhapura),

a pious leader whose name intriguingly translates as 'Elephant Arm' and who possibly introduced the Pattini devi cult to Sri Lanka

Ganesh   popular elephant-headed Hindu deity, associated with the arts, wisdom and removal of obstacles. Also revered by Buddhists, and commonly depicted on Sri Lankan temples associated with both religions.

Gautama Buddha   b?563BC, d483BC. Founder of Buddhism, born Prince Siddhartha in Nepal and attained enlightenment after meditating under the original Bo Tree for 49 days

Gopallawa, William   last Governor General of Ceylon (1962–72) and first (non-executive) President of Sri Lanka (1972–78)

Gregory, Sir William   British governor of Ceylon (1872–77)

Hanuman   Hindu monkey-god and devotee of Prince Rama who helped rescue Sita from captivity on Lanka. Several hills on Sri Lanka are claimed to be relics of a massive chunk of forested Himalayan rock that was carried across by Hanuman to save Rama's wounded brother Lakshmana with the life-restoring herb called Sanjivani.

Harischandra, Walisinghe   b1876, d1913. Negombo-based Buddhist revivalist leader

Ibn Battuta   b1304, d1368. Moroccan traveller who visited most of the Muslim world, and several other regions, over a 30-year career, and ascended Adam's Peak in 1344

Ilanaga   Sinhala king (r?AD38–44 from Anuradhapura), also known as Elunna

Indra   thunderbolt-throwing Hindu Vedic deity reminiscent of the Greek Zeus or Nordic Thor. Revered by Buddhists as the less-warlike deity Sakra.

Jayaweera Astana   King of Kandy (r1411–51), at a time when Kandy was a semi-autonomous vassal of Kotte

Jayewardene, J R   Prime Minister (1977–78) and President (1978–89) of Sri Lanka under whom Sri Jayawardene Kotte replaced Colombo as official capital

Jetta Tissa II   Sinhala king (r?AD332–40 from Anuradhapura)

Kali   terrifying-looking four- or ten-armed Hindu goddess, consort of Shiva, associated with kindness by her devotees but feared as a human flesh-eater by some Sinhala Buddhists

Kalinga Magha   South Indian Hindu founder of the Jaffna Kingdom, captured Polonnaruwa in 1215 and ruled from there until he was ousted in 1236

Kanittha Tissa   Sinhala king (r?AD163–94 from Anuradhapura)

Karaliyadde Bandara   King of Kandy (r1551–81), at a time when Kandy was a semi-autonomous vassal of Kotte

Kasyapa   Sinhala king (rAD477–95), reigned from Sigiriya, where he created the country's most famous royal citadel, despite his unpopularity as the killer of his father Dhatusena

Kataragama   guardian deity of Sri Lanka, recognised by both Buddhists and Hindus; represents the present in Sri Lanka's Buddhist iconography

A2

Kavan Tissa	influential King of Ruhuna, r205–161BC, father of King Dutugamunu of Anuradhapura and his successor Saddha Tissa
Kelani Tissa	King of Kelaniya, a 2nd-century BC polity that stood close to Colombo, remembered mainly as the father of Queen Viharamahadevi of Ruhuna
Kirti Sri Rajasinha	King of Kandy (r1747–81), a highly influential figure who kept the Dutch at bay throughout his reign, played a key role in the Buddhist revival, and built, renovated or made a significant contribution to the décor of several important temples
Knox, Robert	b1641, d1720. Sea captain whose 19 years as a captive in Kandy led to his authorship of a unique book, *An Historical Relation of the Island Ceylon*
Kubera	Hindu deity governing wealth and the semi-divine Yakshas, often depicted as a pot-bellied deformed dwarf
Kumaratunga, Chandrika	first female president of Sri Lanka (1994–2005)
Kutakanna Tissa	Sinhala king (r42–20BC) from Anuradhapura
Kuveni	legendary 5th-century BC Yaksha queen who had two children with Prince Vijaya
Lakshmi	Hindu goddess and wife of Vishnu associated with wealth and prosperity. Also recognised as a deity by Buddhists.
Lilavati	wife of Parakramabahu I who briefly served as queen of Polonnaruwa thrice in the tumultuous period that followed the death of Nissanka Malla
Lipton, Sir Thomas	b1848, d1931. Scottish planter and founder of Lipton's Tea, instrumental in the development of Sri Lanka's tea industry
Mahadathika Mahanaga	Sinhala king (rAD9–21 from Anuradhapura)
Mahanaga	brother and rival of Devanampiya Tissa who founded the offshoot Ruhuna Kingdom in the 3rd century BC
Mahasena	aka Mahasen. Sinhala king (rAD277–304 from Anuradhapura), builder of 16 major reservoirs, including Minneriya, and a staunch Mahayana Buddhist who discriminated against Theravada followers and built the Jetavana Dagoba
Mahinda	first-born son of Emperor Ashoka, and monk who introduced Buddhism to Sri Lanka c250BC
Mahinda IV	Sinhala king (r?AD975–91)
Mahinda V	Sinhala king (r?1002–17), last monarch of Anuradhapura prior to its capture by King Raja-Raja and relocation of the capital to Polonnaruwa; died an exile in an Indian prison in 1029
Maitland, Lt-Gen Thomas	British governor of Ceylon (1805–11) and inadvertent founder of the Mount Lavinia Hotel
Maitreya	revered bodhisattva who has yet to appear on earth but, when he does come, at some undetermined in the future, will achieve complete nirvana and teach the purest dharma

Mara	evil dharmapala demon who tried and failed in seducing the meditating Gautama Buddha with visions of his beautiful daughters
Mayadunne	King of Sitawaka (r1521–81), a fierce rival of Kotte, much of which he annexed to his kingdom in the 1560s, and also a combative opponent of the Portuguese at Colombo
Moggallana I	Sinhala king (rAD496–515 from Anuradhapura), succeeded his unpopular brother Kasyapa after killing him in a battle near his citadel at Sigiriya
Moggallana III	Sinhala king (rAD608–14 from Anuradhapura)
Murugan	alternative name for Skanda/Kataragama
Mutasiva	Sinhala king (r?367–307BC from Anuradhapura), a long peaceful reign during which the ancient city took much of its shape
Natha	Buddhist guardian deity of enigmatic provenance, a rather nebulous figure whose name literally means 'without shape or form' and who is often associated with one or other of the bodhisattvas Maitreya and Avalokiteshvara
Nissanka Malla	Sinhala king (r1187–96 from Polonnaruwa), who built several of the former capital's most impressive buildings including the Lata Mandapa, Hatadage and Rankoth Dagoba
North, Frederick	first British governor of Ceylon (1798–1805)
Pandukabhaya	Sinhala king (r?474–367BC from Anuradhapura), generally credited as the city's founder
Panduvasudeva	Sinhala king (r?504–474BC over the ancient pre-Anuradhapura kingdom of Upatissa Nuwara)
Parakrama II	King of the Indian Tamil state of Pandy who captured and ruled over Polonnaruwa (1212–15)
Parakramabahu I	Sinhala king (r1153–86), also known as Parakramabahu the Great, who unified the island from his capital at Polonnaruwa and is accredited with constructing several of its most impressive buildings
Parakramabahu II	Sinhala king (r1234–69 from Dambadeniya), son of Vijayabahu III, and author of the epic *Kavsilumina*
Parakramabahu V	Sinhala king (r?1344–59 from Gampola)
Parakramabahu VI	Sinhala king (r?1412–67), relocated the capital from Gampola to Kotte at the start of his long and stable reign
Parjanya	Vedic Hindu deity of rain, protector of poets and enemy of fire
Parvati	important Hindu fertility goddess; wife of Shiva and mother of Ganesh and Kartikeya
Pattini	Hindi and Buddhist female guardian deity of Sri Lanka
Polo, Marco	b1254, d1324. Venetian explorer who visited Sri Lanka in 1298, declaring it to be the finest island of its size in the world, and summited Adam's Peak
Prabhakaran, Velupillai	b1954, d2009. Tamil secessionist, founded the LTTE in 1976 and led it until his death in battle in 2009

A2

Premadasa, Ranasinghe	President of Sri Lanka (1989–93) until his assassination by an LTTE suicide bomber
Raja-Raja	Chola king (r985–1014), who conquered Anuradhapura, forced the Sinhala monarchy into exile, and established Jananathamangalam (Polonnaruwa) as his new Hindu-dominated capital
Rajadhi Rajasinha	King of Kandy (r1782–98), incumbent when the Dutch relinquished their coastal possessions to the British in 1796
Rajapaksa, PM 'Mahinda'	President of Sri Lanka (2005–15)
Rajasinha I	King of Sitawaka (1581–92), a warlike figure who deposed and succeeded Dona Catherina of Kandy in the first year of his rule and died in battle in 1592
Rajasinha II	Sinhala king (r1629–87 from Kandy), initiated the treaty with the Dutch that helped enable them to replace the Portuguese as the dominant colonial power on the coast
Rajendra I	Chola king (r1014–44), son of Raja-Raja, who extended Chola rule from Polonnaruwa/Anuradhapura to practically the whole island after leading a military campaign there in 1017
Rama, Prince	central figure of the *Ramayana*, an earthly incarnation of Vishnu considered to be the Supreme Being in some Hindi traditions
Ravana	demonic ten-headed king who legendarily ruled over Lanka for several hundred years prior to being killed by Prince Rama c2500BC
Saddha Tissa	Sinhala king (r137–119BC from Anuradhapura), son of Kavan Tissa of Ruhuna and brother of Dutugamunu
Sakra	Buddhist guardian deity who rules Trayastrimsa (second heaven) atop the legendary Mount Meru
Saman	guardian deity of Sri Lanka whose name means 'rising sun' and is often depicted in the company of a white elephant. Legendarily he started life as a Yakka chief who was preached to by the Buddha at Mahiyanganaya and now inhabits the slopes of Adam's Peak
Sangamitta Thera	sister of Mahinda, daughter of King Ashoka accredited with transporting the Bo Tree to Sri Lanka c249BC
Sangili, King	see Cankili
Saradiel, Deekirikevage	b1832, d1864. Highwayman, preyed on wealthy carriage passengers on the Colombo–Kandy road
Sena I	Sinhala king (rAD846–66 from Anuradhapura), regarded to be the founder of Ritigala monastery
Sena Sammatha Wickramabahu	King of Kandy (r1473–1511), at a time when Kandy was a semi-autonomous vassal of Kotte
Senanayake, D S	first prime minister (1947–52) and 'Father of the Nation', who guided Ceylon to independence
Senarat	Sinhala king (r1604–35 from Kandy)
Shiva	Hindu deity, component of the Trimurti (divine trinity) associated with destruction and regeneration

Siddhartha, Prince	synonymous with Gautama Buddha
Silameghavanna	Sinhala king (rAD614–23 from Anuradhapura)
Sirimeghavanna	Sinhala king (rAD301–28 from Anuradhapura), who received the tooth relic from the Indian Princess Hemamali
Sirisena, Maithripala	President of Sri Lanka (2015–present)
Sita	the central female character in the *Ramayana*, earthly incarnation of Lakshmi and wife of Prince Rama who was abducted to Lanka by Ravana then rescued by her husband and his allies. A paragon of Hindu wifely and feminine virtues.
Skanda	Hindu god of war, son of Shiva, usually regarded to be synonymous with Kataragama
Soma Devi	second wife of King Valagamba, captured in the Tamil invasion of 103BC and exiled to India, but returned to Anuradhapura after her husband recaptured it in 89BC
Taylor, James	b1838, d1892. British planter, who first planted tea on Ceylon, at Loolecondera estate south of Kandy
Tennent, Sir James	Colonial Secretary of Ceylon (1845–51)
Turnour, George	b1799, d1843. British administrator and scholar who deciphered the *Mahavamsa*
Upatissa I	Sinhala king (rAD370–412 from Anuradhapura), accredited with building the precursor to the Parakrama Samudra at Polonnaruwa
Upulvan	guardian deity entrusted with the protection of Sri Lanka by the Buddha. Depicted with a lily-blue body and often associated with Vishnu.
Valagamba	Sinhala king (r103 and 89–77BC, from Anuradhapura), overthrown by Chola invaders a few months into his reign but reclaimed the throne after 14 years. Accredited as the founder of Abhayagiriya Monastery and several cave temples including Dambulla. Also known as Vattagamani Abhaya.
Valli	goddess and consort of Skanda/Kataragama
van Rhee, Thomas	Dutch Governor of Ceylon (1693–95)
Varuna	Hindu deity of water, once the primary god of the Vedic pantheon, but later replaced by Indra
Vasabha	Sinhala king (rAD67–111 from Anuradhapura)
Vibhishana	pure-hearted younger brother of the devilish Ravana; assisted Prince Rama in the rescue of Sita and was later crowned King of Lanka as a token of gratitude
Viharamahadevi	Queen of King Kavan Tissa of Ruhuna, mother of kings Dutugamunu and Saddha Tissa
Vijaya	Sinhala prince/king (r?543–505BC), refugee from India who legendarily founded the Sinhala nation
Vijaya Rajasinha	King of Kandy (r1739–47), aristocratic Tamil brother-in-law of King Vira Narendra Sinha, the last Sinhala
Vijayabahu I	Sinhala king (r1055–1110), who defeated the Chola usurpers at Polonnaruwa in 1055 and restored Buddhism as the state religion
Vijayabahu III	Sinhala king (r1220–34), founder of the Siri Sanga Bo dynasty, established Dambadeniya as the royal capital

Vijayabahu VI	Sinhala king (r1513–21), based at Kotte and granted Portuguese permission to settle at Colombo
Vikrama Pandu	11th-century King of Ruhuna who made Kalutara his temporary capital
Vikrama Rajasinha	Sinhala king (r1798–1815), teenage son of Kirti Sri Rajasinha whose erratic temperament led to him becoming the last monarch of Kandy, exiled by British to India, where he died in 1832
Vikramabahu III	Sinhala king (r1357–74 from Gampola), the first king to build a palace at Kandy
Vimaladharmasuriya I	Sinhala king (r1592–1604 from Kandy), entrenched Kandy as capital by relocating the tooth relic there from Kotte in the first year of his reign
Vimaladharmasuriya II	Sinhala king (r1687–1707 from Kandy)
Vira Narendra Sinha	Sinhala king (r1707–39 from Kandy), died without legitimate issue to go on record as the island's last Sinhala monarch
Vishnu	Hindu deity, usually depicted in blue, component of the Trimurti (divine trinity) associated with preservation; represents the past in Sri Lanka's Buddhist iconography
Wendt, Lionel	b1900, d1944. Multidisciplinary artist known for his photography and efforts to popularise Sri Lankan dance
Wickramasinghe, Martin	b1890, d1976. Prolific novelist, short-story writer, philosopher and essayist widely regarded to be the father of modern Sinhala literature
Wijetunga, Dingiri	President of Sri Lanka (1993–94)
Woolf, Leonard	b1880, d1969. British writer, best known today as the husband of Virginia Woolf but who formerly served as District Administrator of Hambantota over 1908–11
Yama	Vedic Hindu deity associated with death and the underworld, regarded by Buddhists to be a figure of wrath
Yatala	3rd-century BC monarch of Ruhuna, son of its founder Mahanaga
Zheng He	Chinese maritime explorer (b1371, d1433) who sailed into Galle harbour in 1409 and erected a trilingual tablet there

Appendix 3

FURTHER INFORMATION

BOOKS Many books about Sri Lanka are only available at bookshops in Colombo and some are listed here. The Sri Lankan sections in Colombo bookshops will have many others. These include informative CCF and Department of Archaeology publications about most major cultural sites including Dambulla, Sigiriya, Anuradhapura, Polonnaruwa and Kandy, as well as smaller sites such as Ritigala and Mihintale.

General

Arjuna's A–Z Street Guide Arjuna Consulting, 2006. Maps showing every street in Colombo and suburbs, and also in Kandy, Galle, Nuwara Eliya, Anuradhapura, Polonnaruwa, Trincomalee, Batticaloa and Jaffna.

Barlas, Robert, and Wanasundera, Nanda P *Culture Shock! Sri Lanka* Marshall Cavendish International, 2013. A useful explanation of cultural mores.

Meyler, Michael *A Dictionary of Sri Lankan English* Mirisgala, 2011 (*www.mirisgala.net*). Self-published volume with some amazing examples of Sri Lankan English culled from Sri Lankan authors, making an entertaining read as well as a useful reference book.

Roberts, Norah *Galle: As Quiet as Sleep* Colombo, 1993. Details of Galle and the town's personalities of the past.

Health

Wilson-Howarth, Dr Jane *Essential Guide to Travel Health* Cadogan, 2009

Wilson-Howarth, Dr Jane, and Ellis, Dr Matthew *Your Child Abroad: A Travel Health Guide* Bradt, 2014

History

De Silva, K M *A History of Sri Lanka* Penguin India, 2005. The most detailed and authoritative single-volume work on the island's long history, though it stops short in the 1990s.

Sebastian, Anton *Complete Illustrated History of Sri Lanka* Vijitha Yapa 2012. Sumptuously illustrated hardcover coffee-table tome suited both to the casual page-browser and more serious scholars.

Weiss, Gordon *The Cage: The Fight for Sri Lanka & the Last Days of the Tamil Tigers* Vintage, 2012. Readable, balanced and meticulously researched account of the civil war of 1983–2009.

Natural history

De Vlas, J, and De Vlas, J *Illustrated Field Guide to the Flowers of Sri Lanka* Mark Booksellers, 2008.

Ratnayake, H D, and Ekanayake, S P *Common Wayside Trees of Sri Lanka* Royal Botanical Gardens, Peradeniya, 1995. With photographs and details of Sri Lanka's trees.

Warakagoda, Deepal *et al. Birds of Sri Lanka* Helm Field Guides, 2012. The best field guide to Sri Lanka's birds illustrates, describes and shows the distribution of 450-plus species including all endemics, residents, migrants and regular vagrants.

Wijeyeratne, Gehan de Silva *Mammals of Sri Lanka* Bloomsbury 2016. Portable pocket guide showing all the island's large mammal species and several smaller ones.

Wijeyeratne, Gehan de Silva *Naturalist's Guide to the Butterflies & Dragonflies of Sri Lanka* John Beaufoy, 2015.

Wijeyeratne, Gehan de Silva *Sri Lankan Wildlife: A Visitor's Guide* Bradt, 2007. This useful overview of the island's wildlife includes detailed coverage of larger mammals, good sections on other vertebrates and invertebrates, with superb photographs throughout.

Other Asia guides For a full list of Bradt's Asia guides, see w bradtguides.com/shop

Leung, Mikey, and Meggitt, Belinda *Bangladesh* (2nd edition) Bradt Travel Guides, 2012

Lovell-Hoare, Sophie, and Lovell-Hoare, Max *Kashmir: including Ladakh and Zanskar* Bradt Travel Guides, 2014

Thiessen, Tamara *Borneo* (3rd edition) Bradt Travel Guides, 2016

WEBSITES It is surprising how many websites there are devoted to Sri Lanka, or a particular part of it. Type 'Sri Lanka' in the Google search box on the internet, and you will be rewarded with 570,000,000 entries. I have listed hotel websites in the guide. Here are some others to peruse for particular information:

w **colombopage.com** News of Sri Lanka

w **dailymirror.lk** A newspaper website with breaking news posted throughout the day

w **dailynews.lk** A newspaper website

w **gov.lk** Official website of the Government of Sri Lanka

w **island.lk** A daily newspaper website

w **lankalibrary.com** Virtual library and information on Sri Lanka

w **lankapage.com** News about Sri Lanka

w **srilanka.travel** The official website of the Sri Lanka Tourism Development Authority

w **srilankaluxury.com** Concentrates on unique accommodation, rustic as well as luxury

w **srilankan.com** SriLankan Airlines site, with timetable

w **sundaytimes.lk** Good newspaper website

w **theacademic.org** Lanka academic newspaper

INDEX OF ADVERTISERS

Index